D1615567

THE LAW OF PARTNERSHIP IN SCOTLAND

The Law of Partnership in Scotland

by

JAMES BENNETT MILLER

T.D., M.A., LL.B.

Professor of Mercantile Law at the University of Glasgow

Published under the auspices of
THE SCOTTISH UNIVERSITIES LAW INSTITUTE

EDINBURGH
W. GREEN & SON LTD.
1973

First published in 1973

ISBN 0 414 00545 7

Printed in Great Britain
by The Eastern Press Limited
of London and Reading

PREFACE

THE terms of the preface in which an author launches a new work upon the public are at once salutatory and valedictory. They are valedictory in that he may at last take his leave, for a spell at least, of the task which has been his main preoccupation over a number of years; but they are addressed also in salutation to those by whom the book will be read and judged. In the accomplishment of that dual purpose some writers of textbooks upon the law, though not all, have displayed the powers of adroit draftsmanship which may be expected from them; and accordingly there is no shortage of styles, as it were, upon which to model one's own preface. From the rueful to the euphoric there is a wide range of models to suit almost every mood. Even so, to present a treatise on the Scottish law of partnership after the lapse of more than a century entails some speciality of approach which is not entirely or adequately catered for by the elegance of earlier models; for, while there are useful examples of prefaces to books which treat of a new aspect of law or for those which add a fresh volume to the existing literature on a particular topic and for books which refurbish and bring up to date authoritative works of long standing, it is more difficult to find a precedent for the preface to a book which attempts over the waste of so many years to present a treatment of the law of partnership in Scotland in replacement of a work of authority which has remained undisturbed by the activity of parliament and of the courts since 1868. Yet, archaic as some of the passages in that earlier work must now appear to be, no writer on the Scots law relating to partnership can fail to acknowledge his debt to Francis William Clark.

It is true that the impact of parliamentary activity has, over the past century, been more marked than that of the courts. There have, of course, been reported decisions during that period which are of importance, but in relation to the length of the period they have been surprisingly few. In part this may be due to the replacement of the partnership in many instances by the private limited company; but the partnership is still a prevalent form of association in business, particularly in professional or quasi-professional activity, and one cannot escape the conjecture that the limpid prose in which Sir Frederick Pollock clothed the provisions of the Partnership Act 1890 has had an unlooked-for effect; for it seems almost as though the deceptive simplicity, born of clear and elegant expression, of those provisions has in some measure anaesthetised legal thought. That situation, if it exists, produces its problems for the writer. He is at many points thrown back upon decisions reached by the courts prior to the passing of the Partnership Act 1890. There are obvious perils in the use of authority of that kind and these are touched upon in the pages which follow. It remains true, however, that no one can explore the true nature of the law of partnership without resort to these earlier decisions.

Moreover, the Act does not supply, nor does it profess to supply, a complete codification of the law of partnership; and where it neglects to bring a topic within its express regulation the rules of the common law are preserved. Finally, in those matters with which it deals expressly, the Act has treated of the English and the Scottish law and has done so with a minimum of divergent provision. This has been achieved with a remarkable degree of success but, inevitably, where the outlook upon the nature of the partnership itself differs so widely, there are areas in which the *rapprochement* is a rather uneasy one.

It will be seen that, after all, the preface has taken a traditional and foreseeable shape—that of reminding the censorious reader that the author is conscious of the difficulties of the task he has set himself and that in essaying it he is at least as prone to error as the rest of fallible humanity. While he hopes that this book may be of some service to the legal profession and to students of the Scots law, he is only too aware that there will be points at which it will be found wanting in some particular where his diligence and attentiveness have, flagged.

That apology is a necessary and humbling task for any author. It remains to discharge the more pleasant task of expressing gratitude to those without whose advice or assistance this book might bear more blemishes. In particular, the author's thanks are due to the Honourable Lord Kissen and to the late Mr. William Allister Cook who each read the entire work in manuscript and made valuable suggestions for its improvement. While both have thus contributed to any merit which the book may have, neither is in any way accountable for its defects, the responsibility for which lies with the author. It is a great sorrow that Mr. Cook's untimely death has robbed the author of making manifest to his eyes as well as to those of the public the debt which, it is at least consoling to recall, the author acknowledged to Mr. Cook personally on many occasions during the progress of the work.

The book appears under the aegis of the Scottish Universities' Law Institute established with the financial assistance of the Carnegie Trust for the Universities of Scotland. To both the author is indebted for the encouragement of his labours which the Institute's Director, Professor T. B. Smith, provided in his own genial and helpful way. Over the period when the author has been in travail, many of his colleagues have been exposed to the onslaught of his obsession and preoccupation, and they have borne it both manfully and sympathetically. It will, I hope, not be considered graceless if a general expression of gratitude is made to them. Special mention must, however, be made of Mrs. Buchanan and Mrs. Simpson, secretaries to the Faculty of Law of the University of Glasgow, for their assistance, constant, efficient and unabatedly good-humoured, in reducing the author's original manuscript and its innumerable amendments and afterthoughts to the neat and expert typescript in which it was submitted to the publishers. Mrs. Buchanan has added to these benevolent labours by ordering in her superbly competent manner the material collected for the index, while in Edinburgh Miss Stewart has not only read the proofs most meticulously but has also prepared the Table of Statutes and the Table of Cases.

The law is stated as ascertainable from sources available on December 31, 1971, though it has been possible to take notice briefly of some decisions reported in the early months of 1972.

Department of Private Law,   J. BENNETT MILLER.
The University of Glasgow.
November 1972.

It has not been thought necessary to supply a bibliography, since most of the materials cited are familiar. References to Bell's Commentaries on the Law of Scotland and on the Principles of Mercantile Jurisprudence (cited Bell, *Comm.*) are to the seventh edition by John McLaren. Ross's *Leading Cases in the Commercial Law of England and Scotland* are for the sake of brevity cited as Ross, *Commercial Cases.*

CONTENTS

		PAGE
Preface	. . . .	V
Table of Cases	. . . .	xv
Table of Statutes .	. . . .	xliii

CHAPTER I. THE GENERAL ATTRIBUTES OF THE RELATIONSHIP 1
  Definition of partnership 2
  Participation in profits 7
  Salaried partners 12
  Restriction on number of partners . . . 13
  Corporations and firms 14
  Delectus personae 16

CHAPTER II. CAPACITY OF PARTIES TO ENTER THE CONTRACT OF
  PARTNERSHIP 24
  Pupil children 24
  Minors 29
  Insanity 38
  Intoxication 40
  Bankruptcy 41
  Married women 43
  Corporations 44
  Aliens 46

CHAPTER III. THE INDICIA OF THE CONTRACT OF PARTNERSHIP
  Evidence of constitution of partnership . . 51
  Quasi-partnership 60
  The statutory rules 63

CHAPTER IV. ILLEGALITY IN RELATION TO PARTNERSHIPS AND
  ASSOCIATIONS 97
  Introduction 97
  Objects opposed to current notions of morality,
    religion or public policy . . . 98
  Objects illegal by statute 103
  Partnerships initially illegal . . . 105
  Registration of Business Names Act 1916 . 113
  Severability 118
  Concealment of illegality 124
  Restrictive covenants 119
  Claims against illegal partnerships . . . 125

ix

CHAPTER V. HOLDING OUT 127
    Introduction 127
    Holding out as an aspect of the doctrine of
      personal bar 130
    What amounts to holding out a person as a
      partner 131
    The legal effect of holding out . . . 135
    A person knowingly suffering himself to be
      held out as a partner 135
    Holding out by a person of his intention to
      become a partner 142
    Fraudulent inducement to hold oneself out
      as a partner 143
    Problems of holding out arising on a change
      in the composition of the firm . . . 144
    Effect of registration of particulars of firm
      under the Registration of Business Names
      Act 1916 152
    Liability in delict 153
    Liability of the firm in cases of holding out . 154

CHAPTER VI. THE RIGHTS AND DUTIES OF PARTNERS INTER SE
    The limits of the partner's authority . . 158
    The partners as cautioners 159
    Uberrima fides 161
    Actings of partner during the course of the
      partnership 164
    Partner's duty to act honestly . . . 180
    Powers of management 182
    Expulsion 188
    Limitations on the mutual obligations of good
      faith owed among partners . . . 189
    Remedies for breach of the obligations of the
      partners *inter se* 193
    Rights of relief *inter socios* 196
    Right of access to the firm's books . . 198
    Assignation of partner's share . . . 201
    Sub-partnership 203
    Right of the firm to the services of the
      partners 205
    Liability of partners *inter se* in delict . . 206

CHAPTER VII. RIGHTS AND DUTIES OF THE PARTNERS IN
    RELATION TO THIRD PARTIES (CONTRACT) . 207
    Introduction 207
    The business of the firm 208
    Authority in cases of emergency . . . 214
    Admissions and representations made by a
      partner 217
    Notice to one partner is notice to all partners 218
    Execution of written contracts on behalf of
      the firm 220
    Liability of the firm under contracts in writing 224
    Limits of the partner's authority . . . 235

CHAPTER VII. RIGHTS AND DUTIES OF THE PARTNERS IN RELATION TO THIRD PARTIES (CONTRACT)— *continued*

Cases where the third party is placed on his inquiry as to the partner's authority . 248
Inducement to become a partner in the firm 254
Liability on the ground that the firm has had the benefit of the contract . . . 256
Liability of incoming partner for firm's debts 258
Endurance of liability 274
Cautionary obligations undertaken in connection with the firm 278
Revocation of partner's authority during subsistence of the partnership . . . 287
Liability of a partner on dissolution of the firm 288

CHAPTER VIII. RIGHTS AND DUTIES OF THE PARTNERS IN RELATION TO THIRD PARTIES (DELICT AND BREACH OF TRUST) 302
Vicarious liability imposed upon the firm . 302
Liability for penalty 313
Liability for fraud 317
Fraud or breach of fiduciary duty committed with the knowledge of the copartners . 323
Firm receiving benefit from a partner's wrongful act 326
Wrong committed without authority and not in ordinary course of the business . . 335
Partner's wrongful act causing injury to his copartner 338
Liability of firm for partner's breach of trust 339
Joint and several liability in delict . . . 356
Improper employment of trust property for partnership purposes 358
Following the trust money 370

CHAPTER IX. THE PROPERTY OF THE PARTNERSHIP . . . 376
Introduction 376
Partnership property 377
Mode of proof as to partnership property . 382
Heritable estate belonging to the partnership 387
Partnership property as a qualification for voting 392
Difference of treatment of partnership property under Scots and under English law . . 394
Rights of partners *inter se* in the partnership property 398
The partner's lien 406
Assignation of a partner's share . . . 411
Goodwill 419
Trade marks 428
Valuation of goodwill 432

Chapter X. Dissolution and Expulsion . . . 435
  Introduction 435
  Dissolution by expiration of the contractual term or by notice 436
  Partnership at will 437
  Dissolution on death or bankruptcy of one of the partners 444
  Dissolution of the firm compared with a change in its composition 451
  Dissolution upon illegality of the partnership business 453
  Dissolution of partnership by order of the court 455
  Treatment of private limited company as a *quasi*-partnership 474
  Assignation by a partner of his share . . 478
  Arbitration clause as affecting dissolution of the partnership 480
  Expulsion from the partnership . . . 484

Chapter XI. Effects of Dissolution 494
  Effect of dissolution upon contracts . . 494
  Effect of dissolution upon third parties . . 499
  Right of partner to give notice of dissolution . 508

Chapter XII. The Winding Up of the Firm's Affairs . 510
  Continuing authority of the partners for purposes of winding up 511
  Continuance of partnership business . . 517
  Appointment of judicial factor to wind up affairs of the partnership 520
  Effect of arbitration clause in contract of copartnery 523
  Right of partner's representatives in winding up of the partnership 524
  Distribution of assets on final settlement of accounts in winding up 527
  Questions as to property accruing and claims incurred after dissolution which are specially provided for in the Partnership Act 1890 540
  Rights arising where the partnership is dissolved for fraud or misrepresentation . 547
  Agreements based on false accounts . . 552

Chapter XIII. The Firm and the Partners in Bankruptcy 553
  Where the firm is sequestrated while the partners remain solvent 554
  Where the firm is solvent but one of the partners is bankrupt 562
  Where the firm and the partners are all bankrupt 565

CHAPTER XIII. THE FIRM AND THE PARTNERS IN BANKRUPTCY
—*continued*
Identity of the firm for purposes of sequestration 566
Claims against solvent partner when firm's assets have been sequestrated while one or more partners are insolvent and one or more solvent 570
Sequestrated firm a partner in another partnership or joint adventure 571
Challenge of transactions of the partnership 573
The ranking of claims against the partnership 576

CHAPTER XIV. THE LIMITED PARTNERSHIP 583
The constitution of the limited partnership . 585
Registration of the limited partnership . . 590
Change in status from general to limited partner 594
Assignation of share of limited partner . . 595
Applicability of general law of partnership . 597
Matters to be implied in a limited partnership failing agreement to the contrary . . 598
Dissolution 601
Winding up 604

CHAPTER XV. THE JOINT ADVENTURE 607
The limits of the joint adventure . . . 607
Joint ownership distinguished from joint adventure 610
Joint adventure a separate *persona* . . . 611
Differences arising from the inherent nature of the joint adventure 613
Liability in delict 619
Illegality of adventure 621
Rights of the joint adventurers *inter se* . . 623
Compensation of claims 625
The property of the joint adventure . . 630
Termination of the joint adventure . . 631

APPENDIX.
1. The Partnership Act 1890 . . . 636
2. The Limited Partnerships Act 1907 . 646
3. The Limited Partnerships Rules 1907 . 650
4. The Companies Act 1948
   section 429 656
   section 434 656
5. The Companies Act 1967
   Part IV 656
6. The Partnerships (Unrestricted Size) No. 1 Regulations 1968 (S.I. 1968 No. 1222) . . . 658

APPENDIX—*continued*
7. The Partnerships (Unrestricted Size) No. 2 Regulations 1970
(S.I. 1970 No. 835) . . . 659
8. The Partnerships (Unrestricted Size) No. 3 Regulations 1970
(S.I. 1970 No. 992) . . . 659
9. The Partnerships (Unrestricted Size) No. 4 Regulations 1970
(S.I. 1970 No. 1319) . . . 659
10. The Limited Partnerships (Unrestricted Size) No. 1 Regulations 1971
(S.I. 1971 No. 782) . . . 660

Index 661

TABLE OF CASES

A. B., *Petr.* (1884) 22 S.L.R. 294 .... 468, 472, 522
—— *v.* C. D. (1832) 10 S. 523 454
—— *v.* —— 1912, 1 S.L.T. 44 .... 109, 411
A. & M., *Re* [1926] 1 Ch. 274; 95 L.J.Ch. 258 29
Aas *v.* Benham [1891] 2 Ch. 244; 65 L.T. 25 .... 165, 168, 172, 174, 177, 179
Abbott *v.* Smith (1760) 2 W.Bl. 947 357
—— *v.* Sullivan [1952] 1 K.B. 189; [1952] 1 All E.R. 226 493
Abel *v.* Sutton (1800) 3 Esp. 108; 6 R.R. 818 .... 514, 515
Abenheim, *Re* (1913) 109 L.T. 219 .... 3, 95
Aberdeen Ry. Co. *v.* Blaikie (1854) 1 Macq. 461; Ross, *Commercial Cases III*, 338 165
Aberdeen Town & County Bank *v.* Clark (1859) 22 D. 44; 32 Sc.Jur. 20 ... 401
Adam *v.* Adam, 1962 S.L.T. 332 .... 383, 384, 386, 609
—— *v.* Newbigging (1888) 13 App.Cas. 308; 57 L.J.Ch. 1066 ...... 59, 163, 189, 548, 549, 550
Addie *v.* Western Bank of Scotland (1867) 5 M. (H.L.) 80; 39 Sc.Jur. 437 ... 318
Advocate (Lord) *v.* Wemyss (1899) 2 F. (H.L.) 1; [1900] A.C. 48; 7 S.L.T. 172 37
Agace, *Ex p.* (1792) 2 Cox 312; 2 R.R. 49 .... 218, 237, 238, 253, 322
Airth (1602) Mor. 8939 30
Aitchison *v.* Aitchison (1877) 4 R. 899 .... 7, 57–59, 609, 623
Aitken *v.* Charles & Co., 5 Fac. 263; (1830) 8 S. 446 505
Aitken's Trs. *v.* Shanks, 5 Fac. 594; (1830) 8 S. 753 .... 406, 436, 446
Alderson *v.* Pope (1808) 1 Camp. 404n. 143, 144
Aldridge, *Re* [1894] 2 Ch. 97; 63 L.J.Ch. 465 539
Alexander *v.* Kinneir (1632) Mor. 6278 38
—— *v.* Simms (1854) 18 Beav. 80; (1854) 23 L.J.Ch. 721; 104 R.R. 23 407
Alexander's Trs. *v.* Thomson (1885) 22 S.L.R. 828 .... 18, 21, 182, 412, 445
Allan *v.* Gronmeyer (1891) 18 R. 784; 28 S.L.R. 525 521
—— *v.* McLeish (1819) 2 Murray 158 304
Allen *v.* McCombie's Trs., 1909 S.C. 710; 1909, 1 S.L.T. 296 .... 327, 368
Allison *v.* Allison's Trs. (1904) 6 F. 496; 12 S.L.T. 33 .... 65, 84, 85
Alloa (Mags. of) *v.* Wilson, 1913 S.C. 6; 1912, 2 S.L.T. 287 217
Amalgamated Socy. of Ry. Servants *v.* Motherwell Branch of the Socy. (1880) 7 R. 867; 17 S.L.R. 607 101
—— *v.* Osborne [1909] 1 Ch. 163; [1910] A.C. 87 101
Amber Size & Chemical Co. *v.* Menzel [1913] 2 Ch. 239; 82 L.J.Ch. 573 ... 174
American Pioneer Leather Co., *Re* [1918] 1 Ch. 556; 87 L.J.Ch. 493 477
Anderson *v.* Anderson (1857) 25 Beav. 190; 119 R.R. 388 .... 194, 453
—— *v.* Daniel [1924] 2 K.B. 138; 93 L.J.K.B. 97 104
—— *v.* Rutherford, 10 Fac. 282; (1835) 13 S. 488 498
—— *v.* Torrie (1857) 19 D. 356; 29 Sc.Jur. 157 101
Andrews *v.* Mitchell [1905] A.C. 78; 74 L.J.K.B. 333 488
Andrews' & Alexander's Case (1869) L.R. 8 Eq. 176; 20 L.T. 943 6
Anon. (1855) 2 K. & J. 441; 110 R.R. 308 .... 464, 467
Apsey, *Ex p.* (1791) 3 Bro.C.C. 265 .... 358, 363
Arbuckle *v.* Taylor (1815) 3 Dow 160 312
Arden *v.* Sharpe & Francis (1797) 2 Esp. 524; 5 R.R. 748; Ross, *Commercial Cases III*, 505 227
Argo *v.* Smarts (1853) 1 Irv. 250; 25 Sc.Jur. 450 30
Armour *v.* Gibson, Nov. 29, 1774, F.C.; (1774) Mor. 14575 .... 296, 503
Armstrong *v.* Armstrong (1834) 3 Myl. & K. 45; 41 R.R. 10 .... 107, 111, 124, 621
—— *v.* Strain [1952] 1 K.B. 232; [1952] 1 All E.R. 139 .... 319, 320, 340
Arnauld *v.* Boick (1704) Mor. 10159 46
Arrol & Cook *v.* Montgomery, 1 Fac. 424; (1826) 4 S. 499 123
Arundell *v.* Bell (1883) 52 L.J.Ch. 537; 49 L.T. 345 424
Aspell *v.* Seymour [1929] W.N. 152 203
Atkin *v.* Rose [1923] 1 Ch. 522; 92 L.J.Ch. 209 141
Att.-Gen. *v.* Boden [1912] 1 K.B. 539; 81 L.J.K.B. 704 529
—— *v.* Burges (1726) Bunb. 223 313

xv

Att.-Gen. v. Hubbuck (1884) 13 Q.B.D. 275; 53 L.J.Q.B. 146   390
—— v. Weeks (1726) Bunb. 223   313
Att.-Gen. for Ceylon v. Silva (A.D.) [1953] A.C. 461; [1953] 2 W.L.R.
        1185; [1953] 1 Lloyd's Rep. 563   253
Atwood v. Maude (1868) L.R. 3 Ch. 369; 16 W.R. 665   469
Ault v. Goodrich (1828) 4 Russ. 430; 28 R.R. 151   518
Austen v. Boys (1857) 24 Beav. 598; 2 De G. & J. 626; 119 R.R. 264   433
Australia & New Zealand Bank v. Ateliers de Constructions Electriques
        de Charleroi [1967] 1 A.C. 86; [1966] 2 W.L.R. 1216; [1966] 2
        Lloyd's Rep. 463   209
Australian Auxiliary Steam Clipper Co. v. Mounsey (1858) 4 Kay & J.
        733; 27 L.J.Ch. 729   184
Ayton v. Dundee Banking Co. (1844) 6 D. 1409; 16 Sc.Jur. 593 ... 282, 293, 508

BACKHOUSE v. Charlton (1878) 8 Ch.D. 444; 26 W.R. 504   212
Badeley v. Consolidated Bank (1886) 34 Ch.D. 536; (1888) 38 Ch.D. 238 ...   65,
                                                                                          77, 80, 81, 94
Bagel v. Miller [1903] 2 K.B. 212; 72 L.J.K.B. 495   512
Bagshaw v. Parker (1847) 10 Beav. 532; 76 R.R. 198 .... 460, 478
Bailey v. Ford (1843) 13 Sim. 495; 60 R.R. 383   472
Baird v. Lees, 1924 S.C. 83; 1923 S.L.T. 749 .... 474, 475, 522
—— v. Planque (1858) 1 F. & F. 344   132
Baker's Case (1870) L.R. 7 Ch. 115; 41 L.J.Ch. 275   37
Balfour v. Sime (1811) 5 Pat.App. 525   391
Ballantyne v. Evans (1886) 13 R. 652; 23 S.L.R. 447   39
Bank of Australasia v. Breillat (1847) 6 Moore P.C. 152; 12 Jur. 189   212,
                                                                                          229, 245
Bank of England v. Vagliano [1891] A.C. 107; 60 L.J.Q.B. 145   146
Banks v. Gibson (1865) 34 Beav. 566; 34 L.J.Ch. 591   427
Bannatyne v. McIver [1906] 1 K.B. 103; 75 L.J.K.B. 120   257
Barber, Ex p. (1870) L.R. 5 Ch.App. 687; 23 L.T. 230 .... 529, 538
Barfoot v. Goodall (1811) 3 Camp. 147; 3 R.R. 673   300
Baring v. Dix (1786) 1 Cox 213; 1 R.R. 23 .... 472, 474
Barklie v. Scott, 1 Huds. & Br. 83 .... 25, 27, 81
Barnard, Re [1932] 1 Ch. 269; 101 L.J.Ch. 43   597
Barnes v. Youngs [1898] 1 Ch. 414; 67 L.J.Ch. 263 .... 193, 481, 487, 490
Barr v. Lions, 1956 S.C. 59; 1956 S.L.T. 250   428
—— v. Speirs, May 18, 1802, unreptd.; Bell, Com. II, 523   472
Barron v. Mitchell (1881) 8 R. 933; 18 S.L.R. 668   43
Barrow, Ex p. (1815) 2 Rose 255   204
Barton v. Hanson (1809) 2 Taunt. 49; (1809) 2 Camp. 97; 11 R.R. 524;
        Ross, Commercial Cases III, 573   618
—— v. Reed [1932] 1 Ch. 362; 101 L.J.Ch. 219 .... 141, 142
Barwick v. English Joint Stock Bank (1867) L.R. 2 Ex. 259; 36 L.J.Ex.
        147   318
Batchelor v. Dundee Commercial Socy. (1831) 9 S. 549   210
Batchelor's Trs. v. Honeyman (1892) 19 R. 903; 29 S.L.R. 780   286
Battersby v. Smyth (1818) 3 Madd. 110   381
Baumwoll, Manufaktur von Carl Scheibler v. Furness [1893] A.C. 8   334
Baxter v. Brown (1845) 7 M. & G. 198; 66 R.R. 706   392
—— v. Portsmouth (Earl) (1826) 5 B. & C. 170; 2 C. & P. 178 .... 39, 286
Baxter (William) & Son v. Aitchison & Co. (1841) 3 D. 391 .... 56, 158
Bayly v. Schofield (1813) 1 M. & S. 338   511
Beale v. Caddick & Hartland (1857) 2 H. & N. 326, 329; 115 R.R. 564 ...   272
—— v. Mouls (1847) 10 Q.B. 976; 74 R.R. 567   498
Bean v. Sinclair, 1930 J.C. 31; 1930 S.L.T. 423   316
Beard & Co., Re [1915] Hansell Bank Rep. 191 .... 91, 95
Beath v. Campbell Rivers & Co. (1826) 2 W. & S. 25; affg. (1824) 3 S. 353   625
Beavan v. McDonnell (1854) 9 Ex. 309; 96 R.R. 730; (1854) 10 Ex. 184;
        102 R.R. 518   39
Beckham v. Drake (1841) 9 M. & W. 79; (1843) 11 M. & W. 315; 60 R.R.
        678 .... 210, 212, 256
Bedford v. Deakin (1818) 2 B. & A. 210 .... 15G
Belfield v. Bourne [1894] 1 Ch. 521; (1894) 69 L.T. 786   481
Bell v. Marsh [1903] 1 Ch. 528; [1903] W.N. 30   131
—— v. Phyn (1802) 7 Ves. 453; 6 R.R. 148   390

Bellairs v. Ebsworth (1811) 3 Camp. 53; 13 R.R. 750 281
Bellamy & Metropolitan Bd. of Works, Re (1883) 24 Ch.D. 387; 52 L.J.Ch.
    870 347
Bennett v. Blain (1863) 15 C.B.(N.S.) 518; 33 L.J.C.P. 63 392
Bentley v. Bates (1840) 4 Y. & C. Ex. 182; 54 R.R. 465 .... 70, 446
—— v. Craven (1853) 18 Beav. 75; 104 R.R. 373 .... 166, 177
Beresford's Tr. v. Argyll Assessor (1884) 11 R. 818; 21 S.L.R. 544 609
Bergmann v. McMillan (1881) 17 Ch.D. 423; 44 L.T. 794 .... 203, 416
Berton v. Alliance etc. Investment Co. [1922] 1 K.B. 742; 91 L.J.K.B.
    748 .... 141, 142
Bertram v. McIntosh (1822) 1 S. 314 299
Bertram Gardner & Co. (1795) Bell, Com. II, 515 n. 1 567
Besch v. Frolich (1842) 1 Ph. 172; 65 R.R. 363 .... 460, 478
Betts, Re, Burrell v. Betts [1949] 1 All E.R. 568 .... 420, 432
Bevan v. Lewis (1827) 1 Sim. 376; 27 R.R. 205 256
—— v. Webb [1901] 2 Ch. 59; 70 L.J.Ch. 536 198
—— v. —— [1905] 1 Ch. 620; 74 L.J.Ch. 300 .... 170, 171, 381
Beveridge v. Beveridge (1872) 10 M.(H.L.) 1; (1871) 9 M. 886; (1869) 7 M.
    1034 .... 18, 19, 23, 194, 412, 444
Biggs v. Lawrence (1789) 3 T.R. 454; 1 R.R. 740 .... 105, 123
Bilborough v. Holmes (1876) 5 Ch.D. 255; 46 L.J.Ch. 446 150
Binney v. Mutrie (1886) 12 App.Cas. 160; 36 W.R. 129 529
Birch v. Cropper, re Bridgewater Navigation Co. (1889) 14 App.Cas. 525;
    59 L.J.Ch. 122 .... 530, 533
Birchtold, Re [1923] 1 Ch. 192; 92 L.J.Ch. 185 389
Bird v. Boulter (1833) 4 B. & Ad. 443 30
Bishop v. Jersey (Countess) (1854) 2 Drew 143; 100 R.R. 51 347
—— v. Tudor Estates [1952] C.L.Y. 2493; [1952] C.P.L. 807 ...... 153, 298, 503
Biss, Re, Biss v. Biss [1903] 2 Ch. 40; 72 L.J.Ch. 473 170
Blackburn Bldg. Socy. v. Cunliffe Brooks & Co. (1885) 29 Ch.D. 902;
    (1884) 9 App.Cas. 857; affg. (1882) 22 Ch.D. 61 257
Blacks v. Girdwood (1885) 13 R. 243; 23 S.L.R. 161 ...... 147, 148, 150, 506, 507
Blackwood v. Thorburn (1868) 7 M. 318; 41 Sc.Jur. 187 36
Blades v. Free (1829) 9 B. & C. 167; 32 R.R. 620 293
Blair v. Bromley (1847) 5 Hare 542; 71 R.R. 213 .... 332, 341, 368
—— v. Bryson, 10 Fac. 665; (1835) 13 S. 901 .... 210, 225, 226, 228, 245
—— v. Russell, 5 Fac. 76 (1828) 6 S. 836; (1829) 8 S. 72 .... 410, 538
Blair Iron Co. v. Alison (1855) 18 D. (H.L.) 49; 27 Sc.Jur. 614 210,
                                                            211, 221, 222
Blake v. Shaw (1860) Johns. 732; 123 R.R. 318 .... 420, 432
Blakeley's Excrs. (1852) 3 Mac. & G. 726; 87 R.R. 265 294
Blay v. Pollard & Morris [1930] 1 K.B. 628; 99 L.J.K.B. 421 552
Blew v. Wyatt (1832) 5 C. & P. 397; 38 R.R. 826 277
Blisset v. Daniel (1853) 10 Hare 493, 522, 536; 90 R.R. 454 .... 161, 180, 187,
                                                        188, 486, 490, 538
Bloomenthal v. Ford [1897] A.C. 156; 66 L.J.Ch. 253 249
Bloxham & Fourdrinier v. Pell & Brooke (1775) 2 Wm.Bl. 999; Ross,
    Commercial Cases III, 401–402 .... 78, 88
Blyth v. Fladgate [1891] 1 Ch. 337; 60 L.J.Ch. 66 .... 308, 366, 368
Boardman v. Phipps [1967] 2 A.C. 46; [1966] 3 W.L.R. 1009; [1966] 3 All
    E.R. 721 328
Bodenham v. Purchas (1818) 2 B. & A. 39; 20 R.R. 342; Ross, Commercial
    Cases III, 661 283
Bolden v. Fogo (1850) 12 D. 798; 22 Sc.Jur. 341 126
Bolland, Ex p. (1828) 1 Mont. & Ayr. 570 347
Bonbonus, Ex p. (1803) 8 Ves. 540; Ross, Commercial Cases III, 470 212,
                                                            227, 228
Bond v. Pittard (1838) 3 M. & W. 357; 49 R.R. 638 144
Bonnin v. Neame [1910] 1 Ch. 732; 79 L.J.Ch. 388 202
Boorne v. Wicker [1927] 1 Ch. 667; 96 L.J.Ch. 361 421
Booth v. Commercial Bank, May 16, 1823, F.C.; (1823) 2 S. 311 282
—— v. MacKinnon (1908) 15 S.L.T. 848 520
Borthwick v. Wright (1827) 5 S. 293 563
Boston Deep Sea Fishing & Ice Co. v. Ansell (1888) 39 Ch.D. 339; 59
    L.T. 345 367
Boswell v. Selkrig (1811) Hume 350 384
Boulton v. Jones (1857) 2 H. & N. 564; 115 R.R. 695 22
Boulton v. Mansfield (1787) 3 Pat.App. 70 .... 61, 78, 298

Bourdillon v. Roche (1858) 27 L.J.Ch. 681; 114 R.R. 572 347
Bourne, Re, Bourne v. Bourne [1906] 1 Ch. 113; [1906] 2 Ch. 427; 95 L.T.
  131 .... 517, 518
—— v. Freeth (1829) 9 B. & C. 632; 33 W.R. 275 142
Bowden Wire v. Bowden Brake Co. (No. 1) (1913) 30 R.P.C. 580; (1914)
  31 R.P.C. 385 429
Bower v. Swadlin (1738) 1 Atk. 294 277
Bowie v. Watson, MacNight & Co., 15 Fac. 1144; (1840) 2 D. 1061 281
Bowman v. Secular Society [1917] A.C. 406; 86 L.J.Ch. 568 .... 98, 99, 118
Bowsher v. Watkins (1830) 1 Russ. & M. 277; 32 R.R. 210 190
Boyd v. Craster (1864) 10 L.T. 480; 12 W.R. 787 157
Boydell v. Drummond (1808) 2 Camp. 157; 170 E.R. 1114 .... 299, 300
Bradbury v. Dickens (1859) 27 Beav. 53; 122 R.R. 311 421
Bradford Old Bank v. Sutcliffe [1918] 2 K.B. 833; 88 L.J.K.B. 85 ...... 281, 283
Braga v. Taylor, 1930 S.N. 158 572
Brash v. Steele (1845) 7 D. 539; 17 Sc.Jur. 267 304
Bray v. Fromont (1821) 6 Madd. 5; 22 R.R. 224 .... 19, 204, 412
Brember v. Rutherford (1901) 4 F. 62; (1901) 9 S.L.T. 6 135
Brett v. Beckwith (1856) 3 Jur.(N.S.) 31; 26 L.J.Ch. 130 105
Brickmann's Tr. v. Commercial Bank (1901) 38 S.L.R. 766; 9 S.L.T.
  145 579–581
Brinsden v. Williams [1894] 3 Ch. 185; 63 L.J.Ch. 713 366
British Homes Assce. Corpn. v. Paterson [1902] 2 Ch. 404; 71 L.J.Ch.
  872 .... 271, 346
British Legal Life Assce. Co. v. Pearl Life Assce Co. (1887) 14 R. 818;
  24 S.L.R. 589 303
British Linen Co. v. Alexander (1853) 15 D. 277; 25 Sc.Jur. 180 .... 258, 262,
                                                                         615, 617
British Milk Products Co.'s Application [1915] 2 Ch. 202; 32 R.P.C. 453 ... 431
British Mutual Bank Co. v. Charnwood Forest Ry. (1887) 18 Q.B.D. 714;
  56 L.J.Q.B. 449 318
British Nation Life Assce. Assoc., Re (1872) 8 Ch.D. 704; 48 L.J.Ch.
  118 .... 212, 213
Broadbent, Ex p. (1834) 1 Mont. & A. 635; 3 L.J.Bk. 95 446
Brooks v. Brooks (1901) 85 L.T. 453 442
Broome, Ex p., 1 Rose 69 143
Broughton v. Broughton (1855) 5 De G. M. & G. 160; 97 R.R. 284 325,
                                                                         326, 328
Brown v. Adam (Sir C.) (1848) 10 D. 744; 20 Sc.Jur. 253 195
—— v. De Tastet (1819) Jac. 284; 23 R.R. 59 .... 201, 413, 415, 423
—— v. Duncan (1829) 10 B. & C. 93; 39 R.R. 698, 707 104
—— v. Kilsyth Police Commrs. (1886) 13 R. 515; 23 S.L.R. 366 ... 184, 440, 441
—— v. Leonard (1816) 2 Chitty 120; 23 R.R. 744 .... 143, 146, 290, 291
—— v. Oakshot (1857) 24 Beav. 254; 116 R.R. 109 380
—— v. Sutherland (1875) 2 R. 615; 12 S.L.R. 385 197
—— v. Tapscott (1840) 6 M. & W. 119; 9 L.J.Ex. 139 88
—— v. Vidler (1797) 15 Ves. 223; 26 R.R. 95, 96 544
Brown or Drummond v. Macgregor, Feb. 26, 1813, F.C. 304
Brown's Tr. v. Brown (1897) 24 R. 962; 5 S.L.T. 54 29
Bruce (1577) Mor. 8979 .... 25, 28
—— v. Hamilton (1854) 17 D. 265; 27 Sc.Jur. 107 36
Bruce & Co. v. Beat, Dec. 10 1765, F.C.; Mor. 4056 183
Brunswick (Duke) v. Slowman (1849) 8 C.B. 317; 79 R.R. 521 308
Bryan v. Butters (1892) 19 R. 490; 29 S.L.R. 415 .... 210, 211, 229, 247
Brydges v. Branfill (1842) 12 Sim. 369; 56 R.R. 71 .... 346, 368
Bryon v. Metropolitan Saloon Omnibus Co. (1858) 3 De G. & J. 123; 121
  R.R. 35 184
Buchanan (1849) 11 D. 510; 21 Sc.Jur. 149 .... 556, 558
—— v. Glasgow University, 1909 S.C. 47; 16 S.L.T. 421 375
—— v. Lennox (1838) 16 S. 824 630
Bullock v. Chapman (1848) 2 De G. & Sm. 211 426
Burchell v. Wilde [1900] 1 Ch. 551; 69 L.J.Ch. 314 .... 152, 424, 427
Burden v. Burden (1813) 1 Ves. & B. 170; 12 R.R. 210 539
Burdon v. Barkus (1862) 4 De G. F. & J. 42; 3 Giff. 412 381
Burfield v. Rouch (1862) 31 Beav. 241 432
Burgess v. Florence Nightingale Hospital for Gentlewomen [1955] 1 Q.B.
  349; [1955] 2 W.L.R. 533; [1955] 1 All E.R. 511 44
Burland v. Nash (1861) 2 F. & F. 687 273
Burmester v. Norris (1851) 6 Ex. 796; 21 L.J.Ex. 43 .... 212, 256, 395

Burnard v. Aaron & Sharpley (1862) 31 L.J.C.P. 334; 9 Jur.(N.S.) 470 334
Burnell v. Hunt (1841) 62 R.R. 850; 5 Jur. 650 .... 7, 12
Burrows v. Rhodes [1899] 1 Q.B. 816; 68 L.J.Q.B. 545 125
Burton v. Issitt (1821) 5 B. & A. 267 499
—— v. Wookey (1822) 6 Madd. 367; 23 R.R. 249 170
Butchart v. Dresser (1853) 4 De G. M. & G. 542; 10 Hare 453; 102 R.R.
    269 .... 186, 512, 517, 518
Butler v. Butler (1885) 16 Q.B.D. 374; 55 L.J.Q.B. 55 44
Byrne v. Reid [1902] 2 Ch. 735; 71 L.J.Ch. 830 18

CAERPHILLY COLLIERY CO., Re, Pearson's Case (1877) 5 Ch.D. 336; 46
    L.J.Ch. 339 168
Cairncross v. Lorimer (1860) 3 Macq. 827; 22 D.(H.L.) 15; (1860) 3 L.T. 130 629
Cairns v. Walker, 1914 S.C. 51; 1913, 2 S.L.T. 379 101
Calder v. Downie, Apr. 14, 1815, F.C.; affg. Dec. 11, 1811, F.C. ... 25, 26, 34, 81
—— v. Stevens (1871) 9 M. 1074; 43 Sc.Jur. 543 621
Caldicott v. Griffiths (1853) 8 Ex. 898; 91 R.R. 824 5
Camden v. Anderson (1794) 5 T.R. 709 381
Cameron v. McMurray (1855) 17 D. 1142; 27 Sc.Jur. 597 198
—— v. Young (1871) 9 M. 786; 43 Sc.Jur. 437 .... 210, 211, 609, 614
Campbell (1830) 8 S. 625 556
—— v. Calder Iron Co. (1805) Bell, Com. I, 78, n. 3 496
—— v. Campbell (1893) 6 Rep. (ed. Mews) 137 480
—— v. Cruickshank (1845) 7 D. 548; 17 Sc.Jur. 264 .... 150, 276
—— v. McLintock (1803) Hume 755 298
—— v. Mullett (1819) 2 Swanst. 551; 19 R.R. 127 .... 67, 381
—— v. Scotland, Nov. 28, 1778, F.C.; (1778) Mor. 9530 100
—— v. Turner, 20 Fac. 508; (1822) 1 S. 266 31
Campbell's Trs. v. Thomson (1831) 5 W. & S. 16; revg. (1829) 7 S. 650;
    Ross, Commercial Cases III, 383 .... 399, 400, 402
Canadian Pacific Ry. v. Lockhart [1942] A.C. 591; 111 L.J.P.C. 113 308
Candilis (C. G.) & Sons v. Victor (Harold) & Co. (1916) 33 T.L.R. 20;
    [1916] W.N. 424 50
Candler v. Candler (1821) Jac. 225; 23 R.R. 34 109
Carabine v. Carabine, 1949 S.C. 521; 1949 S.L.T. 429 .... 520, 521, 526, 527
Cargill v. Dundee & Perth Ry. Co. (1848) 11 D. 216; 21 Sc.Jur. 51 304
—— v. Muir (1837) 15 S. 408 65
Cargo (The) ex Sultan (1859) Sw. 504 216
Carlyle & Co.'s Creditors' Tr. v. Dunlop's Creditors' Tr. (1777) 2 Pat.App.
    437; affg. (1776) Mor. 14610 578
Carlyon-Britton v. Lumb (1922) 38 T.L.R. 298 166
Carmichael v. Evans [1904] 1 Ch. 486; 73 L.J.Ch. 329 .... 162, 182, 193,
                                                                      465, 489, 490
Carr v. L. & N. W. Ry. (1875) L.R. 10 C.P. 307; 44 L.J.C.P. 109 131
Carrick v. Edinburgh & Glasgow Property Investment Co. (1902) 10
    S.L.T. 105 43
Carron v. Cowan & Co., Nov. 28, 1809, F.C. 46
Carter v. Horne (1728) 1 Eq.Cas.Abr. 17 167
—— v. Palmer (1841) 8 C. & F. 657; 1 Ir.Eq.R. 289 173
—— v. Whalley (1830) 1 B. & Ad. 11, 14; 35 R.R. 199; Ross, Commercial
    Cases III, 635 .... 145, 295, 504
Cassels v. Stewart (1879) 6 R. 936; (1881) 8 R. (H.L.) 1; (1881) 6 App.Cas.
    64 .... 167, 168, 172, 180, 181, 192,
                                          201, 203, 204, 397, 414, 416–418, 479, 510
Catchpole v. Ambergate Ry. (1852) 1 E. & B. 111; 93 R.R. 39 493
Catt v. Howard (1820) 3 Stark. 3; 23 R.R. 751 217
Catto, Thomson & Co. v. Thomson & Son (1867) 6 M. 54; 40 Sc.Jur. 29 ... 342
Cavander v. Bulteel (1873) L.R. 9 Ch. 79; 43 L.J.Ch. 370 .... 203, 408,
                                                                      409, 416, 525
Cavendish-Bentinck v. Fenn (1887) 12 App.Cas. 652; 57 L.J.Ch. 552 177
Central Bank of London, Ex p. [1892] 2 Q.B. 633; 67 L.T. 401 .... 146, 292
Central Ry. of Venezuela v. Kisch (1867) L.R. 2 H.L. 99; 36 L.J.Ch. 849 ... 164
Chandler v. Dorsett (1679) Rep. temp. Finch 431 552
Chapple v. Cadell (1822) Jacob. 537; 23 R.R. 138 188
Charlton & Bagshaw v. Highet, 1923 S.L.T. 493 .... 82, 87, 91, 95
Chatto & Co. v. Piper & Co. (1827) 4 Murray 354 56

Cheap v. Aiton (1772) 2 Pat.App. 283; revg. (1769) Mor. 14573   294
——— v. Cramond (1821) 4 B. & A. 663; Ross, *Commercial Cases III*, 435   79
Cheeseman v. Price (1865) 35 Beav. 142   490
Cheetham v. Ward (1797) 1 Bos. & P. 630; 4 R.R. 741   277
Chippendale, *Ex p.* (The German Mining Co.'s Case) (1853) 4 De
    G. M. & G. 19; 102 R.R. 7 .... 216, 257
Christie v. Royal Bank of Scotland (1839) 1 D. 745; (1841) 2 Rob.App.
    118; Ross, *Commercial Cases III*, 668 .... 144, 283, 293, 508
Chuck, *Ex p., re* Starkey & Whiteside (1832) 8 Bing. 469; 34 R.R. 762 ...   85
Churton v. Douglas (1859) Johns. 174; 123 R.R. 56 .... 421, 425
Ciceri v. Hunter (1904) 12 S.L.T. 293   210
Citizens Life Assce. Co. v. Brown [1904] A.C. 423; 90 L.T. 739   312
City & Suburban Dairies v. Mackenna; Scottish Farmers' Dairy Co. v.
    Mackenna, 1918 J.C. 105; 1918, 2 S.L.T. 155   316
Clark v. Jamieson, 1909 S.C. 132; 16 S.L.T. 450 .... 76, 334, 608
——— v. Leach (1863) 32 Beav. 14; 1 De G.J. & Sm. 409; 32 L.J.Ch. 290 ... 438,
                                                                             492
Clarke v. Bickers (1845) 14 Sim. 639; 65 R.R. 657   352
——— v. Hart (1858) 6 H.L.C. 633; 108 R.R. 231   486
——— v. Shepherd (1821) 1 S. 179; (1823) 2 S. 255 .... 227, 228, 245
Clayton v. Clayton, 1937 S.C. 619; 1937 S.L.T. 318 .... 108. 609, 622, 623
Cleather v. Twisden (1884) 28 Ch.D. 340; 54 L.J.Ch. 408 .... 347, 350
Clegg v. Edmondson (1857) 8 De G. M. & G. 787; 114 R.R. 336 .... 170, 171
——— v. Fishwick (1849) 1 Mac. & G. 294; 84 R.R. 61 .... 170, 171
Cleghorn (1901) 8 S.L.T. 409 .... 461, 522
Clements v. Hall (1858) 2 De G. & J. 173; 119 R.R. 74   170
——— v. Macaulay (1866) 4 M. 583; 38 Sc.Jur. 277 .... 608, 611
——— v. Norris (1878) 8 Ch.D. 129; 47 L.J.Ch. 546 .... 171, 186, 210, 232
Clifford v. Timms [1908] A.C. 12; affg. 77 L.J.Ch. 91 .... 456, 489
Clinton (Lord) *Petr.* (1875) 3 R. 62; 13 S.L.R. 31   29
Clippens Shale Oil Co. v. Scott (1876) 3 R. 651; 13 S.L.R. 429   34
Clough v. L.N.W. Ry. (1871) L.R. 7 Ex. 34; 41 L.J.Ex. 17   453
Clough, *Re*, Bradford Commercial Banking Co. v. Cure (1885) 31 Ch.D.
    324; 55 L.J.Ch. 77   517
Clowes, *Ex p.* (1789) 2 Bro.C.C. 595   561
Clydesdale Bank v. Paul (1877) 4 R. 626; 14 S.L.R. 403 ...... 258, 331, 371, 374
Coasters, *Re* [1911] 1 Ch. 86; 80 L.J.Ch. 89   217
Coats (J. & P.) v. Brown, 1909 S.C.(J.) 29; 1909, 1 S.L.T. 432   124
Cochrane v. Black (1857) 19 D. 1019; affg. (1855) 17 D. 321 ... 359, 541, 544, 545
Cockle v. Whiting (1829) Taml. 55; 32 R.R. 135   200
Cocks v. Nash (1832) 9 Bing. 341; 35 R.R. 547   277
Cofton v. Horner (1818) 5 Price 537   194
Cole v. Handasyde & Co., 1910 S.C. 68; 1909, 2 S.L.T. 358   22
Collen v. Gardner (1856) 21 Beav. 540   209
——— v. Wright (1857) 8 E. & B. 647; 110 R.R. 602, 611 .... 238, 239
Collingwood v. Berkeley (1863) 15 C.B.(N.S.) 145; 8 L.T. 763 .... 139, 143
Collins v. Blantern (1767) 2 Wils. 341, 347   124
——— v. North British Bank (1852) 1 Macq. 369; affg. (1851) 13 D. 349 ...   195
——— v. Young (1853) 1 Macq. 385 .... 521, 523
Collinson v. Lister (1855) 7 De G. M. & G. 634; 109 R.R. 267 .... 219, 233
Commercial Bank of Scotland v. Tod's Tr. (1895) 33 S.L.R. 161   567
Commercial Banking Co. of Sydney v. Mann [1961] A.C. 1; [1960] 3
    W.L.R. 726; [1960] 3 All E.R. 482   231
Commr. of Stamp Duties v. Salting [1907] A.C. 449; 76 L.J.P.C. 87   389
Conquest (1875) 1 Ch.D. 334; 45 L.J.Ch. 336   150
Const v. Harris (1824) Turn. & R. 496; 24 R.R. 108 ...... 166, 183, 185, 186, 187
Cook, *Ex p.* (1728) 2 P.Wms. 500; Mos. 80   566
——— v. Catchpole (1864) 10 Jur.(N.S.) 1068; 34 L.J.Ch. 60   524
——— v. Collingridge (1823) Jac. 607; 23 R.R. 155, 767 .... 190, 191
Cook (J. & H.) v. Alban Expanded Metal & Engineering Co., 1969 S.L.T.
    347   115
Cooke's Circus Bldgs. Co. v. Welding (1894) 21 R. 339; 1 S.L.T. 432   210,
                                                                        232, 233, 609
Cookson v. Cookson (1837) 8 Sim. 529 .... 390, 438
Coomer v. Bromley (1852) 5 De G. & Sm. 532; 90 R.R. 131   347
Coope v. Eyre (1788) 1 H.Bl. 37; 2 R.R. 706; Ross, *Commercial Cases III*,
    407 .... 66, 68
Cooper v. Cooper's Trs. (1885) 12 R. 473; 22 S.L.R. 314   29

Cooper v. Watson (1784) 3 Dougl. 413 422
Cooper & Sons, Re [1937] 1 Ch. 392; [1937] 2 All E.R. 466 .... 63, 475
Copland v. Toulmin (1840) 7 Cl. & F. 349; 51 R.R. 414 .... 401, 402
Coppock v. Bower (1838) 4 M. & W. 361 100
Cork & Bandon Ry. Co. v. Cazenove (1847) 10 Q.B. 935; 74 R.R. 553 ... 37
Cork & Youghal Ry., Re (1866) L.R. 4 Ch. 748; 39 L.J.Ch. 277 257
Cornelius v. Phillips [1918] A.C. 199; 87 L.J.K.B. 246 104
Cornish v. Abington (1859) 4 H. & N. 549; 28 L.J.Ex. 262 131
Corpe v. Overton (1833) 10 Bing. 253; 83 R.R. 422 35
Corse & Anr., Petrs., Dec. 10, 1802, F.C. 200, 391
Cory Bros. & Co. v. Owners of the " Mecca " [1897] A.C. 286; 66 L.J.P.C.
    86 .... 286, 372
Court v. Berlin [1897] 2 Q.B. 396; 66 L.J.Q.B. 714 .... 212, 296
Couston v. Miller (1862) 24 D. 607; 34 Sc.Jur. 302 41
Coventry v. Barclay (1863) 3 De G. & Sm. 320; 9 L.T. 406 .... 529, 537–539
Cox v. Coulson [1916] 2 K.B. 177; 85 L.J.K.B. 1081 75
—— v. Hickman (1860) 8 H.L.C. 268; 9 C.B.(N.S.) 47 .... 4, 61, 65,
                                                        78, 81–83, 130, 214
—— v. Willoughby (1880) 13 Ch.D. 863; 49 L.J.Ch. 237 438
Craig v. Grant (1732) Mor. 8955 ....30, 31
Cran v. Dodson (1893) 1 S.L.T. 354 257
Cranleigh Precision Engineering v. Bryant [1965] 1 W.L.R. 1293; [1964] 3
    All E.R. 289 173
Crawford v. Hamilton (1818) 3 Madd. 251 .... 19, 412, 445
Crawshay v. Collins (1808) 15 Ves. 218; 10 R.R. 61; Ross, Commercial
    Cases III. 622 .... 170, 423, 491, 544
—— v. —— (1820) 1 J. & W. 267; 21 R.R. 168 543
—— v. —— (1826) 2 Russ. 325; 26 R.R. 83 512
—— v. Maule (1818) 1 Swanst. 495; 18 R.R. 126 .... 19, 69, 380, 412, 444
Croft v. Pyke (1733) 3 P.Wms. 180 .... 407, 408, 525
Crooks v. Tawse, Jan. 29, 1779, F.C.; (1779) Mor. 14596 624
Crosbie v. Guion (1857) 23 Beav. 518; 113 R.R. 245 445
Cross v. Williams (1862) 7 H. & N. 675; 31 L.J.Ex. 145 5
Cruickshank v. McVicar (1844) 8 Beav. 106; 68 R.R. 29 549
—— v. Sutherland (1922) 92 L.J.Ch. 136; 128 L.T. 449 .... 433, 529
Crum & Co. v. McLean (1858) 20 D. 751; 30 Sc.Jur. 403 .... 157, 237,
                                                        244, 246, 247
Cruttwell v. Lye (1810) 17 Ves. 335; 11 R.R. 98 421
Culcreugh Cotton Co. v. Mathie (1822) 2 S. 47 221–223
Cullen v. Macfarlane (1842) 4 D. 1522; 14 Sc.Jur. 587 .... 566, 571
Curl Bros. v. Webster [1904] 1 Ch. 685; 73 L.J.Ch. 540 421
Curtis v. Perry (1802) 6 Ves. 739; 6 R.R. 28 381

DADSWELL v. Jacobs (1887) 34 Ch.D. 278, 286; 56 L.J.Ch. 233 198
Daimler Co. v. Continental Tyre Co. [1916] 2 A.C. 307; 85 L.J.K.B. 1333;
    [1915] 1 K.B. 893 .... 47, 453
Dale v. Hamilton (1846) 5 Hare 369; 71 R.R. 127 217
Dalgleish v. Sorley (1791) Mor. 14595; Hume 746 .... 290, 298
Dalrymple v. McGill (1804) Hume 387 304
Dance v. Girdler (1804) 1 Bos. & P.N.R. 34; 8 R.R. 748 283
Daniel v. Rogers [1918] 2 K.B. 228; 87 L.J.K.B. 1149 114
Dann v. Curzon (1910) 27 T.L.R. 163 101
D'Arcy v. Adamson (1913) 29 T.L.R. 367; 57 S.J. 391 488
David v. Ellice (1826) 5 B. & C. 196; 29 R.R. 216 277
David & Mathews, Re [1899] 1 Ch. 378; 68 L.J.Ch. 185 .... 421, 432, 524
Davidson v. Robertson (1815) 3 Dow 218 3
Davidsons v. Ranken (1733) Mor. 7061 276
Davie v. Buchanan (1880) 8 R. 319; 18 S.L.R. 217 .... 381, 609, 632
Davies v. Davies (1837) 2 Keen 534; 1 Jur. 446 190
—— v. Harvey (1874) L.R. 9, Q.B. 433; 43 L.J.M.C. 121 317
—— v. Hodgson (1858) 25 Beav. 177; 119 R.R. 379 .... 420, 424
—— v. Games (1879) L.R. 12 Ch.D. 813; 28 W.R. 16 380
—— v. Makuna (1885) 29 Ch.D. 596; 54 L.J.Ch. 1148 110
Davis v. Davis [1894] 1 Ch. 393; 63 L.J.Ch. 219 .... 66, 80, 88
—— v. Foreman [1894] 3 Ch. 655; 43 W.R. 168 .... 179, 194
Davis & Collett, Re [1935] Ch. 693; 153 L.T. 329 .... 63, 475
Daw v. Herring [1892] 1 Ch. 284; 61 L.J.Ch. 5 441

Dawson v. Beeson (1882) 22 Ch.D. 504; 48 L.T. 407 .... 420, 421
—— v. Counsell [1938] 3 All E.R. 5; 159 L.T. 176 3
Dean v. McDowell (1878) 8 Ch.D. 345; 47 L.J.Ch. 537 ...... 161, 169, 179, 194
De Berkom v. Smith & Lewis (1793) 1 Esp. 29 .... 129, 130
Debtor, A, Re (No. 5 of 1919) (1919) 89 L.J.K.B. 40; [1919] W.N. 293 ... 113
Debtor, A, Re [1927] 1 Ch. 97; 96 L.J.Ch. 28 113
De Bussche v. Alt (1878) 8 Ch.D. 286, 317; 47 L.J.Ch. 381 166
Dennistoun v. Mudie (1850) 12 D. 613; 22 Sc.Jur. 195 35
Dennistown McNayr & Co. v. Macfarlane, Feb. 16, 1808, F.C.; (1808)
    Mor.App. 1 "Tack" No. 15 .... 387, 496
De Ribeyre v. Barclay (1857) 23 Beav. 107, 125; 113 R.R. 54 342
Derry v. Peek (1889) 14 App.Cas. 337; 37 Ch.D. 541 319
Deutsche Bank, Re [1921] 2 Ch. 291; 90 L.J.Ch. 449 47
Devaynes v. Noble (1839) 1 Mer. 529; 34 R.R. 142; Ross, Commercial
    Cases III, 643 144
—— v. ——, Baring's Case (1816) 1 Mer. 611; 15 R.R. 169 .... 342, 368
—— v. ——, Brice's Case (1816) 1 Mer. 620; 15 R.R. 151 293
—— v. ——, Clayton's Case (1816) 1 Mer. 572; 15 R.R. 151; Ross, Com-
    mercial Cases III, 654 .... 272, 283–286, 372
—— v. ——, Houlton's Case (1816) 1 Mer. 616; 15 R.R. 151 293
—— v. ——, Johnes' Case (1816) 1 Mer. 619; 15 R.R. 151 293
—— v. ——, Sleech's Case (1816) 1 Mer. 539, 570; 15 R.R. 151; Ross
    Commercial Cases III, 643 368
Dewar v. Miller, June 14, 1766, F.C.; (1766) Mor. 14569 .... 210, 211
Dickie v. Mitchell (1874) 1 R. 1030; 11 S.L.R. 577 .... 520, 522, 523
Dickinson v. Valpy (1829) 10 B. & C. 128; 34 R.R. 348; Ross, Commercial
    Cases, III, 561 .... 129, 130, 135, 216, 245, 617
Dickson v. Dickson (1821) 1 S. 113 .... 68, 69, 610
—— v. —— (1823) 2 S. 462 185
—— v. National Bank of Scotland, 1917 S.C. (H.L.) 50; 1917, 1 S.L.T.
    318 .... 513, 517
Dixon v. Dixon (1832) 6 W. & S. 228; affg. (1831) 10 S. 178 .... 521, 522
Dodd v. Amalgamated Marine Workers' Union [1924] 1 Ch. 116; 93
    L.J.Ch. 65, 100 198
Doddington v. Hallet (1750) 1 Ves.Sen. 497 406
Dolman v. Orchard (1825) 2 Car. & P. 104 .... 146, 291, 499
Donaldson v. Williams (1833) 1 Cr. & M. 345; 38 R.R. 613 186
Dougall v. Lornie (1899) 1 F. 1187; (1900) 2 F. 1123; 8 S.L.T. 117 286
Douglas (James), Excrs. of, Ex p. [1930] 1 Ch. 342; 99 L.J.Ch. 97 150
Douglas v. Mackenzie, conjoined to Lord Gray etc. (1856) 19 D. 12 326
Douglas, Heron & Co. v. Gordon (1795) 3 Pat.App. 428 .... 494, 512
Downes v. McFie & Co. (1829) 8 S. 246 .... 220, 244
Downman v. Williams (1845) 7 Q.B. 103 239
Downs v. Collins (1848) 6 Hare 418; 77 R.R. 171 445
Dresser v. Norwood (1864) 17 C.B.(N.S.) 466; 34 L.J.C.P. 48 .... 219, 220, 235
Drummond v. Leith Assessor (1886) 13 R. 540; 23 S.L.R. 385 420
Dry v. Davey (1839) 10 A. & E. 30; 50 R.R. 314 281
Duché v. Duché (1920) 149 L.T. 300 198
Duff v. Corsar (1902) 10 S.L.T. 27 .... 182, 196
Dumbarton Steamboat Co. v. Macfarlane (1899) 1 F. 993; 7 S.L.T. 75 421
Dunbar v. Remington, Mar. 10, 1810, F.C. 300
Dundas v. Allan (1711) Mor. 9034 31
Dundonald (Earl) v. Masterman (1869) L.R. 7 Eq. 515; 38 L.J.Ch. 350 ... 344
Dunlop v. Speirs (1776) Mor. 14610; (1777) 2 Pat.App. 437 565
Dunlop's Trs. v. Clydesdale Bank (1891) 18 R. 751; (1893) 20 R. (H.L.) 59   370
Dunne v. English (1874) L.R. 18 Eq. 524 166
Duvergier v. Fellows (1828) 5 Bing. 248; 34 R.R. 578 106
Dyke v. Brewer (1849) 2 C. & K. 828 498

E.W.A., Re [1901] 2 K.B. 642; 70 L.J.K.B. 810 .... 277, 279
Eadie v. MacBean's Curator (1885) 12 R. 660; 22 S.L.R. 422 ... 40, 455–462, 522
Eaglesham & Co. v. Grant (1875) 2 R. 960; 12 S.L.R. 604 92
Ebbett's Case (1870) L.R. 5 Ch. 302; 39 L.J.Ch. 679 37
Eden v. Ridsdales Ry. Lamp & Lighting Co. (1889) 23 Q.B.D. 368; 58
    L.J.Q.B. 579; 61 L.T. 444 168
Edinburgh & District Tramways Co. v. Courtney, 1909 S.C. 99; (1908) 16
    S.L.T. 548 .... 327, 331
Ehrman v. Ehrman (1894) 72 L.T. 17 18

Elder v. Elder & Watson, 1952 S.C. 49; 1952 S.L.T. 112 ...... 475, 476, 478, 523
Electric Telegraph Co. of Ireland (1856) 22 Beav. 471; 111 R.R. 447 474
——, Re, Maxwell's Case (1857) 24 Beav. 321 25
Elliot v. Aitken (1869) 7 M. 894; 41 Sc.Jur. 512 161
Elliott v. Cassils (1907) 15 S.L.T. 190 .... 406, 523
Ellis v. Joseph Ellis & Co. [1905] 1 K.B. 324; 74 L.J.K.B. 229 12
—— v. Schmoeck (1829) 5 Bing. 521; 30 R.R. 725 143
Elton, Hammond & Co. v. Neilson, June 24, 1812, F.C. 281
Emly v. Lye (1812) 15 East 7; 13 R.R. 347; Ross, Commercial Cases III,
    552 .... 244, 256
England v. Curling (1844) 8 Beav. 129; 30 Beav. 376; 68 R.R. 39 168
—— v. Webb [1898] A.C. 758; 67 L.J.P.C. 120 6
English & Irish Church & University Assce. Socy. (1862) 1 Hem. & M.
    85; 7 L.T. 669 83
Essell v. Hayward (1860) 30 Beav. 130, 158; 29 L.J.Ch. 806 .... 464, 478
Essex v. Essex (1855) 20 Beav. 442; 109 R.R. 490 438
European Society Arbitration Acts, Re, ex p. British Nation Life Assce.
    Assoc. (1878) 8 Ch.D. 679 45
Evans v. Drummond (1801) 4 Esp. 89; Ross, Commercial Cases III, 638 ... 151,
                                                                            276, 504
Everet v. Williams, Lindley on Partnership, 13th ed., 130, n. 23; (1725) 9
    L.Q.R. 197; 2 Pothier Obligations, 3n. 97, 102
Ewing v. Osbaldiston (1837) 2 Myl. & C. 53; 45 R.R. 9 ...... 105, 123, 126, 411
Expanded Plugs, Re [1966] 1 W.L.R. 514; [1966] 1 All E.R. 877 475
Eyre, Ex p. (1842) 1 Ph. 227; 65 R.R. 375 347

FANFOLD'S APPLICATION, Re (1928) 45 R.P.C. 325; affg. 45 R.P.C. 199 431
Fairholm v. Marjoribanks (1725) Mor. 14558; Ross, Commercial Cases
    III, 697 .... 204, 412
Fairthorne v. Weston (1844) 3 Hare 387; 64 R.R. 342 .... 193, 490, 491
Falconer v. Thomson (1792) Mor. 16380 .... 24, 25, 29
Falkner, Bell & Co. v. Scottish Pacific Coast Mining Co. (1888) 15 R. 290;
    25 S.L.R. 226 .... 324, 325, 367, 369
Faraday v. Wightwick (1829) 1 R. & M. 45; (1829) Taml. 250 69
Farey v. Cooper [1927] 2 K.B. 384; 96 L.J.K.B. 1046 421
Farhall v. Farhall (1871) L.R. 7 Ch.App. 123; 41 L.J.Ch. 146 145
Farmers' Mart. v. Milne, 1914 S.C. (H.L.) 84; 1914, 2 S.L.T. 153 ... 100, 119, 124
Farquharson Bros. & Co. v. King & Co. [1902] A.C. 325; 71 L.J.K.B.
    667 .... 129, 131, 133
Farr v. Pearce (1818) 3 Madd. 74; 18 R.R. 196 420
Farrar v. Beswick (1836) 1 M. & Rob. 527; 42 R.R. 820 .... 401, 402
—— v. Deflinne (1844) 1 Car. & K. 580 .... 151, 502–504
Faulds v. Roxburgh (1867) 5 M. 373 539
Fawcett v. Whitehouse (1829) 1 Russ. & M. 132; 32 R.R. 163 .... 164, 166
Featherstonhaugh v. Fenwick (1810) 17 Ves. 298; 11 R.R. 77; Ross, Com-
    mercial Cases III, 615 .... 170, 423, 439, 441, 491
Fenston v. Johnstone (1940) 23 T.C. 29; 84 S.J. 305 .... 60, 85
Ferguson v. Mackenzie (1870) 8 S.L.R. 273 194
—— v. Wilson (1904) 6 F. 779; 12 S.L.T. 117 .... 41, 163, 548
Ferguson Bequest Fund (1879) 6 R. 486; 16 S.L.R. 300 100
Fergusson v. Graham's Trs. (1836) 14 S. 871 .... 56, 399, 403, 623, 630
Fife C.C. v. Minister of National Insurance, 1947 S.C. 629; 1948 S.L.T. 63   212
Fildes Bros., Re [1970] 1 W.L.R. 592; [1970] 1 All E.R. 923 .... 63, 475, 477
Findlater v. Duncan (1839) Macl. & R. 911; revg. 15 S. 1304; 16 S. 1150 ...   307
Findlay, Bannatyne & Co.'s Assignee v. Donaldson (1865) 2 M. (H.L.)
    86 .... 538, 539
Finlayson v. Braidbar Quarry Co. (1864) 2 M. 1297; 36 Sc.Jur. 647 237,
                                                                            238, 315
—— v. Fisher (1828) 6 S. 419 142
Fisher v. Taylor (1843) 2 Hare 218; 62 R.R. 84 .... 256, 258
Fisher & Sons, Re [1912] 2 K.B. 491; 81 L.J.K.B. 1246 .... 4, 66
Fitch v. Dewes [1921] 2 A.C. 168; 90 L.J.Ch. 436 120
Fleming v. Ballantyne (1842) 5 D. 305; 15 Sc.Jur. 115 221
—— v. Campbell (1845) 7 D. 935; 17 Sc.Jur. 480 183
—— v. Newton (1848) 6 Bell's App. 175; 20 Sc.Jur. 229 195
Flemyng v. Hector (1836) 2 M. & W. 172; 46 R.R. 553; Ross, Commercial
    Cases III, 585 5

Fletcher v. Grant (1878) 6 R. 59; 16 S.L.R. 15   161
Flowerdew v. Laing (1843) 5 D. 440; 15 Sc.Jur. 220   552
Forrest v. Campbell (1853) 16 D. 16; 26 Sc.Jur. 22 .... 35, 37
Forrester v. Robson's Trs. (1875) 2 R. 755; 12 S.L.R. 464 .... 380, 382,
                                                                       383, 385, 386
Forrester (P. & F.) v. Forbes (Sir W.) & Co. (1798) Bell, Com. II, 515 ...   567
Forster v. Mackreth (1867) L.R. 2 Ex. 163; 36 L.J.Ex. 94   212
——— v. Ridley (1864) 4 De G.J. & S. 452; 11 L.T. 200   539
Forsyth v. Hare & Co., 10 Fac. 35; (1834) 13 S. 42   221
Fort, Re, ex p. Schofield [1897] 2 Q.B. 495; 66 L.J.Q.B. 824 .... 87, 95
Fortune v. Young, 1918 S.C. 1; 1917, 2 S.L.T. 150 .... 159, 237, 238, 239
Foster v. Driscoll [1929] 1 K.B. 470; 98 L.J.K.B. 282 .... 102, 124
Foulds v. Thomson (1857) 19 D. 803; 29 Sc.Jur. 372   622
Fowler v. Paterson's Trs. (1896) 3 S.L.T. 305 .... 609, 619
Fox v. Clifton (1830) 6 Bing. 776; 31 R.R. 536   137
——— v. Hanbury (1776) Cowp. 445   295
Fraser, 1971 S.L.T. 146   559
——— v. Hair (1848) 10 D. 1402; 20 Sc.Jur. 509 .... 106, 454
——— v. Hill (1854) 16 D. 789; (1853) 1 Macq. 392; revg. (1852) 14 D.
   335 .... 56, 106, 411, 454
Freeman v. Cooke (1848) 2 Ex. 654; 76 R.R. 711   131
——— v. Fairlie (1812) 3 Mer. 43; 17 R.R. 7   198
——— v. Gainsford (1865) 18 C.B.(N.S.) 185; 34 L.J.C.P. 95   392
Freeman & Lockyer v. Buckhurst Park Properties (Mangal) [1964] 2 Q.B.
   480: [1964] 2 W.L.R. 618; [1964] 1 All E.R. 630 .... 131, 254
French v. Styring (1857) 2 C.B.(N.S.) 357; 109 R.R. 716   3
Fromont v. Coupland (1824) 2 Bing. 170; 27 R.R. 575   67
Fuller v. Duncan (1891) 7 T.L.R. 305   165

GAIR v. Brewster, 1916 S.C. (J.) 36; 1916, 1 S.L.T. 388   315
Gairdner v. Chalmers (1636) Mor. 9024   31
Galdie v. Gray (1774) Mor. 14598 .... 564, 565
Gallway (Lord) v. Mathew (1808) 1 Camp. 403; 10 R.R. 289; Ross,
   Commercial Cases III, 507 .... 249, 287
Garden, Haig-Scott & Wallace v. Prudential Approved Socy. for Women,
   1927 S.L.T. 393; 1927 S.N. 8   498
Gardiner v. Childs (1837) 8 Car. & P. 345; Ross, Commercial Cases III,
   546 .... 73, 261
Gardner v. Anderson (1862) 24 D. 315; 34 Sc.Jur. 159 .... 134, 138, 140
——— v. McCutcheon (1842) 4 Beav. 534; 55 R.R. 154   169
Garland v. Jacomb (1873) L.R. 8 Ex. 216; 28 L.T. 877 .... **252**
Garner v. Murray [1904] 1 Ch. 57; 73 L.J.Ch. 66 .... 531, 532, 536
Garwood's Trusts, Re, Garwood v. Paynter [1903] 1 Ch. 236   416
Gatherer (1893) 1 S.L.T. 401 .... 83, 85, 526, 527
Gatty v. Maclaine, 1921 S.C. (H.L.) 1; 1921, 1 S.L.T. 51 .... 131, 500
Geddes v. Wallace (1820) 2 Bligh 270; 21 R.R. 66   144
Gedge v. Royal Exchange Assce. Corpn. [1900] 2 Q.B. 214; 69 L.J.Q.B.
   506 .... 126, 621
Gen. Assembly of Gen. Baptist Churches v. Taylor (1841) 3 D. 1030   383
Gibbs v. British Linen Co. (1875) 4 R. 630   257
Gibson v. Glasgow Corpn., 1963 S.L.T. (Notes) 16   205
——— v. Lupton (1832) 9 Bing. 297; Ross, Commercial Cases III, 419   68
——— v. Stewart (1835) 14 S. 166; (1840) 1 Rob.App. 260 ...... 97, 123, 200, 454
Gieve, Re, ex p. Shaw [1899] W.N. 41; 80 L.T. 737   94
Gilfillan v. Henderson, 7 Fac. 385; (1832) 10 S. 523   110
Gillett v. Thornton (1875) L.R. 19 Eq. 599; 44 L.J.Ch. 398   438
Gilpin v. Enderby (1824) 5 B. & A. 954; 1 D. & R. 570   85
Glasgow Heritable Trust v. Inland Revenue, 1954 S.C. 266; 1954 S.L.T. 97   3, 67
Glasgow University v. Yuill's Tr. (1882) 9 R. 643; 19 S.L.R. 429   577
Glassington v. Thwaites (1833) 1 Sim. & Stu. 124; 24 R.R. 153 .... 168, 178
Glen v. Dundas (1822) 1 S. 234   100
Glyn v. Hood (1859) 1 Giff. 328; (1859) 1 De G.F. & J. 334; 114 R.R. 471   201,
                                                                             413
Goddard v. Mills (1929) The Times, Feb. 16, 1929   59
Goldfarb v. Bartlett & Kremer [1920] 1 K.B. 639; 89 L.J.K.B. 258 ...... 513, 517
Goldsoll v. Goldman [1915] 1 Ch. 292; 84 L.J.Ch. 228   120
Goode v. Harrison (1821) 5 B. & A. 147; 24 R.R. 307   37

Goodman v. Whitcomb (1820) 1 J. & W. 589; 21 R.R. 244 467
Goodwin v. Industrial & Gen. Trust (1890) 18 R. 193 .... 499, 513
Gopala Chetty v. Vijayaraghavachariar [1922] 1 A.C. 488; 91 L.J.P.C. 233 200
Gordon v. British & Foreign Metaline Co. (1886) 14 R. 75; 24 S.L.R. 60 ... 312,
                                                                      313, 358
—— v. Commissioners of Police [1910] 2 K.B. 1080 124
—— v. Holland (1913) 82 L.J.P.C. 81; 108 L.T. 385 167
—— v. Howden (1845) 4 Bell 254; revg. (1843) 5 D. 698 .... 106, 411, 454
—— v. —— (1849) 12 D. 253; 22 Sc.Jur. 52 551
—— v. McCubbin (1851) 13 D. 1154; 23 Sc.Jur. 441 514
Gorham v. Thompson (1791) Peake 60; 3 R.R. 650 301
Gough v. Davies (1817) 4 Price 200; 18 R.R. 697 277
Gouthwaite v. Duckworth (1811) 12 East 421; Ross, Commercial Cases III,
    541 .... 73, 261, 262, 614, 618
Gow v. Schulze (1877) 4 R. 928; 14 S.L.R. 581 523
Grace v. Smith (1775) 2 W.Bl. 998; Ross, Commercial Cases III, 400 61,
                                                                   66, 77–79, 88
Gracie v. Prentice (1904) 42 S.L.R. 9; (1904) 12 S.L.T. 15 436
Graham v. Henderson (1802) 4 Pat.App. 421 298
—— v. Hope (1792) Peake 208; 3 R.R. 671 .... 298, 299, 501
—— v. North British Bank (1849) 11 D. 1165; 21 Sc.Jur. 458 195
—— v. Paton (R. & S.) 1917 S.C. 203; 1917, 1 S.L.T. 66 .... 174, 175, 177
Grant, Petr., Dec. 21, 1811, F.C. 568
Gray v. Haig (1855) 20 Beav. 219; 109 R.R. 396 199
—— v. Pearson (1870) L.R. 5 C.P. 568; 23 L.T. 416 6
—— v. Smith (1889) 43 Ch.D. 208; 59 L.J.Ch. 145 427
Gray (Lord) & Ors. Petrs. (1856) 19 D. 1; 28 Sc.Jur. 522 .... 324, 325, 326
Great North of Scot. Ry. v. Urquhart (1884) 21 S.L.R. 377 174
Great Western Ry. v. Rushout (1852) 5 De G. & Sm. 310; 90 R.R. 87 187
Green v. Briggs (1848) 6 Hare 395; 77 R.R. 156 .... 67, 407
—— v. Hertzog [1954] 1 W.L.R. 1309; 98 S.J. 733 536
—— v. Howell [1910] 1 Ch. 495; 79 L.J.Ch. 549 .... 161, 189, 486, 488, 489
Greenaway v. Greenaway (1939) 84 S.J. 43 470
Greenberg v. Cooperstein [1926] Ch. 657; 95 L.J.Ch. 466 .... 6, 13
Greenshield's Case (1852) 5 De G. & Sm. 599; 21 L.J.Ch. 733 447
Gregory v. Patchett (1864) 33 Beav. 595; 11 L.T. 357 183
Grierson, Oldham & Co. v. Forbes, Maxwell & Co. (1895) 22 R. 812; 3
    S.L.T. 65 22
Griffith v. Owen [1907] 1 Ch. 195; 76 L.J.Ch. 92 171
Grimston v. Cunningham [1894] 1 Q.B. 125 179
Giswold v. Waddington (1818) 15 Johns. 57; (1819) 16 Johns. 483 (Amer.) 453, 454
Gunn v. Ballantyne & Co. (1870) 7 S.L.R. 289 74
—— v. Gardiner (1820) 2 Murray 194 304
Gurney v. Evans (1858) 27 L.J.Ex. 166; 117 R.R. 623 245
Guyot-Guenin v. Clyde Soap Co., 1916 S.C. 6; 1915, 2 S.L.T. 244 49

HACKSTON v. Hackston, 1956 S.L.T. (Notes) 38 .... 480, 481, 484
Hadley v. Baxendale (1854) 9 Ex. 341; 23 L.J.Ex. 179 240
Hall v. Barrows (1863) 4 De G.J. & S. 150; 33 L.J.Ch. 204 432
—— v. Hall (1855) 20 Beav. 139 432
Hall (George) & Son v. Platt [1954] T.R. 331; 47 R. & I.T. 713 67
Hallett's Estate, Re (1880) 13 Ch.D. 696; 49 L.J.Ch. 415 .... 371, 372
Halliday v. Watt & Co., 1950 S.L.T. (Sh.Ct.) 58; 66 Sh.Ct.Rep. 246 114
Halsey v. Lowenfeld [1916] 2 K.B. 707; 85 L.J.K.B. 1498 .... 49, 50
Hamer's Devisees (1852) 2 De G.M. & G. 366; 95 R.R. 141 294
Hamilton v. McLauchlan (1908) 16 S.L.T. 341 .... 126, 621
—— v. Main (1823) 2 S. 356 102
Hamlyn v. Houston (John) & Co. [1903] 1 K.B. 81; 72 L.J.K.B. 72 ... 157,
                                                               302, 312, 336
Handyside v. Campbell (1901) 17 T.L.R. 623 .... 471, 554
Hannan v. Henderson (1879) 7 R. 380; 17 S.L.R. 236 .... 449, 451, 511
Hargrove, Ex p. (1875) L.R. 10 Ch. 542; 44 L.J.Ch. 569 6
Harkness v. Graham (1833) 11 S. 760; (1836) 14 S. 1015 36
Harman v. Johnson (1853) 2 E. & B. 61; 95 R.R. 429 ...... 211, 343, 344, 347, 350
Harris, Ex p. (1813) 1 Rose 438; 13 R.R. 65 562
Harrison, Ex p. (1814) 2 Rose 76 67
—— v. Gardner (1817) 2 Madd. 198; 17 R.R. 207 422

Harrison v. Tennant (1856) 21 Beav. 482; 111 R.R. 175 .... 467, 470, 474
—— v. Willis Bros [1966] Ch. 619; 2 W.L.R. 183; 3 All E.R. 753 314
Harse v. Pearl Life Assce Co. [1904] 1 K.B. 558; 73 L.J.K.B. 373 123
Hart v. Alexander (1837) 2 M. & W. 484; 46 R.R. 666 .... 150, 300
—— v. Clarke (1858) 6 H.L.C. 633; affg. (1854) 6 De G.M. & G. 232; 105
    R.R. 171 491
Hartley v. Manton (1843) 5 Q.B. 247; 13 L.J.Q.B. 61 279
Harvey v. O'Dell (R.G.) [1958] 2 Q.B. 78; [1958] 2 W.L.R. 473; [1958] 1
    All E.R. 657 307
Haseldine v. Hosken [1933] 1 K.B. 822; 102 L.J.K.B. 441 125
Hawkins v. Duché [1921] 3 K.B. 226; 90 L.J.K.B. 913 114
Hawksley v. Outram (1892) 3 Ch. 359; 62 L.J.Ch. 215 .... 92, 93, 212, 213
Hawtayne v. Bourne (1841) 7 M. & W. 595; 56 R.R. 806 .... 212, 214–216,
                                                                   256, 395, 599
Hay v. Douglas, 1922 S.L.T. 365 .... 608, 619
—— v. Mair (Kay v. Pollock) Jan. 27, 1809, F.C.; Ross, *Commercial
    Cases III*, 639 .... 296, 505
Hay & Co. v. Torbet, 1908 S.C. 781; 15 S.L.T. 627 .... 283, 286, 372
Hay & Kyd v. Powrie (1886) 13 R. 777; 23 S.L.R. 567 276
Head v. Head, Re Head (No. 1) [1893] 3 Ch. 426; 63 L.J.Ch. 35 150
—— v. Head, Re Head (No. 2) [1894] 2 Ch. 236; 63 L.J.Ch. 549 149
Heap v. Dobson (1863) 15 C.B.(N.S.) 460 616
Heath v. Sansom (1831) 4 B. & Ad. 172, 175; 38 R.R. 237 .... 295, 479, 504
Heaton, Ex p. (1819) Buck. 386 .... 358, 361, 363
Heddel v. Duncan, June 5, 1810, F.C. 30, 31
Heddle's Exrx. v. Marwick & Hourston's Tr. (1888) 15 R. 698; 25 S.L.R.
    553 .... 263–265, 267–270, 273
Hedley v. Bainbridge (1842) 3 Q.B. 316; 61 R.R. 239 211
Heggie v. Heggie (1858) 21 D. 31; 31 Sc.Jur. 14 628
Helme v. Smith (1831) 7 Bing. 709; 33 R.R. 630 67
Helsby v. Mears (1826) 5 B. & C. 504; 29 R.R. 301 498
Henderson v. Mackay (1832) 11 S. 225 .... 101, 110
—— v. Stubbs (1894) 22 R. 51; 2 S.L.T. 288 .... 269, 270, 273
Hendry v. Turner (1886) 32 Ch.D. 355; 55 L.J.Ch. 562 508
Hennessy, Ex p. (1850) 2 Macn. & G. 201; affg. (1849) 3 De G. & S. 191   25
Heritable Securities Investment Assoc. v. Wingates (1891) 29 S.L.R. 904 ...   562
Hermann v. Charlesworth [1905] 2 K.B. 123; 74 L.J.K.B. 620 123
Hesketh v. Blanchard (1803) 4 East 143; Ross, *Commercial Cases III*,
    451 .... 88, 129, 130
Hewitt v. Bonvin [1940] 1 K.B. 188; 109 L.J.K.B. 223 308
Heyman v. Darwins [1942] A.C. 356; 111 L.J.K.B. 241 484
Hichens v. Congreve (1828) 1 Russ. & M. 150n.; 32 R.R. 173 164
Hilckes, Re [1917] 1 K.B. 48; 86 L.J.K.B. 204 48
Hildesheim, Re [1893] 2 Q.B. 357; 69 L.T. 550 95
Hill v. City of Glasgow Bank (1879) 7 R. 68; 17 S.L.R. 17 .... 29, 31
—— v. Clifford [1908] A.C. 12; affg. [1907] 2 Ch. 236 465
—— v. Fearis [1905] 1 Ch. 466; 74 L.J.Ch. 237 .... 420, 424
—— v. Lindsay (1846) 8 D. 472; 18 Sc.Jur. 218 414
—— v. Merricks (1813) Hume 397 311
—— v. Wyllie (1865) 3 M. 541; 37 Sc.Jur. 271 444
Hoare v. Dawes (1780) 1 Doug. 371; Ross, *Commercial Cases III*, 404 ...   68,
                                                                   79, 610
Hoby v. Roebuck (1816) 7 Taunt. 157; 17 R.R. 477 260
Hodges v. London Trams Omnibus Co. (1883) 12 Q.B.D. 105; 550 L.T. 262   426
Hoey v. MacEwan & Auld (1867) 5 M. 814; 39 Sc.Jur. 450 495
Hoggan v. Wardlaw (1735) 1 Pat.App. 148 100
Holderness v. Shackels (1828) 8 B. & C. 612; 32 R.R. 496 .... 406, 410
Hollis v. Burton [1892] 3 Ch. 226; 67 L.T. 146 217
Holme v. Hammond (1872) L.R. 7 Ex. 218; 41 L.J.Ex. 157 .... 4, 83, 244
Holmes Oil Co. v. Pumpherston Oil Co. (1891) 18 R. (H.L.) 52; 28 S.L.R.
    940 481
Holroyd v. Griffiths (1856) 3 Drew 428; 106 R.R. 389 409
Homfray v. Fothergill (1866) L.R. 1 Eq. 567; 14 L.T. 49 510
Hommel v. Hommel (1912) 29 R.P.C. 398; 56 S.J. 399 .... 421, 426
Hookham v. Pottage (1872) L.R. 8 Ch. 91; 27 L.T. 595 421
Horne v. Morrison (1877) 4 R. 977; 14 S.L.R. 584 383–386
Horsbrugh v. Ramsay & Co. (1885) 12 R. 1171; 22 S.L.R. 779 574–576
Hoskins v. Christie (1845) 8 D. 167; 18 Sc.Jur. 63 265
Houghton, Ex p. (1810) 17 Ves. 251; 11 R.R. 73 381

Houghton & Co. v. Nothard, Lowe & Wills [1928] A.C. 1; 97 L.J.K.B. 76   220
Houldsworth v. City of Glasgow Bank (1880) 7 R. (H.L.) 53; 17 S.L.R. 510   318
Howard v. Hudson (1853) 2 E. & B. 1; 22 L.J.Q.B. 341   131
—— v. Patent Ivory Co. (1888) 38 Ch.D. 156; 57 L.J.Ch. 878   263
Howarth v. Brearley (1887) 19 Q.B.D. 303; 56 L.J.Q.B. 543   110
Howbeach Coal Co. v. Teague (1860) 5 H. & N. 151; 120 R.R. 518   187
Hughes v. Sutherland (1881) 7 Q.B.D. 160; 50 L.J.Q.B. 567   381
Hughes & Co., Re [1911] 1 Ch. 342; 80 L.J.Ch. 262 ....   597, 604
Hume v. Bolland (1832) 1 Cr. & M. 130 ....   342, 347
Hunter (1728) Mor. 8964   29
Hunter, Ex p. (1741) 1 Atk. 223   562
Hunter v. Dowling [1895] 2 Ch. 223; 64 L.J.Ch. 713 ....   433, 529, 538
—— v. Evans, Foster & Langton (1830) 9 S. 159 ....   290, 298
—— v. Stevenson (1804) Hume 686   41
Huntington Copper Co. v. Henderson (1877) 4 R. 294; 14 S.L.R. 219   324

I.R.C. v. Falkirk Temperance Café Trust, 1927 S.C. 261; 1927 S.L.T. 87 ... 9, 11
—— v. Lebus's Trs. [1946] 1 All E.R. 476 ....   86, 419
Imperial Loan Co. v. Stone [1892] 1 Q.B. 599; 61 L.J.Q.B. 449 ....   39, 286
Imperial Mercantile Credit Assoc., Liquidators of v. Coleman & Knight
    (1871) L.R. 6 H.L. 189; 42 L.J.Ch. 644 ....   325, 328, 361, 367–369
Inglis v. Austine (1624) Mor. 14562 ....   165, 167
—— v. Smyth's Exrx., 1959 S.L.T. (Notes) 78   383
Inland Revenue v. Livingston, 1927 S.C. 251; 1927 S.L.T. 112   3
Irvine v. Irvine (1851) 13 D. 1367; 23 Sc.Jur. 635 ....   200, 391
Isaacson v. Wiseman (1806) Hume 714   101

JACAUD v. French (1810) 12 East 317; 11 R.R. 390 ....   219, 244
Jackson, Ex p. (1790) 1 Ves.Jun. 131; 1 R.R. 91 ....   263, 273
—— v. Jackson (1804) 9 Ves. 591   380
Jacobs v. Morris [1902] 1 Ch. 816; 71 L.J.Ch. 363   218
Jacomb v. Harwood (1751) 2 Ves.Sen. 265   150
James v. Baird, 1916 S.C.(H.L.) 158; revg. 1916 S.C. 510; 1916, 1 S.L.T. 138   493
James W. Elwell (The) [1921] P. 351; 90 L.J.P. 355   67
Jameson v. Watson (1852) 14 D. 1021; 24 Sc.Jur. 631   517
Janson v. Driefontein Mines [1902] A.C. 484; [1902] W.N. 157 ....   47, 48
Janvier v. Sweeney [1919] 2 K.B. 316; 88 L.J.K.B. 1231   312
Jardine v. Elliot (1803) Hume 684   41
—— v. Macfarlane (1828) 6 S. 564; Ross, Commercial Cases III, 575
                                                  157, 259, 609, 619
Jardine's Trs. v. Carron Co. (1864) 2 M. 1101; 36 Sc.Jur. 316 ....   321, 323
Jarvis, Re [1958] 1 W.L.R. 815; [1958] 2 All E.R. 336   171
Jebara v. Ottoman Bank [1927] 2 K.B. 254; 96 L.J.K.B. 581   214
Jefferys v. Smith (1820) 1 J. & W. 298; 21 R.R. 175   69
—— v. —— (1827) 3 Russ. 158; 27 R.R. 49 ....   417, 479, 510
Jeffreys v. Pinto [1929] 1 Ch. 401; 98 L.J.Ch. 337   112
Jenkins v. Blizard (1816) 1 Stark. 418; 18 R.R. 792 ....   299, 300
Jenkins' Deed of Partnership, Re [1948] 1 All E.R. 471 (sub nom. Jenkins
    v. Reid); [1948] W.N. 98   121
Jennings v. Baddeley (1856) 3 K. & J. 78; 112 R.R. 42   472
—— v. Hammond (1882) 9 Q.B.D. 225; 51 L.J.Q.B. 493   105
—— v. Jennings [1898] 1 Ch. 378; 67 L.J.Ch. 190 ....   421, 432
Johnston v. Clark (1854) 17 D. 228; 27 Sc.Jur. 79   40
—— v. Losh (1844) 6 D. 626 ....   536, 565
Johnston, Sharp & Co. v. Phillips (1822) 1 S.App. 244 ...... 227, 228, 245, 247,
                                                            252, 256
Johnstone v. Pedlar [1921] 2 A.C. 263; 90 L.J.P.C. 181   48
Jones v. Lloyd (1874) L.R. 18 Eq. 265; 43 L.J.Ch. 826 .... 439, 458, 478
—— v. Maund (1839) 3 Y. & C. Ex. 347; 51 R.R. 384   284
—— v. Noy (1833) 2 M. & K. 125; 39 R.R. 160 ....   40, 459, 460
—— v. Welch (1855) 1 K. & J. 765; 103 R.R. 339 ....   460, 461
——, Re ex p. Harper (1857) 1 De G. & J. 180   85
Jonge Klassina (The) (1804) 5 Ch.Rob. 296   48
Joplin v. Postlethwaite (1889) 61 L.T. 629 ....   480, 482
Jopp v. Johnston's Tr. (1904) 6 F. 1028; 12 S.L.T. 279 ....   370, 371
Joy v. Campbell (1804) 1 Sch. & Lef. 328; 9 R.R. 39   125

K/9 MEAT SUPPLIES (GUILDFORD), *Re* [1966] 1 W.L.R. 1112; [1966] 3
All E.R. 320 .... 63, 475
Karmali Abdullah Allarakhia *v.* Vora Karemji Jiwanji (1914) L.R. 42
Ind.App. 48 262
Kay *v.* Johnson (1864) 2 H. & N. 118 224
—— *v.* Johnston (1856) 21 Beav. 536; 111 R.R. 192 .... 66, 407
Kearney *v.* Whitehaven Colliery Co. [1893] 1 Q.B. 700; 62 L.J.M.C. 129
119, 621
Keating *v.* Marsh (1834) 1 Mont. & Ayr. 582, 592 .... 342, 347
Keen *v.* Mear [1920] 2 Ch. 574; 89 L.J.Ch. 513 319
Keighley, Maxsted & Co. *v.* Durant & Co. [1901] A.C. 240; 70 L.J.K.B.
662 271
Keith *v.* Keir, June 10, 1812, F.C. 311
—— *v.* Penn, 15 Fac. 662; (1840) 2 D. 633; Bell, *Com.* II 502 ..... 380, 387,
406, 410, 525, 565, 609, 612, 624, 630
Keith Spicer *v.* Mansell [1970] 1 W.L.R. 333; [1970] 1 All E.R. 462 54,
132, 259
Kelly *v.* Hutton (1868) L.R. 3 Ch. 703; 37 L.J.Ch. 917 ...... 201, 203, 413, 416
Kelner *v.* Baxter (1866) L.R. 2 C.P. 174 263
Kemp *v.* Allan, June 17, 1824, F.C.; (1824) 3 S. 153 .... 293, 299, 508
—— *v.* Glasgow Corpn., 1920 S.C. (H.L.) 73; 1920, 2 S.L.T. 6 101
Kendall *v.* Hamilton (1879) 4 App.Cas. 504; 48 L.J.C.P. 705 .... 506, 507
Kennedy, Dec. 22, 1814, F.C. 209, 227, 247, 252
—— *v.* Lee (1817) 3 Mer. 448; 17 R.R. 110 .... 421, 432
—— *v.* Weir (1665) Mor. 11658 .... 34, 35
Kent *v.* Jackson (1852) 14 Beav. 367; 95 R.R. 8 184
Ker *v.* McKechnie (1845) 7 D. 494; 17 Sc.Jur. 228 149
Kershaw *v.* Matthews (1826) 2 Russ. 62; 26 R.R. 13 445
Kilboy *v.* South Eastern Fire Area Joint Cttee., 1952 S.C. 280; 1952 S.L.T.
332 305
Kilgour *v.* Finlayson (1789) 1 H.Bl. 155 .... 499, 514
Kilpatrick *v.* Kilpatrick (1841) 4 D. 109; 14 Sc.Jur. 46 383
Kilshaw *v.* Jukes (1863) 3 B. & S. 847; 32 L.J.Q.B. 217 83
King *v.* Hamilton (1844) 6 D. 399; 16 Sc.Jur. 207 195
Kingsbridge Flour Mill Co. *v.* Plymouth Grinding Co. (1848) 2 Ex. 718;
76 R.R. 742, 748 256
Kingston, Miller & Co. *v.* Thomas Kingston & Co. [1912] 1 Ch. 575;
81 L.J.Ch. 417 419
Kinnell *v.* Peebles (1890) 17 R. 416; 27 S.L.R. 365 .... 56, 82
Kirchner & Co. *v.* Gruban [1909] 1 Ch. 413; 78 L.J.Ch. 117 .... 179, 194
Kirkintilloch Equitable Coop. Socy. *v.* Livingstone, 1972 S.L.T. 154 336
Kirkpatrick *v.* Sime (1811) 5 Pat.App. 525 200
Kirwan *v.* Kirwan (1836) 2 Cr. & M. 617; 39 R.R. 861 277
Kitchen *v.* Turnbull (1871) 20 W.R. 253 480
Knapman, *Re* (1881) 18 Ch.D. 300; 50 L.J.Ch. 629 203
Knight *v.* Marjoribanks (1848) 11 Beav. 322; 83 R.R. 166 .... 551, 552
Knowles *v.* Zoological Socy. of London [1959] 1 W.L.R. 823; [1959] 2
All E.R. 595 187
Knox *v.* Gye (1872) L.R. 5 H.L. 656; 42 L.J.Ch. 234 191
Kyle *v.* Allan (1832) 11 S. 87 37

LABOUCHERE *v.* Dawson (1872) L.R. 13 Eq. 322; 41 L.J.Ch. 427 421
—— *v.* Wharncliffe (Earl) (1879) 13 Ch.D. 346; 41 L.T. 638 488
Lacey *v.* Hill (1876) 4 Ch.D. 537; 35 L.T. 149 566
Lacy *v.* Wollcott (1823) 2 D. & R. 458; 1 L.J.(o.s.) K.B. 143 .... 295, 520
Laing *v.* Campbell (1865) 36 Beav. 3 539
Laing Bros. & Co.'s Tr. *v.* Low (1896) 23 R. 1105; 4 S.L.T. 109 ...... 65, 90, 91,
128, 570, 571
Laird *v.* Laird (1855) 17 D. 984; 27 Sc.Jur. 505 .... 170, 544
—— *v.* —— (1858) 20 D. 972; 30 Sc.Jur. 582 .... 372, 373
Laird (Wm.) & Co. *v.* Laird & Rutherford (1884) 12 R. 294; 22 S.L.R.
200 .... 217, 380–382, 384–386
Lake *v.* Argyll (Duke) (1844) 6 Q.B. 477 132
Lamb *v.* Evans [1893] 1 Ch. 218; 62 L.J.Ch. 404 .... 173, 174
Lancaster *v.* Allsup (1887) 57 L.T.(N.S.) 53; (1887) W.N. 134 445
Landale *v.* Goodall (1879) 16 S.L.R. 434 .... 193, 194
Lang *v.* Brown (1855) 2 Macq. 93 affg. 15 D. 38 481

Lang v. Brown (1859) 22 D. 113; 32 Sc.Jur. 64 .... 283, 286
Lang & Co. v. McLeod (1830) 8 S. 323 243
Langmead's Trusts, Re (1855) 20 Beav. 20; 7 De G.M. & G. 353; 109
    R.R. 161 .... 408, 409, 525
Lascelles v. Rathbun (1919) 35 T.L.R. 347; (1919) 63 S.J. 410 5
Lauder v. Wingate (1852) 14 D. 633; 24 Sc.Jur. 321 482
Law v Hodson (1809) 11 East 300; 10 R.R. 513 104
—— v. Law [1905] 1 Ch. 140; 74 L.J.Ch. 169 .... 189, 552
—— v. Liddell's Trs. (1862) 24 D. 577; 34 Sc.Jur. 291 538
Law Accident Insce. Socy. v. Boyd, 1942 S.C. 384; 1942 S.L.T. 207 162
Lawes v. Lawes (1878) 9 Ch.D. 98; 38 L.T. 709 530
Lawrence v. Bowle (1846) 2 Ph. 140; 78 R.R. 54 368
Lawrie v. Lawrie's Trs. (1892) 19 R. 675; 29 S.L.R. 525 .... 82, 85
Lawson v. Morgan (1815) 1 Price 303 194
Learmouth v. Leadbetter (1841) 3 D. 1192 195
Leathley v. Spyer (1870) L.R. 5 C.P. 595; 39 L.J.C.P. 299 282
Lee v. Sheard [1956] 1 Q.B. 192; [1955] 3 W.L.R. 951; [1955] 3 All E.R.
    777 205
Leeson v. Holt (1816) 1 Stark. 186; 18 R.R. 758 .... 299, 300
Leggott v. Barrett (1880) 15 Ch.D. 306; 28 W.R. 962 421
Leiper v. Cochran (1822) 1 S. 552 38
Leslie, Re, Leslie v. French (1883) 23 Ch.D. 552; 52 L.J.Ch. 762 407
Leslie v. Lumsden (1856) 18 D. 1046; 28 Sc.Jur. 149 195
Leslie's Reps. v. Lumsden (1851) 14 D. 213; 24 Sc.Jur. 91 194
Leverson v. Lane (1862) 13 C.B.(N.S.) 278; 32 L.J.C.P. 10 .... 245, 252
Levy v. Pyne (1842) Car. & M. 453 211
—— v. Walker (1879) 10 Ch.D. 436; 48 L.J.Ch. 273 .... 425, 427
Lewcock v. Bromley (1920) 37 T.L.R. 48; 65 S.J. 75 218
Lewis v. Haas, 1970 S.L.T.(Notes) 67 475
—— v. Reilly (1841) 1 Q.B. 349; 55 R.R. 262 .... 499, 515
Liardet v. Adams, 1 Mont.Part 112n. 467
Life Assoc. v. Foster (1873) 11 M. 351; 45 Sc.Jur. 240 161
Limpus v. London Gen. Omnibus Co. (1861) 1 H. & C. 526; 32 L.J.Ex. 34 . 311
Lindern Trawler Managers v. W. H. J. Trawlers (1949) 83 Ll.L.R. 131 213
Lindsay v. Barmcotte (1851) 13 D. 718; 23 Sc.Jur. 315 383
—— v. Inland Revenue, 1933 S.C. 33; 1933 S.L.T. 57 102
—— v. Trent (1683) Mor. 6281 39
Lingen v. Simpson (1824) 1 S. & S. 600; 24 R.R. 249 .... 200, 409
Lingood v. Eade (1747) 2 Atk. 505 .... 523, 524
Linwood v. Hathorn (1821) 1 Sh.App. 20; affg. May 14, 1817, F.C. 304
Lipton v. Powell [1921] 2 K.B. 51; 90 L.J.K.B. 366 621
Lister v. Marshall's Tr. 1927 S.N. 55 (O.H.) 190
—— v. Romford Ice & Cold Storage Co. [1957] A.C. 555; [1957] 2 W.L.R.
    158; [1957] 1 All E.R. 125 307
Lister & Co. v. Stubbs (1890) 45 Ch.D. 1; 59 L.J.Ch. 570 167
Little v. Poole (1829) 9 B. & C. 192 104
Liverpool Borough Bank v. Turner (1859) 2 De G.F. & J. 502; 30 L.J.Ch.
    379 381
Livingstone v. Allans (1900) 3 F. 233; 8 S.L.T. 287 .... 609, 611, 630, 634
Lloyd v. Ashby (1831) 2 C. & P. 138; 36 R.R. 454 259
—— v. Freshfield (1826) 2 C. & P. 325; 9 D. & Ry. 19 .... 238, 256
—— v. Grace, Smith & Co. [1912] A.C. 716; 81 L.J.K.B. 1140 318
Loch v. Blackwood (John) [1924] A.C. 783; 93 L.J.P.C. 257 ...... 474, 475, 476
Lock v. Lynam (1854) 4 Ir.Ch. 188 178
Lockhart v. Brown (1888) 15 R. 742; 25 S.L.R. 568 .... 257, 608, 616
—— v. Moodie (1877) 4 R. 859; 14 S.L.R. 548 609
Lodge v. Dicas (1820) 3 B. & A. 611; 22 R.R. 497 277
Logan v. Brown (1824) 3 S. 15 .... 3, 624
Logie v. Gordon (1725) Mor. 14580 184
Logy v. Durham (1697) Mor. 14566 .... 210, 608, 615
London Assoc. for the Protection of Trade v. Greenlands [1916] 2 A.C.
    15; 85 L.J.K.B. 698 6
London Assce. Co. v. Bold (1844) 6 Q.B. 514; 66 R.R. 477 282
L.C.C. v. Tobin [1959] 1 W.L.R. 354; [1959] 1 All E.R. 649 433
London County etc. Properties v. Berkeley Property etc. Co. [1936] 2 All
    E.R. 1039; 155 L.T. 190 .... 320, 321
London Financial Assoc. v. Kelk (1884) L.R. 26 Ch.D. 107; 53 L.J.Ch.
    1025 537
London India Rubber Co., Re (1868) L.R. 5 Eq. 519; 37 L.J.Ch. 235 530

L. & N.W. Ry. Co. *v*. McMichael (1850) 5 Ex. 114; 82 R.R. 898   37
London & Southern Counties Freehold Land Co., *Re* (1885) 31 Ch.D. 223;
     55 L.J.Ch. 224   187
Longworth's Excr.'s Case (1859) 1 De G.F. & J. 17; 29 L.J.Ch. 55   621
Lonsdale Hematite Iron Co. *v*. Barclay (1874) 1 R. 417; 11 S.L.R. 226 ...   192,
                                                                                   414, 417, 418
Lord *v*. Copper Miners Co. (1848) 2 Ph. 740; 18 L.J.Ch. 65   184
Loudon *v*. Elder's Curator, 1923 S.L.T. 226   38
Lovegrove *v*. Nelson (1834) 3 M. & K. 1; 41 R.R. 1 .... 18, 205, 415
Lovell *v*. Hicks (1837) 2 Y. & C.Ex. 472; 6 L.J.Ex.Eq. 85; 47 R.R. 335 ...   255,
                                                                                        332, 341
Low *v*. Lizars (1838) 16 S. 1092 .... 228, 247
Ludgater *v*. Love (1881) 44 L.T. 694 .... 320, 321
Lumsden *v*. Gordon (1728) Mor. 14567   210
Lundie Bros., *Re* [1965] 1 W.L.R. 1051; [1965] 2 All E.R. 692 .... 63, 475
Lyne-Pirkis *v*. Jones [1969] 1 W.L.R. 1293; [1969] 3 All E.R. 738 ..... 123, 423
Lyon *v*. Knowles (1864) 5 B. & S. 751; 10 L.T. 876; affg. (1863) 3 B. & S.
     556   74
—— *v*. Tweddell (1881) 17 Ch.D. 529; 50 L.J.Ch. 571   478
Lyth *v*. Ault (1852) 7 Ex. 669; 86 R.R. 785   277

MACADAM *v*. Martin's Tr. (1872) 11 M. 33; 45 Sc.Jur. 31 .... 370, 371
McAra *v*. Wilson (1848) 10 D. 707; 20 Sc.Jur. 227   44
MacArthur *v*. Croall (1852) 24 Sc.Jur. 170; 1 Stuart 296   304
McArthurs *v*. McBrair & Johnstone's Tr. (1844) 6 D. 1174; 16 Sc.Jur. 513   381
Macartney *v*. Garbutt (1890) 24 Q.B.D. 368; 62 L.T. 368   47
McAulay *v*. Gault, Mar. 6, 1821, F.C.   70
McAulay, Gartly, McDonald & Co.'s Tr. *v*. Renny (1803) Bell, *Com. II,*
     514 .... 25, 26, 34, 81
Macaura *v*. Northern Assce. Co. [1925] A.C. 619; 94 L.J.P.C. 154   202
McBain *v*. Crichton, 1961 J.C. 25; 1961 S.L.T. 209   124
McBay *v*. Hamlett, 1963 S.C. 282; 1963 S.L.T. 18   205
McCarroll *v*. Maguire, 1920, 2 S.L.T. 108, 220 .... 112, 125
McCaul's Creditors *v*. Ramsay & Ritchie (1740) Mor. 14608 .... 406, 608,
                                                                                        612, 624, 630
McConnell *v*. Hector (1802) 3 Bos. & P. 113; 6 R.R. 724   48
McCormick & Carnie *v*. Wilson's Exrs., July 4, 1822, F.C.; (1822) 1 S. 541   427
McCosh *v*. Brown & Co.'s Tr. (1899) 1 F. (H.L.) 86; 7 S.L.T. 253 .... 59, 65,
                                                                                        77, 90, 91
MacCreadie's Trs. *v*. Lamond (1886) 24 S.L.R. 114 .... 193, 194, 463,
                                                                                   529, 537, 540
McCubban *v*. Turnbull (1850) 12 D. 1123; 22 Sc.Jur. 469, 523   581
McCulloch *v*. McCulloch (1731) Mor. 8965   29
—— *v*. ——, 1953 S.C. 189; 1953 S.L.T. 117 .... 468, 520, 522, 526, 527
Macdonald (1789) Mor. 9038   31
McDougall *v*. Arbuthnott (1681) Mor. 9044   36
McEllistrim *v*. Ballymacelligott Co-op. Socy. [1919] A.C. 548; 88 L.J.P.C.
     59   120
McFarlane *v*. Donaldson, 10 Fac. 473; (1835) 13 S. 725 .... 342, 359, 361
—— *v*. Kent [1965] 1 W.L.R. 1019; [1965] 2 All E.R. 376 .... 123, 423
Macfarlane *v*. Nicoll (1864) 3 M. 237; 37 Sc.Jur. 113   123
McFeetridge *v*. Stewarts & Lloyds, 1913 S.C. 773; 1913, S.L.T. 325 ...... 30, 36
McGee *v*. Anderson (1895) 22 R. 274; 2 S.L.T. 433 .... 334–336, 619, 620
McGibbon *v*. McGibbon (1852) 14 D. 605; 24 Sc.Jur. 306   38
McGivan *v*. Blackburn (1725) Mor. 14672   70
Macglashan *v*. Dundee & Perth Ry. Co. (1848) 10 D. 1397; 20 Sc.Jur. 508   304
McGown *v*. Henderson, 1914 S.C. 839; 1914, 2 S.L.T. 66   438
McGregor *v*. Bainbrigge (1849) 7 Hare 164n.; 82 R.R. 48   403
—— *v*. McGregor (1823) 2 S. 461   200
McIntosh & Son *v*. Ainslie (1872) 10 M. 304; 44 Sc.Jur. 178   149
McIver *v*. Humble (1812) 16 East 169, 174   301
Mackay, *Re* (1834) 2 A. & E. 356; 41 R.R. 456   524
—— *v*. Advocate (Lord), 1914, 1 S.L.T. 33   161
—— *v*. Commercial Bank of New Brunswick (1874) L.R. 5 P.C. 412; 43
     L.J.P.C. 31   318
McKeand *v*. Laird's Tr. (1861) 23 D. 846 .... 263–267, 269
Mackenzie *v*. Blakeney (1879) 6 R. 1329   161
McKenzie *v*. Jones (1926) 42 Sh.Ct.Rep. 289   229

Mackenzie v. Macfarlane, 1934 S.N. 16 424
Mackersies v. Mitchell (1872) 10 M. 861; 9 S.L.R. 549 .... 406, 423
McKinlay v. Gillon (1831) 5 W. & S. 468; affg. (1830) 9 S. 90 78
—— v. Wilson (1885) 13 R. 210; 23 S.L.R. 134 .... 285, 286
McKirdy v. Paterson (1854) 16 D. 1013; 26 Sc.Jur. 616 491
McLaren & Co. v. Pendreigh's Tr. (1869) 7 M. 926; 6 S.L.R. 606 .... 567, 568
—— v. Rae (1827) 4 Murray 381 304
McLean v. Rose, 12 Fac. 217; (1836) 15 S. 236 .... 221, 277
Maclean & Son (1824) 3 S. 122 .... 556, 558
McLeod v. Dowling (1927) 43 T.L.R. 655 442
—— v. Howden, 14 Fac. 1135; (1839) 1 D. 1121 .... 229, 247, 248
McLeod v. Thorburn (1839) 1 D. 359 282
Macleod, Re, Mills v. Macleod (1895) 11 T.L.R. 445; (1895) W.N. 97 372
McLeod v. Tosh, 11 Fac. 884; (1836) 14 S. 1058 225–228
McManus v. Fortescue [1907] 2 K.B. 1 240
McMichael v. Barbour (1840) 3 D. 279 31
Macmillan v. Ehrmann Bros. (1904) 21 R.P.C. 357 431
McMurray v. McMurray's Trs. (1852) 14 D. 1048; 24 Sc.Jur. 639 544
McNab v. Lockhart & Hendrie (1843) 5 D. 1014; 15 Sc.Jur. 371 .... 499, 515
Macnab v. Macnab, 1912 S.C. 421; 1912, 1 S.L.T. 127 466
McNair v. Fleming (1812) 5 Pat.App. 639 .... 156, 244
McNair & Co. v. Gray, Hunter & Speirs, Jan. 19, 1803; Hume 753 ... 210, 227, 247
McNaught v. Milligan (1885) 13 R. 366; 23 S.L.R. 236 160
McNiven v. Peffers (1868) 7 M. 181; 41 Sc.Jur. 104 .... 170, 379, 380, 406, 436, 439
Macpherson v. Richmond (1869) 6 S.L.R. 348; 41 Sc.Jur. 288 .... 455, 521
McTaggart's Reps. v. Robertson, 9 Fac. 204; (1834) 12 S. 338 100
McTavish v. Saltoun, Feb. 3, 1821, F.C. 277
McWhannell v. Dobbie (1830) 8 S. 914 .... 406, 427, 436
McWhirter v. Guthrie (1822) 1 S. 319 401
Mac Fisheries v. Harrison (1924) 93 L.J.K.B. 811; 40 T.L.R. 709 131
Macao v. Officers of State (1822) 1 Sh.App. 138 46
Machin v. Bennett [1900] W.N. 146 480
Maddeford v. Austwick (1826) 1 Sim. 89; 27 R.R. 167 .... 189, 552
Maddick v. Marshall (1864) 17 C.B.(N.S.) 829; 11 L.T. 611 .... 136, 139, 143
Magdalena S.N. Co. v. Martin (1859) 2 E. & E. 94 47
Mahmoud and Ispahani, Re [1921] 2 K.B. 716; 90 L.J.K.B. 821 .... 112, 125
Mains & McGlashan v. Black (1895) 22 R. 329; 2 S.L.T. 453 210
Mair v. Wood, 1948 S.C. 83; 1948 S.L.T. 326 .... 3, 206, 313, 338, 354, 355, 358, 493, 579, 608, 612, 613, 619, 620
Malloch v. Duffy (1882) 19 S.L.R. 697 175
Manley v. Sartori [1927] 1 Ch. 157; 96 L.J.Ch. 65 .... 432, 542, 543
Mann v. D'Arcy [1968] 1 W.L.R. 893; [1968] 2 All E.R. 172 ... 46, 211, 212, 254
—— v. Sinclair (1879) 6 R. 1078; 16 S.L.R. 630 .... 83, 296, 505
Manners v. Whitehead (1898) 1 F. 171; 6 S.L.T. 199 .... 41, 163, 189, 547, 549, 551
Mara v. Browne [1896] 1 Ch. 199; 65 L.J.Ch. 225 .... 361, 367
Marsh v. Joseph [1897] 1 Ch. 213; 66 L.J.Ch. 128 .... 231, 346
—— v. Keating (1834) 2 Cl. & F. 250; 8 Bli.(N.S.) 651 ...... 342, 347, 351, 360
Marshall, Re [1920] 1 Ch. 284; 89 L.J.Ch. 204 286
—— v. Colman (1820) 2 J. & W. 266; 22 R.R. 116 .... 185, 194, 467
—— v. Marshall, Feb. 23, 1816, F.C.; Jan. 26, 1815, F.C.; Ross, Commercial Cases III, 611 .... 379, 406, 427, 436, 438, 441, 525
Martyn v. Gray (1863) 14 C.B.(N.S.) 824 .... 133, 136, 139
Mason, Re, ex p. Bing. [1899] 1 Q.B. 810; 68 L.J.Q.B. 466 95
—— v. Paterson (1904) 12 S.L.T. 511 43
—— v. Provident Clothing Co. [1913] A.C. 724; 82 L.J.K.B. 1153 120
Matheson v. Fraser (1820) Hume 758 .... 274, 498
Matthews, Ex p. (1814) 3 V. & B. 125 129
—— v. Ruggles Brise [1911] 1 Ch. 194; 80 L.J.Ch. 42 150
Maude, Ex p. re Braginton (1867) L.R. 2 Ch. 550; 16 L.T. 577 533
Maxton v. Brown, 14 Fac. 398; (1839) D. 367 185
Measures Bros. v. Measures [1910] 1 Ch. 336; [1910] 2 Ch. 248; 79 L.J.Ch. 707 174
Meekins v. Henson [1964] 1 Q.B. 472; [1962] 3 W.L.R. 299; [1962] 1 All E.R. 899 .... 308, 309, 311, 312, 320, 321, 337, 338
Megevand, Re, ex p. Delhasse (1878) 7 Ch. D. 511; 38 L.T. 106 91
Meikle v. Meikle (1895) 33 S.L.R. 362; (1895) 3 S.L.T. 204 120

Melgrave & Melgrave v. Finer, *The Times*, Feb. 18 and June 4, 1959;
[1959] C.L.Y. 2394 481
Meliorucchi v. Royal Exchange Assce. Co. (1728) 1 Eq.Ca.Ab. 8 407
Mellersh v. Keen (No. 1) (1859) 27 Beav. 236; 7 W.R. 629 ... 421, 439,460, 478
Mellis v. Royal Bank of Scotland, June 22, 1815, F.C.; Bell, *Com. II,*
567 .... 225, 555, 569
Melliss v. Shirley Local Board (1885) 16 Q.B.D. 446; 55 L.J.Q.B. 143 104
Mellors v. Shaw (1861) 1 B. & S. 437; 124 R.R. 621 307
Melrose-Drover v. Heddle (1902) 4 F. 1120; 39 S.L.R. 529 .... 420, 421, 426
Melvil v. Arnot (1782) Mor. 8998 38
Menzies' Trs. v. Black's Trs., 1909 S.C. 239; 16 S.L.T. 580 494
Mercantile Bank of Sydney v. Taylor [1893] A.C. 319 277
Mercantile Credit Co. v. Garrod [1962] 3 All E.R. 1103 213
Mercedes Daimler Motor Co. v. Maudslay Motor Co. (1915) 31 T.L.R.
178; [1915] W.N. 54 50
Merryweather v. Moore [1892] 2 Ch. 518; 61 L.J.Ch. 505 174
Mersey Docks v. Gibbs, 11 H.L.C. 686; 1866 L.R. 1 H.L. 93 307
Metcalf v. Bruin (1810) 12 East 400; 11 R.R. 432; 104 E.R. 156 281
Meyer & Co. v. Faber (No. 2) [1923] 2 Ch. 421; 129 L.T. 490 539
Middleton v. Pyper (1935) 51 Sh.Ct.Rep. 20 224
Miles v. Finlay & Co. (1830) 6 Fac. 11; (1830) 9 S. 18 .... 314, 317
Millar v. Craig (1843) 6 Beav. 433; 63 R.R. 134 190
Miller, *Re* [1901] 1 K.B. 51; 70 L.J.K.B. 1 94
—— v. Douglas, Jan. 22, 1811, F.C.; Ross, *Commercial Cases III,* 500 ... 157,
227, 245, 252
—— v. Downie (1876) 3 R. 548; 13 S.L.R. 345 .... 66, 92
—— v. Harvie (1827) 4 Murray 388 304
—— v. Mackay (1862) 31 Beav. 77; (1864) 34 Beav. 295 .... 169, 178
—— v. Mitchell (1860) 22 D. 833; 32 Sc.Jur. 346 .... 237, 243
—— v. Race (1758) 1 Burr. 452 372
—— v. Thorburn (1861) 23 D. 359; 33 Sc.Jur. 180 ...... 264–267, 269, 270, 282
—— v. Walker (1875) 3 R. 242; 13 S.L.R. 143 .... 436, 472, 473, 609, 632
Milliken v. Love & Crawford (1803) Hume 754 .... 274, 276, 498
Mills, *Ex p. Re* Tew (1873) L.R. 8 Ch. 569; 28 L.T. 606 95
Minister of Health v. Stafford [1952] Ch. 730; 2 All E.R. 386 355
Minto v. Kirkpatrick (1833) 11 S. 632 .... 200, 391, 543
Mitchell, *Ex p.* (1808) 14 Ves. 597; 9 R.R. 357 394
——v. Canal Basin Foundry Co. (1869) 7 M. 480; 41 Sc.Jur. 263 626
Moinet v. Hamilton (1833) 11 S. 348 43
Mollison v. Noltie (1889) 16 R. 350; 26 S.L.R. 240 .... 609, 619, 622, 624
Mollwo, March & Co. v. Court of Wards (1872) L.R. 4 P.C. 419 ... 7, 11, 65,
77, 91, 140
Molton v. Camroux (1848) 2 Ex. 487; (1849) 4 Ex. 17; 76 R.R. 669 ...... 39, 286
Montefiore v. Lloyd (1863) 15 C.B.(N.S.) 203; 33 L.J.C.P. 49 282
Montgomery v. Forrester & Co. (1791) Hume 748; (1791) Mor. 14583 ... 184,
474, 477, 608, 632
Montrose (Marquis) v. Livingston (1697) Mor. 9046 36
Moore v. Dempster (1879) 6 R. 930; 16 S.L.R. 535 .... 69, 82, 609
—— v. Knight [1891] 1 Ch. 547; 60 L.J.Ch. 271 .... 332, 341
Moreton v. Hardern (1825) 4 B. & C. 223; 6 D. & R. 275 .... 157, 307, 336
Morgan v. Blyth [1891] 1 Ch. 337; 60 L.J.Ch. 66 308
—— v. Marquis (1853) 9 Ex. 145; 96 R.R. 624 .... 295, 517
Morley v. Newman (1824) 5 D. & R. 317; 27 R.R. 528 524
Morris v. Barrett (1829) 3 Y. & J. 384; 53 R.R. 246 .... 380, 389
—— v. Livie (1842) 1 Y. & C.Ch. 380; 57 R.R. 391 416
—— v. Saxelby [1916] 1 A.C. 689; 85 L.J.Ch. 210 .... 120, 423
Morrison, *Ex p.* (1847) De Gex. 539 187
—— v. Learmont & Co. (1870) 8 M. 500; 42 Sc.Jur. 232 28
—— v. Miller (1818) Hume 720 387
—— v. Morrison (1900) 2 F. 382; 7 S.L.T. 326 419
—— v. Service (1879) 6 R. 1158; 16 S.L.R. 686 .... 54, 56, 62
Morton v. Edinburgh & Glasgow Ry. Co. (1845) 8 D. 288; 18 Sc.Jur. 134 304
Morton's Trs. v. Robertson's J. F. (1892) 20 R. 72; 30 S.L.R. 101 150
Morvah Consols Tin Mining Co., *Re,* McKay's Case (1875) 2 Ch.D. 1 ... 168
Moss v. Elphick [1910] 1 K.B. 846; 79 L.J.K.B. 631 .... 436, 437, 442
Moyes v. Cook (1829) 7 S. 793 155
Muir v. Collett (1862) 24 D. 1119; 34 Sc.Jur. 558 160
—— v. Dickson (1860) 22 D. 1070; 32 Sc.Jur. 495 .... 150, 276, 515
Muirhead v. Borland, 1925 S.C. 474; 1925 S.L.T. 289 .... 602, 604, 606

Munro v. Cowan, June 8, 1813, F.C. 449, 486
—— v. Stein, 1961 S.C. 362 .... 383, 384
Murray v. Hogarth, 10 Fac. 263; (1835) 13 S. 453 496
—— v. Murray, Feb 5, 1805, F.C.; Mor.App. No. 1, "Heritable and
    Moveable " No. 4 391
Murray's Tr. v. McIntyre (1904) 6 F. 588; 11 S.L.T. 759 419
Mustad (O.) & Son v. Dosen (1928) [1964] 1 W.L.R. 109n.; [1963] 3 All
    E.R. 416 173
Mycock v. Beatson (1879) 13 Ch.D. 384; 49 L.J.Ch. 127 .... 548, 549

NAAMLOOZE, KLENE & CO'S APPLICATION (1923) 40 R.P.C. 103 431
Nant-y-Glo & Blaina Iron Works Co. v. Grave (1878) 12 Ch.D. 738; 38
    L.T. 345 168
National Exchange Co. v. Drew & Dick (1855) 18 D. (H.L.) 6; (1855) 2
    Macq. 103 323
—— v. —— (1860) 23 D. 1, 27, 1278; 33 Sc.Jur. 357 237
National Exchange Co. of Glasgow v. Glasgow, Kilmarnock etc. Ry. (1849)
    12 D. 249; 21 Sc.Jur. 181 195
Neilson v. McDougal (1682) Mor. 14551 .... 6, 388, 610
—— v. Mossend Iron Co. (1886) 13 R. (H.L.) 50; (1885) 12 R. 499; 23
    S.L.R. 867 .... 438, 441, 492
—— v. Wilson (1890) 17 R. 608; 27 S.L.R. 505 .... 355, 560
Neilson & Murdoch v. Colquhoun & Rae (1745) Mor. 723 398
Nelmes & Co. v. Montgomery & Co. (1883) 10 R. 974; 20 S.L.R. 662 ... 265–268
Newbigging v. Adam (1886) 34 Ch.D. 582; 56 L.J.Ch. 275 549
New Brunswick Ry. v Muggeridge (1860) 1 Drew & Sm. 363; 30 L.J.Ch.
    242 164
New Mining & Exploring Syndicate v. Chalmers & Hunter, 1912 S.C. 126;
    1911, 2 S.L.T. 386 .... 258, 328–331, 343, 344, 346, 350, 360, 371, 374
Newsholme Bros. v. Road Transport & Gen. Insce. Co. [1929] 2 K.B. 356;
    98 L.J.K.B. 751 220
Newsome v. Coles (1811) 2 Camp. 617; 12 R.R. 756; Ross, Commercial
    Cases III, 634 .... 139, 146, 291, 292
Nicholson v. Ricketts (1860) 2 E. & E. 497; 119 R.R. 816 244
Nicoll v. Christie, 2 Fac. 581; (1827) 5 S. 882 .... 565, 577, 578, 581
Niemann v. Niemann (1889) 43 Ch.D. 198; 59 L.J.Ch. 220 210
Nisbet v. Neil's Tr. (1869) 7 M. 1097; 41 Sc.Jur. 637 221
Nisbet's Trs. v. Nisbet (1871) 9 M. 937; 43 Sc.Jur. 530 39
Noble v. Noble, 1965 S.L.T. 415 .... 433, 529
Nocton v. Ashburton (Lord) [1914] A.C. 932; 83 L.J.Ch. 784 162
Nordenfeldt v. Maxim-Nordenfeldt Guns & Ammunition Co. [1894] A.C.
    535; 63 L.J.Ch. 908 .... 119, 120
Nordisk Insulinlaboratorium v. Gorgate Products [1953] Ch. 430; [1953] 2
    W.L.R. 879; [1953] 1 All E.R. 986 (sub nom. Nordisk Insulin-
    laboratorium v. Bencard) 173
North British Bank v. Ayrshire Iron Co. (1853) 15 D. 782; 25 Sc.Jur.
    466 .... 257, 617
—— v. Collins (1852) 15 D. (H.L.) 29; 1 Macq. 369 552
North Western Salt Co. v. Electrolytic Alkali Co. [1914] A.C. 461; 83
    L.J.K.B. 530 .... 126, 621
Nottidge v. Pritchard (1834) 2 Cl. & F. 379; 33 R.R. 187 198

OGDEN v. Nelson [1905] A.C. 109; 74 L.J.K.B. 433 80
Oldaker v. Lavender (1833) 6 Sim. 239; 38 R.R. 98 538
Olver v. Hillier [1959] 1 W.L.R. 551; [1959] 2 All E.R. 220 .... 474, 481,
    482, 484, 524
Olympia Ltd., Re [1898] 2 Ch. 153; 67 L.J.Ch. 433 166
O'Mealey v. Wilson (1808) 1 Camp. 482; 10 R.R. 742 48
Ord v. Barton (1846) 8 D. 1011; 18 Sc.Jur. 505 385
Orr v. Pollock (1840) 2 D. 1092 .... 609, 611
Osborn v. Barton (1950) 66 T.L.R. (Pt. I) 115; 94 S.J. 15 42
Ottley v. Browne (1810) 1 Ball & Bea. 360 125
Owen v. Delamere (1872) L.R. 15 Eq. 134; 42 L.J.Ch. 232 145
Oxford Benefit Bldg. Socy., Re (1886) 35 Ch.D. 502; 56 L.J.Ch. 98 368

PADON v. Bank of Scotland, 2 Fac. 115; (1826) 5 S. 175 .... 281, 298, 299
Padstow Total Loss Assoc., Re (1882) 20 Ch.D. 137; 51 L.J.Ch. 344 6
Page v. Ratcliffe (1897) 75 L.T. 371; 76 L.T. 63 .... 432, 433, 543
Palmolive Case (1912) 29 R.P.C. 278 431
Pare v. Clegg (1861) 29 Beav. 589; 30 L.J.Ch. 742 98
Parker, Ex p. (1842) 2 Mont. D. & D. 511 273
—— v. McKenna (1874) L.R. 10 Ch. 96, 123; 44 L.J.Ch. 425 166
—— v. Morrell (1848) 2 Ph. 453; 17 L.J.Ch. 226 217
—— v. Walker, 1961 S.L.T. 252 .... 76, 82, 334, 339, 608
Parkin v. Carruthers (1800) 3 Esp. 248; 6 R.R. 828 .... 290, 501
Parkinson v. College of Ambulance [1925] 2 K.B. 1; 93 L.J.K.B. 1066 ... 125
Parnell v. Walter (1889) 16 R. 917; 27 S.L.R. 1 .... 388, 395, 398, 600
Parrington v. Parrington [1951] 2 All E.R. 916; [1951] 2 T.L.R. 918 44
Parsons v. Hayward (1862) 31 Beav. 199; 31 L.J.Ch. 666 170
Paterson (1894) 1 S.L.T. 564 526
—— (Thomas) (1843) 1 Broun 629 99
—— v. Grant (1749) Mor. 14578 .... 447, 449
—— v. Stirling Mags., Mar. 1, 1775, F.C.; (1775) Mor. 9527 100
—— Bros. v. Gladstone (1891) 18 R. 403; 28 S.L.R. 268 .... 144, 157, 210,
                                                                    211, 245, 249
Patersons v. Calder, July 5, 1808, F.C.; Mor.App. 1, Society, No. 4 282
Patten v. Bond (1889) 60 L.T. 583; 37 W.R. 373 372
Pattison v. Ballingall (1874) 12 S.L.R. 68 .... 179, 180
Paul v. Taylor (1826) 4 S. 572 4
Peacock v. Peacock (1809) 2 Camp. 45; (1808) 16 Ves. 49; 10 R.R. 138;
       Ross, Commercial Cases III, 381, 398, 607 ... 62, 187, 401, 402, 441, 512
Pearce v. Chamberlain (1750) 2 Ves.Sen. 33 .... 19, 412, 445
—— v. Foster (1886) 17 Q.B.D. 536; 55 L.J.Q.B. 306 .... 464, 465
Pearson & Son v. Dublin Corpn. [1907] A.C. 351; 77 L.J.P.C. 1 318
Peele, Ex p. (1802) 6 Ves. 602 .... 259, 263, 273
Pemberton v. Oakes (1827) 4 Russ. 154; Ross, Commercial Cases III, 687   281
Pender v. Henderson (1864) 2 M. 1428; 36 Sc.Jur. 663 .... 166, 167, 379, 381
Pennell v. Deffel (1853) 4 De G.M. & G. 372; 102 R.R. 170 .... 370, 371
Perpetual Excrs. & Trustees Assoc. of Australia v. Commr. of Taxes of
       the Commonwealth of Australia [1954] A.C. 114; [1954] 2 W.L.R.
       171; [1954] 1 All E.R. 339 529
Peter Pan Mfg. Corpn. v. Corsets Silhouette [1964] 1 W.L.R. 96; [1963] 3
       All E.R. 402 173
Petrie v. Hannay (1789) 3 T.R. 418 103
Peyton v. Mindham [1972] 1 W.L.R. 8; [1971] 3 All E.R. 1215 .... 123, 423,
                                                                    463, 488
Pharmaceutical Socy. v. London & Provincial Supply Assoc. (1886) 5
       App.Cas. 857; 49 L.J.Q.B. 736 110
Phillips v. Blackhurst, 1912, 2 S.L.T. 254 .... 112, 125
—— v. Phillips (1832) 1 Myl. & K. 649; 36 R.R. 410 .... 380, 389
Phipps v. Boardman [1965] Ch. 992; [1967] A.C. 46; [1966] 3 W.L.R.
       1009; [1966] 3 All E.R. 721 .... 165, 172
Pickard v. Sears (1837) 6 A. & E. 469; 45 R.R. 538 131
Piddocke v. Burt [1894] 1 Ch. 343; 63 L.J.Ch. 246 167
Pillani v. Motilal (1929) 45 T.L.R. 283 145
Pillans v. Harkness (1713) Colles 442 548
—— Bros. v. Pillans (1908) 16 S.L.T. 611 .... 167, 172, 178, 380
Pinto, Leite & Nephews, Re [1929] 1 Ch. 221; 98 L.J.Ch. 211 ... 82, 86, 92, 94
Plews v. Baker (1873) L.R. 16 Eq. 564; 43 L.J.Ch. 212 480
Plotzker v. Lucas, 1907 S.C. 315; 14 S.L.T. 678 224
Plumer v. Gregory (1874) L.R. 18 Eq. 621; 43 L.J.Ch. 616 ... 211, 258, 347, 350
Pocock v. Carter [1912] 1 Ch. 663; 81 L.J.Ch. 232 388
Pole v. Leask (1863) 33 L.J.Ch. 155 209
Polhill v. Walter (1832) 3 B. & Ad. 114; 1 L.J.K.B. 92 238
Pollock v. Burns (1875) 2 R. 497 41
—— v. Paterson, Dec. 10, 1811, F.C. 39, 286
Pomeroy v. Scale (1907) 24 R.P.C. 177 426
Pooley v. Driver (1876) L R. 5 Ch.D. 458; 46 L.J.Ch. 466 .... 7, 11, 65,
                                                                    90, 91, 245
Porter v. Freudenberg [1915] 1 K.B. 857; 84 L.J.K.B. 1001 .... 47, 49, 453
—— v. Taylor (1817) 6 M. & S. 156; 18 R.R. 338 212
Porthouse v. Parker (1807) 1 Camp. 82; 10 R.R. 637 219
Pott v. Eyton (1846) 3 C.B. 31; 71 R.R. 271 132
Poulson, Ex p. (1844) De Gex 79; 9 Jur. 262 .... 363, 368

Powles v. Page (1846) 3 C.B. 16; 71 R.R. 262 219
Prager v. Blatspiel etc. [1924] 1 K.B. 566; 93 L.J.K.B. 410 214
Pratt v. Strick (1932) 17 T.C. 459 .... 92, 93
Price & Logan v. Wise (1862) 24 D. 491 270
Pritchard v. Draper (1831) 1 Russ. & M. 191; 32 R.R. 187 198
Proudfoot v. Lindsay, Jan. 18, 1825, F.C.; (1825) 3 S. 443 ... 225, 226, 228, 245
—— v. Montefiori (1867) L.R. 2 Q.B. 511; 36 L.J.Q.B. 225 219
Pullan v. Koe [1913] 1 Ch. 9; 82 L.J.Ch. 37 374
Pulsford v. Richards (1853) 17 Beav. 87; 99 R.R. 48 549
Punnett, Ex p., re Kitchin (1880) 16 Ch.D. 226; 50 L.J.Ch. 212 420
Pyper v. Christie (1878) 6 R. 143; 16 S.L.R. 67 .... 611, 612, 614, 626, 633

QUARMAN v. Burnett (1840) 6 M. & W. 508; 55 R.R. 717; Ross, *Commercial Cases III*, 266 154
Queensbury Industrial Socy. v. Pickles (1865) L.R. 1 Ex. 1; 35 L.J.Ex. 1   377

R. v. Frankland (1863) L. & C. 276; 32 L.J.M.C. 69 124
—— v. Kupfer [1915] 2 K.B. 321; 84 L.J.K.B. 1021; 112 L.T. 1138 ...... 49, 453
—— v. Manning (1739) 2 Comyns 616 313
—— v. Stranyforth (1721) Bunb. 97 313
—— v. Tankard [1894] 1 Q.B. 548; 63 L.J.M.C. 61 124
Rae v. Neilson (1742) Mor. 716 .... 397, 398
Rainbow v. Howkins [1904] 2 K.B. 322 240
Raleigh v. Hughson & Dobson (1861) 23 D. 352; 33 Sc.Jur. 174 627
Ralli Bros. v. Compania Naviera [1920] 2 K.B. 287; 89 L.J.K.B. 999 102
Rama Corpn. v. Proved Tin & General Investments [1952] 2 Q.B. 147;
    [1952] 1 All E.R. 554 .... 131, 159
Ramsay v. Maxwell (1672) Mor. 9042 36
Ramsay's Exrs. v. Graham, Jan. 18, 1814, F.C. 498
Randall v. Randall (1835) 7 Sim. 271; 40 R.R. 142 390
Randell v. Trimen (1856) 18 C.B. 786; 25 L.J.C.P. 307 238
Rapp v. Latham (1819) 2 B. & A. 795; 21 R.R. 495; Ross, *Commercial Cases III*, 481 .... 332, 340, 342, 360
Rasnoimport V/O v. Guthrie & Co. [1966] 1 Lloyd's Rep. 1 240
Rawlings v. General Trading Co. [1921] 1 K.B. 635; 90 L.J.K.B. 404 621
Rawlins v. Wickham (1858) 3 De G. & J. 304; 121 R.R. 134 ...... 548, 549, 551
Rawlinson v. Clarke (1846) 15 M. & W. 292; 15 L.J.Ex. 171 83
Raynard v. Chase (1756) 1 Burr. 2 109
Reaveley's Case [1848] 1 De G. & S. 550 25
Reddie v. Williamson (1863) 1 M. 228; 35 Sc.Jur. 170 280
Redmayne v. Forster (1866) L.R. 2 Eq. 467; 35 L.J.Ch. 847 .... 203, 416
Redway v. Sweeting (1867) L.R. 2 Ex. 400; 36 L.J.Ex. 185 6
Reed v. White (1804) 5 Esp. 122 276
Regal (Hastings) v. Gulliver [1942] 1 All E.R. 378 367
Regier v. Campbell Stuart [1939] Ch. 766; [1939] 3 All E.R. 235 173
Reid v. Reid, 1938 S.L.T. 415; 1938 S.N. 93 .... 427, 428
—— v. Hollinshead (1825) 4 B. & C. 867; 28 R.R. 488 85
Reid & McCall v. Douglases, June 11, 1814, F.C. 277
Reid's Case (1857) 24 Beav. 318; 116 R.R. 138 25
Religious Tract & Book Socy. v. Inland Revenue (1896) 23 R. 390; 3
    S.L.T. 229 .... 10, 11
Rely-A-Bell Burglar & Fire Alarm Co. v. Eisler [1926] 1 Ch. 609; 95
    L.J.Ch. 345 .... 179, 194
Reversion Fund & Insce. Co. v. Maison Cosway [1913] 1 K.B. 364; 82
    L.J.K.B. 512 257
Reynell v. Lewis (1846) 15 M. & W. 517; 71 R.R. 751 142
—— v. Sprye (1852) 1 De G.M. & G. 660 123
Rhagg, *Re* [1938] Ch. 828 420
Rhodes v. Moules [1895] 1 Ch. 236; 64 L.J.Ch. 122 346
Rice v. Gordon (1848) 11 Beav. 265; 83 R.R. 153 190
Riches, *Re* (1865) 4 De G.J. & S. 581; 11 L.T. 651 252
Ricketts v. Bennett (1847) 4 C.B. 686; 72 R.R. 691 .... 212, 216, 256, 395
Ridgeway v. Brock, 7 Fac. 98; (1831) 10 S. 105 .... 264–266, 269, 270
Ritchie v. Couper (1860) 28 Beav. 344 169
Ritson, *Re*, Ritson v. Ritson [1899] 1 Ch. 128; 68 L.J.Ch. 77 408
Robb v. Forrest (1831) 5 W. & S. 740; affg. (1830) 8 S. 839, 1035 221
—— v. Green [1895] 2 Q.B. 1, 315; 64 L.J.Q.B. 593 174

Roberts v. Eberhardt (1853) Kay 148; 101 R.R. 548 467
Robertson, Petr. (1902) 10 S.L.T. 417 .... 406, 526, 527
—— v. Lockie (1846) 15 Sim. 285; 74 R.R. 80 .... 460, 478
—— v. Oswald (1584) Mor. 8980 36
—— v. Quiddington (1860) 28 Beav. 529 419
Robertson's Creditors (1744) Bell, Com. II, 508, n. 3 396
Robinson v. Anderson (1855) 20 Beav. 98; 7 De G.M. & G. 239; 109 R.R.
    362 .... 401, 403
—— v. Finlay (1878) 9 Ch.D. 487; 39 L.T. 398 430
—— v. Wilkinson (1817) 3 Price 538; 18 R.R. 659 150
Robley v. Brooke (1833) 7 Bli.(N.S.) 90; 38 R.R. 1 402
Robson v. Premier Oil & Pipe Line [1915] 2 Ch. 124; 84 L.J.Ch. 629 49
Rodriguez v. Speyer Bros. [1919] A.C. 59; 88 L.J.K.B. 147 .... 49, 50
Rogers v. Harvey (1858) 5 C.B.(N.S.) 3; 116 R.R. 536 392
Rolfe v. Flower, Salting & Co. (1865) L.R. 1 P.C. 27; 35 L.J.P.C. 13 ... 264, 273
Rolland v. Hart (1871) 6 Ch.App. 678; 40 L.J.Ch. 701 219
Rombach Baden Clock Co. v. Gent (1915) 31 T.L.R. 492; 84 L.J.K.B. 1558 ... 50
Ronbar Enterprises v. Green [1954] 1 W.L.R. 815; [1954] 2 All E.R. 266 ... 120,
                                                                      121, 122
Rooth v. Quin (1819) 7 Price 193; 21 R.R. 744 .... 249, 287, 300
Ross v. Parkyns (1875) L.R. 20 Eq. 331; 44 L.J.Ch. 610 83
Rosslund Cycle Co. v. McCreadie, 1907 S.C. 1208; 15 S.L.T. 271 244
Roumanian, The [1916] 1 A.C. 124; affg. [1915] P. 26 453
Rouse v. Bradford Banking Co. [1894] 2 Ch. 32; [1894] A.C. 586 150
Routh v. Jones [1947] 1 All E.R. 758 423
—— v. Peach (1795) 2 Anstr. 519; (1796) 3 Anstr. 637 524
—— v. Webster (1847) 10 Beav. 561; 76 R.R. 211 426
Rowlands v. Evans (1861) 30 Beav. 302; 31 L.J.Ch. 265 .... 459, 460
Rowley v. Adams (1844) 7 Beav. 391, 548; 2 H.L.C. 725; 64 R.R. 105, 149 ... 190,
                                                                          390
—— v. Horne (1825) 3 Bing. 2; 28 R.R. 551 300
Royal Bank v. Christie (1841) 2 Rob.App. 118 281
Royal Bank of Scotland v. Greenock Bank (1797) 3 Pat.App. 595; affg.
    Nov. 14, 1794, F.C. 157
—— v. Stein Smith & Co.'s Assignees, Jan. 20, 1813, F.C.; Bell, Com.
    II, 515 .... 567, 568
Ruben & Ladenburg v. Great Fingall Consolidated [1906] A.C. 439; 75
    L.J.K.B. 843 .... 157, 318
Ruffin, Ex p. (1801) 6 Ves. 119; 5 R.R. 237 406
Russell v. Austwick (1826) 1 Sim. 52; 27 R.R. 157 178
—— v. Breadalbane (Earl) (1831) 5 W. & S. 256; affg. (1827) 5 S. 891 ... 414
—— v. Glen, 2 Fac. 141; (1827) 5 S. 221 537
—— v. McNab (1824) 3 S. 63 628
—— v. Russell (1874) 2 R. 93; 12 S.L.R. 64 .... 455, 465, 522
—— v. —— (1880) 14 Ch.D. 471; 49 L.J.Ch. 268 ...... 189, 481, 482, 485, 490
Russian Commercial & Industrial Bank v. Comptoir d'Escompte de Mul-
    house [1923] 2 K.B. 630; 92 L.J.K.B. 1053 446
Rust v. Cooper (1777) Cowp. 634; Bell, Com. II, 228–229, n. 6 576
Ryall v. Rowles (1749) 1 Ves.Sen. 348 408
Rye v. Rye [1962] A.C. 496; [1962] 2 W.L.R. 361; [1962] 1 All E.R. 146;
    affg. [1960] 3 All E.R. 810 381

Sadler v. Lee (1843) 6 Beav. 324; 63 R.R. 95 .... 40, 342, 368
St. Aubyn v. Smart (1868) L.R. 5 Eq. 183 345
St. George's Steam Packet Co., Re, Litchfield's Case (1850) 3 De G. & Sm.
    141 25
——, Pim's Case (1849) 3 De G. & Sm. 11 25
St. James's Club, The, Re (1852) 2 De G.M. & G. 383; 95 R.R. 146 5
Salford, Corpn. of v. Lever [1891] 1 Q.B. 168; 60 L.J.Q.B. 39 167
Salter v. Leas Hotel Co., re Salter [1902] 1 Ch. 332; 71 L.J.Ch. 294 432
Salton v. New Beeston Cycle Co. [1900] 1 Ch. 43; 69 L.J.Ch. 20 .... 446, 561
Samuel Bros. v. Whetherly [1907] 1 K.B. 709; [1908] 1 K.B. 184 5
Samuel & Co. v. Brown (1842) 4 D. 1518; 14 Sc.Jur. 583 608
Sander v. Sander (1845) 2 Coll. 276; 70 R.R. 220 460
Sanders v. Parry [1967] 1 W.L.R. 753; [1967] 2 All E.R. 803 173
Saville v. Robertson (1792) 4 T.R. 720; Ross, Commercial Cases III, 518 ... 73,
                                                         261, 262, 608, 618

Sawers *v*. Tradestown Victualling Socy., Feb. 24, 1815, F.C. 6, 300
Sawyer *v* Goodwin (1867) 36 L.J.Ch. 578; 15 W.R. 1008 308
Scarf *v*. Jardine (1882) 7 App.Cas. 345; 51 L.J.Q.B. 612 ...... 129, 130, 146–149,
298, 453, 501, 506, 507
Schaffenhuis *v*. Goldberg [1916] 1 K.B. 284; 85 L.J.K.B. 374 48
Scholefield *v*. Templar (1859) 4 De G. & J. 429; 28 L.J.Ch. 452 .... 371, 374
Schulze Gow & Co. *v*. Bank of Scotland, 1914, 2 S.L.T. 455 48
Scott *v*. Beale (1859) 6 Jur.(N.S.) 559 272
—— *v*. Brown, Doering, McNab & Co. [1892] 2 Q.B. 724; 61 L.J.Q.B.
738 .... 124, 126, 411, 621
—— *v*. Dick, 1909, 2 S.L.T. 118 91
—— *v*. Ker (1832) 6 W. & S. 214 564
Scott's Excrs. *v*. Gillespie (1869) 6 S.L.R. 656 198
Scott's Tr. *v*. Scott (1887) 14 R. 1043; 24 S.L.R. 738 38
Scott's Trs., *Petrs*., 1957 S.L.T. (Notes) 45 388
Scottish Farmers Dairy Co. (Glasgow) *v*. McGhee, 1933 S.C. 148; 1933
S.L.T. 142 .... 120, 121
Scottish Insce. Commrs. *v*. McNaughton, 1914 S.C. 826; 1914, 2 S.L.T.
56 .... 76, 334
Scottish Pacific Coast Mining Co. *v*. Falkner Bell & Co. (1888) 15 R. 290;
25 S.L.R. 226 .... 361, 373
Scrivenor (Home's Tr.) *v*. Home's Trs., 1926 S.L.T. 214; 1926 S.N. 21 572
Seager *v*. Copydex [1967] 1 W.L.R. 923; [1967] 2 All E.R. 415 172
Seligman *v*. Eagle Insce. Co. [1917] 1 Ch. 519; 86 L.J.Ch. 353 49
Selkrig *v*. Dunlop, May 30, 1804, F.C.; (1804) Hume 277 221
Semple *v*. Macnair & Crawford (1907) 15 S.L.T. 448 .... 483, 484
Shaer, *Re* [1927] 1 Ch. 355; 96 L.J.Ch. 282 .... 114, 115
Shand *v*. Henderson (1814) 2 Dow 519 195
Shand & Co. *v*. Winton (1848) 11 D. 162; 21 Sc.Jur. 30 568
Sharp *v*. Milligan (1856) 22 Beav. 606; 111 R.R. 501 .... 210, 232
—— *v*. Taylor (1848) 2 Ph. 801; 78 R.R. 298 125
Sharpe *v*. Carswell, 1910 S.C. 391; 1910, 1 S.L.T. 80 .... 3, 67
—— *v*. Cummings (1844) 2 D. & L. 504; 14 L.J.Q.B. 10 67
Shaw *v*. Benson (1883) 11 Q.B.D. 563; 52 L.J.Q.B. 575 .... 13, 105, 123
—— *v*. Simmons (1883) 12 Q.B.D. 117; 53 L.J.Q.B. 29 13
Shayler *v*. Woolf [1946] Ch. 320; [1946] 2 All E.R. 54 202
Shearer's Tutor, 1924 S.C. 445; 1924 S.L.T. 336 24
Sheil, *Ex p. re* Lonergan (1877) 4 Ch.D. 789; 36 L.T. 270 94
Shiell's Trs. *v*. Scottish Property Investment Co. Bldg. Socy. (1884) 12 R.
(H.L.) 14; 22 S.L.R. 139 210
Sheppard, *Ex p*., *re* Parkers (1887) 19 Q.B.D. 84; 56 L.J.Q.B. 338 369
Sherry *Re*, London & County Banking Co. *v*. Terry (1884) 25 Ch.D. 692;
53 L.J.Ch. 404 283
Shirreff *v*. Wilks (1800) 1 East 48; 5 R.R. 509; Ross, *Commercial Cases*
III, 488 272
Sime *v*. Balfour, Mar. 1, 1804, F.C.; (1804) Mor.App. Heritable & Move-
able No. 3 380
Simmonds *v*. Swaine (1809) 1 Taunt. 549 524
Simpson *v*. Bloss (1816) 7 Taunt. 246 .... 119, 124
—— *v*. Chapman (1853) 4 De G.M. & G. 154; 102 R.R. 61 541
—— *v*. Howden (Lord) (1842) 9 Cl. & F. 61 100
Sims *v*. Brutton (1850) 5 Ex. 802; 20 L.J.Ex. 41 .... 342, 350, 351
Simson *v*. Cooke (1824) 1 Bing. 452; 2 L.J.(O.S.)C.P. 74 281
—— *v*. Ingham (1823) 2 B. & C. 65; 26 R.R. 273; Ross, *Commercial*
Cases III, 689 .... 283, 284
Sinclair & McIntyre's Sequestration (1885) 1 Sh.Ct.Rep. 279 568
Singleton *v*. Knight (1888) 13 App.Cas. 788; 57 L.J.P.C. 106 .... 212, 213
Skipp *v*. Harwood (1747) 2 Swanst. 586 .... 406, 407
Slater, *Ex p*. (1801) 6 Ves. 146 277
—— *v*. Willis (1838) 1 Beav. 354 381
Small *v*. Attwood (1832) Younge 507; 49 R.R. 115 549
Smith, *Ex p*. (1821) 6 Madd. 2; 22 R.R. 224 189
——, *Petr*. (1827) 5 S. 357 .... 568, 569
—— *v*. Anderson (1880) 15 Ch.D. 247; 50 L.J.Ch. 39 3
—— *v*. Bailey [1891] Q.B. 403; 60 L.J.Q.B. 779 153
—— *v*. Blyth [1891] 1 Ch. 337; 60 L.J.Ch. 66 308
—— *v*. Craven (1831) 1 Cr. & J. 500; 35 R.R. 764 .... 256, 259, 616
—— *v*. Everett (1859) 27 Beav. 446; 122 R.R. 484 .... 421, 428
—— *v*. Jeyes (1841) 4 Beav. 503; 55 R.R. 149 .... 194, 467

Smith v. Macbride & Smith (1888) 16 R. 36; 26 S.L.R. 22 .... 421, 426
—— v. Mawhood (1845) 14 M. & W. 452; 69 R.R. 724 104
—— v. Mules (1852) 9 Hare 556; 89 R.R. 573 .... 485, 487, 490
—— v. N.B. Ry. Co. (1850) 12 D. 795; 22 Sc.Jur. 346 220
—— v. Nugent, 1955 S.L.T. (Sh.Ct.) 60; 71 Sh.Ct.Rep. 350 104
—— v. Patrick (1901) 3 F. (H.L.) 14; [1901] A.C. 282; 38 S.L.R. 613 ... 150, 277
—— v. Puller (1820) 2 Murray 342 .... 54, 56
—— v. Smith (1800) 5 Ves. 189; 5 R.R. 22 .... 378, 379
—— v. Watson (1824) 2 B. & C. 401; Ross, *Commercial Cases III*, 442 ... 129, 130
Smyth v. Muir (1891) 19 R. 81; 29 S.L.R. 94 550
Snaith v. Burridge (1812) 4 Taunt. 684; 13 R.R. 731 252
Snodgrass v. Hair (1846) 8 D. 390; 18 Sc.Jur. 176 .... 499, 513, 514
Soar v. Ashwell [1893] 2 Q.B. 390; 69 L.T. 585 374
Solicitor's Arbitration, *Re* A [1962] 1 W.L.R. 353; [1962] 1 All E.R. 772 487
Solly v. Forbes (1820) 2 Bro. & B. 38; 22 R.R. 641 279
Sorley's Trs. v. Graham (1832) 10 S. 319 243
South Wales Atlantic S.S. Co., *Re* (1876) 2 Ch.D. 763; 46 L.J.Ch. 177 ... 14, 105, 125, 453
Spalding (A.G.) & Bros. v. Gamage (A.W.) (1915) 31 T.L.R. 328; 32 R.P.C. 273 429
Spanish Prospecting Co., *Re* [1911] 1 Ch. 92; 80 L.J.Ch. 210 ...... 4, 70, 78, 530
Spence v. Paterson's Tr., July 7, 1812, F.C. 39, 286
Spenceley v. Greenwood (1858) 1 F. & F. 297; 115 R.R. 912 515
Spiers v. Houston's Excrs. (1829) 3 W. & S. 392; Ross, *Commercial Cases III*, 687 .... 281, 283
—— v. Royal Bank, June 22, 1822, F.C.; (1822) 1 S. 516 300
Spittal v. Smith (1829) Taml. 45 552
Spooner v. Browning [1898] 1 Q.B. 528; 67 L.J.Q.B. 339 .... 136, 139
Stables v. Eley (1825) 1 Car. & P. 614 153
Stalker v. Carmichael (1735) Mor. 9455 121
Standard Cameras' Application (the "Robin Hood" Case) (1952) 69 R.P.C. 125 431
Standard Property Investment Co. v. Dunblane Hydropathic (1884) 12 R. 328; 22 S.L.R. 215 559
Stanley & Co. v. Solomon [1932] 2 K.B. 287; affg. [1932] 1 K.B. 611 ... 75, 76, 77
Starrett v. Pia, 1968 S.L.T. (Notes) 28 .... 378, 414
Steel v. Lester (1878) 3 C.P.D. 121; 47 L.J.C.P. 43 .... 307, 336
Steel & Co., *Petrs.* (1855) 18 D. 34 .... 555, 568
Steele v. Stuart (1866) 2 Eq. 84 219
Steinberg v. Scala (Leeds) [1923] 2 Ch. 452; 92 L.J.K.B. 944 35
Stephen's Tr. v. Macdougall & Co.'s Tr. (1889) 16 R. 779; 26 S.L.R. 594 ... 263, 270, 273
Sterry v. Clifton (1850) 9 C.B. 110; 82 R.R. 319 100
Steuart v. Gladstone (1878) 10 Ch.D. 626; 47 L.J.Ch. 423 ... 433, 487, 490, 529
Stevens v. Britten [1954] 1 W.L.R. 1340; [1954] 3 All E.R. 385 314
—— v. South Devon Ry. (1851) 9 Hare 326; 89 R.R. 460 184
Stevenson v. Adair (1872) 10 M. 919; 44 Sc.Jur. 529 30
—— v. Campbell, 11 Fac. 486; (1836) 14 S. 562 243
—— v. Cartonnagen Industrie [1918] A.C. 239; 87 L.J.K.B. 416 .... 49, 50
Stevios Thomopulos v. John Mandilos [1948] A.C. 12 113
Steward v. Blakeway (1869) 4 Ch.App. 603; affg. (1868) L.R. 6 Eq. 479 ... 67, 388, 390, 391
Stewart v. Buchanan (1903) 6 F. 15; 11 S.L.T. 347 ... 51, 59, 64, 77, 81, 90, 91
—— v. Forbes (1849) 1 Mac. & G. 137; 13 Jur. 523 .... 401, 402
—— v. Galloway (Earl) (1752) Mor. 9465 102
—— v. Gibson (1840) 1 Rob. 260; (1835) 14 S. 166 124
—— v. Morrison, Jan. 19, 1779, F.C.; (1779) Mor. 7080 161
—— v. North (1893) 20 R. 260; 30 S.L.R. 235 .... 170, 171, 178, 609, 629
—— v. Simpson, 11 Fac. 49; (1835) 14 S. 72 .... 406, 423, 525
—— v. Snodgrass (1860) 23 D. 187; 33 Sc.Jur. 91 36
Stewart's Tr. v. Salvesen & Co. (1900) 2 F. 983; 8 S.L.T. 64 560
Stewart & McDonald v. Brown (1898) 25 R. 1042; 6 S.L.T. 85 .... 559, 561
Stocken v. Dawson (1848) 17 L.J.Ch. 282; affg. (1845) 9 Beav. 239; (1843) 6 Beav. 371 .... 190, 407, 525, 539, 541, 543
Stone, *Re* (1886) 33 Ch.D. 541; 55 L.J.Ch. 795 95
—— v. Marsh (1827) 5 L.J.(o.s.)K.B. 201; 30 R.R. 420 .... 347, 351
Stott v. Fender & Crombie (1878) 5 R. 1104; 15 S.L.R. 734 .... 90, 92
Strong v. Harvey (1825) 3 Bing. 304 6

Stroud v. Gwyer (1860) 28 Beav. 130; 2 L.T. 400 540
Stroyan v. Milroy, 1910 S.C. 174; 1909, 2 S.L.T. 453 197
Struthers v. Barr (1826) 2 W. & S. 153 400
Sturgeon v. Salmon (1906) 22 T.L.R. 584 479
Suburban Hotel Co. (1867) 2 Ch.App. 737; 36 L.J.Ch. 710 474
Summers v. Solomon (1857) 7 E. & B. 879; 26 L.J.Q.B. 301 157
Sumner v. Powell (1816) 2 Mer. 30; 16 R.R. 136 352
Sutherland v. Morson, Jan. 19, 1825, F.C.; (1825) 3 S. 449 35
Sutherland (Duchess) Re, Bechoff & Co. v. Bubna (1921) 31 T.L.R. 248 ... 48
Sutton & Co. v. Grey [1894] 1 Q.B. 285; 63 L.J.Q.B. 633 .... 75, 76, 77
Swan v. Bank of Scotland (1835) 2 Mon. & Ayr. 661 104
Swire v. Francis (1877) 3 App.Cas. 106; 47 L.J.P.C. 18 318
Syers v. Syers (1876) 1 App.Cas. 174; 35 L.T. 101 91
Sykes v. Midland Bank Excr. & Tr. Co. [1970] 3 W.L.R. 273; [1970] 2 All
    E.R. 471 220
Symington v. Symington's Quarries (1905) 8 F. 121; 13 S.L.T. 509 475

TANCRED ARROL & CO. v. Steel Co. of Scotland (1890) 17 R. (H.L.) 31;
    affg. (1889) 16 R. 440; 27 S.L.R. 463 209
" Tarantella " Tms. (1910) 27 R.P.C. 573 .... 431, 432
Tatam v. Williams (1844) 3 Hare 347; 64 R.R. 325 .... 19, 412
Tattersall v. Sladen [1928] Ch. 318; 97 L.J.Ch. 145 465
Taylor, Ex p., re Grason (1879) 12 Ch.D. 366; 41 L.T. 6 95
—— v. Best (1854) 14 C.B. 487; 98 R.R. 717 47
—— v. Chester (1869) L.R. 4 Q.B. 309; 38 L.J.Q.B. 225 124
—— v. Plumer (1815) 3 M. & S. 562; 16 R.R. 361 371
—— v. Provan (1864) 2 M. 1226; 36 Sc.Jur. 611 .... 40, 41
—— v. Walker [1958] 1 Lloyd's Rep. 490; [1958] C.L.Y. 1647 167
Taylor & Paterson, Petrs. (1840) 2 D. 952 568
Taylor & Sons v. Taylor (1823) 2 S. 157 196
Tennant, Ex p., re Howard (1877) 6 Ch.D. 303; 37 L.T. 284 .... 77, 83
Tennent v. Tennent's Trs. (1870) 8 M. (H.L.) 10; 7 S.L.R. 400 491
Thicknesse v. Bromilow (1832) 2 Cr. & J. 425; 37 R.R. 752 245
Thom v. North British Banking Co. (1850) 13 D. 134; 23 Sc.Jur. 40 626
Thomas v. Atherton (1878) 10 Ch.D. 185; 48 L.J.Ch. 370 224
—— v. Shillibeer (1836) 1 M. & W. 124 277
Thompson v. Brown (1827) Moo. & M. 40; 31 R.R. 710 198
—— v. Percival (1834) 5 B. & Ad. 925; 53 R.R. 187 .... 150, 276
Thomson, Petr. (1893) 1 S.L.T. 59 .... 406, 468, 470, 526, 527
—— v. Bell (1894) 1 S.L.T. 433 91
—— v. Clydesdale Bank (1893) 20 R. (H.L.) 59; 1 S.L.T. 111; (1891) 18
    R. 751 257
—— v. Dove, Feb. 16, 1811, F.C. 100
—— v. Liddell & Co., July 2, 1812, F.C. 161
—— v. Shanks, 15 Fac. 710; (1840) 2 D. 699 .... 5, 6
—— v. Thomson, 1962 S.C. (H.L.) 28; 1962 S.L.T. 109 .... 18, 23, 412, 445
Thomson & Balfour v. Boag & Son, 1936 S.C. 2; 1936 S.L.T. 2 268
Thomson & Co. v. Pattison, Elder & Co. (1895) 22 R. 432; 2 S.L.T. 546 ... 321,
    332, 333
Thomson & Husband v. Mackaile, Feb. 14, 1770, F.C.; Mor. 9519 102
Thorburn v. Ellis, May 24, 1811, F.C. 304
Thornton v. Dixon (1791) 3 Bro.C.C. 199 390
—— v. Howe (1862) 31 Beav. 14; 31 L.J.Ch. 767 98
Thurn & Taxis (Princess) v. Moffitt [1915] 1 Ch. 58; 84 L.J.Ch. 220 453
Thwaites v. Coulthwaite [1896] 1 Ch. 496; 65 L.J.Ch. 238 .... 108, 111, 621
Thynne v. Shove (1890) 45 Ch. 577; 59 L.J.Ch. 509 427
Tingley v. Müller [1917] 2 Ch. 144; 86 L.J.Ch. 625 48
Tinnevelly Sugar Refining Co. v. Mirrlees Watson & Yaryan Co. (1894) 21
    R. 1009; 2 S.L.T. 149 263
Todd v. Emly (1841) 8 M. & W. 505 5
Tomlinson v. Broadsmith [1896] 1 Q.B. 386, 392; 65 L.J.Q.B. 308 212
Toulmin v. Copland (1836) 3 Y. & C. Ex. 655; 51 R.R. 414, 429 198
Towart v. Sellers (1817) 5 Dow 231; 6 Pat.App. 301 39
Tower Cabinet Co. v. Ingram [1949] 2 K.B. 397; [1949] 1 All E.R. 1033 ... 137,
    139, 140, 145, 151, 152, 297, 298, 301, 502, 503, 590
Townsend v. Jarman [1900] 2 Ch. 698, 702, 703; 69 L.J.Ch. 823 .... 152, 427
Traill v. Smith's Trs. & Fernie (1876) 3 R. 770; 13 S.L.R. 489 ... 258, 320, 331

Trego v. Hunt [1896] A.C. 7; revg. [1895] 1 Ch. 462 .... 175, 198, 419–421
Trimble v. Goldberg [1906] A.C. 494; 75 L.J.P.C. 92 .... 168, 181
Troughton v. Hunter (1854) 18 Beav. 470; 104 R.R. 504 .... 426, 508
Trower & Sons v. Ripstein [1944] A.C. 254; [1944] 2 All E.R. 274 65
Trueman v. Loder (1840) 11 A. & E. 589; 9 L.J.Q.B. 165 157
Tully v. Ingram (1891) 19 R. 65; 29 S.L.R. 78 .... 273, 308, 366
Tunley v. Evans (1845) 2 D. & L. 747; 69 R.R. 877 217
Tupper & Carr v. Rowell (1858) 20 D. 758; 30 Sc.Jur. 408 .... 157, 244
Turnbull v. McKie (1822) 1 S. 353 .... 183, 229, 237, 249
Turnell v. Sanderson (1891) 60 L.J.Ch. 703; 64 L.T. 654 480
Turner v. Bayley (1864) 4 De G.J. & S. 332; 34 Beav. 105 199
—— v. Major (1862) 3 Giff. 442; 5 L.T. 600 434
—— v. Reynall (1863) 14 C.B.(N.S.) 328; 32 L.J.C.P. 164 110
Tytler (Walker's Tr.) v. Walker (1883) 10 R. 699; 20 S.L.R. 448 573

Underwood (A. L.) v. Bank of Liverpool & Martins [1924] 1 K.B. 775; 93
    L.J.K.B. 690 220
University of Cambridge v. Baldwin (1839) 5 M. & W. 580; 52 R.R. 850 281
Urquhart v. McPherson (1878) 3 App.Cas. 831 550
Usher v. Dauncey (1814) 4 Camp. 97; 15 R.R. 729 .... 293, 515
Uxbridge Permanent Benefit Bldg. Socy. v. Pickard [1939] 2 K.B. 248;
    [1939] 2 All E.R. 344 157

Vamvakas v. Custodian of Enemy Property [1952] Q.B. 183; [1952] 1 All
    E.R. 629 47
Van Sandau v. Moore (1826) 1 Russ. 441; 25 R.R. 100 439
Van Zetler v. Mason Cattley & Co. (1908) 25 R.P.C. 37 430
Vawdrey v. Simpson [1896] 1 Ch. 166; 65 L.J.Ch. 369 .... 480, 483
Venables v. Wood (1839) 1 D. 659; 14 Fac. 773; Ross, Commercial Cases
    III, 529 .... 72, 74, 259, 260, 261, 609
Ventisei v. Ventisei's Excrs., 1966 S.C. 21 529
Vere v. Dale (1804) Mor. 16389; Feb. 29, 1804, F.C. 29
Vice v. Fleming (1827) 1 Y. & J. 227 287
Victorian Daylesford Syndicate v. Dott [1905] 2 Ch. 624; 75 L.J.Ch. 446 104
Vinall v. Howard [1954] 1 Q.B. 375; [1954] 2 W.L.R. 314; [1954] 1 All
    E.R. 458 104
Vince, Re [1892] 2 Q.B. 478; 61 L.J.Q.B. 836 94
Viney v. Chaplin (1858) 2 De G. & J. 483; 119 R.R. 213 347
Virtue v. Alloa Police Commrs. (1873) 1 R. 285; 11 S.L.R. 140 307
Vulliamy v. Noble (1817) 3 Mer. 593; 17 R.R. 143 .... 144, 145, 293
Vyse v. Foster (1874) L.R. 7 H.L. 318; affg. (1872) L.R. 8 Ch.App. 309 ... 541, 546

Waddle v. Gibson, Jan. 18, 1812, F.C. 30, 35
Wade v. Jenkins (1860) 2 Giff. 509 .... 433, 529
Wakefield Rolling Stock Co., Re [1892] 3 Ch. 165; 61 L.J.Ch. 670 533
Waldie v. Roxburgh (Duke) (1825) 1 W. & S. 1; affg. (1822) 1 S. 367 ... 304
Walker, Re [1905] 1 Ch. 160; 74 L.J.Ch. 86 286
—— v. Davidson (1821) 1 S. 21 274
—— v. I.R.C. [1920] 3 K.B. 648 94
—— v. Law (1872) 11 M. 199; 45 Sc.Jur. 122 .... 393, 394
—— v. McKnights (1886) 13 R. 599; 23 S.L.R. 408 496
—— v. Mottram (1881) 19 Ch.D. 355; 51 L.J.Ch. 108 421
—— v. Reith (1906) 8 F. 381; 13 S.L.T. 660 83
—— v. Smith (1906) 8 F. 619; 13 S.L.T. 907 .... 157, 237, 238, 250, 251
Wall v. Brownlee (1724) Mor. 9035 31
—— v. London & Northern Assets Corpn. [1898] 2 Ch. 469; 67 L.J.Ch.
    596 187
Wallace v. Wallace's Trs. (1906) 8 F. 558; 13 S.L.T. 844 444
—— v. Whitelaw (1900) 2 F. 675; 7 S.L.T. 410 .... 455, 456, 461
—— v. Plock & Logan (1841) 3 D. 1047 .... 161, 277
Wallace, Hamilton & Co. v. Trs. of John Hamilton & Co. (1824) 2 S.App.
    467; affg. June 8, 1821, F.C. (1821) 1 S. 53 171
Wallis v. Russell [1902] 2 I.R. 585 30
Walmsley v. Walmsley (1846) 3 Jo. & Lat. 556; 72 R.R. 129 199

Walter v. Ashton [1902] 2 Ch. 282; 71 L.J.Ch. 839 139
Warlow v. Harrison (1859) 1 E. & E. 309; affg. (1858) 1 E. & E. 295; 117
    R.R. 219, 227 240
Warner v. Cunningham (1815) 3 Dow 76 144
——— v. Smith (1863) 1 De G. J. & S. 337; 32 L.J.Ch. 573 404
Waterer v. Waterer (1873) L.R. 15 Eq. 402; 21 W.R. 508 .... 380, 389
Watson, Ex p. (1809) 16 Ves. 265 .... 129, 130
——— v. Black (1885) 16 Q.B.D. 270; 55 L.J.Q.B. 31 392
——— v. Duncan (1879) 6 R. 1247; 16 S.L.R. 791 381
——— v. Haggitt [1928] A.C. 127; 97 L.J.P.C. 33; 138 L.T. 306 ...... 12, 70, 530
——— v. Park Royal (Caterers) [1961] 1 W.L.R. 727; [1961] 2 All E.R. 346 114
——— v. Smith, Dec. 17, 1806; Hume 756 .... 134, 143
Watt v. Ritchie, Jan. 23, 1782, F.C.; (1782) Mor. 7074 161
Watts v. Brooks (1798) 3 Ves. 612 103
——— v. Driscoll [1901] 1 Ch. 294; 70 L.J.Ch. 157 .... 416, 526
Waugh v. Carver (1793) 2 H.Bl. 235; 14 R.R. 845; Ross, *Commercial*
    Cases III, 426 .... 61, 78, 79, 83, 128, 130
Webster v. Bray (1849) 7 Hare 159; 82 R.R. 44 .... 401, 403
——— v. Webster (1791) 3 Swanst. 490n.; 19 R.R. 258 144
Wedderburn v. Wedderburn (1836) 2 Keen 722; 44 R.R. 331 .... 190, 541,
    545, 546
——— v. ——— (1856) 22 Beav. 84; 111 R.R. 267 428
Weikersheim's Case, *Re* Land Credit Co. of Ireland (1873) 8 Ch.App.
    831; 42 L.J.Ch. 435 393
Weiner v. Harris [1910] 1 K.B. 285; 79 L.J.K.B. 342 60
Weir v. Bell (1878) 3 Ex.D. 238; 47 L.J.Ex. 704 318
Weissenbruch v. Weissenbruch, 1961 S.C. 340; 1961 S.L.T. (Notes) 55 383
Weller v. Denton [1921] 3 K.B. 103; 90 L.J.K.B. 889 114
Welsh v. Knarston, 1972 S.L.T. 96 .... 153, 275, 498, 513
Wemyss v. Australian Co. of Edinburgh (1856) 19 D. 122; 29 Sc.Jur. 59 . 340, 360
——— v. His Creditors (1637) Mor. 9025 .... 34, 35
Wenlock (Baroness) v. River Dee Co. (1883) 19 Q.B.D. 155; 56 L.J.Q.B.
    589 257
West v. Skip (1749) 1 Ves.Sen. 239 .... 406, 407, 525
Westbourne Galleries, *Re* [1971] 1 Ch. 799; [1971] 2 W.L.R. 618; revg.
    [1970] 1 W.L.R. 1378 475
West London Commercial Bank v. Kitson (1884) 13 Q.B.D. 360; 53
    L.J.Q.B. 345 238
Western Bank of Scotland v. Needell (1859) 1 F. & F. 461 504
Weymouth Steam Packet Co., *Re* [1891] 1 Ch. 66; 60 L.J.Ch. 93 533
Wheatly, *Ex p.* Cooke, *Bankruptcy Law*, 8th ed., 534 561
Whetham v. Davey (1885) 30 Ch.D. 574; 53 L.T. 501 .... 201, 203, 413, 526
White, *Ex p.*, *re* Nevill (1871) L.R. 6 Ch. 397; 40 L.J.Bk. 73 .... 358, 363
——— v. McIntyre, 16 Fac. 309; (1841) 3 D. 334 .... 66, 157, 257, 259, 262,
    609, 615, 616, 619, 624
Whitechurch v. Cavanagh [1902] A.C. 117 131
Whitehill v. Bradford [1952] Ch. 236; [1952] 1 All E.R. 115 ... 121, 122, 423, 424
Whiteman v. Sadler [1910] A.C. 514; 79 L.J.K.B. 1050 104
Whiteman Smith Motor Co. v. Chaplin [1934] 2 K.B. 35; 103 L.J.K.B. 328 419
Whitmore, *Ex p.* (1838) 3 Deac. 365; 3 Mont. & Ayr. 627 .... 264, 265, 273
Whitwell v. Arthur (1865) 35 Beav. 140 .... 461, 522
Whitwood Chemical Co. v. Hardman [1891] 2 Ch. 417; 60 L.J.Ch. 428 ... 179, 194
Wilkie v. Dunlop, 9 Fac. 294; (1834) 12 S. 506 35
——— v. Johnstone, Bannatyne & Co. (1808) 5 Pat.App. 191 608
Wilkinson v. Page (1842) 1 Hare 276; 58 R.R. 77 523
Willett v. Blanford (1842) 1 Hare 253; 58 R.R. 61 .... 543, 546
——— v. Chambers (1778) Cowp. 814; Ross, *Commercial Cases III*, 476 ... 342,
    346
Williams, *Ex p.* (1805) 11 Ves. 3; 8 R.R. 62 .... 406, 512
——— v. Jones (1826) 5 B. & C. 108; 29 R.R. 181 .... 106, 591
——— v. Keats (1817) 2 Stark. 290; 19 R.R. 723 .... 146, 290, 291, 301
Williamson v. Hine [1891] 1 Ch. 390; 60 L.J.Ch. 123 169
——— v. Taylor (1898) 14 Sh.Ct.Rep. 303 .... 166, 181
Willis v. Dyson (1816) 1 Stark. 164 .... 249, 287
Wilson v. Glasgow & S.W. Ry. (1850) 13 D. 227; 23 Sc.Jur. 82 195
——— v. Greenwood (1818) 1 Swanst. 471; 18 R.R. 118 512
———, *Re*, Wilson v. Holloway [1893] 2 Ch. 340; 62 L.J.Ch. 781 .... 67, 390
——— v. Laidlaw (1816) 6 Pat.App. 222. *See also* Wilson's (Pettigrew)
    Case 25, 27, 29, 31, 32, 35

Wilson v. Moore (1834) 1 Myl. & K. 337; affg. (1833) 1 Myl. & K. 126; 36
    R.R. 272 .... 368, 369
——— v. Riddell, 1 Fac. 707; (1826) 4 S. 732 361
——— v. Threshie (1825) 4 S. 361 .... 380, 631
——— v. Whitehead (1842) 10 M. & W. 503; 62 R.R. 685 .... 260, 261, 617
——— v. Williams (1892) 29 L.R.Ir. 176 424
Wilson & Fraser v. Nisbet (1736) Mor. 1509 41
Wilson & Meeson v. Pickering [1946] K.B. 422; 175 L.T. 65 131
Wilson & Ors. v. Alexander & Ors. (1807) 5 Pat.App. 182 33
Wilson's (Pettigrew) Case, Bell, Com. II, 514; sub nom. Wilson v. Laidlaw
    (1816) 6 Pat.App. 222 .... 25, 27, 29, 31, 32, 35
Wilsons & Clyde Coal Co. v. English, 1937 S.C.(H.L.) 46; 1937 S.L.T. 523 ... 310
Wiseman v. Easton (1863) 8 L.T.(N.S.) 637 245
Witham v. Teenan's Tr. (1884) 11 R. 776; 21 S.L.R. 520 573
Withers, Birch & Co. v. Cowan, Nov. 16, 1790, unreported; Bell, Com. II,
    540 .... 608, 614, 633
Wood v. Argyll (Duke) (1844) 6 M. & G. 928; 13 L.J.C.P. 96 132
——— v. Scoles (1866) L.R. 1 Ch. 369; 35 L.J.Ch. 547 .... 529, 531
——— v. Wilson (1835) 2 Cr. M. & R. 241; 4 L.J.Ex. 193 523
——— v. Woad (1874) L.R. 9 Ex. 190; 43 L.J.Ex. 153 .... 486, 487, 490, 492
Woodin, Ex p. (1843) 3 Mont. D. & D. 399 363
Worcester Corn Exchange Co., Re (1853) 3 De G.M. & G. 180; 98 R.R.
    98 .... 219, 256
Wotherspoon v. Henderson's Trs. (1868) 6 M. 1052; 40 Sc.Jur. 584 ...... 499, 516
Wray v. Hutchinson (1834) 2 Myl. & K. 235; 3 L.J.Ch. 62 467
Wright v. Gardner's Trs. (1831) 9 S. 721 299
——— v. Outram & Co. (1890) 17 R. 596; 27 S.L.R. 482 312
Wrightson v. Pullan (1816) 1 Stark. 375; 18 R.R. 784 515
Wyld v. Hopkins (1846) 15 M. & W. 517; 71 R.R. 751 142

Yallop, Ex p. (1808) 15 Ves. 60; 10 R.R. 24 381
Yates v. Finn (1880) L.R. 13 Ch.D. 839; 49 L.J.Ch. 188 .... 438, 541
Yenidje Tobacco Co., Re [1916] 2 Ch. 426; 86 L.J.Ch. 1 .... 63, 474, 475,
    476, 490, 522
Yonge v. Toynbee [1910] 1 K.B. 215; 79 L.J.K.B. 208 460
Yorkshire Banking Co. v. Beatson (1880) 5 C.P.D. 109; 49 L.J.C.P. 380 ... 245,
    248
Young, Re, ex p. Jones [1896] 2 Q.B. 484; 65 L.J.Q.B. 681 ...... 90, 91, 93, 94
——— v. Ladies Imperial Club [1920] 2 K.B. 523; 89 L.J.K.B. 563 187
——— v. Smart, 7 Fac. 107; (1831) 10 S. 130 243
——— v. Dougans (1887) 14 R. 490; 24 S.L.R. 363 632

TABLE OF STATUTES

1621 Act (c. 18) 553, 573
1696 Act (c. 5) 449, 508, 553,
         563, 573–575
      Act (c. 25) 382–386
1765 Bank Notes (Scotland)
         Act (5 Geo. 3, c. 49) 314
1772 Bankrupts Act (12 Geo.
         3, c. 47) 556, 557
1800 Bank of England Act (39
         & 40 Geo. 3, c. 28) 111
      Pawnbrokers Act (39 &
         40 Geo. 3, c. 99) ... 106, 107
1828 Statute of Frauds Amend-
         ment Act (9 Geo. 4,
         c. 14) 318
      Bank Notes Act (9 Geo.
         4, c. 23 111
1831 Truck Act (1 & 2 Will.
         4, c. 37) 314–316
1833 (3 & 4 Will. 4, c. 55) ... 381
1839 Bankruptcy (Scotland) Act
         (2 & 3 Vict. c. 41 ... 556
1844 Bank Charter Act (7 & 8
         Vict. c. 32) 111
1845 Registering of British
         Vessels Act (8 & 9
         Vict. c. 89) 381
1853 Betting Act (16 & 17 Vict.
         c. 119) 108
1854 Merchant Shipping Act
         (17 & 18 Vict. c. 104) 381
      Merchant Shipping Re-
         peal Act (17 & 18
         Vict. c. 120) 381
1856 Mercantile Law Amend-
         ment (Scotland) Act
         (19 & 20 Vict. c. 60) 278–
         281. 318
      Bankruptcy (Scotland) Act
         (19 & 20 Vict. c. 79) 559–
         561, 567, 569, 578, 579, 581
1857 Court of Session Act (20
         & 21 Vict. c. 56) ... 455
1862 Companies Act (25 & 26
         Vict. c. 89) 533, 636
      s. 4   6
      s. 79 473
1865 Law of Partnership Act
         (28 & 29 Vict. c. 86) 61,
         76, 82, 83, 86, 91, 583
1868 Court of Session Act (31
         & 32 Vict. c. 100) ... 458
1869 Stannaries Act (32 & 33
         Vict. c. 19)   14
      Debtors Act (32 & 33
         Vict. c. 62) 167
1871 Trade Union Act (34 &
         35 Vict. c. 31) 111
1872 Pawnbrokers Act (35 &
         36 Vict. c. 93) ... 107, 111

1874 Infants Relief Act (37 &
         38 Vict. c. 62) 37, 38
1876 Trade Union Act Amend-
         ment Act (39 & 40
         Vict. c. 22) 111
1880 Judicial Factors (Scot-
         land) Act (43 & 44
         Vict. c. 4) 456
      Debtors (Scotland) Act
         (43 & 44 Vict. c. 34) 560
1881 Newspaper Libel and
         Registration Act (44
         & 45 Vict. c. 60) ... 111
1882 Bills of Exchange Act (45
         & 46 Vict. c. 61) ... 8, 245
1883 Sea Fisheries Act (46 &
         47 Vict. c. 22) 335
1887 Stannaries Act (50 & 51
         Vict. c. 43)   14
      Truck Amendment Act
         (50 & 51 Vict. c. 46) 315
1889 Arbitration Act (52 & 53
         Vict. c. 49) 203
      Interpretation Act (52 &
         53 Vict. c. 63) 44, 387
1890 Partnership Act (53 & 54
         Vict. c. 39)—
      s. 1 ... 2, 5, 7–11, 13, 14, 44,
         54, 58, 100, 205, 395, 447,
            470, 586, 607, 636
      s. 2 .... 53–55, 62–96, 204,
            334, 583, 610, 636
      s. 3 .... 93–96, 637
      s. 4 .... 1, 14, 15, 45, 161,
         196, 197, 222, 223, 276, 278,
         320, 351, 354, 356, 370, 432,
         555, 570, 571, 580, 586, 637
      s. 5 ... 154, 155, 158–160, 207–
         211, 218, 221, 224, 231–236,
         242–244, 248, 251–253, 271,
         302, 306, 307, 313, 323, 333,
         341, 494, 513, 517, 574–576,
            588, 589, 599, 617, 637
      s. 6 .... 207, 637
      s. 7 .... 207, 236, 242,
            243, 638
      s. 8 .... 143, 207, 287, 638
      s. 9 .... 159, 160, 196, 197,
         207, 275, 276, 278, 352–358,
            554, 638
      s. 10 ...... 157, 206, 207, 302,
         303, 306–328, 332–342, 348,
         351, 352, 357, 358, 367, 369,
            455. 493. 620, 638
      s. 11 ...... 207, 303, 304, 318,
         327, 329, 336, 339–352, 358,
            360–369, 638
      s. 12 .... 207, 351, 352,
            356–358, 369, 638
      s. 13 ...... 207, 326, 348, 351,
            360–370, 374, 638

xliii

1890 Partnership Act—*cont.*
      s. 14 ... 12, 80, 127–146, 153,
            154, 290–293, 296, 297, 426,
            427, 444, 500–503, 507, 519,
                            520, 638
      s. 15 .... 207, 217, 218,
                            342, 639
      s. 16 ...... 207, 218–220, 230,
            232–235, 360, 513, 639
      s. 17 ...... 149, 150, 260, 263,
            271–275, 498, 639
      s. 18 .... 280, 281, 639
      s. 19 .... 378, 414,
                      593, 599, 639
      s. 20 .... 65, 67, 377–379,
            381, 383, 384, 387–389, 527,
                            630, 639
      s. 21 ... 65, 67, 377–379, 640
      s. 22 .... 65, 67, 200,
                      389–392, 640
      s. 23 ...... 378, 394, 395, 398,
                452, 599, 600, 640
      s. 24 .... 17, 22, 43, 53,
            182–185, 198, 199, 249, 254,
            287, 400–402, 404, 411, 412,
            453, 530, 539, 557, 581, 599,
                      624, 634, 640
      s. 25 ...... 188, 484, 491, 641
      s. 26 .... 437–439, 441,
                      492, 591, 641
      s. 27 .... 437, 438, 441,
                      442, 593, 641
      s. 28 ...... 198, 220, 633, 641
      s. 29 ...... 164–173, 178, 181,
            192, 193, 379, 434, 641
      s. 30 .... 164, 168, 169,
            177–179, 181, 193, 379, 380
                            642
      s. 31 .... 17, 18, 43, 199,
            201–203, 397, 413–416, 418,
            453, 479, 480, 525, 526, 595,
                            634, 642
      s. 32 ... 3, 40, 436, 442, 443,
            460, 600, 607, 631, 642
      s. 33 .... 41, 44, 294, 295,
            416, 436, 444–452, 480, 553,
                562, 564, 599–601, 642
      s. 34 ...... 453–455, 467, 468,
                            642
      s. 35 .... 40, 44, 186, 229,
            435, 446, 453, 455–478, 480,
            482–484, 490, 491, 524, 554,
                            603, 642
      s. 36 .... 145, 146, 151,
            288–298, 300, 301, 444, 500–
            509, 594, 595, 643
      s. 37 ...... 288, 508, 595, 643
      s. 38 ...... 275, 295, 444, 448,
            460, 498, 512, 513, 517–520,
            539, 553, 564, 604, 643
      s. 39 ...... 406–411, 455, 520,
            521, 524–527, 644
      s. 40 .... 255, 455, 481,
                            540, 644
      s. 41 .... 163, 255, 540,
                      547–551, 644
      s. 42 .... 373, 416, 455,
            540–546, 601, 644

1890 Partnership Act—*cont.*
      s. 43 645
      s. 44 ...... 404, 405, 527–532,
            535–539, 563, 565, 571, 645
      s. 45 .... 2, 455, 586, 645
      s. 46 ..... 1, 8, 127, 154, 206,
            313, 332, 338, 339, 354, 356,
                478, 491, 507, 645
      s. 47 ...... 294, 447–450, 508,
            510, 519, 553, 564, 566, 645
      s. 48 .... 281, 645
      s. 49 645
      s. 50 645
1891 Stamp Act (54 & 55 Vict.
            c. 39) 109
1893 Sale of Goods Act (56 &
            57 Vict. c. 71) 38
1894 Finance Act (57 & 58
            Vict. c. 30) 389
      Merchant Shipping Act
            (57 & 58 Vict. c. 60)   381
1896 Stannaries Court (Aboli-
            tion) Act (59 & 60
            Vict. c. 45) 14
1900 Money-lenders Act (63 &
            64 Vict. c. 51) 112
1905 Trade Marks Act (5 Edw.
            7, c. 15) 428, 431
1907 Limited Partnerships Act
            (7 Edw. 7, c. 24)—
      s. 1 646
      s. 2 646
      s. 3 .... 586, 646
      s. 4 ...... 585, 586, 592, 600,
            601, 646, 657, 660
      s. 5 .... 588, 590, 593,
                            594, 646
      s. 6 ... 586–591, 595–606, 646
      s. 7 .... 590, 594–599,
                            636, 647
      s. 8 .... 588, 590–594, 647,
                            651, 655
      s. 9 .... 586, 591–594,
                      648, 650, 652
      s. 10 ...... 586, 587, 594–596,
                            648, 655
      s. 11 ...... 586, 596, 597, 648,
                      651, 653, 654
      s. 12 .... 597, 649
      s. 13 .... 586, 588, 649
      s. 14 649
      s. 15 .... 590, 593, 649
      s. 16 .... 588, 649
      s. 17 649
      Sheriff Courts (Scotland)
            Act (7 Edw. 7, c. 51)   456
1908 Companies Act (8 Edw. 7,
            c. 12), s. 1 6
      Companies (Consolida-
            tion) Act (8 Edw. 7,
            c. 69)—
      s. 268 606
      s. 286 .... 605, 647
      Sched. 6 647
      Statute Law Revision Act
            (8 Edw. 7, c. 49) ... 640, 645

1913 Bankruptcy (Scotland) Act
(3 & 4 Geo. 5, c. 20)   42,
43, 295, 447, 451, 508, 553,
556, 558–560, 565, 567–569,
574, 577–581, 605
1914 Aliens Restriction Act (4
& 5 Geo. 5, c. 12) ...   47
Status of Aliens Act (4 &
5 Geo. 5, c. 17)   47
Bankruptcy Act (4 & 5
Geo. 5, c. 59)   42,
566, 572
Trading with the Enemy
Act (4 & 5 Geo. 5,
c. 87) 47, 48
1916 Registration of Business
Names Act (6 & 7
Geo. 5, c. 58)   111,
113–117, 152, 153, 297, 298,
301, 427, 590, 593
1919 Aliens Restriction (Amendment) Act (9 & 10
Geo. 5, c. 92)   47
1920 Finance Act (10 & 11
Geo. 5, c. 18) ... 596, 648
Married Women's Pro-
perty (Scotland) Act
(10 & 11 Geo. 5,
c. 64)   44
1921 Trusts (Scotland) Act (11
& 12 Geo. 5, c. 58)   24,
388
1924 Conveyancing (Scotland)
Act (14 & 15 Geo. 5,
c. 27)   30
1925 Settled Land Act (15 & 16
Geo. 5, c. 18)   65
Law of Property Act (15
& 16 Geo. 5, c. 20) ...   65,
391
Former Enemy Aliens
(Disability Removal)
Act (15 & 16 Geo. 5,
c. 43)   47
Guardianship of Infants
Act (15 & 16 Geo. 5,
c. 45)   24
Theatrical Employers Re-
gistration Act (15 &
16 Geo. 5, c. 50) ...   111
1927 Moneylenders Act (17 &
18 Geo. 5, c. 21) ... 111, 112
Statute Law Revision Act
(17 & 18 Geo. 5,
c. 42) ... 47, 117, 152, 447
1928 Racecourse Betting Act
(18 & 19 Geo. 5,
c. 41)   111
1929 Companies Act (19 & 20
Geo. 5, c. 23), s. 357   6
1931 Architects (Registration)
Act (21 & 22 Geo. 5,
c. 33)   659
1933 Solicitors (Scotland) Act
(23 & 24 Geo. 5,
c. 21) 109, 110, 657
Finance Act (23 & 24
Geo. 5, c. 19) ... 596, 648,
651, 654, 655

1934 Betting and Lotteries Act
(24 & 25 Geo. 5,
c. 58) 111, 622, 623
1938 Trade Marks Act (1 & 2
Geo. 6, c. 22) 428–432
Conveyancing Amendment
(Scotland) Act (1 & 2
Geo. 6, c. 24)   30
Coal Act (1 & 2 Geo. 6,
c. 52)   69
1939 War Risks Insurance Act
(2 & 3 Geo. 6, c. 57)   656
Trading with the Enemy
Act (2 & 3 Geo. 6,
c. 89) 47, 48
1943 British Nationality and
Status of Aliens Act
(6 & 7 Geo. 6, c. 14)   47
Coal Act (6 & 7 Geo. 6,
c. 38)   69
1946 Coal Industry Nationalisation Act (9 & 10
Geo. 6, c. 59)   69
National Health Service
Act (9 & 10 Geo. 6,
c. 81)   424
1947 National Health Service
(Scotland) Act (10 &
11 Geo. 6, c. 27) ...   3,
92, 110, 424
Local Government (Scot-
land) Act (10 & 11
Geo. 6, c. 43)   364
Companies Act (10 & 11
Geo. 6, c. 47)—
s. 115   574
s. 116 ... 115, 116, 117, 118
Sched. 9   152
1948 Companies Act (11 & 12
Geo. 6, c. 38)—
s. 117   393
s. 129   585
s. 161   657
s. 222 .... 63, 473, 474,
475, 476, 477
s. 278   441
s. 398 .... 605, 606
s. 399   606
s. 429 .... 13, 586, 656
s. 434 .... 6, 13, 586,
656–659
Sched. I   394
Sched. VII   585
British Nationality Act
(11 & 12 Geo. 6,
c. 56)   47
1949 Legal Aid and Solicitors
(Scotland) Act (12,
13 & 14 Geo. 6,
c. 63) 363, 364
Representation of the
People Act (12, 13 &
14 Geo. 6, c. 68) ...   100,
392
Patents Act (12, 13 & 14
Geo. 6, c. 87) ... 111, 658
Election Commissioners
Act (12, 13 & 14
Geo. 6, c. 90)   100

1949 National Health Service
       (Amendment)   Act
       (12, 13 & 14 Geo. 6,
       c. 93) 3, 92, 643
     Criminal Justice (Scot-
       land) Act (12, 13 &
       14 Geo. 6, c. 94) ...   649
1950 Arbitration Act (14 Geo.
       6, c. 27) 203, 482
1956 Valuation and Rating
       (Scotland) Act (4 &
       5 Eliz. 2, c. 60)   393
     Medical Act (4 & 5 Eliz.
       2, c. 76)   110
1957 Dentists Act (5 & 6 Eliz.
       2, c. 28)   110
1958 Prevention of Fraud (In-
       vestments) Act (6 &
       7 Eliz. 2, c. 45)   657
     Insurance Companies Act
       (6 & 7 Eliz. 2, c. 72)   111
1959 Licensing (Scotland) Act
       (7 & 8 Eliz. 2, c. 51)   316
     Mental Health Act (7 & 8
       Eliz. 2, c. 72)   439,
                          458, 642
1960 Road Traffic Act (8 & 9
       Eliz. 2, c. 16)   104
     Betting and Gaming Act
       (8 & 9 Eliz. 2, c. 60)   111

1962 Finance Act (10 & 11
       Eliz. 2, c. 44)   389
     Law Reform (Husband
       and Wife) Act (10 &
       11 Eliz. 2, c. 48) ...   337
1964 Diplomatic Privileges Act
       (c. 81)   47
1967 Companies Act (c. 81)—
       s. 2   585
       s. 70   111
       s. 119 .... 586, 656
       s. 120 .... 6, 13, 586,
                          656, 658, 659
       s. 121 .... 646, 657, 659
       s. 122   658
       s. 130   111
       Sched. 5   111
1969 Decimal Currency Act
       (c. 19)   645
     Representation of the
       People Act (c. 15) ...   393
     Age of Majority (Scot-
       land) Act (c. 39) ...   29
1970 Income and Corporation
       Taxes Act (c. 10) ...   313
                          314, 585
     Taxes Management Act
       (c. 9)   314
1971 Industrial Relations Act
       (c. 72)   111

Chapter I

THE GENERAL ATTRIBUTES OF THE RELATIONSHIP

In the development of the law of partnership, Scots law though originally basing itself on the *societas* of the Roman law has owed much to English law and to decisions of the English courts. Following the august example of George Joseph Bell, the author of the most complete and exhaustive Scottish treatise on partnership prior to the passing of the Partnership Act 1890,[1] drew heavily upon English decisions for his materials, though he warned the reader against uncritical acceptance of them as persuasive authority in Scotland in a passage which has withstood the onslaught of over a century and which still affords the Scots lawyer prudent counsel.

> " All English decisions, dicta and principles which are ostensibly based on abstract justice or sound commercial polity may be safely followed as precedents; but all such as are either founded on or are mixed up with technicalities are to be distrusted as of very doubtful authority in the Scottish system. English decisions are safe precedents when the circumstances of the case are substantially identical but must be received with great caution when they are merely analogous." [2]

The passing of the Partnership Act 1890, while it did much to foster the assimilation of English and Scots law, still leaves important areas of divergence. Some of these are apparent from the terms of the Act itself, *e.g.* section 4 which preserves the personality of the Scottish firm as distinct from the individual partners, while leaving the English law unaltered in its non-recognition of the separate personality of the firm.[3] But apart from those areas where the terms of the statute themselves put the Scottish reader on his guard, there is a wider and less defined area in which Clark's warning must be heeded. The Partnership Act 1890 is not a complete code of the law of partnership. While it legislates in terse and generally appropriate terms for the broad principles of the law of partnership and has achieved a marked success in reducing the rules of the common law to a simple and brief statement wherever it has chosen to cover the topic, it leaves important areas of partnership law, such as the law relating to the goodwill of partnerships, untouched. Moreover, the Act provides [4] that existing rules of equity and of common law shall continue in force except

---

[1] Clark, *A Treatise on the Law of Partnerships and Joint Stock Companies According to the Law of Scotland.* This remains the only work devoted to a detailed treatment of partnership in Scots law, though later writers on mercantile law have dealt with the subject in more abridged fashion.

[2] *Op. cit.* Vol. I, p. 14.

[3] A feature of the Act which is regretted by Lindley, *Partnership* (13th ed.) p. 5, where it is described as " a defect in the (English) law of partnership."

[4] s. 46.

1

in so far as inconsistent with the express provisions of the Act. An authoritative modern textbook on the law of partnership states that " speaking generally, the Act made no important changes in the law save in respect of the mode of making a partner's share of the partnership assets available for the payment of his separate judgment debts." [5] Though this assessment is made in relation to English law, it follows at least that many of the pre-statute decisions in the English courts may still be appealed to in a proper case as " not inconsistent " with the statute. That is not to say that they can be used to contradict the Act where its language is clear [6]; but since the Act in general has not sought to reform the law of partnership, there will be a considerable volume of pre-statute decisions both in England and in Scotland which may be useful in the interpretation of the words of the statute and also where that wording is obscure or does not entirely cover any particular case. There is thus a field in which a Scottish lawyer may have resort to pre-statute decisions in the English courts as well as in his own. His use of English authority since the passing of the Act will be even more confident. But he will do well to keep Clark's words in mind and he will be happier in his reliance upon such material if the English decision has been reached on broad equitable grounds and not by resort to the technicalities of the common law.

The nature of partnership is defined [7] as " the relation which subsists between persons carrying on a business in common with a view of profit," and that succinct definition is further explained and enlarged by a definition of " business " as including every trade, occupation or profession.[8] There are thus three elements of partnership expressed in the definition— (1) a business, (2) two or more persons engaged in carrying on that business, and (3) a motivation on the part of those persons in seeking a profit. It has been suggested by Sir Frederick Pollock [9] that there is an additional element which is implicit or inherent in the words of the definition, namely (4) an agreement among the persons forming the partnership to participate in the profits earned. Each of these elements deserves closer examination.

" Carrying on a business "

In view of the definition of " business " in section 45 of the Act, virtually any activity of a commercial or professional nature is comprehended in these terms, though in some cases, *e.g.* barristers [10] and advocates, partnerships for the purpose of their profession are prohibited by the code of conduct imposed upon them and in others, *e.g.* medical practitioners

---

[5] Lindley, *op. cit.* p. 4.
[6] On the principle, *leges posteriores priores contrarias abrogant.* Maxwell, *Interpretation of Statutes* (11th ed.) pp. 153 *et seq.*
[7] Partnership Act 1890, s. 1.
[8] *Ibid.* s. 45.
[9] *Digest of the Law of Partnership* (15th ed.) p. 9.
[10] *Annual Statement of the General Council of the Bar,* 1902–03, p. 4.

practising in partnership under the National Health Service [11] conditions are attached to the formation of such partnerships. These special cases apart, the question comes to be—Is the activity one which may be described as a business in the wide sense in which the term is employed in the Act? The activity need not be of a continuing nature since a single commercial adventure is clearly regarded by the Act as falling within its ambit.[12] The view here taken of the effect of the Partnership Act 1890 consorts with that taken under the pre-statute law of Scotland.[13] It also consorts with that taken in Scotland since the Partnership Act 1890 was passed.[14] The joint adventure which will be examined later in more detail is characterised by Bell as " limited to a particular adventure or voyage or course of trade." [15] The term " business " does however imply a course of business activity albeit of a limited nature. The mere ownership of property in common from which profits are drawn is neither a partnership nor a joint adventure, since " property owning is not a trade." [16] Likewise the ownership of shares in a ship does not of itself make the owner a partner with the owners of the remaining shares.[17] In *French* v. *Styring*,[18] joint ownership of a race-horse was held not sufficient to create a partnership between the owners but if in addition to the ownership in common of the property there is some business activity wherein the property so owned is used, the parties will become partners at least so far as that activity is concerned.[19] Thus, though the members of an association which has as its object the purchase of investments for the common benefit of members are not partners, even though they may have powers of realising the investments, changing them and re-investing in other investments, yet if the society were formed to speculate in investments and the real object were to make a profit by buying and selling securities to commercial advantage in the market, the members would be regarded as carrying on a business and hence as partners.[20]

" Persons carrying on a business "

Partnership entails that a business is carried on by a number of persons in association with one another. The title, " sole partner," is thus a

[11] National Health Service (Scotland) Act 1947, ss. 35–37; National Health Service (Amendment) Act 1949, ss. 1–9.
[12] Partnership Act 1890, s. 32: *Re Abenheim* (1913) 109 L.T. 219.
[13] Erskine, *Institute* iii: 3: 29 attempted a distinction in nature between a joint adventure and a partnership which according to Bell, *Com.* II, p. 539, led him to deduce "certain consequences not to be admitted." Bell's view is supported in *Davidson's Appeal* (1815) 3 Dow 218 and by Clark, *op. cit.* Vol. I, p. 44.
[14] *Inland Revenue* v. *Livingston*, 1927 S.C. 251; *Mair* v. *Wood*, 1948 S.C. 83.
[15] Bell, *Com.* II, p. 539.
[16] *Glasgow Heritable Trust* v. *Inland Revenue*, 1954 S.C. 266, *per* Lord President Cooper at p. 284.
[17] *Sharpe* v. *Carswell*, 1910 S.C. 391. See also Underhill, *Principles of the Law of Partnership* (9th ed.) p. 4; *Logan* v. *Brown* (1824) 3 S. 15.
[18] (1857) 2 C.B.(N.S.) 357.
[19] *Dawson* v. *Counsell* [1938] 3 All E.R. 5 (where the business consisted in horse-breeding from a mare).
[20] *Smith* v. *Anderson* (1880) 15 Ch.D. 247, *per* James L.J. at p. 276.

misnomer for the purposes of the law. But the idea of association cannot in every case be arrived at by a simple process of counting the heads of those who occupy themselves in the activities of the business. A number of persons may be engaged in managing a business but purely on behalf of a single individual. In such a case there is no partnership among the individuals so occupied in the management of the business.[21] On the other hand, one individual may run a business on behalf of himself and another or others. In that case a partnership may exist.[22] A so-called " sleeping partner " is nonetheless a partner and is " carrying on a business " for the purpose of section 1, though his activity in that pursuit may be indiscernible to the world beyond the partnership.[23]

" With a view of profit "

In *Re Spanish Prospecting Co. Ltd.*[24] Fletcher Moulton L.J. examined the idea of profit in its legal sense and found that it implies a comparison between the state of a business at two different points in time, which in practice are generally spaced one year apart, in order to ascertain the gain made by the business during the intervening period. To make the comparison accurately, the assets must be valued, and not merely enumerated, at each date since even if they are identical at each date that does not necessarily entail that there has been neither gain nor loss because the market value of the assets may have risen or fallen at the later date of the comparison and will in such circumstances disclose either a profit or a loss over the entire period of comparison. Fletcher Moulton L.J. therefore advanced the view that the strict legal concept of profit might be expressed as follows: " If the total assets of a business at the two dates concerned be compared the increase which they show at the later date as compared with the former, due allowance having been made for capital introduced into or taken out of the business in the meantime, represents in strictness the profits of the business during the period." This view of the meaning of profit, as Fletcher Moulton L.J. himself recognised, is not the view upon which a business man normally assesses his profit for any year of trading. He will value his stock-in-trade at both dates for the purpose of the comparison but he will not normally revalue his fixed assets each year and indeed may often write off from the value of such assets depreciation at a predetermined rate. The reasons for this practice are that no trading is being carried on in the fixed assets and while the business is a going concern any variation in the market value of such assets is unrepresented in cash because the firm is not in a position to realise its fixed assets in order to command the increase in their value. The instance which Fletcher Moulton L.J. was considering was an increase

[21] *Re Fisher & Sons* [1912] 2 K.B. 491; *Holme* v. *Hammond* (1872) L.R. 7 Ex. 218; *Paul* v. *Taylor* (1826) 4 S. 572.
[22] *Cox* v. *Hickman* (1860) 8 H.L.C. 268.
[23] Bell, *Com.* II, 512–513.
[24] [1911] 1 Ch. 92 at pp. 98–101.

in value of an asset which, although it had been regarded as valueless while the company was a going concern, yet was realised at a profit after the company had gone into liquidation. That gain was decided to be a " profit " of the company, so that servants whose remuneration was in some degree determined by a percentage of the profits of the company were entitled to claim in the liquidation for the appropriate share of the gain arising on the realisation of the asset by the liquidator.

The strict view of profit expounded by Fletcher Moulton L.J. is, therefore, not necessarily applicable in terms of the definition in section 1 of the Partnership Act 1890. The section speaks of " persons carrying on a business ... with a view of profit " and the contemplation of profit is envisaged in relation to a going concern. The partnership, in other words, cannot be regarded as " carrying on a business " with its fixed assets. No doubt, were the partnership to be dissolved and on winding up the firm a profit to be realised from the sale of its fixed assets, that profit would, in terms of the views expressed by Fletcher Moulton L.J., be a profit of the partnership and be dealt with accordingly. While that has its relevance elsewhere in a consideration of the legal consequences of partnership,[25] it does not appear to have any bearing on the profit which must be in the contemplation of the parties in terms of section 1.

Moreover, the statutory definition does not make the *occurrence* of a trading profit over any period a necessary requirement for the existence of a partnership. It is sufficient that there be a view of profit. Any element in the definition which made the actual making of a profit a necessary element for the existence of a partnership would be manifestly absurd. The definition is considering the situation where the parties first enter the association and at that stage no actual profit has been made and profits can only be in contemplation. Yet the contemplation of a profit arising from the association is a matter of great importance as it was under the pre-statute law. " It is in virtue of this principle that societies and clubs whose object is not the sharing of profits are not regarded as partnerships." [26] Thus the members of a trade protection society are held not to be partners [27]; nor are the members of clubs formed for political purposes [28] or for social convenience.[29] Such associations are not partnerships and their members will be held liable for their own individual acts alone [30] or at the most for the actings of those who have been empowered as their agents. In the latter case the onus rests on the person seeking to recover to prove that the relation of principal and agent exists, since that is not to be presumed or implied from the mere existence

[25] *Infra* Chap. XII.
[26] Clark, *op. cit.* I, p. 46.
[27] *Caldicott* v. *Griffiths* (1853) 8 Ex. 898.
[28] *Todd* v. *Emly* (1841) 8 M. & W. 505; *Thomson* v. *Shanks & Others* (1840) 2 D. 699; *Flemyng* v. *Hector* (1836) 2 M. & W. 172.
[29] *Re The St. James's Club* (1852) 2 De G.M. & G. 383.
[30] *Cross* v. *Williams* (1862) 7 H. & N. 675; *Samuel Bros. Ltd.* v. *Whetherly* [1907] 1 K.B. 709; [1908] 1 K.B. 184. Compare with *Cross* v. *Williams* (*supra*); *Lascelles* v. *Rathbun* (1919) 35 T.L.R. 347.

of the association.[31]   Both aspects of this rule are implicit in the Scottish
decision of *Thomson* v. *Shanks and Others*.[32]

Apart from there being a prospect of profit in contemplation by the
parties, there must be in contemplation a *community* of profit.   In *Neilson*
v. *McDougal* [33] two parties contracted to buy grain, the seller being taken
bound to deliver equal quantities to each.   It was held that there was no
partnership since *emptio rei facta a pluribus ementibus* was not sufficient
to infer it, there being no community of profit and loss.   Where, however,
a victualling society was set up to purchase goods and supply them to its
members and the public, it was held that the element of community of
profit could be regarded as in contemplation from the stated object of
trading with the public.   The society was therefore a partnership.[34]

Upon this ground that no community of profit and loss is present, it
has been held in England that there is no partnership among the members
of a mutual insurance society.[35]   The reasoning is that in such associations
each member underwrites a policy in return for a premium paid to him.
The policy so underwritten by a number of members of the society is not a
joint venture but a number of separate engagements under which each
underwriter is individually bound.   There is therefore no joint contract
on the part of the society nor is there any joint stock held by it.   The
authorities on this point are all anterior to the statute and it has been
held that such associations come within the meaning of section 4 of the
Companies Act 1862,[36] later represented by section 1 of the Companies
Act 1908, section 357 of the Companies Act 1929 and now by section 434
of the Companies Act 1948 as amended by section 120 of the Companies
Act 1967, since they are regarded as associations formed for the purpose
of carrying on a business " that has for its object the acquisition of gain by
the . . . association . . . or by the individual members thereof."   This line
of authority does not appear to be inconsistent with the decision that
associations of this kind are not partnerships.   The relevant provisions
of the Companies Acts apply to a " company, association or partnership,"
so that an association may be held to offend against those provisions
because it has for its object the acquisition of gain [37] without being necessarily regarded for that reason alone as a partnership.   It is true that such
an association must now be regarded as having a view of profit but the
profit contemplated is not that of the association but of each individual
separately.   Therefore the argument based upon lack of community of
profit appears to be unimpaired.[38]

[31] Lindley, *op. cit.* p. 12, cited with approval in *London Association for the Protection of
Trade* v. *Greenlands Ltd.* [1916] 2 A.C. 15, *per* Lord Parker at p. 39.
[32] *Supra* n. 28.
[33] (1682) Mor. 14551.
[34] *Sawers* v. *Tradestown Victualling Society*, Feb. 24, 1815, F.C.
[35] *Strong* v. *Harvey* (1825) 3 Bing. 304; *Redway* v. *Sweeting* (1867) L.R. 2 Ex. 400; *Gray* v.
Pearson (1870) L.R. 5 C.P. 568; *Andrews and Alexander's Case* (1869) L.R. 8 Ex. 176.
[36] *Ex p. Hargrove* (1875) L.R. 10 Ch. 542; *Re Padstow Total Loss Association* (1882) 20
Ch.D. 137.   A similar question was decided as to mutual loss societies in *Greenberg* v.
Cooperstein [1926] 1 Ch. 657 under the Companies Act 1908, s. 1 (2).
[37] On carrying on a business for acquisition of gain see *England* v. *Webb* [1898] A.C. 758.
[38] Lindley, *op. cit.* pp. 12-13, takes this view.

The necessity for the partners participating in the profits

Though section 1 of the Partnership Act 1890 makes no express mention of it, it has been suggested that the statutory definition implies a fourth element which is not stated therein, namely, that there should not merely be a " view of profit " held by the parties to the association but that they should also have in contemplation the division among themselves in some way of that profit.   That view has been propounded by no less an authority than Sir Frederick Pollock [39] himself and therefore requires careful consideration.   It is perhaps not particularly helpful to appeal to the various definitions of partnership which have been attempted from time to time in different legal systems.   A number of these have been collected in *Lindley on Partnership* [40] and the majority mention the element of division of the profits among the partners.   To the definitions so collected those of Bell [41] and Clark [42] might be added.   The former does not expressly mention division of the profits among the partners, though this may be due to Bell's professed distrust of definitions of partnership in general, " which like all others are proverbially dangerous, seldom useful." [43]   Clark, on the other hand, sees more virtue in the task of defining partnership and his definition comprehends the element of " sharing the profits and losses arising."

Pollock bases his argument chiefly upon the derivation of the words partner and partnership from *partiarius*, one who shares with another. His contention is that the notion of division or sharing of the profits among the partners is inherent in the very word " partnership " which is sought to be defined and therefore must be implied as an element in the statutory definition.   It is in his view of the essence of partnership that the profits of the association be shared among the partners.   While Pollock's argument is advanced chiefly upon the derivation of the word " partnership," it is difficult to resist the conclusion that it is an attempt to supply what was omitted as an express term.   There is authority for the proposition that at common law participation in the profits earned by the association was regarded as of the essence of partnership before the passing of the Partnership Act 1890. [44]   That of itself, however, does not advance the argument for the inclusion of the element as an implied term.   While the Partnership Act 1890 is in the main a measure declaratory of the pre-existing common law, its intention as declared in its title is not so closely restricted.   It is described as " an Act to declare and amend the law of partnership."   It is thus unavailing to appeal to the pre-existing state of the law to supply a deficiency in the wording of section 1, since the wording may have been intentionally devised to amend the former law.   It is

[39] *Digest of the Law of Partnership* (15th ed.) pp. 9 *et seq.*
[40] pp. 14 *et seq.*
[41] *Com.* II, p. 499.
[42] *Op. cit.* I, p. 46.
[43] *Loc. cit.*
[44] *Pooley* v. *Driver* (1876) L.R. 5 Ch.D. 458; *Mollwo March & Co.* v. *Court of Wards* (1872) L.R. 4 P.C. 419; *Burnell* v. *Hunt* (1841) 62 R.R. 850. But see *Aitchison* v. *Aitchison* (1877) 4 R. 899 discussed *infra* Chap. III, pp. 57–59.

submitted that it is equally fruitless to appeal to section 46 which preserves " the rules of equity and common law applicable to partnership " since the saving clause preserves the effect of such rules " except so far as they are inconsistent with the express provisions of the Act."

Are then the rules of the common law, in so far as they tended to import a fourth element into the definition " inconsistent " with those express provisions? The answer is not unattended with difficulty. On the one hand, it might be said that there is nothing essentially inconsistent with the statutory terms in the addition of the common law requirement of the fourth element. To some extent, such an addition might properly be regarded as complementary to, or merely exegetical of, the terms of section 1. On the other hand, section 1 is a defining section. Its purpose is to describe accurately and analytically the legal nature of partnership. In common with other exercises in definition, its purpose must be to some extent to delimit the concept and to restrain it within the bounds of the defining words. In that sense it can be argued that the importation of terms from the common law further to delimit the defined concept is to introduce material which is inconsistent with the provisions of the statute and that it is improper to invoke section 46 to explain the terms of the definition in section 1.

It is still possible, however, to maintain that the use of the word " partnership " in section 1 itself imports the inherent quality of participation among the partners and that the fourth element in the definition is thus supplied by implication. It can be objected to this method of interpretation that it attempts to supply from the word sought to be defined an element which is absent from the definition which is set forth. The process of circular definition by Act of Parliament has been the occasion of sardonic comment in other areas of the law,[45] though this apparently futile approach to the task may be found on examination to be governed by sound practical reasons. It would, however, be difficult to justify a process which sets forth a term to be defined, defines it with apparent exhaustiveness and then returns to the term itself to supply from its " inherent " meaning an aspect which has been omitted from the definition.

Mr. Robertson Christie in his article on " Partnership " [46] expresses the view that the objection to the statutory definition seems hypercritical. After an examination of some of the existing definitions of partnership, including the definition by Bell and the statutory definition, he notes the point that both Bell and the statute omit the element of division of profits among the partners, but assigns no great significance to that. " For, in speaking of persons carrying on business with a view of profit (1890 Act) or ' for the acquisition of gain or profit ' (Bell), it is a fair implication that the gain or profit with a view to which it is carried on is their gain or profit." With respect, it must be said that what is advanced

---

[45] Bills of Exchange Act 1882, s. 2: " ' Banker ' includes a body of persons, whether incorporated or not, who carry on the business of banking."
[46] *Encyclopaedia of the Laws of Scotland*, Vol. 11, para. 14.

as an argument in the passage quoted appears perilously close to a complete begging of the question which is raised for solution, namely is there room for the implication of a borrowed term in what purports to be a defining section? It may indeed be thought that Mr. Christie's approach to the matter leads him into logical difficulty when he continues,[47]

> " It is indeed possible to figure the case of a number of persons combining to carry on some business enterprise with a view to profit but to the devotion of the entire profit to some public or charitable purpose. . . . Were it to occur, it would depend on circumstances whether it was a partnership.[48] If the purpose were publicly and sufficiently identified with the charity or object, probably the individuals carrying on the work would be treated rather as agents for the charity than as agents for each other which latter is the feature of partnership. On the other hand if they were carrying on the business with all the ostensible features of partnership, the relationship would seem to be not the less partnership that the partners agreed to devote their profits when earned to some altruistic or other object."

From that passage it emerges that the writer, having initially taken up the position that the fourth element is present in the statutory definition of partnership by fair implication, is shortly thereafter compelled to the admission that nevertheless a partnership may exist in which the fourth element is absent, *i.e.* it may exhibit the three elements expressly mentioned in section 1 and not comply with the fourth which Mr. Christie considers to be implied in the wording of section 1. If that be a correct interpretation of his meaning, it is an argument for the restrictive interpretation of section 1 since that interpretation, and not Mr. Christie's, will alone permit of all the cases of partnership being covered. On the other hand, if the fourth element is to be implied in the definition, we are left with a definition of partnership to which we must add a mental proviso that cases of partnership may occur which do not comply with that definition in all its requirements. That is a most unhappy situation for a definition to find itself in and indeed is a clear indication that it is not an accurate definition.

Nor does the distinction which Mr. Christie purports to draw between cases where " the purpose is publicly and sufficiently identified with the charity or object," on the one hand, and cases where the individuals are " carrying on a business with all the ostensible features of partnership," on the other, permit us to escape from the dilemma. In the former case the explanation in terms of agency is only partially applicable. It can be appealed to if the charity is envisaged as some sort of charitable association, corporate or unincorporated, but how does an individual become an agent for a charitable object or, for that matter, any other object? It is precisely in this area, where some sort of association of individuals is formed with a view of profit which is to be devoted to the

[47] *Loc. cit.*
[48] *Commissioners of Inland Revenue* v. *Falkirk Temperance Café Trust*, 1927 S.C. 261.

realisation of their aspiration to advance some altruistic or other " object " that the real difficulty over the definition of partnership arises. In that case the argument for the inclusion of the fourth element in partnership appears to break down since it is admitted that a partnership may exist without the presence of that element. Mr. Christie obscures rather than elucidates the issue when he states that " the relationship would seem to be not the less partnership that the partners agreed to devote their profits when earned to some altruistic or other object." In the case as he states it, there can be little dubiety on either view fo the definition in section 1, because he is envisaging a division of the profits among the partners with an agreement among them that the share of each will be devoted to the favoured object. Leaving aside the question whether any individual would be so imprudent as to order his affairs in a manner so fraught with difficulties of taxation, this is not a case where the issue arises, because, whether necessary or not, the element of division of profits among the partners is present and is then governed by a further agreement devoting their respective shares of profits to other than personal ends.

It is where the individuals combine to conduct a business enterprise with a view of profit but without any of them having a personal right to a share of those profits, the whole being allotted *ab initio* to the charitable or other object sought to be advanced, that it becomes necessary to consider whether the association is a partnership in terms of section 1. On that question the state of the authorities makes it difficult to give a definite answer. There has been no decision since the passing of the Partnership Act 1890 which has dealt with the question from the viewpoint of the law of partnership, uncomplicated by the specialties of tax law. In *Religious Tract and Book Society* v. *Inland Revenue*,[49] a society, the object of which was to promote religion by the circulation of tracts and books, engaged in two distinct activities,—(1) they carried on the business of a booksellers' shop and (2) they sold books by means of colporteurs. They earned profits from the booksellers' shop but the colportage activities were not such as could be regarded as a commercial undertaking or carried on at a profit. The colportage could only be carried on with the assistance of the profits earned in the booksellers' shop and of voluntary subscriptions. The society was assessed to income tax on the profits of the booksellers' business and claimed to set against those profits the losses which had been incurred on the colportage activities. It was held that the profits earned in the booksellers' business were trade profits and assessable to income tax and that the losses on the colportage were not deductible therefrom, since the colportage was distinct from the bookselling business and was not in itself of a commercial nature. The case is not particularly helpful on the question of partnership which was not canvassed before the court. Lord Adam [50] said, " I agree with your Lordship that if a party takes to selling books, it does not matter to the Crown what his object is in doing

[49] (1896) 23 R. 390.
[50] *Ibid.* p. 393.

so—whether it is to put profit into his own pocket or having made profit, to expend it in charity or donation." But the case cannot confidently be cited for the proposition that the society was conducting the booksellers' business as a partnership. All it decides is that, for tax purposes, they were not conducting it as a charity.

In *Commissioners of Inland Revenue* v. *Falkirk Temperance Café Trust* [51] a testator conveyed half of the residue of his estate to trustees for the purpose of providing a temperance public house in Falkirk in further-ance of his expressed desire that the leading of a sober life might be made easier for the inhabitants of that town. His trustees used part of the trust funds in setting up a temperance hotel with two cafés, one where the middle classes might entertain themselves with decorous sobriety and one where the working classes might avail themselves of similar entertainment at cheaper prices. The hotel also contained free reading and recreation rooms, and bedrooms, bathrooms and a lecture hall which could be let at moderate charges. The trustees' aim was to make the hotel pay its way without making a profit. Any deficit in the annual returns was supplied from the interest earned by the balance of the trust funds which were invested in securities. On being assessed to income tax on the interest earned by the investments of the trust estate, the trustees claimed exemp-tion on the ground that the interest was part of the income of a charitable trust and was applied to charitable purposes only. The court so held and ruled that though charges were made for the services provided, that did not deprive the trust of its charitable nature. In this case again the question of partnership does not arise. If it had, it may be hazarded that the trustees would not have been regarded by the court as partners since they sought, albeit unsuccessfully, to charge only such prices as would meet the oncost of providing this sombre service to the inhabitants of Falkirk and therefore could not be said to be carrying on a business " with a view of profit."

The indications given in *Religious Tract and Book Society* v. *Inland Revenue* and in *Commissioners of Inland Revenue* v. *Falkirk Temperance Café Trust* do not afford any substantial basis on which to forecast which of the rival interpretations of section 1 of the Partnership Act 1890 the Scottish courts might favour, were the question to arise for decision. On the other hand, the pre-statute cases,[52] where the element of participation by the partners in the profits was regarded as of the essential nature of partnership, offer an equally unsure footing. It is not to be readily assumed that Parliament has inadvertently omitted this aspect from the definition, particularly when the effect of the omission is to broaden the scope of the definition. Perhaps the value of the decisions in *Religious Tract and Book Society* v. *Inland Revenue* and *Commissioners of Inland Revenue* v. *Falkirk Temperance Café Trust* in this context is that they

---

[51] 1927 S.C. 261.
[52] *e.g. Pooley* v. *Driver* (1876) L.R. 5 Ch.D. 458; *Mollwo March & Co.* v. *Court of Wards* (1872) L.R. 4 P.C. 419.

indicate an area of ambivalence which the pre-statute law had not dealt with and thus may suggest a reason for the omission by intent of the fourth element from the definition.

Salaried partners and partners subject to special provisions as to sharing in profits

In addition to the difficulties mentioned above in relation to the importation of Pollock's implied fourth element in the definition of partnership, problems also arise with regard to salaried partners, *i.e.* those whose names appear on the firm's stationery and, where applicable, in the entry relative to the firm in the register of business names, in the character of partners but who, in terms of the contract of copartnery, have no entitlement to share in the profits of the business and no interest in the assets of the firm, but are remunerated for their services by a salary. If it be regarded as an essential element in the definition of partnership that all those associated as partners in the firm should actually participate in the profits, then the salaried " partner " cannot be regarded as in partnership with his associates. He is, however, held out to the public in the character of a partner. It would, of course, be possible to rationalise his position on the ground either (a) that by drawing his salary he is " participating " in the profits or (b) that his liability to third parties in respect of transactions of the firm arises from his knowingly suffering himself to be held out as a partner. Neither rationalisation is entirely convincing. While a salaried partner might, though rather loosely, be described as participating in the profits where he draws his salary from profits earned by the firm, he can hardly be regarded as in any real sense " sharing " in those profits, and in any event his right to his salary will be maintainable against the firm where no profits have been earned or even where a loss has been sustained. Again, if the rationalisation be attempted on the ground that he has been held out as a partner,[52a] that will suffice to render him liable on firm transactions *as if he were a partner* but it will not make him a partner in the firm. Therefore if the fourth element of the definition is to be implied as Pollock suggests, then the salaried " partner " is merely held out in that character and liable on the score of that holding out. He will not, however, be a partner nor will he be entitled to the rights and equities of which a partner may avail himself in questions with his co-partnery. It appears to be the better opinion that although in terms of the contract of copartnery he receives a salary only and does not share in the profits, he is a partner of the firm in terms of the Act.[52b]

Where a partner is entitled under the partnership agreement to a share of profits and a guaranteed minimum yearly sum in the event of his stipulated share of profits in any year being less than that guaranteed

---

[52a] On holding out see Partnership Act 1890, s. 14 (1) and *infra* Chap. V.
[52b] Lindley, *op. cit.* pp. 13–14 commenting on *Watson* v. *Haggitt* [1928] A.C. 127. See also *Ellis* v. *Joseph Ellis & Co.* [1905] 1 K.B. 324. But *cf. Burnell* v. *Hunt* (1841) 5 Jur. 650.

sum, Pollock's implied fourth term in the definition would not give rise to difficulty in regarding him as a partner, but since in the case envisaged he will not be required as among the partners themselves to contribute towards losses, the terms of the agreement as a whole may require to be construed to discover whether the true intention of the parties is to create a partnership.[52c]   Where the agreement provides that the " partner " will receive a stipulated share of the profits earned, and contribute a stipulated share to the losses sustained, in the running of the business but will have no right to share in " capital " profits, *e.g.* those derived from the sale of fixed capital assets of the firm, it is thought that he is clearly to be regarded as a partner whether or not Pollock's fourth term is imported into the definition of partnership in section 1 (1) of the Partnership Act 1890.

Restriction on number of partners

The maximum number of partners under the Companies Act 1948 was ten for banking partnerships [53] and for other partnerships, twenty.[54] Under the Companies Act 1967 [55] the maximum number in the case of banking partnerships is increased to twenty.   In the case of partnerships of solicitors, accountants, whose qualifications are recognised by the Board of Trade, stockbrokers and other bodies which may be specified by the Board of Trade, the number of partners who may be associated in the same firm is now unlimited.   The former maximum of twenty laid down under section 434 (1) of the Companies Act 1948 remains unaltered in cases not expressly exempted under the Companies Act 1967 or added to the exempted classes by the Board of Trade (now the Department of Trade and Industry) in virtue of the powers conferred under that Act.

Any association which exceeds the statutory limit, where one is still applicable, is illegal.   Similarly, a partnership which was originally within the statutory limit of number will become illegal if, by admitting new members, it exceeds the statutory limit, where one is still applicable to it.[56]   In such cases each member of the partnership has unlimited liability for the whole debts of the association.[57]   The members of a Scottish partnership are subject to joint and several liability for the partnership debts [58] and the imposition of unlimited liability on each member of an illegal partnership entails that they may not escape a liability which otherwise would rest upon them as partners merely because their association is an illegal one.   Their liability, however, now becomes a primary one and not accessory as it would be if the partnership itself were legal.   In England where the liability of the partners is a joint one, the rule laid

[52c] This will hold good in the case of the salaried partner also.   See *infra* Chap. III, pp. 84–85.
[53] Companies Act 1948, s. 429.
[54] *Ibid.* s. 434 (1).
[55] s. 120. See the Partnership (Unrestricted Size) No. 1 Regulations 1968 (1968 S.I. No. 1222)—surveyors, auctioneers, valuers, estate agents etc.; 1970 (S.I. 1970 No. 835)—actuaries; 1970 (S.I. No. 992)—consulting engineers; 1970 (S.I. No. 1319)—building designers.
[56] *Shaw* v. *Simmons* (1883) 12 Q.B. 117.
[57] *Shaw* v. *Benson* (1883) 11 Q.B.D. 563; *Greenberg* v. *Cooperstein* [1926] 1 Ch. 657.
[58] *Infra* pp. 159–161.

down in the English decisions [57] imposes a more stringent liability.   But
a creditor who had notice of the illegality cannot recover against the
individual members.[59]

The terms of the first subsection of section 1 of the Partnership Act
1890 are sufficiently wide to embrace not only partnerships but also other
forms of association, such as corporations and limited liability companies
which are treated by the law as different from partnership.   The legal
distinction is preserved by subsection (2) which excludes from the wide
terms of subsection (1) any company or association which is:

(a) registered under the Companies Acts,

(b) formed or incorporated by or in pursuance of any other Act of
     Parliament or Letters Patent or by Royal Charter,

(c) a company engaged in working mines within and subject to the
     jurisdiction of the Stannaries.

The last mentioned of these exceptions relates to the Stannaries
district in England, including all parts of Devon and Cornwall where any
tin works are situated.   " Stannary " (latin, *stannaria*) means a tin mine.
From early times the Stannaries Court regulated questions arising between
the tinners of Devon and Cornwall but the court was abolished by the
Stannaries Court (Abolition) Act 1896 and its jurisdiction transferred to
the county court.   The Stannaries Acts 1869 and 1887 contain provisions
which are still operative relating to the registration of partnerships working
mines in the stannaries.   This excepted case, therefore, has no significance
for the Scots lawyer and even in England it is now rarely met with.[60]

Corporations and firms

In making the distinction between partnerships and other forms of
association, the Partnership Act attempts a provision [61] which will serve
the needs of both the English and the Scottish systems of law.   The needs
to be provided for differ on either side of the border.   Apart from the
speciality of the provision relating to the Stannaries, which is peculiar to
England, the distinction drawn between corporations and companies, on
the one hand, and partnerships, on the other, has different legal consequences in Scotland from those obtaining in England.   In England there
is a clear separation of the corporation or the company registered under
the Companies Acts, with its complete juristic *persona*, from the partnership, where there is no separate *persona* in the firm which remains merely
the aggregate of the *personae* of the individual partners who comprise
it.[62]   The sharpness of the distinction is illustrated in the maxims concerned
with the liability of the corporation, or *universitas—Si quid universitati
debetur singulis non debetur, nec quod debet universitas singuli debent*—as

[59] *Re South Wales Atlantic S.S. Co.* (1876) 2 Ch.D. 763.
[60] Gower, *Modern Company Law* (3rd ed.) p. 8.
[61] s. 1 (2).
[62] Partnership Act 1890, s. 4 (1): " Persons who have entered into partnership with one
     another are for the purposes of this Act called collectively a firm, and the name under
     which their business is carried on is called the firm name."

compared with the maxim relating to the partnership, or *societas—Si quid societati debetur singulis debetur et quod debet societas singuli debent*. In the case of the corporate body the rights and obligations of the corporation are not owed to or by the individual members nor are the individual members liable for the debts and obligations of the corporation. In the case of the (English) partnership the members do not collectively form a distinct and separate person in law and thus the partnership as a collective whole has no capacity of acquiring rights or incurring obligations.

In the case of a Scottish partnership the Act makes detailed and distinctive provision [63]: " In Scotland a firm is a legal person distinct from the partners of whom it is composed, but an individual partner may be charged on a decree or diligence directed against the firm, and on payment of the debt is entitled to relief *pro rata* from the firm and its other partners." In the subsection just quoted the intention is to preserve the salient feature of the common law of Scotland as it existed prior to the passing of the Act. Clark [64] explains the law as follows: " The distinctive or central feature of the Scottish partnership is that it constitutes a *quasi persona* of which the members are agents and sureties, a principle which exactly realizes the notion of a firm entertained by mercantile men both in this country and in England." Clark's claim that the Scots law conforms to the view of partnership held by commercial men is indorsed by the eminent English authority on this branch of the law. Lindley,[65] dealing with the English law as expressed in section 4 (1) of the Act, states, " Partners are called collectively a firm. Merchants and lawyers have different notions respecting the nature of a firm. Commercial men and accountants are apt to look upon a firm in the light in which lawyers look upon a corporation, *i.e.* as a body distinct from the members composing it and having rights and obligations distinct from those of its members. . . . In the mercantile view partners are never indebted to each other in respect of partnership transactions, but are always either debtors or creditors to the firm." And later he continues, " But that is not the legal notion of a firm. The firm is not recognised by English lawyers as distinct from the members composing it." [66]

It will be seen that the Partnership Act in section 4 (2) accurately reflects the essential feature of the firm in Scotland as explained by Clark. The *persona* of the firm is kept distinct and separate from those of the partners composing the firm, but the subsection immediately proceeds to qualify that general statement with two subsidiary propositions which tend to interlace the *personae* of both firm and partners in a way which is entirely unfamiliar in the law of corporations. By the first of those qualifications an individual partner may be charged on a debt or diligence directed against the firm, so that the sharp distinction maintained between the liability of the corporation and those of its individual members is

[63] Partnership Act 1890, s. 4 (2).
[64] *Op. cit.* Vol. I, p. 31.
[65] *Op. cit.* p. 27.
[66] *Ibid.* p. 28.

lost.   By the second qualification any individual partner who has paid a debt of the firm is entitled to relief *pro rata* from the firm itself and from the other partners.   In neither of these qualifications is the major proposition that the firm in Scotland is a legal person destroyed.   In both the separate entity of the firm is implicit; but as a result of both that entity is different in its legal consequences from the juristic *persona* of an incorporated association.

That difference in the legal consequences of regarding the firm as a separate legal person has traditionally been recognised by designating the Scottish partnership, as Clark designated it, a *quasi-persona*.   The description had its attractions as a brief and compendious manner of referring to the incomplete attribution of corporate personality to the Scottish firm, but, like other exercises in the cult of the " *quasi*," it has little else to commend it.   In itself the use of the term "*quasi-persona*" adds nothing to our comprehension of the legal quality of the partnership.   Its sole usefulness is to remind us that there are specialities attached to that kind of legal personality and to exhort us to bear those specialities in mind when we consider the impact of the law upon the notion that the firm is a separate person from its partners.

Any strictures which may be made upon the descriptive value of this excursion in the law of partnership into what Sir Carleton Allen has happily christened " the ghost land of the *quasi* " [67] should not, however, obscure the importance of this " distinctive or central feature of the Scottish partnership " as a legal notion.   England maintains a position apart from most other European countries in her persistent non-recognition of the personality of the firm.   The view of the English law is in conflict with the realities of commercial life and the pressures of the latter have caused some modification of the rigidity of English legal theory, particularly in the treatment by the courts of questions affecting partnership accounts and the administration of partnership assets.   There has been a general relaxation in favour of allowing actions to be brought by or against partners in the firm name.[68]   But in general terms the firm in England has no legal recognition and this has been admitted as a defect in the English law which it would have been desirable to remedy in the Partnership Act 1890 by assimilating the English to the Scots law.[69]

Delectus personae

The circumstances which impel a number of persons to associate themselves in a partnership from their very nature imply that there is a high degree of personal choice based upon the personal attributes of the persons so associating.   Thus Stair,[70] dealing with the termination of the relationship, states,

[67] *Law and Orders* (3rd ed.) p. 351.
[68] For a detailed discussion of those trends, see Lindley, *op. cit.* p. 26.
[69] Lindley, *op. cit.* p. 5.
[70] *Institution* I: 16: 5.

" Society by consent then is finished ... *secondly*, by the death, or incapacity of any of the partners to act in the society; for it being one individual contract of the whole, and not as many contracts as partners, it is like a sheaf of arrows bound together with one tie, out of which, if one be pulled, the rest will fall out, and the personal humour and industry of the partners is so chosen, that it is not supposed to be communicated to their heirs or assignees unless by custom or paction the contrary is proved. Which no doubt is consistent with, though not consequent from, the nature of Society."

This exposition of the basic principle underlying the contract of partnership is followed by Erskine [71] and Bankton. [72] In so far as Stair in the passage quoted makes an exception of cases where " by custom or paction the contrary is proved," his views were followed by succeeding institutional writers. Bell [73] following Pothier regards the principle of the Roman law as having " more of subtility than of good sense " and declares that by the law of Scotland, (1) *delectus personae* bars the admission of new partners " either by succession or by alienation," but (2) " the parties may stipulate that their heirs, or even their assignees, shall be adopted in their room." Even in the second case, he does not regard the principle of *delectus personae* as entirely abrogated.

" But although, in a contract of partnership which admits heirs and assignees, there is less of *delectus personae* than when they are excluded, still a confidence is mutually reposed in the members, that in assigning their shares they will be careful in selection; and at least it would appear that the company might object, on cause shown, to the partner proposed to be introduced, and that the power of assigning or selling the share must be qualified to this effect." [74]

While the Partnership Act 1890 makes special provision that no person may be introduced as a partner without the consent of all existing partners, [75] that is expressed as a rule which is to be effective " subject to any agreement express or implied between the partners." Greater significance may be given to the words of section 31 (1) which provide,

" An assignment by any partner of his share in the partnership ... does not, as against the other partners, entitle the assignee, during the continuance of the partnership, to interfere in the management or administration of the partnership business or affairs, or to require any accounts of the partnership transactions, or to inspect the partnership books, but entitles the assignee only to receive the share of

---

[71] *Institute* III: 3: 22: " As partners are, from a *delectus personae*, or the reciprocal choice they make of each other, united in a kind of brotherhood, no partner could by the Roman law transfer his interest or share in the society to a third person, without consent of the company; but copartneries, even private ones, may now be so constituted by a special article for that purpose, that the partners are left at liberty to transfer their shares to whom they please. If any of the partners shall assume a third person into partnership with him, such assumed person becomes partner not to the company but to the assumer. . . ."
[72] *Institute* I: 22: 15.
[73] *Com.* II, p. 509.
[74] *Ibid.*
[75] Partnership Act 1890, s. 24 (7).

profits to which the assigning partner would otherwise be entitled, and the assignee must accept the account of profits agreed to by the partners."

Even these words do not preclude the possibility of agreement among the partners in the contract of copartnery that a partner may introduce his assignee as a partner of the firm in his place and the Partnership Act has done nothing to assail the views as to the common law expressed by Stair and Bell. A stipulation in the partnership agreement that any partner shall be entitled to introduce another person into the partnership is a prospective consent by the partners to the assumption of that other person as a partner and if they refuse to admit a person so introduced, or to execute any deeds or writings requisite to confer upon that person the rights of a partner, it has been held in the English courts that he will be granted such relief as the courts normally grant to a partner in the circumstances of the particular case, *e.g.* an interdict to prevent his being excluded from the affairs of the business, or an accounting or an order for the execution by the existing partners of any such deeds as may be proper in the particular case or even to a dissolution of the firm.[76]

> " To make a person a partner with two others their consent must clearly be had, but there is no particular mode or time required for giving that consent; and if three enter into partnership by a contract which provides that on one retiring, one of the remaining two, or even a fourth person who is no partner at all, shall name the successor to take the share of the one retiring, it is clear that this would be a valid contract which the court must perform and that the new partner would come in as entirely by the consent of the other two as if they had adopted him by name." [77]

It may be hazarded that the occasions upon which a right of this kind will be stipulated for, while never numerous, will within their own narrow ambit mainly arise in relation to the retirement or death of one of the existing partners, though there is a reported case in England of a stipulation in the contract of copartnery allowing a partner to nominate an infant son to be a partner when he should attain majority.[78] In Scotland the decisions have been mainly concerned with the situation where a right to the trustees or representatives of a deceased partner to be assumed as a partner in his place is stipulated for in the partnership agreement.[79] Much will turn upon the construction of the clause in the partnership agreement conferring the right and the Scottish decisions will be examined more closely later.[80] In England also the general rule that the trustees of a

[76] *Lovegrove* v. *Nelson* (1834) 3 M. & K. 1. Any such entitlement will be conditional upon the party introduced having implemented the conditions laid down in the contract of copartnery for his introduction: *Byrne* v. *Reid* [1902] 2 Ch. 735.
[77] *Lovegrove* v. *Nelson* (*supra*) *per* Lord Brougham.
[78] *Ehrman* v. *Ehrman* (1894) 72 L.T. 17.
[79] *Beveridge* v. *Beveridge* (1872) 10 M.(H.L.) 1; *Alexander's Trs.* v. *Thomson* (1885) 22 S.L.R. 828; *Thomson* v. *Thomson*, 1962 S.C.(H.L.) 28.
[80] *Infra* pp. 19–23.

deceased partner will not be entitled to insist upon being admitted to the partnership in his place has been held to yield to an express term of the partnership agreement.[81] The exceptions are clearly related to the intention of the parties to the contract of copartnery as expressed therein and in *Pearce* v. *Chamberlain*,[81] the Master of the Rolls seems to have gathered the intention of the parties to some extent at least from the circumstances surrounding the parties at the date of entering the contract and not solely from the wording of the contract itself although it is arguable that the terms of the contract themselves gave no express right to Pearce's representatives to be admitted in partnership with the surviving partner.

Even when the contract of copartnery expressly provides that after the death of one of the partners the business will be carried on by the surviving partners and the testamentary trustees of the deceased all difficulties likely to arise are not automatically circumvented. It may not be possible in the light of later authority, to accede to the view propounded by Bell in the passage already quoted [82] that sufficient of the principle of *delectus personae* remains even in such cases to make it possible for the surviving partners to " object, on cause shown, to the partner proposed to be introduced." It may be more confidently asserted that the view of Bankton [83] that " it is generally on account of the personal fitness of all the partners that society is entered into; and therefore, by the death of one, it is dissolved among the rest, if it was not otherwise provided at contracting; but no previous compact can be valid for assuming into copartnership the heir or representative of the partner that shall decease; because it is impossible they can know anything certain about the heir; however, he can be assumed after the predecessor's death," is too widely stated if by that passage he intends to convey the idea that some residual principle of *delectus personae* may prevail even in the face of an express provision of the contract of copartnery. The difficulties attendant upon the personal nature of the partnership relation may, however, have their influence upon the construction of any such provision.

Two problems of construction in particular are inherent in any case where such a clause is before the court for interpretation,—(1) Are the trustees introduced as partners merely to watch over the continuing interest of the deceased partner's estate in the business of the firm or in order to take an active part in the management of the firm? and (2) What is the constitutional position of a body of trustees introduced as a partner in respect of the deceased's interest? An attempt in the contract of copartnery to resolve the problem of the management of the firm, subsequent to the death of one of the partners, was before the court in *Beveridge* v. *Beveridge*.[84] The pursuer entered partnership with his father under a contract

[81] *Pearce* v. *Chamberlain* (1750) 2 Ves.Sen. 33; *Crawford* v. *Hamilton* (1818) 3 Madd. 251; *Bray* v. *Fromont* (1821) 6 Madd. 5; *Crawshay* v. *Maule* (1818) 1 Swanst. 495; *Tatam* v. *Williams* (1844) 3 Hare 347.
[82] *Supra* n. 73.
[83] *Institute* I: 22: 18.
[84] (1872) 10 M.(H.L.) 1.

of copartnery which provided that during the father's lifetime the business would be under his " charge and control " and, after the father's death, that of his brother, Mr. Robert Beveridge, who was not a partner and that the partnership would nevertheless remain in force between the father's trustees and the pursuer, notwithstanding the father's death.   Both parties bound themselves to grant any necessary authority to Mr. Robert Beveridge for the subscribing of obligations on behalf of the copartnery in the course of his management of its affairs.   The father in fact died before the date when the partnership was due to commence under the contract of copartnery.   His trustees, of whom Mr. Robert Beveridge was one, granted full authority to him as manager of the business and, about seven months later, commenced business in partnership with the pursuer.   The business proved successful but friction arose between the pursuer and Mr. Robert Beveridge who, as manager, arrogated to himself powers which the pursuer claimed were beyond those necessary in the management of the business.   The pursuer's complaints were upheld in the Court of Session on a number of issues but the issue which most clearly raised a legal principle was his practice of adhibiting the firm signature to documents instead of signing them as manager on behalf of the firm.   The defenders, the father's trustees, attempted to meet this criticism by contending that Mr. Robert Beveridge, as one of the trustees, was as such a partner in the firm and not merely its accredited manager.   That argument found no support either in the Court of Session [85] or in the House of Lords, where Lord Chelmsford observed,

"But then it is said that he was a partner and that as a partner he had a right to sign for the firm.   Now there were five trustees appointed by Mr. Erskine Beveridge which five trustees were to carry on the business on the death of Mr. Erskine Beveridge.   It is said that each of these five trustees was a separate partner—and, there being power to add indefinitely to the number of partners, there might have been twenty instead of five—and if Mr. Robert Beveridge, by reason of being a partner under these circumstances was fairly entitled to use the partnership name, then each of these five, or those twenty, persons would be similarly entitled to do the same.   And that would certainly be a strong argument against the possibility of such a power having been conferred under the circumstances of a trusteeship of this kind."

Lord Chelmsford then cited the relevant passages of the contract of copartnery to show that the trustees in their collective capacity were the partner of the firm. [86]

The point raised by Lord Chelmsford had been examined when the case was before the Second Division and was dealt with in the opinion of the Lord Justice-Clerk (Patton) who said, [87]

"The implied authority arising in the case of proper partnership

[85] (1869) 7 M. 1034.
[86] (1872) 10 M.(H.L.) at p. 9.
[87] (1869) 7 M. at p. 1041.

appears to me to have no place as far as trustees of a deceased partner are concerned. They have not the interest which a proper partner has; nor has the partner, who is supposed to be bound by their acts, any choice in their nomination. The body may be altered in their number, and in the persons of the trustees; and the *delectus personae*, which so essentially enters into the contract of society, is wholly awanting. That a partner of my own selection shall have the power to act as my accredited agent in the management of the company, and in the matters of the copartnership, is reasonable, and in accordance with what may be fairly presumed to be the nature of the contract. It is otherwise, I think, when we come to consider the position of parties who are really and in point of fact only administrators for others. There is, from the number of the trustees, an impossibility that the trustees as a body should execute the commercial instruments to which I have referred. There might have been one trustee only, and then there would have been no such impossibility. But according to the view which I take of the matter, the position of the party as trustee would not be such as to warrant his subscription of the copartnery firm of a company in which he had interest only as the administrator of the estate of another party."

In a case later decided [88] a contract of copartnery entered into between two parties stipulated that one of them should manage the business of the partnership, receiving a salary for doing so, and that on the death of either partner, the partnership would not be dissolved but that the representatives of the deceased partner should be " entitled to take his room and place in the copartnery with the exception that such representatives shall not be entitled to take the active management or carrying on of the business." The partner who had been the manager died and the surviving partner assumed the management. The representatives of the deceased partner raised an action for declarator that they collectively formed one partner along with the defender and that the defender had no right to assume the management and exclude them therefrom, and for interdict. It was held that they were entitled to a declarator that they collectively formed one partner but that they were not entitled to take part in the management of the copartnery business.

Further consideration will be given to the position of the trustees as collectively a partner of the firm at a later stage.[89] In the present context, the discussion is confined to what has been earlier described as the " constitutional " position of trustees in that situation, and to the interaction of the so-called principle of *delectus personae* upon that position. Taking the question of *delectus personae* first, it should be stated that, whatever its force in the Roman law, it is perhaps misleading to describe it as having the force of a " principle " in Scots, or English, law. It appears rather to be an element to be taken into consideration in arriving at a true

[88] *Alexander's Trs.* v. *Thomson* (1885) 22 S.L.R. 828.
[89] *Infra* pp. 22–23.

construction of the intention of the parties to a contract. This becomes apparent when the various judicial dicta on the subject are considered and analysed. Even the classic case of *delectus personae* mentioned by Bramwell B. in *Boulton* v. *Jones* [90] is susceptible of this explanation. The fact that one contracts with an author to write a book may, in the absence of any other expression in the contract as to authorship of the projected work, imply that there is *delectus personae* and that the contract must be performed personally but that will not be of sufficient force to displace any express terms as to delegation of the task such as might be expected to be present had Dumas subjected himself to such a relationship with his publisher. In the partnership cases which have been considered *delectus personae*, if it be invoked at all, may not be invoked to supply an overriding condition of personal choice of the partner or of personal performance by him of his duties. That such a term will be implied when the contract is silent upon the subject is trite law and finds its expression in section 24 (7) of the Partnership Act 1890. But there is no place for an implied term of that kind, where the parties have expressed an intention otherwise as is clearly recognised in the opening words of section 24.

Yet, though *delectus personae* cannot prevail in a head-on collision with the express terms of the contract, it is discernible that it has had some influence, though indeterminate, upon the manner in which those express terms have been construed by the courts, at least when the terms occur in contracts of partnership. An influence of more significance, however, is the practical difficulty attendant upon the position of trustees who are thus admitted as a " partner." The primary point mentioned by both Lord Chelmsford and the Lord Justice-Clerk that the trustees are collectively to be regarded as a partner does not appear to be redarguable. But once it has been conceded, the legal position of the trustees in the partnership is difficult to explain consistently with the underlying theory of the law of partnership. Too much need not be made of the issue of *delectus personae* raised by the Lord Justice-Clerk, since in the agreement of co-partnery that feature of the normal relationship had been expressly waived and if the initial *delectus* exercisable by the partners was waived in favour of the deceased partner's nomination of his own trustees, there is no very cogent reason in theory for regarding the waiver as ineffective to cover assumed trustees, provided that the clause in the partnership agreement is framed in such a manner as to cover that eventuality. The practical inconvenience of so uncontrolled a waiver affords no certain ground for the court refusing to give effect to its terms where they are clear and unambiguous. Nevertheless, that practical inconvenience is likely to alert the court to a more restricted interpretation of the provision which may be more workable; and equally compelling in the same direction is

---

[90] (1857) 2 H. & N. 564: " Where a contract is made in which the personality of the contracting party is, or may be, of importance, as a contract with a man to write a book, or the like, or where there might be a set-off, no other person can interpose and adopt the contract." Cited with approval in *Grierson, Oldham & Co.* v. *Forbes, Maxwell & Co.* (1895) 22 R. 812 at 814 and *Cole* v. *Handasyde & Co.*, 1910 S.C. 68 at 70.

the impracticability of a body of trustees who are collectively one partner engaging effectively in the commercial transactions of the firm. There is no collective agency which can adhibit the firm signature nor voice, as a collective partner, the views of the body of trustees.

One is, therefore, left with the situation that the trustees have been admitted as a partner without being in any practical sense enabled to act collectively as a partner in the management of the firm's affairs. However their position is regarded, it is clear that their powers as a " partner " are more restricted than are those of an individual who acts as a partner. On the other hand their liability for the obligations undertaken by the firm is not similarly limited and they enjoy the other rights, apart from those of taking part in the management, afforded to the partners under the contract of partnership, including, it is thought, the right to be informed of, and consulted upon, the conduct of the business.

It may, therefore, be possible to regard trustees in this situation as partners, but of a special kind. They presumably cannot be regarded as *quasi* partners since in terms of the partnership agreement their collective status as a partner is expressly recognised, and none of the pre-statute explanations of *quasi* partnership suggests that trustees acting as a collective partner are in this category.[91] Probably the view to be taken is that they are to be recognised collectively as a partner in the eyes of the law but that the practical limitations upon their powers of action preclude them from exercising all the powers which a partner normally enjoys. That, however, is not of itself sufficient to account for the case where an individual is admitted to the partnership in his capacity as trustee of a deceased partner. In *Beveridge* v. *Beveridge*[92] the Lord Justice-Clerk regarded that also as a case where his representative capacity would not warrant him in subscribing documents in the firm name. This dictum was not required for decision on the facts of the case and, with respect, its reasoning is not so clear or so compelling. The dubiety which the court may feel whether an administrator of a deceased partner's estate or other representative of the deceased was really intended by the parties to the contract of copartnery to take the deceased's place as a full partner in the firm is one which may be present in the mind of the court when construing the partnership agreement and may influence them in arriving at the conclusion that some alternative construction must be placed upon the words[93]; but once the words have been interpreted by the courts as entitling a trustee or representative of a deceased partner to be assumed as a partner, it is difficult to see what limitations are imposed upon his acting as a partner simply on account of his representative capacity which was the warrant for his introduction to the partnership in the first place.

[91] On *quasi* partnership see *infra*, Chap. III, pp. 60–63.
[92] As reported in (1869) 7 M. 1034.
[93] *Thomson* v. *Thomson*, 1961 S.C. 255; affd. 1962 S.C.(H.L.) 28 was a case of this kind.

CHAPTER II

CAPACITY OF PARTIES TO ENTER THE CONTRACT OF PARTNERSHIP

IN considering the question whether a contract of partnership has been entered into, as in the case of other contracts, it is necessary to have regard to the capacity of the parties to contract. Contractual capacity of a person may be subjected to legal limitation directly in the sense that his personal capacity to enter the contract in question, or any contract, is restricted. Such questions may arise from the personal qualities of an individual party concerned or from the nature of the legal entity bestowed by the law upon artificial persons such as corporations or companies. Again the capacity of a person to enter a contract may be affected by the fact that he purports to enter the contract not as binding himself to the relationship intended but as agent on behalf of another whom he intends to bind to that contractual relationship. A full treatment of contractual capacity belongs to a study of the law of contract in general.[1] It is inappropriate in the more specialised treatment of the contract of partnership which is undertaken here, and if essayed would inevitably duplicate material treated elsewhere in this series of works on the law of Scotland.[2]

There are, however, situations which can arise in regard to partnership and which are illustrative, or indeed may be the occasion of, specific difficulties in applying the general law of capacity to contract. To such topics this chapter will be confined.

Pupil children

Since pupils are regarded as being incapable of giving consent and hence having no power to contract, contracts made by a pupil, when he has no tutor, or where he has a tutor but purports to contract on his own behalf without reference to that tutor, are void.[3] If the pupil child has a tutor and that tutor purports to act in such manner as to bind his ward to a contract, the contract is voidable by the pupil within the *quadriennium utile* on the proof of lesion.[4] While the tutor has power to enter into ordinary contracts on behalf of a pupil,[5] the tutor is regarded as being in the position of a trustee [6] and as such he can have no implied power

---

[1] See *e.g.* Gloag, *Contract* (2nd ed.) Chaps. V, VI and VII.
[2] *i.e.* the projected work on Contract.
[3] Gloag, *op. cit.* p. 77.
[4] *Falconer* v. *Thomson* (1792) Mor. 16380.
[5] Fraser, *Parent and Child* (3rd ed.) pp. 222 and 307.
[6] Fraser, *loc. cit.*; Trusts (Scotland) Act 1921, s. 2. In *Shearer's Tutor*, 1924 S.C. 445 the statutory words were regarded as not including a father as tutor for his pupil child. But see Guardianship of Infants Act 1925, s. 10: " In Scotland a father or mother acting as tutor of a pupil child . . . shall be deemed to be and always to have been a trustee within the meaning of the Trusts (Scotland) Act 1921."

24

to invest the property of the pupil in speculative projects of trade. Thus it can be affirmed that a party cannot effectively engage himself in a partnership with a pupil child. If the purported contract is with the pupil himself, it may be reduced at the instance of the pupil at any time within the long negative prescription.[7] If it is entered into with the tutor on the pupil's behalf, then the pupil may have the contract of partnership reduced on proof of lesion but in that case he must raise his action within the *quadriennium utile*.[8]

In three early Scots cases, tutors signing a contract of co-partnery on behalf of pupil wards were held to have made themselves partners of the firm in place of the pupil. In *McAulay, Gartly, McDonald & Co.'s Tr.* v. *Renny*[9] a father as tutor executed a contract of partnership on behalf of his son who was eleven years of age. He was held to have made himself a partner in place of his son, who, as pupil, was incapable of entering into the contract. In *Calder* v. *Downie*[10] a similar judgment held the father liable as a partner where he had placed his son aged ten years in a company. In that case the pupil died and when the company became insolvent, an action was raised against the father on the ground that he had made himself a partner in the company. In *Pettigrew Wilson's Case*,[11] according to Bell, the tutor introduced his ward, a boy of fourteen years, into a partnership. The contract was held to be null and the creditors not to be entitled to claim in respect of it.

These cases do not clearly establish any rule in Scots law that parents or guardians who on behalf of pupil children who are their wards purport to enter the latter as partners in a trade, are in all cases themselves liable whether as partners in place of the pupil or as cautioners for him.[12] In an Irish case[13] a father who had paid a sum of money in respect of his infant son's share of the capital of a partnership, on the understanding that during the son's minority the profits would be accounted for to the father, was held not himself to be a partner in place of the infant son. But in *Reid's Case*[14] a father who had transferred shares into the name of his infant son was himself held liable as a contributory. On a consideration of these decisions, Clark[15] professes to have discovered the English law to be as follows:

[7] *Bruce* (1577) Mor. 8979.
[8] Bell, *Principles* § 2098; *Falconer* v. *Thomson* (1792) Mor. 16380.
[9] (1803). Briefly reported in Bell, *Com.* II, p. 514 n. 1.
[10] Dec. 11, 1811, F.C.
[11] Noted by both Clark, *op. cit.* and Bell, *Com. loc. cit.* as unreported. The case is later reported on as *Wilson* v. *Laidlaw* (1816) 6 Pat.App. 222. Bell appears to have been in error in citing the case as one where the father was held personally liable. No question of that sort was raised in the case which was concerned solely with the son's liability. Bell also misrepresented the effect of the decision which certainly did not lay down any rule that the creditors were unable to claim. But this may be explained by the fact that the ward was not a pupil as he states, but a minor. See note appended by the editor of the report at pp. 232–233 and *infra*.
[12] See Clark, *op. cit.* I, p. 23: Menzies, *Lectures on Conveyancing*, p. 409.
[13] *Barklie* v. *Scott*, 1 Huds. & Br. 83. See also *Ex p. Maxwell* (1857) 24 Beav. 321.
[14] (1857) 24 Beav. 318. See also *Reaveley's Case* (1848) 1 De G.& S. 550; *Ex p. Lichfield* (1849) 3 De G. & S. 141; *Ex p. Hennessy* (1849) 3 De G. & S. 191; (1850) 2 Macn. & G. 201; *Pim's Case* (1849) 3 De G. & Sm. 11.
[15] *Op. cit.* I, p. 23.

> " A father or guardian may engage an infant as a partner without
> incurring any responsibility as a partner himself, provided he receive no
> advantage or emolument from the transaction, is not in receipt of any of
> the profits in trust for the infant, and has not induced the company to
> receive the infant by fraudulent representations or by holding out
> his own responsibility. But, on the other hand, if he transfer shares
> from his own name to that of the infant, in order to avoid respon-
> sibility, or even in bona fide at a time when the company is insolvent,
> the transfer will be held null and the father or guardian will still
> remain liable to be made a contributory."

The rules quoted are taken by Clark [16] to be " the true exponent of the
Scotch cases referred to above, in so far as the latter can be taken as
precedents, encumbered as they are with specialities, and only imperfectly
reported."

That Clark is well founded in mistrusting the Scottish decisions as
authority for a general rule that parents or guardians introducing their
pupil wards as partners will themselves incur liability as partners in place
of their wards is sufficiently made out by the report in *Calder* v. *Downie*.[17]
Though the decision in *McAulay, Gartly, McDonald & Co.'s Tr.* v. *Renny* [18]
was urged upon them as conclusive of the question of the father's responsibility as a general principle of law, the court were divided on that point
and the father was only held liable in the special circumstances of the
case, since the majority of the judges (the Lord Justice-Clerk (Boyle),
Lords Glenlee, Craigie and Robertson) were of opinion that the father
had never truly divested himself of the input stock, and that he had
otherwise conducted himself as a partner. The minority (Lords Meadowbank and Gillies) were of opinion that the pursuers had not proved the
father to be a partner and also that he was not personally liable to the
pursuers for having bona fide placed his son as a partner in a trading
company since he had bestowed on him at the same time " a competent
input stock." Lord Robertson, who found with the majority of the
judges, observed that he did so on his view of the facts and if that had been
different, he " might possibly have coincided with the minority in opinion
as to the law."

Calder v. *Downie*, therefore, far from reinforcing the decision in the
earlier unreported decision of *McAulay, Gartly, McDonald & Co.'s Tr.* v.
Renny, detracts at least in some measure from it as an authority for the
generalised proposition sought to be deduced from it and there is justice
in the reporter's cautionary observation that " no decision was given upon
the point of law," though in the state of the authorities it is fortunate
that he did not act upon his other recorded reflection, that " as the case
was decided, it is perhaps an unfit subject for these reports." The meagre
record which we have from Bell's *Commentaries* [19] of the decision in

[16] *Ibid.*
[17] Dec. 11, 1811, F.C.
[18] *Supra*, n. 9.
[19] *Supra* n. 11.

Pettigrew Wilson's Case is of little assistance towards a solution of the problem. According to Bell the purported partnership " was held null, and the creditors not entitled to claim on it." Setting aside the question whether the court, if correctly reported, were right in holding the contract to be " null " instead of merely voidable, there is no word here as to the personal liability of the tutors in the contract of partnership.

It is more dubious whether the principles which Clark enunciates in the passage quoted, and which he considers, with some hesitation, would be adopted in Scots law, are stated with complete accuracy. Of the three requirements of the conduct of the " father or guardian " if he is to escape liability as a partner himself, the second, that " he is not in receipt of any of the profits in trust for the infant " does not derive support from *Barklie* v. *Scott* [20] since in that case the profits of the son's share in the partnership were to be accounted for to the father during the son's infancy, yet the father was held not to be a partner. The other requirements of escaping liability may be accepted less critically but of these only the first requirement, *i.e.* that the father himself receive no advantage or emolument from the transaction, is in any way germane to the problem which Clark is considering. The third requirement, that the father " has not induced the company to receive the infant by fraudulent representations or by holding out his own responsibility," in itself gives rise to independent causes of action against the father either on the ground of fraud or of holding himself out as a partner.[21] Moreover the principle upon which Clark seeks to impose liability upon a father or tutor, *i.e.* " where he transfers shares from his own name to that of the infant, in order to avoid responsibility, or even *in bona fide* at a time when the company is insolvent," while supported by the English authorities, is not particularly illuminating so far as the problem of the pupil's own liability under the transaction is concerned.

The English authorities upon which Clark relies for that proposition are without exception cases where the infant was introduced into a joint stock company. While at the time when the cases were decided, a member of a joint stock company was under an unlimited liability for the debts of the company on the same principle as if he were a partner in a firm, unlike a partner he was not entrusted with any of the management of the company's affairs. Though his rights and liabilities were based upon the law of partnership, since there was no other legal basis upon which they could rest, the demands of the commercial realities behind the crea tion of the joint stock company, reflected in its deed of settlement, introduced ideas, among them that of the contributory, which were neither normal in, nor entirely accounted for by, the partnership relation.[22] When considering partnership in modern times, therefore, the use of the earlier cases relating to joint stock companies must be discreet. At the

[20] 1 Huds. & Br. 83.
[21] On holding out, see *infra*, Chap. V, pp. 127 *et seq.*
[22] For an historical account of the joint stock company and its development into the modern company limited by shares, see Gower, *Modern Company Law* (3rd ed.) Chaps. 2 and 3.

date when the decisions were reported it was possible to integrate them, though rather uneasily, in a *rationale* of the law of partnership since that was the only existing legal relationship under which they could be subsumed. Nowadays, most of the specialities upon which such cases are reported are entirely foreign to the modern partnership and are explicable only in terms of the modern limited company.[23]

The decisions, both Scottish and English, which have just been discussed go very little distance towards clarifying the problem whether a pupil can in fact *be* a partner in any circumstances at all. The question is possibly somewhat academic and unreal in the case of pupils, but it becomes more pressing when the case of minors comes to be considered. If it can be envisaged that a pupil child acting for himself and without the intervention of his tutor would be accepted as a partner in a firm, then the legal relationship would rest upon so insecure a foundation as to be barely discernible as a legal relationship at all. The contract is in legal terms void.[24] It can be challenged not only within the *quadriennium utile* but at any time within the long negative prescription.[25] Any such partnership, therefore, is merely *de facto* and rests upon no legal basis whatsoever. If however the pupil continues in a relation of partnership after he has attained majority and without entering into a new contract of copartnery, it is possible to speculate upon the effectiveness of the agreement entered into by him as a pupil for the purpose of ascertaining his rights and duties as a partner when in majority. It is true that the agreement cannot fasten upon him any liabilities incurred by the firm while he was in minority, or, at least, that he will be able to extricate himself from these liabilities by pleading the nullity of the original agreement. But if his conduct subsequent to majority establishes the parties' intention that they should *then* be associated in partnership, and parties have continued after the majority of the pupil to associate in partnership on the terms of the original agreement with the pupil, it is thought that that agreement, though of itself void, may be looked at in order to work out the terms and conditions upon which he is now associated as a person *sui juris* with his partners. If the agreement under which the pupil originally became a " partner " was entered into on his behalf by his tutor, then, so far as the pupil child is concerned, it is voidable within the

---

[23] The difficulties mentioned are perhaps illustrated in the passage in Bell's *Com.* II, p. 513 of McLaren's edition where he says, " Not only is a pupil incapable of becoming a partner; but even a father as administrator for his son, or the tutors of a minor (?) for their ward, have no power to engage him in a partnership. They may indeed acquire for him a share in a prosperous company; and the partners who enter with them into such a contract will be bound to give him all the benefits thence accruing. But the pupil cannot thus be subjected to the personal responsibility of a partner; and the alienation implied in the contract, if heritage enter into the concern, will be ineffectual, while even the personal contract with the co-partners will be reducible on lesion. In such cases it has been doubted whether the father or the tutor do not for himself undertake all the responsibility of the concern; and it rather seems to be the law that they are to be held personally liable." But see also the note supplied by the learned editor based on *Morrison* v. *Learmont & Co.* (1870) 8 M. 500.
[24] Erskine, *Inst.* I: 7: 14.
[25] *Bruce* (1577) Mor. 8979.

quadriennium utile only, on proof of lesion.[26] The original agreement, if unchallenged during the four years after majority, will stand. If challenged and if the parties remain in association as partners, thereafter, presumably the original agreement will have little or no evidential value as to the contractual terms upon which the parties are now associating and these terms will be construed by the court from the facts and circumstances attendant upon the parties since the pupil attained majority. These submissions are advanced somewhat tentatively and in due recognition of the paradox implied, namely that the void contract may sometimes be considered as one of the elements in the situation from which the new partnership may be spelled out, whereas the voidable contract may not. The paradox, however, is lessened if it is remembered that in the latter case it is only where the original agreement is challenged, and possibly only where it is *successfully* challenged, by the pupil, that its terms cannot be regarded; and in such cases there is no inference that the pupil child intended to associate on the pre-arranged terms after he attained majority.

The air of unreality surrounding a discussion of the situation of a pupil so circumstanced is to some extent dispelled in the case of a minor who during minority has purported to enter a contract of partnership. Several aspects of the rights of a pupil on attaining majority are common to both pupil and minor. These will be discussed in the succeeding paragraphs where the position of the minor is examined.

Minors [26a]

It is clear that a minor, without curators, having full contractual powers,[27] may effectively enter into a partnership[28] even with another minor.[29] These contractual powers are, however, subject to the qualification that any contracts which he makes are, during his minority and for four years after he has attained majority, voidable at his instance on proof of lesion. If the minor has a curator, his contractual powers are more limited. Any contracts which he then makes require the consent of his curator. If the contract is entered into by the minor with consent of his curator, it is as binding as if he had contracted, having no curator.[30] Where the minor has a curator and purports to contract without the consent of

---

[26] Bell, *Principles*, para. 2098: *Falconer* v. *Thomson* (1792) Mor. 16380; *Vere* v. *Dale* (1804) Mor. 16389; *Lord Clinton, Petitioner* (1875) 3 R. 62.

[26a] See Age of Majority (Scotland) Act 1969, under which the period of minority subsists from the expiry of pupillarity until the age of 18 years and not, as formerly, 21 years.

[27] Except to grant any deed, *inter vivos* or *mortis causa*, whereby he alters gratuitously the succession to his heritable property: *Hunter* (1728) Mor. 8964; *McCulloch* v. *McCulloch* (1731) Mor. 8965; but see *Brown's Tr.* v. *Brown* (1897) 24 R. 962.

[28] *Wilson* v. *Laidlaw* (1816) 6 Pat.App. 222; *Hill* v. *City of Glasgow Bank* (1879) 7 R. 68, *per* Lord President Inglis at p. 75.

[29] *Re A. & M.* [1926] Ch. 274.

[30] The contract however is still reducible by the minor within the *quadriennium utile* on proof of lesion: Bell, *Principles*, para. 2098. But where the minor has entered the contract with consent of his curators a higher degree of lesion may require to be proved: *Cooper* v. *Cooper's Trs.* (1885) 12 R. 473, *per* the Lord Ordinary (Fraser) at pp. 487–488.

the curator, " his contracts then require the consent of his curator and, if that is not obtained, are, if not void, at least voidable." [31]   There is some ambivalence in the law on this point as is suggested by the form of words adopted by Gloag on the passage just quoted.   It has been held that a contract of service is not a nullity simply on the ground that the minor has entered into it without the consent of his curator.[32]   The same rule may apply in the case of a contract of apprenticeship, though this has not been expressly so decided.[33]   The general rule, however, appears to be that where a minor, who has curators, contracts without their consent, the contract is void and may be reduced at any time within the period of the long negative prescription,[34] with the possible exception of a contract considered to be beneficial to the minor.[35]   Among the contracts which have been treated as null under this rule, there is no recorded instance of a partnership but there are instances of other contracts of a commercial nature.[36]   It may be observed that a minor, or even a pupil, in circumstances in which he would have no capacity to bind himself in a valid contract for his own behoof may yet act as agent to the end of so binding his principal.[37]   The point is, however, irrelevant to the rule which is under examination, since what is being considered in the agency cases is the effect of the minor's actings upon his principal, assuming, of course, the latter to have full contractual capacity.   Under the general rule as to capacity of pupils or minors to contract the person in non-age may, if he enters into a contract of agency in the circumstances which are being discussed, escape a liability for example, to a third party on the contract which he negotiates for his principal which would be imposed upon an agent of full age and capacity.[38]   It is thought that, on the analogy of the decided cases where contracts of a commercial kind were involved, that a minor who, having curators, enters a contract of partnership without their consent, may be considered to have purported to enter a contract which is a nullity and may be set aside at any time within the long negative prescription.[39]   But that rule is subject to the qualification noticed immediately hereafter.

[31] Gloag, *Contract* (2nd ed.) p. 79.

[32] *Heddel* v. *Duncan*, June 5, 1810, F.C.; *Argo* v. *Smarts* (1853) 1 Irv. 250; *McFeetridge* v. *Stewarts & Lloyds*, 1913 S.C. 773.   In the last mentioned case, the minor was held to have been foris-familiated which would be sufficient to remove him from the curatory of his father.

[33] *Stevenson* v. *Adair* (1872) 10 M. 919.

[34] Stair, *Inst.* I: 6: 33.   Bankton, *Inst.* I: vii: 56.   Erskine, *Inst.* I: 7: 34.   But *cf. Waddle* v. *Gibson*, Jan. 18, 1812, F.C.

[35] Erskine, *Inst.* I: 7: 33 and 41.

[36] *e.g.* a bill of exchange (*Craig* v. *Grant* (1732) Mor. 8955) even though it would otherwise not have been challengeable on the ground of minority and lesion since it had been granted in the course of the minor's trade: a cautionary obligation, or a bond (*Airth* (1602) Mor. 8938).

[37] Fridman, *Agency* (3rd ed.) p. 42; Gow, *Mercantile and Industrial Law of Scotland*, p. 516; *Bird* v. *Boulter* (1833) 4 B. & Ad. 443, *per* Littledale J. at p. 447; *Wallis* v. *Russell* [1902] 2 I.R. 585.

[38] *Bird* v. *Boulter, supra.*

[39] The long negative prescription in such cases is now restricted to 20 years: Conveyancing (Scotland) Act 1924, s. 17, as amended by Conveyancing (Scotland) Act 1938, s. 4.   No allowance is made for the years of minority.

Minor engaging in trade. There is a general rule that, where a minor is carrying on a trade or a profession, the obligations undertaken by him in the course thereof are binding upon him and cannot be escaped upon a plea of minority and lesion.[40] If he grants a bond [41] or becomes party to a bill of exchange for goods supplied to him in the course of his trading [42] he cannot later claim to be restored against these obligations upon the ground of his minority and on proof of lesion. So also it was decided that a loan of money to a minor engaged in trade raises no presumption of lesion and that the onus rests with him to prove that it was not expended for the purposes of his trading or for other purposes which were *in rem versum.*[43] He is likewise liable in damages for loss occasioned by his lack of normal skill or attention in conducting his business.[44] Yet the plea of minority and lesion is excluded only in so far as regards contracts entered into and obligations undertaken in the course of the trade in which the minor is engaged. A cautionary obligation granted by a minor trading as a shopkeeper [45] for the implement of the obligation in a deed, or as a farmer [46] for his father's antecedent obligation under a bill of exchange or even by a minor practising as a solicitor for the price of goods supplied, not to himself, but to another [47] will be reducible on the ground of minority and lesion.

The position in law of a minor engaging in trade is reflected in the manner in which he is treated if he becomes a partner in a trading concern. He is not allowed to plead minority and lesion in regard to transactions with the creditors of the firm.[48] His right of challenge is not, however, removed in a question arising with his partners. This, at least, appears to be the result of the decision in *Wilson* v. *Laidlaw.*[49] The facts of this case were complex. A lease of the coal on Green estate was granted to the father of the appellant but for the use of the appellant, the father's interest being merely as curator for the appellant. The appellant was then about fourteen years of age. The father assumed partners, among

[40] Erskine, *Inst.* I: 7: 38.
[41] *Heddel* v. *Duncan,* June 5, 1810, F.C.
[42] *Craig* v. *Grant* (1732) Mor. 8955; *Campbell* v. *Turner* (1822) 1 S. 266.
[43] *Macdonald* (1789) Mor. 9038.
[44] *McMichael* v. *Barbour* (1840) 3 D. 279. Bankton, *Inst.* I: vii: 78 explains the rule as follows: " A lesion which falls out through the minor's ignorance of the business or employment which he professes will not afford ground of restitution; as a lawyer in point of law, a trading merchant or artificer, in matters that belong to their respective occupations; because, at that rate, they would *propriam allegare turpitudinem,* disgracefully own ignorance of that which they profess to know: and it were to the infinite damage of minors, if such allegations were receivable; for none would employ them if that was the case."
[45] *Wall* v. *Brownlee* (1724) Mor. 9035.
[46] *McMichael* v. *Barbour* (1840) 3 D. 279.
[47] *Dundas* v. *Allan* (1711) Mor. 9034. Contrast the case of *Gairdner* v. *Chalmers* (1636) Mor. 9024.
[48] *Wilson* v. *Laidlaw* (1816) 6 Pat.App. 222: *Hill* v. *City of Glasgow Bank* (1879) 7 R. 68 is not entirely in point since in that case the *quadriennium utile* had expired before the challenge was made.
[49] (1816) 6 Pat.App. 222, referred to by Bell *Com.* II, p. 514 as " *Pettigrew Wilson's Case* " and by Clark, *op. cit.* I, p. 23 under the same citation, though Clark's ascription of the decision to the year 1796 relates to the original interlocutor of the Lord Ordinary (Meadowbank) in this long and complicated litigation.

them Shields, Milligan and Burnside, to work the coal in the lease under
the firm of the Green Coal Company and the appellant, at varying stages
when he was from thirteen to fifteen years of age, was made a party to
these arrangements through the acts of his father which purported to be
on his behalf. Milligan some time after becoming a partner became
bankrupt in 1793 but no steps were taken to end his partnership and the
firm was not dissolved, being carried on under the management of the
father and Shields. Milligan carried on another business, Milligan and
Company, in which the respondent Laidlaw was a partner. Milligan's
trustee sued and obtained decree in absence for certain sums due to
Milligan by the Green Coal Company. The latter acknowledged no
dealings with Milligan & Company, only with Milligan as an individual,
but Milligan had entered certain items in the books of Milligan &
Company as advances to Green Coal Company from the former firm,
apparently in order to conceal cash deficiencies for which he was responsible to Milligan & Company. The respondent Laidlaw, the surviving
solvent partner of Milligan & Company, sued the appellant for the amount
of these advances and the appellant lodged defences denying the claim.
Milligan's trustee also sued for advances of money by Milligan to Green
Coal Company and for his share of the profits of that company. Green
Coal Company was then sequestrated but the sequestration was later
recalled on the appellant's undertaking to pay the debts due to the several
creditors of Green Coal Company. The appellant himself sued for
reduction of his partnership in Green Coal Company on the ground of
minority and lesion. The Lord Ordinary (Meadowbank) reduced the
pretended partnership on the ground that, the appellant having been
introduced to it " while a pupil," it was void *ab initio* but of the appellant's
consent qualified the interlocutor with the reservation that before extract
the appellant should find security for payment of " all the debts contracted
for behoof of the concern during the management of these vitious titles."
On adjustment of the account it appeared that the appellant's father had
docquetted and signed accounts in which the present claim was shown as
a debt due to Milligan & Company. The appellant then paid off the
creditors having claims which he considered were for sums beneficially
and profitably laid out on his estate but he resisted Laidlaw's claim and
brought a further action of reduction of all transactions, deeds, writings,
interlocutors and decrees to his prejudice during his minority. This
action was raised during the *quadriennium utile*, and was conjoined with
the other actions pending. After various procedure before the Lord
Ordinary (Hermand), on a reclaiming petition the Inner House found
that though the appellant and his cautioners were effectually bound to
pay the debts contracted by or on behalf of Green Coal Company, " he
did not thereby undertake to answer the demands of the partners themselves, with whom he had been duly associated while under age, unless
in so far as such demands could be legally and justly maintained against
him, on the footing of his estate being benefited by their operations, or

by the advances made by them during the subsistence of the copartnery."
The legal interest of the proceedings ceases at this point. Milligan's
trustee, in view of the interlocutor, persisted no longer in his claim and
while the respondent Laidlaw continued his action ultimately to the
House of Lords, the issue narrowed to a question whether there was
sufficient evidence of any advance made by Milligan's firm to Green Coal
Company upon which question the Lords returned a negative answer.

Commenting upon the case, Gloag [50] observes, " a minor had been
introduced by his father as a partner in a trading concern which failed.
In an action for a debt due by the firm for money advanced by A,
the minor did not dispute his liability for the firm's debts but averred
that A was in reality a partner, and brought a reduction of the
partnership on the ground of minority and lesion. It was held to
be proved that A was a partner, and that, in a question with him,
the minor was entitled to be relieved of his obligation." That passage reduces the complex and protracted proceedings to a neat
statement of principle delivered with that crystalline clarity which those
of us who studied under the late Professor Gloag remember with affection
and admiration. Perhaps, however, in view of the uneasy treatment
which the case has received even at the hands of such giants as George
Joseph Bell, and of the reporting of the facts of the case, which is at
certain parts rather indeterminate,[51] it may not be presumptuous to
attempt to analyse the case more closely.

The *ratio* of the decision in the Court of Session seems to be two-fold.
(1) The appellant appears to have been treated as a *minor* at the time when
he was introduced into the partnership. Though he is stated to have
been between thirteen and fifteen years of age when the various arrangements were made by his father as to working the coal and is expressly
characterised as a pupil at that stage by Lord Meadowbank, it seems to
be the case that he was fourteen years old when he was introduced to the
partnership with Milligan.[52] As a minor, he could engage in trade and
be held liable for the obligations undertaken in the course of that trade.
(2) The debts contracted by the Green Coal Company represented sums
which had been expended to the benefit of the minor's estate and were
thus *in rem minoris versa*. The interlocutor of Lord Meadowbank at an
early stage of the proceedings did in fact represent his liability to the
creditors as arising *of consent* but that " consent " was granted of necessity
since he had, in the earlier process for recall of the sequestration of Green
Coal Company, only succeeded on condition that he undertook to pay
the firm's creditors. When he sought to have that consent, in addition

[50] *Contract* (2nd ed.) p. 88.
[51] Some supplementary assistance on the facts can be derived from the report of an earlier
episode of the unhappy history of the coal in Green Estate: *Wilson and Others* v.
Alexander and Others (1807) 5 Pat.App. 182.
[52] He is referred to as " then being a minor " by Lord Redesdale (*Wilson* v. *Laidlaw, supra*
at pp. 230–231) but this refers to the date when the adjusted accounts were signed by his
father. In *Wilson and Others* v. *Alexander and Others, supra* he is described as 14 years
of age when the partnership arrangement was made.

to the other proceedings, reduced on the ground of his minority, he was unsuccessful. It would, indeed, be difficult to establish such a proposition as an abstract principle affecting the creditors, since the two-fold ratio of the court's decision seems to conflict with a general and abstract principle of that kind.

Similarly, if the son be a minor and not a pupil, there is no justification for the father or guardian being held to have made himself a partner in place of the minor whom he has introduced into the partnership, even if that legal result can be supported in the case of the introduction of a pupil, on the somewhat suspect authority of the earlier reported decisions.[53] A father or guardian introducing a minor to the firm may of course so conduct himself as to hold himself out personally as a partner in a question with creditors, but there is no inference to be drawn by way of legal principle that by such introduction he has made himself a partner. In *Clippens Shale Oil Co.* v. *Scott and Another*[54] the pursuers sued for a declarator that the first named defender was a partner in the business. They averred that he had signed a contract of copartnery as curator for his son, the second named defender, who was a minor and who also signed the contract. The pursuers also averred that, though when they signed the contract they believed that the minor was to be their partner, immediately thereafter they discovered that the first named defender was really the party who became the partner and implemented his son's obligations under the partnership agreement, the son having betaken himself to the Continent without entering upon his duties with the firm and leaving the first named defender to undertake these duties in his place which the first named defender did. The action was dismissed as irrelevant the court holding that although the facts averred might make the first named defender liable as if he were a partner to third parties, these facts could not constitute him a partner in a question *inter socios*.

Misrepresentation as to age. The protection afforded to a minor by his right of challenge within the *quadriennium utile* of transactions in which he has engaged during minority does not extend to cases where the minor has misrepresented himself as being a major to the party contracting with him.[55] But even in that case the courts will look closely at the circumstances before depriving the minor of his right of challenge. The mis-statement by the minor as to his age will not prove a relevant defence to a plea of minority and lesion unless it can also be shown that there was no ground from the appearance of the minor to disbelieve him[56] and that the mis-statement induced the other party to contract with him.[57] The mis-statement must be directed to the other party to the contract. It is no sufficient answer that the minor represented himself

---

[53] *McAulay, Gartly, McDonald & Co.'s Tr.* v. *Renny* (1803) reported briefly Bell, *Com.* II, p. 514: *Calder* v. *Downie*, Dec. 11, 1811, F.C.: and see *supra* pp. 25–27.
[54] (1876) 3 R. 651.
[55] Stair, *Inst.* I: 6: 44; Erskine, *Inst.* I: 7: 36.
[56] *Kennedy* v. *Weir* (1665) Mor. 11658.
[57] *Wemyss* v. *His Creditors* (1637) Mor. 9025.

elsewhere or to others than the contracting party as *sui juris*.[58] Nor can protection be gained by a declaration in the agreement that the minor is *sui juris*. Such an expedient may indeed be a double-edged weapon since it is prima facie evidence that the other party at least had cause to suspect that he was transacting business with a minor.[59] A minor who from appearance gives the impression of mature years is probably not from that circumstance alone bound to warn the party with whom he seeks to contract that he is a minor; and certainly where his appearance is such that he would not be taken to be in majority and the other contracting party has neglected to seek information on the subject through channels of information which were obviously and readily available, the minor will be allowed to challenge the transactions on the ground of minority and lesion.[60] If the minor fraudulently misrepresents himself as of full age and thereby induces the other party to contract with him he will be barred from later challenging the contract on the ground of minority and lesion, at least if the other party can be shown to have relied upon the representation [61] and where the other circumstances were not such as to put him on his inquiry.[62]

Extent of the minor's right of challenge

If on reaching majority a person seeks to repudiate a contract of partnership entered into during his minority, he must do so unequivocally.[63] Where a minor who has curators engages himself as a partner without their consent, the contract so entered may be treated as null if he chooses so to regard it.[64] In such a case he does not require to reduce the contract. He may rid himself of it by simple repudiation [65] or may plead the circumstances *ope exceptionis* [66] to any claim made upon him under the contract. He may recover contributions which he has made during the supposed subsistence of the contract though not where he has benefited and it is impossible to restore matters *in integrum*.[67] The same rule holds in all cases where a pupil has either engaged himself as partner [68] or has been introduced as such by his tutor.[69] Where a minor who has no curators has entered a contract of copartnership or where, having curators, he

---

[58] *Sutherland* v. *Morson* (1825) 3 S. 449. The minor by misrepresentation of his age obtained the degree of M.D. which would induce a belief by others that he had attained 21 years.
[59] *Kennedy* v. *Weir* (1665) Mor. 11658.
[60] *Dennistoun* v. *Mudie* (1850) 12 D. 613 (minor engaged in speculative transactions on the stock exchange). *Wilkie* v. *Dunlop* (1834) 12 S. 506 which appears to support the view that the minor may in some circumstances be under a duty to warn the other party can equally well be regarded as a case where the minor was held liable on an obligation undertaken in respect of necessaries supplied to him.
[61] *Wemyss* v. *His Creditors* (1637) Mor. 9025.
[62] *Kennedy* v. *Weir* (1665) Mor. 11658.
[63] *Forrest* v. *Campbell* (1853) 16 D. 16.
[64] *Supra* pp. 29–30.
[65] Clark, *op. cit.* I, p. 24; Ersk. *Inst.* I: 7: 34. But contrast *Waddle* v. *Gibson*, Jan. 18, 1812, F.C.
[66] *Wilson* v. *Laidlaw* (1816) 6 Pat.App. 222.
[67] Erskine, *Inst.* I: 7: 41.
[68] *Corpe* v. *Overton* (1833) 10 Bing. 253; *Steinberg* v. *Scala* (*Leeds*) *Ltd.* [1923] 2 Ch. 452.
[69] Gloag, *Contract* (2nd ed.) pp. 77–79.

has entered the contract with their consent and concurrence, it will not be sufficient for him to give intimation to the other contracting parties that he repudiates that contract.[70]   In the older cases it seems to have been regarded as essential that an action of reduction should be raised,[71] though service of the summons within the *quadriennium* was regarded as sufficient.[72]   The modern view is not so insistent upon the necessity for an action of reduction, and a challenge of the contract *ope exceptionis* in an action based upon that contract or upon matters germane to the contract entered by the minor [73] will probably be sufficient.   The challenge may be at the instance of the minor himself, or of his heirs or personal representatives [74] or his creditors [75] or a party deriving title to sue from an assignation by the minor of his right of challenge.[76]   The possibility of a challenge by the minor within the *quadriennium utile* does not, however, afford a ground of action to other parties who, were the minor to have challenged, might found thereon in another question with the contracting party.   In *Blackwood* v. *Thorburn* [77] objection was raised to a person being enrolled as a voter in respect of his occupancy of partnership property.   It was contended that no legal partnership existed since his only copartner was a minor whose curators had not consented to the contract of copartnery.   The objection was repelled, the court holding that it was *jus tertii* to any but the minor to object.

A contract of partnership, like other contracts entered into by a minor, even where the circumstances are such that it is treated as void, is a nullity only if the minor chooses to regard it as such.   When he comes of age he may choose to adopt it when the other parties to the contract remain bound.[78]   " But whichever alternative he chooses to adopt, he must accept it with all its consequences—that is he must either repudiate his connection with the company altogether, in which case he will renounce alike liability and profit; or else he must abide by the company in which case he will share risks as well as gains, according to the maxim, *Qui sentit commodum sentire debet et onus.*" [79]   While, as Clark observes, this question does not appear to have come up for decision in its pure form in the Scottish courts, it may perhaps be supported on the general

---

[70] *Marquis of Montrose* v. *Livingston* (1697) Mor. 9046; *Ramsay* v. *Maxwell* (1672) Mor. 9042; *Stewart* v. *Snodgrass* (1860) 23 D. 187.

[71] *Stewart* v. *Snodgrass, supra.*

[72] *McDougall* v. *Arbuthnott* (1681) Mor. 9044.

[73] *McFeetridge* v. *Stewarts & Lloyds*, 1913 S.C. 773.

[74] *Bruce* v. *Hamilton* (1854) 17 D. 265; Erskine, *Inst.* I: 7: 42.

[75] *Harkness* v. *Graham* (1833) 11 S. 760.

[76] *Robertson* v. *Oswald* (1584) Mor. 8980.

[77] (1868) 7 M. 318.

[78] Clark, *op. cit.* p. 24.   *Quaere* whether this would apply to a pupil entering a contract of partnership, on his own behalf, since he is *ab initio* incapable of consent.   Presumably since in such a case the association continues during his minority, the question on his attaining majority falls to be decided upon the principle stated by Clark though the original " contract " by the pupil could only be appealed to as an adminicle of evidence which, taken with the other circumstances, shows the terms upon which the minor agreed to continue his association.

[79] Clark, *loc. cit.*

proposition decided in *Forrest* v. *Campbell*.[80] The principle was accepted in England even before the passing of the Infants Relief Act 1874[81] that a person who retains a share in a partnership cannot retain it without its incidental obligations.[82] Lindley,[83] commenting on the rule, observes that " the doctrine of holding out is itself sufficient to impose liability on an adult, although he may not long have attained his majority." In *Goode* v. *Harrison*[84] the infant was a partner and known to be such. When he reached majority he neither affirmed nor denied expressly the existence of the partnership, and he was held liable for debts incurred by his copartners *subsequently to the time when he came of age*. The ratio of that case, however, scarcely justifies Clark who uses it to support his view that the law of Scotland would be held to be the same " on the well-known principle of ' Approbate and Reprobate.' "[85] If that principle were applied a party either affirming or neither affirming nor dis-affirming the contract on reaching majority would be held to have approbated the contract so as to have incurred liability for transactions of the firm during his minority and not merely subsequently thereto.

Moreover if the principle enunciated by Lindley[86] were to be applied in Scots law so as to impose liability on the ground of holding out for liabilities incurred by the firm during minority, that might be in direct conflict with the Scots law which allows the period of four years after attaining majority within which to challenge contracts made during minority. Holding out as a principle explaining the liability for the partnership debts appears to be conclusive only as to the liability for firm debts incurred after the minor has attained majority, and it is thought that *Goode* v. *Harrison*[87] is authority for no wider proposition than that. Moreover, holding out may impose liability on a person for firm debts as if he were a partner, but it is not a method by which a partnership may be created. It is in fact a surviving example of the doctrine of *quasi* partnership.[88]

A person who has entered into a contract during minority and who after attaining majority, but within the *quadriennium utile*, ratifies or homologates it, is personally barred from thereafter challenging the contract on the ground of minority and lesion.[89] That ratification or homologation may be inferred from his conduct after attaining majority,[90] though the ratification or homologation, whether express or implied, will be ineffectual if the party against whom it is pleaded was at the time

---

[80] *Supra* n. 63.
[81] 37 & 38 Vict. c. 62. See *L. & N.W. Ry. Co.* v. *McMichael* (1850) 5 Ex. 114.
[82] *Cork and Bandon Railway Co.* v. *Cazenove* (1847) 10 Q.B. 935; *Ebbett's Case* (1870) L.R. 5 Ch. 302; *Cf. Baker's Case* (1870) L.R. 7 Ch. 115.
[83] *Op. cit.* p. 55. On holding out see *infra* Chap. V.
[84] (1821) 5 B. & A. 147.
[85] *Op. cit.* I, p. 25.
[86] *Op. cit.* p. 55.
[87] *Supra* n. 84.
[88] See *infra* Chap. III, pp. 60–63.
[89] Stair, *Inst.* I: 6: 44. *Kyle* v. *Allan* (1832) 11 S. 87; *Forrest* v. *Campbell* (1853) 16 D. 16.
[90] *Lord Advocate* v. *Wemyss* (1899) 2 F.(H.L.) 1.

unaware that he had the right to challenge the contract [91] and must be
an act of his own deliberate and free choice, unaffected by the influence
of other interested parties.[92]   While mere holding himself out as a partner
after attaining majority may not in all circumstances amount to ratification of the contract of partnership as existing during minority, and in
any event will impose liability as a partner rather than establish the
partnership, yet it will go a considerable distance towards such ratification
and in many cases may be taken as implying ratification of the original
contract.   English authority on the subject is unhelpful since the Infants
Relief Act 1874 [93] which does not permit an action based on ratification,
after majority, of a contract made before attaining majority does not
apply to Scotland.

Insanity

" Insanity, in cases of civil rights, must be taken as a question of
degree, and the validity of a contract entered into by a party who has not
been judicially deprived of the control of his property must be judged on a
consideration of the question whether the party's intelligence was sufficient
to enable him to apprehend the particular contract." [94]   Thus while the
broad general proposition that according to the law of Scotland insane
persons are incapable of contracting and their contracts are void is
advanced by the institutional writers,[95] the content of that general
proposition is found on analysis to comprehend two separate principles:
(1) where a party has been adjudged insane and the control of his estate
vested in a curator on his behalf, contracts entered into by that person
are void [96]; and (2) where a person is proved to be insane all contracts
into which he enters are void.[97]   In the application of these two principles
there is need for additional expository rules.   Insanity is a state which
can be established or redargued by evidence and which is not necessarily
constant.   Unlike minority, it is not a status which once established is
fixed and determinable as to its duration.   While, therefore, if a person
is proved to be a lunatic [98] or a congenital imbecile [99] any contracts
which he enters into will be reduced as void, subject to the exceptions that
he will be required to pay a reasonable price for necessaries supplied [1]
and, on the principle of recompense,[2] money advanced to a lunatic may

[91] *McGibbon* v. *McGibbon* (1852) 14 D. 605.
[92] *Melvil* v. *Arnot* (1782) Mor. 8998; *Leiper* v. *Cochran* (1822) 1 S. 552.
[93] s. 2.
[94] Gloag, *Contract*, 2nd ed., p. 93.
[95] Stair, *Inst.* I: 10: 13; Erskine, *Inst.* III: 1: 16.
[96] *Loudon* v. *Elder's curator*, 1923 S.L.T. 226 (O.H.).
[97] *Alexander* v. *Kinneir* (1632) Mor. 6278.
[98] *Loudon* v. *Elder's curator*, *supra*.
[99] Bell, *Com.* I, 132.
[1] Sale of Goods Act 1893, s. 2.
[2] *Scott's Tr.* v. *Scott* (1887) 14 R. 1043, a case relating to money advanced to a pupil.
  Gloag cites *Dig.* xliv: 7: 46: *Furiosus et pupillus obligantur ubi ex re actio venit*, as
  authority for this proposition.   The passage cited does not, however, appear to be in
  point in a question of recompense.   Professor Watson has directed my attention to *Dig.*
  xxvi: 8: 1, xxvi: 8: 5 and xxv: 3: 4 (the last mentioned containing scribal errors) as
  supporting the principle in the case of the *pupillus*.   No clear statement appears as to
  the *furiosus* but presumably he would be subject to the same principle of law.

be recovered if it is proved that the money was expended to the benefit of his estate, insanity of a less pronounced kind may require to be assessed as a matter of degree, to ascertain whether the party possessed sufficient *intellectus* to permit of his understanding the transaction into which he has entered. That an assessment of this nature must be undertaken is shown by the observations of judges,[3] and institutional writers,[4] as to the degree of intellectual capacity required to make a will as compared with that required to transact a bargain.[5] Likewise, the elements of degree and fluctuation in a state of insanity are illustrated in the treatment of contracts entered into during a lucid interval which will be binding,[6] though where a state of insanity has been established the onus will rest upon the person who seeks to treat the contract as binding to prove that it was entered into at a time when the insane person had temporarily recovered.[7]

In Scots law, differing from English law, a lunatic is not bound by a contract into which he has entered merely on the ground that the other contracting party was unaware that he was dealing with a lunatic.[8] If insanity be established and is of such a nature and degree that the insane person is incapable of understanding the contract he entered into, the contract is void.[9]

Supervening insanity

The effect of supervening insanity upon a continuing contract originally entered into when the party in question was sane is in some cases a

---

[3] *Per* Lord Young in *Ballantyne* v. *Evans* (1886) 13 R. 652 at p. 667.

[4] Bell, *Com.* I, 133.

[5] Gloag (*Contract*, 2nd ed., p. 93) has pointed out that the conclusions of Lord Young and Bell on this point are diametrically opposed, and comments, " as the question in both cases is one of capacity to assent, it would seem that the criteria by which it may be judged ought to be the same." The observation is just but it does not assail the idea that these ought to be criteria directed towards the ascertainment of the disabling effect of the particular case of insanity.

[6] Bell, *Com.* I, 132.

[7] *Nisbet's Trs.* v. *Nisbet* (1871) 9 M. 937; *Towart* v. *Sellers* (1817) 5 Dow. 231. See particularly the observations of Lord Kinloch in *Nisbet's Trs.* v. *Nisbet*, *supra* at p. 950 on " general insanity " as opposed to being " thoroughly insane " even though the latter be " only exhibited in a single point." Lord Kinloch, differing from the other judges of the First Division, regarded the case not as one of a lucid interval but as one of a degree of insanity which did not preclude the testator from apprehending the effect of his testamentary directions.

[8] See on the English law, *Imperial Loan Co.* v. *Stone* [1892] 1 Q.B. 599; Lindley, *op. cit.* p. 56.

[9] *Lindsay* v. *Trent* (1683) Mor. 6281. (Fountainhall's report of the case): " If the furiosity be proved, then the deed is simply null." The statement in Clark, *op. cit.* I, p. 26 that " if one contracts with a lunatic *bona fide* and in ignorance of this incapacity and if by reason of *rei interventus* it has become no longer possible to restore matters *in integrum*, the contract will not be held to be a nullity so as to set the lunatic free from the liabilities he has thereby incurred previous to the time when the other partner was made aware of the lunacy " cannot be accepted on the authorities he cites. Of these *Molton* v. *Camroux* (1848) 2 Ex. 487, *Beavan* v. *McDonnell* (1854) 9 Ex. 309 and *Baxter* v. *Earl of Portsmouth* (1826) 5 B. and C. 170 are decided on what Gloag describes as " historical grounds peculiar to the law of England " (*Contract*, 2nd ed., p. 92, n. 2). The Scottish cases cited, *Pollock* v. *Paterson and Others*, Dec. 10, 1811, F.C.; and *Spence* v. *Paterson's Tr.*, July 7, 1812, F.C. are decisions upon the effect of the supervening insanity of a principal upon his agent's mandate.

question attended with doubt.[10]   In cases of partnership, however, the supervening insanity of a partner does not necessarily bring his relationship with the firm to an end.   An occurrence of that kind may be stipulated as a cause of dissolution of the partnership in the agreement of co-partnery, but in the absence of such a provision there is no general statutory power in the remaining partners to terminate the partnership.[11] In the absence of any such provision partners may apply to the court to order the dissolution of the partnership, " when a partner is found lunatic by inquisition, or in Scotland by cognition, or is shown to the satisfaction of the court to be of permanently unsound mind, in either of which cases the application may be made as well on behalf of that partner by his committee or next friend or person having title to intervene as by any other partner." [12]   In a case where under a contract of partnership no active duties in the management of the firm were imposed upon a partner who had become insane and he had merely provided his share of the capital, the court refused to order dissolution of the firm upon the application of the remaining partners, when the *curator bonis* of the insane partner opposed the application.[13]

Where there is no provision in the agreement for dissolution of the firm upon a partner becoming insane or where neither the remaining partners nor the insane partner's representative apply to the court for an order to dissolve the partnership, or where such application is made and is refused by the court, the insane partner, notwithstanding his insanity, will remain entitled to his share of the profits subsequently made in the partnership business.[14]   In *Sadler* v. *Lee* [15] it was held that where a partner became imbecile, but the firm was not dissolved, he was responsible for the misconduct of the other partners in the subsequent management of the business of the partnership.

Intoxication

Since intoxication may result in a complete lack of comprehension, it may produce an incapacity to consent and therefore to contract.[16]   Any question as to the validity of a contract entered into when a party was in an intoxicated state thus involves an examination of the degree of intoxication.   There is no general rule that contracts entered into when under the influence of drink are reducible.   The issue is whether the contract was entered into by the party when he was so intoxicated as to be wholly incapable of understanding business.[17]   Even when complete intoxication has resulted in a contracting party losing " for a time the

[10] See Gloag, *Contract* (2nd ed.) pp. 93–94.
[11] Partnership Act 1890, s. 32.
[12] *Ibid.* s. 35 (*a*).
[13] *Eadie* v. *MacBean's Curator* (1885) 12 R. 660.
[14] *Jones* v. *Noy* (1833) 2 M. & K. 125.
[15] (1843) 6 Beav. 324.
[16] Stair, *Inst.* I: 10: 13; Erskine, *Inst.* III: 1: 18.
[17] *Johnston* v. *Clark* (1854) 17 D. 228; *Taylor* v. *Provan* (1864) 2 M. 1226.

use of reason," [18] the contract is not void but merely voidable [19]; and a party will not be relieved of a contractual engagement made in such circumstances unless he repudiates the contract so soon as he becomes sober and realises what he has done while intoxicated.[20]

A state of partial intoxication where a party has not complete command of his intelligence yet is able to perceive and understand the nature of the business on which he is engaged will afford no ground for his later repudiating the contract, but may vitiate the contract entered into upon other grounds. Thus where two parties purport to enter a contract during a drinking bout, neither party being completely intoxicated, it may yet be possible to plead that in the circumstances no contract was seriously intended.[21] " These were not cases in which it was averred or sought to be proved that either party was in a state of incapacity from drink. The question in these cases was whether the parties had seriously made a bargain, and the court held that they had not, and upon grounds which commend themselves to one's common sense." [22] Again, while there is no principle of law which can be appealed to imposing a duty to refrain from contracting with a man who is partially overtaken in drink, it may amount to fraudulent conduct if one plies a man with drink in order to induce him to enter a contract.[23] In the contract of partnership which is *uberrimae fidei* [24] it seems clear that any such stratagem would be strictly regarded by the courts especially if any false or misleading statements have been made to the party affected by drink.

Bankruptcy

Under section 33 (1) of the Partnership Act, " Subject to any agreement between the partners, every partnership is dissolved as regards all the partners by the death or bankruptcy of any partner." The introductory words of the subsection leave the situation arising from the bankruptcy of a partner to be regulated, if the parties so desire, by the express terms of the partnership agreement. The statutory provision, and the terms of

[18] Stair, *Inst.* I: 10: 13.

[19] *Wilson & Fraser* v. *Nisbet* (1736) Mor. 1509; Gloag, *Contract*, 2nd ed., p. 95.

[20] *Pollock* v. *Burns* (1875) 2 R. 497.

[21] *Jardine* v. *Elliot* (1803) Hume 684; *Hunter* v. *Stevenson* (1804) Hume 686.

[22] *Per* the Lord Justice Clerk (Inglis) in *Taylor* v. *Provan, supra* at p. 1232.

[23] *Couston* v. *Miller* (1862) 24 D. 607.

[24] It may be that the Scots law inherits from the Roman law a " unitary concept " of good faith as Professor T. B. Smith argues, *Short Commentary on the Law of Scotland*, pp. 836–837 and that the notion of *uberrima fides,* implying that the law exacts varying standards of honesty which vary with the particular kind of contract is " hardly a happy one." If these strictures are addressed to the terminology which has been borrowed from England to express the particular duty imposed in certain contracts, *e.g.* partnership, insurance, etc., the criticism may be accepted. The expression *uberrima fides,* however, may be regarded as an attempt to describe compendiously certain contractual relationships in which fiduciary duties are imposed upon the parties contracting in addition to the normal requirement of good faith. The principle requiring *uberrima fides* is clearly laid down in questions *inter socios* in the conduct of the business. In negotiations at the stage of entertaining proposals to enter a partnership, the position is not so clear and the decisions seem to have turned upon the general requirements of the law of contract as to good faith. (*Ferguson* v. *Wilson* (1904) 6 F. 779; *Manners* v. *Whitehead* (1898) 1 F. 171.)

any agreement envisaged between the partners, are concerned with the bankruptcy of a partner occurring during the course of the partnership, and, if an express agreement among the partners so provides, the partnership may continue without dissolution upon the supervening bankruptcy of one of the partners. Where a partner is an undischarged bankrupt, it is a criminal offence for him to obtain credit to the extent of £10 or upwards without informing the person from whom he obtains the credit that he is an undischarged bankrupt.[25] The effect of that provision upon the position of a partner who, as an undischarged bankrupt, is actively engaged in the business of the firm seems problematical. In such transactions as he undertakes on behalf of his firm he must almost unavoidably " obtain credit "[26] but the credit is obtained on behalf of the firm, and though section 182 of the Bankruptcy (Scotland) Act 1913 does not qualify the words " obtains credit " it is perhaps the true construction to place upon them that the offence is committed where the bankrupt obtains credit for himself. The associated offence in the English Bankruptcy Act 1914, s. 155,[27] does not appear in the Scottish Act and it is doubtful whether a Scottish undischarged bankrupt obtaining credit of £10 or upwards for the firm of which he is a partner is guilty of an offence under section 182 of the Scottish Act. However undesirable and inconvenient it may be for a firm to employ about its business a partner who is an undischarged bankrupt, there appears to be no criminal offence involved. If the undischarged bankrupt remains a partner but takes no part in the conduct of the business, this is legal.

Such considerations, however, go to the question of continuity of the partnership relation and are not directly relevant to the capacity of a person so affected to enter the relationship in the first place. Since examination of an undischarged bankrupt's association with that firm, and even with the conduct of the firm's business, appears to disclose no factor which would make the partnership an illegal association, the considerations discussed above have some bearing upon the question of the validity of a contract of copartnery with a person who is an undischarged bankrupt. Apart from the statutory restrictions imposed upon the undischarged bankrupt,[28] the law imposes no limit on his capacity to contract.

[25] Bankruptcy (Scotland) Act 1913 (3 & 4 Geo. V, c. 20), s. 182.
[26] But according to English authority a bankrupt who obtains money on the faith of his promise to supply goods or render services in the future does not " obtain credit " within the meaning of the corresponding section of the English Bankruptcy Act 1914: *Osborn* v. *Barton* (1950) 66 T.L.R. (Part 1) 115.
[27] (4 & 5 Geo. V, c. 59): " Where an undischarged bankrupt— . . . (*b*) engages in any trade or business under a name other than that under which he was adjudicated bankrupt without disclosing to all persons with whom he enters into any business transaction, the name under which he was adjudicated bankrupt, he shall be guilty of a misdemeanour." That provision is regarded by Lindley (*op. cit.* p. 63) as precluding an undischarged bankrupt in England from entering into or joining a partnership which carries on business in any name other than the sole name of the bankrupt, except on disclosure of the fact of bankruptcy to everyone dealing with the firm.
[28] Bankruptcy (Scotland) Act 1913, ss. 178 and 182.

Acquirenda

Where a person who has been sequestrated in bankruptcy continues as a partner or where, after sequestration, he becomes a partner, his trustee in bankruptcy has no right to take up the contract of partnership to the effect of putting himself in the bankrupt's place as a partner. Any such claim on his part will be defeated by the element of *delectus personae* which affects the contract of partnership and in terms of section 24 (7) of the Partnership Act 1890. The trustee will, however, be entitled to claim for the bankrupt's creditors the bankrupt's share in the profits of the firm, when the bankruptcy has occurred during the currency of the partnership. Under section 97 (1) of the Bankruptcy (Scotland) Act 1913 the trustee's act and warrant is equivalent to an assignation of the bankrupt's share in the partnership and will thus entitle the trustee to receive the share of profits to which the bankrupt partner would have been entitled, though the trustee will have no right, during the continuance of the partnership, to interfere in the management of the firm or to require an accounting of the firm transactions or inspect the firm's books. Should a dissolution of the firm occur either on account of the bankruptcy of the partner or for other reasons, the trustee will be entitled to receive the share of the firm's assets to which the bankrupt is entitled under the partnership agreement and to an account for the purpose of ascertaining that share.[29] Where the bankrupt has, subsequently to his sequestration, entered into a contract of partnership, it will be for the trustee's consideration whether he should claim any share of profits of the partnership to which the bankrupt may become entitled as *acquirenda* under the procedure laid down in section 98 of the Bankruptcy (Scotland) Act 1913. It has been decided in several cases in the Outer House that the personal earnings of the bankrupt, if solely the product of his own brain or hands, do not fall within the sequestration as *acquirenda*.[29a] But that rule would not avail a bankrupt partner, since it is restricted to the fruits of his own labours, whether intellectual or physical. Where his earnings are derived partly from the efforts of others, *e.g.* clerks or servants, it has been held that they may properly be treated as *acquirenda*.[29b] It seems to follow that the share of profits derived from the firm by a bankrupt partner would, upon the same ratio, be regarded as falling within the sequestration as *acquirenda*. Where the share of profits represents the bankrupt's sole earnings the trustee will be required to allow to him such portion thereof as is needed for the support of the bankrupt and his dependants by way of *beneficium competentiae*.

Married women

Under the common law, while an unmarried woman might be a partner in a business, if she thereafter married during the course of the partnership

[29] Partnership Act 1890, s. 31.
[29a] *Moinet* v. *Hamilton* (1833) 11 S. 348; *Barron* v. *Mitchell* (1881) 8 R. 933 *per* Lord Fraser.
[29b] *Carrick* v. *Edinburgh & Glasgow Property Investment Co.* (1902) 10 S.L.T. 105; *Mason* v. *Paterson* (1904) 12 S.L.T. 511.

the combined effect of the rule as to coverture, which to all intents
and purposes substituted her husband in her place, and the principle of
delectus personae in partnership was that her marriage operated as a
dissolution of the partnership. Moreover the contracts of a married
woman which were entered without her husband's consent were null and
void except in certain special cases.[30] The Married Women's Property
(Scotland) Act 1920 [31] abolished the right of administration of a husband
in his wife's heritable and moveable estate [32] and provided [33] that a married
woman " shall be capable of entering contracts and incurring obligations
and be capable of suing and being sued, as if she were not married, and her
husband shall not be liable in respect of any contract she may enter into
or obligation she may incur on her own behalf." No contractual incapacity on the part of a married woman now remains. Before the
passing of the Married Women's Property Acts, it was the law that a
married woman could in no circumstances, even if she was possessed of
separate estate, validly contract a partnership with her husband.[34] Since
the passing of the Married Women's Property (Scotland) Act 1920 no
reason appears to subsist why a married woman should not enter into a
contract of copartnery with her husband.[35] In view of the close legal
relationship subsisting between husband and wife, however, an inference
of partnership between them will less readily be drawn where the parties
are husband and wife other than where the parties are not so related.[36]

Corporations

A corporation is a person within the meaning of the Partnership
Act 1890, s. 1.[37] It may be a partner in a firm, provided it is so
authorised by its constitution. A company limited by shares may be a
partner of a firm either in association with other companies so limited or
with individuals.[38] If a limited company or other incorporated body is
a partner of the firm, provisions of the Partnership Act 1890 which are
designed to regulate the terms of a partnership among individuals where
no express provision has been made in the partnership agreement may be
inapplicable or imperfectly applicable. The dissolution of the partnership
on the death of any partner provided for in section 33 of the Partnership
Act 1890 will obviously be inapplicable in the case of a partner who is
an incorporated body and the right to apply to the court under section
35 (*a*) for dissolution of the partnership on insanity of a partner will
likewise be inapplicable to the case of a corporate partner. Other
provisions, such as those contained in section 35 (*b*) (*c*) and (*d*) of the

---

[30] See Clark, *op. cit.* I, pp. 25–26.
[31] 10 & 11 Geo. V, c. 64.
[32] s. 1.
[33] s. 3.
[34] Clark, *op. cit.* I, p. 26; *McAra* v. *Wilson* (1848) 10 D. 707, *per* Lord Ivory at p. 713.
[35] It has been so held in England: *Butler* v. *Butler* (1885) 16 Q.B.D. 374; *Burgess* v. *Florence Nightingale Hospital for Gentlewomen* [1955] 1 Q.B. 349.
[36] *Parrington* v. *Parrington* [1951] 2 All E.R. 916.
[37] Interpretation Act 1889 (52 & 53 Vict. c. 63), s. 19.
[38] Palmer, *Company Law* (21st ed.) p. 128.

Act, which are concerned with the right to apply to the court for dissolution of the partnership on the ground of disability or prejudicial conduct of any partner, may require consideration in drawing up a partnership agreement where one of the partners is a corporate body and it may be desirable to incorporate express provisions in the agreement relating more specifically to the sort of activities carried out by the corporate body or in its name which will entitle the copartners to dissolve the partnership. It will be apparent that where a limited company is a partner of a firm, the force of the application of *delectus personae* to the partnership is to some extent diminished; but in many cases the corporate partner will be a private limited company and the right to transfer its shares will be restricted in its articles of association, thus limiting in some degree the possibility of change in its constituent membership though affording no safeguard if the company is taken over by agreement with other interests. The company, like the other partners, is liable for the debts of the firm without limitation but this affords no ground in law to prohibit a limited company entering a partnership since the unlimited liability thus resulting is a corporate one and does not affect the liability of the members of the company which remains limited to the amount remaining unpaid on their shares. It is doubtful whether a limited company has power to enter into a partnership with other persons unless power to do so is contained in the objects clause of its memorandum of association.[39]

The corporate *persona* of the corporation or company leads to the question whether it is to be regarded as an " alien " and particularly an " alien enemy " being determined upon different criteria other than those applied in the case of an individual. These aspects will be briefly considered at a later stage.[40]

Firm as partner with others in another business

In England the firm has no distinct *persona* apart from the partners comprising it.[41] No legal problem arises, therefore, under English law where the partners of one firm enter collectively into a partnership with others in another business or venture. The partners as individuals and natural persons are entering into that relationship and not the firm as a *quasi* person. In Scotland the situation is less clear since the firm under Scots law is regarded as a *quasi* person distinct from the individual members who comprise it.[42] Clark states that " in England corporations alone can become partners: common law companies and private companies being excluded, by reason of the English law not recognising a *quasi*

---

[39] Lindley (*op. cit.*) p. 61; Palmer, *Company Law* (21st ed.) p. 77, gives a specimen clause. And see *Re European Society Arbitration Acts, ex p. British Nation Life Assurance Association* (1878) 8 Ch.D. 679 at 704. That, however, was a case of a joint stock company of *quasi* corporate *persona*. See *infra* p. 50.
[40] *Infra* pp. 48–50.
[41] Partnership Act 1890, s. 4 (1).
[42] *Ibid.* s. 4 (2).

persona in such associations." [43]   Since the common law company has disappeared and trading concerns of the kind formerly carried on under common law companies are nowadays almost invariably incorporated as companies under the Companies Acts, they need no further attention. Clark's observation still holds good as to English partnerships which having no *persona* in law cannot enter a partnership with others as a firm.[44] It remains for consideration whether the converse is true, that since in Scots law the firm enjoys *quasi* personality, the firm itself may be admitted a partner with other persons under the firm name. It appears clear that this is so. In Scots law

> " one company frequently becomes a member of another company. This is quite legal and the consequences are: 1. That the creditors of the greater company are preferable on the stock of that company to the creditors of the company entering it as a partner: 2. That after applying the company funds to the payment of its debts, the creditors have their claim, as creditors of the included partnership, for the balance unpaid, and not merely as creditors of the individuals who comprise that partnership." [45]

Aliens

A detailed treatment of the capacity of aliens to contract with others is more appropriately placed in other treatises than this.[46]   It is proposed to confine discussion in these pages to questions affecting the right of aliens to enter into partnerships in this country.

> " Some persons, though otherwise capable, are prevented by law from becoming partners or shareholders in this country. Among these, aliens may be specially referred to. An *alien ami, i.e.* the subject of a foreign state at peace with Great Britain, since he can sue actions relating to moveables, may be a partner or shareholder in a British company. But an *alien enemy*—that is, the subject of a foreign state at war with this country—having no right of action either directly or by trustee, is much more unfavourably situated." [47]

The older decisions upon which Clark founds his statement of the law were concerned with the personal qualities and status of the contracting party.[48]   In the case of both the *alien ami* and the *alien enemy* it was the status of the person himself which was regarded. That still holds

---

[43] *Op. cit.* I, p. 28.
[44] The distinction can at times become somewhat artificial. See *Mann* v. *D'Arcy & Others* [1968] 2 All E.R. 172 where a partner entered a joint venture on behalf of his firm with another and was held to have made himself *and his two copartners* partners with that other in a joint adventure.
[45] Bell, *Com.* II, p. 514.
[46] See, for example, Gloag, *Contracts* (2nd ed.) p. 96; Anton, *Private International Law*, pp. 131 *et seq.* In Lindley, *op. cit.* pp. 49–53, 62, there is a useful summarised treatment with a copious citation of the English authorities.
[47] Clark, *op. cit.* I, p. 27.
[48] *Arnauld* v. *Boick* (1704) Mor. 10159; *Carron* v. *Cowan & Co.*, Nov. 26, 1809, F.C.; *Macao* v. *Officers of State* (1822) 1 Sh.App. 138.

good so far as the *alien ami* is concerned, although a considerable amount of legislation [49] since Clark's day deals with the legal attributes of the alien and regulates his sojourn in this country. Otherwise, Clark's statement of the law still holds good. Even the immunity enjoyed by ministers of foreign states accredited to and received by Her Majesty is not directly relevant to their capacity to enter a contract of partnership, though it formerly prevented them from being sued in the British courts in respect of private commercial enterprises in which they had engaged,[50] unless an express condition had been made when the minister was received here, that the immunity was excluded.[51] Since the passing of the Diplomatic Privileges Act 1964 the members of the diplomatic staff of a mission will enjoy no immunity from being sued in a British court in respect of any professional or commercial activity which they carry on in the United Kingdom outside their official duties.[51a] Administrative and technical staff [51b] and, service staff [51c] enjoy immunity for official acts only.

Alien enemies

Both the common law and the legislation introduced to prohibit trading with the enemy during two world wars has altered the attitude adopted towards enemy aliens since Clark wrote. For the purpose of regulation of trading with the enemy, a person will be regarded as an " enemy " if a state of war exists between this country and the country in which he is resident.[52] That principle has been adopted in the legislation regulating trading with the enemy both during the First [53] and the Second [54] World Wars. It thus becomes irrelevant in a case involving trading with the enemy whether the party to the contract is an alien or not and whether he can be regarded as an enemy of this country in the every-day usage of that term. " Trading with the most loyal British subject, if he be resident in Germany, would, during the present war, amount to trading with the enemy." [55] The needs of the country's efforts in war, as protected by the legislation against trading with the enemy, entail that the prohibition attaches also to persons who are neither aliens nor enemies. Thus when a person is resident in an enemy country, the place of his birth or his particular allegiance [56] or his personal

---

[49] British Nationality and Status of Aliens Act 1914 as amended by Statute Law Revision Act 1927, British Nationality and Status of Aliens Act 1943 and British Nationality Act 1948. See also Aliens Restriction Acts 1914 and 1919 and Former Enemy Aliens Disabilities Removal Act 1925.

[50] *Taylor* v. *Best* (1854) 14 C.B. 487; *Magdalena S.N. Co.* v. *Martin* (1859) 2 E. & E. 94.

[51] *Macartney* v. *Garbutt* (1890) 24 Q.B.D. 368.

[51a] Diplomatic Privileges Act 1964, Sched.I Art. 31.

[51b] *Ibid.* Art. 37 (2).

[51c] *Ibid.* Art. 37 (3).

[52] Trading with the Enemy Act 1939, s. 2 (1) (*b*). " Resident " refers to *de facto* residence irrespective of other circumstances: *Vamvakas* v. *Custodian of Enemy Property* [1952] 2 Q.B. 183.

[53] Trading with the Enemy Act 1914 and amending legislation.

[54] Trading with the Enemy Act 1939

[55] *Daimler Co.* v. *Continental Tyre Co.* [1916] 2 A.C. 307, *per* Lord Atkinson at p. 319.

[56] *Janson* v. *Driefontein Mines* [1902] A.C. 484; *Porter* v. *Freudenberg* [1915] 1 K.B. 857; and see *In re Deutsche Bank* [1921] 2 Ch. 291.

feelings of hostility or friendliness towards this country [57] are all irrelevant considerations in deciding whether contracts made with him may be enforced in time of war. Though the earlier decisions upon which Clark's pronouncement was founded were concerned with the nationality and allegiance, as well as with the residence, of a person with whom a person in this country contracted during time of war, even before the Trading with the Enemy Acts 1914 and 1939 the courts had departed from the concept of the alien enemy and concerned themselves with the economic realities of commercial intercourse with *any* person situated in enemy territory during a state of war. In that context the use of the terms " alien " and " enemy " as applied to the contracting party loses its significance. The object of the law is to prevent any trading which may afford assistance to the enemies of the Sovereign and that prohibition the common law would enforce on grounds of public policy irrespective of the terms of the Trading with the Enemy Acts.[58] The basis of the rule is seen in the decision in *Tingley* v. *Muller* [59] where a contract made by a British subject after the outbreak of war with another British subject acting under an irrevocable power of attorney granted in his favour before the war by a German was held to be valid since the fulfilment of the contract did not involve any intercourse with the enemy.

On the same reasoning an alien who comes to this country in time of peace, enters a partnership and abides in this country will not, if war later is declared between this country and the country of which he is a native, find his right as a partner affected by the state of war at least so long as he remains in this country with the permission of the Crown.[60] The same rule will apply if he is resident in a neutral country,[61] whereas even if the partnership consists entirely of British subjects some of whom reside in this country and others in a foreign country with which Britain declares war, the partners abroad become enemies so far as regards their trading [62] and that remains the position even when they have no fixed residence in the enemy country if they have gone there to trade.[63]

It will be observed that there are two different concepts involved in the enemy alien cases, (1) the common law concept of public policy which regards a person as an alien enemy if the result of contracts with him is to render assistance to the Queen's enemies and (2) the disabilities imposed on trading with that enemy as contained in the emergency statutes passed to regulate such activity in time of war. These two are distinct and not to be confused one with the other.[64] In consequence of their enemy

---

[57] *Johnstone* v. *Pedlar* [1921] 2 A.C. 263.
[58] *Janson* v. *Driefontein Mines* [1902] A.C. 484, particularly the judgment of Lord Halsbury.
[59] [1917] 2 Ch. 144. *A fortiori* a policy of marine insurance effected before outbreak of war over a ship engaged in trade with the belligerent nation could be enforced in respect of a loss also occurring before the outbreak of war: *Janson* v. *Driefontein Mines, supra.*
[60] *Schulze Gow & Co.* v. *Bank of Scotland*, 1914, 2 S.L.T. 455; *Schaffenhuis* v. *Goldberg* [1916] 1 K.B. 284.
[61] *Re Duchess of Sutherland, Bechoff & Co.* v. *Bubna* (1921) 31 T.L.R. 248.
[62] *McConnell* v. *Hector* (1802) 3 Bos. & P. 113; *O'Mealey* v. *Wilson* (1808) 1 Camp. 482.
[63] *The Jonge Klassina* (1804) 5 Ch.Rob. 296.
[64] *Re Hilckes* [1917] 1 K.B. 48.

status, and the resultant illegality at common law of commercial intercourse between them, no partnership can be recognised as subsisting
between the subjects of enemy countries and further if two partners
reside in different countries the partnership will be terminated by the
outbreak of war between those countries.[65] The ratio of the principle
being the protection of the national interests of belligerent nations,
however, the British courts would not apply it in their decision of a
commercial question arising between the subject of two different nations
who are at war with each other if Britain herself is neutral in the
conflict.[66] While some executory contracts are not rendered illegal by
the outbreak of war between the countries in which the contracting
parties reside [67] these exceptions are hedged round with restrictions where
there is any possibility of the intercourse with the enemy which is involved
in the contractual relationship affording assistance to the Queen's
enemies. Thus although shares held by an alien enemy in a British
company are not forfeited he may not vote by proxy in respect of them.[68]
Such cases, however, remain closely guarded exceptions to the normal
rule that where at the outbreak of the war a contract is executory in that
mutual obligations rest upon the parties to perform acts in order to complete it, the contract is at an end if either party to it becomes an alien
enemy and that rule is applied in the case of partnerships existing at the
outbreak of war.[69]

During the war debts due prior to its outbreak to a person who has
thereupon become an alien enemy may not lawfully be discharged even
through the medium of a neutral party.[70] In such cases if action is
brought against a debtor by an alien enemy, it is sufficient if the former
lodges the money in court, intimation then being made to the appropriate
authorities.[71] But such debts are not cancelled merely because the
creditor is now an alien enemy, nor are the property rights of an alien
enemy forfeited.[72] Thus when a partnership with an alien enemy was
dissolved, the partners in this country were held bound to account for
the enemy partner's share in the firm's assets and also for a share of the
profits accruing after the dissolution so far as those profits were earned
by the use of the capital held by the enemy partner in the firm at the date

---

[65] *Rodriguez* v. *Speyer Bros.* [1919] A.C. 59; *Stevenson* v. *Cartonnagen Industrie* [1918]
A.C. 239.
[66] *Porter* v. *Freudenberg* [1915] 1 K.B. 857 at pp. 874 *et seq.*
[67] *e.g.* leases, *Halsey* v. *Lowenfeld* [1916] 2 K.B. 707; holding of shares, *Robson* v. *Premier
Oil & Pipe Line* [1915] 2 Ch. 124; life insurance, *Seligman* v. *Eagle Insurance Co.* [1917]
1 Ch. 519. It is not illegal to receive payment of a debt from an alien enemy and to
grant a receipt therefor: *Halsey* v. *Lowenfeld, supra.*
[68] *Robson* v. *Premier Oil & Pipe Line, supra.*
[69] *Stevenson* v. *Cartonnagen Industrie* [1918] A.C. 239; *Rodriguez* v. *Speyer Bros.* [1919]
A.C. 59.
[70] *R.* v. *Kupfer* [1915] 2 K.B. 321.
[71] *Guyot-Guenin* v. *Clyde Soap Co.*, 1916 S.C. 6.
[72] " It is not the law of this country that the property of enemy subjects is confiscated. Until
the restoration of peace the enemy can, of course, make no claim to have it delivered up
to him, but when peace is restored he is considered as entitled to his property, with any
fruits it may have borne in the meantime ": *per* Lord Finlay L.C. in *Stevenson* v.
Cartonnagen Industrie [1918] A.C. 239 at 244.

of dissolution.[73]   It is thought that this is the correct explanation of the rather wider proposition stated by Clark [74]:

". . . a British subject who happens to be detained in a foreign country at war with Great Britain, though he does not thereby lose his right to call his copartners to account, may have to postpone its exercise till the return of peace.   So also a foreigner resident abroad, and holding shares in this country before the declaration of war with the country in which he is resident, does not thereby necessarily incur the forfeiture of their proceeds, but must await the return of peace to make good his claim.   Whether the supervention of war in such cases terminates the partnership relation as from that date, depends on whether the partner is resident in the enemy's country, and whether the contract requires him to take a more active part in the concern than is compatible with such residence."

In that passage Clark deals compendiously with the partnership proper and with the joint stock company.   As has already been mentioned the position of the shareholder in the modern limited company, a position roughly analogous to that of " a foreigner resident abroad and holding shares in this country " referred to by Clark, has been treated as an exceptional case on the lines laid down by Clark.[75]   There appears, however, to be no modern authority which supports his view that a partnership with an alien enemy may escape being dissolved on that ground if the enemy alien's participation in the venture is passive.   In such cases the rule in *Stevenson* v. *Cartonnagen Industrie* [76] would permit the enemy alien on peace returning to demand an accounting from the other partners for his interest in the partnership until its dissolution at the outbreak of war, and for any share of profits in the subsequent conduct of the partnership affairs which is attributed to the use of the capital of the enemy alien in the firm; but that is in no way consistent with the view that the partnership itself continues after the outbreak of war.   The English decisions which appear to militate against that view are not strictly in point, since the apparent relaxation of the rule against the alien enemy being allowed to enforce his rights in the British courts pending a state of war can in these cases be explained on special grounds which do not necessitate any view that the partnership with the enemy alien is continued in wartime.[77]

---

[73] *Stevenson* v. *Cartonnagen Industrie, supra.*
[74] *Op. cit.* I, pp. 27–28.
[75] *Halsey* v. *Lowenfeld, supra.*
[76] *Supra.*
[77] *Rodriguez* v. *Speyer Bros.* [1919] A.C. 59 where an alien enemy was allowed to be conjoined as a co-plaintiff with his British partners in an action to recover a debt due to the firm in order to wind up its affairs.   The decision, however, clearly regards this action as arising from a former partnership, now dissolved.   See also *Mercedes Daimler Motor Co.* v. *Maudslay Motor Co.* (1915) 31 T.L.R. 178; *Rombach Baden Clock Co.* v. *Gent* (1915) 31 T.L.R. 492.   Even in these cases, permission may be refused when the majority of the partners are alien enemies: *C. G. Candilis & Sons* v. *Harold Victor & Co.* (1916) 33 T.L.R. 20.

...

CHAPTER III

THE INDICIA OF THE CONTRACT OF PARTNERSHIP

Evidence of constitution of partnership

Partnership is a consensual contract and may be entered into in any manner in which the interchange of the consent of the parties to the establishment of the relationship can be made manifest.[1] Any contract of partnership alleged to exist between the parties may be looked at from two different points of view. The issue may be brought before the court by a third party who has had dealings with the firm, in which case the only point of importance is to establish the general fact of partnership so that the legal consequences of the relationship in regard to the liability of the firm and of its individual partners may flow from the fact that a partnership has been proved to exist. On the other hand, the question may be raised between the partners themselves. In this case the actual terms of the particular contract of partnership may be of importance beyond the establishing of the general fact of partnership; and indeed in many, though by no means all, of such cases the issue will be mainly concerned with the terms of the contract. These differing approaches create different *desiderata* in terms of prudence, though not of law, as to the mode of bringing the contract into being. For the purposes of both, a written contract of partnership executed in due form by the parties will be the most satisfactory. It will provide the best evidence of the fact of partnership when that fact, if established, is sufficient to dispose of the issue raised in the case.[2] It will also be the most satisfactory means of recording the detailed terms upon which the parties have agreed to enter the partnership relation, particularly where the terms as to contribution of capital, sharing of profits and the like are special and an equality of contribution or share is not provided for.

But, however desirable, it is not necessary that the contract be constituted by a formal deed. It may be evidenced by an exchange of letters between, or among, the partners. Heads of agreement, or a draft or memorandum of the proposed articles of agreement may be produced in evidence of the terms of the partnership agreement, though no such agreement has been executed, if the parties have proceeded to carry on business on the footing of those articles or heads of agreement. The mere existence of a document of that kind will, of itself, be inconclusive as to the terms to which the parties have actually agreed, since proposed

---

[1] Gloag, *Contract* (2nd ed.) p. 191; Bell, *Com.* II, pp. 510–511; Clark, *op. cit.* pp. 43 *et seq.*
[2] But the terms of the written agreement are not always conclusive as to this: *Stewart* v. *Buchanan* (1903) 6 F. 15.

51

heads of agreement may have been drawn up but have been rejected or at least disapproved of in some particulars by one or more of the parties to the association. Nor will the existence of such a document suffice even when coupled with proof of the fact that the parties have proceeded to carry on business in association.

> "It will further be required that some precise sanction shall have been given to the articles or the terms expressed in them. Thus, if they have been transcribed into the books; or if the parties shall be found to have conducted their connection on the peculiar stipulation in question; or if the contract, as contained in the articles, shall be identified by proof of the observance of some characteristic point in those articles; or if the parties shall have settled their accounts conformably to the articles,—such proof may be sufficient to establish the contract according to those terms." [3]

The principle upon which Bell founds this view does not appear with entire clarity in the text. From his introductory observations and particularly his qualification that the parties "have proceeded to trade on that footing, and *res non sunt integrae*," there is a suggestion, however slight and cautious, of the principle of *rei interventus*. But to invoke that principle would be to beg the question, since, if *rei interventus* were to apply, the parties must already have come to an agreement, albeit expressed in terms of such informality as to be unenforceable at law. It is possible to regard the matter as one of homologation or adoption of the heads of agreement and indeed, elsewhere, Bell does advance this explanation.[4] It is, however, probable that he is treating the existence of the unsigned articles coupled with proof of actings of the parties of the nature he specifies as themselves evidencing the agreement of the parties. This they would be sufficient to accomplish since there are no formalities prescribed for the constitution or proof of a contract of partnership. But from the manner in which Bell has ordered his commentary it might be deduced that he was regarding the unsigned articles as a contract in writing set up by later actings of parties, or by surrounding circumstances. This appears from his treatment of the subject in two separate paragraphs, the first, in which the observations upon the articles or heads of agreement occur, dealing with writing as evidencing the contract and the second, headed "Parole or Circumstantial Proof" opening with the words, "where no written contract has been executed . . ."

It is thought that Bell in the passage referred to has been led through the duality of the purpose of his exposition to misplace the unsigned "heads of agreement," treating them as themselves an agreement instead of an adminicle of evidence which along with the actings of parties or the other surrounding circumstances might more properly have been

---

[3] Bell, *Com.* II, p. 511. In the *Principles*, para. 361, Bell is more specific in referring to "articles subscribed by initials and afterwards acted upon; articles written in the ledger or otherwise identified with the trade."

[4] *Principles*, para. 361.

considered in his second paragraph " Parole or circumstantial proof." [5] His own words show clearly that the articles taken by themselves and without supporting evidence of actings of parties or other " circumstantial proof " are not adequate to establish agreement; and it appears that he is more concerned, in the division of the subject which he has made, with the two purposes in regard to which the need for evidence of partnership may arise. If this be a correct interpretation of his thought, the treatment of the unsigned heads of agreement along with the formal contract of partnership or the contract entered by an exchange of letters is explicable on the ground that despite the division into written contracts and contracts not in writing the distinction which he was really concerned to draw was between the evidence of the contract required in cases arising between the partners themselves where, as he earlier points out, it may be of importance to establish not merely the general fact of partnership but also the special terms upon which the partnership has been entered.   It is significant that in his paragraph on " parole or circumstantial proof," Bell is considering those cases in which the general fact of partnership alone is required to be established.[6]

The practical importance of maintaining a distinction between the evidential needs of a case involving a dispute between the alleged partners and those of a case concerned with establishing the general fact of partnership which will allow a third party to treat a specified person as a partner of a particular firm was vital in the law prior to the passing of the Partnership Act 1890. It still has its importance but this has been diminished in two ways.   First, the establishing of the detailed terms of the partnership agreement has been assisted at many points by the statutory implications made where the contract of partnership is itself silent on the point in question.[7]   Secondly, the evidence upon which the general fact of partnership may be established has been to some extent rationalised and codified in the Act.[8]

The latter point is of partial validity only, since the Act confines itself to dealing with the relevance of such facts and circumstances as joint ownership, sharing of gross returns and participation in profits as indicative of partnership and does not attempt to range over the whole field of facts and circumstances which may be relied upon to establish the general fact of partnership.   Thus the sharing of an office and office staff coupled with the keeping of day-books and ledgers intended to cover the joint interests of the parties and letter-books which, though nominally maintained for each party, were recurrently interchanged, the signing of letters in joint names, though not in a firm name, and the rendering of accounts and publication of advertisements in a similar

[5] See also Bell, *Principles*, para. 361 where he speaks of the contract being evidenced by " a solemn written contract of partnership duly authenticated; or a less formal writing; letters exchanged; minutes; articles subscribed by initials and afterwards acted upon . . . ."
[6] See, *e.g.* his reference to the adequacy of such proof to " raise the responsibility as a partner " and the discussion (pp. 511–512) of the position of " dormant partners."
[7] *e.g.* Partnership Act 1890, s. 24.
[8] Partnership Act 1890, s. 2; *infra* pp. 63 *et seq.*

manner were regarded as sufficient to establish that a partnership existed.[9]

The assessment of the evidence of facts and circumstances in a given case in relation to whether they are sufficient to establish the existence of a partnership is of the nature of a jury question, and indeed, in a former age, such questions were tried before a civil jury.[10] Yet, as Clark,[11] observes

> " In one sense it is no doubt a question of fact to be ascertained by a jury or its equivalents whether, in the absence of a written contract or equivalent admission, the partnership relation is established by the facts and circumstances of the case. But this presupposes the possibility of distinctly ascertaining what is of the essence of the contract, or at least of fixing upon some test which shall serve as a means of deciding in all cases whether the facts as established are to be taken as evidence of the existence of a partnership."

The problem posed by Clark is a familiar one. While it is attractively easy to state a distinction between questions of fact and questions of law, the distinction is not always so easily maintained in practice. " Matters of law grow downward into roots of fact and matters of fact reach upward without a break into matters of law." [12] The difficulty is perhaps seen at its clearest when the court decides that a jury could not have reached the conclusion which it did reach save by being perverse or unreasonable —a decision which cannot be arrived at without some judicial assessment of matters of fact, yet which is regarded as a decision on a question of law. Conversely, if the assessment of the facts which are sufficient to establish a partnership relation is a jury question of fact, it is closely connected with the essential nature of the relationship thus established, which is a question of law. It is true that some of the difficulties which Clark and other pre-statute writers experienced on this subject may have been removed by the terms of the statutory definition [13] or, in those cases which are concerned with the holding of joint property, sharing of gross returns and sharing of profits, by the " rules for determining existence of partnership " contained in section 2 of the Partnership Act 1890. The effect of the latter rules will be considered later in this chapter.[14] In the meantime, it may be of advantage to examine such other facts and circumstances as have been regarded as of some relevance in the establishing of the relationship of partnership.

In doing so, care must be taken to analyse the reasoning in the pre-statute cases so that where the absence of an authoritative definition of partnership in the common law can be seen to have influenced the decision to some extent, due consideration is given to any assistance which would

---

[9] *Morrison* v. *Service* (1879) 6 R. 1158.
[10] *e.g. Smith* v. *Puller* (1820) 2 Murray 342.
[11] *Op. cit.* Vol. I, p. 44.
[12] Dickinson, *Administrative Justice and the Supremacy of Law*, p. 55. See *Keith-Spicer Ltd.* v. *Mansell* [1970] 1 All E.R. 462, *per* Harman L.J. at p. 463.
[13] Partnership Act 1890, s. 1; *supra* pp. 7 *et seq.*
[14] *Infra* pp. 63 *et seq.*

have been derived from the statutory definition had the case arisen after the passing of the Act. It may be that the result of this analysis will in many cases be inconclusive, since the definition, whatever else may be said of it, does not err upon the side of undue rigidity and rigour. Although Clark considered that the difficulty he experienced in reconciling some decisions " would be removed, if the legislature had authoritatively defined what constitutes partnership, or if lawyers could have fixed on a definition of that contract, at once exhaustive and practical," [15] and although the legislature has since been obliging enough to accede to his wish, it cannot be said that the definition in the Partnership Act offers any dramatic revelation as to the essential nature of the relationship which had escaped the notice of lawyers prior to the passing of the Act. Cases decided prior to the Act may still have a bearing on similar problems which present themselves today and the virtue of the statutory definition may largely be to exclude the area of uneasy approximation formerly covered by the *quasi* partnership.

Setting aside cases of community of property or in profit and loss as more appropriate to be dealt with in relation to the statutory rules contained in section 2 of the Partnership Act 1890, consideration will first be given to evidence of other features which have been taken into account by the courts in arriving at a decision whether the existence of a partnership has been established. The separation is to some extent artificial since, without some element of sharing in profits and losses, none of the features discussed is likely, by itself, to convince the courts of the existence of partnership. The decision in favour of partnership, when it can be reached, is attained after examination of an interwoven set of facts and circumstances in which the participation of the parties in the financial fortunes of the venture must in some degree be present. Yet it may not be entirely fruitless to examine some of the other *indicia* which in the past have had their influence upon the court's decision.

An element upon which Clark [16] sets great store is the existence of agency among the parties to the association. The point has importance, but in a negative way. If the parties are all actively engaged in carrying on in association a commercial enterprise, it may be difficult to ascribe to them the character of partners if " the circumstances of a con.ract or relation are proved to be such as to exclude the notion of agency, express or implied." [17] Obviously, the mere existence of a relationship of principal and agent between two parties will have no relevance as to their being regarded as partners, but where there is a mutuality in the agency relationship, so that each may stand as either the principal or the agent of the other in the different transactions of the business carried on, it becomes more difficult to describe the relationship in other terms than those of partnership. It is not, however, of itself strong affirmative

---

[15] *Op. cit.* Vol. I, p. 44.

[16] " Agency is inseparable from the partnership relation." *Op. cit.* Vol. I, p. 49.

[17] Clark, *loc. cit.* The " negative " criterion may not have the same validity in a question between an active and a sleeping partner.

evidence of the existence of partnership and the fact that there is a mutuality of agency in the course of business carried on will not by itself set up a partnership where the circumstances show a clear intention of the parties merely to act mutually as agents for each other.[18]　The importance of the aspect of mutuality of agency is rather that, in its absence, a partnership cannot readily be held to exist, at any rate when the other circumstances before the court are that all the parties are actively engaged in the business transactions.

In cases where it is sought to set up a partnership *rebus et factis*, evidence of a witness's belief that the parties were acting in partnership is inadmissible.[19]　The witness should be interrogated as to the circumstances observed by him which tend to show that such a relationship existed.　Statements by the alleged partners themselves as to the existence of a partnership among them may be proved as part of the *res gestae* and a statement to that effect by one of the alleged partners may be proved, though the effect of the admission may be difficult to determine.[20]　In *Fergusson* v. *Graham's Trustees*,[21] much of the proof turned upon admissions, by one of the parties, both in express terms and implicit in his conduct.　The appellant was proved to have admitted in conversation that Graham was to have a share of the profits of the adventure.　It was also proved that Graham had raised an interdict against the appellant delivering the cargo, which was the subject in issue, to a third party on the ground that the cargo was at least in part Graham's property, and that the appellant did not oppose the interdict and admitted that the whole cargo, or part at least, belonged to Graham.　The admissions in this case, however, were received against the appellant who made them and in favour of the respondents who were seeking to establish the fact of partnership which the appellant now denied.　They related, moreover, to the facts and circumstances from which a partnership or joint adventure might be established.　These, however, were admissions received against a party to the action that Graham was a partner, and there was other evidence as to Graham's contribution of capital toward the prosecution of the venture.　The record, issues and verdict in a former action of interdict have been held admissible in a later action where the fact of partnership was in issue, though not between precisely the same parties.[22]

Questions as to businesses managed within a family have given rise to difficult decisions whether a partnership has been established among the members of the family.　In *Kinnell* v. *Peebles*,[23] two sisters had been set up in business by a relative who provided the initial capital on loan. One sister had taken the dominant part in the business, assisted by the other sister, who had for a time conducted the business in the absence

[18] *William Baxter & Son* v. *Aitchison & Company* (1841) 3 D. 391.
[19] *Chatto & Co.* v. *Piper & Co.* (1827) 4 Murray 354.　See also the opinion of the Sheriff Principal (Clark) in *Morrison* v. *Service* (1879) 6 R. 1158.
[20] *Smith* v. *Puller* (1820) 2 Murray 342.
[21] (1836) 14 S. 871.
[22] *Fraser* v. *Hill and Others* (1854) 16 D. 789.
[23] (1890) 17 R. 416.

of her sister. The decision of the court was ultimately against a partner-ship. Its interest lies, however, not so much in the detailed facts and circumstances assessed as in the view taken that, notwithstanding that the facts relative to the inception of the business supported a partnership between the two sisters,[24] the later facts and circumstances as to the conduct of the business negatived the existence of a partnership. The case was a narrow one and it is perhaps too definite a conclusion to draw from it that a business which *rebus et factis* is held to originate as a partnership may later be held by facts and circumstances to have changed its nature. Probably the more correct view of the decision of the Inner House is that, while the circumstances in which the money was put into the business were consonant with a partnership, the facts and circum-stances, as a whole, led to the opposite conclusion.[25]

The problems attendant upon setting up a partnership *rebus et factis* in a family business are further illustrated in *Aitchison* v. *Aitchison*.[26] Among the complicated facts elicited in the voluminous evidence in that case, the following salient points were proved. A large family of brothers and sisters, who resided together, occupied themselves in the various branches of a bakery, cooking and confectionery business which had been developed by them from a small business of a similar nature which had been carried on by their deceased father and in which the funds of his estate had been mainly involved. The father's estate was never distributed among the family who continued to carry on the business without any written agreement as to the terms upon which it was being carried on and under the general superintendence of their mother. The court held that the pursuer, one of the brothers, was entitled to an accounting from his brother, the defender, of his intromissions with the father's trust estate and of the funds realised from or belonging to the family business. In the reasons stated by the court a rather indeterminate attitude was adopted to the issue of partnership. The Lord Ordinary, to whose judgment the Inner House adhered, considered that it was " not proved that there was any proper partnership entered into between Mrs. Aitchison and her sons or any of them " but that the business, under certain modifications at different dates, was carried on at first for behoof of the widow and her family and after the widow's death for the joint behoof of the surviving brothers and sisters [27]; and he concludes,

" Now I think that the facts proved in this case abundantly establish that, although Mrs. Aitchison and her sons . . . may have chosen to call themselves partners, they carried on their business, not for their own behoof alone, but for behoof of all the other members of the family; and that, as these members successively came into the business

[24] *Ibid. per* the Lord Ordinary (McLaren) at p. 418; *per* Lord Shand pp. 420–421.
[25] Lord Shand at p. 421: " In such a case it is impossible to limit one's view to the money put into the business. One must look at the whole circumstances of the case, and, looking at these, I think that the mere contribution of the money is a small matter."
[26] (1877) 4 R. 899.
[27] *Ibid.* pp. 904–905.

and devoted their time and attention to it, they were in reality, though not perhaps in form or in name, partners also." [28]
The Lord Justice-Clerk (Moncreiff) was of the opinion that no case of mercantile partnership had been made out. After examining the facts proved, he continued,

" If I am right in my reading of these writings, the case rests, as I think, on a sufficiently solid foundation, and one more consistent with the proved facts of the case than the theory of a commercial partnership at law. If a family of brothers and sisters, each engaged in their own avocations, agree to live together and throw their separate earnings into a common fund, they will not thereby become partners in the separate trades or callings in which each might be engaged; but still, if they choose, by writing under their hand, to indicate the nature of their arrangement, the joint purse might be equally divisible. Such, I think, is the case here . . ." [29]

The Lord Justice-Clerk, therefore, founded his judgment on the existence of a community of interest among the family and not on partnership. On the other hand, Lord Ormidale founded entirely on the fact that partnership had been established.[30] Lord Gifford, while regarding it as quite legal and competent for the members of a family to enter an agreement of family community, preferred to regard the arrangement established in the case before him as one of partnership, though the interests embraced in it were uncommonly wide. He saw no reason in that, however, for departing from the concept of partnership in favour of that of community.[31]

It is possible to regard *Aitchison* v. *Aitchison* as a case so special on its own facts that it affords little guidance in general principle. It is perhaps better regarded as one which serves to delimit and define the area of association which can properly be considered as a partnership. The Lord Justice-Clerk, in his insistence upon the " mercantile " or " commercial " nature of the partnership relation, emphasised an element of partnership which is significant and still finds its place in the statutory definition in section 1 of the Act, which requires that the parties should be carrying on a business. The illustration which he supplies of a family community is clearly distinguishable from partnership on that ground. That example, however, does not match the facts of the case

[28] *Ibid.* pp. 910–911.
[29] *Ibid.* p. 916.
[30] *Ibid.* p. 919: " In my opinion, therefore, the ground of the defender's liability to account to the pursuer must, if it is to be established at all, be made out on the footing of there having been a partnership between them and their brothers and sisters."
[31] *Ibid.* p. 927: " But I think the compact between the members of this family is really a case of partnership and falls under that category of the law. No doubt it is much wider and broader than mercantile partnerships usually are. It embraced the whole property of all the partners, at least all the property to which they had right by succession from their father and mother, with all its increments and all which each of them had earned or contributed to earn from their early youth upwards. This may be a very uncommon kind of partnership but there is nothing illegal in it. . . . Indeed, community is just a name for a wide and universal partnership which included the whole lives and the whole property and earnings of all the *socii*."

which he is considering. In the illustration which he employs, the parties were employed in entirely separate callings and contributed the gains from those callings to a common family fund. There was no element of their being associated together in carrying on a business. In *Aitchison* v. *Aitchison* a business was carried on in common and with a view of profit. It is true that some members of the family were actively engaged in that business, while others, including the pursuer, were not; but there is no requirement in the statutory definition of partnership or in the common law view of the relationship that all the parties should be actively engaged in the business. It is thought, therefore, that the majority of the judges were well founded in their opinion that the case was essentially one of partnership. If that view is accepted, there is an interesting corollary, since the case is the only one discovered which may be used with any confidence as authority for the proposition that sharing in the profits of the business is not an essential element in partnership. That view, which it is submitted is implicit in the decision, runs counter to the pre-statute decisions in the English courts which tend to support the view that sharing in profits was at common law of the essence of the relationship.[32]

Since the terms of the agreement as a whole are to be looked at, no one provision of an agreement in writing and no one circumstance in an agreement set up *rebus et factis* will be sufficient taken in isolation apart from its context to establish a partnership. An express declaration by the parties that they are partners, though obviously a matter deserving of considerable weight in deciding the question, will not be given effect to if the other terms to which the parties have agreed are not consistent with the subsistence of the legal relationship of partnership.[33] Similarly, where the parties agree to terms which are inconsistent with any relationship other than that of partnership a declaration that they are not to be held to be partners will not of itself be sufficient to destroy the true effect of their agreement.[34]

> " If a partnership in fact exists, a community of interest in the adventure being carried on in fact, no concealment of name, no verbal equivalent for the ordinary phrases of profit or loss, no indirect expedient for enforcing control over the adventure will prevent the substance and reality of the transaction being adjudged to be a partnership; and I think I should add, as applicable to this case, that the separation of different stipulations of one arrangement into different deeds will not alter the real arrangement, whatever in fact that arrangement is proved to be, and no 'phrasing of it' by dexterous draftsmen . . . will avail to avert the legal consequences of the contract." [35]

[32] See Chap. I, and cases cited.
[33] *Goddard* v. *Mills* (1929) *The Times*, Feb. 16, 1929.
[34] *Stewart* v. *Buchanan* (1903) 6 F. 15.
[35] *Per* Lord Halsbury in *Adam* v. *Newbigging* (1888) 13 App.Cas. 308 at p. 315, referred to and reaffirmed by him in the Scottish appeal *McCosh* v. *Brown & Co.'s Tr.* (1899) 1 F.(H.L.) 86 at p. 88.

As an element to be taken into account in deciding what is the true intention of the parties an express declaration that they are not to be held to be partners one with another will have some force but only if it can be read consistently with the other terms to which the parties have agreed.

> " Two parties enter into a transaction and say, ' It is hereby declared that there is no partnership between us.' The court pays no regard to that. The court looks at the transaction and says, ' Is this, in point of law, really a partnership? ' It is not in the least conclusive that the parties have used a term or language intended to indicate that the transaction is not that which in law it is." [36]

That forceful dictum may perhaps be criticised as going too far in stating that the court will pay no attention to the express declaration of the parties.[37] If the terms of the agreement as a whole are not inconsistent with the declaration or even, it is submitted, if the terms of the agreement as a whole are susceptible of more than one meaning as to the legal relationship created, the expressed intention of the parties not to be bound as partners must be given weight to by the court. But the essence of the dictum that it is idle for the parties to seek to avoid the legal consequences of the agreement which they have entered by declaring that in spite of its terms they are not to bear the legal character of partners is unchallengeable.

Quasi partnership

In the pre-statute decisions and textbooks the conception of the *quasi* partnership is sometimes encountered. Clark [38] explains the notion in these words.

> " While liability for company obligations is inseparable from the partnership relation, many cases continually recur in which persons who have not constituted partnership among themselves are still liable to the world as though they had. Such cases are generally classed under the head of *quasi* partnerships, or partnerships as regards third parties."

These words immediately call to mind cases of holding out in partnership and indeed Clark deals with that question in the context of his discussion of the *quasi* partnership.[39] But he also embraces within the description two categories of case which he regards as distinguishable from holding-out cases—(1) those in which a person who has never contracted the partnership relation has made himself liable to the public by participating in the profits of the concern and (2) those in which the liability of persons, not partners, or at least not proved to be partners, for firm obligations has been referred to the doctrine of agency, express or implied, rather than to that of sharing profits. It is clear that in the

[36] *Per* Cozens-Hardy M.R. in *Weiner* v. *Harris* [1910] 1 K.B. 285 at p. 290.
[37] See *per* Wrottesley J. in *Fenston* v. *Johnstone* (1940) 23 T.C. 29 at p. 36.
[38] *Op. cit.* Vol. I, p. 52.
[39] *Ibid.* pp. 57 *et seq.*

common law prior to the passing of the Partnership Act 1890 some difficulty was experienced in supplying a rationale which would satisfactorily account for and reconcile the decisions of the courts in such cases as *Waugh* v. *Carver*,[40] *Boulton* v. *Mansfield*[41] and *Grace* v. *Smith*[42] on the effect of sharing in the profits of a concern as *eo ipso* establishing a partnership and on the reasoning upon which that proposition was based. The reason given by de Grey C.J. in the last-mentioned case, that " everyone who has a share in the profits of a trade ought also to bear his share of the loss; and if anyone takes part of the profit he takes part of that fund on which the creditor of the trader relies for payment," is too widely stated to rest upon any assured logical basis and, apart from the dubiety of the main premiss advanced, it might attach liability as a partner or *quasi* partner upon those who receive remuneration for their services based upon a proportion of the profits or receive a share of the profit as an annuity to the widow of a deceased partner or in repayment of a debt due by, or a loan made to, the firm.

This difficulty was increasingly felt by the courts during the nineteenth century and culminated in what was virtually a restatement of the law by Lord Cranworth in *Cox* v. *Hickman* when he observed[43]:

> " It is often said that the test, or one of the tests, whether a person, not ostensibly a partner, is nevertheless in contemplation of law a partner is whether he is entitled to participation in the profits. This no doubt is, in general, a sufficiently accurate test; for a right to participate in profits affords cogent, often conclusive, evidence that the trade in which the profits have been made was carried on in part for, or on behalf of, the person setting up such claim. But the real ground of liability is that the trade has been carried on by persons acting on his behalf. When that is the case, he is liable to the trade obligations and entitled to its profits or to a share of them. It is not strictly correct to say that his right to share in the profits makes him liable to the debts of the trade. The correct mode of stating the proposition is to say that the same thing which entitles him to the one makes him liable to the other—namely, the fact that the trade has been carried on on his behalf, *i.e.* that he stood in the relation of principal towards the persons acting ostensibly as the traders by whom the liabilities have been incurred and under whose management the profits have been made."

The decision in *Cox* v. *Hickman* did not entirely allay the doubts entertained as to the precise position under the common law, and " Bovill's Act "[44] was passed specifically to deal with those cases where a share of profits was made available to a person who lent money to a trader on condition of the lender receiving a rate of interest fluctuating

[40] (1793) 2 H.Bl. 235.
[41] (1787) 3 Pat.App. 70.
[42] (1775) 2 W.Bl. 998.
[43] (1860) 8 H.L.C. 268 at p. 309.
[44] 28 & 29 Vict. c. 86.

with the profits of the trading concern or receiving a share of the profits of that concern. Similar provision was made in the Act in respect of the remuneration of servants or agents by a share of profits, the payment of annuities based on profits to the widow or children of a deceased partner and the receipt of a share of profits by one who had sold the goodwill of his business to the trading concern. These provisions were later in substance re-enacted though with modification and amendment in the Partnership Act 1890.[45] Ascertainment of the precise effect upon the pre-existing common law of those statutory provisions is not unattended with difficulty and will be attempted later.[46] The immediate purpose is to examine the question whether, and, if so, to what extent, any content remains in the common law concept of a *quasi* partnership since the passing of the Partnership Act.

It is now difficult to discern any remaining content in the idea which is not already covered more appropriately and accurately by the doctrine of holding out. Any further area of doubt under the common law where persons, who were not in fact partners, might yet incur liability as if they were partners, was occasioned, it is submitted, by the fact that there was no authoritative definition of partnership prior to the Partnership Act 1890. The circularity of discussion which this involved is perhaps nowhere more clearly to be seen in Scots law than in the opinion of Clark himself, when Sheriff Principal of Lanarkshire, in the case of *Morrison* v. *Service* [47] where he observes:

" One of the strongest tests of the partnership relation is the existence of mutual agency, by which any one of the alleged partners has the power of binding his fellows or the concern with third parties. This is indeed aptly expressed in the civil law by the brocard, *contractus societatis non secus ac contractus mandati.* Now it seems to me that if there is any one fact more clearly proved than another in the present case it is this, that in a question with the world, the pursuer and defender would have been effectually held liable as copartners. There can be no reason to doubt that orders given or obligations undertaken by either of them within the sphere of a writer's business would have effectually bound the other. *Quasi* partnership therefore undoubtedly existed, but *quasi* partnership has always been held to form a very strong presumption for the existence of actual partnership." [48]

This curiously ambivalent approach seems to be due to the two aspects of the partnership noticed earlier in this chapter.[49] The establishment of a partnership may be sought, as it were, from the outside by a third party

[45] s. 2.
[46] Partnership Act 1890, s. 2, and *infra* pp. 63 *et seq.*
[47] (1879) 6 R. 1158 at p. 1160.
[48] The learned sheriff cited Lindley, *Partnership* (3rd ed.), Vol. I, p. 93, and *Peacock* v. *Peacock* (1809) 2 Camp. 45 in support of his views. His judgment was approved by the Second Division without further observations from the judges.
[49] *Supra* pp. 51–53.

endeavouring to hold a person liable as a partner for a debt incurred by a firm or the firm liable for a debt incurred by the person he alleges to be a partner. This approach seeks to establish the public aspect of the partnership relation, the general fact of partnership, and not the detailed stipulations of the contract of partnership. On the other hand, the relationship of partnership may be sought to be established by one party in regard to those who, he alleges, are his copartners and in such questions *inter socios* it will generally be necessary to do more than merely to establish the general fact of partnership. While these differing approaches are distinguished in the pre-statute works on partnership,[50] they do not seem to have been completely disentangled. The cases where the concept of *quasi* partnership has in the past been appealed to partake of the former nature. It seems therefore that the doctrine of *quasi* partnership no longer has much to contribute to the law since the passing of the Partnership Act 1890. Such difficulties as remain, and these are considerable, are not solved by the creation of an intermediate legal concept of *quasi* partnership and its validity in the present-day law seems to be spent.[51]

The Statutory Rules

The " rules for determining the existence of partnership " are, as already mentioned, contained in section 2 of the Partnership Act 1890 and are as follow—

" 2. In determining whether a partnership does or does not exist regard shall be had to the following rules:

(1) Joint tenancy, tenancy in common, joint property, common property, or part ownership does not of itself create a partnership as to anything so held or owned, whether the tenants or owners do or do not share any profits made by the use thereof.

(2) The sharing of gross returns does not of itself create a partnership, whether the persons sharing such returns have or have not a joint or common right or interest in any property from which or from the use of which the returns are derived.

(3) The receipt by a person of a share of the profits of a business is prima facie evidence that he is a partner in the business, but the receipt of such a share, or of a payment contingent on or varying

---

[50] Bell, *Com.* II, 510–511; Clark, *op. cit.* Vol. 1, p. 43.
[51] Lindley, *op. cit.* (13th ed.) p. 5. The concept is ignored in Underhill, *Law of Partnership* (9th ed.), Pollock, *Law of Partnership* (15th ed.) and in Green's *Encyclopaedia of the Law of Scotland, sub voce* Partnership. The idea of *quasi*-partnership is now employed in a specialised sense in company law where in the winding up of a limited company under the " just and equitable " clause (Companies Act 1948, s. 222(*f*)) if the company is in substance a partnership carried on under the guise of a limited company, grounds which would justify the dissolution of a partnership are regarded as sufficient for the winding up of the company: *Re Yenidje Tobacco Co. Ltd.* [1916] 2 Ch. 426; *Re Davis & Collett Ltd.* [1935] Ch. 693; *Re Cuthbert Cooper & Sons Ltd.* [1937] Ch. 392; *Re Lundie Brothers Ltd.* [1965] 2 All E.R. 692; *Re K/9 Meat Supplies (Guildford) Ltd.* [1966] 3 All E.R. 320; *Re Fildes Bros. Ltd.* [1970] 1 All E.R. 923. See *infra* pp. 474–478.

with the profits of a business, does not of itself make him a partner
in the business; and in particular—

(a) The receipt by a person of a debt or other liquidated
amount by instalments or otherwise out of the accruing profits
of a business does not of itself make him a partner in the
business or liable as such;

(b) A contract for the remuneration of a servant or agent
of a person engaged in a business by a share of the profits of the
business does not of itself make the servant or agent a partner
in the business or liable as such;

(c) A person being the widow or child of a deceased partner
and receiving by way of annuity a portion of the profits made
in the business in which the deceased person was a partner, is
not by reason only of such receipt a partner in the business or
liable as such;

(d) The advance of money by way of loan to a person
engaged or about to engage in any business on a contract with
that person that the lender shall receive a rate of interest varying
with the profits, or shall receive a share of the profits arising
from carrying on the business, does not of itself make the
lender a partner with the person or persons carrying on the
business or liable as such: Provided that the contract is in
writing and signed by or on behalf of all the parties thereto;

(e) A person receiving by way of annuity or otherwise a
portion of the profits of a business in consideration of the sale
by him of the goodwill of the business is not by reason only
of such receipt a partner in the business or liable as such."

The rules stated in section 2 are of obvious importance and will be
examined in detail at a later stage in this chapter. In the first place,
however, it is necessary to consider the general effect of the section as a
whole. As is pointed out in *Lindley on Partnership*,[52] the rules therein
stated are, with one exception, expressed in a negative form; the guidance
given in rules (1) and (2) as to the significance to be attached to the
circumstances therein mentioned presupposes that these circumstances
occur in isolation and provides that any such circumstance shall not
" *of itself* " create a partnership. The same facts, taken in association
with other facts and circumstances, may be of the utmost importance as
eivdence that a partnership exists.[53]   Under the common law, the question
whether a partnership exists between the parties is one which must be

---

[52] 13th ed., p. 65.
[53] " It must now be taken on the one hand to be the law that the receipt by a person of a share
of the profits of a business does not of itself make him a partner; neither does it of itself
make a person a partner that having advanced money in loan he stipulates for a certain
amount of control over the business in order to secure the debt.   But both these things,
receipt of a share of the profits and control of the business, are important elements in
deciding whether there is a partnership or not ": *per* Lord Moncreiff in *Stewart* v.
Buchanan (1903) 6 F. 15 at p. 22.

decided upon the basis of the true contract in which the parties have engaged and in reaching a conclusion as to the true nature of that contract regard must be paid to the real intention of the parties as that intention appears upon a consideration of the whole facts of the case.[54] That governing principle finds no express mention in the Partnership Act 1890, but that it is not displaced by the Act may be deduced with confidence from the terms of the specialised statutory rules themselves and the decisions of the courts subsequent to the passing of the Act.[55]

Rule 1. Co-ownership

The term which has been employed in this cross-heading to denote the general ambience of rule 1 is one of studied neutrality. It may perhaps be ventured without undue rashness that in terms of Scots law the rule concerns itself with those cases where the fact appealed to as evidencing the existence of a partnership is one of holding property jointly or in common ownership. It appears to have been the intention of the statute to cover compendiously in terms appropriate to both the English and the Scots law cases where there is any aspect of joint or common property or ownership. The introductory phrases, "Joint tenancy, tenancy in common" have no counterpart in Scots law and indeed since the passing of the Law of Property Act 1925 [56] tenancies in common cannot subsist and may not be created, save as permitted by that Act or the Settled Land Act 1925.[57] The remaining phrases, "joint property, common property, or part ownership," are more recognisable by a Scottish lawyer. "Common property is a right of ownership vested *pro indiviso* in two or more persons, all being equally entitled to enjoy the uses and services derivable from the subject, and the consent of all being requisite in the management, alteration or disposal of the subject. This common and undivided right is continued either by necessity, if a subject belonging to several be indivisible, or voluntarily, if the subject be divisible, until it shall be divided." [58] Such a right may arise through the operation of the law of partnership,[59] or trust and succession. By whatever means the right has arisen, it may be either (a) a joint, or conjunct, right or (b) simply a right of common property, the holders of the latter right having sometimes been described as "part-owners" as distinct from "joint owners." In *Cargill & Another* v. *Muir* [60] the Lord Ordinary (Moncreiff) said,

---

[54] *Cox* v. *Hickman* (1860) 8 H.L.C. 268; *Mollwo, March & Co.* v. *Court of Wards* (1872) L.R. 4 P.C. 419; *Pooley* v. *Driver* (1876) 5 Ch.D. 458; *Badley* v. *Consolidated Bank* (1888) 38 Ch.D. 238 at p. 258.
[55] See particularly, in Scotland, *McCosh* v. *Brown & Co.'s Tr.* (1899) 1 F.(H.L.) 86; *Allison* v. *Allison's Trs.* (1904) 6 F. 496; *cf. Laing Brothers & Co.'s Tr.* v. *Low* (1896) 23 R. 1105, and, in England, *Trower & Sons* v. *Ripstein* [1944] A.C. 254.
[56] s. 1 (6).
[57] For an explanation of the present position of English tenancies in common and joint tenancies, see Lindley, *op. cit.* pp. 67–68.
[58] Bell, *Principles*, para. 1072.
[59] Partnership Act 1890, ss. 20–22.
[60] (1837) 15 S. 408 at p. 410.

" Heirs portioners are not joint proprietors but, as their name imports, part-owners or portioners. They hold *pro indiviso* while the subject is undivided. But each has a title in herself to her own part or share, which she may alienate or burden by her own separate act. The condition of two joint proprietors in the fee is very different; they have no separate estates, but only one estate vested in both, not merely *pro indiviso* in respect of possession, but altogether *pro indiviso* in respect of the right. The distinction is the same which the Lord Ordinary believes is expressed by English lawyers by the terms joint tenants and tenants in common."

The passage just quoted appears to indicate the design and purpose of the rule. The two introductory English terms, " joint tenancy, tenancy in common," are to be matched with the equivalent Scottish terms, " joint property, common ownership, or part ownership," and to cover the same area of legal rights. It is therefore clear that the intended effect of the rule is that persons who succeed [61] to property jointly or in common or to whom property is given jointly or in common, or by whom it is so acquired, are not by that fact alone to be regarded as partners. The notions of holding property jointly, and of carrying on business in partnership, are not necessarily to be equiparated.[62] When several parties acquire property with the intention of holding it jointly that intention is not of itself sufficient to make them partners.[63] To establish the relation of partnership the parties must have had the intention to enter that relationship over and above the intention simply to acquire the property and hold it either jointly or in common. In some cases the question whether the parties in fact formed that dual intention may be difficult to determine. That difficulty is referred to by Gould J. in *Coope* v. *Eyre* [64] where he says, " Although there may be partnerships in many other instances besides what are merely commercial, as in the case of farms rented by several persons jointly, and of partnerships of attorneys, and the like, yet I think the true criterion is, as stated by Blackstone J. in *Grace* v. *Smith*,[65] ' Whether they are concerned in profit and loss.' " In *Davis* v. *Davis* [66] North J. stated, " It is not the law that partners in business, who are owners of the property by means of which the business is carried on are necessarily partners as regards that property." The facts relied upon as establishing an intention that the parties are partners in regard to the management of the property must therefore apparently amount to more than the use of the common property to house a business

---

[61] *Re Fisher & Sons* [1912] 2 K.B. 491.
[62] *Miller* v. *Downie* (1876) 3 R. 548.
[63] *Kay* v. *Johnston* (1856) 21 Beav. 536.
[64] (1788) 1 H.Bl. 37; also reported Ross's *Commercial Cases* III, 407. Even if it can be established that there is a partnership or a joint adventure in relation to the use of the property this will not necessarily extend to all aspects of the parties' actings in relation to the property and the joint venture: *White* v. *McIntyre* (1841) 3 D. 334.
[65] (1775) 2 W.Bl. 998.
[66] [1894] 1 Ch. 393.

carried on by those partners in association.[67]   Questions of that kind are closely interrelated with questions as to the property of the partnership and will be considered later in that context.[68]

The *ratio* lying behind rule 1 of the statutory rules is that the mere holding of property in common is not a " business." [69]   If then a land-owner is not to be regarded as carrying on a business even though his whole time and energies are devoted to the management of his landed estates, it seems to follow logically that co-owners are not by reason of co-ownership alone carrying on a business and their association in a common purpose cannot therefore be ascribed to partnership.   This will remain the case even if they share in the gross returns secured by the letting or even the development of the common property.   Difficulty, however, arises if there is any suggestion that the common property is being used in a business carried on by the parties in association.   The co-owners of a ship are not by that fact alone to be held to be partners even if they derive benefit from the hiring out of the ship on charter [70] but if they use the ship in the conduct of a business of carriers by sea, they may be partners at least in so far as that business is concerned.[71] Again, if land is held in common and is farmed, each owner taking his share of the gross returns of produce obtained by the use of the land, there is no partnership between the co-owners; but if those gross returns are converted by the co-owners into cash which is used as a common stock to defray the expenses of obtaining the returns and the resultant net profits are then divided, the co-owners may be regarded as partners in the business of farming.[72]   It may be doubtful whether the partnership so established is in the business in which the common property is used, rather than in the common property itself, whether it is, as Lindley expresses it,[72] a partnership " in the profits," but doubt of this kind verges upon the merely semantic when it is recollected (a) that the purpose of rule 1 is to declare the effect of co-ownership as an element indicating the existence of a partnership not necessarily closely confined to a partner-ship in that co-ownership, and (b) that if a partnership in a more general business can be established the real question as to the property held in common will be whether it is property of that partnership, a question which is resolved by the application, not of section 2 but of later sections of the Act.[73]

[67] *Fromont* v. *Coupland* (1824) 2 Bing. 170; *Steward* v. *Blakeway* (1869) 4 Ch.App. 603.
Cf. as a narrow decision of intention to form a partnership, *Sharpe* v. *Cummings* (1844) 2 D. & L. 504; and see *Wilson* v. *Holloway* [1893] 2 Ch. 340; *George Hall & Son* v. *Platt* (1954) 47 R. & I.T. 713.
[68] *Infra* Chap. IX, pp. 388 *et seq.*
[69] " Property-owning is not a trade ": *per* the Lord President (Cooper) in *Glasgow Heritable Trust* v. *Inland Revenue*, 1954 S.C. 266 at p. 284.
[70] *Sharpe* v. *Carswell*, 1910 S.C. 391; *Helme* v. *Smith* (1831) 7 Bing. 709; *Ex p. Harrison* (1814) 2 Rose 76; *Green* v. *Briggs* (1848) 6 Hare 395.
[71] The partnership may be held to subsist as to the co-ownership of the vessel as in *Campbell* v. *Mullett* (1819) 2 Swanst. 551, or merely as to the profits of her employment as in *The James W. Elwell* [1921] P. 368
[72] Lindley, *op. cit.* p. 71.
[73] ss. 20–22.   See *infra* Chap. IX.

In *Hoare* v. *Dawes* [74] a broker had been employed by a number of persons to purchase a consignment of tea, in which the broker and the various persons instructing him were each to have separate shares, since the whole consignment was too large to be handled by any one dealer. The broker, in accordance with the usual practice, advanced 25 per cent. of the price in exchange for which he received warrants for delivery of the tea upon payment of the balance of the price. These he deposited with the plaintiffs who were bankers and who had lent him a sum of money upon the security of the warrants. The price of tea fell so that by the time the balance had to be paid for it the value of the tea represented by the warrants was considerably below the amount of the sum lent by the plaintiffs. In the meantime the broker had become a bankrupt and the persons who had employed him were all either dead or bankrupt, except for the defendants who had undertaken to take two-sixteenths of the consignment and had already paid all that they owed in respect of that share. The plaintiff bank sued the defendants on the ground that they, with the other employers of the broker, were to be considered as partners and jointly and severally liable for the whole price. Lord Mansfield, who was at first inclined to consider the defendants as dormant partners, finally decided that the transaction was not one involving partnership since there was no undertaking by any one of the broker's employers " to advance money for another nor any agreement to share with one another in the profit or loss." The essence of the transaction was thus " merely an undertaking by each, for a particular quantity " of tea.

Partnership in the property or in the profits thereof

At several points in the foregoing discussion a distinction has been suggested as to the ambience covered by the partnership when it has been possible to hold that a partnership exists in a case where co-ownership of property was one of the elements in the situation. It must be confessed that the distinction proposed between a partnership as to the property in co-ownership on the one hand and a partnership merely in relation to the profits derived from the use of the property co-owned is a distinction which it is difficult to keep sharply defined; for, if a partnership as to the profits only is held to subsist, the next logical step is inevitably to consider whether the property itself is in fact partnership property. It is clear that it will not necessarily follow that the common property is partnership property. It may remain a subject of co-ownership rather than partnership even though the co-owners associate in a business partnership to exploit its use. [75] But the interaction of the ideas of partnership and co-ownership so closely concerned with the property

---

[74] (1780) 1 Doug. 371, also reported Ross, *Commercial Cases* III, 404. See also *Coope* v. *Eyre* (1788) 1 H.Bl. 37; Ross, *op. cit.* III, p. 407; *Gibson* v. *Lupton* (1832) 9 Bing. 297; Ross, *op. cit.* III, 419.

[75] *Dickson* v. *Dickson* (1821) 1 S. 113 appears to be a case of this kind but is too sparsely reported to throw much light on the subject.

demands considerable vigilance if the distinctions which require to be made are to be sharply maintained; and not a little of the difficulty attending this difficult area of the law of partnership is attributable to the demands of that vigilance.

The distinction is perhaps most usefully illustrated by reference to cases of co-ownership of mines. The reported Scots decisions upon this subject have been few and none is of recent date.[76] The English decisions have, however, been numerous and throw useful light on the question of co-owners of a mine operating it in partnership. There is, of course, no speciality in the co-ownership of mines which displaces the general principle laid down in rule 1. Common or *pro indiviso* owners of a mine may or may not be associated as partners and the mine itself may or may not be part of the property of a partnership.[77] The fact of co-ownership of a mine will not of itself be sufficient as evidence of the subsistence of a partnership among the co-owners, but where the co-owners of a mine work it themselves it becomes inconvenient to the point of virtual impossibility for them to do so without becoming partners. The tendency has, therefore, been to regard persons who work a mine or a quarry held by them in common ownership as partners rather than merely as common owners *pro indiviso* of the property so worked.[78] If the co-owners are held not to be partners, their rights and liabilities depend upon the law of co-ownership. Each may demand an accounting from the other of what that other has received from the mine over and above his share.[79] Each may transfer his share *pro indiviso* without the consent of the other co-owners.[80]

If on the other hand, the circumstances are such that it is held that the co-owners are working the mine or quarry in partnership, two separate cases of partnership may arise. (1) It may be held that the co-owners are partners both in the mine and in its profits. If so, the co-owners are partners both as to the property held in common and as to the venture in which the property is used. Their rights and liabilities thus are determined by reference to the law of partnership and not the law of co-ownership. It seems to follow that none of the parties will then be able to transfer his share in the common property since it is now held as partnership property and the individual partner's interest therein is no longer a *pro indiviso* share of the property but is a right to a share in the property and profits of the partnership. It has become a personal right to a share in a bundle of assets held by the partnership and he can maintain no right to a *pro indiviso* share of the mine unless the partnership be dissolved, and on a winding up he receives such a *pro indiviso* share

---

[76] *Moore* v. *Dempster* (1879) 6 R. 930 appears to be the latest reported case.

[77] The reference to mines relates only to those which have not been nationalised by the Coal Industry Nationalisation Act 1946 and the antecedent statutes, the Coal Acts 1938 and 1943.

[78] *Jefferys* v. *Smith* (1820) 1 J. & W. 298; *Crawshay* v. *Maule* (1818) 1 Swanst. 495; *Faraday* v. *Wightwick* (1829) 1 R. & M. 45.

[79] *Dickson* v. *Dickson* (1821) 1 S. 113.

[80] Bell, *Principles*, para. 1073; Rankine, *Landownership*, 4th ed., pp. 586–587.

in settlement *pro tanto* of his share in the partnership.[81] (2) The co-owners may be held to be partners in the profits derived from working the mine which is held in common but not to be partners in the mine itself. In such a case the subsistence of a partnership as to the working of the mine will not affect the mutual rights and liabilities of the co-owners in regard to the mine itself. These rights and liabilities will still be determined in accordance with the law of common ownership. Each will thus be entitled to convey his *pro indiviso* share in the mine to a third party without the consent of the other co-owners.[82] Each will be entitled to an accounting from the other co-owners as to the benefits derived from the property without seeking a dissolution of the partnership.[83] Negative points upon which the relationship is distinguished from partnership are—(1) the co-owners do not have implied powers of mutual agency and (2) they share gross returns from the common property and not net profits as in partnership.[84] These and other specialities of treatment will arise on a dissolution of the partnership since the mine itself is not partnership property and will be noticed at the appropriate stage when dealing with the dissolution and winding up of the firm.[85]

Rule 2. Sharing in gross returns

The distinction of gross returns from net profits was important in the common law even before the passing of the Partnership Act 1890. Indeed, it might be argued that rule 2 of section 2 gives a significance to the distinction which reflects the common law without sufficiently appreciating that in view of other provisions of the section [86] the logical need for the preservation of the distinction is no longer clamant. The legal view of the nature of profits is that they are the excess of the value of what is obtained over the expense of obtaining it.[87] In that view of profit there is identity between profits and " net profits," [88] but since gross returns are frequently described as " gross profits " it has become the practice to refer to profits as " net profits " in order to avoid confusion with returns. Persons who agree to share in net profits have necessarily in contemplation the possibility of losses since the share will arise only if the sums expended are less than the returns obtained from the business. On the other hand persons who agree to share in the gross returns of a business do not necessarily have in contemplation any contribution to

---

[81] See Lindley, *op. cit.* p. 73 and n. 59.

[82] According to English law the curious situation arises that in such circumstances the partner may also, without consent, convey his interest in the partnership working the mine. See Lindley, *op. cit.* p. 74 and cases there cited. *Quaere* whether this would apply in Scots law.

[83] *Bentley* v. *Bates* (1840) 4 Y. & C.Ex. 182.

[84] Clark, *op. cit.* I, 50; *McAulay* v. *Gault*, Mar. 6, 1821, F.C.; *McGivan* v. *Blackburn* (1725) Mor. 14672.

[85] *Infra* Chaps. XI and XII.

[86] Notably rule (3), on which see *infra* pp. 77 *et seq.*

[87] *Re Spanish Prospecting Co. Ltd.* [1911] 1 Ch. 92.

[88] But " net profits " may be differently interpreted in different contexts within the same deed: *Watson* v. *Haggitt* [1928] A.C. 127.

losses of that business. In the idea of gross returns what has been expended or advanced to gain these returns is irrelevant. So far as the ascertainment of gross returns is concerned, the sums advanced or expended to achieve them are the responsibility of those who actually advance or expend those sums. While, therefore, a person who is in right to a share in the gross returns of a business may incidentally share in the profits of that business when profits are made, he does not thereby become liable to contribute to losses since he must receive his share of those returns whether or not a loss be incurred. It is the absence of the element of any responsibility for losses which accounts for the rule that sharing in gross returns does not *of itself* provide evidence of partnership since by that fact alone there is no necessary community of interest in both profit and loss which is the hall-mark of partnership.[89]

While those reasons are accepted as the cause of the provision laid down in rule 2, the reasonableness of the rule is questioned by Lindley,[90] at least where a community of capital or common stock exists. It is arguable that the rule owes its origin " less to the difference which exists between net profits and gross returns than to the doctrine which so long confused the whole law of partnership in this country, according to which all persons who shared profits incurred liability as if they were really partners." The reference here is clearly to the *quasi* partnership of the common law.[91] While that doctrine has now been discarded, it is difficult to accept the conclusion of the learned author that the distinction between gross returns and net profits is, therefore, now " of comparatively little importance." Rule 2 will certainly not go far to assist in dis-claiming the existence of a partnership when sharing in gross returns is accompanied by community of capital in the association or a common stock. But rule 2 does not purport to legislate for the case where sharing in gross returns is accompanied by other circumstances which may be regarded as the *indicia* of partnership. The rule is concerned with the fact of sharing gross returns and with that fact considered in isolation, and " whether the persons sharing such returns have or have not a joint or common right or interest in any property from which or from the use of which the returns are derived." These added words in rule 2 appear to do no more than to suggest (a) that sharing in gross returns does not of itself create a partnership and (b) that where the sharing in gross returns is accompanied by circumstances of co-ownership of the nature dealt with in rule 1 those added circumstances will not affect the application of the rule. But if in addition, other facts can be

[89] It may be true, as Clark states (*op. cit.* I, 48), that " liability to share in losses is not, like the right to participate in profits, so essential to the partnership relation that its absence is to be taken as conclusive evidence against the existence of a partnership." But it is clear from Clark's ensuing words that he is here considering stipulations of the partners *inter se* that one or more of their number shall be free of liability for share of a loss, and that he is not challenging the view that responsibility *to third parties* for losses is of the essence of a partnership.
[90] *Op. cit.* p. 76.
[91] See *supra* pp. 60–63.

appealed to as supporting partnership, the fact that the parties share in gross returns will do nothing to militate against the existence of a partnership. The effect of rule 2 is that participation in gross returns is, taken by itself, inconclusive. Cases of partnership may occur where the parties agree to share in gross returns in a fixed ratio and to meet the expenses of the business in a different ratio or in an entirely different manner. It was at one time common in medical partnerships for the partners each to defray individually the expenses which they incurred in respect of transport to and from visits, provision of consulting rooms and instruments, virtually the whole expenses of the medical partnership, and to share in the gross returns of the practice in an agreed proportion.[91a]

Characteristic cases where a share in gross returns is provided as remuneration are (a) the royalties allowed to an author on the sales of his book, (b) provision of a theatre for the performance of a play in consideration of a share of the gross receipts and (c) " half-commission " agreements made by stockbrokers with persons introducing business to them.

(a) *Royalties on book sales.* The criterion in such cases appears to be that the royalties are merely a mode of determining the author's remuneration and afford no evidence of the intention of author and publisher to enter a partnership or joint adventure in the publication of the book. The *ratio decidendi* of the pre-statute cases is, however, not entirely clear and Clark [92] draws a distinction between the Scots law, where such agreements are held not to establish a partnership between author and publisher, and the English pre-statute law, where they are " usually regarded as partnerships confined on the one side to profits only."

It is not entirely clear that either proposition can be maintained unqualifiedly. In *Venables* v. *Wood* [93] the pursuers, a firm of stationers, sold paper to the order of Wardlaw, an Edinburgh bookseller, who became insolvent before he had defrayed the cost of the paper. Part of the paper had been used to print an edition of two works by Wood of which the Edinburgh bookseller was publisher on terms that he pay to Wood for the copyright of the edition " one half of the clear profits in the event of any profit being realised, after allowing a commission of ten per cent. for the sale; but that he was to bear no share of the loss, and that Mr. Wardlaw was to undertake all liability for the risk, as well as the whole responsibility and trouble of the publication." The pursuers sued Mr. Wood for the balance due to them in respect of the paper supplied after deducting a dividend received from Wardlaw's bankrupt estate. They pleaded that Wood was a partner or joint adventurer with Wardlaw in the publication of the works for which the paper had been used and that he was liable therefor as a partnership debt. The paper

[91a] I am indebted to Mr. W. A. Cook for directing my attention to this point.
[92] *Op. cit.* I, 51.
[93] (1839) 1 D. 659.

had been used partly in printing Wood's books and partly in publishing a periodical called the *Secession Magazine* of which Wardlaw was the publisher. The Lord President (Hope) directed the jury that on the evidence led the defender was in point of law entitled to a verdict. On the pursuers' excepting to his direction, the court upheld the direction finding that the object of the agreement was to remunerate Wood for his work and not to set up a partnership or joint adventure between him and Wardlaw.

It will be observed that the share agreed to be taken by Wood was in the " clear profits " and not in the gross returns of the publication. That circumstance, considered along with the pre-statute law whereby participation in profits was commonly regarded as by itself establishing either partnership or at least liability as a *quasi* partner may have been the occasion of the observation made by Ross [94] upon this decision where he comments:

> " In so far as the Court found that there was no joint adventure between the publisher and the author, the soundness of the judgment may be questioned, as it would rather appear that where an author stipulates for a share of the profits of the sale of a work, he becomes a partner in a joint adventure for the sale of that work. In so far, however, as the defender was found not liable, the judgment may be supported on the ground that the paper was not supplied expressly and exclusively for the publication of the work in which he had an interest."

The decision, though cited by Clark as a case of sharing of gross returns now falling under rule 2, is on its facts a case of sharing of " clear," or net, profits now falling under rule 3 of section 2 which has still to be considered.[95] The observations made by Clark upon the *ratio decidendi* more properly should be considered in the context of rule 3. It is significant that in developing his views Ross seeks to support them by citing *Gouthwaite* v. *Duckworth* [96] as authority for his more general proposition that an author stipulating for a share of *the profits* of the sale of a book becomes a partner with the publisher in a joint adventure whereas he cites *Saville* v. *Robertson* [97] and *Gardiner* v. *Childs* [98] as authority for the more specialised proposition that the author is not so liable if the paper was ordered by, and supplied to, the publisher for the publication of all works indiscriminately in which the publisher was engaged and not with particular reference to or exclusive appropriation for the publication of the author's book. All three cases are concerned with agreement to share in net profits of the common venture.

The arrangement whereby an author is remunerable by a royalty on the gross returns, or the sales, of his book is regarded as involving no

---

[94] *Commercial Cases* III, 540–541.
[95] *Infra* pp. 77 *et seq.*
[96] (1811) 12 East 421; Ross, *Commercial Cases* III, 541.
[97] (1792) 4 T.R. 720; Ross, *Commercial Cases* III, 518.
[98] (1837) 8 Car. & P. 345; Ross, *Commercial Cases* III, 546.

prima facie question of partnership.[99]   In view of the terms of rule 2 no
further authority need be cited by post-statute writers.   Where the statement appears in pre-statute treatises it may be supported upon the
analogy of the cases concerned with the let of theatres for dramatic and
other productions referred to in the next paragraph.   It is not supported
by *Venables* v. *Wood*; nor does Clark's view of the distinctive treatment
of authors' royalty agreements in English and in Scots law appear to be
accurately and precisely formed.   So far as those royalties are based
upon gross returns, there does not appear to be any difference between
the view taken of them north or south of the border.   In cases like
Venables v. *Wood*, where the royalties are based upon net profits, there
may be prima facie evidence of partnership, a question which will be
further discussed in relation to rule 3 of section 2.   But Clark's observations upon the case, even when taken in this context, appear to be
superficial in two respects—(1) It is by no means clear that such an
agreement between author and publisher will in Scots law never be
regarded as constituting a partnership or that, as Clark suggests, such a
result " appears to be more consonant to sound principle."   Where the
sole effect of the royalty agreement is to provide remuneration for the
author, that may well be the view taken by the courts, at least in cases
decided under the Partnership Act, but other circumstances may attend
the agreement, as where the publisher stipulates that the risk of loss on
the publication shall be shared with the author of a work of limited
popular appeal or the like.   In that case a strong case for partnership
in a joint adventure may be made out.[1]   (2) Nor, it is submitted, is it
entirely clear that in England alone such contracts will be regarded as
partnerships " confined on the one side " (by which Clark presumably
means, the publisher's side) " to profits only."   The Scottish courts also
may, in the light of the circumstances of such a contract, hold that a
partnership subsists between author and publisher but that the copyright
in the work remains with the author and is not partnership property.

   (b) *Letting of theatres etc. for production of dramatic and other works.*
A number of cases are reported where agreements have been made by
proprietors of theatres or halls to hire these for the purpose of presentation
of dramatic or musical entertainments upon the terms that the proprietor
receive a proportion of the gross receipts taken as payment for admission
to the entertainment.   In *Lyon* v. *Knowles*,[2] Knowles who was the proprietor of a theatre agreed to hire the theatre to Dillon for the production
of dramatic entertainments.   Dillon provided the company of actors,
selected the plays to be performed, managed the performance and chose
the persons employed in the theatre.   Knowles paid for printing and
advertising, lighting of the theatre, the wages of door-keeper and scene-
shifters and hired the services of the band of musicians who provided the

[99] Lindley, *op. cit.* p. 11; Underhill, *op. cit.* pp. 6–7; Clark, *op. cit.* I, 51.
[1] There is an interesting example of a joint literary and publishing venture in *Gunn* v. *Ballantyne & Co.* (1870) 7 S.L.R. 289.
[2] (1863) 3 B. & S. 556. affd. (1864) 5 B. & S. 751.

incidental music regarded as essential in the dramatic presentations. The money paid by the public for admission was collected by Knowles's representatives and Knowles retained one-half of this, paying the other half to Dillon. It was held that these facts did not establish the subsistence of a partnership between Knowles and Dillon. In a case later decided [3] the lessee and manager of a theatre agreed with the manager of a theatrical company to make the theatre available to the latter for the performance of a play. The manager of the theatre was to pay for the lighting and the printing of the play bills while the manager of the theatrical company paid the actors' remuneration and the cost of the scenery. The manager of the theatre received 60 per cent. and the manager of the theatrical company 40 per cent. of the receipts. Again it was held that no partnership existed between them.

In both cases there were circumstances beyond the mere sharing of gross returns and in both cases those circumstances might have been of some significance if the parties had been sharing in profits and not in gross returns. The importance of the distinction is brought out in the words of Swinfen Eady L.J.[4]:

> " Nor can the defendant be fixed with liability on the ground of being a joint adventurer with Mill [the manager of the theatrical company]. Although the gross takings were divided between them, there was not any partnership: each had to discharge his own liabilities in respect of the venture. The travelling expenses, the remuneration of the actors, the cost of the appliances had to be borne entirely by Mill. The theatre rent and outgoings, the cost of lighting and the cost of the play bills were wholly to be borne by the defendant. One of them might have made a profit out of the venture and the other might have made a loss."

(c) " *Half-commission* " agreements. In *Sutton & Co.* v. *Grey*,[5] the defendant, who was not a stockbroker, agreed with a firm of stockbrokers that they would carry through business on the Stock Exchange for clients introduced by Grey to the firm upon the terms that Grey would be paid one-half of the commission earned by the firm on that business and that Grey, in turn, would be liable to the firm for a one-half share of any loss incurred by the firm in respect of it. The Court of Appeal held that the participation in the commission was a sharing in gross returns, not profits, and that accordingly no partnership existed between Grey and the firm of stockbrokers. A similar, though not identical, arrangement was considered by the court in *Montagu Stanley & Co.* v. *J. C. Solomon Ltd.*,[6] and in that case the question of the existence of a partnership was not adumbrated. In both cases the sharing of the commission, being regarded as a sharing of gross returns, would by itself have been insufficient

---

[3] *Cox* v. *Coulson* [1916] 2 K.B. 177.
[4] [1916] 2 K.B. at p. 181.
[5] [1894] 1 Q.B. 285.
[6] [1932] 1 K.B. 611; affd. [1932] 2 K.B. 287.

to establish a partnership in view of the terms of rule 2. In both cases, however, there was the added circumstance of an agreement to share in any loss incurred in connection with the business introduced. Though participation in profit and in loss has been regarded as virtually the badge of partnership [7] there is still even in that context substance in the words qualifying the general rule.[8] When an agreement " to bear a definite share of loss " is taken along with receipt of a share of gross returns, it cannot be said that the conjunction of the two circumstances raises the same conclusion of partnership, whether that conclusion be described as " almost invincible " or merely as " very strong." The most that can be said is that the added factor is one which must be considered, and consideration is given to it in order to discover whether the real intention of the parties was to enter a partnership. In *Sutton & Co.* v. *Grey* [9] the conclusion of the court was that no such intention had existed and that the circumstances were consonant with the intention that the party introducing the business should indemnify the firm accepting it for losses incurred thereon to the extent of one-half of such losses.[10]

The specific cases which have been discussed, while characteristic examples of agreements to share in gross returns, are not exhaustive. Arrangements frequently made in regard to whaling voyages [11] where the crew receive a share of the proceeds of the oil obtained and certain [12] though not all [13] of the arrangements made in regard to share fishing exhibit some features akin to partnership but are not regarded as establishing that relationship since the agreement is in essence one of sharing gross returns.

In considering the cases where the share of the parties to the agreement, or some one or more of them, is a share in the gross returns, no real problem is presented by the stipulation of rule 2 that this circumstance, taken in isolation, is no evidence of partnership; nor does it appear profitable to contradict Lindley's assertion [14] that the rule reflects a distinction of the common law between participation in profits and participation in gross returns which before the passing of Bovill's Act was of considerable importance in view of the prevalence of the doctrine of *quasi* partnership arising *inter alia* from the mere fact of participation

---

[7] Gow, *Mercantile and Industrial Law of Scotland*, p. 542 n. 25: " On the other hand, whatever the verbal and accounting formulae employed, if in fact there is an agreement to share profits and losses the almost invincible conclusion is partnership."

[8] Pollock, *op. cit.* p. 7: " Even an agreement to bear a definite share of loss as well as take a definite share of profit is not necessarily a partnership for the purpose of giving either party the rights of a partner against the other, though an unqualified agreement to share profit and loss is very strong evidence of partnership."

[9] (1894) 1 Q.B. 285.

[10] The same attitude was adopted by the court in *Montagu Stanley & Co.* v. *J. C. Solomon Ltd.* [1932] 2 K.B. 287 though in that case the question of partnership was not argued.

[11] Lindley, *op. cit.* p. 76 and cases there cited.

[12] *Clark* v. *Jamieson*, 1909 S.C. 132.

[13] *Scottish Insurance Commissioners* v. *McNaughton*, 1914 S.C. 826, where the share fishermen shared in the profits and were accordingly held to be joint adventurers though trawlnet fishermen were not so regarded; *Parker* v. *Walker*, 1961 S.L.T. 252.

[14] *Op. cit.* p. 63.

in profits.[15]   It is more difficult to accept Lindley's view that, since the
introduction of the statutory provisions,[16] the distinction is " of comparatively little importance " unless this judgment is based upon a purely
quantitative assessment and merely signifies that cases of a partnership
relation where one or more of the partners draw a share in gross returns
are likely to be of rare occurrence.   The importance of maintaining the
distinction, however, is unaffected by the degree of frequency of occurrence
of the problem, if the problem can in fact occur.

Rule 2, by its terms, suggests that a partnership may be established
where the element of participation in gross returns is accompanied by
other circumstances tending to establish the intention of the parties to
create a partnership, though participation in gross returns by itself will
not establish such a relationship.   The real difficulty is to deduce from
the reported decisions the additional circumstances which will be sufficient
to establish the partnership.   It is clear that co-owners of property who
participate in the gross returns of that property are not thereby to be
regarded as partners since rule 1 expressly states that sharing in the
profits made by the use of the common property will not be sufficient to
establish a partnership relation and *a fortiori* sharing in gross returns of
the property will not have that result.   Nor, apparently, is the circumstance that, in addition to sharing in gross returns, there is an obligation
to bear a share of losses, conclusive of partnership.[17]   The existence of
an obligation of that kind may be consistent with an intention to enter a
legal relationship other than that of partners.   It is probable that on
the analogy of the cases concerned with sharing of profits to be considered
immediately hereafter, evidence of active participation in the control [18] of
the partnership business or of the right of effective intervention [19] in the
management thereof would be accepted as strong evidence of partnership
even in the face of an express stipulation in the agreement that the parties
are not to be held as partners one with the other.[20]   What must be
regarded by the court are the " real contracts and relations of the
parties." [21]   In considering such cases therefore the court will not be
concerned to attribute some doctrinal significance to a particular circumstance or class of circumstances but to spell out from those circumstances
as a whole the real intention of the parties.

Rule 3.   Participation in profits

Lindley [22] has drawn attention to the fact that the rules embodied in
section 2 are universally couched in the negative with one exception.

[15] *e.g. Grace* v. *Smith* (1775) 2 W.Bl. 998; Ross, *Commercial Cases* III, 400.
[16] Particularly Partnership Act 1890, s. 2, rule 3.
[17] *Sutton & Co.* v. *Grey* [1894] 1 Q.B. 285; *Montagu Stanley & Co.* v. *J. C. Solomon Ltd.*
    [1932] 2 K.B. 287.
[18] *McCosh* v. *Brown & Co.'s Tr.* (1899) 1 F.(H.L.) 86.
[19] *Mollwo, March & Co.* v. *Court of Wards* (1872) L.R. 4 P.C. 419; *Ex p. Tennant, re Howard*
    (1877) 6 Ch.D. 303; *Badeley* v. *Consolidated Bank* (1888) 38 Ch.D. 238.
[20] *Stewart* v. *Buchanan* (1903) 6 F. 15.
[21] *Mollwo, March & Co.* v. *Court of Wards, supra per* Sir Montagu Smith.
[22] *Op. cit.* p. 65.

The opening sentence of rule 3 is expressed affirmatively—" The receipt by a person of a share of the profits of a business is prima facie evidence that he is a partner in the business." That affirmative statement is, however, immediately followed by one in the more familiar negative pattern—" but the receipt of such a share, or of a payment contingent on or varying with the profits of a 'business does not of itself make him a partner of the business." Apart from the opening sentence of rule 3, rules 1 and 2 and the sub-rules to rule 3 itself are negative. They deny to the particular fact with which they deal any effect in establishing the relation of partnership if that fact exists in isolation. There is nothing in these negatively expressed rules which requires the circumstances dealt with to be ignored where they occur in conjunction with other circumstances and indeed far from being disregarded such circumstances may be given considerable weight where they exist as one of a set of circumstances from which it is sought to establish the intention of the parties to set up a partnership. On the other hand participation in profit is regarded in legal terms as participation in net profit [23] which in turn implies that the value of the gross benefits gained over a period are debited with the expense of achieving them before they are distributed as net profits. Whatever the adequacy or otherwise of the judicial pronouncements in *Re Spanish Prospecting Co. Ltd.*,[23] as an exposition of the techniques applied in making up the accounts of a trading firm, there is at least in contemplation, when a right to participate in profits of this kind is asserted, that there may in fact be no profits or that there may be losses. It is true that the mere assertion of a right to participate in profits does not by itself logically entail that one has agreed to contribute to losses but it is submitted that it is at least an indication that the participants are involved together in the fortunes of a commercial venture.

It is possibly on that view of the implications of participation in profits that the pre-statute law made so much of this element. Until the corrective applied by Lord Cranworth in *Cox* v. *Hickman* [24] there were frequent pronouncements which seem to follow this line of reasoning as justifying a universal rule that where there was participation in the profits of a business, that alone was sufficient to establish the relation of partnership,[25] and that where the establishment of such a relationship among the parties to the agreement *inter se* was negated by the express terms of their agreement or otherwise by the circumstances of the case, nevertheless, liability to third parties would be imposed on the doctrine of *quasi* partnership.[26]

In considering the difficult, and often apparently conflicting decisions of that epoch it is necessary to keep in mind the two purposes for which the fact of partnership may be sought to be invoked as mentioned at the

[23] *Re Spanish Prospecting Co. Ltd.* [1911] 1 Ch. 92.
[24] (1860) 8 H.L.C. 268 at 309. See *supra* p. 61.
[25] *Grace* v. *Smith* (1775) 2 Wm.Bl. 998; *Bloxham* v. *Pell* (1775) 2 Wm.Bl. 999; *McKinlay* v. *Gillon* (1830) 9 S. 90; affd. (1831) 5 W. & S. 468.
[26] *Waugh* v. *Carver* (1793) 2 H.Bl. 235; *Boulton* v. *Mansfield* (1787) 3 Pat.App. 70.

commencement of this chapter.[27] Even when participation in profits could be held as conclusive proof of partnership it was difficult to do so in the face of express terms of the agreement which were inconsistent with such a conclusion. In questions arising between the partners themselves the rule did not operate to write a contract for the parties entirely different from that which they had entered. In such cases participation in profits was regarded as the conclusive factor when the intention of the parties had to be established *rebus et factis* or where there was nothing of substance, as opposed to mere " ingenuities of draftsmanship," in the express terms of their agreement which was inconsistent with a true intention to be bound to one another as partners. Such cases were concerned with the actual terms of the contract made.[28] But where the parties acting in concert, albeit in an ill-defined relationship to one another, transacted with a third party, that third party could in many cases establish the " general fact of partnership " with its attendant legal consequences by proving participation in the profits of the business. Even so, cases occurred where the third party sued a person who, although he had a right to participate in profits, could not readily be held to be an actual partner.[29] In such cases liability as a partner tended to be imposed upon him under the doctrine of *quasi* partnership,[30] though even the latter liability might be excluded if the facts were entirely inconsistent with partnership.[31]

That survey of the pre-statute law is of importance since it helps to explain another peculiarity of rule 3. In the first two rules of section 2 it is stated that co-ownership and sharing in gross returns respectively do not of themselves " create a partnership." In rule 3 it is stated that the receipt by a person of a share in the profits of a business is prima facie evidence that he is a partner in the business but that the receipt of such a share, or of a payment contingent on or varying with the profits of a business does not of itself make him a partner in the business and in each of the particular cases of exception mentioned in subparagraphs (*a*) to (*e*) of the rule it is stated that the particular circumstance mentioned does not of itself make him a partner *or liable as such.* The intrusion of the new formula in the italicised words may be accounted for in two ways. (1) It may be explained simply upon the ground that whereas rules 1 and 2 express the result of the fact of co-ownership and of sharing in gross returns respectively upon the creation of a partnership, rule 3 takes a different approach. Instead of following the pattern of the preceding rules and stating, " The sharing of profits is prima facie evidence of partnership " the rule personalises the issue by stating, " The *receipt by a person* of a share of the profits of a business is prima facie evidence *that he is a partner* in the business." Having thus introduced the rule, it follows that what is being considered is the effect upon an individual and

---

[27] *Supra* p. 51.
[28] *Cheap* v. *Cramond* (1821) 4 B. & Ald. 663; Ross, *Commercial Cases* III, 435.
[29] *Grace* v. *Smith* (1775) 2 W.Bl. 998.
[30] *Waugh* v. *Carver* (1793) 2 H.Bl. 235.
[31] *Hoare* v. *Dawes* (1780) 1 Doug. 371.

in such a personalised issue it perhaps follows that the absence of that individual's liability as a partner should be emphasised in the excepted cases. If that be the correct explanation, it is surprising that the words " or liable as such " were not added in the second clause of the general part of rule 3 of which the sub-rules (*a*) to (*e*) are particular instances. (2) The alternative explanation is that the particular instances in sub-rules (*a*) to (*e*) of rule 3 are all cases where under the pre-statute law liability might have been imposed upon an individual on the ground of *quasi* partnership. This appears to be the better explanation and thus the exceptions in these sub-rules represents the statutory abrogation of the doctrine of *quasi* partnership except in cases of holding out which are separately and expressly legislated for later in the Act.[32]

One further general point deserves notice before the detailed situations covered by the rule are surveyed. There is an apparent inconsistency between the two clauses of the main rule itself. If the receipt of a share of the profits of a business is prima facie evidence that the recipient is a partner in that business it is difficult to give effect to the succeeding clause, " but the receipt of such a share . . . does not of itself make him a partner in the business," without destroying the major proposition of the rule. It must be confessed that the Act in this particular falls short of the generally high standard of draftsmanship which it otherwise displays. The awkwardness of the apparent contradiction has given rise to some difficulty in the courts. The words were considered by North J. in *Davis* v. *Davis*.[33] In the result the court took an indulgent view. " These phrases appear somewhat conflicting," said North J.,[34] " but I do not think there is any real difficulty in understanding them, because the matter was clearly explained by the Court of Appeal in *Badeley* v. *Consolidated Bank*. It is true that that case was decided before the Act of 1890 was passed, but the Act seems to give effect to what was there laid down." *Badeley* v. *Consolidated Bank* [35] decided that if it is established that two persons are sharing in the profits of a business, that fact, in the absence of explanation, leads to the conclusion that the business is carried on by them in partnership. If, however, participation in the profits is merely one of a set of relevant facts, all the circumstances must be considered in arriving at the real intention of the parties. It is thus erroneous to regard the fact of participation in profits as raising a presumption of partnership which then must be rebutted by evidence of other circumstances. North J., therefore, interpreted rule 3 in the light of the pre-existing law which he assumed that the Act intended to reproduce. He said[36]:

[32] s. 14 (1).
[33] [1894] 1 Ch. 393.
[34] *Ibid.* at p. 398.
[35] (1888) 38 Ch.D. 238.
[36] *Davis* v. *Davis, supra*, at p. 399. If participation in profits were regarded as raising a presumption of partnership the customers of a trader who agreed to distribute part of his profits among them, as in *Ogden Ltd.* v. *Nelson* [1905] A.C. 109, might have to rebut the presumption that they were partners of the trader. That case, however, is perhaps more properly considered as one of sharing in gross returns.

" Adopting then the rule of law which was laid down before the Act, and which seems to me to be precisely what is intended by sect. 2 (3) of the Act, the receipt by a person of a share of the profits of a business is prima facie evidence that he is a partner in it, and if the matter stops there it is evidence upon which the court must act. But, if there are other circumstances to be considered, they ought to be considered fairly together; not holding that a partnership is proved by the receipt of a share of profits unless it is rebutted by something else; but taking all the circumstances together, not attaching undue weight to any of them, but drawing an inference from the whole."

Badeley v. *Consolidated Bank* [37] was considered in Scotland in *Stewart* v. *Buchanan*.[38] Though no reported Scottish decision has dealt expressly with the apparent conflict in rule 3, it is thought the construction placed upon the rule by North J., which has remained undisturbed for over three-quarters of a century, would probably be adopted in Scotland.

Participation in profits prima facie evidence but not conclusive

Though many pre-statute cases placed in undue prominence the element of participation of profits as evidence of partnership, the peculiarly baffling conflict of pre-statute authority on this point which has earlier been referred to is sufficient indication that even before the passing of the Act the receipt of a share of profits was not regarded as a conclusive test of partnership. Lindley [39] declares that even before the Act " it was well settled " that no conclusive test could be based upon the receipt of a share of profits alone.[40] The causes of a conflict amounting almost to complete confusion have already been touched upon.[41] In addition, while *Cox* v. *Hickman* [42] did much to destroy the doctrinal view of participation in profits, it was not until the decision in *Badeley* v. *Consolidated Bank* [43] that the fact of sharing in profits was clearly explained as one which, taken by itself, was prima facie evidence of partnership but which was not a conclusive test whether partnership existed if there were other relevant facts to be considered, and which did not even go so far as to raise a presumption of partnership which had to be rebutted. Despite the plethora of dicta from the English courts which were freely called in aid of argument in the Scottish cases of the late nineteenth century, Scottish judges seem usually to have preferred to take an overall

[37] (1888) 38 Ch.D. 238.
[38] (1903) 6 F. 15. Though Lord Trayner (at p. 22) observed that the case " goes further than I would be prepared to follow in at least one respect," it appears that the *ratio decidendi* of the Scottish case is consonant with the proposition deduced from *Badeley* v. *Consolidated Bank*.
[39] *Op. cit.* pp. 78–79.
[40] Unfortunately the Irish case cited by way of example, *Barklie* v. *Scott*, 1 Huds. & Br. 83, might well have been decided otherwise in Scotland upon different grounds. See *McAulay* v. *Renny* (1803) Bell, *Com.* II, 514, *Calder* v. *Downie*, Dec. 11, 1811, F.C.; affd. April 14, 1815, F.C. See also *supra* pp. 25–27.
[41] *Supra* pp. 60–62.
[42] (1860) 8 H.L.C. 268.
[43] (1888) 38 Ch.D. 238.

view of the terms of the agreement or of the facts and circumstances establishing it, with the object of determining what was the real intention of the parties to the agreement.[44] Since the passing of the Partnership Act 1890, and indeed since the passing of Bovill's Act,[45] the cases in which partnership has been held not to exist despite participation in the profits, have been mainly concerned with the particularly instanced examples in sub-rules (a) to (e) of rule 3. That is understandable, since those instances were selected as the cases where a rigorous application of the " participation in profits " test of partnership would most frequently result in hardship if not injustice. They remain, however, instances or illustrations of the general effect of rule 3 and other sets of circumstances may occur where participation is one of the circumstances, yet on overall consideration the court may conclude that the real intention of the parties was not to create a partnership.

The general effect of rule 3 having been examined, some consideration should now be given to each of the particular cases mentioned in sub-rules (a) to (e). It will be noticed that these cases are not strictly " exceptions " to rule 3 as they are sometimes described. In reality, they fall within the general rule as explained above and afford particular though not exhaustive [46] instances of collocations of circumstance in which the prima facie evidence of the receipt of a share of profits is displaced in favour of a consideration of those circumstances as a whole.

(a) *Receipt of a debt etc. by instalments or otherwise out of the accruing profits of a business*

No reported decision has turned on this particular type of case. It is an instance where presumably the intention of the parties to arrange for settlement of a debt and not to carry on business in a partnership may be fairly readily discerned. It is to be kept in view, however, that the wording of sub-rule (a) is governed by the immediately preceding words of rule 3 and that accordingly the debt may be paid off by instalments " contingent on or varying with the profits " of the business. It may therefore be agreed that a stipulated share of the profits shall be received by the creditor and applied over a period in extinction of his debt. The most common arrangement of this kind will relate to sums advanced on loan to a firm upon such terms but this is dealt with as a separate case under the Act.[47] Until the decision in *Cox* v. *Hickman* [48] the position of creditors who agreed to an arrangement under which their debts would be repaid out of the profits of the business of the debtor

---

[44] *Moore* v. *Dempster* (1879) 6 R. 930; *Lawrie* v. *Lawrie's Trs.* (1892) 19 R. 675; *Kinnell* v. *Peebles* (1890) 17 R. 416. Participation in losses, although not in itself conclusive, is a feature of great importance and may be decisive in many cases; *Parker* v. *Walker*, 1961 S.L.T. 252.

[45] 28 & 29 Vict. c. 86.

[46] *Pinto Leite & Nephews* [1929] 1 Ch. 221; *Charlton & Bagshaw* v. *Highet*, 1923 S.L.T. 493 (O.H.).

[47] s. 2 (3) (d) and *infra* pp. 87 *et seq.*

[48] (1860) 8 H.L.C. 268.

firm was not regarded as entirely clear. In *Cox* v. *Hickman* the question arose for decision whether creditors who were scheduled in a deed of arrangement whereby they were to receive payment of their claims from the profits of the debtor's business were liable for obligations undertaken by the trustees under the deed of arrangement in carrying on the debtor's business for the purposes of the deed. In the House of Lords the problem was treated as one of agency and the fact that the profits of the business were to be shared by the scheduled creditors was held insufficient to establish that the trustees were the authorised agents of the creditors.[49] But the fact that the creditors were entitled to a share of profits only to the amount of their several debts was stressed to distinguish the case from *Waugh* v. *Carver* [50] where the total extent to which the creditor was entitled to take his share of profits was undefined. As has been mentioned earlier,[51] the implications of the decision in *Cox* v. *Hickman* have been (correctly) regarded as much wider than the actual point decided. The particular point decided, and followed in a number of later decisions,[52] has been embodied in section 2 (3) (*a*) of the Act.

(b) *Remuneration of a servant or agent by a share of the profits of the business*

Like the other provisions of the section this sub-rule is declaratory of the pre-existing common law. Even prior to the passing of Bovill's Act and the Partnership Act 1890 there was no necessary implication that servants or agents whose remuneration was determined proportionately to the profits earned in the business in which they were employed were to be regarded as partners in that business. The matter was one to be decided on the basis of the true intention of the parties as gathered from the terms of the agreement considered as a whole.[53] The terms of section 2 (3) (*b*) have the same legal effect. In *Walker* v. *Reith* [54] arrangements made by the owner of a manufacturing business provided that after his death certain of his employees should have a " prospective interest " in the profits of the business and in the business itself " if acquired by them." It was further provided that these interests would not vest in the employees until the owner's capital had been entirely paid out, that no employee was entitled to sell or dispose of his interest, that the whole of the net profits should be divided among the chosen employees who were to receive 10 per cent. thereof in cash, the remaining 90 per cent. being credited to their accounts with the firm until the whole of the owner's capital had been paid out, and that, upon the capital having been paid out along with a sum representing the price of the factory and any

[49] *Mann* v. *Sinclair* (1879) 6 R. 1078 which has features apparently conflicting with that view is to be distinguished. In that case the question raised was the trustee's title to sue as representing the whole body of creditors rather than some of those creditors and not others.
[50] (1793) 2 H.Bl. 235; Ross, *Commercial Cases* III, 426.
[51] *Supra* p. 61.
[52] *Kilshaw* v. *Jukes* (1863) 3 B. & S. 847; *Re English and Irish Church and University Assurance Society* (1862) 1 Hem. & M. 85; *Holme* v. *Hammond* (1872) L.R. 7 Ex. 218.
[53] *Ex p. Tennant, re Howard* (1877) 6 Ch.D. 303; *Ross* v. *Parkyns* (1875) L.R. 20 Eq. 331; *Rawlinson* v. *Clarke* (1846) 15 M. & W. 292; *Gatherer* (1893) 1 S.L.T. 401 (O.H.).
[54] (1906) 8 F. 381.

amounts due upon the accounts of deceased, retired or bankrupt employees, the owner's trustees should convey the business and factory to the surviving employees, those employees being entitled at any time to purchase the business on paying the sum at credit of the deceased owner in the firm's accounts. While the business was to be carried on by the employees, substantial powers of control were retained in the hands of the owner's trustees. On these arrangements coming into operation after the owner's death it was held that the employees were not partners in the business but servants of the owner's testamentary trustees. The decision was reached upon an overall consideration of the intention as evidenced by the agreement as a whole. Walker, who was one of the employees concerned, appealed an assessment to income tax made upon him on the basis, as contended by the Inland Revenue, that he was a partner of the business and that his emoluments should be assessed upon the full amount of his " prospective " share of profits, not merely on the 10 per cent. which he was entitled to receive in cash. Much of the argument was concerned with special features of tax law, but it does not appear from the report that the terms of section 2 (3) (b) were invoked in favour of his contention that no partnership existed and Lord Stormonth-Darling giving the judgment of the court made no mention of the statutory provision, presumably regarding them as having no application in the circumstances of the case.

On the other hand, in *Allison* v. *Allison's Trustees*,[55] the pursuer was regarded as a partner where he was appointed to manage his brother's business at a yearly salary with allowance for house rent and a share of the profits amounting to three-eighths thereof. The Lord President (Kinross) described the agreement as " not a mere contract of service . . . but a complex contract implying partnership as well as service." [56]

Salaried partners

A situation sometimes arises where a partner is assumed into the firm upon the terms that he has a fixed salary in addition to a share in the profits. In the case of a junior partner, the salary payable may represent the minimum remuneration payable if his share of profits in any year falls below that level. The detailed arrangements may vary considerably but it is a common problem in all such arrangements to decide whether the true intention is to create a partnership, or merely to employ a servant with an entitlement to remuneration varying with the profits of the business. If it is to be held that a partnership has been created, there must be circumstances beyond the mere entitlement to a share of profits which provide evidence of the intention to enter that relationship. An agreement which in addition to providing for a share in profits as remuneration for the services rendered gives an interest in the capital or stock of the firm, will often be regarded as establishing an intention to

[55] (1904) 6 F. 496.
[56] *Ibid.* p. 500.

enter a partnership.[57] Averments that the party introduced into the business has contributed to, or holds a share of, the capital of the firm will be regarded as significant as to the intention to create a partnership [58]; but even if there has been no contribution to the capital and no portion thereof has been credited to the person with whom the agreement has been made, it has been held sufficient to create a partnership that the party introduced into the business is to share in the profits arising from the development of certain land which was the property of the firm,[59] and participation in the profits with in addition a share in the goodwill of the business was held sufficient to establish a partnership in *Lawrie* v. *Lawrie's Trs.*[60] If sufficient *indicia* of partnership are found to be present to justify the court in holding the relationship established an express disclaimer by the parties of that relationship will not receive effect, at least in a question with third parties.[61]

Where a so-called " partner " receives a salary for his services and the agreement is entirely silent as to participation in the profits, other *indicia* of the partnership relationship must be looked for. Liability for a share of the losses incurred in the business would be an element of some importance, though in most agreements with " salaried partners " it is unlikely to appear in that specific and restricted manner. That element may, however, be present in the wider concept that there is agreement that each of the parties will have power by his actings to bind the others and conversely that each will be bound by the actings of the others. If that element, which Clark [62] described as standing " *mutually* to each other in the relation of principal and agent," be present the court will give great weight to it. If it be absent, the court will in most cases hold the relationship created to be other than a partnership.[63]

(c) *Receipt by the widow or child of a deceased partner, by way of annuity, of a portion of the profits*

In *Re Jones, ex p. Harper* [64] a contract of copartnery provided that on the death of either partner the survivor should, during the joint lives of himself and the widow of the deceased partner, pay to her at her option either a fixed annuity out of the profits or one-quarter share of the profits of the business continued by him. The decision, which is,

---

[57] *Reid* v. *Hollinshead* (1825) 4 B. & C. 867; *Ex p. Chuck, re Starkey & Whiteside* (1832) 8 Bing. 469; *Gilpin* v. *Enderby* (1824) 5 B. & A. 954.
[58] *Allison* v. *Allison's Trs. (supra)*.
[59] *Fenston* v. *Johnstone* (1940) 23 T.C. 29. This, however, was a case where the parties were bound both to share in profit and to contribute to loss and therefore the agreement was strongly indicative of partnership.
[60] (1892) 19 R. 675.
[61] " Now such a disclaimer as we have in this case may of course have some effect on the rights *inter se* of those who subscribe to it, the partners, but it cannot change the character of what is in essence a partnership, at any rate as regards third parties . . .": *per* Wrottesley J. in *Fenston* v. *Johnstone (supra)* at p. 36.
[62] *Op. cit.* I, p. 50.
[63] *Gatherer* (1893) 1 S.L.T. 401 (O.H.).
[64] (1857) 1 De G. & J. 180.

of course, prior to the passing of either Bovill's Act or of the Partnership Act 1890 was concerned with the question whether the widow was entitled to claim on the bankrupt estate of the surviving partner for the fixed annuity or for the agreed share of the profits of the business as continued by him. It was held that she could not and the reasoning adopted by the court suggested that she was regarded as being a partner in the business. This was one of the cases where Bovill's Act [65] expressly declared that the relation of partnership was not to be held to have been created and the substance of that provision is now enacted in section 2, rule 3 (*c*) of the Partnership Act 1890. This sub-rule appears to have given little cause for litigation. *Commissioners of Inland Revenue* v. *Lebus's Trustees* [66] is one of the few cases upon the question which have been before the court since the passing of the Partnership Act 1890 and the facts in that case were special. Under the articles of partnership it was provided that in the event of Mr. Lebus's death, the business should be continued for ten years and his share of the capital should remain in the business for that period. Mr. Lebus by his will bequeathed to his trustees one-quarter of the profits of the business in trust to pay the same to his widow. The trustees were his widow and the continuing partners in the business. For the tax year ending April 5, 1939, the widow's share of profits was substantial but, through financial stringency, the business was unable to pay her any part of that share. The question arose whether the widow's assessment to surtax should include a sum representing her share of the profits of the business. The court held that she was not a partner in the business and that none of its assets belonged to her. Moreover, there was no ground for saying that the partners were trustees of the business or of any part of its assets for the widow. She could not, therefore, be said to have received any income therefrom unless and until she received her share of the profits.

Commissioners of Inland Revenue v. *Lebus's Trustees* is, however, not a case which falls readily within the terms of sub-rule (*c*) of rule 3 of section 2, and indeed the statutory rules are nowhere referred to in the judgments. It is rather a case concerned with payment for goodwill of a business in which the difficulties have been increased by the somewhat loose terminology favoured by Mr. Lebus in his testamentary arrangements.[67] It may more usefully be regarded as a case which illustrates the view that on a true construction of rule 3 the cases particularly mentioned in sub-rules (*a*) to (*e*) are not to be taken as exhaustive [68] and that the court may give weight to circumstances other than those there particularly mentioned in applying the second phrase of rule 3, " but the receipt of such a share, or of a payment contingent on or varying with the profits of a business, does not of itself make him a partner in the business."

[65] 28 & 29 Vict. c. 86, s. 3.
[66] [1946] 1 All E.R. 476.
[67] See *infra* p. 419.
[68] *Re Pinto Leite & Nephews* [1929] 1 Ch. 221; Pollock, *op. cit.* p. 7; and see *supra* p. 82.

(d) *Loan to a business on condition of the lender receiving a rate of interest varying with the profits or a share of the profits of the business*

The wording of the sub-rule should be carefully considered. It declares that " the advance of money by way of loan " upon terms related to the profits earned by the business or in consideration of a share in those profits shall not of itself make the lender a partner in the business or liable as such. So far as the statutory sub-rule is concerned the only transaction envisaged is a direct loan from the lender to the person " engaged or about to engage in " the business and other methods whereby that person may be facilitated financially through the intervention of another party are not covered by sub-rule (d) even where that party stipulates for a share in the profits in return for the assistance which he has afforded.[69]

In cases where an advance of money has been made to a business and it is claimed that this has been made " by way of loan," the possibilities of setting up an agreement of an equivocal kind need hardly be stressed. Whatever be the nature of the transaction to which it is ascribed, a contribution to the capital of the firm has been made and, were it possible for the parties later to prove facts and circumstances tending to explain that contribution as a loan to the business, the " lender " might escape liabilities to third parties to which he should be subjected. Sub-rule (d) therefore adds a proviso that the contract under which the loan is made to the business must be in writing and signed by or on behalf of all the parties thereto. While the broad intention of the legislature in introducing the proviso is reasonably clear, it is possible to be more dubious as to its implications in all their aspects. If the advance of money by way of loan is made on consideration that the lender receives a share of the profits of the business or a rate of interest which varies with those profits, and that circumstance is not of itself sufficient to make the lender a partner, provided that the contract is in writing and signed by the parties, does it follow that, where there is no such written contract signed by or on behalf of the parties, the lender is prima facie to be regarded as a partner? Smith L.J. in *Re Fort, ex p. Schofield*[70] took that view. " If the benefit of the section is desired by the lender," he said, " then, under the proviso, the contract must be in writing." The dictum, which was *obiter*, seems to be in accord with the intention lying behind the proviso. Indeed if the effect of the proviso is not that assigned to it by Smith L.J., it is difficult to suggest any meaning which the words can usefully bear. Nevertheless, Underhill[71] considers that the dictum of Smith L.J. cannot be supported since, if it were correct, " it would follow that a person who never was a partner, but only a creditor, and with regard to whom the only scintilla of evidence of partnership is participation in profits, is, in the absence

[69] *e.g.* where a party has given a guarantee to a bank upon consideration of the latter affording overdraft facilities to the business and has stipulated for a share in profits in return for that service: *Charlton & Bagshaw* v. *Highet*, 1923 S.L.T. 493 (O.H.).

[70] [1897] 2 Q.B. 495 at 501.

[71] *Op. cit.* pp. 19–20.

of a written and signed contract, to be deemed a partner notwithstanding the express words of section 2 that the receipt of profits is not of itself sufficient."

If this criticism is to be accepted, it follows that the words of the proviso to sub-rule (d) must be regarded as otiose and indeed it is recognised by Underhill [72] that " it is difficult to give any meaning to the proviso, unless its effect is that indicated by the learned Lord Justice." It is submitted that the courts would not readily adopt Underhill's view if the result is to destroy any meaning which can be ascribed to the proviso. Moreover, Underhill's view of the consequence of accepting the dictum of Smith L.J. is itself based upon the learned author's inter-pretation of the section, and he appears to construe sub-rule (d) in isolation. His argument appears to be that if participation in profits is not of itself sufficient to create a partnership but only provided that the contract is in writing and signed, then, if there is no such contract, participation in profits in the circumstances mentioned *will* create a partnership. While this contention is maintainable if the words of sub-rule (d) are considered by themselves and without reference to the general effect of rule 3, it is submitted with diffidence that that is an approach to the construction of the sub-rule which is unlikely to find favour with the courts; for sub-rule (d) is but a particular illustration of the effect of the general rule expressed in the introductory words which comprise rule 3. If no contract such as is required by sub-rule (d) exists, then the case becomes one to which the general terms of rule 3 apply and participation in profits does not automatically make the lender a partner. It is prima facie evidence of partnership but " if there are other circumstances to be considered, they ought to be considered fairly together." [73]   Underhill's view of the effect of the proviso is based on construing sub-rule (d) in isolation as an exception to the general terms of rule 3 rather than construing the rule as a whole, regarding the sub-rule as a particular illustrative instance. With respect it is thought that the latter is the correct approach to the construction of the section.

Sub-rule (d) has its origins in two aspects of the common law: (1) that persons who agree to share the profits of a venture in which they engage together are prima facie partners even if their agreement expressly provides that they shall be liable for losses up to the amount which they have agreed to contribute but no further [74]; and (2) that while the laws against usury were in force, there was a tendency to hold parties in effect to their bargain by regarding what was in reality a loan, but one which was illegal under the laws against usury, as a contract of partnership and accordingly untainted with the illegality which would have attached to it as a contract of loan. In *Bloxham and Fourdrinier* v. *Pell and Brooke* [75] there was a

[72] *Op. cit.* p. 19.
[73] Per North J. in *Davis* v. *Davis* [1894] 1 Ch. 393 at 399–400; and see *supra* pp. 80–81.
[74] *Brown* v. *Tapscott* (1840) 6 M. & W. 119.
[75] Davy, *arguendo* in *Grace* v. *Smith* (1775) 2 Wm.Bl. 997; Ross, *Commercial Cases* III, 400 at pp. 401–402. In *Hesketh* v. *Blanchard* (1803) 4 East 143; Ross, *Commercial Cases* III, 451 the liability of the lender in such circumstances was based on the doctrine of *quasi* partnership.

partnership for seven years between Brooke and Pell. At the end of one year it was agreed to dissolve the partnership though no express dissolution took place. An agreement was made between the partners which narrated that, Brooke wishing to have the profits of the business for himself and Pell wishing to relinquish his interest in the trade and profits, it was agreed that Brooke would grant a bond for £2,485 in favour of Pell, the sum which Pell had contributed to the partnership, with interest at 5 per cent. per annum; and that was done. It was also agreed that Brooke would pay Pell £200 per annum for six years if Brooke lived so long, in lieu of the profits of the business, Pell having liberty to inspect the books. Brooke became bankrupt before he paid any sum to Pell under the bond or agreement. Pell was then sued in respect of a debt incurred by Brooke in the course of the business. Lord Mansfield held that Pell was a secret partner. It was a device to make more than legal interest of money and if it was not a partnership it was a crime. " And it shall not be in the defendant Pell's mouth to say, ' It is usury, and not a partnership.' "

The first of those two aspects of the pre-statute common law is still effective [76] while the second is not. Yet the interaction of the two aspects has had a significant influence upon the terms of the sub-rule. The first is particularly important since it indicates how very indeterminate is the line between partnership and loan under certain agreements. While community of profit and loss is a circumstance strongly suggestive of partnership it does not follow that where there is agreement among the parties that one shall indemnify the others against losses to be incurred the possibility of a partnership existing is thereby denied.[77] But if a person is indemnified not only against the excess of losses over the contributions which he has made but also against loss of those contributions themselves, the contract is a mere " contrat de société simulé " and is in reality a contract of loan.[78] The two passages quoted define

---

[76] Lindley, *op. cit.* p. 83.

[77] Pothier, *Contrat de Société*, para. 21: " Ce que nous venons de dire, qu'on peut, sans blesser l'équité, convenir que l'un des associés supportera une moindre part, ou même ne supportera aucune part dans les pertes, ne doit pas s'entendre en ce sens que cet associé aura part au profit de chacune des affaires qui auront été avantageuses à la société, sans porter rien de la perte que la société a soufferte dans celles qui lui ont été désavantageuses, ce qui seroit manifestement injuste: mais cela s'entend en ce sens, qu'après la dissolution de la société, on fera un état de tous les gains que la société a faits, et un état de toutes les pertes qu'elle a enterprises; et que si le total des gains excède le total des pertes, cet associé prendra sa part dans l'excédent; et que si au contraire le total des pertes excède celui des gains, cet associé n'aura ni profit ni perte: *neque enim lucrum intelligitur, nisi omni damno deducto*; *neque damnum nisi omni lucro deducto* (Cod. civ., art. 1855)."

[78] Pothier, *op. cit.* para. 22: ". . . En général toutes les fois qu'un particulier fait un prétendu contrat de société avec un marchand qui l'associe à son commerce pour une certaine somme d'argent qu'il apporte à ce marchand, lequel s'oblige de la lui rendre à la fin de la société, sans que ce particulier supporte aucune part dans la perte si la société ne réussit pas, et à la charge qu'il aura une certaine part dans le gain; quelque modique que soit cette part dans le gain, en conséquence de ce qu'il ne porte rien de la perte, et soit que cette part soit assurée à une certaine somme par chacun, ou soit qu'elle ne le soit pas, un tel contrat doit passer pour un contrat de société simulé, qui n'a été fait que pour déguiser un prêt usuraire que ce particulier vouloit faire au marchand de la somme d'argent qu'il lui a remise."

the areas of partnership and loan respectively in terms which are acceptable in both the English and the Scottish courts.   Since the abolition of
the laws against usury the need for the tendency to be detected in the
older English cases to ascribe such cases wherever possible to partnership
in order to avoid the consequences of holding them to be usurious loans
has disappeared and the British courts are now free to adopt the pure
Gallic logic of Pothier's approach.

Sleeping partners

On the other hand, if the true relationship between the parties is that
of partners, though one of the partners is a " sleeping " or dormant
partner he will not be able to escape being treated as such merely by
cloaking the transaction with the outward semblance of a loan.   That
was the law even before the passing of the Partnership Act 1890 [79] and
it still continues to be the law, in spite of the terms of sub-rule (d).[80]
Since a sleeping partner is one whom parties outside the partnership do
not know to be a partner and who does not take any part in the business
which would cause him to appear to third parties in the character of a
partner, the question whether a person who lends money to a business
under an agreement in terms of which he participates in the profits is to
be held to be a mere creditor of the business or a sleeping partner in it is
often difficult to answer.   The entire terms of the agreement require to
be carefully considered and even where there are conditions which allow
him facilities to superintend the conduct of the business, these must be
treated with caution before they are accepted as *indicia* of partnership.
Thus the circumstance that the lender is to have a right to participate in
the profits will justify a right on his part to an accounting therefor and
to inspect the books of the business without these rights being necessarily
regarded as *indicia* that he is a partner [81]: nor will terms of the agreement
which give the lender a measure of superintendence over the conduct of
the business [82] necessarily be so regarded.   It is, therefore, dangerous to
rely too strongly on the occurrence of unusual powers in the lender as
evidencing that he is a partner.   If on a consideration of the agreement
as a whole, including the unusual powers, the true intention of the parties
is found to be that these powers are conferred on the lender merely for the
adequate security of the sums which he has advanced, the lender will not

[79] *Pooley* v. *Driver* (1876) 5 Ch.D. 458.
[80] See, *e.g.*, *McCosh* v. *Brown & Co.'s Tr.* (1899) 1 F.(H.L.) 86; *Stewart* v. *Buchanan* (1903) 6
F. 15.
[81] *Laing Bros. & Co.'s Tr.* v. *Low* (1896) 23 R. 1105.
[82] In *Laing Bros. & Co.'s Tr.* v. *Low* (*supra*) the lender was to receive a monthly statement
showing the quantity of jute in stock and to arrive and this was coupled with a condition
that the business was not " to purchase or have at any time in their possession a larger
stock of jute than one or two months' supply in excess of yarns sold."   In *Re Young, ex p.
Jones* [1896] 2 Q.B. 484, the lender was given sole control and management of the business,
with the option (which he did not exercise) of becoming a partner.   See also *Stott* v.
Fender & Crombie (1878) 5 R. 1104.

be regarded as a partner in the business.[83]   On the other hand, if the true interpretation of the agreement as a whole is that the so-called lender has embarked the advance at risk in the business or that the advance while described as a loan really represents his contribution to the capital thereof, he will be regarded as a partner in the business.[84]   A declaratory term in any such agreement that the lender is not to be held to be a partner in the business will be disregarded if it is inconsistent with the true nature of the agreement taken as a whole.[85]

The relationship of lender to, and partner in, a business are not in all cases mutually exclusive.   Cases may occur where the same party may be held to bear the relation of both partner and creditor of the same business.[86]

As has been mentioned [87] sub-rule (d) is concerned with the direct advance of money from the lender to the business.   Where a person facilitates the business in the acquisition of finance, e.g. by guaranteeing the repayment of sums advanced to a business by a bank and in return for that stipulates that he shall receive a share in the profits, sub-rule (d) has no application [88] and the question whether by entering the agreement he has made himself a partner in the business will be answered by determining whether on a consideration of the agreement as a whole, the true intention was to create a partnership relation.[89]   In arriving at a conclusion in such a case the courts will derive no help from the rules laid down in section 2 of the Partnership Act 1890, save in so far as the general terms of rule 3 thereof afford assistance.   In deciding such cases, the general considerations to which the courts will give weight will be similar to those assessed in cases of direct advances of money on loan to a business.   Conditions in the agreement stipulating for superintendence of the conduct of the business by the party guaranteeing the advances may perhaps receive more weight than in the case of a direct loan in holding a partnership to have been established.   Such conditions are perhaps more readily to be accounted for in terms of a lender's security for the sums which he has advanced than of a guarantor seeking some control over the extent of his liability under the guarantee where the

---

[83] *Laing Bros. & Co.'s Tr.* v. *Low, supra*; *Mollwo, March & Co.* v. *Court of Wards* (1872) L.R. 4 P.C. 419; *Re Young, ex p. Jones, supra*. On the other hand, the courts have placed considerable weight on unusual provisions and powers in agreements drafted to secure the benefit of Bovill's Act: *Re Megevand, ex p. Delhasse* (1878) 7 Ch.D. 511 (loan to firm coupled with a power to dissolve the partnership and a provision that the profits and losses should be divided in certain proportions between the borrowers and the lender); *Syers* v. *Syers* (1876) 1 App.Cas. 174 (loan to business on terms that borrowers should execute a deed of partnership " to be drawn up under Bovill's Act " under which the lenders received a share of the profits); *Pooley* v. *Driver* (1876) 5 Ch.D. 458 (a complicated and carefully drawn agreement under which, however, it might turn out that when repayment of the loans fell due, not only was there nothing outstanding to repay but the " lenders " might have to refund part of what they had already received).

[84] *Pooley* v. *Driver* (1876) 5 Ch.D. 458; *McCosh* v. *Brown & Co.'s Tr.* (1899) 1 F.(H.L.) 86; *Stewart* v. *Buchanan* (1903) 6 F. 15.

[85] *Stewart* v. *Buchanan, supra*; see also *Scott* v. *Dick* 1909, 2 S.L.T. 118.

[86] *Thomson* v. *Bell* (1894) 1 S.L.T. 433 (O.H.).

[87] *Supra* p. 87.

[88] *Charlton & Bagshaw* v. *Highet*, 1923 S.L.T. 493 (O.H.).

[89] *Charlton & Bagshaw* v. *Highet, supra*; *Re Beard & Co.* [1915] Hansell Bank.Rep. 191.

relevant information may be obtained from the bank as creditor. The point is, however, of doubtful validity and certainly the pre-statute cases in Scotland in which the facilities afforded to the business have been by way of cautionary obligation have tended to be decided in favour of some relationship other than partnership.[90]

It will also be noticed that the sub-rule does not cover the case where a person lends money to a business upon condition that a third party shall receive a share of the profits. The recipient of the share will however not *eo ipso* be held to be a partner.[91]

(e) *Participation in profits in consideration of the sale of the goodwill of a business*

This sub-rule has much in common with sub-rule (*d*) which has been discussed in the immediately preceding pages, so that occasionally the two sub-rules may overlap to some extent. In *Hawksley* v. *Outram* [92] the essence of the agreement, which was of a special and complex kind, was that a firm agreed to sell its business, worth £20,000 as estimated, the purchaser being taken bound to pay its existing debts. If those debts did not exceed £15,000 the sellers were to be entitled to a share of the profits calculated on the basis of a capital sum of £5,000 which was described as deferred capital and was to participate in the profits only after interest at 10 per cent. had been credited to the other capital employed in the business. Special arrangements were made for deduction from the deferred capital of £5,000 if the debts of the former business exceeded £15,000 and the sellers were entitled to have the amount of their " deferred capital " so ascertained secured by the purchaser's bond. The purchaser sued for specific performance of the agreement and was met by the defence *inter alia* that the agreement was in effect a partnership between sellers and purchaser. It was held that the agreement did not create a partnership. It was an agreement for the sale of a business at a price, part of which was undetermined and had to be ascertained, that portion when ascertained carrying a specified share of profits until it was paid.

In *Pratt* v. *Strick* [93] a medical practitioner sold [94] the goodwill of his practice but agreed with the purchaser to remain resident in the house from which the practice was carried on for a period of three months and introduce the purchaser to the patients of the practice. During that period he was entitled to one-half of the profits and liable for one-half of the expenses of the practice. The court held that this agreement did not

---

[90] *Stott* v. *Fender & Crombie* (1878) 5 R. 1104; *Eaglesham & Co.* v. *Grant* (1875) 2 R. 960; *Miller* v. *Downie* (1876) 3 R. 548.
[91] *Re Pinto, Leite & Nephews, ex p. Olivaes* [1929] 1 Ch. 221.
[92] [1892] 3 Ch. 359.
[93] (1932) 17 T.C. 459.
[94] The present position as to medical partnerships and the sale of medical practices is affected by the National Health Service (Scotland) Acts 1947 and 1949. The provisions of the Acts and their effect on medical partnerships are examined in Lindley, *op. cit.* Appendix 5, pp. 893–907.

create a partnership between seller and purchaser but was an agreement for an outright sale of the practice.

The possible area of confluence between sub-rules (*d*) and (*e*) is illustrated in *Hawksley* v. *Outram* (*supra*) where the unascertained balance of the price was to be left in the business and to carry with it a right to participate in profits. Such a case could not, however, have been readily brought within the terms of sub-rule (*d*) as " the advance of money by way of loan to a person engaged or about to engage in any business." Nor could *Pratt* v. *Strick* (*supra*) be covered by any of the sub-rules but sub-rule (*e*). In *Re Young, ex p. Jones* [95] a person lent £500 to another for use in the latter's business. It was agreed that the lender should have sole control and management of the business and the option of a partnership within a specified time. Meanwhile he would be entitled to a weekly sum from the profits in return for the use of his money, the borrower being entitled to draw the same weekly amounts. The borrower became bankrupt before the lender had exercised the option and before the time for exercising it expired. The borrower was held not to be a partner. This case, unlike two immediately above considered, is predominantly one under sub-rule (*d*) in which the option of a partnership was not a circumstance which the court considered as sufficient, taken in conjunction with the lender's right to participate in profits, to establish a real intention to create a partnership. Indeed the option may have been regarded as tending to negative the parties' intention to enter into a partnership at the date when the loan was granted and, as it were, to postpone any real intention of partnership until the option should be exercised.

The similar, or at least analogous, features of the cases arising under sub-rules (*d*) and (*e*) are further suggested by the provisions of the Partnership Act [96] relating exclusively to these two sub-rules:

" 3. *Postponement of rights of persons lending or selling in considera-tion of share of profits in case of insolvency.* In the event of any person to whom money has been advanced by way of loan upon such a contract as is mentioned in the last foregoing section, or of any buyer of a goodwill in consideration of a share of the profits of the business, being adjudged a bankrupt, entering into an arrangement to pay his creditors less than twenty shillings in the pound, or dying in insolvent circumstances, the lender of the loan shall not be entitled to recover anything in respect of his loan, and the seller of the good-will shall not be entitled to recover anything in respect of the share of profits contracted for, until the claims of the other creditors of the borrower or buyer for valuable consideration in money or money's worth have been satisfied."

The intention behind the statutory words is reasonably clear. If a

[95] [1896] 2 Q.B. 484: and see *supra* p. 90.
[96] s. 3.

lender of money or the seller of the goodwill of a business chooses to stipulate for a right to participate in the profits in return for the use of his money or as an element in the price paid for the goodwill, he has to some extent involved himself in the fortunes of the business and whether he is to be regarded as a partner in the particular circumstances or not, the facilities he has afforded to the business by the loan or by his accept-ance of payment of the purchase price, or part of it, on deferred terms are facilities which become a part of the capital used in the business. That this is the reasoning underlying the section is perhaps supported by the decision in the English courts that a contract under which a person is entitled to receive a fixed sum out of the profits of the business is regarded as equivalent to " such a contract as is mentioned in the foregoing section," *i.e.* a contract that he shall receive " a share of the profits " as provided in section 2 (3) (*d*) [97]; and it has been held that the lender's " share of profits " under a contract such as is provided for in section 2 (3) (*d*) cannot be deducted in arriving at the profits of the business upon which the firm is assessed to excess profits tax.[98] Moreover, if the terms of an agreement under which it is sought to make the interest on the loan vary in some ratio to the profits are unintelligible and so held to be void in this respect, the element of involvement of the lender in the fortunes of the business has gone; section 3 will not operate in such a case and the lender will be allowed to claim and rank with the other creditors for the amount of his loan.[99]

Section 3 is, however, concerned only with the ranking of the lender or seller in competition with the ordinary creditors of the business. His ranking is postponed to that of the ordinary creditors but his claim is not disallowed. Moreover, though the section declares that the lender " shall not be entitled to recover anything in respect of the share of profits contracted for . . . until the claims of the other creditors . . . have been satisfied " this does not appear to deprive him of his right to retain [1] or to foreclose upon [2] any security which he has for the loan.[3] Since section 2 (3) (*d*) does not apply to the case where a lender advances money to a business on condition that a third party receives a share of the profits, section 3 likewise does not apply and the third party may claim and rank for his share of the profits in competition with the ordinary creditors.[4] It is thought that by a parity of reasoning a person who stipulates for a share of the profits of a business in return for accepting liability as guarantor or cautioner of a loan made by a third party to the business will be entitled to rank for his share of profits along with the

---

[97] *Re Young, ex p. Jones* [1896] 2 Q.B. 484.
[98] *Walker* v. *Commissioners of Inland Revenue* [1920] 3 K.B. 648.
[99] *Re Vince* [1892] 2 Q.B. 478; *Re Gieve, ex p. Shaw* [1899] W.N. 41 and 72.
[1] *Ex p. Sheil, re Lonergan* (1877) 4 Ch.D. 789.
[2] *Badeley* v. *Consolidated Bank* (1886) 34 Ch.D. 536; (1888) 38 Ch.D. 238.
[3] It is doubtful whether he is entitled to institute sequestration. See *Re Miller* [1901] 1 K.B. 51 where the point is developed in argument.
[4] *Re Pinto Leite & Nephews, ex p. Olivaes* [1929] 1 Ch. 221.

ordinary creditors.   Section 2 (3) (*d*) does not apply to that case [5]: hence it is not covered by section 3.

Where a lender has originally advanced the money upon condition that he receive a share of the profits, a subsequent variation of the agreement replacing his right to a share of profits with a right to interest on the loan at a fixed rate will not serve to free him from the disability imposed by section 3 [6] unless there is an entire novation by repayment of the original loan and a new loan upon the changed terms. [7]

Cases may occur where the lender splits the amount of the advance, or advances the money on two separate occasions, stipulating for a share of profits in the one case and a fixed rate of interest in the other.   Such an expedient may readily lend itself to use as a mere device to avoid the full disability imposed by section 3 and thus be a fraud upon the ordinary creditors of the business.   Where there is no element of fraud in the transaction and sums have been bona fide advanced on loan in return for a fixed rate of interest, section 3 is not applied and the borrower may rank in competition with the ordinary creditors for the sums lent on these terms. [8]   Where the transaction is used as a mere device to avoid the application of section 3 to the loan with intent to defraud the ordinary creditors, it has not been decided what the attitude of the courts might be.   It has been suggested [9] that the device would probably be defeated by holding the lender liable as a partner, though this seems dubious since it is not clear that the added circumstance of the resort to the device might in all cases be regarded by the court as supporting the proposition that by resorting to it the parties had evinced their true intention to create a partnership.   An alternative approach [10] is that the lender might be held to be within section 3 in respect of the total amount of the loan. It seems more probable that the courts might adopt this attitude, looking to the substance of the transaction rather than to any colourable device which cloaked its real nature, particularly in cases where a small sum was advanced in return for a large share of profits and at the same time a large sum was advanced upon a fixed rate of interest.

The wording of section 3 in some respects falls short of the generally high standard of draftsmanship displayed in the Act.   It was argued in *Re Fort, ex p. Schofield,*[11] that as section 3 applied only to loans " upon such a contract as is mentioned " in section 2 (3) (*d*) and since in section 2 (3) (*d*) it was provided that any such contract should be in writing and signed by or on behalf of all the parties to it, a loan, made to a business on condition of a right to a share in the profits which was not the subject

[5] *Charlton & Bagshaw v. Highet,* 1923 S.L.T. 493 (O.H.); *Re Beard & Co.* [1915] Hansell Bank.Rep. 191.
[6] *Ex p. Taylor, re Grason* (1879) 12 Ch.D. 366; *Re Stone* (1886) 33 Ch.D. 541; *Re Hildesheim* [1893] 2 Q.B. 357; *Re Mason* [1899] 1 Q.B. 810.
[7] *Re Abenheim, ex p. Abenheim* (1913) 109 L.T. 219.
[8] *Re Tew, ex p. Mills* (1873) L.R. 8 Ch. 569; *Re Mason, ex p. Bing* [1899] 1 Q.B. 810.
[9] Lindley, *op. cit.* pp. 96–97.
[10] Lindley, *op. cit. eodem loco.*
[11] [1897] 2 Q.B. 495.

of an agreement in writing or if it was so subject, was governed by a written agreement which was not signed by all the parties, was not struck at by section 3.   The court, however, held that section 3 would apply. In construing section 2 (3) (*d*) Smith L.J. said,[12]

> " The words ' on a contract ' in their ordinary meaning apply to a contract whether written or oral.   All that (*i.e.* the first) part of [section 2 (3)] (*d*), therefore, describes this case.   Then there is a proviso as follows: ' Provided that the contract is in writing, and signed by or on behalf of all the parties thereto.'   In my opinion the true meaning of the whole is that the first part which describes the contract includes both written and oral contracts, but that the benefit is given only if the contract is in writing."

It is thought that this interpretation would be followed in the Scottish courts were the question to come before them for decision.   Not only does the construction of the words of section 3, " such a contract as is mentioned " in section 2 (3) (*d*) accord better with the sense of section 2 (3) (*d*) read as a whole, but it avoids the manifest absurdity of placing a lender whose right to a share of profits rests upon a written contract in a worse position as to ranking for his share than one who has no such written agreement.[13]

[12] *Ibid.* at p. 501.
[13] In the course of his opinion, Smith L.J. observed that if a lender desired the benefit of s. 2 (3) (*d*) the contract must be in writing.   For criticism of this *obiter dictum* in Underhill, *op. cit.* p. 19 see *supra* pp. 87–88.   Underhill's criticism on that point appears to be misconceived.   It is submitted that this dictum of Smith L.J., albeit *obiter*, is also unchallengeable.

CHAPTER IV

ILLEGALITY IN RELATION TO PARTNERSHIPS AND ASSOCIATIONS

WHEN parties associate themselves in a partnership the object of which is to effect some purpose which is contrary to law or the object of which is lawful but is sought to be achieved in a manner prohibited by law, the contract of partnership so entered into is a *pactum illicitum*, and the courts will refuse to lend judicial assistance to a party who seeks to enforce his rights thereunder.[1] The fact that, in adhering to this principle, the courts may give effect to a plea by one of the parties setting up the illegality in order to avoid a claim by the other for what has been contracted to be provided will not alter the view taken by the courts, for, as Lindley [2] has forcefully put it:

"However ungracious and morally reprehensible it may be for a person who has been engaged with another in various dealings and transactions to set up their illegality as a defence to a claim by that other for an account and payment of his share of the profits made thereby, such a defence must be allowed to prevail in a court of justice. Were it not so, those who—*ex hypothesi*—have been guilty of a breach of the law would obtain the aid of the law in enforcing demands arising out of that very breach; and not only would all laws be infringed with impunity but, what is worse, their very infringement would become a ground for obtaining relief from those whose business it is to enforce them."

Without entering into a discussion of the judgment of relative values implied in the sentence last quoted, a matter upon which it might be perplexing to reach a definite conclusion, the basis of the rule is sufficiently justified by either of the consequences ascribed to its neglect. Yet the principle operates in an area of human conduct where one may expect at times narrow and difficult questions to arise for decision. There is little difficulty in applying the rule to the notorious claim by one of a partnership of two highwaymen for an accounting of the profits of the business, an unreported case which was long regarded as apocryphal but has been found to have been brought in the English courts.[3] When the issue can be presented in terms of a contract so flagrantly *contra bonos mores* the result can be

[1] Gloag, *Contract* (2nd ed.) pp. 585–586.
[2] *Op. cit.* p. 146; and see *Gibson* v. *Stewart* (1828) 6 S. 733; affd. (1840) 1 Rob. 260.
[3] For a full account, see (1893) 9 L.Q.R. 197. The case (*Everet* v. *Williams*) is also noticed in some detail in Lindley, *op. cit.* p. 130 n. 23. It seems to have been mentioned originally in a footnote in Evans' translation of *Pothier on Obligations* Vol. II, p. 3.

97

forecast with confidence. The cases which arise for decision in more modern days, however, seldom present themselves in the stark terms of the *Highwaymen's Case*. In these cases a number of associated problems may require solution and these are analysed in the pages which follow.

Objects opposed to current notions of morality, religion or public policy

" All associations, of whatever nature they may be, which have for their object an undertaking or line of business forbidden by the current notions of morality, religion or public policy, are illegal; and the law, apart from punishing the promoters, or members, will hold their acts to be nullities." [4]   Thus an association formed for the purpose of reviling, ridiculing or subverting the established religion of the country has been regarded as illegal in England.   The authorities cited by both Clark and Lindley in support of that proposition [5] reveal on examination that the rule is somewhat more involved than appears from the simple proposition stated by them.   The first of the decisions cited [6] was to the effect that an association, known as the National (later Rational) Community Society, though attacked as having as its objects the propagation of natural religion to the injury of revealed religion, the abolition of all moral restraint in the actings of mankind and the destruction of the institution of private property was, on a consideration of its rules, regarded by Lord Romilly M.R. as one which, though " based upon irrational principles " and seeking " to realise a visionary and unattainable object," was not to be considered as founded " for the purpose of propagating irreligious and immoral doctrines in the ordinary and proper use of these words." [7]   The case, therefore, is no authority for the proposition derived from it by Clark and Lindley, though that proposition may perhaps be deduced from it.   In the second case cited,[8] a trust for the purpose of " printing and publishing the sacred writings " of Joanna Southcote was held to be a charitable trust and it was observed that in respect of such a trust for printing and circulating works of a religious tendency the court makes no distinction between one sect and another unless their tenets include doctrines adverse to the foundation of all religion or subversive of all morality.

Neither decision can be confidently appealed to for a rule that an association formed with the object of " overturning the established religion " [9] is illegal, unless " the established religion " is regarded as meaning no more than the Christian faith, without regard to the particular sect professing it.[10]   Even with that qualification, the rule may be difficult to apply in all cases.   It is possible to regard the rule as not partaking of

---

[4] Clark, *op. cit.* I, p. 17.
[5] *Pare* v. *Clegg* (1861) 29 Beav. 589; *Thornton* v. *Howe* (1862) 31 Beav. 14.
[6] *Pare* v. *Clegg* (*supra*).
[7] *Ibid.* at p. 601.
[8] *Thornton* v. *Howe, supra.*
[9] Clark, *op. cit.* I, p. 17.
[10] Lord Dunedin took this view: *Bowman* v. *Secular Society Ltd.* [1917] A.C. 406 at p. 433.

the nature of a rule of public policy which may fluctuate with the opinions of the age but rather as " a definite rule of law that any purpose hostile to Christianity is illegal." In such a view, " the opinions of the age may influence the application of the rule but cannot affect the rule itself." [11] That view, expressed by Lord Finlay, was not approved by the other judges in *Bowman* v. *The Secular Society* and it is difficult to see how any court could admit it in these days when public discussion of fundamental issues of Christianity is widely engaged in both in print and other mass media of communication. It would be otherwise if the material published was of a scurrilous or outrageous character as to amount to blasphemy. Even then the issue is not entirely clear. While, in the case of *Thomas Paterson*,[12] the Lord Justice-Clerk (Hope) held that the Bible and the Christian religion were part of the law of the land, and that whatever vilified them was an infringement of the law, he expressly reserved the question whether it was blasphemy to vilify them, and that question was unanimously answered in the negative by the House of Lords in *Bowman* v. *The Secular Society*.[13] If a campaign against the Christian religion were the object of an association, it is unlikely that the object itself, as opposed to the conduct of the campaign, would be expressed in scurrilous or vilificatory terms. If it were, then the object might be regarded as blasphemous and if blasphemy is still to be regarded as a crime in Scotland it would on that score be regarded as illegal. If as has been suggested [14] blasphemy is no longer a crime and blasphemous publications which are indecent will be dealt with as indecent publications and blasphemous statements which are made in circumstances likely to cause a breach of the peace will be dealt with as breaches of the peace, then the possibility of holding an association to be illegal upon its proposed objects seems to be remote, though the question remains for later consideration whether it may be held illegal on the score of the conduct of the activities of the association.

" Subverting the constitution "

Similar difficulties may arise in applying the general rule that an association formed with the object of " subverting the constitution " [15] is illegal. While it can scarcely be open to doubt that where parties enter an association with treasonable or seditious objects that association is illegal, Clark's phrase suggests a wider connotation for the rule, particularly since treasonable or seditious activities are crimes and thus fall more appropriately under the branch of the rule treating of associations formed for the perpetration of crimes in general. It has been held that the tenets of a religious society which required its members to refuse to vote or to take the oath of allegiance were not such as to render the society an illegal

---

[11] *Per* Lord Finlay L.C. (dissenting) in *Bowman* v. *The Secular Society* (*supra*) at p. 432.
[12] (1843) 1 Broun 629.
[13] [1917] A.C. 406.
[14] See Gordon, *Criminal Law* p. 935; Macdonald, *A Practical Treatise on the Criminal Law of Scotland* (5th ed.) p. 153.
[15] Clark, *op. cit.* I, p. 17.

one.[16]   The older cases of associations formed for trafficking in the sale of public offices are perhaps examples of a wider connotation which may properly be given to the words quoted [17] and though in this context the word " constitution " may be inappropriate, the courts have viewed associations of parties to defeat the intention of the law as to appointment to offices as illegal.[18]

Public policy

To some extent cases which might be considered under the preceding paragraph may more appropriately be dealt with along with many other cases not so to be considered under the more compendious heading of public policy.   According to Gloag [19] " contracts tending to interfere with the ordinary course of the internal administration of the country are illegal."   It is submitted, with respect, that this is a notion to which it is difficult to apply any precise meaning, at least as regards partnerships or associations formed with such an object in view.[20]   Associations which have the object of improperly influencing the conduct of elections will be illegal.[21]   Many such instances may constitute offences under election law [22] and thus be more appropriately considered as examples of associations illegal by statute.[23]   An association of town councillors who agreed to vote at an election of magistrates in accordance with the wishes of the majority of their members and secured their observance of these terms by their bond was held to be a *pactum illicitum*.[24]   The cases last

[16] " *The Ferguson Bequest Fund Case* " (1879) 6 R. 486.   " Indeed I consider it to be inconsistent with the principles of religious toleration, and with the modern constitutional views of personal liberty which secure to every member of the community freedom of thought and opinion, and freedom in expressing thought and opinion, so long as this freedom does not expand or degenerate into mischievous action, and is not used to incite others to violate law, or to outrage public morality or public decency.   But I cannot see how the avoidance of occasions to take oaths, and abstention from voting for members of Parliament can be in any sense a violation of law or an outrage on public morality or decency ": *per* Inglis L.J.C. at p. 515.

[17] *Sterry* v. *Clifton* (1850) 9 C.B. 110, cited by Clark, *loc. cit.* in support of this, was decided on its facts in favour of the legality of the partnership; but it sufficiently appears from the report that, had the agreement been regarded as " trafficking in public offices," the court would have held the partnership illegal.   See also *Thomson* v. *Dove*, Feb. 16, 1811, F.C.

[18] *McTaggart's Representatives* v. *Robertson* (1834) 12 S. 338 (agreement between competing candidates for trusteeship in a sequestration that one withdraw in favour of the other on understanding that he receive half the estate's commission).   See also *Farmer's Mart. Ltd.* v. *Milne*, 1914 S.C.(H.L.) 84.

[19] *Contract* (2nd ed.) p. 565.

[20] It will be appreciated that as far as a partnership is concerned the illegal object must be associated with a purpose of profit.   Otherwise the association will not fall within the definition of partnership in the Partnership Act 1890, s. 1.

[21] *e.g. Campbell* v. *Scotland* (1778) Mor. 9530 (bribery); *Glen* v. *Dundas* (1822) 1 S. 234 (bond securing an elector's vote); *Coppock* v. *Bower* (1838) 4 M. & W. 361 (agreement to stifle an election petition).

[22] Representation of the People Act 1949, ss. 140 and 141; Election Commissioners Act 1949, ss. 9 and 10.

[23] *Infra*, pp. 103 *et seq.*

[24] *Hoggan* v. *Wardlaw* (1735) 1 Pat.App. 148; *Paterson* v. *Magistrates of Stirling* (1775) Mor. 9527. In these cases the resulting election was held to be null. Presumably if rights *hinc inde* among the associates themselves had arisen, the courts would not have lent assistance for their enforcement.   But in *Simpson* v. *Lord Howden* (1842) 9 Cl. & F. 61 a contract with a landowner to buy off his opposition to a private Bill was held not to be illegal even though the landowner was a member of Parliament and the contract might be regarded as one which bound him as to the manner in which his vote would be cast in Parliament.

cited illustrate a general principle that it is illegal and against public policy for an elected member of Parliament or an elected representative, or possibly any representative on an authority or board to agree to cast his vote as dictated or possibly merely influenced by another person or body.[25]

Other aspects of public policy which result in the association being regarded as illegal are the treatment at common law of partnership with an alien enemy,[26] contracts which obstruct the course of justice, such as an agreement between a solicitor and a messenger-at-arms under which the solicitor was to receive the fees of the messenger for the official duties of the latter and in return to pay him an annual salary,[27] or to concert a scheme to institute a bogus prosecution for purposes of advertising publicity[28] or to indemnify a person in respect of any penalties imposed on him by a court of criminal jurisdiction.[29] Partnerships for the purpose of smuggling dutiable goods into this country are likewise illegal[30] even though the party maintaining his rights is a foreign national, at least if he had knowledge that the goods which he supplied were intended to be smuggled.[31] So far as smuggling goods into this country is concerned, the illegality of the partnership might be ascribed to the contravention of the revenue statutes rather than to the more general concept of public policy. But a joint adventure to smuggle dutiable goods into a foreign country in contravention of its revenue laws is likewise illegal. In *Cairns* v. *Walker*[32] a firm of merchants in Grangemouth had, without the knowledge of the owners but with the connivance of the captain, supplied goods to the steward of a ship sailing with coal from Grangemouth to Buenos Aires. The goods were supplied on credit and were to be paid for by the steward out of the proceeds of his trading with them. Such trading, to be successful, involved the smuggling of the goods at the port of destination in the Argentine Republic, as the merchants were aware. The goods were discovered by the customs authorities at Buenos Aires and a fine was imposed on the ship and paid by the shipowners' agents at Buenos Aires. The shipowners raised an action against the supplier of the goods for the loss incurred to them in paying the fine, on the ground that the supplier had without their knowledge been a party to the wrongful use of the ship for smuggling. In that action they were successful.

It is important to appreciate that in this case the court found no evidence

[25] *Amalgamated Society of Railway Servants* v. *Osborne* [1909] 1 Ch. 163; [1910] A.C. 87, *per* Lord Shaw at p. 106; *Kemp* v. *Corporation of Glasgow*, 1920 S.C. (H.L.) 73.
[26] *Supra* Chap. II, pp. 46 *et seq.*
[27] *Henderson* v. *Mackay* (1832) 11 S. 225.
[28] *Dann* v. *Curzon* (1910) 27 T.L.R. 163.
[29] *Anderson* v. *Torrie* (1857) 19 D. 356; *Amalgamated Society of Railway Servants* v. *The Motherwell Branch of the Society* (1880) 7 R. 867, *per* Lord Young at p. 873.
[30] Bell, *Principles*, para. 42 and cases there cited.
[31] *Isaacson* v. *Wiseman* (1806) Hume 714 (knowledge not inferred from mere fact that gin was supplied from Norway for import to Scotland in small ankers, known as " smuggle ankers ").
[32] 1914 S.C. 51.

of a joint adventure, or partnership, between the supplier of the goods and the ship's steward.[33] The interest of the supplier in the " adventure " was simply that he, as seller of the goods, relied on the steward smuggling them to obtain ultimately the price.[34] That interest was, however, held to be sufficient to make him a party to a legal wrong committed upon the shipowners. The liability of the supplier of the goods would have been established a fortiori, had he been a copartner or co-adventurer in the disposal of the smuggled goods, but it may be questionable whether that circumstance would have tainted the association itself with illegality unless it was the sole object of the association.

Associations for immoral or illegal purposes

A partnership formed for a purpose regarded as *contra bonos mores*, according to " the current notions of morality " is illegal.[35] Thus a partnership in the profits derived from robbery,[36] or from prostitution,[37] or from using one's interest to obtain a pardon for a person convicted of murder [38] would be illegal, as also would be a partnership whose object was to procure marriages for profit.[39] Any association formed with the purpose of obtaining profits from, or being parties to, the commission of a crime is illegal, and the illegality inheres in the partnership even where the crime is committed in a foreign and friendly country, though the rule in that case is grounded on a different aspect of public policy, since to recognise the association as legal in this country would be contrary to the principles of international comity.[40] A distinction has been drawn in respect of partnerships having the object of contravening the revenue laws of a foreign country, though the English decisions which establish it are now of doubtful authority.[41] It will be appreciated, however, that the decisions in *Lindsay* v. *Inland Revenue* and *Foster* v. *Driscoll* [42] turned upon activities which were not merely a breach of the revenue laws of the United States of America but were a violation of the 17th amendment of the U.S. Constitution. Cases of illegality on the ground of contravening current notions of morality, tend in modern times to merge with those where the

[33] *Ibid., per* the Lord Ordinary (Skerrington) at pp. 54–55.

[34] *Ibid., per* Lord Salvesen at p. 59; Lord Guthrie at p. 60.

[35] *Infra* pp. 105–106. In any event the illegality of a partnership affords no ground of defence to an action by a third party, who does not know of the illegality, against the firm or partners. See *infra* p. 105 and the partners may be assessed to tax on the profits made: *Lindsay* v. *Inland Revenue*, 1933 S.C. 33.

[36] *Everet* v. *Williams, supra* n. 3.

[37] *Hamilton* v. *Main* (1823) 2 S. 356.

[38] *Stewart* v. *Earl of Galloway* (1752) Mor. 9465.

[39] *Thomson and Husband* v. *Mackaile*, Feb. 14, 1770, F.C.

[40] *Foster* v. *Driscoll* [1929] 1 K.B. 470; and see *Lindsay* v. *Inland Revenue*, 1933 S.C. 33.

[41] *Ralli Bros.* v. *Compania Naviera* [1920] 2 K.B. 287, *per* Scrutton L.J. at p. 300.

[42] Cited *supra* n. 40. In *Lindsay* v. *Inland Revenue*, the point for decision was whether the venture was a " trade " assessable to income tax and the court so held on the ground that it was no less a trade for that purpose because it had been conducted illegally. If the issue before the court had been a claim by one partner against his copartners for his share of the profits, the question of the legality of the association would have arisen for decision since in those circumstances it might affect the enforceability of the claim.

illegality consists in the forming of a purpose forbidden by statute, or by statutory instrument.   The area covered by the latter cases is wider than that covered by the notion of activities *contra bonos mores.*   At least it is hoped that this observation may be made without undue cynicism.   The notions of morality current today, as opposed to those in Clark's time, may partake more of the nature of social ethics postulating that it is one's duty as a moral member of a community to obey its laws, however little of merit one may find in them personally, simply because they *are* laws.

Objects illegal by statute

A distinction between an object which of itself offends against " the current notions of morality " and one which, while forbidden by statute, would not be illegal in the absence of the statutory provision, was at one time maintained in England on the theory of a distinction between *mala prohibita* and *mala in se.*[43]   The distinction is noted by Clark as obsolete [44] and is dismissed by Lindley as one which " has very properly long ceased to be recognised as of any value for legal purposes." [45]   Indeed it is difficult to preserve any meaningful distinction between what is " illegal " because it is prohibited by statute from what is " illegal " in the sense that it is forbidden by the common law unless there is imported into the discussion an ethical element which is not strictly relevant.   Since the duty of the courts is to administer the law, it cannot be doubted that they will regard as illegal any object which is prohibited by the law whether by statute or at common law.

Yet there may be a qualified sense in which the vestiges of the doctrine may still be seen.   When illegality arises under the provisions of a statute it is axiomatic that the illegality will be decided on a construction of the statutory provisions.   Clark takes notice of the distinction maintained under English law between statutory provisions " which are strictly prohibitory, and such as are merely directory." [46]   He does not commit himself to a view that this approach would be taken in Scots law and indeed the relevance, if not the meaning, of the distinction is not easy to discern in a question whether a partnership which infringes a statutory provision in its objects is illegal.   The distinction is, however, preserved in the English law as at present existing.   " Again, though a statute may in terms apparently prohibit an act or omission and affix a penalty in case of disobedience, it does not necessarily follow that all transactions to which the penalty attaches are illegal.   They are so if the statute is really prohibitory—as is the case if the penalty is imposed for the protection of the public—but they are not so if the true construction of the statute is that the

[43] *Watts* v. *Brooks* (1798) 3 Ves. 612; *Petrie* v. *Hannay* (1789) 3 T.R. 418.
[44] *Op. cit.* I, p. 18.
[45] *Op. cit.* p. 130.
[46] *Op. cit.* I, p. 18.

penalty is, as it were, the price of a licence for doing what the statute apparently forbids." [47]

The distinction noted by Clark between " prohibiting " and " directory " provisions inadequately represents the sophistication of the idea as explained in the passage above quoted, and appears to be of little assistance in deciding whether a particular contract is illegal and unenforceable in view of the provisions of a particular statute. It verges upon the unintelligible as a criterion of such illegality since there appears to be no clear antithesis for that purpose between a prohibitory provision and one which is " merely directory." The question whether a particular contract is illegal on the ground of infringing the statutory provision must, it is submitted, still be solved whether the statute prohibits the making of the contract or directs that the contract must be made only in a manner other than that in which the parties have in fact entered into it. In both cases it is assumed that the statutory provision has not expressly declared the contract to be illegal and unenforceable [48] and what has to be undertaken in either case is a construction of the provision in the whole context of the Act which contains it in order to discover from the intent of the statute whether it be implied that a contract entered into in contravention of the provision is thereby tainted with illegality so as to be unenforceable.

In that task of construction, the rule as expounded by Lindley [49] is of more recognisable assistance, but it is thought that the importance of the distinction is still much over-emphasised. It is noteworthy that the only authorities cited in support of the construction that the provision for the statutory penalty is merely the price of a licence to infringe the statutory provision all date from the first half of the nineteenth century and moreover are all concerned with revenue statutes.[50] The foregoing examination suggests that the Scottish courts might be disinclined to accept the somewhat bogus inflation of the distinction as a legal rule which is binding upon them. Certainly there is no reported decision in Scotland which lends any clear support to the view that any such " rule " exists. The rule of law involved is that the construction of the statutory provision must be

---

[47] Lindley, op. cit. p. 131. The terms of the statute were construed as prohibitory in *Melliss* v. *Shirley Local Board* (1885) 16 Q.B.D. 446; *Whiteman* v. *Sadler* [1910] A.C. 514; *Cornelius* v. *Phillips* [1918] A.C. 199. They were regarded as imposed in the interest of the public in *Little* v. *Poole* (1829) 9 B. & C. 192; *Law* v. *Hodson* (1809) 11 East 300; *Victorian Daylesford Syndicate* v. *Dott* [1905] 2 Ch. 624 at 629; *Anderson Ltd.* v. *Daniel* [1924] 1 K.B. 138. The statutory penalty was regarded as imposed in the interests of the revenue in *Swan* v. *Bank of Scotland* (1835) 2 Mon. & Ayr. 661; *Smith* v. *Mawhood* (1845) 14 M. & W. 452. For fuller citation of authority, see Lindley, *loc. cit.* and the earlier English cases cited by Clark, *op. cit.* I, pp. 18–19.

[48] The statutory provision may, on the contrary, expressly *preserve* the enforceability of the contract. See Road Traffic Act 1960, s. 68 (5) which abrogates the effect of the decisions in *Vinall* v. *Howard* [1954] 1 Q.B. 375 and *Smith* v. *Nugent*, 1955 S.L.T.(Sh.Ct.) 60 in which a contravention of the provisions of the prior statutes and Regulations had been held to make the contract of sale unlawful and unenforceable.

[49] *Supra*, n. 47.

[50] See, in addition to *Swan* v. *Bank of Scotland* and *Smith* v. *Mawhood* cited *supra* n. 47, *Brown* v. *Duncan* (1829) 10 B. & C. 93, a decision which is criticised in any event as one in which " it may be doubted whether the statutes in question were properly construed by the court." Lindley, *op. cit.* p. 131.

arrived at by considering it in the context of the statute as a whole. In
that exercise a judge may find that the effect of the statutory words upon
him is such that he cannot regard them as implying any taint of illegality
in a contract which offends against the statutory provision and in the mental
processes which lead him to test that conclusion it may be that he is influenced by an impression that what the statute intends is merely to exact a
price for non-compliance, though it is thought that the occasion for such a
view in modern statutes may be infrequent. The significant point, however,
seems to be that in a system untrammelled with the earlier English
precedents, it appears unsatisfactory and even unhelpful, to treat that
mental process of arriving at a meaning for the statutory words as if it
were a rule of law; and the Scottish courts may be expected to avoid so
regarding it.[51]

In the cases involving illegality under statute which have been examined
and in those which are subsequently discussed, it is important to keep in
view the different cases of illegality which may occur in a partnership,
since it is a continuing contractual relationship. A partnership may be
an illegal association because it has been formed for a purpose declared
illegal by statute, or it may become an illegal association if its purposes,
or some of them, are later infected by a supervening illegality under a
statutory provision, or, again, a particular object of the partnership or a
particular provision of the contract of copartnery may be held illegal and
unenforceable if the occasion arises to put it into effect.

Partnerships initially illegal

In the first case, the firm and its partners may not enforce *inter socios*
rights and obligations which arise under the contract of partnership into
which they have entered in pursuance of an illegal purpose [52] even where the
agreement for partnership has been partly performed,[53] nor may a third
party sue the firm and its partners under a contract which he has made
with them in the knowledge of the illegality involved in it.[54] But an
illegality attaching to the purposes of the partnership will not afford a
defence to the firm against a claim by a third party under a transaction
which he has carried through with the firm in ignorance of any illegality
inhering in the firm or its objects. " For instance, a shipbuilder might sue
[the members of an illegal partnership] for the price of a ship which was to
be used in the Red Sea slave trade, so long as he was not aware of the
illegal object." [55] In questions *inter socios,* where it can be established

---

[51] That is not to say that the Scottish courts will not in appropriate cases have regard to the
consideration whether the provision is designed for the protection of the public in general
or of a particular class of the public, a circumstance which may be of importance in certain
cases. See *infra*, p. 112.
[52] Gloag, *Contract* (2nd ed.) pp. 585–586; Lindley, *op. cit.* p. 145; *Biggs* v. *Lawrence* (1789)
3 T.R. 454; *Shaw* v. *Benson* (1883) 11 Q.B.D. 563; *Jennings* v. *Hammond* (1882) 9 Q.B.D.
225.
[53] *Ewing* v. *Osbaldiston* (1837) 2 Myl. & C. 53.
[54] *Re South Wales Atlantic Steamship Co.* (1876) 2 Ch.D. 763.
[55] Underhill, *Principles of the Law of Partnership* (9th ed.) p. 26; and see *Re South Wales
Atlantic S.S. Co.* (*supra*) *per* Mellish L.J. and *Brett* v. *Beckwith* (1856) 3 Jur.(N.S.) 31.

that a partnership if and when it is entered into will be illegal, then any contract concerned with bringing about its formation will also be held to be illegal.[56]

On the other hand, the illegality must inhere in the very purpose of the association.[57] This principle is one which has given rise to difficulty in a number of cases concerned with partnerships for a business of pawn-broking, so conducted that they infringed the provisions of the Pawn-brokers Act 1800 [58] that the names of those engaged in the business of pawnbroking must appear in the licence, over the door of the premises where the business is conducted and on the pawn tickets. While the business of pawnbroking is now of no great significance in the national economy, it is perhaps worth devoting some space to the consideration of the decisions relating to pawnbroking as illustrative of the general principle involved, rather than in recognition of the importance of the activity nowadays. In a number of Scottish and English cases the point was considered whether a partnership between two persons for the purposes of a pawnbroking business was reducible as illegal where the name of one of the partners did not appear as required by the Act. In *Gordon* v. *Howden* [59] the Court of Session held that the partnership was not reducible though the partnership agreement provided that the business would be carried on by one only of the partners and that his name alone would be painted above the door of the business premises, the court taking the view that the whole tenor of the contract and the acting of the partners thereunder suggested that concealment was not intended. On appeal the House of Lords did not share that view and reversed the judgment.[60] In a later decision in the Court of Session [61] a case went to trial on an issue whether the pursuer was a partner of a pawnbroking business. His name did not appear on the pawn tickets or in the licence or over the door of the premises. The presiding judge refused to stop the trial and held that it was competent to prove by parole evidence or by facts and circumstances whether the alleged partnership had been created. An exception was taken to that direction and was allowed. On appeal to the House of Lords, that decision was reversed and the exception to the direction of the Lord Ordinary was disallowed. In that case, however, the issue of illegality did not yet arise since it had first to be established that the parties were in partnership. In *Fraser* v. *Hair* [62] it was held in an action of accounting by an alleged partner against his co-partner that averments, that he was a partner of a pawnbroking firm which was carried on under a firm name, that he was known and treated as a partner by the public and

---

[56] *Williams* v. *Jones* (1826) 5 B. & C. 108 (premium agreed to be paid by defendant on assumption as partner with defendant in an illegal partnership); *Duvergier* v. *Fellows* (1828) 5 Bing. 248.
[57] Clark, *op. cit.* I, 18.
[58] 39 & 40 Geo. III, c. 99 s. 23.
[59] (1843) 5 D. 698.
[60] (1845) 4 Bell 254.
[61] *Fraser* v. *Hill* (1852) 14 D. 335; revd. (1853) 1 Macq. 392.
[62] (1848) 10 D. 1402.

acted as such, were relevant in spite of the infringement of the Pawn-brokers Act 1800 since there was no contract to conceal the name. It was also held that the pursuer was not bound to take upon himself the onus of proof that a contract had been entered into to carry on the business as publicly known and avowed partners, since that was presumed until a contract providing for a concealed partnership was proved.

These cases sufficiently reveal the problem of ascribing a statutory illegality to a partnership where the terms of the contract of partnership are of themselves neutral as to the motives of the partners. The problem and the proper approach to its solution were neatly and clearly expressed by the Lord Chancellor, Lord Brougham, in an English decision upon the same statutory provision.[63] He said,

> " If as in the present instance we have before us a contract of partner-ship wholly silent upon the statutory obligation to make the names public over the door, we have no right to argue from the omission that an infraction of the law was intended. . . . If, again, such a contract, legal in itself, has been made, nothing done afterwards, how illegal so ever, can operate to make the contract unlawful. But where the acting of the parties is illegal: where, the contract being silent, the law is broken under it, though not by force of it, there arises a very natural suspicion that the written articles, though true so far as they go, do not contain the whole truth and that another agreement was entered into, collateral with the one in writing, and to which the illegal acting may be referred."

Those decisions are cited in illustration only of the general principles governing the statutory illegality of a partnership. Since they were decided under the Pawnbrokers Act 1800, which made it unlawful to enter an agreement to carry on a pawnbroking business in partnership if *it was part of the agreement that the names of some of the partners would be concealed*, they are of doubtful authority as to the legality or otherwise of a modern partnership in pawnbroking. The statutory provision which now governs the matter requires every pawnbroker to have his name legibly printed over the door of every shop or place where he carries on business.[64] It is therefore doubtful whether any of the considerations examined in the earlier cases are now strictly relevant. If they are not, the further point arises that while the business is one which is being illegally conducted so long as the provisions of the Pawnbrokers Act 1872 are infringed, it may be difficult on that score alone to characterise the partnership itself as an illegal one, without taking into account to some extent the considerations mentioned by Lord Brougham in *Armstrong* v. *Armstrong*.[65]

The whole question whether an illegality is inherent in the purposes for which it is entered into or is merely an incident in the conduct of the

---

[63] *Armstrong* v. *Armstrong* (1834) 3 Myl. & K. 45.
[64] Pawnbrokers Act 1872, s. 13.
[65] *Supra* n. 63.

business of a partnership originally entered into for a purpose in itself legal can be one of fine and difficult decision, upon the facts of any particular case, as is brought out clearly in the words of Lord Brougham. It would be manifestly absurd to hold a partnership unenforceable as one entered into for illegal purposes on the score merely that in the conduct of its business one of the partners has offended against the provisions of a statute or has committed some other act of an illegal nature.[66]   On the other hand the possibility that the agreement of partnership which is produced and which contains no indication of a purpose to conduct the business in an illegal manner is free from the taint of illegality cannot in every case be accepted at its face value.   There will certainly be no presumption in such cases that there is an undisclosed collateral agreement as to carrying on the business of the partnership in an illegal way.   In *Thwaites* v. *Coulthwaite*,[67] a case where the plaintiff sued for an accounting of the profits of a partnership in a bookmaker's business and was met by the defence that the partnership was a *pactum illicitum*, Chitty J. approached the decision of the matter in two stages.   " The first question that arises is this: Is the business of bookmaking necessarily illegal? That is to say, must it necessarily be carried on in such a manner as to fall within the provisions of this statute?" [68]   Having answered that question in the negative, he continued, " The next question is whether the parties intended or contemplated that the partnership business should be carried on in a manner prohibited by the statute.   If they did, the partnership was illegal, even though nothing definite might have been said at the time the partnership contract was entered into as to the mode of carrying on the business." [69]   In a Scottish case [70] a similar approach was taken to a defence of *pactum illicitum* raised in an action by three pursuers against the defender for payment of the balance due under a contract whereby the four parties had contributed equally to the purchase of a ticket in a foreign lottery.   The ticket was taken in the defender's name and any proceeds were to be divided equally among the four.   On an examination of the problem the court found that the contract as averred by the pursuers was capable of lawful performance but that, having regard to the different account of the transaction which the defender gave in his pleadings, it was impossible to sustain or to repel his plea of *pactum illicitum* until the facts relating to the transaction had been established in proof.

Infringement of Statutory Provisions designed to ensure that a particular type of business is carried on by properly qualified persons

" With reference, however, to those statutes which prohibit unqualified

---

[66] " But proof that a firm has been guilty of an unlawful act is not sufficient to bring the firm within the class of illegal partnerships; for if this were enough, every partnership which does not pay its debts, or which commits any tort, or is guilty of culpable negligence would be illegal, which is obviously absurd."   Lindley, *op. cit.* p. 127.
[67] *Thwaites* v. *Coulthwaite* [1896] 1 Ch. 496; *Clayton* v. *Clayton*, 1937 S.C. 619.
[68] *i.e.* the Betting Act 1853 (16 & 17 Vict. c. 119).
[69] *Thwaites* v. *Coulthwaite, supra* at p. 498.
[70] *Clayton* v. *Clayton, supra.*

persons from carrying on certain trades or businesses, it may be observed that such statutes are not infringed by an unqualified person who does nothing more than share the profits arising from those trades or businesses, if they are in fact carried on by persons who are duly qualified. The unqualified person is not within the mischief of the statutes in question and the partnership of which he is a member is not therefore illegal." [71] The statements though expressed with great generality should be applied with caution to any particular case. It is no doubt correct in so far as it merely seeks to declare that in construing a statutory provision of that nature there is no necessary implication to be drawn that it is intended to render illegal a partnership entered into with an unqualified person if that person takes no active part in the business. [72] But the matter remains one of a true construction of the terms of the statute as a whole. The statute itself may expressly forbid association with any unqualified person or, in some cases, the association may be illegal at common law.

Solicitors. That qualification is clearly illustrated in the case of a solicitor entering into a partnership with an unqualified person. In *A.B.* v. *C.D.* [73] Lord Skerrington observed, " Though the point was disputed by pursuer's counsel, I cannot doubt that an agreement between a qualified law agent and an unqualified person for carrying on the business of a law agent in partnership is illegal and void both at common law and under the Stamp Act 1891, s. 43. Further, the illegality is not, in my opinion, obviated by making the unqualified person a mere sleeping partner with no right to interfere as regards the conduct of the details of the legal business." The statutory illegality referred to by Lord Skerrington is now made a matter of clear and express provision. [74] The illegality at common law referred to by Lord Skerrington is more difficult to support by direct authority. It would appear to originate in the principle that such an arrangement is a potential " obstruction of the course of justice " or possibly a " contract tending to interfere with the ordinary course of the internal administration of the country " and thus illegal as being against public policy. [75] The cases which have in Scotland been concerned with the illegality of an association of this kind for the purpose of carrying on a solicitor's business have not, however, dealt with the situation where an unqualified person was a dormant partner in the business. In both cases the unqualified person was actively associated in the business and so the

---

[71] Lindley, *op. cit.* p. 130; and see Clark, *op. cit.* I, p. 19; " It must be observed that as regards such statutes as require certain businesses or trades to be carried on by duly qualified persons, and no others, their provisions do not strike against partnerships with dormant partners unqualified, so long as the active partners are within the requirements."

[72] That seems to be the proposition justified by the authorities cited by Lindley and Clark. See *Raynard* v. *Chase* (1756) 1 Burr. 2; *Candler* v. *Candler* (1821) Jac. 225; 23 R.R. 34.

[73] 1912, 1 S.L.T. 44 (O.H.) at p. 45.

[74] Solicitors (Scotland) Act 1933, s. 38: " Any solicitor who shall share with any unqualified person any profits or fees or fee derived from any solicitor's business transacted by him shall be guilty of an offence under the Act. . . ." The section excepts from its general provisions a share of profits paid to a retired partner, or as the price of the goodwill of a solicitor's business, to the widow of a deceased partner, etc.

[75] Gloag, *Contract* (2nd ed.) pp. 565 and 566. See also *supra*, p. 101.

precise nature of the objection at common law to an unqualified partner in a solicitor's business is not explained.[76]

Medical practitioners. No person may recover any charge in any court of law for any medical or surgical advice or attendance or for the performance of any operation or for any medicine which he has both prescribed and supplied unless he prove upon the trial that he is registered under the Medical Act 1956.[77] It is a punishable offence wilfully and falsely to pretend to be, or to take or use the name or title of, a physician, doctor of medicine, licentiate in medicine and surgery, bachelor of medicine, surgeon, general practitioner or apothecary or any name, title, addition or subscription implying that he is registered under the Act or recognised by law as such.[78] While the National Health Service (Scotland) Acts 1947 to 1953 prohibit the sale of the goodwill of a practice providing general medical services under the Acts, and thus involve special treatment of such transactions there is no provision of the National Health Service (Scotland) Acts or of the Medical Act 1956 which renders a partnership of medical practitioners illegal. Moreover, there is no provision in any of these Acts analogous to the prohibition in the Solicitors (Scotland) Act 1933 [79] against association in partnership with unqualified partners. If one member of the firm is registered, the partnership appears to be legal under the statutes,[80] though an unregistered partner may not lawfully act as physician, surgeon or apothecary.[81] It appears, therefore, that a medical partnership which in addition to its registered and active members contains dormant partners who are not so qualified is not thereby rendered an illegal partnership.

Dentists. In the case of dentists, on the other hand, no person is entitled to practise or hold himself out, whether directly or by implication, as practising or as being prepared to practise dentistry unless he is a registered dentist or a registered medical practitioner and contravention of this provision is an offence under the statute.[82] The terms of the National Health Service Acts add nothing which has a relevant bearing upon the legality of a partnership for carrying on a dentist's practice where some of the partners are qualified and some are not. There has been no decision upon the effect of section 34 of the Dentists Act 1957 upon the legality or otherwise of such a partnership. It is thought that such an association might be held to be illegal under the section since the unqualified person could be regarded as holding himself out by implication as prepared to practise dentistry whether he in fact did so practise or not.

[76] See *Gilfillan* v. *Henderson* (1832) 10 S. 523 (agreement by a country agent to employ an Edinburgh agent, to advance him sums of money on loan and to take a share of the profits of the business of the Edinburgh agent); *Henderson* v. *Mackay* (1832) 11 S. 225 (agreement between a solicitor and a messenger-at-arms whereby the former received the fees earned by the latter and paid him an annual salary).
[77] Medical Act 1956, s. 27.
[78] *Ibid.*, s. 31.
[79] s. 31.
[80] *Turner* v. *Reynall* (1863) 14 C.B.(N.S.) 328, *per* Erle C.J. at p. 334.
[81] *Howarth* v. *Brearley* (1887) 19 Q.B.D. 303; *Davies* v. *Makuna* (1885) 29 Ch.D. 596; *Pharmaceutical Society* v. *London & Provincial Supply Association* (1886) 5 App.Cas. 857.
[82] Dentists Act 1957, s. 34.

It may be, however, that the courts would approach the question in the manner adopted by Lord Brougham in *Armstrong* v. *Armstrong*.[83]

Other statutory provisions regulate the activities of bankers,[84] bookmakers,[85] insurers,[86] moneylenders,[87] newpaper proprietors,[88] patent agents,[89] pawnbrokers,[90] theatrical employers [91] and trade unions.[92]

The effect of these various statutory restrictions is considered in more detail in *Lindley on Partnership*.[93] Two general observations may be made upon them. (1) In considering the statutory provisions it will be found that they are of two kinds. In some cases they may make provision for registration or some similar expedient as a condition of the lawful conduct of the business in question. The requirement of registration or other requirement ensuring publicity is usually imposed upon the individual who engages himself in the particular activity, though this is not always so.[94] The requirement of registration of the individual practitioners is universal in the case of professional men but even in these cases the terms of the relevant statute must be closely construed in order to determine whether the intention of the provision is to forbid the association of such individuals in partnership with individuals who are not so registered or is merely to prohibit the unregistered partners from taking an active part in the business of the firm.

(2) The statute may attach an illegality to certain contracts or transactions in the course of the conduct of the business rather than prescribe prerequisite conditions for the initiation of such a business. Provisions of the former nature may if they are contravened create a situation where a particular transaction entered into will be regarded as illegal and therefore unenforceable, but they will seldom have the effect of rendering illegal a partnership entered into for the purpose of a business of the kind in which these transactions have been carried through.[95] Provisions of the latter

[83] (1834) 3 Myl. & K. 45. See *supra* p. 107.
[84] Bank Charter Act 1844, s. 21. The Bank of England Act 1800, s. 15, and the Bank Notes Act 1828 both relate to note issues in England and have been considerably modified by subsequent legislation.
[85] Racecourse Betting Act 1928; Betting and Lotteries Act 1934; Betting and Gaming Act 1960; and see *Thwaites* v. *Coulthwaite, supra* n. 67.
[86] Insurance Companies Act 1958, as amended by the Companies Act 1967 ss. 70 and 130 and Schedule 5.
[87] Moneylenders Act 1927.
[88] Newspaper Libel and Registration Act 1881, s. 8.
[89] Patents Act 1949, s. 88.
[90] Pawnbrokers Act 1872, s. 13.
[91] Theatrical Employers Registration Act 1925.
[92] A trade union means " an organisation of workers which is for the time being registered as a trade union " : Industrial Relations Act 1971, s. 61 (3). It was formerly supposed that a trade union could not be a partnership in view of the proviso to s. 23 of the Trade Union Act 1871 as amended by the Trade Union Act 1876, s. 16. Both these Acts are now repealed by the Industrial Relations Act 1971 and the question discussed by Lindley, *op. cit.* p. 144 is thus rendered obscure.
[93] pp. 131–144.
[94] *e.g.* it is imposed on the individual by the Moneylenders Act 1927, s. 1. But the requirements of the Pawnbrokers Act 1872, s. 13, would, it is thought, be complied with by painting the name of the firm above the door if the firm is registered under the Registration of Business Names Act 1916.
[95] See *supra* pp. 107–108. A joint adventure for a single transaction or a series of transactions which offended against the statute might, however, be held an illegal association.

kind may have the effect that the partnership is illegal *ab initio* with the result that even where the business dealings of the partnership have in no way offended against statutory provisions of the former kind, the partners will not be allowed to enlist judicial aid in enforcing their rights under the partnership agreement.[96]

The courts have in appropriate cases distinguished between statutory provisions which render transactions illegal in the general public interest, on the one hand, and those which create an illegality with the object of protecting a particular class of the public, on the other hand.   In *Phillips* v. *Blackhurst* [97] the Lord Ordinary regarded the Moneylenders Act 1900 as one passed for the protection of a particular class of the public, namely borrowers.   While, therefore, a loan made by an unregistered money-lender is illegal and the courts will lend no assistance to enforce it, the Lord Ordinary held that the disability thus imposed did not preclude a member of the class intended to be protected from applying to the court for recovery of securities which he had deposited with an unregistered moneylender in respect of the illegal transaction of loan.   The principle upon which that decision is based is unexceptionable but its value as an aid in the construction of such provisions may be diminished by the difficulty of applying the initial distinction.   In *McCarroll* v. *Maguire*,[98] Lord Sands held that an order fixing the maximum price chargeable for whisky was issued for the protection of consumers from the imposition of extortionate prices and that a purchaser might therefore recover the excess which he had paid above the prescribed maximum.   In the English courts an order of very similar import dealing with fertilisers and foodstuffs was regarded as having been issued in the general interest of the state and not for the protection of a particular class of the public.   A purchaser for a price which exceeded the maximum prescribed was therefore not entitled to sue for recovery.[99]   The apparent conflict between these two decisions may perhaps be resolved on the reasoning that in the Scottish case the whisky was an end product which must ultimately reach a particular section of the public, *i.e.* those who drink whisky, while in the English case the farm fertilisers and foodstuffs were themselves used in food production and thus the control of the price chargeable for them might be regarded as a relevant factor in the economy of the nation as a whole. But even if this can be accepted as the true basis upon which the conflicting decisions of the Scottish and English courts may be distinguished, it sufficiently emphasises the point that there may be a wide marginal area where it will be difficult to draw a firm line of distinction.

[96] The two distinct types of provision occur in the Moneylenders Act 1927.   In the first place contravention of s. 1 (1) by inclusion of a partner who does not hold a licence in his true name and in respect of the address at which the business of the firm is carried on, may render the partnership illegal.   On the other hand, an individual transaction in the course of the partnership business which contravened the statute, *e.g.* one brought about through a canvasser (*Jeffreys* v. *Pinto* [1929] 1 Ch. 401) may itself be reduced as illegal.
[97] 1912, 2 S.L.T. 254 (O.H.).
[98] 1920, 2 S.L.T. 108; affd. 1920, 2 S.L.T. 220.
[99] *Re Mahmoud and Ispahani* [1921] 2 K.B. 716.

Registration of Business Names Act 1916

Under this Act every firm having a place of business in the United Kingdom and carrying on business under a business name which does not consist of the true surnames of all the partners who are individuals and the corporate names of all partners who are corporations, without any addition other than the true Christian names of individual partners or the initials of such Christian names, must be registered [1] with the Registrar of Business Names within fourteen days of commencement of business or of the occurrence of any change in the composition of the firm which renders registration necessary under section 1.[2] For the purposes of the Act a business includes a profession [3] but the acquisition of property by two or more persons in part ownership or ownership in common will not of itself be regarded as carrying on a business even where the owners share in the profits arising from a sale of the property.[4] Thus even where a firm as originally composed is not required to register under the Act, on a change of partners, the original firm name being continued, registration will often become requisite. In addition the Act requires registration in the case of (a) every individual having a place of business in the United Kingdom and carrying on business under a business name which does not consist of his true surname without any addition other than his true Christian names or the initials thereof, (b) every individual or firm having a place of business in the United Kingdom, who, or a member of which, has either before or after December 22, 1916, the date of the passing of the Act, changed his name except in the case of a woman in consequence of marriage and (c) every firm, individual or corporation having a place of business within the United Kingdom and carrying on business wholly or mainly as nominee or trustee of or for another person or other persons or another corporation, or acting as general agent for any foreign firm.[5]

Disability on default in registration

If default occurs in supplying the particulars required under the Act, the defaulter is precluded from enforcing his rights under or arising out of any contract made or entered into by him or on his behalf in relation to the business in respect of which the particulars should have been supplied, by any action or other legal proceeding either in the business name or otherwise. The disability persists during the time when he is in default.[6] Where the defaulter is a firm, the disability applies to claims against third parties and not to the right of one partner to sue another.[7] No disability arises until the time allowed for registration has expired [8]; nor does its

[1] Registration of Business Names Act 1916, s. 1.
[2] *Ibid.* s. 5.
[3] *Ibid.* s. 22.
[4] *Ibid.* s. 1, proviso (iv). The meaning of the term " business " generally is discussed in *Re a Debtor* [1927] 1 Ch. 97.
[5] *Ibid.* ss. 1 and 2. A " foreign firm " means any firm, individual or corporation whose principal place of business is situate outside Her Majesty's dominions (s. 22).
[6] *Ibid.* s. 8.
[7] *Stevios Thomopulos* v. *John Mandilos* [1948] A.C. 12.
[8] *Re a Debtor (No. 5 of 1919)* (1919) 89 L.J.K.B. 40.

application extend beyond the actual defaulter to a trustee in bankruptcy or other person claiming under the defaulter.[9]

Extent of the disability. The disability relates to *enforcement* of rights arising from contracts entered into when the business is in default. It does not render such contracts void, and a defaulter, while precluded from enforcing his rights by legal proceedings, is not banned from asserting his rights of ownership in goods which he has in fact obtained under a contract made while he was in default. Thus in *Daniel* v. *Rogers*[10] the defendant had sold his business and stock in trade to Miss Fantini. She defaulted in her duties of furnishing the particulars to be registered in terms of the Act. The seller's creditors attached the stock in trade on the ground that Miss Fantini's title to them was invalid by reason of her default. The court, however, held that she was not prevented by the Act from asserting her rights of ownership in goods in her possession even though she had purchased those goods under a contract which she would not have been allowed to enforce. It has also been held in the sheriff court that section 8 of the Registration of Business Names Act 1916 does not disable a defaulter from suing to enforce a right which accrued before any default in registration had taken place[11]; nor do the terms of the section affect the right of any other person to initiate proceedings to enforce his rights under a contract entered into with the defaulter.[12] Moreover, if any such proceedings are raised by a third party against the defaulter, the defaulter himself may then enforce in those proceedings, by way of counter-claim, set-off or otherwise, any rights which he has in respect of that contract against the third party.[13]

Relief from disability.[14] The Court of Session or a judge of that court may, on application by the defaulter for relief from the disability imposed by the Act, grant such relief on being satisfied that the default is accidental or due to inadvertence or some other sufficient cause or that on other grounds it is just and equitable to grant the relief.[15] While the power to grant relief is liberally exercised in appropriate circumstances, it is not granted automatically upon application.[16] The application may be made and relief granted after an action has been commenced or even apparently after judgment has been signed.[17] It may be granted on the application of the trustee in bankruptcy of the defaulter.[18] The relief granted by the court may be either general or as respects any particular contracts, on the condition that the defaulter pays the costs of the application and upon such

---

[9] *Hawkins* v. *Duché* [1921] 3 K.B. 226.
[10] [1918] 2 K.B. 228.
[11] *Halliday* v. *Watt & Co.*, 1950 S.L.T.(Sh.Ct.) 58.
[12] Registration of Business Names Act 1916, s. 8 (1) (*b*).
[13] *Ibid.* s. 8 (1) (*c*).
[14] *Ibid.* ss. 8 (1) (*a*) and 23 (1).
[15] See *Hawkins* v. *Duché* [1921] 3 K.B. 226 (foreign name wrongly spelled); *Weller* v. *Denton* [1921] 3 K.B. 103 (defaulter ignorant of Act and need for registration and other party knew he was the proprietor of the business and was not misled).
[16] *Watson* v. *Park Royal (Caterers) Ltd.* [1961] 1 W.L.R. 727.
[17] *Re Shaer* [1927] 1 Ch. 355.
[18] *Hawkins* v. *Duché (supra).*

other conditions as the court may impose.[19] It will not be granted save on such service and publication of the application as is ordered by the court and it will be refused in respect of a contract if any party to that contract proves to the satisfaction of the court that, if the Act had been complied with, he would not have entered into the contract.[20] If granted the relief from the statutory disability is retrospective so that the contract affected is restored *ab initio* to one enforceable in law and all subsequent proceedings in respect of it are validated.[21] If any proceeding to enforce any contract is initiated by a defaulter in the sheriff court, the sheriff may grant the relief from the statutory disability in so far as respects the contract in issue before him.[22]

Misleading names

The Registrar of Business Names shall refuse to register any business name under which the business of a firm or individual is carried on if it contains the word " British " or any other word which, in his opinion, is calculated to lead to the belief that the business is under British ownership or control and where he is satisfied that the nationality of the persons by whom the business is wholly or mainly owned or controlled is at any time such that the name is misleading. The registrar has likewise the power to remove a name from the register on those grounds. Appeal lies from the decision of the registrar to the Board of Trade, now the Department of Trade and Industry, whose decision is final.[23] The registrar's power to refuse registration has now been extended " to any name which is in his opinion undesirable." [24]

Offences and penalties

An offence is committed where any firm or person who is required by the Act to furnish a statement of particulars or of any change in particulars makes default without reasonable excuse in doing so within the time and in the manner specified in the Act and every partner in the defaulting firm or the person who is himself so in default is liable on summary conviction to a fine not exceeding £5 for every day during which the default has continued. In addition the court will order the persons in default to furnish a statement of the required particulars or change in particulars to the registrar within a specified time.[25] It is likewise an offence punishable on summary conviction with imprisonment for a term not exceeding three

---

[19] Registration of Business Names Act 1916, s. 8 (1) (*a*).
[20] *Ibid.* Where the other parties to the contract did not offer to prove this, but averred an association between an individual partner of the defaulting firm and a named solicitor whom they believed to be in partnership with him, the court refused an inquiry on the strength of that averment; but it is still for the petitioner to satisfy the court that he is entitled to relief: *J. & H. Cook and Another* v. *Alban Expanded Metal & Engineering Co. Ltd.*, 1969 S.L.T. 347 (O.H.).
[21] *Re Shaer* [1927] 1 Ch. 355.
[22] Registration of Business Names Act 1916, ss. 8 (2), proviso, and 23.
[23] *Ibid.* s. 14.
[24] Companies Act 1947, s. 116 (1).
[25] Registration of Business Names Act 1916, s. 7.

months or a fine not exceeding £20 or both such imprisonment and fine, for a person to sign a statement required to be furnished under the Act which to his knowledge contains any matter which is false in any material particular.[26]   In addition the Department of Trade and Industry may require any person to furnish to them such particulars as appear to them necessary in order to ascertain whether that person or the firm of which he is a partner should be registered or whether any alteration should be made to the registered particulars.   In the case of a corporation the Department may require the secretary or any other officer of the corporation performing the duties of secretary to supply such particulars.   If any person when so required either fails to supply such particulars as it is in his power to give or furnishes particulars which are false in any material particular, he is liable on summary conviction to imprisonment for a time not exceeding three months or to a maximum fine of £20 or to both.[27]

The Registration of Business Names Act 1916 is silent as to the consequences where a firm commences or continues to carry on business after the registrar has refused to register its name or has removed it from the register.   The Companies Act 1947 now provides,[28]

> " Where registration of a business name is refused under section 14 [of the Registration of Business Names Act 1916], any person carrying on business under that name in such circumstances as to require registration under the Act shall be liable under section seven thereof to the same penalties as if he had without reasonable excuse made default in furnishing a statement of particulars with respect to that name."

The lacuna in the Registration of Business Names Act 1916 is thus filled so far as regards the carrying on of business under a name which the registrar has refused to register.   Section 116 of the Companies Act 1947, however, leaves still in doubt the consequences of continuing to carry on business under a name which the registrar has ordered to be removed from the register as " undesirable."   There is no statutory provision which declares that to be punishable as an offence.   If the firm has not been in default up to the time when the registrar refuses to register the name or when he removes it from the register, there is likewise no express provision in the Act as to the consequential duties imposed upon a firm which has complied with the statutory requirements up to that time and so is not in default.[29]   It is also possible that the original period of fourteen days allowed for registration may have elapsed before the name has been refused by the registrar.   Almost certainly that period will have elapsed in any case where the registrar removes a name from the register.   In such cases there is no period specified under the Act within which the business must

---

[26] *Ibid.* s. 9.
[27] *Ibid.* s. 10 (1).
[28] s. 116 (2).
[29] It will be appreciated that it does not necessarily follow that because the name is " undesirable " in the opinion of the registrar, it is in any particular " false " to the knowledge of the person who signed the statement (Registration of Business Names Act 1916, s. 9).

be registered under an amended name. In discussing this point, Lindley [30] expresses the opinion that the firm will be allowed a reasonable time after receiving notice of the refusal or removal of the name by the registrar or of the decision of the Department on appeal from the registrar's decision to submit an alternative name for registration and that, until a reasonable time has elapsed, the firm is not in default. " If the firm promptly changed its name a reasonable time might be fourteen days from the date of the change. . . . If it did not promptly change its name, the court by analogy might consider fourteen days from the time of such notice a reasonable time."

Publication of true names

" Every individual and firm required by the Act to be registered shall, in all trade catalogues, trade circulars, show cards, and business letters on or in which the business name appears and which are issued or sent by the individual or firm to any person in any part of His Majesty's dominion, have mentioned in legible characters—

(a) in the case of an individual, his present Christian name or the initials thereof and present surname, any former Christian name or surnames,[31] his nationality if not British [32]; and

(b) in the case of a firm, the present Christian names or the initials thereof and the present surnames, any former Christian names and surnames [31] and the nationality if not British [32] of all the partners of the firm or, in the case of a corporation being a partner, the corporate name." [33]

If a default is made in compliance with that provision, the individual defaulter [34] or, in the case of a defaulting firm, every partner thereof is guilty of an offence and is liable on summary conviction for each offence to a fine not exceeding £5.[35] In England and Ireland proceedings for this offence require to be instituted with the consent of the Board of Trade,[36] now the Department of Trade and Industry. This provision is not made applicable to Scotland presumably because of the more ordered system of prosecution by the state for offences which obtains in Scotland.

While it has proved convenient to discuss in this context the statutory provisions as to registration of business names, it remains a point for consideration whether a firm which defaults in compliance with those

---

[30] *Op. cit.* p. 40.
[31] In the case of natural-born British subjects the former Christian name or surname need no longer be stated where it has been changed or disused before the person bearing the name had attained the age of 18 years or has been changed or disused for a period of not less than 20 years: Companies Act 1947, s. 116 (4) (a).
[32] This requirement is no longer effective: *ibid.* s. 116 (3).
[33] Registration of Business Names Act 1916, s. 18 (1), as amended by the Statute Law Revision Act 1927 and annotated with reference to amendments introduced by the Companies Act 1947, s. 116.
[34] In the case of a corporation, in default, every director, secretary or officer of the corporation who is knowingly a party to the default is guilty of the offence (s. 19).
[35] Registration of Business Names Act 1916, s. 18 (2).
[36] *Ibid.* s. 18 (2), proviso.

provisions is to be regarded as being on that score an illegal association. It is thought that in spite of the disabilities imposed upon defaulting firms and of the statutory offences created by the Act, a defaulting firm cannot be so regarded. The effect of the disabilities imposed is not to render any contracts affected by the default void, but merely unenforceable; and even where such disability exists it affects merely the direct enforcement of the contract. It does not render null all rights which may have been acquired under the contract despite the default [37] as would be the case were the defaulting firm to be treated as an illegal association. In view of the special nature of the effect of the disabilities expressly imposed upon the contracts of the defaulting firm, there appears to be little relevance in an examination of the statutory offences created to discover whether these are devised for the protection of persons dealing with the firm or in the general interests of the state, since if the statutory disabilities disclose, as, it is submitted, they do, that the firm is not to be treated as an illegal association because of default, then the nature of the provisions as to the statutory offences will not displace that view.

Illegality of partnership through exceeding the maximum number of members permitted by statute

This aspect has already been dealt with in Chapter 1 [38] to which the reader is referred.

Severability

It does not follow that because one or more clauses in a contract of copartnery are illegal, the partnership will itself be held to be an illegal association. [39] Not all the clauses in a contract of copartnery are concerned with the objects of the partnership and therefore, in some cases, e.g. a restrictive covenant, the clause itself may embody a *pactum illicitum* and be unenforceable without rendering the partnership itself illegal. In other cases, a clause of the partnership agreement may provide for an illegal object but on a construction of the clause in relation to the other declared objects of the partnership, the court may regard the offending clause as one which does not necessarily involve the illegality of the association. The point was discussed in relation to a company, some of the objects of which involved a denial of Christianity. [40] While a case relating to the construction of the objects clause of a company incorporated under the Companies Act presents features which are in no way analogous to those affecting a similar question arising in regard to a partnership, [41] certain of the dicta of the judges suggest that they have a wider application. In that case Lord Buckmaster said, [42]

---

[37] *Supra* p. 114.
[38] *Supra* pp. 13–14.
[39] Lindley, *op. cit.* p. 127.
[40] *Bowman* v. *Secular Society Ltd.* [1917] A.C. 406.
[41] See *e.g.* Lord Parker of Waddington at p. 443; Lord Buckmaster at p. 477.
[42] *Ibid.* at p. 477.

" I cannot accede to the argument that the later purposes in the memorandum, which, taken alone, must be regarded as proper and lawful objects, become unlawful because they are associated with the first purpose of the memorandum. If an unequivocal act be lawful in itself, the motive with which it is performed is immaterial; and if it be said that all the lawful purposes are instruments by which the first purpose may be effected, this, as it seems to me, may be an argument for showing that the first purpose is lawful but it cannot establish that the later purposes are unlawful."

In the difficult area of illegality as assailing " the established religion," *i.e.* Christianity, and also in view of the reliance placed by the judges upon the corporate entity of the company, any tendency to apply this reasoning generally to a partnership, some of the objects of which are illegal, must be cautiously argued. Yet the principle involved appears to be applicable in its broadest sense to such a case. If a partnership is formed having objects one of which is unlawful while the others are in themselves lawful, and if the latter and lawful objects can be regarded as severable from the former and unlawful one, it may be argued that the partnership is a lawful association, so far as its lawful and severable objects are concerned.[43]

The general criterion of severability in England was stated by A. L. Smith L.J. in *Kearney* v. *Whitehaven Colliery Co.*[44] in these words: " If the consideration is tainted with illegality, either in whole or in part, all the promises depending on that consideration must fail; but if the consideration be not tainted with illegality, either wholly or in part, then if one of the several promises depending upon it be illegal and the others legal, the legal promises stand." The wording, while appropriate as indicating a general criterion by which severability may be determined, is not easily adaptable to meet the case of a partnership the objects of which are in one instance illegal while legal in the others. A more fruitful approach to such cases may be to employ the test usually applied in cases where it is sought to establish that the parties are not *in pari delicto* and expressed in a general proposition in the headnote to *Simpson* v. *Bloss* already cited.[45]

Restrictive covenants

A detailed treatment of this subject would be inappropriate in a specialised study of partnership. Such notice as is taken of the topic will be confined to the effect of restrictive covenants expressed in a contract of copartnery. The general principle may be stated in the words of Lord Macnaghten.[46]

[43] Lindley, *op. cit.* p. 127, takes this view. It also derives some support from dicta of Lord Dunedin in *Farmers' Mart Ltd.* v. *Milne,* 1914 S.C.(H.L.) 84 at p. 87, where, quoting the headnote of *Simpson* v. *Bloss* (1816) 7 Taunt. 246, he says: " ' The test whether a demand connected with an illegal transaction is capable of being enforced at law is whether the plaintiff requires any aid from the illegal transaction to establish his case.' . . . Now, taking that test here, it seems to me to solve the whole matter. The pursuers have solved it for themselves, because they cannot get the accounting they seek without getting it through the aid of that very clause which I have already said is illegal."

[44] [1893] 1 Q.B. 700 at p. 714.

[45] *Supra,* n. 43.

[46] *Nordenfeldt* v. *Maxim-Nordenfeldt Guns and Ammunition Co.* [1894] A.C. 535 at p. 565.

" The public has an interest in every person's carrying on his trade freely, so has the individual. All interference with individual liberty of action in trading, and all restraints of trade of themselves, if there is nothing more, are contrary to public policy, and therefore void. But there are exceptions: restraint of trade and interference with individual liberty of action may be justified by the special circumstances of an individual case. It is a sufficient justification, and indeed it is the only justification, if the restraint is reasonable—reasonable, that is, in reference to the interests of the parties concerned, and reasonable in reference to the interests of the public, so framed and so guarded as to afford adequate protection to the party in whose favour it is imposed, while at the same time it is in no way injurious to the interests of the public."

It is therefore no part of public policy that *all* restrictive covenants are to be treated as illegal. Illegality will attach to those which are framed more widely than is reasonably necessary to protect the interest which the covenant is framed to protect. The principle thus involves an assessment of the degree of protection which is reasonable and that assessment may be based upon the nature and extent of the business which it is designed to safeguard [47] or the relationship subsisting between the parties to the covenant [48] or, as in most cases, a combination of both factors. In regard to the relationship between the parties to the covenant, the law has made a broad distinction between covenants imposed by a master upon his servant and covenants imposed on the seller of the goodwill of a business in favour of the purchaser. In the first case the master will not be allowed to enforce a restrictive covenant which is devised to protect him from competition by a person leaving his employment, or if that is the only possible effect of the restrictive covenant, whether or not designed with that in view.[49] In the second case, the purchaser may protect himself from the competition of the seller of the goodwill of the business, but if the restrictive covenant framed to effect this is wider than the safe-guarding of the goodwill reasonably demands, it may be objected to.[50]

Restrictive covenants in a partnership agreement

Restrictive covenants included in a partnership agreement have been regarded in England as similar in effect to those entered into between a seller of goodwill and the purchaser thereof.[51] In Scotland, a clause in a partnership agreement entered into by booksellers provided that if either partner declined to renew the agreement at its expiry upon the terms previously agreed, he would be prohibited from taking any part in any business of

[47] *Nordenfeldt* v. *Maxim-Nordenfeldt Guns and Ammunition Co.* (*supra*).
[48] The line of authority in England culminating in *Fitch* v. *Dewes* [1921] 2 A.C. 168 maintaining a distinction based on relationship of the parties appears now to be adopted in Scotland: *Scottish Farmers Dairy Co.* (*Glasgow*) *Ltd.* v. *McGhee*, 1933 S.C. 148.
[49] *Mason* v. *Provident Clothing Co.* [1913] A.C. 724; *Morris* v. *Saxelby* [1916] 1 A.C. 689; *McEllistrim* v. *Ballymacelligott Co-operative Society* [1919] A.C. 548; *Fitch* v. *Dewes, supra.*
[50] *Goldsoll* v. *Goldman* [1915] 1 Ch. 292; *Meikle* v. *Meikle* (1895) 33 S.L.R. 362.
[51] *Ronbar Enterprises* v. *Green* [1954] 1 W.L.R. 815.

booksellers within the City of Glasgow. This was found to be a lawful provision and not assailable on the ground of restraint of trade.[52] That decision, however, was prior to the trend of authority in England distinguishing for the purpose of the validity of a restrictive covenant the relationship of master and servant from that of vendor and purchaser of the goodwill of a business. It was issued in an epoch when the test applied was whether the restriction was wider than was reasonably necessary for the protection of the party in whose interest it was imposed, irrespective of the relationship of that party to the party subjected to the restriction. Since the decision in *Scottish Farmers Dairy Company (Glasgow) Ltd.* v. *McGhee* [53] the English authorities for the distinctive treatment of restrictions on the basis of the contractual relationship of the parties may probably be regarded as acceptable by the Scottish courts but there is as yet no Scottish decision which makes it clear whether in Scotland a restrictive covenant in a partnership agreement will generally be regarded as falling within the vendor and purchaser category, as in England,[54] or the master and servant category, or perhaps an intermediate category between these two.

It is thought that the approach of the Scottish courts to a restrictive covenant occurring in a partnership agreement would be unlikely to be based upon a general rule categorising partnership cases as pertaining to the vendor and purchaser class of restrictive covenant but rather would be to arrive at a conclusion as to the appropriate way to treat the covenant upon a construction of the terms of the partnership agreement as a whole. Indeed it is doubtful whether this is not a more correct view of the English authorities cited than the general statement made in *Lindley on Partnership* [55] " it is now clearly settled that the court takes a far stricter and less favourable view of covenants in restraint of trade entered into between master and servant than it does of similar covenants between vendor and purchaser, and for this purpose covenants entered into between partners generally fall under the second group." The difference in the treatment by the courts of the two main categories is, of course, not disputed and is borne out by a number of English decisions [56] but the decisions relied on for regarding restrictive covenants between partners as falling generally within the vendor and purchaser category do not appear entirely to support the proposition. Both were decisions relating to restrictive covenants occurring in medical partnerships. In *Re Jenkins' Deed of Partnership* [57] the restraint was imposed not upon the partner but upon his wife who was also a qualified medical practitioner, though not in partnership along with her husband and one Reid. It was held that on a true construction of the deed the relationship between the wife and the partnership should be regarded as analogous to employer and employee for the purpose of determining

[52] *Stalker* v. *Carmichael* (1735) Mor. 9455.
[53] *Supra* n. 48.
[54] *Re Jenkins' Deed of Partnership* [1948] W.N. 98; *Whitehill* v. *Bradford* [1952] Ch. 236. See Lindley, *op. cit.* pp. 458–459.
[55] *op. cit.* pp. 458–459.
[56] *Ronbar Enterprises Ltd.* v. *Green* [1954] 1 W.L.R. 815 and cases therein cited.
[57] [1948] W.N. 98; reported *sub nom. Jenkins* v. *Reid* [1948] 1 All E.R. 471.

the validity of the restrictive covenant imposed upon her and the covenant was held to be invalid.   In *Whitehill* v. *Bradford* [58] a partnership agreement among four doctors imposed a restrictive covenant of considerable range both in duration and in area of operation upon a partner who retired from the practice.   The restrictive covenant was in this case considered as if it had arisen between vendor and purchaser.   Evershed M.R. observed,[59] " In cases arising between vendor and purchaser, of mutual covenants between professional men, the test of reasonableness must at the end of all remain.   But in the last mentioned class of case there is always a proper subject-matter for protection, and that protection comprehends that which it does not comprehend in master and servant cases, namely protection against competition."

It seems, therefore, that the English decisions cited by Lindley go no further than to suggest that the attitude of the courts towards a restrictive covenant appearing in a partnership agreement will be determined on a true construction of the deed itself.   In some cases the situation surrounding the partners when the restrictive covenant comes into effect will clearly place the covenant in the category of one between vendor and purchaser. In *Ronbar Enterprises Ltd.* v. *Green* [60] a partnership was entered into between the plaintiff company and the defendant to carry on the business of publishing a weekly newspaper, the plaintiff company having purchased a 40 per cent. interest in the newspaper from the defendant for £10,000. A clause in the deed of partnership provided that in certain events either partner had the right to determine the partnership and to purchase the other partner's share in which case " the partner whose share is purchased shall not for five years from such date (*i.e.* the date of determining the partnership) directly or indirectly carry on or be engaged or interested in any business similar to or competing with the business of the partnership." On the plaintiff company determining the partnership and purchasing Green's share in terms of the partnership deed, Green found employment as a writer with another periodical of similar character and make-up.   The plaintiff company were successful in their application for an injunction against Green.   That case, however, can be regarded as a straightforward one between vendor and purchaser, and the fact that the sale was occasioned by the operation of the terms of a partnership deed raises no material point of distinction.

The dictum of the Master of the Rolls in *Whitehill* v. *Bradford*, above quoted,[61] however, raises a wider issue and suggests that the courts in England will be prepared to regard mutual covenants in a partnership, or at least in a partnership between professional men, as analogous to a restrictive covenant imposed on the vendor in the sale of the goodwill of a business.   The analogy presumably is justified by the greater degree of protection which a professional practice of doctors or solicitors, for

[58] [1952] Ch. 236.
[59] *Ibid.* at p. 246.
[60] [1954] 1 W.L.R. 815.
[61] *Supra* nn. 58 and 59.

example, may reasonably require in view of the confidential nature of the relationship of the partners with their patients or clients. Thus what would be invalid in a restrictive covenant in a contract of service, as designed to protect the master from competition on the part of his former servant, may become a reasonable measure for the protection of a professional practice in a partnership case and thus more analogous to the view taken in the vendor and purchaser cases.[61a] That view might well prevail even when the restriction is imposed by the partnership deed on a junior partner, whose conditions otherwise under the deed may be more closely analogous to those of an employee, or on a salaried partner. Even so, the dictum of the Master of the Rolls excludes by implication restrictive covenants imposed mutually on the partners of a commercial business and affords no support for the view that restrictions in partnership agreements are generally to be regarded as analogous to those between vendor and purchaser.

Partners not in pari delicto

There is a general principle of the law relating to *pacta illicita* that when the parties are not *in pari delicto* the less blameworthy party may found upon the illegality.[62] The principle applies where one party to the illegal transaction has been able to compel the other to join in committing the illegal act and, in Scotland, has been applied mainly in cases where a creditor has demanded and obtained from his debtor a secret preference in consideration of acceding to a composition arrangement,[63] but the principle has been applied in other circumstances by the English courts.[64]

The application of the rule to cases of illegal partnership is doubtful and difficult, since in most cases arising between the members of an illegal partnership it will not be easy to regard the individual partners otherwise than *in pari delicto*.[65] In such cases judicial assistance will not be granted to enable a party to the illegal association to enforce his rights and " the necessary consequence of the refusal of judicial assistance in the expiscation of rights resulting from an illegal agreement is that the party who has gained an advantage is entitled to keep it. If a partnership be illegal, one partner may have defrauded the other but no action of accounting is admissible." [66]

In questions arising between the illegal partnership and third parties the rule is, however, seen to operate. While the illegal firm may not sue for the enforcement of transactions entered into with third parties,[67] an

[61a] But that will not prevent such covenants being closely inspected to see whether they are reasonable: *Lyne-Pirkis* v. *Jones* [1969] 1 W.L.R. 1293; *McFarlane* v. *Kent* [1965] 1 W.L.R. 1019; *Peyton* v. *Mindham* [1971] 3 All E.R. 1215.

[62] Gloag, *Contract* (2nd ed.), pp. 587–588.

[63] *Arrol* v. *Montgomery* (1826) 4 S. 499; *Macfarlane* v. *Nicoll* (1864) 3 M. 237.

[64] *Harse* v. *Pearl Life Assurance Co.* [1904] 1 K.B. 558; *Hermann* v. *Charlesworth* [1905] 2 K.B. 123; *Reynell* v. *Sprye* (1852) 1 De G.M. & G. 660.

[65] See *e.g. Ewing* v. *Osbaldiston* (1837) 2 Myl. & C. 53; *Stewart* v. *Gibson* (1835) 14 S. 166; (1840) 1 Rob. 260.

[66] Gloag, *Contract* (2nd ed.), pp. 585–586.

[67] *Biggs* v. *Lawrence* (1789) 3 T.R. 454; *Shaw* v. *Benson* (1883) 11 Q.B.D. 563.

illegal partnership in England may prosecute a person for theft of its property [68] or a member of the partnership for embezzling its funds.[69] Though such prosecutions in Scotland will not normally depend upon the partnership's title to prosecute, in theory it is thought that in the event of the state refusing to prosecute, the illegal partnership would be entitled to apply for criminal letters to bring a private prosecution.[70] It is possible to regard the English decisions as in a wide sense the exception made in respect of parties who are not *in pari delicto*. If that proposition can be supported, it would be possible to extend the reasoning to cover the right of an illegal partnership to sue a third party in the civil courts for damages in respect of a delict committed against the partnership though this is not entirely borne out by authority. It may possibly be deduced, however, from the general proposition in *Simpson* v. *Bloss* [71] that a demand connected with an illegal transaction is unenforceable if the claimant requires any aid from the illegal transaction to establish his case, but not otherwise, a rule which was expressed by Mellor J. in *Taylor* v. *Chester* [72] in the words, " The true test for determining whether or not the plaintiff and the defendant were *in pari delicto* is by considering whether the plaintiff could make out his case otherwise than through the medium and by the aid of the illegal transaction to which he was himself a party." [73]   Thus if the illegality of the association does not affect any contract on which the party claiming redress is compelled to rely in order to establish his right, it is not open to the defender to plead that illegality in defence to the claim, because it does not follow that, because money has been obtained in breach of some legal provision, the person in whose possession that money is will be entitled to retain it.[74]

Concealment of illegality

Where it is established that the purposes for which a partnership was formed are illegal, the legal effects of that illegality will follow even if the true purpose has been concealed [75] and even where the deed of partnership has been drawn up formally and has succeeded in presenting itself as *ex facie* legal, parole evidence will be admitted to establish the true facts which taint the association with illegality.[76]

Fraudulent misrepresentation inducing party to enter an illegal contract

The exception made in respect of a party who is not *in pari delicto* does

---

[68] *R.* v. *Frankland* (1863) L. & C. 276.
[69] *R.* v. *Tankard* [1894] 1 Q.B. 548.
[70] *J. & P. Coats Ltd.* v. *Brown*, 1909 S.C.(J.) 29; see also *McBain* v. *Crichton*, 1961 J.C. 25, where the application was refused since the only wrong alleged by the complainer was of a general and public nature.
[71] (1816) 7 Taunt. 246.
[72] (1869) L.R. 4 Q.B. 309 at p. 314.
[73] See also *Scott* v. *Brown, Doering, McNab & Co.* [1892] 2 Q.B. 724. These cases were considered and approved by Lord Dunedin in the Scottish appeal, *Farmers' Mart Ltd.* v. *Milne*, 1914 S.C.(H.L.) 84.
[74] *Gordon* v. *Commissioners of Police* [1910] 2 K.B. 1080.
[75] *Stewart* v. *Gibson* (1840) 1 Rob. 260; *Armstrong* v. *Armstrong* (1834) 3 Myl. & K. 45.
[76] *Collins* v. *Blantern* (1767) 2 Wils. 341; *Foster* v. *Driscoll* [1929] 1 K.B. 470.

not apply to the case where he has been induced to enter into a contract which is illegal and has an element in it of moral turpitude, by misrepresentations which do not relate to the legality of the contract. In such a case the party deceived has no claim under the contract nor can he claim damages from the party who deceived him.[77] Where he is induced to enter a contract, which is prohibited in the interests of the public, by misrepresentations which fraudulently represent the facts as such that the contract entered into would not have been prohibited by law had those representations been true, he will likewise be unable to enforce a claim under the contract.[78] In any case where a party is induced by misrepresentation of another to believe that the contract to be entered into is not illegal or immoral, he may claim damages from the party whose misrepresentations induced him to enter the contract.[79] These rules appear to be irreconcilable with the principle that if one party to an illegal contract is not *in pari delicto* with the other he may be allowed to recover what he has paid under the contract. Certainly in the case of misrepresentations as to the legality of the contract, the party misled by them is allowed to claim damages against the party who has deceived him though he is not allowed to found a claim for recovery of sums paid under the contract upon the ground that the contract is illegal. In the case where the misrepresentations have not been directed to the legality or otherwise of the proposed contract it can be argued that the parties are in fact *in pari delicto* in the sense that both have agreed to be involved in an immoral or illegal contract and therefore on the principle *ex turpi causa non oritur actio* neither is allowed to enforce a claim against the other. That principle, however, has no application as a defence by an executor of a deceased partner against a claim by the creditors, legatees or other beneficiaries in succession to the deceased's estate. Even if the funds of the deceased held by the executor represent the profits derived by the deceased from an illegal partnership, that circumstance has no relevance to the accountability of the executor for the funds which he holds as representative of the deceased even where the executor himself has been one of the deceased's partners in the illegal venture.[80]

Claims against illegal partnerships

The illegality of a partnership does not of itself prevent a creditor from suing the partnership. If a third party transacts business with an illegal partnership he is not involved *in turpi causa* unless he is aware of the illegality and seeks to enforce a claim arising from a transaction which he knows is infected with the illegality of the partnership.[81]

[77] *Parkinson* v. *College of Ambulance Ltd.* [1925] 2 K.B. 1.
[78] *Re Mahmoud and Ispahani* [1921] 2 K.B. 716; compare *Phillips* v. *Blackhurst*, 1912, 2 S.L.T. 254; *McCarroll* v. *Maguire*, 1920, 2 S.L.T. 108, at p. 110.
[79] *Burrows* v. *Rhodes* [1899] 1 Q.B. 816; *Haseldine* v. *Hosken* [1933] 1 K.B. 822.
[80] *Joy* v. *Campbell* (1804) 1 Sch. & Lef. 328; 9 R.R. 39. But if no account has been settled with the deceased's partner, it would appear that his executor *qua* partner may rely on the illegality and refuse to account to the deceased's estate for the profits made: *Ottley* v. *Browne* (1810) 1 Ball & Bea. 360; *cf. Sharp* v. *Taylor* (1848) 2 Ph. 801; 78 R.R. 298.
[81] *Re South Wales Atlantic Steamship Co.* (1876) 2 Ch.D. 763.

Objection on ground of illegality taken by the court ex proprio motu

When the illegality of the contract appears *ex facie* thereof it is *pars judicis* to take notice of that illegality even where it has not been pleaded by the parties.[82]

Actings upon illegal contract

An agreement for an illegal partnership will not be enforced even if it has been partly performed.[83] But where actings of the parties have followed upon an illegal contract, one of these parties will not be allowed to plead the illegality of the contract in order to secure for himself an advantage which would have been denied to him under the illegal contract.

" To him who pleads and brings before the court the illegality of this agreement I apprehend the appropriate and conclusive legal answer is—assume the agreement to be, as you say, illegal, it is the one you acted under, and the only understanding on which you were allowed to act; and the very policy of the law to which you now appeal as discountenancing such agreements is best advanced by holding that if you have no claim under that agreement, you have none at all, and have thrown away your money and services in the hope of an illegal profit." [84]

[82] *Hamilton* v. *McLauchlan* (1908) 16 S.L.T. 341; *Scott* v. *Brown* [1892] 2 Q.B. 724; *Gedge* v. *Royal Exchange Assurance Corporation* [1900] 2 Q.B. 214; *North Western Salt Co.* v. *Electrolytic Alkali Co.* [1914] A.C. 461.
[83] Lindley, *op. cit.* p. 127; *Ewing* v. *Osbaldiston* (1837) 2 Myl. & C. 53; 45 R.R. 9.
[84] *Bolden* v. *Fogo* (1850) 12 D. 798, *per* Lord Justice-Clerk Hope at p. 804.

CHAPTER V

HOLDING OUT

THE contract of partnership has much in common with the contract of
agency, and, as in the law of principal and agent, circumstances may arise
in which a party may be regarded as being held out as an agent, so there are
circumstances in which a person who is not in fact a partner may be
regarded as holding himself out or having been held out by others as a
partner of a firm. The doctrine of holding out is said to be based in both
cases on the equitable principle of personal bar or estoppel. In cases of
agency it has been explained in these words—" The salient feature of
agency by estoppel is that no agency . . . is actually created thereby;
true agency arises by agreement only. The principal may be estopped
from denying that another is his agent and his relationship with third
parties may be affected by the acts of such person; but, without more, the
relationship of principal and agent does not arise between him and his
apparent agent." [1]

In partnership while agency is an essential element in the legal concept
the agency involved is of the kind described by Clark [2] as " mutual "
agency, *i.e.* the partners may in different transactions stand at one time in
the relationship of agent one to another and at other times as principal.
In Scotland, where the firm is recognised as a person distinct from the
parties who comprise it, one might have expected separate treatment of
the doctrine of holding out, first, from the standpoint of the liability of a
person who is held out, or who suffers himself to be held out, as a partner,
and, secondly, from the standpoint of the liability of a firm which has held
out a person as a partner. The first of these aspects alone is provided for
in the Partnership Act 1890.[3] The second is nowhere expressly mentioned
in the Act and must therefore be regarded as left *sub silentio* to be governed
by the general rules of the common law and of equity.[4] The basic
reasoning involved in that approach appears clear when the two
aspects of the relation are more closely analysed; for it is in the first of
these aspects only that the peculiarity of the law of partnership, the mutual
agency, arises. In the second aspect the issue raised is a clear issue of
agency proper.

Section 14 (1) of the Partnership Act 1890 provides—

" Every one who by words spoken or written or by conduct
represents himself, or who knowingly suffers himself to be represented,

[1] Bowstead, *Agency* (13th ed.), p. 20.
[2] *Op. cit.* I, 50.
[3] s. 14 (1).
[4] Partnership Act 1890, s. 46.

127

as a partner in a particular firm, is liable as a partner to anyone who
has on the faith of any such representation given credit to the firm,
whether the representation has or has not been made or communicated
to the person so giving credit by or with the knowledge of the apparent
partner making the representation or suffering it to be made."

That subsection is declaratory of the pre-statute law as explained by
Eyre C.J. in *Waugh* v. *Carver* [5] in these words—

> " Now a case may be stated in which it is the clear sense of the
> parties to the contract that they shall not be partners, that A is to
> contribute neither labour nor money, and, to go still farther, not to
> receive any profits. But if he will lend his name as a partner he
> becomes as against all the world a partner, not upon the ground of the
> real transaction between them, but upon principles of general policy,
> to prevent the frauds to which creditors would be liable, if they were
> to suppose that they lent their money upon the apparent credit of
> three or four persons, when in fact, they lent it only to two of them,
> to whom without the others they would have lent nothing."

The effect of the subsection is not to create a partnership between the
firm and the person so held out. The statutory words deal with the case
where no such partnership can be held to have been created and where
by the holding out a person is held liable for the transactions in which
he has been so held out as if he were a partner of the firm. That distinction
also reflects the pre-statute law and is clearly brought out in the judgment
of Eyre C.J. in *Waugh* v. *Carver*.[6] His words, it is true, do not express this
idea as clearly as might be desired since he still speaks of the holding out
as something which " constituted themselves partners in respect to other
persons," but the difficulty is one of expression only, since, it being conceded that no partnership has been created between the persons concerned,
the " constitution " of themselves as partners " in respect to others,"
cannot refer to the creation of a partnership but to a relation which, at the
time when Eyre C.J. spoke, would have been described as a *quasi* partnership, and however little content is now left in that concept in the modern
law of partnership [7] there is little violence done to the essential meaning of
the liability arising on holding out if one describes as a *quasi* partnership
a relation in which a person who is not in fact a partner, finds himself
liable to third parties as if he were one. It is in fact the same idea which
was later stated by Lindley L.J., " No person who does not hold himself
out as a partner is liable to third persons for the acts of those whose profits
he shares unless he and they really are partners." [8]

---

[5] (1793) 2 H.Bl. 235; 3 Ross's *Commercial Cases* 426 at p. 433.
[6] *Supra*. See particularly 3 Ross, *Commercial Cases* at p. 434. " ... it is plain upon the
construction of the agreement, if it be construed only between the Carvers and Giesler,
that they were not, nor ever meant to be partners. ... But the question is, whether they
have not, by parts of their agreement, constituted themselves partners in respect to other
persons?"
[7] *Supra* Chap. III, pp. 60–63.
[8] *Op. cit.* p. 82, quoted by Lord Kinnear in *Laing Bros. & Co.'s Trustee* v. *Low* (1896) 23 R.
1105 at p. 1110.

A wider connotation which might be given to the words of Eyre C.J. as suggesting that a partnership is created or " constituted " in any respect by holding out is contained in the words " he becomes *as against all the world* a partner." The same approach can be detected in dicta in other decisions of the same period.[9] But in the phrase " against all the world " may be discovered the point of departure from the essential idea of the doctrine of holding out which is perhaps the source of the confusion. Parke J. makes the point in his judgment in *Dickinson* v. *Valpy* [10] where he says, " If it could have been proved that the defendant had held himself out to be a partner, not to the world, for that is a loose expression, but to the plaintiff himself, or under such circumstances of publicity as to satisfy a jury that the plaintiff knew of it and believed him to be a partner, he would be liable to the plaintiff in all transactions in which he engaged and gave credit to the defendant upon the faith of being such partner." [11]

The point, which may have been unduly laboured, is made in criticism of the mode of expression chosen by Eyre C.J. rather than of the soundness of the decision which he reached; but it is of some importance in the initial consideration of the doctrine of holding out to rid the mind of any suggestion, latent or otherwise, (1) that holding out can ever create a partnership and (2) that holding out can be founded upon by any save those who were aware of it and acted in reliance upon it. Both points are brought out in the terms of section 14 (1) of the Partnership Act 1890 and indeed are clearly apprehended and stated by writers on the common law of partnership prior to the passing of the Act. Thus Clark [12] explains the doctrine as follows:

> " Here persons who are not partners, and who may not be entitled
> to share profits or to exercise any of the other rights of the partnership
> relation, render themselves liable to creditors of a company or firm,
> by reason of their having, prior to the contracting of the debt ... held
> themselves out as partners, that is to say, done or permitted something
> to be done, which naturally led to the conclusion that their credit was
> pledged to the concern—that they were its guarantees, or that it was
> their agent. This doctrine is indeed a necessary consequence of the
> law of principal and agent, whereby if any man hold out another as

[9] *e.g. per* Ellenborough C.J. in *Hesketh* v. *Blanchard* (1803) 4 East 143; 3 Ross, *Commercial Cases* 451 at p. 453, " *Quoad* third persons it was a partnership: for the plaintiff was to share half the profits. But as between themselves it was only an agreement for so much, as a compensation for the plaintiff's trouble, and for lending Robertson his credit." See also *Scarf* v. *Jardine* (1882) 7 App.Cas. 345; *Ex p. Watson* (1809) 16 Ves. 265; *Ex p. Matthews* (1814) 3 V. & B. 125; *De Berkom* v. *Smith & Lewis* (1793) 1 Esp. 29.

[10] (1829) 10 B. & C. 128 at p. 140. In *Smith* v. *Watson* (1824) 2 B. & C. 401, Best J. also observes the distinction in the words " The question is not whether he is liable to third persons as a partner, but whether he had a joint interest in this property. There are many cases where a person may be liable to third persons as a partner and yet not have any interest in the property."

[11] The point is also made by Lord Lindley in *Farquharson Bros. & Co.* v. *King & Co.* [1902] A.C. 325 at 341 (a case relating to holding out in agency): " The holding out must be to the particular individual who says he relied on it, or under such circumstances of publicity as to justify the inference that he knew of it and acted upon it."

[12] *Op. cit.* I, p. 57.

his agent, he is bound by that other's acts within the sphere of the agency. It is also a consequence of the principle that the partners are guarantees for the company obligations."

At the same time marginal cases may occur where the facts relied on may be regarded either as establishing a holding out of a person as a partner or as establishing the fact that a partnership has been created. Such cases are often concerned in some degree with the feature that the person whose position in regard to the firm is being considered, has to some extent and upon some basis, received a share of the profits of the firm. In such cases the facts relied on may go far towards establishing a partnership rather than a mere holding out of a person as a partner, and it was in the difficult area of distinction to which such cases give rise that most of the earlier discussions already referred to were taken.[13] Of such cases, Story observed, "The distinction as thus presented does certainly wear the appearance of no small subtlety and refinement, and scarcely meets the mind in a clear and unambiguous form; for the question must still recur. When may a party properly be said to have ' an interest in the profits as profits'? When, also, may it properly be said, that ' the interest in the profits is mutual ' and that ' each person has a specific interest in the profits as a principal trader '? " [14] It will be observed that Clark in the passage quoted [15] sets aside from consideration in the context of holding out any question of participation in profits and confines attention to cases of persons " who are not partners and who may not be entitled to share profits or to exercise any of the other rights of the partnership relation." That is not to say that Clark regarded sharing in profits as in every case establishing a partnership. Its force was probably stronger in that direction in Clark's time than it later came to be regarded in the light of decisions such as *Cox* v. *Hickman* [16] but there were still cases of participation in profits which Clark would not have regarded as establishing the creation of a partnership. Such cases equally were not subsumed by him under the doctrine of holding out but rather under the concept of *quasi* partnership. Indeed it is such cases of " no small subtlety and refinement " which may have given rise to the concept of *quasi* partnership, though since the passing of the Partnership Act 1890 there seems to be no need to distinguish them from holding out cases where the facts do not establish actual partnership.[17]

Holding out as an aspect of the doctrine of personal bar

The liability of an individual who has been held out as a partner is usually ascribed to the doctrine of personal bar or estoppel: and indeed the wording of section 14 (1) of the Partnership Act 1890 suggests a strong

[13] See *Waugh* v. *Carver* (*supra* n. 5); *Hesketh* v. *Blanchard* and other cases cited *supra* n. 9; *Dickinson* v. *Valpy* and *Smith* v. *Watson, supra* n. 10.
[14] *Story on Partnership*, p. 30.
[15] *Supra* n. 12.
[16] (1860) 8 H.L.C. 268.
[17] *Supra* Chap. III, pp. 60–63.

affinity with this doctrine. The analogy, however, is not a perfect one and holding out in partnership is perhaps more properly regarded as a special aspect of holding out in the general law of agency. It is true that in agency the notion is often itself ascribed to personal bar or estoppel. But it is essential to the doctrine of personal bar that the person pleading it must have acted on the representation and have so acted *to his detriment*.[18] That latter condition has been applied in several of the decisions in holding out in agency.[19] But in other agency cases all that is referred to is acting on the faith of the representation or altering one's position as a result thereof.[20] The terms of section 14 (1) suggest that the latter view is adopted by the section in regard to holding out in partnership, since the section refers to " anyone who has on the faith of any such representation given credit to the firm." It is true that by so acting the third party may frequently have acted to his detriment but the section does not make this a requirement of his claiming against the person held out as a partner. Moreover, even in agency, it is thought to be the better view that " there need be no more than an entering into the contract on the faith of the representation." [21] In partnership the point will infrequently be of practical importance in a case of holding out under section 14 (1), since in most cases the third party will seek his recourse against the person held out only where he is unable to obtain satisfaction from the firm itself and its actual partners. But if the liability of the individual held out rests upon a modified application of the dotrine of personal bar or upon an analogous but separate doctrine of holding out as distinct from personal bar, it may be necessary to keep that fact in view later when discussing the case of the liability of the firm for the acts of a person whom it has held out as a partner, a case where the terms of section 14 (1) are not applicable.[22]

What amounts to holding out a person as a partner

Section 14 (1) of the Partnership Act 1890 describes broadly two types of holding out, (a) a holding out by words spoken or written by, or by conduct of, the individual representing himself to be a partner, and (b) cases where the individual " knowingly suffers " himself to be so held out by others. The distinction on first sight appears to be one between active and passive behaviour on the part of the person held out to be a partner and it seems to be so treated by Lindley.[23] On analysis, however, it is

[18] *Gatty* v. *Maclaine*, 1921 S.C.(H.L.) 1, *per* Lord Birkenhead at p. 7.
[19] *Howard* v. *Hudson* (1853) 2 E. & B. 1; *Carr* v. *L. & N.W.Ry.* (1875) L.R. 10 C.P. 307; *Whitechurch* v. *Cavanagh* [1902] A.C. 117; *Farquharson Bros. & Co.* v. *King & Co.* [1902] A.C. 325; *Bell* v. *Marsh* [1903] 1 Ch. 528; *Mac Fisheries Ltd.* v. *Harrison* (1924) 93 L.J.K.B. 811; *Wilson & Meeson* v. *Pickering* [1946] K.B. 422.
[20] *Pickard* v. *Sears* (1837) 6 A. & E. 469; *Freeman* v. *Cooke* (1848) 2 Exch. 654; *Cornish* v. *Abington* (1859) 4 H. & N. 549; *Rama Corporation* v. *Proved Tin & General Investments* [1952] 2 Q.B. 147; *Freeman & Lockyer* v. *Buckhurst Park Properties (Mangal) Ltd.* [1964] 2 Q.B. 480.
[21] See for a brief discussion of the point in relation to agency, *Bowstead on Agency* (13th ed.) pp. 251–253 and particularly pp. 252–253.
[22] See *infra* pp. 154–157.
[23] *Op. cit.* pp. 101–102.

not easy to characterise all the cases in which the individual has " knowingly suffered " himself to be held out as a partner by others as purely passive conduct. It may be necessary to examine such cases more closely in order to determine whether the acquiescence of the individual is to be regarded as an authorisation or endorsement by him of the representations made about him by others, in which case it is not a true case of " knowingly suffering " the representations but a case where the individual's own conduct represents him to be a partner,[24] or a case of mere non-remonstrating acquiescence which might be truly described as passive behaviour and regarded as a case falling under the statutory words " knowingly suffers."

Words or conduct

What will be regarded as amounting to holding out in any case is a question of fact, to be determined as a jury question. Thus in two practically contemporaneous cases the Duke of Argyll was sued as liable through holding himself out as intending to pay for work ordered to be done on behalf of a society of which he was advertised as the president, and in which he had acted as president at a meeting of the society and had signed some of the resolutions passed at that meeting. In the first case [24] the jury held these facts as sufficient evidence of his holding himself out and their verdict was for the plaintiff. In the second case [25] another jury on the same facts found for the defendant. The court refused to disturb the verdict in either case. Where there is evidence that an individual, not being a partner, has represented to others that he is in fact a partner or that he has so conducted himself as to create that belief in the minds of the person with whom he has transacted business on behalf of the firm, he is clearly liable as if he were a partner in terms of section 14 (1). The representations which he makes either by his words or his conduct must, however, be made before the transaction has been entered into with the third party; otherwise he will not be held liable as a partner upon the contract which he has entered into on behalf of his alleged firm,[26] because if the representation relied upon is subsequent to the entering of the contract with the firm, it cannot be said that the latter took place in reliance by the third party on the credit of the person so holding himself out as a partner. Moreover the representation made must have been known to the third party who now seeks to hold him liable as if he were a partner. In *Pott* v. *Eyton* [27] A who was concerned in a colliery built and stocked a shop in the vicinity for the supply of goods to the colliers and their families. He opened the shop in 1830 and put B in charge of the business, receiving 7 per cent. of the gross sales while B took the remainder of the profits. A's name appeared above the shop and in the excise licences. Until 1834 the goods required to stock the shop were purchased and paid

[24] *Wood* v. *Duke of Argyll* (1844) 6 M. & G. 928. See, however, the observations of Harman L.J. on this case in *Keith Spicer Ltd.* v. *Mansell* [1970] 1 All E.R. 462 at p. 463.
[25] *Lake* v. *Duke of Argyll* (1844) 6 Q.B. 477.
[26] *Baird* v. *Planque* (1858) 1 F. & F. 344.
[27] (1846) 3 C.B. 31.

for either by A or on his behalf but in that year it was agreed that B in future would purchase all the goods and that A's interest in the business would be reduced to 5 per cent. of the gross sales in consequence. Following on that agreement B, who had several other shops, opened an account with a bank which later failed. At the date of the failure the balance due to the bank on B's account exceeded £2,000. No evidence was led for the bank that the credit had been given to A by them or that they had been aware that his name stood above the shop or that they had supposed him to be a partner when the debt was contracted. On the assignees of the bank suing both A and B for recovery, the jury found that no partnership existed between A and B and that A had not been held out as a partner. The court refused to disturb that verdict.

The *ratio* of that decision appears to be reflected in the terms of section 14 (1). If the third party seeking to hold a person liable as having held himself out as a partner did not in fact know of his words or conduct which fostered that belief, then the third party has not been misled by the representation and therefore he cannot be said in the words of section 14 (1) to have given credit to the firm " on the faith of any such representation." That is not to say, however, that the representation relied upon must be directly addressed to the third party. " There may be a holding out without any direct communication by words or conduct between the parties. One who makes an assertion, intending it to be repeated and acted upon, or even under such circumstances that it is likely to be repeated and acted upon by the third person, will be liable to those who afterwards hear of it and act upon it." [28] What is regarded is not a contractual or other relationship between the third party and the person holding himself out as a partner but a situation in which the third party may claim that he had acted in reliance upon the state of facts represented. The third party in order to substantiate that claim must be able to establish that the holding out was communicated directly to him or was made " under such circumstance of publicity as to justify the inference that he knew of it and acted upon it." [29] The possibility that a representation made to A may be repeated to other persons and thus extend the scope of the representation originally made was the issue before the court in *Martyn* v. *Gray* [30] where the person holding himself out or permitting himself to be held out as a partner, wished to conceal his name and was referred to as a person of substance who did not wish to have his name disclosed. He was referred to in the terms authorised by him yet incurred liability as a partner on being identified by those who had given credit to the firm on these representations; not only so but he was held liable to persons to whom those representations had not originally been made. " If the defendant informs

---

[28] Pollock, *Law of Partnership* (15th ed.) p. 54. In terms of the Partnership Act 1890, s. 14 (1), liability as a partner is imposed in a case of holding out " whether the representation has or has not been made or communicated to the person so giving credit by or with the knowledge of the apparent partner making the representation or suffering it to be made."
[29] *Per* Lord Lindley in *Farquharson Brothers & Co.* v. *King & Co.* [1902] A.C. 325 at 341.
[30] (1863) 14 C.B.(N.S.) 824.

AB that he is a partner in a commercial establishment, and AB informs
the plaintiff, and the plaintiff believing the defendant to be a member of the
firm supplies goods to them, the defendant is liable for the price. If the
party is not named, or even if his name is refused, but at the same time
such a description is given as sufficiently identifies the person, the result is
the same as if his name had been given as a partner." [31]

It is clear that facts and circumstances which are averred in support of
a plea that a person has held himself out as a partner may on occasion be
regarded as sufficient to establish that this person was in fact a partner.
The distinction between the two possible results is not maintained as a
question of law but as one of fact. Thus in *Gardner* v. *Anderson and
Another* [32] in an action against A and B for the price of goods supplied to
AB & Company, the issues for the jury were (1) Was A a partner of AB
& Company? and (2) Did he hold himself out or allow himself to be held
out as such? The facts proved were that A and B carried on business as
A & Company for three years. A then retired from the business and B
intimated to the pursuers and others, with A's knowledge, that the business
would continue under the firm of AB & Company. A took no steps to
intimate that he was not the person whose name appeared in the new firm,
and evidence was led that the pursuers had understood the change to
amount merely to the introduction of B's name in the firm. The jury
found for the defender A on the first issue that he was not a partner of the
new firm but against him on the second issue, holding that A had held
himself out as a partner in the new firm. A moved for a rule to show
cause why that verdict, so far as it found for the pursuers on the second
issue, should not be set aside as contrary to the evidence, arguing that there
was no evidence of any holding out except the appearance of A's name in
the new firm name and that the pursuers should have been put on their
inquiry by a circular from B which showed that the firm of A & Company
of which A had been a partner had come to an end. The court refused
to disturb the verdict.

On the other hand, cases may occur where it is possible to hold a person
liable on the ground that he in fact is a partner in the firm, even though
there are no circumstances in which holding out of him as a partner can
be established. In *Watson* v. *Smith* [33] it was averred that a brother who
traded under a firm name had induced a younger brother to sign a contract
of partnership which was not thereafter acted upon by the younger
brother. The agreement was later cancelled and had at no time been
known to the pursuers who transacted business with the firm. These
averments, however, were irrelevant to support a plea by the younger
brother that he was not liable for a bill granted by his elder brother under
the firm name during the existence of the agreement. The decision was
not one of holding out because the younger brother was not in fact held out

[31] *Ibid. per* Williams J. at p. 841.
[32] (1862) 24 D. 315.
[33] Dec. 17, 1806.

to the person as a partner. It was a straightforward case where an actual partnership had been established with the consequence that the younger member was in fact a member of the firm and liable for the firm debt.

The legal effect of holding out

While a person who holds himself out as a partner will be subjected to the same liability for the firm debt in question as if he were a partner, that liability is merely analogous to the liability incurred by an actual partner; it is not co-extensive with it. Thus liability will be imposed upon a person holding himself out as a partner only for those transactions of the firm in which he has been so held out.[34] An actual partner may be held liable for all transactions in the ordinary course of the business of the firm.[35] The distinction in the legal results attendant upon actual partnership as opposed to holding oneself out as a partner may also arise from the type of action before the court. Thus in *Brember* v. *Rutherford* [36] the respondent had obtained a decree in absence against the firm of *Brember & Company* on which he caused a charge for payment to be executed against the complainer " as one of the partners of Brember & Company . . . as such partner and as an individual." The complainer presented a note of suspension of the charge, on the ground that there was no warrant for the execution of diligence against the complainer. The respondent pleaded *inter alia* that since the complainer by his actings had held himself out (1) as owner and (2) as partner of the business and since the respondent had relied on his name and credit, the note of suspension should be refused. The Lord Ordinary (Stormonth-Darling) held that no actual partnership had been established but he was of opinion that Brember had held himself out as a partner and he found the charge orderly proceeded.[37] On appeal the Second Division reversed that judgment and held that the charge must be suspended. Lord Trayner said,[38]

> " The Lord Ordinary is of opinion, and I agree with him, that it has been proved that he (Brember) is not a member of the firm. That is conclusive of the whole matter, for if the complainer is not a partner, there is no warrant for the charge complained of. . . . I offer no opinion as to whether the complainer held himself out as a partner and thus made himself liable for the company's debts. That is not the question here. The question is—Does the charge proceed on a sufficient warrant? and I am of opinion that it does not."

" Knowingly suffers "

It might be argued that section 14 (1) in providing for holding out (a) by words or conduct of the person held out and (b) by knowingly suffering

---

[34] *Dickinson* v. *Valpy, supra* n. 10.
[35] *Infra* Chap. VII, pp. 243 *et seq.*
[36] (1901) 4 F. 62.
[37] For a fuller report of the proceedings before the Lord Ordinary, see (1901) 9 S.L.T. 6.
[38] (1901) 4 F. 62 at p. 64.

himself to be so held out is legislating for two distinct classes or case (a) where the defender has held himself out as a partner and (b) where he is so held out by others.   On closer analysis of the words of the subsection this is not entirely borne out.   The words or conduct referred to in the first branch of the subsection may in certain circumstances embrace cases where the defender has in fact been held out by others but has authorised that holding out.   Such authority need not be express; it may be inferred from the defender's conduct.[39]   The conduct from which such authorisation may be inferred may take many forms.   It may consist in statements which the defender has made, even when he did not intend them to be repeated [40] or from his being an assenting party to resolutions passed.[41]   It may, in effect, arise from any conduct on the defender's part which unequivocally implies that the other person who held him out as a partner did so with his authority.

Such cases, however, though they depend upon the representations made by persons other than the defender himself are not truly *passive* cases of holding out nor, it is submitted, do they depend upon the second branch of section 14 (1).   What are to be regarded in the holding out in such cases are the words or conduct of the defender himself as referable to the representations made by other persons.   They are thus true cases of *active* holding out under the first branch of the subsection.

The point is of importance since if that be not the correct view and all cases of holding out by others are cases of passive holding out, then they will fall under the second branch of section 14 (1) and be governed by the words " knowingly suffers."   These words are productive of considerable difficulty in their proper ambit and it seems unnecessary to add to that difficulty by bringing within their scope cases where the defender has by his own words or conduct authorised others to represent him as a partner. It may be answered that if he has so authorised them, then he must be held to have knowingly suffered the representations made. But that does not logically follow since the " authority " spelled out from the conduct of the defender will not necessarily be equiparate with the representations made.   It is thought that any such equiparation is entirely destroyed by decision in *Martyn* v. *Gray*.[42]   In the relevant passage in Lindley [43] after dealing with the case of the defendant held out by others, the next paragraph, under the cross heading " knowingly suffering," proceeds, " A further question arises under section 14 of the Partnership Act 1890 as to the meaning of ' knowingly suffers.' "   If by that passage it is intended to suggest that the words " knowingly suffers " will govern the cases in the preceding paragraph of his work, it is respectfully submitted this is not a true construction of the section.

[39] *Spooner* v. *Browning* [1898] 1 Q.B. 528.
[40] *Martyn* v. *Gray* (1863) 14 C.B.(N.S.) 824.
[41] *Maddick* v. *Marshall* (1864) 17 C.B.(N.S.) 829.
[42] *Supra* n. 40.
[43] *Op. cit.* pp. 102–103.

The second branch of section 14 (1) should be regarded as covering only those cases of holding out by other persons in which the defender has remained entirely passive. It is concerned with cases where, with no conduct of the defender offering any foundation for the suggestion that he has authorised the holding out, or even where the defender's conduct negates any such authority, he has been held out by others as a partner in a firm. If no knowledge of the representations made about him can be ascribed to the defender, then he must escape liability in terms of section 14 (1).[44] But what will amount to knowledge for this purpose and if knowledge can be ascribed to the defender what steps may he take on acquiring that knowledge in order to dis-embarrass himself of the legal consequences? The treatment of the word " knowingly " in the phrase " knowingly suffers " has been somewhat uneasy, probably since the section itself attempts to be declaratory of what was a rather indeterminate notion in the pre-statute common law. In a pre-statute decision in England [45] it seems to be regarded as the law that the mere fact that a person knows that another person is falsely representing him to be a partner will not make him liable if such representations are made entirely without authority, " for there is no legal duty to stop another from lying." [46] It is difficult to see how such a proposition can survive in view of the express terms of section 14 (1), and it is thought that the Scottish courts would not readily regard that decision as persuasive authority. More difficulty arises over the exact interpretation of " knowingly." It seems reasonable to regard it as importing more than " carelessly " and it has been held in England that mere carelessness will not suffice to impose liability.[47] It may be possible to argue from that decision that even when the means of knowledge are at the defender's disposal he has not knowingly suffered the holding out merely because he carelessly neglects to avail himself of those means. The degree of carelessness involved in *Tower Cabinet Co.* v. *Ingram* [47] was, however, minimal. It is difficult to see any real lack of care in the use of the means of knowledge available where a retired partner had not scrupulously examined every letter heading in the firm's existing stock of stationery to ensure that the instructions given to block out his name on them have been adhered to without exception. Yet the decision does indicate that knowledge must be brought home to the defender and, perhaps, that there is little or no room for conceptions like " constructive knowledge " in the terms of section 14 (1).

The real problem in such cases, as Lindley states,[48] is what steps a person must take, when it comes to his notice that he has been held out as a partner by others, before he can dis-embarrass himself of the allegation that he has knowingly suffered the holding out. Is it enough if he

[44] Lindley, *op. cit.* pp. 101–102; Pollock, *op. cit.* p. 52; *Fox* v. *Clifton* (1830) 6 Bing. 776 at 794.
[45] *Fox* v. *Clifton, supra.*
[46] Pollock, *op. cit.* p. 53.
[47] *Tower Cabinet Co.* v. *Ingram* [1949] 2 K.B. 397.
[48] *Op. cit.* p. 103.

remonstrates with those who have so held him out or must he publicise his dissent by advertisement or by seeking an interdict against the offenders? Though cases of this kind may be expected not to have been infrequent, the law is by no means clear. It has been held in the Scottish courts that a party whose name is held out without his consent must take immediate action to have it withdrawn or by some other means inform the public that he is not a partner and that, if he remain silent, he may be found liable to parties who transacted with the firm on the faith of the representation as if he were in fact a partner thereof.[49]   In the case in question, the Lord President (McNeill) stated,

> " A circular was issued on 13th September, 1858, intimating ' that the business hitherto conducted under the firm of James Anderson and Company will, after this date, be carried on under the firm of James Anderson, Crichton and Company.' These gentlemen in Belfast (*i.e.* the pursuers) say they understood that this intimation related, not to a change of persons in the firm, but to a change in the name of the firm merely, by the introduction of Crichton's name.   I cannot say that that was not a natural supposition.   It appears that the circular was communicated to Anderson and that he afterwards dealt with the firm under the name of Anderson, Crichton and Company; and it does not appear that he made any communication to the effect that he was no longer a partner; or that he was not the Anderson whose name was in the firm; or that he insisted upon his name being taken out of the firm; or that he had any reason to suppose that a different person of the name of Anderson was meant.   In his evidence he says that the name Anderson in the new firm was not his name, and that he never consented to the use of his name.   But he admits that he never objected to it, and says only that he ' thought it might be a Mr. Anderson with whom Crichton had been formerly employed.'   That is somewhat equivocal." [50]

It is possible to argue from that dictum of the Lord President that in Scots law at least several courses of action, short of seeking an interdict against those representing that he was a partner, might be regarded as sufficient to allow him to escape liability as such.   If the defender, so soon as he learned of the use of his name, had intimated to the persons that he was not the Anderson referred to in the firm name, it appears clear that the pursuers could not have held him liable as having knowingly suffered himself to be held out as a partner and that he might escape liability even on a transaction which had been entered into with the firm after the circular had reached them but before the defender's disclaimer had arrived in their hands.   If the defender " insisted upon his name being taken out of the firm " presumably that insistence could only be made effective by his seeking an interdict against the firm.   It is more difficult

[49] *J. & C. Gardner* v. *Anderson and Another* (1862) 24 D. 315.   See *supra* p. 134.
[50] *Ibid.* at p. 319.

to see how a mere objection on his part to the use of his name would relieve him of liability unless that objection was communicated not only to the firm but also in some manner to those doing business with the firm. Too much should not be read into the passage quoted since in the case in which it was delivered Lord President McNeill's words were directed to discovering whether there was material upon which a jury could properly have arrived at the verdict that the defender had suffered himself to be held out as a partner. It may, however, be reasonable to deduce from his words that steps short of seeking an interdict may, if brought to the third party's notice without delay, relieve him from liability.[51]

It appears that the wording of the second branch of section 14 (1) perhaps goes beyond what was laid down in the pre-statute cases which appear to have based the defender's liability where he had been held out as a partner by others upon aspects of his conduct which might be said to have authorised, expressly or impliedly, the representations made by persons other than himself.[52] While the Partnership Act 1890 in section 14 (1) has introduced the idea of knowingly suffering a holding out by others, it has not defined the meaning of that phrase and cases since the passing of the Act have not arisen to elucidate it.[53] In *Walter* v. *Ashton*,[54] Byrne J. said, " If a man allows his name to be held out to the public as being the person responsible for the transaction in question, he can be held liable in consequence of this holding out or in consequence of his conduct, although he may not have originally authorised the act because he has not taken the steps which he should take to stop the unauthorised use of his name."

The general principle is not too difficult to state but, once it has been allowed to introduce an entirely passive state on the part of the person held out, questions arise first, as to the means by which he may extricate himself from the position of being passively held out and, second, if he has so extricated himself the effect of that upon transactions which have already taken place on the faith of the representations made and before he has had the opportunity of correcting them. Neither question has been exhaustively dealt with by the courts since the passing of the Partnership Act 1890. The first question, which has been discussed in the preceding paragraphs, can possibly be answered to some extent by the application of the word " knowingly " in " knowingly suffers " as that word has been interpreted in *Tower Cabinet Company* v. *Ingram*.[55] No person who is held out as a partner by others will be liable as a partner on that account

---

[51] In *Newsome* v. *Coles* (1811) 2 Camp. 617, Lord Ellenborough held that the defendants were not bound to apply for an injunction. That, however, was a special case in that the use of the defendants' names in the firm had continued after its dissolution had been communicated to the firm's customers.

[52] *Newsome* v. *Coles, supra; Spooner* v. *Browning* [1898] 1 Q.B. 528; *Collingwood* v. *Berkeley* (1863) 15 C.B.(N.S.) 145; *Maddick* v. *Marshall* (1864) 17 C.B.(N.S.) 829; *Martyn* v. *Gray* (1863) 14 C.B.(N.S.) 824.

[53] With the exception of *Tower Cabinet Co.* v. *Ingram* [1949] 2 K.B. 397 discussed *infra* pp. 152–153.   [54] [1902] 2 Ch. 282 at p. 294.

[55] [1949] 2 K.B. 397; and see *supra* p. 137.

unless he knows that he is being so held out.[56] It appears from the English decisions that " knowingly " will be fairly strictly interpreted and that even if his lack of knowledge originated in carelessness he is not to be held as having knowingly suffered the holding out,[57] though it is difficult in Scots law to reconcile that rule with the case of *J. & C. Gardner* v. *Anderson and Another*.[58] On the other hand, once knowledge has been attributed to him, and before he has taken any steps, whatever those may be, to establish that he is not " suffering " the representations made about him by others, what is his liability for any transactions between third parties and the firm in that interim period? If he delays to take the appropriate steps to extricate himself from liability, it is clearly possible to argue that during such delay he has knowingly suffered the representations, but the practical realities of the situation in which he is placed entail that there will inevitably be some lapse of time between the holding out coming to his notice and the steps taken by him to show that he dissociates himself from the holding out, even if he acts with reasonable urgency. During that interim period, however short, transactions may take place between the firm and third parties on the faith of the holding out. It is thought that there must be a reasonable time given to the defender after the representations have come to his knowledge in which to make manifest in some way his dissent, and that he will not be held liable for transactions with the firm which have taken place during that reasonable time. To decide otherwise in these circumstances would be to impose liability upon him for a holding out of which he admittedly had knowledge but which he had been given no reasonable opportunity to controvert. That would undoubtedly be in conflict with the common law as it existed before the passing of the Partnership Act 1890,[59] and it is thought that in interpreting the words " knowingly suffers " in section 14 (1) the court might regard it as controlling not only the point of time at which the knowledge was acquired but also that at which the defender had a reasonable opportunity to communicate his disclaimer of the representations which had come to his knowledge. The defender cannot properly be held to have " suffered " something which he has taken reasonable steps to disclaim.

The interpretation of the word " suffers " may also have a considerable bearing on the kind of action which will be demanded of the defender if he seeks to avoid the liability which will otherwise rest upon him as a result of the representations of others. No reported decision appears to have

---

[56] Lindley, *op. cit.* pp. 101–102; Pollock, *op. cit.* p. 53.

[57] *Tower Cabinet Company* v. *Ingram, supra.*

[58] *Supra* n. 49. Though this decision is pre-statute that increases rather than diminishes its force since the pre-statute cases mainly appear to lay stress on the defenders having authorised the holding out by other persons, and the suggestion made by the Lord President in *J. & C. Gardner* v. *Anderson and Another* that the defender was put on his inquiry whether his name was being falsely held out has therefore considerable interest.

[59] See *e.g. Mollwo, March & Co.* v. *Court of Wards* (1872) L.R. 4 P.C. 419 at p. 435: " Where a man holds himself out as a partner, or *allows* other parties to do it, he is then properly estopped from denying *the character he has assumed*, and upon the faith of which creditors may be presumed to have acted " (italics supplied).

had this question under consideration. Lindley [60] considers that the present state of the law affords no clear guidance and adds that " until the law is settled prudence suggests such an application (*i.e.* for injunction) after remonstrance has proved useless." It is implied in that view that there may be some interval of time during which remonstrance has taken place and before an injunction or interdict has been applied for and that, notwithstanding that, the defender will not be held liable for transactions occurring during that period on the ground that he has not knowingly suffered the holding out. It is thought for the reasons previously advanced [61] that that is a correct view; and if during that period the defender has confined himself to " remonstrance " with those who are so holding him out, it may well be that, on their persisting despite his remonstrance, he will only extricate himself from liability on the ground of knowingly suffering the holding out, if he applies for interdict against the parties so holding him out. If he brings to the notice of third parties who are dealing with the firm on the faith of the representations, the fact that he dissents from them, he will be free from liability to them upon subsequent transactions and he may be free from liability under transactions which have already taken place on the faith of the holding out, if he communicated with the third parties concerned with reasonable promptitude after the holding out had come to his knowledge. But there are obvious perils in ensuring that the defender has in fact communicated directly with all third parties whose dealings with the firm may involve him in liability and a public advertisement of his disclaimer of association with the firm will likewise require to be proved to have been brought to the notice of the third parties affected.

The absence of authority as to the interpretation of the word " suffers " in section 14 (1) had led to a reference by the editors of the later editions of *Lindley on Partnership* to the cases reported on the effect of the word when included in a covenant undertaken by the lessee on a lease.[62] In *Barton* v. *Reed* [63] Luxmoore J. said:

> " The word ' suffer ' is a wide term. It seems to me to be wider than the word ' permit.' . . . The word in the case before me is ' suffer ' and at any rate that must cover allowing something to be done which the covenanter had the complete power to prevent. It is said that a covenant not to suffer a thing to be done imposes no liability on the covenanter to take legal proceedings to prevent the thing being done. I think that is putting the case too high."

As to the necessity to raise legal proceedings in order to avoid being held as " permitting " an infringement of the covenant, Atkin L.J. said in an earlier case,[64]

[60] *Op. cit.* p. 102.
[61] *Supra* p. 140.
[62] *Op. cit.* p. 103 n. 28.
[63] [1932] 1 Ch. 362 at p. 375.
[64] *Berton* v. *Alliance etc. Investment Co.* [1922] 1 K.B. 742 at p. 761. See also *Atkin* v. *Rose* [1923] 1 Ch. 522, *per* Lawrence J. at pp. 532–533.

" For my part I am inclined to think that in certain circumstances a man may permit the continuance of an act if he can prevent it by taking legal proceedings and refrains from doing so. . . . But all the circumstances must be taken into account, and where there is a reasonable doubt whether legal proceedings to stop an act will be successful, where, for example, the person has taken legal advice and comes to the conclusion that he could not reasonably expect legal action to be successful, then he does not permit the act by abstaining from legal proceedings."

The dangers of construing a word occurring in a statute by reference to cases which interpret the same word in an entirely separate context are apparent; nor do the qualifications mentioned by Atkin L.J. readily appear applicable to a case where a person has been falsely held out by others as a partner, since if the false holding out can be established it is difficult to envisage circumstances in which his resort to legal proceedings to restrain other persons from persisting in it would be likely to be attended with failure. Nevertheless, the decisions are interesting for the view taken of the scope of the word " permit " [65] and the wider scope of the word " suffer," [66] and it may be that on the analogy of these decisions where a person has remonstrated without success with those who hold him out as a partner he will be required to initiate proceedings for inter-dict if he is to escape liability, at least if he has not made his disclaimer known to third parties who may transact business with the firm on the faith of the holding out.

Holding out by a person of his intention to become a partner

If the words or conduct relied on by a third party merely evince the intention of the defender to become a partner in a firm, that is not holding himself out in such circumstances as to impose liability upon him as a partner in that firm.[67] " As persons intimating an intention to become partners are not taken to be such until their intention has given place to performance, so neither do those who hold themselves out as intending partners incur the liability which would attach to them if they held themselves out as partners *de facto*." [68] An inchoate partnership arrangement will afford no relevant basis for an action for damages by one of the parties involved against the other who refuses to proceed with the partnership.[69] It is, therefore, not a circumstance upon which a third party can justly claim to rely in doing business with a firm that another person has by words or conduct held himself out as having the intention to become a

---

[65] *Berton* v. *Alliance etc. Investment Co.* (*supra*).
[66] *Barton* v. *Reed* (*supra*).
[67] *Bourne* v. *Freeth* (1829) 9 B. & C. 632; *Reynell* v. *Lewis* (1846) 15 M. & W. 517; *Wyld* v. *Hopkins* (1846) 15 M. & W. 517.
[68] Clark, *op. cit.* I, p. 59.
[69] *Finlayson* v. *Fisher* (1828) 6 S. 419 where averments that the defender, after verbal communings with the pursuer as to entering a partnership and after instructions had been given to draw up the contract, refused to execute it were held irrelevant to support a claim for implement of the contract or alternatively damages.

partner in that firm. Equally, it would appear that a person who has knowingly suffered himself to be so held out, will not be subjected to liability on that ground.

Fraudulent inducement to hold oneself out as a partner

" It is no defence against an action on the ground of liability from holding out, that the defender was induced so to do by the fraudulent representations of parties other than the pursuer." [70]   An inducement whether fraudulent or by way of irresponsible promises which causes a person to hold himself out or suffer himself to be held out as a partner is an irrelevant consideration in a question with third parties who have acted on the faith of the holding out and have had no part in the fraud or the promises [71]; for, even if the person so held out holds an indemnity from those to whom he lends his name, he will yet be liable to third parties who have acted on the faith of the representation since his name has no less induced them to act in reliance on his credit.   Indeed Lindley takes the view that even where the existence of such an indemnity is known to the third party it does not legally follow that he ought to escape liability because they are aware of it.   " His name does not induce credit the less on account of his right to be indemnified by others against any loss falling in the first instance on himself; and although, in the case supposed, he cannot be believed to be a partner, the lending of his name does justify the belief that he is willing to be responsible to those who may be induced to trust to him for payment." [72]   Lindley, however, notices the case of *Alderson* v. *Pope* [73] in which Lord Ellenborough held " that where there was a stipulation between A, B & C who appeared to the world as copartners, that C should not participate in the profits and loss and should not be liable as a partner, C was not liable as such to those who had notice of this stipulation, and that notice to one member of the firm was notice to the whole partnership."   On that decision Lindley comments [74] that the words " should not be liable as a partner " are ambiguous and is of the opinion that if they mean that C was to be indemnified by A & B the decision was in error whereas " if they meant that C would not be liable at all to third parties for the acts of A & B, then a more difficult question would arise, but the decision would be in accordance with the Partnership Act 1890, s. 8. . . . " [75]

It is perhaps unnecessary to invoke the aid of section 8 to support the

---

[70] Clark, *op. cit.* I, p. 59. In addition to the decisions referred to *infra*, Clark cites *Watson* v. *Smith,* Dec. 17, 1806; Hume 756 as authority. That case, however, was not one of holding out, but of actual partnership.

[71] *Collingwood* v. *Berkeley* (1863) 15 C.B.(N.S.) 145; *Maddick* v. *Marshall* (1864) 17 C.B. (N.S.) 829; *Ellis* v. *Schmoeck* (1829) 5 Bing. 521; *Ex p. Broome,* 1 Rose 69.

[72] Lindley, *op. cit.* pp. 100–101, citing *Brown* v. *Leonard* (1816) 2 Chitty 120.

[73] (1808) 1 Camp. 404.

[74] *Op. cit.* p. 101.

[75] " If it has been agreed between the partners that any restriction shall be placed on the power of any one or more of them to bind the firm, no act done in contravention of the agreement is binding on the firm with respect to persons having notice of the agreement."

pre-statute decision in *Alderson* v. *Pope*. The fact that a third party is aware that a person held out as a partner is entitled to be indemnified by his copartners does not necessarily conflict with his character as a partner, since if he were *de facto* a partner his right to be indemnified would not make him any less a partner nor allow him to escape liability as such to third parties.[76] If, however, a third party is aware that a person whose name is lent to a concern is in no way to be liable as a partner to those who deal with the firm, it is difficult to see how he can be said to be held out as a partner under section 14 (1) or how third parties dealing with the firm can claim to have given credit to the firm on the faith of the holding out.   Even if the knowledge is ambiguous, it could be argued that a third party is put on his inquiry before he relies upon the representation.[77]

Problems of holding out arising on a change in the composition of the firm

When a partnership has been dissolved by the death or retirement of one of the partners, the remaining partners may continue to carry on the business under the firm name used by the former partnership. Where the dissolution of the former firm has been occasioned by the death of one of its partners the Act expressly declares [78]

> " Provided that where after a partner's death the partnership business is continued in the old firm-name, the continued use of that name or of the deceased partner's name as part thereof shall not of itself make his executors' or administrators' estate or effects liable for any partnership debts contracted after his death."

It will be observed that the subsection is concerned with the exclusion of any personal liability on the part of the executors of the deceased partner on the score of that holding out.   Since death operates as a dissolution of the partnership and is regarded as a public fact there is no necessity for notice to the creditors of the firm regarding the death in order to extricate the estate of the deceased partner from " liability for firm debts contracted subsequently to the death."   There is no room for the application of the doctrine of holding out in such cases.[79]   In the common law prior to the passing of the Partnership Act 1890 it was considered that if the name of the deceased parter was continued in his firm by his executor, the estate would be bound for subsequent debts and the executor would render himself liable to the beneficiaries.[80] The case of *Vulliamy* v. *Noble*,[81] upon

---

[76] " But there is nothing to prevent one or more partners from agreeing to indemnify the others against loss, or to prevent full effect from being given to a contract of partnership containing such a clause of indemnity."   Lindley, *op. cit.* p. 83, citing *Bond* v. *Pittard* (1838) 3 M. & W. 357; *Geddes* v. *Wallace* (1820) 2 Bligh 270.

[77] As he was, for another reason, considered to be put on his inquiry in *Paterson Bros.* v. *Gladstone* (1891) 18 R. 403.

[78] s. 14 (2).

[79] *Christie* v. *Royal Bank of Scotland* (1839) 1 D. 745; (1841) 2 Rob.App. 118; *Warner* v. *Cunningham* (1815) 3 Dow 76; *Webster* v. *Webster* (1791) 3 Swanst. 490 n.; *Devaynes* v. *Noble* (1839) 1 Mer. 529.   And see Lindley, *op. cit.* p. 108; Clark, *op. cit.* I, p. 59.

[80] Clark, *loc. cit.*

[81] (1817) 3 Mer. 593.

which Clark relied for the proposition was special on its facts and rather supports the more limited proposition that if a partner appoints his co-partner as his executor and then dies, and if the executor continues to carry on the business, his actings in so doing, or some of them, may be regarded as referable not to him *qua* partner but *qua* executor of the deceased partner and in consequence subject the assets of the deceased to liability for debts contracted by the business after his death.   Such a case is described by Lindley [82] as " quite exceptional," and it seems clear that the Partnership Act 1890, s. 14 (2), entirely destroys the generality of the statement made by Clark.   It is equally true that the statutory words will not exclude liability in the special circumstances on which *Vulliamy* v. *Noble* was decided, though normally the fact that the executor is the surviving partner of the firm will not of itself impose liability on the deceased partner's estate for debts incurred subsequently to his death. [83]

Retired partner

In this case there is much more scope for the application of the doctrine of holding out, " Where a person deals with a firm after a change in its constitution, he is entitled to treat all apparent members of the old firm as still being members of the firm until he has notice of the change." [84] It is, however, expressly provided [85] that a notice in the *London Gazette*, in the case of a firm having the principal place of business in England or in the *Edinburgh Gazette* in respect of a firm having its principal place of business in Scotland, will be sufficient notice to those who have had no dealings with the firm prior to the dissolution or change notified therein. Where persons have had prior dealings with the firm before the date of dissolution or change, notice thereof to such persons must be established to have been in fact given. [86]   While these rules suggest counsels of prudence to a retiring partner, failure to observe them will not auto-matically entail that he has been held out as a partner after he has retired. The doctrine remains an equitable one and therefore if a partner is not known by the third party to have been a partner in the firm before his retirement, it will not be necessary to give notice of retirement to that third party in order to avoid the retired partner becoming liable to him for firm debts contracted after his retirement, [87] even when, subsequent to his retirement, the third party discovers that he was formerly a partner. [88]   A retiring partner is, however, liable for debts which are incurred in order to complete a transaction entered into before his retirement.   Liability in that case does not arise under the provisions of section 14 or section 36 of

[82] *Op. cit.* p. 632.
[83] *Farhall* v. *Farhall* (1871) L.R. 7 Ch.App. 123; *Owen* v. *Delamere* (1872) L.R. 15 Eq. 134.
[84] Partnership Act 1890, s. 36 (1).
[85] *Ibid.* s. 36 (2).
[86] *Pillani* v. *Motilal* (1929) 45 T.L.R. 283.
[87] Partnership Act 1890, s. 36 (3); *Carter* v. *Whalley* (1830) 1 B. & Ad. 14.
[88] Bowstead, *Agency* (13th ed.) pp. 454–455; *Tower Cabinet Co.* v. *Ingram* [1949] 2 K.B. 397. In that case, the words of s. 36 (3) of the Partnership Act 1890 were construed as becoming effective from the date of retirement.

the Partnership Act 1890 but is founded on the general doctrine of holding
out, as it applies in agency. A person who accredits an agent, in this case
the firm, is personally barred from denying the existence of that agency in
a question with a third party who has acted upon the faith of the agency
before he has had any notice of revocation of the authority.[89]

Apparent partner

It may appear from the firm name that a person is a member of the firm,
and the continued use of that firm name after he has retired will amount to
a representation that he is still a partner. As in other cases of holding
out the question is one of fact but the retired partner's liability as a partner
in such circumstances will continue if he fails to give due notice of his
retirement in terms of section 36 of the Partnership Act 1890. If he has
given due notice of his retirement but either authorises or knowingly
suffers the remaining partners to carry on the business under the former
firm name from which it appears that he is a partner, his position is more
doubtful. On this question little or no help is obtained from the Scottish
decisions, but the English law is discussed by Lindley [90] who cites a number
of English pre-statute decisions [91] in illustration. It is difficult to detect
any useful general consideration from an examination of these decisions
which will serve as a guide where the distinguishing line may be drawn
between cases involving the former partner in liability and those where he
escapes liability. The only safe generalisation to make is that since holding out is to be decided as a question of fact, it is for the court in each
case to assess the facts as a jury might regard them. Moreover, it is at
least doubtful whether the pre-statute decisions offer any help even of that
general nature in cases arising after the passing of the Partnership Act
1890. Such cases will now be decided upon an interpretation of sections
14 and 36 of the Partnership Act 1890 and, though pre-statute decisions
may be consulted in arriving at a true construction of statutory provisions,[92]
the usefulness of the pre-statute authorities above cited [93] for this purpose
does not seem to be great.

Change of partners

When a partner retires from the firm and a new partner is assumed in
his place, the firm name continuing unchanged, it can be argued that the
general considerations as to whether the retired partner continues to be
held out as a partner apply. Lindley, however, sounds a warning note
against too uncritical an application of the doctrine.

[89] *Scarf* v. *Jardine* (1882) 7 App.Cas. 345; Bowstead, *op. cit.* pp. 454–457.
[90] *Op. cit.* pp. 105–107.
[91] *Williams* v. *Keats* (1817) 2 Stark. 290; *Dolman* v. *Orchard* (1825) 2 Car. & P. 104; *Brown* v.
Leonard (1816) 2 Chitty 120, all cases where liability was imposed on the former partner.
In *Newsome* v. *Coles* (1811) 2 Camp. 617 and *Ex p. Central Bank of London* [1892] 2 Q.B.
633, a case which was decided on the pre-statute law in spite of the date of the report, where
the former partner escaped liability.
[92] *Bank of England* v. *Vagliano* [1891] A.C. 107, *per* Lord Herschell at pp. 144–145.
[93] *Supra* n. 91.

" Suppose A and B carry on business under the name of X & Co. Neither A nor B holds himself out as a member of that firm to anyone who does not know his connection with it.   If therefore, A retires from the firm, and gives no notice of his retirement, he will still be liable to old customers who knew of his connection with X & Co. and who continue to deal with it on the faith that A is still a member of it: but A will incur no liability to new customers of X & Co. who have never heard of him. Further, if on A's retirement C joins B, and B and C carry on business as X & Co., even an old customer of X & Co. who goes on dealing with it without notice of A's retirement or C's ad-mission, cannot truly say that A ever held himself out as a partner with C or with both B and C; and, consequently, even an old customer cannot maintain an action against A, B and C jointly for a debt con-tracted by X & Co. after A's retirement.   The old customer can, in the case supposed, sue A and B on the ground that he dealt with X & Co. on the faith of A and B being still the members of that firm; or he can sue B and C on the ground that they are his real debtors; but he must elect between A and B on the one hand and B and C on the other." [94]

The view propounded by Lindley in the passage above quoted is founded upon the decision in *Scarf* v. *Jardine* [95] where the facts were some-what similar to those set forth in the quotation.   In *Scarf* v. *Jardine*, however, while the customer of the old firm continued to deal with and became a creditor of the new firm, having received no notice either of the retirement of A or of the assumption of C as a partner, he was thereafter made aware of these facts and sued the new firm for the debt thus incurred to him and on their bankruptcy, proved against their estate.   He later attempted to recover the same debt against A, the partner of the old firm, who had retired but it was held that, since he had elected to sue the new firm, he could not subsequently sue A who was not a member of the new firm.   The authority of *Scarf* v. *Jardine* as illustrative of the law on both sides of the border is much diminished by the observations which fell from the judges in the Scottish case of *Blacks* v. *Girdwood and Another* [96] where the facts were similar to those in *Scarf* v. *Jardine* save that the credi-tor, in lodging his claim in the sequestration of the new firm, reserved his claim against the partner of the old firm who had retired and later with-drew his claim in the sequestration before it was ranked and raised an action against the retired partner.   The court held that, even if the pursuer had been bound to elect between the old and the new firms, he had not in fact made that election and was therefore entitled to recover from the retired partner.   In so deciding the court were not necessarily to be re-garded as either approving or disapproving of the decision in *Scarf* v. *Jardine*; but the Lord Justice-Clerk (Moncreiff) examined the doctrine of election propounded in the English decision and observed,[97]

[94] Lindley, *op. cit.* p. 107.
[95] (1882) 7 App.Cas. 345.
[96] (1885) 13 R. 243.   [97] *Ibid.* at p. 248.

" I do not think that there is any doctrine in the law of Scotland corresponding to that recognised in the law of England and founded upon the distinction between a claim resulting from estoppel and a claim on contract; the effect of which I understand to be that a creditor in right of the two claims cannot claim in respect of both, but must make his election, so that one obligant, who is not the less the debtor, escapes altogether from the obligation which he had incurred. I do not think that that doctrine is in accordance with the law of Scotland. . . . "

That view was concurred in by Lord Young [98] and Lord Craighill [99] though Lord Rutherford Clark, while concurring in the decision in the case, commented

" With regard to the general question, if I felt myself bound to decide it, I should have held that the decision in the case of *Scarf* was authoritative and binding upon me; for I can see no difference between the law of England and that of Scotland in the matter of partnership which would entitle me to reject the decision as inapplicable. . . . At the same time, while I should have followed it, I should have thought that in doing so I was departing from the well-known law of Scotland on the subject." [1]

The opinions of the majority in *Blacks* v. *Girdwood and Another*, though *obiter*, are weighty. They proceed, however, upon the assumption that the judges in *Scarf* v. *Jardine* were applying rigorously a technical rule of pleading in English law and on that basis, the majority of the Scottish judges found the decision inapplicable in Scotland. It is not so clear that they would have so regarded the more refined *ratio* suggested for the English decision by Lindley where he states,[2] " The reason why he could not have (held the retired partner liable) was that J(ardine) did not in fact contract with the new firm upon the faith that S(carf) was a member of it. If it had been proved that J had so contracted he could, it is apprehended, have sued S and the other members of the new firm and have proved S to have been a partner by estoppel." This *ratio* becomes more acceptable in terms of Scots law but it is thought that the " election " which is made the foundation of the decision in *Scarf* v. *Jardine* and is accepted as such by Lindley,[3] is more satisfactorily explained as a novation by the customer of his contract. That in fact is suggested in the case of *Scarf* v. *Jardine* itself as a *ratio* for the decision.[4] It involves an agreement between the customer, the partner who has retired and the new firm by means of which a new agreement is made substituting a new obligation for that formerly

---

[98] *Ibid.* at pp. 249–250.
[99] *Ibid.* at p. 251.
[1] *Ibid.* at p. 252. The Lord Ordinary (Kinnear) had earlier affirmed in somewhat stronger terms that " the principles upon which they (the Judges in *Scarf* v. *Jardine*) proceeded are common to the law of both countries " (*ibid.* p. 246).
[2] *Op. cit.* p. 233.
[3] *Op. cit.* pp. 107–108; p. 233.
[4] (1882) 7 App.Cas. 345 at p. 351.

held against the old firm. Such a novation or, more precisely, delegation, may, but need not, be express. It may be implied from a course of conduct of dealings between the customer and the new firm.[5] But it is to be noticed that the delegation may speak with one of several different voices in the circumstances under consideration. It may release the retired partner; it may accept in place of his obligation, the obligation of the continuing partners of the firm as formerly constituted or it may accept in place of the original obligation, the obligation of the continuing partners with the added obligation of the new partner who had joined them.[6] If that is the correct interpretation of the decision of *Scarf* v. *Jardine*, it is thought that it may be regarded as persuasive authority in a case before a Scottish court. Its application will, however, be much more limited than it would be if the decision proceeded upon a doctrine of election between a claim based on estoppel and one based on contract, as Lord Moncreiff regarded it: for, if it is based rather upon delegation, and the delegation is not matter of express agreement, the courts will be slow to infer it from a course of dealing. " It is laid down by all the authorities that delegation is not to be presumed, and I think the doctrine even goes further, and that there is a strong presumption against it " [7] and " the narrowest cases with regard to novation and delegation occur when there is a change in a business, either complete by the transference of the business to another, or partial, by the retirement of a partner with or without the introduction of a new one." [8] The liability of the retired partner for a debt due by the firm at the time he retired will rarely be discharged on the ground that the customer must be held to have accepted the obligation of the firm as newly constituted by the continuing partners in place of his original claim and only in exceptional cases. The substitution will be upheld if the delegation is in express terms and was also upheld in *Ker* v. *McKechnie* [9] where a customer had a balance at credit on account with a firm of bankers and after having notice of the death of one of the partners of the bank, subscribed a docquet written in the books of the bank to the effect that his account had been settled and the balance paid to him while simultaneously obtaining a credit receipt for the balance standing to his credit. The court, by a majority, took the view that this transaction was reasonably explained only on the footing that the customer had discharged his claim against the representatives of the deceased partner.[10] The fact that the customer has accepted interest from the new

[5] Partnership Act 1890, s. 17 (3).

[6] *Scarf* v. *Jardine, supra* n. 4.

[7] *Per* Lord President Inglis, *McIntosh & Son* v. *Ainslie* (1872) 10 M. 304 at p. 309.

[8] Gloag, *Contract* (2nd ed.) p. 259.

[9] (1845) 7 D. 494.

[10] The decision was described as a narrow one and the customer's act in signing the docquet was probably the determining feature. In England the fact that a customer has taken a new deposit receipt for a former one after he was aware of the death of one of the partners has been held not to amount to delegation, while if the customer in these circumstances transfers his balance at his credit on current account to a deposit receipt on the request of the continuing partner this will amount to delegation (*Re Head* [1894] 2 Ch. 236).

firm will not by itself be sufficient to infer delegation [11] nor will the fact
that he has accepted a dividend on the bankruptcy of the new firm.[12] The
cases examined have been concerned with the question of delegation where
it is contended that a new obligation has been accepted for the original
obligation of a deceased partner and his co-partners. If the partner has
retired and a new partner has been assumed in his place the inference
that the customer who accepts the obligation of the new firm has relin-
quished his claim against the retired partner is more possible to draw,
where he obtains the obligation of the newly assumed partner as a result.[13]
But the adoption by the creditor of the new firm as his debtor will not of
itself alone deprive him of his rights against the old firm.[14] That circumstance is no more than an element tending to furnish evidence of an
agreement to take the obligation of the new firm in place of the former
obligation. It will, therefore, have no such effect if the creditor in adopting the new firm expressly reserves his rights against the old firm,[15] or
where the creditor did not know that the retired partner was a member of
the old firm and thus liable under the original obligation, since in these
circumstances he cannot be taken to have had the intention of discharging
the obligation of that person.[16] On the other hand, where the creditor
knows of the change in the composition of the firm and continues to deal
with it over a long period making no claim on the retired partner, that will
be strong evidence of delegation.[17] But each case will be decided on the
whole circumstances pertaining to it and the tendency of the courts in
such cases is to lean in favour of the creditor. Thus it has been held that
any significance to be attached to the actings of the creditor will vary
according to the view which the court takes as to the degree of familiarity
with business displayed by the creditor.[18] In deciding such questions an
important factor is that in accepting the obligation of the new firm the
creditor has obtained the obligation of any newly assumed partner as it
were in exchange for the obligation of the old partner which he has released.
It is thus important to decide whether the creditor who has continued a
course of dealing with the new firm is entitled to hold the newly assumed
partner liable for the debts of the former firm. This question is examined
at a later stage.[19]

[11] *Campbell* v. *Cruickshank* (1845) 7 D. 548; *Muir* v. *Dickson* (1860) 22 D. 1070; *Morton's Trs.* v. *Robertson's Judicial Factor* (1892) 20 R. 72.
[12] *Morton's Trs.* v. *Robertson's Judicial Factor, supra* (since the death of the partner in this case occurred in July 1890, the provisions of s. 17 (3) of the Partnership Act 1890 did not apply); *Smith* v. *Patrick* (1901) 3 F.(H.L.) 14 (a case decided after the passing of the Partnership Act 1890).
[13] *Bilborough* v. *Holmes* (1876) 5 Ch.D. 255.
[14] *Re Head, Head* v. *Head* [1893] 3 Ch. 426; *Rouse* v. *Bradford Banking Co.* [1894] 2 Ch. 32; [1894] A.C. 586; *Matthews* v. *Ruggles Brise* [1911] 1 Ch. 194.
[15] *Bedford* v. *Deakin* (1818) 2 B. & Ald. 210; *Jacomb* v. *Harwood* (1751) 2 Ves.Sen. 265; *Blacks* v. *Girdwood and Another* (1885) 13 R. 243.
[16] *Robinson* v. *Wilkinson* (1817) 3 Price 538.
[17] *Thompson* v. *Percival* (1834) 5 B. & Ad. 925 at pp. 932–933; *Hart* v. *Alexander* (1837) 2 M. & W. 484; *Ex p. Executors of James Douglas* [1930] 1 Ch. 342 at p. 350.
[18] *Conquest* (1875) 1 Ch.D. 334.
[19] *Infra* Chap. VII, pp. 258 *et seq.*

Sleeping partner

The term " sleeping " or " dormant " partner is used in a variety of meanings, so that it is difficult to apply any general rule of law to the class without first defining the term. Clark states, " Dormant or sleeping partners are properly such as, whether known or unknown, have no power of agency to bind the firm; but, while liable for its obligations and entitled to share profits, are passive as to its management." [20] In the same passage of his work on *Partnership*, Clark notes that the phrase is frequently used also to denote " latent " partners, *i.e.* those whose existence is not known to the world but who, sharing in the profits, are either *de facto* partners, or are liable as though they were and who normally are concerned in the management of the firm's affairs along with those whose names appear as its partners, and *quasi* partners who, though not partners *inter socios*, are yet liable for the obligations of the firm " by reason of something which they have done or permitted to be done." [21] The position of such partners will be examined in more detail at a later stage [22] when the distinction drawn by Clark may require to be kept in view. In the context of holding out, however, the special features which require consideration arise from the fact that there is no disclosure to those dealing with the firm of the connection of the " partner " with the firm. It follows, therefore, that such rules as may be propounded will apply to latent partners and also to sleeping partners if their existence as members of the firm is not disclosed. The same rules will have no application to a person who has held himself out, or knowingly suffered himself to be held out, as a partner since his connection, real or fictitious, with the firm has then been disclosed to the persons who transact business with the firm and, since the other instances of *quasi* partnership which are mentioned by Clark no longer are extant in the law,[23] *quasi* partners are not embraced within the principles which are stated in the following paragraph.

Where a sleeping, or dormant, partner retires and the firm name does not disclose that he was a partner, then it cannot be said that the continued use of the same firm name after his retirement in any way holds him out or represents him as a partner of the firm; but if customers who dealt with the old firm were aware of his connection with it, the continued use of the name of the old firm will operate as a holding out of him as a continuing partner *to such customers* and in order to extricate himself from liability for the obligations of the new firm he must give to such persons due notice that he has retired.[24] But where the firm name of the old firm merely comprises the surname of the retiring partner and the subse-

---

[20] *Op. cit.* I, p. 67.
[21] A person who holds himself out as a partner or knowingly suffers himself to be so held out might therefore be subsumed under the description of a *quasi* partner though the wider connotations of the term have disappeared from the law since the passing of the Partnership Act 1890. See *supra* Chap. III, p. 60.
[22] *Infra* Chap. XI, pp. 499 *et seq.*
[23] *Supra* pp. 60–63.
[24] Partnership Act 1890, s. 36; *Evans* v. *Drummond* (1801) 4 Esp. 89; *Farrar* v. *Deflinne* (1844) 1 Car. & K. 580; *Tower Cabinet Co.* v. *Ingram* [1949] 2 K.B. 397.

quent words, " and Company," it has been held that the continued use
of that name will not normally hold the retiring partner out as continuing
as a partner of the firm or liable as such.[25]   It is emphasised that these
principles are rigidly confined to the case where the question is whether
an undisclosed partner who has retired is to be considered as continuing
to be held out as a partner in the firm.   In that context they give rise to
little difficulty.   They are not, however, to be regarded as enunciating any
rule as to the ostensible authority with which a sleeping partner endows
his copartners as to the management of the firm's business, while he in
fact continues to be a partner, albeit a sleeping partner, of the firm.   Such
questions are concerned with a different type of holding out, namely the
holding out by a principal of a person as his authorised agent and will
be examined at a later stage.[26]

Effect of registration of particulars of firm under Registration of Business Names Act 1916

The Registration of Business Names Act 1916, in imposing the duty
upon certain firms of registering particulars as to the firm and the members
who comprise it, makes no direct impact upon the doctrine of holding
out in partnership.   The Act is concerned to ensure that the particulars
are registered in appropriate cases and to impose sanctions where its
provisions are not observed.   There is some relevance, however, to the
law of holding out (first) in the provisions which require any firm the name
of which does not consist of the names of all the partners, to register the
names of its partners [27] and any changes in the firm [28] and (secondly)
in the requirement that such firms must disclose the names of the partners
on trade catalogues, trade circulars and business letters on which the firm
name appears.[29]   It is obvious that, in general, these provisions lessen the
danger of a person who is not a partner being held out as one, though
they do not entirely obviate the risk, and the Act gives no remedy on the
ground that its provisions have been contravened.

The provisions which have been referred to, however, have some
bearing upon the position of the liability of a retiring partner to persons
who transact business with the firm after he has retired.   No liability
will be incurred by the retiring partner merely on the ground that he has
not personally verified that on his retirement the entire existing stocks of
the firm's letter headings have had his name as partner of the firm
blocked out.   Thus when a firm communicated with a third party regarding a transaction upon a sheet of their writing paper on which the retired
partner's name had not been deleted, the retired partner was not regarded
in these circumstances as having " knowingly suffered " the holding out.[30]

[25] *Townsend* v. *Jarman* [1900] 2 Ch. 698; *Burchell* v. *Wilde* [1900] 1 Ch. 551.
[26] *Infra* Chap. XI, pp. 499 *et seq.*
[27] s. 1.
[28] s. 6.
[29] s. 18 as amended by the Statute Law Revision Act 1927 and the Companies Act 1947,
      Sched. 9, Part II.
[30] *Tower Cabinet Co.* v. *Ingram* [1949] 2 K.B. 397.

Liability would, however, have been imposed on him if he had authorised the use of that writing paper.[31]   Again where a retiring partner does not personally ensure that his name is removed from the particulars registered in the Register of Business Names in relation to the firm from which he is retiring, he will not on that ground alone be held liable as a partner of the continuing firm in a question with new creditors.[32]   In *Bishop* v. *Tudor Estates* [33] a firm of estate agents which was registered under the Registration of Business Names Act 1916 had been dissolved.   The business continued to be carried on under the same firm name by one of the former partners.   The retired partner had failed to inform the registrar of the change and the plaintiff had seen a certificate of registration showing the names of the two partners.   It was held by Denning and Hodson L.JJ. affirming the decision of Barry J. that the retired partner had held himself out as a partner in terms of section 14 (1) of the Partnership Act 1890. It does not, however, appear to be arguable that the converse will hold good and that the registration of the particulars of a change in the composition of the firm, will amount to a notice thereof to the former customers of the firm or to the public at large.[33a]   The register is a public one in the sense that it may be consulted by any member of the public upon payment of a fee but the contents of the register are not published by the registrar.   Before a third party could be barred from holding the retired partner liable it would be required to be brought home to him that he had consulted the register prior to entering the transactions, had knowledge of the change and thus did not deal with the firm in reliance on the retired partner's credit.

Liability in delict

The doctrine of holding out is based upon the concept that a third party has entered into contractual relationship with the firm in reliance on the credit of the person held out to be a partner.   There is therefore no sound foundation in theory for extending the application of the doctrine so as to impose liability on a person held out as a partner for the delicts or *quasi* delicts committed in the course of the firm's business.   No reported case in Scotland lends any support for the proposition that a person will be liable in such circumstances because he has held himself out as a partner.   In the English courts one early case [34] decided that a retired partner was liable for damage done by a cart which was the property of his former firm and upon which his own name still appeared.   In *Smith* v. *Bailey* [35] it was later decided that the ground of decision of the earlier case as reported could not be supported; and indeed it is difficult to see in what sense a party who complains that his property has been damaged by

---

[31] *Ibid.*
[32] *Ibid.*
[33] [1952] C.L.Y. 2493; also reported in [1952] *Current Property Law* 807.
[33a] See *Welsh & Another* v. *Knarston & Others*, 1972 S.L.T. 96.
[34] *Stables* v. *Eley* (1825) 1 Car. & P. 614.
[35] [1891] 2 Q.B. 403.

collision with a cart which has been negligently driven can argue that he gave credit to a person whose name appeared upon the cart. The appearance of his name on the cart may be regarded as one of a series of facts and circumstances to which regard must be paid in deciding whether he is in fact a partner of the firm to whom the cart belongs and if he is held to be a partner, then he may be liable along with his copartners vicariously for the fault of the servant of the firm who negligently drove the cart but there is no warrant for the plaintiff in such cases maintaining an action against him on allegations that he has been held out as a partner since the plaintiff cannot bring himself within the class of persons to whom that principle applies, namely, those who have altered their condition on the faith of the holding out being true.[36]

Liability of the firm in cases of holding out

Section 14 of the Partnership Act 1890 deals exclusively with the liability of the individual who has been held out as a partner for the obligations of the firm and is silent upon the question of the liability of the firm for the debts incurred by an individual whom the firm has itself held out as a partner. It has been earlier suggested that the reason for this omission is that the firm's liability in such cases rests upon the general law affecting principal and agent and exhibits no features which are peculiar to the law of holding out in partnership.[37] If that explanation be accepted, the question of liability of the firm in these cases is not one which falls to be regulated in terms of the Partnership Act 1890. Alternatively, if it is agreed that holding out of an individual by the firm as a partner exhibits features which are attributable to the law of partnership alone, and which have not been detected by the writer, then liability in such cases has been left to be regulated by the pre-existing common law.[38]

The general principles of agency are applied to the relationship of a partner with his firm.

> " Every partner is an agent of the firm and his other partners for the purpose of the business of the partnership; and the acts of every partner who does any act for carrying on in the usual way business of the kind carried on by the firm of which he is a member bind the firm and his partners, unless the partner so acting has in fact no authority to act for the firm in the particular matter, and the person with whom he is dealing either knows that he has no authority, or does not know or believe him to be a partner." [39]

In the case of a person who is an actual partner of the firm, then, his author-

---

[36] *Quarman* v. *Burnett* (1840) 6 M. & W. 508. See also Clark *op. cit.* I, p. 58: " But in as much as the ground of liability is, that credit has been obtained by means of the party's name, it is necessary that the holding out shall have taken place, and that the creditor shall have been in the knowledge thereof prior to his entering into the contract sued upon, otherwise it could not be said that he had been misled by the conduct of the supposed partner."

[37] *Supra* p. 127.

[38] Partnership Act 1890, s. 46.

[39] Partnership Act 1890, s. 5.

ity to bind his principal in the obligations which he undertakes as a partner is clearly stated and the section also provides that, in spite of any limitations placed on his authority to impose liability on the firm as his principal, he has an ostensible [40] authority which may exceed the limits imposed *inter socios* and which may be relied upon, in a question with the firm, by a third party who transacts business with him as such partner and without knowledge of the limits placed upon his authority. The effect of the section upon the dealings of an actual partner in the business of his firm must be deferred for further discussion at the appropriate place [41] but for the moment it is sufficient to draw the inference from section 5 that if an individual is held out by a firm as a " partner " of that firm, he is in effect being held out as an agent for the firm. It follows that the firm so holding him out will be held liable for the transactions into which he enters with third parties who transact with him as if he were a partner and on the faith of the representations made by the firm to that effect.

That principle is apparent from the opinions of the judges in *Moyes* v. *Cook* [42] though the report of the case is imperfect and presents puzzling features. The case appears to have arisen from an arrestment lodged by a creditor of the person held out in the hands of the firm of which he was represented to be a partner. In an action of furthcoming raised by the creditor, the magistrates, after proof, held that the debtor was not a partner and that the firm had no funds or effects belonging to him. On advocation of the cause, the Lord Ordinary sustained the decision of the magistrates, but his decision was reclaimed against when the First Division held it proved that the debtor had been held out as a partner. It is difficult to see how that fact militated against the decision of the magistrates. The fact that the debtor had been held out as a partner of the firm did not entail that the firm held any of his funds or effects and indeed effectively disposed of any contention that the arrestment had attached any share in the partnership belonging to the debtor, since *ex hypothesi* the fact that the debtor had been held out as a partner clearly demonstrated that he was not in fact a partner. The court appears to have conflated the issue raised before the magistrates on the arrestment, upon which it is respectfully submitted that the magistrates and the Lord Ordinary had arrived at the correct decision, with a wider issue not raised in the proceedings for the furthcoming, namely that the firm was liable for the original debt contracted by the person held out which formed the basis of the arrestment in the hands of the firm. Lord Craigie indeed, in the single sentence which is reported as his opinion even further widened the issue. He said, " If the case is to be viewed as one of fraud, there are sufficient grounds for subjecting the company in payment of the debt." Lord Gillies said,

---

[40] The terminology in this area of law is ill-defined. See Bowstead, *Agency* (13th ed.), pp. 249 *et seq.*, where the editors prefer to describe the authority here in question as an " apparent authority." The term " ostensible " has, however, been so commonly used to describe it that it has been retained here.

[41] See *infra* Chap. VII, pp. 208 *et seq.*

[42] (1829) 7 S. 793.

" This is not a question between partners.   It is a question between the
company and the public.   If the company hold out a rich man as a partner,
the company will be liable as if he were so; and in like manner, if a rich
company hold out a poor man as a partner, they shall be responsible as
if he were truly so."

While the facts upon which the decision is reported to be based appear
to be imperfectly narrated, the statement of principle in Lord Gillies'
opinion appears to be of general application.   It is, however, perhaps
rather widely stated.   The question arising in cases where the firm has
held out an individual as a partner is not truly a question between the
firm *and the public* but between the firm and those third parties who have
transacted business with the party so held out in reliance upon the representations of the firm that he was a partner and therefore authorised to
bind the firm as its agent in his dealings with third parties.   No doubt,
had the circumstances in which the original debt was contracted been
reported upon, Lord Gillies' reference to " the public " might be read in
that sense.

In these cases of holding out by the firm of an individual as partner,
it is particularly important to examine closely the circumstances of the
transaction between the third party and the person held out before holding
the firm liable thereon.   In all such cases neither the holding out by
itself nor even that holding out coupled with knowledge thereof by the
third party will be conclusive as to the firm's liability.   In addition it must
be established that the third party contracted with the person held out
as a " partner " and not as an individual.   In other words the simple
issue of holding a person out as a partner is overlaid with the additional
question whether, since to represent a person as a partner is to hold him
out as the agent of the firm, his subsequent conduct is to be regarded as
referable to his agency or as referable to his own private affairs.   That
question arises also for decision in cases involving the actings of an actual
partner as imposing liability upon his firm,[43] and it is an equally important
feature in the cases involving this aspect of holding out as a partner.   Thus
when a banker had discounted bills accepted by a person trading under a
company name in Greenock part of whose business related to the affairs
of a venture in Nassau which he conducted in partnership with a person
in London and part of which was his own separate business, it was held
that, since the banker had discounted other bills similarly accepted on
behalf of the partnership, the London partner was liable upon the bills.[44]
It is possible, indeed, to take the view that once it has been proved that a
person has been held out as a partner of the firm and that the third party
dealing with him has done so in reliance on that representation, the question
of the firm's liability must be decided upon precisely the ground which
would suffice to impose liability upon them for the actings of an actual
partner; and that the criteria used by the courts in determining whether

[43] *Infra* Chap. VII, pp. 243 *et seq.*
[44] *McNair* v. *Fleming,* July 5, 1805, F.C.; Feb. 5, 1807, F.C.; affd. (1812) 5 Pat. 639.

the actual partner of a firm has contracted with a third party within his apparent or ostensible authority [45] as a partner and more fundamentally whether he has entered into the transaction as a partner or as an individual, [46] are equally applicable in the case of a person held out by the firm as a partner.

The question whether a firm which holds out a person as its partner will be liable vicariously for the wrongful acts and negligence of that person which cause loss or injury to a third party does not appear to have been raised in any of the reported cases. It is thought that such cases may also depend upon the fundamental idea that the firm in holding him out as a partner is in effect holding him out as an agent. [47] Third parties who deal with him on the faith of the firm's representations will, it is thought, be entitled to hold the firm liable for the wrongful acts committed by the person held out as a partner provided that the act is committed within the ambit of the dealings which fall within his apparent authority even though he has no authority to do what he has done. [48] That will apply even to forgery if the forgery is perpetrated during the performance of business within his apparent authority [49] but not where the transaction is beyond the scope of the apparent authority. [50] It seems, however, that the fact that the person is merely held out as a partner and is not *de facto* a partner will set some limit upon the vicarious liability of the firm for his delicts and *quasi* delicts. While the firm will be vicariously liable for the wrongful acts and omissions of one of its partners acting in the ordinary course of the business of the firm or with the authority of his copartners, [51] so that the firm may be liable in an action of damages for loss and injury caused by the negligent driving of a partner about the firm's business, [52] it is difficult to ascribe such liability to a firm which has held a person out as a partner, since the injured party cannot claim that he in any way relied upon the holding out. Any vicarious liability of the firm will be in no way distinguishable from such as may arise in agency.

[45] *Paterson Bros.* v. *Gladstone* (1891) 18 R. 403; *Walker* v. *Smith* (1906) 8 F. 619.

[46] *Royal Bank of Scotland* v. *Greenock Bank*, Nov. 14, 1794, F.C., affd. (1797) 3 Pat. 595; *Miller* v. *Douglas*, Jan. 22, 1811, F.C.; *Jardine* v. *McFarlane* (1828) 6 S. 564; *White* v. *McIntyre* (1841) 3 D. 334; *Crum & Co.* v. *McLean* (1858) 20 D. 751; *Tupper & Carr* v. *Rowell* (1858) 20 D. 758.

[47] " The principal having delegated the performance of a certain class of acts to his agent, it is not unjust that he, being the person who has appointed an agent, and who will have the benefit of his efforts if successful, should bear the risk of his exceeding his authority in matters incidental to the doing of the acts the performance of which has been delegated to him ": *per* Collins M.R. in *Hamlyn* v. *John Houston & Co* [1903] 1 K.B. 81 at pp. 85–86. See also Atiyah, *Vicarious Liability in the Law of Torts*, p. 117.

[48] *Boyd* v. *Craster* (1864) 10 L.T. 480; *Summers* v. *Solomon* (1857) 7 E. & B. 879; *Trueman* v. *Loder* (1840) 11 A. & E. 589.

[49] *Uxbridge Permanent Benefit Building Society* v. *Pickard* [1939] 2 K.B. 248.

[50] *Ruben & Ladenburg* v. *Great Fingall Consolidated* [1906] A.C. 439.

[51] Partnership Act 1890, s. 10.

[52] *Moreton* v. *Hardern* (1825) 4 B. & C. 223.

CHAPTER VI

THE RIGHTS AND DUTIES OF PARTNERS *INTER SE*

THE rights and duties of the members of a partnership *inter se* will in many respects be the result of the express terms of the contract which has been entered into among them or the terms which may be implied therein as a result of the circumstances in which the contract has been entered into or in accordance with the provisions of the Partnership Act 1890; but, overriding the terms of the contract, and indeed to a considerable degree determinative whether the contract actually is one of partnership, is the concept of agency which is essential to the relationship. " Every partner is an agent of the partnership; and his rights, powers, duties and obligations are in many respects governed by the same rules and principles as those of an agent. A partner virtually embraces the character of both principal and agent." [1] It is this quality of mutual agency where " two or more persons stand *mutually* to each other in the relation of principal and agent, —that is to say, where each of them is capable of binding and being bound by the others," [2] which is productive of most of the legal specialities of the relations of partners among themselves. [3]

The mutuality of the partners' position as in turn principal and agent can be discerned in section 5 of the Partnership Act 1890—

> " Every partner is an agent of the firm and his other partners for the purpose of the business of the partnership; and the acts of every partner who does any act for carrying on in the usual way business of the kind carried on by the firm of which he is a member bind the firm and his partners, unless the partner so acting has in fact no authority to act for the firm in the particular matter, and the person with whom he is dealing either knows that he has no authority, or does not know or believe him to be a partner."

The limits of the partner's authority

Even where the partnership establishes that a partner transacting with a third party had no actual authority to do so and the unauthorised act of the partner was not later ratified, the third party may in certain circumstances rely upon the ostensible [4] authority of the partner as described in

---

[1] Story, *Partnership*, p. 1.

[2] Clark, *op. cit.* I, p. 50.

[3] In certain circumstances a mutual agency may exist without a partnership being inferred from it: *William Baxter & Son* v. *Aitchison & Co.* (1841) 3 D. 391. The existence of mutal agency is therefore not conclusive evidence of a partnership but the absence of mutual agency will be strong evidence that no partnership exists.

[4] A better term would be " apparent." Though " ostensible " is generally used to denote this type of case, it is also sometimes used to denote an " implied " authority which is an actual authority implied by the law to exist as well as an " apparent " authority where *ex hypothesi* no authority in fact exists.

section 5. The section in effect provides for, and delimits, that authority in two broad propositions:

(1) An act done by a partner on behalf of his firm, if it is done in order to carry on the partnership business in the usual way will prima facie bind the firm and the other partners, even if the act was not authorised by them; whereas

(2) if such act was not done for carrying on the partnership business in the usual way the firm and the other partners prima facie are not bound by it. These propositions are, however, further refined and qualified in the section. The first is qualified in that if the partner in fact had no authority to bind the firm in the particular transaction and the third party dealing with him knew that he had no such authority or did not know or believe him to be a partner at all, and therefore did not deal with him on the footing that he was a partner, the prima facie liability of the firm and the other partners is displaced and they are not liable for the act. The second proposition is subject to the qualification that the firm and the other partners will be liable for an act of the partner which was not done for carrying out the partnership business in the usual way, if the partner so acting has actual authority from his copartners to do so or if they subsequently ratify his act. While both propositions are broadly concerned with the " authority " of a partner as agent for his firm, the first deals with his apparent,[5] or ostensible, authority and thus is in essence one which concerns the relations of the firm and its partners with third parties since it deals with a situation where the partner's act is unauthorised in a question arising among the partners themselves. The second deals with circumstances where an act which does not fall within the partner's apparent authority may yet be binding upon the firm and his copartners either because it is within his actual authority, express or implied,[6] or because it has later been ratified by the firm. Detailed examination of both propositions is more appropriately to be undertaken when the relationship of the firm with third parties is considered,[7] since both are primarily designed to delimit the area of apparent authority of the partner and questions of apparent authority are essentially questions arising between the principal and third parties.[8]

The partners as cautioners

It is sometimes said that the rights and obligations of the partners in addition to their dependence upon the concept of mutual agency, are also to some extent ascribable to cautionry.[9] In section 9 of the Partnership Act 1890 it is provided—

[5] " Apparent authority which negatives the existence of actual authority ": *Rama Corporation* v. *Proved Tin & General Investments* [1952] 2 Q.B. 147 at p. 149.
[6] " Where it results from a manifestation of consent that he should represent or act for the principal expressly or impliedly made by the principal to the agent himself."—Bowstead, *Agency* (13th ed.) Art. 22 (1) (*a*), pp. 61–62. See further on implied authority Arts. 28–30, pp. 72–82.
[7] *Infra* Chap. VII, pp. 241 *et seq.*
[8] Bowstead, *op. cit.* p. 63.
[9] Bell, *Comm.* II, p. 507; *Fortune* v. *Young*, 1918 S.C. 1; Lillie, *The Mercantile Law of Scotland* (6th ed.), p. 225.

" Every partner in a firm is liable jointly with the other partners, and in Scotland severally also, for all debts and obligations of the firm incurred while he is a partner; and after his death his estate is also severally liable in a due course of administration for such debts and obligations, so far as they remain unsatisfied, but subject in England or Ireland to the prior payment of his separate debts."

Setting aside for consideration at a later stage the treatment of the estate of a deceased partner,[10] it is clear from the terms of section 9 that in Scotland a partner is liable *in solidum* for the firm debts. That liability rests upon the partners " more as guarantors than as principals." [11] That entails that the individual partners are conditional debtors if the firm does not discharge its obligations when due and perhaps is slightly inconsistent with, or at least modifies, the concept that the partners *themselves* stand on a mutual footing of principal and agent, one with another as is provided in section 5. It may be that the desire of those responsible for the drafting of the Act to notice the peculiarities of the Scots law with the utmost brevity and compendiousness within the framework of an Act designed primarily to codify the English law has resulted in a slight logical inconsistency in the presentation of the Scots law on this topic, though it must be confessed that the logical distinction between the two concepts is not always clearly preserved in the decisions of the Scottish courts prior to the passing of the Act.   Nor does it seem possible to resolve the inconsistency on the reasoning advanced by Clark [12] that " according to the theory of Scottish law, the partners are agents for the *quasi* person of the firm, and not mutually for each other; and the liabilities they incur are not for the obligations of each other, but for those of the firm in consequence of their being its guarantees or sureties," because there is nothing in the general law affecting the relationship of the agent with his principal, be the latter the firm or his copartners, which would entail that the partner *as agent* accepted responsibility as a cautioner for his principal.   It appears that in both England and Scotland the relationship is merely analogous to agency or perhaps more properly that it is one of agency to which has been added the obligation of standing cautioner for the debts of the principal.

The responsibility of the individual partners at once [13] arises when the firm fails to pay its debts but in order to recover from the individual partner, the debt must first be constituted against the firm.[14]   If the firm has been dissolved all the former partners within the jurisdiction must be called in the action for recovery of the debt.[15]   Where one of the partners has paid a firm debt, he is entitled to claim relief *pro rata* from his co-

---

[10] *Infra* pp. 293–294.
[11] Bell, *Comm loc. cit.*
[12] *Op. cit.* I, p. 297.
[13] Bell, *Comm.* II, p. 507.
[14] Bell, *Prin.* § 356.
[15] *McNaught* v. *Milligan* (1885) 13 R. 366; *Muir* v. *Collett* (1862) 24 D. 1119.

partners.[16] In cases where one partner admits the liability of the firm while the others dispute it, the court will grant decree against him and reserve his claim of relief against the firm and his copartners. In such a case it will not be necessary first to constitute the claim against the firm.[17] A bill of exchange or promissory note by the firm in the firm name constitutes the debt represented by it against the firm and each partner individually and, on the appropriate steps having been taken, is a warrant for the execution of diligence against each individual partner.[18]

Uberrima fides

There is a considerable weight of authoritative statement supporting the view that partnership is a contract *uberrimae fidei*. Clark [19] and Bell [20] both describe it as a contract of " exuberant trust." In *Green v. Howell*,[21] Cozens-Hardy M.R. said, " Partnership is a contract in which *uberrima fides* is required." On the other hand, other judicial dicta refer to a fiduciary relationship [22] or an especial degree of good faith [23] as of the essence of partnership. At times the notions of *uberrima fides* and fiduciary duty are conflated and presented as if they were equivalents.[24] Any use of the terms " *uberrima fides* " and " fiduciary relationship " as interchangeable is liable to lead to confusion. The concept of *uberrima fides* is an importation in Scots law from the law of England and from the general mercantile law of the late eighteenth century and involved the introduction of the rule, not formerly applicable in Scotland, that in contracts of insurance an especial duty of full disclosure of material facts was imposed.[25] The principle of full disclosure thus introduced is one which affects the attitude of the parties at the time of negotiating the terms of the contract into which they are about to enter. The concealment or misrepresentation of material facts, therefore, strikes at the validity of the contract itself.[26] In the insurance cases and in the other cases in Scots law where *uberrima fides* has been held to import a duty of disclosure,[27]

---

[16] Partnership Act 1890, s. 4. (2).
[17] *Elliot* v. *Aitken* (1869) 7 M. 894.
[18] *Thomson* v. *Liddell & Co.*, July 2, 1812, F.C.; *Wallace* v. *Plock & Logan* (1841) 3 D. 1047.
[19] *Op. cit.* I, p. 182.
[20] *Comm.* II, p. 508.
[21] [1910] 1 Ch. 495.
[22] " The fiduciary relation which partners owe to one another ": *Dean* v. *McDowell* (1878) 8 Ch.D. 345, *per* Cotton L.J. at p. 354.
[23] *Blisset* v. *Daniel* (1853) 10 Hare 493, *per* Page Wood V.-C. at p. 522.
[24] *Per* James L.J. in *Dean* v. *McDowell*, *supra* at p. 350: " It is quite clear that in partnership matters there must be the utmost good faith and that there is to that extent a fiduciary relation between the parties."
[25] See Gloag, *Contract* (2nd ed.), pp. 496–497 and the argument reported in the cases of *Stewart* v. *Morrison* (1779) Mor. 7080 and *Watt* v. *Ritchie* (1782) Mor. 7074 cited by Gloag.
[26] *Life Association* v. *Foster* (1873) 11 M. 351, *per* Lord President Inglis at p. 359; Gloag, *op. cit.* p. 497.
[27] *e.g. Fletcher* v. *Grant* (1878) 6 R. 59 (agreement to marry); *Mackay* v. *Lord Advocate*, 1914, 1 S.L.T. 33 at 37–38 (duty to disclose any exceptional difficulty known to the employer when inviting tenders for execution of work); *Mackenzie* v. *Blakeney* (1879) 6 R. 1329 (failure by client instructing stockbroker in the sale of shares to inform latter that they were not saleable on the stock exchange).

there is no support for the proposition that there is a continuing duty of disclosure during the activities which the contract itself regulates.   Even the duty of an insured under an indemnity policy such as a fire insurance policy, to disclose subsequent material facts relating to the risk arises in consequence of the periodic renewal of the contract of insurance and does not affect the validity of the subsisting contract.[28]   But in the contract of partnership the duty of disclosure may be imposed either (1) at the stage of negotiating and entering the contract itself or (2) in the course of the actings of the partners under the contract of partnership which has been entered into.   In by far the greater number of cases where *uberrima fides* has been invoked, the issue has arisen as to the actings of the parties under the contract.

Uberrima fides and fiduciary relationship

It is apparent that in the concept of *uberrima fides* there is included the idea that a fiduciary relationship subsists between the parties; but a fiduciary relationship alone will not suffice to explain the full extent of the duties imposed by a requirement of *uberrima fides*.   While the more exigent principle (*uberrima fides*) may be regarded as comprehending the less exigent (fiduciary duty), there is no clear authority for holding the converse to be true, or even for holding the two to be equivalents.   The distinction is firmly drawn by Gloag,[29] and indeed it is difficult to see how the notion of *uberrima fides* has come to be applied to the actings of the partners in the partnership business unless on the very insufficient ground that many of the cases have been concerned with disclosure by a partner to his co-partners of material facts.   But if such non-disclosure were to import a requirement of *uberrima fides* the consequence of that non-disclosure would be to render the contract of partnership in itself voidable, and that argument has never been advanced in such cases and indeed is obviously untenable.[30]   Moreover, while the element of fiduciary relationship in contract is not to be regarded as confined to a category of cases to which that feature has been traditionally attributed but may be extended to other and analogous situations in the law of contract,[31] there is no authority for a similar extension of the application of the doctrine of *uberrima fides* in Scots law, and indeed it has been suggested that this doctrine has been recognised in Scots law at the expense of some violence to the fundamental principles on which the law of Scotland is founded.[32]

---

[28] *Law Accident Insurance Society Ltd.* v. *Boyd & Another*, 1942 S.C. 384.

[29] *Contract* (2nd ed.).   Compare Chap. XXX (Contracts *Uberrimae Fidei*) and Chap. XXXI (Contracts by Parties in Fiduciary Positions).

[30] It may be that a failure by a partner to disclose material facts to his co-partners will be a ground for dissolution of the contract.   It has certainly been held in England that dishonest conduct of a partner (even when unconnected with the business of the partnership) will justify dissolution: *Carmichael* v. *Evans* [1904] 1 Ch. 486.   But it has never been held to make the contract of partnership voidable.

[31] *Nocton* v. *Lord Ashburton* [1914] A.C. 932 *per* the Lord Chancellor (Haldane).

[32] Smith, *A Short Commentary on the Law of Scotland*, pp. 835–837.   See also *op. cit.* pp. 297–298.

If that view be correct, it is an added argument against any extension of the application of the doctrine in Scots law.

Negotiations or proposals to enter a partnership. On the whole it may be argued that there is no very convincing case made out for the explanation of the incidence of the rights and duties arising between partners *inter se* during the course of the partnership in terms of the doctrine of *uberrima fides*. That doctrine, however, is prima facie, at least, more readily applicable to the dealings between parties which lead up to their entering into partnership with one another. If a new partner is assumed into a business and has been induced to become a partner by misrepresentation as to the nature and resources of the business, he will be entitled to reduce the contract, and recover any capital which he has contributed to the firm, even though the misrepresentation was not fraudulent. In *Ferguson* v. *Wilson* [33] the Lord Justice-Clerk (Macdonald) said,

> " There having been misrepresentation, will it save the defender from a judgment rescinding the contract that no fraud has been proved? I do not think so. The pursuer asks nothing but that it be rescinded, and to that I consider him to be entitled. I adopt the language of Lord Watson in the case of *Adam* v. *Newbigging* holding it to apply directly to this case. He says: ' I entertain no doubt that these representations, although not fraudulently made, are sufficient to entitle the respondent to rescind the agreement. . . . He relied, and was entitled to rely, upon the assurances which he had received as to the satisfactory condition of the business, until he became aware of the true state of the facts '."

In the absence of fraud or deceit in the representations made, the incoming partner will have no relevant ground of action in damages [34]; his remedy is to reduce the contract and claim restitution of the capital which he had been induced to contribute. The decisions cited, however, do not depend upon any speciality of the law of partnership but apply the general principles of the law of contract. The Partnership Act 1890 provides in section 41—

> " Where a partnership contract is rescinded on the ground of the fraud or misrepresentation of one of the parties thereto, the party entitled to rescind is, without prejudice to any other right, entitled—
>
> (*a*) to a lien on, or right of retention of, the surplus of the partnership assets, after satisfying the partnership liabilities, for any sum of money paid by him for the purchase of a share in the partnership and for any capital contributed by him, and is
>
> (*b*) to stand in the place of the creditors of the firm for any payments made by him in respect of the partnership liabilities, and
>
> (*c*) to be indemnified by the person guilty of the fraud or making the misrepresentation against all the debts and liabilities of the firm."

---

[33] (1904) 6 F. 779 at p. 783. See also *Adam* v. *Newbigging* (1888) 13 App.Cas. 308 at p. 320.

[34] *Manners* v. *Whitehead* (1898) 1 F. 171.

It is not clear from any reported decision whether an existing trader or partner owes a duty of disclosure of all material facts to a person who is contemplating entering into partnership with him. It has been suggested that since that duty lies upon the promoter of a company who invites the public to subscribe for shares therein, " it must almost necessarily be held that it lies equally on one who invites an individual to join him in partnership." [35] There are undoubtedly points of analogy between the two cases. For example if one of the parties to a proposed partnership has in the course of negotiating the purchase of property for the intended firm, received a commission, he is liable to account for it to the firm when it has been formed.[36] But it will be observed that the remedy of the aggrieved party in such circumstances as in similar cases arising with the promoters of joint stock companies,[37] is to demand an accounting for the profit made. There is no right on the part of the aggrieved party to treat the contract of association as voidable, as would be the case, *e.g.* in a contract of insurance where the proposal form did not disclose all material facts. The doctrine of *uberrima fides* would if applicable render the contract of association voidable and not merely allow the aggrieved party to insist upon an accounting. It is thought, therefore, that the analogy drawn by Gloag from the case of the company promoter goes no further than to establish a fiduciary relationship between the parties [38] and does not warrant the imputation of the doctrine of *uberrima fides* unless that term is loosely used as equivalent to fiduciary duty.

Actings of partners during the course of the partnership

Under section 29 of the Partnership Act 1890 it is provided—

" (1) Every partner must account to the firm for any benefit derived by him without the consent of the other partners from any transaction concerning the partnership, or from any use by him of the partnership property, name or business connection.

(2) This section applies also to transactions undertaken after a partnership has been dissolved by the death of a partner, and before the affairs thereof have been completely wound up, either by any surviving partner or by the representatives of the deceased partner."

In the immediately succeeding provision of the Act, in section 30, it is further provided—

" If a partner, without the consent of the other partners, carries on any business of the same nature as, and competing with, that of the firm, he must account for and pay over to the firm all profits made by him in that business."

---

[35] Gloag, *Contract* (2nd ed.) p. 507.
[36] *Fawcett* v. *Whitehouse* (1829) 1 Russ. & M. 132.
[37] *Hichens* v. *Congreve* (1828) 1 Russ. & Myl. 150; *New Brunswick Ry.* v. *Muggeridge* (1860) 1 Drew. & Sm. 363; *Central Ry. of Venezuela* v. *Kisch* (1867) L.R. 2 H.L. 99.
[38] Indeed this is later recognised by Gloag himself; for he treats the relationship of " promoter and company " under the heading of " Contracts by Parties in Fiduciary Positions ": *Contract* (2nd ed.), Chap. XXXI, pp. 517–518.

The two sections, taken together, place the partner in a fiduciary position analogous to that occupied by an agent in regard to his principal, and as in the case of agency the emphasis in the prohibition is upon the secret nature of the profit. In that restricted sense it may be said that there is a duty upon a partner in his dealings with his copartners of disclosure of material facts,[39] and it assuredly assumes that equitable rules apply to the parties in association so as to ensure that " they shall zealously act and co-operate for the common good, and that they shall not place their individual interests before those of the company."[40] But it is impossible to argue from that premise that the partners are under a universal duty of disclosure of material facts such as would be imposed upon them if their obligations and duties were governed by the principle of *uberrima fides* or " exuberant trust " and indeed the decisions on this part of the law fall far short of establishing any such proposition.

Secret profits. The terms of section 29 (1) of the Partnership Act 1890 reflect the position of the partner as agent for his firm.

> " It is quite clear that if an agent uses property with which he has been entrusted by his principal so as to make a profit for himself out of it, without his principal's consent, then he is accountable for it to his principal. . . . Likewise with information or knowledge which he has been employed by his principal to collect or discover, or which he has otherwise acquired for use of his principal, then again if he turns it to his own use so as to make a profit by means of it for himself, he is accountable." [41]

But the fact that a partner has engaged in an activity which has brought him profit will not by itself render him accountable to his co-partners for that profit in every case. Section 29 (1) confines his duty to account to cases of benefit derived by him without the consent of the other partners " from any transaction concerning the partnership " or " any use by him of the partnership property, name or business connection." The subsection clearly reflects the words of Lindley L.J., as he then was, in *Aas* v. *Benham* [42] but in the sentence following upon his enunciation of that principle, Lindley L.J. adds " To hold that a partner can never derive any personal benefit from information which he obtains as a partner would be manifestly absurd." It has been held that a partner is not accountable to the firm for profits made by him where the assets of the firm had not been employed in acquiring these profits.[43] On the other hand, the terms of the contract of copartnery may affect the question whether the partner

[39] *Inglis* v. *Austine* (1624) Mor. 14562.
[40] Clark, *op. cit.* I, p. 182.
[41] *Phipps* v. *Boardman* [1965] Ch. 992, *per* Lord Denning M.R. at pp. 1018–1019. See also Lord Guest in the same case on appeal: [1967] A.C. 46 at p. 115. " It is a rule of universal application that no one, having such duties to discharge, shall be allowed to enter into engagements in which he has, or can have, a personal interest conflicting, or which may conflict, with the interests of those whom he is bound to protect " *per* Lord Cranworth, L.C. in *Aberdeen Railway* v. *Blaikie Bros.* (1854) 1 Macq. 461 at p. 471.
[42] [1891] 2 Ch. 244 at pp. 255–256.
[43] *Fuller* v. *Duncan* (1891) 7 T.L.R. 305.

is accountable or not. Where the contract stipulated that " the salary or other benefit derived by either partner from any office he may hold during the continuance of the partnership shall be treated as forming part of the profits," it was held that the pay and allowances earned by a partner as an officer in the Army were due to be accounted for to the firm on a true construction of the contract.[44] In a sheriff court case, however, the contract of copartnery obliged the defender to devote his whole time and attention to the business of the firm and not to engage in any other business without the pursuer's consent. The partnership carried on a wine and spirit business in Glasgow. The defender purchased other licensed premises in another part of Glasgow which he carried on for his own behoof. It was held that the profits earned thereby were not accountable to his partner, the pursuer, since neither the partnership assets nor its business connection were used in the business which the defender had acquired.[45]

" *Any benefit derived.*" Those words are very wide in their import. They will render the offending partner accountable to the firm for a commission received when purchasing property on behalf of the firm.[46] Nor may he retain for his own benefit a profit which he has made by selling goods which are his own property to the firm if he has not the consent of his copartners to the transaction [47] or in concluding the negotiations which have been entrusted to him by his firm on more advantageous terms than those which he was authorised to accept.[48] The duty to account for such benefits arises from the fact that they have been taken clandestinely without the knowledge of his copartners and to remove the obligation of the partner to account for the profit, the knowledge in the possession of his copartners must be full and complete. In *Dunne* v. *English* [49] the defendant pleaded that his copartner, the plaintiff, had knowledge of the benefit derived by the defendant and there was evidence that the plaintiff was aware that the defendant had some interest in the purchase additional to his share in the known profit of £10,000 made by the firm. The plaintiff, however, did not actually know what the precise extent of that interest was and since the defendant had to that extent gained a personal benefit which was not disclosed to his copartner, it was held that the latter might claim a share in the undisclosed profit. The case makes it clear also that when a partner is authorised to sell the property of the firm at a specified price, he cannot plead that authority as implying a waiver on the part of his copartners of their right to share in the profit from a more advantageous price if that has been secured.[50]

These principles have much in common with the law of agency and

---

[44] *Carlyon-Britton* v. *Lumb* (1922) 38 T.L.R. 298.
[45] *Williamson* v. *Taylor* (1898) 14 Sh.Ct.Rep. 303.
[46] *Pender* v. *Henderson* (1864) 2. M. 1428; *Fawcett* v. *Whitehouse* (1829) 1 Russ. & M. 132.
[47] *Bentley* v. *Craven* (1853) 18 Beav. 75.   [48] *Dunne* v. *English* (1874) L.R. 18 Eq. 524.
[49] (1874) L.R. 18 Eq. 524 and see *Const* v. *Harris* (1824) Turn. & R. 496, *per* Lord Eldon L.C. at p. 525.
[50] *Dunne* v. *English* (*supra*); *Parker* v. *McKenna* (1874) L.R. 10 Ch. 96; *De Bussche* v. *Alt* (1878) 8 Ch.D. 286, 317; *Re Olympia Ltd.* [1898] 2 Ch. 153.

indeed in *Cassels* v. *Stewart* [51] Lord Blackburn ascribed the doctrine as applying in partnership to the fact that the partner is an agent and as such owes to his firm the duties which an agent owes to his principal. " One partner cannot be permitted to retain a benefit for himself to the exclusion of his partners in relation to any matter connected with the partnership in which they were interested as well as he." [52] The principle has often been said to rest upon the fiduciary nature of the duties owed by a partner to his firm. The circumstances in which such a duty may arise must, however, be closely regarded. In *Piddocke* v. *Burt*,[53] Chitty J. expressed the opinion that he would be straining the law if he held that a partner receiving money on account of himself and his copartners received it in a fiduciary capacity towards his copartners. In making that pronouncement, however, the learned judge was considering the competency of enforcing an order for payment of money received by a writ of committal or attachment under the English Debtors Act 1869 and his dictum is to be read as referable to that technical point of English procedure and not as denying the broad fiduciary duty imposed upon the partner to account for the money so received by him to his copartners.[54] The true basis of the general rule is that where a partner has secured a clandestine personal benefit in transacting the business of his firm he has been guilty of " a breach of faith with his copartners," [55] and the same reasoning was applied in the English courts in *Carter* v. *Horne* [56] where the plaintiff and the defendant agreed to contribute equally to the purchase of land, the defendant being entrusted with the negotiations. The land was encumbered for debt which was to be discharged out of the money paid for the purchase. In the course of the negotiations the defendant arranged with the creditors in these incumbrances that certain sums due thereunder for interest would not be claimed and the creditors agreed with the defendant that the advantage of these allowances would be for his own individual benefit. It was held that he must account for them to the plaintiff since the purchase was for the equal benefit of both parties and on a mutual trust between them. No case appears to be reported upon the liability of a partner receiving a bribe from a third party to induce the partner to enter a contract on behalf of his firm with the third party, but it can scarcely be in doubt that the rules applicable in agency would apply. The firm may recover the bribe from the partner who received it [57] and any damages sustained from the partner and the party bribing him jointly and severally,[58] and the firm may rescind the contract.[59] If the bribe

---

[51] (1881) 8 R.(H.L.) 1 at p. 7.
[52] *Per* the Lord Ordinary (Mackenzie) in *Pillans Bros.* v. *Pillans* (1908) 16 S.L.T. 611 at p. 614.   [53] [1894] 1 Ch. 343 at p. 346.
[54] See *per* Lord Atkinson in *Gordon* v. *Holland* (1913) 82 L.J.(P.C.) 81 at p. 88.
[55] *Per* L.J.-C. Inglis in *Pender* v. *Henderson* (1864) 2 M. 1428 at p. 1440.
[56] (1728) 1 Eq.Cas.Abr. 17. See also *Inglis* v. *Austine* (1624) Mor. 14562 and the cases on agency cited in Lindley, *op. cit.* p. 339, n. 23.
[57] *Lister & Co.* v. *Stubbs* (1890) 45 Ch.D. 1.
[58] *Corporation of Salford* v. *Lever* [1891] 1 Q.B. 168.
[59] *Taylor* v. *Walker* [1958] 1 Lloyd's Rep. 490. See also Bowstead, *Agency* (13th ed.), art. 116, pp. 370–372.

received is not in money but in property the partner will be liable for the highest value which the property had while in his possession.[60]

"*Any transaction concerning the partnership.*" The fiduciary duty of good faith is operative within the sphere of activity of the business carried on in association.[61] Thus where three persons entered a partnership to purchase certain land and re-sell it, and two of the partners acquired adjacent ground, it was held that the third partner was not entitled to an accounting for the profit made on the re-sale of the adjacent ground.[62] Similarly the purchase by one partner of the share of another in the firm was held in the English pre-statute decisions not to be any part of the business of the firm.   Where the contract of copartnery did not forbid such a purchase, it was permissible for one partner to acquire the share without informing the remaining partners and without giving them an opportunity to acquire the share.[63] It is possible that the authority of these decisions is assailed by the terms of section 29 (1) which renders the partner liable to account for profit made in " any transaction concerning the partnership." Whereas the earlier cases proceed upon the *ratio* that the partner is accountable for profit only on those transactions which form part of the business of the firm, it would be difficult to regard a purchase or acquisition upon any other terms of the share of a partner otherwise than as a " transaction concerning the partnership "; but the point does not appear to have been decided.[64]

It will be noticed that what is in question under section 29 (1) is the partner's liability to account to his copartners for any profit which he has made. This is important. It may be that the action complained of is otherwise a breach of the contract of copartnery, either in its express terms, or in those implied in the contract by law.   Section 29 (1) does not preclude the normal remedies available on a breach of contract. But even had the two partners in *Trimble* v. *Goldberg*[65] been forbidden by the contract of copartnery to purchase the ground adjacent to that sought to be acquired by the partnership, it would not have followed necessarily that the third partner might have claimed an accounting under section 29 since the purchase was not a transaction affecting the partnership under the first subsection nor could it be regarded as carrying on a business which competed with that of the firm under section 30.[66]

---

[60] *McKay's Case* (1875) 2 Ch.D. 1; *Nant-y-Glo & Blaina Iron Works Co.* v. *Grave* (1878) 12 Ch.D. 738; *Pearson's Case* (1877) 5 Ch.D. 336; *Eden* v. *Ridsdale's Railway Lamp & Lighting Co. Ltd.* (1889) 58 L.J.Q.B. 579.

[61] *Aas* v. *Benham* [1891] 2 Ch. 244, *per* Lindley L.J. at p. 255. See *supra* pp. 165–166.

[62] *Trimble* v. *Goldberg* [1906] A.C. 494.

[63] *Glassington* v. *Thwaites* (1833) 1 Sim. & Stu. 124; *England* v. *Curling* (1844) 8 Beav. 129.

[64] Gloag, however, takes the view that the statutory words do not include the acquisition of a partner's share and that no trust for the remaining partners is inferred. (Citing *Cassels* v. *Stewart* (1879) 6 R. 936; (1881) 8 R.(H.L.) 1.) *Contract* (2nd ed.), p. 519, n. 4.

[65] [1906] A.C. 494.

[66] In fact the acquisition in question was not forbidden by the articles of partnership. In some cases a question might arise as to use of information gained in conducting the partnership business (on which see *infra* pp. 172–173); but this element was not present in the case.

" *Or from any use by him of the partnership property, name or business connection.*" In *Dean* v. *McDowell,*[67] Thesiger L.J. described the principles governing the relations of the partners *inter se* as follows—

" The first of those principles is that a partner shall not derive any exclusive advantage by the employment of the partnership property. . . . The second principle is that a partner is not to derive any exclusive advantage by engaging in transactions in rivalry with the firm. . . . The third principle is that a partner is not allowed in transacting the firm's affairs to carry on for his sole benefit any separate trade or business which, were it not for his connection with the partnership, he would not have been in a position to carry on."

The second of those three principles is separately provided for in the Partnership Act 1890 and will be considered later.[68]   The first, and to some extent the third, are reflected in the words from section 29 (1) which head this paragraph.

Use of the partnership property.   A partner has no right to employ the partnership property in a private speculation of his own and if he derives any personal profit or advantage from so doing he must account for it to his copartners.   Thus a ship of which the plaintiffs and the defendant were part-owners and the defendant was the master was used by the parties in trading.   The defendant also traded on his own account.   He claimed that he had used his own private capital in that trading and that there was a custom allowing shipmasters to trade for their own benefit.   The court, however, held that he must account for the profit which he had made to the other part-owners since he had no right to employ the partnership property in trading for his own private benefit and the profit he had made was derived at least partially from the employment of the ship which was not the defendant's exclusive property.[69]   In *Miller* v. *Mackay* [70] it was held that, in the absence of any agreement, express or implied, a part-owner or partner in ships who acted as ship's husband was not entitled to charge the usual commission against the partnership.[71]   But on inquiry into the whole circumstances, it was later found [72] that by agreement among the part-owners, one of them who was a member of a firm of ship-brokers was allowed to entrust the duties of ship's husband to that firm on the usual terms.   The shipbrokers in turn had employed one of the part-owners of the ships to do the work for them.   It was held that the usual remuneration must be awarded to the firm of shipbrokers and that the part-owner was entitled to retain for his own use any remuneration which he had received from his employment with the shipbrokers.

[67] (1878) 8 Ch.D. 345 at p. 355.
[68] Partnership Act 1890, s. 30, quoted *supra* p. 164 and see *infra* pp. 178 *et seq.*
[69] *Gardner* v. *McCutcheon* (1842) 4 Beav. 534.
[70] (1862) 31 Beav. 77.
[71] A similar decision was reached in respect of profits made by one of the partners in the supply of ship's stores: *Ritchie* v. *Couper* (1860) 28 Beav. 344.   See also *Williamson* v. *Hine* [1891] 1 Ch. 390.
[72] *Miller* v. *Mackay* (1864) 34 Beav. 295.

On the same *ratio,* where one of the partners bartered goods in exchange for supplies of a substance in which the partnership were dealers, he was not entitled in an accounting with his copartners, to charge the selling price of the goods bartered, but must charge such goods at the cost price.[73]   If a partner carries on business for his own account employing the stock-in-trade, goodwill, and premises belonging to the firm he must account to the firm for the profit made.[74]

Leases

A number of cases have been concerned with circumstances in which a partner has obtained in his own name a renewal of the lease of a property occupied by the partnership. It was decided in *Featherstonhaugh* v. *Fenwick* [75] that two of the partners of a firm who obtained a renewal of the lease of the partnership premises and thereupon dissolved the partnership with the object of precluding the remaining partner from having any interest in the lease, could not be permitted to do so and that the new lease was to be regarded as part of the firm's assets in the winding up.   Similarly in Scotland, a partner who before the expiry of the lease of the partnership premises and without notice to his copartner obtained a new lease in his own name and, on termination of the partnership, carried on the same business as an individual from the premises, was bound to communicate a share of the profit made to his former partner.[76]   The rule is based upon the principle that in the renewal of such leases a partner " clearly owes a duty to his copartners not to acquire any special advantage over them by reason of his position." [77]   The special advantage need not be one which is obtained clandestinely.   Where a partner gives notice of dissolution of a partnership at will, at the same time announcing his intention to renew the lease of the partnership premises for his own benefit, he is not permitted to acquire the benefit of the lease for his own advantage even where the landlord has objected to renew the lease to any of the partners except him.[78]   The right of the remaining partners to demand an accounting of the profit obtained by the partner who has renewed the lease for his own benefit may be asserted by the representatives of a partner whose interests have been prejudiced by that transaction.[79]   Indeed, it seems that the right to object to the transaction need not have originally accrued to the deceased himself, and that his executor might call for an accounting where the surviving partners renewed the lease for their own benefit on the broader principle that parties interested jointly with others in the lease

---

[73] *Burton* v. *Wookey* (1882) 6 Madd. 367.
[74] *Laird & Others* v. *Laird* (1855) 17 D. 984; *Crawshay* v. *Collins* (1808) 15 Ves. 218; *Parsons* v. *Hayward* (1862) 31 Beav. 199.
[75] (1810) 17 Ves. 298.
[76] *McNiven* v. *Peffers* (1868) 7 M. 181.
[77] *In re Biss, Biss* v. *Biss* [1903] 2 Ch. 40, *per* Romer L.J. at p. 61.   See also *Bevan* v. *Webb* [1905] 1 Ch. 620, *per* Warrington J. at p. 625.
[78] *Clegg* v. *Edmondson* (1856) 8 De G.M. & G. 787.
[79] *Stewart* v. *North* (1893) 20 R. 260; *Clegg* v. *Fishwick* (1849) 1 Mac. & G. 294; *Clements* v. *Hall* (1858) 2 De G. & J. 173.

cannot by renewing it secure the benefit for themselves to the exclusion of those others.[80]

The general principle above enunciated is not universally applicable. " I am not prepared to say that in no case can a partner contract for a new lease to be granted to himself of property which is in the lease to the partnership without the lease being held to be subject to trusts for the benefit of the partnership." [81] Circumstances may conceivably arise in which the courts would be prepared to assert that a partner so renewing a lease was under no obligation to account to his copartners for the benefit which has accrued to him thereby. No guidance as to the nature of the circumstances which would bring about this result can be obtained from the reported decisions. It has been held that a partner who purchases for himself the reversion of a lease, assumed to belong to his firm, is entitled to retain it for his own benefit.[82] The purchase of the reversion of a lease, however, is not *in pari casu* with the case of a partner renewing in his own name a lease which has been held by his firm since a person who purchases the reversion does not do so in virtue of any existing interest in the lease.[83]

Where a claim arises against a partner who has obtained renewal of the lease for his own benefit it must be made with reasonable promptitude. In *Stewart* v. *North* [84] the court held that a partner who had used the business connection to obtain a lease of the business premises and plant was accountable to his copartner for the profits earned but decided that the trustee on the sequestrated estate of the copartner was barred by *mora* from insisting on the claim. The same legal result is achieved in England by the plea of laches.[85] Where a partner renews a lease against the will of his copartners, he cannot compel them to treat the property in the lease as firm property in the absence of agreement requiring them to do so.[86]

Use of the firm name

The provision of section 29 (1) of the Partnership Act 1890 as to the liability of a partner to account to the partnership for profit made by him personally through the use of the firm name reflects the common law and gives rise to little difficulty. In Scotland it has been held that a partner who embarks upon private trading and uses the firm name to do so is accountable to the firm for the profits made.[87] Such cases often merge with those relating to use of the firm's property already discussed and with those involving the use of the business connection which are

---

[80] *Clegg* v. *Fishwick* (*supra*). It would appear, however, that in such a case the deceased partner's interest must continue in the firm without dissolution of the firm occurring upon the death of the partner.
[81] Per Turner L.J. in *Clegg* v. *Edmondson* (1856) 8 De G.M. & G. 787 at p. 807.
[82] *Bevan* v. *Webb* [1905] 1 Ch. 620.
[83] *Griffith* v. *Owen* [1907] 1 Ch. 195. [84] (1893) 20 R. 260.
[85] *Clegg* v. *Edmondson* (*supra*); *Re Jarvis* [1958] 2 All E.R. 336.
[86] *Clements* v. *Norris* (1878) 8 Ch.D. 129.
[87] *Wallace Hamilton & Co.* v. *Trs. of John Hamilton & Co.*, June 8, 1821, F.C.

dealt with immediately hereafter. In a case decided by Lord Mackenzie in the Outer House [88] a partnership was entered between two persons for the purpose of carrying on a bolt and nut business. The firm had not commenced business though both partners were in the meantime drawing a salary. One partner purchased a rivet, bolt and nut business and raised the money himself to finance the purchase. There was, however, no clear agreement between him and his copartner that the business so acquired had not been bought on behalf of the partnership. It was held that the business must be regarded as acquired for the partnership and that the purchaser was bound to account to his copartners for the profits made therein.

Use of the business connection

The aspect of this provision of section 29 (1) with which the decisions have most frequently been concerned is the benefit which a partner has derived from his own connection with the firm, and particularly from the use of information which he has obtained in the course of conducting the firm's business. To hold that a partner can never derive any personal benefit from information which he has obtained as a partner would be to generalise the rule to a point where it would become manifestly absurd.[89] For example, a partner may in the course of conducting the business of his firm obtain insight and expertness in a particular branch of law, or science or affairs. If he writes a treatise embodying the information obtained as a result of that experience, he is not accountable to the partnership for the profits made on publication of the book.

It is in this area of using information obtained in the course of the business of the firm that most questions of difficulty arise. The fundamental principle originates in an analogy with the obligations of an agent to his principal in such matters. " These cases proceed upon the ground that a partner, being an agent (for I think it is because he is an agent that the fiduciary character arises) makes a profit out of the concerns of his principal and as acting for him, he must communicate it to his principal; he cannot make a profit out of his principal's business for himself. As I have said, a partner is an agent, and the principle applying to him is a branch of the general rule which applies to agents." [90] In *Phipps* v. *Boardman* [91] the rule is clearly stated that an agent is accountable to his principal in circumstances where the agent has turned to his own use and profit information or knowledge " which he has been employed by his principal to collect or discover or which he has otherwise acquired for the use of his principal." The law on this subject, it has been said,[92] does not depend upon any implied contract but on the broad principle of equity

[88] *Pillans Bros. & Others* v. *Pillans* (1908) 16 S.L.T. 611.
[89] *Aas* v. *Benham* [1891] 2 Ch. 244, *per* Lindley L.J. at p. 256.
[90] *Cassels* v. *Stewart* (1881) 8 R.(H.L.) 1, *per* Lord Blackburn at p. 7.
[91] [1965] Ch. 992, *per* Lord Denning M.R. at pp. 1018–1019; and see [1967] 2 A.C. 46, *per* Lord Guest at p. 115.
[92] *Seager* v. *Copydex Ltd.* [1967] 1 W.L.R. 923, *per* Lord Denning M.R. at p. 931.

" that he who has received information in confidence shall not take unfair advantage of it " and make any use of it to the prejudice of him who gave it without obtaining his consent. Thus where the proprietors of a trades directory employed canvassers to obtain advertisements from traders for insertion in the directory, those canvassers were not entitled to use the material or information obtained during that employment for the purpose of assisting the publication of a rival directory even after they had ceased to be employed by the first mentioned concern.[93] The same principle has been applied to persons granted a licence to manufacture and sell articles under a patent who obtained in confidence advance information as to a new design which they endeavoured to use to their own advantage.[94]

But there are exceptions to the applicability of the principle. In *Nordisk Insulinlaboratorium* v. *Gorgate Products Ltd.*,[95] a Danish corporation deposited insulin in an English bank shortly before the outbreak of war. When the German forces invaded Denmark, the corporation became an alien enemy and the property vested in the Custodian of Enemy Property who sold the insulin to the defendants. The defendants had been selling agents for the Danish corporation before the war and they now re-sold the insulin at a profit. It was held that, since they had not acquired any special or secret knowledge about the insulin while they were the agents of the corporation, they were under no fiduciary duty to account for the profit made on the re-sale. That decision may with reason be regarded as one arrived at on special facts and as support for no more than the limited proposition that where an agency comes to an end through the principal becoming an enemy alien, the agent will not be liable to the principal for any profits which the agent subsequently makes in dealing with the property of the principal since such dealings do not properly arise from the agency but upon a purchase from the custodian of enemy property and a re-sale. The agent certainly does not escape from his fiduciary obligation merely because his agency has been terminated, before the profit has been made.[96] The emphasis in the decisions cited, is, however, upon *confidential* information obtained by the agent in the course of transacting his principal's business. If the information is readily available to the public, no fiduciary duty arises upon the agent making use of it for his own benefit.[97] Further if the information which the agent uses is not confidential or secret to the business of his principal but is merely the general understanding of the trade which he has gained while acting as agent, he is not accountable to the principal for profits which he subsequently makes in that trade even though they may be to some extent referable to the information he has thus acquired.

---

[93] *Lamb* v. *Evans* [1893] 1 Ch. 218. See also *Sanders* v. *Parry* [1967] 2 All E.R. 803.
[94] *Peter Pan Manufacturing Corporation* v. *Corsets Silhouette Ltd.* [1964] 1 W.L.R. 96.
[95] [1953] Ch. 430.
[96] *Carter* v. *Palmer* (1841) 8 C. & F. 657; *Regier* v. *Campbell-Stuart* [1939] Ch. 766.
[97] *O. Mustad & Son* v. *Dosen* [1964] 1 W.L.R. 109n. (a case decided in 1928); *Cranleigh Precision Engineering Ltd.* v. *Bryant* [1965] 1 W.L.R. 1293 at pp. 1314–1319.

Applicability of the rule in cases of partnership

The general rule above discussed in relation to agency is applicable in questions arising between partners, so that a partner may not use for his own exclusive benefit information obtained by him in his dealings with the partnership business or because of his connection with the firm as a partner. The rule, however, strikes only at transactions for his individual advantage which are within the scope of the business of his firm. If he infringes that rule he is liable to account to the firm and his copartners for any profit he has made in the offending transaction. If, however, he makes a profit from the use of such information in transactions which are not within the scope of the firm's business, he is allowed to retain that profit and need not account for it to the firm and his copartners.[98] The exception to the general rule of accountability strikes one as much more pointed and specific than any analogous exception in the law of principal and agent. In *Aas* v. *Benham* [98] it is difficult to see the same decision as readily applicable where the relationship is not one of partnership, as it was in that case, but one of agency. The case decided that where a partner of a firm of shipbrokers used information which he had obtained in carrying on the business of his firm for the purpose of facilitating the formation of a shipbuilding company, and received payment for his services and also a salaried directorship from the new company, he was not accountable to his copartner in the firm of shipbrokers for the payment and salary so received since he was held to have used the information in the furtherance of a matter completely outside the ambit of the firm's business. It is difficult to detect in the reported decisions on agency proper as clear an exception to the agent's accountability to his principal in respect of profits made from the use of information similarly obtained,[99] though the opinions of the judges in *Graham* v. *R. & S. Paton* [1] suggest that the ambit of the rule in Scotland at least is restricted in agency cases as well as in those in which partnership is involved. In that case Lord Mackenzie said,[2]

> " There is little authority upon the subject, but such as there is establishes, in my opinion, these propositions: (1) A servant shall use all reasonable means to advance his master's interests within the sphere of his employment; (2) a servant shall not do anything to injure his master's business. I am unable to find authority for the proposition that a servant may not, while in the employment, enter into a contract for the purchase of the commodity in which his master deals, with a view to re-sale at a profit for his own behoof. It may be that, in nine cases out of ten, such an act would be a breach of one or both of the two propositions above stated.

---

[98] *Aas* v. *Benham* [1891] 2 Ch. 244.
[99] See *Amber Size & Chemical Co.* v. *Menzel* [1913] 2 Ch. 239; *Measures Bros. Ltd.* v. *Measures* [1910] 2 Ch. 248; 1 Ch. 336; *Robb* v. *Green* [1895] 2 Q.B. 1, 315; *Lamb* v. *Evans* [1893] 1 Ch. 218; *Merryweather* v. *Moore* [1892] 2 Ch. 518; *Great North of Scotland Ry.* v. *Urquhart* (1884) 21 S.L.R. 377.
[1] 1917 S.C. 203.
[2] *Ibid.* at pp. 209–210.

But apply this test to the present case. Suppose that instead of the potatoes being bought at Girvan they had been bought in Jersey, and that it had been shown that the defenders' firm (the employers) never dealt in Jersey potatoes. Would that have been a breach of the servant's engagement? According to the defenders' argument it would. This carries the law further than the authorities warrant."

As will be apparent from the passage quoted the point for decision in *Graham* v. *R. & S. Paton* was whether there had been a breach of an agreement of service which justified the dismissal of the servant by the employers; and as distinct from a contract of agency, a contract of employment has not been included among those relationships which involve fiduciary duties.[3] Too much may, however, be made of a rigid classification in such cases. The category, under which a particular agreement is subsumed, does not necessarily or logically exclude features which are more appropriate to other contractual relationships. Under certain contracts of service the servant may be called upon to act as agent for his master, and that was the situation in the case under consideration, and in a sense in the Outer House decision which was cited in argument.[4]

Theoretical grounds for a distinction between the rule as applying in partnership and that applying in agency

It remains true, however, that the application of the Scottish cases on dismissal from employment rests on a somewhat uneasy analogy with agency and that they cannot too confidently be relied upon to support the proposition that, in agency as opposed to partnership, profit made by the agent from the use of confidential information gained in the course of his principal's business need not be communicated to the principal if that profit has accrued from activities in a sphere entirely outside the scope of the principal's business.[5] As a practical issue the question is unlikely to arise in agency except in a form so extreme as to make any attempt by the principal to enforce the rule of accountability too unrealistic to be stateable; and this may account for the lack of guidance in the reported decisions. In the absence of any such authoritative pronouncement, it is desirable to consider whether there is any general ground in the legal theory of partnership which would itself justify a distinction from agency in this particular. Two possible grounds suggest themselves—(1) there is the distinction that partnership is *mutual* agency, " that partners are at once principals and agents " which is advanced by Lindley [6] as a factor to be kept in mind when using the decisions on agency in the context of partnership, and (2) there is the view expressed by Clark [7] that the rule that a

---

[3] See *e.g.* Gloag, *Contract* (2nd ed.), Chap. XXXI.
[4] *Malloch* v. *Duffy* (1882) 19 S.L.R. 697.
[5] Gloag (*Contract*, 2nd ed., p. 522, n. 8), however, appears to regard *Graham* v. *R. & S. Paton* (*supra*) as throwing light upon the application of the rule in agency.
[6] *Op. cit.* p. 343, n. 41, citing *Trego* v. *Hunt* [1895] 1 Ch. 462 at p. 466; [1896] A.C. 7 at p. 26.
[7] *Op. cit.* I, p. 184.

partner cannot carry on for his own benefit a business which would compete with his firm is questionably applicable in Scots law since the firm in Scots law possesses a *quasi persona* distinct from the individual partners " and they, accordingly, may, like third parties, stand to it in the relation of debtors and creditors." Neither appears a very compelling reason in theory to account for an exception to the rule in partnership which is not applicable in agency. The mutuality of the agency involved in partnership is undoubtedly an important feature in the resulting relationships which arise among the partners but it is difficult to see it as a feature which accounts for a modification of a principle otherwise applied in agency without modification. Though it is true that a partner may at one and the same time stand in the relation of agent to his copartners in respect of matters which he has transacted for the firm and in the relation of principal in respect of the matters which his copartners have so transacted, it is the former of those relationships taken in isolation which is to be considered when deciding whether he is accountable to the firm and his copartners for a profit which he has made as an individual, and there appears to be no aspect of mutuality which affords a sound basis in theory for a distinction in the application of the general rules of agency in that aspect of his conduct. Indeed it is doubtful whether Lindley, in the observation quoted, intends to suggest such a proposition or to do more than to draw attention to the peculiarity of the agency relationship arising among partners as a general consideration to be borne in mind when applying decisions on agency in partnership cases.

With regard to the point made by Clark, while it is important to remember that in Scotland the partner is an agent for a firm which is itself a *quasi* person in law, it must be observed with respect that the conclusion which he attempts to base upon that does not logically follow.

> " It is difficult therefore to see," he writes,[8] " why they (partners) should not be able to act and transact with it on the same footing as strangers, and why contracts entered into with them should not be equally binding. It may be said that they stand to each other or the company in the relation of trustees, and therefore cannot make profit by their mutual transactions. But it must be observed that they are trustees only *quoad* the funds which the society *de facto* possesses, not as regards such as it may be desirable for it to possess, but which it does not yet possess. It does not therefore appear that there is any good reason to hold that, according to the law of Scotland, a partner may not supply the company with an article of which it stands in need, on the same terms of advantage to himself as if he were dealing with strangers."

It is no doubt true that a partner is not in the position of a trustee for his firm, save in respect of any property of the firm which he may hold in his own name,[9] and that there is a *persona* in the firm under Scots law which is

---

[8] *Op. cit.* I, p. 184.
[9] See *infra* Chap. IX.

entirely separate from the *personae* of the individuals who are partners of the firm, but an individual partner remains an agent for his firm no less than in England he is an agent for his copartners; and if he is an agent for the firm, it seems impossible to maintain, as Clark does, that he is entitled to supply his own goods to the firm and retain for himself a profit on the transaction, unless he has the consent of his copartners to his doing so.[10]

On examination of the whole question there appears to be no entirely satisfactory reason why the rule that a partner may retain a profit made from the use of information obtained by him through his connection with the firm if that profit is made as a result of transactions outwith the scope of the firm's business should be regarded as reflecting a principle exclusively applicable to partnership. It seems rather that the rule is more readily recognisable as applicable in cases of partnership where the criterion of the scope of the business of the principal, the firm, is often more determinate in character than would be the case in general agency. But even in the latter case, it is thought that a principal would not be permitted to claim for an accounting of the profit made by his agent from the publication of a book in which the results of experience gained and information obtained in conducting the principal's business affairs were drawn upon by the author, at least where the publication was such as to involve no disclosure of identifiable confidential information [11]; and it seems that on a parity of the reasoning of Lord Mackenzie in *Graham* v. *R. & S. Paton*,[12] that a profit made by an agent through the use of information obtained in the course of transacting his principal's business but earned in a transaction outside the scope of his principal's business might properly be retained by the agent.

Profits made by a partner as an individual from his connection with the firm

" A partner, moreover, is not allowed, in transacting the partnership affairs, to carry on for his own sole benefit any separate trade or business which, were it not for his connection with the partnership, he would not have been in a position to carry on." [13] The rule is grounded in the principle that since he is under obligation to use his best endeavours for the firm he cannot divert those efforts to his own personal gain. If he does so then he does so at the detriment of the firm as is pointed out by Lindley.[14] It will be noticed, however, that the " detriment " here to be regarded is to be distinguished from the narrower view of detriment in the sense that the partner is competing with the firm, which is expressly dealt with in section 30 of the Partnership Act 1890. It is not necessary that the partner should conduct, or associate himself in the conduct of, a rival business, for him to

---

[10] Gloag, *Contract* (2nd ed.), p. 523. This general principle of agency is the true basis of the decision in the English decisions on a similar question arising in partnership: *Bentley* v. *Craven* (1853) 18 Beav. 75; *Cavendish-Bentinck* v. *Fenn* (1887) 12 App.Cas. 652.
[11] The reasoning of the judgment of Lindley L.J. in *Aas* v. *Benham* [1891] 2 Ch. 244 at p. 256 appears to be equally applicable to a case of agency.
[12] 1917 S.C. 203 at pp. 209–210.
[13] Lindley, *op. cit.* p. 344.
[14] *Loc. cit.*

be accountable to the firm for profits made by him " from any use by him of the partnership . . . business connection " under section 29 (1). In most cases there will be an element of competition or rivalry with the firm because the partnership connection will most readily lend itself to use in making a profit for the individual partner within the scope of the trade carried on by the firm; but the partner will be liable to account under section 29 (1) for the profit made on an isolated transaction of that nature without its requiring to be established that he has been conducting a " business " in competition with that of his firm. Section 29 (1) states that he shall be liable to account for profit made from *any* use by him of the firm connection which suggests even wider extension of the principle of accountability, and that view is supported by the decision in the pre-statute case of *Russell* v. *Austwick* [15] where a number of persons agreed to carry on business as carriers between London and Falmouth, expressly stipulating that no partnership would subsist among them, each being individually responsible for the carriage over a defined portion of the route. The business so conducted included the carriage of bullion from Falmouth and Plymouth to London. Austwick, who was a party to the agreement, subsequently entered a contract with the Mint to carry supplies of a newly issued silver coinage from London to various towns in the Home Counties. His duties under that contract did not involve his carry-ing the coinage on any part of the road between London and Falmouth and indeed the freightage rate was increased over that obtaining in the London/Falmouth contract because of the increased risk of carriage on these roads. Yet it was held that the second agreement was to be con-sidered as made on account of all the persons interested in the first agree-ment. The officers of the Mint had entered into it in view of their connection with the parties under the first agreement or because of their confidence in them.[16]

Business competing with that of the partnership

A partner is also accountable to the firm for all profits made by him in a business " of the same nature as, and competing with, that of the firm " unless he has the consent of the other partners to his carrying on such business.[17] The emphasis is upon carrying on a *competing* business without the consent of his copartners. It is in such cases that the partner is account-able to the firm for the profit made by him in the business, and he is so accountable whether he conducts the rival business openly or secretly.[18]

---

[15] (1826) 1 Sim. 52.
[16] A similar result was reached in the Irish courts in *Lock* v. *Lynam* (1854) 4 Ir.Ch. 188 where the plaintiff and defendant agreed to share the profit and loss from contracts for supplies to the forces and the defendant entered into several contracts with others to share the profit and loss of similar contracts made by them. But see *Miller* v. *Mackay* (1864) 34 Beav. 295, *supra* p. 169.
[17] Partnership Act 1890, s. 30.
[18] *Glassington* v. *Thwaites* (1833) 1 Sim. & Stu. 124. In *Stewart* v. *North* (1893) 20 R. 260 the principle of accountability in such cases was recognised though the partner's claim was defeated by *mora*. See also *Pillans Bros.* v. *Pillans* (1908) 16 S.L.T. 611.

But if he conducts a business which is not connected with the business of the firm and does not compete with it, he is not accountable to the firm for the profits he makes therein, even if he does so without the consent of his copartners,[19] and even if he has undertaken not to engage in any other business than that of the firm.[20]   In the latter case, though he is in breach of his contract of partnership, and therefore subject to an action for damages,[21] his conduct is not such as to entitle his partners to demand an accounting of the profits which he has made.

In *Pattison* v. *Ballingall*[22] a contract of copartnery fixed the respective shares of the partners and provided that if the junior partner was the survivor, he might competently continue to carry on the business under the firm name, in which case he would undertake liability to make certain payments to the representatives of the deceased senior partner, but only after setting aside a yearly minimum amount from the profits as his own share. On the death of his senior partner, the survivor decided, after consultation with the principal clients of the firm, not to carry on the business of the firm.   Instead, he entered a partnership with another firm, where his share fell considerably below the sum allotted to him under the former deed of copartnery.   It was held that he was under no obligation to account to the representatives of his former partner or to make any payment to them in respect of the business which his clients had transferred to the firm which he had joined.   The facts in that case were very special.   In particular it was clear that if the junior partner had not taken the advice of the principal clients of the old firm, that firm would simply have lost their business since the clients were urging upon the junior partner the necessity of " connecting himself with some established firm in Perth whose experience and character would be a sufficient guarantee to those clients that their business would be well conducted." [23]   Again it was established that the junior partner, by associating himself in the new firm, made no profit and indeed suffered at least a notional loss and accordingly there was no purpose in going into an accounting " because an accounting is very useless which does not result in payment." [24]   Even so, this case may properly be regarded as the extreme limit within which a partner may escape a liability to account. The court in effect decided the question in favour of the partner on a view that he had reached an honest decision in no way influenced by any devious attempt to evade his responsibilities under the former partnership [25] but they were also influenced by the fact that he was making no " profit " from his associating himself with the rival firm.   Indeed the question whether he might be accountable if he were to make such a profit in the

[19] *Aas* v. *Benham* [1891] 2 Ch. 244.
[20] *Dean* v. *Macdowell* (1878) 8 Ch.D. 345.
[21] *Rely-A-Bell Burglar & Fire Alarm Co.* v. *Eisler* [1926] 1 Ch. 609; *Whitwood Chemical Co.* v. *Hardman* [1891] 2 Ch. 417; *Grimston* v. *Cunningham* [1894] 1 Q.B. 125; *Davis* v. *Foreman* [1894] 3 Ch. 655; *Kirchner & Co.* v. *Gruban* [1909] 1 Ch. 413.
[22] (1874) 12 S.L.R. 68.
[23] *Ibid. per* the Lord President (Inglis) at p. 70.
[24] *Ibid. per* the Lord President at p. 71.
[25] *Per* Lord Deas at p. 71; Lord Ardmillan *loc. cit.*

future was reserved.[26]   It is difficult to see how such an accounting could
be imposed if at a future date the new firm by accession of business was in
a position to pay the partner an enhanced sum by way of share of profits,
since that accruing business could in no sense be regarded as the business
of the former firm, nor could the former junior partner be said to be " competing " with a non-existent business.   Lord President Inglis expressly
recognises this point though Lord Deas is content to dispose of the difficulty on the ground that it lies in the future and " there probably never
may be sufficient profits to put Mr. Ballingall in that position."

Partner's duty to act honestly

The case of *Pattison* v. *Ballingall* discussed above is perhaps more
appropriately considered as reflecting the wider rule that a partner who
seeks to benefit himself by a transaction at the expense of the firm " will
be required to show, not only that he has the law on his side, but that his
conduct will bear to be tried by the highest standards of honour." [27]   That
general principle is easier to state than to apply.   The difficulty is discernible in *Pattison* v. *Ballingall* and has been commented upon in more recent
decisions in the Scottish and English courts.   In *Cassels* v. *Stewart* [28] the
contract of copartnery prohibited the assignation by any of the partners
of his share in the firm and provided that any such assignation granted in
the contravention of that stipulation would be null and void " so far as
regards the company or other individual partners who shall not be obliged
to pay any attention thereto."   The contract further provided that on the
death, insolvency or retirement of any partner, the remaining partners
should have the option of buying his interest at the amount standing to his
credit at the last balance.   At the relevant time the firm consisted of three
partners, Reid, Cassels and Stewart with equal shares.   Reid and Stewart
entered an agreement whereby Stewart purchased Reid's share.   This was
not disclosed to Cassels, and Reid continued ostensibly as a partner until
his death about seven years later.   In that period the business of the firm
increased in prosperity.   On Reid's death, the agreement came to Cassel's
knowledge and he sued Stewart to compel him to communicate the benefit
derived from the latent arrangement with Reid.   The action was unsuccessful.   In the view of the court the prohibitory clause in the contract did not
affect a sale of a partner's beneficial interest either to a stranger or to a
copartner, provided that the terms of the arrangement did not oblige the
firm or the other copartners to take cognisance of it.   The rule which
requires a partner to communicate any benefit derived by him to the firm
was not applicable to the case of one partner purchasing the share of
another partner since he was not thereby dealing with an asset or liability
of the firm or carrying through transactions in the line of the firm's
business.

[26] *Per* the Lord President at p. 71, *per* Lord Deas at p. 71.
[27] Lindley, *op. cit.* p. 335, citing *Blisset* v. *Daniel* (1853) 10 Hare 522, 536.
[28] (1881) 8 R.(H.L.) 1.

" It would have been better," said Lord Blackburn,[29] " if Mr. Cassels had been informed of it while it was going on. I generally think it is advisable, as a matter of prudence as well as on other grounds, to let everything be above board; and therefore I say it would have been better that he should have been told that Mr. Reid had made that arrangement; but his not having been told about it did no harm whatever, and inasmuch as even supposing harm had resulted from it, Mr. Reid would have been liable for that harm, that cannot entitle Mr. Cassels to say that as against Mr. Stewart the benefit arising from the purchase of Mr. Reid's share is to be given partly to Mr. Cassels."

In *Trimble* v. *Goldberg* [30] the facts upon which the case was decided did not admit of the distinction drawn in *Cassels* v. *Stewart* that the transaction was not concerned with the firm's assets but with a partner's share in the firm. The firm in the English case consisted of three partners who had purchased certain plots of building land and shares in a company with the purpose of re-selling them. Most of the building plots owned by the firm were in a certain district and two of the partners, without the knowledge of the third, purchased other building lots in the same district for their own account. The third partner's claim to share in the benefit of that purchase was rejected since it was held that the purchase was not within the scope of the partnership business nor in competition with it, nor was it forbidden by the agreement of partnership. Even had it been so forbidden, that it did not necessarily entail that the third partner was entitled to share in the profit from the purchase.[31]

In considering the effect of these cases upon a general rule of law exacting the " highest standard of honour " in a partner's dealings with the firm and his copartners it is important to recognise that the question before the court in all three cases was a claim by the partner excluded that the benefit of the transaction complained of should be communicated to him, and that there is no foundation for a claim for this special remedy in section 29 (1) or section 30 of the Partnership Act 1890 or in the pre-statute law which these sections reflect. The situation of the pursuer in such a case then comes to be that of a party complaining of a breach of contract and seeking the normal remedy of an award of damages. If the pursuer in *Cassels* v. *Stewart* had sued on those grounds, then as may be seen from the words quoted from Lord Blackburn's judgment,[32] it would be necessary for him to show injury which might be assessed in an award of damages, which Lord Blackburn held he was unable to establish. Moreover, in that case the action was possibly directed against the wrong defender, since it was primarily Reid's conduct as the seller of the share which was the cause of Cassel's injury and not that of Stewart who was the purchaser. Again in *Trimble* v. *Goldberg*, even assuming an implied term

[29] *Ibid.* at p. 8.
[30] [1906] A.C. 494.
[31] See also *Williamson* v. *Taylor* (1898) 14 Sh.Ct.Rep. 303.
[32] *Supra*, n. 29.

of the agreement of partnership requiring the highest standard of honour among the partners in their dealings one with another, it would be difficult for the plaintiff to qualify a claim for damages *for breach of that agreement* on the sole ground that the defendants had made a profitable bargain from which he was excluded and which in no way involved the use of the partnership property or dealings in competition with the firm.

The real criterion in the application of the rule to such cases seems to be to have regard to the effect of the conduct upon the firm itself. The partners are under a duty to employ the highest standard of honour in their dealings with each other and with the firm, a notion which may be variously expressed in terms of a fiduciary duty or a duty to exhibit *uberrima fides*, at least if the last-mentioned phrase is used less as a legal term of art and more as a figurative use of language or an approximate legal analogy. But the notion, however expressed, must be handled with caution since it too readily lends to a broad and indiscriminate application which is not supported by authority.

Duty of honesty in dealings with third parties

The importance of applying the test of the effect of the dealings upon the firm is illustrated in the further aspect of the partner's duty that he must be honest in his dealings with third parties. While the conduct here regarded is in relation to third parties, the duty to preserve standards in that conduct is owed by the partner to the firm and his copartners. The basis of the rule is that conduct which offends in this respect is detrimental to the interests and reputation of the firm. Therefore the duty of honesty in his dealings with third parties is not confined to those dealings in which the partner engages in the normal course of the firm's business but affects his actings in matters entirely extraneous to the affairs of the firm where that conduct is liable to reflect adversely upon the firm.[33]

Powers of management

In the absence of any agreement, express or implied, to the contrary, every partner may take part in the management of the partnership business.[34] That right to take part in the management may be restricted by the terms of the contract of copartnery [35] which may provide that only certain partners shall conduct the management of the business or that some partners shall have the sole management of one department of the business and others of the other. While such agreed restrictions are binding upon the partners *inter se* and thus reflect the agreed terms as to the authority committed to any particular partner as an agent of the firm, they will not be effectual in a question with a third party who deals with the partner, as an

[33] *Carmichael* v. *Evans* [1904] 1 Ch. 486.
[34] Partnership Act 1890, s. 24 (5).
[35] As in *Duff* v. *Corsar* (1902) 10 S.L.T. 27 (O.H.). A body of trustees representing a deceased partner were held entitled on a construction of the contract of copartnery to a declarator that they collectively formed one partner but not that they were entitled to take any part in the active management—*Alexanders Trs.* v. *Thomson* (1885) 22 S.L.R. 828.

agent of his firm without knowledge of any restriction on his apparent authority.[36]

Powers exercisable by the majority of the partners.   Section 24 (8) of the Partnership Act 1890 provides—

> " Any difference arising as to ordinary matters connected with the partnership business may be decided by a majority of the partners, but no change may be made in the nature of the partnership business without the consent of all existing partners."

The terms of the subsection are subject to any agreement, express or implied, between the partners to the contrary.   They express the provisions which the law will infer as to the powers of the majority if the agreement entered into among the partners themselves has not provided otherwise. In confining the powers of the majority in such circumstances to the decision of " ordinary matters connected with the partnership business," the subsection is in accordance with the pre-existing common law.   Thus Clark [37] recognises the position of the majority in the following rules which bear out the terms of section 24 (8) and in some respects elaborate upon those terms:

> " 1. Where the instrument of formation has not otherwise provided, the will of the majority is the will of the company in all matters within the sphere of its operations.
>
> " 2. The will of the majority is not the will of the company to any effect beyond or in opposition to the purposes of its formation, and does not in such cases bind a dissenting minority, however small.
>
> " 3. When the members are equally divided, the will of the company is presumed to be in favour of the existing state of matters, which consequently remains unaltered.
>
> " 4. The will of a majority is only the will of the company when all the members have voted, or have had it in their power to vote, and when a *bona fide* opinion has been given after due consideration.
>
> " 5. When in the instrument of formation rules have been prescribed for ascertaining the will of the company, it can only be declared by resolutions in the passing of which these rules have been observed."

While the general rules stated by Clark in paragraph 1 and 2 above quoted are in accordance with section 24 (8) of the Partnership Act 1890 the proposition stated in Rule (1) was regarded as not entirely free from doubt in the pre-statute decisions.[38]   Several Scottish decisions, however, lend support to the rule as stated by Clark.   In *Fleming* v. *Campbell* [39] the directors of a cemetery company purchased lands for the company and later sold them with the concurrence of a majority of the shareholders, on

---

[36] *Turnbull* v. *McKie* (1822) 1 S. 353; *Bruce & Co.* v. *Beat,* Dec. 10, 1765, F.C.
[37] *Op. cit.* I, p. 189.
[38] See *e.g. Gregory* v. *Patchett* (1864) 33 Beav. 595; *Const* v. *Harris* (1824) Turn. & R. 496.
[39] (1845) 7 D. 935.

the score that the lands were not suitable for the purposes of the company. A dissentient shareholder brought a note of suspension of the sale on the ground that there was no power in the contract of copartnery which allowed the majority so to act but the court held that the majority had such power and refused the application.   A majority of the partners were also held to have the power to dissolve a partnership against the wishes of the minority, on the ground that they considered it likely to be unprofitable.[40]

Similar decisions were reached in the English courts. On the other hand, the second branch of section 24 (8) that " no change may be made in the nature of the business without the consent of all existing partners " was also recognised as a principle of the common law before the passing of the Act.[41] In English law it is explained on broad equitable lines. " Each partner is entitled to say to the others, ' I became a partner in a concern formed for a definite purpose, and upon terms which were agreed upon by all of us, and you have no right, without my consent, to engage me in any other concern, nor to hold me to any other terms, nor to get rid of me, if I decline to assent to a variation in the agreement by which you are bound to me and I to you.' "[42]   In dealing with the rule as it applies in Scots law, Clark lays special emphasis on the *quasi persona* of the partnership in Scotland as the *ratio* for the rule.   " In cases of this kind, the company as an artificial person cannot be said to have any volition at all, because they lie beyond the sphere of action for which it was created. The will of a majority, however large, does not therefore represent the will of the company; for *ex hypothesi* it has no will to represent."[43] Too much may be made of the distinction between the two systems which Clark attempts to draw; nor is it entirely apt to regard the English rule as resting " on those general grounds of justice and expediency of which, taken as a whole, the Scotch doctrine must be regarded as the artistic embodiment."[44] It is submitted that both systems base the rule upon the same " general grounds of justice and expediency."   To postulate that the Scottish law has laid a more secure foundation in legal theory for the doctrine because it recognises a *quasi* personality in the firm which is not recognised in England, entails either (1) that the doctrine of *vires* appropriate in the case of statutory corporations has in some manner, left unexplained, become applicable to a Scottish unincorporated body where, as in the case of a firm, it is regarded as a *quasi* person at law or (2) that in Scotland the *quasi* personification of the firm has added yet another legal person falling under the " general grounds of justice and expediency " which in England affect the partners

[40] *Logie* v. *Gordon* (1725) Mor. 14580; *Montgomery* v. *Forresters & Co.* (1791) Mor. 14583; *Brown* v. *Kilsyth Police Commissioners* (1886) 13 R. 515.
[41] *Kent* v. *Jackson* (1852) 14 Beav. 367; *Bryon* v. *Metropolitan Saloon Omnibus Co.* (1858) 3 De G. & J. 123; *Australian Auxiliary Steam Clipper Co.* v. *Mounsey* (1858) 4 Kay & J. 733; *Lord* v. *Governor & Company of the Copper Mines* (1848) 2 Ph. 740; *Stevens* v. *South Devon Ry.* (1851) 9 Hare 326.
[42] Lindley, *op. cit.* p. 334.
[43] Clark, *op. cit.* I, p. 191.
[44] *Ibid.*

alone. There appears to be no legal authority for the former of those two alternatives. As to the second, it adds little to the solution of questions between a majority and a minority of the partners that the firm itself may in Scotland be regarded as a *quasi* person in its own right. There appears to be no valid distinction in legal principle to be drawn between such cases as *Maxton* v. *Brown* [45] in Scotland and *Const* v. *Harris* [46] in England.

While there appears, therefore, to be no distinction between the treatment of such cases under English and under Scottish law and while the terms of section 24 (8) of the Partnership Act 1890 appear to be declaratory of the common law existing prior to the passing of the Act, so that pre-statute decisions may be of some value in the application of the subsection in modern cases, the clear dichotomy laid down in the subsection was not always discernible in some of the earlier English decisions. This has led to the guarded utterance of Lindley that the doctrine laid down in section 24 (8) " was probably so before the Act, but the point was not settled." [47] An examination of the apparently conflicting decisions suggests that the divergence arises not so much from any resistance in theory to the principles laid down in section 24 (8) but rather from the ambivalence of the distinction there sought to be drawn. It is one thing to lay down a distinction between disputes " arising as to ordinary matters connected with the partnership business," on the one hand, and a change in the nature of the partnership business, on the other. It is not always so clear on which side of the dividing line a case arising in practice will lie. It may be regarded as an ordinary matter connected with the partnership business to make provision for the manner in which that business is to be conducted and in so doing a majority of the partners may decide the extent to which any partner acting alone may bind the firm. If the contract of copartnery makes no express provision regulating the matter, however, it may not be regarded as within the power of a majority to impose greater restriction upon the authority of one partner than on that of another. Such a decision would not be an " ordinary matter connected with the partnership business " since in the absence of express provision it is implied that every partner may take part in the management of the partnership business [48] and all therefore have an equal right to take part in the management. [49] The primary question in all such cases must be whether the resolution of the majority is or is not within the limits of the contract of copartnery. [50]

The apparent conflict among the pre-statute decisions when it is not resolved upon considerations of the nature just mentioned, may on occasion be found to arise from the application of the rules 3 to 5 in the passage quoted from *Clark on Partnership*. [51] Though these rules are not

[45] (1839) 1 D. 367.
[46] (1824) Turn. & R. 496.
[47] *Op. cit.* p. 333, n. 13.
[48] Partnership Act 1890, s. 24 (5).
[49] See Lindley, *op. cit.* p. 333; *Dickson* v. *Dickson* (1823) 2 S. 462; *Marshall* v. *Colman* (1820) 2 J. & W. 266.
[50] Clark, *op. cit.* I, p. 192.
[51] *Supra* p. 183.

specifically laid down in the Partnership Act 1890, they are regarded as still operative.

Presumption in favour of status quo where partners are equally divided. This rule which reflects a general principle of the Roman law,[52] has been applied in the law of partnership on both sides of the border. It entails that where there is an equal division of voices among the partners on a matter arising in the ordinary course of the partnership business, regard must be had to the state of affairs which actually exists and those who advocate the continuance of that state of affairs must prevail. In *Donaldson* v. *Williams* [53] it was held that in a partnership of two, one partner could not dismiss a servant against the wishes of the other; and on a parity of reasoning a partner who objected to his copartner's engaging a new servant would prevail since his view was in accordance with the *status quo*. The same principle seems to have been applied in a case where one of two partners was not allowed to insist that when the existing lease of the partnership premises had expired, the lease should be renewed and the business continued from the old premises.[54] In that case the partnership itself had not expired and the force of the decision as persuasive authority in Scotland in the face of the doctrine of tacit relocation, may be dubious. If, however, the landlord has given due notice of termination of the lease at its expiry, but is still prepared to treat with the firm for its renewal upon altered terms, then it may be that the partner who opposes the renewal would be entitled to prevail.

The rule is, however, much restricted in its application since a partner who refuses to consent to acts which are clearly necessary for the proper carrying on of the firm's business may provide grounds for an application by his copartner to the court for the dissolution of the partnership.[55] Again if the firm has previously bound itself, then, on an equality of votes among the partners, those who favour the implementation of the obligation undertaken will prevail over those who favour the breach of it.[56]

Bona fide opinion after consideration of the minority view. The fourth rule enunciated by Clark has been otherwise expressed by Lord Eldon,[57] as follows—

> " That is the act of all which is the act of the majority, provided all are consulted, and the majority are acting *bona fide*, meeting not for the purpose of negativing what any one may have to offer, but for the purpose of negativing what, when they are met together, they may after due consideration think proper to negative. For a majority of partners to say, we do not care what one partner may say: we, being

[52] *In re communi, neminem dominorum jure facere quicquam, invito altero, posse.* Digest, X: 3:28.
[53] (1833) 1 Cr. & M. 345.
[54] *Clements* v. *Norris* (1878) 8 Ch.D. 129.
[55] Partnership Act 1890, s. 35 (*d*); *Butchart* v. *Dresser* (1853) 4 De G.M. & G. 542.
[56] *Butchart* v. *Dresser, supra.*
[57] *Const* v. *Harris* (1824) Turn. & R. 496 at p. 525.

the majority, will do what we please, is, I apprehend, what a court of
equity will not allow."

What the law will regard as prevailing over the view of the minority is not
the mere force of the combined view of the majority but the force of that
view arrived at after due consideration of the best interests of the firm in
process of which consideration the view of the minority must be honestly
weighed and considered. Though no doubt the views of all the partners
may be collected in any manner in which they can be communicated, yet
the most satisfactory way in which to arrive at a *bona fide* decision of the
partners will be to call a meeting of all the partners at which the divergent
views may not only be expressed but discussed one against the other. The
rule is a corollary of the principle that " the good faith of the partners is
pledged mutually to each other that the business shall be conducted with
their actual personal interposition, so that each may see that the other is
carrying it on for their mutual advantage." [58]   Thus where the majority
have arrived at a decision at a meeting to which all the partners were not
called or at which some did not attend, it will not suffice for the majority
to adduce evidence that even if all partners had been present the majority
would still have been able to pass the resolution which supported their
view, because if all partners had been present it is possible that the views of
one or more of the absent partners might in the ensuing discussion at the
meeting have influenced the view taken by the majority.[59]

Observance of prescribed procedure for arriving at majority decision. In
his fifth rule Clark deals with the case where the contract of copartnery has
prescribed rules for the procedure to be adopted in " ascertaining the will
of the company." Such procedural rules may provide, for example, that
not less than a prescribed number of the partners must be present at the
meeting at which the majority decision is taken. In such cases the procedure laid down must be followed. In the illustrative case mentioned, it
would not be sufficient to validate the decision of a majority of those present
at a meeting of partners at which less than the prescribed number of
partners was present, that it could be established that the required number
of partners was summoned to the meeting and that those who were absent
could not have converted the majority into a minority even if they had
attended.[60] The cases in which the contract of copartnery will prescribe
procedure for the holding of partners' meetings, apart from in some
instances declaring the intervals at which they will be held, are not likely
to be frequent and the law comprised in Clark's fifth rule has been developed mainly in relation to unincorporated bodies such as joint stock

---

[58] Lindley, *op. cit.* p. 331; *Peacock* v. *Peacock* (1808) 16 Ves. 49, *per* Lord Eldon at p. 51.
See also generally on the rule *Blisset* v. *Daniel* (1853) 10 Hare 493; *Great Western Ry.* v.
Rushout (1852) 5 De G. & Sm. 310; *Wall* v. *London & Northern Assets Corpn.* [1898] 2
Ch. 469; Clark, *op. cit.* I, pp. 195–196.
[59] *Const* v. *Harris, supra*; *Ex p. Morrison* (1847) De Gex 539.
[60] *Re London & Southern Counties Freehold Land Co.* (1885) 31 Ch.D. 223; *Howbeach Coal
Co.* v. *Teague* (1860) 5 H. & N. 151; *Ex p. Morrison* (1847) De Gex 539; *Young* v. *Ladies
Imperial Club Ltd.* [1920] 2 K.B. 523; *Knowles* v. *Zoological Society of London* [1959] 1
W.L.R. 823.

companies and clubs and to incorporated bodies. If, however, a contract of copartnership were to lay down rules for the convening and conduct of meetings of the partners, it can scarcely be doubted that any majority decision to be enforceable against the minority of the partners must be arrived at in accordance with the prescribed procedure, since the basic principle remains the same, *viz.*: " that as the company owes its existence to the will of its members, it lay with them to determine at its formation in what manner its will was to be ascertained; and that the rules laid down in the instrument of formation were conditions of the contract, in virtue of which the members agreed to form themselves into an association." [61]

Expulsion

The considerations above discussed with regard to the circumstances in which a decision of the majority of the partners may be upheld as one taken *bona fide* in the interests of the firm and all its partners will also apply where the majority exercise a power expressly conferred upon them by the deed of partnership. Thus in the absence of an express provision in the contract a majority of the partners has no power to expel a member of the firm on any ground whatsoever,[62] nor may the majority sell the shares of the dissentient minority of the partners.[63] Where an express clause in the contract confers on the majority a power to expel a partner, then both the grounds on which expulsion may be justified in terms of the contract and the procedural requirements there laid down for the exercise of the power will be strictly construed by the courts to guard against the abuse of such powers and the hardship which may result from the exercise of them. The requirements of the law governing the valid exercise of such a power of expulsion are more appropriately considered at a later stage [64] but, as illustrative of the partners' duty to deal faithfully and honestly with each other, it should be observed that the mere justification of the expulsion under the wording of the clause conferring the power will not avail the majority who have exercised that power, where the expelled partner can show that the expulsion clause has been used against him for an oblique motive and not *bona fide* in the interests of the partnership. In *Blisset* v. *Daniel*,[65] where the expulsion clause was in wide and general terms and where those invoking it were not required to give reasons for its exercise or to conduct any meetings or deliberations before exercising it, it was proved that they wished to rid themselves of their partner, not for any benefit of the firm from a commercial point of view, but because he had opposed the wishes of one of his copartners who had then prevailed upon the other partners to sign the notice of expulsion under threat of himself leaving the firm. That notice of expulsion was kept secret from the partner

---

[61] Clark, *op. cit.* I, p. 196; Story, *Partnership*, s. 123.
[62] Partnership Act 1890, s. 25.
[63] *Chapple* v. *Cadell* (1822) Jacob 537.
[64] *Infra* Chap. X, pp. 484 *et seq.*
[65] (1853) 10 Hare 493.

concerned until he had been induced to sign certain accounts which would be binding on him in the event of his expulsion. On those facts the court held the purported notice of expulsion to be void and restored the partner to his right as a member of the firm. " A clause like this enabling one partner to expel the other cannot be relied on unless there is good faith: it cannot be used if the motive is really to get an undue advantage over the other partner by purchasing him out on unfavourable terms." [66] The control of the courts over a power of expulsion may be affected by the terms of the clause conferring the power. They will be powerless if the power is expressed to be exercisable at the pleasure of one of the partners.[67]

Limitations on the mutual obligations of good faith, owed among partners

In the foregoing pages of this chapter, it has sufficiently appeared that the cardinal and overriding principle governing relations *inter socios* is the maintenance of a high standard of fairness in the dealings of partners, one with another. That principle has been variously described as resting upon the principle of *uberrima fides* or on fiduciary duty, though the use of either expression is rather to be justified as a figure of speech than as a legal term of art, and perhaps the descriptive phrase used by Lindley that the conduct of the partners one to another " will bear to be tried by the highest standard of honour," [68] is the most satisfactory way of describing those obligations of good faith which arise from the peculiarities of the partnership relation. That standard of conduct is expected of a person when negotiating for the formation of a partnership [69] and during the subsistence of the partnership itself. " The defendant, being the person whose business it was to keep the accounts of the concern, could not in fairness deal with the plaintiff for the share of the profits of the concern without putting him in possession of all information which he himself had with respect to the state of the accounts between them." [70] These propositions are but applications of the general principle to the special case of financial negotiations entered into between partners or intending partners themselves.

Yet in this area of the law there are certain qualifications of the application of the general principle. It has been said that if one partner be entrusted with the entire management of the partnership concern and he withdraws money for his own use which he duly and openly enters in the partnership books, " this is not a fraud which will entitle the joint estate to prove against the separate; it would be otherwise if by the entries in the books he disguises the transaction, or wholly omits and conceals it." [71]

---

[66] *Green* v. *Howell* [1910] 1 Ch. 495, *per* Cozens-Hardy M.R. at p. 507.
[67] *Russell* v. *Russell* (1880) 14 Ch.D. 471. The power was one to dissolve the firm but the conditions attached to its exercise made it very similar to a power of expulsion.
[68] *Op. cit.* p. 335.
[69] *Adam* v. *Newbigging* (1888) 13 App.Cas. 308; *Manners* v. *Whitehead* (1898) 1 F. 171.
[70] *Maddeford* v. *Austwick* (1826) 1 Sim. 89, *per* Sir John Leach V.-C. at p. 93. See also *Law* v. *Law* [1905] 1 Ch. 140.
[71] *Hay, ex p. Smith* (1821) 6 Madd. 2, *per* Sir John Leach V.-C.

Further, when the duties once owed to a copartner become owed to the representatives of a deceased copartner, the situation is not so clear. It is settled law that the remaining partners may purchase the share of a deceased partner from his executors. Where these executors are not themselves partners of the firm, they may arrange with the surviving partners as to the manner in which the deceased partner's share shall be ascertained or that it is to be held to be valued at an agreed sum. The creditors of the deceased partner or the persons beneficially interested in his estate may not maintain an action against the surviving partners based upon the obligation of conducting themselves according to the highest standards of honour which they owed to the deceased while in life. The agreement so made between the partners and the executors may be attacked only on the ground of fraud or collusion.[72] If there be no fraud or collusion but the executors have failed to obtain from the partners the true value of the deceased's interest in the partnership, no action will lie at the instance of the beneficiaries or creditors against the partners, though the executors themselves may be answerable if they have failed in their duty.[73]

On the other hand, where the executor of the deceased partner is himself a partner in the firm, the double capacity in which he is required to act may result in a conflict of interest and of duty. In such cases the courts regard any arrangement made by him as to the disposal of his deceased partner's share much more strictly and will frequently set aside any such arrangement upon the application of the persons interested in the deceased partner's estate. The arrangements will be set aside and reduced where they have involved the granting of releases by the beneficiaries in ignorance of the true state of the partnership accounts [74] or where errors are proved in the accounts.[75] They have also been reduced where they have involved the taking over of the deceased partner's share at a valuation which has later been shown to have been inadequate.[76] In such cases, there were factual grounds established for the setting aside of the agreement made, but the mere existence of the conflict of interest has been held sufficient to set aside the transaction.[77]

In cases such as *Cook* v. *Collingridge*,[77] however, where the sole ground of challenge is the conflict of interest arising through the executor's acting also in the capacity of partner of the concern, the *ratio* of the principle depends upon his duties as executor rather than as partner. As Lord Eldon observed, " One of the most firmly established rules is that persons

[72] *Davies* v. *Davies* (1837) 2 Keen 534; *Bowsher* v. *Watkins* (1830) 1 Russ. & M. 277.
[73] The court will, however, be reluctant to find the executors liable where in a case of difficulty they have acted bona fide in what they regarded as the best interests of the estate: *Rowley* v. *Adams* (1844) 7 Beav. 391; 2 H.L.C. 725.
[74] *Wedderburn* v. *Wedderburn* (1836) 2 Keen 722; 44 R.R. 331.
[75] *Millar* v. *Craig* (1843) 6 Beav. 433.
[76] *Stocken* v. *Dawson* (1843) 6 Beav. 371; (1845) 9 Beav. 239; *Rice* v. *Gordon* (1848) 11 Beav. 265.
[77] *Cook* v. *Collingridge* (1823) Jac. 607, *per* Lord Eldon at p. 621. The same approach was taken in the Scottish case *Lister* v. *Marshall's Trs.*, 1927 S.N. 55 (O.H.) where the emphasis was laid on the defender having received a benefit from the trust. In that case the claim was unsuccessful, being held to have been barred by *mora*.

dealing as trustees and executors must put their own interest entirely out of the question, and this is so difficult to do in a transaction in which they are dealing with themselves that the court will not inquire whether it has been done or not, but at once says such a transaction cannot stand." Such cases, therefore do not afford authority for imposing duties upon the executor *qua* partner in transactions relating to the share of his deceased partner. His duties are owed in his capacity as executor and his position as a partner of the concern merely establishes his personal interest which is in conflict with those of the beneficiaries in the estate which he administers as executor. The wider question whether a surviving partner is to be regarded as a trustee in his dealings with the representatives of his deceased copartner was considered in *Knox* v. *Gye*.[78] Lord Westbury said in his judgment in that case, " Another source of error in this matter is the looseness with which the word ' trustee ' is frequently used.   The surviving partner is often called a ' trustee,' but the term is used inaccurately.   He is not a trustee, either expressly or by implication.   On the death of a partner the law confers on his representatives certain rights as against the surviving partner, and imposes on the latter correspondent obligations.   The surviving partner may be called, so far as these obligations extend, a trustee for a deceased partner; but when these obligations have been fulfilled, or are discharged, or terminate by law, the supposed trust is at an end," [79] and at a later point in his judgment, Lord Westbury observed, " There is nothing fiduciary between the surviving partner and the dead partner's representative, except that they may sue each other in Equity.   There are certain legal rights and duties which attach to them; but it is a mistake to apply the word ' trust ' to the legal relation which is thereby created." [80]   One is left with the impression that the sharp difference of opinion between Lord Westbury and Lord Hatherley is one of expression only and might have disappeared if Lord Hatherley had chosen to define what he meant by the phrase " fiduciary duty."   Even so, it is sufficient justification for Lord Westbury's plea for accurate use of terms and avoidance of legal metaphors.   The notion that there is in any real sense a general fiduciary duty owed by the surviving partners to the representatives of the deceased partners seems inconsistent with the decision in *Cook* v. *Collingridge* [81] but in that case no claim was made against the surviving partners who were not executors of their deceased copartner.

Limits of partner's duties of disclosure to copartners

While the imposition of a high standard of honour in transactions among partners in the conduct of the business of the firm has been sufficiently established, in at least one Scottish decision there is authority for the view that a distinction may be drawn between those transactions and

---

[78] (1872) L.R. 5 H.L. 656.
[79] *Ibid.* at p. 675.
[80] *Ibid.* at p. 676, but see Lord Hatherley's dissenting opinion at pp. 678–679.
[81] *Supra* p. 190.

transactions which are in some measure referable to the partner's own personal affairs, even when the latter have some bearing upon his position as a partner.   In *Lonsdale Hematite Iron Co.* v. *Barclay*,[82] the partnership deed provided that if any partner failed to pay his instalments of capital when due, the other partners had the option of declaring his interest in the firm at an end, refunding to him any sum he had paid up.   The deed also provided that any partner might assign his share, if he first offered it to the company and then to the individual partners.   One of the partners failed to pay his contribution when due but later raised funds by agreement to assign his share to a third party.   The company accepted from him payment of his contribution.   He then offered his share to the company and to his copartners who rejected the offer, whereupon he assigned the share in terms of his agreement with the third party.   The value of his share had by then risen sharply and the company sought to have the transaction set aside, (1) because they had been kept in ignorance of the agreement to assign, knowledge of which would have allowed them to declare the share forfeited, and (2) because the terms on which the offer of the share to the company and its partners was made, were so exorbitant as to amount to a fraud on the company.   The court held, however, that there was no obligation to disclose the agreement since the company had no concern with the manner in which a partner raised his capital and that the partner was entitled to offer his share at any price he pleased to the company provided he did not thereafter assign it to a stranger at a lower price.

The same line of distinction may perhaps be discerned in *Cassels* v. *Stewart* [83] where the court held that the rule which requires a partner dealing with an asset or liability of the company or transacting in the line of the company's business to communicate any benefit derived by him to the company, did not apply to the case of a partner purchasing the interest of one of his copartners.   In both the decisions last cited the actual terms of the partnership deed had to be construed by the court, and therefore any general exception to the rule on the authority of the decisions must be cautiously regarded.   There is, however, in both decisions the suggestion that certain activities of the partner in regard to raising money to permit of his contributing his share of the capital or otherwise increasing his interest in the capital of the firm are not to be regarded as within the general scope of the overriding principle of accountability but rather to be treated as transactions referable to the partner as an individual and not falling within the statutory description of transactions " concerning the partnership," [84] though it must be confessed that the distinction is maintainable only upon a narrow construction of the statutory words.

Dishonest or immoral conduct not connected with the firm's business

There is a wider obligation upon the partners not so to conduct themselves in matters outside of the scope of the firm's business as adversely to

[82] (1874) 1 R. 417.
[83] (1881) 8 R.(H.L.) 1.   [84] Partnership Act 1890, s. 29 (1).

affect the reputation and business of the firm. This has been described by Lindley [85] as a general duty to be honest in his dealings with third parties. In *Carmichael* v. *Evans* [86] a partner was held to be in breach of that duty when he was convicted of travelling without a ticket with intent to avoid paying his fare. The partnership deed itself may expressly provide that action may be taken by the copartners on the ground of immoral or scandalous conduct of a partner, and it has been held competent to invoke such a clause in the case of a partner keeping a mistress. [87] Such cases raise no issues of accountability to the other partners but are rather concerned with the right of the other partners to dissolve the partnership [88]; and indeed *Barnes* v. *Youngs* [89] was chiefly concerned with the sufficiency of the notice of dissolution.

Remedies for breach of the obligation of the partners inter se

A failure by a partner to discharge the obligations to his copartners imposed upon him by the contract of partnership or implied in terms of the Partnership Act 1890 or under the common law will involve him in a breach of his contract. In cases where his conduct offends against section 29 or section 30 of the Act, the Act itself imposes upon him the obligation to account to his copartners for the benefits received by him. While the courts will entertain an action by one partner against another for an accounting, the English courts of equity were formerly averse from interfering in questions arising otherwise between one partner and another unless to order dissolution of the partnership or, if already dissolved, to order the final winding up of its affairs. The same judicial attitude can be seen in *MacCredie's Trustees* v. *Lamond* [90] where, on a winding up of a partnership on the death of a partner, the surviving partners claimed damages on averments that he had not attended to the business of the partnership. The Lord Ordinary (Fraser) held that, if the deceased partner was either unwilling or unable to perform his part of the contract of copartnery, the remaining partners should have sought their remedy by dissolution of the partnership. But the universal application of such a rule would in some cases involve that the non-offending partners might have to submit to a continuing wrong or, as the only possible alternative, to a dissolution of the partnership. The English courts have held that they will not allow a partner to derive any advantage from his own misconduct by placing his copartners in that dilemma. [91] On the other hand, the court will not interfere in a question between partners merely where there is disagreement among them. In the partnership relation, every partner is expected to

[85] *Op. cit.* p. 336.
[86] [1904] 1 Ch. 486.
[87] *Barnes* v. *Youngs* [1898] 1 Ch. 414.
[88] See *infra* Chap. X.
[89] *Barnes* v. *Youngs* [1898] 1 Ch. 414.
[90] (1886) 24 S.L.R. 114. See also *Landale* v. *Goodall* (1879) 16 S.L.R. 434.
[91] *Fairthorne* v. *Weston* (1844) 3 Hare 387.

exhibit tolerance towards his copartners and temporary differences, even when amounting to squabbles, will not be regarded by the courts as sufficient ground for a dissolution of the partnership or an interdict against the offending partner,[92] and questions of disputes as to management and general disagreement have been held to be insufficient as grounds of an action for damages between partners.[93]

The state of the authorities indicates that there is no support for an unqualified rule that the courts will refuse to grant a remedy in such cases save by way of ordering a dissolution of the partnership or its winding up or by way of ordering an accounting between the partners. The English courts still show reluctance to grant an injunction at the instance of one partner against another whose conduct is in breach of the contract of partnership, since the continuing relationship of confidence which should exist among the partners is in conflict with such a proceeding.[94] But where a breach of the contract of copartnery has taken place and the plaintiff can show resulting injury and loss to himself, the courts have on occasion awarded damages.[95]

While the technicalities of some of the English decisions in equity cannot readily be translated in terms of Scots law, the earlier Scottish decisions exhibit a somewhat similar approach to the question when an action is maintainable by some partners against others of their number who offended against the terms of the partnership agreement in the conduct of the firm's affairs. The decision in *MacCredie's Trustees* v. *Lamond* already referred to [96] and in *Beveridge's Trustees* v. *Beveridge* [97] sufficiently indicate the reluctance of the Scottish courts to intervene in the affairs of the partnership either by making an award of damages after the partnership has been dissolved [98] or even by ordaining the offending partners to concur in settling balance sheets of past years or to have new balance sheets adjusted at the sight of the court.[99] While in some cases the Scottish courts have found averments by a member of fraud in the management of the company relevant to support an action for damages against the offending directors [1] and have even expressed the opinion that that remedy is not removed by express wording of the contract of copartnery vesting the management in certain members as directors and providing that those directors were not bound to divulge the transactions of the company to the members who were not to have access to the books, since that provision was not pleadable

[92] *Marshall* v. *Colman* (1820) 2 J. & W. 266; *Smith* v. *Jeyes* (1841) 4 Beav. 503; *Lawson* v. *Morgan* (1815) 1 Price 303; *Cofton* v. *Horner* (1818) 5 Price 537; *Anderson* v. *Anderson* (1857) 25 Beav. 190; *Landale* v. *Goodall* (1879) 16 S.L.R. 434.
[93] *Ferguson* v. *Mackenzie* (1870) 8 S.L.R. 273.
[94] *Rely-A-Bell Burglar & Fire Alarm Co.* v. *Eisler* [1926] 1 Ch. 609; *Whitwood Chemical Co.* v. *Hardman* [1891] 2 Ch. 417; *Davis* v. *Foreman* [1894] 3 Ch. 655; *Kirchner & Co.* v. *Gruban* [1909] 1 Ch. 413.
[95] *Dean* v. *Macdowell* (1878) 8 Ch.D. 345.
[96] (1886) 24 S.L.R. 114. See *supra* p. 193.
[97] (1871) 9 M. 886; (1872) 10 M.(H.L.) 1.
[98] *MacCredie's Trs.* v. *Lamond, supra.*
[99] *Beveridge's Trs.* v. *Beveridge, supra.*
[1] *Leslie's Reps.* v. *Lumsden* (1851) 14 D. 213.

against averments of fraud,[2] the courts would require very clear and precise averments of fraud to entertain the action.[3]

The Scottish courts have also been reluctant to grant the remedy of interdict at the instance of a dissenting minority against a majority of the partnership. In *Brown* v. *Sir C. Adam* [4] interdict was granted against a majority who wished to apply deposits on shares in the partnership towards the expense of obtaining a special Act, the first application for which had been unsuccessful. The general rule, as stated by Clark,[5] is that " interdict is competent at the instance of companies against their partners, and of partners against their companies, when it is shown that either of them are doing, or intending to do, something injurious to the rights and interest of the other." The most frequent cases of successful application for interdict are where some of the partners have complained that the company has departed from the provisions of the agreement upon which it was formed [6] or where complaints are made of misapplication of the funds of the firm.[7] Most of such cases have occurred in relation to actions by a minority of the shareholders in a joint stock company against the majority; and even in such cases the propriety of granting interdict has been carefully considered.[8] In private partnerships, the remedy is available when some partners of the firm are about to transgress the provisions, express or implied, of the contract of copartnery; and in order to be successful the remedy must be sought before the threatened transgression has taken place. If the act has already taken place, the remedy sought must be by way of declarator.[9] Nor may interdict be obtained upon mere averments of fear that the acts will be perpetrated without averment of reasonable grounds for apprehension.[10]

Apart from those general requirements, the courts will always show some reluctance to award interdict in proceedings between partners of private firms.

> " In general, the courts are slow to interfere between the members of private copartneries; for it is evident that unless the partners agree to bear and forbear with each other's infirmities of temper, peculiarities of disposition, or occasional deviations from what may be deemed the strict line of duty, all combined action is impossible; and experience has shown that when disagreements of an important kind arise and are likely to continue, a dissolution of the partnership will generally be found the most desirable, and perhaps the only effectual remedy. When, however, the improprieties complained of are of a serious

[2] *Collins* v. *North British Bank* (1851) 13 D. 349; affd. 1 Macq. 369. The averments were, however, found irrelevant to found an action based on fraud.
[3] *Leslie* v. *Lumsden & Others* (1856) 18 D. 1046.
[4] (1848) 10 D. 744.
[5] *Op. cit.* I, p. 375.
[6] *Brown* v. *Sir C. Adam, supra; Learmonth* v. *Leadbetter* (1841) 3 D. 1192.
[7] *Wilson* v. *Glasgow & South Western Ry.* (1850) 13 D. 227.
[8] *National Exchange Co. of Glasgow* v. *Glasgow & Ardrossan Ry.* (1849) 11 D. 571; *Graham* v. *North British Bank* (1849) 11 D. 1165.
[9] *Fleming* v. *Newton* (1848) 6 Bell App. 175; *Shand* v. *Henderson* (1814) 2 Dow 519.
[10] *King* v. *Hamilton* (1844) 6 D. 399.

kind, and would make themselves felt notwithstanding dissolution, or if that cannot be brought about, the interference of the court by interdict will generally be obtained." [11]

A number of instances of improprieties of conduct which have been held to justify an interdict are cited by Clark mainly upon the authority of decisions on the granting of injunction by the English courts since the author considers that " the grounds upon which injunction is granted in England are for all practical purposes the same in relation to the present subject as those which warrant interdict in Scotland." [12]   While the view stated may be accepted as a proposition in general terms, some caution is required in applying the English authorities which he cites since, apart from the impropriety of conduct which was involved, in most cases regard was had to the further overriding consideration that a partner should not be allowed by his own misconduct to compel the innocent partners in every case either to condone that misconduct or to seek a dissolution of the firm.[13]   Clark's recognition of the same equitable consideration is expressed in different and perhaps more restricted terms where he writes of improprieties of a serious kind which would make themselves felt notwithstanding dissolution or where dissolution cannot be brought about.[14]   It is probably the law in Scotland as in England that the impropriety of conduct will justify the Court granting interdict if it can be restrained without compelling the partners to seek a dissolution of the firm.[15]

In all such questions, however, the courts will be required to construe the express terms of the contract of partnership before they may decide upon the granting of interdict and in cases like that of *Duff* v. *Corsar* [16] the decision to refuse the remedy of interdict may be said to proceed from the terms expressly agreed between the parties rather than from a general reluctance to interfere in the management of the partnership or indeed may arise from a combination of both considerations.

Rights of relief inter socios

In Scotland as a corollary of the special provision of the Act that the Scottish firm " is a legal person distinct from the partners of whom it is composed " it is provided [17] that " an individual partner may be charged on a decree or diligence directed against the firm, and on payment of the debts is entitled to relief *pro rata* from the firm and its other partners." This provision must be read along with the more general statement of the legal liability of partners contained in section 9 of the Partnership Act 1890:

" Every partner in a firm is liable jointly with the other partners, and in Scotland, severally also, for all debts and obligations of the

[11] Clark, *op. cit.* I, p. 572.
[12] *Ibid.* pp. 572–573.
[13] Lindley, *op. cit.* pp. 493–494.
[14] See the passage quoted *supra* pp. 195–196.
[15] *Taylor & Sons* v. *Taylor* (1823) 2 S. 157.
[16] (1902) 10 S.L.T. 27.
[17] Partnership Act 1890, s. 4 (2).

firm incurred while he is a partner; and after his death his estate is also severally liable in a due course of administration for such debts and obligations, so far as they remain unsatisfied, but subject in England or Ireland to the prior payment of his separate debts."

In this chapter what is studied is the position of the partners *inter se* during the subsistence of the relationship created by the contract of co-partnery. A more detailed consideration of the position of the retired or the deceased partner must be left to a later stage.[18] The rights of relief provided for among existing partners must, however, be considered; and in spite of the general nature of the principle enunciated in both the sections of the Partnership Act above quoted, that generality may be qualified by the particular situation obtaining in a particular case. Thus where A and B were the sole partners of a firm and accepted bills of exchange for the purposes of the firm's business, A met the bills when they were presented for payment and sued B for one-half of the amount paid by him. So far the case appeared a typical one which would be regulated by section 4 (2) of the Partnership Act 1890. Prior to A's action being raised, however, the partnership was dissolved and a judicial factor appointed for the purpose of winding it up. B pleaded that his liability to A should not be determined apart from the state of account between the partners in the partnership. A's action was sisted to await the results of the accounting in the judicial factory.[19] On the other hand, general arguments seeking to escape responsibility under section 4 (2) or section 9 must be closely regarded. In *Brown* v. *Sutherland*[20] a bill was drawn by one partner on certain other partners as trustees for an unregistered company in respect of a debt due by that company to the drawer. The bill was accepted by the drawees without qualification. On the drawer executing a charge for payment, the acceptors raised a suspension of the charge on the grounds (1) that they were liable *qua* trustees only, and (2) that the drawer, being a partner along with them, was liable with them *pro rata* for the amount in the bill. The court held that the charge was competent since the acceptors' signatures were unqualified and even if their liability was *qua* trustees only they had not averred that there were no funds of the association in their hands.

What section 4 (2) of the Partnership Act 1890 is concerned with is payment of a firm debt by one of the partners out of his personal funds. If he is merely the paying hand and applies the money of the firm toward satisfaction of the firm debt no claim for relief *pro rata* can arise at his instance against the other partners. It has been decided in England that, where a partner owes a personal debt to a third party to whom the firm is also indebted and makes a payment to that party from the money of the firm without specifying the account in respect of which the payment is made,

[18] *Infra* Chap. VII.
[19] *Stroyan* v. *Milroy*, 1910 S.C. 174.
[20] (1875) 2 R. 615.

the payment will be taken to have been made on account of the partnership debt.[21]

Right of access to the firm's books

In the absence of any agreement, express or implied, to the contrary—" The partnership books are to be kept at the place of business of the partnership (or the principal place, if there is more than one) and every partner may, when he thinks fit, have access to and inspect and copy any of them." [22]   While that provision is governed by the introductory words of section 24 that the rules enunciated in the subsections which follow may be displaced by agreement, express or implied, among the partners, a general obligation, not so qualified, is imposed in section 28:

> " Partners are bound to render true accounts and full information of all things affecting the partnership to any partner or his legal representatives."

Where the partner's right to inspect the books of the firm is not restricted under the agreed terms of the partnership, he may exercise the right through an agent whom he appoints for the purpose [23] so long as no reasonable objection can be taken by the other partners to the agent so appointed.[24]   When a partner seeks to inspect the books through an agent, his right of inspection by those means is qualified, and the court may refuse it on the ground that the assistance of an agent is not reasonably required in the particular circumstances [25] or that it is intended to conduct the inspection for an improper purpose.[26]   An agent may be required to sign an undertaking that no improper use will be made of the information gained from the inspection of the firm's books.[27]   A partner's right to inspect the books, as well as the derivative right of his agent, is for the proper purposes of informing himself as to the affairs of the firm so as to acquaint himself with his own position as a partner thereof and he is not entitled to make use of information so acquired for an improper purpose.[28]

Agreed restriction on partner's right to inspect accounts.   It is not sufficient to deny to a partner his right of inspection of the books and accounts that his copartner chooses to keep the relevant information in a private ledger which also contains entries relating to private transactions of his own with which his partner has no concern.[29]   If a partner attempts

---

[21] *Thompson* v. *Brown* (1827) Moo. & M. 40; *Pritchard* v. *Draper* (1831) 1 Russ. & M. 191; *Nottidge* v. *Pritchard* (1834) 2 Cl. & F. 379.
[22] Partnership Act 1890, s. 24 (9).   In regard to implied agreement as to the arrangements in a partnership the books of the firm may themselves constitute the appropriate evidence of such agreement and that evidence may be contradicted only in exceptional circumstances: *Scott's Exors.* v. *Gillespie* (1869) 6 S.L.R. 656.
[23] *Cameron* v. *McMurray* (1855) 17 D. 1142, *per* Lord Deas at pp. 1143–1144; *Bevan* v. *Webb* [1901] 2 Ch. 59.
[24] *Dadswell* v. *Jacobs* (1887) 34 Ch.D. 278.
[25] *Dodd* v. *Amalgamated Marine Workers' Union* [1924] 1 Ch. 116.
[26] *Duché* v. *Duché* (1920) 149 L.T. 300.
[27] *Bevan* v. *Webb* [1901] 2 Ch. 59.
[28] *Trego* v. *Hunt* [1896] A.C. 7; *Bevan* v. *Webb, supra.*
[29] *Freeman* v. *Fairlie* (1812) 3 Mer. 43; *Toulmin* v. *Copland* (1836) 3 Y. & C.Ex. 655.

to deny the right of his copartner by making it ineffective, by keeping no books of account at all or keeping them in an unintelligible form or destroying or withholding them, then on an accounting being ordered by the court, the court will allow a presumption as to matters *in dubio* in favour of the partner seeking the accounting and against the partner whose negligence or misconduct has rendered it impossible for proper books to be produced.[30]   It may be however, that, where neglect to keep proper books of account has given rise to the claim for an accounting, both partners are equally at fault, in which case there is no place for a presumption of the kind mentioned.

On the other hand, a partner may expressly agree that he will accept balance sheets prepared by his copartners as correct for the purpose of determining his share of the profits and will not have the right to inspect the books himself.   If so, he will be held to that agreement [31]; and it is expressly provided in the Partnership Act 1890 [32] that the assignee of a partner's share shall not, during the continuance of the partnership, have any right to require accounts of the partnership transactions or to inspect the books.

The nature and extent of the partner's share in the firm

While it will be necessary to revert to the subject in more detail at a later stage when examining the nature of partnership property,[33] some explanation of the general nature of the share of a partner in the partnership is called for when the rights of the partners *inter se* are under consideration.   " The partnership property, or joint-stock, is . . . held by all the partners jointly for the uses of the company, and one of the consequences of this is, that all heritable property belonging to the company is moveable *quoad* succession, for the only right in it which any partner possesses is a mere *jus crediti*." [34]   The share of a partner in the assets of the partnership is thus to be distinguished from the ownership of a share in a ship.[35] In the latter case, where the part owner is registered as such, he has a right of property *pro indiviso* in the ship and the right of the registered holder of each share in the ship is a separate and independent right and is both freely alienable as such by transfer to a third party and transmissible as such in the succession on the death of the part owner to his representatives.   The effect of this distinction can be seen in the nature and extent of the partner's share.   Thus, if no special agreement is made governing the share of each partner, all the partners in an ordinary partnership have an interest in the entirety of the partnership property,[36] but no partner has the right to any particular asset or assets comprised within the totality of the partnership

[30] *Walmsley* v. *Walmsley* (1846) 3 Jo. & Lat. 556; *Gray* v. *Haig* (1855) 20 Beav. 219.
[31] *Turner* v. *Bayley* (1864) 4 De G.J. & S. 332.
[32] s. 31 (1).
[33] *Infra* Chap. IX.
[34] Clark, *op. cit.* I, p. 178.
[35] Bell, *Comm.* II, pp. 544–545.
[36] Partnership Act 1890, s. 24 (1); and see *infra*, Chap. IX.

property to the exclusion of the other partners [37]; and that applies both during the continuance of the partnership as a going concern and after the dissolution of the partnership.[38] " What is meant by the share of a partner is his proportionate interest in the partnership assets after they have been all realised and converted into money, and all the partnership debts and liabilities have been paid and discharged." [39] It follows that whether the partnership assets consist in heritage or not, the partner's share in the partnership, being a share of the bundle of rights comprised in the partnership property after payment and discharge of the firm's liabilities, is on the doctrine of conversion moveable in nature, or, in terms more appropriate to Scottish legal theory, it is moveable in nature as a *jus crediti* rather than a *pro indiviso* right. This view is supported by a preponderance of pre-statute authority in England [40] and received unanimous support from such authority in Scotland [41]; and it is now enacted in section 22 of the Partnership Act 1890 which reads—

> " 22. Where land or any heritable interest therein has become partnership property, it shall, unless the contrary intention appears, be treated as between the partners (including the representatives of a deceased partner), and also as between the heirs of a deceased partner and his executors or administrators, as personal or moveable and not real or heritable estate."

It will be noticed that the general rule expressed in section 22 will be displaced if " the contrary intention " of the partners is apparent, so that where there is agreement, express or implied, that land forming part of the partnership property shall not be sold, that will exclude the application of the doctrine of conversion under English law.[42] The same considerations will not necessarily apply under the Scottish concept of the partner's share as a *jus crediti* but a fuller examination of this aspect of the question is more appropriately undertaken at a later stage when the property of the partnership is being considered.[43]

Distribution of the profits of the partnership and incidence of losses upon the partners inter se

This has an obvious and important bearing on the rights and liabilities of the partners *inter se*. For convenience of treatment, however, and to avoid unnecessary repetition it has been discussed in relation to the general subject of the property of the partnership.[44]

[37] *McGregor* v. *McGregor* (1823) 2 S. 461 (firm books); *Lingen* v. *Simpson* (1824) 1 S. & S. 600; *Cockle* v. *Whiting* (1829) Taml. 55.
[38] *Gopala Chetty* v. *Vijayaraghavachariar* [1922] 1 A.C. 488; but *cf. Gibson* v. *Stewart* (1835) 14 S. 166; (1840) 1 Rob. 260.
[39] Lindley, *op. cit.* pp. 366–367.
[40] Lindley, *op. cit.* p. 370, and cases there cited.
[41] *Corse & Anr., Petrs.*, Dec. 16, 1802, F.C.; *Kirkpatrick* v. *Sime* (1811) 5 Pat.App. 525; *Minto* v. *Kirkpatrick* (1833) 11 S. 632; *Irvine* v. *Irvine & Others* (1851) 13 D. 1367.
[42] Lindley, *op. cit.* p. 371, and cases there cited.
[43] See *infra* Chap. IX, pp. 389–391.
[44] See *infra* Chap. XI, pp. 527 *et seq.*

Assignation of partner's share

Section 31 of the Partnership Act 1890 provides—

" (1) An assignment by any partner of his share in the partnership, either absolute or by way of mortgage or redeemable charge, does not, as against the other partners, entitle the assignee, during the continuance of the partnership, to interfere in the management or administration of the partnership business or affairs, or to require any accounts of the partnership transactions, or to inspect the partnership books, but entitles the assignee only to receive the share of profits to which the assigning partner would otherwise be entitled, and the assignee must accept the account of profits agreed to by the partners.

" (2) In the case of a dissolution of the partnership, whether as respects all the partners or as respects the assigning partner, the assignee is entitled to receive the share of the partnership assets to which the assigning partner is entitled as between himself and the other partners, and, for the purposes of ascertaining that share, to an account as from the date of the dissolution."

The position of the assignee as laid down in section 31 of the Partnership Act 1890 reflects the common law principle that " no one can be introduced into a copartnery without the consent of all the members." [45] An assignee of a partner's share does not, therefore, become a partner in the firm, but since his right to the share in the partnership so assigned is recognised, it was a matter of some doubt prior to the passing of the Partnership Act 1890 whether the assignee might demand an accounting from the partners. In some English cases his right to an accounting appears to have been upheld,[46] whereas in others the right appears to have been denied.[47] In Scotland, the pre-statute common law appears to have reflected the terms of the section. In *Cassels* v. *Stewart*,[48] Lord Justice-Clerk Moncreiff said,

" It cannot be disputed, upon the decided cases, that, although there is a *delectus personae* in the contract of copartnery, any partner may, if he chooses, assign his own share to a third party, as long as that does not interfere with the conduct of the company, or the respective rights and interests of the partners. There is nothing to prevent this at common law, nor is there anything to prevent it in this contract of copartnery. All that is provided there about the assignment of shares in the copartnery is this, that the company shall not be bound to take any notice of transactions of that kind. And so long as the company are not called upon to take any notice of them there is no violation of this provision of the contract."

It seems, therefore, that, possibly because of the express invocation in

---

[45] Clark, *op. cit.* I, p. 60.
[46] *Whetham* v. *Davey* (1885) 30 Ch.D. 574; *Glyn* v. *Hood* (1859) 1 De G.F. & J. 334; *Kelly* v. *Hutton* (1868) L.R. 3 Ch. 703.
[47] *Brown* v. *De Tastet* (1819) Jac. 284. See also cases on rights of sub-partners, *infra*.
[48] (1879) 6 R. 936 at p. 945. The decision was affirmed on appeal (1881) 8 R.(H.L.) 1.

Scots law of the concept of *delectus personae*, the doubts arising from the pre-statute English decisions, find no place in the pre-statute common law of Scotland and that section 31 of the Partnership Act 1890 is an accurate statement of the Scots law prior to the passing of the Act. In any event section 31 has now settled the rights of the assignee in regard to an accounting from the partners. During the subsistence of the partnership he has no right to demand an accounting or even to inspect the books of the firm. Any such rights are vested in the assigning partner alone and are subject to the terms of the partnership agreement, express or implied. Upon a termination of the continuing relation of the partnership, however, by a dissolution of the firm, the assignee becomes a person whose rights are affected by the dissolution, without there being any justification for restricting these, as being in conflict with the relationship which must subsist while the partners are carrying on the business in association, and the assignee, on a dissolution, has the right to an account of the share falling to him by virtue of the assignation. It should be noticed that this right is a statutory one. It is not affected by the terms of the contract of copartnery, so that where, on the dissolution of the partnership, the contract of copartnery provides for arbitration in the event of differences arising among the partners, the assignee is not bound to submit to arbitration nor will he be bound by an accounting awarded in an arbitration among the partners to which he is not a party,[49] though, if he permits the question to be raised before the arbiter without objecting, he cannot subsequently dispute the arbiter's authority to decide the point.[50] In the case of an assignee of a partner's share, it will not be sufficient that a question relating to the amount of that partner's share has been referred by the partners to arbitration unless possibly he has received notice of the intention to do so and intimates no objection on his part. The contract of copartnery may, however, extend the scope of the matters to be referred to cover differences arising between the partners and persons claiming through or under a particular partner. It is suggested, though not decided, in the case of *Bonnin* v. *Neame* [51] that if the arbitration clause in terms includes persons claiming under the partners, such persons will be bound by it, but Lord Greene M.R. in *Shaylor* v. *Woolf* [52] appears to advance a view which is with difficulty reconciled with that proposition. In dealing with the argument that a contract, not one of partnership, could not be assignable because of the existence of an arbitration clause, Lord Greene said,

> " The question whether an arbitration clause prevents a contract from being assignable must depend upon the intention of the parties and the nature of the contract will, of course, be very important. Quite apart from an arbitration clause, if the nature of the contract is one which is incapable of assignment, owing to its personal nature,

[49] *Bonnin* v. *Neame* [1910] 1 Ch. 732.
[50] *Macaura* v. *Northern Assurance Co., Ltd.* [1925] A.C. 619.
[51] *Supra* n. 49.
[52] [1946] Ch. 320 at pp. 322–323.

there is no question of the assignability of the arbitration clause; but that an arbitration clause is assignable in its nature seems to me to be quite clearly contemplated by section 4 of the Arbitration Act 1889 [53], and it has been recognized in this court in . . . *Aspell* v. *Seymour*.[54] "

The effect of an arbitration clause in a partnership agreement which purports to bind not only the partners but those claiming through them may still be doubtful on the present state of the English authorities. On Lord Greene's reasoning it might be argued that even where third parties are in terms included within its scope, the clause will not bind the third party. The " intention of the parties " might be said to be a matter of express statement but the " parties " of whom that might be said are the partners themselves and not a third party who is an assignee of one of the partners. On the other hand the right which that third party takes upon assignation is subject to the limitations imposed upon the assigning partner. The real difficulty perhaps arises from the concept that the assignee has in terms of the Partnership Act 1890 a right to an accounting which is statutory and independent of the contract of copartnery. If that principle is followed to its logical outcome, the wording of the clause of arbitration in the contract of copartnery is of doubtful binding force on the assignee.

The restrictions imposed by section 31 on the rights of an assignee are imposed " during the continuance of the partnership." Apart from the denial of his right to an accounting or to inspect the books, he has no right to interfere in the management or administration of the partnership business during its continuance. Prima facie, therefore, there can be no question of his being a partner of the firm or even of his being held out as such partner by reason only of the assignation. But if the partners, in spite of their right to ignore the assignation for the purposes of the partnership, were to permit him to interfere in the management, a question would arise whether on the facts of the case they had received him as a partner or had held him out as such to third parties. Apart from that possibility, however, the assignee is in no position to take any effective steps against the partners in order to protect his right. The assignation confers no more than a right to payment of what on the basis of the accounts of the partnership may be due to the assigning partner.[55] Moreover he takes that right subject to the rights of the partners other than that of the assigning partner and is affected by their rights arising subsequently to the assignation.[56] He cannot escape that consequence even by intimating the assignation to the firm when it is granted.[57]

Sub-partnership

Arising from the implication of *delectus personae* in the partnership

[53] See now Arbitration Act 1950, s. 4 (1). On the Scottish position, see Irons & Melville, *Law of Arbitration in Scotland*, pp. 349–350.   [54] [1929] W.N. 152.
[55] *Cassels* v. *Stewart* (1881) 8 R.(H.L.) 1; *Whetham* v. *Davey* (1885) 30 Ch.D. 574.
[56] *Cavander* v. *Bulteel* (1873) L.R. 9 Ch. 79; *Re Knapman* (1881) 18 Ch.D. 300.
[57] *Bergmann* v. *McMillan* (1881) 17 Ch.D. 423; *Cavander* v. *Bulteel, supra*; *Kelly* v. *Hutton* (1868) L.R. 3 Ch. 703; *Redmayne* v. *Forster* (1866) L.R. 2 Eq. 467.

relation, an agreement made by one of the partners with a third party to share the proceeds of his share in the firm will create, as it were, a sub-partnership, or a partnership within the original partnership, but it will not make that third party a partner of the original firm. *Socius mei socii meus socius non est*.[58] The rule was expressed by Lord Eldon in these words, "I take it to have been long since established that a man may become a partner with A, where A and B are partners, and yet not be a member of that partnership which existed between A and B." [59] While such an agreement of sub-partnership infers the existence of another partnership to which the sub-partnership is subordinate and may involve a sharing between the sub-partners of profits which are derived from that other partnership, that sharing of profits is referable only to the partner's share which forms the subject of the sub-partnership and is a relevant consideration only in deciding whether a sub-partnership has been established. It is not relevant to establish a partnership between the original partners of the firm and the third party.[60] Though receipt of a share of the profits of a firm is prima facie evidence of partnership under the Partnership Act 1890,[61] it is expressly provided that the receipt of such a share " does not, of itself, make him a partner in the business," and while the subsection goes on to provide for particular instances when the receipt of a share of the profits is not " of itself " evidence of partnership, those illustrations cannot be regarded as exhaustive in view of the wording of the subsection as a whole.[62] The third party, therefore, is not by reason of the sub-partnership introduced as a partner into the original firm but he likewise incurs no liability for the debts of that firm by reason of sharing in its profits in terms of the sub-partnership.[63]

Delectus personae

The *ratio* governing the application of the rules which have been examined as to the rights of the assignee of a partner's share and as to those of a person with whom a partner has engaged in a sub-partnership is in each case explicable in terms of the personal relations involved in a contract of partnership. That emerges clearly from the discussion of the sub-partnership but it also lies at the root of the special treatment accorded to assignees, as can be perceived in the approach to the question by Lord Justice-Clerk Moncreiff in *Cassels* v. *Stewart*.[64] Yet the *delectus personae* which may be said to be characteristic of the partnership relation is an inference to be drawn when the parties are otherwise silent as to their intention. The nature and extent of the implication in favour of *delectus personae* have already been examined in some detail,[65] and it is sufficient at

---

[58] *Fairholm* v. *Marjoribanks* (1725) Mor. 14558. See Pothier, *Traité du Contrat de Société*, para. 91.
[59] *Ex p. Barrow*, (1815) 2 Rose 255.
[60] *Ex p. Barrow, supra.*
[61] s. 2 (3).
[62] See *supra* Chap. III, pp. 81–82.
[63] *Fairholm* v. *Marjoribanks, supra; Bray* v. *Fromont* (1821) 6 Madd. 5.
[64] (1879) 6 R. 936 at p. 945. See *supra*, p. 201.
[65] *Supra* Chap. I, pp. 16 *et seq.*

this stage to note that there is nothing in the Partnership Act 1890 or in the common law which will preclude a partner from introducing into the partnership a person to whom he has assigned his share, provided his existing partners have consented and there " is no particular mode or time required for giving that consent," [66] so that the requisite consent of his partners might be given in a clause in the partnership agreement which provided for a right of introduction on retirement or after death. In the case of the sub-partnership, a qualification of the implied *delectus personae* among the original partners is more difficult to envisage, since in a clear case of sub-partnership the partner concerned can be shown to have intended to enter a relationship with the third party which is independent of the original partnership relation. But the facts and circumstances in cases where a sub-partnership may be in issue are not always, or indeed often, clear, and will always require close scrutiny to determine whether they may be regarded as evincing an intention by all parties that the third party shall be received as a partner into the partnership.

Right of the firm to the services of the partners

While the partners are under obligations of the stringent nature discussed in this chapter in their conduct of the business of the partnership, the fact that those services are lost to the firm will not be a relevant ground of action for damages by the firm and its remaining partners against a third party who by his negligence has caused the personal injuries to the partner which have deprived his firm of his services, even when the firm can aver that loss of profit has resulted therefrom.[67] In England the action *per quod servitium amisit* which is available in certain circumstances to an employer in respect of loss of his employee's services through injury, is not extended by analogy to the case of a partnership.[68] In Scotland where the same form of action is not maintainable [69] the claim cannot be received as relevant, the more so since the partnership is in Scotland a separate legal *persona*.[70]

Liability of the firm and its partners to income tax

An important aspect of the rights and liabilities of the partners *inter se* is concerned with the assessment of and liability for income tax assessed upon the earnings of the firm. The questions arising on this context, however, are complicated and, moreover, the association which may be treated as a " partnership " for purposes of income tax is not necessarily identical with that which is defined as a partnership under section 1 of the Partnership Act 1890. For these reasons consideration of this question is deferred to a later stage when it can be examined in isolation.[71]

[66] *Lovegrove* v. *Nelson* (1834) 3 M. & K. 1, *per* Lord Brougham.
[67] *Gibson & Others* v. *Glasgow Corporation*, 1963 S.L.T. (Notes) 16.
[68] *Lee* v. *Sheard* [1956] 1 Q.B. 192, *per* Denning L.J. at p. 196.
[69] But see *McBay* v. *Hamlett*, 1963 S.L.T. 18 (husband and wife).
[70] *Gibson & Others* v. *Glasgow Corporation*, *supra*, *per* Lord Hunter.
[71] These questions will be discussed in a supplement to this volume.

Liability of partners inter se in delict

" Where, by any wrongful act or omission of any partner acting in the ordinary course of the business of the firm, or with the authority of his copartners, loss or injury is caused to any person, *not being a partner in the firm*, or any penalty is incurred, the firm is liable therefor to the same extent as the partner so acting or omitting to act." [72]

This section provides in general for the vicarious liability of the partnership for the wrongful acts of the individual partners but in the words for which italics have been supplied that liability is excluded in the case of injury being caused to one partner by the wrongful act or omission of another partner. In *Mair* v. *Wood and Others* [73] the argument was advanced that the right of a partner to claim against his copartner in such circumstances existed in the pre-statute common law of Scotland and in view of section 46 of the Partnership Act 1890 could not be held to have been taken away by mere implication in section 10. The Lord President (Cooper) examined the state of the pre-statute law of Scotland as to the vicarious liability of the firm for the wrongful act or negligence of one of its partners and found no warrant for holding that in the common law of Scotland a firm was so liable for the partner even when acting in the ordinary course of the firm's business. The reservation made in section 10, therefore, correctly states the Scots law and the firm may not be held vicariously liable for the injury caused to one partner by the wrongful act or negligence of another acting in the ordinary course of the firm's business. The Scottish rule is thought to apply, possibly *a fortiori*, in English law.[74] The individual partner would, of course, be liable to his copartner for his wrongful act or neglect.

[72] Partnership Act 1890, s. 10.
[73] 1948 S.C. 83. The case was one of joint adventure but the court held that there was no feature of a joint adventure which distinguished it in this respect from a case of partnership.
[74] See Lindley, *op. cit.* p. 188.

CHAPTER VII

RIGHTS AND DUTIES OF THE PARTNERS
IN RELATION TO THIRD PARTIES

Contract

THE importance of the idea of agency in the partnership relation has been
stressed in the immediately preceding chapter dealing with the rights and
duties of partners *inter se*.[1] Its bearing upon the relationship of the
partners and their firm with third parties is even more pronounced and
indeed the discussion in Chapter VI of the actual and apparent authority
of the partners and the effect of section 5 of the Partnership Act 1890 may
be regarded as a preliminary setting of the scene for a more detailed
examination of those questions in the present context. The approach,
however, differs slightly. In considering the relations of the partners
inter se the mutuality of the relationship of principal and agent existing
among the partners is the point which needs greatest emphasis. In the
question of rights and duties arising in relation to third parties that point,
while it may never be lost sight of, yields somewhat in importance to the
general concept of a particular partner acting as agent for his copartners
and the firm and so binding them as a consequence of his dealings with
third parties. In those dealings, the apparent authority conferred upon a
partner under section 5 of the Act is of importance as are section 15 as to
the effect of admissions and representations made by a partner concerning
the partnership affairs, and section 16 as to the effect of notice given to a
partner who habitually acts in the partnership business. But those sections do not by themselves exhaust the circumstances in which issues of
liability to third parties may arise. Along with them must be considered
sections 6 to 9 relating to liability in contract and sections 10 to 13 relating
to liability *ex delicto*. In this chapter it is proposed to deal with obligations arising from contract. Obligations arising from delict will be
considered in the immediately succeeding chapter.

According to the law of Scotland a firm may itself incur obligations
since it is a *quasi* person. The obligations so incurred may be owed to the
members of the firm or to third parties. The former type of obligation
has been discussed in the preceding chapter. In this chapter attention is
focused on obligations owed by the firm to third parties. But in both
cases the obligations are the obligations of the firm itself; they " must be
regarded as the proper obligations of the association viewed as a separate
person, and not as the joint and several obligations of the partners." [2]

---

[1] *Supra* pp. 158–159.
[2] Clark, *op. cit.* I, p. 241.

While the obligations of the firm connote that the partners, individually, are also liable therefor, the obligation of the individual partner is for the debt of the firm. He does not directly himself incur liability but is bound with his copartners *singuli in solidum* as a cautioner for his firm.[3]

Yet the firm as an artificial person can transact its business through the agency of individuals only. These agents are the partners of the firm or those other individuals who have been empowered by the firm, *i.e.* by the partners acting in name of the firm, to act on the firm's behalf. The position of the individual partner is thus conveniently explained in terms of agency.

> " Every partner is an agent of the firm and his other partners for the purpose of the business of the partnership; and the acts of every partner who does any act for carrying on in the usual way business of the kind carried on by the firm of which he is a member bind the firm and his partners, unless the partner so acting has in fact no authority to act for the firm in the particular matter, and the person with whom he is dealing either knows that he has no authority, or does not know or believe him to be a partner." [4]

That statement not only raises the question of the mutuality of the agency so created and of the limits of the individual partner's authority, it also raises the question how such limits of the partner's authority may be imposed and indeed how the firm may transact dealings which are not " for the carrying on in the usual way business of the kind carried on by the firm."

The partner's authority as agent for his firm

The general basis of the partner's authority is to be found in section 5 of the Partnership Act 1890 quoted above. Some consideration of its terms was attempted in Chapter VI [5] where its bearing upon rights and duties of the partners *inter se* was examined. The relevance of the section to the partners' rights and duties in relation to third parties, however, is of much greater significance and demands a more detailed and exhaustive examination of the terms of the section.

The business of the firm

Section 5 declares that " every partner is an agent of the firm and his other partners for the purpose of the business of the firm." In that general statement of the partner's actual authority, the Act has avoided the form of words later used to describe the case where the partner has no actual authority but may be represented or held out to third parties as possessing apparent authority. It is in the latter case that the section resorts to the use of the words " for carrying on in the usual way business of the kind carried on by the firm of which he is a member." There is, therefore,

[3] Bell, *Comm.* II, p. 507; Clark, *op. cit.* I, p. 241.
[4] Partnership Act 1890, s. 5.
[5] *Supra* pp. 158–159.

nothing in section 5 which, in the relationship of the partners *inter se*, precludes the partners from setting bounds to the actual authority exercisable in the firm's affairs by any one or more of their number; and any partner whose actual authority is so limited will be in breach of the contract of copartnery if he transgresses the boundaries of his actual authority even to effect a transaction which is " for carrying on in the usual way business of the kind carried on by the firm." In discussing section 5 Lindley comments, " It will be observed that the extent of a partner's authority to bind the firm is related to things done 'in the usual way' of the 'business of the kind carried on', where no actual authority or ratification can be proved. This probably means the same thing as saying that what is necessary to carry on the partnership business in the usual way is the test of the partner's implied authority to bind the firm." [6] That is true but, as expressed, it is submitted with respect, it contains only a partial truth. It may well be that an agreement of partnership which is entirely silent as to the authority of the individual partners to transact on behalf of the firm will be regarded as impliedly conferring upon them authority to do on behalf of the firm what is necessary, or even usual, to carry on its business in the usual way. Conversely if the transaction is one which has not been in the usual course of business of the firm the third party will not be permitted to rely on an implied authority in the partner to transact that business. [7] It may even be that where express restrictions are placed upon the actual authority of an individual partner to bind the firm those restrictions may be read subject to implication that to the restricted powers are added those which are consequential to the exercise of those restricted powers. But it appears nowhere as the intention of the Partnership Act 1890 that the actual authority of an individual partner should, in a question among the partners themselves, be generally extended by implication. [8] Moreover, where the agreement of partnership has expressly limited the authority of a partner, any further implied content in that limited authority will not be referable in general terms to " carrying on in the usual way business of the kind carried on by the firm " but, on the normal principles applicable in agency, will be confined to doing what is necessarily or normally incidental to the acts authorised to be done. [9]

---

[6] Lindley, *op. cit.* pp. 160–161.

[7] This rule may deny authority to the act of a partner which would otherwise be regarded as within his implied authority. *E.g.* a partner in a commercial firm has implied authority to draw and accept bills of exchange on behalf of the firm (*infra* p. 210) but in *Kennedy*, Dec. 22, 1814, F.C. it was held that a firm was not bound to retire a bill granted by one of the partners under the firm name without the privity of his copartners since it was granted in respect of a transaction which was not in the ordinary course of their business. The bill was drawn for value in soda and there had been no prior transaction in soda between the firm and the payees.

[8] This appears to be recognised in Lindley, *loc. cit.* but reads uneasily along with the reference in the same passage to the partner's " implied authority." There can be no implication of the existence of an actual authority in the teeth of an express restriction in the contract. *Expressum facit cessare tacitum*: *Tancred Arrol & Co.* v. *Steel Co. of Scotland* (1889) 16 R. 440; affd. (1890) 17 R.(H.L.) 31.

[9] *Pole* v. *Leask* (1860) 28 Beav. 562 at 574–575; *Collen* v. *Gardner* (1856) 21 Beav. 540; *Australia & New Zealand Bank* v. *Ateliers de Constructions Electriques de Charleroi* [1967] 1 A.C. 86.

Where the terms of the contract of partnership are such that a term may be implied therein as to the general authority of the individual partners to bind the firm, the apparent authority of the partner under section 5 to bind the firm by any act for carrying on in the usual way business of the kind carried on by the firm may be appealed to in order to embrace it by implication within the actual authority of the partner and indeed the courts have shown some readiness so to treat the question.   In the pre-statute cases the " ostensible " authority of the individual partner was normally assessed in relation to the type of business carried on by the firm though it is not always clear from the decisions whether the courts regarded that ostensible authority as an implied part of the partner's actual authority or merely as an apparent authority held out to third parties and thus barring the firm from denying it in subsequent proceedings raised by the third party who has acted upon the faith of it.   Thus the partners of a trading firm have an ostensible authority to borrow money on behalf of the firm,[10] to draw or accept bills of exchange,[11] to accede to a composition contract,[12] to purchase goods of the type dealt in by the firm,[13] and to engage servants and labour,[14] but not, in the normal case, to undertake cautionry,[15] to submit a dispute to arbitration,[16] or to take shares in satisfaction of a debt due to the firm.[17]   It has been held in England that one partner has no authority to bind the firm to a lease of a house for the purposes of the partnership business.[18]   In Scotland a similar question came before the courts in *Cooke's Circus Buildings Co.* v. *Welding*,[19] a case decided subsequent to the passing of the Partnership Act 1890 in which the court held both the partners in a joint adventure liable in payment of the rent stipulated for in a lease signed by one of the partners.   The claim made by the landlords in the lease, which was one for three years, was in respect only of the period during which the premises had in fact been occupied for the purpose of the joint adventure and the court had no difficulty in finding both partners liable on these special facts.   Lord Trayner, however, expressed the view that, had it been necessary for him to do so, he would have held the lease binding on the partners in the joint adventure for the whole period of its duration.[20]   It appears, though it is not so expressly stated, that his Lordship's view, which was not endorsed by the other

---

[10] *Dewar* v. *Miller* (1766) Mor. 14569; *Cameron* v. *Young* (1871) 9 M. 786; *Paterson Bros.* v. *Gladstone* (1891) 18 R. 403; *Bryan* v. *Butters* (1892) 19 R. 490.

[11] *Blair Iron Co.* v. *Allison* (1855) 18 D.(H.L.) 49.

[12] *Mains & McGlashan* v. *Black* (1895) 22 R. 329.   Though the issue in this case arose after the passing of the Partnership Act 1890 the terms of s. 5 do not appear to have been before the court.

[13] *Logy* v. *Durham* (1697) Mor. 14566.

[14] *Beckham* v. *Drake* (1841) 9 M. & W. 79; *Batchelor* v. *Dundee Commercial Society* (1831) 9 S. 549; *Ciceri* v. *Hunter* (1904) 12 S.L.T. 293.

[15] *McNair* v. *Gray Hunter & Speirs* (1803) Hume 753; *Blair* v. *Bryson* (1835) 13 S. 901; *Shiell's Trs.* v. *Scottish Property Investment Co. Building Society* (1884) 12 R.(H.L.) 14, *per* Lord Blackburn at p. 23.

[16] *Lumsden* v. *Gordon* (1728) Mor. 14567.

[17] *Niemann* v. *Niemann* (1889) 43 Ch.D. 198.

[18] *Sharp* v. *Milligan* (1856) 22 Beav. 606; and see *Clements* v. *Norris* (1878) 8 Ch.D. 129.

[19] (1894) 21 R. 339.

[20] At p. 348.

judges, was based upon the terms of section 5 of the Partnership Act 1890.

It seems clear that in the pre-statute decisions the question of the partner's implied authority to bind the firm has depended at least to some extent upon the nature of the business carried on by the partnership. Since the passing of the Act, the terms of section 5 as to the partner's apparent authority have had considerable influence upon judgments as to the extent of the implied authority to be considered as contained in the actual authority.[21] The question whether a particular transaction entered into by an individual partner may be regarded as concerned with carrying on the partnership business in the way in which businesses of its kind are usually carried on may, therefore, arise in relation to a partner's actual authority and not merely in relation to the authority which he has been held out to others as possessing. Evidence both as to the nature of the partnership business and as to the practice of persons engaged in that type of business will have a relevant bearing on the answer to that question; but as has been pointed out by Lindley [22] if the question is posed in the abstract, no answer can be supplied unless the act in question can be said, having regard to what is usual in business generally, to be one which is required for the prosecution of *any* business or is one which is not required for the prosecution of any business whatsoever. The range of acts which may be unhesitatingly allotted to one or other of those categories is limited and it may be said of that approach to the question that it would provide an answer only in those cases where there is likely to be no serious dispute. The question, which is likely to give rise to doubt, is whether an act which is not usual in the carrying on of all businesses universally is yet usual in the particular type of business carried on by the firm concerning whom the question is raised; and there is no general or abstract answer to such a question, since " the nature of the business and the practice of those who carry it on (usage or custom of the trade) must be known before any answer can be given." [23]

If the implied authority which has already been stated to exist in a partner of a trading company [24] is contrasted with that possessed by a partner of a firm of solicitors, the application of the words quoted above may be clearly seen. While a partner of a trading firm has implied authority to draw or accept bills of exchange [25] or to borrow money on behalf of the firm,[26] a partner of a firm of solicitors has no implied authority as to these activities.[27] A broad distinction may be drawn between trading and non-trading partnerships, between " general commercial partnerships " and those formed for professional or other non-trading purposes.

---

[21] See particularly *Mann* v. *D'Arcy* [1968] 2 All E.R. 172. [22] *Op. cit.* p. 162.
[23] Lindley, *loc. cit.* [24] *Supra* p. 210.
[25] *Blair Iron Co.* v. *Allison, supra* n. 11.
[26] *Dewar* v. *Miller* and other cases cited *supra* n. 10.
[27] *Hedley* v. *Bainbridge* (1842) 3 Q.B. 316; *Levy* v. *Pyne* (1842) Car. & M. 453; *Harman* v. *Johnson* (1853) 2 E. & B. 61 (negotiable instruments); *Plumer* v. *Gregory* (1874) L.R. 18 Eq. 621 (borrowing).

Thus Story [28] makes a general distinction of that kind and includes within the ostensible authority of a partner in a general commercial firm (1) the pledging and (2) the selling of the goods of the firm, (3) purchasing goods on behalf of the firm, (4) borrowing money for the purposes of the firm, (5) contracting and paying debts on behalf of the firm and (6) accepting, transferring, negotiating and arranging for the discounting of negotiable instruments. That statement of the law was approved in *Bank of Australasia* v. *Breillat* [29] but the list is not to be regarded as exhaustive. It is rather a list of the powers which, it may be inferred, are exercisable by a partner in a general commercial firm and which are not to be embraced by implication within the actual authority of a partner of a non-trading firm. Partners of all firms, whatever their nature, may have implied authority to engage servants for the conduct of the firm's business, [30] to grant receipts for the payment of debts due to the firm [31] and to engage solicitors to recover debts due to the firm or to defend an action raised against the firm. [32] Partners in a non-trading firm will have no implied authority to draw, accept, endorse, transfer or discount negotiable instruments on behalf of the firm [33]; nor may they borrow money on behalf of the firm [34] or pledge partnership property [35] without actual express authority.

More generally it may be deduced from the cases that the particular circumstances as to the nature and the scope of the particular partnership business in question must be considered, and on occasion examination of the nature of the act of the individual partner must be made closely and analytically. As a general rule it has been stated that " a partner has no implied authority to make his copartners partners with other persons in another business." [36] This proposition is generally acceptable and its application may be illustrated in many of the cases relating to *delectus personae*. [37] But the general rule does not dispense with the necessity of paying close regard to the actual nature of the partner's act even where it has resulted in his making his copartners partners with another person in a joint venture. In *Mann* v. *D'Arcy and Others* [38] D'Arcy, who was

---

[28] *Law of Agency* (9th ed.) pp. 139–141.
[29] (1847) 6 Moo.P.C. 152.
[30] *Beckham* v. *Drake* (1843) 11 M. & W. 315. It is doubtful, however, whether it is competent for a partner himself to enter a contract of service with his own firm: *Fife County Council* v. *Minister of National Insurance*, 1947 S.C. 629.
[31] *Porter* v. *Taylor* (1817) 6 M. & S. 156.
[32] *Court* v. *Berlin* [1897] 2 Q.B. 396; *Tomlinson* v. *Broadsmith* [1896] 1 Q.B. 386.
[33] *Backhouse* v. *Charlton* (1878) 8 Ch.D. 444. For this purpose a post-dated cheque has been regarded as on the same footing as a bill of exchange: *Forster* v. *Mackreth* (1867) L.R. 2 Ex. 163.
[34] Even a partner in a trading firm will not have implied authority to borrow money on its behalf unless the nature of the business is such that it cannot be carried on in the usual way in the absence of that power: *Hawtayne* v. *Bourne* (1841) 7 M. & W. 595; *Burmester* v. *Norris* (1851) 6 Ex. 796; *Ricketts* v. *Bennett* (1847) 4 C.B. 686.
[35] The power to pledge the firm's goods or other property depends upon the existence of the power to borrow on behalf of the firm: *Ex p. Bonbonus* (1803) 8 Ves. 540.
[36] Lindley *op. cit.*, p. 180, citing *Singleton* v. *Knight* (1888) 13 App.Cas. 788; *Hawksley* v. *Outram* [1892] 2 Ch. 359; *Re British Nation Life Assurance Association* (1872) 8 Ch.D. 704.
[37] *Supra* Chap. VI, pp. 204–205. See also on *delectus personae* Chap. I, *supra* pp. 16 *et seq.*
[38] [1968] 2 All E.R. 172.

the active partner in a firm in which he and the other two defendants were partners, agreed with the plaintiff " to go on joint account " with him on the purchase and resale of a consignment of potatoes forming part of the cargo of the *Anna Schaar*, the purchase and resale thereof being under the control of D'Arcy's firm. This was in effect an agreement for a partnership between D'Arcy's firm and the plaintiff in that single venture. Megarry J., however, held that the arrangement made by D'Arcy with the plaintiff was essentially one for sharing profit and loss on a transaction of purchase and resale of potatoes and was therefore something done for carrying on " in the usual way business of the kind carried on " by D'Arcy's firm, who were produce merchants. Though a partner has no authority to make his copartners partners with another person in another business,[39] D'Arcy had authority to bind and did bind his firm to the partnership with the plaintiff in this single venture, which was regarded by the court as itself part of the business of the firm. In *Lindern Trawler Managers* v. *W. H. J. Trawlers* [40] the scope of the business of the firm was under consideration. The firm had been formed to promote a company to own and manage trawlers and an individual partner was held to have authority to engage agents to manage a trawler. Since no *de facto* authority to do so existed, this must be regarded as a case of ostensible, in the sense of apparent, authority and thus more relevant to the study of the relations between the partners and third parties, but it may also be deduced from the decision that, had there been no *de facto* restriction upon the partner's authority, the engagement of agents to manage the trawler would have fallen within his actual, though implied, authority.

Sleeping partners

The position of the dormant, or sleeping, partner in regard to his liability for the acts of his copartners requires special consideration. Since a dormant partner himself takes no part in the active management of the firm and since his existence is not disclosed, the general underlying principle of mutual agency in partnership is of imperfect application. A dormant partner, as Lindley points out,[41] may be either (1) an undisclosed principal who carries on a business by means of partners or agents, or (2) a person who merely shares in the profits of a business which is carried on by others on their own account. That, however, is merely to say that a person who participates in the profits of a business may do so under terms and conditions which will amount to a partnership and cause him to be regarded as a partner although one who himself takes no active part in the management of the business. In that case the active partners carry on the business as agents on behalf of the firm and of the dormant partner as an undisclosed principal. On the other hand the terms upon which he

---

[39] *i.e.* the *ratio decidendi* of *Singleton* v. *Knight*; *Hawksley* v. *Outram* and *Re British Nation Life Assurance, supra* n. 36.
[40] (1949) 83 Ll.L.Rep. 131. *Mercantile Credit Co.* v. *Garrod* [1962] 3 All E.R. 1103 is also an illustration of this point.
[41] *Op. cit.* p. 160.

participates in profits may not be referable to partnership at all.   In that
case he is not a dormant or sleeping partner and his relationship with the
firm is explicable on other grounds, *e.g.* as a lender to, or creditor of the
firm.   In the former case the dormant partner will be liable for the actings
of his partners and agents in the course of carrying on in the usual way
business of the kind carried on by the firm though that liability is imposed
upon him rather by the law of principal and agent than by any speciality
of the law of partnership.   In the latter case where the participation in
profits is not held to be in itself sufficient to set up a partnership and the
other circumstances either do not support the intention of the parties to
enter a partnership or negate such intention,[42] then the dormant partner
(so-called) is in reality neither partner nor principal.   The persons who
carry on the firm's business do so on their own account and not as agents
with actual or apparent authority from him and there is thus no room for
the application of the doctrine of the undisclosed principal.

Authority in cases of emergency

The partner's authority as agent for his firm and copartners is to do
what is usual in the carrying on of business of the type carried on by the
firm.   There is no implication from that authority that he has an added
power to do an unusual act on behalf of the firm where circumstances of
urgency or emergency appear to call for the performance of that act.   In
a case concerned with agency, and not with partnership,[43] the nature of
the firm's business was such that there was no need to borrow money in
order to carry it on in the usual way.   Extraordinary circumstances
occurred in which money was needed to save the firm's property from ruin
and the agent of the firm borrowed money on its behalf to avert disaster.
The court held that the firm was not liable for the money so borrowed.
The principle laid down in the English decision cited above is regarded by
Clark as forming part of the law of Scotland.   " Hence there is no implied
power to do what, though not necessary, is convenient or beneficial, or
what, though unusual, may be defended on the head of urgency.   To do
such things requires the authority of the principal, that is, in the case of a
partnership, of the whole or at least a working majority of the partners." [44]
The principle, as applied in the English courts, may to some extent owe
its origin to the restricted application in England of the doctrine of agency
of necessity to a few exceptional cases already well recognised in the law.[45]
The corresponding legal concept in Scotland is that of *negotiorum gestio*,
" the management of the affairs of one who is absent or incapacitated from
attending to his affairs, spontaneously undertaken without his knowledge,
and on the presumption that he would, if aware of the circumstances, have

---

[42] *e.g. Cox* v. *Hickman* (1860) 8 H.L.Cas. 268.
[43] *Hawtayne* v. *Bourne* (1841) 7 M. & W. 595.
[44] Clark, *op. cit.* I, p. 199.
[45] McCardie J. in *Prager* v. *Blatspiel etc. Ltd.* [1924] 1 K.B. 566 took the view that the doctrine
was no longer so restricted but that view did not commend itself to Scrutton L.J.: *Jebara*
v. *Ottoman Bank* [1927] 2 K.B. 254 at p. 270.

given a mandate for such interference." [46] The Scottish idea is thus expressed in more general terms than the English one, which arises from particular types of case. It may, therefore, be wider in its ambit, though it will embrace the cases carried by the English doctrine of agency of necessity. [47] It is more difficult to accede to the view of Powell [48] that *negotiorum gestio* is merely a species of agency of necessity, since the wider concept is not readily embraced within the narrower one unless that is taken to signify that the restricted cases recognised in English law as covered by the doctrine of agency of necessity, while they do not justify the proposition that the doctrine of *negotiorum gestio* has been received in English law, yet in certain instances are typical though limited applications of that concept. In any event the problem raised in such cases as *Hawtayne* v. *Bourne* (*supra*), strictly speaking, is not one of *negotiorum gestio* where initially the person acting for another has no relationship but rather one where a person, already an agent, is regarded by the law as having had a greater or more extensive authority to deal with an emergency. [49] In both types of case there is the common feature of an appeal to necessity as justifying an act which the " agent " would otherwise be unauthorised to perform and it is possible to regard the English law of agency of necessity and the Scots law of *negotiorum gestio* as ideologically identical while regarding the Scots law based as it is upon principle derived from the Roman law as susceptible of a freer application in those cases where no initial relationship of principal and agent has existed and where the principle of *negotiorum gestio* approximates to the setting up of a quasi-contractual relationship based on the principle of restitution. The English law, on the other hand, tends to be more rigid in its application and to resist any attempt to extend the principle to classes of case beyond those to which there is precedent for applying it. Thus, though it has been said that " there is no authority which would preclude, in Scotland, the application of the rules of *negotiorum gestio* to cases dealt with in England under the head of agency of necessity " [50] it is also to be observed that the principle of agency of necessity has been developed independently and on more narrow and technical lines. [51]

The real question raised by the acceptance of *Hawtayne* v. *Bourne* [52] as authoritative in Scotland, is whether the Scottish principle of *negotiorum gestio* will operate in emergency to extend the authority already confided in one who is originally an agent of the persons whose affairs require urgently to be dealt with by powers which are not embraced within the agent's actual or ostensible authority. In *Hawtayne* v. *Bourne* it was decided that the resident agent appointed by the directors of a mining

[46] Bell, *Principles*, s. 540.
[47] Gow, *Mercantile and Industrial Law of Scotland*, p. 521.
[48] *The Law of Agency* (2nd ed.) pp. 410 *et seq.*
[49] Bowstead, *Agency* (13th ed.) pp. 29–34.
[50] Gloag, *Contract* (2nd ed.) p. 335.
[51] *Loc. cit.*
[52] (1841) 7 M. & W. 595.

company to manage the mine had no implied authority to borrow money
upon their credit in order to pay arrears of wages due to the labourers in
the mine who had obtained warrants of distress upon the materials belonging to the mine for the satisfaction of such arrears, and further that he
had no such power in any other case of necessity however pressing. The
question whether the power to borrow was within the implied or apparent
authority of the resident manager had not been put to the jury at the trial
but the trial judge had told the jury that they might infer an authority in
the agent, not only to conduct the general business of the mine, but also,
in case of necessity, to raise money for that purpose. He was not upheld
on appeal. Parke B.[53] said,

> " I am not aware that any authority is to be found in our law to
> support this proposition. No such power exists except in the cases,
> alluded to in the argument, of the master of a ship and of the acceptor
> of a bill of exchange for the honour of the drawer. The latter derives
> its existence from the law of merchants: and in the former case the
> law, which generally provides for ordinary events and not for cases
> which are of rare occurrence, considers how likely and frequent are
> accidents at sea. . . . "

It will be observed that Parke B. regards the cases of agency of necessity
as of a closely limited class to which the case before him did not belong;
nor is it possible on analysis to deduce any general principle that agency
of necessity will arise as a sort of *quasi* contract where the *gestor* was a
person who initially had no authority whatsoever as agent from the
" principal " but will not operate where the *gestor* was initially an agent
and seeks to extend the scope of his authority by appealing to the necessity
of the particular situation: for while the master of the ship referred to in
the first example given by Parke B. may be regarded as initially in the
position of an agent for the owners of the vessel,[54] the acceptor for honour
of a bill of exchange need not stand in any such initial relationship to the
drawer.

    It is therefore possible to argue that the persuasive authority of
Hawtayne v. *Bourne* in Scots law is dubious, since the result which Parke
B. was unable to reach *via* the English law of agency of necessity might
possibly be reached in Scotland *via* the principle of *negotiorum gestio*.
The passage quoted from *Clark on Partnership* [55] which relies exclusively
upon the English authorities [56] may, therefore, imperfectly reflect the law
of Scotland. The point is, however, probably of more significance in

[53] *Ibid.* at pp. 659–660.
[54] But not usually of the cargo owner; yet he may in emergency hypothecate the cargo: *The
Cargo ex Sultan* (1859) Sw. 504.
[55] *Supra* p. 214.
[56] On examination of the authorities cited by Clark in support of the passage quoted it will
be found that the Scottish decisions all relate to the denial of any authority to do what is
" convenient or beneficial," whereas his statement that there is no power to do " what,
though unusual, may be defended on the head of emergency " rests on the authority of the
English cases, *Hawtayne* v *Bourne, supra, ex p. Chippendale* (1853) 4 De G.M. & G. 19;
Dickinson v. *Valpy* (1829) 10 B. & C. 128; and *Ricketts* v. *Bennett* (1847) 4 C.B. 686.

legal theory than in practice, since in a question between partners it must be rarely that circumstances can arise where the partners cannot consult together as to the steps which should be taken to meet an emergency.[57]

Admissions and representations made by a partner

The Partnership Act 1890, s.15, reads as follows—

" An admission or representation made by any partner concerning the partnership affairs, and in the ordinary course of its business, is evidence against the firm."

The admission or representation must be made by a person in his character as a partner.   It is not sufficient that he is a partner at the time when it is sought to bring the evidence of the admission or representation before the court, if it was made before the person making it became a partner of the firm.[58]   While the section provides that admissions and representations made by a partner shall be evidence against the firm, it does not declare them to be *conclusive* evidence and they are not necessarily conclusive. Thus where an action is raised against the partners of the firm an admission made by one of the partners in answer to interrogatories has been held in England not to be evidence against the others unless they have been allowed the opportunity of contradicting it [59] and the English courts have refused to order a partner to pay trust money into court on an admission, contained in the pleadings and answers to interrogatories of his co-partner, which he has himself denied.[60]   Section 15, however, is not in its terms designed to cover the last case, since the admission made did not relate to the ordinary course of the partnership business.[61]

On the other hand, admissions and representations made by a partner may be made in circumstances which raise a plea of personal bar at the instance of the third party affected by them and thus preclude the firm from denying the state of affairs represented in the admission or representations.   To advance a plea of personal bar the third party must establish that he acted in reliance upon the statement to his own detriment [62]; for the essence of a plea of personal bar is that " owing to the action of one party the other party has been put in a worse position than he would otherwise have been in." [63]   Moreover, the admission or representation by the partner must be as to a matter within his actual or apparent

---

[57] Though if the *gestor* has ultroneously involved himself in the transaction of another party's affairs he may claim reimbursement *quantum lucratus* from that other party: Erskine, *Inst.* III: 3: 52.

[58] *Tunley* v. *Evans* (1845) 2 D. & L. 747; 69 R.R. 877; *Catt* v. *Howard* (1820) 3 Stark. 3; 23 R.R. 751.

[59] *Parker* v. *Morrell* (1848) 2 Ph. 453; *Dale* v. *Hamilton* (1846) 5 Hare 369.

[60] *Hollis* v. *Burton* [1892] 3 Ch. 226.

[61] It is to be noted that s. 15 is of little assistance in a question arising between an individual partner and his firm regarding property held in the name of the individual partner but alleged by the firm to be held in trust for the firm.   The trust must be proved by writ or oath of the defender, even if he is a partner: *William Laird & Co.* v. *Laird and Rutherford* (1884) 12 R. 294.   See *infra* Chapter IX.

[62] *Re Coasters Ltd.* [1911] 1 Ch. 86.

[63] *Magistrates of Alloa* v. *Wilson*, 1913 S.C. 6, *per* Lord President Dunedin at p. 12.

authority, the latter being related in section 15, as in section 5, of the Partnership Act 1890 to the partnership affairs " and in the ordinary course of its business." The firm will, therefore, not be bound by a representation by one of its partners that he has authority to do something which does not fall within the ambit of his apparent authority as warranted by the nature of the firm's business [64]; nor, it is thought, will the firm be bound by the representation of one of its partners that the firm's business is more extensive, or is different in nature, from what it is in reality.[65]

" Notice to one partner is notice to all partners "

Section 16 of the Partnership Act 1890 provides—

> " Notice to any partner who habitually acts in the partnership business of any matter relating to partnership affairs operates as notice to the firm, except in the case of a fraud on the firm committed by or with the consent of that partner."

The terms of section 16 reflect the general principles of the law of agency which have been more elaborately expressed [66] as follows:

> " (1) When any fact or circumstance, material to any transaction, business or matter in respect of which an agent is employed, comes to his knowledge in the course of such employment, and is of such a nature that it is his duty to communicate it to his principal, the principal is deemed to have notice thereof as from the time when he would have received such notice if the agent had performed his duty, and taken such steps to communicate the fact or circumstances as he ought reasonably to have taken. Provided that
>
> (a) where an agent is party or privy to the commission of a fraud upon or misfeasance against his principal, his knowledge of such fraud or misfeasance, and of the facts and circumstances connected therewith, is not imputed to the principal; and
>
> (b) where the person seeking to charge the principal with notice knew that the agent intended to conceal his knowledge from the principal, such knowledge is not imputed to the principal.
>
> (2) Knowledge acquired by the agent otherwise than in the course of his employment on the principal's behalf, or of any fact or circumstance which is not material to the business in respect of which he is employed, is not imputed to the principal."

The general principle sought to be enunciated by section 16 of the Partnership Act 1890 is tolerably clear and is borne out by the more general statement of the position as between agent and principal in the passage

---

[64] *Ex p. Agace* (1792) 2 Cox 312; *Jacobs* v. *Morris* [1902] 1 Ch. 816.
[65] The third party could not successfully rely on such a representation in contradiction of his own knowledge of the firm and its normal business: *Ex p. Agace* (*supra*), whereas if he has no knowledge of the firm and its business, he is in effect dealing with an agent whose authority, actual or apparent, is unknown to him and such an agent cannot bind his principal by misrepresenting his authority to the third party. See *e.g. Lewcock* v. *Bromley* (1920) 37 T.L.R. 48. The point is discussed in Lindley, *op cit.* pp. 192–193.
[66] Bowstead, *Agency* (13th ed.) p. 355.

just quoted. If a firm secures the benefit of a transaction negotiated by one of its partners, it is not permitted to put itself in a more advantageous position than that in which the partner would have been, if he had been acting as a principal, by pleading its own ignorance of what that partner himself knew.[67] The section is, however, silent as to the date at which such notice is imputed to the firm. In the law of agency, notice is imputed to the principal as from the time when he would necessarily be expected to have received the information, had the agent performed his duty.[68] The wording of section 16 simply states that notice to the partner " operates as notice to the firm." It is possible to regard this as implying that notice to the partner operates as *simultaneous* notice to the firm without any question arising as to the lapse of any period which the agent (the individual partner) might reasonably require in order to pass on the information to his firm, since in the normal conduct of the affairs of a partnership there should not arise in practice any occasion for delay in transmitting the information to the other partners though the realities of the relationship make it difficult to postulate that such complete exchange of information will take place among the partners. The interpretation is also not entirely to be supported on these grounds, at least if section 16 is to be regarded as declaratory of the pre-existing law, since if two firms have a partner common to both, then notice which is imputable to one of the firms is also imputable to the other if the information is referable to the business of the latter firm.[69] It can thus occur that the knowledge of an individual partner of one firm is imputed to that firm and to its partners, including the common partner, and by reason of his imputed knowledge will be imputed to the second firm of which he is also a partner. If the decisions in the earlier cases are to be regarded as reflected in the terms of section 16, it is probably to be interpreted as implying that notice to a partner operates as simultaneous notice to the firm. In none of the decisions, including those dealing with knowledge imputed through a common partner, does the question whether that notice is simultaneous appear to have been expressly considered, but since the decision in such cases appears to proceed upon the principle that knowledge of one partner is knowledge of all,[70] no question of an intervening period for transmission of the knowledge among the partners seems to arise. It is thought that the terms of section 16 of the Partnership Act 1890 preserve this principle and are to be interpreted as imputing the knowledge of a partner to the firm and his copartners without notice by him to the other partners. While such knowledge will be imputed to the remaining partners they may still have a remedy against a partner who has failed to communicate the knowledge which he has obtained, since he may be regarded as in breach

---

[67] *Collinson* v. *Lister* (1855) 7 De G.M. & G. 634.
[68] *Dresser* v. *Norwood* (1864) 17 C.B.(N.S.) 466; *Proudfoot* v. *Montefiori* (1867) L.R. 2 Q.B. 511; *Rolland* v. *Hart* (1871) 6 Ch.App. 678.
[69] *Steele* v. *Stuart* (1866) 2 Eq. 84; *Porthouse* v. *Parker* (1807) 1 Camp. 82; *Re Worcester Corn Exchange Co.* (1853) 3 De G.M. & G. 180; *Jacaud* v. *French* (1810) 12 East 317; *Powles* v. *Page* (1846) 3 C.B. 16.
[70] See *per* Tindal C.J. in *Powles* v. *Page, supra* at p. 30.

of his duties to them as laid down in section 28 of the Partnership Act 1890.[71]

" The knowledge of one partner is the knowledge of all partners "

While this rule may, as has been suggested above, imply that any knowledge acquired by a partner in the conduct of and relevant to the firm's affairs is simultaneously to be imputed to the firm and his co-partners and while the words " operates as notice to the firm " in section 16 may bear the same interpretation, the knowledge as imputed to the firm and its other partners is constructive, not actual. As Lindley states,[72] it would be absurd to hold that a firm has actual knowledge of everything done by each of its partners. The effect of the rule is simply that a third party who requires to establish that the firm had knowledge of a particular matter may generally do so by proving that notice was given to one of its partners who habitually acts in the business of the firm and that on that being proved the firm may not plead the fact that some of its members were unaware of the fact to evade liability on the ground of the knowledge of another, or others, of its members by whose acts the firm is bound or the benefit of whose acts the firm claims.[73] The rule thus again depends to some extent upon the apparent authority of the partner to whom the notice has been given and this entails that the third party must be able to show that he relied upon that apparent authority.[74] Section 16 recognises this by stipulating that the notice which shall operate as notice to the firm is " notice to any partner who habitually acts in the partnership business." It is, however, not clear from the terms of the section whether the partner must in fact be occupied upon the affairs of the partnership at the time when he receives the notice. There is no decision in a partnership case which is directly in point on this question. On the analogy of agency it may be that in commercial cases the principal will have impliedly imputed to him the knowledge acquired by his agent even when that knowledge is not acquired in his character as agent.[75]

Execution of written contracts on behalf of the firm

The general rule is that the proper method of binding an unincorporated

---

[71] " Partners are bound to render true accounts and full information of all things affecting the partnership to any partner or his legal representatives." See *supra* pp. 198–199.

[72] *Op. cit.* p. 165.

[73] It has been held that a solicitor advising a partnership on a lease sufficiently discharges his duty by tendering his advice to the partner who consulted him and is under no obligation to inform all the partners of his advice: *Sykes and Others* v. *Midland Bank Executor and Trustee Co. Ltd. & Others* [1970] 2 All E.R. 471.

[74] *Underwood (A.L.) Ltd.* v. *Bank of Liverpool and Martins Ltd.* [1924] 1 K.B. 775; *Houghton & Co.* v. *Nothard Lowe & Wills Ltd.* [1928] A.C. 1. The Scottish cases *Downes* v. *McFie & Co.* (1829) 8 S. 246 and *Smith* v. *N.B. Railway Co.* (1850) 12 D. 795 may perhaps be explained upon the same *ratio*.

[75] *Dresser* v. *Norwood* (1864) 17 C.B.(N.S.) 466; but only apparently if it was the agent's duty to disclose the facts coming to his knowledge to the principal: *Newsholme Bros.* v. *Road Transport & General Insurance Co.* [1929] 2 K.B. 356.

association is for all the members to sign individually. In the case of partnerships, Clark [76] considers that the rule should be adhered to " in all contracts of importance, particularly such as do not fall within the ordinary sphere of the company's line of business—*e.g.* where a cash credit bond is signed by a company as sureties." That rule will conveniently cover the case where limits are set upon the individual partner's authority to bind the firm, if those limits are set forth in a formal writing, since in that case they will appear in the contract of copartnery or in a supplementary minute thereto, and will be subscribed by all the individual partners in their own names. Where the transaction is a mercantile one but one which is not plainly referable to the sphere of the business usually carried on by the firm, as in the example given in the passage quoted, it would be prudent to have the document subscribed by one of the partners in the firm name and by all the partners in their individual names, though if the obligation is clearly expressed as an obligation of the firm it would be sufficient if each partner adhibit his individual signature.

In the case of mercantile documents which clearly fall within the scope of the usual business carried on by the firm, the rule is not rigidly applied. In such cases an individual partner has implied authority to bind the firm,[77] and the firm will be bound by the adhibiting of the firm name by any partner, or by his signing his own name *per procurationem* of the firm. A distinction is drawn by Clark between a firm name which " includes the name of one or more individuals " and a descriptive name which does not include the names of individuals. In the former case it is sufficient if the individual partner adhibit the firm name to the document [78] but in the latter case " signature by the descriptive name without joinder of the signing partner as agent would not, it is thought, be enough." [79] An individual partner may, however, sign his own name *per procurationem* of his firm which he may designate by a descriptive name, provided that the firm is usually known by that descriptive name.[80]

The distinction drawn by Clark is in accordance with usual practice in such matters, but it is more difficult to state the precise legal principle which supports it. The basis upon which the distinction rests is to be discovered in the treatment of the joint stock company and is so treated by Bell in contrast with the position under a private partnership. ". . . Although a joint stock company cannot in Scotland sue or be sued by the descriptive name, as a private partnership may by its firm; and although the partners cannot, by subscribing that name, bind the company; the company have been allowed to sue or be sued in

---

[76] Clark, *op. cit.* I, p. 242.

[77] Partnership Act 1890, s. 5; *Robb* v. *Forrest* (1830) 8 S. 839; *Forsyth* v. *Hare & Co.* (1834) 13 S. 42; *McLean* v. *Rose* (1836) 15 S. 236.

[78] *Selkrig* v. *Dunlop*, May 30, 1804, F.C.   Such a document if written and in the handwriting of a partner and signed by him in the firm name is regarded as holograph of his firm: *Nisbet* v. *Neil's Tr.* (1869) 7 M. 1097.

[79] Clark, *op. cit.* p. 243; Bell, *Prin.* § 399; *Culcreugh Cotton Co.* v. *Mathie* (1822) 2 S. 47.

[80] *Fleming* v. *Ballantyne* (1842) 5 D. 305; *Blair Iron Co.* v. *Alison* (1855) 18 D.(H.L.) 49.

the descriptive name, with the addition of the names of all or some of the partners." [81] It will be noticed that what Bell is chiefly concerned to explain is the right of an unincorporated association to sue or to be sued in its descriptive name with the addition of the names of a number of representative members. That aspect of the question will be examined later.[82] It does not, however, relate to the question of the proper subscription of a partnership obligation where the firm name is a descriptive one. The partnership may be itself distinguished from the joint stock company in that (1) all the members of the partnership have implied power to transact in the name of the firm, not merely the directors, trustees or managers as in the case of the joint stock company and (2) the firm name, descriptive or otherwise has been recognised by statute in the case of a partnership.[83] As distinct from the unincorporated association the partnership is further distinguished in that it possesses in Scots law a *quasi persona.*[84]

In examining the opinion expressed with some caution by Clark that an individual partner may not validly execute a document obligatory upon his firm, even when the transaction is within his implied authority as a partner, by merely adhibiting the firm name to it when it is a descriptive name, it is possible to adopt two differing lines of approach. On the one hand one may deduce the rule as to signature from the rule prevailing in Clark's time as to the mode in which a firm bearing a descriptive name may sue or be sued. While the two are not necessarily identical there is an analogy to be drawn between the mode in which an obligation may be incurred by a firm and the mode in which it may be enforced against it. That analogy seems to be invoked by Clark,[85] and he is supported in his view by the decision in *Culcreugh Cotton Company* v. *Mathie.*[86] Though the decision turned upon title to sue, the brief note by the reporter of the *ratio decidendi* states that the court held that there was a clear distinction between the case where a mercantile company sued under its firm name *by which it granted obligations* (as Douglas Herron & Company or the like) and where it sued under a mere descriptive name as in the case under consideration. While the decision, therefore, does not itself support Clark's view, there is a clear indication in the reasoning by which it was reached that the analogy relied on by Clark was recognised by the court. In *Blair Iron Company* v. *Alison*,[87] it was pleaded that where a promissory note was signed thus—" Blair Iron Company, Alexander Alison," the firm signature " Blair Iron Company " was merely descriptive and was not binding on the partners of that

---

[81] Bell, *Prin.* § 399.
[82] *Infra* pp. 222–223.
[83] " Persons who have entered into partnership with one another are for the purposes of this Act called collectively a firm, and the name under which their business is carried on is called the firm name "—Partnership Act 1890, s. 4 (1).
[84] Partnership Act 1890, s. 4 (2).
[85] *Op. cit.* I, pp. 242–243.
[86] (1822) 2 S. 47.
[87] (1855) 18 D.(H.L.) 49.

company. The Lord Chancellor (Lord Cranworth) said that there was nothing in the objection that the promissory note was signed with the descriptive name of " The Blair Iron Company " and by Alexander Alison, and not " The Blair Iron Company *per* Alexander Alison." Any form of signature whereby it was indicated that the note was granted by Alison as the acting partner of the firm was sufficient to bind the company. The rule that the adhibiting by a partner of a descriptive firm name to the document is not in itself sufficient, as it would be in the case of a proper firm name composed of the names of individuals, seems to be implicit on that decision though the Lord Chancellor does not reveal the provenance of that rule.

It is possible to regard the rule as based upon the analogy referred to in *Culcreugh Cotton Company* v. *Mathie* [88] or merely upon mercantile practice which has itself become recognised in the form of a legal rule. Even if it be justified by analogy with the procedural requirements of suing or being sued in the descriptive name, the analogy throws little light upon the legal principle upon which it is founded.

It is thus difficult to discern with any certainty a basic principle in legal theory which will satisfactorily account for the treatment of the descriptive name as an invalid execution of a document. No assistance is to be obtained from the Partnership Act 1890 which is neutral on the point, merely providing in section 4 (1)—

> " Persons who have entered into partnership with one another are for the purposes of this Act called collectively a firm, and the name under which their business is carried on is called the firm name."

It is true that the subsection in no way precludes the use of a descriptive name as the firm name but nowhere in the Act is there any provision which distinguishes a descriptive name from any other firm name in legal effect or indeed which stipulates as to the force and effect to be given to a document to which a partner has adhibited the firm name.

It may be preferable, therefore, to regard the rule as based upon practice. Whatever the doubts which may be entertained as to the analogy between the rule as to execution of documents and the rule as to the manner in which the firm may sue or be sued it is clear that as a matter of commercial practice the execution of a document on behalf of a firm by the mere adhibiting of a descriptive name by a partner is not likely to be accepted as valid. It may be argued that there is little to distinguish this from the adhibiting of a firm name consisting of the names of individuals none of which names is now possessed by the present partners of the firm. Legal rules are not always entirely logical, particularly if they have grown out of practice. As a matter of practice the rule appears now to be regarded as axiomatic. In the latest edition of Burns' *Conveyancing Practice* [89] it is stated, when considering the

---

[88] *Supra* n. 86.
[89] Fourth Edition (1957) by Professor F. MacRitchie, p. 91.

provisions to be made in the contract of partnership as to the firm name, " This will be specified. Where it is descriptive, *e.g.* Dalkeith Coal Company, it ought to be stated how letters, cheques, etc. are to be signed, whether the Dalkeith Coal Company *per* John Smith or Thomas Brown, or by any individual partner as director, manager, secretary or otherwise."

Liability of the firm under contracts in writing

The contracts which are binding upon a firm may be made in any manner in which a valid agreement between the firm as a *quasi* person and the third party may be established. It is, therefore, possible for a partner acting within his authority, actual or apparent, to bind his firm to a contract whether arrived at orally or in writing. The implications of this will be examined later in this chapter. For the moment attention is directed solely to the problems arising as to contracts undertaken in writing on behalf of the firm. Two questions may arise as to the liability of the firm under contracts entered into in writing, and both are reflected in the terms of section 5 of the Partnership Act 1890. Under that section the authority of an individual partner to bind the firm is limited to transactions which are " for the carrying on in the usual way business of the kind carried on by the firm." If, therefore, the partner enters into a transaction which does not fall within the usual scope of carrying on the firm's business, then prima facie the firm is not bound in the obligations which he so incurs. The broader implications of this rule will be considered later. At this stage it is necessary to examine the particular results arising where a transaction which is not for carrying on in the usual way the business of the firm is entered into in writing. The view of Clark as to the state of the law prior to the passing of the Partnership Act 1890 has already been noticed,[90] and it is probably true that since the passing of that Act the valid execution of a document binding the partnership to an obligation of that kind should be by all partners signing the document. There are however several points which are worthy of attention. First, where a document of this nature is signed in the firm name by an individual partner, it may be later ratified by the remaining partners so as to give rise to a binding obligation on the partnership.[91] Secondly, even where all the partners individually sign their names to a document of this nature, it is essential that the obligation thus undertaken should be clearly one of the partnership and not merely a collective obligation of the partners as individuals; for in the latter case, the firm itself will not be bound[92]; and if an individual partner subscribes his own signature to a bond granted by the firm for a cash credit to be kept in the name of the firm, he may be bound thereby not only as a partner

---

[90] *Supra* p. 221.
[91] See *e.g. Thomas* v. *Atherton* (1878) 10 Ch.D. 185.
[92] *Plotzker* v. *Lucas*, 1907 S.C. 315; *Kay* v. *Johnson* (1864) 2 H. & N. 118. A promissory note signed by two individuals who were partners of a bankrupt firm has been held in the sheriff court not to vouch a claim against the firm and averments as to prior transactions were held irrelevant in *Middleton* v. *Pyper* (1935) 51 Sh.Ct.Rep. 20.

but as an individual.[93]   Thirdly, where an individual partner signs the firm name to a document it is still possible for the court to look at the circumstances of the transaction to see if they are such as to render the firm liable.

Whether the written contract binds the firm

In a number of early decisions [94] the report suggests that even where a contract has been entered into in writing in the name of the firm, the court may in certain circumstances hold that the firm is not bound thereby. It is important to analyse these decisions closely to discover whether they support, as at first reading of the reports they appear to do, an equitable jurisdiction in the court to relieve the firm of liability in such cases where it is just and equitable to do so.   In *Proudfoot* v. *Lindsay*,[94] a promissory note for £1,000 had been granted in favour of Proudfoot by Charles Archer & Son in exchange for a loan of that sum.   The partners of Charles Archer & Son were Charles and William Archer.   They, along with John Archer and one, Gray, were partners in a firm known as the Perth Foundry Company.   Charles Archer & Son fell into arrear with payment of the interest on their note and they prevailed upon Proudfoot to cancel their note and accept in lieu thereof a promissory note for the same amount granted by the Perth Foundry Company.   That note was signed by John Archer, as manager, and Charles and William Archer as partners of the Perth Foundry Company.   The remaining partner, Gray, was not informed of the transaction which was not entered in the company's books, nor were the payments of the interest which were thereafter regularly made on the note.   On the sequestration of the Perth Foundry Company, Proudfoot claimed to rank as a creditor for the sum in the promissory note but the court held that it was not a debt of the firm.   In *Blair* v. *Bryson*,[94] Bryson accepted a bill drawn on him by Blair & Morrison originally carried on by John Blair and William Morrison but the partners of whom at the material time were Robert Blair, son of John Blair who was now deceased, and William Morrison. Some months later Morrison died insolvent and shortly afterwards Robert Blair also died.   Bryson sued John Blair's representatives and Robert Blair founding on the bill which he had accepted and a letter to him from Blair & Morrison acknowledging that his acceptance on the bill was one for which he had " received no value."   It was proved that neither the signature of the firm name as drawers of the bill nor on the letter of acknowledgment were in the handwriting of Robert Blair, that no entry appeared in the firm's books regarding the bill, though there was an account kept there between the firm and Morrison but that in a private book kept by Morrison such an entry appeared.   It was also proved that between Bryson and Morrison as an individual there

---

[93] *Mellis* v. *Royal Bank of Scotland,* June 22, 1815, F.C.
[94] *Proudfoot* v. *Lindsay* (1825) 3 S. 443; *Blair* v. *Bryson* (1835) 13 S. 901; *McLeod* v. *Tosh* (1836) 14 S. 1058.

had been similar transactions and that on Morrison's death Bryson had ranked as a creditor on his individual estate. The court adhered to the interlocutor of the Lord Ordinary (Moncreiff) who had assoilzied the defenders. Lord Medwyn said, " This is a case of a company obligation and it is necessary for the respondent to make out that it was applied for a company debt which the circumstances of the case show that it was not. . . . There is thus prima facie evidence against the respondent, and he would require to bring contrary evidence to take off the presumption which hence arises." In *McLeod* v. *Tosh* [94] George and John Tosh carried on business in partnership under the firm name of George Tosh & Son. In 1826 an acknowledgment of receipt of £40 from McLeod was signed in the firm name which was adhibited by John Tosh. In 1828 the firm was dissolved and in the published notice thereof it was stated that the business was to be carried on by John Tosh who was authorised to receive and discharge sums due to the firm and who undertook to pay all debts. McLeod thereafter rendered an account to John Tosh as an individual including the sum of £40 therein. In October 1828, an arrangement was come to between McLeod and John Tosh whereby McLeod gave Tosh a memorandum in which the £40 was entered as one of Tosh's own individual debts. Tosh on his part acknowledged in a letter affixed to the memorandum that he had himself borrowed the sums mentioned in the memorandum and granted his own bill for £172 to McLeod which was expressly declared by Tosh to include the £40. Tosh was sequestrated in December 1828 and McLeod ranked as a creditor. He made no application to George Tosh, who continued solvent, for payment of the £40. In June 1833 he raised an action against George Tosh and John Tosh founding on the acknowledgment granted in the firm name and requiring payment of the £40 after deduction of the dividends received from John Tosh's estate. The court in the circumstances adhered to the interlocutor of the sheriff which assoilzied the defenders.

It is thought that none of these decisions affords any basis for a general legal doctrine that the court may relieve the firm from obligations validly entered into where it is just and equitable to do so. On analysis of the facts in each case, the decision is found to turn upon a more restricted principle of law. Thus in *Proudfoot* v. *Lindsay* the promissory note granted by the Perth Foundry Company was clearly not a transaction " the carrying on in the usual way business of the kind carried on by the firm." It was of the kind described by Clark as " such as do not fall within the ordinary sphere of the company's line of business "; and therefore required the signature of all members of the firm.[95] The absence of Gray's signature on the note and the fact that the transaction was kept entirely secret from him are sufficient of themselves to account for the decision. In *Blair* v. *Bryson* the circumstances may be thought

[95] Clark, *op. cit.* I, p. 242.

to come nearer to establishing a general equitable principle, but the court merely decided that, on the past history of dealings between Morrison & Bryson, in view of the fact that the transaction was entered in Morrison's private books and not in the books of the partnership and since Bryson himself had recognised Morrison as his creditor by ranking on his individual estate, there was proof that the obligation which purported to be a firm debt was really a private debt of Morrison's and no countervailing evidence had been led by Bryson to displace that view of the facts.[96] *McLeod* v. *Tosh* was a clear case of novation and was so regarded by the court after a careful consideration of the facts in view of the presumption against novation.

In some early decisions, however, the foundation of the reasoning on which the court relieved the firm from liability is not so clearly reported. Where it was sought to suspend a charge against a partner of a firm on a bill accepted in name of the firm at the instance of a third party who actually had taken the bill in satisfaction of a private debt owed by the partner individually to the third party, the court passed the bill in order to ascertain whether the holder of the bill was a *bona fide* onerous indorsee. It was later held that he was, and the bill was orderly proceeded.[97] The bill was therefore regarded as binding upon the firm but there is a clear inference that it would not have been binding if the indorsee had not taken in good faith and for onerous consideration. This is borne out by English authority.[98] In *McNair & Company* v. *Gray Hunter & Speirs*[99] a partner who granted a guarantee in the firm name for dealings by himself and his mother in goods in which the firm did not deal was held not to have bound the firm thereby; and in *Kennedy*[1] a bill drawn " for value in soda " was accepted by a partner in the firm name as guarantee for the debtor in the transaction. It was held that the bill could not be recovered from the firm since the transaction was not of the ordinary course of its business and was not entered in the firm's books; and in *Johnston Sharp & Company* v. *Phillips*[2] a bill granted by a partner in the firm name for a private debt was held not to be binding on the firm.

That there may be cases, even in relation to negotiable instruments, where the adhibiting of the firm name by one of the partners will not bind the firm is well settled. But these cases do not establish any principle that if a partner uses the partnership name for his own private ends, then the firm will not be bound because the benefit accrues to the individual partner and not to the firm. Even where an incidental

[96] See *supra* p. 226.
[97] *Clarke* v. *Shepherd* (1821) 1 S. 179; (1823) 2 S. 255. On the firm's liability on bills see *infra* pp. 244–245.
[98] *Ex p. Bonbonus* (1803) 8 Ves. 540 (firm held liable, the creditor in the bill being innocent of the fraud); *Arden* v. *Sharpe & Gilson* (1797) 2 Esp. 524 (firm not liable since indorsee had been told to keep the transaction secret from the other partner, which was held sufficient to have made indorsee aware of the fraud).
[99] Jan. 19, 1803, F.C.
[1] Dec. 22, 1814, F.C.
[2] (1822) 1 S.App. 244. See also *Miller* v. *Douglas*, Jan. 22, 1811, F.C.

advantage is derived by the firm, that will not necessarily result in the firm being bound.[3] The true principle upon which such cases are decided is stated by Lord Chancellor Eldon,[4]

> " There is no doubt now the law has taken this course; that if, under the circumstances, the party taking the paper can be considered as being advertised in the nature of the transaction, that it was not intended to be a partnership proceeding, as if it was for an ante-cedent debt, prima facie it will not bind them; but it will, if you can shew previous authority or subsequent approbation; a strong case of subsequent approbation raising an inference of previous positive authority. In many cases of partnership and different private concerns it is frequently necessary for the salvation of the partnership that the private demand of one partner should be satisfied at the moment; for the ruin of one partner would spread to the others who would rather let him liberate himself by dealing with the firm. The nature of the subsequent transactions, therefore, must be looked to, as well as that at the time."

The equitable principle announced in these words is more limited than one which would allow the courts to apply general considerations of what justice and equity would demand as between the third party and the firm. Yet it is the only principle of law which may be appealed to with certainty on the question. Where the cases appear to extend the principle further they are found on examination to derive not from any general principle of the law of partnership but from the nature of the transaction itself as established in proof[5] or from a different and more specific rule of partnership law,[6] or from doctrines derived from the general law of contract.[7] The limited principle laid down by Lord Eldon in *Ex parte Bonbonus*[8] reflects partly the legal doctrine of the apparent authority of the partner[9] and partly the effect of later actings of the partners which may be held to have ratified a transaction entered into by an individual partner who had no authority actual or apparent to bind the firm in that transaction. Lord Eldon's point is well taken that the measure of the firm's liability will not necessarily be assessed on a consideration of the features of the transaction entered into by the individual partner in isolation but upon a consideration of that transaction in the light of subsequent actings of the partnership. The commercial exigencies of a relation such as partnership may well entail upon occasion that partners will, by their actings, even if not expressly, ratify what has

---

[3] *Johnston Sharp & Co.* v. *Phillips* (1822) 1 S.App. 244. On liability of the firm *quantum lucratus*, see *infra* Chap. VIII, pp. 256–258.
[4] *Ex p. Bonbonus* (1803) 8 Ves. 540 at pp. 544–545.
[5] *e.g. Blair* v. *Bryson* (1835) 13 S. 901; *Clarke* v. *Shepherd* (1821) 1 S. 179; (1823) 2 S. 255. The more complex case of *Low* v. *Lizars* (1838) 16 S. 1092 is another example of the same nature.
[6] *e.g. Proudfoot* v. *Lindsay* (1825) 3 S. 443.
[7] Such as *e.g.* novation: *McLeod* v. *Tosh* (1836) 14 S. 1058.
[8] *Supra* n. 4.
[9] See passage from his judgment above quoted.

been done by an individual partner in the firm name, even when without authority and sometimes when done for his private benefit to the detriment, or even in fraud, of his firm. It may be the decision of the remaining partners in such a case to have the offending partner make redress within the partnership itself rather than repudiate his actings publicly. The offending partner may not, of course, rely upon such clemency being shown to him [10] but if it in fact is shown, the transaction will become binding upon the firm.

Where the reported decisons support any doctrine that the partnership will not be held bound to an obligation entered in the firm name by a partner for his private benefit, it is only upon a principle of the restricted application discussed above that those decisions may be reconciled with the numerous decisions that the firm will be held bound by a transaction entered into by a partner, within the scope of his apparent authority, even where the firm offers to prove that the transaction was for the private benefit of the partner and not for the benefit of the firm. Thus in *Turnbull* v. *McKie* [11] a partner was held liable for a bill subscribed by another partner who acted as manager and who signed the bill *per procurationem* of the firm. He had no authority to grant bills but the bill in question was for goods of the description of those in which the firm traded.[12] *Bryan* v. *Butters Brothers & Company*,[13] a case more frequently cited for a wider principle, also supports the liability of the firm where the partner has entered a transaction for his own benefit and decided further that, where the partner had no actual authority to enter the transaction for the firm though it was within his apparent authority, the objection could not be taken that the writ in question was signed not by the partner but by the firm's cashier on his instructions. In spite of a characteristically vigorous dissenting judgment of Lord Young, the court held that, though the partner in question had no actual authority to borrow the money in question, he could authorise the firm's cashier to sign the acknowledgment of the loan on behalf of the firm and that the writing so signed was the writ of the firm.

Rei interventus

In the circumstances which have been under discussion and in other cases yet to be discussed where a partner in his dealings on behalf of the firm has exceeded his apparent authority, the situation may arise that the firm is imperfectly bound in a contract with a third party. In general cases of imperfect obligation, the doctrine of *rei interventus* may, in

---

[10] His partners, if so minded, might apply to the court for dissolution of the partnership on the ground that he " has been guilty of such conduct as, in the opinion of the court, regard being had to the nature of the business, is calculated to prejudicially affect the carrying on of the business "—Partnership Act 1890, s. 35 (*c*).

[11] (1822) 1 S. 353.   See also *McLeod* v. *Howden* (1839) 1 D. 1121; *McKenzie* v. *James* (1926) 42 Sh.Ct.Rep. 289.

[12] Hence it was within the apparent authority of a partner of a trading firm to grant bills for transactions in the goods: *Bank of Australasia* v. *Breillat* (1847) 6 Moore P.C. 152 at p. 193.

[13] (1892) 19 R. 490.

appropriate circumstances, be invoked to perfect the obligation. The doctrine has been given its classical statement by Bell in a familiar passage in the *Principles* [14] where he states that *rei interventus* " is inferred from any proceedings not unimportant on the part of the obligee, known to and permitted by the obligor to take place on the faith of the contract as if it were perfect; provided they are unequivocally referable to the agreement, and productive of alteration of circumstances, loss, or inconvenience, though not irretrievable." The doctrine is a general doctrine in the law of contract; hence it is applicable to contracts undertaken by or on behalf of a firm, as is recognised by Clark.[15] Beyond mentioning the applicability of the doctrine to contracts of a firm, however, Clark does not develop the theme. It is, therefore, left somewhat in doubt whether he intends merely to remind us of the applicability of a general principle to be kept in mind, *e.g.* that contracts of service with a partnership, though informally entered into may be set up *rei interventu* so that there is no longer *locus poenitentiae*, or whether he desires to direct attention to the doctrine as worthy of particular study in the context of partnership.

From the words of Bell's definition it may be deduced that special problems in regard to the doctrine may arise in partnership and indeed the nature of these problems is reflected in the example given in the passage quoted from *Clark on Partnership*: for if *rei interventus* is to be inferred from " proceedings . . . known to and permitted by the obligor to take place," then, where the obligor is a firm, the questions arise— whose knowledge may be imputed to the firm and whose permission is to be regarded as the permission of the firm for the purpose? The obvious answer is in each case, that of a partner. As to knowledge, the Partnership Act 1890 in section 16 provides—

> " Notice to any partner who habitually acts in the partnership business of any matter relating to partnership affairs operates as notice to the firm, except in the case of a fraud on the firm committed by or with the consent of that partner."

Permission of the firm, like any other act relating to the business, may be granted on behalf of the firm by its agents, the partners, under section 5. It might therefore appear that the application of the doctrine of *rei interventus* was readily applicable by reason of the agency of the partners in the firm's affairs. Even so, there are questions which require closer examination.

The knowledge of a partner is not imputed to the firm under section 16 where a fraud is perpetrated on the firm either by, or with the consent of, that partner. Knowledge of the transaction by the individual partner who entered into it for his own private ends will therefore not suffice to

---

[14] § 26.
[15] *Op. cit.* I, p. 245: " If a contract be merely pending between a firm and a stranger, any one of the partners may rivet it indissolubly *rei interventu, e.g.* by accepting on the part of the company delivery of goods in relation to which the sale had not been formally completed."

raise a plea of *rei interventus* against the firm, nor, of course, will any
" permission " to be inferred from his dealing with the third party be
regarded as " permission " by the firm in terms of Bell's definition. The
question remains whether another partner who accepts for the firm
goods sold under a contract made without authority by his partner (to
use Clark's example) is to be regarded as having perfected the contract
on behalf of the firm *rei interventu*. If the other partner is the only other
partner in the firm it might be said that his intervention in the matter
effected a complete agreement with the firm: if he is only one of a number
of other partners then it is difficult to see how his actings can validate
an unauthorised transaction which would require the consent of all the
partners for its validation. In these cases, it appears unsound to appeal
to the principle of *rei interventus*. What is really being postulated is a
ratification by the firm of the actings of the offending partner. It is at
least doubtful whether ratification in such a case may take place unless
with the consent of all the remaining partners [16] and since ratification
can only take place where the ratifying party has knowledge of the
circumstances, the knowledge of the firm for this purpose must amount
to the knowledge of all the remaining partners.[17]

It is therefore difficult to envisage the operation of the doctrine of
rei interventus in the circumstances mentioned by Clark, *i.e.* where it is
invoked to perfect a transaction which is imperfect initially as being beyond
the apparent authority of the partner dealing on behalf of the firm. Even
if there be only two partners and the remaining partner subsequently
does some act in relation to the transaction which induces the third party
to believe that the obligation of the firm has been perfected, the act of
the remaining partner is more conveniently regarded as one of ratification.
He must of course have knowledge of the circumstances in order to ratify,
but knowledge must equally be proved if *rei interventus* is to operate [18];
and the result of invoking that doctrine would merely be to accept the
burden of establishing that the subsequent acts of the third party " took
place on the faith of the contract as if it were perfect." No such additional
onus of proof would be required if the contract is regarded as ratified.

---

[16] Ratification will require consent of all the partners if the transaction is not within the
partner's apparent authority: Clark *op. cit.* I, p. 250; Lindley *op. cit.* p. 167. If the transaction is within the apparent but beyond the actual authority of the partner the firm will
be liable irrespective of ratification (Partnership Act 1890, s. 5). But if the firm wishes to
ratify the transaction, it is thought that all the other partners must consent to the extension
of the actual authority of the transacting partner—Lindley, *op. cit.* pp. 207–208.

[17] Lindley, *op. cit.* p. 167; *Marsh* v. *Joseph* [1897] 1 Ch. 213. Any such ratification may
not be a partial ratification of the transaction; *i.e.* the ratifying copartner may not
select the part of the transaction which it is in his interest to ratify and reject the
remainder which conflicts with his interests: *Commercial Banking Company of Sydney* v.
Mann [1960] 3 All E.R. 482.

[18] In the 10th edition of Bell's *Principles* § 26 the learned editor adds the comment, " But it
must be added that the knowledge or permission of the obligor is not necessarily actual
knowledge or express permission, for one who signs and gives forth an imperfect contract
knowing that the other party relies on it, must be held to have assented to his acting upon it
in the way contemplated." While the " permission " of the remaining partner may be
implied, if not express, it is thought that the observations as to " knowledge " of the remaining partner are inapplicable in the circumstances under consideration.

There remain for consideration those cases where *rei interventus* may be pleadable against the firm in accordance with the general principles of the law. Such cases will be concerned with contracts of imperfect obligation entered into by the firm itself. In other words, the imperfection will not result from lack of authority to contract on behalf of the firm but from lack of observance of the formal requirements of the law when purporting to make the contract. *Rei interventus* may therefore be expected to occur in relation to contracts made on behalf of the firm for the lease or sale of heritage, for engagement of servants and in other similar cases where neglect of the legal formalities in making the contract would allow the firm to resile, were it not for the principle of *rei interventus*. Viewed in that light, the only problems to be discussed as peculiar to partnership are those concerned with what is to be regarded as knowledge of or permission by the firm. There do not appear to be any reported decisions which are helpful on this point and any tentative answer must be sought in the general principles laid down in the Partnership Act 1890 and in the common law.

Knowledge of the firm

Section 16 of the Partnership Act 1890 provides that notice to any partner who habitually acts in the partnership business of any matter relating to the partnership affairs operates (except in certain cases of fraud) as notice to the firm. It will be observed that the wording of this section is more widely framed than that of section 5. Where the partner is the hand of the firm in transacting the firm's business, he is restricted, in the absence of actual authority of wider import, to activities " for carrying on in the usual way business of the kind carried on by the firm "; but where he is the medium through which the firm obtains its collective knowledge, it is sufficient that the partner be one who habitually acts in the partnership business and that the information imparted to him should relate " to the partnership affairs." Section 16 is thus more demanding than section 5 in that the partner falling under it must be habitually engaged in the conduct of the firm's business, whereas section 5 provides, with appropriate qualification as to his authority, that *every* partner is an agent of the firm. Once the partner may be regarded as qualified under section 16, however, the knowledge which he obtains and which will be imputed to the firm, is not restricted to matters which he would have apparent authority to transact under section 5, *i.e.* matters for carrying on the firm's business in the usual way, but will cover " any matter relating to partnership affairs." Thus while a partner, in the absence of express authority, has no apparent or implied authority to contract on behalf of the firm for the lease of a house for purposes of the partnership,[19] if the firm has contracted to take such premises on lease by an improbative writing and if the landlord has on the faith thereof

---

[19] *Sharp* v. *Milligan* (1856) 22 Beav. 606; *Clements* v. *Norris* (1878) 8 Ch.D. 129. But *cf.* on its special facts *Cooke's Circus Buildings Co.* v. *Welding* (1894) 21 R. 339.

incurred expenditure in adapting the premises for the firm's needs, the firm may well be confronted by a plea of *rei interventus* in which the landlord founds upon an individual partner's knowledge of the expense which the landlord had incurred, even though that partner alone could not validly have entered into the lease on behalf of his firm.

A situation in regard to *rei interventus* which is peculiar to partnership might arise where the third party has proceeded on the faith of a contract in writing purporting to be by the firm but where the contract is imperfectly binding upon the firm since the firm name had been adhibited by an individual partner and the subject matter of the contract does not lie within his apparent or his actual authority as agent of the firm. This point was adumbrated in *Cooke's Circus Buildings Company* v. *Welding* [20] but was not disposed of since the court found it possible to decide the case on other grounds. Were such a case to arise for decision it would be possible to argue from a literal interpretation of section 16, that the knowledge of the partner who had unauthorisedly entered the contract of lease in the name of his firm is to be imputed to the firm and thus if the partner knew of the landlord's expenditure on the premises, that knowledge would be sufficient to cure the original imperfection by binding the firm to the contract *rei interventu*. That construction though possible is not likely to find favour in the courts, since it is inconsistent with, and indeed partially destructive of, the provisions of section 5 of the Act and a construction which will allow the statute to be read as a consistent whole, is more likely to be adopted. Lindley [21] treats section 16 as laying down the principle that " if a firm claims the benefit of a transaction entered into by one of its members, it cannot effectively set up its own ignorance of what that member knew, so as to be in a better position than he himself would have been in had he been dealing on his own account as a principal." [22] Later in dealing with the same subject, he adds,

> " When it is said that notice to one partner is notice to all, what is meant is (1) that a firm cannot, in its character of principal, set up the ignorance of some of its members against the knowledge of others of whose acts it claims the benefit, *or by whose acts it is bound*; and (2) that when it is necessary to prove that a firm had notice, all that need be done is to show that notice was given to one of its members who habitually acts in the partnership business. The expression means no more than this; and although every person has notice of what he himself does, *it would be absurd to hold that a firm has notice of everything done by each of its members*."

And again [23] he states, ". . . if a partner exceeds his authority, and it is contended that the firm is bound by what he has done, on the ground

[20] *Supra* n. 19.
[21] *Op. cit.* p. 165.
[22] *Collinson* v. *Lister* (1855) 7 De G.M. & G. 634; 20 Beav. 356.
[23] *Op. cit.* p. 167.

that it has ratified his acts, evidence must be given to prove that at the time of the alleged ratification, his copartners knew of those acts. It would be absurd if, in such a case, knowledge by him was equivalent to knowledge by them." It is thought that the construction placed by Lindley upon section 16 and on the rules of the common law which it is designed to reflect, will be the construction which the courts would be most ready to adopt. At the same time, the wording of the section seems susceptible of a wider construction and it is only the absurdity to which that construction might lead which militates against it. It will be noticed that the difficulty is not entirely removed by the qualifying words of section 16, " except in the case of a fraud on the firm committed by or with the consent of that partner." These words will adequately meet the case where a partner had used the firm name in an unauthorised transaction which in reality he had entered into for his own benefit, but they do not afford any solution where the situation is that the partner has acted for the firm but without authority and the third party now seeks to cure his lack of authority by appealing to his knowledge as knowledge imputable to the firm under section 16.

" *Any partner who habitually acts in the partnership business.*" The precise import of those words has not been pronounced upon by the courts. The general intention of the section seems clear. If the know-ledge of an individual partner as to the partnership affairs is to be imputed to the firm, that partner must be one who is engaged, if not from day to day, at least with recognisable accustomedness in the firm's affairs. It would obviously be unintended by the section that the knowledge of a person who is not recognisable as an active partner of the firm, as, for example, a dormant partner, should be treated as knowledge of the firm itself. It is thought that the words of the section demand no more than that, but the question has been raised by Lindley [24] whether section 16 requires not only that the partner should habitually act in the partnership business but that he should have been so acting when his knowledge was acquired. Any matter concerning partnership which is regarded as worthy of question by Lindley is deserving of earnest con-sideration by those who follow him as students of the subject; and the reason for his doubts are readily appreciable. A man in his day-to-day activities sustains various characters and performs various functions and in any one of these characters or functions he may attain knowledge of particular facts. Is the knowledge obtained by partner A, who habitually acts in the business of his partnership of A B C & Company, while A is concerned in the administration as trustee of the estate of the deceased D, to be imputed as knowledge of his copartners B and C and of his firm A B C & Company? There are obvious objections to such an interpretation, and section 16 provides that notice to any *partner* who habitually acts in the partnership business of any matter relating to the partnership affairs operates as notice to the firm. It may thus be argued

[24] *Op. cit.* p. 165 n. 39.

that what section 16 is concerned with is notice to A in his character as a partner, and not items of information which may come his way as trustee of the deceased D. That would be a desirable and workable interpretation of the section; yet the knowledge which a man owns is not kept by him in water-tight compartments in his mind and it is barely conceivable that knowledge granted by A in whatever character which relates to affairs of his firm of A B C & Company will not be used by him in his habitual activities in the business of his firm. It is possibly therefore the better construction to regard section 16 as stressing the qualification that the partner should habitually act in the business of the firm but not in requiring *sub silentio* and by implication that he should have been so acting when he acquired the knowledge in question.[25] That construction would have the advantage that it would obviate the necessity of the court inquiring as to the character in which he received the notice, a judicial exercise which may on occasion present its problems, the solution of which may not always be readily arrived at by evidence acceptable at law.

The limits of the partner's authority

Some examination of questions as to a partner's actual authority, express or implied, and his apparent authority to bind the firm was necessary in Chapter VI [26] as relevant to the rights and duties of the partners *inter se*. These questions are, however, more generally encountered in cases involving the individual partner and his firm with third parties and a more detailed examination of them was left to be undertaken at this stage and in that context. The key section of the Partnership Act 1890 is section 5 which has already been commented upon [27] and the terms of which are repeated here for convenience of reference:

> " 5. Every partner is an agent of the firm and his other partners for the purpose of the business of the partnership: and the acts of every partner who does any act for carrying on in the usual way business of the kind carried on by the firm of which he is a member bind the firm and his partners, unless the partner so acting has in fact no authority to act for the firm in the particular matter, and the person with whom he is dealing either knows that he has no authority, or does not know or believe him to be a partner."

It has been submitted that what section 5 is concerned with is the *apparent* authority of the partner, *i.e.* the authority which a third party dealing with him is entitled to assume that he possesses. Some writers have regarded the section as concerned with the implied authority of the

---

[25] In the general field of agency the point is also *in dubio*. " Knowledge acquired by the agent otherwise than in the cause of his employment on the principal's behalf . . . is not imputed to the principal " (Bowstead, *Agency* (13th ed.) p. 355). But it appears that if such knowledge was present to the agent's mind at the time of the transaction it will be imputed to the principal.—*Dresser* v. *Norwood* (1864) 17 C.B.(N.S.) 466.

[26] *Supra* pp. 158–159.

[27] *Supra* pp. 158–159.

partner, *i.e.* the authority with which he is clothed by implication in the absence of any express authority to act,[28] and section 5 may in certain cases support the contention that where the partnership agreement is silent as to the authority of a partner in a particular matter that matter, if it falls within the terms of the section, is also within the partner's actual, though implied, authority. Questions of that kind, however, are essentially questions among the partners themselves as to authority to act and it is clear from the wording of the section that it is primarily concerned with questions arising between the firm and third parties. In such questions it is not sufficient to relieve the firm from liability that a partner acting in any matter " for the carrying on in the usual way business of the kind carried on by the firm " should in fact be prohibited in his actual authority from transacting such affairs. His firm may only escape liability for his actings in such a case if the third party dealing with him knows that he has no authority or does not know or believe him to be a partner of the firm. In introducing the state of knowledge or belief of the third party in this way, section 5 is clearly bringing into play equitable considerations which are directly referable to apparent authority, only indirectly referable to actual, but implied, authority and not referable in any way to expressly conferred authority.

Effect of partner exceeding his apparent authority

Section 7 of the Partnership Act 1890 provides:

" 7. Where one partner pledges the credit of the firm for a purpose apparently not connected with the firm's ordinary course of business, the firm is not bound, unless he is in fact specially authorised by the other partners: but this section does not affect any personal liability incurred by an individual partner."

The effect of the section is to place the third party on his guard if the transaction is not " apparently connected with the firm's ordinary course of business," *i.e.* not within the partner's apparent authority. In such circumstances the firm will not be bound by the partner's actings unless he was in fact specially authorised by his copartners. The effective steps to be taken by the third party thus placed on his inquiry will be discussed in the ensuing paragraphs. For the moment the position of a third party who has relied upon the partner having authority for his dealings is under examination. In such a case the firm will have no liability but the section expressly provides that its terms do not affect any personal liability incurred by an individual partner. That personal liability may arise in different ways and on different grounds. In the first place, the third party may not be able to establish that he dealt with the partner in his character as a partner of the firm. A, who is a member of the firm A B & Company, contracts with C for the purchase of goods not usually dealt in by his firm. C makes no inquiry of the firm as to A's authority and in fact A has no such

28 See *e.g.* Lindley, *op. cit.* pp. 160–161.

authority, and has intended the transaction for his own private benefit. In that case A is personally bound to C in the contract which he has entered into with him.   The mere fact that A also sustains a separate character as a partner of A B & Company is in that case irrelevant to the nature of the obligation which he has undertaken.   Such cases may often in practice involve consideration of the whole circumstances and a factual judgment arrived at on a balancing of the circumstances may partake more of the nature of a verdict of a jury than of a decision upon purely legal grounds.[29]

On the other hand, the individual partner may have clearly evinced to the third party his intention to enter the unauthorised transaction on behalf of the firm, e.g. by ordering goods in the firm's name or by subscribing the firm's name to an obligatory document.   If the firm is able to escape liability on the transaction on the ground that it was beyond the apparent authority of the partner, the partner will still be personally liable to the third party in the transaction.[30]   The precise ground on which that personal liability is based is not clearly stated.   It can be argued that the partner has warranted his authority to act for the firm and is liable in damages to the third party for breach of that warranty.   This appears to be implied in the view taken by Clark who states, " If a partner contract avowedly on behalf of the firm, and it afterwards turns out that the firm is not liable, in respect that he had no authority, either express or implied, to bind it by such a transaction, he will be liable to indemnify the creditor for whatever loss may have been sustained, whether it may be attributable to fraud or an innocent mistake." [31]   But of the cases which he cites in support of his statement, the only Scottish decision [32] appears to have been decided on the ground that the transaction in dispute had been with the managing partner of the firm as an individual and not as a partner.   *Ex parte Agace* [33] was a case where the partner could be held personally responsible in damages to the third party on the ground of his fraudulent conduct.   In that case one of two partners granted bills in the name of the firm in payment of his own private debt.   The third party inquired of him whether his copartner knew of the transaction and he untruthfully answered that his copartner both knew and had consented to it.   The firm were not held liable on the bills on the ground that the third party was not a holder for value without notice of the transacting partner's lack of authority,[34] but there was personal liability of the offending partner to the third party for fraudulent representation.   The third case cited by

[29] Clark, *op. cit.* I, p. 249; *Turnbull* v. *McKie* (1822) 1 S. 353; *Miller* v. *Mitchell* (1860) 22 D. 833; *National Exchange Co.* v. *Drew & Dick* (1860) 23 D. 1; *Crum & Co.* v. *McLean* (1858) 20 D. 751.

[30] *Fortune* v. *Young*, 1918 S.C. 1; *Crum & Co.* v. *McLean* (1858) 20 D. 751; *Walker* v. *Smith* (1906) 8 F. 619.

[31] *Op. cit.* I, p. 247.

[32] *Finlayson* v. *Braidbar Quarry Co.* (1864) 2 M. 1297.

[33] (1792) 2 Cox 312.

[34] The transaction was clearly not within the partner's authority and the false statement as to his authority was not referable to the carrying on of the firm's business in the usual way. For further discussion on this point see *infra* pp. 252–254.

Clark [35] established the proposition that when a third party endeavours to hold a firm liable in a transaction which has not prima facie been authorised by the firm, then he must establish the grant of actual authority for the transaction.   If that cannot be done, then no case is established against the firm no matter that the third party may not have known what dealings were so authorised and what dealings were not.   In such a case the firm did not mislead the third party and if he relied on the representations of the partner and was misled by them, any remedy which he has must lie against that partner personally.   In this comment upon this case, Lindley clearly regards the ground of that personal liability to be the partner's breach of his warranty of authority; for he concludes his observations with the words, " Just as when an agent untruly represents his authority, a person dealing with him acquires no right against the principal, but must look to the agent for indemnity." [36]

The cases appear to show differing approaches to the personal liability of the partner where he has exceeded his authority.   That difference in approach, it is thought, may be explained by the differing circumstances in which an exceeding of his authority by a partner may come before the courts.   In some cases, the facts are such that the court will be prepared to hold that the true intention of the parties was that the contract was one with the partner as an individual and not with the firm.   In such cases there is little difficulty in finding a basis in contract for the partner's personal liability even where he has purported to contract in the firm's name. [37]   But in other cases the partner may deal ostensibly for the firm but in excess of his authority and the third party may either accept his assurance that he has in fact authority to enter the transaction on behalf of his firm or may simply assume that he has such authority from the fact that he is a partner. Here there is no clear basis in contract for the personal liability of the partner.   Where the third party relies upon the representations of the partner himself and these are fraudulent, an action for damages may be raised against the partner on the fraud, [38] but where the partner has innocently misrepresented the extent of his authority or where the third party has himself raised no question as to that authority, [39] some other basis must be found for holding the partner personally liable and the third party must base his claim upon the partner's breach of warranty of his authority as a partner, and therefore agent, of his firm.   That principle applies in all cases of agency.

" Where a person, by words or conduct, represents that he has

---

[35] *Lloyd* v. *Freshfield* (1826) 2 C. & P. 325.
[36] Lindley, *op. cit.* p. 208.
[37] *Finlayson* v. *Braidbar Quarry Co.* (1864) 2 M. 1297 and *Walker* v. *Smith* (1906) 8 F. 619 are cases of this kind.   *Fortune* v. *Young*, 1918 S.C. 1 may also, possibly, though with more difficulty be so regarded.
[38] *Randell* v. *Trimen* (1856) 18 C.B. 786; *Polhill* v. *Walter* (1832) 3 B. & Ad. 114; *West London Commercial Bank* v. *Kitson* (1884) 13 Q.B.D. 360.   These are all cases on agency. The liability of the offending partner in *Ex p. Agace* (1792) 2 Cox 312 can be supported on this ground.
[39] *Lloyd* v. *Freshfield* (1826) 2 C. & P. 325; and on agency *Collen* v. *Wright* (1857) 8 E. & B. 647.

authority to act on behalf of another, and a third party is induced by such representation to act in a manner in which he would not have acted if such representation had not been made, the first-mentioned person is deemed to warrant that the representation is true, and is liable for any loss caused to such third party by a breach of such implied warranty, even if he acted in good faith, under a mistaken belief that he had such authority." [40]

While in the earlier cases there may be detected a tendency to regard the partner (or agent) as having entered a personal contract in place of that ostensibly made for his principal, if it subsequently was established that he had no authority to act for his principal,[41] that was not found upon prolonged examination to be a satisfactory solution in terms of legal theory and the present view is that the agent or partner is liable in such cases on a collateral contract which he makes at the time when he entered the contract ostensibly for his principal or firm. Under that collateral contract he warrants that he has authority.[42] It has been said that " the warranty does not apply where the representation is one of law and is made innocently, though there may be great difficulty in distinguishing representations of fact from representations of law." [43] It is thought that questions of law in relation to a partner's authority will arise infrequently, if at all. If the question relates to his apparent authority it is in essence a jury question as to what is covered by the carrying on in the usual way business of the kind carried on by the firm. If the question relates to the partner's actual authority it will almost invariably be a factual question, though in this case a question of law may be envisaged as arising, e.g. where the court has to decide which one of a number of constructions is to be placed upon the provisions of the partnership agreement as to the partner's actual authority to bind the firm. Where the question arises in regard to a partner's warranty of his apparent authority, if the apparent authority covers the transaction the third party can hold the firm liable so that there will be no occasion for him to invoke the partner's warranty of authority and, even should circumstances be envisaged in which occasion arose for invoking the warranty, it would afford no advantage to the third party to invoke it since *ex hypothesi* he could establish no loss. If the firm should subsequently prove insolvent, the partner would not incur liability under the warranty on that score, since his liability to the third party under his collateral contract of warranty is for loss to the third party which arises from the partner having no authority, *i.e.* under the normal rule that damages recoverable in respect of breach of contract are restricted to those which are sustained as a natural and probable consequence of

[40] Bowstead, *Agency* (13th ed.) p. 397.
[41] *Fortune* v. *Young*, 1918 S.C. 1 seems slightly tinged with this doctrine. See the observation of the Lord Justice-Clerk (Scott Dickson) at p. 6: " A partner who signs an obligatory document outwith the scope of his copartnery does not bind the firm, but he undoubtedly binds himself." And on agency generally see *Downman* v. *Williams* (1845) 7 Q.B. 103.
[42] *Collen* v. *Wright* (1857) 8 E. & B. 647. See also Bowstead, *op. cit.* pp. 397–398.
[43] Bowstead, *op. cit.* p. 400.

the breach or which are of a kind which both parties might reasonably expect to result as a probable consequence of that breach.[44]

Warranty in cases of apparent authority

Where the transaction in question is covered by the partner's apparent authority though, by his actual authority, he is prohibited from entering into it, the application of the doctrine of warranty of authority has proved troublesome, and there are dicta in the English cases that in such circumstances there is no implied warranty of authority at all. In *Rainbow* v. *Howkins* [45] Kennedy J., after distinguishing an earlier case,[46] observed, " Here the answer to the plaintiff's claim on the ground of breach of warranty or misrepresentation of authority is that there was none. The defendant's principal was as much bound as if he had made the bargain himself. . . ." That case concerned an auctioneer's apparent authority to sell on behalf of his principal without reserve and was later doubted in *McManus* v. *Fortescue* [47] where Fletcher Moulton L.J. said, " A principal, therefore, who gives authority to an auctioneer to sell subject to a reserve price gives no power to the auctioneer, either expressly or impliedly, to accept a less price. The case of *Rainbow* v. *Howkins*, so far as it is inconsistent with this view, cannot be regarded as in harmony with well established principles." [48] But the disapproval of the earlier decision voiced by Fletcher Moulton L.J. related to the extent of the apparent authority and not to the dictum that where apparent authority existed there was no room for the agent's warranty of authority, and in *V/O Rasnoimport* v. *Guthrie & Co. Ltd.*,[49] Mocatta J. reiterated the view expounded by Kennedy J.,

> " It will be noticed that the authorities relied on . . . are all cases in which a third party had sued the principal; there had been no actual authority given by the principal to the agent, and the question of the principal's liability turned upon whether or not the agent had ostensible authority. If he had, then the principal was held liable. In such a case no question of breach of warranty of authority arises. It is only when the agent has no actual or ostensible authority, that the third party need look for his remedy to the agent and rely, if he can, on breach by that agent of his implied warranty of authority."

It is clear that the dicta of Kennedy and Mocatta JJ. reflect the practical outcome of the particular situations which they are considering. In this context the choice by Mocatta J. of the words, " It is only when the agent has no actual or ostensible authority that the third party *need look* for his remedy to the agent . . ." is significant. If there *is* actual, or

[44] *Hadley* v. *Baxendale* (1854) 9 Ex. 341 at p. 354.
[45] [1904] 2 K.B. 322 at p. 326.
[46] *Warlow* v. *Harrison* (1858) 1 E. & E. 295, affd. (1859) 1 E. & E. 309.
[47] [1907] 2 K.B. 1.
[48] *Ibid.* at pp. 6–7.
[49] [1966] 1 Lloyd's Rep. 1 at p. 10.

ostensible, or apparent authority in the agent or the partner, then he has accomplished what he purported to third party he would accomplish. He has bound his principal or his firm in contractual liability to the third party so that the latter would be unable to qualify any claim for damages in respect of breach of warranty of authority. It may be questioned whether the dicta are intended to go further than this but it may be that both judges considered that the doctrine of warranty of authority had no place in legal theory in the circumstances which they were considering. If so, that view may be theoretically maintained only in relation to cases where the liability of the principal for the agent's acts arises under the apparent authority which they have held out the agent as possessing. For if the liability of the principal arises because it has been established that the agent had actual or ostensible (in the sense of implied) authority, there appears to be no ground in theory or in logic for regarding the fact that the agent has been proved actually to possess the authority as precluding the possibility in theory of his warranting that he possessed it at the time when he entered the transaction with the third party. If, however, he had no actual authority, express or implied, and the principal has been held liable because he has held the agent out as authorised to deal with third parties and therefore is barred from later setting up the true facts in a question with a third party who has done business in reliance on that holding out, it might be argued that the principal's liability had nothing whatever to do with the agent's authority but was established by an equity which personally barred him from denying his liability as principal and therefore was irrelevant in a question of the agent's warranty of authority. It is thought that this argument is faulty. While it is true that the liability ultimately established in the principal does not derive from the agent's authority and indeed proceeds from the hypothesis that no such authority in fact existed, yet the agent in purporting to transact with the third party on behalf of his principal is himself representing that he has authority for his actings. If we were to accede to the view that the warranty of authority had no place in cases of apparent authority, then where the third party made an unsuccessful attempt to hold the principal liable on that ground the third party would have no recourse against the agent unless he could sue him in delict. There is nothing in the reported decisions or in the books which supports such a view and it is not a view which is supported by the dicta of Kennedy and Mocatta JJ. In those dicta what is being considered is the relevance of the agent's warranty of authority in cases where liability has been successfully established against the principal, and it seems clear that the judges are merely pointing out that if liability has been established against the principal there can be no claim for loss under the warranty against the agent, since what the agent warranted has been achieved.

Extent of the partner's apparent authority

The limits of the apparent authority to act on behalf of his firm are laid down in section 5 of the Partnership Act 1890 and have already been discussed.[50] It will be noticed that, in terms of section 5, every partner is the agent of his firm for the transaction in the ordinary course of the business carried on by the partnership. If he is acting within those limits a third party may, if he knows him to be a partner, assume that he has the requisite authority even if he has no knowledge of the actual limits of the authority conferred upon him by the firm and his copartners. Even where his actual authority has been narrowly limited to certain aspects of the ordinary business of the firm, whether on account of a division of duties among the partners or of a provision of the partnership that transactions of importance will be carried through only by the more senior of the partners or the like, the firm will still be liable to a third party who deals with a partner whose authority is so limited in a matter falling within the ordinary business of the firm, provided the third party knows or believes him to be a partner and deals with him in good faith and without notice of any such restriction. Where the transaction does not fall within the scope of " carrying on in the usual way business of the kind carried on by the firm " and is thus beyond the limits of the partner's apparent authority as laid down in section 5, it will not be sufficient, in order to impose liability on the firm, that the third party pleads that he had no knowledge of the actual authority of the partner with whom he dealt. In that case he may hold the firm liable only if he can establish that a wider authority, embracing the sort of transaction which he has entered into with the partner, has in fact been entrusted to the partner in question by his copartners.[51] In the first case notice to the third party of the lack of actual authority is relevant and material whereas in the second case it is immaterial.

In the first case, once the third party is able to establish that he knew the partner to be a partner of the firm and that he dealt with him in the ordinary course of that firm's business, he is in a position to treat the partner as an agent of the firm and to apply the usual rules of agency to the transaction. That entails that the firm, like any other principal, may be rendered liable for the actings of its partner, like any other agent, on the basis that those actings were authorised by the other partners, or may reasonably be assumed by a third party to have been so authorised. Since section 5 provides that they are assumed prima facie to have authorised acts done for carrying on the business in the usual way, they may escape liability for such acts of a partner only if they can establish that the authority assumed to exist under section 5 did not in fact exist and that the third party knew that it did not exist and thus might not avail himself of the assumption provided for in the section. In the second case, however, no prima facie assumption of authority is provided for in section 5. The act of the partner is one which is not for the carrying on in the usual way business of the kind carried on by the firm. The partner must, therefore,

---

[50] *Supra* pp. 208 *et seq.*
[51] Partnership Act 1890, s. 7.

like any agent, satisfy the third party that actual authority has been conferred upon him to deal with the matter in question, and if the third party chooses to deal with the partner without being so satisfied or after inadequate inquiry, then he will not be able to hold the firm liable for the transaction. In such a case, his ignorance of the extent of the partner's authority will not be pleadable by him against the firm since he is not entitled, without knowledge of the partner's actual authority, to assume that the partner has any authority to deal with the matter at all.[52]

Liability of firm for acts within apparent authority of partner

The kinds of transaction which may be regarded as entered into " for carrying on in the usual way business of the kind carried on by the firm " have already been examined.[53]   It will be noticed that in terms of section 5 of the Partnership Act 1890 the third party is entitled to rely on the apparent authority of the partner with whom he contracts unless he knows that the partner has no authority to transact the business or he does not know or believe him to be a partner.   The knowledge or at least the reasonably held belief that a person with whom one is dealing is a partner of the firm which is to be held liable in the transaction is essential if one is to be able to treat his actings as those of an agent for his firm, and the question whether a man transacted as an individual or as a partner is a question of fact. Its determination is assisted by no presumptions of law and it is a matter to be decided as a jury question.[54]   The reported cases in which this question has been disposed of are therefore more properly regarded as guides to the probable weight which will be assigned by the courts to different facts and circumstances than as enshrining any principle of law apart from the very general one that if the transaction can be shown to have been concluded on the faith of the credit of the partner, not as such partner but as an individual, then he alone, and not his firm, will be bound by it, even if the third party knows that he also sustains the character of a partner in his firm.[55]   The cases cited are concerned with agency and are those referred to by Clark [56] in his explanation of the application of the law in partnership.   In so far as they are regarded as vouching the limited proposition above advanced, they are as unexceptionable in agency as they are in partnership cases.   Clark, however, appears to extend the rule in agency beyond the somewhat axiomatic limits above expressed when he states,[57] " If a contract be made with a man on his own credit, he cannot escape from personal liability by showing that it was known at the time that he was acting as agent for another; and if in such a case the transaction was

[52] Partnership Act 1890, s. 7.
[53] *Supra* pp. 208–214.
[54] Clark, *op. cit.* I, p. 247; *Miller* v. *Mitchell* (1860) 22 D. 833.
[55] *Young* v. *Smart* (1831) 10 S. 130; *Stevenson* v. *Campbell* (1836) 14 S. 562; nor, of course, may the " partner " escape his personal liability by pleading that it was known to the third party that he was a partner: *Lang & Co.* v. *McLeod* (1830) 8 S. 323; *Sorley's Trs.* v. *Graham* (1832) 10 S. 319.
[56] *Op. cit.* I, p. 246.
[57] *Ibid.* pp. 245–246.

specially concluded on the credit of the agent alone, the principal will not be bound, even though his existence was disclosed at the date of the contract." The latter part of that statement enlarges the issue much beyond the area of discussion and it is by no means clear that it accurately reflects the modern law of agency which, it is thought, would allow the third party a right of election whether he proceed against the agent or the principal in such circumstances.[58] So far as the law of partnership is concerned section 5 of the Partnership Act 1890 clearly restricts the cases where the firm may escape liability for acts within the apparent authority of the partner to those where the third party knows of the relevant restriction on the partner's actual authority or where he did not " know " the partner to be such (in which case the intention to deal with him as a private individual is clear) or where he did not " believe " him to be a partner, in which case the " belief " is presumably to be interpreted as a belief on reasonable grounds that he was not acting in his capacity as a partner in the transaction in question.[59] If the partner makes it clear that he is contracting not as a partner but as an individual, then he alone is liable on the transaction even if the firm receive in actual fact the entire benefit of the transaction.[60]

Evidence tending to establish that the transaction is with the partner as an individual

Many of the reported cases which illustrate this are concerned with liability on bills upon which the firm name does not appear and where it is sought to impose liability on the firm for the bills on the ground that the transactions represented by the bills were partnership transactions.[61] These cases are not the most certain guides as to the principles generally applicable in partnership law since there is superimposed upon the law of partnership the special consideration appertaining to the law of negotiable instruments. In the case of negotiable instruments the signature of the name of the firm on the bill or promissory note is equivalent to the signature by the person adhibiting it of the names of all persons liable as partners in the firm, but subject to that exception and to the exception that a person who signs a bill in a trade or assumed name is liable thereon as if he had signed it in his own name, no person is liable as drawer, indorser

---

[58] See Bowstead, *Agency* (13th ed.) pp. 289–290.

[59] See the judgment of Cockburn C.J. in *Nicholson* v. *Ricketts* (1860) 2 E. & E. 497 and of Cleasby B. in *Holme* v. *Hammond* (1872) L.R. 7 Ex. 218 upon which the concluding words of s. 5 of the Partnership Act 1890 are thought to be founded. (Lindley, *op. cit.* p. 159; Pollock, *Digest of the Law of Partnership* (1st ed.) pp. 24–25. See also the Supplement to *Lindley on Partnership* (published 1891) p. 27.)

[60] *Emly* v. *Lye* (1812) 15 East 7; *Crum & Co.* v. *McLean* (1858) 20 D. 751; *Tupper & Carr* v. *Rowell* (1858) 20 D. 758. These cases, however, all relate to liability on bills, the circumstances of which are, to some extent, special. See immediately succeeding paragraph. As to possible liability of the firm *quantum lucratus*, see *infra* pp. 257–258.

[61] See cases cited in n. 60 and also *McNair* v. *Fleming* (1812) 5 Pat.App. 639; *Downes* v. *McFie* (1829) 8 S. 246; *Jacaud* v. *French* (1810) 12 East 317; *Nicholson* v. *Ricketts* (1860) 2 E. & E. 497; *Holme* v. *Hammond* (1872) L.R. 7 Ex. 218; *Rosslund Cycle Co.* v. *McCreadie*, 1907 S.C. 1208.

or acceptor of a bill who has not signed it as such.[62] Where the firm name is adhibited to the bill by a partner, then, that signature will be deemed to be the signature of all persons who are partners of the firm,[63] and the firm and its partners will be liable on the bill, provided that it was within the apparent authority of the partner to adhibit the signature of the firm name as a party to the bill.[64] When therefore a bill is drawn, indorsed or accepted in the firm name by a partner in a trading firm a third party taking that bill is entitled to regard the signature of the firm name as being within the partner's apparent authority, and if the bill should fall into the hands of a holder in due course, the presumption as to the partner's authority becomes absolute [65] and it is then immaterial whether the bill was in fact granted for partnership purposes or not. Where the name of the firm and the name of one of its partners are the same, and a bill is granted by that partner in the common name, the signature is prima facie deemed to be that of the firm but the presumption may be rebutted by proof that the bill was not granted for the purposes of the partnership or with the authority of the firm. In that case the intention or belief of the person taking the bill is immaterial, and the firm will not be liable even to a bona fide holder for value.[66] On the other hand if a bill is granted in the firm name by a partner within his apparent authority but the person taking the bill knows that it was granted without authority, then he, as opposed to a holder in due course, cannot hold the firm liable in the bill. This may be seen from the decisions involving the granting of a bill by a partner in the firm name and using it in settlement of a private debt.[67] It seems to follow, therefore, that when decisions which have negated the liability of firms upon negotiable instruments are sought to be used in support of a view taken as to the liability of the firm on transactions in general, it may be possible to regard the evidence which has led the courts in such cases to negative the liability of the firm as helpful in a more general context while those cases concerned with negotiable instruments where the courts have treated the evidence as insufficient to elide the liability of the firm will require to be examined closely and critically in order to discover whether the reasoning upon which the court reached its decision really reflects any consideration of general application in partnerships or is rather concerned with the special liabilities falling on the firm in consequence of the law relating to negotiable instruments.

In deciding whether a particular transaction has been entered into with

---

[62] Bills of Exchange Act 1882, s. 23.

[63] *Pooley* v. *Driver* (1876) 5 Ch.D. 458 (secret partner); *Gurney* v. *Evans* (1858) 27 L.J.(Ex.) 166 (person held out as a partner).

[64] As in the case of a partner in a trading firm—*Bank of Australasia* v. *Breillat* (1847) 6 Moore P.C. 152 at p. 194; but not a non-trading firm—*Dickinson* v. *Valpy* (1829) 10 B. & C. 128 at p. 137; *Thicknesse* v. *Bromilow* (1832) 2 Cr. & J. 425.

[65] *Bank of Australasia* v. *Breillat, supra*; *Clarke* v. *Shepherd* (1821) 1 S. 179; (1823) 2 S. 255; *Wiseman* v. *Easton* (1863) 8 L.T.(N.S.) 637.

[66] *Yorkshire Banking Co.* v. *Beatson* (1880) 5 C.P.D. 109.

[67] *Leverson* v. *Lane* (1862) 32 L.J.C.P. 10; *Paterson Bros.* v. *Gladstone* (1891) 18 R. 403; *Proudfoot* v. *Lindsay* (1825) 3 S. 443; *Blair* v. *Bryson* (1835) 13 S. 901; *Johnston Sharp & Co.* v. *Phillips* (1822) 1 S.App. 244; *Miller* v. *Douglas*, Jan. 22, 1811, F.C.

a partner on behalf of the partnership or on his own private account, the courts seem generally to have approached the question on a consideration of all the circumstances much as they would expect those circumstances to be considered and evaluated by an intelligent jury. Thus in *A. W. Crum & Company* v. *McLean* [68] the issue was whether machinery which had been supplied on the order of one Wilson, a partner with the defender in the firm of Wilson & McLean, had been supplied by the pursuers to the partnership or on Wilson's own private account. The firm had been dissolved since the transaction and Wilson was bankrupt at the date of raising the action which was brought against the firm and McLean, " an individual partner of that concern." It was admitted that the machinery had been supplied on the order of Wilson during the subsistence of the partnership and that it was intended for the purpose of his constructing a machine which he had devised for stenting and drying cloths, a process in the firm's business of calenderers, and for which he had obtained a provisional protection for six months. Evidence was led from McLean that the machine belonged to Wilson, was never used by the firm and was not included in the firm's assets at dissolution, that the pursuers were indebted to the firm at the date of dissolution in a sum which was uplifted from them by Wilson without any claim being made by them against the firm for the machinery until the latter part of March 1854. McLean had no knowledge of the claim until that time, and he believed that the goods were ordered by Wilson for his own use and on his own account. In his evidence, Wilson maintained that the goods were ordered for the firm and that the machine which he constructed was reckoned as part of the firm's assets on dissolution. He was sequestrated on March 11, 1854. At no time had the pursuers demanded payment from him individually. They had rendered no account until February 1854 when they rendered it against the firm. Evidence was also led that in the scroll day-book kept by the pursuers the relevant entries appeared in a ledger account under the individual name of Wilson but this had been in subsequent entries deleted and " Wilson & McLean " written in above it. In expressing his concurrence in the judgment of the court upon which he had earlier entertained doubt, Lord Deas stressed the points that Wilson had intended to patent the machine, that the pursuers had paid what they owed to the dissolved firm of Wilson & McLean without set-off of the claim now made, that Wilson had had receipts granted in his favour for payments made for other parts of the same machine furnished after the formation of the partnership and that the pursuers' altered day-book showed that they had become conscious that " they had not a proper and true hold of the company as they wish to make out." The firm was therefore not liable and McLean was assoilzied.

Considerations similar to those discussed above, or at least some of those considerations, have weighed with the court in other cases where the

[68] (1858) 20 D. 751.

liability of the firm has been negated and the debt has been held to be a private debt of the partner, but it is for the court to assess the selective weight of such considerations in a particular case before it, and no one of the factual considerations present in *A. & W. Crum & Company* v. *McLean* [68] may be treated as decisive of the issue or even as raising any presumption of fact or law which requires to be rebutted.   Thus evidence *ex facie* of the firm's books was disregarded by the court in *Low* v. *Lizars* [69] on evidence contained in an accountant's report that the true position was otherwise.   In a number of earlier cases the evidence before the court was such that the issue might be disposed of on the basis that the transaction in question was not within the partner's apparent authority. In *McNair & Company* v. *Gray, Hunter & Speirs,* [70] a guarantee granted by a partner in the firm name in respect of a debt owed by himself and his mother for goods in which the firm did not deal was held not to be binding on the firm.   In these cases the question of the partner's apparent authority and the question whether the transaction was for his own account and not for that of the firm tend to converge, in that the court may decide on the facts that the true intention of both parties was that the transaction was for the partner's private account and hence not within his apparent authority as a partner, but the facts which may satisfy the court that a particular transaction was not one for carrying on the business of the firm in the usual way and that accordingly the third party is not entitled to rely on the apparent authority of the partner need not go so far as to establish that the transaction was intended for the partner's private account.   It is possible to reconcile the decisions in those early cases with *Bryan* v. *Butters Bros. & Co.* [71] on this ground though in *Kennedy* [72] the report does not clearly maintain the distinction and indeed lays emphasis on facts which suggest that the court was holding the transaction to be one for the partner's private account, *i.e.* that no entry respecting it had appeared in the books of the firm.   The fact that some advantage is derived by the firm from the transaction will not necessarily preclude the court from holding on other grounds that the transaction was truly entered into for a private debt of the partner. [73]   In *McLeod* v. *Howden* [74] the court held that the firm was liable on a cash credit obtained by one partner in his own name, which was also the firm name, upon which that partner alone drew until the credit was exhausted.   The reasoning of the court as shown in the judgment of the Lord Justice-Clerk (Boyle) suggests that in this case the court has gone much further in attributing liability to the firm than in the other reported cases concerning what is to be regarded as a firm debt and not a private debt of the partner, but what is probably implicit in that judgment is a different principle already noticed in relation

[68] (1838) 16 S. 1092.
[70] Jan. 19, 1803, F.C.   See also *Kennedy*, Dec. 22, 1814, F.C.
[71] (1892) 19 R. 490.
[72] *Supra* n. 70.
[73] *Johnston Sharp & Co.* v. *Phillips* (1822) 1 S.App. 244.
[74] (1839) 1 D. 1121.

to the liability of the firm on bills, *i.e.* if a partnership business is carried on in the name of one of the partners, as the firm name, the signature of that partner will prima facie be taken as evidencing liability of the firm.[75] While that rule has been announced in relation to negotiable instruments there appears no reason why it should be restricted to such cases and the reasoning in *Yorkshire Banking Co.* v. *Beatson* [75] does not seem inapplicable to cases of documents other than negotiable instruments. The observations of the Lord Justice-Clerk in *McLeod* v. *Howden* [74] as to the identity of the designation of the grantee in the cash credit, *viz.* " Daniel Munro, pawnbroker," with the firm name as appearing on a sign-board outside the business premises suggests that the decision may more properly be considered as an illustration of this principle.

Cases where the third party is placed on his inquiry as to the partner's authority

" In the absence of notice to the contrary, the public are entitled to deal with every known partner of a firm on the assumption that he is vested with such powers as are necessary or usual in carrying on the business in the usual way." [76] Those words of Clark's still accurately reflect the law as it is stated in section 5 of the Partnership Act 1890, but the introductory and qualifying words, " in the absence of notice to the contrary " [77] require further examination. The qualification only applies where the third party is appealing to the apparent authority of the partner. The doctrine which imposes liability on the firm for acts within the apparent authority of the partner is an equitable doctrine which allows the third party to plead that the firm has held out the partner as possessing authority in certain matters, defined in section 5 as those " for the carrying on in the usual way business of the kind carried on by the firm," and is therefore personally barred from setting up in defence of a claim by the third party restrictions upon that apparent authority which had not been revealed by them to the third party. If, therefore, a third party contracts with a partner regarding a matter which is not for the carrying on in the usual way business of the kind carried on by the firm, then it will be useless to plead that he had no knowledge that the partner was precluded from binding the firm to the contract since the third party cannot bring the transaction within the class of those which he was entitled to expect the partner to have authority to complete.[78] But where the transaction in question lies within the scope of the apparent authority of the partner, though in terms of the conditions of the partnership it does not lie within his actual authority, the knowledge of the third party is highly material because he is in that case claiming the

---

[75] *Yorkshire Banking Co.* v. *Beatson* (1880) 5 C.P.D. 109; and see *supra* p. 245.
[76] Clark, *op. cit.* I, p. 247.
[77] Compare the words of s. 5: " unless the partner . . . has in fact no authority to act for the firm in the particular matter, and the person with whom he is dealing either knows that he has no authority, or does not know or believe him to be a partner."
[78] Lindley, *op. cit.* p. 208, and see *supra* pp. 241–243.

benefit of an equitable doctrine which allows him to assume an authority reposed in the partner where none in fact has been conferred,[79] and to avail himself of that equity, the third party must be himself deserving of the equitable consideration which he seeks at the hand of the court.[80] What then will amount to knowledge on the part of the third party which will preclude him from relying upon the apparent authority of the partner? Obviously, where the fact has been already brought to his notice by the firm, he will be unable to hold the firm liable if he chooses, in spite of this, to deal with the partner in a matter covered by the restrictions so brought to his notice. Where the defendant sent a circular to the third party instructing him not to supply goods to the firm of which the defendant was a partner without the defendant's written order, and the third party, notwithstanding this, supplied goods to the defendant's partner without such written instructions, the defendant as a partner of the firm was held free from liability for the price of the goods.[81] A public notice that the partner's authority to transact on behalf of the firm is terminated [82] or that his copartner will not be liable for a partner's transactions [83] has been held to be effective to preclude liability of the firm to third parties who have seen the notice.[84]

Short of such direct and express notice, the third party may be precluded from relying on the apparent authority of the partner because the circumstances of the transaction itself are such that they would put a reasonable man on his guard so that he would think it right to inquire as to the partner's authority to enter into it. In *Paterson Brothers* v. *Gladstone* [85] a partner in a building firm who was prohibited in terms of the deed of partnership from signing bills on behalf of the firm, adhibited the firm signature to promissory notes in favour of a moneylender with whom he discounted them at a rate of interest of 40 per cent. per annum. The notes were not granted in the course of the firm's business or for purposes of that business and the proceeds were applied by the partner to his own use. The moneylender charged the firm for payment and the firm brought a suspension of the charge. It was held that the loss incurred

[79] *e.g. Turnbull* v. *McKie* (1822) 1 S. 353.
[80] As in the case of agency, the third party " cannot hold the principal liable if he did not believe that the agent had authority despite the appearance of authority."—Bowstead, *Agency* (13th ed.), p. 252. See *Bloomenthal* v. *Ford* [1897] A.C. 156.
[81] *Willis* v. *Dyson* (1816) 1 Stark. 164.
[82] *Rooth* v. *Quin* (1819) 7 Price 193.
[83] *Lord Galway* v. *Matthew* (1808) 1 Camp. 403.
[84] It may be doubted whether notices of that kind are entirely effective, without a dissolution of the firm. In the absence of a provision in the partnership agreement giving the majority power to abrogate the authority of any partner, it seems that such a step might require a unanimous decision of the partners which in the circumstances might be difficult to achieve. On the other hand, there is a question of degree involved, since, subject to the express or implied provisions of the partnership agreement, a majority of the parners have power to decide " any difference arising as to ordinary matters connected with the partnership business " (Partnership Act 1890, s. 24 (8)) and notice of a decision, so reached, that certain acts relating to the firm's business, shall in future be done by a specific partner only, might probably be effective against a third party who transacts such business with a partner not so specified. For further discussion of this point, see *infra* pp. 287–288.
[85] (1891) 18 R. 403.

through the fraudulent granting of the notes fell upon the moneylender who had discounted them in suspicious circumstances, without inquiry and not on the firm and its partners who were ignorant of the transaction which was not a transaction in the course of the firm's business or on its behalf. The Lord President (Inglis) observed [86]

". . . (the moneylender) must have had suspicions aroused that things were not all right when a firm of builders in good repute required to borrow at 40 per cent. He must have known that the strain would be such as very shortly to bring any ordinary business to an end and that it was not a likely thing that a firm in good repute would find it necessary to resort to him for such a purpose. It was quite in Mr. Gladstone's power to ascertain whether Robert Paterson was dealing fairly by him and with his copartners and whether his action was authorised by the firm. But he abstains from inquiry of any kind and is satisfied to take his 40 per cent. and incur all risks."

The duty of inquiry imposed upon the third party where the circumstances of the transaction are such as should put him on his guard exists even where the obligation granted in the name of the firm is one which is in no way extraordinary in the usual course of business. In *Walker* v. *Smith*,[87] Smith, a partner of a firm of solicitors, arranged with Miss Walker, through her solicitor, for a loan of £400 to himself and granted a bond and a disposition in security of certain ground annuals in respect of the loan. The titles to the ground annuals which were delivered along with the bond and disposition in security to Miss Walker's solicitor, were not in Smith's name and Smith gave Miss Walker's solicitor a letter of obligation in the name of his firm to record and to deliver a disposition in Smith's favour of the ground annuals. The amount of the loan was then released to Smith but no valid title in his favour was completed so that the bond and disposition in security was ineffectual. Miss Walker then sued Smith's partners to recover the amount of the loan to Smith in respect of the letter of obligation granted in the firm name. She was unsuccessful, the court holding that her solicitor was not entitled to take it as being Smith's " implied mandate " as a partner to bind his firm in an obligation relating to his own property. The Lord President (Dunedin) after remarking upon the normal practice of legal firms in settling conveyancing transactions of granting letters of obligation to complete uncompleted matters, continued,[88]

" But while this is so, I do not think it is possible to extend the rule so as to cover such an obligation as was undertaken by Smith in the present case. When Black (*i.e.* Miss Walker's solicitor) received the titles he saw that Smith had no right whatever to assign the ground

[86] *Ibid.* at p. 407.
[87] (1906) 8 F. 619.
[88] *Ibid.* at p. 624.

annuals, and to say that in these circumstances he bound his firm to produce a title which was the foundation of the borrower's right is to go entirely outside the ordinary mandate of the partner of a firm of law agents."

Lord Dunedin's words might be interpreted as ruling that it is not within the apparent authority of a partner in a firm of solicitors to grant his firm's obligation that the title of a client will be completed, recorded and delivered. While it is an undesirable proceeding, it is by no means unknown in practice and even though knowledgeable solicitors neither grant nor accept such obligations with alacrity, it might be difficult to contend that they were not granted for carrying on in the usual way business of the kind carried on by the firm. It is thought that the feature of the transaction which Lord Dunedin intends to emphasise is that Smith was purporting to grant his firm's obligation in respect of the title to his own property and that this should have put Miss Walker's solicitor on his inquiry. That interpretation is reinforced by his later observation that Miss Walker's solicitor " was put on his guard when he received the original titles, and he should never have trusted to Smith's undertaking that his firm would produce what it was not its business to supply."

Walker v. *Smith* is therefore a case which should be regarded not as governed by application of the general limits of apparent authority in section 5 of the Partnership Act 1890 but as an illustration of the principle expressed by Lindley, " A person who knows that a partner is using the credit of the firm for a private purpose of his own, knows that he is using it for a purpose prima facie outside the limits of his authority." [89] Indeed the cases where the courts have held that the third party should have been put on his inquiry as to the partner's authority through his knowledge of unusual or suspicious circumstances attending the transaction are no more than a special application of the general rule that he may not rely upon the apparent authority of the partner if he in fact knew of relevant restrictions upon the scope of that apparent authority. The third party does not know factually that the partner has no authority to enter into the unusual transaction with him but he has prima facie notice through his knowledge of those unusual features that the transaction is one which is not embraced within the apparent authority of the partner, an authority which is confined to " carrying on in the usual way business of the kind carried on by the firm. . . ." The third party in such circumstances is consequently unable to rely upon the apparent authority of the partner and must make inquiry in order to satisfy himself that actual authority is held for the transaction. [90] Where the transaction is such that it discloses to the third party that the partner is using the credit of his firm in furtherance of a private transaction of his own, the third party may not remain passive and supine if he is to hold the firm liable on the transaction.

[89] Lindley, *op. cit.* p. 210.
[90] Partnership Act 1890, s. 5.

It will not be sufficient for him to establish that the partner's apparent authority covers the drawing of bills of exchange on behalf of the firm, if in the particular transaction in question a partner in a trading firm purports to grant the firm's bill in settlement of a private debt of his own, unless the third party can also establish that the bill was in fact granted with the authority of the other partners of the firm.[91] Even if the partner is a bona fide holder for his own use of a negotiable instrument granted by his firm and a third party takes the instrument from the partner in settlement of a private debt of the latter, the transaction raises a prima facie inference that it is irregular and a fraud on the other partners which the third party must rebut before he may enforce payment from the firm.[92] Similarly, even where it is within the apparent authority of the partner to pledge the goods of the partnership for the purposes of the firm's business, a third party may not rely on that apparent authority in a case where the partner has pledged the goods for private purposes of his own and this rule will hold where two firms are jointly interested in goods and one of those firms pledges the documents of title with a bank in security of sums borrowed on a separate account of that firm. The bank cannot hold the goods as against the other firm if it knew the real facts when it accepted the pledge.[93]

Representations by a partner as to his apparent authority

In transactions of such a kind as to arouse doubts in the mind of the third party regarding the apparent authority of the partner with whom he is dealing, it sometimes occurs that the third party makes his inquiry and seeks his reassurance from the partner with whom the transaction is being arranged. In such cases the third party's inquiries will often be directed to ascertaining the nature and extent of the business activities of the firm since that information will have an obvious bearing on the scope of the partner's apparent authority. When in response to such inquiries the partner misrepresents to the third party the nature of the partnership business or falsely represents it as being more extensive than it really is, it is improbable that the third party will be permitted to rely upon those representations as sufficient to admit of his holding the firm liable on the transaction. The representation of the partner as to the nature and extent of the firm's business cannot readily be regarded as an act for the carrying on in the usual way of business of the kind carried on by the firm in terms of section 5 of the Act, and thus does not fall clearly within his apparent authority. It might be contended

---

[91] *Miller* v. *Douglas*, Jan. 22, 1811, F.C.; *Kennedy*, Dec. 22, 1814, F.C.; *Johnston Sharp & Co.* v. *Phillips* (1822) 1 S. App. 244; *Leverson* v. *Lane* (1862) 13 C.B.(N.S.) 278; *Re Riches* (1865) 4 De G.J. & S. 581.

[92] *Leverson* v. *Lane, supra*; *Re Riches, supra.* A bona fide holder for value into whose hands the bill or note comes does not require to rebut this inference: *Garland* v. *Jacomb* (1873) L.R. 8 Ex. 216.

[93] *Snaith* v. *Burridge* (1812) 4 Taunt. 684; nor, presumably, could the bank do so, if, short of actual knowledge of the facts, there were features of the transaction which should have led them to seek confirmation of it from the other firm.

that the partner has actual, though implied, authority from his co-partners to inform third parties with whom he seeks to bring the firm into contractual relations as to the nature and extent of the firm's business. That attempted distinction between what is embraced within the actual authority by implication and what is within the apparent authority even if not within the actual authority is attractive theoretically but it is thought that an argument on those lines might not find favour with the court. While section 5 is concerned primarily with the apparent authority of the partner,[94] what is there laid down has a considerable bearing upon what may be implied within the actual authority. The limits set by the section on the apparent authority may be wider than those which it may be possible to imply as actually authorised in a particular case, but it would be difficult to contend that the actual authority which a partner may be regarded by implication as possessing can, in the general case, exceed what a third party is entitled to assume as the authority of the partner, i.e. his apparent authority. It may be that, in special cases, a partner's actual authority to exceed the limits of his apparent authority may be implied from facts and circumstances, such as previous actings of the partners,[95] but such considerations are unlikely to be relevant in many cases where the third party seeks to rely upon representations made by the partner with whom he is dealing as to the nature or extent of the business in which the partnership is concerned. Certainly if the third party has any knowledge whatsoever of the nature and extent of the business as normally carried on by the firm, he cannot rely on the representations of the partner [96]; for then having been put on his inquiry as to whether the partner is authorised to bind the firm in the transaction in question, he has not taken reasonable steps to ensure that his suspicions are unfounded and his doubts resolved. Where the third party has no previous knowledge of the firm at the time when the transaction is proposed by the partner, there is no reported decision on the law of partnership which is helpful on the question whether he may hold the firm liable on the strength of the representations made by the partner as to the nature or extent of its business, but on the basis of the general principles of agency it is difficult to see how he could succeed; for he is merely relying upon the word of the agent that he, the agent, has authority to bind his principal, and if the agent's representations as to his authority are false, the principal is not bound thereby.[97] Since the false representation of the partner as to the nature or extent of the business of the firm is as to a matter which delimits the apparent authority which third parties

---

[94] *Supra* pp. 208 *et seq.*

[95] Such cases might come close to including the act within the apparent authority of the partner.

[96] *Ex p. Agace* (1792) 2 Cox 312.

[97] " All ' ostensible ' authority involves a representation by the principal as to the extent of the agent's authority. No representation by an agent as to the extent of his authority can amount to a ' holding out ' by the principal." *Att.-Gen. for Ceylon* v. *Silva* (A. D.) [1953] A.C. 461 at p. 479.

may assume that he possesses, it is difficult on the analogy of agency to
see how any such misrepresentation will result in the firm being liable to
the third party. " A representation by the agent that he has authority
cannot create apparent authority, unless the agent has been expressly or
impliedly authorised to make representations as to his authority and so
enlarge the scope of his actual authority." [98] The qualifying clause in
the sentence just quoted raises the same issue which has been discussed
earlier in the paragraph in relation to the partner's misrepresentation, and
it is as difficult to envisage its application where an agent attempts to
increase the scope of his apparent authority by misrepresenting the nature
of his principal's business as it is in the case of a similar misrepresentation
by a partner as to the nature of the partnership business. The cases
which have given rise to the need for the qualifying words are concerned
with another issue entirely. They are based upon decisions to the effect
that even if an agent has not been appointed by the principals to carry
through the duties a third party dealing with him may rely upon his
possessing the ostensible authority of an agent of that particular kind if
the principals by their actings have publicly recognised him in the character
of such agent.[99]

Inducement to become a partner in the firm

The carrying on in the usual way of business of the kind carried on by
the firm does not entail the introduction of additional partners to the
membership of the firm. It is therefore not within the apparent authority
of an existing partner to make overtures to a third party or to seek to
induce him to join the firm. A partner requires actual authority from
the firm to bind it by such actings and if he offers a partnership to a third
party, the remaining partners are not bound by that offer unless they
have authorised the making of it or later ratify it.[1] The situation where
a partner involves his firm and copartners in a joint adventure with others
is to be distinguished. Here the rule is that a partner, without the consent
of his copartners, may not involve them in a partnership *in a different type
of business* from that carried on by his firm. If, however, the involvement
is in a joint adventure which is itself merely a means of carrying on the
ordinary business of the firm, it may be within a partner's authority to
bind his copartners in an arrangement of that kind.[1a] That, however, is
distinguishable from committing his copartners to accept a new partner
into the existing partnership which can never be within his implied
or his apparent authority. Moreover, if one of the partners fraudulently induces a third party to join the firm, that fraud will not
be imputed to the firm in the absence of express authority to the

---

[98] Bowstead, *Agency* (13th ed.), p. 250.
[99] *Freeman & Lockyer* v. *Buckhurst Park Properties (Mangal) Ltd.* [1964] 2 Q.B. 480.
[1] " No person may be introduced as a partner without the consent of all existing partners."
—Partnership Act 1890, s. 24 (7).
[1a] *Mann* v. *D'Arcy and Others* [1968] 2 All E.R. 172; and see *supra* pp. 212–213

partner to bring in an additional partner or of their ratification of the fraud when the remaining partners become aware of it. The mere assumption of the new partner will not of itself amount to ratification of any fraud perpetrated by the negotiating partner, but where the new partner has contributed money to the firm, then the remaining partners may not retain the money, in the knowledge of that fraud, without being held to have ratified the fraud itself and thus making themselves parties to it and liable for it. Accordingly, they will be liable to repay the money.[2] That principle is independent of, and should be distinguished from, the rights under section 40 of the Partnership Act 1890 of a partner who has paid a premium on entering a partnership. Section 40 provides

> " Where one partner has paid a premium to another on entering into a partnership for a fixed term, and the partnership is dissolved before the expiration of that term, otherwise than by the death of a partner, the court may order the repayment of the premium, or of such part thereof as it thinks just, having regard to the terms of the partnership contract and to the length of time during which the partnership has continued . . ."

except where the dissolution (a) is held to be due to the misconduct of the partner who paid the premium, or (b) is in terms of an agreement among the partners which makes no provision for a return of any part of the premium. Section 40 is concerned with " premiums," i.e. sums of money paid by the incoming partner to the others already established in business for their private account and as a consideration of his being assumed a partner in that business. Section 40 is, thus, not concerned with any question of fraud in inducing the incoming partner to enter the partnership nor, in theory at least, any liability of the partnership as such, since the premium is paid to the existing partner or partners as individuals and not to the firm, but rather it is concerned with the equitable treatment of such a premium where it has been paid on the understanding that the partnership will endure for a fixed term and it has been prematurely dissolved.

Section 41, however, does deal with the right of a partner to recover any money paid by him for purchase of a share in the partnership and any capital contributed by him, if the partnership contract is rescinded on the ground of fraud or misrepresentation of one of the partners thereto. The principle announced in *Lovell* v. *Hicks*,[2] however, exists independently even of section 41, since under the section the rights arise on a rescission of the contract of partnership, and hence a dissolution of the firm, whereas the partner might assert his right under the rule in *Lovell* v. *Hicks* during the subsistence of the partnership.

Since sections 40 and 41 are both concerned with rights arising in

[2] *Lovell* v. *Hicks* (1837) 2 Y. & C.Ex. 472.

dissolution of the firm detailed consideration of them is deferred until they may be examined in that context.[3]

Liability on the ground that the firm has had the benefit of the contract

" It is an erroneous but popular notion that if a firm obtains the benefit of a contract made with one of its partners, it must needs be bound by that contract. Now, although the circumstance that the firm obtains the benefit of a contract entered into by one of the members tends to show that he entered into the contract as the agent of the firm, such circumstance is no more than evidence that this was the case, and the question upon which the liability or non-liability of the firm upon a contract depends is not—Has the firm obtained the benefit of the contract? but—Did the firm, by one of its partners or otherwise, enter into the contract? " [4]

The principle applies equally in Scots law and was upheld in *Johnston Sharp & Co.* v. *Phillips.*[5] In that case a partner granted a bill in the firm name for a private debt but the firm itself was alleged to have derived some benefit from the transaction. They were not, however, held liable on the bill. In *Emly* v. *Lye,*[6] a partner drew bills in his own name and had them discounted by an agent of the firm. He obtained the proceeds from the agent and paid them into the firm's account. The firm was held to have no liability either for the bills or for their proceeds. No loan had been made to the firm and there was no contract with it. The only ground upon which it could be sought to impose liability on the firm was that the partner who was liable on the bills had later applied the proceeds for the benefit of his copartners as well as of himself, and that was an insufficient ground of liability on the part of the firm.[7]

The principle is a fundamental one and is recognised by Clark as forming part of the law of Scotland. After discussing the borrowing powers of a common law company, he continues,[8]

" It does not, however, follow that because the company has had the benefit of money borrowed by one of its partners or by its directors, the lender shall have recourse against the company *ipso jure.* The real question in such cases is, whether the loan was or was not made to the company. The fact that it received the proceeds is certainly strong, but not conclusive, evidence of its being a party to the contract; for the lender may have dealt with the partner

---

[3] *Infra,* Chap. XII, pp. 540 *et seq.*

[4] Lindley, *op. cit.* p. 225, founding on the judgment of Rolfe B. in *Beckham* v. *Drake* (1841) 9 M. & W. 79 at pp. 99–100.

[5] (1822) 1 Sh.App. 244.

[6] (1812) 15 East 7.

[7] See also *Bevan* v. *Lewis* (1827) 1 Sim. 376 and (as to loans to a partner) *Smith* v. *Craven* (1831) 1 Cr. & J. 500; *Hawtayne* v. *Bourne* (1841) 7 M. & W. 595; *Burmester* v. *Norris* (1851) 6 Ex. 796; *Ricketts* v. *Bennett* (1847) 4 C.B. 686; *Re Worcester Corn Exchange Co.* (1853) 3 De G.M. & G. 180; *Fisher* v. *Taylor* (1843) 2 Hare 218 (goods supplied to a partner); *Kingsbridge Flour Mill Co.* v. *Plymouth Grinding Co.* (1848) 2 Ex. 718; *Lloyd* v. *Freshfield* (1826) 2 C. & P. 325.

[8] *Op. cit.* I, p .219 (n.8a).

or the directors on their own credit solely, and the partners or the directors may have gone into the transaction in order to enable them to pay a debt due by them to the company, or to enter a transaction with it on their own account. The onus, therefore, of proving that the loan was made to the company rests on the lender."

Liability of the firm quantum lucratus

In the preceding paragraph, the subject under discussion was the liability of the firm *under the contract made by the partner* on the sole ground that the firm has derived a benefit from that contract. Though the liability of the firm will be negatived if it is asserted on that ground without more, it does not follow that the firm will necessarily escape all liability to the third party. But any liability which may be imposed upon it will rest, not on the partner's contract, but on the equitable principle of recompense which has been described by Stair [9] as " recompense of what we are profited by the damage of others, without their purpose to gift." The dangers of indiscriminate application of this equitable doctrine have been indicated by Gloag.[10] The doctrine does not provide a general claim by a creditor under a contract with A against B on the ground that B has ultimately benefited. " There is no such doctrine in the law of Scotland as that every person who has profited by work done under a contract is to be liable for the work so done." [11] But the principle is applicable where it can be established that the relationship between A and B is that of agent and principal.[12] Even so, the principle must be applied with caution in cases of partnership. Where a partner is under obligation to contribute some specified property to the capital of the firm and obtains that property on his own credit from a third party, the firm will not be liable *quantum lucratus* to the third party.[13] In that case, the firm's authority to the partner is not in question. The firm is in fact a creditor in the partner's obligation to contribute the property and a creditor is not bound to inquire as to the means by which his debtor has put himself in a position to discharge his obligation.[14] But where money is borrowed by a partner in name of his firm, though without authority, and that money has been applied in paying off the debts of the firm, the third party who lent the money has an equitable claim to repayment of the amount which he can prove was so applied by the firm, even if he knew when he lent the money that it was borrowed without authority.[15] The rule will apply in the case of money borrowed which is applied for any other lawful purpose of the firm.[16] Lindley

[9] *Inst.* I: 8: 2.   [10] *Contract* (2nd ed.), pp. 319 *et seq.*
[11] *Cran* v. *Dodson* (1893) 1 S.L.T. 354, *per* Lord Kyllachy.   [12] Gloag, *op. cit.* p. 330.
[13] *White* v. *McIntyre* (1841) 3 D. 334; *Lockhart* v. *Brown* (1888) 15 R. 742.
[14] *N.B. Bank* v. *Ayrshire Iron Co.* (1853) 15 D. 782; *Gibbs* v. *British Linen Co.* (1875) 4 R. 630; *Thomson* v. *Clydesdale Bank* (1891) 18 R. 751; (1893) 20 R.(H.L.) 59.
[15] *Reversion Fund & Insurance Co.* v. *Maison Cosway Ltd.* [1913] 1 K.B. 364.
[16] *Ex p. Chippendale (The German Mining Co.'s Case)* (1853) 4 De G.M. & G. 19; *Re Cork & Youghal Ry.* (1866) L.R. 4 Ch. 748; *Blackburn Building Society* v. *Cunliffe Brooks & Co.* (1882) 22 Ch.D. 61; (1884) 9 App.Cas. 857; (1885) 29 Ch.D. 902; *Baroness Wenlock* v. *River Dee Co.* (1883) 19 Q.B.D. 155; *Bannatyne* v. *McIver* [1906] 1 K.B. 103.

explains the doctrine as it has been developed in the English courts as founded partly on the right of the lender to stand in equity in the place of those creditors of the firm whose claims have been paid off by his money; and partly on the right of the borrowing partner to be indemnified by the firm against liabilities bona fide incurred by him for the legitimate purpose of relieving the firm from its debts or of carrying on its business.[17] It will be seen that the English doctrine has been developed with a more specialised reference to the particular circumstances than the Scottish doctrine of recompense. The result of the Scots law resting upon a principle of the broad and general kind described by Stair is that it must be applied to any particular case with great caution.[18] The English doctrine will be applied only in a case which falls under one or other of the two principles mentioned in the passage last quoted from Lindley and the English decisions, though they proceed upon the basis of a more narrowly defined principle, may yet be helpful in applying the broader based Scottish doctrine to those cases in partnership where it may be appropriately applied.[19] There is, moreover, adequate authority for the application of the principle of recompense in Scottish cases of agency.[20] In such cases it is well settled that where money has been obtained by an agent by unauthorised use of the principal's credit and has been used by the agent for the purposes of the principal or to meet the principal's obligations, the principal may not escape liability to the third party purely on the ground that the agent had neither actual nor apparent authority from him to obtain the money. He will require to recoup the third party to the extent to which he has been enriched by the application of the money obtained from the third party.

Liability of incoming partner for firm debts

It is a consequence of the rule that partners are jointly and severally liable for the debts and obligations of the firm itself, that their liability depends upon the firm as a *quasi* person having been in existence when the debts or obligations were incurred. The liability of the partners is an accessory one as cautioners for their firm and accordingly their liability does not arise until the date of formation of the firm. Where a number

---

[17] Lindley, *op. cit.* pp. 226–227. Though the words " for the legitimate purpose . . . of carrying on its business " might suggest that the partner's actings fall within his apparent authority and that there was therefore no need for the equitable doctrine, borrowing for the declared purpose of increasing the partnership capital (*Fisher* v. *Taylor* (1843) 2 Hare 218) or any form of borrowing where the firm is normally carried on without borrowing as in the case of a firm of solicitors (*Plumer* v. *Gregory* (1874) L.R. 18 Eq. 621) will require actual authority from, or ratification by, all the partners since the borrowing is not within the scope of the ordinary business of the firm. A power to borrow will fall within the apparent authority of the partner only when " its exercise is necessary for the transaction of the partnership business in the ordinary way " (Clark, *op. cit.* I, pp. 215–216).

[18] Gloag, *Contract* (2nd ed.), pp. 319–320.

[19] The doctrine of recompense has however been recognised in a Scottish case relating to the liability of the firm for the delict of a partner. See *New Mining Syndicate* v. *Chalmers & Hunter*, 1912 S.C. 126. *Infra* Chap. VIII, pp. 326–330.

[20] *British Linen Co.* v. *Alexander* (1853) 15 D. 277; *Traill* v. *Smith's Trs.* (1876) 3 R. 770; *Clydesdale Bank* v. *Paul* (1877) 4 R. 626.

of individuals have in prospect the formation of a partnership among themselves, it may happen that before the partnership is actually formed they have reached an agreement among themselves as to the respective contributions to be made by each to the capital of the firm when formed and a third party may provide the goods which one of the intending partners has undertaken to contribute or lend him the money which he has agreed to contribute to the capital of the partnership when it is formed. In that case the third party has no claim against the partnership when it subsequently comes to be formed, but must recover from the individual to whom he afforded these facilities.[21] Even if it can be proved that the goods or the money thus made available were applied to the purposes of the proposed partnership, the third party is still in the position of having contracted with the individual and not with the partnership and the firm is not concerned in the transactions by means of which a partner has put himself in a position to contribute what he has agreed to contribute to the firm and will not be liable upon such a transaction even when it occurs after the partnership has been formed and the individual entering the transaction with the third party has at the date of that transaction become a partner. In the last mentioned case, the firm will only be liable if the contract with the third party has proceeded upon the credit of the firm either expressly or by implication.[22]

Where the transaction has taken place before the partnership has been created, there is no *quasi* person in existence who may be liable for it and the other persons who propose to become partners are therefore not bound, since theirs is a secondary or accessory liability for the firm's liability even if in the particular circumstances an existing firm could be held liable. If, however, those who propose to become partners have lent themselves to the transaction which their associate has entered into with the third party, so that the latter has contracted in reliance upon them they will be held liable upon it but their liability in that case will arise on agency existing prior to the formation of the partnership and not as cautioners for a debt of the firm.[23] According to Clark,[24] " partners may also become liable for the debts and obligations of their copartners, though entered into before formation of the firm, if after that event such obligations, or the transactions of which they are the consequences, have been adopted, ratified or homologated by the company." The cases cited in support of that statement hardly bear it out. *Lloyd* v. *Ashby* [25] was not a case of ratification by the firm of an antecedent obligation by persons who proposed to join in forming the firm; it was rather a substitution of the firm's obligation, contained in its bill, for the

[21] Clark, *op. cit.* I, pp. 292–293; *White* v. *McIntyre* (1841) 3 D. 334, where the judges accepted the persuasive authority of English cases such as *Smith* v. *Craven* (1831) 1 Cr. & J. 500.
[22] *Jardine* v. *Macfarlane* (1828) 6 S. 564; *Venables* v. *Wood* (1839) 1 D. 659; *White* v. *McIntyre, supra.*
[23] *Ex p. Peele* (1802) 6 Ves. 602, *per* Lord Eldon. See also *Keith Spicer Ltd.* v. *Mansell* [1970] 1 W.L.R. 333.
[24] *Op. cit.* I, p. 293.
[25] (1831) 2 C. & P. 138.

former obligation undertaken by the persons proposing to form the partnership. *Hoby* v. *Roebuck* [26] seems to support a quite different rule from that which Clark seeks to ascribe to it. The case really decides that partners continue liable in the covenants entered into by them in a lease of the partnership premises even though the firm may have been dissolved since the lease was granted, and not, as Clark asserts, that " a person who became partner with the lessee of a house after the commencement of the lease and jointly agreed with him to pay additional rent for additional accommodation was found liable as a partner for the whole rent." While the facts as stated by Clark are so far as they go correct, his view of the nature of the case appears to be erroneous. There was in *Hoby* v. *Roebuck* no question of the obligations being undertaken otherwise than as partnership obligations and the case is therefore more correctly regarded as an illustration of the rule in section 17 (2) of the Partnership Act 1890, *viz.*—" A partner who retires from a firm does not thereby cease to be liable for partnership debts or obligations incurred before his retirement." [27]

It appears more consistent with authority that the cases which Clark regards as ratification by the firm after formation are, where they do not involve the subsequent substitution of the firm's obligation for the individual obligations previously undertaken, more properly regarded as cases where on the facts the court has decided that the original obligation was undertaken as a partnership one. The relation of partnership may be inferred from the actings of the partners and the formation of a partnership may in some cases be inferred from the agreements made by the intending partners. The English decisions appear to support this view. These decisions admittedly turn on the aspect of agency involved in partnership rather than on that of caution which is peculiar to Scots law but the same principle may be derived from agency. " The agency of each partner commencing with the partnership, and not before, it follows that the firm is not liable for what may be done by any partner before he becomes a member thereof." [28] Thus in *Wilson* v. *Whitehead* [29] three parties agreed that one should be the publisher of a book, another should be editor and the third should be the printer and should find the paper for the publication, charging it to the partnership account at cost price. The profits of the publication were to be divided equally among the three parties. The printer ordered and received the paper and the supplier later sued the editor and the publisher for the price. It was held that they were not liable since the printer was not authorised to purchase the paper except on his own account and the supplies which he had bought might have been used for another book. [30] There is some

---

[26] (1816) 7 Taunt. 157.
[27] See Lindley, *op. cit.* p. 255. On the liability of a partner after retirement, see *infra* pp. 263 *et seq.*
[28] Lindley, *op. cit.* p. 236.
[29] (1842) 10 M. & W. 503.
[30] See also *Venables* v. *Wood* (1839) 1 D. 659 and the comments upon that decision in Ross, *Leading Cases on the Commercial Law*, III, p. 529.

difficulty in reconciling that decision with *Gardiner* v. *Childs* [31] where in similar circumstances a partnership was held to exist so as to impose liability for the price of the paper upon the copartner. But that case was decided upon a jury verdict and Lord Denman C.J. in his charge to the jury left them with this direction—" You will say whether you think that at the time when those goods were furnished the defendants were partners in the concern for whose benefit they were furnished. If you think they were, then you will find for the plaintiffs; if you think the plaintiffs have not made this out to your satisfaction, then you will find your verdict for the defendants."

The discrepancy between the decisions in *Wilson* v. *Whitehead* and *Gardiner* v. *Childs* may therefore be reasonably accounted for by the differing view taken in each case on the purely factual issue whether the transaction entered into was a partnership one or otherwise. [32] The view here propounded as to the effect of these decisions is fortified when the contrasting decisions of *Saville* v. *Robertson* [33] and *Gouthwaite* v. *Duckworth* [34] are studied. These cases are closely similar on their facts. In both the parties had an agreement for a joint adventure in goods, and it was attempted to hold one of the parties who had not ordered the goods liable to pay for them because he was a partner of the person who did in fact order them and the goods were supplied and used for the purposes of the joint adventure. In both cases it was pleaded in defence that the goods were ordered before the commencement of the partnership and the defendant was consequently not liable for the purchase. Yet in the first case the defence prevailed while in the second it failed and the defendant had to pay. In *Saville* v. *Robertson* a number of parties agreed to share in the profit or loss arising in a joint adventure in goods. The kind of goods to be dealt in was to be fixed by a majority of the parties but each party's share in the adventure was restricted to the amount of the goods ordered and shipped by himself and he was not to be liable for goods ordered and shipped by any of his co-adventurers. The court held that in these circumstances no partnership commenced until the goods were on board ship. Each partner was to contribute his share of the goods and his copartners were not liable to third parties who furnished him with the means whereby he made contribution of his share. On the other hand, in *Gouthwaite* v. *Duckworth*, two persons, Browne and Powell, who were in partnership owed money to Duckworth. All three agreed to join in an adventure for the purchase and sale of goods. Browne and Powell were to purchase and pay for the goods and ship them. The proceeds of sale were to be remitted to Duckworth who, after deducting

---

[31] (1837) 8 Car. & P. 345.

[32] In commenting on *Venables* v. *Wood, supra,* a case somewhat similar to *Wilson* v. *Whitehead,* Ross (*op. cit.* p. 541) observes, " If however the paper had been ordered by the publisher expressly for the publication of the work in which the defender had an interest, then it may be thought that the defender would have been liable, as the circumstances of the case would have then very nearly resembled those of *Gardiner* v. *Childs.*"

[33] (1792) 4 T.R. 720.

[34] (1811) 12 East 421.

the amount owed to him by Browne and Powell, was to share equally with them the profit of the adventure. If there was a loss, Duckworth was to share in it. Browne purchased the goods on credit and all three co-adventurers were held liable to pay for them. The goods were purchased for the adventure in terms of the agreement, and while it was not intended that Duckworth should pay for the goods, the adventure in which he had associated himself began when the goods were purchased and he was in consequence liable since the price was a debt of the partnership. In commenting upon this decision Lindley [35] observes that it is difficult to reconcile it with *Saville* v. *Robertson* [33] if it rested on grounds of partnership and implied agency resulting therefrom: " for it is not easy to see how any partnership existed prior to the purchase of the goods." If, however, the decision was based upon an agency independent of the partnership, then although it was agreed that Browne and Powell were to pay for the goods, that might be construed merely as a stipulation which was effective as between them and Duckworth and " did not necessarily exclude the inference that as Browne and Powell were to buy for the adventure, they were at liberty to procure the goods on the credit of all concerned." Lord Dunedin, however, in *Karmali Abdullah Allarakhia* v. *Vora Karemji Jiwanji* [36] discussed these decisions and reconciled them on the basis that *Saville* v. *Robertson* was not, while *Gouthwaite* v. *Duckworth* was, a partnership transaction. Lord Dunedin said [37]: " Their Lordships think that the law on these matters is accurately stated in the well-known judgment of Lord Ellenborough in *Gouthwaite* v. *Duckworth*. In saying ' the law ' it would perhaps be more accurate to say, a statement of the criterion which is to be applied to the particular facts of each case in order to see whether the transaction is or is not a partnership transaction." Later in his judgment he added, [38] " It may be and often is a difficult matter to say on which side of the line thus indicated the facts of a particular case fall and cases will be found illustrating both results." [39] That such a decision on the facts may at times be difficult is clear from the cases which have been examined. But it will not be simplified by appealing to any principle of ratification, as Clark appears to suggest. [40] It is not easy to see how a firm which is a *quasi* person may ratify what has been done in its name before it had even that qualified corporate existence. It may, it is true, *adopt* such transactions by granting a fresh obligation in its own name to replace the earlier one but a mere ratification in such a case would it is thought add nothing to the original transaction. At least this appears arguable from the general principles of agency. " The only person who has power effectively to ratify an act is the person

[35] *Op. cit.* p. 238.
[36] (1914) L.R. 42 Ind.App. 48.
[37] *Ibid.* at p. 54.
[38] *Ibid.* at p. 55.
[39] Lord Dunedin referred to *British Linen Co.* v. *Alexander* (1853) 15 D. 277 as " on the lines of *Gouthwaite's* case " and *White* v. *McIntyre* (1841) 3 D. 334 as " on the lines of *Saville's* case."
[40] *Op. cit.* I, p. 293. See *supra* p. 259.

in whose name or on whose behalf the act purported to be done, and it is necessary that he should have been in existence and capable of being ascertained at the time when the act was done, and competent at that time and at the time of ratification to be the principal of the person doing the act; but it is not necessary that he should be known, either personally or by name, to the person doing the act." [41]   While the English rule is confined to cases of incorporated companies which may not ratify acts purporting to be done on their behalf before they were incorporated, it is reasonable to argue by analogy that in Scotland where a partnership is recognised as a *quasi* person transactions purporting to be done on its behalf before it is formed may not be ratified by it, though as in the case of the incorporated company it may make a new contract in the same terms as the former one which may be established by facts and circumstances such as the actings of parties, including the firm. [42]

Liability of a partner joining an established firm

" A person who is admitted as a partner into an existing firm does not thereby become liable to the creditors of the firm for anything done before he became a partner." [43]   Even if the new firm constituted by the assumption of the new partner acquires the entire assets of the firm which previously existed, that fact will not necessarily entail that the new firm and the newly assumed partner will be liable for the debts of the former business, [44] though it will be a circumstance to which the court will give weight in deciding as to liability.   Though the English authorities require to be treated with caution since at points they proceed to some extent upon the doctrine of consideration, [45] a similar line of approach may be detected in these cases.   There is no doubt that under both systems of law such an agreement may be established by indirect evidence. [46]   In England, it has been said, the courts lean in favour of such an agreement and are ready to infer it from comparatively slight evidence. [47]   Indeed they were prepared at one time to infer it whenever the incoming partner agreed with the other partners to treat such debts as debts of the new firm.   That reasoning has, however, been criticised by Lindley, [48] who points out that the agreement which requires to be established in such cases is an agreement between the incoming partner and the creditor, not one among the partners themselves.

[41] Bowstead, *Agency* (13th ed.), pp. 40–41.   And see *Kelner* v. *Baxter* (1866) L.R. 2 C.P. 174; *Tinnevelly Sugar Refining Co.* v. *Mirrees Watson & Yaryan Co.* (1894) 21 R. 1009.
[42] *Howard* v. *Patent Ivory Co.* (1888) 38 Ch.D. 156.
[43] Partnership Act 1890, s. 17 (1).
[44] *Stephen's Tr.* v. *Macdougall & Co.'s Tr.* (1889) 16 R. 779; *Heddle's Exrx.* v. *Marwick & Hourston's Tr.* (1888) 15 R. 698 at p. 706.
[45] See, for example, Lindley, *op. cit.* p. 240: " In order to render an incoming partner liable to the creditors of the old firm, there must be some agreement, express or tacit, to that effect entered into between him and the creditors and founded on some sufficient consideration."
[46] *Heddle's Exrx.* v. *Marwick & Hourston's Tr.* (*supra*); *McKeand* v. *Laird's Tr.* (1861) 23 D. 846; *Ex p. Jackson* (1790) 1 Ves.Jun. 131; *Ex p. Peele* (1802) 6 Ves. 602.
[47] Lindley, *op. cit.* p. 240; *Ex p. Jackson, supra*; *Ex p. Peele, supra*.
[48] *Op. cit.* pp. 240–241.

The approach of the Scottish courts appears to be differently conceived. In some of the decisions it seems that the liability of the new partner for the debts of the old firm has been based upon the fact that the new firm has taken over the assets of the former firm and that the new partner has made no, or slight, contribution to the capital of the new firm. This leads Dr. Gow [49] to state that in Scots law " the prime principle is that the partners in the existing firm cannot be allowed to prejudice their creditors by dissolving that firm and conveying its assets to the new partnership without the latter assuming responsibility for the liabilities of the old." It must be said that certain passages in the judgments of the Lord President (Inglis) in the cases, *Miller* v. *Thorburn* [50] and *McKeand* v. *Laird's Trustee* [51] strongly suggest a broadly based equitable doctrine of that kind; and Lord Cowan expresses the notion very clearly in *Miller* v. *Thorburn* [52] when he says, " I concur in the principle given effect to by the cases of *Ridgeway* and *McKeand* that in the general case, where the whole estate of a company is given over to and taken possession of by a new concern or partnership, the business being continued on the same footing, the estate goes to the new company *suo onere*—that is the liabilities go along with the effects. To sustain any other principle might result in the greatest injustice. This is the general presumption, although there may be special circumstances in particular cases not admitting of its application." Lord Shand generalised the rule even more widely in these words: " If a person grants a universal disposition in favour of another party, in so far as this is gratuitous and not for value, it can only be under burden of the obligations for which that party is liable." [53]

There is little in the English decisions which suggests a broadly based equitable rule of that kind. The emphasis appears to be almost entirely upon an agreement, either express or tacit, with the creditors affected by the selling up of the new firm. In the English case [54] most nearly resembling the Scottish decisions which have just been discussed, that emphasis is clearly shown. In that case two persons, Warwick and Clagell, entered a partnership. Warwick had had prior business dealings with certain merchants and he notified them of the partnership, and asked them to make up their accounts and transfer any balance at credit or debit of him personally to an account with the partnership. In carrying through these requests, a debt of Warwick's was debited to the partnership and a bill was drawn on the firm for the amount of the debit. The bill was accepted by the firm but was dishonoured on presentation. In the supervening bankruptcy of the partnership it was held that the debt had become the debt of Warwick and Clagell jointly and that their joint liability had been accepted by the creditor in lieu of Warwick's sole liability.

[49] *Mercantile & Industrial Law of Scotland*, p. 550.
[50] (1861) 23 D. 359.
[51] (1861) 23 D. 846.   See also *Ridgeway* v. *Brock* (1831) 10 S. 105.
[52] *Supra cit.* at p. 362.
[53] *Heddle's Exrx.* v. *Marwick & Hourston's Tr.* (1888) 15 R. 698 at pp. 709–710.
[54] *Ex p. Whitmore* (1838) 3 Deac. 365; and see *Rolfe & Others* v. *Flower, Salting & Co.* (1865) L.R. 1 P.C. 27.

In *Ex p. Whitmore* the creditor was requested to debit the new firm in place of his former debtor and complied with the request. There was then a basis for ascribing the liability of the new firm and the incoming partner to an implied agreement to which the creditor was a party. In the Scottish cases,[55] no such request was addressed to the creditor and it is more difficult to regard him as a party to any agreement express or implied with the new firm. The taking over by the new firm of the assets of the old firm arises from agreement between the former debtor and the new firm, and beyond the fact of that agreement having been made and affecting the interests of the creditor there is no element in the Scottish cases which involves the creditor in the agreement nor was he notified of it. Gloag, nevertheless, regards the taking over of the assets as a " fact from which the court may draw the inference that the new firm has agreed to be liable to the creditors of the old." [56] That such an agreement may be and has been inferred in such circumstances by the Scottish courts is clearly supported by authority but the agreement so inferred still remains an agreement to which the creditor is a *tertius*. It is this aspect of the Scottish cases which has led the courts to adopt the equitable doctrine noticed by Dr. Gow [57] as the basis of the decision. Yet even the equitable doctrine is not entirely satisfactory in all cases where the new firm has taken over the assets of the former debtor. It will not always be compelling in equity to impose liability on the incoming partner in such circumstances. In *Nelmes & Company* v. *Montgomery & Company & Others*,[58] Montgomery who carried on business as a tobacconist and billiard-room keeper, assumed Loudon as a partner. Under the deed of partnership the capital of the firm was fixed at £158, whereof £68 was contributed by Montgomery and £90 by Loudon. There was no provision as to the existing stock in trade and assets of the business. Montgomery, having subsequently become bankrupt, Nelmes & Company, a firm of billiard-table makers, sued Loudon, the solvent partner, for the price of two billiard-tables supplied to Montgomery about one year before the partnership was entered into. It was held that Loudon was not liable for the price of the tables.

If the ground of liability in such circumstances rested upon an implied agreement that the new firm, and the incoming partner, undertook liability for debts previously incurred in the business, there was obviously little in the facts of this case which would serve as a basis for any such implied agreement. It was not a term of the contract of copartnery that the partnership took over the assets of the former business, though admittedly the billiard-tables in question were used in the business of the partnership. Moreover, Loudon, the incoming partner, had made a

[55] *Ridgeway* v. *Brock* and *McKeand* v. *Laird's Tr.*, *supra* n. 51; *Miller* v. *Thorburn*, *supra* n. 50 and *Heddle's Exrx.* v. *Marwick & Hourston's Tr.*, *supra* n. 44; and see also *Hoskins* v. *Christie* (1845) 8 D. 167.
[56] Gloag, *Contract* (2nd ed.), p. 267.
[57] *Supra* n. 49.
[58] (1883) 10 R. 974.

proportionately significant contribution to the capital of the partnership by paying his share of £90 and if the billiard-tables were to be regarded as in fact taken over by the partnership, it would be difficult to argue that there was any implied agreement on his part to undertake liability to the manufacturers for the cost of them. The main interest of the case lies in the observations made upon the broad doctrine of liability which had been expounded in the judgments on the earlier cases of *Ridgeway* v. *Brock, McKeand* v. *Reid* and *Miller* v. *Thorburn.* In examining these cases, the Lord Justice-Clerk (Moncreiff) [59] said,

> " I cannot, however, separate these dicta from the facts of the cases in which they were uttered, and I find that in both cases the parties to the new copartnery had indicated their intention of becoming liable for business debts by taking over the assets and stock of the former concern; and by treating these debts as due by the firm. The judgment in the case of *McKeand,* expressly proceeds on the direct obligation of the partners, and Lord Wood in his opinion in *Miller's* case states that such was the ground of judgment in that case. But I am not to be supposed to hold that the creditors of a trader who forms a partnership with another person have anything of the nature of a *nexus* over the stock in trade with which the original trader has been carrying on business. I concede that the circumstances under which, and the mode in which, a new partner enters a business may raise a presumption that he intends to assume liability for the debts of the old business. But here we have not a case of that kind. In the first place no trade was carried on which could be made the subject of stipulation in a deed of copartnery as to making over the stock of a going concern to a new partnership. The truth is, there was no going concern or stock in trade made over in this case in any reasonable sense. It does not even appear that these tables belonged to the new concern. This tobacconist—Montgomery—had set up a billiard table in his shop, and finding that it attracted customers, he conceived the idea of taking a larger place and putting in two new billiard tables, and he afterwards got a partner to assist him in the business."

His Lordship referred secondly to the point that there was no word in the deed of copartnery as to a transfer of property in the tables and appointments to Loudon nor any suggestion that Loudon thought they had been transferred or assumed liability for their cost. Lords Craighall and Rutherford Clark also found that the facts in the case did not involve their deciding it in a manner which would throw doubt on the soundness of the dicta in the earlier cases cited. Lord Young, however, was more uncompromising. " The contention for the pursuers," he said,[60] " comes to nothing short of this, that a man who joins any trader as a partner becomes

[59] *Nelmes & Co.* v. *Montgomery & Co. & Others* (1883) 10 R. 974 at pp. 978–979.
[60] *Ibid.* at p. 980.

liable in consequence of the debts which that trader owes so far as connected with the business which he has carried on.   Is there any authority
for that, or any principle?   I should say none, and it seems to me irrational
on the statement of it.   Such liability would go as far back as it is possible
to prove the debts."

In *Heddle's Executrix* v. *Marwick & Hourston's Trustee* [61] the point was
again considered by the court.   In that case the whole assets of a going
concern were taken over by a new partnership, the incoming partners contributing no capital.   It was held that the presumption was that the
liabilities were taken over with the assets and that the new partnership
assumed liability for all the trade debts contracted by the former business.
The Lord President (Inglis) observed,[62]

> " Although in the recent case of *Nelmes* opinions were expressed by
> some of their Lordships of the Second Division which the Lord
> Ordinary thinks are at variance with the views in the two previous
> cases to which I have referred, I cannot help thinking that the differ-
> ence is more apparent than real, and that if another case raising the
> same kind of question which occurred in the cases of *McKeand* and
> *Miller* comes to be considered by the court, it will be found that the
> law to be applied is very much the same as was enunciated by the
> Judges in the former cases . . ."

In all the cases cited, apart from *Nelmes & Company* v. *Montgomery
& Company and Others*, the new partner had been given a partnership without having contributed any substantial sum to the capital of the firm and
where the new partnership took over the assets of the former business it was
held that they, and consequently the new partner, must be presumed to
have taken over the liabilities of the former business also. *Nelmes & Company* v. *Montgomery & Company and Others* differs in two respects from
the other cases; (1) in that case the new partner did in fact make a contribution to the capital of the partnership; and (2) it was not established that the
new partnership had in fact taken over the assets of the former business.
In the state of authority at this point it might have been questioned whether
the liability of the incoming partner for the debts of the old business was
elided by either one of those two elements appearing in the arrangements
for the new partnership or whether there required to be, as there was in
Nelmes & Company's case, a combination of both elements.   It can
reasonably be deduced that if the assets of the old business are not taken
over, the new partnership will not be held liable for the debts of the old
business since the principle under which that liability has been imposed is
that such assets are presumed to have been taken over *cum onere*.   But
though *Nelmes & Company* did not decide the point and indeed expressly
found that no taking over of assets had been established, that case was
regarded as affording support for the proposition that the taking over of

[61] (1888) 15 R. 698.
[62] *Ibid.* at p. 710.

the assets was of itself no ground for imposing liability on the new firm and the incoming partner, and would only do so if the arrangements with the incoming partner were such that he acquired gratuitously, or at least for inadequate consideration, a share as partner in the new firm of the assets taken over. Gloag took that view of the decision,[63] and the same view was adopted in *Thomson & Balfour* v. *Boag & Son* [64] where the earlier authorities were reviewed. The Lord President (Normand) said,[65]

> " It is a settled principle of law that, when the whole assets of a going concern are handed over to a new partnership and the business is continued on the same footing as before, the presumption is that the liabilities are taken over with the stock. ... The principle is that it would be inequitable to allow a trader to injure his trade creditors by assuming a partner and handing over his whole trading assets to the new partnership without liability to pay the trade debts. But this presumption must not be extended beyond the circumstances to which it properly applies. In *Heddle's Executrix*, Lord Shand pointed out (at p. 710) that, if a partner comes into a business, paying in a large sum of capital and the other partners merely put in their shares of a going business as their share of the capital, special circumstances might have to be proved in order to impose liability on the new partner for transactions entered into before he became a partner. If, again, the new partnership is carried on on the basis that there shall be no liability for the prior debts and no right to collect sums due to the individual partners or the old partnership in respect of prior transactions, the presumption is, I think, displaced."

It will be noticed that the first of the exceptions mentioned by Lord Normand involves a question of degree. If the incoming partner pays in a " large sum of capital " while the others merely contribute their shares of the existing business, the new partner may be absolved from liability for prior debts of the business. In deciding what is a " large sum " for this purpose, the court will look at the sum contributed in proportion to the capital of the partnership. In *Thomson & Balfour* v. *Boag & Son* the value of the stock, plant and goodwill of the existing business was stated to be approximately £700. Though there was no actual conveyance of those assets to the new partnership in the contract of copartnery, they were in fact handed over. The incoming partner paid in all £340 as his contribution to the capital of the partnership. That was regarded as a " real and substantial " contribution and sufficient to exempt the incoming partner from the liability imposed upon such partners where they had paid no sum into the capital of the firm and thus had given no consideration for the transfer of the assets to the new firm. That approach is consistent with the views expressed *obiter* in *Nelmes & Company* v. *Montgomery & Company & Others* [66] where the capital of the new partnership was stated to be

---

[63] *Contract* (2nd ed.), p. 267, n. 6.
[64] 1936 S.C. 2.
[65] *Ibid.* at p. 10.
[66] (1883) 10 R. 974.

£158 whereof £68 was contributed by Montgomery and was represented by the assets taken over from the business previously carried on by him and £90 was contributed in cash by the incoming partner, Loudon. Though the question is not expressly dealt with in either case, it appears to be a reasonable inference that where the incoming partner has made a payment in cash as a contribution to the capital of the firm but one which is not regarded as " substantial " in relation to the capital employed in the firm's business, including the assets taken over, the court would not find in the mere fact that a payment of this kind has in fact been contributed any compelling reason for releasing the incoming partner from liability for the debts of the old business.

The conclusions to be drawn from the authorities examined appear to be that the Scottish courts have approached the question of the liability of an incoming partner in such cases on the basis that the circumstances surrounding the creation of the partnership and the transfer of the assets to it from the former business raise a presumption of continuing liability on the part of the new firm for the debts of the former business and, in appropriate circumstances, the imposition of liability on an incoming partner for such debts. The theory that this liability is grounded in an implied agreement to undertake such liability to creditors of the old business, while it receives support from the dicta of some of the judges in the earlier cases and is advanced by Gloag,[67] cannot comfortably be maintained in the face of the decision in *Henderson* v. *Stubbs Limited*.[68] In that case the purchaser of a business undertook expressly in the agreement for the purchase " to pay and discharge all the present and future liabilities of the vendors in connection with the business." A creditor of the old business sued the purchasers for payment of a debt due to him by the vendors. The action was held to be irrelevant because the pursuer was not a party to the agreement for purchase of the business and he had no *jus quaesitum tertio* under it. If the creditor is *tertius* in an express agreement between the old business and the company taking over its undertaking that the latter will assume liability for the former's debts, the theory cannot explain the decisions in such cases as *Ridgeway* v. *Brock, Miller* v. *Thorburn, McKeand* v. *Reid* and *Heddle's Executrix* v. *Marwick & Hourston's Tr.* where the agreement has to be inferred from the actings of the parties; for in none of these decisions can it be argued that the agreement so inferred was one with the creditor, since the actings on which it is based were actings to which he was in no sense a party and of which he may indeed have had no knowledge whatsoever. Even the suggestion that by such actings the new firm " adopted " the liability on the former debts [69] will not serve to explain the liability incurred to the creditors if adoption is used as a legal term of art

---

[67] *Per* Lord Adam in *Heddle's Exrx.* v. *Marwick & Hourston's Tr.* (1888) 15 R. at pp. 706–707, *per* L. President Inglis at p. 710; Gloag, *Contract* (2nd ed.), p. 267.

[68] (1894) 22 R. 51.

[69] *Per* Lord Adam in *Heddle's Exrx.* v. *Marwick & Hourston's Tr., supra* at pp. 706–707: " I think in all cases it is a question of circumstances, and that it must be established by presumption, or by proof of facts, and circumstances, that the new firm agreed to adopt the old debts and to become liable for them."

since if it has taken place it is inferred from the actings of the parties. It is in fact a special instance of personal bar by conduct and where the conduct is referable to the agreement between the old business and the new partnership as it is in the cases under consideration, that adoption of liability may not be pleaded by the creditor. The true ground of liability it is submitted is that " if the new firm takes over the stock-in-trade and the book debts and whole business of the old firm and the goodwill of that business, equity requires that they shall take over its obligations." [70]

It should also be noticed that the presumption arising in equity from such transactions is not concerned primarily with the liability of the incoming partner, though that may arise as a corollary. The basic principle behind the presumption is that a trader may not defeat his existing trade creditors simply by transferring his trade assets to a new concern and that if he attempts to remove his assets from the grasp of his creditors in this way, the person to whom they are transferred will be presumed to take these assets under burden of the existing liabilities. The transferee of the assets may be a new partnership consisting of the partners of the former business with one or more additional and incoming partners as was the case in *Ridgeway* v. *Brock* and *Miller* v. *Thorburn*. On the other hand, the assets may be transferred from the old business to a new partnership of which none of the partners of the old firm, or only some of them, are members [71] or to a concern which has no connection whatsoever with the former business. [72] In the last case there is no room for the application of the equitable doctrine since they can have recourse for payment of their debts to the price which is in the hands of their debtor [73] and the like reasoning would support the view that unless some at least of the partners of the former business continue as members of the new firm the doctrine is inapplicable, since if none of them is a member of the new firm, then the old firm is simply a seller of its business to the new firm and the price received by the old firm is available in its hands and in the hands of its partners to meet the claims of its creditors. In these cases, even where the purchasers agree with the vendors to pay the liabilities of the old firm that is a contract with the old firm and not with its creditors who are not parties to it. In order that the purchasers may become liable to the creditors an undertaking by the purchasers to the creditors themselves will require to be proved and even in that case the liability of the old firm will not be elided unless delegation of the liability can be pleaded and established. The essential equity of the doctrine arises from the fact that in the new partnership the trader is parting with his trade assets to a new concern in which he still remains a partner and where his contribution to the capital of the new partnership consists in his assets so taken over by them. If the

---

[70] *Per* Lord Shand in *Heddle's Exrx.* v. *Marwick & Hourston's Tr., supra* at p. 709. The essentially equitable nature of the presumption is also brought out in the judgment of Lord Shand in *Stephen's Tr.* v. *Macdougall & Company's Tr.* (1889) 16 R. 779 at p. 787.
[71] *Price & Logan* v. *Wise* (1862) 24 D. 491.
[72] *Henderson* v. *Stubbs Ltd.* (1894) 22 R. 51.
[73] *Ibid. per* Lord Shand at p. 55.

taking over of the assets is upon an arrangement whereby those coming to the new partnership themselves make no payment, or an insubstantial payment, to the capital, then the trader has parted with his assets to the prejudice of his trade creditors and those assets are presumed to have been taken over by the new partnership on the basis that it and its partners including the incoming partners are liable for the prior trade debts; but where the incoming partners have made a real and substantial contribution to the capital of the new partnership, the new firm may still be liable under the equitable doctrine but the incoming partners are not so liable since there is then no equitable consideration so far as they are concerned to render them liable for debts of the partnership incurred on transactions prior to the date of their becoming partners.

Other aspects of liability of incoming partner for previous transactions of the firm

When a new partner is assumed into an existing firm it is clear from the terms of section 17 (1) of the Partnership Act 1890 that he does not by reason of that fact alone render himself liable to the creditors of the firm for anything done before he became a partner. The wording of the section is cautiously expressed, however, and does not preclude the possibility that an incoming partner may in special facts and circumstances be held so liable. From the date when he enters the partnership he will of course be liable under section 5 for the transactions of the firm but his entry into the partnership does not in any way establish that he has authorised the past transactions of the firm either expressly or impliedly; nor can he be said to have ratified such transactions merely by joining the firm, because ratification would entail that those carrying through the original transaction purported to act on his behalf though with imperfect or with no authority from him, and the very fact of his later introduction to the partnership will destroy any such argument if the fact of his being a partner is the sole ground upon which it is claimed that the former partners professedly acted on his behalf.[74] A more difficult question may arise in respect of transactions initiated before he entered into partnership but completed only after that date. So far as his liability *ex contractu* is concerned, he will normally be liable on such transactions, though section 17 (1) of the Partnership Act 1890 will not of itself impose that liability, since it is expressed negatively and does not involve the proposition that the incoming partner *eo ipso* will be liable on new transactions so as to preclude the possibility of his avoiding liability on these. Thus, when the creditor, after the introduction of the new partner, clearly continues to deal with the former trader and refuses to deal with the new firm, the incoming partner will not be bound.[75] Again, where the incoming partner is in terms of

---

[74] *Keighley, Maxsted & Co.* v. *Durant & Co.* [1901] A.C. 240.
[75] *British Homes Assurance Corporation Ltd.* v. *Paterson* [1902] 2 Ch. 604. There was the added feature of that case, which will be present in many cases of the kind, that the money derived from the transaction never came into the possession of the new firm, on which see *infra* Chap. VIII.

section 17 (1) free from liability for the former debts of the firm, he will not be rendered liable if after he becomes a partner his copartners give a bill or note in name of the new firm for the former debt which they alone incurred.   That amounts to a fraud upon the incoming partner and he will not be liable on the bill or note to a holder with notice of the fraud.[76]   On the same reasoning it is probably the law that the incoming partner will not be liable for a debt contracted before he entered the partnership on the strength of an account subsequently adjusted by his copartner with the creditor in which that debt is admitted as due from the present firm,[77] but in that case the incoming partner may be liable if his own conduct is such that a novation of the contract with the creditor can be established.   Where there is an open running account with the creditor, which commenced prior to his introduction to the partnership and continues with the new firm, the incoming partner may incur liability to pay the balance due thereon, and that liability may exist even though the payments made by the new partnership of which he is a member are sufficient to discharge the part of the account which represents liability on transactions carried through since he became a partner.[78]   The effect of the rule in *Clayton's* case [79] should be kept carefully in mind where partial payments are made towards the indebtedness due on any such running account.   Under that rule the creditor is not entitled without express stipulation to ascribe general payments on account which have not been expressly ascribed to particular items by the debtor or the creditor, to the later items in the account so as to show himself as a creditor in respect of the earlier items, nor is the debtor entitled to ascribe a general payment on account to subsequent rather than earlier items of the account.   The prejudice which may enure to an incoming partner through the application of the rule to a running account commenced before he became a partner and continuing thereafter is obvious. While the rule in *Clayton's* case may not be applied to the prejudice of the incoming partner without his consent, either express or implied, he must be watchful that he does not appear to assent to any treatment of the running account which will allow the rule to operate since then he may find that payments made by the new partnership are ascribed to the debts of the old and the balance outstanding on the account is in respect of items incurred since the date of his becoming a partner.   The rule in *Clayton's* case may only be applied with consent either express or tacit of the incoming partner.   If that consent cannot be established, then a creditor of the former concern who continues to deal with the new firm has no right to appropriate a payment made by an incoming partner to a debt incurred by his copartners prior to his becoming a partner or indeed to treat the account of the old firm and the account of the new firm as one continuous running account and apply *Clayton's* rule so as to ascribe a general

---

[76] *Shirreff* v. *Wilks* (1800) 1 East 48.
[77] Lindley, *op. cit.* p. 242.
[78] *Beale* v. *Caddick & Hartland* (1857) 2 H. & N. 326; *Scott* v. *Beale* (1859) 6 Jur.(N.S.) 559.
[79] *Devaynes* v. *Noble, Clayton's Case* (1816) 1 Mer. 572.

payment made by the new firm to the earlier items in the combined running account.[80]

A similar question may arise as to the liability *ex delicto* of an incoming partner, where a transaction was commenced before he became a partner and not completed until after he had become a partner.   If in these circumstances one of his copartners is guilty of negligence during the period when the transaction is being completed under the auspices of the new firm, the Lord Ordinary (Kyllachy) in *Tully* v. *Ingram* [81] stated the view that the incoming partner would be liable; but opinions on this point were reserved in the Inner House.

It is also to be kept in view that if an incoming partner agrees to accept liability for debts incurred by the firm prior to his assumption as a partner, there is nothing in section 17 (1) of the Partnership Act 1890 to prevent this.   In the normal case, however, any such agreement will be among the partners themselves and will not involve the incoming partner in direct responsibility to the creditors of the firm but will rather render him liable in relief *pro rata* to any of his copartners who have been called upon to pay the debt and have done so.   If the incoming partner is to be liable directly to the creditors of the former firm, agreement to that effect must be entered into between him and the creditors themselves.[82]   An agreement of that sort may be in express terms or it may be tacitly implied in the actings of parties.   In most cases where the issue arises in practice, it is likely to arise not from the terms of any express agreement with the creditors but on indirect evidence as to the circumstances of the particular case. The English courts have in the past been inclined to infer the existence of an agreement of this nature from circumstances in themselves not strongly indicative of the agreement,[83] and at one time would give effect to it in cases where the incoming partner agreed with his copartners to accept the liability.[84]   The existence of an agreement to that effect with his copartners is a circumstance upon which it is obviously erroneous to found as evidencing an agreement with the creditors.[85]   Nor are the specialities of the Scots law of *jus quaesitum tertio* such as to assist the Scottish courts in arriving at such a conclusion.[86]   It is thought that the circumstances which a Scottish court will accept as indicative of an agreement of this kind will be required to be at least unequivocal in their indication of the agreement.   In some cases the courts in Scotland may be able to avail themselves of the equitable doctrine laid down in cases like *Heddle's Executrix* v. *Marwick & Hourston's Trustee*,[87] but even in that context the circumstances will be closely examined.[88]   There appears to be no suggestion in the

---

[80] *Burland* v. *Nash* (1861) 2 F. & F. 687.
[81] (1891) 19 R. 65.   [82] *Henderson* v. *Stubbs Ltd.* (1894) 22 R. 51.
[83] *Ex p. Jackson* (1790) 1 Ves.Jun. 131; *Ex p. Peele* (1802) 6 Ves. 602; *Rolfe* v. *Flower, Salting & Co.* (1865) L.R. 1 P.C. 27; *Ex p. Whitmore* (1838) 3 Deac. 365.
[84] Cooke's *Bank Law* (8th ed.), p. 534.
[85] *Ex p. Peele, supra*; *Ex p. Parker* (1842) 2 Mont. D. & D. 511.
[86] *Henderson* v. *Stubbs Ltd.* (1894) 22 R. 51.
[87] (1888) 15 R. 698.   This case and the other authorities are discussed *supra* pp. 263–271.
[88] See *e.g. Stephens' Tr.* v. *Macdougall & Co's Tr.* (1889) 16 R. 779.

reported decisions that they will take an unduly benign view of the circumstances in order to arrive at the conclusion that the incoming partner has agreed with the creditors to accept responsibility for their claims against the former business and indeed since the agreement may in some cases, though not all, amount to delegation and in most cases the agreement will at the very least have the effect of involving an additional obligant in the original obligation, fairly strict standards of proof are likely to be demanded.

Endurance of liability

A partner's liability to the creditors of the firm may arise in respect (1) of acts done by his copartners while the mutual agency subsisting between them and him was still in existence or (2) of future acts of those who were formerly his copartners and who after he has in some way disengaged himself from the partnership continue the business formerly carried on by him and them in partnership.

Liability for past acts. Since in these cases the former partner prima facie at least has undertaken liability for what has been done in the name of the partnership of which he was a member, the onus of proof that this liability no longer exists will rest upon him. Thus in relation to a partner who has retired, section 17 (2) of the Partnership Act 1890 provides—" A partner who retires from a firm does not thereby cease to be liable for partnership debts or obligations incurred before his retirement." A partner who has retired from the firm will remain liable for transactions carried through while he was a partner unless he can prove circumstances, beyond the mere fact of his retirement, which justify the conclusion that he is no longer liable on those transactions. In other words, ". . . the liability for past engagements survives the severance of the partnership relation, and as regards the public terminates only by implement or satisfaction; while in a question with the *socii*, it may be brought to an end by arrangement, even before the company obligation has been extinguished." [89] In the case of liabilities incurred while the partner was still a member of the firm, therefore, the fact of the partner's subsequent retirement will not serve to extinguish his responsibility for these obligations: nor will the fact that he has retired with the consent of his copartners, that he has duly notified his retirement to the creditor in the obligation, that he has lodged with the remaining partners sums sufficient to discharge the obligations taking them bound to pay the debts within a stated time, and that he has been granted by his former copartners a full discharge from liability in respect of such obligations, taken separately or in combination, suffice to extinguish his liability to third parties for the debts.[90] These elements are all related to the arrangements under which the partner has retired from the firm, and since section 17 (2) provides that he does not " thereby," *i.e.* by his retirement,

[89] Clark, *op. cit.* I, p. 306.
[90] *Milliken* v. *Love* (1803) Hume 754; *Matheson* v. *Fraser* (1820) Hume 758; *Walker* v. *Davidson* (1821) 1 S. 21.

cease to be liable, the retired partner must be able to point to other features which have a more direct bearing upon the relationship of his former firm with third parties in order to escape liability. Obviously if he had made an agreement with the creditor or creditors in question that he will no longer be held liable upon their claims, he will be free. In certain circumstances the fact of his bankruptcy or his death may be relevant matters for consideration but since these are perhaps better studied in conjunction and since the death of the partner raises issues which are divorced from those implicit in his retiring from the firm they are deferred for treatment at a later stage. Apart from these cases there must be circumstances from which it may be inferred that the debt in question has been discharged as regards the firm or some arrangement short of that to which the creditor of the firm is a party, *e.g.* delegation of the liability as debtor in the obligation.

But there must be something more to appeal to beyond the mere fact that the partner has retired from the firm. In *Welsh and Another* v. *Knarston and Others* [90a] an action for damages based on professional negligence was raised against the partners of a firm of solicitors. The firm was instructed in 1966 to act for the pursuers in regard to their claims for injuries sustained in a road accident which occurred in September 1965. The claims were negligently allowed to become time-barred since no actions had been raised by September 1968. In the meantime two of the defenders had ceased to be partners, one as from September 30, 1967, and the other as from February 28, 1968. These partners pleaded that they were not liable for actings of the firm after the respective dates of their retirement from the firm. In his judgment the Lord Ordinary (Lord Stott) considered the effect of sections 9 and 17 (2) of the Partnership Act 1890 neither of which he regarded as apt in the circumstances of the case. " No doubt the commitment to prosecute the defenders' claim for damages was an obligation of the firm incurred while all the defenders were partners, but to say that they are to be liable for it would be an odd way of describing responsibility for pursuing the claims to a conclusion." The Lord Ordinary preferred to regard the case as falling under section 38 of the Act which provides for the continuing authority of the partners to bind the firm after its dissolution so far as may be necessary to wind up the affairs of the partnership and to complete transactions begun but unfinished at the time of the dissolution.[90b] " The obligation to prosecute the pursuers' claim was a continuing one and if, as I think, there was an obligation on each and all of the partners to continue to attend to the pursuers' original instructions until they had either withdrawn from the case or the transaction was at an end, they must in my opinion continue to be liable for the negligent omission to raise an action even although the partnership had meanwhile been dissolved." The court, accordingly, allowed a proof before answer on these issues.

[90a] 1972 S.L.T. 96.
[90b] See *infra* Chap. XII, pp. 511 *et seq.*

Discharge of the firm's obligation. The liability of the partners for the firm's obligation is a joint and several one. In Scotland all the partners are bound jointly and severally if payment has not been made by the firm itself.[91] In Scotland, therefore, the partners are joint and several cautioners for the firm.[92] It follows from the accessory character of that liability that if the debt has been paid by the firm the accessory liability of the partners flies off and thus all the partners, including the partner who has since retired, are free from liability. The firm may, however, in special circumstances be released from liability for its debt without paying it. Here again in the normal case the general principle will apply and the partners as cautioners will be released by the release of the principal debtor, the firm.[93] But where the discharge by the creditor of the firm is upon a delegation of the liability for the obligation of the firm, as where the firm is a debtor to a third party and is at the same time a creditor of one of its partners in an equivalent or larger amount, and the creditor agrees to accept that partner as his debtor in place of the firm, then the firm will be discharged but the partner will remain bound in the obligation. Though in such cases it is convenient to talk of the partner as remaining bound in the firm's obligation, in legal theory and in actual fact he is bound in a separate and distinct obligation which has arisen under delegation. As a result the partner in such a case will not have a right of relief against the firm and his copartners under section 4 (2) of the Partnership Act 1890, since his claim for relief will be met with a plea of compensation or set-off on the part of the firm.[94] As the basis for the avoidance of liability in such cases is delegation, and delegation is never to be presumed (indeed the presumption may be against delegation),[95] the conduct of the creditor must admit of no other interpretation than that he assented to the substitution of a new debtor for the old, so that unless the creditor has assented to the arrangement, an agreement between a former firm and a new partnership whereby the new firm has agreed to take over the assets and undertake the liabilities of the old firm will not amount to delegation.[96] This principle is not in conflict with what has already been said as regards the equitable principle under which a new firm taking over the assets of a former business may in certain circumstances be held liable for the debts of that business.[97] In these cases there is no question of the creditor being held to have accepted the new partnership as his debtor by delegation. What is secured to him by the equitable doctrine is the super-added obligation of the new partnership. In England there have been a number of decisions upon

[91] Partnership Act 1890, s. 9.
[92] *Supra* Chap. VI, pp. 159–161.
[93] Clark, *op. cit.* I, p. 307.
[94] *Davidsons* v. *Ranken* (1733) Mor. 7061; *Thompson* v. *Percival* (1834) 5 B. & Ad. 925; *Evans* v. *Drummond* (1801) 4 Esp. 89; *Reed* v. *White* (1804) 5 Esp. 122.
[95] *Hay & Kyd* v. *Powrie* (1886) 13 R. 777.
[96] *Muir* v. *Dickson* (1860) 22 D. 1070; *Milliken* v. *Love* (1803) Hume 754; *Campbell* v. *Cruickshank* (1845) 7 D. 548.
[97] *Supra* pp. 258 *et seq.*

similar questions.[98]   While the cases just cited illustrate the application of
the same principle in England and may therefore be cited as persuasive
authority, due allowance must be made for the difference in the English law
of contract before the result announced in the decision may be regarded as
applicable in Scotland.   In certain of the cases [99] where the decision of the
English court was against liability having been imposed by delegation on
the partnership continuing after the retirement of the former partner,
the decision in Scotland might have been in favour of delegation since the
English court were strongly influenced by lack of consideration for the
agreement to accept the new firm and debtor, even if the agreement on
the part of the creditor were held to be established, while a Scottish court,
untrammelled by that technical rule, would not have been precluded from
deciding in favour of delegation on proof of the creditor's assent.[1]

Termination of joint and several liability

According to English law the discharge of one partner from an obligation of the firm may release the other partners also and terminate the firm
obligation.   The principle applied is that " whether the obligation be
joint, or joint and several, it has only to be performed once; and performance by any one of the persons obliged is available as a defence to a second
demand made against the others." [2]   So stated the principle appears to be
clearly applicable in Scots law and indeed to be almost axiomatic.   In
Scots law, however, payment by one of the partners cannot be enforced
unless the debt has first been constituted against the firm,[3] but where the
firm debt is constituted by a bond, a bill of exchange or a decree, any
partner may be sued individually for it or may be charged for payment of
it.[4]   The English law, however, goes further than this and lays down that
a *release* of one partner from a partnership debt discharges all the others;
" for where several persons are bound jointly, or jointly and severally, a
release of one is a release of them all." [5]   Commenting on the English
rule, Clark states that it does not operate in Scotland.[5a]   He cites no authority for this proposition and no case reported either before or after the date

[98] *e.g. Lodge* v. *Dicas* (1820) 3 B. & Ald. 611; *David* v. *Ellice* (1826) 5 B. & C. 196; *Thomas* v. *Shillibeer* (1836) 1 M. & W. 124; *Kirwan* v. *Kirwan* (1836) 2 Cr. & M. 617; *Gough* v. *Davies* (1817) 4 Price 200; *Blew* v. *Wyatt* (1832) 5 C. & P. 397.
[99] *e.g. Lodge* v. *Dicas, supra; David* v. *Ellice, supra.*
[1] See Clark, *op. cit.* I, pp. 273–274, where he also notices the later decision *Lyth* v. *Ault* (1852) 7 Ex. 669 as apparently evidencing a tendency on the part of the English courts to apply the doctrine of consideration in cases of this nature. See also *Smith* v. *Patrick* [1901] A.C. 282 and Lindley, *op. cit.* p. 271.
[2] Lindley, *op. cit.* p. 256 and cases there cited.
[3] *Reid & McCall* v. *Douglases,* June 11, 1814, F.C.
[4] *McTavish* v. *Saltoun,* Feb. 3, 1821, F.C.; *McLean* v. *Rose* (1836) 15 S. 236; *Wallace* v. *Plock* (1841) 3 D. 1047.
[5] Lindley, *op. cit.* p. 267, citing *Re E.W.A.* [1901] 2 K.B. 642; *Bower* v. *Swadlin* (1738) 1 Atk. 294; *Ex p. Slater* (1801) 6 Ves. 146; *Cheetham* v. *Ward* (1797) 1 Bos. & P. 630; *Cocks* v. *Nash* (1832) 9 Bing. 341; *Mercantile Bank of Sydney* v. *Taylor* [1893] A. C. 319. The principle does not apply where there is a covenant not to sue one of several joint obligants; for though such a covenant in a case where there is only one debtor is regarded as a release of the debtor, it does not operate as a release to persons taken bound in a joint obligation apart from those who are parties to the covenant.—Lindley, *op. cit.* p. 267 and cases there cited.
[5a] *Op. cit.* I, p. 276.

when he wrote illustrates it or contains any dictum which might be used in support of it. Nevertheless, he asserts that " it would seem never to have been doubted that in our law the discharge of one partner does not operate as a release to the others." He ascribes the difference between the two systems to two broad divergences in legal theory. First, in the law of cautionary obligations, while the English law was that release of one of several co-cautioners was a release to them all, the Scots law originally did not have that effect and the claim against the copartners was diminished only to the extent of the share of the obligation undertaken by the released cautioner.[6] Secondly, Clark directs attention to the distinctive features of the Scots law of partnership whereby the obligations of that firm are not, as in England, the joint and several obligation of the partners, but are the obligations of the firm for which the partners are jointly and severally cautioners.[7] He therefore discusses the point whether the amendment of the Scots law of cautionry by the Mercantile Law Amendment (Scotland) Act 1856 [8] under which a discharge of one of several co-cautioners, without the consent of the remaining co-cautioners, is a discharge of them all, " has by implication introduced the English rule into our partnership law." He dismisses this on the ground that the Mercantile Law Amendment (Scotland) Act 1856 applies to persons bound as cautioners *eo nomine* and does not extend to those who become cautioners by implication of law.[9]

The force of Clark's argument, therefore, lies in his invocation of the earlier common law that the discharge of one co-obligant does not release the others whether they are bound jointly or jointly and severally, save to the extent to which the debt for which they are bound has been satisfied.[10] The fact that this rule has been altered, " where two or more parties shall become bound as cautioners for any debtor," [11] does not appear to militate against that contention as Clark himself argues; but the point is difficult and abstruse and no firm conclusion may be stated upon it in the absence of authority.

Cautionary obligations undertaken in connection with the firm

If the continuing obligation which is under examination is itself one of cautionry, then, since it will clearly come within the terms of section 9 of the Mercantile Law Amendment (Scotland) Act 1856, the English rule will apply to it and if one of the partners is released, all are released, but even in this case the rule will yield to the intention of the parties as evidenced by the words of the release. Thus if the release is so drawn as to show that it was intended as a benefit to the grantee personally and is not to be pleadable by him in an action at the instance of the grantor

[6] Bell, *Com.* I, 376.
[7] *Cf.* Partnership Act 1890, ss. 4 (2) and 9.
[8] s. 9.
[9] This question is discussed by Clark, *op. cit.* I, pp. 276–277.
[10] Bankton, I, 24, 2.
[11] Mercantile Law Amendment (Scotland) Act 1856, s. 9.

against him jointly with his co-obligants, then those co-obligants will not be discharged.   The principle that all are released in such a case apparently in English law creates a presumption only which will be rebutted by clear express words to the contrary effect in the release itself.[12]   In spite of the approximation of the two systems of law brought about by section 9 of the Mercantile Law Amendment (Scotland) Act 1856, it is thought that *Solly* v. *Forbes* would have been decided on a different basis in Scotland. In that case the defendants, Forbes and Ellerman, were partners, and were as such indebted to the plaintiffs.   They had stopped payment and on consideration of a payment made by Ellerman, the plaintiffs released him from all further demands.   The release, to which Forbes was not a party, expressly declared that nothing contained in it would affect the plaintiffs' rights against Forbes either separately or as a partner with Ellerman or against the joint estate of both.   It was held that the release was no bar to an action against Forbes and Ellerman to recover the debt.   Now as Forbes had not consented to the arrangement, it is submitted that the earlier common law of Scotland in those matters will rule since section 9 of the Mercantile Law Amendment (Scotland) Act 1856 expressly confines the introduction of the general rule in England (release of one is release of all) to cases where the co-cautioner has not consented to the release and so far as the terms of the release itself might be pleaded before the Scottish courts, they could not be pleaded to extend the liability of Forbes who was not a party to the release.   Forbes would thus, it is thought, have been able to plead immunity from Solly's claim to the extent that the release to Ellerman had not reflected payment by Ellerman of his share of the joint indebtedness, in other words the extent to which Forbes might be said to have been prejudiced by the granting of the release.   On that *ratio* the decision of the Scottish courts might have been the same as that of the English court but for a different reason.   Ellerman in consideration of his discharge agreed to pay £3,000 of which he paid down £600 and granted bills for £100 each payable successively over the next twenty-four months. In the event of any two of those bills remaining unpaid, the release was to be null and void and any sums which had been paid by Ellerman were to be transferred by the plaintiffs to the credit of the partnership of Forbes and Ellerman.   Thus the only prejudice which Forbes could plead would be that the £3,000 in all did not fully represent Ellerman's share of the indebtedness of the partnership.   Since the report is unfortunately silent as to the total amount of the indebtedness of the partnership it is impossible to speculate on this point but it is fair to say that the judgment in the English court proceeded entirely upon that basis of a true construction of the intention of the parties to the release, and if that were to be taken as the true *ratio* of the decision it appears almost accidental that Forbes received justice; for had the court construed the document as intended to grant Ellerman a complete release, Forbes might have been prejudiced by an

---

[12] *Solly* v. *Forbes* (1820) 2 Bro. & B. 38; *Re E.W.A.* [1901] 2 K.B. 642; *Hartley* v. *Manton* (1843) 5 Q.B. 247.

intention to which he was never a party. It may be that this point did
not present itself as a practical issue to the English court, as it would have
done in Scotland because if Ellerman had been released absolutely, he
could not have been joined with Forbes as a defendant in the action and
since the Scottish concept of a separate *quasi persona* in the firm does not
obtain, an action against Forbes alone for the balance would not be
competent.[13]

Changes in the firm as affecting continuing guarantees

By section 18 of the Partnership Act 1890 it is provided—

> " A continuing guaranty or cautionary obligation given either to
> a firm or to a third person in respect of the transactions of a firm is,
> in the absence of any agreement to the contrary, revoked as to future
> transactions by any change in the constitution of the firm to which, or
> of the firm in respect of the transactions of which, the guaranty or
> obligation was given."

The section translates into terms of partnership law the general principle
in the law of cautionry that an act upon the part of the creditor which alters
the risk of the cautioner without his consent will discharge the cautioner
from future liability under the cautionary obligation. The cautioner's
obligation " cannot be extended beyond the person to or for whom it was
undertaken," unless with the cautioner's consent.[14] His liability will
exist up to the date of the purported change but as regards the future it will
be terminated as, for example, where the principal debtor or the creditor
has died.[15] If, therefore, he grants a cautionary obligation in favour of a
firm, the document must be examined to discover whether he had in
contemplation that changes may occur in the firm and undertook the
obligation not only to the firm as constituted at the time when the obligation was entered into but also to the firm as it might later be constituted
after changes had occurred in its composition. Section 7 of the Mercantile
Law Amendment (Scotland) Act 1856 provided that the intention might
" appear either by express stipulation or by necessary implication from
the nature of the firm or otherwise." Although section 18 of the Partnership Act 1890, which replaces that provision, uses the more general and
less pointed expression " in the absence of agreement to the contrary,"
that alteration in wording is not to be taken as restricting the proof of
intention to cases where an express provision appears in the contract of
cautionry. The intention may still be shown by necessary implication
from the nature of the firm. Since the partnership are the creditors and
the caution is granted in their favour as guaranteeing the ability of their
debtor to pay, any implied intention that the guarantee will continue after a

---

[13] Though in England the firm is still regarded as having no *persona* distinct from the partners
who compose it, the rule has now been to some extent relaxed to permit of actions being
brought by, or against, partners in the firm name.—Lindley, *op. cit*. pp. 25–26.
[14] Gloag & Irvine, *Rights in Security*, p. 863.
[15] *Reddie* v. *Williamson* (1863) 1 M. 228.

change in the partnership will often depend on its nature, *e.g.* where it is a banking partnership.[16]   If an agreement to that effect may be spelled out of the cautionary obligation and the obligation is a continuing one, then the cautioner will not be discharged from liability simply because changes later occur in the composition of the firm in favour of which he originally granted the cautionry.   But if that intention may not be established from the terms of the cautionary obligation, then he will be bound by it only for so long as the firm remains unchanged.   Changes may occur through the death [17] or retirement [18] of a partner or through the assumption of a new partner [19] and any of those will have the effect of terminating the liability of the cautioner.   He will, however, remain bound in respect of his liabilities which arose before the change took place and that liability will not be discharged by the transfer of the debt to the new firm.[20]   The law laid down in section 18 of the Partnership Act 1890 [21] is declaratory of the principles of construction applied both in England and in Scotland in the pre-existing common law.[22]   The earlier decisions, both Scottish and English,[23] may, therefore, be appealed to with confidence.

Cautionary obligations in respect of the debts of a firm

Section 18 covers not only cautionary obligations granted *to* a firm but also those granted to a third party *in respect of the transactions of a firm*. The first branch of the section, which has already been considered, deals with the case where a firm, such as, for example, a banking partnership, takes a cautionary obligation from a person in respect of the firm's claim against their debtor.   In the second branch the cautioner is guaranteeing to a third party the conduct of the firm itself.   Though the earlier Scottish authorities were not entirely clear on the point, it was decided by the House of Lords in *Royal Bank* v. *Christie* [24] that in the absence of express or implied agreement to the contrary a continuing guarantee for the transactions of a firm will not render the cautioner liable for transactions carried through after a change in the constitution of the firm has occurred.   In *Royal Bank* v. *Christie*, the change was brought about by the death of one of the partners.   In another Scottish pre-statute decision the rule had been applied where the change consisted in the retirement of a partner.[25] Section 18 of the Partnership Act 1890 is thus in this respect also declaratory of the pre-existing common law in Scotland and also in England.[26]

---

[16] See Bell, *Com.* I, p. 387; Gloag & Irvine, *Rights in Security*, p. 930.

[17] *Elton, Hammond & Co.* v. *Neilson*, June 24, 1812, F.C.; *Pemberton* v. *Oakes* (1827) 4 Russ. 154.

[18] *Metcalf* v. *Bruin* (1810) 12 East 400; *Dry* v. *Davey* (1839) 10 A. & E. 30.

[19] *Spiers* v. *Houston's Exrs.* (1829) 3 W. & S. 392; *Bowie* v. *Watson* (1840) 2 D. 1061.

[20] *Bradford Old Bank* v. *Sutcliffe* [1918] 2 K.B. 833.

[21] Replacing in rather more explicit terms s. 7 of the Mercantile Law Amendment (Scotland) Act 1856 which was repealed by the Partnership Act 1890, s. 48.

[22] See Gloag & Irvine, *Rights in Security*, p. 928.

[23] A full citation of the English decisions is given in Lindley, *op. cit.* p. 45.

[24] (1841) 2 Rob.App. 118.

[25] *Padon* v. *Bank of Scotland* (1826) 5 S. 175.

[26] *Bellairs* v. *Ebsworth* (1811) 3 Camp. 53; *University of Cambridge* v. *Baldwin* (1839) 5 M. & W. 580; *Simson* v. *Cooke* (1824) 1 Bing. 452.

What will amount to necessary implication that the cautioner intended to continue to be liable despite a change in the constitution of the firm whose transactions he has guaranteed will necessarily differ from the implication to be drawn in the case where the firm itself is the creditor whose claim is guaranteed.   In a case where a party has guaranteed the conduct of the firm, the courts will require very cogent grounds before they hold that there was an implied intention on the part of the cautioner to remain bound in spite of changes in the debtor firm.   There is an obvious altera- tion in the risk which the cautioner originally accepted and, where he has not expressly provided for his continuing liability in spite of changes in the partnership, when a person undertakes a cautionary obligation in respect of another person, the courts will not necessarily infer an intention that the cautioner is surety for his conduct as a partner when he later enters into partnership and will certainly not find that the cautioner in these circumstances had any intention to guarantee the conduct of the person with whom the partnership was contracted.[27]   Thus the defendant exe- cuted a bond by which he undertook that the agent of an insurance company would pay to the plaintiffs, the insurance company, all money received by him for policies of assurance effected with the plaintiffs. Before he executed the bond the defendant received a letter informing him that the agent was about to enter into a partnership with another person to act as agents for the plaintiffs and some four months later the partner- ship was entered into.   The firm subsequently became indebted to the plaintiffs in respect of money collected by them as agents but the defendant was held free from liability in respect of transactions subsequent to the formation of the partnership.[28]

The cautioners may be liable in respect of transactions carried through subsequently to a change in the composition of the debtor firm if the terms of the cautionary obligation show, expressly or impliedly, that such con- tinuing liability was in the contemplation of the parties [29] and to establish an implied intention of that sort the cautionary obligation may be read in the light of the circumstances surrounding the parties at the time of entering into it.[30]   The cautioner may also be held liable where, in the knowledge that the creditor is continuing to advance money to the firm after the alteration has taken place and on the faith of the guarantee, his conduct is such as to imply that he had consented to remain liable.[31]

Change occurring upon incorporation of the firm.   In addition to a change in the firm consequent upon a change in the partners who compose

---

[27] *London Assurance Co.* v. *Bold* (1844) 6 Q.B. 514; *Montefiore* v. *Lloyd* (1863) 15 C.B.(N.S.) 203.

[28] *Montefiore* v. *Lloyd, supra.*

[29] *Patersons* v. *Calder,* July 5, 1808, F.C.; *Booth* v. *Commercial Bank* (1823) 2 S. 311; *Leathley* v. *Spyer* (1870) L.R. 5 C.P. 595.

[30] *Leathley* v. *Spyer, supra.* The *ratio decidendi* of that case may, however, be otherwise, since in addition to the original guarantee there was a subsequent letter which could be construed as a renewal of the guarantee.

[31] *Ayton* v. *Dundee Banking Co.* (1844) 6 D. 1409; *McLeod* v. *Howden* (1839) 1 D. 1121; *Miller* v. *Thorburn* (1861) 23 D. 359.

it, the firm may become an entirely distinct legal *persona* by being incorporated as a limited liability company.   In such a case the newly incorporated body does not assume liability for the debts of the former partnership and unless an agreement between the incorporated company and the creditors of the former partnership is established, the partners of the former firm remain liable.[32]   Similarly the transformation of the firm into a limited liability company is an alteration in the identity of the firm and will discharge a cautioner for the firm.[33]

Appropriation of payments under guarantee.   Where the cautioner has guaranteed operations by the partnership upon an account current with the creditor and though a change in the partnership has freed the cautioner from liability for further transactions on the account current, dealings between the new firm and the creditor continue upon the same account current, the rule in *Clayton's* case [34] will apply and payments made into the account after the change will be presumed to be appropriated towards the repayment of the sum due on the account at the date of the revocation of the guarantee.   The arrangement has been that the transactions of the old and the new firms are embraced within one continuous running account, and payments made by the new firm may have the effect of diminishing or entirely repaying the balance which was outstanding on the account at the date of the change for which the cautioner was liable at that date.[35]   It is, therefore, a matter of great practical importance to ensure that if a change in the firm has had the effect of revoking for the future a guarantee of the former firm's dealings upon a current account and it is desired to preserve recourse against the cautioner, the current account with the old firm should be brought to a balance at the date of the change and a new account opened for the future transactions of the new firm with the creditor.[36]   In the general application of the rule in *Clayton's* case even if the former account is continued for the transactions of the new firm it will be open to the new firm when making a payment to stipulate that it shall be applied to the indebtedness arising from the later transactions but an incoming partner relying on this would have imposed upon him an almost impossible task of vigilance, and, in any event, where the change in the firm occurs through the death or retirement of one of the partners, the remaining partners continuing their dealings with the creditor, the presumption of that rule may not be available.   The law is expounded by Bayley J. in *Simson* v. *Ingham.*[37]

" The general rule," he said, " is that the party who pays money has a right to apply that payment as he thinks fit.   If there are several

---

[32] See *e.g. Hay & Co. and Another* v. *Torbet,* 1908 S.C. 781.
[33] *Dance* v. *Girdler* (1804) 1 Bos. & P.N.R. 34.
[34] *Devaynes* v. *Noble, Clayton's Case* (1816) 1 Mer. 572.
[35] *Bodenham* v. *Purchas* (1818) 2 B. & Ald. 39; *Lang.* v. *Brown* (1859) 22 D. 113; *Spiers* v. *Houston's Exrs.* (1829) 3 W. & S. 392; *Christie* v. *Royal Bank* (1839) 1 D. 745; affd. (1841) 2 Rob.App. 118.
[36] *Re Sherry, London & County Bank* v. *Terry* (1884) L.R. 25 Ch.D. 692; *Bradford Old Bank* v. *Sutcliffe* [1918] 2 K.B. 833.
[37] (1823) 2 B. & C. 65 at pp. 72–73.

debts due from him, he has a right to say to which of those debts the payment shall be applied. If he does not make a specific application at the time of payment, then the right of application generally devolves on the party who receives the money. But there is a third rule, *viz.* that where one of several partners dies and the partnership is in debt, and the surviving partners continue their dealings with a particular creditor, and the latter joins the transactions of the old and new firms in one entire account, then the payment made from time to time by the surviving partners must be applied to the old debt. In that case it is to be presumed that all the parties have consented that it should be considered as one entire account and that the death of one of the partners has produced no alteration whatever. In this case the partner died in September 1814. If in the ordinary course of business a monthly account had been sent in, stating the transactions before and after the death of the partner, as forming part of one entire account, and the balance as due from the survivors, in that case the creditor would have been precluded and would have had no right to have said that the payments made subsequently to the death of the partner should be applied to any but the old account."

In the case in question, Bayley J. went on to distinguish the facts, in that the bankers did not send in any account after the death of the partner until November and then sent in two distinct accounts. Though they had made entries *in their own books* treating the account as one account, they were not precluded by that from expressing to the debtors in November " their dissent from making the whole one entire account." It would have been otherwise if the entries had been made in a book "kept for the common use of both parties, as a passbook and that had been communicated to the opposite party."

Right to combine accounts. It has been said that it follows from the decision in *Simson* v. *Ingham* that a creditor of the firm may, when a change occurs in that firm, decide whether the outstanding balance due to him on his account with the old firm shall form an item in his account with the new firm.[38] That statement, however, is thought to be too wide unless it is taken as strictly referable to the context in which it is made. The question will most frequently arise in connection with the bank accounts of the old and the new firms. If it is the intention of the bank to hold a retiring partner or the representatives of a deceased partner liable for the balance due at the date of retirement or death, the banker's duty on receiving notice of the retirement, or on the death, of the partner is to stop operations on the partnership account and demand settlement. If he does not do so, the rule in *Clayton's* case will apply.[39] In that sense the decision whether to combine the accounts is the bank's, since if they close the account and demand settlement, the partners have no plea which they can competently argue against this, whereas if the bank agrees to continue

[38] Lindley, *op. cit.* p. 264; and see *Jones* v. *Maund* (1839) 3 Y. & C.Ex. 347.
[39] Wallace & McNeil, *Banking Law* (8th ed.) p. 78.

the account with the remaining partners, they are not likely to have any grounds to take exception to that. But if the change in the firm involves the introduction of incoming partners, the bank's " decision " to blend the accounts by allowing the new firm to continue to operate on the account formerly kept for the old firm may be prejudicial to the incoming partners and it is thought that the bank could not impose any such decision without their consent, though if the bank's decision were to stop operations on the account of the old firm and open an account with the new firm, that may accurately be described as a decision of the bank so far as regards the closing of the old account, but the opening of an account with that bank by the new firm would not arise from the bank's " decision " but from the consent of the new firm to the opening of the account.

Intention of the parties as rebutting the rule in Clayton's case. Before the rule in *Clayton's* case may be invoked there must be in existence between the parties an " account current." The typical account current is a banking account kept by the bank for its customer and that was the type of account with which *Clayton's* case was concerned. It has, however, been recognised that accounts of similar character, although not occurring in business of a strictly banking type, may be held to be accounts current. The Lord President (Inglis) in *McKinlay* v. *Wilson* [40] described the features of an account current between traders, in these words:

> " I think I am right in saying that the present is an account-current, and for several reasons. Not only were the transactions of a very varied description—the articles being chiefly horses—but there was the selling one day by the pursuer to the defender, and the other day by the defender to the pursuer, and these went to meet one another in this current account, and quite naturally, according to the course of dealings, because there was a credit entry to meet a debit entry within a day or two of its being made. There was a variety in the mode in which the sales and purchases were made. Sometimes the parties had an arrangement that horses brought from Ireland by the pursuer were to be at the command of the defender if he chose to take them at the prices which had been paid for them, plus a charge of £2 additional as a kind of commission to the pursuer for buying the horses. Sometimes it would appear that there was an arrangement to divide the profits upon the horses so bought and handed to the defender. In these circumstances, I think, it cannot be said that there are two accounts for things sold and delivered, one in which the pursuer is creditor and one in which he is debtor."

On the other hand, for the rule in *Clayton's* case to apply, there must be something of the nature of an account current in existence and where the account is simply for goods supplied against which the debtor is credited with general payments made " on account " from time to time, then, even

[40] (1885) 13 R. 210 at pp. 215–216.

where the account discloses that the creditor has at times helped the debtor over a temporary difficulty with financial aid and charged him interest for that facility, it is not an account current.[41]   Indeed, it seems that the mode of making out the account may have a bearing on the decision whether it is an account current. " The account . . . is not stated as a proper account current at all. It first contains a record of all the goods sold or advances made . . . and next below that a record of the payments made. . . . Each of these columns is added up, the one deducted from the other, and a balance struck." [42]   While, if the account is carried forward from day to day as a running account and displays the features referred to by Lord President Inglis in *McKinlay* v. *Wilson*,[43] it may be regarded as an account current, trade accounts will not generally be so regarded even if cast in the form of a current account,[44] but an account between solicitor and client in which debits and credits arising from transactions carried through on behalf of the client are entered in running account will be treated as an account current.[45]

Even if the account is held to be an account current, the application of the rule in *Clayton's* case merely raises a presumption which may be redargued, not merely by proof of express appropriation of a payment to a later item of account, but also by inference from a general course of dealing which is proved to have been resorted to by the parties.[46]

Insanity of partner

If a partner becomes insane but the fact of his insanity is not made known to the third parties dealing with him or with his firm and is not apparent to them, his apparent authority to bind the firm and his liability for the firm obligations undertaken by his copartners remain unaffected.[47] Where, however, he has been cognosced as insane and a *curator bonis* appointed, he may no longer dispose of his property or affect it by his contracts.[48]   His power to bind the firm may therefore be terminated by that process as formerly was the case in England upon his being found insane by inquisition or upon a receiver being appointed on his estate.[49] Many of the problems which arise as to the supervening insanity of a partner are related to the right of his copartners to dissolve the partnership and this aspect will be dealt with more appropriately at a later stage.[50]

[41] *Hay & Co. and Another* v. *Torbet*, 1908 S.C. 781.
[42] *Ibid. per* Lord Ardwall at p. 788.
[43] *Supra* n. 40.
[44] *Cory Bros. & Co.* v. *Owners of the "Mecca"* [1897] A.C. 286; *Dougall* v. *Lornie* (1899) 1 F. 1187; *Batchelor's Trs.* v. *Honeyman* (1892) 19 R. 903.
[45] *Lang* v. *Brown* (1859) 22 D. 113.
[46] *Per* Lord Ardwall in *Hay & Co. and Another* v. *Torbet*, 1908 S.C. 781 at pp. 790–791.
[47] Clark, *op. cit.* I, p. 26; *Pollock* v. *Paterson*, Dec. 10, 1811, F.C.; *Spence*, July 7, 1812, F.C.; *Baxter* v. *Earl of Portsmouth* (1826) 5 B. & C. 170; *Molton* v. *Camroux* (1848) 2 Ex. 487; *Imperial Loan Co.* v. *Stone* [1892] 1 Q.B. 599.
[48] Gloag, *Contract* (2nd ed.) p. 94.
[49] *Re Walker* [1905] 1 Ch. 160; *Re Marshall* [1920] 1 Ch. 284.
[50] *Infra* Chap. X, pp. 456–461.

Revocation of partner's authority during subsistence of partnership

There are two aspects of this question. In the absence of express or implied agreement to the contrary, the majority of the partners of the firm have power under section 24 (8) of the Partnership Act 1890 to impose their will " as to ordinary matters connected with the partnership business." In the exercise of that power they may vary the terms of the authority conferred upon any partner and it is thought that the majority might resolve that, in future, actings of a specified nature shall be carried through, not by one partner alone, but by two or more partners,[51] though, to be effective against a third party, he would require to have notice of the restricted terms of the agreed actual authority.[52] If the majority were to resolve that one or more of the copartners should henceforth have no authority to bind the firm in any transactions of the partnership business, it is dubious whether such a resolution would be valid in the absence of an agreed term conferring such power of revocation upon the majority; for, unless the partnership agreement has expressly or by implication provided otherwise, " every partner may take part in the management of the partnership business." [53] If, therefore, the majority purported to deprive him of that right by a total revocation of his authority, that could not be regarded as " a difference arising as to ordinary matters connected with the partnership business." It rather falls under the description of a change in the nature of the partnership business which requires the consent of all existing partners.[54]

The other aspect of the matter—whether a partner may revoke his copartners' authority to bind him during the continuance of the partnership—is subject to an equal scarcity of authority. The Partnership Act makes no pronouncement whatever on this point. After some fluctuation of view, the editors of the latest edition of *Lindley on Partnership* express the opinion that " on general principles it would seem that unless he is in a position to dissolve the firm, a notice that he will no longer be bound by their acts will be inoperative." [55] That view proceeds upon the reasoning that a notice which a person has no right to give can avail him nothing, but, with respect, the reasoning seems rather circular in nature since it leads back to the point *de quo quaeritur*. The authorities cited by Lindley [55] all appear to deal with notice given that a partner will not accept liability for certain types of actings by his copartner, *e.g.* by his accepting bills or signing promissory notes in name of the firm. Such cases would now come within section 8 of the Partnership Act 1890. They do not appear

[51] Lindley, *op. cit.* p. 243; *supra* pp. 182–188.
[52] Partnership Act 1890, s. 8.
[53] Partnership Act 1890, s. 24 (5).
[54] Partnership Act 1890, s. 24 (8); and see *supra* p. 249.
[55] Lindley, *op. cit.* p. 243, citing *Vice* v. *Fleming* (1827) 1 Y. & J. 227; *Willis* v. *Dyson* (1816) 1 Stark. 164; *Rooth* v. *Quin* (1819) 7 Price 193; *Lord Galloway* v. *Mathew* (1808) 1 Camp. 403; 10 East 264. The view taken in the 5th and earlier editions prepared by the original author was that " the agency of each partner . . . may be determined by notice at any time during the continuance of the partnership; for his power to act for the firm is not a right attaching to him as partner independently of the will of his copartners . . ." (5th ed., p. 210).

to have much bearing upon the real question posed—whether during the continuance of a partnership one of the partners may revoke his copartner's authority to bind him through transactions which the copartner has carried through apparently within the scope of carrying out in the usual way business of the kind carried on by the partnership. It is submitted that on general principles that revocation will be ineffective but the " general principles " appealed to do not appear to be those to which Lindley has regard or, at least, are not those reflected in the authorities which he cites. The general principle involved is that which has already been examined in regard to the first aspect of this topic. While the partnership is in existence, and in the absence of agreement to the contrary, every partner is entitled to take part in the management of the firm's business. Hence no single partner may by his own act deprive any one or more of his copartners of that right.[56]

Liability of a partner on dissolution of the firm

In most cases problems of the liability of the individual partner arise where a dissolution of the firm has taken place or where he has retired from the firm. The Partnership Act 1890, s. 36, provides—

" 36.—(1) Where a person deals with a firm after a change in its constitution, he is entitled to treat all apparent members of the old firm as still being members of the firm until he has notice of the change.

(2) An advertisement in the *London Gazette* as to a firm whose principal place of business is in England or Wales, in the *Edinburgh Gazette* as to a firm whose principal place of business is in Scotland, and in the *Dublin Gazette* as to a firm whose principal place of business is in Ireland, shall be notice as to persons who had not dealings with the firm before the date of the dissolution or change so advertised.

(3) The estate of a partner who dies, or becomes bankrupt, or of a partner who, not having been known to the person dealing with the firm to be a partner, retires from the firm, is not liable for partnership debts contracted after the death, bankruptcy, or retirement respectively."

Section 37 provides—

" 37. On the dissolution of a partnership or retirement of a partner any partner may publicly notify the same, and may require the other partner or partners to concur for that purpose in all necessary or proper acts, if any, which cannot be done without his or their concurrence."

It has been said [57] that section 36 (1) reiterates the common law rule of agency that a person known to be agent for another continues to have

---

[56] In certain circumstances, however, he may seek his remedy by dissolving the firm. In that case any partner may publicly notify the dissolution of the partnership. Partnership Act 1890, s. 37 and see the immediately succeeding paragraph.
[57] Lindley, *op. cit.* p. 244.

apparent authority as agent until the revocation of that authority is made known. Since the sort of agency involved in partnership is mutual agency, in which a partner may at one time be acting as agent for the firm and at another may with the firm and his copartners be the principal for whom one member has acted as agent, the principle of the law of agency which is applied in section 36 (1) might perhaps be more appropriately expressed as follows:

> " Where a principal, by words or conduct, represents or permits it to be represented that an agent is authorised to act on his behalf, he is bound by the acts of the agent, notwithstanding the determination of authority otherwise than by the death or bankruptcy of the principal to the same extent as he would have been if the authority had not been determined, with respect to any third person dealing with the agent on the faith of any such representation, without notice of the determination of his authority." [58]

The statement here quoted seems more apt to indicate precisely the two-fold nature of the problem which may arise upon a change in the constitution of the firm where no notice has been given of the change. In the first place, the partner who has left the firm, by retirement, remains liable for the firm debts. He does not, however, do so because the remaining partners continue to be his agents until the revocation of their authority is made known but because, through his words or conduct, he represents or holds himself out as still being a partner of the firm. Secondly, on the other hand, although the point is not so frequently raised in the reported decisions, the situation may result in a continuing and unlooked for liability on the part of the firm as newly constituted, since the partner who has retired may still bind the firm in transactions with third parties if the retired partner purports to act on behalf of the firm and the third party with whom he deals has had no notice that he is no longer a partner.

Notice required to relieve retiring partner from future liability for firm

> " As the public has been led to regard the concern as guaranteed by the credit of each of the partners, the retirement of any of their number will not be held to relieve him from liability for the subsequent acts of the remaining partners who still carry on the concern; nor will its entire dissolution have this effect if some of the former partners still appear to prosecute the business as before. To effect this, the public must in some legal manner be certiorated that the retiring partner no longer guarantees the company as formerly; or, in the language of the English law, has withdrawn the agency which he had previously conferred on the other partners to bind him within the sphere of the company's action. Hence results the general rule, that to destroy liability for future acts, *notice* is indispensable." [59]

[58] Bowstead, *Agency* (13th ed.) Art. 145, pp. 454–455.
[59] Clark, *op. cit.* I, p. 309.

The liability in these circumstances is treated by Lindley as distinguishable from that incurred by a retired partner who holds himself out or knowingly suffers himself to be held out as continuing as a partner of the firm.[60] Cases of holding out of a retired partner as continuing in partnership will, of course, frequently arise in circumstances where both elements are present, *i.e.* no notice has been given of the change *and* the retiring partner has also otherwise been held out as a partner in the firm, but there are also cases where the retiring partner has been held liable for future debts of the firm on the sole ground that he has failed to give notice of his retirement, without any question of his having subsequently held himself out as a partner or knowingly suffered himself so to be held out by others. For example, if a person, known to be a partner, retired and no notice of that is given, he is liable to be sued upon a promissory note made by his former partner in name of the firm even though the person taking the note had no prior dealings with the firm.[61] In many cases where the dissolution of the firm has not been brought to notice of third parties, both that element and the further element that the former partner has either held himself out [62] or has knowingly suffered himself to be held out [63] as continuing as a partner have contributed to the decision.

In a case where notice of dissolution has been duly given, the former partner may still find himself liable for future debts incurred by the firm. In that case the sole ground of liability will be that by allowing himself to be held out, as a partner, he has by his conduct represented that state of facts to exist and is barred from subsequently setting up a different state of facts to the detriment of a third party who had dealt with the firm in reliance on his representation.[64] A former partner in those circumstances is no different from an entire stranger to the partnership who has so held himself out. But it may be argued that where due notice of dissolution has been given, a former partner so holding himself out presents to the third party dealing with him a situation in which the third party should be upon his inquiry as to the true state of affairs. That may be the circumstance which occasions the following expression of doubt: " If he gives due notice of his retirement, but authorises or knowingly suffers his late partners to continue to carry on business under the old name, it would appear somewhat doubtful whether or not he will by such conduct incur liability under the doctrine of holding out." [65] As is indicated by the

---

[60] Lindley, *op. cit.* pp. 105–106.

[61] *Parkin* v. *Carruthers* (1800) 3 Esp. 248. The Scottish case *Dalgleish* v. *Sorley* (1791) Mor. 14595 is also one decided on the *ratio* that where there was no notification of the change, the former partner remained liable to a third party since he had taken no steps publicly to revoke the authority committed by him to his former copartners.

[62] *Brown* v. *Leonard* (1816) 2 Chit. 120 (where the former partner suffered his name to continue in the firm and undertook to be responsible for the note).

[63] *Williams* v. *Keats* (1817) 2 Stark. 290. In that case though the dissolution of the firm was advertised in the *Gazette*, the bill which bore a date prior to the dissolution was accepted on behalf of the firm after that date. The former partner had, despite the advertisement, " allowed his name to remain over the shop in the Poultry " as a partner. See also *Hunter* v. *Evans, Foster & Langton* (1830) 9 S. 159.

[64] Partnership Act 1890, s. 14 (1); and see *supra* Chap. V.

[65] Lindley, *op. cit.* p. 105.

learned author the answer must now depend upon the true construction of sections 14 and 36 of the Partnership Act 1890; but it must be kept in mind that these sections are concerned with two entirely distinct situations in the partnership. Section 36 is concerned with the method whereby on a dissolution, a former partner may disengage himself from liability for future actings of the continuing association of which he was formerly a member. But section 14 is concerned with the circumstances in which a person *who is not a member of the partnership* may yet be held liable as if he were a partner. There is therefore nothing logically unacceptable in applying the doctrine of holding out to a former partner who has by means of section 36 extricated himself for the future from partnership in the continuing firm, though in practical terms, a third party may find it difficult to establish that he has " on the faith of any such representation given credit to the firm." [66] The authorities discussed by Lindley [67] seem to bear this out. In *Williams* v. *Keats* [68] the holding out consisted in the fact that a retired partner had not prevented his name remaining above the door of the shop with that of his former partner. Notice of his retirement had been duly advertised in the *Gazette* but the court still held the retired partner liable; for there was no evidence that the third party in fact knew of the dissolution of the firm. On the other hand, in *Dolman* v. *Orchard*,[69] it does not appear from the report that notice of dissolution had been given; otherwise the facts were similar to those in *Williams* v. *Keats.* In *Brown* v. *Leonard* [70] the plaintiff had actually been informed by the defendant that he, the defendant, was no longer a partner of the firm but that his name was to continue in the firm for a time. The former partner was held liable on a promissory note granted by the firm after his retirement; but he appears to have given his personal undertaking to the plaintiff that the note would be honoured. In *Newsome* v. *Coles*,[71] Thomas Coles and three of his sons carried on business as Thomas Coles & Sons. After the father's death the three sons continued the business under the old firm name for some years. The partnership was then dissolved, notice of the dissolution appearing in the *Gazette* and also being sent to the correspondents of the firm. Two of the sons then established a new business while the third continued the old business alone but under the old firm name. The plaintiff had had no dealings with the partnership prior to its dissolution but he had not seen the notice in the *Gazette.* He attempted to hold all three brothers liable on a bill accepted on behalf of Thomas Coles & Sons by the third brother after the date of dissolution. The other two brothers had not held themselves out to the plaintiff as partners of Thomas Coles & Sons nor had they authorised the use of the firm name by the remaining brother. The plaintiff's case was that they

[66] Partnership Act 1890, s. 14 (1).
[67] *Op. cit.* pp. 105–107.
[68] (1817) 2 Stark. 290.
[69] (1825) 2 Car. & P. 104.
[70] (1816) 2 Chit. 120.
[71] (1811) 2 Camp. 617.

knew that the old name was being used and did nothing to prevent it. That argument failed, the court holding that they were not bound to take any steps to prevent the third brother using the old name.[72]   As in all cases the decision whether a person has held himself out as a partner is one of fact,[73] the difficulty of reconciling those pre-statute decisions should not be overstressed.   At the same time, they do not afford much help in interpreting sections 14 and 36 of the Partnership Act 1890.   The construction of those sections will, it is suggested, be more likely to be the true one if the purpose of each is clearly distinguished from the outset and if it is recognised that where the requirements of section 36 have been observed that has the effect of publicly declaring that the former partner is now a stranger to the partnership.   The implied authority which as a partner he formerly committed to his copartners to act in the business of the partnership is now revoked.   But it does not logically follow as a result that he cannot hold himself out or be held out as a partner, since even a stranger to the partnership may so hold himself out or be held out.   The real difficulty in such cases is what will amount to holding out in the case of a person who has severed his connection with the firm and has given due notice of the fact.   The point is clearly brought out in the judgment of Lord Ellenborough [74] where he says,

> " It is not pretended that the defendants George or Charles Coles ever interfered with the business carried on by William after the dissolution of the partnership, or by any act whatsoever authorised him to use the firm under which they had traded together.   I am therefore of opinion that they are not liable for that firm being used by him without their authority.   Ample notice had been given of the dissolution of the partnership; and after that it was the duty of persons taking securities in the name of Thomas Coles & Sons to inquire who were designated by that firm."

Actings of former partner binding as respects the continuing firm

Where due notice has not been given of the dissolution of the firm, it would seem that on a parity of reasoning the firm itself may find itself bound by transactions entered into in its name by a former partner.   Section 36 of the Partnership Act 1890 is silent upon this aspect but that is not surprising since that section is solely concerned with the means by which the former partner may free himself from liability for future transactions of the firm.   But since the contract of partnership is one of mutual agency, the same doctrine which requires public notice to be given of the revocation by the former partner as principal of any authority to the continuing partners to act as his agents must also require public notice to be given of

---

[72] For a discussion of the possible effect on this decision of the statutory words " knowingly suffers " in s. 14 (1) of the Partnership Act 1890, see *supra* Chap. V, pp. 135–139. And see also *Ex p. Central Bank of London* [1892] 2 Q.B. 633.
[73] See *supra* Chap. V, p. 132.
[74] *Newsome* v. *Coles* (1811) 2 Camp. 617.

the revocation by the firm and of his copartners of his authority to act as agent for the firm, and it seems that where no such notice is given, the firm may be held liable for a transaction which a former party has purported to effect on behalf of the firm, if no notice has been given to third parties that he is no longer a partner.

Cases where no notice is required

Section 36 (3) of the Partnership Act 1890 provides for three exceptions to the general rule under section 36 that the statutory notice must be given if a partner whose connection with the firm is severed upon a dissolution is not to continue to be liable for the future transactions of that firm.

1. *Death.* On dissolution of the partnership through the death of a partner, the rule laid down in section 36 (1) does not apply and there is no necessity for notice to be given under section 36 (2) in order to relieve the estate of the deceased partner from liability for future transactions of the firm.[75] In this provision section 36 (3) declares the pre-existing common law in both Scotland [76] and England,[77] although Clark finds some difficulty in detecting the reason for the exception.[78] " It is perhaps more correct to say," he concludes, " that death is a public fact, which soon makes itself generally known; and that, were the common rule requiring notice to be enforced, the representatives of deceased persons would be continually exposed to fraud and injustice." The basis of the English rule, upon which section 36 seems to have been framed, is that the authority of an agent is terminated by his principal's death, whether the third party knew of it or not.[79] In virtue of that rule it is deduced that the estate of the deceased principal cannot be bound under the doctrine of apparent authority. The deceased partner is therefore not an " apparent member " of the firm in terms of section 36 (1) of the Partnership Act 1890.[80]

While the death of a partner frees him from liability for subsequent transactions of the firm, his estate still remains liable for obligations of the firm while he was a partner; and his death does not have retroactive effect so as to free the surviving partners from liability for engagements which he entered into for the firm during his life and which are not implemented until after his death. In *Usher* v. *Dauncey* [81] one of the partners drew a bill of exchange in blank in the firm name of the partnership payable to their order. He indorsed it in the firm name and handed it to a clerk to be filled up and negotiated as the finances of the firm required.

[75] Partnership Act 1890, s. 14 (2) and s. 36 (3).
[76] *Kemp* v. *Allan* (1824) 3 S. 153; *Christie* v. *Royal Bank* (1839) 1 D. 745; 2 Rob.App. 118; *Ayton* v. *Dundee Bank* (1844) 6 D. 1409.
[77] *Vulliamy* v. *Noble* (1817) 3 Mer. 593; *Devaynes* v. *Noble, Johnes' Case* (1816) 1 Mer. 619; *Brice's Case* (1816) 1 Mer. 620; *Houlton's Case* (1816) 1 Mer. 616.
[78] *Op. cit.* I, pp. 311–312.
[79] *Blades* v. *Free* (1829) 9 B. & C. 167.
[80] It seems clear that s. 36 reflects this doctrine. See Lindley, *op. cit.* pp. 245–246. The harshness of the doctrine as applied in agency has led to a more critical examination of it, particularly since in many of the earlier authorities where the rule was propounded, the possibility of apparent authority was not examined. See Bowstead, *Agency* (13th ed.) p. 447.
[81] (1814) 4 Camp. 97.

After his death, the bill was filled up and negotiated. The surviving partners were held liable as drawers of the bill to a bona fide indorsee for value although no part of the value came into their hands. Lord Ellenborough said, " The power must be considered to emanate from the partnership, not from the individual partner, and therefore after his death the bill might still be filled up to bind the survivors." [82]

It will, of course, be kept in view that section 36 is concerned with the liability of a deceased partner to the creditors of the firm. It does not necessarily follow that the estate of the deceased partner will be free from liability to his surviving copartners where they, in ignorance of his death, have incurred obligations subsequent to the death. While the doctrine will probably apply if those circumstances are all that are established,[83] the liability of the deceased partner to his copartners will depend upon the agreement which he has made with them.[84]

2. *Bankruptcy.* Under section 36 (3) of the Partnership Act 1890, where one of the partners " becomes bankrupt," his estate is not liable for partnership debts contracted after the date of his bankruptcy. In the application of the Act to Scotland the bankruptcy of a firm or of an individual means " sequestration under the Bankruptcy (Scotland) Acts and also in the case of an individual the issue against him of a decree of *cessio bonorum.*" Moreover, the Partnership Act 1890 expressly provides that nothing in its provisions " shall alter the rules of the law of Scotland relating to the bankruptcy of a firm or of the individual partners thereof." [85] The effect of section 36 (3) is therefore that on an individual partner's estates having been sequestrated in bankruptcy his authority as a partner is, without further notice, at an end. He is regarded as no longer able to grant authority for the acts done by his copartners in the firm name and his estate is not liable for transactions after the date of his sequestration in bankruptcy.

Section 36 (3), however, does not state that his sequestration brings the partnership to an end, and while it is elsewhere provided [86] that " every partnership is dissolved as regards all the partners by the . . . bankruptcy of any partner," that provision is fenced by the qualification that it is subject to any agreement between the partners. There is nothing to prevent the partners from making it a term of the contract of copartnery that the partnership will continue notwithstanding the bankruptcy of any individual partner. If they so agree, a partner who is sequestrated in bankruptcy will still come within the terms of section 36 (3) and his sequestrated estate will not be liable to a claim by a third party in respect of a transaction of the firm subsequent to the date of his bankruptcy. If as a continuing partner he himself has carried through the transaction on

---

[82] See also *Cheap* v. *Aiton* (1769) Mor. 14573; reversed 2 Pat.App. 283.
[83] *Cheap* v. *Aiton* (1772) 2 Pat.App. 283; *Blakeley's Exors.* (1852) 3 Mac. & G. 726; *Hamer's Devisees* (1852) 2 De G.M. & G. 366.
[84] See *infra* Chaps. X and XI.
[85] Partnership Act 1890, s. 47.
[86] Partnership Act 1890, s. 33 (1).

behalf of the firm, the firm will not be bound by it, since in terms of the proviso to section 38 of the Partnership Act 1890 " the firm is in no case bound by the acts of a partner who has become bankrupt." That occurs as a proviso to a section which relates to the continuing authority of the partners to bind the firm after a dissolution of the partnership, but the proviso is expressed in the widest terms and may perhaps be construed as terminating the bankrupt partner's authority to bind the firm even in the case where the partnership is not dissolved.[87] In practice, it is difficult to envisage a case in which the agreement of copartnery for a professional or trading firm would expressly provide for the continuance of the partnership with a bankrupt partner, and the saving clause in section 33 (1) has probably in contemplation unincorporated companies with transferable shares.[88]

In cases where, in spite of the bankruptcy of a partner, the remaining partners hold themselves out as still in partnership with him, they will be liable for his dealings as if he and they were still partners [89]; and while the bankrupt partner is absolved from liability for the acts of his partners subsequent to the date of his bankruptcy, his solvent copartners may bring the firm's transactions to a conclusion and dispose of the partnership property in terms of the contract of copartnery.[90]

In the consideration of questions relating to bankruptcy, the English decisions must be carefully analysed before they are applied to a Scottish case. Since the firm in Scotland is a *quasi* person distinct from its members, it may remain solvent, though some of the partners have been rendered notour bankrupt and sequestrated in bankruptcy. If, however, any of the partners have been rendered notour bankrupt for a firm debt, that will suffice to constitute the notour bankruptcy of the firm itself.[91]

3. *Retirement of a latent partner.* Section 36 (3) also exempts from liability for future debts of the partnership " the estate . . . of a partner who, not having been known to the person dealing with the firm to be a partner, retires from the firm." The pre-existing common law in Scotland was supposed to differ from the common law of England which is reflected in the words of the section. The English common law proceeds upon the basis that if the partner were not known to be a partner, there is no reason in equity why he should be required to give notice of his retirement to third parties in order to escape liability for future debts of the firm, since the public in transacting with the firm do not do so in reliance upon the credit of a partner of whose existence they are unaware.[92] The rule was frequently expressed in the terms that if a dormant partner retired from the firm, he was not liable for future obligations of the firm, even if no public

---

[87] The section is so construed by Lindley, *op. cit.* pp. 701–702.
[88] In the case of such companies, Lindley, *op. cit.* p. 579 expressed the view that an agreement that the company shall continue despite the bankruptcy of one of the members, need not be express but may be inferred from the nature of the company.
[89] *Lacy* v. *Wollcott* (1823) 2 D. & R. 458; Partnership Act 1890, s. 38.
[90] *Fox* v. *Hanbury* (1776) Cowp. 445; *Morgan* v. *Marquis* (1853) 9 Ex. 145.
[91] Bankruptcy (Scotland) Act 1913, s. 6.
[92] *Carter* v. *Whalley* (1830) 1 B. & Ad. 11; *Heath* v. *Samson* (1831) 4 B. & Ad. 172.

notice of his retirement was given. In Scotland, after a decision which was consonant with that rule [93] the decision in *Hay* v. *Mair* [94] was thought to overrule the earlier decision and thus create a difference between the Scottish and the English common law. The difference, however, is, as Clark points out,[95] more apparent than real and arises from the rather specialised use of the term " dormant partner " in England. A person may be a " dormant partner," *i.e.* he may take no part in the management of the firm, without being a secret, or latent, partner. If he is known to be a partner, albeit a dormant one, third parties dealing with the firm do so to some extent at least on the faith of his credit and in such a case, if he retires from the firm, he must, in common with any other known partner of the firm, give public notice of his retirement if he wishes to protect himself from liability for future obligations of the firm. That is precisely the point which *Hay* v. *Mair* decides and the same rule applies in England, though the use of the term " dormant partner " to describe what section 36 (3) styles " a partner . . . not having been known to the person dealing with the firm to be a partner " creates an apparent, though on examination insubstantial, point of difference between the systems.[96] In *Court* v. *Berlin*,[97] two latent partners who retired from the firm were held liable to a solicitor who was retained by the third, and active, partner to raise an action for recovery of a debt due to the firm. Since the latent partners were held liable for the expenses of the action incurred subsequently to their retirement and since the solicitor when instructed was unaware of the existence of the latent partners, this decision appears to conflict with those previously considered. It is probably distinguishable on the ground that the original instructions to the solicitor, which were given before the retirement of the latent partners, represented a mandate to him to act on behalf of the firm until he had brought the action to a conclusion. Hence the expenses incurred subsequently to the retirement of the latent partners were referable to the original instructions given by the active partner on behalf of the firm, including at the material time the two latent partners.

Effect of notice of retirement upon subsequent holding out

It has already been submitted that even where due notice of retirement has been given, this will not entirely preclude the possibility of the retired partner being held liable as if he were a partner under section 14 (1) of the Partnership Act 1890,[98] and it has also been suggested that though it be theoretically possible for a retired partner to hold himself out or knowingly suffer himself to be held out as a partner even in such circumstances, the

[93] *Armour* v. *Gibson* (1774) Mor. 14575.
[94] Jan. 27, 1809, F.C.
[95] *Op. cit.* I, p. 315. See also *Mann* v. *Sinclair* (1879) 6 R. 1078, *per* Lord Shand at p. 1088 and the comments of Professor J. Campbell Lorimer in the Supplement to *Lindley on Partnership* (1891), pp. 96–97.
[96] This use of the term " dormant partner " persists in England to this day in spite of its ambiguity. See Lindley, *op. cit.* p. 247 n. 98: " A dormant partner known to a few persons to be a partner is not dormant as to them."
[97] [1897] 2 Q.B. 396.
[98] *Supra* pp. 290–292.

fact that due notice has been given of his retirement under section 36 will in some cases present an obstacle to the holding out being established to the satisfaction of the court. It is thought that this may be the true *ratio* of *Tower Cabinet Company* v. *Ingram*.[99] In that case due notice of the defendant's retirement had been given under section 36 (2) of the Partnership Act 1890 but subsequently a third party, who had had no previous dealings with the firm, received an order from the firm which by inadvertence was written upon a sheet of the firm's former stock of writing paper upon which the defendant's name still appeared as one of the partners. The defendant was absolved from liability on the transaction. Lindley [1] explains the *ratio decidendi* on the reasoning that since, at the date of the defendant's retirement, the provisions of section 36 (2) of the Partnership Act 1890 had been observed, the defendant was relieved under those provisions from liability in respect of subsequent transactions of the firm. That reasoning, by itself, however, does not satisfactorily dispose of the plea that in the subsequent transaction the defendant had " knowingly suffered " himself to be held out as a partner, and on the facts of the case it is thought that the decision rests less uneasily upon the arguments (1) that since due notice of retirement had been given under section 36 (2) the former connection of the defendant with the firm could not be appealed to as supporting the alleged subsequent holding out, (2) that any such holding out must be established as in the case of holding out by, or of, a stranger to the firm, and (3) on the facts of the case, the court was not prepared to find that the defendant had knowingly suffered himself so to be held out.

Effect of the Registration of Business Names Act 1916

In practical terms, the problems concerned with the latent partner may be said to have been lessened by this Act, since if its provisions are complied with, the names of all existing partners will either appear in the firm name or may be ascertained by inspection of the register. Where, however, the entries in the register are defective and do not strictly comply with the provisions of the Registration of Business Names Act 1916 problems may still arise. It is obvious that the special rules of the common law in regard to latent partners may continue to apply in cases where a dormant partner's name is omitted from the relevant entry on the register in respect of the firm. On the other hand, the mere fact a partner's name has not been removed from the register upon his retirement will not necessarily involve him in liability for future transactions of the firm on the ground that he has " knowingly suffered " himself to be held out as a partner under section 14 (1) of the Partnership Act 1890,[2] nor apparently will that by itself suffice to render him " known to the person dealing with the firm to be a partner " in terms of section 36 (3) of the same Act.[3] In terms of

---

[99] [1949] 2 K.B. 397.
[1] *Op. cit.* p. 247.
[2] *Tower Cabinet Co.* v. *Ingram, supra.*
[3] *Ibid.*

the Registration of Business Names Act 1916,[4] any change of membership, by death, retirement or otherwise, of a firm to which the Act applies must, of course, be registered; but it seems that, in order to impose liability upon the member who has severed his connection with the partnership, that fact must be supported by evidence of circumstances which support the inference that he has been a party to, or at least has had knowledge of, the failure to register the change.[5]   Perhaps, the most direct effect of the entry in the register upon the problems concerned with liability of a partner who had retired is that it may be impossible, and will certainly prove difficult, for him to maintain that he was a latent partner where his name has appeared on the register.   It certainly would appear that it would be impossible for him to make that claim in a question with a third party who has in fact consulted the register before dealing with the firm; and in such a case, the retiring partner would, it is submitted, require to give notice under section 36 (2) of the Partnership Act 1890 in order to escape future liability on transactions of the firm with that third party.[6]

What amounts to effective notice

While the retirement of a latent partner need not be notified, since he was not known before his retirement to be a partner and thus third parties could not have relied upon the credit afforded to the firm through his association with it, the situation is different when a known or apparent partner retires, or where a partnership among several known partners has been dissolved.   In these cases third parties who have previously dealt with the firm have known and relied upon the fact that the firm consisted of its original members and they are entitled to assume that its membership remains unchanged until they receive notification to the contrary.[7]   Moreover, persons who had no dealings whatsoever with the firm prior to the change are entitled to assume that it exists as formerly constituted, or as it is sometimes expressed with all its " apparent members "[8] until some notification is given of the change.[9]   In the former case, the customer can point to a course of dealing with the old firm.   He is thus in a stronger position to maintain that his continued dealings took place upon the faith of the constitution of the firm as known to him from those prior dealings than is a member of the public who commences dealing with the firm after the unnotified change has taken place.   The customer of the former firm has, therefore, always been regarded as entitled to more specific notice than a person who had no prior dealings with the firm.[10]

---

[4] ss. 3 and 6.
[5] *Tower Cabinet Co.* v. *Ingram, supra.*
[6] See Lindley, *op. cit.* p. 248, citing *Bishop* v. *Tudor Estates* [1952] C.L.Y. 2493.
[7] *Scarf* v. *Jardine* (1882) 7 App.Cas. 345, *per* Lord Selborne at p. 349; Partnership Act 1890, s. 36.
[8] See *e.g.* Partnership Act 1890, s. 36 (1).   For the meaning of " apparent members " see *Tower Cabinet Co.* v. *Ingram* [1949] 2 K.B. 397; *Bishop* v. *Tudor Estates* [1952] C.L.Y. 2493.
[9] *Dalgleish* v. *Sorley* (1791) Hume 746; *Boulton* v. *Mansfield* (1787) 3 Pat.App. 70; *Graham* v. *Henderson* (1802) 4 Pat.App. 421; *Campbell* v. *McLintock* (1803) Hume 755; *Hunter* v. *Evans* (1830) 9 S. 159.
[10] *Padon* v. *Bank of Scotland* (1826) 5 S. 175; *Graham* v. *Hope* (1792) Peake 208.

In the case of customers of the old firm it was stated by Lord Ellen-borough [11] that the usual and proper course was to send circular letters to all who had previously had dealings with the firm. Under the common law, sufficient notice was given to persons who had had no prior dealings with the old firm if the change had been notified by advertisement in the *Edinburgh Gazette* and in the local newspapers.[12] As has been previously stated [13] the distinction as to the type of notice required in each case is preserved in section 36 (2) of the Partnership Act 1890, but adequate notice to the public generally, as distinct from former customers, is now given by advertisement in the *Edinburgh Gazette* alone.

Special notice. While in the case of persons who had previous dealings with the old firm, notice by advertisement without more particular notice to the customer concerned will be of little avail in most cases,[14] both at common law and under the Partnership Act 1890, however, if it can be proved that notice has actually been received by the customer, no matter by what means, that will suffice to release the retired partner from liability for transactions subsequent to that notice. Section 36 (1) of the Partnership Act 1890 merely provides that the customer must receive " notice of the change." The Act nowhere requires that any particular form of notice must be received by him. At common law, while Lord Ellenborough mentioned a circular letter to the customer as a usual and proper way of giving notice,[15] he did not lay that down as the only means whereby notification might be made to the customer nor has any such rule been laid down in any other decision. Whether or not the customer has received notice is a question of fact. For purposes of proof, notification by circular letter has obvious advantages, particularly since when the firm can prove that the circular has been posted, the *onus* then rests upon the customer to prove that it never reached him.[16] But even in relation to a customer advertisement will be sufficient if it can be proved that the customer has in fact seen the advertisement, and, as in the case of a party who had no prior dealings with the old firm, evidence that the customer in question took in the newspaper in which the notice appeared will go some way towards establishing that he knew of the change advertised in it.[17] No particular form of wording is required in the notice, if it adequately communicates to the customer that the particular change has taken place.[18] Other facts from which it may be inferred that the change has actually come to the knowledge of the customer may be established. " In truth the question of sufficient notice to customers is one of fact, to be determined by a jury or its equivalents." [19] Thus the general notoriety of the change

---

[11] *Jenkins* v. *Blizard* (1816) 1 Stark. 418.
[12] Clark, *op. cit.* I, p. 310.
[13] *Supra* p. 298.
[14] *Graham* v. *Hope* (1792) Peake 208.
[15] *Jenkins* v. *Blizard, supra* n. 11.
[16] *Padon* v. *Bank of Scotland* (1826) 5 S. 175; *Jenkins* v. *Blizard, supra.*
[17] *Leeson* v. *Holt* (1816) 1 Stark. 186; *Boydell* v. *Drummond* (1808) 2 Camp. 157; *Kemp* v. *Allan* (1824) 3 S. 153; *Wright* v. *Gardner's Trustees* (1831) 9 S. 721.
[18] *Bertram* v. *McIntosh* (1822) 1 S. 314.
[19] Clark, *op. cit.* I, p. 310.

in the firm and the execution of powers of attorney to the new firm were held sufficient to justify a jury in finding that an old customer had knowledge of the change.[20]   Indeed, Bell states that " an obvious change of firm is notice, for it puts the creditor on his guard to inquire as at first." [21] In tha' passage, Bell appears to be referring to a change in the firm name, and to that extent the statement is borne out by authority.[22]   If the statement is taken in a wider significance to mean any circumstance whereby a change in the constitution of the partnership itself is made obvious to those dealing with the partnership, it is difficult to find any decision in point, as Clark observes.[23]   The absence of authority, it is thought, does not detract from Bell's statement, but rather indicates the unlikelihood of such circumstances arising in practice for decision; for the " obviousness " of the change in the partnership other than a change in the firm name will frequently depend upon the very circumstances upon which a jury might find that the customer had received adequate notice of the change, in which case consideration of the question whether he was put on his inquiry will be rendered otiose.   Thus the cases which Bell mentions in support of his contention that an obvious change will put the customer upon his inquiry may equally be treated as material upon which a jury might find that the customer had actually received adequate notice of the change.   For example a change in the name of a firm of bankers which appeared *ex facie* of the cheques used by their customers was held to be sufficient notice to an old customer drawing his cheques on the new form supplied,[24] and Bell is of opinion that a similar change in the invoices rendered by a trading partnership to its customers would have the same effect,[25] though this is perhaps more dubious.

Notice by advertisement. Public notice by advertisement in the *Edinburgh Gazette* will now be sufficient in the case of persons who have had no prior dealings with the firm, whether they have seen the advertisement or not.[26]   Advertisement in any other newspaper will not have that effect.   In that case, as in the case of *Gazette* notices in a question with customers, the advertisement will only be regarded as adequate notice if it can be established that the party in question in fact saw it.[27]   In these circumstances the fact that the jury are satisfied that the advertisement was seen by the creditor of the firm will suffice even where no notice appeared in the *Gazette*.[28]   Evidence that the third party concerned took the newspaper concerned is admissible though it is not conclusive upon the question whether he saw the advertisement itself.[29]   If notification of the change

[20] *Hart* v. *Alexander* (1837) 2 M. & W. 484.
[21] *Com.* II, p. 530.
[22] *Dunbar* v. *Rimington*, Mar. 10, 1810, F.C.
[23] *Op. cit.* I, p. 310.
[24] *Barfoot* v. *Goodall* (1811) 3 Camp. 147.
[25] Bell, *Com.* II, 530–531.   [26] Partnership Act 1890, s. 36 (2).
[27] *Sawers* v. *Tradestown Victualling Society*, Feb. 24, 1815, F.C.; *Leeson* v. *Holt* (1816) 1 Stark. 186; *Boydell* v. *Drummond* (1808) 2 Camp. 157.
[28] *Rooth* v. *Quin* (1819) 7 Price 193.
[29] *Jenkins* v. *Blizard* (1816) 1 Stark. 418; *Rowley* v. *Horne* (1825) 3 Bing. 2; *Speirs* v. *Royal Bank of Scotland* (1822) 1 S. 516.

to the party in question can be established by other means, advertisement in the *Gazette* is not an indispensable formality.   In *McIver* v. *Humble* [30] the altered name of the firm was painted upon its counting house, the business of the former firm was removed for purposes of winding up and circulars were sent to the customers of the old firm.   These circumstances were held sufficient without advertisement in the *Gazette* in a question with a third party who had not been a customer of the old firm and who was not proved to have received any more specific notice.   On the other hand advertisement in the *Gazette* will not relieve a retiring partner from liability in the future if he has in some manner counteracted its effect by his conduct, as where he allows the name of the old firm to remain above the door of the premises in which the new firm is now carrying on business. [31]

Registration of Business Names Act 1916.   Since actual notice of the change, however brought to the knowledge of the third party, is all that need be established, the provisions of the Registration of Business Names Act 1916 may be relevant in some cases.   Where a firm to which the Act applies has observed the statutory provisions regarding the appearance of the names of the partners upon the letter-headings and other trade communications emanating from the firm this will be an element in establishing that due notice has been given of the change to a third party who has received documents of that kind from the firm.   Indeed, as has been already mentioned, Scottish opinion of great authority exists to the effect that such a circumstance, or at least one closely analogous to it, places the third party upon his inquiry before he may maintain that he was entitled to rely upon the credit of former partners of the firm. [32]   Registration of a change in the composition of the firm in the Register of Business Names is not regarded as equivalent to notice in terms of section 36 of the Partnership Act 1890 or of the common law [33] though if the third party can be proved to have consulted the register and inspected the relevant entry that would probably be regarded as sufficient notice to him.

[30] (1812) 16 East 169.   *Cf. Gorham* v. *Thompson* (1791) Peake 60.
[31] *Williams* v. *Keats* (1817) 2 Stark. 290.
[32] Bell, *Com.* II, 530–531.   *Tower Cabinet Co.* v. *Ingram* [1949] 2 K.B. 397 does not conflict with that view.
[33] Lindley, *op. cit.* pp. 109–110.

CHAPTER VIII

RIGHTS AND DUTIES OF THE PARTNERS IN RELATION TO THIRD PARTIES

Delict and Breach of Trust

THE liability of the firm for the wrongful act or omission of one of the partners is governed by the general rule laid down in section 10 of the Partnership Act 1890—

> " 10. Where, by any wrongful act or omission of any partner acting in the ordinary course of the business of the firm, or with the authority of his copartners, loss or injury is caused to any person not being a partner in the firm, or any penalty is incurred, the firm is liable therefor to the same extent as the partner so acting or omitting to act."

It is clear that in terms of section 10 vicarious liability is imposed upon the firm in respect of the delicts and *quasi* delicts of individual partners thereof. The vicarious liability thus imposed upon the firm in section 10 is, moreover, rooted in the relationship of agency existing between the partners and the firm in section 5 of the Partnership Act 1890; for there appears little doubt that the justification for the existence of that vicarious liability rests upon the principle of agency. This is clear from the words of Collins M.R. in *Hamlyn* v. *John Houston & Co.*,[1] a case where the liability of a firm for the tort of its partners was under consideration. " The principal," he said, " having delegated the performance of a certain class of acts to the agent, it is not unjust that he, being the person who has appointed the agent, and who will have the benefit of his efforts if successful, should bear the risk of his exceeding his authority in matters incidental to the doing of the acts the performance of which has been delegated to him." [2]

In order that responsibility may be imposed upon a principal for the delict of his agent, or on a master for the delict of his servant, one of three factual states of circumstances must have existed.

(1) The principal, as the master, must have authorised the commission of the act; or

(2) the act must have been done on his behalf and later ratified by him; or

(3) the act must have been committed by the agent, or the servant, in the course of his employment and as a part of it.

In the first two cases the issue is not one of vicarious liability but of *direct* liability upon the principle *qui facit per alium facit per se.* It is only in the third case that the special social and equitable considerations expressed in

---

[1] [1903] 1 K.B. 81.
[2] *Ibid.* at pp. 85–86.

the maxim *respondeat superior* will arise.[3]   Section 10 of the Partnership Act 1890 clearly covers all three situations of fact by the words " acting in the ordinary course of the business of the firm or with the authority of his copartners."   In the latter case where he acts " with the authority of his copartners " the firm's liability is direct and personal under the maxim *qui facit per alium facit per se*.   That authority may consist in the fact that the firm has authorised the individual partner to commit the wrongful act prior to its being committed or in the fact that the firm has later ratified a wrongful act committed by a partner and thus made it the act of the firm. In the case where the individual partner commits the wrongful act when " acting in the ordinary course of the business of the firm," the liability of the firm is vicarious under the maxim *respondeat superior*.[4]

Vicarious liability of the firm

It has been said [5] that " the liability of partners for fraud and misappropriation of property entrusted to the firm has been established [in England] since the eighteenth century, but vicarious liability for partners in pure tort entered English law relatively late; and there is ground for thinking that Baty [6] may well have been right in regarding the statutory foundation of such liability in the Partnership Act 1890 [7] as based on a very slim foundation."   Consideration of cases of fraud and of misappropriation of property entrusted to the firm may be set aside for closer examination when the provisions of section 11 of the Partnership Act 1890 are considered.[8] In the remainder of cases of delict it cannot be said that Scots law was in advance of English law.   Even in mid-nineteenth century, the doctrine of vicarious liability of the firm, if it is discerned at all, appears in a fragmentary and unrationalised form.   The most cursory reading of the relevant passages in Clark's treatise on *Partnership* [9] will convince the reader that the doctrine was, at the time when Clark wrote in 1866, somewhat perilously poised between a rationalisation based upon the contractual consequences of the agency relationship and one in which the writer seems to be groping

---

[3] See Gow, *Mercantile and Industrial Law of Scotland*, pp. 727–728 (where the liability of the employer for the act of his employee is examined); Atiyah, *Vicarious Liability in the Law of Torts*, Chap. 1, pp. 3–11 (where the ideas of personal liability and vicarious liability are analysed and contrasted).

[4] While this analysis is in a broad sense a true one, the fact that vicarious liability of the firm rests upon the application of the principle in agency makes the precise significance of the doctrine somewhat uncertain or at least inelegant, since in questions of agency " the clear dichotomy between contract and tort . . . even now is not as clear as is sometimes assumed."—Bowstead, *Agency* (13th ed.) p. 327.

[5] Atiyah, *op. cit.* p. 116.

[6] *Vicarious Liability*, p. 46.

[7] s. 10.

[8] *Infra* pp. 339 *et seq.*

[9] Vol. I, pp. 252–264.   In *British Legal Life Assurance Co. Ltd.* v. *Pearl Life Assurance Co. Ltd.* (1887) 14 R. 818 vicarious liability of the defender company for the wrongs committed by its officials was invoked to support an interdict against their uttering or publishing defamatory matter which had already been published by their officials without the knowledge of the company.   The sheriff substitute (Campbell Smith) clearly held that vicarious liability was established.   The Lord President (Inglis) at p. 822, however, based the grant of interdict on the fact that when the libel had been brought to their notice, the company did not take " instant and very energetic steps to put a stop to " it, and thus brought the case under the *ratio* of direct, rather than vicarious, liability.

for a wider explanatory principle which remains just beyond his grasp.[10] In examining cases of liability of the firm for the delict of the partner or agent Clark distinguishes two situations where the firm may be liable: (1) where the act is done in the course of carrying out an engagement which the principal has undertaken to fulfil, and the party with whom he has contracted is injured thereby. " In cases of this kind," he comments, " the liability to [sic] the principal arises not from the delict of the agent, but from the fact that loss or damage had arisen to the obligee, from the obligor having either failed to fulfil his obligation, or having carried it out in an improper manner." [11]   Apart from the typographical error in that passage where the words " to the principal " should read " of the principal," the cases which are cited to illustrate the rule are concerned either with misappropriation of funds entrusted to the firm, which will be considered separately when examining the provisions of section 11 of the Partnership Act 1890,[12] or with cases where carriers are under a contractual obligation to convey passengers safely and through the recklessness or improper conduct of the servants of the carrier the passengers suffer injury.[13]   But in such cases it is necessary to establish that the delict was committed by the servant in the course of and as a part of the obligation undertaken.[14] (2) The second case of liability of the principal which Clark mentions is " when, in the course and as a part of carrying out the directions of his principal, the agent has committed a delict whereby some of the public have been injured."   Under this category he subsumes cases where the servant in the course of his duties drives his master's vehicle carelessly and injury is suffered as a result by a member of the public, or when the servant carries out the instructions of the master carelessly or improperly and thereby causes damage to the property of a third party or where the servant negligently fails to warn the public to keep out of the way of danger and one of the public sustains injury.   In such cases Clark ascribes the liability of the master or the principal to " that implied contract or obligation which everyone is held to make with the public, whereby when he does or orders anything to be done, he undertakes that it shall be done with due regard to the safety and interests of the lieges." [15]

As a rationalisation of the doctrine of *respondeat superior*, whether that

---

[10] It is difficult, even nowadays, to escape entirely from contractual overtones when discussing vicarious responsibility for delict in partnership or agency cases, since the area in which the liability is imposed is to some extent apt to be conflated with the scope of the authority of the partner or agent.   See *e.g.* Walker, *Delict*, p. 80, and Bowstead, *Agency* (13th ed.) p. 327.

[1] *Op. cit.* I, p. 262.

[2] *Infra* pp. 339 *et seq.*

[13] *Brown* v. *Macgregor*, Feb. 26, 1813, F.C.; *Allan* v. *McLeish* (1819) 2 Murray 158; *Gunn* v. *Gardiner* (1820) 2 Murray 194; *Brash* v. *Steele* (1845) 7 D. 539; *MacArthur* v. *Croall* (1852) 24 Sc.Jur. 170.   See also the railway cases, *Morton* v. *Edinburgh & Glasgow Ry. Co.* (1845) 8 D. 288; *Macglashan* v. *Dundee & Perth Ry. Co.* (1848) 10 D. 1397; *Cargill* v. *Dundee & Perth Ry. Co.* (1848) 11 D. 216.

[14] Clark, *op. cit.* I, pp. 262–263, citing *Linwood* v. *Hawthorn*, May 14, 1817, F.C.; (1821) 1 S.App. 20; *McLaren* v. *Rae* (1827) 4 Murray 381; *Miller* v. *Harvie* (1827) 4 Murray 388; *Dalrymple* v. *McGill* (1804) Hume 387; *Thorburn* v. *Ellis*, May 24, 1811, F.C.; *Waldie* v. *Roxburgh* (1822) 1 Sh. 367; (1825) 1 W. & S. 1.

[15] *Op. cit.* p. 263.

doctrine be examined strictly in regard to the partnership or more generally, it is clear that Clark's theory of a liability arising under contract or
under implied contract leaves something to be desired. In the first category of cases which he considers, he is dealing with circumstances where
the wrongful or defective performance by the partner produces a breach
of a contractual obligation owed by the firm to a third party. His reference in that context to the " delict " of the servant (or partner) is confusing
since, while admittedly the partner might himself be sued personally in
delict, the firm's liability is grounded on contract. In the second category
of cases Clark adds to the confusion by rationalising clear cases of vicarious
liability in delict by postulating as a contractual obligation upon the firm
something which upon his own exposition is clearly seen to be founded not
on contract but upon a duty to avoid injuring others, with whom one has
no contract, through wrongful acts or negligence. It is equally true that
other attempted rationalisations where the theory propounded has perhaps
involved a more strenuous effort to explain away the legal difficulties of the
conception, such as the control exercised by the master or the principal
over the activities of the servant or the agent, or his benefit from the work
done by the person for whom he is held vicariously liable, or his power of
selection of that person, are also subject to criticism in that they all at some
points fall short of a satisfactory explanation of the doctrine in all its
aspects. In some ways the traditional theory of identification, *i.e.* that the
master and the servant are so identified that the act of the latter is the act of
the former, which has been the most roughly handled by its critics,[16] if
regarded in a somewhat more sophisticated way than that in which it was
originally advanced, has the most to commend it. Certainly, in the context of partnership and in other cases of collective and artificial *personae*,
there is a strong connection between the notion of group unity and that of
vicarious liability and the existence of the one is a " powerful reason for the
acceptance of " the other.[17] No theory which may be advanced, however,
will be free from attack at some points.

> " It is no longer possible (if it ever was) to approach the problem by
> inquiring into the ratio of the rule *respondeat superior*. A mixture of
> ideas has inspired many unconvincing judicial efforts to find a scien-
> tific basis for the maxim, and I note that some of these have been dis-
> missed in a recent work as ' rhythmical inanities.' What was once
> presented as a legal principle has degenerated into a rule of expediency,
> imperfectly defined, and changing its shape before our eyes under the
> impact of changing social and political conditions." [18]

Even the most widely advocated modern theory, the loss-distribution
theory, which did not come within Lord President Cooper's survey, is no
more likely to appeal to the reflective as entirely satisfactory. This theory,

---

[16] *e.g.* Baty, *Vicarious Liability*, p. 147, where it is described as an " inane fiction."
[17] Glanville Williams, 20 M.L.R. 234.
[18] *Per* Lord President Cooper in *Kilboy* v. *South Eastern Fire Area Joint Committee*, 1952
S.C. 280 at p. 285.

much favoured by modern American writers, bases itself upon the postulate that in most cases the employer who is required to pay damages for the wrongful act of his servant does not in fact pay these entirely from his own pocket. The liability is in actual fact distributed over a wide section of the community partly through resort to insurance against " employers' liability " and partly because more and more employers nowadays are not individuals but incorporated bodies such as limited companies and public and local authorities. That theory is of course immediately fallible when considered in relation to the application of the doctrine of partnership. Even taken, however, in terms of the area of business in relation to which it has been advanced, it is productive of the paradox that it is precisely in the area where the law did *not* recognise vicarious liability that the principle of loss-distribution was first widely recognised, *e.g.* in the area of workmen's compensation for industrial accidents, and it is also noticeable that the theory does not satisfactorily account for the restrictions placed by the law upon the application of the doctrine *respondeat superior*. If the principle of loss-distribution be accepted, it is difficult to understand why vicarious liability should exist only for wrongful acts committed by the servant within the scope of his employment.[19]

"*Any wrongful act or omission of any partner acting in the ordinary course of the business of the firm . . .*"   The form of words used in section 10 in defining the firm's liability for the wrongful acts of its partners should be contrasted with the words used in section 5 when defining the limits of the partner's agency for his firm and thus the firm's liability in contract for the acts done by that partner in terms of his agency. In section 5 the acts of the partner which bind the firm contractually are those done " for carrying on, in the usual way, business of the kind carried on by the firm." In section 10 the wrongful act or omission by the partner must arise while he is " acting in the ordinary course of the business of the firm." The firm's vicarious liability for the wrongful act of one of its partners, therefore, is not related to what a third party might reasonably expect to have been within the authority of a partner carrying on business of the kind carried on by the firm. The wrongful act must be related to the course of the firm's actual business. The distinction is no less important because the contrasted words tend to be treated as roughly equivalent in meaning. It is, for example, not unusual to hear section 5 expounded as if the act of the partner in order to bind the firm contractually must " be one done in relation to the partnership business." [20]   But while that statement is partially true, it ignores the fact that the firm may still be bound in contract by an act of its partner which is unrelated to its actual business but which is more generally related to the kind of business which the firm carries on. It is in section 10, dealing with the firm's liability for wrongful acts, that the relation of the act to the actual business of the firm is emphasised.

---

[19] For an interesting and full discussion both of the traditional theories and of the loss-distribution theory, with a citation of much of the modern legal writing on this subject, see Atiyah, *Vicarious Liability in the Law of Torts*, Chap. 2.

[20] Underhill, *Principles of the Law of Partnership* (9th ed.) p. 57.

In section 10, therefore, the Act has passed from consideration of contractual liability of the firm to consideration of some type of vicarious liability in delict; and the resemblance of idea expressed in the words " in the ordinary course of the business of the firm " to the formula familiar in the treatment of a trader's vicarious liability for his servant—" within the scope of his employment "—is significant.   The force of the words used in section 10 is clear if we attempt to use them as a sort of measure of the partner's authority, as is the purpose of the words used in section 5; for if section 10 were so regarded it would be difficult to see how a wrongful or negligent manner of transacting the business of the firm could be regarded as falling within the partner's authority, be it express, implied or even apparent.   Any such attempted analogy with liability in contract breaks down, and indeed the whole doctrine of vicarious liability in delict was at one time imperilled by the logical answer to that analogy, that a master could not be held impliedly to have authorised a wrongful performance of the duties committed to his servant.[21]   The correct approach seems clearly to be to subsume the firm's liability in such cases under the doctrine *respondeat superior*, a doctrine which has been accounted for in different ways but which appears ultimately to derive its force from the social expediency which imposes upon him who takes the benefit arising from the activities of those he has employed about his business a corresponding liability for the injury suffered by third parties through wrongful or negligent performance of the matters so committed.[22]   And section 10, in confining the firm's liability to acts " in the ordinary course of the business of the firm," appears to be appealing to the doctrine of vicarious liability as it is known in other relationships, where it is untinged with any overtones of a contractual nature such as might be implied in an explanation founded upon authority of the partner.

Both before and after the passing of the Partnership Act 1890, the vicarious liability of the firm has been recognised in such circumstances. Thus the firm and all its partners were held liable for the negligence of one partner in driving for the firm and in the ordinary course of its business a coach belonging to the partnership,[23] and a similar liability has been imposed in the case of negligent handling of a ship belonging to the firm.[24] Where the firm is under a duty to keep a mine shaft in proper order, the firm will be held liable for the consequences of the neglect of that duty even though the superintendence of the shaft was entrusted exclusively to one of the partners.[25]   Again when writs had been irregularly executed by one

---

[21] That view was upheld in *Findlater* v. *Duncan* (1839) McLean & Robson's App. 911; late departed from in *Mersey Docks & Harbour Board Trustees* v. *Gibbs* (1866) L.R. 1 H.L. 93 and *Virtue* v. *Commissioners of Police of Alloa* (1873) 1 R. 285.

[22] See *supra* pp. 303–306.

[23] *Moreton* v. *Hardern* (1825) 4 B. & C. 223.   A right of indemnity may, however, exist in the other partners against the partner driving the coach.   See *Lister* v. *Romford Ice & Cold Storage Co. Ltd* [1957] A.C. 555; *Harvey* v. *R. G. O'Dell and Another* [1958] 2 Q.B. 78 (both cases concerned with master and servant).

[24] *Steel* v. *Lester* (1878) 3 C.P.D. 121.

[25] *Mellors* v. *Shaw* (1861) 1 B. & S. 437.

of two partners, both partners were held liable.[26]   A firm of solicitors and
its partners are liable for the negligence of one of the partners in advising
a client of the firm [27]; but in this case the liability is contractual rather than
delictual.[28]

"*Or with the authority of his copartners.*"   Section 10 of the Partnership Act 1890 imposes liability upon the firm for the delict of a partner,
not only where the delictual act was in the ordinary course of the firm's
business, but also where it was done with the authority of his copartners.
The principle on which the liability arises in the latter case is not *respondeat
superior*, but the maxim often associated with it, *qui facit per alium facit
per se*.   Though the two operate in a similar field of law and are often
cited rather indiscriminately, it is thought that they involve quite distinct
principles.   *Respondeat superior* is a much broader principle and is properly invoked in support of vicarious liability in its widest sense.   The
issue raised in the maxim *qui facit per alium facit per se* is a much narrower
one.   The principle is that no one can escape liability for a wrongful act
by employing another person to commit it for him.   In such a case the
person instructing or authorising the wrongful act to be committed by
another is not vicariously, but directly,[29] liable for the consequences.   Thus
the maxim *qui facit per alium facit per se*, though sometimes treated as if it
were an exception to the principle *culpa tenet suos auctores*, is in reality an
illustration of that principle, since he who instructed or authorised the
wrong to be done is the " author " of the wrong and is liable for the fault.[30]
The distinction here attempted to be drawn between the vicarious liability
imposed where the partner commits a wrong, " acting in the ordinary
course of the business of the firm " and the direct liability of the firm which
arises where the partner committing the wrong does so " with the authority
of his copartners," is brought out in the judgment of Winn J. in *Meekins* v.
Henson,[31] where he said,

> ". . . speaking purely hypothetically, and coming now to the sphere
> of defamation, I can well imagine that at a conference of partners of a
> firm, the decision might be taken that a letter should be written, either
> specifically stating A, B or C, or comprising A, B and C in a general
> way, in the treatment to be given to the subject in the letter decided on
> by the conference as a matter of principle.   Moreover, one can well
> imagine in slightly different terms that information might be given by
> one partner to another in such terms or by such account that he, as a

---

[26] *Duke of Brunswick* v. *Slowman* (1849) 8 C.B. 317; 79 R.R. 521.
[27] *Blyth* v. *Fladgate* [1891] 1 Ch. 337; *Morgan* v. *Blyth* [1891] 1 Ch. 337; *Smith* v. *Blyth* [1891]
    1 Ch. 337.
[28] The firm in its contract with its client impliedly undertakes to exercise a professional
    standard of care.   As compared with liability in delict, a higher degree of liability may,
    therefore, rest on the partners.   See *Tully* v. *Ingram* (1891) 19 R. 65, *per* Lord Kyllachy
    (incoming partner); *Smith* v. *Blyth* [1891] 1 Ch. at p. 366; *Sawyer* v. *Goodwin* (1867) 36
    L.J.Ch. 578 (representatives of deceased partner).
[29] *Canadian Pacific Ry.* v. *Lockhart* [1942] A.C. 591, *per* Lord Thankerton at p. 599;
    Hewitt v. *Bonvin* [1940] 1 K.B. 188, *per* du Parcq L.J. at p. 195.
[30] See Smith, *Short Commentary on the Law of Scotland*, pp. 684 *et seq.*; Gow, *Mercantile
    and Industrial Law of Scotland*, pp. 727–728.
[31] [1962] 1 All E.R. 899 at p. 902.

reasonable man, should foresee that that information would produce a publication of a kind defamatory to some stranger by one of the other partners.

" In the evidence in the present case it was said . . . that another letter dated June 20, 1958, was written by Mr. Sayers in draft and then shown by him to Colonel Henson, his senior partner, for approval. . . . There again is another hypothetical example of the manner in which one partner . . . might be directly and personally responsible for the defamatory terms, and the publication, of a letter which he did not himself write or dictate or put in the outgoing post."

Cases where the wrongful act of a partner is expressly authorised by his co-partners may be expected to be rare save in the field of fraud which is the subject of later examination.[32] They may, however, occur in circumstances of abuse of process by the firm and in *Meekins* v. *Henson*,[33] the issue arose in relation to a defamatory letter signed by one of the partners in the firm name. In that case it was pointed out that liability might be imposed upon the copartners, or some of them, irrespective of the terms of section 10 of the Partnership Act 1890. The words " or with the authority of his co-partners " in that section were read to mean that for the firm to be liable *all* the remaining copartners must have authorised the wrongful act, though if one partner authorised his copartner to write the defamatory letter he would be liable along with the writer of the letter. Indeed, in cases of defamation and probably also of malicious prosecution, the situation may arise, as it did in *Meekins* v. *Henson*, that the malice required in order to impose liability can be established against one of the partners only. In *Meekins* v. *Henson* the partner who actually published the defamatory letter (Mr. Sayers) and one of his copartners (Mr. Valder) were held to be free from liability since the occasion upon which the copy of the letter complained of was communicated to the borough treasurer was a privileged one and they had acted without malice. Malice was established, however, against the remaining partner (Colonel Henson) and he alone was held answerable in damages to the plaintiff. It is clear that Winn J. treated the question as one of direct liability and quite apart from the terms of section 10. He said,[34] " . . . Mr. Sayers and Mr. Valder and Colonel Henson were entitled in law to make this publication, provided that they entertained no malice, were actuated by no malice in making the publication. By that test, Mr. Sayers and Mr. Valder did not abuse the privilege; the privilege is not destroyed so far as either of them is concerned by malice; *per contra* it is destroyed by proof which the jury had accepted in the case of Colonel Henson, that he was actuated by malice."

At an earlier stage in his judgment [35] Winn J. after quoting the terms of section 10, proceeded to say,

---

[32] *Infra* pp. 317 *et seq.*
[33] *Supra* n. 31.
[34] *Meekins* v. *Henson* [1962] 1 All E.R. at p. 903.
[35] *Ibid.* at p. 901.

" This provision in the statute was clearly necessary for several reasons. For example, a partner might be driving negligently the motor car of the partnership on partnership business and it would be desirable in those circumstances that not only he but also his partners should be liable to the same extent as he was to an injured person.   Similarly, a partner might be guilty of fraudulent misrepresentation, causing damage, in the course of the partnership business.   Moreover, since no partner is the servant or employee of any other partner, or of the partnership, merely by reason of the existence of the partnership relationship, the ordinary doctrine of *respondeat superior* does not apply to render liable the other partners; but this provision (*i.e.* section 10) produces, as I see it, an equation, for the purpose which I have just referred to as ' necessary,' of members of a partnership firm with employers.   Then since under the well known doctrine expressed in particular in *Wilsons & Clyde Coal Co. Ltd.* v. *English* [36] there are certain personal duties and obligations which an employer owes to his workmen, so, where workmen are the employees of a partnership firm, there might be under section 10, over and above the ground of liability on the footing of *respondeat superior*, a liability of the individual partners, if some personal duty to a workman were not to be performed.   Furthermore, any partner may be liable for any personal tort.   Thus a contrast can be seen between liability falling directly on a man who is a partner in a partnership firm and liability falling on him because he is an employer or principal whose employee or workman or agent has done a tortious act.   In my judgment, section 10 of the Partnership Act 1890 deals only with such secondary liability as the liability of one for the act of another who is acting in the course of his employment or as agent for him; as I have expressed it, it equates the position of a partner in those respects with that of an employer or principal."

Since in the case before him Winn J. was concerned to distinguish the vicarious, or, as he terms it, " secondary," liability of the firm from the direct liability of a partner for his own wrongful act, he has confined his analysis to making this broad contrast.   Even so, his analysis is helpful as a reminder that section 10 of the Partnership Act 1890 is not exhaustive on the question of the liability of the partners.   In England where the firm has no separate *persona*, and where the liability of the partnership for the tort of a partner is imposed upon his copartners, it is easy to see why Winn J. was so pre-occupied with the broad distinction which he made as to the effect of section 10, since that section may create a situation within the partnership where *all* the partners become liable for the tort of one partner but does not displace the operation of the common law under which one, or some, of the members of the partnership may be held directly liable for a wrongful act committed at the hand of one of them, while section 10 may be ineffective to impose a " secondary " or vicarious liability upon all of

[36] 1937 S.C.(H.L.) 46.

them, because some element in the composition of the wrongful act, such as malice, is not present in the persons of *all*, as distinct from *some*, of the partners. That analysis holds good with equal force in Scots law where the vicarious liability under section 10 is imposed upon the firm but in view of the introduction of this *quasi* person in Scots law, it will be necessary to carry the analysis of section 10 a stage further than Winn J. found necessary, or indeed relevant, in *Meekins* v. *Henson*; for section 10 deals not only with the vicarious liability of the firm in Scots law for the wrongful act of one of its partners " acting in the ordinary course of the business of the firm " but also for what it has been submitted [37] is the *direct* liability of the firm where the wrongful act has been committed " with the authority of his copartners." In the latter situation, the introduction of the firm as a separate person, while generally regarded as a more realistic approach to the legal problems of partnership, yet involves the Scots lawyer in a close examination of what may be taken to be " the authority of his copartners " so as to impose direct liability upon the firm on the principle *qui facit per alium facit per se*. In many cases involving the delict of a partner, the authorisation of the wrongful act or of the negligent course of conduct will clearly infer direct liability for the consequences thereof; but where a variable personal factor, such as malice, is a necessary component in the delict, then authorisation of the act itself by a partner, against whom that component of malice cannot be established, will not necessarily be regarded as " authority " for the wrongful act so as to render the firm liable under section 10; and the possibility of the firm itself being held liable will not, it is thought, preclude a Scottish court from arriving in appropriate circumstances at the same decision as was reached by Winn J. in *Meekins* v. *Henson*.

Liability for the wilful wrong of a partner

It has been held in England that a wilful wrongful act of a partner does not as a rule impose liability upon his firm.[38] It is difficult to maintain that proposition in the face of the express terms of section 10 of the Partnership Act 1890, " by any wrongful act or omission of any partner," which appear wide enough to embrace all wrongful acts whether wilful or not and in addition unwitting acts of negligence or omission. Even in the decisions reported before the passing of the Partnership Act 1890 it was recognised that a wilful tort committed by a partner in the course of transacting the business of the firm would impose liability on the firm,[39] and the test whether the act, albeit a wrongful means of doing so, was designed to accomplish something which in the ordinary course of the firm's business it was sought to accomplish, was also applied before the passing of the Partnership Act. Thus Clark regards as applicable in partnership the principle in *Keith* v. *Keir*,[40] a master and servant case, in which the master

[37] *Supra* p. 308.
[38] Lindley, *op. cit.* p. 188.
[39] *Limpus* v. *London General Omnibus Co.* (1861) 1 H. & C. 526.
[40] June 10, 1812, F.C. See also *Hill* v. *Merricks* (1813) Hume 397.

instructed his servants to clear part of his own property of timber. In
doing so the servants set fire to the timber and the fire spread to timber
growing on the property of an adjoining proprietor. The master was held
liable.[41] Since the passing of the Partnership Act 1890 the same test has
been applied in partnership cases. In *Hamlyn* v. *John Houston & Company* [42] where it was part of the firm's business to obtain information by
lawful means concerning the contracts made by competitors of the firm,
one of the partners bribed a clerk of a competing business in order to
obtain the information. The firm was held liable in damages.[43] Both
before and after the passing of the Partnership Act 1890 the firm has been
held liable in damages for defamation or slander by one of its partners if
occurring within the course of conducting the ordinary business o the
firm.[44] It is probable that the problems apparently arising as to "wilful
torts " of a partner are more problems of semantics than of law, and that,
in using the expression, the intention is not to contrast wrongful acts which
are deliberate with those which are inadvertent but rather to contrast
wrongs which arise from the conduct of the partner as an individual from
those which he commits in the ordinary course of and within the relevance
of the firm's business. If that be so, then the rule advanced as to the
" wilful " tort of the partner, interpreted in that sense, may be read consistently along with section 10 of the Partnership Act 1890 and indeed adds
little to the terms of that section, save in one particular. It is perhaps significant that the example given by Lindley [45] of the application of the rule
is of malicious prosecution by a partner of a third party on a charge of
stealing partnership property. In that case the firm is not answerable in
damages unless all the copartners are privy to the malicious prosecution.[46]
It may be that the rule, therefore, is no more than an alternative, and perhaps slightly inadequate, statement of the proposition which may be
derived from *Meekins* v. *Henson*,[47] namely, that section 10 is not exhaustive
of the cases in which liability may fall upon the partners of a firm for the
wrongful acts of a copartner and that where an element such as malice is
a component part of the delict there may be vicarious liability within the
partnership imposed upon some of its members against whom malice can
be established while in the case of others of the partners against whom
malice cannot be established, these will not be vicariously liable. The
occurrence of differing degrees of vicarious liability within the partnership
is more in accord with the principles of English law founding upon the
theory that each partner is the agent of his copartners. In Scotland, it
would be more in line with the principles of the common law to regard
each partner as an agent of the firm, his copartners being liable as secondary

[41] Clark, *op. cit.* I, p. 263.
[42] [1903] 1 K.B. 81.
[43] See also *Janvier* v. *Sweeney* [1919] 2 K.B. 316.
[44] *Gordon* v. *British & Foreign Metaline Co.* (1886) 14 R. 75; *Citizens Life Assurance Co.* v. *Brown* [1904] A.C. 423; *Wright* v. *Outram & Co.* (1890) 17 R. 596.
[45] *Op. cit.* p. 188.
[46] *Arbuckle* v. *Taylor* (1815) 3 Dow 160.
[47] [1962] 1 All E.R. 899; and see *supra* pp. 308–311.

obligants, or cautioners for the firm, in which case the difficulty above noticed would not arise.[48] But it appears probable that the principle of mutual agency among the partners themselves has now been introduced into Scots law by the opening words of section 5 of the Partnership Act 1890,—" Every partner is an agent of the firm *and his other partners* . . . ," so that differing liability may conceivably arise within a Scots partnership also. Nor is that possibility removed merely on the ground that the firm itself is in Scotland the person on whom vicarious liability is imposed, the partners, though liable jointly and severally, being so liable only under the accessory obligation of cautionry which they undertake for their firm [49]; for the vicarious liability which is under consideration in such cases as are being here examined is not the vicarious liability of the firm for its partner under section 10, but the vicarious liability of a principal for his agent at common law which arises from the existence of a mutual agency among the partners.[50]

Liability for penalty

Section 10 of the Partnership Act 1890 imposes vicarious liability on the firm not only for the loss or injury caused to a third party by the wrongful act or omission of a partner but also for " any penalty " if incurred. There are a number of English decisions which even before the passing of the Act laid down the rule that where a partner in conducting the partnership business infringes the revenue laws so as to incur a penalty, that penalty may be imposed upon the firm and his copartners even though they may not have given authority for, or been parties to, the offence committed by that partner.[51] Though no case appears to have been reported where a firm has been held liable in penalty consequent upon a fraudulent return made by one of its partners of the income of the partnership, it is thought that on the analogy of the cases cited immediately above, the firm and its partners would all be held liable. The income tax in respect of any trade or profession carried on by two or more persons jointly is computed and stated jointly and independently of any other tax chargeable upon them, a joint assessment being made in the partnership name.[52] The partners may claim their tax relief according to their respective shares and interests in

---

[48] Nor the other difficulty adumbrated in Lindley's original commentary on the Partnership Act 1890 as to liability in a case where one partner in the ordinary course of the firm's business makes a statement which he believes to be true but which his copartners know to be false.—*Supplement to the Law of Partnership* (published 1891) p. 34.

[49] Walker, *Delict*, p. 139; Bell, *Prin.* § 356; *Comm.* II, 508; *Gordon* v. *British & Foreign Metaline Co.* (1886) 14 R. 75; *Mair* v. *Wood*, 1948 S.C. 83 at p. 89.

[50] It is doubtful whether s. 46 of the Partnership Act 1890 assists in restricting the effect of s. 5 upon the former common law of Scotland. S. 46 saves the rules of the common law " applicable to partnership except so far as they are inconsistent with the express provisions of this Act." It can be argued (1) that s. 5 *is* inconsistent with the former Scots law of partnership, though (2) while the rule displaced by s. 5 is, properly regarded, one of agency and not one of partnership, it would still come within the terms of s. 46 because as a rule of agency it was " applicable to partnership."

[51] *R.* v. *Stranyforth* (1721) Bunb. 97; *Att.-Gen.* v. *Burges* (1726) Bunb. 223; *Att.-Gen.* v. *Weeks* (1726) Bunb. 223; *R.* v. *Manning* (1739) 2 Comyns 616.

[52] Income and Corporation Taxes Act 1970, s. 152.

the partnership, " and any such claims which are proved may be dealt with
in the same manner as in the case of several interests." [53]   The effect of
those provisions is that the partnership, both in England and in Scotland,
is treated for tax purposes as if it were a legal person distinct from the
partners, although under English law it is not so regarded for other purposes, and the tax assessed is a liability of the partnership which is joint
but not several.[54]   In the Taxes Management Act 1970 [55] it is provided that,
in the case of incorrect returns, whether fraudulently or negligently made,
a penalty may be imposed not exceeding the aggregate of £50 and the
amount of the difference between (a) the amount [56] of income tax and
capital gains tax actually payable and (b) the amount which would have
been payable on the basis of the incorrect return.   That penalty is imposed
on the person making the return.   There is express provision for imposing
the penalty for an incorrect return made by a company upon the company
itself,[57] but for this purpose " company " does not include a partnership.[58]
Nevertheless, in Scotland at least, the firm is a separate person at law and
since under section 10 of the Partnership Act 1890 the liability for any
penalty incurred is imposed upon the firm where the penalty has been incurred in respect of the wrongful act or omission of any partner " acting
in the ordinary course of the business of the firm," there would appear to
be a liability on the firm for the penalty imposed in respect of an incorrect
return for tax purposes.   The return of the profits of the firm is the responsibility of the " precedent partner " and is made by him on behalf of his
copartners and himself, whereas the individual partners all make separate
returns, each of his own income, in which allowances are claimed.[58a]   It
would appear, therefore, that in claiming allowances and reliefs, each individual partner is acting on his own behalf and not in the ordinary course
of the business of the firm, though in making the return of profits of the
firm the precedent partner is acting in the ordinary course of the firm's
business and his copartners may be involved along with him in liability
for penalty in the event of a false return.[59]

In regard to penalties imposed under the Truck Acts it is expressly
provided [60]—

> " No person shall be liable to be convicted of any offence against
> this Act, committed by his or her copartner in trade and without his
> or her knowledge, privity or consent; but it shall be lawful when any

[53] Income and Corporation Taxes Act 1970, s. 26.
[54] *Stevens* v. *Britten* [1954] 3 All E.R. 385; but *cf. Harrison* v. *Willis Brothers* [1965] 1 All E.R.
583; [1965] 3 All E.R. 753.
[55] s. 95.
[56] In the case of fraud, twice that amount.
[57] Taxes Management Act 1970, s. 96.
[58] *Ibid.* s. 118 (1); Income and Corporation Taxes Act 1970, s. 526 (5).
[58a] Taxes Management Act 1970, s. 9.
[59] In *Miles* v. *Finlay & Co.* (1830) 9 S. 18, the court held that a petition and complaint that a
firm and its cashier and clerk had issued unstamped cheques or notes and had thus incurred
penalties under the Act 5 Geo. 3, c. 49, ss. 3 and 7, was incompetent so far as directed
against the firm.   This decision does not appear to have been in mind when the effect of
s. 10 of the Partnership Act 1890 on the pre-existing Scots law was under consideration.
[60] Truck Act 1831 s. 13.

penalty, or any sum for wages, or any other sum is ordered to be paid
under the authority of this Act, and the person or persons ordered to
pay the same shall neglect or refuse to do so, to levy the same by distress
and sale of any goods belonging to any copartnership, concern or
business in the carrying on of which such charges may have become
due or such offence may have been committed; and in all proceedings
under this Act to recover any sum for wages it shall be lawful in all
cases of copartnership for the justices, at the hearing of any complaint
for the non-payment thereof, to make an order upon any one or more
copartners for the payment of the sum appearing to be due; and in
such case the service of a copy of any summons or other process, or of
any order, upon one or more of such copartners shall be deemed to
be a sufficient service upon all."

This section is not entirely consistent with section 10 of the Partnership
Act 1890 although in some cases the results achieved by it will be indistinguishable from those under section 10, *i.e.* the monetary penalty imposed for the infringement may be exacted from the firm and the other
partners though they did not authorise the infringement and though they
were not parties to it.   The formula employed in section 10 of the Partnership Act 1890, however, goes further than that used in section 13 of the
Truck Act 1831; for, under the Partnership Act, it is thought that section
10 imposes vicarious liability on the firm for the infringement itself and thus
the firm may be charged with the offence along with the offending partner,[61]
whereas under section 13 of the Truck Act 1831 the possibility of conviction of any partner who is not a consenting party to the offence is expressly
excluded,[62] though on default by the offending partner in paying the
penalty imposed on conviction the property of the partnership may be
subjected to diligence for recovery of that penalty.   The question thus
arises—does the wider formula employed in section 10 of the Partnership
Act 1890 extend the liability for the offence so that the firm itself may be
charged with it?   The point has not been the subject of any reported decision since the passing of the Partnership Act, but it is thought that section
10 would be powerless to attain such a result in view of the express and
restrictive terms of section 13 of the Truck Act 1831.   In general terms the
doctrine of vicarious responsibility with which section 10 is concerned has
no place in the criminal law of Scotland.[63]   Generally, in cases where it is
sought to charge the firm vicariously with an offence, it will be necessary
to show that *mens rea* is not a concomitant part of the offence charged.
Where the offence is a statutory one the express words of the statute will
frequently impose vicarious responsibility either expressly or by implication; *e.g.* in contrast to section 13 of the Truck Act 1831, the Truck Amendment Act 1887 provides [64]—

[61] ". . . the firm is liable therefor *to the same extent* as the partner as acting or omitting to
    act "—Partnership Act 1890, s. 10 (italics supplied).
[62] See *Finlayson* v. *Braidbar Quarry Company and Others* (1864) 2 M. 1297.
[63] *Gair* v. *Brewster*, 1916 S.C.(J.) 36, *per* the Lord Justice-General (Strathclyde) at p. 38.
[64] s. 6.

> " No employer shall, directly or indirectly, by himself or his agent, impose as a condition, express or implied, in or for the employment of any workman any terms or conditions as to the place at which, or the manner in which, or the person with whom any wages or portion of wages paid to the workman are or is to be expended. . . ."

The vicarious liability for the offence is there expressly provided for as it is also in other statutes such as the Licensing (Scotland) Act 1959.[65] Again the creation of the statutory offence may give rise to an implication of a vicarious responsibility for its commission.

> " If a trader is, in virtue of statutory restrictions, allowed to carry on his trade only under certain conditions, the trader is, in my opinion, answerable for any breach of those conditions committed in the course of his trade. A breach is none the less committed in the course of *his* trade because the actual delinquent is a servant or other person acting within the authority committed to him by the trader." [66]

The relevance of that dictum to the case of a partnership is apparent but its application depends upon the wording creating the statutory offence itself and not upon any general principle of vicarious guilt which may be thought to be discernible in section 10 of the Partnership Act 1890. Although the concluding words of that section are widely expressed in very general terms—" Where . . . any penalty is incurred, the firm is liable therefor to the same extent as the partner so acting or omitting to act "—it is thought that these words are not strong enough to bear the construction that in any case where a partner has committed a statutory offence in the course of conducting the firm's business the firm itself may be charged along with the delinquent partner. It is significant that the wording of the section renders the firm liable " therefor," *i.e.* for the penalty and not for the offence which occasioned that penalty. In certain statutory offences such vicarious guilt will be provided for expressly or by implication when the words in section 10 add nothing to the legal nature of the offence. But if the section were construed as postulating an overriding principle of vicarious guilt of the partnership for the partner's offence, that would be impossible to reconcile with cases where the possibility of conviction on grounds of vicarious liability has been expressly precluded in terms of the statute creating the offence [67] and would co-exist uneasily with statutory provisions creating an offence in the construction of which there is no room for the assertion that the concomitant of *mens rea* is unnecessary in the commission of the offence.

If these views are well founded, it remains to discover what construction must then be placed upon the words of section 10 of the Partnership Act 1890 in regard to the liability of the firm for a " penalty " incurred as a

[65] See ss. 121, 139, 142 and 150.
[66] *Per* the Lord Justice-General (Clyde) in *Bean* v. *Sinclair*, 1930 J.C. 31 at p. 36. But *cf. City & Suburban Dairies* v. *Mackenna*; *Scottish Farmers' Dairy Co.* v. *Mackenna*, 1918 J.C. 105.
[67] *e.g.* Truck Act 1831, s. 13.

result of the wrongful act or omission of one of its partners. It was probably the intention of those who framed the provisions of the Act to go no
further than to impose on the firm pecuniary liability for the penalty incurred by the partner should the latter neglect, or refuse, or be unable, to
pay. Even that construction goes beyond what has been regarded by most
writers as the scope of section 10 which has almost uniformly been regarded
as confined to an expression of the firm's vicarious liability in the case of
delict or tort.[68] Of those writers, Lindley alone appears to have given any
thought to the implications of the words " or any penalty is incurred " in
section 10 and his treatment of the question is confined to the statement
that where in the conduct of the firm's business one partner is guilty of a
breach of the revenue laws, all the partners are jointly and severally answerable for the consequent penalties though they have not themselves authorised or been parties to the infringement [69]; and his statement of the law is
not based on any detailed consideration of section 10 but on a number of
decisions prior to the passing of the Act. While too much may be read
into the use of the word " penalty " in the section, it is difficult to account
for the intrusion into the section at all unless it is intended to impose on
the firm a vicarious liability in two distinct cases (a) where the partner's
wrongful conduct causes loss or injury to a third party and thus gives rise
to a claim for damages and (b) where his wrongful conduct involves an
offence for which a penalty may be exacted. It is a trifle difficult to
explain why the vicarious responsibility under (b) should have been provided for, particularly under a section the side-note of which reads
" Liability of the firm for wrongs." If, as appears possible, it was intended, however inelegantly, to cover the earlier English decisions as to
breach by a partner of the revenue laws [70] and the liability of a guardian
of the poor where his partner sold goods furnished for purposes of parish
relief,[71] then if it has been effective for that purpose, the pre-statute law of
Scotland may have been amended or at least modified without the fact
having been noticed at the time.[72]

Liability for fraud

The terms of section 10 of the Partnership Act 1890 are in themselves
sufficient to impose liability on the firm for frauds committed by one of the
partners while conducting the ordinary course of the business of the firm
and even though the other partners are themselves innocent of the fraud
committed, they cannot escape liability on the ground that they did not
authorise their partner to perpetrate the fraud or indeed that they were

---

[68] See e.g. Lindley, op. cit. pp. 187–188; Underhill, Principles of the Law of Partnership
(9th ed.) pp. 62 et seq.; Fridman, Law of Agency (3rd ed.) p. 281; see also Mr. Robertson
Christie's article in Green's Encyclopaedia of the Law of Scotland, Vol. 11, sub voce Partnership, para. 91, where, however, the words " or any penalty is incurred " are omitted from
the text of s. 10 as quoted by him.
[69] Lindley, op. cit. p. 188.
[70] Supra n. 51.
[71] Davies v. Harvey (1874) L.R. 9 Q.B. 433.
[72] Miles v. Finlay & Co. (1830) 9 S. 18; and see supra n. 59.

entirely unaware that it had been perpetrated. Section 10 provides for a
general liability of a vicarious nature on the part of the firm in respect of
wrongful acts or omissions of its partners in the ordinary course of its
business and there is no distinction to be drawn between fraud and any
other wrongful act which the partner may commit.[73] This view has prevailed after considerable fluctuation of judicial opinion on the general
question whether an action for damages may be brought against the principal for a fraud perpetrated by his agent in the course of his employment.[74]
That fluctuation in opinion which was occasioned by the dilemma,
that, while the elements required to establish a case of fraud are such
that it is difficult to hold a person liable for fraud unless he has actually perpetrated it, it is equally difficult to make any meaningful distinction between
a fraud and any other wrong which an agent may commit, has now for a
long time been resolved. An action will lie against the principal if the
fraud of the agent has been committed in the course of his employment [75]
but no action will lie against the principal if the fraud was not committed
within the agent's course of employment.[76]

The general principle thus arrived at in the law of agency is such that it
is aptly covered for the purposes of the law of partnership by the general
words of section 10.[77] Fraud, however, is a compendious term and its
manifestations may occur under a variety of circumstances. Among those
circumstances the Partnership Act 1890 has selected frauds involving the
misapplication of money or property for special treatment,[78] and in these
special circumstances special rules have been devised as to the liability of
the firm and its partners for the fraud of any one member. These will be
considered later. At this stage the effect of the more generalised statement of section 10 will alone be considered in so far as it may be invoked
in a case in which the fraud of an individual partner is alleged. It is
thought, however, that the terms of section 10 do not impose a liability on
the firm for a fraudulent representation made by a partner as to the
" character, conduct, credit, ability, trade or dealings " of any person unless
made in writing and subscribed by the person making the representation,
i.e. the firm or by some person duly authorised by that person.[79] In
England where the matter is governed by the Statute of Frauds Amendment Act 1828, s. 6, the representation must not only be in writing but

---

[73] *Mackay* v. *Commercial Bank of New Brunswick* (1874) L.R. 5 P.C. 412.
[74] *Barwick* v. *English Joint Stock Bank* (1867) L.R. 2 Ex. 259; *Weir* v. *Bell* (1878) 3 Ex.D.
   238; *Swire* v. *Francis* (1877) 3 App.Cas. 106; *Houldsworth* v. *City of Glasgow Bank* (1880)
   7 R.(H.L.) 53; *Mackay* v. *Commercial Bank of New Brunswick, supra* n. 73; *Addie* v.
   Western Bank of Scotland (1867) 5 M.(H.L.) 80.
[75] *Pearson & Son Ltd.* v. *Dublin Corporation* [1907] A.C. 351; *Lloyd* v. *Grace, Smith & Co.*
   [1912] A.C. 716.
[76] *British Mutual Bank Co.* v. *Charnwood Forest Ry.* (1887) 18 Q.B.D. 714; *Ruben* v. *Great
   Fingall Consolidated* [1906] A.C. 439.
[77] Lindley in the commentary attached to s. 10 in his *Supplement to Lindley on Partnership*
   (1891) p. 34 accepted that view though contenting himself with stating as to the law in
   agency generally that while the general law had not been so conveniently declared it was
   " the better opinion that a firm is liable in an action of damages for the fraud of any agent,
   whether a partner or not, acting within the limits of his authority."
[78] s. 11.
[79] Mercantile Law Amendment (Scotland) Act 1856, s. 5.

must also be signed by all the partners and the signature of one partner will bind no one but himself.[80]   In Scotland that additional requirement is not imposed and the signature of the firm name by one of its partners will render the firm liable.   It seems clear, however, that in spite of the wide terms of section 10 of the Partnership Act 1890, the firm will only be liable if the representation is in writing and bears to be made in the name of the firm.[81]

The nature of fraud

Even when fraud is considered in relation to a partnership after excluding the special problems attendant upon the misapplication of money or property by a partner, there are aspects which present difficulty of a more general kind.   These arise from the fact that fraud by its very nature involves an assessment of the conduct of an individual.   That conduct must involve his making a representation which is false and is known by the person making it to be false, or is false and is made by that person recklessly and without in fact any real belief that the statement which he makes is true.[82]   When several persons are joined in an association such as a partnership, there is no room for ascribing to the conduct of any one of them an element of, as it were, *constructive* fraud in which the fraudulent element in his conduct is derived from the knowledge not of himself but of his partners of the true facts which make his statement a misrepresentation. This aspect which might be regarded as in a sense the converse of the situation legislated for in section 10 caused Lindley difficulty on his first consideration of the effect of section 10 of the Partnership Act 1890.   " A difficult question of liability in an action for damages may still arise," he wrote,[83] " if one partner in the ordinary course of the business of the firm makes a statement which he bona fide believes to be true but which his co-partners know to be false."   So far as the general law of agency is concerned that difficulty is removed by the case of *Armstrong* v. *Strain* [84] where an owner of a bungalow, in the knowledge of defects in its foundations, instructed agents to effect a sale of the bungalow.   The agents, in ignorance of the true state of affairs, innocently misrepresented the condition of the bungalow to the plaintiff thereby inducing him to purchase it. It was held that the knowledge of the owner could not be combined with the statement of the agents to establish a constructive fraud on the part of the owner.   That decision, however, does not exhaust the possibilities to be considered in the relation of partnership.   The association among the individual partners is a more closely knit one than that existing between principal and agent and in Scotland confers on the partnership itself a *quasi*-personality in law.   Even in England where the firm is not recognised as a person distinct from the individual members of the firm, it has been

[80] Lindley, *op. cit.* p. 192 and cases there cited.
[81] See *Keen* v. *Mear* [1920] 2 Ch. 574.
[82] *Derry* v. *Peek* (1889) 14 App.Cas. 337.
[83] *Supplement to Lindley on Partnership* (1891) p. 34.
[84] [1952] 1 K.B. 232.

recognised that the peculiarly close and continuing association among the partners will not permit of the decision in *Armstrong* v. *Strain* being applied to its full effect in every case. Thus it is suggested by Singleton L.J.[85] that where a partner who is ignorant of the adverse features is also reckless in not consulting with his copartners before making the representation, that will amount to a fraudulent misrepresentation by the firm. If a partner who is aware of the true facts authorises his copartner who is unaware of them to make the false statement, then the authorising partner is himself clearly answerable in fraud, but it has been stated that his conduct would also amount to fraud by the firm,[86] and that if a partner who is aware of the facts deliberately stands aside in the knowledge, expectation or hope that his copartner, who is unaware of the facts, will, albeit innocently, falsely represent the situation, that will be imputed as a fraud to the firm.[87] It is thought that there may be difficulty in reconciling these views with the decision in *Meekins* v. *Henson* [88] in which Winn J. appears to distinguish within the partnership differing degrees of responsibility among individual partners for the wrong done. In that case Winn J. was concerned with the question whether there was malice sufficient to render the firm liable for a defamatory statement made on a privileged occasion and his reasoning may therefore not be entirely applicable to cases of fraud of the kind now considered. Yet the analysis which he makes is closely concerned with the position of one partner who, though himself actuated by malice, does not himself publish the defamatory material but stands by in the knowledge that it will be published by his copartner, and in the result he held that each of the three partners of the firm had his own individual state of knowledge of the defamatory publication and that it should be regarded as a publication by each partner, but that since malice had been established against one of these partners only, liability in damages attached to him alone. The implications of that decision are interesting because it proceeds upon the premiss which is recognised and expressed by Winn J. that in order to set up a personal liability which arises from a duty owed by a partner personally or from an act in which he was actively involved, the person injured need not rely on section 10 of the Partnership Act 1890, even where the act was done by the hand of his copartner. There is no great difficulty in accepting that proposition. Section 10 deals with the vicarious responsibility of a firm for the wrongful acts of a partner. Thus it involves, in England directly, and in Scotland inferentially under section 4 (2) of the Partnership Act, that each copartner is himself liable in damages for the wrong committed; but it does not follow that section 10 exhausts the cases in which the association among the partners may give rise to a liability upon the part of one of them for an act committed by the

[85] *Armstrong* v. *Strain* [1952] 1 K.B. 232 at p. 244. See, however, *Traill* v. *Fernie and Others* (1876) 3 R. 770, where it was held that a principal could not benefit from the fraud of his agent.
[86] Lindley, *op. cit.* p. 190, citing *London County etc. Properties Ltd.* v. *Berkeley Property etc. Co. Ltd.* [1936] 2 All E.R. 1039.
[87] *Ludgater* v. *Love* (1881) 44 L.T. 694.
[88] [1962] 1 All E.R. 899, discussed *supra* pp. 308 *et seq.*

hand of another of them.   The real difficulty involved in carrying that
proposition to its logical conclusion lies in the differing degrees of responsibility which may be created within the firm among the individual partners
for an act done in the ordinary course of the business of the firm.   If the
legal quality of that responsibility is to vary from partner to partner on an
assessment of his personal attitude to and knowledge of circumstances
affecting the commission of the act, then that doctrine would, it seems, go
some way towards destroying the views expressed in earlier English cases
and endorsed by Lindley as to the imputation of a fraud committed at the
instance of an innocent partner where another partner in full knowledge
of the facts has either actively authorised the act or passively encouraged
its commission.   It may be doubted whether the difficulty foreseen by
Lindley originally upon his examination of the terms of section 10 [89] has
been entirely removed by the views expressed in the latest edition of his
treatise,[90] and in Scotland, where a suitable case for decision on the point
does not yet appear to have been before the court, the view which may commend itself is not easy to forecast.   The opinion may be ventured that on
balance the Scottish courts may favour the views expressed in *London
County Freehold and Leasehold Properties Ltd.* v. *Berkeley Property Investment Co. Ltd.*[91] and *Ludgater* v. *Love* [92] on considerations (a) of the general
purpose and intent of section 10 of the Partnership Act 1890 and (b) of the
difficulty of reconciling the Scottish theory of the independent *quasi persona*
of the firm with varying degrees of vicarious responsibility of the individual
partners.   The latter point, however, is not entirely satisfactory because it
appears from a reading of the judgment in *Meekins* v. *Henson* that Winn J.
was not in fact concerned with vicarious but with direct responsibility of
the partners or some of them.

   In some of the earlier Scottish decisions fraudulent misrepresentation
by one or more of the partners has been imputed to the partnership.[93]
The attitude of the Scots law to questions of fraud committed by a partner
is perhaps more clearly referred to in *Thomson* v. *Pattison, Elder & Company* [94] a case in which it was held that it is incompetent to sue a firm for
damages on the ground of fraud, unless the names of the partners alleged
to have committed the fraud are specified.   The case as presented was
otherwise lacking in specification and after a debate on the relevancy the
action was dismissed.   The Lord President (Robertson) in the course of
his judgment said:

   " Fraud is a personal matter and can only be committed by an individual.   It is true that others than individuals may become liable for
   the frauds of individuals, but that does not affect the essentially personal nature of the act giving rise to the liability.   Now, this record

[89] *Supra* p. 313 n. 48.
[90] *Op. cit.* pp. 189–190.
[91] [1936] 2 All E.R. 1039.
[92] (1881) 44 L.T. 694.
[93] *e.g. Jardine's Trs.* v. *Carron Co.* (1864) 2 M. 1101.
[94] (1895) 22 R. 432.

does not allege the acts complained of against any individual at all. Accordingly, it is not by a mere euphemism that this case differs from and falls short of a case of fraud. Had the pursuer said that such a conspiracy had been entered into by someone named, one of the partners of Pattison, Elder & Company, I could quite understand the firm being concluded against, as being liable for a fraud committed by a partner in the region of his mandate. But on this record the basis of such a case is awanting." [95]

It is thought that these words of the Lord President, although *obiter dicta*, go some way towards dispelling the difficulty which has been under discussion and suggesting the attitude which the Scottish courts may adopt. Fraud is a " personal matter " in the sense that, for its perpetration, it depends upon the actions and the mental state of an individual. When it is committed, however, by an individual whose position is reasonably regarded as entitling him to bind another or others by his actions, as a partner, his firm, then the fraud is imputed to his firm even where the other members of the firm were not parties to that fraud. If that be so, and it has never been seriously doubted, then the fraud involved in a partner with the material knowledge either authorising or standing by and permitting a copartner innocently to make a misrepresentation is nonetheless fraudulent on the part of the partner with the material knowledge. It is, of course, " personal " to him in that it is in his individual personality that the concomitants of the fraud are lodged in his person. But by his conduct he has nonetheless committed a wrongful act in the ordinary course of the firm's business and the firm is liable for it under section 10 of the Partnership Act 1890.

Untrue statements as to partner's authority or as to the nature and extent of the firm's business [96]

An apparent inconsistency arises in the rule that if a partner who is apparently acting beyond the limits of his authority falsely represents that he is acting with the consent of his copartners, they and the firm are not bound by that representation.[97] The inconsistency is, however, more apparent than real. If the partner has been acting beyond the limits of his apparent authority, it cannot be said that he has been acting in the ordinary course of the business of the firm and therefore the basis of vicarious liability under section 10 is destroyed. The same may be true of the case where a partner makes misrepresentations as to the nature of the business of the firm or that it is more extensive than it really is, where Lindley [98] holds the view, though it is unsupported by judicial authority, that the firm and his copartners will not be answerable for the misrepresentation. But this case, like the former one, has really little to do with the terms of section 10

---

[95] *Ibid.* at pp. 436–437.
[96] See *supra* Chap. VII, pp. 252–254.
[97] *Ex p. Agace* (1792) 2 Cox 312.
[98] *Op. cit.* p. 193.

of the Partnership Act 1890. It is possible to describe the partner's act as a wrongful one but the measure of liability in respect of it arises rather under section 5 than for tort and delict under section 10. The delinquent partner is in fact in breach of his warranty of authority and that ground of action can only give rise to an award of damages against him personally. Section 10 is, however, concerned with an entirely separate issue, though one which, in Scotland at least, is bound up with the notion of the firm as a person distinct from the individual partners comprising it. Since the firm so regarded is an artificial person, the acts ascribed to it are of necessity the acts of individuals who carry on activities as the hand of the firm. This has a direct bearing upon the responsibilities of the firm for the fraudulent misrepresentations of one of its partners who may properly be regarded as the hand of the firm itself in the transactions affected, *i.e.* where he is acting in the ordinary course of the business of the firm, as it is expressed in section 10. The point is clearly brought out in the judgment of the Lord Chancellor (Lord Cranworth) in *National Exchange Company* v. *Drew and Dick* [99]—

> " The company, as an abstract thing, can represent and do nothing. It can only act by its managers. When, therefore, the directors, in the discharge of their duty, fraudulently . . . for the purpose of misleading others as to the state of the concerns of the company, represent the company to be in a different state from that in which they know it to be, and the persons to whom the representation is addressed act upon it in the belief that it is true, I cannot think that society can go on without treating that as a misrepresentation by the company. Otherwise companies of this sort would be in this extraordinary predicament —that they might employ, nay must employ, agents to carry on their concerns, and that those agents might make representations, be they ever so false and ever so fraudulent, and yet, nevertheless, that the company might and must benefit by those misrepresentations without being at all liable to be told, that is your fraud."

Fraud or breach of fiduciary duty committed with the knowledge of the co-partners

Where a fraudulent misrepresentation is made by one partner as to the affairs of the firm and his copartners are aware both that he has made the misrepresentation and that it is fraudulent, there is of course no need to invoke the principle of vicarious responsibility in order to impose liability on the firm and his copartners. That situation is provided for in section 10 in the words " or with the authority of his copartners " but the liability then imposed is a direct and not a vicarious liability. In cases of fraud, as in cases of other wrongful acts, no person may escape liability merely by permitting another to act wrongfully on his behalf. *Qui facit per alium facit per se.* It is to be observed, however, that the doctrine in partnership

[99] (1855) 2 Macq. 103 at pp. 124–125. See also *Jardine's Trustees* v. *Carron Co.* (1864) 2 M. 1101.

cases may be carried further and may affix to the firm the liability for the breach of a fiduciary duty which the individual partner owed to the third party if that duty was undertaken in the affairs of the firm and with the knowledge of his copartners. Thus when a partner, with the knowledge of his firm, accepted a fiduciary position in regard to a limited company in the latter's purchase of a mine and introduced to the limited company a seller from whom commission was paid to his firm, the firm was held liable to repay the commission.[1] The fiduciary duty did not rest upon the firm. It was personal to the partner, but his association with the firm placed the partner in a position where he owed two conflicting duties, one to the limited company of which he was a director and to which he introduced the seller of the mine, and another and directly conflicting duty to his own firm who stood to gain substantially if these particular sellers were success-ful in disposing of their mine to the limited company.[2] That, however, is a situation which, while it may be the ground of a claim against the partner of the firm, does not of itself establish a conclusion for an order against his firm for the return of the commission secretly received from the sellers, and if such an order be sought against the partner personally, it can be answered that he personally received no commission, it being paid to his firm. This point was fully argued before the court who held, however, that the firm was liable to repay the commission. Lord Mure said,[3]

" The circumstance that the question is here raised with the firm of Falkner, Bell & Company and not directly with Mr. Walker [the partner], which is the main distinction I see between this and the case of *Huntington* cannot, in my opinion, be held to make any difference in the application of the general rule, more particularly in a case where, as here, the firm were throughout quite well aware that their leading partner was acting as a director of the [limited] company. The firm, in a question of this description, cannot, in the view I take of it, be in any better position than the partner himself who assumed the fiduciary character, and the general rule has been applied by this Court in the case of a firm of law agents in which the whole Court was consulted. I refer to the case of *Paterson's Trs.*[4] . . . where one of a firm which acted as agents for a trust estate was himself one of the trustees for whom the firm acted, and an objection was on that ground taken to the accounts of the firm. It was not disputed that the objection must have been sustained had the trustee been sole agent for the trust; but it was contended that the objection was obviated by the circumstance that it was not the firm but only one of the partners who had acted as trustee. There was some difference of opinion on the bench, but the great majority of the Court were agreed that the objection was well founded, and disallowed the claim of the firm."

[1] *Falkner, Bell & Co.* v. *Scottish Pacific Coast Mining Co. Ltd.* (1888) 15 R. 290.
[2] *Huntington Copper Co.* v. *Henderson* (1877) 4 R. 294.
[3] *Falkner, Bell & Co.* v. *Scottish Pacific Coast Mining Co. Ltd., supra* at p. 304.
[4] *Lord Gray and Others, Petitioners* (1856) 19 D. 1.

Lord Adam reached the same conclusion. He said,[5]

> " The only remaining question is whether, if Walker was in that position, his firm of Falkner, Bell & Company are bound to repay [the commission]? Upon that question I think we are perfectly within the authority of the case of the *Imperial Mercantile Association* v. *Coleman.*[6] That case decided, and I think quite rightly decided, that where parties in the position of a company are implicated in a breach of trust by one of its partners and take the benefit of that breach of trust, they are just as much bound to repay any sum they may have got in that way as the individual partner whose active agency procured this money."

It is not entirely clear from the decision precisely what circumstances must be present if the firm is to be answerable for the breach of fiduciary duties owed by a partner as an individual. It is essential that the firm, *i.e.* the other partners, should be aware of the fiduciary position occupied by the partner. Both Lord Mure and Lord Adam laid stress on this element in *Falkner, Bell & Company* v. *Scottish Pacific Coast Mining Company Ltd.* and while in the passage quoted from Lord Mure's judgment, the words, " more particularly in a case where, as here, the firm were throughout quite well aware that their leading partner was acting as a director . . ." seem susceptible to a possible interpretation that he considered knowledge not to be essential in every case where the firm might be held answerable, that interpretation is not in accord with Lord Adam's judgment where he clearly restricts the application of the principle to cases where the partnership is implicated in the partner's breach of trust. Lord Mure's qualifying words are insufficient to bear the weight of the argument that they extend the principle to cases where the firm was unaware of the partner's fiduciary position. In the case which he was considering, the knowledge of the firm was clearly established and the better interpretation of the form of words which he used is that he was cautiously avoiding delivering an opinion upon a situation which he was not called upon to decide in the case before him. In all probability that caution arose from the fact that he based his judgment on the decision of the whole court in *Lord Gray and Others, Petitioners.*[7] In that case words were used by some of the judges as to the policy of the rule against a trustee " making a profit " out of his trust.

In *Broughton* v. *Broughton* [8] it was held that if one of the partners of a firm of solicitors is a trustee, his firm cannot claim payment for its services as solicitors to the trust since the disability of one of the partners extends to them all. The Lord Chancellor (Lord Cranworth) criticised the statement of the principle as insufficiently enunciated by saying that a trustee

---

[5] *Falkner, Bell & Co.* v. *Scottish Pacific Coast Mining Co. Ltd., supra* at p. 306.

[6] *Liquidators of the Imperial Mercantile Credit Association* v. *Coleman & Knight* (1871) L.R. 6 H.L. 189.

[7] (1856) 19 D. 1.

[8] (1855) 5 De G.M. & G. 160.

shall not be able " to make a profit of his trust." " The rule really is," Lord Cranworth continued, " that no one who has a duty to perform shall place himself in a situation to have his interests conflicting with that duty; and a case for the application of the rule is that of a trustee himself doing acts which he might employ others to perform, and taking payment in some way for doing them." To disable a firm of which the trustee is a partner from taking payment for its services, apart from reimbursement of out-of-pocket expenses, clearly entails that the fiduciary character of the partner is extended to cover his firm and the extension is justified upon the ground that the " principle and policy " of the rule demand it. On that view certain of the judges in *Lord Gray and Others* founded their judgment.[9] The decision therefore clearly imposes the liability for the fiduciary duty of the partner upon his firm but there is nothing in its facts or in the facts of *Broughton* v. *Broughton* [10] which supports the view that this result will arise if the firm is unaware of the fiduciary character in which the partner acts. In the trustee cases the only authority which the partner can have for instructing his firm to act as solicitors is that he is a trustee in the trust to which they are required to render their services. But in the area of activity covered by trading partnerships it is conceivable that a partner may owe to a third party a fiduciary duty, of which the firm is entirely unaware. If he personally receives financial benefit in breach of that fiduciary duty, it is difficult to see in what sense his firm, who has received nothing and knows nothing of the fiduciary duty or of its breach, may be identified with the partner. Section 10 of the Partnership Act 1890 will impose no liability because the partner's " wrongful act " is neither in the ordinary course of the business of the firm nor is it authorised by his copartners.[11]

Firm receiving benefit from a partner's wrongful act

The cases discussed in the preceding pages have been concerned with the extension of the fiduciary character of the partner to his firm so that the firm may be ordered to repay to the party to whom the partner's fiduciary duty is owed a monetary benefit received by the firm as a result of its partner's breach of that duty. Inevitably, therefore, in these decisions the constant factor is present that the firm has " benefited " by the breach, since the question raised in them of the firm being called upon to " repay " can scarcely arise unless the firm has in the first instance received something which it can be ordered to repay. Cases, however, may be envisaged where the fact of the firm having received some benefit from the partner's wrongful conduct is not directly the consequence of the partner's wrongful act or where the firm has received the benefit innocently and in ignorance of any wrongful act of the partner which may have been in some degree

---

[9] See (1856) 19 D. 1, *per* Lord Wood at pp. 9–10; *per* the Lord Justice-Clerk (Hope) in the conjoined case of *Douglas* v. *Mackenzie* at p. 12.
[10] *Supra* n. 8.
[11] Liability in these cases may be more correctly attributed to implication of the copartners in a partner's breach of trust—Partnership Act 1890, s. 13. See *infra* pp. 358 *et seq.*

the contributing cause of the benefit accruing.   In such cases the terms of
section 10 of the Partnership Act 1890 are no longer a relevant consideration.   The partner's wrongful act which has contributed to the receipt by
the firm of the benefit has not been committed while he was acting in the
ordinary course of the business of the firm nor has it been committed with
the authority of his copartners.   If in any such case liability may be imposed upon the firm, it will be necessary to invoke more general principles
of the common law to substantiate that liability.   Two such principles
exist and may be applied in certain circumstances so as to impute liability
to the firm.   These are—

(1) the principle of following the trust money in the hands of the firm;
and

(2) the principle of recompense by the firm *quantum lucratus*.

The first of these will come into operation when goods or money held in
trust have been misapplied and is therefore considered hereafter when the
terms of section 11 of the Partnership Act 1890 are considered.[12]   The
second is of more general application and may in appropriate cases infer a
liability on the firm even where the partner's wrongful act has not been
committed in the ordinary course of the business of the firm.

Quantum lucratus

This ground of liability rests in Scots law upon a *quasi*-contractual
claim for recompense.   It therefore may be traced to the reception into
our system of law of the Roman law classification of obligations as those
arising *ex contractu, quasi ex contractu, ex maleficio* and *quasi ex maleficio*.[13]
While under the Roman law, the *quasi*-contractual obligation was a rationalised concept of considerable significance within the system, *quasi* contract
as received in the Scottish legal system cannot be said to have the same
significance or indeed to have any very definite meaning at all.   The
classification of obligations in the Roman law was early rejected [14] in
Scotland as misleading but the use of the term " *quasi* contract " has been
retained to describe certain obligations which arise on equitable considerations and are distinguished from an obligation to make reparation for a
wrongful act.[15]   Among the obligations so characterised as *quasi*-con-
tractual is the obligation of recompense under which a person who has
gained by the lawful act of another, performed without any intention to
make a gift to the first person, is in certain circumstances bound to recompense that other person to the extent of his gain (*quantum lucratus*).[16]   It
will be noticed that the attribution of a *quasi*-contractual nature to the
obligation owed at once places that obligation entirely outside the purview
of section 10 of the Partnership Act 1890.   It has no concern with liability

---

[12] *Infra* pp. 339 *et seq.*
[13] Justinian, *Inst.* III, 13.
[14] Stair, I, 3, 2; Bell, *Prin.* § 525; and see *Allen v. McCombie's Trs.*, 1909 S.C. 710.
[15] Gloag, *Contract* (2nd ed.) p. 319.
[16] Bell, *Prin.* § 538, as restricted in its application by the Lord President (Dunedin) in
Edinburgh and District Tramways Co. Ltd. v. Courtenay, 1909 S.C. 99 at p. 105.

or vicarious liability for wrongful acts. On the contrary its classification as a *quasi* contract is intended to stress that the obligation arises on grounds entirely distinct from those of reparation.

While the doctrine of recompense in Scots law gives the appearance of introducing a characteristic feature of Scots, as compared with English, law, the manner in which the doctrine has been developed with regard to equitable considerations has resulted in little difference, save that of terminology, between the two systems of law, at least where the principle has to be applied in the partnership relation. Thus Lindley [17] explains the English law as follows: " If a member of a firm is a director of a company and with the knowledge of his copartner enters into a contract with the company out of which the firm makes a profit, both he and his partner will be liable to account to the company for the whole of such profit unless the director, when he entered into the contract, made a full and sufficient disclosure of his interest therein." It is tempting to regard the principle of English law so stated as solving the problems raised in earlier paragraphs as to the extension of the fiduciary character of the partner to his firm in cases where that fiduciary duty has a bearing also upon the conduct of the ordinary course of the business of the firm, but though the Scottish judgments are not well defined on this point, possibly because they rely to a considerable extent on English authority, they show no clear intention to explain the basis of the firm's liability as that of recompense but rather to associate the firm in liability for the partner's breach of trust or other fiduciary duty; and Lindley himself does not subsume the corresponding English rule, as to the extension of the fiduciary duty to cover the firm, under the statement of principle just quoted, but deals with it as falling under another general principle altogether, *viz.* that what a person has no right to do himself, he cannot acquire right to do by associating others with him.[18] That principle while not entirely adequate to explain the cases which have been examined on the subject, since it is concerned with the position of the individual partner whereas the decisions themselves are concerned with the position of the firm, is at least clearly one which operates within the ambit of reparation for a wrongful act committed by the partner. It does not set up an equitable obligation of recompense for a benefit unjustifiedly obtained at the expense of a third party.

But it is thought that even within the restricted field of the obligation of recompense, the English rule as laid down by Lindley [19] does not go so far as the Scots law has gone in applying the equity of recompense. The point was considered by the Scottish Courts in *New Mining & Exploring Syndicate Limited* v. *Chalmers & Hunter* [20] and though it was not necessary to decide it in order to dispose of the case, the judges uttered observations which are helpful as to the application of the principle. In that case

[17] *Op. cit.* p. 206, citing *Imperial Mercantile Credit Association* v. *Coleman & Knight* (1871) L.R. 6 H.L. 189; *Boardman* v. *Phipps*, [1967] 2 A.C. 46.
[18] *Op. cit.* p. 297, citing *inter alia Broughton* v. *Broughton* (1855) 5 De G.M. & G. 160.
[19] *Supra* n. 18.
[20] 1912 S.C. 126.

Chalmers, while in practice as a solicitor on his own account, was appointed salaried secretary to the syndicate. He then entered into partnership with Hunter under an agreement that each partner should devote his whole time and attention to the business of the firm and that " all fees . . . salaries and other emoluments, payable to either party individually " should be credited to the firm. Chalmers continued thereafter as secretary for some five months after which the firm were appointed secretaries. During Chalmers' tenure of office, entries were made in the firm's book connected with the company's business and Chalmers paid into the current bank account of the firm sums which he received from the public in payment of shares applied for in the company. These totalled £925 of which only £175 was received by the company. On Chalmers later absconding it was found that he had, without the knowledge of the partner, embezzled a considerable sum of money from the company. His partner, Hunter, admitted liability on the part of himself and the firm, for sums embezzled after the date when the firm became secretaries of the company, but denied liability for sums embezzled by Chalmers after the partnership was formed and before he had been replaced as secretary by the firm. The court assoilzied the firm and Hunter from the conclusions as to these last mentioned embezzlements on the ground, which will be later examined, that the money embezzled had not been received by the firm " in the course of its business." [21] The only alternative ground of liability was that of recompense in that the money ultimately embezzled from the company had been entered in the books of the firm and to the credit of the overdrawn current account of the firm. Dealing with this point, Lord Mackenzie said,[22]

" From one point of view it may no doubt be represented that the firm took a gratuitous benefit from these payments to credit of its bank account. At the date of the first of the payments the account was overdrawn to the extent of £2,601–12–7 and the argument is that the amount of the overdraft was extinguished *pro tanto* by the payment in of the £300. If, however, the debit side of the account is examined, it is found that at the close of the banking operations on the 7th of November, the day when the £300 was paid in, so far from the overdraft being diminished, it was increased to the figure of £2,934–14–10. The pursuers, however, say, We have charged you, the firm, with receipt of £300 of the company's money—you do not discharge yourselves of the receipt of that money by merely pointing to the fact that cheques were drawn the same day which *in cumulo* are much more than sufficient to draw out the amount paid in. This in the ordinary case would appear to me to be a formidable argument. I have come, however, to be of the opinion that it is sufficiently met by the evidence led for the defender. It is conclusively proved that Chalmers drew out of the firm's bank account for other than firm purposes sums amounting to £1,840. It is also proved that throughout the whole of the

[21] See Partnership Act 1890, s. 11 (*b*), and *infra* p. 343.
[22] 1912 S.C. 126 at p. 138.

period in question he was in debt to the firm for upwards of £1,000. There is a want of specification about both these items of evidence. When, however, it is said that Chalmers was throughout a debtor to the firm for the amount stated, I think it may fairly be held to mean that he had drawn out by upwards of £1,000 more than he had put in, including in his payments to credit the amount of the pursuers' money. This being the case, it is impossible, in my opinion, to say that the firm took a gratuitous benefit to the extent of the £300. If the succeeding payments are scrutinised in the same way, the same considerations, I think, apply to them."

While the decision in *New Mining & Exploring Syndicate Limited* v. *Chalmers & Hunter* did not impose a liability on the firm in the circumstances of that case, it is implicit in that decision that, if the court had held that the firm derived a gratuitous benefit from the partner's wrongful act, the firm would have been held liable *quantum lucratus*. That is apparent in the reasoning adopted by Lord Mackenzie in the passage from his judgment quoted above and it is emphasised in a later part of his judgment where he expounds the rule that where circumstances exist which suggest that a gratuitous benefit has occurred, the onus rests on the firm to disprove it. " An onus is put on the defender by the pursuers when they prove that money belonging to them was paid into the bank account—the onus being to show that the firm was not enriched thereby." [23]   In the case under consideration, the court considered that the onus had been discharged by the firm.   The case was likened to one where a partner of the firm puts cash into the firm's safe for a limited period and then takes it out again. " The fact that the money has been deposited in the safe does not *per se* benefit the firm." [24]   The analogy is not entirely compelling.   To deposit cash *in specie* in the firm's safe, and later to abstract it therefrom, will admittedly not benefit the firm, *unless the firm has in the interval had the use of the money*.   But it is precisely that the firm had the use of the money, notionally at least, in reducing the balance overdrawn on its bank account which provides the interest of the decision in *New Mining and Exploring Syndicate Limited* v. *Chalmers & Hunter*.   It is still possible for the firm to discharge the onus resting on them to prove that they had not been enriched thereby, but the onus will obviously be a much more exacting one than in the analogical case figured by Lord Mackenzie.

No profit by fraud

In a passage appearing with this side-note Gloag [25] suggests that the rule that no person is entitled to profit by another's fraud is not a true case of recompense but closely resembles it. If there be any virtue in sub-classification of this kind then clearly the liability of the firm for the sums embezzled

[23] *Ibid.* at p. 138.
[24] *Per* Lord Mackenzie *eodem loco*.
[25] *Contract* (2nd ed.) p. 332.

by its partner fall under the more specialised rule rather than under the general principle of recompense. If Chalmers' fraud had resulted in a gain to his firm of Chalmers & Hunter at the expense of the New Mining & Exploring Syndicate Limited, then the firm of Chalmers & Hunter would have been ordered to make restoration to the syndicate to the extent to which the firm had been enriched; and the mere fact that the firm had been in no way involved in Chalmers' fraud would have afforded no ground of defence against a claim for restoration to that extent. It may be that the right to restoration in such circumstances depends not upon the *quasi* contract of recompense but upon an analogous principle of equity, but recompense itself though described as a *quasi* contract is little more than the assertion of an equitable right to restoration of that which one person has unjustly gained at another's expense. While in terms of historical legal theory there may be justification for treatment of cases like *New Mining & Exploring Syndicate Limited* v. *Chalmers & Hunter* as distinct from, though analogous to, cases of recompense proper, that distinction is to a large extent justified only upon the argument that the doctrine of recompense represents a reception in Scots law of the Roman law of *quasi*-contractual obligations. That contention is not entirely supported in modern legal theory,[26] and there appears to be little to be gained by subjecting a general equitable principle to artificial distinctions and classification of this kind. The real problem attendant upon the application of the principle is a wider one. It is that not every gain by A at the expense of B will allow B his right to demand restoration as was pointed out by Lord Kames.[27] Thus if some disaster destroys a large stock of a specific commodity held by one merchant the resulting scarcity of the commodity may cause the stocks held by another merchant to appreciate in value. The first merchant has incurred a loss as a result of which the second merchant has been enriched. Yet the equitable principle will not operate to permit the first merchant to claim from the second restoration to the extent that the second merchant has been enriched.[28] It is interesting to notice the qualifying statement in the passage quoted from the *Principles of Equity* as to the supporting of a low " degree of intimacy " between the loss and the enrichment resulting to another with circumstances in which the persons are " otherwise strongly connected." [29] The later decisions arising in the field of partnership [30] and of agency [31] may possibly be rationalised within a general equitable principle on those broad lines. Certainly where the party who has been enriched is called upon to restore to another the amount by which that other

---

[26] See *Edinburgh & District Tramways Co. Ltd.* v. *Courtenay*, 1909 S.C. 99 and *supra* p. 327.
[27] " The connection between the loss and the gain may be more or less intimate: and its different degrees of intimacy ought to be carefully noted. When this connection is found in the highest degree, there is scarce requisite any other circumstance to oblige one to apply his gain for making up another's loss: in its lower degrees no duty arises, unless the persons be otherwise strongly connected "—Kames, *Principles of Equity* (4th ed.) p. 101.
[28] Kames, *op. cit.* p. 102.
[29] *Supra* n. 27.
[30] *New Mining and Exploring Syndicate Ltd.* v. *Chalmers & Hunter (supra)*.
[31] *Clydesdale Bank* v. *Paul* (1877) 4 R. 626. See also *Traill* v. *Smith's Ts.* (1876) 3 R. 770.

party's loss has enriched him, there appears to be no very compelling distinction to be drawn between the legal principles which are applied when the case properly falls under the category traditionally regarded as " *quasi* contractual " and those falling under the principle that one must not profit from another's fraud. In both cases what is being considered is whether, and how far, a loss incurred by one person has to be recouped by another who, albeit innocently, has been enriched thereby, and if the application of the equitable principle is to be justified, then it must be shown at least prima facie that the second party has been enriched as a result. But where a prima facie case to that effect is established and the case is in other respects brought within the equitable principle of restoration, then the defender who alleges that he was not in fact the gainer must accept the onus of displacing the prima facie case of enrichment.

Personal nature of fraud and its effect on vicarious liability

From what has been said in the preceding pages it may be concluded that, although as has been recognised in many of the reported cases the perpetration of a fraud involves a personal element peculiar to the person perpetrating it, that fact alone will not preclude the possibility of vicarious liability being imposed upon the firm for the fraud of a partner under section 10 of the Partnership Act 1890. Apart from cases where the co-partners have authorised the perpetration of the fraud and so incur direct liability under section 10 and the cases considered in the immediately preceding paragraphs where the firm has been enriched as a result and under the residual common law left undisturbed by the Partnership Act 1890 [32] the firm is liable to the victim in restoration *quantum lucratus*, a number of decisions clearly establish that in fraud as in other wrongful acts committed by a partner in the ordinary course of the business of the firm, the firm itself and the copartners may be held answerable for the loss or injury incurred by him through the commission of the fraud.[33] The importance of the idea of fraud as personal to the person who commits it does not therefore consist in its affording a defence to the vicarious liability of the firm, but it is an idea which still retains some importance in the law of partnership. While the firm may be held vicariously liable in fraud it will not be sufficient to aver that the firm itself committed that fraud. The names of the partner or partners alleged actually to have committed the fraud in the ordinary course of the firm's business must be specified. The point is clearly and succinctly brought out in the judgment of Lord Kinnear in *Thomson* v. *Pattison Elder & Company and Another* [34] a case where it was alleged that while the second named defender was acting exclusively as a commercial traveller for the pursuer he agreed with Pattison Elder & Company to divert to them from his master business which he

[32] s. 46.
[33] *Rapp* v. *Latham* (1819) 2 B. & A. 795; 21 R.R. 495; *Lovell* v. *Hicks* (1837) 2 T. & Cr.Ex. 472; *Blair* v. *Bromley* (1847) 5 Hare 542; *Moore* v. *Knight* [1891] 1 Ch. 547.
[34] (1895) 22 R. 432 at p. 437.

secured while acting for his master, the pursuer. The action was laid against the firm of Pattison Elder & Company and one Swann, the pursuer's commercial traveller as defenders jointly and severally. Lord Kinnear said,

> " In many cases it is convenient, and not inaccurate, to ascribe to a firm the actions of commission or omission of one of the partners acting within the scope of his authority but . . . actions based on fraud fall within a different category. Fraud is always personal and though a firm may be responsible for the individual fraud of one of the partners acting within the scope of his authority, it is incompetent to charge the firm generally with the fraud. Here we do not know how many partners there are in the firm sued, and it would be contrary to justice and procedure to allow a charge of fraud against an indefinite number of persons, without specification of any particular person who had committed the fraud, to go to trial." [35]

Though the grounds of action in this case arose after the passing of the Partnership Act 1890 there is no evidence in the report that section 10 was referred to either in the arguments or in the judgments. The reason may lie partially in the fact that the written pleadings were so framed as to cause some perplexity in the mind of the court as to the precise ground of action. Both the firm and the commercial traveller were sued jointly and severally but upon the averments prima facie there appeared no common ground of liability. The commercial traveller was clearly liable in breach of a contractual liability to his employer, the pursuer, but no such contractual obligation rested on the defender firm, nor would such an obligation, had it existed necessarily have justified a conclusion against both defenders jointly and severally. The only ground of action which could effectively be pleaded as common to both defenders was that of fraud. But so far as the firm was concerned, the fraud which they perpetrated on the pursuer, can only consist in their entering an agreement with the pursuer's traveller to divert to them from the pursuer business which was rightfully the latter's, and if that agreement were to be such as to impose obligations on the firm, it must be one properly entered into by a partner or partners under the authority committed to them in section 5 of the Partnership Act 1890. Thus the determination of whether the firm was liable in fraud turned upon the question whether there was an actual or apparent authority under section 5 to enter an agreement on behalf of the firm which probably accounts for Lord Kinnear's repeated use of the words " within the scope of his authority " in his judgment. But once the authority has been postulated to exist, that does not dispose of the question since the agreement with the commercial traveller *per se* will afford no rights to the pursuer. His case must proceed a step further and contend by this agreement which under section 5 is a binding agreement on the firm, a wrong has been done for which the firm is liable under section 10.

[35] See also the judgment of the Lord President (Robertson) at p. 436.

Liability of the firm for partner's wrongful acts other than fraud

Where a firm is sued in respect of the wrongful act of one of its partners, the terms of section 10 of the Partnership Act 1890 clearly impose that liability provided (1) that the partnership relation in fact existed at the time of the commission of the wrong and (2) that the wrongful act was committed in the ordinary course of the business of the firm or with the authority of the copartners. If the pursuer is unable to prove facts and circumstances which are sufficient to establish a case of partnership, then the persons whom he has sued in the character of a " firm " have of course no case to answer, but the facts and circumstances proved may be such as to establish a prima facie case of partnership, in which case the onus will rest upon the defenders to adduce further evidence which is inconsistent with partnership if they are to escape liability.[36] In many cases, however, the alternative association set up may be that of master and servant or principal and agent when vicarious liability may, though not necessarily will, be maintainable against the defenders even within the alternative relationship for which they contend. Thus where the parties concerned are involved in " share-fishing " activities it may be a matter of some nicety of decision whether they are so engaged as partners or as employers and employees,[37] but though the vicarious liability of a firm for its partner is not imposed upon terms precisely identical with those affecting the vicarious liability of a master for his servant, there is approximation enough to ensure that when the association is one of employer and employee the liability sought to be placed upon the firm in terms of partnership may at least be imposed upon the dominant person in the association, the employer, and in most cases it will be for the purposes of securing *his* liability that the question of partnership has been raised. More difficult questions may arise where a fishing boat is given out " on deal " by the owner, since here the question is whether the owner is a partner in a joint adventure or is rather in the position of an owner who has chartered by demise his ship to others for their purposes, when no ground of liability could be maintained against the owner for a wrongful or negligent act in the management or navigation of the vessel.[38] In such cases it may be essential, if liability is to be imposed on the owner, to establish a partnership between him and those using his boat for purposes of fishing. Thus in *McGee* v. *Anderson*,[39] where an arrangement of this kind was involved, the defender, who was the owner of the boat, was held to be a partner in a joint adventure along with those to whom he gave it out " on deal," since under his agreement with them he was to receive a stipulated proportion of the net profits [40] of the fishing

[36] Partnership Act 1890, s. 2; and see *supra* Chap. III.
[37] *Clark* v. *Jamieson*, 1909 S.C. 132; *Scottish Insurance Commissioners* v. *McNaughton*, 1914 S.C. 826; *Parker* v. *Walker*, 1961 S.L.T. 252.
[38] *Baumwoll, Manufaktur von Carl Scheibler* v. *Furness* [1893] A.C. 8; *Burnard* v. *Aaron & Sharpley* (1862) 31 L.J.C.P. 334.
[39] (1895) 22 R. 274.
[40] So described by Lord Trayner at p. 277, though according to the findings of the sheriff substitute, he was entitled to two-fifteenths of the gross earnings after deduction of the cost of the crew's food and the pier dues.

expedition.   He was accordingly held liable in damages to the pursuer when the crew of his fishing vessel, apprehensive that their nets would be fouled, wrongfully cut the head-rope of the nets of another fishing vessel and caused her the loss of the rope, thirty-seven nets and accompanying buoys. Once the partnership had been held to be established Lord Trayner disposed of the question of the defender's liability in the following terms:

> " It was said, further, that the defender Anderson could not in any view be liable for the delict or wrong of the joint adventurers, because he had not authorised it.   But then the thing done was in pursuance of the joint adventure; it was done to protect the joint adventure, and to enhance the joint profit, and all profited by it more or less. Anderson cannot take the benefit of the act by which profit was earned or secured (as he has done in point of fact), and then repudiate the act or means by which that profit was gained."

Wrong committed without authority and not in the ordinary course of the business

Lord Trayner's words above quoted lead naturally to the examination of the second possible defence to a liability vicariously imposed upon the firm, that the wrongful act was not one committed in the ordinary course of the firm's business or with the authority of the copartners.   Although the wrongful act complained of was committed in 1893, strangely enough, no reference is made either in the arguments, as reported, or in Lord Trayner's judgment, which was concurred in by the other members of the court, to the terms of section 10 of the Partnership Act 1890.   Lord Trayner's opinion, however, is as consistent with section 10 as it is with the pre-statute common law of Scotland.   On analysis of his judgment, he disposes of the plea that the wrongful act did not have the defender's authority by pointing out that " it was done for the benefit of all concerned and all concerned shared that benefit according to the terms of their joint bargain."   Those words, it is submitted, answer the difficult question posed by the wording of section 10, " any wrongful act or omission of any partner acting in the ordinary course of the business of the firm," namely, can a wrongful act ever be in the ordinary course of the business of the firm?   The difficulty is one which is familiar in other fields of vicarious responsibility and has already been adverted to in general terms.[41]   It becomes even more apparent on a consideration of the facts in *McGee* v. *Anderson*,[42] where on first impression the act of cutting the head-rope of the other vessel's nets, while it may have been done in a reasonable apprehension of disaster, yet can only be described as " in the ordinary course " of the business of a fishing expedition if the words quoted are used in a highly specialised sense.   It is true that under the Act then in force [43] and the Convention attached to it [44] cutting of the nets of another fishing boat

[41] See *supra* p. 307.
[42] *Supra* n. 39.
[43] Sea Fisheries Act 1883.
[44] Art. 20.

is permissible if necessary to clear the nets of the crew so acting but, while those provisions legalise in certain circumstances what would otherwise be an illegal act, they do little to stamp that act, even when permitted, with the character of one done " in the ordinary course "; and Lord Trayner does not rely upon them for any such purpose.   Instead, he speaks of an act done " for the benefit of all concerned " in the partnership.   That is an approach which is consonant with decisions prior to the Partnership Act 1890 both in Scotland and in England,[45] and it is in that sense that the wording of section 10 of the Partnership Act 1890, however fallibly expressed, must be read.[46]

Merging of the ideas of delict and authority in section 10

It has been rightly said that section 10 of the Partnership Act 1890 is " solely concerned with tort " and that section 11, which will be considered later, " deals in a somewhat curious way with a mixture of tortious and contractual liability." [47]   That should not, however, obscure the point which has been earlier noticed [48] that while section 10 is concerned solely with the liability of the firm in delict and *quasi*-delict, the determination of that vicarious liability will to some extent involve an examination of the delinquent partner's position in relation to his firm at the time when the wrongful act was committed.   The firm will be liable for the negligent driving of one of its partners where he causes injury to a third party while driving one of the firm's hired cars in the ordinary course of the business of the firm, but it will not be liable to a third party who is injured through the negligence of its partner when he is driving his own car for his own purposes.   And, inevitably, considerations of the position of the delinquent partner at the time of the wrongful act may be extended to cover questions of the real nature of his activities at that time; for the delinquent partner's business activities may not be exclusively confined to the business of his firm and in some cases it may be a difficult decision whether the activity upon which the delinquent partner was engaged falls within the ordinary course of the business of the firm or was attributable to his own business interests.[48a]   Cases may be envisaged where the conduct of the delinquent

---

[45] See *e.g.* in England, *Moreton* v. *Hardern* (1825) 4 B. & C. 223; and *Steel* v. *Lester* (1878) 3 C.P.D. 121; and in Scotland, see Clark, *op. cit.* I, 253–254.

[46] " [S. 10] states the application to partners of a general rule of the law of principal and agent," Lindley, *Supplement* (1891) p. 33, but the wording of s. 10 does not materially assist in explaining the difficulty inherent in the legal notion of a principal's liability for his agent's delict.   See Bowstead, *Agency* (13th ed.) pp. 326 *et seq.*   It seems that the ground of liability which is sought to be expressed in s. 10 is not so much whether the wrongful act was *done* in the ordinary course of the business of the firm but whether it *arose* during the conduct by the partner of business the transaction of which fell within the ordinary scope of his duties.   That explanation would accord with the view taken by Lord Trayner in *McGee* v. *Anderson supra* and with the words used by Collins M.R. when discussing the vicarious liability of partners in *Hamlyn* v. *John Houston & Co.* [1903] 1 K.B. 81 at pp. 85–86: " The principal having delegated the performance of a certain class of acts to his agent, it is not unjust that he, being the person who has appointed the agent, and who will have the benefit of his efforts if successful, should bear the risk of his exceeding his authority in matters incidental to the doing of the acts the performance of which has been delegated to him."

[47] Atiyah, *Vicarious Liability in the Law of Torts*, p. 117.   [48] *Supra* pp. 306–307

[48a] For an examination of the partner's activities in relation to the firm's business see *Kirkintilloch Equitable Cooperative Society* v. *Livingstone*, 1972 S.L.T. 154.

partner at the material time may be regarded as designed to further both the firm's interests and private interests of his own which are unconnected with his firm.   In such cases, section 10 affords no very precise guidance and there is no reported case which throws light on the interpretation which might be put on the section by the courts.   It seems probable that the judicial approach will be to attempt to assess whether the activity was carried out in the ordinary course of the firm's business to any material extent.   If so, it is thought that the firm will be held vicariously liable. There is nothing in section 10 which requires that the partner should have been acting *exclusively* in the ordinary course of the business of the firm.

   " *To the same extent as the partner so acting or omitting to act.*"   These words have already been considered in association with the words " or any penalty is incurred," when it was submitted that they are insufficient to bear an interpretation that they connote a vicarious liability of the firm for conviction of a crime or offence committed by a partner though they may impose a liability on the firm to pay a monetary penalty imposed on that partner if he defaults in payment.[49]   The concluding words of section 10 may, however, have a restrictive effect upon the liability of the firm.   Since the firm is to be liable " to the same extent as the partner so acting or omitting to act," it appears to follow that if the delinquent partner enjoys some personal immunity from being sued in damages for his wrongful act, the firm and his copartners will also escape liability since the measure of their vicarious liability is stated to be co-extensive with his direct liability and if that is non-existent, there is no basis under section 10 for the firm's liability. Thus in jurisdictions where husband and wife may not sue each other in delict, a wife will be unable to sue the firm where her husband's negligence in the conduct, as a partner, of the firm's business has caused her loss. This difficulty does not now arise in England or in Scotland [50] where it is possible for husband and wife to sue each other in delict but it has still some significance in other circumstances.   It will be impossible to hold the firm *qua* firm liable for tort which involves the ingredient of malice if the partner on whose conduct the claim is based was guiltless of malice even though others of the copartners were so actuated.[51]   It has been suggested that it is not clear why the firm and the innocent partner cannot be held vicariously responsible for the partner or partners who were motivated by malice and indeed in *Meekins* v. *Henson,*[51] where one of the partners, though not the partner who actually sent the defamatory document, was ultimately held personally liable in damages, it is difficult to discern the ratio for the exclusion of the firm's liability.   Though the partner, exhibiting malice, did not actually publish the defamatory material, he stood by and let the partner do so in innocence.   It seems clear that in doing so he committed a wrongful act against the plaintiff, and indeed a considerable part of the judgment in the case is devoted to establishing that proposition. Equally it seems difficult to argue that the wrongful act of the partner

---

[49] *Supra* pp. 313–317.   [50] Law Reform (Husband and Wife) Act 1962.
[51] *Meekins* v. *Henson* [1962] 1 All E.R. 899.

actuated by malice was not one done in the ordinary course of the business of the firm. There would, therefore, seem to have been no obstacle to holding the firm vicariously liable, but the point is not mentioned in argument or in the judgment and may not have been open on the pleadings.[52] The facts in *Meekins* v. *Henson* were, however, somewhat special and do not appear to impugn the proposition that where a partner without malice issues defamatory matter in the course of the firm's business, the firm will be equally entitled to plead in defence the lack of malice on the part of that partner, even if some one or more of the other partners, had they defamed the pursuer, would have been guilty of malice. But to maintain the defence successfully the firm may have to prove that those other partners knew nothing of the acting of the partner who issued the defamation and were in no way implicated with him in it.

Partner's wrongful act causing injury to his copartner

Section 10 of the Partnership Act 1890 expressly excepts from the vicarious liability of the firm liability for the wrongful act or omission of a partner which causes loss or injury to one of his copartners.[53] Though the terms of the section exclude liability for a delict committed against a partner, the question of such liability is not precluded if it be found to exist at common law and if any such liability at common law may be regarded as preserved under section 46 of the Act as not " inconsistent with the express provisions " of the Act. This question was considered in *Mair* v. *Wood*,[54] where one of the partners in a joint adventure in sea-fishing was injured as a result of the negligence of one of his copartners in failing to replace the engine room floor boards of the fishing vessel after removing them in order to clear an obstruction which was fouling the propeller. It was held that no liability for the act of the delinquent partner attached to the firm in those circumstances.

Two points were considered in the judgments —(1) did the common law prior to the passing of the Act impose vicarious liability on the firm where a partner has been injured through the delict of a copartner and (2) if the firm had that liability at common law, has it been displaced by express terms of section 10 as being inconsistent with the continuing of the common law rule on force and effect?

On the first question the court held that no such rule could be invoked from the common law of Scotland as it existed prior to 1890. It had been argued that the possibility of the firm's liability was precluded by the doctrine of *confusio*. The court did not regard that as a compelling argument, since the application of the doctrine of *confusio* could not be pleaded to defeat the possibility of the firm's liability, the liability of the partners for a

---

[52] See Atiyah, *op. cit.* p. 119.
[53] " Where by any wrongful act or omission of any partner acting in the ordinary course of the business of the firm, or with the authority of his copartners, loss or injury is caused to any person *not being a partner in the firm*, . . . the firm is liable therefor to the same extent as the partner so acting or omitting to act."—Partnership Act 1890, s. 10 (italics supplied).
[54] 1948 S.C. 83.

debt of the firm being a subsidiary or ancillary one [55]; but there is " no warrant for holding that by the common law of Scotland a firm is liable to one partner for injury or loss due to the negligence of another (or indeed due to any wrong committed by another) when acting within his implied mandate —much less when acting beyond the scope of that mandate." [56]

Although in terms of the decision, the second question was unnecessary for the disposal of the case, the Lord President expressed the view that had such a rule existed in the common law, he would not have regarded the terms of section 10 of the Partnership Act 1890 as sufficient to abrogate that rule by implication. [57]   Lords Carmont and Russell concurred in the judgment of the Lord President, but Lord Keith [58] reserved his opinion upon the effect of the words, " not being a partner in the firm," occurring in section 10 though since his view as to the first question agreed with those of the other judges, he found it unnecessary to decide the point.   While the views expressed as to the effect of section 10 on the previous law, had that law differed from the rule laid down in section 10, are *obiter*, the fact that these views are not completely unanimous, indicates that the provisions of section 46 of the Partnership Act 1890 preserving the common law so far as not inconsistent with the express provisions of the Act may in particular cases prove difficult to apply.

Liability of firm for partner's breach of trust

In terms of section 11 of the Partnership Act 1890—

" In the following cases; namely—

(a) Where one partner acting within the scope of his apparent authority receives the money or property of a third person and misapplies it; and

(b) Where a firm in the course of its business receives money or property of a third person, and the money or property so received is misapplied by one or more of the partners while it is in the custody of the firm;

the firm is liable to make good the loss."

Before examining the words of the section in detail it is important to study its general scope and effect.   The section is clearly concerned with fraudulent conduct by a partner or partners but its application is limited to conduct in relation to the money or property of a third party which has been entrusted to the firm.   Section 11 is therefore not exhaustive on the question of the firm's liability for the fraud of one of its partners as has been seen when considering the terms of section 10; nor are the more general terms of section 10 entirely inapplicable where the fraud is concerned with the money or property of a third party.   If money or property of a

---

[55] See *per* the Lord President (Cooper) at pp. 86–87.

[56] *Per* the Lord President, *ibid.* at p. 87.   The liability of the individual partner who commits the wrongful act is, of course, not elided; and where the partner is, in terms of the partnership agreement, under obligation to provide safe working conditions for his copartners, he may be personally liable to one of them who is injured as a result of his failure to discharge his contractual obligation.—*Parker* v. *Walker*, 1961 S.L.T. 252.

[57] *Ibid.* p. 88.   [58] *Ibid.* at p. 91.

third party has been obtained by a firm through the misrepresentation of one of its partners, the firm will be liable to restore or refund it, and, apparently, it will be unnecessary to establish in such a case that the partner's misrepresentation was fraudulent in addition to being false.[59] Such cases do not fall entirely within the ambit of section 11 which is concerned exclusively with the misapplication of money or property which has either been placed by a third party in the custody of the firm itself or which has been entrusted by him to a partner of that firm in his character as such partner.   Thus in *Rapp* v. *Latham* [60] Parry and Latham were in partnership as wine and spirit merchants.   Rapp employed the firm to buy wine for him on commission and to sell it for him as occasion arose when this might be done to his profit.   Parry alone conducted the firm's business and he falsely and fraudulently misrepresented to Rapp that he had carried through purchases and sales of wine on Rapp's behalf and remitted him balances said to be due on the pretended sales.   In all Rapp advanced £126,000 to the firm for the purchase of wines and he had received back on account of the pretended sales £130,000, but there was still a large balance unaccounted for.   Parry claimed that this balance had been invested for Rapp in the purchase of pipes of wine, and Rapp's action was directed against Parry and his copartner, Latham, for recovery of that balance.   In point of fact, no purchase of wine had ever been made on behalf of Rapp and no sales carried through on his behalf; and Parry's representations had been false and fraudulent throughout.   It was argued on behalf of Latham that the fictitious transactions created by Parry could not be regarded as partnership transactions since they were not " in the ordinary course of the business of the firm " but the court held that Latham was bound by his partner's representations and could not be heard to plead that Parry had represented to be real what was in fact fictitious.

The decision in *Rapp* v. *Latham* was one based on the law as existing prior to the passing of the Partnership Act 1890 and it must be confessed that there is some difficulty in bringing it within the terms either of section 10 or of section 11 of that Act.   It does not readily fall under section 10 for the reason just advanced.   It can be regarded as falling under section 11 (*a*) since it is possible to argue that it was within the scope of Parry's apparent authority as a partner to carry through dealings of the kind which he falsely represented to Rapp he was conducting and in the course of those fictitious dealings he received *qua* partner of the firm money amounting to £126,000 from Rapp.   But Rapp's action was not for the refund of that money which is the extent of the firm's liability under section 11.[61]

---

[59] *Armstrong* v. *Strain* [1952] 1 K.B. 232, *per* Singleton L.J. at p. 244; Lindley, *op. cit.* p. 190.

[60] (1819) 2 B. & Ald. 795.   And see the Scottish case *Wemyss* v. *Australian Company of Edinburgh* (1856) 19 D. 122.

[61] This may be questioned as an over-simplified interpretation to be placed on the words of s. 11, " the firm is liable to make good the loss."   See *infra* p. 341.   But in the context of the present discussion the distinction between the liability imposed by s. 10 and that imposed by s. 11 seems to be relevant.   In *Wemyss* v. *Australian Company of Edinburgh* (*supra* n. 60) the averments were held relevant to support issues that the company was liable in an accounting to the pursuer for the dividends earned on stock in the Bank of New

He had already been refunded £130,000 and his claim was for a " balance " which Parry had falsely assured him was invested in wine. The action was thus not one seeking from the firm refund of the money entrusted to Parry while " acting within the scope of his apparent authority." Rather, it was based upon Parry's fraud and sought damages for the loss to the plaintiff which arose therefrom. To support a claim of that kind the appropriate section to invoke since the passing of the Act is section 10 and not section 11. This view, however, does not dispose of the difficulty in applying section 10 to such cases; yet it is clear that, in the pre-statute cases at least, vicarious liability was imposed on the firm in such cases.[62] In *Blair* v. *Bromley*[63] the Lord Chancellor (Cottenham) decided for liability of the firm on the ground that where persons who have a duty to perform, represent to third parties interested in the performance of that duty, that it has been performed, they make themselves liable for the consequences of non-performance. Since one partner may bind another in any transaction within the limits of the partnership association, so he may bind his co-partner by an act which albeit not in itself constituting a contract is still in equity considered as having all the same consequences. The *ratio* attributed to the decision in that case is probably that which most conveniently covers those cases where section 10 will operate, if at all, somewhat uneasily. It will be noticed, however, that there is a tendency for the firm's liability in delict in terms of section 10 to be tinged with considerations more appropriate to the partner's apparent authority as agent of his firm under section 5. The difficulty in drawing a clear line between contract and delict in these questions has already been referred to.[64] It is, moreover, possible to regard *Blair* v. *Bromley*, on its facts, as a case which would now fall under section 11 (*b*) of the Partnership Act 1890, since the third party's money which was ultimately misapplied by one of the partners had been placed to the credit of the bank account of the partnership, although without the knowledge of the other partner, and later embezzled by the delinquent partner.

Liability for false accounts rendered by one of the partners

Though the principle enunciated by the Lord Chancellor in *Blair* v. *Bromley* would now be unnecessary in view of the terms of section 11 (*b*) of the Partnership Act 1890, its ambit, and in particular its appeal to equitable considerations, are much wider than the facts of that particular case would now require. It may have some bearing on the decision of the much discussed question whether accounts rendered by one partner which disclose that the money of a third party is in the hands of the firm when in fact that money has been misapplied, are to be imputed to the firm of which he is a partner. The issues raised in such a case are not governed by section 11

South Wales which the company's manager had undertaken to purchase from money entrusted to him by the pursuer for that purpose.
[62] See *Lovell* v. *Hicks* (1837) 2 Y. & C.Ex. 472; *Blair* v. *Bromley* (1847) 5 Hare 542.
[63] *Supra* n. 62. And see *Moore* v. *Knight* [1891] 1 Ch. 547.
[64] *Supra* pp. 336–338.

of the Partnership Act 1890. They involve an application of sections 10 and 15 of the Act, the former sounding in vicarious liability of the firm for the wrongful act of a partner committed in the ordinary course of the business of the firm while the latter rests upon the contractual basis of agency and may be argued to be applicable to the false accounts as a " representation " [65] made by the delinquent partner and thus providing evidence against the firm. Perhaps on account of these differing approaches to a possible liability of the firm, the pre-statute cases are not always consistent in decision.[66] Both section 10 and section 15 apply only where the false representation is made in the ordinary course of the business of the firm. In addition section 15 provides that it must be a representation " concerning the partnership affairs." Though the added requirement of section 15 is deserving of consideration in cases where it is sought to apply the section, it is thought that circumstances in which an act which does not concern the partnership affairs is to be regarded as one committed in the ordinary course of the business of the firm must be of rare occurrence; and Lindley's view [67] that " if the accounts relate to the matters within the scope of the partnership business the firm is bound by them " is probably correct.[68]

The scope of liability under section 11

It cannot be too strongly emphasised that the scope of section 11 is restricted. In this respect it is in marked contrast to section 10. Section 11 is dealing in specific terms with wrongful acts relating to misapplication of money or property and it has already been mentioned that, in considering such matters in relation to a firm and its partners a mixture of delictual and contractual notions may be called into play. It is hardly surprising that the matters dealt with in section 11 should have been thought deserving of special and separate treatment since the interdependence of the firm and its partners make such questions of especial importance and indeed occupied the attention of the courts on frequent occasions prior to the passing of the Partnership Act 1890.[69] Under section 11 two cases involving the liability of the firm are distinguished—

(1) Where the partner himself receives the money or property and misapplies it; and

(2) Where the money or property reaches the custody of the firm and while in its custody is misapplied by one of the partners.

---

[65] " An admission or representation made by any partner concerning the partnership affairs, and in the ordinary course of its business, is evidence against the firm."—Partnership Act 1890, s. 15.

[66] *Rapp* v. *Latham* (1819) 2 B. & Ald. 795; *Devaynes* v. *Noble, Baring's Case* (1816) 1 Mer. 611; *Marsh* v. *Keating* (1834) 2 Cl. & F. 250 and *De Ribeyre* v. *Barclay* (1857) 23 Beav. 107, 125, all affirm liability. But *contra* see *Hume* v. *Bolland* (1832) 1 Cr. & M. 130; *Sims* v. *Brutton* (1850) 5 Ex. 802.

[67] *Op. cit.* p. 192.

[68] The accounts concerned must, of course, be the accounts of the firm. The private books of one of the partners cannot be a representation or admission under s. 15 and as a general rule cannot be held to be the writ of the firm: *Catto, Thomson & Co.* v. *Thomson & Son* (1867) 6 M. 54.

[69] *e.g. McFarlane* v. *Donaldson* (1835) 13 S. 725; *Willett* v. *Chambers* (1778) Cowp. 814; 3 Ross L.C. 476; *Sadler* v. *Lee* (1843) 6 Beav. 324; *Keating* v. *Marsh* (1834) 1 Mont. & Ayr. 582, 592.

The criterion of liability of the firm is different in each of these cases. In the first case the partner himself receives the money or property from the third party and therefore, before any question of the firm's liability can arise, it must be shown that the partner concerned was apparently acting as a partner and not as an individual. In the second case the money or property has been received by the firm and is in its custody. Therefore the preliminary question posed in the former case as to the partner's apparent authority does not arise. But it will be noted that if the firm is to be liable for the misapplication by a partner of the money or property while in the firm's keeping, it is required under section 11 (*b*) of the Partnership Act 1890 that the money or property must initially have reached the firm's keeping in the course of its business and this has been held to mean the *ordinary* course of its business.[70] The scope of this may, of course, vary at different stages of the firm's history as is illustrated in *New Mining & Exploring Syndicate Limited* v. *Chalmers & Hunter* where the ordinary course of the business of a firm of solicitors during the period when one of the partners in his office as secretary of the pursuer company received and credited to the firm sums subscribed by third parties for shares, did not include the receipt of such money so as to make the firm liable for its misapplication under section 11 (*b*), whereas it was conceded that at a later period when the firm itself was appointed secretary, the money so received by it and misappropriated by Chalmers was recoverable from the firm under that section as having been received " in the course of the business."

Money received by a partner " acting within the scope of his apparent authority "

These cases which arise under section 11 (*a*) raise few difficulties of comprehension. Essentially they are the sort of cases which might arise in a partnership of solicitors or of merchant bankers where the day-to-day running of the partnership business will involve the entrusting by third parties to a partner of the firm of sums of money in circumstances where the third party regards the partner as the hand of the firm. Section 11 (*a*) in such cases raises the question—was the money received by the partner within the scope of his apparent authority from the firm to do so? and that question may be approached in two ways. In the first place, one may pose the question—was the purpose for which the money was entrusted to the partner a purpose which it was within the scope of the business of the partnership to implement? In this approach, an interaction between section 11 (*a*) and section 11 (*b*) begins to become apparent. If the purpose for which the partner received the money is not a purpose within the scope of the ordinary business of the firm then prima facie the firm will not be liable for its defaulting partner.[71]

[70] *New Mining & Exploring Syndicate Ltd.* v. *Chalmers & Hunter*, 1912 S.C. 126. " In no proper sense, however, can it be said that a firm's business includes matters as to which the firm has no right or duty to concern itself," *per* Lord Skerrington at p. 131.

[71] *Harman* v. *Johnson* (1853) 2 E. & B. 61; *New Mining & Exploring Syndicate Ltd.* v. *Chalmers & Hunter, supra.*

But though that is the first question to be asked and though the express terms of section 11 (*a*) appear to be satisfied if an answer is obtained to that question, it is not in fact the *only* question to be asked in many cases. Section 11 (*a*) implies this when it refers to the scope of the apparent authority of the delinquent partner; for, if liability may be imposed on the firm on the ground that the money was received by the partner " acting within the scope of his apparent authority," *a fortiori* the firm will be held liable if the partner had actual authority from his copartners to receive the money or property. That liability will be imposed if actual authority can be established whether or not the receipt of the money or property was within the apparent authority of the partner. Thus in *Harman* v. *Johnson* [72] the headnote states correctly the *ratio* of the decision as that the receipt by a partner of a firm of attorneys of money from a client of the firm for the purpose of investing it when a good security offered itself for investment " is not an act within the scope of the ordinary business of an attorney so as, *without proof of actual authority from his partners*, to render them liable for the money so deposited." (Italics supplied.) The decision depended on its facts on the court's finding as to the scope of the ordinary course of the business of a firm of " attorneys " and is in no way a guide to the scope of the business of a modern firm of solicitors.[73] Moreover the actual authority of the partner to receive the money or property on behalf of the firm need not be an express authority from his copartners, even when that actual authority is not comprised within his apparent authority. Thus in *Earl of Dundonald* v. *Masterman* [74] it was held that money received by one member of a firm of solicitors in the course of management and settlement of the affairs of a client of the firm is money paid to the firm in the course of its professional business and that, consequently, the members of the firm are liable to make good any loss occasioned through the negligence or dishonesty of the partner by whom the money was received. The decision is important since it corrects any tendency to appeal too uncritically to the rather old-world approach taken in *Harman* v. *Johnson* and it may well be that in the light of present-day conditions of a solicitor's practice the receipt by one partner of money for a client of the firm is without need for further proof to be regarded as a transaction within the scope of that partner's apparent authority as being one in the ordinary course of the business of the firm. It will be observed, however, that *Earl of Dundonald* v. *Masterman* did not so decide. The *ratio decidendi* on which the distinction was based was that the Earl of Dundonald had employed the firm to arrange his affairs which had become embarrassed. There was thus a course of

---

[72] (1853) 2 E. & B. 61.

[73] This case which drew a distinction between the business of attorneys and the business of scriveners in such affairs is not cited as in any way relevant to the determination of the scope of the ordinary business of a firm of modern solicitors. Nor, it is thought, does *New Mining & Exploring Syndicate Ltd.* v. *Chalmers & Hunter* (*supra*) lend any support to that view. *Harman* v. *Johnson* is cited merely to illustrate the rule that " apparent authority " is not the sole test. For solicitors, see *Earl of Dundonald* v. *Masterman* (1869) L.R. 7 Eq. 515.

[74] (1869) L.R. 7 Eq. 515.

dealing in receiving and making payments on his behalf and the particular payment received by the partner was one received in the course of the performance of duties which the firm had undertaken. From that course of dealing, therefore, an actual authority was implied under which the partner received the money for the firm.

Cases falling within the terms of section 11 (b)

The discussion of the points raised immediately above illustrates the tendency for section 11 (*a*) in its logical extension to merge imperceptibly into section 11 (*b*), because where the partner receives the money within his apparent authority the third party is entitled to assume that he receives it as the hand of the firm and where he does so with actual authority he does in fact receive it as the hand of the firm. It is thought, however, that on a true construction of section 11 even the receipt by a partner with actual authority to do so on behalf of the firm remains firmly within section 11 (*a*). Section 11 appears to be concerned with the physical receipt of the money or property and where section 11 (*b*) deals with a case " where a firm in the course of its business receives the money or property of the third person " those words must be satisfied by tracing the third party's money or property into the actual custody of the firm itself. Section 11 appears to be designed to cover two different grounds on which the firm may find itself liable. Under (*a*) it is held liable because the partner has received the money while acting within the scope of his apparent authority or (as has been suggested) with actual authority from his copartners. In such cases the act of receiving the money is imputed to the firm and liability will be imposed on the firm when the money so received has never been placed by the partner in the firm's keeping but has been misapplied by him after receiving it and without having placed it to the credit of the firm at all. Section 11 (*b*), however, envisages that the money received from the third party has actually come into the keeping of the firm and that while in the firm's custody, one of the partners misapplies it.

Pre-statute decisions

Both aspects of section 11 are declaratory of the common law existing prior to the passing of the Act. It has been held repeatedly that the receipt of money by a partner acting within the scope of his apparent authority is receipt of the money by his firm who are liable to the third party for the misapplication of that money by the partner who received it even where the firm and his copartners never actually received the money into their custody and where the copartners had no knowledge that their partner had received it.[75] It is important to establish that the transaction under which the partner received the money was one which the third party entered into with him in his character as a partner of the firm and not as an individual. Even if the transaction may be regarded as falling within the scope of the business of the firm, no vicarious liability will attach to the

[75] *St. Aubyn* v. *Smart* (1868) L.R. 5 Eq. 183.

firm if in point of fact the partner and the third party concerned dealt with each other as individuals.[76] In most cases, however, the decision will turn upon the question whether the partner receiving the money was acting within the scope of his authority since that will often be the only circumstance which can be adduced as evidence of the intention of the parties to the transaction. In examining that question the authority of the partner may be measured by consideration of the scope of the ordinary business of the firm as in *Brydges* v. *Branfill* [77] where one partner of a firm of solicitors connived at a fraud committed by a client in obtaining money out of the Court of Chancery thus depriving the parties for whom the money was held of their right to the money. The money was obtained by the delinquent partner under a power of attorney and then handed over to the client who was a client of the firm. Although the remaining partners were innocent of the fraud and in fact did not know that it had been committed, they were held liable to restore the money to those who had been deprived of it through the fraud.[78] Frequently the court will have under consideration not only the scope of the business ordinarily carried on by firms of the same kind as the firm involved, but additional factors based on the course of dealing in the particular transaction or a course of dealing in the past with the particular client or customer who seeks to hold the firm liable. When the nature of the particular transaction is looked at, the court may examine the nature of the dealings with the third party subsequent to the actual receipt of the money.[79] In other cases the former course of dealing of the firm with the particular client may be looked at in addition to the general course of dealing by the firm with clients similarly circumstanced to the client who had been defrauded. In *Rhodes* v. *Moules* [80] a partner in a firm of solicitors on the instructions of a client of the firm obtained a loan for him on a mortgage of the client's estate but, by falsely representing to the client that collateral security was required by the lender, he received from the client share warrants payable to bearer which he misappropriated, and then absconded. His copartners knew nothing of the fraud or the deposit of the share warrants. Nevertheless, they were held liable to restore to the client the value of his share warrants on the ground that the transaction was a partnership one, since (a) the firm on previous occasions had actually received the same share warrants through their delinquent partner for the same purpose as was avowed in the transaction under consideration, *i.e.* in order to procure loans for the client and (b) the firm had

---

[76] *New Mining & Exploring Syndicate Ltd.* v. *Chalmers & Hunter*, 1912 S.C. 126 is regarded by Lindley (*op. cit.* p. 196) as authority for this proposition though the opinions of the judges hardly bear it out. The point is more clearly brought out in *British Homes Assurance Corporation* v. *Paterson* [1902] 2 Ch. 604.

[77] (1842) 12 Sim. 369.

[78] But *cf. Marsh* v. *Joseph* [1897] 1 Ch. 213.

[79] *Willett* v. *Chambers* (1778) Cowp. 814, where, in a case involving the misapplication by a partner of money received from a client to invest on mortgage, Lord Mansfield founded on the fact that a bill for the work done in respect of the fictitious mortgage had been made and rendered by the offending partner in the name of his firm and had been paid to a partner innocent of the fraud.

[80] [1895] 1 Ch. 236.

been in the habit of receiving bearer bonds from such clients. In that case, therefore, the decision that the particular transaction was a partnership one rested partly upon the element that it was embraced within the general scope of the firm's business and partly on the additional factor that, in the history of the firm's dealings with the particular client, it was established that transactions of a similar kind had taken place with the same securities.[81]

When the decisions prior to the Partnership Act 1890 relating to the liability of the firm for money of a third party misappropriated by a partner *while in the custody of the firm* are considered, the importance of the distinction made in section 11 (*b*) is emphasised. If at the time of the misappropriation by the partner the money was not actually in the firm's custody, the firm will escape liability[82] unless vicarious liability for the partner's acts can be imputed to the firm on the ground that these acts were within the scope of the partner's apparent authority. In the cases arising under section 11 (*b*) the principle to be applied is entirely independent from that of vicarious liability. The principle in these cases is that since the firm has in the course of the business received into its custody the money or property of the third party and has parted with the possession thereof without the authority of the third party, the firm is responsible to restore to the third party his money or property. On the strength of that principle it in no way diminishes the liability of the firm that the property or money was originally obtained from the third party by improper conduct of one of the partners, even if the firm is not responsible for that conduct under section 11 (*a*), so long as the partner so obtaining it has placed it in the hands of his firm. The principle is illustrated in a number of decisions arising from the forgeries or frauds of one Fauntleroy, a partner in the banking house of Marsh & Company.[83] Fauntleroy forged powers of attorney from customers of the bank empowering him to sell their stock. He instructed a broker to sell the stock and the broker remitted the proceeds to the credit of Fauntleroy's firm with Martin Stone & Company with whom Marsh & Company had an account. Fauntleroy then presented to Martin Stone & Company a cheque signed by himself in the name of his firm, drew out the sum at credit and applied it to his own use. Marsh & Company were held liable. The sale of stock for its customers and the receipt of the proceeds of sale on their behalf were within the scope of the business of Marsh & Company, who had received the proceeds of sale in the usual way by having them placed to their credit with Martin Stone & Company. The fact that the other partners did not know of the receipt of the proceeds did not avail Marsh & Company as a defence. With ordinary diligence they might have

[81] Contrast *Cleather* v. *Twisden* (1884) 28 Ch.D. 340. And compare generally, on the questions of transactions regarded as not within the scope of the partner's authority, *Viney* v. *Chaplin* (1858) 2 De G. & J. 483; *Bourdillon* v. *Roche* (1858) 27 L.J.Ch. 681; *Harman* v. *Johnson* (1853) 2 E. & B. 61; *Plumer* v. *Gregory* (1874), 18 Eq. 621; *Re Bellamy & Metropolitan Board of Works* (1883) 24 Ch.D. 387.

[82] *Coomer* v. *Bromley* (1852) 5 De G. & Sm. 532. See also *Bishop* v. *Countess of Jersey* (1854) 2 Drew. 143; *Ex p. Eyre* (1842) 1 Ph. 227.

[83] *Stone* v. *Marsh* (1827) 6 B. & C. 551; *Keating* v. *Marsh* (1834) 1 Mont. & Ayr. 582; *Marsh* v. *Keating* (1834) 2 Cl. & F. 250; *Ex p. Bolland* (1828) 1 Mont. & Ayr. 570; *Hume* v. *Bolland* (1832) 1 Cr. & M. 130.

gained knowledge of the receipt of the money and the source from which it came. They were not aware of these facts because they chose to rely implicitly on Fauntleroy. Moreover, Fauntleroy's fraud in misappropriating the money was no defence to the firm once the money had been received into the firm's custody.

"*In the course of its business.*" The fact that the money or property of a third party has been received into the custody of the firm will not by itself be sufficient to render the firm liable if the money or property is misapplied by a partner of the firm. In addition to receipt of the money or property section 11 (*b*) requires that it should have been received in the course of the business of the firm. Mere receipt by the firm in the sense that money, for example, is employed in its business by one of the partners and thus becomes immixed with the firm's own funds will not involve the firm in liability for the misapplication of the money unless the other partners of the firm had notice of a breach of trust involved in such actings by another partner.[84] The liability imposed on the firm under section 11 (*b*) is one which is closely associated with the authority of the individual partners. Even before the passing of the Partnership Act 1890 the circumstance that the receipt by the firm of the money must be in the course of the firm's business was regarded as highly important and material. In the *Fauntleroy* fraud cases,[85] for example, not only were the proceeds of Fauntleroy's frauds " received " by his firm through being placed to the credit of the firm's account with Martin Stone & Company but it was emphasised that it was within the scope of the firm's business to sell stock for customers and to receive the proceeds of sale on their behalf. Consequently, where the partners, other than the delinquent partner, were unaware of the receipt by the firm of the money, the firm was none the less liable since the means of knowledge were at their command and if, instead of informing themselves by these means, the other partners chose to rely upon their partner, Fauntleroy, they and the firm could not escape liability on the ground of their ignorance.

It will be noticed that in section 11 (*b*) the qualifying words are " in the course of its business " whereas in section 10 the words used are " acting in the ordinary course of the business of the firm." The reason for the variation in wording is not easy to explain. It is true that section 10, dealing with the vicarious responsibility for the delict or *quasi* delict of its partners, requires some limiting concept which will correspond to the idea of the scope of the employment which is applied when the doctrine is considered in relation to the vicarious liability of a master for his servant, while on the other hand section 11 (*b*) is concerned, at least to some extent, with a prima facie liability of a contractual kind which falls upon the firm when it has received into its custody the money or property of a third party. The accepted analytical view of sections 10 and 11 is that while section 10 is concerned with the general responsibility of the firm in tort or delict,

---

[84] Partnership Act 1890, s. 13. See *infra* pp. 358 *et seq.*
[85] *Supra* n. 83.

section 11 endeavours to find an explanation for the firm's liability in the cases covered by the section in some form of contractual obligation of care.[86] Consequently, in considering the ambit of section 11, it has been said,

> " The principle underlying this section is that in order that a firm may be liable for the misapplication of money by one of its members, some obligation on the part of the firm to take care of the money must be shown. A receipt of the money by the firm prima facie imposes this obligation: but where there is no receipt by the firm, there is prima facie no obligation on its part with respect to the money in question. Thus, the firm must be treated as receiving what any partner receives as its real or ostensible agent, *i.e.* in the course of transacting the business of the firm. In a case of this sort it is immaterial whether the other partners know anything about the money or not; for *ex hypothesi*, it is in the custody of one who must be regarded as their agent. On the other hand, the firm cannot be treated as receiving what one partner receives otherwise than as its real or ostensible agent, unless the money actually comes into the possession or under the control of the other partners. Agency being excluded in such a case as the last, the money cannot be considered as in the possession or under the control of the innocent partners, unless they know that it is so, or unless they are culpably ignorant of the fact." [87]

The difficulty about the passage above quoted is that the analysis of the terms of section 11, though perceptive and illuminating, does not even inferentially explain why, if the receipt by the firm of money of a third party raises a prima facie obligation on the firm's part to take care of it, there is any need for the qualifying words, " in the course of its business " at all. If a third party writes a letter to a firm, remitting money to the firm to invest for him, then it is difficult to see on the theory advanced by Lindley why it should be a condition of the firm's liability that the receipt of money by the firm in such circumstances should be in the course of the firm's business, because if the firm be unwilling to transact the business for which the third party has remitted his money, the firm should immediately refund it to him. It is here that the interaction of section 11 (*a*) with section 11 (*b*) becomes important albeit that the section sets these out as two independent and distinct propositions; for, when one speaks of receipt by the firm, some individual, usually a partner, must act as the hand of the firm. He must peruse the letter, take a decision whether the firm will accept the instructions in it, and either credit the remittance to the firm's account or refund it to the third party. In some cases, the decision whether to " receive " the money will be one in which all the partners will be consulted and will participate, but these cases are unlikely to raise issues for determination by the courts. The circumstances which have been before

---

[86] Lindley, *op. cit.* pp. 187–188 and p. 194.
[87] Lindley, *op. cit.* p. 194.

the courts have generally been that an individual partner has " received "
the money on behalf of the firm without the knowledge of his copartners
and has in some way misapplied it after it has been so received. In these
circumstances it is attractive to regard the qualifying words " in the course
of its business " as in some way limiting the liability of the innocent partners on the ground that unless a remittance made payable to the firm is for
a purpose in the course of the business of the firm, those innocent copartners are not " culpably ignorant " if they remain unaware that the
remittance has been lodged to the credit of the firm's bank account and so
" received " by the firm. There is indeed some support for that view in
New Mining & Exploring Syndicate Ltd. v. *Chalmers & Hunter.*[88] In
several of the English decisions, the same point is stressed where a partner
has received money from a third party in connection with a transaction
unconnected with the business of the firm or not in the course of such business. In *Harman* v. *Johnson* [89] the partner received the money for the
purpose of investing it on mortgage when a good occasion presented itself.
His firm was a partnership of attorneys and the court held that no evidence
had been adduced to establish that it was part of the business of such a
firm to act as " scriveners," *i.e.* persons acting as depositaries of money
awaiting investment. If the money had been received for investment in a
specific mortgage, that would have been regarded as in the course of the
business of a firm of solicitors, or attorneys, and the firm might have been
held liable for subsequent misapplication of the money; but since the purpose for which the money was received was not shown to be in the course of
the firm's business, the firm was not liable where the partner receiving the
money later misapplied it. Such cases suggest that the real purpose of the
words " in the course of its business " occurring in section 11 (*b*) is to
emphasise that when an individual partner " receives " the money as the
hand of the firm and places it to the credit of the firm, liability will be imposed on the firm only if the money is received for a purpose connected
with the business of the firm. The distinction between section 11 (*a*) and
section 11 (*b*) is that in the former case although the partner acts ostensibly
as a partner, the money never reaches the firm at all. In the pre-statute
cases on which section 11 (*b*) appears to be founded where the money has
been credited to the firm in connection with a transaction in the course of its
business, knowledge of the fact that the money has been so received by the
firm is imputed to the other partners with a resulting obligation on the
firm to safeguard that money from misapplication while in its custody. If
the money is " received " for a purpose not in the course of the firm's
business, no such knowledge is imputed to the other partners, though, if
such knowledge can in fact be established, the firm will be liable if the
money is misapplied while in its custody.[90] The principle governing the
distinction of the two cases is not entirely convincing. It is difficult to see

---

[88] 1912 S.C. 126.   In that case the court seems to have regarded the words " in the course of
    its business " as meaning " in the *ordinary* course of its business."
[89] (1853) 2 E. & B. 61.   See also *Plumer* v. *Gregory, Cleather* v. *Twisden, supra* n. 81.
[90] *Sims* v. *Brutton* (1850) 5 Ex. 802.

why the innocent partners should be regarded as in knowledge of the receipt of the money in the former case yet not in the latter case which equally appears in the books of the firm and indeed is from its circumstances a transaction more likely to draw attention to itself. To hold the innocent partners " culpably ignorant " if they are unaware of the facts in the former case yet free from liability in the latter case is consonant with reason only if the decision is explained in terms of agency, and if it be so explained, it depends partially at least on the actings of the partner being within the scope of his apparent authority under section 11 (a) rather than on an obligation arising from the mere receipt of the money by the firm under section 11 (b). That this area of the law is uneasily poised is evident when the pre-statute decisions are considered; and the decision in *Sims* v. *Brutton* [90] contrasted with the *Fauntleroy* fraud cases.[91]

Liability imposed on the partners

Vicarious liability has been discussed in this chapter on the basis of the liability imposed upon the firm for the acts of a delinquent partner. In view of the separate *persona* of the firm in Scotland the terms of sections 10 and 11 make this consonant with legal theory. In both sections the firm itself is made liable for the partner's acts in the appropriate circumstances, but the firm in English law is merely a collective description of the partners [92] whereas in Scotland the firm is " a legal person distinct from the partners of whom it is composed." [93] Under both systems there is a consequential liability on the partners of the firm, but whereas in England the liability imposed on the firm simply connotes a personal liability on the partners, in Scotland it has traditionally been regarded as a secondary liability on the partners for the obligation of the firm itself. Section 12 of the Partnership Act 1890 sets out a compendious provision designed to apply with equal force in both countries—" Every partner is liable jointly with his copartners and also severally for everything for which the firm while he is a partner therein becomes liable under either of the two last preceding sections."

It is to be noticed that section 12 excludes from its purview questions of breach of trust which are not dealt with in either of the preceding sections, 10 and 11, but in the succeeding section 13. Liability for breach of trust by one of the partners is not controlled by the Partnership Act 1890 but is left to be governed by the general law as it existed when the Act was passed.[94] Section 12 is concerned with the liability of the copartners for the tort or fraud of a partner or for his misapplication of money or property which has been received on behalf of or which is in the custody of the firm. Moreover, in the application of section 12 it is important to distinguish those obligations which arise from contract and those which arise from

[91] Particularly *Stone* v. *Marsh* and *Marsh* v. *Keating, supra* n. 83.
[92] Partnership Act 1890, s. 4 (1).
[93] *Ibid.* s. 4 (2).
[94] *Infra* pp. 358 *et seq.*

delict or tort.   The liability of the partners for obligations which arise from
contract is governed, not by section 12, but by section 9 which reads—

> " Every partner in a firm is liable jointly with the other partners,
> and in Scotland severally also, for all debts and obligations of the
> firm incurred while he is a partner; and after his death his estate is also
> severally liable in a due course of administration for such debts and
> obligations, so far as they remain unsatisfied, but subject in England
> or Ireland to the prior payment of his separate debts."

For the English lawyer the importance of the distinction between contractual cases under section 9 and delictual cases under section 12 is that in
the former the liability is joint [95] whereas in the latter it is joint and several.
In Scotland this ground of distinction is of no significance since in both
types of case the liability of the partners is joint and several.   The contractual liability, however, must still be distinguished from the delictual
since, although both result in joint and several liability, the *ratio* upon
which that liability is imposed differs in the two cases.   In Scotland the
basis of the joint and several liability in contract of the partners is explained
by Bell [96]:

> " To third parties each partner is responsible for the whole debts
> of the concern.   In legal language they are liable *singuli in solidum*,
> and more as guarantors than as principals.   But they are not . . .
> entitled to the benefit of discussion.   The non-payment on the part of
> the company at once raises their responsibility.   Like other mercantile
> guarantors, they are conditional debtors if the debt is not paid at the
> day "; and in a later passage [97]:
> " It is a consequence of this separate existence of the company as
> a person that an action cannot directly and in the first instance be
> maintained against a partner for the debt of the company.   The
> demand must be made first against the company, or the company must
> have failed to pay, or have dishonoured their bill, before the partner
> can be called on."

On the other hand, the basis of the joint and several liability imposed
in section 12 is that " partners are jointly and severally liable in the same
way and to the same extent as other principals and masters for the torts of
their agents and servants acting within the scope of their authority or
employment." [98]   That annotation is in accord with the legal position in
England but does not seem equally apt as far as Scots law is concerned.
Sections 10 and 11 expressly impose the vicarious liability upon the firm
and in Scotland where the firm is a separate *persona* from the partners
composing it, the sections do not of themselves inferentially impose a

[95] The partners of an English firm may, of course, by their contract with a third party accept
joint and several liability, but where the statutory joint liability alone is imposed the
estate of a deceased partner will not be liable: *Sumner* v. *Powell* (1816) 2 Mer. 30; *Clarke*
v. *Bickers* (1845) 14 Sim. 639.
[96] *Com.* II, 507.
[97] *Ibid.* II, 508.
[98] Lindley, *Supplement* (1891) p. 36.

liability upon the individual copartners as is the case in England where
" the firm " is simply a convenient collective description of the individual
copartners. In his note on the section so far as affecting Scots law,[99]
Professor Lorimer does not examine this point in detail but refers the
reader to his annotation of section 9.[1] In his commentary on section 9,
Lorimer considers the question whether the effect of section 9 is that the
joint and several liability of the copartners in Scotland now arises immediately and in the first instance against a partner for a firm debt without its first having been constituted against the firm, as was required by the
pre-existing Scots law as expounded by Bell.[2] He expresses the opinion
that section 9 will not be held to have that effect. That opinion has been
consistently held by later writers.[3] All these writers baldly state the position to be that which existed in Scotland prior to the passing of the Act
and none bestows even a passing glance at the doubt raised by Lorimer.
Equally none (except Professor Walker) has cited any decision of the
courts in Scotland subsequent to the passing of the Act which supports
his view.

In the face of unanimity among such distinguished persons and having
also in mind the emphasis which has from generation to generation been
laid upon that view by those more humbly employed in the instruction of
future practitioners, it appears rash, if not presumptuous, to express even
the merest scintilla of doubt. Yet bare assertions of the sort encountered
in the textbooks leave one with the uneasy feeling that one may be observing the emergence of a twentieth-century mythology on this subject. That
uneasiness is the writer's excuse for pursuing the topic. It is possible to
seek reassurance in two ways. In the first place, one can examine again
the reasoning by which Lorimer came to his hesitant and modestly advanced
opinion that section 9 should not be interpreted as displacing the earlier
principle of Scots law that a firm debt must first be constituted against the
firm and that the liability of the partners therefor, although joint and
several, was of a secondary nature similar to that of a cautioner for the
principal debtor. Lorimer set out the arguments for each of the two conflicting interpretations which are possible. In favour of an interpretation
of section 9 which reads it as altering the former law so as to impose a joint
and several liability on the partners which is primary in nature, he referred
(a) to " the scope of the Act, which is imperial, and designed to declare
and amend the law applicable to the three kingdoms," (b) to the precise
terms of the section itself " and the fact that, though Scotland is mentioned
in it, no qualification of the liability in this particular is introduced and
none exists in England." In favour of the view that section 9 does not
disturb the secondary nature of the joint and several liability of the partners, he argues that the doctrine in Scots law of the separate *persona* of the

---

[99] *Eodem loco.*
[1] *Ibid.* pp. 32–33.   [2] *Supra* p. 352.
[3] Gloag, *Contract* (2nd ed.) p. 205; Gow, *Mercantile & Industrial Law of Scotland*, p. 548;
Bell, *Prin.* (1899 ed.) § 356; Lillie, *Mercantile Law of Scotland* (6th ed.) p. 247; Walker,
Delict, p. 139.

firm is recognised and continued elsewhere in the Act [4] and that, according to Bell, the secondary nature of the partners' joint and several liability is a consequence of that doctrine.[5]   Moreover, under the Act the rules of the common law are continued in force " except so far as they are inconsistent with the express provisions of this Act." [6]   According to Lorimer's view no inconsistency can be appealed to.   The joint and several liability of the partners is not denied by the common law of Scotland.   All that appears from the common law is an appended qualification that the joint and several liability is of a secondary nature and that qualification is based on a principle elsewhere sanctioned in section 4 (2) of the Act.   These are respectable arguments for reaching the conclusion which he reaches, that on the whole " the latter view appears to be the better opinion." [7]   The " qualification," however, is an important one and it is difficult to draw the line at a point where it is a mere innocuous gloss on the liability imposed by section 9 and where it introduces matter of such a substantial nature as to make the common law " inconsistent " with that express provision of section 9.

In this dilemma of doubt, the second course appears to be to make a close study of the cases on partnership decided since 1890 in the hope that some judicial authority may be gleaned which will assist in the removal of doubt. Even if some assistance can be found in these decisions, that will merely provide the answer to the correct basis of the liability of the partners for the contractual obligations of the firm since that is the question legislated for in section 9.   It may, therefore, be necessary further to compare and contrast that liability with the liability of the partners for the delictual obligations of the firm.   The most thorough examination which the nature of the partners' liability has received since the passing of the Partnership Act 1890 is at the hands of Lord President Cooper in *Mair* v. *Wood*,[8] a case concerned with liability in delict, but one in which the Lord President took occasion to examine the basic nature of the relationship between a firm and its partners.

> " It is fundamental to the Scots law of partnership," he said,[9] " that the firm is a legal *persona* distinct from the individuals who compose it.   This rule, which dates from the seventeenth century, has been expressly preserved by the Partnership Act [1890], section 4 (2); and it is the source of most of our distinctive rules both of substantive law and of procedure. . . .   One of the leading consequences of the doctrine of the separate *persona* is the principle that a firm may stand in the relation of debtor or creditor to any of its partners, and the rule of process that a partner cannot be sued for a company debt until that

[4] Partnership Act 1890, s. 4 (2).
[5] Bell, *Com.* II, 508.
[6] Partnership Act 1890, s. 46.
[7] Lindley, *Supplement* (1891) p. 82.
[8] 1948 S.C. 83.
[9] *Ibid.* pp. 86–87.

debt has first been constituted against the firm, *Neilson* v. *Wilson*.[10] Partners are of course liable jointly and severally in a question with a firm creditor for the obligations of the firm, but the theory of Scots law views them as being so liable only *subsidiarie*, the partners being in substance guarantors or cautioners for the firm's obligations, and each being entitled on payment of a firm debt to relief *pro rata* from the others.   The matter is so put in Bell's *Principles*, section 356, and *Commentaries* (7th ed.) Vol. ii, p. 508, and in the *Encyclopaedia, s.v.* ' Partnership,' xi, 29.

" Consequently it involves no conflict with the doctrine of *confusio* to allow a partner to take decree against the firm of which he is a partner, because the partner's liability for a firm debt is not a primary liability, and it is one in respect of which he enjoys a right of relief against his copartners. (*Gloag on Contract* (2nd ed.) p. 276 and authorities there cited.)   It is only at the second stage, when the firm debt comes to be met by the individual partners, that *confusio* would operate; and it would then operate only to the effect of preventing the pursuer from recovering from his copartners that proportion of the firm debt for which as a partner he is liable in a question with his copartners."

That passage has been quoted at length, including Lord Cooper's observations on the plea of *confusio* advanced by the defenders, since the view of the fundamental nature of the liability is illustrated and, it is thought, rendered more abundantly clear by Lord Cooper's treatment of that defence.   It is true that the Lord President, in the course of his judgment, nowhere considers the effect of express provisions of section 9 of the Partnership Act 1890.   That is hardly surprising because the case before the court in *Mair* v. *Wood* was one of delictual liability and not of contractual liability with which alone section 9 is concerned.   Nevertheless, the Lord President's reasoning clearly discloses his view that the joint and several liability of the partners for a contractual obligation of the firm is accessory, and not primary, in nature, and it must be inferred from that reasoning that he regards the words of section 9 as qualified by the Scottish common law doctrine as to the liability of the partners.   The force of that view is compelling on two mutually reinforcing grounds, apart altogether from the eminence of the judge who pronounced it.   (1) There is the point emphasised by the Lord President that the Partnership Act itself recognises the separate *persona* of the partnership; so that when the terms of section 9 come to be interpreted in the Scottish courts, that interpretation will be preferred which gives effect to the provisions of the statute as a whole.[11] The implications of recognition of the separate *persona* of the firm militate against the notion that the joint and several liability imposed on the partners in section 9 is to be regarded as primary and unqualified, since, as the

[10] (1890) 17 R. 608, *per* Lord President Inglis at p. 612; Maclaren's *Court of Session Practice*, p. 208; Gloag, *Contract* (2nd ed.) pp. 205–206.
[11] *Incivile est nisi tota lege perspecta una aliqua particula ejus praeposita judicare vel respondere*: *Dig.* I, 3, 24.   See *Minister of Health* v. *Stafford* [1952] Ch. 730.

Lord President points out, the doctrine of the separate *persona* of the firm is itself the source of the principles (a) that the liability of the partners is of an accessory or subsidiary nature and (b) that in order to impose that liability on the partners, the debt must first be constituted against the firm.   (2) The common law doctrine of a joint and several liability which is accessory in nature may thus be regarded as consistent with the express provisions of the Partnership Act 1890 and thus preserved by section 46. If it were to be taken as inconsistent with the provisions of section 9, that could be done only at the expense of creating a further inconsistency with section 4 (2).   Since the words of section 9 are neutral as to the nature of the joint and several liability imposed on the partners, it appears that the qualification imported by the Scottish common law is not inconsistent with them whereas to regard section 9 as displacing the Scottish common law doctrine of partnership would itself involve a serious conflict with the terms of section 4 (2).

Joint and several liability in delict

While the joint and several liability of the partners for the contractual obligations of the firm may thus be regarded as an accessory liability in Scotland in spite of the absence of any such qualifying terms in section 9 of the Partnership Act 1890, that does not, of itself, dispose of the problem as to joint and several liability in delict as provided for in section 12.   The terms of that section have already been quoted [12] and it will be noticed that in section 12 as in section 9 the wording accords more easily with the underlying common law in England than in Scotland.   Indeed the ordering of the two sections seems to be devised with the primary object of explaining the essential distinction in English law between the liability of the partner in contract on the one hand and in tort on the other hand.   In regard to the obligations of the firm arising *ex contractu* every partner is in England liable jointly with the other partners for the debts contracted while he is a partner and after his death his estate is also severally liable.   In regard to torts of the firm, however, the partners are liable, not only jointly, but also severally.   As a result, the plaintiff who sues upon a debt or a contractual obligation of the firm must bring one action against the members of the firm.   He is not allowed to bring several actions against them.   He need not call all the members of the firm as defendants but if he chooses to omit some of them, he loses his rights against the partners whom he has omitted, though the court may, on the motion of any of the defendants to his action, order the partners so omitted to be added as co-defendants in the action. A plaintiff who sues upon a tort of the firm may issue separate writs against each partner.   He may issue those separate writs either contemporaneously or successively and, if successively, then if the defendant to his first action becomes bankrupt, he is not precluded, upon the score of having sued that partner alone, from raising a second action against another

---

[12] *Supra* p. 352.

partner.[13]   That distinction does not entail any difference between the law of England and the Scots law as to the extent of the liability of any partner for a debt of his firm.   In England, as in Scotland, " every member of an ordinary partnership is liable to the utmost farthing of his property for the debts and engagements of the firm." [14]   But the route by which this destination is reached in England bears no resemblance to the legal theory underlying the unlimited liability of a partner in Scotland.   In England the law ignores the firm as an entity separate and distinct from the persons composing it and treats the debts and engagements of the firm as those of the individual partners.   Thus if judgment be obtained against the partners for a joint (a " firm ") debt, the creditor need not do diligence against the property of the firm before he has recourse to the property of an individual partner; nor need he do diligence against all the partners *pro rata*.   He may choose any one or more of the partners and levy execution on him or them until he has received satisfaction of the sum in his judgment decree, leaving questions of contribution among the partners as a whole to be settled subsequently *inter se*.[15]   That is the obverse side of the principle of joint liability as explained by Underhill.[16]   The joint liability of the partner in no way limits the *extent* of his liability but in order to impose that unlimited liability upon him the creditor must sue him jointly with such other members of the firm as he intends to hold liable.   When the third party founds upon a tort which is imputable to the firm, he is not subject to the rule of joint liability which requires him to sue all the partners jointly under pain of being held to have excused any partner whom he does not conjoin in his action.   The liability of the partners in tort is joint *and several* under section 12 of the Partnership Act 1890.   Hence he may sue the partners separately and even successively.   This distinction drawn by the English law is not explained by any of the English works of authority.   It seems possible, however, that it is yet a further consequence of the English legal theory which identifies the firm with the individual partners comprising it, so that where section 10, for example, declares that when a third party has been occasioned loss or injury by any wrongful act or omission of any partner acting in the ordinary course of the business of the firm, *the firm* is liable therefor, that in English terms is tantamount to saying that the individual partners are so liable.   Thus a situation arises under English law where the partners, as individuals, are liable as joint tortfeasors, or co-delinquents, with the legal result that they are jointly and severally liable to the victim in reparation.[17]

Basis of the partners' liability in delict under Scots law

It will be obvious that, as with section 9, the position of the partners in

[13] Underhill, *Principles of the Law of Partnership* (9th ed.) p. 71.
[14] Lindley, *op. cit.* p. 234.
[15] *Abbott* v. *Smith* (1760) 2 W.Bl. 947, *per* de Grey C.J. at p. 949.   [16] *Supra* n. 13.
[17] In the great majority of cases of vicarious liability both the principal (the firm) and the delinquent partner will be liable as joint tortfeasors and thus all will be liable *in solidum* to the victim. See Atiyah, *Vicarious Liability in the Law of Torts*, p. 421.   For the similar position in Scots law, see Walker, *Delict*, pp. 119 *et seq.*

Scots law with regard to their liability for a wrongful act imputed to the firm may not be disposed of upon the theory which has been advanced to account for it in English law. In Scotland the situation of the copartners themselves as co-delinquents with the erring partner is not so readily ascertainable, since the firm itself is a *quasi* person in law and, both in terms of the underlying principles of Scottish legal theory and of the wording of sections 10 and 11 of the Partnership Act 1890, it is the firm itself, and not the individual partners, which appears in the light of the co-delinquent. When section 12 of the Partnership Act 1890 imposed upon every partner a liability " jointly with his co-partners and also severally for everything for which the firm while he is a partner therein becomes liable under either " section 10 or section 11, the question whether the common law of Scotland has been silently revolutionised by these words is just as clamant, and is perhaps even more difficult to answer, than it was in relation to section 9. It is clear, however, from his judgment in *Mair* v. *Wood*[18] that Lord President Cooper regards the liability of the partners for a wrong imputed to their firm as of the same order as their liability for a contractual obligation of their firm. The partners are, in his view, in the nature of guarantors or cautioners for the firm. As such, their joint and several liability is an accessory liability and is distinguishable from the joint and several liability which would be imposed on them were they regarded in the light of co-delinquents rather than cautioners. In particular, it would appear to follow from the distinction that the victim cannot, as he can in England, raise separate and successive actions against the partners for reparation. He must constitute his claim against the firm before he has any claim against the individual partners as cautioners for the firm.

Improper employment of trust property for partnership purposes

The liability of one partner for a breach of trust committed by his co-partner is not strictly a partnership liability in the same sense in which a vicarious liability of the firm may arise under section 11 of the Partnership Act 1890.[19] The knowledge of the offending partner that he is in breach of trust is not the knowledge of his firm and in order that the firm and his co-partners may be held liable, further evidence must be led to establish that they had notice of the breach.[20] It is not sufficient of itself to impose liability on his copartners that the offending partner's breach of trust has involved the use of the trust funds in the partnership business though that feature will have an obvious bearing in some cases to establish knowledge on the part of the copartners. To establish that knowledge, it will usually be relevant to consider the nature of the partnership itself and the use made of the trust money in the partnership business. In *Cochrane* v.

---

[18] 1948 S.C. 83. See also *Gordon* v. *British & Foreign Metaline Co.* (1886) 14 R. 75.
[19] Pollock, *Digest of the Law of Partnership* (5th ed.) p. 48; Lindley, *op. cit.* p. 204.
[20] *Ex p. Apsey* (1791) 3 Bro.C.C. 265; *Ex p. White, re Nevill* (1871) L.R. 6 Ch. 397; *Ex p. Heaton* (1819) Buck. 386.

Black and Another,[21] the defenders were the partners of a firm who were also trustees under a testamentary trust. The testator had left the bulk of his estate in the hands of the firm and, in spite of his directions, to realise his estate after his death and invest it in specified types of security, the partner/trustees allowed it to remain with the firm and interest at 5 per cent. per annum was paid thereon. The partner/trustees were held to be in breach of trust and were ordered to account for and pay to the beneficiaries " any profits made on the funds so employed over and above the five per cent. of interest paid to the pursuers " and it was remitted to an accountant to examine the books and report " what amount of profit, if any, was made on the proportion of the capital in trade representing the trust funds and by the defenders in their trade during said period, after deducting 5 per cent. per annum from the profits on said proportion of capital, if profit was made. . . ." After receiving the accountant's report, the court directed him further in these terms—

> " Finds that in ascertaining the amount of profits made on the trust funds belonging to the pursuers employed by the defenders in their trade no fixed sum, whether stated in the docquets to the balance sheets or otherwise, is to be taken as the amount of the proper capital or stock of the company of J. Black and Company in reference to which the trust money as it may stand at the commencement of any yearly or half-yearly period is to be rated and to share in profits with the partners on that sum as a proportion of such divisible capital: And find that in ascertaining at any particular date the amount of the capital or fund by which, together with the trust monies, the profits (if any) for the succeeding period of a year or half year is to be held to have been made, there is to be taken into account not only the amount of what may be found to be the proper input stock or funds of the partners employed in the trade of the company but all other funds or monies, whether consisting of money regularly borrowed on loan or obtained in any other way in order to be employed in the business, and which have accordingly been invested and employed in it, and on which the trade has truly been carried on for the period in question: Find that the stock or funds employed in the trade, including the trust money, and by which the profit is held to have been made as aforesaid, being ascertained, the share of the profit to be assigned to the pursuers is to be in the proportion which the amount of the trust money bears to the whole amount of the said stock or fund. . . ."

In that case, however, although there were other copartners who were not trustees, they were not sued and the interlocutors of the court were directed toward ascertaining what the partner/trustees as trustees were due to make good to the beneficiaries in the trust. On the other hand in *Macfarlane* v. *Donaldson* [22] a firm of solicitors and the individual partners were held

---

[21] (1855) 17 D. 321; (1857) 19 D. 1019.
[22] (1835) 13 S. 725.

liable for the intromissions of one of the partners who was factor *loco tutoris* to a pupil child and who, to the knowledge of his copartners, immixed the funds belonging to the factory with the funds of the firm.

The law announced in the earlier decisions cited is now reflected in section 13 of the Partnership Act 1890—

"If a partner, being a trustee, improperly employs trust property in the business or on the account of the partnership, no other partner is liable for the trust property to the persons beneficially interested therein;

Provided as follows:

(1) This section shall not affect any liability incurred by any partner by reason of his having notice of a breach of trust; and

(2) Nothing in this section shall prevent trust money from being followed and recovered from the firm if still in its possession or under its control."

Distinction to be drawn between section 11 and section 13

There is a resemblance in the situations which are regulated under section 11 and section 13 respectively since under both sections money or property of a third party has been misapplied. A clear distinction must, nevertheless, be preserved as to the situation which each section attempts to govern; otherwise it will be difficult to reconcile the principle stated in section 11 and the earlier decisions on which it is founded.[23] In cases of liability under section 11, the money has reached the hands of the firm in the ordinary course of its business. Under section 13 that is not the case. The money has reached the firm's hands as a result of a breach of trust. There is, consequently, no room for the application of the principle of implied or apparent authority in cases under section 13. If liability is to attach to the firm in these cases an entirely different principle must be appealed to and it will not be enough to establish that the firm has had the benefit of the trust funds.[24] If the firm is to be held liable for the partner's breach of trust, the firm itself must be implicated in that breach of trust; and for the firm to become so implicated it will be necessary to establish that all the partners were aware of the source of the funds or at least knew that the funds did not belong to the partner who applied them in the running of the firm's business. In cases arising under section 13, such knowledge on the part of one partner is not imputed to his copartners under section 16 of the Partnership Act 1890 because the constructive notice provided for in section 16 arises in closely qualified circumstances. The knowledge of one partner to be imputed to his copartners must (a) be the knowledge of a partner " who habitually acts in the partnership business " and (b) it must be concerned with a " matter relating to the partnership

---

[23] *e.g. Rapp* v. *Latham* (1819) 2 B. & Ald. 795; *Wemyss* v. *Australian Company of Edinburgh* (1856) 19 D. 122; *Marsh* v. *Keating* (1834) 2 Cl. & F. 250.

[24] The firm may be held liable *quantum lucratus*: see *New Mining & Exploring Syndicate Ltd.* v. *Chalmers & Hunter*, 1912 S.C. 126. But that is distinguishable from imposing a vicarious responsibility on the firm for the breach of trust.

affairs," and a breach of trust by an individual who happens also to be a partner has no relation to the partnership affairs.

The basis of implication in the partner's breach of trust rests, therefore, on having knowledge of it and the knowledge required is actual, not constructive, knowledge of the individual partners. This can be clearly seen if the wording of section 13 is compared with that of section 11. Whereas section 11 refers to the liability of the firm for the misapplication of money received by a partner " within the scope of his apparent authority " or received by the firm " in the course of its business," section 13 does not in terms refer to the liability of the firm at all. It provides that " no other partner " is liable for his copartner's breach of trust subject to proviso (1) which preserves the liability of the other partner " by reason of his having notice " of the breach of trust. What is required for liability under section 13 is knowledge which can be imputed to the other partner individually, and knowledge so imputed to him will not affect his other copartners who are equally with him innocent of the original breach of trust. If those other partners are unaware of the breach, liability will not extend to them.[25] " It is not within the scope of the implied authority of a partner in such a business that he should so act as to make himself a constructive trustee, and thereby subject his partner to the same liability." [26] On the other hand there is nothing in section 13 to *preclude* liability of the firm for a partner's breach of trust; but if the firm is to be held liable, then knowledge on the part of *all* the copartners must be established. " Where parties in the position of a company are implicated in a breach of trust by one of its partners, and take the benefit of that breach of trust, they are just as much bound to repay any sum they may have got in that way as the individual partner whose active agency procured the money." [27]

In determining what will amount to knowledge on the part of a co-partner who is innocent of the perpetration of the breach of trust, the circumstances of each case will, naturally, govern the decision so that the reported decisions offer little more than the most general guide. In *McFarlane* v. *Donaldson* [28] liability was imposed upon the other partner and his firm for the breach of trust of his copartner on the ground of implication in the breach. This clearly appears from the judgment of the Lord Ordinary (Lord Fullerton) who states—

> " The present, however, is a special case, and it appears to the Lord Ordinary to warrant the application of a different principle from that which seems, upon very reasonable grounds to have been adopted in the decision referred to.[29] Messrs. Low and Rutherford were the

[25] *Ex p. Heaton* (1819) Buck. 386.
[26] *Per* Lord Herschell in *Mara* v. *Browne* [1896] 1 Ch. 199 at p. 208.
[27] *Per* Lord Adam in *Scottish Pacific Coast Mining Co. Ltd.* v. *Falkner Bell & Co.* (1888) 15 R. 290 at p. 306. See also *Liquidators of Imperial Mercantile Credit Association* v. *Coleman & Knight* (1871) L.R. 6 H.L. 189.   [28] *Supra* p. 359 n. 22.
[29] *i.e. Wilson* (1826) 4 S. 732, where it was held that where the parties were willing to take the risk of paying the partner as a trustee in his individual capacity without seeing his title completed, the firm as solicitors for the partner in his capacity as trustee were not bound to interpel, or warn, them from doing so.

agents in the application to the court for the appointment of one of the firm, Mr. Low, as factor *loco tutoris* and curator bonis. It was their duty to know, and they must be presumed to have ascertained, whether caution had been found, and the act extracted, before proceeding one step further, as agents for Mr. Low, in that character. Still more was it their duty to ascertain that fact before they, as agents, countenanced the payment to, and the appropriation by, Mr. Low of large sums of money, which he was entitled to receive only in that character. Now, it follows, from the entries in their books, that the company must be held to have been cognisant, not only of Mr. Low assuming that character in dealing with Mr. McFarlane and Donaldson's trustees, but of those trustees paying large sums of money, on the reliance of his title having been complete. Not only are the revisal of the discharge, the meeting with Mr. McFarlane for the purpose of signing the discharge, and the various letters addressed to Mr. McFarlane in relation to the transference of the shares of the minors, entered as articles of charge in the company's books, but various of the payments received by Mr. Low, as curator, are entered in the company's books at the credit of the minors, under the designation of ' Donaldson's executors.' In short, it rather appears from the books that, although Mr. Low was appointed the factor and curator, the business charges of his actings in that capacity truly formed part of the profits of the company."

In examining the words of Lord Fullerton it is important to regard them as a recital of elements to which weight may be given in imputing the knowledge to Low's copartner which will render him liable, rather than as a recital of duties incumbent upon Low's firm and copartner. The form of expression, which the Lord Ordinary chose to adopt in the earlier part of the extract quoted from his judgment, might suggest otherwise but must be taken in context and, in particular, in association with the circumstance that any " duty " to ensure that caution was found and the act extracted was imposed upon them " before they countenanced the payment to Mr. Low." In the latter part of the judgment as quoted it becomes clear that the case hovers uncertainly between what would now-a-days be a section 13 liability and a section 11 responsibility of the firm. The earlier considerations advanced all point towards a liability on the ground of knowledge of Low's breach of trust but the later considerations and particularly those regarding the articles of business charges in the firm's accounts and the view that those business charges " truly formed part of the profits of the company " rather tend towards establishing that the money obtained by Low in breach of trust and credited to the minors in the firm's books was money received by the firm in the course of its business and would thus support a case against the firm under section 11.

It may be useful to examine and contrast the cases in which the courts have held that no liability attaches for the breach of trust except to the individual partner who has committed the breach. The most arresting contrast is perhaps to be found in *Ex parte Heaton* [30] where a father and his sons were partners. The sons were trustees under a will and in breach of trust they applied the trust funds in their charge to the purposes of the firm's business. The firm became bankrupt and it was held that the claim of the beneficiaries for the money so appropriated in breach of trust could not be proved against the joint estate of the bankrupt partners unless it were first established that the money was used for the purposes of the firm's business with the knowledge of the father who was not a trustee. The court directed inquiry to be made into this aspect. In *Ex parte Apsey* [31] a partner in a firm was an assignee in bankruptcy and applied part of the bankrupt's assets towards paying debts of his firm. In the subsequent bankruptcy of the firm, the amount so used in paying the firm's debts was not allowed to be proved against the joint estate. In *Ex parte White, re Nevill* [32] a firm, Towle & Company, arranged with Nevill, a partner of Nevill, Jourdain & Company, to sell their goods. He paid the sums received by him into, and discharged the sums due to his suppliers by payments by his own firm out of, a private account which he kept with his own firm. On Nevill, Jourdain & Company becoming bankrupt, Towle & Company sought to prove against the joint estate for the amount standing to Nevill's credit in that account, but they were held to have no right to follow the money since they had employed Nevill as an individual to act as agent for them.

In general, therefore, knowledge on the part of those partners who are not involved in the perpetration of the actual breach of trust is requisite if they are to be held liable along with the partner who committed it. Actual knowledge of the breach need not in every case be established against the partner. If it is reasonable to regard a partner as being aware that trust funds are being used in the business of the partnership, he will then be under an obligation to inquire and to satisfy himself that the trust in question empowers the trustees to apply the trust funds in that manner and he will be held liable, if he neglects to do so, and the funds are lost through application to these purposes in breach of trust. [33]

Effect of Solicitors' Accounts Rules

So far as partnerships of solicitors are concerned requirements of considerable stringency have been introduced since the passing of the Partnership Act 1890. These are contained in the Solicitors (Scotland) Accounts Rules 1952, [34] as amended by the Solicitors (Scotland) Accounts Rules (Amendment) Rules 1963 and the Solicitors (Scotland) Accounts Rules (Amendment) Rules 1965. The Rules apply [35] to every solicitor holding

---

[30] (1819) Buck. 386.
[31] (1791) 3 Bro.C.C. 265.
[32] (1871) L.R. 6 Ch. 397.
[33] *Ex p. Woodin* (1843) 3 Mont.D. & D. 399; *Ex p. Poulson* (1844) De Gex 79.
[34] Made by the Council of the Law Society of Scotland and approved by the Lord President of the Court of Session under the Solicitors (Scotland) Act 1949, s. 20.
[35] Solicitors (Scotland) Accounts Rules 1952, r. 2 (1).

a practising certificate except for a solicitor [36] employed as solicitor to a Minister of the Crown, or a governmental department or as an assistant or officer appointed to act under the direction of such solicitor [37] or in the employment in an office connected with the administration of a local authority or a statutory undertaking or a designated body to which he has been appointed, by the authority or the statutory undertakers or the person responsible for the management of the body, by reason of his being a solicitor.[38]   A local authority means a county council, town council or district council " or a combination of such councils "; " statutory undertakers " are as defined in the Local Government (Scotland) Act 1947, section 379 (1), i.e. " any persons (including a local authority) authorised by any enactment or statutory order or any scheme made under or confirmed by an enactment to construct, work or carry on any railway, light railway, tramway, road transport, water transport, canal, inland navigation, dock, harbour, pier or lighthouse undertaking or any undertaking for the supply of gas, electricity, hydraulic power or water." A " designated body " means any body, whether corporate or unincorporate, for the time being designated by the Council of the Law Society of Scotland for the purposes of section 20 of the Solicitors (Scotland) Act 1949.[39]

The effect of the rules is to ensure that money held for or received on behalf of a client by the solicitor shall " without delay " be paid into a bank account—the " client account "—kept separate from the bank account in which money belonging to the solicitor is lodged.   Exception is made in the case of sums of £50 or less,[40] and in the case of cash receipts paid without delay to the client or to a third party on his behalf,[41] cheques or drafts indorsed over in the ordinary course of business to the client or to a third party on his behalf and not passed by the solicitor through a bank account,[42] payment without delay into a separate bank account opened in the name of the client or of some person named by him,[43] where the client for his own convenience requests the solicitor in writing not to lodge the sum received in client account,[44] where the sum is received for or to account of a debt due to the solicitor from the client or in repayment of money expended by the solicitor on the client's behalf [45] or where the money is received by the solicitor expressly on account of a professional account incurred by the client or to account of an agreed fee for the business done for him.[46]

---

[36] *Ibid.* r. 3.
[37] Solicitors (Scotland) Act 1949, s. 20 (2) (*a*).
[38] *Ibid.* s. 20 (2) (*b*).   In both excepted cases the exemption applies only to moneys received, held or paid by him " in the course of that employment " where he is employed by a Minister of the Crown or a government department and " in the course of his employment in such office " where he holds an office connected with the administration of a local authority, statutory undertaking or designated body.
[39] *Ibid.* s. 20 (2).
[40] Solicitors (Scotland) Accounts Rules 1952, r. 4 (1).
[41] *Ibid.* r. 7 (*a*).
[42] *Ibid.* r. 7 (*b*).
[43] *Ibid.* r. 7 (*c*).
[44] *Ibid.* r. 7 (*d*).
[45] *Ibid.* r. 7 (*e*).
[46] *Ibid.* r. 7 (*f*).

These rules are imposed in the interests of the standing of the profession as a whole in the eyes of the public. A written complaint of breach of them may give rise to an investigation by a person appointed by the Council of the Law Society of Scotland to ascertain whether the Rules are being complied with, or the Council may, on their own motion, initiate such an investigation.[47] The Solicitors (Scotland) Accounts Rules 1952 will have an obvious effect in reducing in practice the incidence of cases within partnerships of solicitors of inadvertent misappropriation of funds belonging to clients and possibly will to some extent minimise the already rare cases where a partner of intent misappropriates them. They may therefore have a bearing on cases where liability may arise either under section 11 or section 13 of the Partnership Act 1890; and in considering whether the innocent partners are implicated under section 13 it may be a relevant circumstance to be taken into account that under the Rules each partner of a firm of solicitors has placed upon him the responsibility for securing compliance by the firm with the provisions of the Rules.[48] That responsibility is imposed as a matter of professional conduct within the context of the Rules and would not, it is thought, be necessarily conclusive in a case where the court is called upon to decide whether knowledge of a breach of trust should be imputed to a partner under section 13, but it appears to be a factor with a bearing upon the decision. To that extent the Rules might be appealed to in cases arising under section 13. Otherwise, the view has been expressed in relation to the similar regulations affecting solicitors in England that " the provisions of section 13 of the Partnership Act 1890 are not affected, since the regulations and the compensation fund in question are in essence a domestic concern of the solicitors' profession. Their relevance is, first, that the regulations operate to prevent firms of solicitors and each member thereof from falling into error or actionable wrongdoing, and, secondly, that a breach of them for which one solicitor partner is responsible as between the partners may possibly constitute a breach of the obligation between partners to be just and faithful to each other, or otherwise found a case for dissolution or other relief against the partner in default." [49] If the previously mentioned additional factor of relevance on section 13 cases is kept in view it is possible, respectfully, to agree with the opinion quoted. The Rules are not designed to alter or amend the basic liability arising in partnership under section 13 of the Partnership Act 1890 but are designed as a matter of domestic regulation within the profession to ensure proper handling of clients' money, and public confidence in the profession. In the latter design they are supplemented by the Guarantee Fund [50] established to compensate clients of solicitors for pecuniary loss incurred by them " by reason of dishonesty on the part of a solicitor or any servant of any solicitor, in connection with the practice of the solicitor, or any trust of which the

---

[47] *Ibid.* r. 9.
[48] *Ibid.* r. 10.
[49] Lindley, *op. cit.* p. 203.
[50] Set up under the Scottish Solicitors' Guarantee Fund Rules 1951.

solicitor was or is a trustee." [51] The two aspects of the design are, however, interwoven since it is evident that if the profession as a whole undertakes to guarantee the actings of its individual members, adequate rules must be promulgated to ensure the proper keeping of accounts to prevent the immixing of clients' money with the money of the firm; and these Rules have their effect in controlling cases of inadvertent misapplication of clients' money under section 11 of the Partnership Act 1890 as well as breach of trust by a solicitor partner under section 13.[52]

Advice by a firm of solicitors leading to a breach of trust

Section 13 is concerned with the liability, or otherwise, of partners in a firm for a breach of trust committed by one of their number. The partners in a firm of solicitors may be called upon to advise a body of trustees, without themselves being trustees, as to such matters as the investment of trust funds and if the advice tendered is erroneous the trustees may be implicated in a breach of trust through following it. In many such cases, the solicitor tendering the advice, and his firm, may be answerable to the trustees in a claim for damages for professional negligence [53]; but if no such claim can be maintained, the area of liability of the solicitor, and his firm, is not extended by reason of section 13 of the Partnership Act 1890. In *Brimsden* v. *Williams* [54] a trustee sought the assistance of a partner in a firm of solicitors in order to invest the trust funds in a mortgage. The firm of solicitors also acted for the mortgagors. The partner consulted by the trustee knew that the money to be advanced on mortgage was trust money and the security offered was improper in character and insufficient in value for such a purpose. But the trustee did not request the advice of the solicitor partner on these aspects. He acted on his own responsibility in accepting the security. The title deeds of the property which was to be the subject of the mortgage were held by a bank as security for an overdraft and the trust money advanced on the mortgage was to be paid to the bank who would then give up their charge and deliver the title deeds to the solicitor. This was accomplished by the trustee handing the solicitor a cheque for the money advanced which the solicitor paid into his firm's banking account, next day giving the banker who held the title deeds his firm's cheque for the same amount and in return receiving the title deeds. The

[51] The Scottish Solicitors' Guarantee Fund Rules 1951, r. 2 (1).

[52] Mr. W. A. Cook, a former president of the Law Society of Scotland, has drawn my attention to the fact that the Law Society of Scotland have taken the view in a number of cases that, where funds of a trust of which one partner of a firm of solicitors was a trustee were embezzled, the other partners were liable to make good the loss. Mr. Cook observes, " The explanation may be that in these cases the firm were factors to the trust, so that moneys received by the trustee partner would be received by him ' in the course of his practice ' in terms of r. 2 (1) of the Solicitors (Scotland) Accounts Rules 1952. It was the duty of all the partners to comply with the Rules and accordingly to see that the moneys were lodged in a client account. If moneys were not so lodged or were later improperly withdrawn it may be that the innocent partners, looking to their duty to comply with the Accounts Rules, could not maintain that they had no notice of the breach of trust."

[53] *Blyth* v. *Fladgate* [1891] 1 Ch. 337; *Tully* v. *Ingram* (1891) 19 R. 65. And see *supra* p. 308 n. 28.

[54] [1894] 3 Ch. 185.

investment thus made was in breach of trust and it later resulted in a loss to the trust whereupon one of the beneficiaries sought to hold the solicitor, who was then the sole surviving partner of his firm, liable therefor. The court, however, held that the actings of the solicitor were solely in his character as agent for the trustee and that he was not implicated in the breach of trust.[55]

Liability of firm where a partner is a director of a company

The directors of a limited company owe to the company duties of a fiduciary nature in administering the company's affairs and where in the management of the company's affairs a director secures for himself an unauthorised or an undisclosed profit, he may be called upon by the company to account for that profit to them.[56]   While the position of the director is not in all respects that of a trustee for the company, breach by him of his fiduciary duties to the company raises a situation analogous to that arising on breach of trust.   Where a partner of a firm holds office as director of a company and with the knowledge of his copartners enters into a contract with the company from which his firm makes an undisclosed profit, he and his firm and copartners will be held liable to account to the company for the profit so earned.[57]   The implications of the decisions cited were more fully examined at an earlier stage in this chapter [58] when liability of the firm under section 10 of the Partnership Act 1890 was under consideration.   Though certain of the reported decisions appear to be a trifle ambivalent, it is thought that the true *ratio decidendi* of such cases is that the remaining partners of the firm, either through actual knowledge or through imputable knowledge, are regarded as implicated in the breach of duty of their partner who is the director and that his breach of duty is regarded as equivalent to a breach of trust.   Though the point does not appear to have been before the courts since the passing of the Partnership Act 1890, it seems probable that any such case arising in the future may be decided on an application of the terms of section 13 of the Act.   Section 10 appears entirely inappropriate both in regard to its ambit and in regard to the remedy available to the third party thereunder.

Joint and several liability of partners

While the Partnership Act 1890 provides explicitly for the joint and several liability of the partners when they are answerable under either section 10 or section 11, it is silent as to the nature of their liability when

[55] In *Mara* v. *Browne* [1896] 1 Ch. 199 a similar decision was reached though on the facts it is conceivable that an action for damages would have lain against the firm of solicitors if it had not been barred by the Statute of Limitations.
[56] *Regal (Hastings) Ltd.* v. *Gulliver and Others* [1942] 1 All E.R. 378; *Boston Deep Sea Fishing & Ice Co.* v. *Ansell* (1888) 39 Ch.D. 339.
[57] *Falkner Bell & Company* v. *Scottish Pacific Coast Mining Company Ltd.* (1888) 15 R. 290; *Liquidators of the Imperial Mercantile Credit Association* v. *Coleman & Knight* (1871) L.R. 6 H.L. 189.
[58] *Supra* pp. 323–326.

they are answerable under proviso (1) to section 13. The general rule of law is that persons who are implicated in a breach of trust are jointly and severally liable to the beneficiaries for the loss incurred even though, as among themselves, differing degrees of blame may attach to each.[59] On this basis it is stated that " if partners are implicated in a breach of trust, their liability is joint and several." [60] It is not possible to accept that statement entirely uncritically so far as Scots law is concerned. The leading Scottish decision [61] goes no further than to assert that all *trustees* who are implicated are jointly and severally liable for breach of trust. It is true that where a partner who is a trustee commits a breach of trust to the knowledge of his copartners by misapplying the trust funds under his charge to the purposes of the partnership, his copartners may be said to be implicated in his breach of trust, and they may be answerable for a breach of duty to the beneficiaries as a result. But they do not become co-trustees with their partner as a consequence of their being implicated in his breach of trust; and unless some general rule of the law of trust can be invoked which imposes joint and several liability upon all implicated in a breach of trust, *whether trustees or not*, then it is impossible to ascribe that liability to the partners of the trustee upon the general principles of the law of trusts. There appears to be a general rule of that nature in England and Sir Frederick Pollock clearly held the view that liability of one partner for another partner's breach of trust was not a partnership liability.[62] But the authorities cited in *Lindley on Partnership* [63] cannot all be regarded as supporting the rule.[64] In cases such as *Blyth* v. *Fladgate* the action is based on professional negligence on the part of a member of a firm of solicitors. *Blair* v. *Bromley* might now be brought within the ambit of section 11 of the Partnership Act 1890 rather than section 13. It is submitted that the decision in *Devaynes* v. *Noble, Sleech's Case* may be similarly explained although in most of the foregoing cases dicta are to be found which suggest that the equitable rule applied was that a breach of trust imputable to a firm always has created a joint and several obligation upon the partners to make it good. *Brydges* v. *Branfill* concerned the liability of the firm for a partner's fraud; and in *Re Oxford Benefit Building Society* directors of a limited company who had improperly paid out dividends were held liable jointly and severally " as upon a breach of trust " to repay the sums improperly paid as dividends. *Sadler* v. *Lee* raised an issue of liability similar to that decided in *Blair* v. *Bromley*. In none of these cases does the equitable rule that all implicated in a breach of trust are liable therefor jointly and severally appear to be involved save upon

---

[59] *Lawrence* v. *Bowle* (1846) 2 Ph. 140; 78 R.R. 54; *Allen* v. *McCombie's Trs.*, 1909 S.C. 710.
[60] Lindley, *op. cit.* p. 206.
[61] *Allen* v. *McCombie's Trs., supra.*
[62] *Digest of the Law of Partnership* (5th ed.) p. 48.
[63] *Loc. cit.*
[64] *Blyth* v. *Fladgate* [1891] 1 Ch. 337 at p. 353; *Re Oxford Benefit Building Society* (1886) 35 Ch.D. 502; *Imperial Mercantile Credit Assn.* v. *Coleman* (1871) L.R. 6 H.L. 189; *Devaynes* v. *Noble, Sleech's Case* (1816) 1 Mer. 539; *Baring's Case* (1816) 1 Mer. 611; *Sadler* v. *Lee* (1843) 6 Beav. 324; *Brydges* v. *Branfill* (1842) 12 Sim. 369; *Blair* v. *Bromley* (1847) 2 Ph. 354; *Wilson* v. *Moore* (1832) 1 Myl. & K. 126; *Ex p. Poulson* (1844) De Gex 79.

arguments of analogy. In *Wilson* v. *Moore*, however, the liability appears to have been based upon that rule and the same principle appears from *Ex parte Sheppard, re Parkers.*[65]

So far as Scots law is concerned, the decision in *Liquidators of Imperial Mercantile Credit Association* v. *Coleman & Knight* is perhaps the most persuasive since it was cited with approval in the similar Scottish case of *Falkner Bell & Company* v. *Scottish Pacific Coast Mining Company Limited.* These cases have already been discussed at some length [66] and the opinion has been expressed that the *ratio decidendi* cannot be consistent with any ground of liability other than for a partner's breach of fiduciary duty. While the expressions " trust " and " fiduciary duty " are not interchangeable, it may at least be asserted that every trustee owes fiduciary duties to the beneficiaries in the trust and to that extent the decision in those cases may justify the application of the more general principle of English equity in all cases of breach of trust in Scotland. Perhaps the only safe generalisation to be made is that in Scotland, as in England, there has been a tendency to regard a firm which is implicated in a partner's breach of trust as liable jointly and severally along with the offending partner, but the precise process of reasoning whereby that conclusion is reached is not clearly explained. There is at times a tendency to invoke the rule as applied in cases of delict, such as fraud, but that will not serve, since the Partnership Act 1890 has expressly provided for joint and several liability in such cases while the Act remains silent as to the nature of the firm's liability for a partner's breach of trust. When thus thrown back on the common law, the student again tends to find the purported rule of equity supported in a rather equivocal manner. Most of the cases in which the joint and several liability of the firm has been imposed have been cases of a partner's fraudulent conduct. Many cases of breach of trust will involve fraud or fraudulent misapplication of trust moneys but these are cases in which the pre-existing equitable rule of joint and several liability is not required since they fall under either section 10 or section 11 of the Partnership Act and joint and several liability is expressly imposed by section 12. Another prevalent situation in which the question of a partner's breach of trust is appealed to is where the firm is implicated in an irregular investment of the trust funds amounting to a breach of trust by a partner who is a trustee, or who is in a position of trust in regard to the investor. These cases have usually arisen with respect to partnerships of solicitors or bankers, where the joint and several liability may be justified on contractual grounds, at least in Scotland.[67] Perhaps it may be unrewarding, if not imprudent, to attempt to assign an overriding joint and several liability in all cases of a breach of trust by a partner without examining the circumstances of the

---

[65] (1887) 19 Q.B.D. 84.

[66] See *supra* pp. 323–326 and p. 367.

[67] Cases of breach of trust consisting of improper investment of the trust funds will not come within the scope of s. 13 of the Partnership Act 1890 unless the funds are invested so as to be " employed in the business or on the account of the partnership." The significance of these words is discussed *infra* p. 370.

breach. The Act, in section 13, imposes liability on the firm and its partners when they are implicated in the breach of trust; and in most cases falling to be decided in the Scottish courts, the essence of the association involved in a partnership and preserved in section 4 (2) of the Partnership Act 1890 will be adequate to ensure that the liability so imposed will be a joint and several one.

Following the trust money

In considering the responsibility of a firm and its partners for a co-partner's breach of trust, attention has been paid exclusively to the terms of proviso (1) to the section. There is another ground of recovery, however, which may be effective against the firm, though in this case it is not theoreti-cally based upon the firm's liability along with its partner for the original breach of trust. Proviso (2) reads—

> " (2) Nothing in this section shall prevent trust money from being followed and recovered from the firm if still in its possession or under its control."

It will be recollected that section 13 begins by a general denial of the liabil-ity of any other partner where his copartner, " being a trustee, improperly employs trust property in the business or on the account of the partner-ship." Unless the partner-trustee so employed the trust property, there would be no element in his conduct which would raise the question of liability of his firm or his copartners, since if the impropriety of his conduct lay in his employing the trust funds for purely private and personal ends no question of the liability of his firm and copartners could conceivably arise.

Since the section is thus restricted in terms to an improper employment by the partner-trustee of the trust property in his firm's business or on its account, in many cases it may be possible for the beneficiaries to trace the trust funds and identify them in the hands of the firm itself. In such cases the beneficiaries are entitled to restoration of the trust funds upon the equitable doctrine of following the trust money. That doctrine may pro-vide an additional remedy against the offending trustee himself [68] but it may also be taken against those who hold the money through the trustee,[69] but not where the party claiming it through the trustee has acquired it in good faith and for value, or where the trustee has used the trust funds in payment of his own debts and his creditor has taken payment in good faith.[70] Thus, in cases where the firm, *i.e.* all the partners, cannot be shown to be implicated in the partner's breach of trust, it may still be possible for the beneficiary to follow the trust money into the hands of the firm and demand its restoration, if he can establish (1) that the trust money is still in the hands of the firm and (2) that the firm did not obtain it by

---

[68] Bell, *Com.* I, 286; *Macadam* v. *Martin's Trs.* (1872) 11 M. 33; *Pennell* v. *Deffel* (1853) 4 De G.M. & G. 372 at p. 388.
[69] *Jopp* v. *Johnston's Tr.* (1904) 6 F. 1028.
[70] *Dunlop's Trs.* v. *Clydesdale Bank* (1891) 18 R. 751; (1893) 20 R.(H.L.) 59.

purchase for value and without notice of the breach of trust. It has been pointed out by Professor T. B. Smith [71] that, while English law is lacking in the general principle of Scottish equity, *nemo debet ex alieno damno lucrari*,[72] the English decisions upon following the trust money have influenced the Scots law on this subject.[73] English decisions as to following the trust money in the hands of a firm may therefore be treated as of persuasive authority, and the general principle stated by the Lord Chancellor (Campbell) in an English case [74]—" I consider it to be an established principle that a person cannot avail himself of what has been obtained by the fraud of another, unless he is not only innocent of the fraud, but has given some valuable consideration "—was cited with approval by Lord Shand in *Clydesdale Bank* v. *Paul* [75] and in *New Mining & Exploring Syndicate Limited* v. *Chalmers & Hunter* [76] by Lord Skerrington, who equiparated the principle with the " common ground of equity " to which Stair ascribed the Scottish principle *nemo debet ex alieno damno lucrari*.[77]

Extent of the right to follow the trust funds

Since the trust property may not only change hands but may also have changed its identity or shape in the hands of the person to whom it is traced, it is necessary to examine the rights of the beneficiary to trace the trust property through the various changes which have occurred to it while in the hands of the recipient and by this process of identification to establish his claim to it. This process of identification has been explained as " a particular illustration of the general doctrine of subrogation." [78] " It makes no difference in reason or law into what other form, different from the original, the change may have been made, . . . for the product of or substitute for the original thing still follows the nature of the thing itself, as long as it can be ascertained to be such, and the right only ceases when the means of ascertainment fails." [79] The qualification expressed in the final words of the passage quoted is important. The right to follow the funds continues as long as their identity is preserved, *i.e.* as long as the trust funds can be distinguished from other funds in the hands of the same person. The identification of the fund need not be by means of identifying the individual assets comprising the original fund but by indicating a separate and independent fund, readily distinguishable from all other funds held by the

[71] *Short Commentary on the Law of Scotland*, p. 574.
[72] A doctrine which has been regarded as the basis in Scots law of the right to follow the trust money: *New Mining & Exploring Syndicate Ltd.* v. *Chalmers & Hunter*, 1912 S.C. 126, *per* Lord Skerrington.
[73] In particular *Re Hallett's Estate* (1880) 13 Ch.D. 696; *Pennell* v. *Deffel* (1853) 4 De G.M. & G. 372, both cases cited with approval in *Jopp* v. *Johnston's Tr.* (1904) 6 F. 1028 and the latter English decision also in *Macadam* v. *Martin's Trs.* (1872) 11 M. 33.
[74] *Scholefield* v. *Templer* (1859) 4 De G. & J. 429.
[75] (1877) 4 R. 626 at pp. 628–629.
[76] 1912 S.C. 126 at p. 133.
[77] Stair, *Inst.* I, 6, 33.
[78] Menzies, *The Law of Scotland affecting Trustees* (2nd ed.) § 1289.
[79] *Per* Lord Ellenborough in *Taylor* v. *Plumer* (1815) 3 M. & S. 562 at p. 574.

person accountable. This entails that the property against which the right to follow is maintained must be capable of being traced back by successive stages to actual property originally held in trust for the claimant. In *Re Macleod, Mills* v. *Macleod,*[80] a person conveyed property to trustees. Owing to an error on the part of the solicitors employed by him in the business the property thus conveyed to the trustees proved to be of less value than it should have been. The truster sued the solicitor and obtained an award of damages against him for negligence. The trustees were not allowed to recover this sum from the truster as part of the trust estate. Their claim to follow the trust property failed since they were unable to trace the sum represented by the award of damages back to actual trust property held by them. The trust funds do not lose their identity simply by having been converted into cash or notes so long as they remain distinguishable. If, however, the cash or notes are put into circulation they lose their identity with the trust funds and so cannot be followed further.[81] Where the person holding the trust funds has blended the trust money with his own, " he cannot be heard to say that he took away the trust money when he had a right to take away his own money." [82] The equity of that rule can scarcely be gainsaid. If a person intermingles in his own bank account funds which are his own and funds for which he is accountable as a trustee, be it a constructive trustee or otherwise, then, in the payments which he makes for his own purposes from that bank account, he may not claim that he has misappropriated the trust funds in that account towards paying his private debts, until he has exhausted that part of the sum at credit of his bank account which is represented by his own funds. He must be held to have expended in the first place what he had a right to expend, namely, his own funds.[83]

Right to profits earned by the trust funds

The right of the party following the trust estate to recover not only that estate but also any profits which may have been earned by the employment of it in breach of trust was strongly negatived by Lord President McNeill in a partnership case.[84] He there dealt expressly with the case where the profits were made by the employment of the trust funds in the business of a partnership, one of the partners being a trustee in the trust estate. " If none of the partners had been trustees, the beneficiaries could not, I think, have got these profits from the parties who made them. But here one of the partners was a trustee; the others were not. . . . Some of the profits were made by the trustee; the rest of the profits by persons who were not trustees. . . . We have no ground for holding that the other partners

[80] (1895) 11 T.L.R. 445. See also *Patten* v. *Bond* (1889) 60 L.T. 583.
[81] *Miller* v. *Race* (1758) 1 Burr. 452, *per* Lord Mansfield at p. 457.
[82] *Per* Jessel M.R. in *Re Hallett's Estate* (1880) 13 Ch.D. 696 at pp. 727–728.
[83] Nor will the rule in *Clayton's Case* (*Devaynes* v. *Noble* (1816) 1 Mer. 572) avail him since that rule is " a mere presumption " which gives way to " evidence of circumstances from which a contrary intention must be presumed ": *Re Hallett's Estate, supra*; and see *Cory Brothers & Co.* v. *Owners of the " Mecca "* [1897] A.C. 286; *Hay* v. *Torbet,* 1908 S.C. 781.
[84] *Laird* v. *Laird* (1858) 20 D. 972 at p. 981.

who earned these profits must disburse them. . . . The liability of a
trustee arises from his position, the gain having been made through
his position. The other partners here did not hold that position." [85]
The Lord President next considered whether the trustees were liable
to account to the beneficiaries for the profits where these had not been
made by the trustees themselves but by persons who owed no
fiduciary duties to the beneficiaries. He held not. " I cannot hold
that [the partner-trustee,] in his fiduciary character, is to be liable
to account for profits made by other parties who were not in a fiduciary character, nor do I see how the beneficiaries can get from him profits
which he did not make, and which he is not entitled to exact from the
parties who did make them." The case under consideration was one in
which a former partner of a trading company died leaving a settlement
under which he appointed one of the partners to act along with other persons as his trustees. He also directed his funds to be realised and divided
within twelve months. The partner alone accepted the office of trustee but
a year later assumed co-trustees. The capital of the deceased invested in
the firm remained with the firm for several years to the profit of the firm.
The interlocutor pronounced by the First Division found *inter alia* that the
partner-trustee was not liable to account for any profits arising from the
use by the firm of the trust funds except so far as these had enured to him
personally as a partner of the firm. [86]   There is an apparent conflict between
this decision and the case of *Scottish Pacific Coast Mining Company Limited*
v. *Falkner Bell & Company*. [87]   In the later decision *Laird* v. *Laird* does not
seem to have been before the court for consideration and admittedly the
facts were different in that *Laird* v. *Laird* was concerned with the profit
made by the firm from the use of trust money which one of their partners
as a trustee had left invested with it, in breach of trust, while *Scottish
Pacific Coast Mining Company Limited* v. *Falkner Bell & Company* concerned an undisclosed profit made by a firm in the course of the formation
of a company of which one of the partners was a promoter. In neither
case, however, was the firm or the remaining partners under any fiduciary
duties. Yet in the later case the partners were apparently held to be constructively placed in the same fiduciary position as the promoter-partner
while, in the former, the partners were not regarded as owing the same
fiduciary duties as did the partner-trustee. [88]

Nature of the right to follow the trust money

It should be noticed as a matter of particular importance in the type of

---

[85] *Ibid. loc. cit.*
[86] Under the Partnership Act 1890, s. 42 (1), the estate of the deceased partner might claim
" such share of the profits made since the dissolution as the court may find to be attributable to the use of his share of the partnership assets " or alternatively interest at 5 per
cent. per annum on the amount of such share.
[87] (1888) 15 R. 290.
[88] But it could be argued that the partners in *Laird* v. *Laird* having the means of knowledge
that the trust funds were employed in the firm should be regarded as implicated in the
breach of trust. A possible ground of distinction is that they did not necessarily know
that the trust funds were so employed *in breach of trust*.

cases which may arise in connection with a partnership that in all cases where the right of a beneficiary to follow the trust money in the hands of a third party is involved, the third party must be shown to have been constructively affected by the trust originally attaching to the property followed. This situation can be distinguished, however, from that of a third party, such as the co-partner of a trustee, who has become implicated in his partner's breach of trust and as a consequence incurs liability therefor in terms of proviso (1) to section 13 of the Partnership Act 1890. The right of the beneficiary to follow the trust money in the hands of a firm, one of the partners of which is a trustee, arises irrespectively of the question whether the firm, through the knowledge of all the other partners of the breach of trust, has become liable. But it is not a right *in rem* as would be the case if a person exercised the right to follow his own property in the hands of another.[89] Were it so, a beneficiary claiming the right to follow trust property would require to establish that it remained in its original shape in the hands of the third party, and, as has already been stated it is not necessary for the beneficiary to establish this except in so far as it is necessary to identify the property now held with that originally held in trust. The doctrine of subrogation is applicable to the right of the beneficiary to follow the trust property, and this entails that his right is one *in personam* against the third party who is affected by the trust.[90]

The third party, however, must be a person who is affected by the trust, *i.e.* since he is not himself a trustee, he must hold the property as a constructive trustee. Such a constructive trust may arise (1) where an express trustee has acquired in his character as trustee property other than that expressly conveyed to him in trust [91]; (2) where funds which are affected by a trust come into his hands either gratuitously or with notice of the breach of trust involved [92]; or (3) where a sum of money in the hands of the owner becomes payable to an express trustee.[93] While it is conceivable that a partnership may be affected by a constructive trust arising as a result of any one of those situations, the only situation with which proviso (2) to section 13 of the Partnership Act 1890 is concerned is the second, since the object of that proviso is to exclude *inter alia* from the general denial of a firm's liability for the breach of trust of its partner the liability to submit to the right of the beneficiary to follow the trust property which is in the firm's hands as a result of the breach. This right of the beneficiary may, therefore, be a supplementary remedy when the firm is itself implicated in its partner's breach of trust or it may be the only remedy of the beneficiary where the firm has no notice of the breach but

---

[89] *Pullan* v. *Koe* [1913] 1 Ch. 9.

[90] Menzies, *The Law of Scotland affecting Trustees* (2nd ed.) § 1270.

[91] *Soar* v. *Ashwell* [1893] 2 Q.B. 390, *per* Bowen L.J. at p. 396.

[92] *Scholefield* v. *Templer* (1859) 4 De G. & J. 429, *per* the Lord Chancellor (Campbell) at p. 433; see also *Clydesdale Bank* v. *Paul* (1877) 4 R. 626, *per* Lord Shand at p. 628; *New Mining & Exploring Syndicate Ltd.* v. *Chalmers & Hunter*, 1912 S.C. 126, *per* Lord Skerrington at p. 133.

[93] See Menzies, *op. cit.* § 1272, and his observations in n. 6 to that section.

the partner has applied the trust funds in the business of the firm and the firm has thus received them into its hands gratuitously.

The firm in becoming affected by such a constructive trust does not, however, become liable along with the partner-trustee for the discharge of the latter's duties as express trustee.   It is a trustee to the extent that it has a duty to account to the beneficiary for the trust funds in its possession but it is under no general liability to answer for its partner's personal failure to perform his duties as an express trustee.[94]

---

[94] Hence, though a sum of money, in the hands of a person as owner, is affected with a constructive trust when it becomes payable to the (express) trustee in a trust, he is not answerable if he pays it to the trustees and they misapply it: *Buchanan* v. *University of Glasgow*, 1909 S.C. 47 at p. 54.

CHAPTER IX

THE PROPERTY OF THE PARTNERSHIP

QUESTIONS as to the property of the firm may arise either purely as an issue between the partners themselves or they may involve the added element of competition with the rights of strangers to the partnership. Bell maintains this distinction when he writes that, while the contract of partnership itself has the effect of a conveyance of property to the firm (a *titulus transferendi dominii*), this does not obviate the need for completion of the transference of that property by means of delivery, possession or intimation, as may be appropriate to vest that property in the partners of the firm.[1] " Where the question is between the partners and their representatives, as to what shall be considered as the estate of the company, but without involving any competition with third parties, whatever falls under the fair construction of the contract will, as a personal right, belong to the company and its creditors. But where there arises a competition, depending on the question of real right, it will be determined according to the criterion of real right which the law has appointed in the case of transference." [2] The distinction is the familiar one between a *jus ad rem* and a *jus in re*. In the former case, the *jus ad rem* will be regulated by the intention of the parties to the contract of copartnery, while in the latter case, where third parties claim a competing *jus in re*, that right will be displaced only by a completed real right in the firm or in a partner, or some other person, on behalf of the firm.

In any question involving partnership property there are thus a number of contributing factors in the determination of the issue, and it is necessary to be clear in what sense and for what purposes the term " partnership property " is being used. Where the question arises among the partners themselves, their intention is the ruling factor; yet even here questions may arise when the property is held in the name of one or more of the members of the firm or in the name of other persons who are not partners, whether the property so held is to be regarded as partnership property. In such cases, no less than in those cases where there are competing claims to the property by the partnership on the one hand and by third parties on the other, the right to the property as partnership property must be established by admissible and appropriate evidence. Indeed, the proof of the right of the firm to property held by a person who is alleged to hold it on behalf of the firm has given rise to some decisions which are not always easy to reconcile.[3]

---

[1] Bell, *Com.* II, 501.
[2] *Ibid.* II, 502.
[3] See *infra* pp. 382 *et seq.*

In terms of the Partnership Act 1890, s. 20—

" 20.—(1) All property and rights and interests in property originally brought into the partnership stock or acquired, whether by purchase or otherwise, on account of the firm, or for the purposes and in the course of the partnership business, are called in this Act partnership property, and must be held and applied by the partners exclusively for the purposes of the partnership and in accordance with the partnership agreement.

" (2) Provided that the legal estate or interest in any land, or in Scotland the title to and interest in any heritable estate, which belongs to the partnership shall devolve according to the nature and tenure thereof, and the general rules of law thereto applicable, but in trust, so far as necessary, for the persons beneficially interested in the land under this section.

" (3) Where co-owners of an estate or interest in any land, or in Scotland of any heritable estate, not being itself partnership property, are partners as to the profits made by the use of that land or estate, and purchase other land or estate out of the profits to be used in like manner, the land or estate so purchased belongs to them, in the absence of agreement to the contrary, not as partners, but as co-owners for the same retrospective estates and interests as are held by them in the land or estate first mentioned at the date of the purchase."

Property

This word is not defined in relation to its use for the purposes of the Partnership Act 1890. It is not, apparently, used in the Act as a legal term of art and must be construed in an ordinary, everyday sense.[4] The term will, therefore, embrace all assets of the firm, including the goodwill of the business carried on by it.[5]

" Partnership property "

It is clear from the terms of section 20 (1) of the Partnership Act 1890 that the partners may by agreement *inter se* decide what shall, and what shall not, be regarded as partnership property. The general rules set forth in sections 20 and 21 of the Act apply where no agreement has been expressly made or may be implied as existing among the partners by which the application of the statutory rules to the partnership concerned is excluded. Where a question arises whether any property is to be treated as partnership property, it will not be sufficient to determine that question according to the general rules laid down in section 20 and the succeeding sections of the Partnership Act 1890. The stamping of any property with the character of partnership property has important results so far as the

---

[4] *Queensbury Industrial Society* v. *Pickles* (1865) L.R. 1 Ex. 1, *per* Bramwell B. at pp. 4–5.
[5] For " goodwill " see *infra* pp. 419–428.

mutual rights and duties of the partners are concerned and these rights and duties are created by the intentions of the parties to the partnership agreement or, where the agreement itself is silent, by the implications made as to them by the Act itself.   These mutual rights and duties may be varied only with the consent of all the partners and such consent may be either express or inferred from a course of dealing.[6]   The whole circumstances must be examined in order to discover whether any agreement exists which qualifies, or varies the effect of, the statutory rules.   Though there is a strong presumption that what is bought with partnership money is partnership property that presumption is a rebuttable one.[7]   It may be proved, for instance, that the money was lent by the firm to a particular partner and thus did not have the character of partnership property when it was invested by him.[8]   It is also to be considered whether the special treatment of the Scottish firm as a *persona* distinct from the individual partners who comprise it has any effect to create a different concept of the partnership property of a Scottish, as compared with an English, firm.   The difference in the treatment of the firm results in a difference in the treatment of the rights of the partners in the property of the firm,[9] but that aspect of the question is not relevant in a discussion of the problem of what is comprehended within the partnership property itself.   It will make no difference to what is described as partnership property either in terms of section 20 or in terms of the partnership agreement that the right of the firm and its partners to such property may be differently explained under Scots, as compared with English, law.[10]

Property " acquired . . . on account of the firm "

The wording of section 20 of the Partnership Act 1890 is very wide.   It covers all acquisitions of property on account of the firm " whether by purchase or otherwise."   Its purpose is to include within the section as partnership property not only that which has been originally contributed to the partnership stock, but also all assets which have been added thereto during the continuance of the partnership.   When property has later been acquired by purchase on account of the firm, there is a presumption that the property so acquired is partnership property.   Section 21 of the Partnership Act 1890 provides—

> " 21. Unless the contrary intention appears, property bought with money belonging to the firm is deemed to have been bought on account of the firm."

It will be noticed (1) that the presumption introduced by section 21 relates only to one mode of acquisition of property and moreover the presumption

---

[6] Partnership Act 1890, s. 19.   And see *Starrett* v. *Pia*, 1968 S.L.T.(Notes) 28.
[7] Lindley, *op. cit.* pp. 351–352.   Partnership Act, 1890, s. 21
[8] *Smith* v. *Smith* (1800) 5 Ves. 189.
[9] See *infra* pp. 394–398.
[10] The distinction is, of course, important for other purposes and is examined hereafter in relation to s. 23 of the Partnership Act 1890 (a section which is not applicable to Scotland). See *infra* pp. 394 *et seq.*

operates only where the purchase is made " out of money belonging to the firm," [11] and (2) that the presumption may be rebutted by proof of a contrary intention on the part of the partners. The acquisitions on account of the firm which may be regarded as partnership property under section 20 of the Partnership Act 1890 are extended beyond those which have resulted from purchase " with money belonging to the firm " to those acquired by purchase on account of the firm or otherwise " on account of the firm, or for the purposes and in the course of the partnership business." These words will cover not only assets acquired by purchase on account of the firm where the purchase price has not actually been paid out of money belonging to the firm and assets acquired by accrual to the original partnership property for the purposes and in the course of the conduct of the partnership business but also any property which one of the partners may have acquired personally in breach of his obligation of *uberrima fides* owed to his copartners and his firm. Thus under section 29 of the Partnership Act 1890—

" 29.—(1) Every partner must account to the firm for any benefit derived by him without the consent of the other partners from any transaction concerning the partnership, or from any use by him of the partnership property, name, or business connection.

(2) This section applies also to transactions undertaken after a partnership has been dissolved by the death of a partner, and before the affairs thereof have been completely wound up, either by any surviving partner or by the representatives of the deceased partner." [12]

The firm may also receive partnership property by acquisition otherwise than through purchase by claiming an accounting under section 30 of the Partnership Act 1890 against a partner who has, without the consent of his copartners, carried on a business of the kind carried on by the firm and competing with it.[13]

Contrary intention

Both the general provisions as to the partnership property in section 20 and the presumption raised as to property purchased out of money belonging to the firm are subject to the overriding consideration of the actual intention of the partners. In the eliciting of the true intention of the partners in cases under section 20, the question will usually be whether the property has originally been brought into the partnership stock or has later been " acquired . . . for the purposes and in the course of the partnership business." The wording is cumulative in effect and it cannot be said

---

[11] See *Smith* v. *Smith* (1800) 5 Ves. 189.
[12] Erskine, *Inst*. III, 3, 20; Bell, *Com*. II, 502; *Marshall*, Jan. 26, 1815, F.C. and Feb. 23, 1816, F.C.; *Pender* v. *Henderson* (1864) 2 M. 1428; *McNiven* v. *Peffer* (1868) 7 M. 181. And see *supra* Chap. VI, pp. 164 *et seq.*
[13] " If a partner, without the consent of the other partners, carries on any business of the same nature as and competing with that of the firm, he must account for and pay over to the firm all profits made by him in that business ": Partnership Act 1890, s. 30. See *supra* Chap. VI, pp. 164 *et seq.*

that it affords much help in the solution of the most difficult problem which has frequently come before the court, namely, whether land which has been conveyed to persons who are partners and is used by them for the purpose of the partnership business is partnership property [14] since it does not necessarily follow that land which is used for the partnership business has been acquired for those purposes and in the course of the partnership business. In Scotland it has been held that the mere use of heritable property for the purposes of the partnership is not sufficient to stamp the property with the character of partnership property. In *Wilson* v. *Threshie*,[15] where the property had not only been used for the purposes of a joint adventure but had actually been purchased by the joint adventurers, the court still held upon an assessment of the whole circumstances of the case that it was not partnership property.[16] The terms of the feudal title, however, will be disregarded if there is evidence, such as, for example, entries in the books of the firm, establishing that the property truly belongs to the firm,[17] or evidence establishing that the property was itself the subject of the partnership, or joint adventure.[18] Similar questions may arise as to other types of property standing in the name of one or more of the partners but claimed as partnership property on the ground that it was acquired " on account of the firm, or for the purposes and in the course of the partnership business." In *Pillans Brothers* v. *Pillans* [19] one of three brothers, who had signed a contract of copartnery for the conduct of a rivet, bolt and nut business, acquired in his own name a rival business of the same nature and was held in the circumstances of the case to have acquired it on behalf of the firm as partnership property.[20] Similar questions have arisen in the case of a life insurance policy effected in name and on the life of one of the partners and payable to his " executors, administrators and assigns," but forming the security for an advance of money to the firm by whom the premiums were paid,[21] to a patent held in names of two persons one of whom only was a partner of the firm which claimed the patent as partnership property,[22] to a lease of the partnership premises acquired by one of the partners in his own name,[23] and to commissions or discounts obtained by one of the partners in connection with

[14] See *e.g. Morris* v. *Barrett* (1829) 3 Y. & J. 384; *Brown* v. *Oakshot* (1857) 24 Beav. 254; *Phillips* v. *Phillips* (1832) 1 Myl. & K. 649; *Jackson* v. *Jackson* (1804) 9 Ves. 591; *Crawshay* v. *Maule* (1818) 1 Swanst. 495; *Waterer* v. *Waterer* (1873) L.R. 15 Eq. 402; *Davies* v. *Games* (1879) L.R. 12 Ch.D. 813.
[15] (1825) 4 S. 361.
[16] See also *Sime* v. *Balfour* (1804) Mor. (App. Heritable & Moveable) No. 3.
[17] *Keith* v. *Penn* (1840) 2 D. 633.
[18] *Keith* v. *Penn* (1840) 2 D. 633.
[19] (1908) 16 S.L.T. 611.
[20] The business for which the three brothers had entered into partnership had not commenced operations at the date of the acquisition. It is thus doubtful whether the other brothers could have called for an accounting of the profits made in the business acquired in terms of s. 30 of the Partnership Act 1890. The " rival business " was of the same nature as that proposed to be carried on under the contract of copartnership but was not " competing " with it since in fact no business was as yet carried on in partnership.
[21] *Forrester* v. *Robson's Trs.* (1875) 2 R. 755.
[22] *Laird & Co.* v. *Laird & Rutherford* (1884) 12 R. 294. But as to this case see *infra* pp. 382–387.
[23] *McNiven* v. *Peffers* (1868) 7 M. 181.

the business of the firm.[24]   In the older cases regarding the ownership of ships, there was difficulty in applying the same general principles to ships registered in the name of one partner only but claimed as partnership property on the ground that it had been bought with partnership money, used for the purposes of the partnership and treated by the partners as partnership property.   It had been settled in the English courts that a ship belonged exclusively both in law and in equity to the person or persons who were registered as her owners and to no one else.[25]   That position was reflected in the earlier legislation as to shipping.[26]   Those earlier provisions were, however, repealed [27] and were replaced by those of the Merchant Shipping Act 1854 [28] under which there was no corresponding provision that a bill of sale should have no effect unless registered under the Act. This is the position today [29] and thus where a similar question now arises as to partnership property in a ship the partner registered as owner would be deemed to hold the property as a trustee for his firm.[30]   In all these cases the question arose *inter socios* and prima facie the partner was deemed to hold it on behalf of the firm.[31]   Where, however, the property is in the hands of third parties it will require to be delivered, actually or constructively, or assigned to the firm with intimation to the third party before it may be regarded as partnership property.

Due regard must also be paid to the words of section 20 (1) of the Partnership Act 1890, " . . . acquired . . . on account of the firm."   These words are necessary to ensure that the section does not bring within the partnership property assets acquired by a partner entirely apart from the partnership and as personal property.   Moreover, even if an advantage which has been obtained by a partner is connected with the partnership affairs, he is not under an obligation to account for it to the firm, if it was in fact conferred on him for his own personal benefit.   When a ship which was the property of three partners, one of whom was French, the remaining two being American, was captured by a British cruiser and compensation was paid to the Americans only, the French partner being expressly excluded from the arrangement, it was held that the compensation so paid belonged to the American partners alone and that the French partner could maintain no claim to share in it.[32]

[24] *Pender* v. *Henderson* (1864) 2 M. 1428.
[25] *Slater* v. *Willis* (1838) 1 Beav. 354; *Battersby* v. *Smyth* (1818) 3 Madd. 110; *Camden* v. *Anderson* (1794) 5 T.R. 709; *Curtis* v. *Perry* (1802) 6 Ves. 739; *Ex p. Yallop* (1808) 15 Ves. 60; *Ex p. Houghton* (1810) 17 Ves. 251.
[26] 3 & 4 Will. IV, c. 55, ss. 31 and 34; 8 & 9 Vict. c. 89; *McArthurs* v. *McBrair & Johnstone's Tr.* (1844) 6 D. 1174.
[27] Merchant Shipping Repeal Act 1854.
[28] ss. 55 and 57.   See *Watson* v. *Duncan* (1879) 6 R. 1247.
[29] Merchant Shipping Act 1894, ss. 56 and 57.
[30] *Hughes* v. *Sutherland* (1881) 7 Q.B.D. 160; *Liverpool Borough Bank* v. *Turner* (1859) 2 De G.F. & J. 502.   And see *Davie* v. *Buchanan* (1880) 8 R. 319.
[31] Except in the case of *Laird & Co.* v. *Laird & Rutherford* (1884) 12 R. 294 on which see below pp. 385–386.
[32] *Campbell* v. *Mullett* (1819) 2 Swanst. 551.   See also *Rye* v. *Rye* [1960] 3 All E.R. 810; disapproved on the facts but affirmed on different legal grounds [1962] A.C. 496; *Burdon* v. *Barkus* (1862) 3 Giff. 412; affd. (1862) 4 De G.F. & J. 42; *Bevan* v. *Webb* [1905] 1 Ch. 620 at p. 631.

Mode of proof

When it is alleged that property held in name of an individual *ex facie* absolutely is truly held as property of a partnership, it is a question which has been before the courts on several occasions whether the allegation amounts to one of trust, thus requiring to be proved by writ or oath of the party in whose name the property is held.[33] The decisions are not easy to reconcile one with another. In *Forrester* v. *Robson's Trustees* [34] it was doubted if the Act 1696, c. 25, applied in partnership cases. The Lord Justice-Clerk (Moncreiff), however, stated,

> "If the proof taken is competent, it seems to establish beyond doubt that Robson never had any individual interest in the policy. He had an interest as partner of the firm of Forrester & Robson and also as a partner of the joint adventure constituted by the transaction, but beyond that he had no interest in the policy. He was put forward by the joint intervention of the two firms of Forrester & Robson and George Cowie & Sons . . .
>
> "With regard to the competency of the proof where the allegation is not trust but partnership, the Act 1696 [c. 25] does not apply. The fact that a partner holds on behalf of the company may be proved *prout de jure*." [35]

That view was concurred in by Lord Neaves and Lord Ormidale, but Lord Gifford expressed some doubt as to it and preferred to rest his opinion on the ground that the proof which had been offered satisfied the requirements of the Act 1696, c. 25.[36] In *Laird & Company* v. *Laird & Rutherford* [37] the Lord President (Inglis) observed,

> "Again it is said that the Act [1696, c. 25] does not apply because one of the defenders is a partner of the pursuer's firm and we have been referred to cases which show that where a right is taken in name of a partner and is claimed for the firm, the case comes under the law of partnership, and not of trust, and that proof *prout de jure* is allowable. I do not think it is necessary to go back upon the cases which have been cited in support of that contention because I agree with the Lord Ordinary that they have no application here. There was no ' deed of trust ' [38] in any of them, there was nothing in the nature of a right granted in favour of an alleged trustee in absolute terms such as we find here." [39]

But it was held in *General Assembly of the General Baptist Churches* v.

---

[33] Act 1696, c. 25.
[34] (1875) 2 R. 755.
[35] *Ibid.* at p. 759.
[36] *Ibid.* at p. 760.
[37] (1884) 12 R. 294.
[38] "That no action of Declarator of Trust shall be sustained as to any Deed of Trust made for hereafter, except upon a Declaration or Back Bond of Trust lawfully subscribed by the person alleged to be the Trustee and against whom or his heirs or assignees the Declarator shall be intented, or unless the same be referred to the Oath of Party *simpliciter* ": Act 1696, c. 25.
[39] *Ibid.* at p. 297.

Taylor [40] that an averment that money deposited in the bank in name of a partner really belongs to the firm may be proved parole, apparently on the reasoning that the averment is one of partnership and not one of trust. [41] In *Munro* v. *Stein* [42] the Lord Ordinary (Wheatley) held that where an agreement of partnership had been entered into under which a dance hall belonging to one of the partners was to form part of the partnership property but that partner had died before the actual conveyance of the dance hall to the partners as trustees for the firm had been executed, it was competent to prove by parole that the dance hall was partnership property and that, on the evidence of the case, it had been so proved. He founded his judgment as to the admissibility of parole evidence on the fact that an equal partnership in the business conducted in the dance hall had come into existence; and he added, [43]

> " A different situation might have arisen if the situation had been that the deceased was alleged to have brought the heritable property into the partnership agreement after the partnership had been constituted. That situation does not arise and accordingly I do not require to consider the line of authority, and apparently conflicting authorities, as to whether property acquired in his own name by a partner, for alleged behoof of the partnership, has to be regarded as an act of trust with the limitations of proof thereof prescribed by the Act 1696, c. 25, or can be proved *prout de jure* as an element of the partnership."

In *Adam* v. *Adam* [44] a heritable property was purchased by a wife and the title taken in her husband's name in order that a public-house could be operated as a joint adventure on the premises, the certificate for the licensed premises being in the husband's name. The Lord Ordinary (Johnston) held, distinguishing the previous decisions to the contrary, [45] that proof of the averment that the heritable property was held in trust for the joint adventure was restricted under the Act 1696, c. 25, to the writ or oath of the defender. In the proceedings before him Lord Johnston had to consider three main grounds of contention as to the admissibility of parole proof—(1) that the Act 1696, c. 25, did not apply where the parties were husband and wife, (2) that it did not apply since the parties were joint adventurers and the question was thus one of partnership and not one of trust, and (3) that the application of the Act 1696, c. 25, was excluded by the terms of section 20 of the Partnership Act 1890. As to the first of those contentions, the issue raised is not one with which this treatise is concerned and it may suffice to say that Lord Johnston repelled it following earlier Outer House decisions. [46] As to the second contention, he

[40] (1841) 3 D. 1030.
[41] See also *Horne* v. *Morrison* (1877) 4 R. 977; *Kilpatrick* v. *Kilpatrick* (1841) 4 D. 109.
[42] 1961 S.C. 362.
[43] *Ibid.* at p. 369.   [44] 1962 S.L.T. 332.
[45] *General Assembly of Baptist Churches* v. *Taylor* (1841) 3 D. 1030; *Kilpatrick* v. *Kilpatrick* (1841) 4 D. 109; *Lindsay* v. *Barmcotte* (1851) 13 D. 718; *Forrester* v. *Robson's Trs.* (1875) 2 R. 755; *Horne* v. *Morrison* (1877) 4 R. 977.
[46] *Inglis* v. *Smyth's Executrix* (1959) S.L.T.(Notes) 78; *Weissenbruch* v. *Weissenbruch*, 1961 S.C. 340.

founded upon the dicta of Lord President Inglis in *Laird & Company* v. *Laird & Rutherford* which have already been quoted.[47] He accepted the distinguishing feature of the partnership cases on the point as being the presence or absence of a " deed of trust." If there was a " deed of trust," the Act 1696, c. 25, applied; if not, the question was one of partnership and parole evidence was admissible. In the case before him there was a " deed of trust," *i.e.* the conveyance to the husband of the heritable property purchased from the wife's resources. The third contention was that the Act 1696, c. 25, had been modified by section 20 (1) and (2) of the Partnership Act 1890. Lord Johnston said that if it had been the intention to modify the Act 1696, c. 25, by those means he would have expected to find some reference to the Act 1696, c. 25, in section 20 of the Partnership Act 1890 but no such reference could be discovered. That fact was not necessarily fatal to the contention but on examination of section 20 of the Partnership Act 1890 he found that it provided that partnership property must be applied for the purposes of the partnership and that the title to heritable estate belonging to a partnership devolves according to the general rules of law but in trust for the persons beneficially interested. " The 1696 Act, Cap. 25, deals with something quite different, the limitation of the modes by which a trust may be proved." [48] The pursuer also attempted to support his third contention by the decision in *Munro* v. *Stein* [49] but in that case " the reason for the non-application of the Act 1696, Cap. 25, was not that its application was avoided by section 20 of the Partnership Act 1890 but that the prerequisites to the application of the Act 1696, Cap. 25 . . . did not exist." [50]

The apparent conflict of authority on the question cannot be resolved on any ground of distinction which looks only to the question whether the partner holds the property on some title *ex facie* of which he appears as absolute owner. In *Horne* v. *Morrison*,[51] another case in which Lord President Inglis delivered the leading judgment, one of the joint adventurers held the property which was alleged to be the property of the joint adventure upon just such a title. The *ratio* upon which the Act 1696, c. 25, applies or is inapplicable is a subtler one and involves, as Lord Johnston said, an examination of the question whether the prerequisites of its application are present. Those prerequisites are clearly stated in *Boswell* v. *Selkrig* [52]: " This enactment was obviously meant for those cases where, for some reason of convenience, and in pursuance of an agreement of parties, the documents or investiture of some right—for instance, the title deeds of a house, the tack of a farm, the bond for a sum of money—have been taken in the name of one of the parties as if for himself, though truly in trust for the other party to whom the beneficial interest in the

[47] *Supra* n. 37.
[48] *Adam* v. *Adam*, 1962 S.L.T. at p. 333.
[49] 1961 S.C. 362.
[50] *Eodem loco.*
[51] (1877) 4 R. 977.
[52] (1811) Hume 350.

subject truly belongs." It is a " document or investiture " of that nature which is referred to by Lord President Inglis in *Laird & Company* v. *Laird & Rutherford* [53] when he distinguishes that case by the fact that it was concerned with a " deed of trust." The deed of trust to which he referred was the letters patent themselves [54] which stood in the names of Laird, the partner, and Rutherford who was not a partner. But the " deed of trust " so considered has its origin in some agreement between the parties to constitute such a trust holding. In many of the partnership cases where property held by one of the partners in his own name is claimed by the firm as partnership property that element of agreement to create a trust is lacking. Instead the situation is frequently one of mandate—

> " Just as if a law agent were verbally authorised to go to a public sale and purchase an estate for a client, and nothing was said as to the name in which the purchase should be made. The agent might, in such a case, purchase the estate in his own name, and afterwards become a consenting party to a disposition being granted to his client. . . . But if the agent should take it into his head to say that he had made the purchase for himself that would raise a mere question of verbal mandate, which might be proved *prout de jure*." [55]

In many of the partnership cases where a partner acquires property in his own name but it is claimed that he did so " on account of the partnership " the issue will resolve itself clearly into one of his performance of his mandate from his firm. No question will arise as to the application of the Act 1696, c. 25, since the prerequisite of its application will be absent. There has been no agreement among the parties to create a trust under which the property is held and proof *habili modo* as to the mandate and the execution of it will be allowed. Where, however, there is a " deed of trust," where the firm has for convenience agreed that the partnership property be held in the name of one of its partners, where, as it has been expressed,[56] " the action is really and in substance a declarator of trust," the prerequisites of application of the Act 1696, c. 25, are present and proof of the alleged trust will be restricted to writ or oath.[57] The case of *Forrester* v. *Robson's Trustees* [58] does not, it must be admitted, fall easily within this *rationale* and it may be that the doubts expressed by Lord Gifford in that case are well founded and that on its facts it should be considered as one where the evidence before the court was admissible under the Act 1696, c. 25, or at least that there was sufficient evidence of an admissible nature to establish the firms' right to the policy as partnership property. It is also to be recollected that in the most cogent of decisions arising in the field of partnership where the proof was restricted in terms of the Act

[53] (1884) 12 R. 294.
[54] *Ibid. per* Lord Shand at p. 297.
[55] *Per* Lord Deas in *Horne* v. *Morrison* (1877) 4 R. 977 at p. 979. See also *per* Lord Shand at p. 980.
[56] See J. Robertson Christie *Encyclopaedia of the Laws of Scotland*, Vol. 11, *sub voce* " Partnership " § 112.
[57] *Ord* v. *Barton* (1846) 8 D. 1011; *Laird & Co.* v. *Laird & Rutherford* (1884) 12 R. 294.
[58] (1875) 2 R. 755.

1696, c. 25,[59] the issue was not a clear-cut one between a partner of the firm and the firm itself since the patent in that case was held in the names of Laird who was a partner and Rutherford who was not. To what extent that special feature influenced the decision that there was an agreement among the parties to create a trust cannot be stated with any certainty since the point is not directly dealt with in any of the judgments delivered in the case. It is a matter which may be thought to have some bearing on the determination of the question and its force is sufficient to have occasioned a tentative qualification of the rule by at least one writer.[60] On the whole, and particularly in view of the Outer House decision in *Adam* v. *Adam* [61] which is reported subsequently to the date of Mr. Robertson Christie's reservation, it may be the better opinion that the principle in *Laird & Company* v. *Laird & Rutherford* will apply even where the sole person or persons " in the record of title " are partners, provided that the circumstances are such as clearly to establish an agreement among the partners that the property be held by one or more of their number in trust for the firm and that the decision in *Forrester* v. *Robson's Trustees* may be accounted for on its own facts without doing violence to that rule. While a partner may owe fiduciary duties to his copartners, it is submitted that by itself that is not sufficient to deprive him of the protection of the Act 1696, c. 25, in cases where the prerequisites for the application of that Act are present. A partner's fiduciary duties are associated with his conduct of the affairs of the partnership, and if he acquires property in the course of his conduct of those affairs which he later seeks to claim as his own, the question which then arises is one as to the due discharge by him of the authority committed to him by the firm—a question in regard to which proof *prout de jure* is admissible. That is not a question with which the Act 1696, c. 25, is concerned because, for the Act to apply, a party must be in the position of having entrusted property to another,[62] which is an entirely different question from a case where the real issue is whether a partner is claiming to retain as his own property something which he acquired as the agent for his firm. Yet it is possible to envisage cases occurring within the partnership relation where the holding of particular property in the name of one of the partners is in no way clearly explicable in terms of his mandate from his firm. In such cases the claim of the firm to the property must rest on the ground that for reasons of convenience or otherwise the property was entrusted to be held in the name of the individual partner. But there is little in the relationship of partners to make such a claim any less ambivalent than it is in the general cases of undisclosed trusts which are legislated for in the Act 1696, c. 25. Individual partners hold their own individual property and even if some connection

---

[59] *Laird & Co.* v. *Laird & Rutherford, supra.*

[60] " But on the other hand if the action is really and in substance a declarator of trust, the proof will be restricted to proof by writ or oath even although the pursuers are a firm and the defender is one of the partners of it—at least where the latter is in the record of title associated with someone who is not a partner."—J. Robertson Christie, *loc. cit.*

[61] 1962 S.L.T. 332.

[62] *See per* Lord President Inglis in *Horne* v. *Morrison* (1877) 4 R. 977.

of that property with the business of the firm may be traced, that will not necessarily be in every case destructive of the claim of the partner to it as his own property. Indeed if the general rule of restriction of proof in cases of trust were held inapplicable in partnership, the relationship itself might expose a partner to a considerable danger of vexatious litigation at the instance of his copartners in which he might have to vindicate his right to his own property against a partnership claim founded upon general indications of right based upon the partnership association without any but the vaguest support for the claim.

Heritable estate belonging to the partnership

In its terms so far as applicable in English law section 20 (2) of the Partnership Act 1890 refers to " the legal estate or interest in any land." The term " land " includes " messuages, tenements and hereditaments, houses and buildings of any tenure." [63] For purposes of Scots law the subsection introduces an explanatory gloss " or in Scotland the title to and interest in any heritable estate." The wording is thus sufficient to cover all types of heritable property and it is provided that " the title to and interest in any heritable estate which belongs to the partnership shall devolve according to the nature and tenure thereof." The general rules of law are declared applicable but the title or interest will devolve " in trust, so far as necessary, for the persons beneficially interested in the land under this section." The effect of the subsection is that in England if several of the partners are seised of land forming part of the partnership property as joint tenants, the legal estate will accrue, on the death of one to the surviving partner or partners.[64] In Scotland, if the beneficial estate has been established by appropriate evidence to belong to the firm, then the partner or partners holding that estate do so in trust for the firm. The trust upon which they hold is in the first place for the creditors of the firm and secondly for the partners according to their respective rights under the partnership agreement.[65] It has been held that a lease may be validly granted in favour of a firm in the firm name.[66] A title to heritable estate which is owned by the partnership is taken in name of individuals as trustees for the firm, in general the appropriate practice being to take the title in favour of the partners by name, and the survivors or survivor of them as trustees for their firm,[67] and it has been suggested that the title of the firm to leasehold property should be taken in similar fashion to obviate the risk that the lease may be regarded as having lapsed on the dissolution of the firm.[68]

[63] Interpretation Act 1889, s. 3.
[64] Lindley, op. cit. pp. 367–368.
[65] See the opinion of the Lord Ordinary in Keith v. Penn (1840) 2 D. 633: " He supposes it will not be disputed that if an heritable subject be really made part of the stock of a trading company and be used by them as such, it will be liable to the claims of the company's creditors in preference to those of the more personal creditors of the individual partners."
[66] Dennistoun McNayr & Co. v. Macfarlane, Feb. 16, 1808, F.C.
[67] Morrison v. Miller (1818) Hume 720.
[68] Encyclopaedia of the Laws of Scotland, Vol. 11, sub voce " Partnership " § 114.

Where the title to the heritable property of a firm is taken in name of the individual partners simply as trustees for their firm and the partners have died, the testamentary trustees of the deceased partners may petition the court for authority to complete title to the property, but only if they are entitled to the possession of the property for their own absolute use or have derived their title from a person so entitled.[69] The petition in the case cited was submitted in terms of section 24 of the Trusts (Scotland) Act 1921 and the proceedings were continued to allow the petition to be amended and brought under section 22 of the same Act.

Co-owners in heritable estate used by the partnership

Heritable property which is occupied and used by a partnership will not necessarily be partnership property. The property may be occupied by the firm as tenant of one of its partners where the circumstances will raise no question of its being partnership property.[70] More difficult questions arise where the property is owned by the partners and is used by them to make profits. The mere fact that they are co-owners does not of itself make them partners *as to the property* and thus the fact that the co-owners are associated as partners in a business which makes profits from the use of the joint property will not render that joint property partnership property.[71] The question whether the co-owners of the property are partners as to that property must be determined on the facts and circumstances of the case, and unless there are circumstances in addition to the fact of joint ownership which evince the intention of the owners to associate themselves as partners as to the property owned,[72] their relation will not be ascribed as partnership.[73] In the case where the parties are held to be co-owners of the heritable estate but are partners as to the profits made by its use and where they purchase other land or estate out of those profits to be used in like manner without agreement as to how the acquired property is to be treated, it will be held by them as co-owners, and not as partners, and their respective rights and interests as co-owners will be determined on the basis of their rights and interests in the original land or estate at the date when the further purchase is made.[74] There appears to have been no reported Scottish decision which reflects this rule in its entirety. The subsection appears to be based on the decision in *Steward* v. *Blakeway*,[75] but the application of the rule depends upon the inference drawn by the court as to the manner in which the parties intend to treat the acquired property, and from the facts of other English cases a different

[69] *Scott's Trs., Petitioners*, 1957 S.L.T.(Notes) 45.
[70] A let of that kind, however, will prima facie be deemed to be for the duration of the partnership and not merely from year to year.—*Pocock* v. *Carter* [1912] 1 Ch. 663.
[71] Stair, *Inst.* I: 16: 1; Erskine, *Inst.* III, 3, 12; Bell, *Com.* II, 544; *Prin.* § 351; *Neilson* v. *McDougal* (1682) Mor. 14, 551.
[72] *Parnell* v. *Walter* (1889) 16 R. 917.
[73] *Supra* Chap. III, pp. 66–68.
[74] Partnership Act 1890, s. 20 (3).
[75] (1869) 4 Ch.App. 603; (1868) L.R. 6 Eq. 479.

inference was drawn, thus causing the acquisition to be dealt with as partnership property.[76]

Effect of the distinction on incidence of estate duty

It seems clear that the terms of section 20 (3) of the Partnership Act 1890 lay it down that if co-owners, or in Scotland *pro indiviso* proprietors, of some heritable subject capable of commercial use associate themselves as partners in order to exploit the commercial potential of their property, that will not of itself make the property partnership property nor will the fact that they devote the profits made in partnership or part of them to purchase of further heritable subjects render the acquisition partnership property in the absence of agreement among them to the contrary. It has been pointed out [77] that this rule had important results in the case of partnerships working heritable subjects situated abroad, such as a tea plantation. If the agreement among the partners evinced their intention that the property is partnership property, each partner's interest therein is moveable [78] in nature, being a right to share in it along with the other assets of the firm. On his death the partner's estate thus became assessable to estate duty on his share in the partnership according to the law of the country of his domicile.[79] But if the partnership association was confined to the cultivation or working of the property situated abroad and the deceased partner was a *pro indiviso* owner thereof along with his copartners his interest in the property was an interest as owner of land and thus assessable to estate duty according to the law of the country where it is situated.[80] The law as to this has now been altered. In the case of deaths occurring on or after August 1, 1962, heritable property situated abroad is assessable to estate duty in this country where the owner died domiciled in Great Britain though the death duties payable in the country where the heritable property is situated will be credited against the British estate duty.[81]

Conversion of heritable into moveable estate

Section 22 of the Partnership Act 1890 reads—

" 22. Where land or any heritable interest therein has become partnership property, it shall, unless the contrary intention appears, be treated as between the partners (including the representatives of a deceased partner) and also as between the heirs of a deceased partner

---

[76] *Morris* v. *Barrett* (1829) 3 Y. & J. 384; *Waterer* v. *Waterer* (1873) L.R. 15 Eq. 402; *Phillips* v. *Phillips* (1832) 1 Myl. & K. 649.
[77] By Mr. Robertson Christie, *Encyclopaedia of the Laws of Scotland*, Vol. 11, *sub voce* " Partnership " § 114.
[78] See below pp. 390–391.
[79] Finance Act 1894, s. 2 (2).
[80] Finance Act 1894, s. 2 (2); *Coms. of Stamp Duties* v. *Salting* [1907] A.C. 449; *Re Birchtold* [1923] 1 Ch. 192.
[81] Finance Act 1962, ss. 28 and 29. In cases concerning foreign property the division to be made is between moveable and immoveable property not between real property and personal property.

and his executors or administrators, as personal or moveable and not real or heritable estate."

The rule announced in this section reflects the doctrine favoured in the majority of the former English decisions [82] though a number of pre-statute decisions in the English courts conflicted with that doctrine.[83] It will be noticed that the section is general in its application. There is thus no longer room for the distinction previously maintained between land which has been purchased out of partnership assets and land which has become the property of the partnership in other ways.[84] If the land has become partnership property in any way, then in England the equitable doctrine of conversion applies, that doctrine being founded on the reasoning that the right of each partner is represented by his share of the partnership assets after they have been realised in a winding up of the partnership and applied in the first place in discharging the debts and liabilities of the partnership. It follows, therefore, that on considerations of equity a partner's share in a partnership, whether the partnership property consist of land or not, is regarded as personal property and not real estate in any question arising between the real and personal representatives of the partner, unless that equitable conversion is inconsistent with the agreement among the partners.[85] Section 22 of the Partnership Act 1890 is, however, concerned exclusively with the question of lands or heritable interests which have become partnership property, and has no application to land which, although in fact held by partners, is held by them not in their character as partners but as co-owners or *pro indiviso* proprietors.[86]

Application of section 22 in Scotland. While the application of the doctrine has been explained in terms which are peculiar to the English legal system and are unfamiliar in Scots law, there is little doubt that the section sufficiently reflects the common law of Scotland and does no real violence to it. In Scots law it is possible to see the same basic equity at work and, although the terms and concepts used to explain it differ from those employed in the law of England, it can be affirmed that the same equitable notion is inherent in both systems of law. Bell explains the peculiarity so far as Scots law is concerned by reference to the *pro indiviso* right in the partnership property which is vested in the partners in the first place for the creditors of the firm and thereafter for the partners themselves. " The stock or common fund," he writes,[87] " is held by the partners *pro indiviso*. And,

" 1. This *pro indiviso* right implies, as between the parties themselves, a right of retention in each partner over the stock, for the

---

[82] *Steward* v. *Blakeway* (1868) L.R. 6 Eq. 479; affd. (1869) 4 Ch.App. 603; *Re Wilson, Wilson* v. *Holloway* [1893] 2 Ch. 340; and *per* Bowen L.J. in *Attorney General* v. *Hubbuck* (1884) 13 Q.B.D. 275 at p. 289.
[83] *Thornton* v. *Dixon* (1791) 3 Bro.C.C. 199; *Bell* v. *Phyn* (1802) 7 Ves. 453; *Randall* v. *Randall* (1835) 7 Sim. 271; *Cookson* v. *Cookson* (1837) 8 Sim. 529.
[84] See *e.g. Cookson* v. *Cookson, supra.*
[85] Lindley, *op. cit.* pp. 370–371.
[86] *Rowley* v. *Adams* (1844) 7 Beav. 548; *Steward* v. *Blakeway, supra* n. 82.
[87] *Com.* II, 501.

advances which he may have made to the company, or for any debt due by the company, for which he may be made responsible.

" 2. It also implies, in relation to the public at large, creditors of the company, a trust in the several partners, as joint trustees, for payment in the first place of the company debts. And on this point rests, 1. The preference which the creditors of the company have over the company funds: none of the partners, nor any one in their right, as individual creditors or otherwise, being entitled to more than the reversion after the purposes of that trust are fulfilled. And, 2. The peculiarity, that heritable subjects belonging to and held by a company are considered not as heritable in succession, but as moveable, consisting of the *jus crediti* only.

" 3. In this respect, the contract of partnership has the effect of a direct conveyance of property to the company of whatever is engaged to be given, or by clear evidence is contributed to the uses of the company by any of the partners to whom it belongs. The contract does not indeed supersede the necessity of the completion of the transference by tradition or otherwise, but it operates as a conveyance (*titulus transferendi dominii*), which, when followed by tradition, possession, intimation, and the other methods of completing a transference by law, vests the property in the partners jointly for the purposes already expressed. . . ."

The doctrine as explained by Bell may be seen in a long line of Scottish authority.[88]

" Unless the contrary intention appears "

These saving words in section 22 have been explained in terms of English law as meaning that the rule in the section will apply only in the absence of intention of the partners to the contrary. If there is agreement, express or implied, that the land belonging to the partnership shall not be sold, then the view is advanced that the principle of conversion set out in section 22 is excluded,[89] though the effect of the Law of Property Act 1925 [90] in treating the equitable interests of joint tenants or tenants in common or legal estate in land held by or in trust for joint tenants or tenants in common as personal estate leads to a doubt " whether the partners can by agreement alter the character of their equitable interests except by putting an end to them by a partition of the land." [91]

In Scotland where the equity of the partner's share in the property of the firm is explained in terms of a trust giving rise to equitable interests in third parties who are creditors of the firm as well as in the partners themselves, it is difficult to see how a contrary intention of the partners may

---

[88] *Corse & Anr., Petrs.*, Dec. 16, 1802, F.C.; *Murray* v. *Murray*, Feb. 5, 1805, F.C.; *Balfour* v. *Sime* (1811) 5 Pat.App. 525; *Minto* v. *Kirkpatrick* (1833) 11 S. 632; *Irvine* v. *Irvine* (1851) 13 D. 1367.
[89] Lindley, *op. cit.* p. 370, citing *Steward* v. *Blakeway* (1869) L.R. 4 Ch.App. 603.
[90] ss. 28 and 36.
[91] Lindley, *op. cit.* p. 371.

override the general principle of section 22. Of course if the true intention of the partners is that the heritable subjects are held by them as co-
owners and not as partnership property, that will be given effect to. But
that is not a " contrary intention " as to the treatment of an asset which is
ex hypothesi partnership property. It is a contrary intention as to the
essential question, are those heritable subjects partnership property at
all; and section 22 does not make provision for that case, since, as has been
above stated,[92] it is concerned exclusively with the case where " any land
or heritable interest therein has become partnership property." It is
thought that the Scottish courts might experience difficulty in giving
effect to a contrary intention of the partners within the ambit of section
22. In cases where it is contended that a contrary intention as to the
treatment of heritable subjects forming partnership property is to be
inferred from the actings of parties or the facts and circumstances of the
case, a Scottish court may resolve its difficulty by showing a reluctance
amounting to a virtual refusal to draw the inference contended for; but if
the court were to be called upon to consider a contrary intention clearly
and expressly declared in the contract of partnership, it is submitted that
unless it could construe the provision as excluding the heritable subjects
from the partnership property altogether, it would have grave difficulty in
giving effect to it so as to refuse to apply the general equity in section 22 to
the property in question, albeit that section 22 seems to envisage that such
a course may be adopted by the court.

Partnership property as a qualification for voting

The question whether a partner's share of the real estate forming partnership property affords him a qualification for exercising the parliamentary
franchise was the subject of considerable discussion formerly when the
franchise depended upon the ownership of real estate or at least when one
of the qualifications was the ownership of real estate. It was settled in
England that if a partner had no interest in real estate forming part of
the partnership property, apart from his right to the free proceeds arising
from its sale, that conferred no qualification.[93] On the other hand, if he
would otherwise have had a qualification as a joint tenant or tenant in
common, the doctrine of conversion reflected in section 22 of the Partnership Act 1890 did not deprive him of that qualification.[94] These questions,
so far as the parliamentary franchise is concerned, need no longer trouble
us since that franchise is now based upon a residential qualification only.[95]
In Scotland, however, the local government franchise might be exercised
by persons who, though not resident in the area, owned or occupied
property of a yearly value of at least £10 therein,[96] and it was further
provided that—

[92] *Supra* p. 389.
[93] *Watson* v. *Black* (1885) 16 Q.B.D. 270; *Bennett* v. *Blain* (1863) 15 C.B.(N.S.) 518; *Freeman*
v. *Gainsford* (1865) 18 C.B.(N.S.) 185.
[94] *Baxter* v. *Brown* (1845) 7 M. & G. 198; *Rogers* v. *Harvey* (1858) 5 C.B.(N.S.) 3.
[95] Representation of the People Act 1949, s. 1 (1).   [96] *Ibid.* s. 2 (1) (*a*) (ii).

" Where in Scotland any lands and heritages are owned or occupied by two or more persons jointly and the aggregate yearly value of such lands and heritages is not less than the amount produced by multiplying ten pounds by the number of owners or occupiers, as the case may be, each of them shall be treated as owning or occupying, as the case may be, lands and heritages of the yearly value of ten pounds." [97]

It was thus possible for questions of the sort discussed in relation to the former parliamentary franchise to arise in regard to the non-resident local government franchise of the partners of a Scottish firm for which they claimed to qualify on the ground of lands and heritages belonging to the partnership in the local government area.   This qualification of the owner of heritable subjects in Scotland was, however, based upon his liability to be rated in respect of them and when owners' rates in Scotland were abolished in 1956 the qualification of the owner to exercise the local government franchise was consequentially repealed.[98]   Even the local government franchise, therefore, was then only exercised on the ground of *occupation* of the subjects and problems as to the quality of the rights of *ownership* of partners in lands and heritages of the partnership can no longer arise as a practical issue.   The non-resident qualification has now been entirely abolished.[98a]   It has been held that voting rights arising as a result of a firm's subscription to an infirmary permit one partner only to vote at any meeting of the institution though he requires no written mandate from his firm to do so.[99]   In spite of the rule of English law that a partnership is not a legal entity distinct from its members, it has been held in England that a firm may be registered under the partnership name as a shareholder of a limited company [1] and *a fortiori* this applies in Scotland where the separate legal *persona* of the firm is recognised.   The right of the individual partners to vote at meetings of the company in respect of the shares held by the partnership may depend upon the mode in which the firm has chosen to appear on the register of members of the limited company.   If the shares belonging to the partnership are entered on the register of members in the names of the individual partners [2] the voting rights of the partners as joint holders will be regulated by the Articles of Association of the company; and in most cases it is provided that the vote of the senior holder who tenders a vote shall be accepted to the exclusion of the other joint holders, seniority for this purpose being determined by

[97] *Ibid.* s. 5.
[98] Valuation and Rating (Scotland) Act 1956, s. 35.
[98a] Representation of the People Act 1969, s. 15.
[99] *Walker* v. *Law* (1872) 11 M. 199.
[1] *Re Land Credit Co. of Ireland—Weikersheim's Case* (1873) 8 Ch.App. 831.
[2] In the case of a limited company registered in Scotland the fact that the partners hold for their firm may be noted on the register but in the case of a limited company registered in England or Wales no such notice of trust may appear on the register—Companies Act 1948, s. 117.

the order in which their names stand in the register of members.[3] Where the firm itself appears on the register of members the provisions of the Articles of Association are unlikely to be of assistance in determining the rights of the partners thereof to vote in respect of the shareholding, and no reported decision appears to have dealt with the point. In Scotland it is thought that the *ratio* of the decision in *Walker* v. *Law* [4] might be applied and that any one of the partners would be entitled to vote in respect of the firm's holding but that there would be no entitlement for more than one partner to vote in respect thereof at any meeting of the company. It has been held that one partner alone may vote on behalf of the firm at meetings of creditors of a bankrupt debtor of the firm.[5] In such questions the issue seems to be not that the property in respect of which the partner exercises voting rights is partnership property, but rather that it falls within his implied mandate as a partner to act as the agent of the firm in acts relating to the firm's affairs or property.

Difference in the treatment of partnership property under Scots and under English law

This subject has already been touched upon at an earlier stage in this chapter but is deserving of more specific analysis. Perhaps the most convenient way to introduce the essential nature of the distinction is to consider the terms of section 23 of the Partnership Act 1890, a section which does not apply to Scotland. Section 23 reads—

" 23.—(1) After the commencement of this Act a writ of execution shall not issue against any partnership property except on a judgment against the firm.

" (2) The High Court, or a judge thereof, or the Chancery Court of the county palatine of Lancaster, or a county court, may, on the application by summons of any judgment creditor of a partner, make an order charging that partner's interest in the partnership property and profits with payment of the amount of the judgment debt and interest thereon, and may by the same or a subsequent order appoint a receiver of that partner's share of profits (whether already declared or accruing) and of any other money which may be coming to him in respect of the partnership, and direct all accounts and inquiries, and give all other orders and directions which might have been directed or given if the charge had been made in favour of the judgment creditor by the partner, or which the circumstances of the case may require.

" (3) The other partner or partners shall be at liberty at any time to redeem the interest charged, or in the case of a sale being directed, to purchase the same.

" (4) This section shall apply in the case of a cost-book company as if the company were a partnership within the meaning of this Act.

" (5) This section shall not apply to Scotland."

[3] See Companies Act 1948, 1st Sched., Table A, Part I, Art. 63.
[4] *Supra* p. 393 n. 99. [5] *Ex p. Mitchell* (1808) 14 Ves. 597.

Before that section was enacted a separate judgment creditor of an individual partner could under English law levy execution not only against that partner's separate property but also against the property of any firm in which his debtor was a partner.[6] The difficulties attendant upon this rule were indicated by Lord Lindley in the last edition of his work on *Partnership* for which he was personally responsible where the former law was fully examined.[7] Section 23 of the Partnership Act 1890 met those criticisms by adopting a procedure already available in England in the case of public companies. The separate judgment creditor of a partner can no longer levy execution on the property of the partnership on a judgment obtained against one partner only but he can obtain an order charging the interest of the partner in the assets of the firm with payment of the judgment debt and he may enforce the charge by obtaining an order for sale of the partner's interest or for the appointment of a receiver. In remedying the former law, section 23 extended its provisions to cover the case of cost-book mining companies [8] though the provisions of the Partnership Act 1890 do not otherwise apply to such companies.[9]

Section 23, however, is expressly excluded from application to the Scottish partnership and the simple explanation that this is because the Scots law before the passing of the Act was not liable to the criticisms levelled at the English law is not acceptable without further examination, since Lord Kinnear in *Parnell* v. *Walter*,[10] a Scottish case arising before the passing of the Partnership Act 1890, declared that the law of England as proved in the proceedings in that case was precisely the same as the law of Scotland, and that it followed that particular debts due to the firm could not be taken in execution by the creditor of a partner for a private debt. The question at issue in that case, however, was not one of levying execution in England against the partnership property. It was a case of arrestment to found jurisdiction in Scotland against a partner of a firm in an action for damages for alleged slander by him where the funds held by the arrestee belonged to the firm of which the defender was a partner and he had no other property in his possession in which the defender had an interest. The proof as to the English law adduced from Mr. W. O. Danckwerts and Mr. Brodie Innes for the defenders and Mr. Lumley Smith and Mr. William Graham for the pursuers was that

" the property belonging to a partnership, according to English law . . . is in the individual partners—the partnership having no separate *persona*; but it is only the legal estate of which the individual partners have the property, their beneficial interest does not give them individually any right to the specific property of the partnership, but only

---

[6] Lindley, *op. cit.* p. 379.
[7] *Lindley on Partnership* (5th ed.) pp. 356 *et seq.*
[8] *i.e.* companies engaged in working mines on what is described as the " cost-book " or " ready money " principle. See *Hawtayne* v. *Bourne* (1841) 7 M. & W. 595; *Burmester* v. *Norris* (1851) 6 Ex. 796; *Ricketts* v. *Bennett* (1847) 4 C.B. 686.
[9] Partnership Act 1890, s. 1 (2).
[10] (1889) 16 R. 917.

to a share of the surplus assets on a realisation. Hence an execution creditor of an individual partner could not take part of the partnership property in satisfaction of his debt; he could only force a dissolution and recover payment out of the share found due to his debtor."

After considering this evidence the Lord Ordinary (Kinnear) came to the conclusion that the law of England and the Scots law are at one on this point. He added,[11]

"It is said that the rule of our law, by which the separate creditors of an individual partner cannot arrest debts due to the copartnery, arises from a principle which is not recognised in England, inasmuch as the law of that country does not treat the firm as a separate person distinct from its members. But it is not, in my opinion, because of the mere impersonation of the firm that its assets cannot be arrested by the creditors of a partner, but because the partner has no separate share in the assets which is capable of being attached by that diligence. The principle is that a partner has no right to claim any particular portion of the assets as belonging exclusively to him, and neither his assignees nor his separate creditors can have any higher right against the joint property than the debtor or cedent from whom they derive their interest. The true ground, therefore, is that which is stated in Lord Pitfour's note, quoted by Mr. Bell,[12] when he says that the creditors of the partner can only affect his share of the balance after payment of the copartnery debts. The proposition maintained for the pursuer is a very startling one, because it comes to this, that the separate creditor of any partner of an English trading firm may arrest funds belonging to the firm which he may find situated in Scotland, and carry them off for the satisfaction of his separate debt. There is no authority in the law of Scotland for that proposition. . . ."

Lord Kinnear's views were expressed in relation to the use of the diligence of arrestment and though somewhat generally expressed are to be read in that context. It is no doubt strictly accurate to say that the view taken by the Scots law as to the nature of a partner's right in the property of the firm does not originate merely in the separate *persona* of the Scottish firm, but it does not necessarily follow that, the "impersonation" of the firm being disregarded, the English and Scots law may be regarded as at one on the question of the nature of the partner's right in partnership assets. In Scotland the legal estate is held by the firm itself, or if it is in the hands or the name of a partner it is held by him in trust for the firm. In both cases there is a person at law who is entitled to the beneficial interest in the property. Moreover as a consequence of the separate entity of the Scottish firm the interest of any partner of the firm may be arrested by his separate creditors but it must be so attached by arrestment in the hands of the firm as a separate person.[13] The diligence by means of which a

[11] *Ibid.* at p. 925.
[12] In *Robertson's Creditors* (1744) unreported referred to Bell, *Com.* II, 508 n. 3.
[13] Bell, *Com.* II, 508.

partner's interest may be attached is arrestment, and not poinding, because
the assets of the partnership in which the partner's interest subsists are
either held by the firm itself or by the partners on behalf of the firm [14] and
" the share of each partner is a portion of the *universitas*; it forms a
debt or demand against the company, so as to be arrestable in the hands of
the company." [15] Arrestment may be used to attach the interest of the
partner in the firm while the firm is a continuing concern but to be made
effective the arrestment must be followed by an action of furthcoming
which cannot be raised until the dissolution of the partnership. [16] The
arrestment, indeed, places the arrester in a similar position to that of an
assignee of a partner's share [17] and cannot carry with it any right of partnership other than the right to pursue a division of the assets. He does not
himself become a partner nor is he entitled to nominate a partner in place
of his debtor. [18] The debtor remains a partner of the firm and his rights
and interests continue to be regulated by the partnership agreement;
consequently if a definite term is fixed for the endurance of the partnership
the arresting creditor has no means available to him for enforcing an earlier
dissolution of the partnership though he may secure for himself the whole
of the sums accruing to his debtor as partner during the continuance of the
partnership and the other partners have no right to object to this. [19] In
the case of a partnership at will, it has not been decided in the Scottish
courts whether the arresting creditor has the power to dissolve the partnership either at his own hand or by compelling his debtor to exercise his
right to dissolve the firm. In practice the contract of copartnery often
makes provision for the dissolution of the firm on the bankruptcy of a
partner and even where that provision does not appear in the contract, the
difficulty and inconvenience of conducting the affairs of the partnership
under the shadow of a continuing arrestment of a partner's share may
prove pressing enough to compel the partners to seek some kind of
settlement with the arresting creditor.

It is in the application of the law of partnership property for the
purposes of the Scottish diligence of arrestment that Lord Kinnear found
the similarity between the English and the Scottish concepts of the nature
of the partner's right. Since the beneficial interest of a partner in an
English firm is not in any specific asset of the firm but in his share of the
totality of these assets on their realisation and after discharging the liabilities of the partnership, it is possible for the separate creditor of a
partner to arrest in the hands of the partnership the interest of his debtor
and this will be competent whether the partnership be an English or a
Scottish one. But he will not be entitled to attach by an arrestment
founded on his claim against an individual partner funds due to the

[14] Erskine, *Inst.* III, 3, 24.
[15] Bell, *Com.* II, 536.
[16] Erskine, *Inst.* III, 3, 24.
[17] Partnership Act 1890, s. 31. See *infra* pp. 411–418.
[18] *Rae* v. *Neilson* (1742) Mor. 716.
[19] *Cassells* v. *Stewart* (1879) 6 R. 936, *per* Lord Gifford at p. 956.

partnership itself in the hands of a third party,[20] and he will not be able to execute a poinding of partnership property for the same reason or an adjudication, since the partner's share in the partnership property is moveable, not heritable, in nature.[21] In England before the passing of the Act, the forms of diligence available to the creditor of a partner permitted him to levy execution against the partnership property on a judgment obtained against an individual partner, notwithstanding that what was held as partnership property by the partners jointly was the legal estate in that property only and the beneficial interest of each individual partner was, as in Scotland, his right to share in the proceeds of realisation of the partnership assets. While it may be argued that the distinction between the partner's right in England and in Scotland depends more upon the technicalities of the pre-statute procedure in England for enforcing a judgment obtained against an individual partner than upon the nature of the right itself and the effect of the Scottish doctrine of the firm as a separate *persona*, that argument is not entirely convincing since the interposition of the *persona* of the firm in Scotland removes the difficulty arising in England as to a legal estate in the persons of the partners which differs from their beneficial interest. This is discernible in the terms of the remedial section of the Partnership Act 1890 itself since, though the judgment creditor of an individual partner may now obtain no more than " an order charging that partner's interest in the partnership property and profits," the court order may direct a sale of the interest or appoint a receiver in respect of it, whereas, in Scotland, as has been explained, the arresting creditor can assert no greater right than is reposed in his debtor. The whole question of the nature of the partner's right in partnership property is a difficult area of law in which the two systems of law show an apparent though partial convergence at some points and a divergence in others. It would be too much to claim on the strength of the points of convergence referred to by Lord Kinnear that the two systems of law are " at one," [22] since the approach of each system to the problem is entirely different and indeed it could be said that if Scots and English law had been identical on the subject, the necessity for the introduction of section 23 to govern the position in England without similar provision made applicable in Scotland would become difficult to explain.

Rights of the partners inter se in the partnership property

In the absence of agreement, express or implied, among them to the contrary, the partners are entitled to share equally in the partnership property. This rule, or presumption, of equality of treatment of the partners is of long standing in both the English and Scottish systems of law but, as was perhaps to be expected, the older decisions are somewhat uneasily based so far as their rationalisation is concerned. In *Campbell's*

[20] *Parnell* v. *Walter* (1889) 16 R. 917.
[21] *Rae* v. *Neilson* (1742) Mor. 716; *Neilson and Murdoch* v. *Colquhoun and Rae* (1745) Mor. 723.
[22] *Supra* p. 395 n. 10.

Trustees v. *Thomson* [23] the Court of Session held that " according to the law of Scotland the presumption was for equality." Earlier, Bell had somewhat elaborated on that doctrine, stating that " the presumption is that in the opinion of the parties their several contributions are equalised, though it may be impossible or difficult to state in what the equality consists." [24] The " contributions " to which Bell refers are those of property or money or skill or labour made by the respective partners and it would clearly be inequitable that contributions of property and money, or either of them, should be taken exclusively as the yardstick by which a partner's share in the firm is measured. Other things such as his personal skill or labour, his connection and the personal qualities which cause him to be respected by, or to enjoy the confidence of, others may well be important and valuable contributions to the partnership although they are not capable of being quantified in money or money's worth. It is, therefore, not inequitable that there should be a " presumption " for equality of treatment if by " presumption " all that is meant is that in the absence of agreement, express or implied, the partners should be treated as equal partners. As was observed by the Lord President (Hope) in *Campbell's Trustees* v. *Thomson*,[25] " It is immaterial that no capital was contributed, because a person's mind and exertions may be more valuable than capital." But the Lord President was there considering the case of a partnership in a profession, where his words had an added force.[26] Even so, the proceedings in the Court of Session were not entirely unambiguous and appear at one point to be contending for a general presumption in favour of equality while elsewhere [27] it is stated, " But suppose the case were sent to a Jury, the result must be a verdict finding equality because there is confessedly no evidence as to the extent of the share; and in the absence of evidence, it is the duty of the Judge to tell the Jury that they must find equality, so that a remit to the Jury Court is superfluous." In the House of Lords, Lord Brougham said that the jury would only have recourse to the presumption of equality in the last resort and for want of evidence. The House of Lords reversed the decision of the Court of Session and directed the Court of Session to send an issue to the jury court to ascertain what in all the circumstances of the case was the fair share to which the partner was entitled.[28] In a subsequent case relating to a joint adventure, the shares of the co-adventurers were held to be equal in the absence of any circumstances indicating an agreement among them that the shares were to be in different proportions.[29] The amount of capital contributed by the respective partners, taken by itself, was held not to be conclusive as to the proportion in which the losses and gains of the partnership were to be

[23] (1829) 7 S. 650 and, on appeal, (1831) 5 W. & S. 16.
[24] Bell, *Com.* II, 503.
[25] (1829) 7 S. 650 at p. 652.
[26] *Ibid. per* Lord Balgray at p. 652.
[27] *Per* Lord Gillies at p. 653.
[28] (1831) 5 W. & S. 16.
[29] *Fergusson* v. *Graham's Trs.* (1836) 14 S. 871.

shared.[30]   That decision presumably reflected the reiterated view which
has been expressed that a contribution of property or money on the part of
one partner may be balanced by the contribution by another of his
personal qualities such as his skill and industry,[31] but it is not entirely
satisfactory, possibly because the situation envisaged, where the only
circumstance which can be proved and which has a bearing upon the
intention of the partners as to their respective shares is the amount of their
input capital standing in isolation, is a somewhat unreal one and unlikely
to be encountered in practice.[32]   In England the effect of a similar tract of
pre-statute authority has been summarised in the following passage—

> " In the event of a dispute between the partners as to the amount
> of their shares, such dispute, if it does not turn on the construction of
> written documents, must be decided like any other pure question of
> fact; and it has been decided that if there is no evidence from which
> any satisfactory conclusion as to what was agreed can be drawn, the
> share of the partners will be adjudged equal." [33]

The Scottish authorities which have been examined do not entirely coincide
with the view taken in the earlier English authorities.   There is a greater
emphasis in the Scottish cases on a general presumption in favour of equal
shares, yet on analysis the decisions appear to recognise that this is an
over-simplified view.   Certainly since the passing of the Partnership Act
1890 there is no room for the unrestricted application of such a presumption in the face of the provisions of section 24 (1) of the Act.

Section 24 (1) of the Partnership Act 1890

This section reads—

> " 24. The interests of partners in the partnership property and
> their rights and duties in relation to the partnership shall be deter-
> mined, subject to any agreement express or implied between the
> partners, by the following rules:
>> (1) All the partners are entitled to share equally in the capital
>> and profits of the business and must contribute equally towards
>> the losses whether of capital or otherwise sustained by the firm. . . . ''

It is clear that where there is no other indication from the circumstances
of the case from which an inference may be drawn as to the proportions
in which the partners have agreed to share in the capital and profits of the
firm, they will be held to share equally therein.   In some cases this may
operate so as to raise doubts as to the equity of the results but no other rule
suggests itself as more equitable.   Ideally, it might be contended that in

---

[30] *Struthers* v. *Barr* (1826) 2 W. & S. 153.

[31] Erskine, *Inst.* III, 3, 19: *Campbell's Trs.* v. *Thomson* (1829) 7 S. 650, *per* Lord President
Hope at p. 652; Bell, *Com.* II, 503.

[32] Even if such a situation occurs, the amount of the input capital will now be an important
element under the Partnership Act 1890, s. 24 (1) (see below p. 401 n. 34).

[33] Lindley, *op. cit.* p. 372 and cases there cited.

every case the share to which a partner is entitled should be proportionate to the amount which he contributes to the partnership but, as has already been indicated, the contribution which a partner makes is not necessarily a contribution of money or property and where it consists in making available personal qualities of skill, connection, character or services there is no ready means of assessing these in terms of money so as to work out a ratio between the shares of different partners. In many businesses the input of capital by the respective partners to the common stock of the firm may be of great importance but if that be so, one would expect to find its importance recognised in the terms of the actual agreement among the partners as to their shares, where the partners have contributed differing amounts of capital. To attempt, on a consideration of the nature of the business alone, to evaluate the relative importance for the conduct of that business of contributions of money and property as against those of skill, labour and the like and then to quantify the latter in terms of money would lead to a most subjective decision in cases where it was called for. It, therefore, appears doubtful whether the views expressed by Professor Lorimer upon the effect of section 24 (1) are entirely sound.[34] If there is utterly no indication otherwise from the circumstances that the partners have agreed to take unequal shares, then the fact that they have contributed differing amounts of capital will not, taken in isolation, suffice to establish an agreement among them to receive unequal shares and to contribute unequal amounts to losses. " Whether, therefore, partners have contributed money equally or unequally, whether they are or are not on a par as regards skill, connection or character, whether they have or have not laboured equally for the benefit of the firm, their shares will be considered as equal, unless some agreement to the contrary can be shown to have been entered into." [35] In a decision in such circumstances there is probably less violence to the intention of parties in assuming from their silence that they have agreed that they intended their various contributions to be reduced to an equality in money terms and to share on the ratio thus brought out.

Evidence of agreement to accept unequal shares

Any agreement among the partners whereby inequality in their shares in the firm is stipulated for may be in express terms but it may also be implied from the actings of the parties themselves and such an agreement may be inferred from the conduct of the partners and the entries in the

---

[34] " Under this subsection it is thought that the amount of input capital, though an important element, will not be conclusive. If there be no other circumstance to throw light (a case not very likely to occur) it may determine the proportion . . .": *Supplement to Lindley on Partnership* (1891) p. 64.

[35] Lindley, *op. cit.* p. 373; and see *Stewart* v. *Forbes* (1849) 1 Mac. & G. 137; *Webster* v. *Bray* (1849) 7 Hare 159; *Copland* v. *Toulmin* (1840) 7 Cl. & F. 349; *Robinson* v. *Anderson* (1855) 20 Beav. 98; 7 De G.M. & G. 239; *Peacock* v. *Peacock* (1809) 2 Camp. 45; *Farrar* v. *Beswick* (1836) 1 M. & Rob. 527. See also *McWhirter* v. *Guthrie* (1822) 1 S. 319; *Aberdeen Town & County Bank* v. *Clark* (1859) 22 D. 44 and the Scottish decisions earlier cited.

books of the firm [36] or otherwise from the mode in which the partners have in fact dealt with each other.   The material which is established in evidence as to conduct of the partners must, however, be such as to allow an agreement for unequal shares to be inferred.   What is required is proof of circumstances which lead to the conclusion that the partners did in fact intend, or from the general habit or custom of their trade and business must fairly be presumed to have intended, to share in unequal proportions. The issue is thus of the nature of a jury question but the question of fact to be decided is whether circumstances have been proved which lead to such an inference.   " The real difficulty lies in holding that, where there is an inequality in the stock, or skill, or services, or experience, of the different partners, any one or more of those circumstances alone, or in conjunction with other circumstances, equally indeterminate and equivocal, should overcome the ordinary presumption of law of equality of shares between the partners." [37]   In some of the earlier cases [38] doubt appears to be thrown on the existence of the presumption of equality as a doctrine of the common law.   In *Peacock* v. *Peacock* [38] Lord Ellenborough seems to have considered that in such circumstances of " indeterminate inequality " there was no presumption of law governing the case and that the shares of the partners would be adjudged *ex aequo et bono* as upon a claim *quantum meruit*.   That view was disapproved by Lord Eldon [39] and in any event could not now be maintained in the face of the terms of section 24 (1) of the Partnership Act 1890.   It is, therefore, all the more important to examine the facts set up in order to see whether they really evince a clear intention of the partners to take unequal shares. Inequality in the contribution of capital, or skill or services may by themselves be indeterminate circumstances " which might be urged with more or less effect upon a jury, but which carried no certainty as to the positive intent or contract of the parties. . . ." [40]   On the other hand if it were proved that by the custom of any particular trade or business there was a general rule that the share taken by a partner was fixed upon his capital or that one should receive *e.g.* a fourth share and another three fourths on account of inequality of skill or experience, that may control the application of the presumption as to equal shares because it may amount to presumptive evidence that the partners intended to contract on the usual and customary terms.   If an agreement exists as to unequal shares, this will not be displaced by the fact that some of the original partners have retired.   If there is no evidence of agreement among the remaining partners to the contrary, the inference to be drawn is that the shares of the retiring partners are taken over by those remaining in the proportions in which the remaining partners originally shared in the partnership. [41]

[36] *Stewart* v. *Forbes* (1849) 1 Mac. & G. 137.
[37] Story, *Commentaries on the law of Partnership* (6th ed.) p. 35 n. 3.
[38] *Campbell's Trs.* v. *Thomson* (1831) 5 W. & S. 16; *Peacock* v. *Peacock* (1809) 2 Camp. 45.
[39] *Peacock* v. *Peacock* (1808) 16 Ves. 49.   See also *Farrar* v. *Beswick* (1836) 1 M. & Rob. 527 per Parke B.
[40] Story, *loc. cit.*
[41] *Robley* v. *Brooke* (1833) 7 Bli.(N.S) 90; *Copland* v. *Toulmin* (1840) 7 Cl. & F. 349.

Presumption in favour of equality applicable in partnership as to a single transaction

Where the contract creates a partnership as to an isolated adventure and not for the carrying on of a continuing business the rule that in the absence of agreement express or implied to the contrary the partners in the venture take equal shares is applicable. The Partnership Act 1890 makes no distinction in this respect between an arrangement of that sort, known as a joint adventure, and an ordinary partnership [42]; and the presumption of equality of shares was applied in such cases even before the passing of the Act. In *Fergusson v. Graham's Trustees* [43] a series of facts and circumstances were proved upon which the court held that the partners were equal partners in a joint adventure. That decision could only have been reached by the application of the presumption, since among the facts and circumstances proved was one of those circumstances of inequality described by Story as "indeterminate," *i.e.* that Graham had advanced money to retire bills for the price of the cargo which was the subject-matter of the joint adventure " up to fully two thirds of the whole." In the English case, *Robinson v. Anderson,* [44] two solicitors who were not in partnership with one another were jointly retained to defend certain actions. They were paid separately for the work which each had done and they had done unequal amounts of work in the defence of the actions. But since there was no evidence sufficient to establish agreement between them as to the proportions in which they were to share the remuneration, it was held that they were entitled to equal shares. The Master of the Rolls (Sir John Romilly) said,[45] " It is, in point of fact, a limited partnership [46] for a particular sort of business. Assuming nothing to have been said as to the manner in which the profits were to be divided, it appears to me to follow as a necessary consequence of law that they are to be divided equally between them. And although one may do more business and have exerted himself more than the other, yet if nothing is said on the subject of profits, the presumption is that they are to be equally divided between them." [47] A further question of some difficulty may arise where two parties agree to associate in a joint adventure without any agreement as to their respective shares of profits, and one of the parties so contracting is a firm while the other is an individual. Let it be assumed that the firm itself comprises two partners. Does the presumption as to equality of shares operate so as to give one half to the firm and one half to the individual associated with the firm in the adventure or so as to give one third

[42] See *infra* Chap. XV, pp. 623–624.

[43] (1836) 14 S. 871.

[44] (1855) 20 Beav. 98.

[45] *Ibid.* at p. 102.

[46] The Master of the Rolls is, of course, referring to the limited nature of the objectives of the joint adventure and not to the concept of the limited partnership later introduced in the Limited Partnerships Act 1907.

[47] See also *Webster v. Bray* (1849) 7 Hare 159; and *McGregor v. Bainbrigge* referred to in a note to *Webster v. Bray* (*supra*) at p. 164.

share to each of the individual persons associated in the adventure? This question must be determined on a consideration of the circumstances in which the agreement was made. If it appears from those circumstances that the joint adventure was entered into between the firm itself on the one part and the individual third party on the other, there are two *socii* only in the adventure, and the firm and the individual will each receive one half share,[48] but if the true intention of the parties as ascertained from the agreement was that the partners of the firm and the third party all entered into the adventure as individuals, then each will be entitled to a one third share.

Meaning of equality of share and contribution

In applying the presumption as to equality in partnership cases close regard must be had to the ambit and meaning of equality in this context. The Partnership Act 1890 [49] provides that " all the partners are entitled to share equally in the capital and profits of the business and must contribute equally towards the losses whether of capital or otherwise sustained by the firm." In its normal use in partnership affairs the capital of a firm is distinct from its property. The capital of the partnership is a term used to denote the aggregate of the sums contributed by the partners for the purpose of carrying on the business of a partnership. It is thus not equiparate to the assets or property of the firm which will vary during the conduct of the business and it is really represented by the amounts at credit of the partners on capital account. That amount may not, in the case of any partner, be the sum originally contributed by him as capital. He may owe money to the firm which is set off against his contribution or on the other hand he may have advanced further money to the firm not as his contribution of capital which he places at risk in the business of the firm but as a loan to the firm.[50]

It seems clear that neither the common law presumption as to equality nor section 24 (1) of the Partnership Act 1890 is to be taken as applicable to the capital of the partnership in that sense, at least where the circumstances show that the partners have made contributions which are unequal one with another. It cannot be maintained that the effect of section 24 (1) is that on a settlement of accounts among the partners, capital contributed in unequal shares by the partners is to be aggregated in one sum which will then be divided among the partners in equal shares. Such a proposition is in direct conflict with the terms of section 44 of the Partnership Act 1890 which states—

" 44. In settling accounts between the partners after a dissolution of partnership, the following rules shall, subject to any agreement, be observed:
(a) Losses, including losses and deficiencies of capital, shall be paid first out of profits, next out of capital, and lastly, if

[48] *Warner* v. *Smith* (1863) 1 De G.J. & S. 337.
[49] s. 24 (1).
[50] See Lindley, *op. cit.* pp. 347–348.

       necessary, by the partners individually in the proportion in which they were entitled to share profits;

  (b) The assets of the firm including the sums, if any, contributed by the partners to make up losses or deficiencies of capital, shall be applied in the following manner and order:

     1. In paying the debts and liabilities of the firm to persons who are not partners therein;

     2. In paying to each partner rateably what is due from the firm to him for advances as distinguished from capital;

     3. In paying to each partner rateably what is due from the firm to him in respect of capital;

     4. The ultimate residue, if any, shall be divided among the partners in the proportion in which profits are divisible."

The Partnership Act 1890 appears, therefore, to distinguish between the capital of the firm, *i.e.* the sums contributed by the partners and placed at risk in the venture and the property or assets of the firm; as to the share in the profits and the contribution to the losses which occur in the running of the business, in the absence of agreement, the presumption is for equality since the circumstances that the original contributions to capital are unequal is " indeterminate and equivocal " as governing any partner's right to share in the fortunes of the partnership business. On the other hand, the fact that the contributions of capital are unequal is not indeterminate and equivocal in a question as to settling with the partners for sums standing to their credit on capital account. On the contrary it is a determining and conclusive factor in the settlement. But it does not follow that where the sums originally contributed as capital, or part of them, are lost in the running of the business the same element of unequal contribution to that capital should be taken as determining the proportions in which the partners must bear that loss. The question then in issue is not the rights of the partners in the sums which originally stood to their credit on capital account but the right which they are held to have to share in the fortunes of the firm, and here the presumption of equal shares in losses as well as profits [51] may operate even where the contributions to capital were unequal. The question of settlement of accounts among the partners is more properly treated in a discussion of the dissolution and winding up of the firm, and the terms of section 44 are hereafter examined more closely in that context.[52] For the moment it is sufficient to emphasise the distinction between a final settlement of accounts in which an unequal contribution of capital will be recognised and given effect to in the accounting, and a sharing in profit and losses during the currency of the partnership in which the presumption for equality may apply even where the

---

[51] " The partners are, by the general law of partnership, equal sharers of stock on the dissolution of the company and equal participators of profit and of loss, where there is no special contract relative to this matter."—Bell, *Com.* II, 503. In the first part of that statement, " stock " must refer to the property of the firm, not to the contributions to input capital.

[52] See *infra* Chap. XII, pp. 531 *et seq.*

losses incurred by the partnership in the conduct of its business are reflected in losses on the capital account of the various partners.

The partner's lien

In section 39 of the Partnership Act 1890 it is provided—

" 39. On the dissolution of a partnership evei y partner is entitled, as against the other partners in the firm and all persons claiming through them in respect of their interests as partners, to have the property of the partnership applied in payment of the debts and liabilities of the firm, and to have the surplus assets after such payment applied in payment of what may be due to the partners respectively after deducting what may be due from them as partners to the firm; and for that purpose any partner or his representatives may on the termination of the partnership apply to the Court to wind up the business and affairs of the firm."

The right conferred in that section reflects the position under the pre-existing common law. It has been likened to " an equitable lien on the partnership property for the purpose of having it applied in discharge of the debts of the firm "; and " a similar lien on the surplus assets for the purpose of having them applied in payment of what may be due to the partners respectively after deducting what may be due from them, as partners, to the firm." [53]   This equitable lien, or right, or quasi-lien, does not resemble in all its particulars other liens recognised by the law, but even before the passing of the Partnership Act 1890 its existence was recognised in a number of decisions in the English courts.[54]   A similar principle was recognised in the earlier Scottish decisions when the right was usually described as one of retention.[55]   It will be observed that the right of lien cannot be invoked to any practical effect save on the dissolution of the partnership. It cannot be called into practical effect during the subsistence of a continuing partnership. When the partnership is dissolved and its affairs require to be wound up or the share of a partner ascertained and paid out, however, the right conferred in section 39 comes into being and in order to make it effective, any partner may apply to the court to have the affairs of the partnership wound up [56] and where partnership property falls to be divided among the partners any one of them is entitled to insist on a public sale thereof.[57]   If, however, a valuation has been agreed among them a sale will not thereafter be ordered by the court.[58]

[53] Lindley, *op. cit.* p. 375.
[54] *West* v. *Skip* (1749) 1 Ves.Sen. 239; *Skipp* v. *Harwood* (1747) 2 Swanst. 586; *Doddington* v. *Hallet* (1750) 1 Ves.Sen. 497 at pp. 498–499; *Ex p. Ruffin* (1801) 6 Ves. 119; *Ex p. Williams* (1805) 11 Ves. 3; *Holderness* v. *Shackels* (1828) 8 B. & C. 612.
[55] *McCaul's Creditors* v. *Ramsay & Ritchie* (1740) Mor. 14608: *Keith* v. *Penn* (1840) 2 D. 633.
[56] Partnership Act 1890, s. 39; and see *Thomson, Petitioner* (1893) 1 S.L.T. 59; *Robertson, Petitioner* (1902) 10 S.L.T. 417; *Elliott* v. *Cassils* (1907) 15 S.L.T. 190.
[57] *Marshall* v. *Marshall*, Feb. 23, 1816, F.C.; *Aitken's Trs.* v. *Shanks* (1830) 8 S. 753; *McWhannell* v. *Dobbie* (1830) 8 S. 914; *Stewart* v. *Simpson* (1835) 14 S. 72.
[58] *Mackersies* v. *Mitchell* (1872) 10 M. 861; *McNiven* v. *Peffers* (1868) 7 M. 181.

Extent of the property affected

During the subsistence of the partnership, the right, while it cannot be put into effect, attaches to all partnership property and the substitution of new stock for old will not entail the loss of the right.[59] When the partnership has been dissolved, however, the right attaches only to such assets as were partnership property at the date of dissolution. It will not attach to stock in trade and other property which has thereafter been acquired by those who continue to carry on the business where it is carried on by the surviving partners after a dissolution caused by the death or bankruptcy of one of the original partners. But to the extent mentioned, the right of the deceased or bankrupt partner will continue to be available to his representatives until his share has been ascertained and provision has been made by the other partners for paying it.[60] Since both under the common law and under section 39 of the Partnership Act 1890 the right attaches only to the property of the partnership, it is important to ensure before the right is asserted that the property affected is of that kind; for if the partnership subsists as to the profits only and the property by the use of which those profits are made does not belong to the partnership but to one or more of the partners to the exclusion of their copartners then the right of a partner under section 39 of the Partnership Act 1890 will attach only to the profits of the partnership and not to the property which produced those profits, nor will those of the partners who are co-owners of the property to the exclusion of the others enjoy a similar right *inter se* because mere co-ownership does not of itself confer the equitable right or lien which is conferred upon partners.[61]

Debts in respect of which the right may be asserted

Section 39 of the Partnership Act 1890 is concerned with the right in the partners which, on the dissolution of the firm, attaches to the partnership property and the right thus extends " to whatever is due to or from the firm by or to the members thereof as such." [62] In asserting the right, therefore, to deduct the debt of a partner before applying the surplus assets of the partnership in payment of what may be due to him,[63] it is necessary to examine the nature of the debt so proposed to be deducted. Where the partner concerned has borrowed money belonging to the partnership, the other partners will have the right to deduct or retain from the amount paid to him the debt thus incurred by their copartner to the partnership.[64] On the other hand where a partner has borrowed money

---

[59] *Stocken* v. *Dawson* (1845) 9 Beav. 239; affd. (1848) 17 L.J.Ch. 282; and see also *West* v. *Skip, Skipp* v. *Harwood* both cited *supra* n. 54.

[60] *Stocken* v. *Dawson, supra.*

[61] *Re Leslie, Leslie* v. *French* (1883) 23 Ch.D. 552; *Kay* v. *Johnston* (1856) 21 Beav. 536, though the part owner of a ship has a somewhat similar right to have the gross freight earned applied first to defray the expenses incurred in earning it: *Alexander* v. *Simms* (1854) 23 L.J.Ch. 721; *Green* v. *Briggs* (1848) 17 L.J.Ch. 323.

[62] Lindley, *op. cit.* p. 378.

[63] See Partnership Act 1890, s. 39.

[64] *Meliorucchi* v. *Royal Exchange Assurance Co.* (1728) 1 Eq.Ca.Ab. 8; *Croft* v. *Pyke* (1733) 3 P.Wms. 180.

which is not partnership money from his copartners for his own personal purposes it has been held in England that on his bankruptcy his assignees are entitled to his share in the partnership as ascertained without deduction of the sum borrowed from his copartners.[65] While that decision entailed that the solvent partners had to pay to the bankrupt partner's estate the full amount of his share and thereafter to prove against the bankrupt estate for the sum lent to the bankrupt partner, the hardship thus caused to them does not affect the essential correctness of the decision, since the equitable right of retention only arises as to partnership property and in the case in point it was not partnership property in the shape of a debt owed by the bankrupt partner to his firm but the property of his copartners not as partners but as individuals which was concerned.

Persons against whom the right may be asserted

It is clear from the terms of section 39 of the Partnership Act 1890 that the right where it exists may be made effective against the partner concerned but it is also pleadable against the executors or trustee in bankruptcy of the partner or an assignee of his share. Section 39 makes the right available not only against the partners but also " all persons claiming through them in respect of their interests as partners." [66] The principle has been applied in the English courts in *Re Ritson, Ritson* v. *Ritson* [67] where one of two partners charged his own real estate in security of a debt due by the partnership. On his death he left the real estate to his son and the residue, including his share in the partnership, to his children. The assets of the partnership were sufficient to pay all debts and liabilities of the partnership and the residuary legatees contended that the firm debt should be discharged out of the real estate charged with it. This contention was not favoured by the court who held that the share of the partnership bequeathed to them under residue was merely the deceased's share in the surplus of the partnership assets after payment of all the partnership debts including the debt secured over the real estate and that since the surviving partner could have insisted that the assets of the firm be applied in payment of the firm's debts, the devisee of the real estate had the same right against the executors and the residuary legatees of the deceased partner.

The limits of the principle should, however, be noted. The terms of section 39 will not include among the persons claiming through a partner in respect of his interest as a partner a person who in good faith purchases from one of the partners specific property belonging to the partnership and such a purchaser will acquire a good title to the property albeit that prior to the sale the other partners may have had an equitable right of retention which would attach on dissolution of the partnership.[68] " To hold . . . that this lien could be enforced against persons purchasing

[65] *Ryall* v. *Rowles* (1749) 1 Ves.Sen. 348; *Croft* v. *Pyke* (1733) 3 P.Wms. 180.
[66] See *Croft* v. *Pyke, supra* (executor); *Cavander* v. *Bulteel* (1873) L.R. 9 Ch. 79 (assignee).
[67] [1899] 1 Ch. 128.
[68] *Re Langmead's Trusts* (1855) 20 Beav. 20.

partnership property would be in effect to prevent any sale of that property without the consent of the whole firm and would practically stop all partnership trade." [69]   The distinction should be noted, however, between a bona fide purchase of specific property or goods which form part of the partnership property and a purchase, equally in good faith, of a partner's share in the firm, since in the latter case the purchaser takes the share subject to the rights or liens of the other partners which may attach to it. [70]

Circumstances in which right may be lost

Since the right afforded by section 39 of the Partnership Act 1890 is made effective against " the property of the partnership " it follows that if the property against which it is asserted has lost that character the right itself is lost.   The cases in which such a change in the character of partnership property may be expected to occur are somewhat restricted since the right can be made effective only on the dissolution of the partnership and the occasions for a change in the nature of partnership property after that event has occurred are not wide-ranging.   Nevertheless if the partnership property is converted into the separate property of one of the partners the rights of his copartners under section 39 over that property will be lost. On a dissolution of partnership it may be agreed among the partners that the partnership property, or some of it, be divided among the partners and assets of the partnership, to the agreed value of their respective proportions handed over to them *in specie*, while agreed arrangements are made among them for the payment of the debts and liabilities of the firm in some manner not involving the realisation of the partnership assets so transferred and the application of the proceeds of realisation thereof toward payment of these debts and liabilities.   If the partnership property is divided among the partners in terms of that agreement but the debts and liabilities of the firm are not paid in terms of the other arrangements agreed to, the right against the property now in the hands of a partner as a result of the agreement has been lost and his copartners cannot insist upon such property being restored to the common stock of the partnership and applied in terms of section 39 in discharge of the debts and liabilities of the firm. That, at least, was the law in England before the passing of the Partnership Act 1890. [71]   The same principle has been applied in the English courts when two partners consign goods for sale and instruct the consignee to credit the proceeds of the sale in equal shares to their separate accounts without any reserve.   On that being done neither party was allowed to assert a right against the share so credited to the other, though if the goods so consigned had remained the joint property of the partners the case would have been otherwise decided, [72] and even where the facts are similar to those on which the decision is founded, the transfer to each partner

[69] Lindley, *op. cit.* p. 377.
[70] *Cavander* v. *Bulteel* (1873) L.R. 9 Ch. 79.
[71] *Lingen* v. *Simpson* (1824) 1 S. & S. 600.   See also on this point *Re Langmead's Trusts* (1855) 7 De G.M. & G. 353, *per* Turner L.J. at pp. 360–362.
[72] *Holroyd* v. *Griffiths* (1856) 3 Drew. 428.

may be made subject to the right or lien, in which case it will not be lost.[73]

Though no reported decision in the Scottish courts appears to deal with the losing of the right under section 39 if the partnership property is converted into separate property of the individual partners, it is thought that the English decisions just cited would be received as persuasive authority in the Scottish courts. The common law of Scotland before the passing of the Act was in consonance with the English law in regard to the application of the assets of the firm on a dissolution of the partnership.[74] As in England, and as reflected in section 39 of the Partnership Act 1890, the rules as to distribution of the partnership property on dissolution, laid down by the common law, yield to the terms agreed by the partners whether the agreement be expressed in the contract of copartnery itself or be inferred from the books and usage of the partnership.[75] Any such agreement among the partners will not, however, affect the rights of the firm's creditors to be paid preferably out of the firm's property, but the claims of the partners on the surplus assets of the partnership, after the firm's debts have been discharged, are preferable to any claim of a personal creditor of an individual partner on those surplus assets of the firm.[76] It has been questioned whether the concluding words of section 39, " and for that purpose any partner or his representatives may on the termination of the partnership apply to the Court to wind up the business and affairs of the firm " do not permit a partner or his representatives to insist on the appointment of a judicial factor to wind up the firm's affairs, in disregard of the former principles of the Scots common law [77] and to that extent the section may not entirely reflect the pre-existing law. This point is more relevant in a discussion of the general law governing the dissolution and winding up of partnerships and is treated elsewhere in this book.[78] In so far as section 39 is concerned with the lien or right over the partnership property there is nothing in the pre-existing Scots law which is inconsistent with the premiss on which that right is based and since both logically and in terms of the express provisions of the section the right is attached to partnership property only, it seems that the reasoning behind the earlier English decisions on conversion of the partnership property is equally applicable in Scotland.

---

[73] This was the situation in *Holderness* v. *Shackels* (1828) 8 B. & C. 612.

[74] " 3.   The common property thus converted [*i.e.* realised], with the pecuniary funds when collected, forms a fund over which the creditors of the concern have a primary and preferable claim, and it must be so applied, in the first place, before any partner or his assignee or representatives can claim a share.
   " 4.   In taking an account between the partners themselves, the state of the stock is to be taken as at the dissolution (death, for instance), and the proceeds thereof until it is got in; and each is to be allowed whatever he has advanced to the partnership, and is to be charged with what he has failed to bring in, or has drawn out more than his just proportion ": Bell, *Com.* II, 535.

[75] *Anderson Blair* v. *Russell* (1828) 6 S. 836.

[76] *Keith* v. *Penn* (1840) 2 D. 633.

[77] See *Supplement to Lindley on Partnership* (1891) p. 104.

[78] See *infra*, Chap. XII, pp. 520 *et seq*.

Illegality of partnership as affecting right

It has been held in England that if the partnership is itself illegal,[79] the members of the partnership have no lien upon or right against the common property of the concern or upon the share of any of their co-partners therein.[80] The rule is equally applicable in Scots law on the application of the general principle *ex turpi causa non oritur actio* and *in turpi causa melior est conditio possidentis*, the latter maxim being more parti-cularly in point, since under section 39 of the Partnership Act 1890 questions of right to property are involved. In any event, a partner in an illegal partnership who asserted his rights under section 39 would be in the posi-tion of seeking the assistance of the court in maintaining a claim based upon a *pactum illicitum* and the general principle is clearly applicable that " if a plaintiff cannot maintain his cause of action without showing, as part of such cause of action, that he has been guilty of illegality, then the courts will not assist him in his cause of action." [81] It has been repeatedly held in Scotland that if a partnership is illegal, no action of accounting is maintainable by one partner against the other, even if the defender has defrauded the pursuer,[82] and *a fortiori* it appears that the right of lien afforded under section 39 of the Partnership Act 1890—a right closely associated with the accounting for the partnership assets on a dissolution of the partnership and indeed dependent upon the settlement of accounts in the partnership—is similarly precluded. It will however be possible to assert the right if it arises from an agreement among the partners which itself is not tainted with the illegality.[83]

Assignation of a partner's share

It has already been mentioned [84] that on the principle of *delectus personae* which applies in partnership, the intention of the partners when entering the partnership, in the absence of provision to the contrary, is considered to be that the partnership will subsist among the parties to the contract of copartnery and them alone. No person may be introduced into the firm as a partner unless all the existing partners consent [85] but cases may occur where what might be termed an anticipatory consent by the partners is evinced by the terms of the partnership deed itself as where the partners, or some of them, have stipulated in the agreement of partner-ship that in the event of death, for example, the executors or representatives of the deceased partner will have the right to be admitted to partnership

---

[79] *Supra*, Chap. IV.
[80] *Ewing* v. *Osbaldiston* (1837) 2 Myl. & C. 53.
[81] *Scott* v. *Brown* [1892] 2 Q.B. 724, *per* A. L. Smith L.J. at p. 734.
[82] *Fraser* v. *Hill* (1852) 14 D. 335; *Gordon* v. *Howden* (1843) 5 D. 698, rev. on appeal (1845) 4 Bell 254; *A.B.* v. *C.D.*, 1912, 1 S.L.T. 44.
[83] Lindley, *op. cit.* p. 379. But it is difficult to see how in that case the " lien " can be said to arise under the law of partnership and under s. 39 of the Partnership Act 1890 since the partnership itself is illegal. It appears that what is here considered is some form of equitable lien created by an agreement among the partners entirely independent of, and separate from, the partnership agreement.
[84] *Supra* Chap. I, pp. 16–18.
[85] Partnership Act 1890, s. 24 (7).

with the surviving partners.[86] The same principle is applied where a partner transfers his share in the partnership to a third party. He is not permitted to introduce his assignee by this means as a partner in the firm without the consent of all existing partners. In England the rule is clearly based upon the principle that all partners must consent to the assumption of a new partner into the firm.[87] In Scotland the same principle is applied to the case of an assignation by a partner of his share to a third party. Even where a partner actually assumes another person into partnership, rather than merely assigning his share in the firm to him, the third party thus assumed becomes a partner not of the firm, but of the individual partner who assumes him. " The company are not bound to regard the second contract formed by the assumption which is limited to the share of the partner assuming. He still continues with respect to the company the sole proprietor of that share and must sustain all actions concerning it." [88] *Socius mei socii non est socius meus*.[89]

Nevertheless, an assignation by a partner of his share in the partnership in favour of a third party is a transfer of a *jus crediti* even although it does not confer on the assignee the legal status of a partner in the firm. On a dissolution of the firm when the share assigned to him falls to be ascertained and paid out, the assignation of that share has obvious and important consequences. While the partnership is a going concern, the position of the assignee is more ambivalent. On the one hand, on the principle *assignatus utitur iure auctoris*, he is entitled to stand in the shoes of the cedent in so far as the right assigned is concerned; but, on the other hand, if that general principle as to the position of the assignee were applied without modification to the assignation of a share in a partnership, that principle would collide with a principle of equal validity and force in the law of partnership—that mutual confidence among partners is of the essence of the legal relationship and that while a person may repose that confidence in a partner whom he has chosen, he may obviously be reluctant to accord it to any other person who, without his assent, is proposed to stand in that relationship to him. Therefore while the partnership is a going concern, the extent of the right and powers conferred upon a third party as assignee of a share in a partnership must be anxiously considered in order to ensure that any rights and powers so conferred do not put him in the position of interfering in the management of the firm's affairs, a right jealously reserved to the partners themselves [90] and inferentially not

---

[86] *Beveridge* v. *Beveridge* (1872) 10 M.(H.L.) 1; *Alexander's Trs.* v. *Thomson* (1885) 22 S.L.R. 828; *Thomson* v. *Thomson*, 1962 S.C.(H.L.) 28. As to the difficulty of executors or trustees acting collectively as a partner under such a right, see Chap. I, pp. 21–23.

[87] *Pearce* v. *Chamberlain* (1750) 2 Ves.Sen. 33; *Crawford* v. *Hamilton* (1818) 3 Madd. 251; *Bray* v. *Fromont* (1821) 6 Madd. 5; *Crawshay* v. *Maule* (1818) 1 Swanst. 495; *Tatam* v. *Williams* (1844) 3 Hare 347.

[88] Ersk. *Inst.* III, 3, 22.

[89] *Fairholm* v. *Marjoribanks* (1725) Mor. 14558. See also Dig. 17: 2: 20.
   " Qui admittitur socius ei tantum socius est qui admisit, et recte, cum enim societas consensu contrahatur, socius mihi esse non potest quem ego socium esse nolui: quid ergo si socius meus eum admisit ei soli socius est "; Pothier, *Traité du Contrat de Société* § 91.

[90] Partnership Act 1890, s. 24 (5).

to be entrusted to any one else without their consent.[91] In the English case law prior to the passing of the Partnership Act 1890 that ambivalence was reflected in the doubt which existed whether the assignee of a share in the partnership was entitled to call upon the partners of his cedent for an accounting while the firm was still a going concern.[92] The rights of an assignee of a share in a partnership are now laid down in section 31 of the Partnership Act 1890:

> " 31.—(1) An assignment by any partner of his share in the partnership, either absolute or by way of mortgage or redeemable charge, does not, as against the other partners, entitle the assignee during the continuance of the partnership, to interfere in the management or administration of the partnership business or affairs, or to require any accounts of the partnership transactions, or to inspect the partnership books, but entitles the assignee only to receive the share of profits to which the assigning partner would otherwise be entitled, and the assignee must accept the account of profits agreed to by the partners.
>
> (2) In case of a dissolution of the partnership, whether as respects all the partners or as respects the assigning partner, the assignee is entitled to receive the share of the partnership assets to which the assigning partner is entitled as between himself and the other partners, and for the purpose of ascertaining that share, to an account as from the date of the dissolution."

Section 31 therefore resolved the doubt which formerly existed in the English law as to the right of an assignee to call for an accounting from the partners of the firm. During the continuance of the partnership his rights under the assignation are rigorously qualified in deference to the principle that it is in conflict with the basic nature of partnership that any person should be permitted to take part in the conduct of the affairs of the partnership without the consent of all the partners; in other words, the principle that partnership is a contract involving *delectus personae*. That principle has been upheld to a dramatic degree, almost to the extent of placing the assignee in an unprecedentedly weak position so long as the partnership continues in existence, and so far at least as English law is concerned, in view of the earlier conflicting decisions, section 31 may have altered the law. The pre-statute Scots law is not favoured with the same wealth of authority, even if conflicting authority, as is the English law but the opinion may be hazarded that section 31 entirely reflects the earlier Scots law. Certainly the view propounded by Erskine [93] supports that opinion, and it is further reinforced by judicial dicta in the case of *Cassells*

---

[91] It is instructive to compare the position of the assignee of a share of a general partnership with that of the assignee of a limited partner's share in a limited partnership under the Limited Partnerships Act 1907. See *infra* Chap. XIV, pp. 595–596.

[92] *Whetham* v. *Davey* (1885) 30 Ch.D. 574; *Glyn* v. *Hood* (1859) 1 Giff. 328; *Kelly* v. *Hutton* (1868) L.R. 3 Ch. 703 were decided in favour of such a right. *Brown* v. *De Tastet* (1819) Jac. 284 and the cases decided on the maxim *socius mei socii socius meus non est* (see *supra* p. 412) were decided adversely to the existence of the right.

[93] *Inst.* III, 3, 22.

v. *Stewart* [94] where Lord Moncreiff stated, " It cannot be disputed upon
the decided cases that, although there is a *delectus personae* in the contract
of copartnery, any partner may, if he chooses, assign his share to a third
party as long as that does not interfere with the conduct of the company,
or the respective rights and interests of the partners.   There is nothing to
prevent this at common law " [95]; and in the same case Lord Gifford
said,[96] " But, further, even an out-and-out assignation of Reid's interest
was quite lawful, provided Reid continued a partner, and fulfilled all the
conditions of the contract."   The view of the Scots common law, therefore, accords with the law laid down in section 31 of the Partnership Act
1890.   The assignation is legal but the cedent remains the partner, exercising his rights as such.   To complete the assignee's right to the share
assigned and to prefer him over the cedent's creditors, the assignation must
of course be intimated to the firm or to all the partners thereof unless the
cedent has assigned his share to his copartner and he and his assignee are
the only partners of the firm, when intimation would be otiose and
unnecessary.[97]   But the assignation remains an assignation of a share in
the partnership not of the status and quality of a partner.[98]

While section 31 of the Partnership Act 1890 may therefore be claimed
to be in consonance with the pre-existing Scots law, there are aspects of the
wording of the section which merit close attention.

Effect of contrary agreement.   While the words of section 31 are general
and unqualified they must be construed along with the provisions of the
Partnership Act 1890 as a whole and that construction is to be preferred
which so interprets the various sections that they are not mutually destructive.   In particular, regard must be had to the terms of section 19 of the
Act which provides—

> " 19. The mutual rights and duties of partners, whether ascertained
> by agreement or defined by this Act, may be varied by the consent of
> all the partners, and such consent may be either express or inferred
> from a course of dealing." [99]

It will therefore be perfectly competent for the partners to provide in their
contract of copartnery or by supplementary minute of agreement that any
partner may assign his share in the partnership,[1] and that the assignee
shall become a partner by virtue of the assignation (if duly intimated) or
that the assignee shall enjoy higher rights as to inspecting the books of the
partnership or as to an accounting from the partners than are afforded him
under section 31; and if that is done the agreement of the partners will

---

[94] (1879) 6 R. 936.
[95] *Ibid.* at p. 945.
[96] At p. 955.
[97] *Hill* v. *Lindsay* (1846) 8 D. 472, *per* Lord Fullerton at p. 480.
[98] See in addition for the earlier Scots law, *Russell* v. *Earl of Breadalbane* (1827) 5 S. 891;
    aff. (1831) 5 W. & S. 256: *Lonsdale Hematite Co.* v. *Barclay* (1874) 1 R. 417.
[99] *Starrett* v. *Pia*, 1968 S.L.T.(Notes) 28.
[1] In *Lonsdale Hematite Co.* v. *Barclay* (1874) 1 R. 417 the partnership agreement allowed the
    partners to assign their share on condition that they first offered them to the firm and their
    partners. See also *Cassells* v. *Stewart* (1879) 6 R. 936.

supplant the terms of the section. That is entirely in accordance with the underlying legal principles; for section 31 is not concerned with a limitation of the assignee's rights upon general and dogmatic grounds but with preventing a third party from exercising powers over the affairs of a partnership merely by virtue of his holding an assignation of a share therein and without the consent of all the partners. Consequently if partners enter into an agreement under which they undertake to admit to the partnership any person whom one of the partners introduced into the partnership whether by assignation of his share or otherwise, there is nothing in the Partnership Act 1890 nor in the general law of partnership which prevents a partner from doing so [2]; nor does the doctrine of *delectus personae* militate against that, since *delectus personae* is based upon the implication by law that the contract has been entered into in reliance on the personal qualities of the person with whom the contract is made and will therefore yield to proof that in terms of the agreement no such reliance upon individual qualities can be established. For instance, the contracts which provide the classic *delectus personae* are the engagement of an author to write a book or of an artist to paint a picture; yet it would have been difficult, it is submitted, to contend that a contract with Dumas for a new tale of the swash-buckling adventures of the three musketeers would have involved *delectus personae* to the extent of excluding the participating hacks employed by that author in his literary activities or that a contract with Rubens for one of his pictures would have excluded the contribution to the finished work of the efforts of his *atelier*. In such cases, at least in the heyday of the artists concerned, their method of working was so notorious as to render the implication of *delectus personae* in its most rigidly legalistic terms untenable; and where by the express terms of a contract of copartnery the parties agree in advance to assume a person introduced by one of the partners, it will be otiose to invoke the general principle of *delectus personae* in the face of express agreement which waives any such principle in the copartnery.

" *As against the other partners.*" It will be observed that section 31 of the Partnership Act 1890 governs only the legal relationship between the assignee of a partner's share and the other partners in the firm. It does not deal with the rights of the assignee against the assigning partner. The latter rights are governed by the general law without modification in terms of the Partnership Act 1890. An assignee of a share in a partnership may therefore compel the assigning partner to account to him for all profits which he, the assigning partner, may have received.[3] Again, while the terms of section 31 appear to preclude an assignee from obtaining, in a question with the partners of the firm, during the continuance of the partnership, sums to which the assigning partner is entitled but which are not *stricto sensu* profits,[4] the terms of the assignation may render the

---

[2] *Lovegrove* v. *Nelson* (1834) 3 M. & K. 1.
[3] *Brown* v. *De Tastet* (1819) Jac. 284.
[4] " . . . but entitles the assignee only to receive the share of profits to which the assigning partner would otherwise be entitled . . ." : Partnership Act 1890, s. 31 (1).

cedent liable to account to his assignee for any such sums. It is also to be noticed that in a question with the partners the assignee under section 31 of the Partnership Act 1890, even where he has intimated his assignation to the firm, does not thereby acquire a right to the assigning partner's share as it stood at the time when the assignation was intimated. His right is still subject to claims which subsequently arise against his cedent at the instance of the other partners.[5] In terms of the assignation, however, the assigning partner may, in a question with his assignee, be subject to a more rigorous liability.[6] On dissolution of the partnership, on the other hand, the assignee has the right " to receive the share of the partnership assets to which the assigning partner is entitled as between himself and the other partners." [7] His right is not restricted as it is in the case of a continuing partnership to the assigning partner's share of profits and he has the right to an accounting from the other partners " as from the date of dissolution." The situation on a dissolution of the partnership is more appropriately considered elsewhere in this treatise.[8] For the moment it is sufficient to notice that in distinction from the position under a continuing partnership the assignee's rights are not affected by any sale of, or agreement for valuing or otherwise dealing with, the assigning partner's share which has been made among the partners after the dissolution and the intimation of the assignation.[9] Finally section 31 (2) of the Partnership Act 1890 affords to the assignee the higher rights in the case of a dissolution of the partnership " whether as respects all the partners or as respects the assigning partner." Unless the partnership agreement provides otherwise, the death or bankruptcy of any partner dissolves the partnership.[10] If, therefore, the assigning partner dies or is made bankrupt and the remaining partners continue the partnership business, a dissolution has nonetheless occurred so far as the assigning partner is concerned and his assignee will then be entitled to his cedent's share in the partnership assets and to receive an accounting. Since he has had assigned to him the share of the assigning partner, then, if the remaining partners continue the partnership business using the assigning partner's capital, a right may arise in the assigning partner to such share of the profits made since the dissolution and until settlement of accounts with him as the court may find attributable to the use of his capital or alternatively to interest of 5 per cent. per annum on the amount of his share of the partnership assets,[11] and that accruing right would, it is thought, be available to the assignee.

---

[5] *Bergmann* v. *McMillan* (1881) 17 Ch.D. 423; *Morris* v. *Livie* (1842) 1 Y. & C.Ch. 380; *Cavander* v. *Bulteel* (1873) L.R. 9 Ch. 79; *Kelly* v. *Hutton* (1868) L.R. 3 Ch. 703; *Redmayne* v. *Forster* (1866) L.R. 2 Eq. 467.
[6] *Cassells* v. *Stewart* (1879) 6 R. 936, *per* Lord Gifford at p. 955 citing Lindley (3rd ed.) I, p. 698; see now Lindley, 13th ed. pp. 384–385.
[7] Partnership Act 1890, s. 31 (2).
[8] *Infra* Chap. X, pp. 478–480; Chap. XII, pp. 523–526.
[9] *Watts* v. *Driscoll* [1901] 1 Ch. 294. But see *Re Garwood's Trusts, Garwood* v. *Paynter* [1903] 1 Ch. 236 (payment of salaries to partners for work done on winding up).
[10] Partnership Act 1890, s. 33 (1).
[11] Partnership Act 1890, s. 42 (1).

Effect of assignation where there is a right to assign

It has been decided in the English courts that where the terms of the partnership agreement allow a partner unconditionally the right to assign his share, then the partner may by transfer of his share rid himself of all liability arising between himself and his copartners for transactions entered into subsequently to the date of intimation of the assignation to the firm, even if the assignee is a man of straw.[12] The basis of that decision is not easy to follow since in the same decision it is recognised that the assignation itself in such circumstances does not make the assignee a partner and liable as such for the subsequent liabilities of the firm, the other partners being required to recognise him as a partner or permit him to act as such before he can assume that character.   Accordingly there does not appear to be any novation of the contract of copartnery involved in the exercise of the assigning partner's unconditional right to assign his share; nor is it entirely satisfactory to regard such an assignation exercised as of right, as notice to the other partners of his intention to terminate the partnership.   Indeed, he may have a clear intention to continue as a partner for example, where he has assigned his share in security of a temporary loan made to him by the assignee.   On the other hand, it sometimes occurs that a right to assign his share is conferred under the partnership agreement on a partner as a method by which he may retire from the partnership and realise his capital in the partnership.[13]   It appears possible that the court in *Jefferys* v. *Smith* [12] regarded the question as one of that nature and spelt out from the agreement an intention of the partners that an assignation of a partner's share which was notified to the firm in terms of the partnership agreement was designed for the purpose of the assigning partner's severing his association with the partnership and retrieving the capital which he had contributed in which case the intimation of the assignation may be regarded as inferentially a notice of termination of the partnership.   If that be the correct rationalisation of the decision—and it must be confessed that the terms of the report cannot be said unqualifiedly to support it—then *Jefferys* v. *Smith* [14] may be regarded as not inconsistent with Scots law; but if the English decision is authority for the more general proposition advanced earlier in this paragraph, there is difficulty in reconciling it with the general observations on the effect of the assignation in *Cassells* v. *Stewart* [15] and with the decision in *Lonsdale Hematite Company* v. *Barclay*.[16]   While neither of the Scottish cases is directly in point (1) since in neither was the right to assign made unconditional [17] and (2) in neither case did the assigning partner intimate the

[12] *Jefferys* v. *Smith* (1827) 3 Russ. 158.
[13] *Lonsdale Hematite Co.* v. *Barclay* (1874) 1 R. 417 is a case of that kind, although there the right to assign was subject to a right of pre-emption by the firm or its partners.
[14] *Supra* n. 12.
[15] (1879) 6 R. 936.
[16] (1874) 1 R. 417.
[17] In *Cassells* v. *Stewart*, *supra*, the partners were prohibited from assigning their shares and any such assignation was declared to be " of no force, strength or effect as regards the company or other individual partners who shall not be obliged to pay any attention thereto."

assignation to the firm,[18] yet the real question for decision is the effect to be given to an intimation to the firm of the assignation of a share and in the determination of that question the fact that the right to assign was unconditional does not seem to have any general and direct relevance. Its only bearing, it is submitted, is as an element from which an intention of the partners may be inferred that under the particular partnership deed in question a notice of assignation was in effect a notice of retiral.

Effect where the other partners accept the assignee as a partner

Where the other partners accept the assignee as a partner in place of the assigning partner the resultant situation is not expressly dealt with in section 31 of the Partnership Act 1890. It may be, however, that the wording of subsection (1) of that section throws some light by way of implication on the question. The subsection is expressed in such a way that it restricts in a question with partners who do not consent to receive the assignee into the partnership what might otherwise be the full effect of the assignation, and it may be contended that where the other partners consent to his introduction as a partner the result is to remove that specially imposed restriction and to give the assignee the entitlement to " interfere in the management or administration of the partnership business or affairs," *i.e.* to act as a partner. That implication which appeared to Professor Lorimer to be inherent in the terms of the subsection [19] seems to be reasonable. In terms of the general law an assignation of a share in a partnership involves the transfer to the assignee of a *ius crediti* which is not confined merely to the right to draw the share of profits effeiring to the cedent but is a bundle of the concomitant rights and duties of a partner including his *pro indiviso* right to a proportion of the partnership property and his right to participate in the management of the business of the firm. In recognition of the peculiar closeness of the partners' relationship one to another, the subsection has placed a restriction upon what would otherwise be the full legal effect of the assignation and if the other partners consent to waive that restriction, the assignation is restored to its full effect and carries with it the right to assumption as a partner. The point has not been decided in any reported case but it is not a mere academic or artificial one; for if the effect of the consent of the other partners be as above contended, then the assigning partner himself will have no right to exclude his assignee from the partnership when the other partners have consented to his assumption. The terms of the second subsection of section 31 of the Partnership Act 1890 are neutral upon this point, since in terms of that subsection it is a basic assumption that the assignee has not been assumed into the partnership prior to the dissolution of the partnership, because otherwise his right to an accounting would arise from the date of his assumption and not from the date of dissolution as is provided.

---

[18] In *Cassells* v. *Stewart*, the assignation came to light on the death of the assigning partner, in *Lonsdale Hematite Co.* v. *Barclay* as a result of an action at the instance of the assignee against the assigning partner in which the latter was ordered to assign the share.

[19] *Supplement to Lindley on Partnership* (1891) p. 79.

Goodwill

The goodwill of a business is a capital asset which is not confined to those businesses which are carried on in partnership. To that extent it may be said that it is not a peculiarity of the partnership relation which it is relevant to consider in a study of the law of partnership. Nevertheless, goodwill is a concept which requires particular consideration in the light of the law of partnership since the relation of the partners *inter se* may have some effect upon it.

The nature of goodwill. The term "goodwill" has been adopted from commercial practice and does not possess any precise legal connotation. It is clear that goodwill is associated with a continuing business and has no meaning except in that connection,[20] though in *Robertson* v. *Quiddington* [21] there was a legacy of goodwill without any share in the business being bequeathed. Goodwill is concerned with the assessment of the advantage which an established business may, as opposed to a similar business which has just commenced operations, be expected to possess in attracting customers or in retaining them. The elements of which it is composed are various, some attaching to its local situation, in which case they are often to be excerpted from the price received for business premises or for a lease thereof, some to the personality of the person by whom the business has been conducted and some to the trade connection of an established business in which the established relations with persons from whom the business purchases its stock are equally to be regarded with those it has established with persons to whom it sells its goods.[22] Goodwill in any particular case may be ascribed to any one or more of these elements.[23]

> "It is the connection formed, together with the circumstances, whether of habit or otherwise, which tend to make it permanent, that constitutes the goodwill of a business. It is this which constitutes the difference between a business just started, which has no goodwill attached to it, and one which has acquired a goodwill. The former trader has to seek out his customers from among the community as best he can. The latter has a custom ready made. He knows what members of the community are purchasers of the articles in which he deals, and are not attached by custom to any other establishment." [24]

That dictum, which has regard mainly to the elements of trade connection and possibly personal reputation, may be supplemented by another definition in which the element of local situation of the business is stressed.

---

[20] *Kingston, Miller & Co.* v. *Thomas Kingston & Co.* [1912] 1 Ch. 575.

[21] (1860) 28 Beav. 529. It is, of course, equally possible to be bequeathed a share of the profits of a business without any share of its assets, including its goodwill: *C.I.R.* v. *Lebus's Trs.* [1946] 1 All E.R. 476.

[22] *Morrison* v. *Morrison* (1900) 2 F. 382, *per* Lord President Balfour at p. 383.

[23] *Murray's Tr.* v. *McIntyre* (1904) 6 F. 588. See the figurative exposition by Scrutton L.J. in *Whiteman Smith Motor Co.* v. *Chaplin* [1934] 2 K.B. 35 at p. 50, sometimes described as the "cat and dog" basis, though it also brings in the analogy of the rat and was supplemented with the rabbit by Maugham L.J.

[24] *Per* Lord Herschell in *Trego* v. *Hunt* [1896] A.C. 7 at p. 17.

Goodwill is " the advantage which is acquired by an establishment beyond the value of the capital and fixtures employed therein, in consequence of the general public patronage which it receives from habitual customers on account of its local position, or reputation of celebrity and comfort, or even from ancient partialities." [25]   If an established business is sold, its goodwill may have a marketable value but whether such value attaches or not is a question of fact.[26]   In some cases the goodwill, though attributable to all, or at least more than one, of these elements, may have no real value save in so far as it is associated with the conduct of the business from its habitual premises and in certain circumstances the goodwill of a business is so closely connected with the particular premises from which the business is conducted that it has been held in England that a bequest of the premises carried with it the goodwill, though not expressly mentioned,[27] and even vice versa [28] though a construction of that kind has been placed upon the bequest only where the context strongly supports it.[29]

Sale of goodwill as affecting continuance in business.   Whatever the elements comprised in the goodwill of any particular business, its value to a purchaser will depend in varying degree, but in most cases significantly, upon his being allowed to carry on the business which he has bought without competition from those who previously conducted it. That practical commercial fact has been recognised in a general context by the law which, though it does not go so far as to imply an obligation on the seller not to set up in the same business in the same locality, yet controls him in the use of the firm name, if it differs from his own,[30] or in canvassing orders from his former customers.[31]   Where a business has been conducted by a partnership, the mere fact that the partnership has been dissolved does not of itself entail that the partners must cease from carrying on business of the kind formerly conducted by the partnership.[32]   Since, as has already been mentioned, the fact that a person has sold the goodwill of his business does not carry with it any implied obligation that he will refrain from setting up in a similar trade of business in the same neighbourhood in which his former business is carried on, the terms of any agreement under which a partnership is dissolved and the share of one partner who retires is acquired by the other should be express and detailed and should contain such restrictions on the future business activities of the retiring partner as are reasonable and necessary for the protection of the goodwill of the business formerly carried on in partnership; for if the agreement is merely in the general terms that the partnership will be dissolved and one partner will purchase the share of the other and be entitled

[25] *Per* Lord Fraser in *Drummond & Another* v. *Assessor for Leith* (1886) 13 R. 540 at p. 541.
[26] *Hill* v. *Fearis* [1905] 1 Ch. 466.   [27] *Ex p. Punnett, re Kitchin* (1880) 16 Ch.D. 226.
[28] *Blake* v. *Shaw* (1860) Johns. 732; *Re Rhagg* [1938] Ch. 828.
[29] *Re Betts, Burrell* v. *Betts* [1949] 1 All E.R. 568.
[30] *Melrose-Drover Ltd.* v. *Heddle* (1902) 4 F. 1120.
[31] *Trego* v. *Hunt* [1896] A.C. 7.   See generally on this point Gloag, *Contract* (2nd ed.) p. 299.
[32] *Dawson* v. *Beeson* (1882) 22 Ch.D. 504; *Farr* v. *Pearce* (1818) 3 Madd. 74; *Davies* v. *Hodgson* (1858) 25 Beav. 177.

to continue the business on his own account, the retiring partner will not be restrained by law from setting up a similar business in the same neighbourhood.[33] He may advertise the fact that he is setting up the new business [34] and he is permitted to deal with customers of his former firm if they offer to deal with him without solicitation from him to do so.[35] But he is not permitted to canvass for or solicit orders from the customers of his former firm [36] even if they have dealt with him since the dissolution of the firm and the sale of his share therein.[37] He is likewise restricted from holding himself out as continuing the business of which he has sold his share of the goodwill. Therefore, an interdict may be raised against him if he carries on the new business under the same name as that in which the former business was carried on when he sold it, or in a name which so closely resembles it as to mislead the public into the belief that it is the former business.[38] However, he is generally entitled to conduct the new business under his own name, even though that was the name under which he conducted the former business of the partnership but if he can be shown to be making a dishonest use of his own name to pass himself off as though he were still conducting the original business, an interdict will lie against him.[39] Where a restriction as to the dishonest use of the business name is imposed by law, it is justified on the ground of an implied obligation on the part of the defender not to derogate from his own grant. Where the former business has been sold by a trustee in bankruptcy [40] or other similar arrangement on the bankruptcy of the firm,[41] where the defender has been expelled from the firm [42] or where the sale is by executors of the partner [43] or by the court in an application for dissolution of the partnership,[44] the restriction will not apply.

Agreement not to continue in same business. From the general principles governing the matter, it will be appreciated that on a dissolution of partnership involving the retiral of a partner on terms that he is bought out by the remaining partner or partners who will continue the partnership business, it will be advisable to include in the agreement of dissolution an express restrictive covenant by the retiring partner. In drawing the covenant attention must be given to the limits of reasonableness which must be observed if the courts are to be asked to enforce it, though

[33] *Dumbarton Steamship Co.* v. *Macfarlane* (1899) 1 F. 993; *Kennedy* v. *Lee* (1817) 3 Mer. 448; *Mellersh* v. *Keen* No. 1 (1859) 27 Beav. 236; *Bradbury* v. *Dickens* (1859) 27 Beav. 53; *Smith* v. *Everett* (1859) 27 Beav. 446.
[34] *Hookham* v. *Pottage* (1872) L.R. 8 Ch. 91; *Labouchere* v. *Dawson* (1872) L.R. 13 Eq. 322.
[35] *Leggott* v. *Barrett* (1880) 15 Ch.D. 306; *Curl Brothers* v. *Webster* [1904] 1 Ch. 685.
[36] *Trego* v. *Hunt* [1896] A.C. 7; *Re David & Matthews* [1899] 1 Ch. 378.
[37] *Curl Brothers* v. *Webster* [1904] 1 Ch. 685.
[38] *Melrose-Drover Ltd.* v. *Heddle* (1902) 4 F. 1120; *Churton* v. *Douglas* (1859) Johns. 174.
[39] *Melrose-Drover Ltd.* v. *Heddle, supra*; *Smith* v. *Macbride & Smith* (1888) 16 R. 36; *Churton* v. *Douglas, supra*; *Hommel* v. *Hommel* (1912) 29 R.P.C. 398; *Hookham* v. *Pottage* (1872) L.R. 8 Ch. 91.
[40] *Walker* v. *Mottram* (1881) 19 Ch.D. 355; *Cruttwell* v. *Lye* (1810) 17 Ves. 335.
[41] *Farey* v. *Cooper* [1927] 2 K.B. 384.
[42] *Dawson* v. *Beeson* (1882) 22 Ch.D. 504.
[43] *Boorne* v. *Wicker* [1927] 1 Ch. 667.
[44] *Jennings* v. *Jennings* [1898] 1 Ch. 378 at p. 389.

restrictions laid on the seller of a business, or on a partner retiring on dissolution of the firm, are not objectionable on the sole ground that the object of the restriction is to protect the business from competition.[45]   In certain cases an agreement not to carry on business in competition with his former partners has been implied from the agreement entered into as to dissolution or some other agreement, without any express restrictive covenant having been included.   Such cases generally turn upon the true intention of the parties as evinced on a construction of the terms of their agreement.   In arriving at that construction the English courts appear to have regarded the actual agreement in a fairly broad way.   Thus in *Cooper* v. *Watson* [46] two persons entered a partnership as brewers for a period of eleven years.   The partnership agreement provided that either would be at liberty " to quit the trade and mystery of brewing " on giving to the other six months' notice and that the other partner would then be at liberty to continue the trade on his own account.   The court held that it was implied in that agreement that the partner who retired from the firm after giving such notice was not entitled to continue thereafter in the trade of brewing at all.   In *Harrison* v. *Gardner* [47] the implied obligation was derived from the arrangements made for the dissolution of the firm conjoined with the actings under that agreement.   The partners had agreed that it would be referred to an arbiter to decide what sum should be paid in respect of goodwill by the continuing to the retiring partner.   The arbiter made his award on the basis that the retiring partner would not set up a new business in the street in which the partnership business was conducted.   These circumstances were held sufficient to justify the grant of an injunction restraining the retiring partner from doing so.   While the cases cited establish the proposition that the court may in appropriate circumstances find that an implied condition that he will not carry on business in opposition to the firm has been agreed to by the retiring partner, they afford no very certain guide on the question of the circumstances in which such an agreement will be implied.   Since the decision will in all cases involve an assessment of the true intention of the partners, each case as it occurs may be expected to present its own features of construction or otherwise, so that it would be unrealistic to expect much assistance from the precedents as to the view which may be taken in any future case.   The cases cited appear to have gone to the limits in supporting the existence of an implied agreement and it is possible that the Scottish courts would be more cautious in drawing the inference that such an implied agreement is undertaken.   The case of *Harrison* v. *Gardner* [47] is particularly interesting since the arbitral award did not expressly impose on the retiring partner a condition that he would not continue in business, when it could clearly be argued that by referring the issue to arbitration both parties agreed to implement whatever award the arbiter competently made, but merely

[45] See generally on restrictive covenants, Gloag, *Contract* (2nd ed.) pp. 569–576.
[46] (1784) 3 Dougl. 413.
[47] (1817) 2 Madd. 198.

assessed the value of the goodwill on the basis that the retiring partner's right to continue in business was subject to a geographical limitation.

Where a restrictive covenant is expressly stipulated for in the partnership deed, the courts may have to decide the question whether it is to be treated on the analogy of a restriction imposed by an employer on his employee, or of a purchaser upon the vendor of a business.[47a] It has been held that where the restrictive covenant is imposed upon the assumption of a new partner into the business it will be construed strictly against the partners assuming him as if they were employers.[47b] Where the covenant is made by a retiring partner on the sale of his interest to the continuing partner it is construed as one between vendor and purchaser.[47c]

Goodwill as partnership property

It has been stated that where goodwill exists in the business of a partnership each partner is entitled to insist on its being realised and, if the surviving or continuing partners continue to carry on the business without a settlement, an accounting for the goodwill may be insisted upon even after the lapse of a considerable period of years.[48] Two apparently conflicting rights are dealt with in that statement and they were reconciled by the Lord Justice-Clerk (Moncreiff) in *McKersies* v. *Mitchell and Others* [49] where he said,

> " In short these cases [50] did decide that a surviving partner could not insist on a valuation, and was bound to submit to a sale; but they did not decide that the surviving partner, on the one hand, and the representative of a deceasing partner on the other, could not settle accounts on the footing they thought mutually advantageous; nor was there any principle on which such a doctrine could rest, provided the settlement were one not liable to challenge on the ground of collusion or manifest or known inequality and injustice, amounting to fraud."

In dividing partnership property, including goodwill, among the partners, any partner is entitled to have it brought to public sale and is not bound to fix a value at which he will either part with his own, or take the other partners' shares, even though some years have elapsed since the dissolution of the partnership, provided its affairs have not been wound up.[51] But

---

[47a] *Morris* v. *Saxelby* [1916] 1 A.C. 689.
[47b] *Macfarlane* v. *Kent* [1965] 2 All E.R. 376.
[47c] *Whitehill* v. *Bradford* [1952] 1 All E.R. 115. See also *Routh* v. *Jones* [1947] 1 All E.R. 758 (a case involving a service agreement) and *Lyne-Pirkis* v. *Jones* [1969] 3 All E.R. 738 and *Peyton* v. *Mindham* [1971] 3 All E.R. 1215 (partnership agreements). All these cases concerned general medical practices and the restrictive covenant had to be construed in order to discover whether it was limited to a restraint on conduct of general medical practice or extended to practice as a medical consultant since the latter restraint is not reasonably required to protect a general medical practice.
[48] Green's *Encyclopaedia of the Laws of Scotland*, Vol. 11 s.v. *Partnership* § 165.
[49] (1872) 10 M. 861 at p. 864.
[50] His Lordship founded his judgment on a consideration of *Crawshay* v. *Collins* (1808) 15 Ves. 218; *Featherstonhaugh* v. *Fenwick* (1810) 17 Ves. 298; *Brown* v. *De Tastet* (1819) Jac. 284.
[51] *Stewart* v. *Simpson or Stewart* (1835) 14 S. 72.

there is nothing to prevent him agreeing to a valuation as a basis of the shares of the partners and if he does so he may be barred from later insisting upon a sale. The goodwill of a partnership business may turn out to be unsaleable and worthless for the purposes of anyone save a former partner who wishes to carry on and continue the business formerly carried on by the partnership.[52] It is probably from that standpoint that many of the reported cases on goodwill should be regarded rather than in an attempt to discover a more general proposition that in certain types of business, *e.g.* professional concerns such as a firm of solicitors, no element of goodwill is present in the partnership property, although certain judicial dicta appear to favour the more general approach.[53] Certainly if an attempt is made to find a general rule excluding goodwill from the assets of businesses of any particular type that attempt is unlikely to be successful in view of the conflicting decisions. Thus in *Wilson* v. *Williams* [54] no item was allowed in respect of goodwill in the accounts of a stock-broker's business since it was held to have no saleable value, whereas in *Hill* v. *Fearis* [55] it was held that goodwill was an asset of a similar business. The position in regard to a solicitor's business has already been referred to. Despite dicta to the effect that such a business possesses no goodwill [56] yet in *Burchell* v. *Wilde* [57] it was assumed that such a business had goodwill of possible saleable value. In the case of medical practices carried on under the national health service, it is laid down that the goodwill of such practices is of no saleable value since it may not be sold.[58] Yet in spite of this it appears to remain an asset of a medical partnership.[59] In spite of the difficulty created by the decision last cited, which seems to stem rather from the special features of the provisions of the National Health Service Act 1946 than from any general principles of law in relation to partnership or to goodwill, it appears that the most consistent reading which can be given to the authorities is that where, in the business of any partnership, whatever its nature, the goodwill can be shown to have a saleable value it will be regarded as an asset comprised within the partnership property but where, for any reason, such as the lack of any effective restriction on the partners to continue in business in competition with the firm after severing their connection with it, the goodwill of the partnership business cannot be said to command any value as a saleable asset it cannot effectively be taken into accounting in the partnership books and therefore does not have a real claim to be regarded as partnership property so that an individual partner may not insist on a sale of an asset which is virtually valueless. The difficulty and ambivalence of the decisions may

---

[52] *Davies* v. *Hodgson* (1858) 25 Beav. 177.
[53] See, *e.g. Mackenzie* v. *Macfarlane*, 1934 S.N. 16 where Lord Wark expressed the opinion that a firm of law agents had no realisable goodwill and that the firm name was not an asset which must be sold on dissolution.
[54] (1892) 29 L.R.Ir. 176.
[55] [1905] 1 Ch. 466.
[56] *Mackenzie* v. *Macfarlane, supra.* See also *Arundell* v. *Bell* (1883) 52 L.J.Ch. 537.
[57] [1900] 1 Ch. 551.
[58] National Health Service (Scotland) Act 1947, s. 36.
[59] *Whitehill* v. *Bradford* [1952] Ch. 236.

perhaps be accounted for in some cases by the fact that while the goodwill of the firm's business may not be saleable, in the sense that it is unlikely to command a price if offered for public sale, it may yet be considered to be of some value to those of the original partners who continue to carry on the business of the original firm; and in such cases the alternative expedient of an agreed valuation for goodwill on a dissolution of the partnership seems to be the only effective solution. It has been said [60] that in many such cases the only real element of goodwill attaches to the business premises in which the business of the partnership has been conducted. That observation is justifiable in many cases, particularly in partnerships in trade; but the goodwill attaching to the use of the firm name is perhaps as frequent an issue in partnership cases.

Use of the firm name

A person who acquires the goodwill of a business acquires rights in the name under which that business was previously carried on. This is often an important factor in preserving his effective right to the goodwill which he has acquired and may be essential to preserve for him the value of the other elements making up the goodwill of the business, such as the business connection and the business premises of the former business. The purchaser of the goodwill has the right to the use of the firm name,[61] not merely the right to describe himself as carrying on business as a successor to the former business,[62] and he may interdict others from using the firm name.[63] Where the firm name includes the name of a partner who has severed his association with the partnership, the continued use of the former name by those who continue the business presents difficulty. There are really two distinct problems involved: (1) if the former business was conducted under the name of the erstwhile partner, e.g. A.B. and Company, is A.B. upon severing his connection with the partnership permitted to set up a rival business using his own name and therefore the firm name of the business which he has left? and (2) may A.B. on severing his connection with the business insist that it be no longer carried on under his name by those continuing to conduct the business, so as to ensure that he is involved in no liability for the continuing activities of the business?

There is no simple and universal answer to the first of those questions. Clark expresses the view that " it seems settled law, that when the goodwill of a business has been sold, the seller may recommence a similar business in the immediate neighbourhood of the old premises; the only restrictions on this right being, that in the case of a firm the sellers shall not assume the old name, or represent themselves as the successors of the former concern." [64] That passage reflects the situation arising when goodwill is sold without any restrictive clause being included in the agreement as to

[60] Lindley, op. cit. p. 466.
[61] Levy v. Walker (1879) 10 Ch.D. 436.
[62] Churton v. Douglas (1859) Johns. 174.
[63] Levy v. Walker, supra; Churton v. Douglas, supra.
[64] Op. cit. I, p. 431.

the sellers' right to continue in business [65] and the general prohibition of the sellers using the name of a business which is an element of the goodwill which has been sold.[66] It does not, however, deal expressly with the situation where the name under which the former business was conducted is the name of one of its partners who has either joined with his co-partners in selling the goodwill to a third party or has retired from the partnership leaving his former partners to continue to carry on the business of the partnership. In these cases the general prohibition stated by Clark collides, so far as that partner is concerned, with his right to carry on business under his own name; for that *per se* will not be regarded as a derogation from his grant in selling the goodwill or in the agreement under which he retires, leaving his former partners to carry on the business.[67] The cases, however, suggest that he will be so prohibited if it is proved that his use of his own name is part of a fraudulent intent to pass himself off as still carrying on the former business,[68] and if he were to represent himself as the successor of the former business, he would clearly come under that excepted case. Other circumstances may suffice to establish an intention to pass himself off as conducting the former business, as, for instance, where he has assumed a name for both private and business purposes and later sells the goodwill of the business carried on by him under his assumed name. In that case he will be restrained by the court from setting up a new business under his assumed name.[69] This is, however, an area of the law regarding which it is still possible to echo Clark's plaint that " it cannot be denied that the principles of this branch of partnership law are as yet far from being fixed or definite " [70] and the advantages of clear and express agreement among the parties upon such points cannot be too strongly emphasised.

In a consideration of the second and related question as to the continued use of a firm name which consists of the name of a person who has severed his association with the firm, an important factor is the right of such a person to protect himself from liability on the ground that he " knowingly suffers himself to be represented as a partner " [71] in the firm by permitting his name to continue as the firm name under which the business continues to be carried on.[72] There are no reported Scottish decisions which have a direct bearing on this question but the principle adopted in the English courts is that a sale by the retiring partner of his interest in the goodwill carries with it the right of the purchasers to use the former name even if it is that of the retiring partner, provided it is not so used to expose the latter to any real risk of liability for the continuing

---

[65] *Supra* pp. 420–421.
[66] *Supra* p. 421.
[67] *Melrose-Drover Ltd.* v. *Heddle* (1902) 4 F. 1120.
[68] *Hommel* v. *Hommel* (1912) 29 R.P.C. 398; *Smith* v. *Macbride & Smith* (1888) 16 R. 36.
[69] *Pomeroy Ltd.* v. *Scale* (1907) 24 R.P.C. 177.
[70] *Op. cit.* I, p. 432.
[71] Partnership Act 1890, s. 14 (1).
[72] *Routh* v. *Webster* (1847) 10 Beav. 561; *Bullock* v. *Chapman* (1848) 2 De G. & Sm. 211; *Troughton* v. *Hunter* (1854) 18 Beav. 470; *Hodges* v. *London Trams Omnibus Co.* (1883) 12 Q.B.D. 105.

activities of the business [73] and that the right to use the former business name is not qualified in terms of the agreement under which the goodwill was sold.[74] What circumstances will be sufficient to establish to the satisfaction of the court that the seller is exposed to real risk through the continued use of the name cannot be laid down as a matter of law and must be treated as a question of fact in each case [75] and it is possible that the Registration of Business Names Act 1916 may have some effect in reducing the risk.[76] It will generally not be regarded as sufficient to establish such a risk that the former business name consists of a surname with the added words " and Company " and the owner of the surname has not used that firm name save in connection with the former business. In such a case a continued use of the firm name by the former partners will not normally expose him to risk.[77]

Continued use of name after the death of former partner

It is expressly provided in the Partnership Act 1890, s. 14 (2)—

" (2) Provided that where after a partner's death the partnership business is continued in the old firm name, the continued use of that name or of the deceased partner's name as part thereof shall not of itself make his executors or administrators estate or effects liable for any partnership debts contracted after his death."

The possibility of a liability of a deceased partner on the doctrine of holding out through a continued use of his name as part of the firm name is therefore excluded if that is the sole circumstance invoked as evidence of holding out. The executors of a deceased partner will consequently not be allowed to apply for an order restraining the continued use of the former name on the ground that they are exposed to risk by its continued use. To establish a right to such an order, the executors will need to aver that the order is necessary in making effective the general right to have the partnership assets, including the goodwill, sold for the common benefit.[78] " When a firm is dissolved by death, it would appear that the goodwill, whether it be of real or speculative value, if it is sold at all, must be sold for the behoof of all concerned; that is to say, the surviving partners cannot dispose of it for their own benefit, but must share its proceeds with the representatives of their late partner." [79] The older decisions state the principle in terms of broad legal theory but in practice the realities of the situation may well be governed by other considerations. Since the surviving partner or partners may carry on the business on their own

---

[73] *Townsend* v. *Jarman* [1900] 2 Ch. 698; *Burchell* v. *Wilde* [1900] 1 Ch. 551.
[74] *Townsend* v. *Jarman, supra.*
[75] See *Thynne* v. *Shove* (1890) 45 Ch. 577; *Gray* v. *Smith* (1889) 43 Ch.D. 208; *Levy* v. *Walker* (1879) 10 Ch.D. 436; *Banks* v. *Gibson* (1865) 34 Beav. 566.
[76] See *supra* Chap. V, pp. 152–153.
[77] Lindley, *op. cit.* pp. 470–471; *Townsend* v. *Jarman, supra; Burchell* v. *Wilde, supra.*
[78] *McCormick & Carnie* v. *Wilson's Exrs.* (1822) 1 S. 541; and see Clark, *op. cit.* I, p. 431.
[79] Clark, *loc. cit.*; and see *McCormick & Carnie* v. *Wilson's Executors, supra; Marshall* v. *Marshall,* Feb. 23, 1816, F.C.; *McWhannell* v. *Dobbie* (1830) 8 S. 914; *Reid* v. *Reid,* 1938 S.L.T. 415.

account, the fact that they may theoretically be bound to realise the firm's name as part of the goodwill and account to their former partner for his share of the proceeds will in many cases lack practical effect; for if the surviving partners are in a position to continue the former business the firm name is unlikely to have any saleable value as an asset. As is pointed out by Lindley [80] the surviving partners will in such circumstances acquire all the benefit of the goodwill but not by survivorship as something which belongs to them to the entire exclusion of the deceased partner's executors. If that were so the surviving partners might sell the goodwill for their own benefit whenever it had a saleable value and they do not have this right. [81] The interaction of the right to continue the use of the partnership name and the saleable value of the goodwill of the business must be kept in mind since, although that right is an important element, and sometimes the most important element in goodwill, it may be acquired separately from goodwill in its more general connotation. [82]

Trade marks

The right to use the trade marks of the business has a relation to the goodwill of that business and originally that connection was regarded as so close that trade marks, although assets of the firm which are saleable on dissolution of the firm like any other of its assets, could not be assigned to or apportioned among persons who were not entitled to the business concerned with the goods in respect of which the trade marks were registered. [83] Those provisions have now been repealed by the Trade Marks Act 1938, under which registered trade marks are, and are deemed always to have been, assignable and transmissible either in connection with the goodwill of a business or not [84]; and a registered trade mark is so assignable or transmissible either in respect of all or of some (but not all) of the goods in respect of which it is registered. [85] Where the trade marks are unregistered they may also be assigned and transmitted in the same way if at the time of the assignment or transmission of the unregistered trade mark it is or was used in the same business as a registered trade mark and if it is or was assigned or transmitted at the same time and to the same person as that registered trade mark and in respect of goods all of which are goods in relation to which the unregistered trade mark is or was used in that business and in respect of which that registered trade mark is or was assigned or transmitted. [86]

[80] Op. cit. pp. 467–468.
[81] Smith v. Everett (1859) 27 Beav. 446; Wedderburn v. Wedderburn (1856) 22 Beav. 84. In Reid v. Reid, 1938 S.L.T. 415 the widow of a partner in a solicitor's firm was allowed a proof of her averments against the continuing partner that the goodwill of the business was an asset for which he must account to her. The continuing partner was, however, executor of her late husband's estate and she brought her action for accounting against him in that capacity.
[82] Barr v. Lions, 1956 S.C. 59.
[83] Trade Marks Act 1905, ss. 22 and 23.
[84] Trade Marks Act 1938, s. 22 (1).
[85] Ibid. s. 22 (2).
[86] Ibid. s. 22 (3).

The underlying theory upon which the earlier law proceeded was that a trade mark was taken by the general public to indicate that goods bearing that mark were associated exclusively with a particular business and that when that association was broken, it was contrary to public policy to recognise the continuance of any exclusive right to the mark. Thus the rule was evolved under the common law and reflected in the earlier legislation that a trade mark and the goodwill of the business to which it was related must be assigned together.[87] While the effect of section 22 has been to displace that general principle and to permit the assignation of registered trade marks either in connection with the goodwill of the business or not, it is the validity of the assignation alone which is there considered. If, therefore, the effect of any assignation is to render the trade mark so assigned deceptive, it may be that the registration of the trade mark will be expunged from the register on that ground as invalid.[88] The benefit of the assignation might thus be lost to the assignee although the assignation in his favour is not challengeable under section 22 of the Trade Marks Act 1938. So far as unregistered trade marks are concerned, they are assignable with the same freedom as registered trade marks, only if they are assigned along with registered marks at the same time and to the same assignee and under the conditions *inter alia* that the marks both registered and unregistered are used in the same business and registered or used for the same goods.[89] Section 22 (3) presents some difficulties. If the right which is invaded by a use of a trade mark intended to lead to a passing off, is a right of property, then the property in question may subsist in the trade mark itself or in the goodwill of the business in the course of which the trade mark is used. In *A. G. Spalding & Brothers* v. *A. W. Gamage Ltd.,*[90] Lord Parker suggested that the better view was that the right invaded in such circumstances was a right of property in the goodwill of the business. Though that decision is prior to the passing of the Trade Marks Act 1938, its *ratio* which is concerned with the basis of the action of " passing off " [91] is unaffected by the Act. But if the right of property invaded is regarded as exclusively in the goodwill, it becomes difficult to ascribe any meaning to the provision in section 23 (3) of the Trade Marks Act 1938 that if carried through in terms of the subsection an assignation of an unregistered trade mark may be valid in spite of the fact that it is not assigned " in connection with the goodwill of a business." [92] Yet the enforcement of an assignee's rights in an unregistered trade mark must be by means of an action for passing off and in that

---

[87] For a fuller account of the earlier law on this point see Kerly, *Law of Trade Marks and Trade Names* (9th ed.) §§ 482–487.
[88] *Bowden Wire Ltd.* v. *Bowden Brake Co.* (No. 1) (1913) 30 R.P.C. 580, *per* Buckley L.J. at p. 593; but see also (1914) 31 R.P.C. 385 where the opinions of the judges in the House of Lords suggest that the view of Buckley L.J. is a minority one. See also Kerly, *Law of Trade Marks and Trade Names* (9th ed.) §§ 529–530.
[89] Trade Marks Act 1938, s. 22 (3).
[90] (1915) 31 T.L.R. 328; 32 R.P.C. 273.
[91] See Kerly, *Law of Trade Marks and Trade Names* (9th ed.) Chap. 17 and particularly § 713.
[92] Trade Marks Act 1938, s. 23 (1) imported under the terms laid down in s. 23 (3) of the same Act.

action the assignee will require to establish that the mark in question exclusively denotes his goods which entails that he prove that he owns the goodwill attaching to the unregistered trade mark. " Thus the effect of section 22 (3), though apparently drawn on the assumption that a trade mark is a form of property distinguishable from goodwill, seems really to be that tribunals concerned are required to recognise in the cases covered by the section that one element of goodwill, compendiously described as ' an unregistered trade mark,' can be assigned without the entire goodwill, and that, in such cases, the assignee, when requiring to prove that the mark distinguishes his goods either in a passing-off action, or on an application to register,[93] can rely on user by a predecessor in *title* to the trade mark to the same extent as he could, before the passing of the Act, rely on user by a predecessor in *business*." [94]

Splitting of rights in trade marks

The provisions of section 23 (1) to (3) of the Trade Marks Act 1938, if uncontrolled, might validate the division of trade mark rights by assignation in such manner that the same or similar trade marks are used by different parties in a way which is likely to lead to deception. This situation is met by section 22 (4) which invalidates transactions where " there would in the circumstances subsist, or have subsisted, whether under the common law or by registration, exclusive rights in more than one of the persons concerned to the use, in relation to the same goods or description of goods, of trade marks nearly resembling each other or of identical trade marks, if, having regard to the similarity of the goods and of the trade marks, the use of the trade marks in exercise of those rights would be, or have been, likely to deceive or cause confusion," though a proviso to the subsection permits the splitting of trade mark rights by assignation where the concurrent rights created as a result are confined to rights to export the goods to different markets. Provision is made in section 22 (5) for certification by the Registrar of Trade Marks that a proposed " splitting assignation " does not contravene the provisions of section 22 (4).

Joint ownership of trade marks

The above mentioned restrictions do not preclude the joint ownership of a trade mark and persons may be entered upon the register as joint proprietors provided that their relations *inter se* are such that no one of them is entitled as between himself and the other or others to use it except—
  (a) on behalf of both or all of them or
  (b) in relation to an article with which both or all of them are connected in course of trade.[95]
It was recognised in *Robinson* v. *Finlay* [96] that it is possible to have a trade

[93] Trade Marks Act 1938, ss. 9 and 10.
[94] Kerly, *op. cit.* § 491.
[95] Trade Marks Act 1938, s. 63.
[96] 1878) 9 Ch.D. 487. See also *Van Zeller* v. *Mason Cattley & Co.* (1908) 25 R.P.C. 37.

mark indicating a joint adventure, if all the joint adventurers are connected with all the goods to which the trade mark is applied. Under the Trade Marks Act 1905 parties were entitled to joint registration in respect of a trade mark but only when all the goods which bore the mark were dealt with by each of the parties so registered.[97] Under section 63 of the Trade Marks Act 1938 the right of joint proprietors to be registered is clearly recognised and partners and joint adventurers will therefore be so entitled where they seek registration in respect of the trade marks of the firm. The firm name itself may be registrable as a trade mark if it is " represented in a special or particular manner." [98] This condition appears to be intended to disallow registration of the firm name in such manner that another trader might infringe it simply by an honest use of his own name in trading.[99] Representation in a special or particular manner relates to the manner in which the name itself is presented to the public, for example where the name " Robin Hood " was presented with the initial letter R incorporating the device of an archer and the final letter D incorporating the device of a target, or where the name " Fanfold Ltd." appeared in block letters, " Fanfold " in the form of a curve, " Ltd." in smaller type below and the whole name underlined by a scroll.[1] The signature of the applicant for registration or of some predecessor in his business may be registered as a trade mark [2] but the representation of a descriptive name in the form of a " signature " does not qualify on that ground nor is it registrable as a name " represented in a special or particular manner," [3] nor when the name is an adopted trade name and not the signature of an existing firm.[4] In these cases the presentation of the name is regarded not as a " signature " but as the representation of the name in ordinary handwriting.[5]

When joint proprietors have been registered in respect of a trade mark the registration has effect in relation to any rights to the use of the trade mark vested in the joint proprietors " as if those rights had been vested in a single person." [6] The effect of this provision has been described as ' ' obscure " [7] and it does not appear to be the happiest mode of expressing the intention of Parliament in providing for joint ownership of trade marks. Section 63 however does make it clear that a trade mark registered in the names of joint proprietors may properly be used only on goods " with which both or all of them are connected in the course of trade " and the view has been expressed that " it would seem to follow upon

---

[97] " Tarantella " Tms. (1910) 27 R.P.C. 573; Naamlooze, Klene & Co.'s Application (1923) 40 R.P.C. 103; Palmolive Case (1912) 29 R.P.C. 278. See Trade Marks Act 1938, s. 63.
[98] Trade Marks Act 1938, s. 9 (1) (a).
[99] Ibid. s. 8.
[1] Standard Cameras Ltd.'s Application (the " Robin Hood " Case) (1952) 69 R.P.C. 125; Fanfold Ltd.'s Application (1928) 45 R.P.C. 199, 325.
[2] Trade Marks Act 1938, s. 9 (1) (b).
[3] British Milk Products Co.'s Application [1915] 2 Ch. 202.
[4] Macmillan v. Ehrmann Bros. Ltd. (1904) 21 R.P.C. 357.
[5] British Milk Products Co. Ltd.'s Application, supra.
[6] Trade Marks Act 1938, s. 63.
[7] Kerly, op. cit. § 596.

general principles that any one of the proprietors, who did not authorise an infringing use of the mark, could sue upon it." [8] Though the Trade Marks Act 1938 is generally applicable to Scotland subject to certain modifications,[9] the only provision under which the partnership property in a trade mark may be recognised occurs in section 63 which is framed upon the English legal theory that there is no separate *persona* in the firm. It appears therefore that the trade marks of a Scottish firm should be registered in the names of the partners under section 63 though it might be contended that since the firm is recognised under section 4 (2) of the Partnership Act as having in Scotland a separate *persona* from the partners, a Scottish firm may itself be the applicant for registration of its trade marks.[10] If that contention were to be upheld, the dubiety of the provisions of section 63 of the Trade Marks Act 1938 as providing for a case where one of the joint proprietors is himself the infringer of the trade mark by using it in connection with goods belonging to him individually [11] could be overcome so far as a Scottish partnership is concerned.

Provisions as to valuation of goodwill

What has been discussed on the preceding pages is sufficient to stress the importance of making clear and express provision in the partnership deed as to the disposal of the firm name and goodwill on the dissolution of the firm. It has been held in a number of decisions that the goodwill of a business is to be taken as comprehended in the more general expression " assets," " property," " effects " or stock of the partnership [12]; and such decisions appear to be in accord with the general concept of goodwill. It is even possible that the element of the goodwill of a partnership derived from its local situation may be carried under a right conferred in the partnership agreement to share in the proceeds of realisation of the firm's premises. [13] Nevertheless, there are certain English decisions which have held that where the agreement secures to a retiring partner a share in the property or the effects of the partnership, or places an obligation on the remaining partners to take over his share in such property or effects, that will not entitle him to receive anything in respect of goodwill.[14] It will therefore be better to avoid any chance of ambiguity and to mention the word " goodwill " itself in any agreement where it is intended to secure to the partner a right to participate in its proceeds. The formula, very

---

[8] *Ibid. loc. cit.*

[9] Trade Marks Act 1938, ss. 66 (1) and 68 (3).

[10] " Any person claiming to be the proprietor of a trade mark used or proposed to be used by him who is desirous of registering it must apply in writing to the Registrar . . ." : Trade Marks Act 1938, s. 17 (1).

[11] But perhaps it is to be inferred that in such a case the remaining proprietor or proprietors may sue for an interdict against the offending proprietor: *Tarantella Tms.* (1910) 27 R.P.C. 573.

[12] *Manley* v. *Sartori* [1927] 1 Ch. 157; *Re David & Matthews* [1899] 1 Ch. 378; *Jennings* v. *Jennings* [1898] 1 Ch. 378; *Page* v. *Ratcliffe* (1897) 75 L.T. 371; *Hall* v. *Barrows* (1863) 4 De G.J. & S. 150; *Salter* v. *Leas Hotel Co.* [1902] 1 Ch. 332.

[13] *Blake* v. *Shaw* (1860) Johns. 732; *sed contra Burfield* v. *Rouch* (1862) 31 Beav. 241; *Re Be ts, Burrell* v. *Betts* [1949] 1 All E.R. 568.

[14] *Hall* v. *Hall* (1855) 20 Beav. 139; *Kennedy* v. *Lee* (1817) 3 Mer. 448.

widely used, that on retirement, the value of the retiring partner's share will be taken as that shown in the last balance sheet of the firm will not entitle him to have the goodwill valued and his share thereof included in the payment in settlement if the goodwill is not in fact included in the balance sheet and it has been the practice not to include it in the partnership accounts.[15]

Valuation of goodwill

The normal method of valuation of goodwill is to compute it at a given number of years' purchase of the annual profits, though variations on this method occur and in some businesses goodwill has been calculated upon a number of years' purchase of receipts.[16] Even when the terms of the partnership agreement provide that a retiring partner shall be paid in respect of his interest in goodwill, it may be relevant to take into account the agreed duration of the partnership itself. Thus where a partner retired two days before the expiry of the period of endurance of the partnership expressly stipulated for in the agreement, then, in spite of a provision that a retiring partner would be paid by those continuing in the firm the market value of his share and interest in the business and in its goodwill, it was held that the goodwill thus to be valued was the goodwill of a business which would end on the expiry of the agreed term of endurance and the interest of the retiring partner in the goodwill was therefore to be valued at a nominal sum.[17] The terms of an agreed stipulation as to payment for goodwill must be closely regarded to construe the intention of the parties. In *Wade* v. *Jenkins* [18] the partnership agreement provided that the value of the goodwill should be £6,000, and should belong to the partners in the proportions in which they were entitled to capital. It was further stipulated that the value of the goodwill would not be brought in to any accounting between the partners. One of the partners died and his representatives were held entitled to his share of the goodwill, since the court construed the last mentioned stipulation, when taken along with the others, as applying only to an accounting during the continuance of the partnership.[19] The stipulation as to disposal of the goodwill may be made in the agreement for dissolution of the partnership, rather than in the partnership agreement. In such cases it is often, though not always, connected with sale of the goodwill of the business and where one of the partners attempts to infringe an agreement of that kind by conducting a

---

15 *Hunter* v. *Dowling* [1895] 2 Ch. 223; *Steuart* v. *Gladstone* (1878) 10 Ch.D. 626. As to the right of the executors of a deceased partner to have assets appearing in the balance sheet valued for the purpose of ascertaining his share see *Cruickshank* v. *Sutherland* (1922) 92 L.J.Ch. 136; *Noble* v. *Noble*, 1965 S.L.T. 415.
16 *Page* v. *Ratcliffe* (1897) 75 L.T. 371. See *L.C.C.* v. *Tobin* [1959] 1 W.L.R. 354 for the valuation where goodwill is compulsorily acquired.
17 *Austen* v. *Boys* (1857) 24 Beav. 598; 2 De G. & J. 626.
18 (1860) 2 Giff. 509.
19 While the approach of the court to the construction of the partnership deed can be discerned, it still leaves some doubts unresolved. Would a similar view have been taken as to a *retiring* partner's right and if so what purpose is to be attributed to the stipulations of the deed?

business on his own account before the goodwill has been sold and thus renders it less saleable, the other partner or partners may obtain an order to restrain him from the course of conduct.[20]

[20] *Turner* v. *Major* (1862) 3 Giff. 442. In that case the partner was employing the assets of the partnership in the conduct of his business and could now have been compelled to account for the profit made by him under the Partnership Act 1890, s. 29. The fact that this alternative remedy is available does not, it is thought, render the remedy by way of interdict incompetent.

CHAPTER X

DISSOLUTION AND EXPULSION

ONE of the distinctions between the partnership as a *quasi* corporate entity and a fully corporate body lies in the fact that the latter, having been created by a " public act " of some kind, continues in existence until dissolved by some similar public act, whereas the partnership, which is created by the consent of the partners, may be dissolved likewise by their consent.[1] The doctrine of perpetual succession, *i.e.* that independently of the vicissitudes of the individual corporators, the corporation continues to exist as a separate legal entity until terminated by some act of an overt, or public, authority dissolving it, has no place in the law of partnership.[2] While the partners in a Scottish firm are associated in a relationship to which the Scots law has accorded some of the attributes of a separate *persona* at law, the concept is not pressed to its uttermost logical conclusion in legal theory, and that refusal to follow the theory of the corporation to its logical conclusion in the case of partnership is itself respectably grounded in a logical application of legal theory. The partnership, unlike the corporation, requires no more than the consent of the partners for its creation. Hence, it " dissolves by the consent and mutual act of the parties in terms of the contract." [3] Yet an association has existed among individuals and in Scotland that association has been given some of the attributes of a legal person; and therefore it is necessary that fairly precise legal rules should be devised to regulate, in England, the termination of that association, and, in Scotland, not only the termination of the association, but also the dissolution of the *quasi* person which the law recognises that association to possess. Perhaps nowhere in the law of partnership is the artificiality of the approach of the English common law in refusing to regard the firm as a separate person more apparent than in the tract of the law which deals with the dissolution of the partnership; for although English law steadfastly persists in regarding the partnership as no more than an agglomeration of the individual partners who compose it, yet, when faced with the problem of the termination of the contract of partnership, it is forced to concede that there is something to be dissolved, namely, the association among those individual partners and that can be propounded only in terms which recognise that in fact the firm is something other than merely the individuals who comprise it, something more than a contractual relationship among them. That situation is, indeed, recognised

---

[1] Erskine, *Inst.* I: vii: 64: Bell, *Comm.* II, 521.
[2] Even when a partnership is dissolved by order of the court, the grounds on which the order will be made are such that in the circumstances continuing consent to be bound together in the partnership relationship no longer exists. See Partnership Act 1890, s. 35, and *infra* pp. 455 *et seq.*
[3] Bell, *Comm.* II, 521.

435

pragmatically, if not in theory, by the English law and as a consequence it becomes possible to legislate for the rules governing the dissolution of a partnership in terms which are appropriate to both Scottish and English law, although in Scotland what is being dissolved is not only the contract but the personified association which is created by it, while in England what is dissolved or terminated is a contractual relationship alone.

Dissolution by expiration of the contractual term or by notice

Section 32 of the Partnership Act 1890 provides—

" 32. Subject to any agreement between the partners, a partnership is dissolved—

(a) If entered into for a fixed term by the expiration of that term:

(b) If entered into for a single adventure or undertaking, by the termination of that adventure or undertaking:

(c) If entered into for an undefined time, by any partner giving notice to the other or others of his intention to dissolve the partnership.

In the last-mentioned case the partnership is dissolved from the date mentioned in the notice as the date of dissolution, or, if no date is so mentioned, as from the date of the communication of the notice."

Expiration of the fixed term of the partnership. A partnership for the joint lives of the partners will be regarded as a partnership for a fixed term which expires on the death of the first deceasing partner.[4] Any such inference, however, will yield to the express terms of the agreement made by the partners, and it will be possible by the agreement to provide that the death of one of the partners will not occasion the dissolution of the partnership itself.[5] If the term of endurance of the partnership is not expressly stipulated for in the contract, the term may be inferred from other circumstances surrounding the parties to the contract. But these circumstances will require to establish with reasonable certitude that the intention of the parties was in fact to set a term to the endurance of the contract, and not merely to create a partnership at will.[6] Thus it has been held that the duration of a lease of the premises occupied by the partnership will not be a conclusive indication of an intention to place the same term of endurance upon the contract of partnership itself. The partnership may be dissolved before the lease has expired and the unexpired lease sold in the winding up of the partnership assets.[7] On the other hand, the duration of the lease of the partnership premises, when taken in conjunction with other circumstances, as, for example, when the premises are occupied for the purposes of a joint adventure, may be of considerable significance in fixing the term of endurance of the partnership association.[8]

[4] *Moss* v. *Elphick* [1910] 1 K.B. 846.
[5] See Partnership Act 1890, s. 33 (1), and *infra* pp. 444–445.
[6] See *infra* pp. 437–438.
[7] *Marshall,* Feb. 23,1816, F.C.; *McNiven* v. *Peffers* (1868) 7 M. 181; *Aitken's Trs.* v. *Shanks* (1830) 8 S. 753; *McWhannell* (1830) 8 S. 914.
[8] *Miller* v. *Walker* (1875) 3 R. 242, *per* the Lord President (Inglis) at p. 249. See also *Gracie* v. *Prentice* (1904) 12 S.L.T. 15.

Partnership at will

In the Partnership Act 1890, section 27, it is provided—

" 27.—(1) Where a partnership entered into for a fixed term is continued after the term has expired, and without any express new agreement, the rights and duties of the partners remain the same as they were at the expiration of the term, so far as is consistent with the incidents of a partnership at will.

(2) A continuance of the business by the partners or such of them as habitually acted therein during the term, without any settlement or liquidation of the partnership affairs, is presumed to be a continuance of the partnership."

Therefore, although partnership is dissolved " by the consent and mutual act of the parties in terms of the contract " [9] and will therefore be dissolved on the expiration of the time appointed by the parties for the endurance of the partnership, it may be renewed or continued by tacit consent of the partners. The principle resembles that of tacit relocation of leases and of contracts of service but its application in partnership is to be distinguished. Whereas in leases and contracts of service the effect of tacit relocation is to renew the contract for a further period equal to the original term of endurance or from year to year if the original term of endurance was for a year or more, its effect in partnership is to engage the parties " as partners for an indefinite time, and so dissoluble at pleasure." [10] The continuing association thus becomes a partnership at will under section 27 of the Partnership Act 1890.

But section 27, though clear and direct in its terms, leaves important practical points unresolved. It is not by any means clear which provisions of the original agreement are, and which are not, " consistent with the incidents of a partnership at will." It is clear that a clause in the original partnership agreement which precluded a partner from terminating the partnership would be inconsistent with a continuing partnership at will, since under section 26 (1) of the Partnership Act 1890—

" Where no fixed term has been agreed upon for the duration of the partnership, any partner may determine the partnership at any time on giving notice of his intention so to do to all the other partners."

On the other hand, a provision that a partnership will be dissolved " by mutual consent " of the partners is inconsistent with a partnership at will under section 26 of the Partnership Act 1890 since, for a partnership at will to exist, there must be no fixed term agreed for the endurance of the partnership and the provision as to dissolution " by mutual consent " creates a fixed term in the absence of any mutual agreement to dissolve, *i.e.* for the joint lives of the partners.[11] Section 26 (1) reflects the settled

---

[9] Bell, *Comm.* II, 521.
[10] *Ibid.* p. 521.
[11] *Moss* v. *Elphick* [1910] 1 K.B. 846.

rule as to the position in a partnership at will.[12]   In *Neilson* v. *Mossend Iron Company* [13] the rule laid down in section 27 of the Partnership Act 1890 was applied in the case of a partnership originally entered into for a fixed term and thereafter continued without any express new agreement; but one of the stipulations in the original agreement as to dissolution of the partnership was held to be applicable to the termination of the original partnership only and to be totally inconsistent with the continuing partnership at will.   Similarly, in the English courts, it has been decided that a right of expulsion provided for in the original contract may not be exercised after the expiration of the term of endurance of that original contract.[14] On the other hand, an arbitration clause may be consistent with an agreement for a continuing partnership at will [15] and there will be cases where the consistency or otherwise must be determined by a construction of the clause in question in order to discover the true intention of the parties to the original agreement.[16]   This is clearly brought out in the cases concerning the applicability of a clause in the original agreement conferring a right of pre-emption.[17]

> " It is true that, in any particular case, the right of pre-emption may be so specially conditioned as to be capable of exercise only at the expiration of the original contract, or it may be created in such terms as to show that the bargain of parties was that it should apply solely at the period of the expiry of the contract so as to exclude it from being carried into a partnership at will; but if the parties by the original contract do no more than simply agree that, on a winding-up of the affairs of the partnership taking place at its expiry, the partner shall have the right of pre-emption as an alternative to open sale, I can see nothing to prevent the right being carried forward." [18]

It is not sufficient to render a provision of the original contract inconsistent with a partnership at will that it provides for events occurring during the term of the partnership, or " during the partnership."   Such expressions will not of themselves be construed as limiting their effect to the term of endurance stipulated for in the original agreement of partnership.[19]

Notice of dissolution

To bring to an end a partnership at will a " notice in writing, signed by the partner giving it, shall be sufficient for this purpose." [20]   The Act does not stipulate that notice in writing shall be necessary but merely that it

---

[12] *Marshall* v. *Marshall*, Jan. 26, 1815, F.C.; Feb. 23, 1816, F.C.   See also Bell, *Comm.* II, 520.
[13] (1885) 12 R. 499; (1886) 13 R.(H.L.) 50.
[14] *Clark* v. *Leach* (1863) 32 Beav. 14.
[15] *Gillett* v. *Thornton* (1875) L.R. 19 Eq. 599.
[16] *McGown* v. *Henderson*, 1914 S.C. 839; *Cookson* v. *Cookson* (1837) 8 Sim. 529; *Yates* v. *Finn* (1880) 13 Ch.D. 839.
[17] See cases cited in n.16 and *Essex* v. *Essex* (1855) 20 Beav. 442; *Cox* v. *Willoughby* (1880) 13 Ch.D. 863.
[18] *McGown* v. *Henderson*, *supra*, *per* Lord Cullen at pp. 843–844.
[19] See the cases above cited n. 16 and n. 17.
[20] Partnership Act 1890, s. 26 (2).

shall be sufficient; moreover the provision is made in relation to cases " where the partnership has originally been constituted by deed." That provision does not appear to displace the normal rule of evidence— *unumquodque eodem modo dissolvitur quo colligatur.* There is nothing conflicting with that general rule in the provisions of section 26 (2). In the case of a partnership constituted by agreement by word of mouth, it is probable that a verbal notice of dissolution, if sufficiently established by proof as to its terms, would be regarded by the courts as adequate notice. That, indeed, appears to be borne out by a dictum of Sir William Grant M.R. in *Featherstonhaugh* v. *Fenwick.*[21] Nevertheless, since the Act, in express terms, has declared a criterion of sufficiency, albeit restricted in its application, it will be prudent to give notice of dissolution in writing and it will be certainly unwise to give notice of dissolution otherwise than in writing if the original contract of partnership was itself in writing. To be effective, the notice must be explicit in its terms.[22] It may be prospective [23] but, once given, it may not be withdrawn without the consent of all the partners.[24] The notice will receive effect even though one of the partners to whom it is addressed is a lunatic. In that case, however, it has been decided in England that it will only be carried into effect after recourse to the court.[25] Though the notice may be prospective in its terms, there is no statutory provision as to the period of notice which must be given or that it should be reasonable notice. In a case decided before the passing of the Partnership Act 1890, Sir William Grant M.R. stated that there was no requirement of a reasonable period of notice in order to terminate a partnership at will.[26] On the other hand, it is stated by Erskine [27] that no partner may dissolve the partnership unfairly and merely to aggrandise his personal interest. These two statements are not, of course, mutually destructive; for it is possible to give immediate notice of dissolution without thereby securing, or intending to secure, an unfair personal advantage as distinct from one's view of the interests of the firm as a whole. But it does not follow from that fact that no reasonable period of notice is required that, as a consequence, a notice of dissolution given from unfair motives of personal interest is thereby rendered effective at law. The distinction is made by Bell,[28] who states that " although in such cases the dissolution cannot be prevented, the beneficial effect of it will be communicated to the partnership; the acquisition will be held as

---

[21] (1810) 17 Ves. 298 at p. 307: " [in the case of a partnership at will] any partner may say, ' It is my pleasure on this day to dissolve the partnership.' "
[22] *Van Sandau* v. *Moore* (1826) 1 Russ. 441.
[23] *Mellersh* v. *Keen* (1859) 27 Beav. 236.
[24] *Jones* v. *Lloyd* (1874) L.R. 18 Eq. 265.
[25] *Mellersh* v. *Keen, supra.* Similarly, the consent required by the other partners to the withdrawal of a notice of dissolution is still required when one of them is a lunatic: *Jones* v. *Lloyd, supra.* The English procedures are now affected by the Mental Health Act 1959, but the relevant provisions are not applicable in Scotland save in so far as to render effective the administration by the English courts of the affairs of an English lunatic.
[26] *Featherstonhaugh* v. *Fenwick* (1810) 17 Ves. 298.
[27] *Inst.* III, 3, 26.
[28] *Comm.* II, 522–523; and see *McNiven* v. *Peffers* (1868) 7 M. 181.

partnership property at the time of the dissolution." Nevertheless, these general observations as to the inapplicability of a fixed or a reasonable period of notice in a partnership at will yield on occasion to the intention of the parties as ascertained on a construction of the original agreement of partnership. In *Brown* v. *Kilsyth Police Commissioners* [29] under the original articles of partnership it was provided that the company should endure for a period of twenty-one years, that, before the expiry of that period, the endurance of the association might be extended to any further number of years which the partners might consider proper, and that they might dissolve the partnership, either before the expiry of the original period or before the expiry of the extended period, on a resolution to that effect having been carried at two meetings of the company specially convened for the purpose and held at an interval of one month. The company continued to carry on business after the expiry of the original period of twenty-one years but without any express agreement as to the continuance of the partnership. It thus became a partnership at will and it was held that the provision as to the procedure whereby the dissolution of the company was to be brought about was inapplicable as inconsistent with a partnership at will. [30] The Lord Ordinary (McLaren), however, was of the opinion that in the case of the company in question, while the extension of the original period of endurance continued it as a partnership at will, it could not be dissolved by immediate notice by a partner or partners. The company was managed by directors who were elected at annual meetings and made up annual accounts; and in these circumstances Lord McLaren was of opinion that it could not be dissolved in the middle of a financial year unless the terms of the original provision in the articles of partnership were observed. No comment was made by the judges in the Inner House upon that view. Its effect, if it be sound, appears to be that, in the particular case, the partnership at will continued from year to year and not for an undefined period terminable by giving notice of dissolution. Some difficulty may be experienced in accepting the logic of Lord McLaren's view that the company might still be dissolved during a financial year if the meetings stipulated for took place. That provision was made expressly in regard to a dissolution occurring during the original period of the company's existence or during the prolongation of its existence for a further term under the procedures laid down. It is difficult to disagree with the view expressed in the Inner House that the provision as to dissolution contained in the articles of partnership was inapplicable where the company continued in existence as a partnership at will. In any event, whether or not the circumstances of that case warrant Lord McLaren's conclusion that the partnership might be dissolved " at will " but only on the termination of each financial year, his view does no real violence to the views expressed as to notice in general in the English cases; for he says nothing to displace the rule that, albeit on the completion of any

[29] (1886) 13 R. 515.
[30] *Ibid.* at p. 520.

financial year, any partner may give notice of dissolution to take instan-
taneous effect. The circumstances in *Brown* v. *Kilsyth Police Commissioners*
were closely related to the situation of the joint stock company, rather than
the partnership proper, and are unlikely to occur in a modern partnership.[31]
    Though at one time the view was taken in Scotland that, to be effective,
the notice of dissolution must give reasonable notice,[32] the English law
has long been settled that no question of reasonable notice is involved and
that, in the case of a partnership at will, " any partner may say, ' It is my
pleasure on this day to dissolve the partnership.' " [33]   That result is now
borne out in Scots law in the case of *Neilson* v. *Mossend Iron Company*.[34]
In that case Lord Watson said, " The main distinction between the old
contract and the new . . . consists in this, that the latter is a contract
determinable at will.   It is an implied term of such a contract that each
partner has the right instantly to dissolve the partnership whenever
he thinks proper." [35]   Where, however, the agreement of partnership,
which was for a period of ten years, expressly provided for dissolution
thereof on one partner giving six months' notice to the other, and the
partnership was continued beyond the term stated in the original agreement, it was held that that provision was consistent with the existence
of a partnership at will within the meaning of section 27 (1) of the
Partnership Act 1890.[36]   Stirling L.J. said that " the question is not
merely one of verbal construction but whether the provisions as to
the consequences of the termination of the original partnership are in
their essence applicable or inapplicable to a partnership at will." [37]
Thus, even where the intention of the parties, that a provision in the
original agreement is to be carried forward into the extended period of
the partnership as to which no agreement has been expressly made, may
be ascertained from a construction of the terms of the original agreement,
that provision will have no force under section 27 (1) unless it is consistent
with a partnership at will as envisaged by that section and by section 26.
While the emphasis on the two conditions to be satisfied is deserving of
attention, the distinction drawn between them should not be allowed to
obscure the very close interrelation of the two; for, where a partnership is
continued beyond its stated term without further agreement and thus must
be held under section 27 to be a partnership at will, the court in construing
the original agreement to ascertain the true intention of the parties as to

---

[31] In such cases the association will probably take the form of a limited company and the
members may resolve by special resolution that it be wound up.   Companies Act 1948,
s. 278 (1) (*b*).

[32] *Marshall* v. *Marshall*, Jan. 26, 1815, F.C.

[33] *Featherstonhaugh* v. *Fenwick* (1810) 17 Ves. 298 at p. 307.   See also *Peacock* v.
Peacock (1808) 16 Ves. 49.

[34] (1886) 13 R.(H.L.) 50.

[35] *Ibid.* at p. 54.   See also *per* Lord Fitzgerald at p. 56; " If it terminates by a partner
saying, as in words like those put in the case of *Featherstonhaugh* v. *Fenwick*, ' It is my
pleasure on this day to dissolve the partnership,' then *ipso facto* it ceases to exist as a
partnership."

[36] *Daw* v. *Herring* [1892] 1 Ch. 284.

[37] *Ibid.* at p. 288.

which provisions are to be carried forward into the new period of partnership, must inevitably be influenced by the consideration whether any such
provision can in fact co-exist along with a partnership at will.   Indeed the
only case in which a dichotomy of the two conditions might be maintained
appears to be where on a construction of the provisions of the original
agreement the court is able to deduce an intention of the parties that an
extension of the original term is itself *sub silentio* to be for a fixed term,[38]
and thus removed from the ambit of section 27 (1) of the Partnership Act
1890.[39]   In *Brooks* v. *Brooks* [40] the provision as to six months' notice was
associated with a further provision that on termination of the partnership,
whether by such notice or by effluxion of time, the partner in whose favour
the provision was made should have the right to purchase the other
partner's share at a valuation.   Farwell J. observed,

> " Then it is said that . . . the clause here is preliminary to the effluxion
> of time provisions, and that the antecedent portion of the clause gives
> an option or power to buy on giving six calendar months' notice; or,
> on the other hand, that it is necessary here to come to the opinion
> that that is confined to the partnership term and that, the rights being
> to be determined on six calendar months' notice, the provisions are
> inconsistent with a partnership at will when it can be determined
> at any moment.   But I do not think it is necessary to consider
> that, because it is wholly distinct from the other portion of the clause.
> First this power is given.   Then it goes on to provide for the event of
> the power being exercised or the event of the determination by
> effluxion of time, and then the valuation is to take place.   This is the
> only mode pointed out for ascertaining the respective rights on
> determination of the partnership.   I see no difficulty in holding,
> therefore, that the clause is applicable to the case of a partnership
> at will." [41]

Communication of notice

It is clear, however, that where a partnership which has been continued
beyond its original term is sought to be terminated under section 32 (*c*) of
the Partnership Act 1890 by a partner " giving notice . . . of his intention to
dissolve the partnership," that notice does not receive effect until it has been
communicated to the other partners.   Section 32 is concerned with two
things, (1) dissolution and (2) the date from which dissolution becomes
effective.   In *McLeod* v. *Dowling* [42] the partnership deed contained a provision that if either partner died during the term of the partnership, the

---

[38] Using these words in their wide sense: see *e.g. Moss* v. *Elphick* [1910] 1 K.B. 846.
[39] It is true that s. 27 (1) prescribes a partnership at will where a partnership is continued
   after its term has expired " without any express new agreement " thus suggesting that if
   nothing is done at the expiry of the original period the continuing partnership becomes
   a partnership at will; but it is submitted that there is nothing in these words to prevent
   the parties having entered into such an express agreement as to continuance in their
   original agreement.
[40] (1901) 85 L.T. 453.
[41] *Ibid.* at p. 454.   [42] (1927) 43 T.L.R. 655.

surviving partner would be exclusively entitled to the business and goodwill of the partnership. The original term of the partnership was seven years, but it was continued thereafter without any new agreement. McLeod posted a notice to Dowling terminating the partnership as from the date of the notice, *viz.* March 23, 1927. Dowling received the notice at 10 a.m. on March 24 but in the meantime McLeod had died at 3.15 a.m. on the same day. Russell J. held that the partnership had been dissolved by McLeod's death, and not by the notice, and Dowling accordingly was entitled to the business and goodwill. " Section 32 did not come into operation as to sub-head (c) until notice had been received by the defendant. By that time the partnership had been dissolved by the death of McLeod." [43]

Effect on third parties. The termination of a partnership at will by notice given by one of the partners to the others is often for practical purposes indistinguishable from his retirement from the firm under an agreement with his copartners that they will be entitled to continue to carry on the firm's business in the firm name. In some cases where the notice of dissolution is followed by actual dissolution and winding up the situation is clearly distinguishable both in legal theory and in practice but the partner's notice of dissolution of a partnership at will may arise from no other motive than that he wishes personally to sever his association with the firm and no longer to bear any responsibility for the future conduct of its affairs. In these circumstances the remaining partners may wish themselves to continue the firm and its business, and the partner who has given notice of termination may see no objection to their doing so provided he is no longer liable along with them. The practical situation thus closely resembles the position arising on the retirement of a partner from a firm under a clause in the contract of partnership which provides for his doing so while the firm itself continues under the direction of the remaining partners. But the theoretical situation where a partnership at will is dissolved by one of the partners giving notice to the others is very different. " The effect . . . is to determine the partnership at the date when the notice takes effect, *i.e.* to dissolve it, not merely to let him drop out, leaving the remaining partners *ipso facto* to carry on the business as a new firm. *Cum aliquis renunciaverit societati, solvitur societas.*" [44] The firm is dissolved and the partner who has given the notice of termination is entitled, with the others, to have his share dealt with in the manner which is appropriate on a dissolution. As regards third parties, however, the partner who has given notice of termination of a partnership at will is not *ipso facto* liberated as a result from liability for the future. Even if, following upon the notice, the firm is in fact dissolved and wound up, he will remain liable along with his copartners for future transactions entered

---

[43] *Ibid.* at p. 656.
[44] J. Robertson Christie, *Encyclopaedia of the Laws of Scotland*, Vol. 11, *sub voce* Partnership s. 139.

into for the purposes of winding up the affairs of the firm.[45]   The effect of
the notice is to dissolve the firm but on dissolution the courts will hold
the parties bound as partners one to another so far as is necessary for
those purposes.[46]   In these conditions he is liable in his character as a
partner but he may also incur liability as an " apparent partner " [47] or
through being held out, or knowingly suffering himself to be held out, as a
partner.[48]   Considerations of that sort, however, have a more general
relevance to questions arising on the dissolution of the firm for whatever
cause this may have been brought about, and they will accordingly be
deferred for examination at a later stage.[49]

Dissolution on death or bankruptcy of one of the partners

Section 33 of the Partnership Act 1890 *inter alia* provides—

" 33.—(1) Subject to any agreement between the partners, every
partnership is dissolved as regards all the partners by the death or
bankruptcy of any partner."

It will be noticed that the subsection will receive effect only if the partners
have not agreed otherwise in the partnership deed or in their contract,
however it has been reached, as to the creation of the partnership.   An
example of agreement that a partnership should continue in spite of the
death of a partner occurred in *Hill* v. *Wyllie* [50] where in a contract of
copartnery for a term of nineteen years it was provided that " in the event
of the death of either of the parties during the currency of this contract,
the copartnership shall not come to an end, but the surviving partner
shall continue to carry on the business along with the representatives of
the deceasing partner."   In his judgment, in which the remaining judges
of the Second Division concurred, the Lord Justice-Clerk (Inglis) observed,

" I think the clause renders the contract of copartnership binding not
only on the partners, but also on their representatives, in this sense and
to this effect, that on the decease of a partner his representatives are
bound to become partners, and to take the place of the deceasing
partner.   It is quite different from the cases in which the representatives of deceasing partners are entitled to become partners if they
choose.   If that had been intended, these clauses would have been
expressed in the usual way.   This is an unusual clause but it is quite
clear what the partners meant." [51]

The more " usual " provisions to which the Lord Justice-Clerk referred are
explained by Bell,[52] and are provisions whereby one of the partners may,

[45] Partnership Act 1890, s. 38.
[46] *Wallace* v. *Wallace's Trs.* (1906) 8 F. 558; *Crawshay* v. *Maule* (1818) 1 Swanst. 495
    and 523.   For fuller examination of the effect of the Partnership Act 1890, s. 38, and
    the relevant decisions see *infra* pp. 499 *et seq.*
[47] Partnership Act 1890, s. 36 (1) and see *infra* pp. 505–507
[48] Partnership Act 1890, s. 14 (1). *Supra* Chap. V.
[49] See *infra* Chap. XI, pp. 449 *et seq.*
[50] (1865) 3 M. 541.   See also *Beveridge* v. *Beveridge* (1872) 10 M.(H.L.) 1.
[51] *Ibid.* at p. 543.
[52] *Comm.* II, 524.

with his death in contemplation, appoint a person to succeed him as partner. That type of provision occurs in the agreement of partnership considered in *Alexander's Trustees* v. *Thomson* [53] where the clause provided
that the representatives of a deceased partner should be " entitled to take
his room and place in the copartnery with this exception that such representatives shall not be entitled to take the active management or carrying
on of the business." In cases where the provision confers an entitlement
on a person to succeed the deceased in his place as partner, if that person
does not choose to accept, then the death of the person who appointed him
to succeed as partner will operate as a dissolution of the partnership.[54]
That, at least, is the view maintained by Bell [55] and to some extent it is
supported inferentially by the dictum of Lord Justice-Clerk Inglis which
has been quoted. But that dictum does not endorse the legal consequences
which Bell deduces from the distinction drawn. Though some support
appears to be given by the decision in *Kershaw* v. *Mathews* [54] the appointment by the deceasing partner is usually made in virtue of a provision that
on his death the business will be carried on by the remaining partners along
with the person nominated by the deceased, and it is at least questionable
whether on a true construction of that provision the failure, or refusal,
of the nominee to take up the partnership necessarily involves its dissolution, since it may be argued that the intention of the parties is that the
partnership will not be dissolved on the death of the partner. The learned
editor of the seventh edition of Bell's *Commentaries* observes that " the
doctrine stated . . . is obviously open to grave objections and little reliance
can be placed upon it."

If, however, there is no agreement among the partners to the contrary,
the rule in section 33 (1) obtains and the partnership is dissolved by the
death of any partner. The subsection reflects the earlier law in England
and in Scotland. In England the rule was stated in a number of early
decisions [56] and the fact that a partnership is entered into for a term of
years during the currency of which the death occurs is not of itself enough
to displace the rule.[57] In Scotland, Bell states the rule as follows [58]:

> " The whole society is dissolved by the death of one or more of the
> partners. If the heir be entitled by the contract to take the place of
> his ancestor, or if the partnership be declared to subsist notwith-
> standing the death of any one, there is no dissolution. But otherwise
> the heir is, on the one hand, entitled to take his ancestor's share of the

[53] (1885) 22 S.L.R. 828. But *cf. Thomson* v. *Thomson*, 1961 S.C. 255; affd. 1962 S.C.(H.L.)
28 where a provision that on the death of either partner the control of the business should
be in the hands of the surviving partner with the proviso that either partner might
nominate his widow to his share was held not to operate as a nomination of the widow
as a partner.
[54] *Kershaw* v. *Mathews* (1826) 2 Russ. 62.
[55] *Comm.* II, 524.
[56] *e.g. Pearce* v. *Chamberlain* (1750) 2 Ves.Sen. 33; *Crawford* v. *Hamilton* (1818) 3 Madd.
251; *Crosbie* v. *Guion* (1857) 23 Beav. 518.
[57] *Crawford* v. *Hamilton, supra; Downs* v. *Collins* (1848) 6 Hare 418; *Lancaster* v. *Allsup*
(1887) 57 L.T.(N.S.) 53.
[58] *Comm.* II, 524.

stock and profits, after deducting the responsibilities of the company:
as he will, on the other hand, be liable, in representing his ancestor,
to all the debts of the concern as at his ancestor's death."

It was likewise held in Scotland that the fixing of a term of endurance
for the partnership was not of itself sufficient to prevent dissolution on the
death taking place during the term.[59] The underlying principle is that,
in the absence of agreement to the contrary, the parties to a contract of
partnership envisage that all the parties shall be alive and take part during
its continuance.

Where one of the partners is a corporate body, the *ratio* of the principle
may possibly be extended to cover its ceasing to exist even though the idea
of natural death is inept in the case of an artificial person of that nature.
It has been held that the dissolution of the corporation or its extinction
by operation of the law of the country in which it is incorporated is analogous to death in the case of an individual.[60] But it has been pointed out
that as the existence of the company depends on legal rather than natural
conditions, the corporation may in one country be regarded as dissolved
while in another country it is regarded as continuing in existence.[61] In
spite of the sort of difficulties which may arise occasionally as to the application of the analogy, the view that " the dissolution of a corporation will,
in the absence of agreement to the contrary, dissolve a firm in which it
is a partner," [62] appears to be sound; and it seems clear that if dissolution
does not take place *ipso facto* on that ground the extinction or dissolution
of the corporation/partner would at least afford a basis for an application
for an order of the court dissolving the partnership under section 35 (*b*)
or 35 (*f*) of the Partnership Act 1890.[63]

Bankruptcy

The provision for dissolution of the firm on the bankruptcy of any
partner is likewise guarded with the introductory words " subject to any
agreement between the partners." It is at first glance perplexing to attempt
to envisage cases of an ordinary partnership where the partners are concerned to provide that one of their number who has become bankrupt
should continue to act along with the others as a partner; but in the former
law the special case of the unincorporated joint stock company tended to
modify the rule that bankruptcy of any member would dissolve the company. In England mining partnerships seem to have been exempted from
the rule [64]; and the bankruptcy of a shareholder in an unincorporated
company with transferable shares may have dissolved the company so far
as he himself was concerned but in the opinion of Lindley did not dissolve

59 *Aitken's Trs.* v. *Shanks* (1830) 8 S. 753.
60 *Salton* v. *New Beeston Cycle Co.* [1900] 1 Ch. 43.
61 *Russian Commercial & Industrial Bank* v. *Comptoir d'Escompte de Mulhouse* [1923] 2 K.B.
630.
62 Lindley, *op. cit.* pp. 578–579.
63 For discussion of s. 35 of the Partnership Act 1890 see *infra* pp. 456 *et seq.*
64 *Ex p. Broadbent* (1834) 1 Mont. & Ayr. 635; *Bentley* v. *Bates* (1840) 4 Y. & C.Ex. 182.

it so far as regards the other shareholders *inter se*.[65] No decisions of the Scottish courts to a like effect appear to have been reported, and indeed the result in *Greenshield's Case* [65] is one for which it would be appropriate to make express provision in the articles of the unincorporated joint stock company. If, in England, a general exception of such companies from the rule that the bankruptcy of any member dissolved the company itself was previously in existence, that exception has now been removed by section 33 of the Partnership Act 1890 in the rare cases when such a company may continue to be regulated under the Act.[66] It may be possible to read too much into the statutory words " subject to any agreement between the partners " in this context. It has been pointed out to the writer by Mr. W. A. Cook that it is a usual provision in partnership contracts that a partner who has become bankrupt is to be treated as if he had died and his share is to vest in the other partners. It may be that the introductory words of section 33 (1) are intended (so far as bankruptcy is concerned) to do no more than preserve the force of that sort of provision. If so, however, the meaning of " bankruptcy " in terms of the statute may differ from the meaning assigned to it in the partnership agreement.[67]

While, in the absence of agreement among the partners, the bankruptcy of any partner will dissolve the partnership, section 33 does not explain the term " bankruptcy." Under the earlier Scots law mere insolvency of a partner did not dissolve the partnership [68] but sequestration of a partner's estates in bankruptcy did have that effect since it transferred to the trustee for creditors all the partner's rights and thus produced what Bell described as incapacity by bankruptcy. On the same reasoning Bell was of the opinion that the granting by a partner of a trust deed for creditors would have the effect of dissolving the firm.[69] Section 47 of the Partnership Act 1890, however, now provides a definition of the term " bankruptcy " in the application of the Act to Scotland, though no similar definition is provided for the term in England. Section 47 reads—

" 47.—(1) In the application of this Act to Scotland the bankruptcy of a firm or of an individual shall mean sequestration under the Bankruptcy (Scotland) Acts, and also in the case of an individual the issue against him of a decree of *cessio bonorum*.

(2) Nothing in this Act shall alter the rules of the law of Scotland relating to the bankruptcy of a firm or of the individual partners thereof."

The process of *cessio bonorum* was later abolished [70] and thus the bankruptcy of any partner in terms of section 33 of the Partnership Act 1890 is now defined as the sequestration of his estates in bankruptcy under the Bankruptcy (Scotland) Act 1913. Nor, it is thought, do the words of

[65] Lindley, *op. cit.* p. 579; *Greenshield's Case* (1852) 5 De G. & Sm. 599.
[66] See Partnership Act 1890, s. 1 (2).
[67] See immediately succeeding paragraph.
[68] *Paterson* v. *Grant* (1749) Mor. 14578.
[69] Bell, *Comm.* II, 524.
[70] Bankruptcy (Scotland) Act 1913, s. 191 and Sched. I, and Statute Law Revision Act 1927.

subsection (2) of section 47 saving " the rules of the law of Scotland relating to the bankruptcy of a firm or of the individual partners " permit of any wider view of the circumstances in which the bankruptcy of a partner will bring about the dissolution of the firm. Even if Bell's statement of the earlier Scots law be correct and the granting of a trust deed for creditors by the partner would formerly have had the same effect as the sequestration of his estates,[71] the saving words of subsection (2) do not appear apt to carry that rule forward into the period subsequent to the passing of the Partnership Act 1890 since (1) Bell's opinion is advanced tentatively and is unsupported by authority, so that it is questionable whether it represents a rule of the law of Scotland existing prior to the passing of the Act, and (2) in any event the terms of section 47 (2) can hardly be invoked to vary the express definition of " bankruptcy " which is given in section 47 (1). That definition is pointed directly at section 33 (1) and section 38 which are the only places in the Act apart from section 47 where bankruptcy is mentioned.

The rules of the law of Scotland relating to the bankruptcy of a firm or of its partners

The object of section 47 (2) of the Partnership Act 1890 appears to be to conserve the special treatment accorded by Scots law to the firm and its partners in cases of bankruptcy—a treatment which is necessitated because of the fact that the firm in Scotland is regarded as a person distinct from the individual members. Thus a firm may be sequestrated while the individual partners remain solvent. Conversely one or more of the partners may be sequestrated while the firm itself remains solvent. Sequestration of the estates of a firm, on the one hand, and of the individual partners, on the other, are entirely separate proceedings. The most significant aspect of the Scots law on this subject relates to the ranking of creditors on the sequestrated estates and is derived from the doctrine of the separate *persona* of the firm and the accessory obligation of the individual partners as cautioners or co-obligants in the debts of the firm. The details of these matters will be considered more deeply at a later stage but the salient points are summarised for convenience here to assist the reader in forming his own view as to the correct interpretation of the saving clause in section 47 (2) of the Partnership Act 1890. These are—

(1) that in the sequestration of the estates of the firm, the creditors of the firm rank for the full amount of their respective debts to the exclusion of the separate creditors of the partners;

(2) that they may also rank, along with the creditors of the individual partners in the sequestrated estate of the individual partners, for the balance of the firm debt after valuing and deducting the claim against the sequestrated estate of the firm and the claim against the other partners so far as the last mentioned are liable in relief to the bankrupt partner;

[71] Bell, *Comm.* II, 524.

(3) that a claim on the sequestrated estate of a partner may, however, be made only by third parties who are proper creditors of the firm, and not by a creditor of the firm who is also a partner of it;

(4) that, in the sequestration of a partner, the firm is entitled to a ranking for any sum due in respect of the bankrupt partner's contribution to capital, sums overdrawn from the firm on account of profits and the like; and where the firm's estates themselves have been sequestrated the trustee in the firm's estate may so rank; but the right of the trustee will not prejudice the claim of the firm's creditors to a ranking against the bankrupt partner's estate under paragraph (2) above;

(5) that where the firm is sequestrated the individual partners are not entitled to a ranking on the sequestrated estate for over-advances made by them to the capital of the firm, but must claim against their copartners on a mutual accounting; and

(6) that where the estate of an individual partner has been sequestrated, his creditors have a claim against the firm to the extent of the bankrupt partner's share and interest in the firm after deduction of firm debts.[72]

It is submitted, therefore, that the purpose of section 47 (2) is expressly to conserve the rules in bankruptcy peculiar to Scotland arising from the separate *persona* of the firm and its partners and that it should not be construed as in any way countenancing the dissolution of a firm on a partner granting a trust deed for creditors. Section 47 (1) clearly confines dissolution to the case where the estates of the partner are sequestrated and there appears to be no room for extension of those clear words by an analogy which, even in the pre-statute law was dubious, and now in terms of the Partnership Act 1890 appears to be untenable.

Insolvency of partner

It has already been stated that the mere insolvency of a partner did not dissolve the firm under the earlier Scots law.[73] It is clear that even notour bankruptcy of a partner in terms of the Act of 1696, c. 5, did not of itself alone bring about a dissolution.[74] Section 33 (1) of the Partnership Act 1890 has made no change in the law in this respect. But insolvency or notour bankruptcy of a partner or his granting a trust deed for his creditors is frequently expressly declared in the partnership agreement to dissolve the partnership[75] and will be given effect notwithstanding that the partner offers later to pay his creditors and thus establish his solvency. In a case where the partnership agreement provided for dissolution of the partnership on a partner's "declared insolvency," and where the partner had issued a circular intimating that he had suspended payment and convening a meeting of his creditors, the Lord President (Inglis) observed of the provision in question,

---

[72] On these rules generally see Bell, *Comm.* II, 547 *et seq.*; Goudy, *Bankruptcy* (4th ed.) pp. 577 *et seq.* The subject of bankruptcy of the firm and its partners is examined in more detail in Chap. XIII.
[73] *Paterson* v. *Grant* (1749) Mor. 14578.
[74] Bell, *Comm.* II, 524.
[75] See *Munro* v. *Cowan*, June 8, 1813, F.C.; *Hannan* v. *Henderson* (1879) 7 R. 380.

"But it is said that this is an irritancy which may be purged at the bar. I have some doubt whether it is an irritancy. It is so, no doubt, in this sense, that it puts an end to certain rights as well as obligations. But assuming it to be an irritancy, it is in the most proper sense a conventional irritancy and the ordinary rule of law is that conventional irritancies must be enforced according to their terms. . . . But this was, besides, a most reasonable stipulation, for the meaning of it was that the partnership was to cease, not because a man has not paid his debts, but because he is publicly known to have become an insolvent trader. That has a prejudicial effect on the business of which the insolvent trader is a partner. That is the reason why the termination of the partnership in these circumstances is so frequently stipulated for. Therefore such an irritancy never can be purged. The mischief is done, and never can be undone. The partner would come in again to the concern with a damaged commercial reputation, and that is the very thing which the provision was intended to prevent." [76]

Proceedings against a partner equivalent to bankruptcy proceedings but instituted in a foreign country

While the Partnership Act 1890 has defined "bankruptcy" in so far as its provisions are applied in Scotland, it has not similarly defined the term in the case of England. This has given rise to speculation as to the effect of proceedings against a partner of an English firm which are equivalent to an English bankruptcy. No decision has been reported on the question but the opinion has been stated [77] "that such proceedings would cause a dissolution, at any rate if taken in the country in which the bankrupt partner is domiciled." That view has considerable cogency where, as in England, the words of section 33 (1) of the Partnership Act 1890 stand alone in regulating the circumstances which *ipso facto* will bring about a dissolution, and where these words simply refer to the "bankruptcy of any partner." In Scotland, it is submitted, the question is foreclosed from speculation since there "bankruptcy" is equated with sequestration [78] and thus there is no possible reading of the combined provisions of the Act which would permit foreign proceedings in bankruptcy to be made the occasion of a dissolution of the firm. On the other hand, "In England the term 'bankruptcy' is used exclusively to express judicial divestiture of the debtor." [79] It can therefore be argued that the true construction of effect of section 47 (1) of the Partnership Act 1890 is merely to equate "bankruptcy" in Scotland with "bankruptcy" in England for the purposes of the Act. If that be the true construction of section 47 (1) there is no specialty of Scots law which appears to displace the English rule.

[76] *Hannan* v. *Henderson, supra* at p. 383.
[77] Lindley, *op. cit.* p. 580.
[78] Partnership Act, s. 47 (1).
[79] Goudy, *Bankruptcy* (4th ed.) p. 16.

Date of dissolution arising from bankruptcy or death

Section 33 (1) of the Partnership Act 1890 states the happenings which will bring about a dissolution of the firm but it does not specify the date from which the dissolution will take effect. There is, of course, no difficulty in the case of a dissolution on the death of a partner. It will take effect from the date when that death occurred. In the case of a dissolution arising through the bankruptcy of a partner, that has been equated in Scotland to his sequestration under the Bankruptcy (Scotland) Acts. Thus the date on which the dissolution takes effect will be that on which sequestration of the bankrupt partner's estate is deemed to commence and take effect, *i.e.* the date of the first deliverance on the petition for sequestration.[80]

Dissolution of the firm compared with a change in its composition

In discussing the circumstances in which the death or bankruptcy may *eo ipso* dissolve the firm it is important to draw as precisely as possible a line of distinction between dissolution of the firm in the sense in which those terms are employed in section 33 of the Partnership Act 1890 and other arrangements made among the partners under which one or more of the partners may be dropped from the partnership in certain eventualities while the partnership itself continues to be carried on by the remaining partners who are unaffected by those eventualities under agreed conditions as to payment to the partners affected of their shares. In the latter case the agreed provision has the effect that on the event occurring he simply ceases to be a partner and provision is made for ascertainment and payment of his share of the firm's assets at that date by the firm as a continuing concern.[81] That situation is to be contrasted with the case where an eventuality befalling an individual partner, such as his death or his bankruptcy, brings about a dissolution of the firm, when the rights and liabilities of *all* the partners fall to be determined as if the firm were to cease to exist and to be wound up. The distinction becomes a somewhat artificial one since even in that situation the partners who are unaffected by the eventuality may agree among themselves to continue to carry on the business of the firm and such agreement may be inferred from the very fact of their continuing to carry on the business. In that case only the partner or partners affected on whom the event has befallen will be " paid out," just as in the case of the expiration of the original stipulated term of the partnership, where some of the partners continue to carry on the business, only the partners who give notice of termination of the partnership will be paid out; but in either case the amount of their shares will be based upon their rights on a dissolution of the partnership and not on any conventional mode of settling their shares stipulated in the partnership agreement. In all these cases what has occurred may be described as a dissolution of the firm; even when one or more partners drop out of the partnership under

[80] Bankruptcy (Scotland) Act 1913, s. 41.
[81] See *e.g. Hannan* v. *Henderson* (1879) 7 R. 380.

pre-arranged provisions that the business of the firm will continue to be carried on by the remaining partners under the firm name in agreed arrangements as to payment of the retiring partner's share, there has been a change in the composition or membership of the firm. The old firm has disappeared and is succeeded by a new firm. That situation is apparent under English law where the firm is no more than a collective title for the individual partners who comprise it, but even in Scots law where a *quasi* personality is accorded to the firm itself that quality of legal personality does not carry with it the attribute of perpetual succession which is a feature of a fully corporate body, and thus a change in the membership of the firm means a new firm. It is possible therefore to employ the term " dissolution " in two different senses, first in its strict sense as denoting an occasion when the firm ceases to exist and is wound up and, secondly, when the firm as previously constituted ceases to exist but is continued in practical terms of business by some of the original partners and under the original firm name with or without addition of new partners; and there may be an intermediate situation where the law regards the circumstances which have occurred as having brought about the dissolution, in the strict sense, of the firm but some of the partners *de facto* continue to carry on the business under the firm name in which case they must satisfy the rights of the partners who no longer are associated in the business as if the old firm had been dissolved and wound up. In this chapter which is concerned with the firm in dissolution and winding up the term dissolution will normally be used in its first and stricter sense. Nevertheless, there are passages in the judgments in reported cases and in the authoritative textbooks where the two senses of the term are employed indiscriminately and where, indeed, on occasion they tend almost imperceptibly to merge one with the other.

Partner suffering his share to be charged for his separate debt

Section 33 (2) of the Partnership Act 1890 provides—

" 33.—(2) A partnership may, at the option of the other partners, be dissolved if any partner suffers his share of the partnership property to be charged undei this Act for his separate debt."

Although the subsection does not in express terms state that it is inapplicable to Scotland, it will be observed that the " charge " which gives the other partners the option to dissolve the partnership is one made " under this Act," and the provision made under the Partnership Act 1890 for a charge against the interest of a partner in respect of a debt owed by him as an individual [82] is expressly stated to be inapplicable to Scotland.[83] It follows that section 33 (2) is itself unavailable in Scotland as a ground for he dissolution of the partnership, and the problems which arise in England

[82] Partnership Act 1890, s. 23.
[83] *Ibid.* s. 23 (5).

as to what may be regarded as an exercise of the option by the other part-ners,[84] within what time the option may be exercised [85] and whether the other partners must be unanimous in exercising the option [86] do not arise in Scotland. Neither the arrestment [87] nor the assignment of a partner's share [88] in Scotland is comprehended within the provisions respecting a charge of his interest in the firm for his separate debt and neither gives an option to the other partners to dissolve the firm, though either may form the ground for an application to the court for an order to dissolve the partnership under section 35 (f) of the Partnership Act 1890.[89]

Dissolution upon illegality of the partnership business

Section 34 of the Partnership Act 1890 provides—

> " 34. A partnership is in every case dissolved by the happening of any event which makes it unlawful for the business of the firm to be carried on or for the members of the firm to carry it on in partner-ship."

The section is concerned with an illegality supervening after the partnership has been constituted [90] and the two most probable events which will give rise to a supervening illegality are a change in the law and an outbreak of war with its consequential restrictions on trading with the enemy. The former of these may be concerned either with the nature of the business carried on in the partnership or with the capacity of the partners, or some of them, to conduct such a business. The latter will most frequently be concerned with a partnership which upon outbreak of hostilities is found to comprise among its members enemy aliens and the continuance of which would therefore involve infringement of the statutes prohibiting trading with the enemy. Section 34 in its terms covers both eventualities, and reflects the earlier law of England. Thus where a partnership existed between two persons residing, and carrying on trade, in different countries, and war was proclaimed between those countries, it was held that the partnership between them was dissolved on account of the supervening illegality of the association.[91] The implications of such supervening illegality upon questions of contract in general were considered and ex-plained in a number of decisions during the First World War [92] and in *R.* v. *Kupfer* [93] the provisions in section 34 of the Partnership Act 1890 were

---

[84] *Scarf* v. *Jardine* (1882) 7 App.Cas. 345 at p. 361; *Clough* v. *L.N.W. Ry.* (1871) L.R. 7 Ex. 34.

[85] *Anderson* v. *Anderson* (1857) 25 Beav. 190; *Scarf* v. *Jardine, supra* at pp. 360–361.

[86] Lindley, *op. cit.* p. 581; Partnership Act 1890, s. 24 (8).

[87] See *supra* Chap. IX, pp. 394–398.

[88] *Ibid., eodem loco*; and see Partnership Act 1890, s. 31.

[89] See *infra* pp. 473–474. The application might be founded on section 35 (c) or (d) in certain cases.

[90] For illegality in general see *supra* Chap. IV, pp. 105 *et seq.*

[91] *Griswold* v. *Waddington*, 15 Johns. 57; an American case cited in *Story on Partnership* § 315. See also *In re S. Wales Atlantic Steamship Co.* (1876) 2 Ch.D. 763.

[92] See *e.g. Porter* v. *Freudenberg* [1915] 1 K.B. 857; *Princess of Thurn & Taxis* v. *Moffitt* [1915] 1 Ch. 58; " *The Roumanian* " [1915] P. 26; affd. [1916] 1 A.C. 124; *Daimler Co.* v. *Continental Tyre Co.* [1916] 2 A.C. 307.

[93] (1915) 112 L.T. 1138.

held to operate to bring about a dissolution of a partnership in circumstances very similar to those of the American decision in *Griswold* v.
Waddington referred to above. These cases, however, so far as they illustrate the rule in its particular application to the dissolution of the partnership are concerned with a supervening illegality under the second branch
of section 34 making it illegal for the members of the firm to carry on its
business in partnership. Questions of more complexity arise when the
supervening illegality is incurred under the first branch of the section, *i.e.*
where it supervenes owing to the " happening of any event which makes it
unlawful for the business of the firm to be carried on." Where the illegality which arises attaches to the actual business carried on, it will usually
arise through a change in the law, but it does not necessarily follow in every
case that if by a change in the law it becomes unlawful to carry on a business
of a certain kind, every partnership created before the change in the law to
conduct the business of that kind will be dissolved by virtue of section 34.
If the partnership has been formed for the purpose of carrying on that
business and that alone, the wording of section 34 is such that the partnership
must be regarded as dissolved by the change in the law. The application
of the section becomes a trifle more obscure where the firm carries on a
number of businesses of different kinds and by a change in the law one of
those businesses is rendered unlawful. It is arguable that the wording of
section 34 is not appropriate to impose dissolution of the partnership in
that case, since the event, *i.e.* in this case the change in the law, which happened has not made it unlawful for the business of the firm to be carried on
but merely for a certain aspect or certain aspects of that business to be
carried on and if the other aspects which remain lawful despite the supervening change in the law are entirely separate from those which are now
unlawful it may still be lawful for " the business of the firm " to be carried
on; but if the aspects which have become unlawful are so interwoven with
those aspects which remain lawful that cessation of the unlawful activities
involves cessation of the business as a whole, section 34 will probably
impose a dissolution on the firm.[94]

There does not appear to be any reported decision under the earlier
Scottish common law which deals with the position on a supervening
illegality affecting the firm or its partners. The effect of an original illegality as voiding the contract of partnership was upheld in a number of
the earlier Scottish decisions,[95] some of which have already been discussed.[96] There does not appear to be any underlying difference in the
theoretical approach of the English and Scottish systems upon a question
of this nature[97] and in any event the law so far as the partnership is

---

[94] This conclusion appears justifiable on general grounds of theory and of construction of
s. 34 and is supported by Lindley, *op. cit.* p. 582.
[95] See *e.g. A.B.* v. *C.D.* (1832) 10 S. 523; *Gordon* v. *Howden* (1845) 4 Bell App. 254; *Fraser*
v. *Hair* (1848) 10 D. 1402; *Fraser* v. *Hill* (1854) 16 D. 789; (1854) 1 Macq. 392; *Gibson* v.
Stewart (1840) 1 Rob.App. 260.
[96] *Supra* Chap. IV.
[97] See Gloag, *Contract* (2nd ed.) pp. 340 *et seq.*

concerned has been assimilated in both countries by section 34 of the Partnership Act 1890. Apart from the question of severability of the business of the firm into those activities which have been rendered unlawful by a supervening change in the law and those which remain lawful in spite of that change, the more general point should be noticed that what section 34 is characterising as unlawful and therefore involving a dissolution of the firm is " the business of the firm," *i.e.* the inherent purpose for which the partnership was created and to achieve which its business is conducted. The section does not strike at some particular act of the firm or of its partners which is in itself unlawful, whether under the law as originally existing or by reason of a supervening change in the law, which amounts to no more than a particular mode, in itself unlawful, whereby a lawful activity has been carried out.[98]

Dissolution of partnership by order of the court

In section 35 of the Partnership Act 1890 provision is made in a number of cases for dissolution of the partnership by order of the court made upon the application of the partners, or some of them. Under section 45 of the Act, it is provided that unless the contrary intention appears, the expression " court " when used in the Act includes every court and judge having jurisdiction in the case. The word " court " appears in four sections of the Partnership Act 1890 in addition to its mention in section 45 and the first occasion of its use in section 35.[99] So far as application for an order under section 35 is concerned, prior to the passing of the Act, the Court of Session frequently entertained summary applications for dissolution of partnerships and the appointment of judicial factors to wind up the business of the firm.[1] Such applications fell within the ambit of " summary petitions and applications to the Lords of Council and Session which are not incident to actions actually depending at the time of presenting the same " and as such were brought before " the Junior Lord Ordinary officiating in the Outer House " in terms of the Distribution of Business Act 1857.[2] A summary application of that kind, however, may not in every case be the appropriate, or indeed the competent, form of process in which questions as to dissolution of a partnership under section 35 of the Partnership Act 1890 should be tried. In cases where the parties are in dispute as to matters which require investigation or inquiry, before the court can adjudicate upon the right to an order for dissolution, an action of declarator may be the appropriate form of process.[3] There is no jurisdiction in the sheriff court to appoint a judicial factor on the estate of a partnership, the power

[98] Otherwise the whole basis for s. 10 of the Partnership Act 1890 would disappear.
[99] The other sections are ss. 39, 40 and 42 of the Partnership Act 1890. On ss. 40 and 42 see *supra* p. 255 and *infra* pp. 540 *et seq.* respectively. On s. 39 see *infra* pp. 460 *et seq.*
[1] *Eadie* v. *McBean's Curator Bonis* (1885) 12 R. 660; *Russell* v. *Russell* (1874) 2 R. 93; *Macpherson* v. *Richmond* (1869) 41 Sc.Jur. 288; and see *per* the Lord President (Balfour) in *Wallace* v. *Whitelaw* (1900) 2 F. 675 at p. 678.
[2] s. 4. See now Rules of Court, Chap. IV, n. 207 (A) (ii) under which they are to be presented to the Outer House and lodged in the Petition Department.
[3] See *Wallace* v. *Whitelaw, supra, per* the Lord President, *loc. cit.*; *Eadie* v. *McBean's Curator Bonis* (1885) 12 R. 660 at p. 669.

of the sheriff as to appointment of judicial factors being restricted to the appointment of factors *loco tutoris* and *curatores bonis* [4] but it is now competent, when the process is by way of action of declarator, to bring the action in the sheriff court,[5] though if, in addition to an order for dissolution of the partnership, the appointment of a judicial factor is concluded for, the action will require to be brought in the Court of Session. While a summary petition for an order for dissolution of the partnership and appointment of a judicial factor is available where the parties are not at variance as to the facts and while in some applications of that nature questions even as to the facts have been disposed of, albeit with some reservation as to the appropriateness of the procedure,[6] an action of declarator coupled with a conclusion for dissolution of the partnership appears to be the most appropriate form of procedure and, where there is no need for winding up under a judicial factor, as when there are surviving, competent and reliable partners who are prepared to do the work, the action would appear to be competent in the sheriff court. The line of distinction between the cases where a summary application is appropriate and those where an action of declarator should be brought was drawn by Lord McLaren in *Wallace* v. *Whitelaw*,[7]

> " When the facts on which dissolution is sought are capable of instant verification, as, for example, when a partner has been sequestrated, or where the deed of partnership limits the duration of the partnership to the period of the partners' lives, and there is evidence of the death of one of the partners, where, in fact, the evidence pointing to the remedy of dissolution is indisputable, I should say that it was convenient and not incompetent to combine a prayer to this effect with a petition for the appointment of a judicial factor to wind up the business of the co-partnery. But if the partnership is in existence, and its business is prosperous, and there is no apparent cause for a dissolution, except a desire on the part of one of the partners to get rid of a copartner, to say that a dissolution of partnership could be obtained by means of a summary petition and on the report of an accountant from whose conclusions there is practically no appeal, would be to sanction a procedure so monstrous that I do not think a parallel to it could be found in any legal system that I know of."

Grounds upon which the court may order dissolution

Section 35 of the Partnership Act 1890 reads—

> " 35. On application by a partner the Court may decree a dissolution of the partnership in any of the following cases:
>> (*a*) When a partner is found lunatic by inquisition, or in Scotland by cognition, or is shown to the satisfaction of the court to be of

---

[4] Judicial Factors (Scotland) Act 1880, ss. 3 and 4.
[5] Sheriff Courts (Scotland) Act 1907, s. 5 (1).
[6] *Eadie* v. *McBean's Curator Bonis, supra, per* Lord Shand at p. 669.
[7] (1900) 2 F. 675 at p. 678.

permanently unsound mind, in either of which cases the application
may be made as well on behalf of that partner by his committee or
next friend or person having title to intervene as by any other
partner;

(b) When a partner, other than the partner suing, becomes in
any other way permanently incapable of performing his part of the
partnership contract;

(c) When a partner, other than the partner suing, has been
guilty of such conduct as, in the opinion of the court, regard being
had to the nature of the business, is calculated to prejudicially
affect the carrying on of the business;

(d) When a partner, other than the partner suing, wilfully or
persistently commits a breach of the partnership agreement, or
otherwise so conducts himself in matters relating to the partnership
business that it is not reasonably practicable for the other partner
or partners to carry on the business in partnership with him;

(e) When the business of the partnership can only be carried on
at a loss;

(f) Whenever in any case circumstances have arisen which, in
the opinion of the court, render it just and equitable that the
partnership be dissolved."

Insanity of partner

The pre-existing Scots law was laid down by Lord President Inglis in
Eadie v. *McBean's Curator Bonis* [8] where he states, " There can be no
doubt that under ordinary circumstances where two or more persons are
engaged in business together as partners, and all of them are expected, or
by the deed of copartnery bound, to take an active management of the
business, the permanent insanity or incapacity of one of the partners
operates a dissolution of the partnership." [9]   In the case in question,
however, the court did not grant an order for dissolution.   Under the
terms of the contract of copartnery the duties of the incapacitated partner
were (a) to provide initially the greater part of the capital of the business
and (b) to sign the cheques and indorse the bills of the firm, but in the
event of his indisposition the continuing part of his duties mentioned under
(b) would be carried out by the other partners.   He was incapacitated
from taking further part in the partnership business through a stroke of
paralysis and a *curator bonis* appointed.   The court, however, refused a
petition for the dissolution of the partnership since it was not a condition
of the partnership agreement that he should give his personal services to
the business.

It will be noticed that two points of apparent divergence occur between
the wording of section 35 (a) of the Partnership Act 1890 on the one hand,
and the pre-statute Scots law as reflected in the dictum of the Lord

[8] (1885) 12 R. 660.
[9] *Ibid.* at p. 665.

President in *Eadie* v. *McBean's Curator Bonis* and the decision itself in that
case, on the other.   In the first place, Lord President Inglis speaks of " the
permanent insanity or incapacity " of the partner as the proper ground for
dissolution.   In its application to Scotland, section 35 (*a*) speaks of a partner "found lunatic . . . by cognition" or " shown to the satisfaction of the
court to be of permanently unsound mind."   Cognition of the insane is
regulated by the Court of Session Act 1868 and the Rules of Court,
Chapter III, section 7.   In terms of the Court of Session Act 1868 [10]
the definition of insanity is that " such person shall be deemed to be
insane if he be furious or fatuous, or labouring under such unsound-
ness of mind as to render him incapable of managing his affairs."   Under
that definition it is not essential that the condition be a permanent state.
If, however, the insanity of the partner is sought to be established otherwise
than by a retour of cognition [11] the court must be satisfied on the evidence
presented that the partner is of permanently unsound mind and presumably
must be so satisfied even when a *curator bonis* has been appointed on the
petition of a near relative of the partner or other party with an interest to
present the petition.   For the purposes of such a petition the definition
of insanity above quoted is sufficient, and it does not need to be established
that the condition is permanent.   In these circumstances, however, the
court in the absence of a retour of cognition, will require satisfaction that
the partner is " of permanently unsound mind."   He will be considered as
of permanently unsound mind when the evidence shows a reasonable
ground for supposing a recovery to be hopeless, or at least very improbable,
during the remainder of the time for which the partnership contract is to
endure.[12]   The earlier English authorities, though based on different
procedures as to lunacy, are helpful in the general principles upon which
the courts proceeded in partnership cases.   Since the passing of the Mental
Health Act 1959 different procedures and provisions apply in England, the
" nominated judges " [13] under the Act have power to dissolve any partnership of which a " patient " is a member [14] and a " patient " is a person
regarding whom the judge is satisfied, after considering the medical
evidence, that he is incapable, by reason of mental disorder, of managing
and administering his property and affairs.[15]   As a result of these provisions, which do not apply in Scotland, the former situation in England
where the court might accept a finding by inquisition that a partner was
lunatic as sufficient to warrant an order dissolving the partnership but
must in other cases be satisfied that the partner was of permanently unsound mind, no longer obtains and cases decided in England after the
passing of the Mental Health Act 1959 will afford no sure guidance in
Scotland where the provisions of that Act do not in this respect apply.

---

[10] s. 101.
[11] Rules of Court 205.
[12] *Jones* v. *Lloyd* (1874) L.R. 18 Eq. 265.
[13] Mental Health Act 1959, s. 100.
[14] *Ibid.* s. 103 (1) (*f*).
[15] *Ibid.* s. 101.

The second point of apparent dissimilarity between the earlier law of Scotland and section 35 (*a*) of the Partnership Act 1890 rests in the fact that under the earlier Scots law as expounded in *Eadie* v. *McBean's Curator Bonis* [16] the court had regard to the conditions imposed by the partnership agreement upon the incapacitated partner before coming to a decision whether or not to order dissolution and, indeed, as a result of that consideration, refused the prayer of the petitioner in the particular case before them. Section 35 (*a*) makes no express mention of that feature but the omission creates no real distinction. The section is so framed that it confers a discretion upon the court whether an order will be granted in such cases or not and the court is not bound *ex debito justitiae* to dissolve the partnership. The discretionary nature of the statutory power is sufficiently indicated by the opening words of the section—" On application by a partner the court *may* decree a dissolution of the partnership . . ." (Italics supplied); but it is reinforced by the words of section 35 (*b*) " Becomes *in any other way* permanently incapable of performing his part of the partnership contract." Construing the two provisions together, it is clear that insanity is treated as merely one type of incapacity and that in both cases what is to be regarded by the court is the effect of that incapacity, whether it be from insanity or any other cause, upon the partner's ability to implement his part of the partnership agreement.

Dormant partner. Since the reason for the court granting an order for dissolution in the case of insanity is the permanent incapacity of the lunatic to perform what he has undertaken to perform under the contract of copartnery,[17] a dormant partner who in terms of the partnership agreement is under no duties as to the management and conduct of the business would not by becoming insane give occasion for an order for dissolution of the firm save in most exceptional circumstances.[18]

Date of dissolution where order granted on ground of insanity.

" The insanity of a partner is a ground for the dissolution of the partnership because it is immediate incapacity: but it may not in the result prove to be a ground of dissolution, for the partner may recover from his malady. When a partner therefore is affected with insanity, the continuing partner may, if he thinks fit, make it a ground of dissolution, but in that case . . . he must obtain a decree of the court. . . . If he carry on the partnership business in the expectation that his partner may recover from his insanity, so long as he continues the business with that expectation or hope, there can be no dissolution." [19]

This treatment of the partnership relation appears to view the question of dissolution as something to the detriment of the insane partner which will not be visited upon him if his copartner chooses to continue in partnership with him in the hope of his recovery or if the incapacity does not affect

[16] (1885) 12 R. 660.
[17] *Eadie* v. *McBean's Curator Bonis, supra*; and see *Jones* v. *Noy* (1833) 2 M. & K. 125.
[18] *Eadie* v. *McBean's Curator Bonis, supra*; and see Lindley, *op. cit.* p. 586.
[19] *Jones* v. *Noy* (1833) 2 M. & K. 125; and see *Rowlands* v. *Evans* (1861) 30 Beav. 302.

the performance of the incapacitated partner's part of the contract.[20] There is an unresolved conflict between this view and the general view of partnership as involving mutual agency among the partners; for, under the general law of agency, it has been held that insanity of the principal terminates the agency even when unknown to the agent.[21] Thus it might be argued that where a partnership was continued by the copartner in spite of his partner's insanity the authority of the copartner so continuing to bind the insane partner in transactions carried out in the course of the firm's business had been revoked. There would be a continuing authority to bind the insane partner in transactions necessary for the winding up of the firm's affairs[22] but not where the affairs of the firm were carried on in the ordinary course without dissolution. The reported decisions on this point seem to have approached the question exclusively from the viewpoint whether the insane partner has a right to share in the profits made while the business was so continued[23] and the question does not appear to have been raised in any case that the insanity of a partner might revoke the authority of his copartners to bind him in firm transactions which proved disadvantageous. As the law stands, however, the position of an insane partner in this respect must be taken to be an exception from the general law of agency in that his insanity, since it does not *per se* dissolve the partnership, does not revoke the mutual agency which exists in the continuing relation of partnership.[24]

These considerations have their bearing upon the date from which a dissolution of partnership on the ground of a partner's insanity will take effect. Except in the case of a partnership at will, the court in ordering dissolution on this ground will make it effective from the date of the order and will not ante-date its effect.[25] In the case of a partnership at will, where notice to dissolve has been given, the order will be made as at the date of the notice.[26] When it is provided in the partnership agreement itself that the partnership will be dissolved on the insanity of any of the partners and a dissolution is carried through under that provision,[27] then any subsequent order as to dissolution pronounced by the court on that ground will date from the actual dissolution of the partnership and not from the date of the order.[28]

[20] The same attitude appears to be adopted in *Eadie* v. *McBean's Curator Bonis, supra*, but the court will not appoint a manager to carry on the concern for the benefit of the insane partner's estate even when the partnership might be carried on advantageously to all partners under this arrangement; *Rowlands* v. *Evans, supra.*

[21] *Yonge* v. *Toynbee* [1910] 1 K.B. 215.

[22] Partnership Act 1890, s. 38.

[23] *Jones* v. *Noy, supra*; *Eadie* v. *McBean's Curator Bonis, supra.*

[24] See Lindley, *op. cit.* p. 586, n. 74.

[25] *Besch* v. *Frolich* (1842) 1 Ph. 172; *Sander* v. *Sander* (1845) 2 Coll. 276; *Jones* v. *Welch* (1855) 1 K. & J. 765.

[26] *Mellersh* v. *Keen* (1859) 27 Beav. 236, and see Partnership Act 1890, s. 32. In this case the intervention of the court is to ensure the adequacy of the notice to the insane partner and not to determine whether his insanity is a ground for dissolution.

[27] A dissolution under an express provision in the agreement may be effected despite the insanity of the partner: *Robertson* v. *Lockie* (1846) 15 Sim. 285.

[28] *Robertson* v. *Lockie, supra*; *Bagshaw* v. *Parker* (1847) 10 Beav. 532.

Representation of interest of insane partner. When an application is made to the court by the remaining partners for an order of dissolution on the ground of the insanity of a partner, the *curator bonis* of the insane partner is entitled to appear in the interest of the insane partner,[29] and if there is no *curator bonis* a *curator ad litem* will be appointed by the court.[30] Under section 35 (*a*) of the Partnership Act 1890, the application to the court may be made " as well on behalf of that [insane] partner by his committee or next friend or person having title to intervene as by any other partner." The terms " committee or next friend " relate exclusively to the former English procedure, but a " person having title to intervene " is an expression which is apt to cover the right of a tutor-at-law, tutor dative or *curator bonis*.

Expenses of application. When the order for dissolution is made by the court, expenses of the application are directed to be paid out of the assets of the partnership.[31] When an application for an order for dissolution has been dismissed the Scottish cases unfortunately do not state in the reports the manner in which the expenses of the application were disposed of.[32] Since the application in these cases has been successfully opposed, it is thought that normally award of expenses will follow upon success and that the partners applying for dissolution will be found liable in the expenses thereof.

Partner permanently incapable of performing his part of the partnership contract

Section 35 (*b*) reflects the general principle governing the issue of an order for dissolution and the terms of section 35 (*a*) as to dissolution on the ground of a partner's insanity may be said to be merely one particular example of the application of that general principle. The principle that dissolution of the partnership should be granted when a partner becomes in any way permanently incapacitated from performing his part under the partnership agreement was recognised in the pre-statute common law both in England and in Scotland. The incapacity must, however, be permanent. Thus in the English case of *Whitwell* v. *Arthur* [33] a dissolution was sought on the ground that one of the partners had suffered a paralytic stroke and had thus been incapacitated from carrying out his duties as a partner. The application was unsuccessful because the medical evidence showed that the partner's condition was improving and that his incapacity was in all probability only temporary. In the pre-existing Scots law the same considerations apply. Bell observes,[34]

" There is no line of distinction by which it shall be ascertained how long a term of inability shall justify measures of this description. A

[29] *Eadie* v. *McBean's Curator Bonis* (1885) 12 R. 660.
[30] *Cleghorn* (1901) 8 S.L.T. 409.
[31] *Jones* v. *Welch* (1855) 1 K. & J. 765; *Cleghorn* (1901) 8 S.L.T. 409.
[32] See *Eadie* v. *McBean's Curator Bonis* (1885) 12 R. 660; *Wallace* v. *Whitelaw* (1900) 2 F. 675.
[33] (1865) 35 Beav. 140.
[34] *Comm.* II, 525.

broken leg or an accidental blow may incapacitate a partner for a time
as much as insanity, and the one may be as temporary as the other; and
perhaps the nearest approximation to be made to a rule on the subject
is that a remedy and relief will be given only where the circumstances
amount to a total and important failure in those essential points on
which the success of the partnership depends."

The same principle is expounded by Lord President Inglis in *Eadie* v.
McBean's Curator Bonis [35] in terms sufficiently general to cover all cases
of permanent incapacity and not merely that resulting from insanity [36];
and Pothier in his *Traité du Contrat de Société* [37] develops the idea explained
by Bell in greater detail.   The general nature of the rule regarding incapacity is reflected in section 35 of the Partnership Act 1890 when one considers clause (*a*) and clause (*b*) of that section in relation one to another;
for while clause (*a*) deals exclusively with insanity as a ground of dissolution of the partnership, it is immediately followed by clause (*b*) which
similarly affords a ground of dissolution where a partner *in any other way*
becomes permanently incapable of performing his duties in the partnership.
One important difference is, however, to be noticed as between the two
clauses.   Whereas under clause (*a*) the partnership may be dissolved on
the application of some person entitled to intervene on behalf of the insane
partner as well as by any other partner, under clause (*b*) a partner incapacitated otherwise than by insanity is not allowed himself to apply for
an order for dissolution founding on his own incapacity.   The reason for
the distinction is nowhere clearly explained in the English or Scottish
decisions but it seems to be an application of the principle, *qui societatem
in tempus coit, ei ante tempus renuntiando, socium a se, non se a socio
liberat.* [38]   A partner who dissolves the partnership before the expiration
of the agreed period of its endurance or in bad faith may be sued by his
copartners for the loss incurred through his renunciation of his part of
the contract by purported dissolution of the partnership.   On the other
hand, if, after such an invalid renunciation of the partnership, the firm
itself has through its remaining partners made a profit, the partner who has

---

[35] (1885) 12 R. 660 at p. 665.
[36] In any event *Eadie* v. *McBean's Curator Bonis* dealt with incapacity from a paralytic
seizure.
[37] § 142.   "Lorsqu'un marchand de bois a contracté une société avec un tonnelier pour
faire et vendre des tonneaux, à laquelle société le marchand devoit apporter le bois et le
tonnelier son travail seulement pour faire les tonneaux: ce tonnelier étant depuis devenu
paralytique, et incapable par-conséquent de faire des tonneaux, cette société cesse-t-elle
en ce cas?   Et peut on dire que le tonnelier n'a plus de quoi y contribuer?   Non; car
en se chargeant par le contrat de faire des tonneaux, il s'est chargé de les faire, non
precisément par lui-même, mais soit par lui, soit par ses ouvriers: il peut encore, quoique
paralytique, les faire faire par ses ouvriers, et il a par-conséquent de quoi contribuer à la
société ce qu'il a promis d'y contribuer (*Code Civil*, article 1865, § 4).
   Quid, si le marchand qui n'a contracté que par la confiance qu'il avoit dans l'habileté
de cet ouvrier, avoit mis une clause dans le contrat de société, que ce tonnelier ne pourroit
faire faire les tonneaux par d'autres que par lui?   En ce cas on peut dire que la société est
éteinte, puisque la chose que cet associé a promis d'apporter à la société, est éteinte:
car ce n'est pas seulement la façon des tonneaux, mais son travail personnel qu'il a promis
d'apporter à la société, et qu'il ne peut plus y apporter.   Le marchand fera néanmoins
prudemment de lui signifier une rénonciation à la société."
[38] *Diges* L: 65: 6.

renounced the contract before the expiry of its agreed duration or in bad faith cannot himself be heard to plead the invalidity of his own purported act of dissolution of the partnership.[39]   Therefore, when it is within the discretion of the court to order the dissolution of a partnership upon grounds relating to the incapacity or the misconduct of one of the partners, the court will not in the normal case hear an application from the partner whose own incapacity or misconduct forms the ground of the application since he continues bound in the association until his partners apply for an order to dissolve it.[40]   An exception is made where the partner has become incapacitated through insanity and his business affairs fall under the administration of a *curator bonis* or similar functionary.   But in cases of incapacity from other causes the incapacitated partner, while prevented from taking an active part in the business, may yet be able to administer his own affairs and protect his own interests if he remains a partner, *e.g.* where he is physically crippled or disabled, and where he in effect incapacitates himself, *e.g.* by absenting himself from the business for prolonged periods or by refusal to take his part in the conduct of the partnership affairs, that is to be regarded rather in the light of his misconduct than his incapacity and it is manifestly inequitable that he be allowed to plead his own misconduct in support of his intention to dissolve the partnership against the wishes of his copartners.   The real difficulty lies in the attempted distinction between the effect of incapacity through insanity and incapacity through physical deformity or disease, for the two may tend to merge. Pothier's workman who has become paralysed has suffered a physical incapacity.   He is no longer able physically to perform his part of the partnership agreement if that agreement insisted upon his personal performance of the work.   But a paralytic seizure may deprive the partner of the power of communication through loss of speech and loss of power in his hands to write, while his mental faculties may still be unimpaired, and it is a question of some nicety whether such a case truly falls within section 35 (*a*) or (*b*) of the Partnership Act 1890.   The partnership agreement may expressly provide for dissolution of the partnership on the incapacity of a partner to perform his duties in the partnership, conferring on the active partner the right to serve notice of dissolution on the incapacitated partner if his incapacity endures for a specified period.   In *Peyton* v. *Mindham* [40a] the clause provided that if either partner was incapacitated from " performing his fair share of the work of the [medical] practice for more than nine consecutive calendar months . . . it shall be lawful for the other by notice to determine the partnership."   One partner suffered a cerebral haemorrhage and only returned to work a day before the expiry of the nine months' period, when he was restored in health but still restricted as to the active part which he might take in the practice.   The active partner, some eight days later, after receiving information as to the

---

[39] Pothier, *Traité du Contrat de Société* § 154.
[40] *Macredie's Trs.* v. *Lamond* (1886) 24 S.L.R. 114.
[40a] [1971] 3 All E.R. 1215.

incapacitated partner's condition, served notice of dissolution upon him. The incapacitated partner served a counter-notice on the active partner alleging persistent breaches of the partnership agreement by the active partner. It was held that a " fair share of the work of the practice " meant a share which the incapacitated partner might reasonably have been expected to undertake if he had not been incapacitated. The notice given by the active partner was therefore valid and the later counter-notice was of no effect.

Conduct prejudicially affecting the carrying on of the business

As it was originally drafted, section 35 (c) confined itself to the case where a partner had become liable to a criminal prosecution and the only decisions reported prior to the passing of the Act were concerned solely with that type of case.[41]   There is no reported case in Scotland of a similar nature but Bell [42] considered that uncontrollable habits of intoxication in a partner of a gunpowder factory would create such risks as to be a ground for dissolution of the partnership by the court.   Indeed he considered that the risks were such as to warrant the immediate entering of an act of dissolution in the firm's books.   In the form in which section 35 (c) has been enacted the ground of dissolution is extended beyond liability to criminal prosecution to cover any conduct which " in the opinion of the court, regard being had to the nature of the business, is calculated to prejudicially affect the carrying on of the business."   Since the ground of the application in this case is that the partner is " guilty " of conduct of the kind mentioned it is to be interpreted as confined to conduct in which the partner knowingly or wilfully engages so that an attempt to commit suicide while suffering from temporary insanity was not regarded as justification for an order for dissolution in Anon.[43]   While neglect, or negligent discharge, of a partner's duties under the partnership agreement may afford a ground of application for a dissolution order even where not wilful, this would be more appropriately considered under section 35 (d) of the Partnership Act 1890.[44]   The conduct founded upon in an application under section 35 (c) need not however be connected directly with the affairs of the partnership if, having regard to the nature of the partnership business, it is calculated to be to its prejudice.   If a partner in a firm engage in gambling transactions on the stock exchange, that may well be conduct affording a ground of dissolution of the partnership, even though the transactions are in no way connected with the business of the partnership.[45]   Conduct which infringes accepted professional standards in such a way as to lead to the censure of the partner by the governing body of the profession or to the

---

[41] See Essell v. Hayward (1860) 30 Beav. 158.   But an unreported case was referred to in argument in Anon. (1855) 2 K. & J. 441 where the partnership was dissolved on the ground of immoral conduct of one of the partners.
[42] Comm. II, 525.
[43] (1855) 2 K. & J. 441 at p. 446.
[44] See infra pp. 466–470.
[45] Pearce v. Foster (1886) 17 Q.B.D. 536.

removal of his name from the register of those professionally qualified will also found an application for a dissolution order.[46] It is thought that the words " calculated to prejudicially affect " used in section 35 (c) are not those most apt to convey the meaning which, in the light of pre-statute decisions, it may be intended to reflect.   The use of the word " calculated " in this connection could be regarded as requiring that in undertaking the conduct complained of the partner had intended or " calculated " its prejudicial effect upon the business of the partnership.   This, however, does not appear to be the construction placed upon the words by the courts. In *Carmichael* v. *Evans* [47] Carmichael, a partner of a firm of drapers, was convicted of travelling on a railway without a ticket with intent to avoid payment.   Under the partnership agreement it was provided that the partnership could be dissolved if any partner was guilty of a flagrant breach of any of his duties.   The remaining partners took Carmichael's conviction as occasion for the dissolution of the partnership under that provision and Carmichael applied for an injunction against them.   The court, however, refused to grant the injunction.   They held that since Carmichael's conviction involved dishonesty it fell within the provision of the partnership agreement and justified the remaining partners in giving notice of dissolution of the partnership.

In that case, as in the other cases noticed in relation to section 35 (c),[48] the issue before the court arose upon the terms of an express provision in the contract of copartnery.   These decisions are therefore of slender assistance in arriving at a view of the construction which the courts would place upon that part of the section.   Indeed, when the contractual provisions employed in the partnership agreements before the courts in these different cases are analysed and compared, it will be found that they have in view circumstances, or conduct, in which elements both of section 35 (c) and (d) are comprised.   They cannot, therefore, assist in the construction of the phrase " calculated to prejudicially affect " occurring in section 35 (c) since they are concerned with a provision which conflates conduct under that part of the section with conduct under section 35 (d) where the limiting words, if they be regarded as limiting words, do not appear.

The Scottish decisions in so far as they raise issues relevant to section 35 (c) of the Partnership Act 1890 are inconclusive.   In *Russell* v. *Russell* [49] it was held that the marriage of a female copartner dissolved the partnership but was not a sufficient reason for the appointment of a judicial factor for the purpose of winding up the firm.   The decision, while anachronistic

---

[46] *Hill* v. *Clifford* [1907] 2 Ch. 236; *Clifford* v. *Timms* [1908] A.C. 12. See also *Tattersall* v. *Sladen* [1928] Ch. 318.
[47] [1904] 1 Ch. 486.   Higgins (*The Law of Partnership in Australia and New Zealand* (2nd ed.) pp. 189–190) considers that " calculated " indicates the probable effect on the firm's business reputation; but it is unnecessary to prove that the conduct had an adverse effect. See *Pearce* v. *Foster, supra.*
[48] *Clifford* v. *Timms* [1908] A.C. 12; *Hill* v. *Clifford* [1907] 2 Ch. 236; *Tattersall* v. *Sladen* [1928] Ch. 318.
[49] (1874) 2 R. 93.

in modern law both in respect of the earlier view of the capacity of married women to administer their separate property and because it is a decision prior to the passing of the Partnership Act 1890, may still be of some slight assistance by way of analogy since the *ratio* on which the dissolution of the partnership was held to be justified was that in the state of the law then existing the property of a married woman was subjected to the control of her husband. The marriage of a female partner was to be considered as conduct calculated to affect prejudicially the partner's performance of her part of the partnership contract. It introduced into effective control of her share a person who was not in the contemplation of the parties to the partnership agreement and thus offended against the essential character of that agreement as one involving *delectus personae*. In *Macnab* v. *Macnab* [50] two of the partners of a firm presented a petition for dissolution of the partnership under section 35 of the Partnership Act 1890 on averment that the third partner was of intemperate habits, that when under the influence of drink he had been violent in conduct and language to his copartners and had assaulted them both, that he absented himself from the business for considerable periods and neglected his duties in connection with the firm. The partnership agreement stipulated that he would devote his whole time and attention to the business. The petition for dissolution was therefore grounded on (1) conduct under section 35 (c) and (2) persistent breach of the partnership agreement and conduct otherwise falling under section 35 (d) and on general grounds that it would be just and equitable to dissolve the partnership under the power contained in section 35 (f). The partner complained of, however, lodged answers denying the averments as to his conduct; and the court did not deliver judgment on the effectiveness of the grounds of dissolution, since, while it was held that procedure by petition was competent, it was held inexpedient in the circumstances, the parties being at variance on matters which required investigation by proof which would be better conducted in an ordinary action. The petition was accordingly dismissed.

Title to sue. It will be noticed that in an application under section 35 (c) as in one under section 35 (b), the application must be at the instance of a partner who is innocent of the conduct which is the subject of complaint.

Persistent breach of partnership agreement or other conduct destroying mutual confidence

This ground of application for a dissolution order, contained in section 35 (d), is in line with the decisions prior to the passing of the Partnership Act 1890. While what is regarded is conduct by the offending partner which renders it impracticable for the business to be carried on in partnership with him, the limitation imposed by the wording of section 35 (d) must be noted. What is struck at is (a) wilful and persistent breach of

[50] 1912 S.C. 421.

the partnership agreement and (b) conduct in other respects and in matters relating to the partnership business. In both cases the actings of the offending partner must be such that " it is not reasonably practicable for the other partner or partners to carry on the business in partnership with him." In the first place, it should be noted that what is involved is a partner's activity in some shape or form. It is conceivable that the continued presence of a particular partner in the firm may prove injurious to the credit of the firm or may cause loss of custom, but neither of these eventualities forms a ground for dissolution under section 35 (*d*). If the objections to a partner's continued presence in the firm supervene as a result of his having been discovered in discreditable conduct, even though that conduct is unrelated to the carrying on of the partnership business, then it may be possible for the other partners to apply for an order under section 35 (*c*). If the objections arise from his irascibility or tactlessness, then what is being complained of is his personal disposition rather than his conduct and section 35 (*d*) affords no ground for dissolution in that respect. In both cases it is possible that the business will be prejudicially affected but unless that can be established and an application made under section 35 (*c*), there will be no ground of dissolution which will necessarily arise under section 35 (*d*). It is perhaps in the area of the personal attributes of the partner as evinced in his dealings with his copartners that the line of distinction becomes most difficult to draw. The court will not feel itself called upon to interfere in mere squabbles within the partnership and the bad temper or the offensive or troublesome conduct of a partner will not be regarded as justifying an order for dissolution of the partnership.[51] To justify interference by the court in these circumstances the results of the disputes must have been to preclude the petitioning partners effectively taking part in the management of the firm [52] or the aspect of the conduct which is the subject of complaint must be such as to disrupt that mutual confidence among the partners which is of the essence if they are to continue together in business under the relations of partnership.[53] Section 35 (*d*) is concerned with conduct which makes it not reasonably practicable for the business to be carried on in partnership and, no doubt, it is a matter of degree when differences and disputes within a partnership reach that point. It has been held that " the misconduct must be such as to affect the business not merely by shaking its credit in the eyes of the world, but by rendering it impossible for the partners to conduct their business together according to the agreement which they have entered." [54] Where misconduct has gone so far as to shake the credit of the firm it may be thought that other grounds of dissolution more easily to be established will be provided in many cases under section 34 (*e*) and the implication in the statement above

---

[51] *Goodman* v. *Whitcomb* (1820) 1 J. & W. 589; *Marshall* v. *Colman* (1820) 2 J. & W. 266; *Wray* v. *Hutchinson* (1834) 2 Myl. & K. 235; *Roberts* v. *Eberhardt* (1853) Kay 148.
[52] See cases cited *supra* n. 51.
[53] *Smith* v. *Jeyes* (1841) 4 Beav. 503; *Harrison* v. *Tennant* (1856) 21 Beav. 482; *Liardet* v. *Adams*, 1 Mont. Part. 112 n.
[54] Lindley *op. cit.* p. 588, citing *Anon.* (1855) 2 K. & J. 441.

quoted that this circumstance must exist and be taken into account with other difficulties before an order will be made under section 34 (*d*) does not appear to be borne out by the reported decisions. In *A.B., Petitioner*,[55] a case which was decided before the passing of the Partnership Act 1890, a partner of a firm of solicitors petitioned for an order for dissolution of the partnership on averments that as a result of his copartner's extravagance the firm was drifting into bankruptcy. The conduct which was thus sought to be made the grounds for dissolution is poised between that which now would be covered by section 35 (*c*) and section 35 (*d*) of the Partnership Act 1890 and it would have been valuable to have had even a pre-statute decision in the point. But the petitioner died pending hearing of his application and, on his trustees and executors craving to be sisted in his place after his death, their application was refused by Lord Kinnear in the Outer House. In *Thomson, Petitioner*,[56] where the petitioning partner complained that his copartner had obtained money by signing the firm name on a cheque and then disappearing with the proceeds, there was little difficulty in finding that the conduct averred came within section 35 (*d*) as destroying the mutual confidence which should exist between the partners and an order for dissolution was granted and a judicial factor appointed to wind up the partnership effects. In a case which was decided upon its special facts rather as to interim protection of the partnership assets than in regard to a dissolution under section 35 (*d*) [57] the petitioning partner applied for sequestration of the partnership and the appointment of a judicial factor, on averments that because of protracted disputes with her son, who was the only other partner and who managed the partnership business, she had served six months' notice on him to dissolve the partnership. As she was unable to supervise personally the manner in which the firm's assets might be dealt with during the currency of the notice and subsequently in the process of winding up the partnership affairs and as she had reasonable grounds for apprehension that they might be dissipated or impaired while under her son's control, she applied for an interim order appointing a judicial factor which the Lord Ordinary granted. The son reclaimed and in the supervening circumstances brought to the notice of the court when the parties were heard, it was found that the judicial factor had taken little or no effective action to preserve the firm estate *ad interim* and that the parties had themselves in the interval concluded an agreement for settlement of their disputes and for the winding up of the firm independently of the judicial factor. In view of the laxity of the proceedings of the judicial factor under the interim order the court considered that the winding up must be completed regularly at the sight of the court and for that object the interim appointment was made final. It is clear that on its facts, that decision has no direct bearing upon the application of section 35 (*d*) of the Partnership Act 1890. It was not a case where a partner

---

[55] (1884) 22 S.L.R. 294.
[56] (1893) 1 S.L.T. 59.
[57] *McCulloch* v. *McCulloch*, 1953 S.C. 189. This case is considered later in relation to winding up. See *infra* pp. 521–522.

petitioned the court for an order to dissolve the firm. Rather it was a case where, having taken action to dissolve the partnership after the appropriate period of notice under the partnership agreement, the partner giving the notice invoked the assistance of the court in protecting the assets of the partnership and her own interest therein. Nevertheless, it is rather difficult to account for the petitioning partner's election to serve notice of dissolution rather than to apply for an order for dissolution under section 35 (*d*), an application which might have been conjoined with a request for appointment of a judicial factor to wind up the firm. It seems that if the petitioning partner's averments that she was excluded by her son's conduct from any effective supervision of what was done by him in the partnership were sufficient to move the Lord Ordinary to grant the interim appointment of the judicial factor, they would have been equally persuasive to move him to grant an order for dissolution. Indeed on logical grounds, her choice of remedy is difficult to appreciate. If the disputes were mere squabbles and would not lead the court to hold that there was a real breakdown in mutual confidence between the partners, it may be understandable that she chose to avail herself of a contractual right to terminate the partnership, but, if so, it is difficult to understand how it might be argued that mere squabbles which did not entail a real breakdown in mutual confidence might be averred in support of an application for interim preservation of the partnership assets. While, if (as it seems probable the court would have held) the facts as to the disputes were adequate to raise a case of conduct in matters relating to the partnership business which made it not reasonably practicable for her to carry on business in partnership with her son, it is difficult to see why she did not seek an order for immediate dissolution of the partnership which would have obviated the necessity for measures to preserve the partnership estate, at least in so far as these were *ad interim*.

It will be obvious from the foregoing discussion that it is difficult, if not indeed impossible, to announce what may be regarded as misconduct entitling the other partners to an order for dissolution in the shape of a general rule which is more definite in its terms than section 35 (*d*) of the Partnership Act 1890. Undoubtedly the most difficult area in which to apply the section is in the case of disputes or quarrels arising among the partners. Such quarrels will not of themselves move the court to intervene, but a state of habitual hostility between partners such as led to mutual accusations of gross misconduct may well be regarded by the court as evincing a destruction of that mutual confidence which ought to subsist among partners [58] and thus to justify order under section 35 (*d*). Other types of conduct which are complained of under that part of the section must have some relation to the partnership business [59] and must likewise be productive, or probably productive, of a breakdown in mutual

---

[58] *Atwood* v. *Maude* (1868) L.R. 3 Ch. 369, *per* Lord Cairns at p. 373.
[59] Conduct complained of under s. 35 (*c*) need not, however, be so related. See *supra* pp. 464–465.

confidence.[60] Where the conduct complained of involves the actual misappropriation by a partner of partnership funds,[61] or even maladministration through carelessness in neglecting to account for sums which he has received in respect of business which he has conducted for the firm, there should be little difficulty in bringing it within the terms of section 35 (*d*) of the Partnership Act 1890. In both cases the conduct is clearly related to the partnership affairs and even in the case of neglect to account for sums received it is destructive of mutual confidence, whereas if actual dishonesty has taken place, the destruction of that confidence is clearly and completely consequential upon it.

Partnership business carried on at a loss

Since partnership is the relation " which subsists between persons carrying on a business in common with a view of profit " [62] it is, by definition, the intention of the partners that the association will result in profit and not in loss. It is, however, no logical result of the application of that definition of the relationship that if a loss be incurred, that by itself will dissolve or terminate the contract of partnership.[63] The vicissitudes of commercial life are such that that interpretation of the definition of partnership would render the basis of the relationship so uncertain and impermanent that it would be virtually impossible to treat of the legal implications of the partnership in any meaningful manner. Yet it remains an element in the definition of partnership that the partners should carry on the business in common with a view of profit and it is possible to envisage circumstances overtaking a partnership in which it will no longer be reasonably possible for the partners to cling to the belief that their continuing association will be " with a view of profit." In such circumstances one of the essential features of the partnership has disappeared and since any continuing association of the members of the firm will lack one of the elements which contribute to its being regarded as a partnership, it is apparent, in theory at least, that for any such continuing association to be persisted in as a partnership presents legal difficulty. The determination of the point of time, however, when the partners have finally departed from the conduct of the business with a view of profit, as distinct from nursing a business which is, at the moment, and even over a considerable period, showing a loss, with a view to an ultimate profit, is a commercial decision rather than a legal one. Thus there is no general principle in law that a partnership will automatically cease to be regarded by the law as such on an overall view by the courts as to the potentiality of the particular business to earn a profit. Any such doctrine would involve the court in taking a commercial view of a partnership business, which might not be shared by the partners actively engaged in that business. In that

---

[60] *Harrison* v. *Tennant* (1856) 21 Beav. 482; *Greenaway* v. *Greenaway* (1939) 84 S.J. 43.
[61] *Thomson, Petitioner* (1893) 1 S.L.T. 59.
[62] Partnership Act 1890, s. 1 (1).
[63] The " badge of partnership " is the immediate purpose of making profit on the part of the partners and not the actual fortunes of the firm. See Gow, *Mercantile and Industrial Law of Scotland*, p. 540.

situation it is not surprising that the law has not involved the courts in decisions of that kind. On the other hand, the partners themselves may find a situation developing in the business of the firm which enforces upon them as a purely business decision that the business can no longer be continued save at a loss; and it is obviously desirable that in that situation a partnership which has been entered into with a view of profit should be dissolved. Inevitably, in coming to a business decision of that kind, at any given moment of time, the partners may not be unanimous. Some may take the view earlier than others. In that they may be correct and the others over-sanguine as to future prospects of the business; yet it is possible that those favouring the view that the business can no longer in the long term be carried on save at a loss may conceivably be unduly pessimistic. With these considerations in view, it seems clear that making the future circumstances of the firm a ground for dissolution, as is enacted in section 35 (e) of the Partnership Act 1890, is the only approach which the law can usefully adopt in such cases.

It will be recollected that section 35 (e) permits the court to decree the dissolution of a partnership ". . . when the business of the partnership can only be carried on at a loss." Admittedly, these words entail that the court will still be required to adjudicate on the commercial potentialities of a particular business, sometimes, though not necessarily always, in the face of conflicting views held by different partners of the firm. Where the application is made by the partners unanimously, the situation will be one with which the court is by experience and expertise well equipped to deal. The conflicting rights and interests of the firm, its creditors and its partners are matters implicit in an application of this kind for dissolution which are peculiarly within the competence and the control of the courts. Where, however, the courts are entertaining an application by some of the partners who consider that the firm can only be carried on at a loss and that is opposed by other partners who maintain that it may still in the future be carried on at a profit, the decision is a more difficult one. Indeed if the words of section 35 (e) were literally construed, the court would be faced with an almost superhuman task. It would indeed be an Olympian decision which maintained that a business could *only* be carried on in the future at a loss in the face of the evidence and representations of some of those actively engaged in that business that it will ultimately break through to a profit. In these circumstances, the construction placed upon section 35 (e) by the English courts [64] will be regarded as highly persuasive in the Scottish courts, *i.e.* that what the words of section 35 (e) must be construed to mean is that there is a real practical impossibility that the business will make a profit in future. In that case Farwell J. refused an application by one partner in a firm of stevedores and riggers who alleged that the partnership could only be carried on at a loss. The firm was in fact making a loss at the time of the application but this was attributed by the partners who opposed the application in part to the mismanagement of the plaintiff

[64] *Handyside* v. *Campbell* (1901) 17 T.L.R. 623.

himself and in part to his protracted absence from the business due to illness. Farwell J. considered that if there were special circumstances, as he held there were in the case before him, to which the loss could be attributed and if the loss could not be traced to any inherent defect in the business, the court could not infer an impossibility that profit would be earned by the business.[65] This ground of dissolution was also recognised in the decisions on the basis of the law prior to the passing of the Partnership Act 1890, some of which may be still of assistance in delimiting the field within which the rule operates. Thus it was held to justify an order for winding up that the capital of the firm as originally contributed had been exhausted, that some of the partners were either unable or unwilling to contribute further capital or to advance more money to the firm and that the business could not continue, save at a loss, unless such further resources were made available to the firm.[66] It is not essential in such cases to prove that the business is actually insolvent or even financially embarrassed. If after all the terms of the partnership agreement as to contribution of capital and the like have been implemented, the result of continuing the business will be to incur certain loss, then the court will, on the application of any partner, grant an order for the dissolution of the firm.[67] In the pre-statute Scottish decision of *Miller* v. *Walker* [68] a joint adventure in a lead mine had been unsuccessfully pursued for three years. The court held that one of the two partners involved was entitled to put an end to the joint adventure since " the said mine has not hitherto yielded any profit " and " there is no reasonable prospect of profits being realised in the future." If the firm is in fact clearly insolvent and becoming more so for every day of its continuance in business the English courts will interfere on a motion to do so and will appoint a person to sell the business and wind up the affairs of the partnership.[69] In similar circumstances the Scottish courts will entertain an application for an order for dissolution and for appointment of a judicial factor. It will not necessarily be sufficient to obtain such an order from the court that the firm is by reason of a partner's extravagance " drifting into bankruptcy." [70] While the case cited cannot because of its special facts be relied on for any definite view of the attitude which the court would take to an application on those grounds it seems tolerably clear that the application would not readily fall within section 35 (*e*) of the Partnership Act 1890 for there is not implicit in the averments that the firm is drifting into bankruptcy as a result of a partner's extravagance any necessary conclusion that " the business of the partnership can only be carried on at a loss."

[65] *Ibid.* at p. 624.
[66] *Jennings* v. *Baddeley* (1856) 3 K. & J. 78.
[67] *Jennings* v. *Baddeley, supra*; *Baring* v. *Dix* (1786) 1 Cox 213; *Bailey* v. *Ford* (1843) 13 Sim. 495.
[68] (1875) 3 R. 242. See also *Barr* v. *Speirs*, May 18, 1802, unreported; see Bell, Com. II, 523.
[69] *Bailey* v. *Ford, supra.*
[70] *A.B. Petitioner* (1884) 22 S.L.R. 294. In that case, however, the petitioning partner had died before the petition was heard and the Lord Ordinary refused the application of his executors to be sisted in his place.

Date of dissolution

When an order is made by the court for the dissolution of a partnership under section 35 (*e*) there appears to be no reported case which lays it down that the effective date of the dissolution shall be at any particular time. Presumably the court will order dissolution with effect from the date of the order pronounced, though where the petitioner asks for interim preservation of the partnership assets the court might in some cases ante-date the dissolution. In *Miller* v. *Walker* [71] the Lord President stated that the partner applying to the court was not entitled to put an end to the joint adventure at a day's notice but was entitled to have it settled in the course of the action that the adventure was to be brought to an end. In that case the remedy sought was a declarator that the initial agreement of partnership in the joint adventure " has all along been and is now null and void and that the same has now fallen and come to an end . . . ," two conclusions for declarator which are perplexing to reconcile. From the opinions of the judges it appears that the two conclusions were, or at least were treated as, alternatively for reduction of the agreement or for declarator that it was at an end. On the second of these conclusions, the Lord President (Inglis) said,[72] " Now the case which is alleged on the part of the pursuers is that nothing has been made out of this mine during the three years it has been worked, and that there is no reasonable prospect of anything being made out of it. If that be so, the pursuers are entitled to put an end to the adventure. They are not entitled to do so at a day's notice but they are entitled to have it settled in the course of the action that the adventure is to be brought to an end." In the result the inter-locutor pronounced stated *inter alia* " Find that in these circumstances the pursuers are entitled to put an end to the joint adventure. . . . Therefore find, decern and declare that the said contract of joint adventure has come to an end. . . ." [73]

Circumstances rendering it just and equitable that the partnership be dissolved

The power under section 35 (*f*) to the court to make an order dissolving the partnership in circumstances which make it " just and equitable " to do so, is the final power succeeding on a number of clauses conferring power to order dissolution on more specific grounds. In this treatment of dissolution of the partnership, the Partnership Act 1890 appears to follow the pattern of the Companies Act 1862.[74] It is therefore probable, although the point does not appear to have been raised in regard to section 35 (*f*) of the Partnership Act 1890, that that clause of the section will not be construed *ejusdem generis* with the preceding clauses of section 35 following the analogy of the construction by the courts of the similar provisions in

---

[71] (1875) 3 R. 242.
[72] *Ibid.* at pp. 249–250.
[73] *Ibid.* p. 253.
[74] s. 79 (5). Now Companies Act 1948, s. 222 (*f*).

the Companies Acts.[75]   The ambit of section 35 (*f*) is on any view of its
terms very wide and general.   *Olver* v. *Hillier* [76] appears to be the only
reported case in which the just and equitable rule has been invoked in
support of an application for an order to dissolve a partnership and the
report is not particularly helpful on this aspect.   The application was
grounded on section 35 (*d*) and (*f*) and the only averments noticed by the
court [77] were to the effect that the defendant had so conducted himself in
matters relating to the partnership business that it was not reasonably
practicable for the plaintiff to carry on the business in partnership with
him.   That averment falls clearly within section 35 (*d*) and indeed practically repeats its wording.   The plaintiff, however, pleaded further that
in the circumstances, it was just and equitable that the partnership be
dissolved and though the report is silent as to the nature of these circumstances, the court to some extent recognised the case as falling under
section 35 (*f*) in directing attention to the difficulty of transferring to the
arbitrator the power, expressly conferred upon the court, of deciding
whether it is just and equitable that the partnership should be dissolved.[78]

Section 35 (*f*) is not clearly reflected as a ground for dissolution in the
cases decided before the passing of the Partnership Act 1890 and indeed it
appears to be the accepted view [79] that it is intended to extend the scope of
the court's power in this respect by conferring on the court a discretionary
power to dissolve the partnership in cases not covered by section 35 (*a*) to
(*e*) and not therefore clearly traceable in the pre-existing law.   The pre-
statute decisions are therefore of uncertain help on this point though in
Montgomery v. *Forrester* [80] there is indication of the court directing the
dissolution of a joint adventure in circumstances which were not expressly
quadrate with any of the grounds of dissolution afforded under section
35 (*a*) to (*e*).   Any earlier decisions which have been appealed to as
illustrating the application of the " just and equitable " doctrine tend to
merge into one or other of the grounds of dissolution previously specified
in section 35 [81] and it is difficult to speculate what circumstances not at least
ejusdem generis with the more specific grounds mentioned earlier in the
section are comprised within section 35 (*f*).

Treatment of private limited company as a quasi-partnership

Oddly enough, the situation in which the courts have given most

---

[75] See *Suburban Hotel Co.* (1867) 2 Ch. 737 (proceeding on Companies Act 1862, s. 79 (5));
Re Yenidje Tobacco Co. [1916] 2 Ch. 426 at p. 435; *Baird* v. *Lees*, 1924 S.C. 83 (Companies
(Consolidation) Act 1908, s. 129 (vi)); *Loch* v. *John Blackwood Ltd.* [1924] A.C. 783
(proceeding on a section of the Companies Act of Barbados expressed in terms similar
to Companies Act 1948, s. 222 (*f*)).
[76] [1959] 2 All E.R. 220.
[77] The real point at issue was whether the application for dissolution should be stayed in
view of the terms of the arbitration clause in the partnership agreement.   On this see
infra pp. 480–484.
[78] *Olver* v. *Hillier*, *supra*, *per* Roxburgh J. at p. 221.
[79] See Lindley, *op. cit.* pp. 590–591; Green's *Encyclopaedia of the Laws of Scotland*, Vol. 11
sub voce " Partnership " § 148.
[80] (1791) Hume 748.
[81] See *e.g.* Lindley, *op. cit.* p. 591 citing *Harrison* v. *Tennant* (1856) 21 Beav. 482; *Electric
Telegraph Co. of Ireland* (1856) 22 Beav. 471; *Baring* v. *Dix* (1786) 1 Cox 213.

consideration to the wording of section 35 (*f*) of the Partnership Act 1890 has been where the application has been for the winding up of private limited companies. There is a tract of authority in both the Scottish and the English courts to the effect that where the private limited company is, in substance, a partnership and where the circumstances averred in the application would have justified an order for the dissolution of a partnership under section 35 of the Partnership Act 1890 the court may order the winding up of the limited company on the ground that it is " just and equitable " to do so in terms of section 222 (*f*) of the Companies Act 1948 or the corresponding provision in earlier Companies Acts.[82] In such cases, however, the rights of the partners must be determined within the framework of the company's articles of association and if the conduct complained of is conduct which is lawful in terms of the articles of association then the court will require to be satisfied that there was a lack of probity in the conduct of the company's affairs which is the subject of complaint.[83] But later cases have extended the application of the rule. As was stated by Megarry J.[84] " As it is the contract between the parties which is of importance, then it seems to me that one must have regard not merely to what the articles say, but also to what the parties are shown to have agreed in any other manner." A detailed consideration of this topic so far as affecting the winding up of private limited companies has no relevance in this treatise.[85] What is of direct relevance is the effect of any such decisions in elucidating the circumstances in which the court will grant an order for dissolution of a *partnership* under section 35 (*f*) of the Partnership Act 1890. It will be noticed that while the cases cited are all applications for winding up under the " just and equitable " rule [86] it does not necessarily follow that the circumstances on which the court founded its order for winding up the limited company themselves fall under the " just and equitable " rule in section 35 (*f*) of the Partnership Act 1890. When considering whether it is just and equitable that an order be made for the winding up of a limited company which has in effect been a mask for what in substance is truly a partnership, the court will give weight to any circumstances which would have justified an order for dissolution under section 35 of the Partnership Act 1890 had the business been conducted under a partnership agreement. But these circumstances need not fall under section 35 (*f*). Circumstances which would justify the dissolution of a partnership under section 35 (*a*) to (*e*) may equally receive weight in

---

[82] *Re Yenidje Tobacco Co. Ltd.* [1916] 2 Ch. 426; *Symington* v. *Symington's Quarries Ltd.* (1905) 8 F. 121, *per* Lord McLaren at p. 130; *Loch* v. *John Blackwood Ltd.* [1924] A.C. 783; *Re Davis & Collett Ltd.* [1935] Ch. 693; *Baird* v. *Lees*, 1924 S.C. 83; *Elder* v. *Elder & Watson Ltd.*, 1952 S.C. 49.

[83] See *per* Lord President (Cooper) in *Elder* v. *Elder & Watson Ltd., supra* at p. 55.

[84] *Re Fildes Brothers Ltd.* [1970] 1 All E.R. 923 at p. 926. See also *Lewis* v. *Hass & Another,* 1970 S.L.T. (Notes) 67.

[85] On this point see, in addition to the cases above cited, *Re Cooper & Sons* [1937] 1 Ch. 392; *Re Expanded Plugs Ltd.* [1966] 1 W.L.R. 514; *Re K/9 Meat Supplies (Guildford) Ltd.* [1966] 1 W.L.R. 1112; *Re Lundie Brothers Ltd.* [1965] 1 W.L.R. 1051; *Re Westbourne Galleries* [1971] Ch. 799.

[86] Companies Act 1948, s. 222 (*f*).

coming to a decision whether it is just and equitable to wind up a limited
company of that kind. Indeed many of such decisions have been chiefly
concerned with the question whether there has been a destruction of confidence among the parties so that it is not reasonably practicable for the
applicant to continue to carry on business in association with the other,
or others, which is the case covered (in a partnership) by section 35 (d) of
the Partnership Act 1890.[87] Many of them involve a deadlock in the
conduct of the company's affairs or an oppressive exclusion of the applicant
from his rights. Such cases give no real guide on the question of the true
construction and content of section 35 (f) of the Partnership Act 1890.
Yet there is indication in some of the judicial pronouncements that section
35 (f) will be read to cover a wider area than that covered in section 35
(a) to (e). In *Elder* v. *Elder & Watson Ltd.*[88] the Lord President said,
"Where the 'just and equitable' jurisdiction has been applied in cases
of this type, the circumstances have always, I think, been such as to warrant
the inference that there has been, at least, an unfair abuse of powers and an
impairment of confidence in the probity with which the company's affairs
are being conducted, as distinguished from mere resentment on the part of
a minority at being out-voted on some issue of domestic policy." In *Re
Yenidje Tobacco Company Ltd.*[89] Lord Cozens-Hardy M.R. said, "If ever
there was a case of deadlock I think it exists here: but whether it exists or
not, I think the circumstances are such that we ought to apply, if necessary,
the analogy of the partnership law and to say that this company is now in a
state which could not have been contemplated by the parties when the
company was formed and which ought to be terminated as soon as
possible." In both dicta the words used are of wide and general implication. It is true that it might be possible to bring "impairment of
confidence in the probity with which the company's affairs are being
conducted" within the analogy of section 35 (d) of the Partnership Act
1890, and even Lord Cooper's more general phrase "abuse of powers"
should, it is thought from its context in his judgment, be related to the
sort of conduct which, in a partnership, would be complained of under
that subsection.[90] While the power of the court to give weight under
section 35 (f) to conduct in a partnership which, though not readily to be
subsumed under any of the preceding clauses (a) to (e) of the section, should
yet in equity be held to justify a dissolution appears to be recognised in the
expressions used by the judges in the winding-up cases, it is important to
distinguish the occasions when the judge is referring to the "just and
equitable" doctrine which justifies his granting an order under section 222

---

[87] *Re Yenidje Tobacco Co. Ltd.*, *supra*; *Loch* v. *Blackwood Ltd.*, *supra*; *Elder* v. *Elder &
Watson Ltd.*, *supra*, *per* the Lord President at p. 56.
[88] 1952 S.C. 49 at p. 55.
[89] [1916] 2 Ch. 426 at p. 432.
[90] The distinction drawn in the passage quoted between abuse of power and impairment of
confidence on the one hand and "mere resentment at being outvoted" on the other,
suggests this; and elsewhere in his judgment the Lord President relates the conduct he is
considering particularly to analogous conduct in a partnership falling under s. 35 (d) of
the Partnership Act 1890. See *Elder* v. *Elder & Watson Ltd.*, 1952 S.C. 49 at p. 56.

(*f*) of the Companies Act 1948 and which permits him to consider the company as if it were a partnership, from the cases where, having done so, he is proceeding to consider whether, treating the company as being in substance a partnership, he then examines the conduct complained of to determine whether it falls within the scope of section 35 of the Partnership Act 1890. In none of the cases considered can it be maintained that the court applied section 35 (*f*) to the conduct of the affairs of the company. In most of them section 35 (*d*) would have justified the order in the case of a partnership. Perhaps the only inference which can be drawn with safety is that in the company winding-up cases the courts were careful to keep open the question of the conduct which under section 35 (*f*) would justify the dissolution of a partnership and in applying section 35 to the case of winding up before them made no further use of section 35 (*f*) than to support any imperfection in the analogy (1) between equating conduct occurring between members of a company and conduct occurring between partners and (2) between the articles of association of the company and the agreement of partnership between the partners. That said, however, the general words used by Lord Cozens-Hardy M.R. in the passage above quoted tend to suggest a broader basis for an order of dissolution than is contained in clauses (*a*) to (*e*) of section 35 of the Partnership Act 1890; and since he expressly founded that proposition upon " the analogy of the partnership law " it is possible to argue that he was then envisaging that cases might occur in partnership which did not justify an order under the earlier clauses of the section but would fall within the terms of section 35 (*f*). The possibility of the court having urged upon it in a future case circumstances of some cogency as calling for a dissolution of the partnership, while at the same time those circumstances do not fall within the ambit of section 35 (*a*) to (*e*), can readily be envisaged. It is not so easy to particularise with prophetic insight what those cases might be. Oddly enough, the only reported decision which appears to have followed the broad principle enunciated by Lord Cozens-Hardy is the early Scottish decision in *Montgomery* v. *Forrester* [91] where the court ordered the dissolution of a joint adventure on the ground that a ship purchased by the joint adventurers had, after trial, been found to be unsuitable for the purposes of the joint adventure. On the analogy of the decisions reached in applications for winding up of private limited companies, it appears that in applying the "just and equitable" jurisdiction the court will take into consideration the terms of the partnership agreement but those terms will not fetter the court in the exercise of its discretion.[92] In issues of this kind, it will obviously be relevant to consider the contractual terms existing among the parties,[93] but the conduct complained of, while possible to be

---

[91] (1791) Hume 748.

[92] *Re American Pioneer Leather Co. Ltd.* [1918] 1 Ch. 556.

[93] Though the contractual terms may not be confined to the provisions of the partnership agreement, just as in the case of a company they may not be confined to the articles of association. See *per* Megarry J. in *Re Fildes Brothers Ltd.* [1970] 1 All E.R. 923 at p. 926.

justified by appeal to a contractual provision, may yet be an abuse of the power conferred by that provision.[94]

Date of dissolution under section 35 (f)

There is no mention in the statutory provision as to the date when the court order effecting the dissolution will be made operative. In view of the wide discretion as to what is " just and equitable " as supporting an order for dissolution, there may be room for argument that the same discretionary considerations may affect the date from which the court makes the order effective. The rule of the pre-existing law was that where an order of the court is necessary for the dissolution of the partnership the dissolution will, in the absence of special reasons, be effective from the date of the order.[95] That rule appears to be preserved in terms of section 46 of the Partnership Act 1890. It will be observed, however, that the rule is qualified so that account may be taken of special circumstances and in the exercise of its discretionary jurisdiction under section 35 (f) there is room for the court deciding upon a date other than the date of the order, if the interests of equity and justice demand it.[96] The normal rule will, however, be that the dissolution is made effective from the date of the order.

Cases where notice of dissolution served prior to application under section 35

In some cases the partnership will have been dissolved by notice prior to the application to the court under any of the grounds mentioned in section 35, and the real question decided in the order of the court will be whether the occasion for the service of notice of dissolution was justified. In cases where the decision of the court is favourable to the right to a dissolution in the circumstances, and the notice has been effectual, the order of the court will make the dissolution effective from the date of the purported dissolution by notice of the partner or partners. That rule will apply whether the notice was given under a partnership at will[97] or under a special provision of the partnership agreement.[98]

Assignation by a partner of his share

Though the point was not much canvassed in the earlier decisions, it would appear that prior to the passing of the Partnership Act 1890 the assignation by a partner of his share in the firm accompanied by notice thereof to his partners operated as a dissolution of the partnership, at

[94] See per the Lord President in Elder v. Elder & Watson Ltd., 1952 S.C. 49 at p. 55 and supra p. 476.
[95] Lyon v. Tweddell (1881) 17 Ch.D. 529; Besch v. Frolich (1842) 1 Ph. 172.
[96] Essell v. Hayward (1860) 30 Beav. 158.
[97] Mellersh v. Keen (1859) 27 Beav. 236.
[98] Robertson v. Lockie (1846) 15 Sim. 285; Bagshaw v. Parker (1847) 10 Beav. 532; Jones v. Lloyd (1874) L.R. 18 Eq. 265.

least where it was a partnership at will.[99]   The position in England was obscure where the partnership was for an agreed period of endurance, though the decisions as to this aspect of the law may be considered to have depended to some extent at least upon the special circumstances of the cases concerned.[1]   In Scotland it was the law even before the passing of the Partnership Act 1890 that an assignation by a partner of his share to a third party was in no sense improper.   Erskine states that " if any of the partners shall assume a third person into partnership with him, such assumed person becomes partner, not to the company, but to the assumer. The company are not bound to regard the second contract formed by the assumption, which is limited to the share of the partner assuming.   He still continues, with respect to the company, the sole proprietor of the share, and must sustain all actions concerning it." [2]   In *Cassels* v. *Stewart* [3] words fall from the judges which make it abundantly clear that there was nothing in the Scottish common law to prevent a partner assigning his share to a third party " as long as that does not interfere with the conduct of the company " (*per* Lord Moncreiff) or provided that the assigning partner " continued a partner and fulfilled all the conditions of the contract " (*per* Lord Gifford).   The important point lies in the qualifying words, which suggest that, despite the strong assertion of a partner's right to assign his share, the Scots law did not in practical terms differ widely from the English common law.   The dilemma for the common lawyer in both countries was that, on the one hand, while the assignation did not sever the association of the assigning partner with the partnership, it left him with little or no interest in the business of the partnership and on that score the continuing copartners might justly contend that they had not in contemplation when they entered the partnership the prospect of continuing in partnership with a person who had no real interest in the partnership business. On the other hand, where an agreed period of duration had been placed on the partnership, to hold that intimation of an assignation of a partner's share automatically dissolved the partnership would be to allow a partner who assigned his share by that means to dissolve a partnership which otherwise he would not be entitled to dissolve.

Assignation of share under section 31 of the Partnership Act 1890.   This section has already been noticed.   Its effect is to declare clearly that the effect of such an assignation is to give the assignee no right as against the other partners, during the continuance of the partnership, to intervene in the management or to require an accounting.   But section 31 expressly envisages that a partnership will continue despite the assignation, and nowhere in the Partnership Act 1890 is such an assignation made a ground

---

[99] *Sturgeon* v. *Salmon* (1906) 22 T.L.R. 584. For a discussion in a Scottish case as to the significance of intimation of the assignation see *Cassels* v. *Stewart* (1881) 8 R.(H.L.) 1.

[1] See *e.g. Heath* v. *Sansom* (1831) 4 B. & Ad. 175 (where the assignment was by one partner to his only copartner); *Jefferys* v. *Smith* (1826) 3 Russ. 158 (where in terms of the partnership agreement the shares were transferable).

[2] Erskine, *Inst.* III: 3: 22.

[3] (1879) 6 R. 936 *per* Lord Moncreiff and Lord Gifford in the Court of Session. The judgment was later affirmed on appeal to the House of Lords (1881) 8 R.(H.L.) 1.

of dissolution of the partnership. It seems clear, therefore, that *per se* the
fact that a partner has assigned his share will not entitle his copartners to
dissolve the partnership.[4] Much less will it afford to the assigning partner
any ground for himself dissolving the partnership. The assignation might,
however, be taken into consideration by the court as a circumstance to
be weighed in deciding whether an order should be made for dissolution
of the partnership under section 35 (*f*). In many partnerships which are
for an agreed term of endurance, the agreement itself will provide expressly
that in the event of assignation by any partner of his share, the remaining
partners may treat the assignation as a ground for dissolution. Such a
clause will be treated as conferring an option on the other partners to
dissolve the firm even where the clause states that the firm shall " stand
dissolved " in such an event.[5] In no circumstances will the assignee be
permitted to plead the assignation as a ground of dissolution.

Arbitration clause as affecting dissolution of the partnership

There is nothing in the law of partnership which affects the general
principle that where the parties have agreed to the disposal of questions
arising between them by arbitration, the decision of such questions should
be left to the adjudicator who has been selected by the parties. Thus if the
partners have submitted a disputed question whether the partnership
should be dissolved to an arbiter, that arbiter will have the power to award
a dissolution of the partnership.[6] In Scotland it has been decided that the
arbiter is not ousted merely because an action between the partners arising
out of the partnership agreement is pending in court; and that the power
given to the court to order dissolution under section 35 of the Partnership
Act 1890 does not exclude the matter of the dissolution of the partnership
being submitted to arbitration.[7] In England, where arbitration proceedings are more rigorously controlled by the courts, if proceedings are
brought in court, the court has a discretion to refuse a stay of those proceedings which is moved for on the ground that the parties have agreed to
submit the question to arbitration, and it was stated in one case [8] that a
question of dissolution was not a suitable one to be left to an arbitrator to
decide. That, however, in view of other reported decisions in the English
courts, cannot be regarded as a general proposition of law but rather as
what has been termed " a proposition of good sense," [9] *i.e.* on the facts
of the case the court exercised its discretion to refuse a stay of proceedings,
since those facts related to a dissolution of the partnership and where such

---

[4] The provisions of s. 31 may usefully be contrasted with the terms of s. 33 (2) which (in
England) expressly provides for dissolution at the option of the other partners if any
partner suffers his share to be charged for his separate debt.

[5] *Campbell* v. *Campbell* (1893) 6 Report (ed. Mews) 137.

[6] *Plews* v. *Baker* (1873) L.R. 16 Eq. 564; *Kitchen* v. *Turnbull* (1871) 20 W.R. 253; *Vawdrey*
v. *Simpson* [1896] 1 Ch. 166; *Machin* v. *Bennett* [1900] W.N. 146.

[7] *Hackston* v. *Hackston and Anr.*, 1956 S.L.T. (Notes) 38.

[8] *Joplin* v. *Postlethwaite* (1889) 61 L.T. 629; and see *Turnell* v. *Sanderson* (1891) 60 L.J.Ch.
703.

[9] *Russell on Arbitration* (18th ed.) p. 167.

a question is disputed that may induce the court to refuse a stay of proceedings.[10]   In a case where the articles of partnership between A and B provided that if the business should not be conducted to B's satisfaction he should have power to give notice to A to terminate the partnership and also that any difference in relation to the partnership should be referred to arbitration, B gave A notice of termination under the articles and A sued B alleging fraud for a declaration that the notice was void and for an order restraining B from announcing the dissolution of the partnership.   B moved the court to have these matters referred to the arbitrator in terms of the arbitration clause and, since A had failed to make out a prima facie case of fraud to the satisfaction of the court, it was held that the dispute between the partners must be so referred.[11]

In view of the difference in the law of arbitration in Scotland, the English decisions upon the effect of an arbitration clause in a deed of partnership must be received with some caution, and in particular those cases which depend for their *ratio decidendi* upon a discretionary power in the court to refuse to stay proceedings in court on the ground of an agreement to submit the question to arbitration cannot be applied in Scotland where the court asserts no such discretionary power,[12] and where the submission is regarded as a contract " by which the parties commit to the entire and exclusive cognisance of the Arbiter or Arbiters the whole matters submitted. . . ."[13]   Some of the English decisions, however, proceed upon more general considerations of legal principle and may be of persuasive authority in the Scottish courts.   Thus it will be necessary to examine the arbitration clause itself to ensure that on a true construction of its terms it is habile to cover the submission of a dispute as to the dissolution of the partnership.   Where the partnership deed provides for arbitration if during the continuance of the partnership or at any time thereafter difference should arise " in regard to the construction of any of the articles herein contained, or to any division, act or thing to be made or done in pursuance hereof, or to any other matter or thing relating to the partnership affairs," it was held that the terms of the arbitration clause conferred power on the arbitrator to award dissolution of the partnership and to order the return of a premium paid by one of the partners as provided for in section 40 of the Partnership Act 1890.[14]   A similar construction was placed upon a clause providing that " all disputes which shall either during the partnership or afterwards arise between the partners . . . touching this agreement . . . or any account, valuation or division of assets . . . shall be referred to a single arbitrator." [15]   In *Hackston* v.

[10] *Barnes* v. *Youngs* [1898] 1 Ch. 414; *Olver* v. *Hillier* [1959] 2 All E.R. 220.   But see *Belfield* v. *Bourne* (1894) 69 L.T. 786; *Melgrave & Melgrave* v. *Finer, The Times* Feb. 18 and June 4, 1959.
[11] *Russell* v. *Russell* (1880) 14 Ch.D. 471.
[12] Irons & Melville, *Arbitration* p. 128; *Holmes Oil Co.* v *Pumpherston Oil Co. Ltd.* (1891) 18 R.(H.L.) 52.
[13] *Per* Lord Cranworth L.C. in *Lang* v. *Brown* (1855) 2 Macq. 93.
[14] *Belfield* v. *Bourne* (1894) 69 L.T. 786.
[15] *Olver* v. *Hillier* [1959] 2 All E.R. 220, though in that case the English court in its discretion refused to stay proceedings in court.

Hackston and Another [16] the clause was expressed in the wide terms frequently used in Scottish agreements of partnership—" if any question, dispute or difference shall arise between the parties . . . as to the meaning of these presents or their rights or liabilities hereunder or in the winding up of the partnership or any other matter, thing or claim relating to or arising out of the partnership or the affairs thereof during its subsistence or after its termination, the same shall be referred to the decision of the arbiter." That clause was held to confer on the arbiter the power of issuing an award as to the dissolution of the partnership.

Questions of fraud

It has been held [17] that even where the terms of arbitration clause are wide and general covering " any difference which shall arise between the partners " that clause will not exclude action in court by one partner against his copartner on the ground of illegal, fraudulent and malicious violation and breach of the contract by attempting to create a fictitious bankruptcy and destroy the partnership. The same principle was noticed, though on the facts of the particular case it was not applied in the English case of *Russell* v. *Russell* [18] where the court held that the plaintiff had not made out a prima facie case of fraud. An ancillary submission of the kind which has been under examination is to be construed having due regard to the nature of the deed in which it is embodied [19] but no reported case appears to have been decided in England directly upon that general principle and such cases would probably now be disposed of under the express power given to the English courts to order that the agreement to arbitrate shall cease to have effect and to revoke any submission of the dispute so far as is necessary to enable the charge of fraud to be investigated by the court.[20]

Cases of dissolution under section 35 of the Partnership Act 1890

Since section 35 of the Partnership Act 1890 confers on the court the power to dissolve a partnership upon application on any of the grounds specified in the section, the argument has been advanced in several cases that an award of dissolution of the partnership by an arbiter on any of those grounds is not valid even where the arbitration clause is drawn in very wide terms, since the Partnership Act 1890 confides the jurisdiction to deal with such questions in the courts. That view seems to be rejected in the judgment of Roxburgh J. in *Olver* v. *Hillier* [21] where after considering the dictum of Bowen L.J. in *Joplin* v. *Postlethwaite*,[22] he said,[23]

[16] 1956 S.L.T. (Notes) 38.
[17] *Lauder* v. *Wingate* (1852) 14 D. 633.
[18] (1880) 14 Ch.D. 471. See *supra* p. 481.
[19] Irons & Melville, *Arbitration*, p. 73.
[20] Arbitration Act 1950, s. 24 (2).
[21] [1959] 2 All E.R. 220.
[22] (1889) 61 L.T. 629 at p. 632: " Now, one of the matters to be determined here is, whether or not the partnership should be dissolved. It does not seem to me that that is a matter which should be determined by arbitration."
[23] [1959] 2 All E.R. at p. 221.

" Against that, counsel for the defendant very properly cited *Vawdrey* v. *Simpson*.[24] In that case, Chitty J. granted a stay. It does not seem to me (though the position is not clear) that the relief there was sought under para. (*f*) of section 35 but only under para. (*d*). At any rate Chitty J. did not advert to a difficulty which troubles me, *viz*., the difficulty of transferring to the arbitrator the power expressly conferred on the court of deciding, not what the facts are, but whether, on the facts as found, it is just and equitable to decree a dissolution. I do not say that, as a matter of construction, the contract may not have that effect, or it may be that the contract has ousted that section altogether as a matter of pure construction."

Having raised the doubt, however, Roxburgh J. did not dispel it but proceeded to refuse a stay of the court proceedings on the grounds that " the dissolution of a partnership which involves the exercise of a judicial discretion under section 35 (*f*) and which may involve the appointment of a receiver and manager, is again a matter which perhaps is more conveniently left in the hands of the court."

It seems clear that where the ground of dissolution occurs under section 35, paragraphs (*a*) to (*e*) of the Partnership Act 1890, no real question can be raised as to the arbiter's power to award dissolution on these grounds if the question has clearly been referred to his decision by the agreement of the partners. No real question is raised as to this in English law and the only questions which remain in such circumstances are (1) whether the terms of the submission themselves are to be construed as covering the point in dispute (a consideration which has equal validity in Scots law) and (2) whether the court should, in a case where the submission in fact covers the point at issue, exercise its discretion to refuse a stay of proceedings in court on that dispute on the ground that the issue will be more conveniently investigated by the court. That discretionary exercise is not so clearly vouched for in the Scottish courts as it is in England, though, no doubt, there may be circumstances where a Scottish court might refuse to sist proceedings before it to await arbitration, for example where the application before the court is not only for the dissolution of the partnership but also for the appointment of a judicial factor. It remains to be considered whether the " just and equitable " jurisdiction conferred on the court in virtue of section 35 (*f*) of the Partnership Act 1890 may properly be committed by agreement of the parties to the decision of the arbiter. In Scotland it was held by Lord Mackenzie in *Semple* v. *Macnair & Crawford*[25] that the arbiter had no power to award the dissolution of the partnership which was a matter for the court. The terms of the arbitration clause in that case were not so wide and general as in the examples previously quoted[26] and the point that these terms could not be construed to cover an award of dissolution was apparently conceded by counsel for the

[24] [1896] 1 Ch. 166.
[25] (1907) 15 S.L.T. 448.
[26] *Supra* p. 482.

objectors, who submitted, however, that the facts of the dispute which was the occasion of the application for the dissolution order were committed to the decision of the arbiter, although the actual order must be made by the court. In *Hackston* v. *Hackston and Another* [27] Lord Wheatley held that on a construction of the terms of the arbitration clause before him the arbiter had the power to award dissolution. He did not regard *Semple* v. *Macnair & Crawford* as establishing a general proposition that the power to order dissolution under section 35 was reserved to the courts and could not in appropriate circumstances be exercised by an arbiter. He held, following *Heyman* v. *Darwins Ltd.*[28] that phrases such as " disputes arising out of the contract " do not cover disputes as to whether the contract was entered into or whether it was void *ab initio,* or whether it sets out the true intention of the parties but if the parties are agreed that a binding contract was made and the dispute which has arisen necessitates recourse to the contract for its resolution then it is a dispute arising out of the contract and falls within the arbiter's powers of award.[29]

The grounds on which it was claimed that the partnership should be dissolved in *Hackston* v. *Hackston and Another* seem, however, to fall within section 35 (*d*) of the Partnership Act 1890 and thus the point raised, but not decided, in *Olver* v. *Hillier* [30] is not finally disposed of in the Scottish decision. There must, of course, be hesitation in taking the view that a jurisdiction which is expressly committed to the court and is to be exercised upon the court's view of what is "just and equitable" may readily be assumed by an arbiter in place of the court. But in theory there seems little to distinguish this from the power of the parties to submit *any* dispute over which the jurisdiction of the courts extends to a private arbiter of their own choosing. The special nature of the duty confided to the courts under section 35 (*f*) of the Partnership Act 1890 will, it is thought, entail that any arbitration clause under which it is claimed that the jurisdiction has been ousted in favour of an arbiter will be strictly and even jealously construed; but the question appears to be one of construction rather than one involving a general legal principle that it is improper or unacceptable that an arbiter should be permitted to decide such a question.

Expulsion from the partnership

In the absence of express agreement among the partners conferring the power, no majority of the partners of a firm has the power to expel a partner.[31] A power to expel, however, must be distinguished from special provisions as to dissolution of the partnership which place the power to dissolve the partnership on certain events occurring in the hands of a single partner of the firm. Thus where the partnership agreement confers power

---

[27] 1956 S.L.T. (Notes) 38.
[28] [1942] A.C. 356 particularly *per* Lord Simon at pp. 366–367 and Lord Macmillan at pp. 373–374.
[29] See *Russell on Arbitration* (18th ed.) p. 69.
[30] [1959] 2 All E.R. 220.
[31] Partnership Act 1890, s. 25.

upon one of the partners to dissolve the firm if the conduct of the business, or the results of the business, should not be to the satisfaction of one of the partners designated in the agreement, that is not equivalent to a power of expulsion, and is to be distinguished from such a power. In that case " You give the power to a single partner in terms which show that he is to be the sole judge for himself, not to acquire a benefit but to dissolve the partnership, and in such a case he may exercise the decision capriciously and there is no obligation upon him to act as a tribunal or state the grounds on which he decides." [32] In spite of the distinction, however, it must be confessed that there is a rather indeterminate area where the frontiers of the expulsion cases and the dissolution cases meet. Where the partnership agreement expressly provides that a partner may be expelled for certain conduct or in certain events the application of the general principles governing the exercise of the power of expulsion is clear. Where, however, the provision is expressed as a power to " terminate " the partnership in certain circumstances the treatment of this provision by the courts appears to vacillate between regarding it as a power of expulsion and one of " cancellation " or dissolution of the partnership for certain reasons founded upon the conduct of a copartner. Now, where a power to " terminate " or dissolve a partnership is exercised by the copartners in respect of the conduct of the offending partner it may often occur that on such termination the partners who have sought termination of the partnership will themselves continue in business but without the offending partner. The situation thus comes very close, in practical terms, to that arising when a partner is expelled particularly when, as is usual in provisions in regard to expulsion, the expelled partner is to have his share paid out on the same terms as if he had retired from the firm.[33] But while the practical result of the two procedures may sometimes amount to much the same thing so far as the excluded partner is concerned, in legal terms the distinction must be preserved since if what has been exercised is truly a power to expel, the exercise of that power will be subject to a stricter scrutiny by the courts than the exercise of a power to terminate [34] and in any event upon the terms of the partnership agreement itself the rights of an expelled partner may not, and often will not, coincide with those of a partner whose conduct has occasioned the termination. Where the partner has been expelled, it is to be expected that the consequences of his expulsion will be stipulated for in the partnership agreement and in view of the nature of expulsion he will normally be " paid out " as if he were a retiring partner. But if his conduct causes the other partners to terminate their partnership with him, that partnership will be dissolved and the offending partner's rights, in the absence of agreement to the contrary, will be treated as in a dissolution and winding up of the firm which may produce a different result.

[32] *Per* Jessel M.R. in *Russell* v. *Russell* (1880) 14 Ch.D. at p. 480.
[33] See *e.g. Smith* v. *Mules* (1852) 9 Hare 556.
[34] See *infra* pp. 487 and 529–530.

Power of expulsion construed strictly

Clauses providing for a power to expel a partner are construed *strictissimi juris* and the partners " who seek to enforce them must exactly pursue all that is necessary in order to enable them to exercise this strong power." [35] The underlying reason for the rule is the abuse to which such powers render themselves subject and the hardship to the expelled partner. The court may therefore decline to give effect to an expulsion of a partner even where there is power under the partnership agreement to expel, if the expelled partner is able to establish that his copartners, though purporting to act under the power in the expulsion clause, have in fact used that power not in order to preserve the interests of the firm but to advance private interests or from private motives of their own, unconnected with the interests of the firm as such. An abuse of power of that nature is directly opposed to the general standards of honourable conduct which should exist among the partners and destructive of the mutual confidence which is a characteristic feature of the relationship.[36] Needless to say, if the power to expel is provided for in very general terms and without detailed specification of the procedures to be followed the expelled partner will find this an impediment in his task of establishing to the satisfaction of the court that his copartners have in fact abused their power. But even in these cases the challenge may prove successful. In *Blisset* v. *Daniel* [37] the partnership agreement provided for expulsion by the holders of two thirds of the shares in an unincorporated company of any partner by giving him notice in writing under their hands of such expulsion in the following form—

" We do hereby give you notice that you are hereby expelled from the partnership of John Freeman and Copper Company.
Witness our hands this   day of   ."

The clause did not require the partners to state their reasons for the expulsion nor did it stipulate for any requirements by way of meetings of, or deliberations among, the partners before the notice was served. The partners in fact advanced no reasons and merely served the notice in the prescribed form. In the action by the expelled partner, however, he was able to show that they wished to get rid of him, not for the good of the firm, but because he opposed the appointment of the son of one of the partners as a co-manager with his father and that the father had then faced the other partners with the alternative that either he or the partner who objected to the arrangement must go. Thus prevailed upon, behind the back of the objecting partner, the other partners signed the notice of expulsion but before serving it, they induced the partner to sign accounts in order that he would be bound by them after he was expelled, while

---

[35] *Clarke* v. *Hart* (1858) 6 H.L.C. 633, *per* Lord Chelmsford at p. 650. See also *Munro* v. *Cowan*, June 8, 1813, F.C.; *Blisset* v. *Daniel* (1853) 10 Hare 493.
[36] *Blisset* v. *Daniel, supra; Wood* v. *Woad* (1874) L.R. 9 Ex. 190; *Green* v. *Howell* [1910] 1 Ch. 495.
[37] (1853) 10 Hare 493.

concealing from him at that stage their intention to expel him.   The notice of expulsion was held void and the partner restored to his rights as a partner of the firm.

Notice of expulsion

There is no general statutory requirement as to the form or sufficiency of notice to be given to the expelled partner.   He must obviously receive notice in some form of his partners' intention before he can be effectively expelled.   The provision of the partnership agreement under which the power is exercised may itself expressly or by implication provide for the type of notice to be given and, if so, that must be strictly observed.   If a notice of expulsion is served which is invoked under the clause providing for the power of expulsion, that notice cannot be invoked as a notice of dissolution of the partnership under another clause of the agreement [38]; and the power may not be exercised without the concurrence of all those who in terms of the agreement are required to concur in its exercise.[39] Thus where the partnership agreement provided that on the ground of certain aspects of the conduct of a partner, his copartners were entitled to dissolve the partnership by giving notice to the offending partner upon which notice the partnership should cease and be dissolved as if the offending partner had retired, A took exception to certain conduct of B.   The partnership consisted of A, B and C, the last named being B's son, A then gave notice to B and C under the power in the partnership agreement although C had in fact done nothing on which A could found for this purpose.   It was held that A could not expel B without the concurrence of C, nor had he the right to dissolve the firm as far as C was concerned. But as C had adopted the notice after it was given, A was likewise precluded from treating the partnership as a continuing one and had actually brought about its dissolution though not a dissolution as provided for in the partnership agreement and hence not involving the consequences of a dissolution under that agreement.[40]

Right of partner to be heard before expulsion

The right of a partner to receive notice of the items of complaint against him and to be heard in explanation or justification of his conduct will depend upon the terms of the clause conferring the power of expulsion. The earlier English cases have been cited as supporting a general rule that a partner must be afforded a full opportunity of explaining his conduct before he is expelled.[41]   In England at least, the rule can no longer be expressed in terms of that generality.   In order that the delinquent partner may claim the right to a hearing by his partners in explanation of his

[38] *Smith* v. *Mules* (1852) 9 Hare 556.
[39] *Smith* v. *Mules, supra*; *Steuart* v. *Gladstone* (1878) 10 Ch.D. 626.
[40] *Smith* v. *Mules, supra.*   See also *Re a Solicitor's Arbitration* [1962] 1 All E.R. 772.
[41] *Wood* v. *Woad* (1874) L.R. 9 Ex. 190; *Steuart* v. *Gladstone* (1878) 10 Ch.D. 626; *Barnes* v. *Youngs* [1898] 1 Ch. 414.

conduct and also, it seems, to notice of the offences alleged against him by his partners, it is necessary that the expelling partners should be in the position of adjudicators of his conduct, or, as it has been otherwise expressed, of " the tribunal to decide whether an event has happened justifying his expulsion." [42]   Where the clause in the partnership agreement provided that a partner who was guilty of a flagrant breach of his duties, might be expelled by his copartner subject to a right of appeal to the arbitrator named in the partnership agreement, his copartner in good faith served on him notice that he was expelled without giving him an opportunity to explain the conduct to which exception had been taken. It was held that this was a valid notice of expulsion.[43]   The situation was explained as follows—

> " It seems to me that the fair reading of this clause, is this . . . The plaintiff, one of the two partners, believes and asserts that there has been a breach entitling him to determine the partnership.   He gives notice of that, but he does not in any way act in a judicial character.   All he does is to start the proceedings, leaving it open to the defendant in the action, the present appellant, to appeal to the domestic tribunal which the parties have agreed upon—namely, the arbitrator, to decide in the event which has happened.   If that is not sufficient, then by the ordinary procedure of the court, the court has to decide whether the event has happened which justifies the expulsion. . . .   Is there any line of authorities . . . binding us to hold that the notice is altogether bad and that all proceedings thereunder must be disregarded because the plaintiff did not give the defendant an opportunity of explanation or did not more carefully specify the grounds for his expulsion?   I am not aware that there is any such authority binding us to take that view." [44]

Though no reported decision in Scotland deals with this point, it is thought that the English decisions will be regarded as of persuasive authority.   The exact ambience of the rule must however be closely scrutinised. *Green* v. *Howell* [43] does not absolve the partners who are exercising a power of expulsion from giving the offending partner notice of the allegations made against him and a fair opportunity of a hearing in every case.   If they themselves are placed in the position of the " tribunal " and have themselves to adjudicate upon their copartner's conduct as justifying his expulsion, the rule in the older cases will be applied and the expelling partners, in common with other tribunals adjudicating upon such issues,[45] will be required to observe in relation to the offending partner these elements of the doctrine of natural justice.   But where the adjudication

---

[42] Lindley, *op. cit.* p. 445.

[43] *Green* v. *Howell* [1910] 1 Ch. 495.

[44] *Ibid., per* Cozens-Hardy M.R. at p. 505.   See also *Peyton* v. *Mindham* [1971] 3 All E.R. 1215.   While this was strictly a case of dissolution, the power given to the active partner to terminate the partnership, coupled with the effect of the restrictive covenant on the partner receiving the notice, made it very similar to an expulsion.

[45] *Labouchere* v. *Wharncliffe* (1879) 13 Ch.D. 346; *D'Arcy* v. *Adamson* (1913) 29 T.L.R. 367 (Clubs); *Andrews* v. *Mitchell* [1905] A.C. 78.

is placed in the hands of another tribunal and not in the hands of the partners themselves, then service of notice of expulsion by the partners, without affording the opportunity for a hearing, does not offend against natural justice because no exercise of judicial power is involved. All the partners have done, by their notice, is to raise an issue which, if he so desires, the offending partner may have adjudicated upon by the arbitrator. That view of the position appears at first sight to run counter to certain decisions of the English courts,[46] but these cases when examined will be found to be concerned, not with the expulsion of a partner, but with a dissolution of the partnership consequent upon his conduct. The distinction has already been noted and will be examined more closely in the immediately succeeding paragraph.

Distinction between expulsion and dissolution

Where the partnership agreement provides a power to dissolve the partnership on complaint of improper conduct of a partner, the terms on which that power is conferred may make the results of its exercise approximate to the practical consequences of an expulsion.[47] Nevertheless, the legal situation remains entirely distinguishable, since in the exercise of a power to dissolve the partners are asserting a right which may be challenged in the courts or, if the partnership agreement so provides, before the arbiter selected for the purpose. The approximation in practical consequences of the exercise of the two different powers has, however, led to cases involving an exercise of either being grouped together somewhat indiscriminately.[48] In neither of the cases just cited did any question arise that the partners before serving notice should particularise to the offending partner the conduct complained of or afford him an opportunity of explaining his conduct and, if these cases were correctly regarded as expulsion cases, they would go a considerable way towards establishing that the expelling partners were in no circumstances under obligation to observe those requirements. The view has already been expressed that this is not a rule which would be likely to be applied in Scots law; nor, it is submitted, is it a view which can possibly be advanced in English law on the strength of the decision in *Green* v. *Howell*.[49] The cases of *Carmichael* v. *Evans* and *Clifford* v. *Timms* [50] cannot be adduced in support of a general rule of that nature since in neither of these cases were the partners, when exercising their power to dissolve the firm, placed in the position of adjudicating on the partner's conduct. To adopt the words of Cozens-Hardy M.R., all they are doing is " to start the proceedings " [51] leaving it to the delinquent partner to challenge them if he thinks fit in the appropriate tribunal whether

[46] *Clifford* v. *Timms* (1908) 98 L.T. 64; *Carmichael* v. *Evans* [1904] 1 Ch. 486.
[47] See *supra* pp. 484–485.
[48] See *e.g.* the treatment of *Carmichael* v. *Evans* [1904] 1 Ch. 486 in Lindley, *op. cit.* pp. 446–447 and of that decision and *Clifford* v. *Timms* (1908) 98 L.T. 64 in Ivamy, *Case-book on Partnership* pp. 44–46.
[49] [1910] 1 Ch. 495.
[50] *Supra* n. 46.
[51] *Green* v. *Howell* [1910] 1 Ch. 495 at p. 505.

that be the courts or the arbiter appointed under the agreement.   There is
nothing in the way of a judicial exercise of power involved in their serving
a notice of dissolution and consequently there is no room for the application of the doctrine of natural justice to their actings.   Added force is
given to the distinction which is sought to be drawn, when the case of a
power to expel in the event of a partner failing or omitting to discharge part
of his duties is concerned.   When, for example, it is provided that, in the
event of his omitting to enter in the books of account of the partnership the
moneys received by him on behalf of the firm, he may be expelled, the
power will not normally be held to be validly exercised unless the omission
was intentional.[52]   No such rule appears to obtain where the same conduct
justifies a dissolution in terms of the express provisions of the partnership
agreement [53]; and it is certainly not pleadable in answer to an application
for a dissolution order under section 35 (*d*) of the Partnership Act 1890
where the basis of the application does not rest upon whether the misconduct was deliberate but rather whether it is such " that it is not reasonably
practicable for the other partner or partners to carry on the business
in partnership with him."   In such cases it is only necessary to show that
the confidence of the applicant in his copartner has been destroyed and
that the applicant himself has not caused that impairment of confidence.[54]

Requirement of good faith

In exercising a power to expel a partner, his copartners must act in
good faith; otherwise the purported expulsion may be held void and the
partner restored to his rights in the partnership.[55]   Since partners are
bound to exhibit to each other perfect good faith in the conduct of the
affairs of the partnership, the same standard of conduct is demanded where
they are acting, not under a power to expel, but under a power conferred
upon some members of the firm to dissolve the partnership upon the
misconduct of another partner or other partners.[56]   Where the power to
dissolve the firm requires for its exercise the assent of all the partners and
one of the partners withholds that assent, an attempt to compel the dissentient to agree to a dissolution by conduct which makes life in the partnership intolerable for him is a breach of the good faith which is owed by
partners, one to another; and if at all possible the court will remedy such
conduct and grant redress to the partner affected by it without dissolving
the partnership.   In *Fairthorne* v. *Weston* [57] one of the partners behaved

---

[52] *Smith* v. *Mules* (1852) 9 Hare 556.
[53] *Cheeseman* v. *Price* (1865) 35 Beav. 142.
[54] " All that is necessary is to satisfy the court that it is impossible for the partners to place
    that confidence in each other which each has a right to expect, and that such impossibility
    has not been caused by the person seeking to take advantage of it." Lindley, *op. cit.*
    p. 589. Quoted with approval in *Re Yenidje Tobacco Co. Ltd.* [1916] 2 Ch. 426 at
    p. 430.
[55] *Blisset* v. *Daniel* (1853) 10 Hare 493; *Wood* v. *Woad* (1874) L.R. 9 Ex. 190; *Steuart* v.
    Gladstone (1878) 10 Ch.D. 626; *Russell* v. *Russell* (1880) 14 Ch.D. 471; *Barnes* v. *Youngs*
    [1898] 1 Ch. 414.
[56] *Carmichael* v. *Evans* [1904] 1 Ch. 486.
[57] (1844) 3 Hare 387.

in a manner intended to drive the other to dissolve the firm, since in respect of the conduct the partnership business could not be carried on properly. Instead of dissolving the partnership, however, the plaintiff applied for an account of the transactions of the partnership since the date of the last settled accounts and the appointment of a receiver. The defendant argued that the plaintiff's only available remedy was to seek dissolution of the partnership but the court allowed the application, observing that if the defendant's argument were upheld, a partner might, for his personal ends and in fraud of his copartner, compel the latter either to dissolve the partnership or to be ruined by persistent violations of the partnership agreement. The equity of the decision is apparent and it seems probable that a Scottish court would exhibit the same reluctance to allow a partner to gain his ends as a result of his own misconduct. Yet the only remedy provided to the innocent partner under the Partnership Act 1890 in such circumstances is an application to the court for the order for dissolution of the partnership.[58] Of itself that does not militate against the decision in *Fairthorne* v. *Weston* since there is nothing inconsistent with the express provisions of the Partnership Act 1890 in the rule applied in that case.[59] The alternative remedy afforded to the applicant in the English case, so far as it involved the appointment of a receiver, is not available in Scotland. The principle observed in the decision might, however, be applied in Scotland if the applicant, instead of dissolving the firm, sought a form of redress which the court in Scotland is empowered to grant, *e.g.* an accounting coupled with an interdict against continuance in the misconduct.

Proceedings similar in effect to expulsion

In the absence of express agreement, the partners have no right to expel one of their number and, though section 25 mentions expulsion alone, they will likewise have no power, in the absence of express provision, to declare the share of a partner forfeit or to force him to leave the firm on his being paid the share which is due to him. If the partnership agreement is silent as to any such rights, then a dissolution of the firm is the only method by which a partner may be compelled to sever his association with it against his will.[60] There is, however, nothing unlawful in persuading a partner to leave the partnership of his own volition.[61] If, however, it can be shown that these arrangements were made by the continuing partners in bad faith, or were achieved by them through the exercise of undue influence upon the partner who has quitted the firm or that it was part of a scheme to expel him from the firm, the partner adversely affected may be restored to his rights in the firm although that appears only inferentially from the judgments in *Tennent* v. *Tennent's Trustees*.[61] That

[58] s. 35 (*d*); and see *supra* pp. 466–470.
[59] Partnership Act 1890, s. 46.
[60] *Hart* v. *Clarke* (1854) 6 De G.M. & G. 232; (1858) 6 H.L.C. 633; *Crawshay* v. *Collins* (1808) 15 Ves. 218; *Featherstonhaugh* v. *Fenwick* (1810) 17 Ves. 298.
[61] *Tennent* v. *Tennent's Trs.* (1870) 8 M.(H.L.) 10; *McKirdy* v. *Paterson* (1854) 16 D. 1013.

case was a very special one dealing with a most unusual agreement whereby a partner in consideration of the payment of his debts renounced his interest in the partnership on the condition *inter alia* that his copartner should have power at his discretion to repone him as a partner. The agreement stemmed from considerations of his copartner, who was his father, having regard to its effect in relation to his dispositions of his fortune among his family and the court refused to reduce the agreement on any of the grounds above mentioned which were pleaded against it.

Effect of expulsion clause after expiration of stipulated term of the partnership

When the stipulated term of endurance of the partnership has expired and the partnership has continued without notice of dissolution and without a fresh agreement being entered into the rights and duties of the partners remain the same as they were at the expiration of the term, so far as is consistent with the incidents of a partnership at will.[62] Under a partnership at will any partner has the right to determine the partnership at any time on giving notice of his intention to do so to his copartners.[63] Presumably upon the consideration that the nature of a partnership at will is inconsistent with the existence of a power of expulsion, it has been held in England that where power to expel is provided for in the partnership agreement and the partnership is continued after the expiry of its agreed term of endurance, the power of expulsion is no longer exercisable.[64] On an application of the general observations made in *Neilson* v. *Mossend Iron Company* [65] as to clauses which are inconsistent with a partnership at will, it appears that a power to expel a partner could not under Scots law be carried forward into the contract implied in the continuing partnership.

Wrongful expulsion

Since an invalid notice of expulsion of a partner is of no effect, it has been held in England that the partner against whom the purported expulsion was directed may not recover damages for wrongful expulsion.[66] The logic of that decision seems to rest upon the view that no one can suffer damage from a notice of expulsion from a partnership which does not in fact achieve what it purports to do, namely, expel him. But that logic, if indeed it be implicit in the decision, is assailable for the correction of the expelling partners and the restoration of the expelled partner to his rights do not either singly or in combination logically entail that the wronged partner has not suffered damage or injury as a result of the invalid notice particularly if it has been followed by some public announcement that he has left the firm. The essential fallacy caused some difficulty to

---

[62] *Ibid.* s. 27 (1).
[63] Partnership Act 1890, s. 26.
[64] *Clark* v. *Leach* (1863) 32 Beav. 14.
[65] (1886) 13 R.(H.L.) 50.
[66] *Wood* v. *Woad* (1874) L.R. 9 Ex. 190.

two of the judges involved in it [67] and to later writers.[68] In *Lindley on Partnership* [69] an attempt is made to support the rule by associating it with the principle in *Abbott* v. *Sullivan* [70] that, " in the absence of malice, the mere fact that persons may have acted *ultra vires* is not in itself tortious." No reported Scottish decisions appear to be in point, but it is difficult to envisage the possibility that any case occurring in the future would be decided upon that *ratio*. It appears more probable that the Scottish courts would grant a remedy by way of damages only (1) if the partner could prove that he had in fact suffered damage through the wrongful expulsion and (2) that the act of expelling him was done maliciously or without probable cause. It seems that the damage suffered would in most cases be damage to reputation, since any other damages effeiring to deprivation of his rights in the partnership would be in most cases effaced by his being restored against the wrongful expulsion. It is thought that the expelling partners might in such circumstances be protected by qualified privilege [71] and that no action for damages would lie if they used the power of expulsion honestly but mistakenly, even where the purported expulsion had been notified to persons who were customers of the firm, provided that the notification went no further than to announce that the " expelled " partner was no longer a partner. If an action for damages can be raised in such circumstances, it must be raised against the partners who were involved in the expulsion personally. There is no vicarious liability imposed on the firm itself in such circumstances.[72]

[67] *Ibid. per* Cleasby B. at p. 199 and Pollock B. at p. 201. See also *Catchpole* v. *Ambergate Ry.* (1852) 1 E. & B. 111.
[68] See Lindley, *op. cit.* p. 447.
[69] *Ibid. eodem loco.*
[70] [1952] 1 K.B. 189.
[71] " A communication honestly made upon any subject in which a person has an interest, social or moral, or in reference to which he has a duty, is privileged if made to a person having a corresponding interest or duty ": *per* the Lord President (Strathclyde) in *James* v. *Baird*, 1916 S.C. 510 at p. 517.
[72] Partnership Act 1890, s. 10; *Mair* v. *Wood*, 1948 S.C. 83.

CHAPTER XI

EFFECTS OF DISSOLUTION

WHEN a partnership has been dissolved the association of the partners in the firm for the purpose of carrying on business is terminated. There is thus no authority in any of the partners under section 5 of the Partnership Act 1890 to enter into fresh transactions on behalf of the firm and his co-partners so as to bind them in such dealings. In the conduct of the partnership business prior to dissolution, however, assets will have been acquired and debts incurred by the partnership and the firm may also at the date of dissolution be under a continuing obligation in terms of contracts entered into prior to dissolution, the effect of which extends beyond the date of dissolution. The process in which such matters are finally disposed of is an entirely separate one from the dissolution itself and is known as the winding up of the firm. That distinction is, of course, essential for the practical needs of the situation and was clearly recognised in the Scottish common law. " The partnership is dissolved in so far as the power of contracting new debts is concerned, but continued to the effect of levying the debts, paying the engagements of the company, and calling on the partners to answer the demands." [1] In the dissolution and the subsequent winding up of the partnership, the rights of third parties will often be concerned and it is therefore necessary to examine (a) the effects of dissolution of the partnership and (b) the legal rules as to winding it up.

Effect of dissolution upon contracts

The contracts entered into by the firm in the conduct of the partnership business are not as a general rule affected by the subsequent dissolution of the partnership. Though no fresh contracts can be entered into after the dissolution, the partners remain liable for all the obligations incurred in the firm's name up to the date of dissolution. There may, however, be exceptions to that general rule. It will always be a question for the court to construe the contract in question to discover whether an obligation of a continuing nature undertaken by the firm will continue to bind the partners after the firm has been dissolved. In *Menzies' Trustees* v. *Black's Trustees* [2] the three partners of a firm of solicitors carried on business without any formal deed of copartnery. They had, however, signed a document entitled " Memorandum of Basis of Distribution of Profits of Menzies Black & Menzies, W.S." in which it was provided that " in the event of any partner dying or becoming incapacitated from active business there shall be paid to such partner, or his widow if she survives him "

---

[1] Bell, *Comm.* II, 527; see also *Douglas Heron & Co.* v. *Gordon* (1795) 3 Pat.App. 428.
[2] 1909 S.C. 239.

certain stated allowances " for a period of five years after such death or incapacity but no longer." After the death of the senior partner, the remaining two partners continued to carry on the business and paid to the widow of the senior partner the allowance stipulated for in her case. About five months after the death the surviving partners dissolved the partnership by mutual consent. Each set up business on his own account and between them they retained virtually the whole practice of the dissolved firm. It was held that what was contemplated was that if the surviving partners carried on the business the allowance would be paid to the widow out of the profits of the business, and that there was no continuing personal obligation on the part of each of the surviving partners to pay the allowance after the partnership had been dissolved.[3] " Of course, if the partnership had been dissolved with the fraudulent purpose of defeating a third party's interest, a serious question would arise, which—like every case of fraud—would require to be dealt with on its own merits." [4]

Similarly, where the contract entered into prior to dissolution involves *delectus personae* that may be a ground for holding it to be terminated by dissolution of the partnership unless the contract provides otherwise. The application of the concept of *delectus personae* in such partnership cases is, however, not entirely clear. It has been decided that a contract of service between a firm and its servant is terminated by dissolution of the partnership.[5] In that case the dissolution was occasioned by the death of one of the partners but certain passages in the judgments suggest that it is the dissolution of the employing partnership, irrespective of the cause of that dissolution, which is, on the ground of the legal *persona* of the firm, equated with the death of an individual employer.[6] The Lord President (Inglis) said, " This seems a purely personal contract, and one that cannot exist after the death of the employer; or, what is the same thing, the dissolution of the partnership by the death of one of the partners." [6] But the Lord President's words, with which both Lords Curriehill and Ardmillan concurred, are not free from ambiguity as to the effect upon the contract of a dissolution through some other cause than death; and Lord Deas [7] said, " The question here, however, is not as to the effect of the death of a master, but as to the effect of the dissolution of a mercantile company. I do not think the cases are in all respects the same." He went on to consider the possibility that the effect of dissolution by the death of a partner is different in some respects from that of voluntary dissolution which may take place at any time, but found the distinction between " voluntary " and " involuntary " too insubstantial to form the basis of a legal principle [8] and regarded the question whether the servant should receive compensation, and if so the amount, as a jury question to be

---

[3] *Ibid. per* Lord Low at p. 243.
[4] *Ibid. per* the Lord Justice-Clerk (Macdonald) at p. 242.
[5] *Hoey* v. *MacEwan & Auld* (1867) 5 M. 814.
[6] *Ibid.* at p. 817.
[7] *Ibid.* at pp. 818–819.
[8] In particular he found difficulty in placing a dissolution by reason of bankruptcy firmly within the category of a voluntary or an involuntary dissolution.

decided on the circumstances of the case after proof. Lord Deas represented a minority view in the case in question yet the judgment of the
majority is itself qualified in terms which destroy to some extent the legal
basis upon which it purports to proceed; for the court held the servant
entitled to his salary for the year ending after the death of the partner
which caused the dissolution, the award, described as " this concession," [9]
being, however, modified by deduction of the servant's earnings from his
own business after the dissolution of the firm. In some cases the personification of the firm may entail that on its dissolution its rights under a lease
will lapse. It has been held competent to take a lease of heritable property
in the firm name alone [10] but if that be done it appears that the lease will
lapse on dissolution of the partnership.[11] Mr. Robertson Christie has
suggested that this may be cured if the lease is taken in the names of the
individual partners as trustees for their firm [12] but it appears difficult to
support this opinion in view of the decision in *Walker and Another* v.
McKnights & Another [13] where the lease was taken in just such a manner yet
was held to have lapsed. The Lord President (Inglis) referred to the case
of *Campbell* v. *Calder Iron Company* as cited by Bell [14] to support his statement that " where a lease is granted to a company with an exclusion of
sub-tenants and assignees, the bankruptcy of the company puts an end to
the lease " and thereafter observed,[15] " Now, putting that case entirely out of
view, in the first place, I think that his dictum is in itself irresistibly well
founded in principle, for it is a fundamental rule in the law of partnership
that when a company is sequestrated it is thereby *ipso facto* dissolved; and
if a company which is a tenant is a dissolved company, it no longer exists,
except for the purpose of the partners who may be left winding up the
business. How then can a company in such a position be a tenant, which
requires that the holder of the lease should possess capital etc.? There is
no *persona* to represent the tenant at all. . . ." It will be observed, however, that the lease under consideration excluded sub-tenants and assignees.
Since the individual partners were stated in the lease to be the sole partners
of the firm and to hold the tenancy " as trustees for the said company and
the partners present and future thereof " it was argued that these words
implied a power of assignation on the assumption of new partners and
were thus inconsistent with the absolute prohibition of sub-tenants and
assignees which the lease purported to impose. The Lord President saw
no real inconsistency in this but the point is perhaps more satisfactorily
dealt with by Lord Shand [16] who regarded the conflicting provisions as

---

[9] *Ibid. per* the Lord President at p. 818.
[10] *Dennistown McNayr & Co.* v. *Macfarlane* (1808) Mor.App. " Tack " No. 15; *Murray* v.
Hogarth (1835) 13 S. 453 and see *supra* Chap. IX, pp. 387–388.
[11] Rankine, *Leases* (3rd. ed.) p. 86; Paton & Cameron, *Landlord & Tenant* pp. 63–64; and
see *Campbell* v. *Calder Iron Co.* (1805) Bell, *Comm.* I, 78; *Walker* v. *McKnights* (1886) 13
R. 599.
[12] *Encyclopaedia of the Laws of Scotland*, Vol. 11, *sub voce* " Partnership " § 157.
[13] *Supra* n. 11.
[14] *Comm.* I, 78.
[15] *Walker & Anr.* v. *McKnights & Anr.* (1886) 13 R. 599 at p. 602.
[16] *Ibid.* at p. 603.

affording, in an appropriate case, occasion for a construction of the provisions of the lease as a whole. " It might be contended that the true meaning of the agreement was that the company was not to be entitled to assign to an entirely new party, but that at the same time they were not prevented from assuming new partners "; but in the circumstances of the case no such question arose.   The *ratio* of the decision on the broad lines advanced by the Lord President, however, rests rather uneasily on the view of the effect of dissolution which he propounds since it is possible to use his reasoning to argue (a) that the exclusion of sub-tenants and assignees makes no real difference to the decision because the firm being dissolved there was no tenant or alternatively no *persona* for whom the tenancy was held in trust and hence there was no real tenant under whom a sub-tenant could hold the lease or from whom he could receive an assignation; and (b) that a supervening change in the constitution of the firm does not itself involve a dissolution of the firm as formerly constituted.   In the state of the report, therefore, it is imprudent to rely upon the case as authority for the lapse of a tenancy on dissolution of the partnership which holds it except in a case where the lease expressly excludes sub-tenants and assignees.[17]

Effect of dissolution generally on contracts involving delectus personae. Apart from the specific contracts above discussed, there is some difficulty in finding reasonable occasion for the application of the rule affecting contracts involving *delectus personae* in cases where a dissolution of the partnership has occurred, unless an extremely rigid and literal view is taken of the personification under Scots law of the firm itself.   This may be one of the rare instances where the approach of the English law to the partnership more readily meets the actualities of the situation.   For when a firm which has bound itself to a third party in a contract involving *delectus personae* is dissolved before that contract has been implemented, the partners of that firm remain bound to implement it in the course of the winding-up; and to regard that contract as terminated by dissolution of the firm by reason of a *delectus personae* under which the firm is the chosen contracting party and not the individual partners who comprise the firm and who continue bound by the contract appears to be a view singularly lacking in substance and in common sense.   In considering this aspect of the question it is important to have regard both to the position of the party who advances the plea and to the circumstances in which it is advanced.   It is unlikely that the personification of the Scottish firm would induce a Scottish court to accede to a plea by its partners that after dissolution they are no longer bound in a firm contract because it involves a *delectus* of the *persona* of the firm as opposed to its partners.   Nevertheless, *delectus personae* may have its application even on the plea of the partners, where there has been a change in the constitution of the firm.   " There is . . . no doubt that every change in the constitution of a firm whether by the death or retiral of an existing partner or the introduction of a new partner involves a change of the *persona* with

[17] Paton & Cameron, *op. cit.* pp. 63–64.

EFFECTS OF DISSOLUTION

important results on existing contracts. Contracts involving any element of
delectus personae are thereby terminated." [18]   In the case of an incoming
partner section 17 (1) of the Partnership Act 1890 provides that he does not
by his introduction to the partnership alone become liable to the creditors
of the firm for anything done before he became a partner [19] but that section
does not exclude his liability for debts arising upon a contract entered into
before his assumption into the partnership if they are really new debts
arising since he became a partner.[20]   When, therefore, new contracts are
made after the introduction of a new partner in pursuance of a course of
dealing which was previously carried on under certain arranged terms, the
presumption is that the new contract or order is impliedly subject to the
previously arranged terms so as to bind the new partner to it on those
terms.[21]   When a firm of solicitors had carried through business for an
agreed scale of fees on behalf of clients and later assumed a new partner, it
was not open to that partner, or his firm, to plead that *delectus personae*
terminated the previous arrangement and that the work which the new
partner carried through for the society must be remunerated according to
the scale of charges applicable to clients in general.[22]

New contracts.   As has already been stated, after dissolution of the
partnership, no new contracts may be entered into on behalf of the firm.
This rule which existed in the common law of both England and Scotland
is now reflected in the concluding words of the first paragraph of section
38 of the Partnership Act 1890 where the continuing authority of the partners to bind the firm is expressly limited to such actings " as may be necessary to wind up the affairs of the partnership and to complete transactions
begun but unfinished at the time of the dissolution, but not otherwise."   It
will be seen from the terms of the authority granted in section 38 that two
questions may be raised as to the authority of any partner purporting to
conduct business on behalf of the firm after dissolution.   In the first place
it is to be determined whether the transaction is one which really consists
in the completion of an unfinished contract entered into before the date of
dissolution or is an entirely new engagement.   If it can be shown that the
contract was entered into prior to dissolution then the firm and its partners
are bound by it and any partner [23] has authority to act on behalf of the
firm in the implement of the unfinished contract and the firm and his copartners will be bound by his actings.[24]   But in the second place, the
authority of the partner in dealing with the affairs of the firm after its dissolution may be determined by an entirely different criterion,—whether
the actings were " necessary to wind up the affairs of the partnership."   It

---

[18] *Garden, Haig-Scott & Wallace* v. *Prudential Approved Society for Women,* 1927 S.L.T.
393, *per* Lord Constable at p. 396.
[19] *Supra* Chap. VII, pp. 271 *et seq.*
[20] *Dyke* v. *Brewer* (1849) 2 C. & K. 828.
[21] *Helsby* v. *Mears* (1826) 5 B. & C. 504; and see *Beale* v. *Mouls* (1843) 10 Q.B. 976.
[22] *Garden, Haig-Scott & Wallace* v. *Prudential Approved Society for Women, supra* n. 18.
[23] Except a bankrupt partner—Partnership Act 1890, s. 38; and see *infra* pp. 519–520.
[24] *Milliken* v. *Love & Crawford* (1803) Hume 754; *Ramsay's Exrs.* v. *Grahame,* Jan. 18, 1814,
F.C.; *Matheson* v. *Fraser* (1820) Hume 758; *Anderson* v. *Rutherford* (1835) 13 S. 488.
See also *Welsh and Another* v. *Knarston and Others,* 1972 S.L.T. 96.

is upon this second criterion of the partner's authority that a receipt granted by a partner in the firm name to a debtor of the firm is valid and binding upon the firm.[25]   The two criteria of the partner's authority may, however, at times tend to lead to different results and it is in these cases that decisions of some nicety are involved.   Thus it has been held that no partner after dissolution can bind the firm by an admission of liability for a debt which has not been constituted against the firm prior to its dissolution [26] or, without being expressly authorised to do so, sign the firm name on a bill of exchange.[27]   Again if there is no agreement to the contrary, the account of a firm is not a continuing one after dissolution but is closed at that date, and if necessary a new account opened for the period of the winding-up.[28] It is in those apparently simple and direct applications of the two criteria that the sophisticated interaction of them begins to become apparent.   On the one hand, it is not within the authority of a partner after dissolution of the partnership to bind the firm and his copartners by bill of exchange even for a debt of the firm existing before the dissolution, or in other words even if the purpose is " to embody debts in bills after dissolution," because that would alter the onus of proof and might subject the firm to summary diligence, neither of which elements is clearly referable to the criterion of necessity in the winding up of the partnership affairs.[29]   But where a partner who is engaged in winding up the firm's affairs, dispenses with notice of dishonour of a bill of the firm, that may be held to be an act within the ambit, as reasonably delimited, of administration of the firm's affairs in the winding-up and therefore binding against the firm and its copartners.[30] Moreover, what an individual partner may not have the authority to do for his firm after dissolution may not be outwith the scope of what is permitted to the firm as a whole during the process of winding up; and so in regard to bills of exchange the normal rule is that after dissolution no acceptance or endorsation may be made on behalf of the firm unless all the partners join in it.[31]

Effect of dissolution upon third parties

Members of the public who are, or who may become, customers of a firm have clearly an interest in being made aware of the retirement of partners therefrom or of the dissolution of the firm.   That interest will be seen at its clearest where the business of the partnership continues to be carried on by some of the former partners in circumstances which may disguise, or obscure, from the knowledge of third parties the fact that the constitution of the firm itself has changed, *e.g.* by some of the partners continuing to

---

[25] Bell, *Comm.* II, 534.
[26] *McNab* v. *Lockhart* (1843) 5 D. 1014.
[27] *Snodgrass* v. *Hair* (1846) 8 D. 390; *Goodwin* v. *Industrial & General Trust* (1890) 18 R. 193; *cf. Lewis* v. *Reilly* (1841) 1 Q.B. 349.
[28] *Wotherspoon* v. *Henderson's Trs.* (1868) 6 M. 1052.
[29] *Snodgrass* v. *Hair* (1846) 8 D. 390; *Kilgour* v. *Finlyson* (1789) 1 H.Bl. 155; *Dolman* v. *Orchard* (1825) 2 C. & P. 104.
[30] *Burton* v. *Issitt* (1821) 5 B. & Ald. 267.
[31] Bell, *Comm.* II, 534.

carry on the business under the old firm name. A person who has not been alerted to the change in the constitution of the partnership may deal with it in reliance upon the credit of the firm as originally constituted and he may place more reliance upon the credit of those of the original partners who no longer are associated with the new firm than he does upon the credit of those who continue to carry on the partnership business. In any event the situation has changed to his detriment since in the firm as originally constituted he had the supporting credit of all the partners for any dealings with the firm, whereas if he deals with the new firm with knowledge of its constitution, he has the supporting credit of some of these only, with or without the additional credit of incoming partners, or in some cases, it may be, the supporting credit of entirely new partners with whom he has not been accustomed to deal or of whom he has not the same detailed knowledge. It is probably because of this universal feature which arises in partnership in situations which call for the application of a principle analogous to that of personal bar in other commercial relationships that in the law of partnership the same strict proof of prejudice does not seem to be required of a party pleading the principle.[32] Moreover, in the case of a partnership, knowledge of the change in the partnership is not to be imputed to a third party merely because he was formerly a customer of the firm as originally constituted and has continued to deal with it after the change has occurred. It must be established by some means that the knowledge has been brought home to him.

Apparent partner

These principles are applied in their widest sense under section 14 (1) of the Partnership Act 1890 where, under the broad doctrine of holding out, *any* person who represents himself to third parties as being a partner of a firm or who knowingly suffers himself so to be represented is liable to those third parties in the transactions effected under such representations as if he were a partner of the firm.[33] Where, however, a third party carries through a transaction with a firm after a change in its constitution, a more particular situation arises specially provided for in section 36 of the Partnership Act 1890 which reads as follows—

" 36.—(1) Where a person deals with a firm after a change in its constitution he is entitled to treat all apparent members of the old firm as still being members of the firm until he has notice of the change.

(2) An advertisement in the *London Gazette* as to a firm whose principal place of business is in England or Wales, in the *Edinburgh Gazette* as to a firm whose principal place of business is in Scotland, and in the *Dublin Gazette* as to a firm whose principal place of business is in Ireland, shall be notice as to persons who had not dealings with the firm before the date of the dissolution or change so advertised.

---

[32] Contrast the definition of personal bar in *Gatty* v. *Maclaine*, 1921 S.C.(H.L.) 1 at p. 7, with the principle of holding out in partnership, Partnership Act 1890, s. 14 (1), and see *supra* Chap. V, pp. 130–131.
[33] See *supra* Chap. V.

(3) The estate of a partner who dies, or who becomes bankrupt, or of a partner who, not having been known to the person dealing with the firm to be a partner, retires from the firm, is not liable for partnership debts contracted after the date of the death, bankruptcy, or retirement respectively."

The liability of an apparent partner under that section, while it has an obvious relation to liability under the general doctrine of holding out, is a very limited application of that doctrine. It arises from the principle that when an apparent partner retires or where a partnership is dissolved, those who have had dealings with the firm prior to the change in its constitution may still assume that the partnership continues unchanged until they receive notice in the appropriate way of the change.[34] Third parties who have had no prior dealings with the firm are also entitled to assume that it remains unchanged until they receive notice to the contrary.[35] In the latter case only, notice in the *Edinburgh Gazette* is sufficient notice in terms of section 36 (2) of the Partnership Act 1890. The statutory provision is merely as to the sufficiency of such notice to persons who have had no prior dealings with the firm; it does not preclude the possibility of proving by other means that any such person has in fact received notice of the change and even a notice in the *Gazette* may be ineffective if its terms are proved to be in conflict with facts and circumstances which indicate that the partnership remains in actual fact unchanged.[36]

Apparent members of the firm

The meaning to be attached to this phrase has already been examined.[37] The word " apparent " is not happily used to express the idea with which section 36 seems to be concerned, because it suggests a possible interpretation that what is meant is a partner apparent as such to the public at large without special reference to the person actually dealing with the firm; and that view of the meaning of the section might be reinforced by the consideration that it has been thought necessary to provide especially in section 36 for the " apparent " partner, thereby suggesting that there is in that section a different basis for the liability from that in section 14 (1) where a person held out as a partner is responsible only to persons who contract with the firm in reliance on the fact that he has been so held out. That there is a distinction between section 36 and section 14 (1) is undeniable but it may be regarded as a distinction in the ambit of the respective sections rather than one as to the basis of the liability which is incurred. Section 14 (1) deals generally with the doctrine of holding out and includes within its terms any person held out whether that person has at any time

---

[34] *Scarf* v. *Jardine* (1882) 7 App.Cas. 345, *per* Lord Selborne at p. 349; Partnership Act 1890, s. 36. As to the perils of too slavish an application of the principles of the English law of agency applied in that case to a Scottish firm, see *supra* Chap. V, pp. 147 *et seq.*

[35] *Graham* v. *Hope* (1792) Peake 208; *Parkin* v. *Carruthers* (1800) 3 Esp. 248.

[36] See *supra* Chap. V, pp. 144–146.

[37] See *supra* Chap. V, p. 146.

been a partner or not.   Section 36, on the other hand, seeks to examine the
doctrine as applied to the case of a person who has formerly been a partner
and to provide more precise guidance as to the means he must adopt if he
is to ensure that he may not in the future be liable on the ground of " holding out " because he has never disclosed his termination of his association
with the partnership.   It might have been better if section 36 had confined
itself to the machinery to be used to avoid that continuing liability, without
attempting to explain in terms of the " apparent member " the continuing
liability which was to be avoided and which, it is thought, could quite
properly have been left to be regulated under the general doctrine laid down
in section 14 (1).   Explanation of that continuing liability had, however,
been made in terms of the apparent partner in earlier English decisions,[38]
and in introducing, perhaps somewhat uncritically, that explanation in
section 36, the Partnership Act 1890 has raised the doubt whether the
references to the liability of " apparent members of the firm " in section 36
postulate a different theoretical approach from that of the general doctrine of holding out in section 14 (1); in other words there is an ambiguity
whether " apparent members " is intended to apply to former partners,
who, by their names forming part of the firm name or in some other way,
appear to the public at large to be members of the firm, or apply to partners
who are known by the third party to have been members of the original
firm without that third party having been apprised of their retirement from
the firm.   This question was discussed in *Tower Cabinet Company Ltd.* v.
Ingram [39] where counsel for the company argued that section 36 (1) of the
Partnership Act 1890 is concerned with the case where it is apparent to the
world that a man is a partner in a firm.   Subsection (2), he contended, was
equally concerned with the position of partners who are apparent to the
world as such.   Both subsections were concerned, in his view, with that
particular case and reflected the distinction drawn in *Farrar* v. *Deflinne* [40]
between " notorious partners " and those who are " profoundly secret
members of the partnership."   That construction of the section did not
find favour with the court.   " In my reading of the subsection, ' apparent
members ' means members who are apparently members to the person who
is dealing with the firm, and they may be apparent, either by the fact that
the customer has had dealings with them before, or because of the use of
their names on the notepaper, or from some sign outside the door, or
because the customer has had some indirect information about them...." [41]
In the same case the Lord Chief Justice (Lord Goddard) said, " In my
opinion the words ' all apparent members' in section 36, subsection (1),
mean all members apparent to the person dealing with the firm." [42]
    It might be suggested that the foregoing discussion on the interpreta-
tion of the words " apparent partner " is largely academic and indeed

[38] Notably *Farrar* v. *Deflinne* (1844) 1 Car. & K. 580.
[39] [1949] 2 K.B. 397.
[40] (1844) 1 Car. & K. 580.
[41] [1949] 2 K.B. 397, *per* Lynskey J. at p. 403.
[42] *Ibid.* at p. 405.

that view was at one time propounded by Lindley himself.[43] Some support is also lent to it by the meagre terms of the report of *Bishop* v. *Tudor Estates* [44] where liability was apparently imposed upon a retired partner under section 14 (1) of the Partnership Act 1890 rather than under section 36. The retiring partner had failed to inform the Registrar of Business Names of the dissolution of the partnership as a result of his retirement and, since the plaintiff had seen a certificate of registration on which the retired partner's name appeared along with that of his former copartner, it was held that this amounted to a holding out under section 14 (1) by the retired partner of himself as a continuing partner of his former firm. It might be argued from this that the retired partner by his omission to rectify the register was holding himself out as an apparent partner to the public at large; but the terms of the report, though frugal, expressly mention the fact that the plaintiff had personal knowledge of the entry on the register. Accordingly, the case can be reconciled with the opinions expressed by Lynskey J. and by the Lord Chief Justice in *Tower Cabinet Company Limited* v. *Ingram.*[45]

The dormant partner

It is a consequence of the view which has been propounded as to the meaning of " all apparent members of the firm " in section 36 (1) of the Partnership Act 1890 that if the words " apparent member " are equated to the words " known by the third party to be (or to have been) a member," then the dormant partner, one who is not known to be a partner, does not come within the scope of section 36 (1) at all. He is in the category of the " profoundly secret " partner referred to by Cresswell J. in *Farrar* v. *Deflinne* [46] and notice of his retirement is not required to free him from liability to those dealing thereafter with the firm since those continuing to deal with the firm do not do so, and in fact have never done so, in reliance upon his credit being available in support of the credit of the firm. Nonetheless, a dormant partner who has in some way become known to a few persons as a partner will not be a dormant partner so far as they are concerned; and to

---

[43] *Supplement to Law of Partnership* (1891) p. 96. If the more limited interpretation be accepted as correct, former partners whose names do not appear in the firm name may still be under liability to third parties who know them to have been partners and who have received no notice of the change: *Kay* v. *Pollock*, Jan. 27, 1809, F.C. in which *Armour* v. *Gibson* (1774) Mor. 14575 was held to have been wrongly decided. The principle reflected in the Partnership Act 1890, s. 36 is based upon equitable considerations which in some respects are closely related to liability on the ground of holding out, and this may account for some of the apparent inconsistencies of the earlier decisions; for if notice of dissolution has been given to third parties the future dealings for which any partner may be held liable are limited to those necessary to wind up the firm. He will be liable for such dealings in his character as a partner and not merely " as if he were a partner," as would be the case in a holding out. But in his dealings with a firm which he knows to be dissolved, the third party is put on his guard and will not be entitled to hold a partner other than the partner he deals with to a more extended liability unless he has reasonable grounds for assuming that the transaction into which he has entered is within the limits of those necessary for the winding up of the firm's affairs.

[44] [1952] C.L.Y. 2393.

[45] *Supra* p. 502 nn. 41 and 42.

[46] (1844) 1 Car. & K. 580.

free himself from any future liability to these persons, he will require to bring to their notice the fact that he is no longer associated with his former firm.[47]   This rule is recognised in terms of section 36 (3) of the Partnership Act 1890 which, in addition to excepting from continuing liability the estate of a partner who dies or becomes bankrupt, also frees from liability a partner who, *not having been known to the person dealing with the firm to be a partner*, retires from the firm.

This view of the effect of section 36 upon the continuing liability of dormant partners is entirely consistent with the English common law on the subject.[48]   In the earlier cases decided in Scotland prior to the passing of the Partnership Act 1890, the same view does not appear to have been taken of the position of the dormant partner.   The difference in approach is clearly brought out in a passage in Bell's *Commentaries* [49] where it is stated,

> " It often happens that a person possessed of capital wishes to employ it on mercantile profit, without being willing that his concern with the trade should be known.   He may as a dormant partner accomplish his object; and while the trade is prosperous, his secret may be kept, and his object attained.   But a reverse of fortune ought to lead to a disclosure.   And when his interest is discovered, such dormant partner will be liable fully as a partner. . . .   The rule rests on reasons of strict justice, as well as of policy and general expediency, since, by a bargain to take part of the profit, the dormant partner becomes actually, or by possibility at least, a participator of that fund on which the creditors rely for payment.   He is either a partner, or guilty of a usurious contract,[50] and has empowered another to act for him in a contract of loss and gain, to the consequences of which he must be responsible."

These words, however, bear no direct relevance to the question of the continuing liability of a dormant partner who has retired from the firm without giving notice of his retirement to customers of the business.   On this question Bell states at a later point in his exposition of the law,[51] " It is said in the English books to have been held by Lord Kenyon [52] that there is no necessity for advertising the dissolution of a secret partnership.   But in the only case of the kind which has occurred in Scotland, it was held that in anonymous partnership, if known to any one person, publication is necessary."   It will be noticed that Bell's qualifying words, " if known to

---

[47] *Evans* v. *Drummond* (1801) 4 Esp. 89; *Carter* v. *Whalley* (1830) 1 B. & Ad. 14; *Farrar* v. *Deflinne, supra.*

[48] *Heath* v. *Sansom* (1831) 4 B. & Ad. 172; *Carter* v. *Whalley* (1830) 1 B. & Ad. 11, where the dormant partner was not known to be a partner and escaped liability.   See the cases cited in the preceding note as to dormant partners known to be partners to some third parties.   *Western Bank of Scotland* v. *Needell* (1859) 1 F. & F. 461 is difficult to reconcile as reported but is probably a case of the latter category.

[49] II, 511.

[50] That dilemma is now a false one and may well have been false when Bell wrote those words.   See *supra* Chap. VII, pp. 295–296.

[51] *Comm.* II, 533.

[52] *Evans* v. *Drummond* (1801) 4 Esp. 89.

any one person," do not amount to a reflection of the English rule previously discussed. In England, a dormant partner whose character as such becomes known to a few third parties, will continue liability *to those third parties only* until he gives them notice that he is no longer associated with the partnership. But Bell appears to suggest that, in the earlier Scots law, if a dormant partner was known to be such to any person, he must notify his retirement publicly to avoid continuing liability to all third parties dealing with the firm after his retirement, and in that he is borne out by the decision which he cites.[53] The basis of the Scots rule appears to be that where the dormant, or latent, partner was known to any persons outside the partnership, there was no means of knowing how far that knowledge might have spread. The point was raised in argument in the subsequent case of *Mann* v. *Sinclair* [54] but it was unnecessary to decide it since on the facts the court held that sufficient notice had been given to third parties to free the dormant partner from liability. Lord Deas noted the fact that the " doctrines laid down in Scotland and those laid down in England do not quite agree." [55] If it had been necessary to decide which view was the better, his Lordship, like Sir Roger de Coverley, could see a great deal to be said on both sides. Lord Shand was more forthcoming and observed,[56] " I shall only say that if the question should hereafter arise, unless it can be shown to have been very conclusively determined, I should be disposed, as a result of the argument we have heard, to give great weight to the reasoning on which the English rule to a different effect is based."

If, indeed, it be possible to maintain from these indications that the earlier Scots law can be firmly distinguished in doctrine from the contemporaneous English law on this topic, it also appears irresistible that any such distinction has been erased in favour of the English doctrine by section 36 of the Partnership Act 1890; and it does not appear possible at this date to rely upon the earlier authorities to support a different Scottish legal doctrine.[57]

Effect of notice on third party's rights

While under both English and Scots law, the principle in section 36 (1) of the Partnership Act 1890 is recognised to the effect that third parties are entitled to assume that the liability of an apparent partner continues until knowledge to the contrary has been brought home to them, the theoretical approach to the basis of that liability as reflected in the pre-statute decisions differs in each system. In England, the basis of liability was explained as similar to that obtaining in agency, where a principal who has established

---

[53] *Kay* v. *Pollock* reported as *Hay* v. *Mair & Others*, Jan. 27, 1809, F.C. In a supplemental note the learned editor of the 7th ed. of the *Commentaries* observes, " This also appears to be the law in England." With great respect that view appears to be misconceived for the reasons stated above in the text. But see *Aitken* v. *Charles & Co.* (1830) 8 S. 446.
[54] (1879) 6 R. 1078.
[55] *Ibid.* at p. 1086.
[56] *Ibid.* at p. 1088.
[57] See Bell, *Prin.* (10th ed.) § 386.

an agency and held a person out to the public as his agent, will continue
liable on transactions effected by that agent until he gives notice that the
agency has been terminated.[58] In the English courts, that has been held to
imply that a third party creditor of the firm has merely the right of election
whether, in the case of a firm debt incurred before notice of the change has
been given, he will sue the retired partner or those who have continued the
business and incurred the debt.[59] That view, however, as is pointed out
by the learned editor of Bell's *Principles*,[60] rests on the theory of the English
law that a partnership debt is due by each of the partners as joint, not
joint and several, contractors. A partner who has retired without giving
notice of his retirement is accordingly not liable under a joint contract made
subsequent to his retirement to which he is not a party, " but on the distinct
and inconsistent principle of estoppel." In Scots law, on the other hand,
although personal bar on the ground of holding himself out as a partner
might equally operate against the partner who has retired, " his liability is
truly founded on a continuing guarantee, or joint and several liability
for the obligations of a firm which is a separate legal *persona*, the guarantee
or liability not ceasing until he has duly intimated its termination." The
distinction between the two legal systems is clearly brought out in *Blacks* v.
Girdwood & Forrest [61] where one of two partners of the defender firm
retired in 1878 but did not give notice of his retirement to customers of the
firm until 1884. In the meantime the other partner continued the business
under the same firm name and assumed a new partner. The new firm became bankrupt in 1884 after the date of notification of the retired partner's
withdrawal from the firm. A customer of the former partnership had had
dealings with the new firm in 1883, still believing the retired partner to be
a partner of the business. On the bankruptcy, he lodged a claim in the
sequestration, reserving his claim against the retired partner. He later
withdrew his claim before ranking and raised an action against the retired
partner for the firm debt. The case bears a strong resemblance on its facts
to *Scarf* v. *Jardine* [62] and the retired partner founded on the latter decision
and pleaded that the pursuer was bound to elect between the old and the
new firms and that by lodging his claim in the sequestration of the new
firm he had made his election. The court held that, even if the pursuer had
been bound to make his election he had not in fact done so and was therefore entitled to recover from the defender. In considering the question
whether there was any duty upon the pursuer to elect between the old and
the new firms, Lord Young said, ". . . according to the law of Scotland it is
not a question of electing between the partners of the new firm and the
partners of the old, but of the liability as a partner of the new firm of a
person who, the creditor had reason to believe, was a partner of it, though

---

[58] *Scarf* v. *Jardine* (1882) 7 App.Cas. 345. For the general rule in agency, see Bowstead,
Agency (13th ed.) pp. 454–455.
[59] *Scarf* v. *Jardine*, *supra*, *per* Lord Selborne at p. 350; *per* Lord Blackburn at pp. 357–358;
and see Lindley, *op. cit.* p. 233.
[60] 10th ed. § 383; and see *Kendall* v. *Hamilton* (1879) 4 App.Cas. 504.
[61] (1885) 13 R. 243.
[62] (1882) 7 App.Cas. 345.

in fact he was not. I do not read the reasoning of the House of Lords in [*Scarf* v. *Jardine*] as applicable to the law of Scotland. It proceeds on a law of partnership and rules of pleading which are essentially different from ours." [63] While the legal theory of the liability of the retired partner according to the pre-statute law of each country is differently based, section 36 (1) of the Partnership Act 1890 seeks to apply a common formula to both legal systems in the rule that a person who deals with a firm after a change in its constitution " is entitled to treat all apparent members of the old firm as still being members of the firm until he has notice of the change." It is possible to embrace within that formula both the English and the Scottish theory of the retired partner's liability and the wording of section 36 (1) is inconsistent with neither theory. It seems, therefore, that in Scottish cases the pre-existing theory of liability is preserved under section 46 of the Partnership Act 1890 and that accordingly the reasoning in English cases such as *Scarf* v. *Jardine* and *Kendall* v. *Hamilton* will not be entirely acceptable in a Scottish court. These English decisions and others like them may be used in support of the general doctrine of holding out under section 14 (1) which is a doctrine common to both systems of law; but if they are invoked as explaining the effect of section 36 (1) the divergency of the underlying legal theory in Scotland and in England renders the decisions valueless for Scottish purposes.[63] Indeed the English principle of election tends to make section 36 (1) for English purposes merely a specific case of the wider principle of holding out under section 14 (1) of the Partnership Act 1890, whereas in Scotland section 36 (1) produces a liability which is to some extent differently based from that in section 14 (1).

Cases where no notice is required

Section 36 (3) of the Partnership Act 1890 excepts from the continuing liability imposed under section 36 (1) cases where the change in the constitution of the firm has been caused by the death or bankruptcy of a partner or where the partner withdrawing from the firm is a dormant, or latent, partner. The last of these cases has already been considered.[64] In providing that no notice of death or bankruptcy need be given in order that the estate of the deceased or bankrupt partner shall escape continuing liability for the transactions of the firm, section 36 (3) is in accordance with the pre-statute law of Scotland. The death of a partner is regarded as a public fact. " The opinion has certainly prevailed very generally, that no notice is necessary; that the partnership, according to the common course of the law, is dissolved by death; that those who deal with the company are held to know the state of their debtor; and that the publication of all deaths, according to the common custom of the world, places this sort of

---

[63] *Blacks* v. *Girdwood & Forrest*, *supra* at pp. 249–250. The Lord Justice-Clerk (Moncreiff) at p. 248 and Lord Craighill at p. 251 concurred in that view. Lord Rutherford Clark at p. 252, while concurring in the judgment, stated that had he required to do so, he would have held *Scarf* v. *Jardine* as authoritative and binding upon him.

[64] *Supra* pp. 503–505.

information within the reach of ordinary care and vigilance." [65]   The rule
stated by Bell is supported by the earlier Scottish decisions [66] and it will be
noticed that knowledge of the death on the part of the third party is not
requisite.   The estate of the deceased partner will be free from liability on
subsequent transactions with the firm even when, at the date of these transactions, the third party mistakenly believed the partner to be alive and still
to be a member of the firm.

   Bankrupt partner.   Section 36 (3) also dispenses with the need for notice
in the case of a partner " who becomes bankrupt."   The basis of the rule is
the same as in the case of death.   The bankruptcy is regarded as a public
fact.   It is important, however, to bear in mind the restricted application
of the term " bankruptcy " as used in the Act in relation to Scotland.   In
the Partnership Act 1890 the bankruptcy of a firm or of an individual,
in its application to Scotland, means sequestration under the Bankruptcy
(Scotland) Acts.[67]   Sequestration in bankruptcy is a circumstance of which
public notice is given in the *Edinburgh Gazette* [68] and thus may be regarded
as a matter of public notice.   On the other hand, no notice is required to
be publicised as to a state of notour bankruptcy under the Act of 1696, c. 5.
The notour bankruptcy of a partner does not, therefore, free him from
continuing liability for transactions of the firm.   That distinction reflects
the state of the law in Scotland prior to the passing of the Partnership Act
1890.[69]

Right of partner to give notice of dissolution

   Section 37 of the Partnership Act 1890 provides—

   " 37.   On the dissolution of a partnership or retirement of a
   partner any partner may publicly notify the same, and may require
   the other partner or partners to concur for that purpose in all necessary or proper acts, if any, which cannot be done without his or their
   concurrence."

In England the pre-existing common law was to require the signatures of all
the partners to a notice in the *London Gazette* relating to a change in the
partnership and to give a right of action against a recalcitrant partner at
the instance of his copartner or copartners to compel him to sign the
notice as concurring therein.[70]   The wording of section 37 appears to be
designed to reflect that position of affairs.   In Scotland, there has never
been anything in the law or in practice to prevent a retired partner himself
notifying his retirement either by an advertisement in the *Edinburgh Gazette*

---

[65] Bell, *Comm.* II, 529; *Christie* v. *Royal Bank of Scotland* (1839) 1 D. 745; (1841) 2 Rob.App.
    118; *Aytoun* v. *Dundee Bank* (1844) 6 D. 1409.
[66] *Kemp* v. *Allan* (1824) 3 S. 153.   See also *Christie* v. *Royal Bank of Scotland* (1839) 1 D.
    745; (1841) 2 Rob.App. 118; *Aytoun* v. *Dundee Bank* (1844) 6 D. 1409.
[67] Partnership Act 1890, s. 47 (1).
[68] Bankruptcy (Scotland) Act 1913, s. 44.
[69] See Bell, *Comm.* II, 530.
[70] *Hendry* v. *Turner* (1886) 32 Ch.D. 355; *Troughton* v. *Hunter* (1854) 18 Beav. 470.   The
    contract of copartnery may, however, give power to any partner to sign such a notice
    on behalf of himself and his copartners.

or elsewhere or by a circular letter announcing his retirement. Notice of that kind if carried through in accordance with the requirements of section 36 (2) of the Partnership Act 1890 will be sufficient for the protection of the retired partner, even though his copartners have not signed the notice as concurring.   It appears that if a written notice signed by a partner, attested by two witnesses and intimating the retirement of that partner from the firm is presented for insertion in the *Edinburgh Gazette*, it cannot be refused.[71]   But if the notice is in the form of an announcement of the dissolution of the firm, the duly attested signatures of all the partners will be required by the *Gazette* office, on the principle, apparently, that an individual partner is entitled only to notice for his own protection of his retirement and the dissolution of, or change in, the firm which that involves so far as he personally is concerned.   He is not entitled at his own hand and without the concurrence of his copartners to notify a dissolution *quoad* the other partners who may be continuing to carry on the partnership business.

[71] Bell, *Comm.* II,533 adding as the reason—" for that is a right which he is entitled at a moment's notice to exercise, and by which alone he can in some cases save himself from ruin."

CHAPTER XII

THE WINDING UP OF THE FIRM'S AFFAIRS

AT the beginning of Chapter XI the distinction between the dissolution of the partnership and the period ensuing during which its affairs are wound up was touched upon and indeed throughout that chapter, where the effects of dissolution of the partnership are under examination, it is impossible to separate that consideration entirely from the process of winding up, since such a separation would in many cases present a most unreal and artificial picture of the law regarding the effect of dissolution of the partnership upon the rights of third parties. Yet the process of winding up will not inevitably follow upon every dissolution of a partnership. Where the dissolution merely involves a change in the constitution of the firm, as, for example, through the retirement, death or bankruptcy of one or more of the partners, the agreement of partnership may itself provide that on any such occurrence the firm shall not be wound up but shall continue under the direction of the remaining or surviving partners, suitable provision having been made for the shares of the retiring, deceased or bankrupt partners to be paid to them. Thus in the case of the retirement of a partner, the agreement may provide that he may sell his interest in the partnership. Usually such a right of sale will be fairly rigorously restricted in view of the peculiarly close relationship of association which exists among partners, but if the right is conferred without restriction then the partner may sell to whomsoever he pleases and on giving his copartners notice of his withdrawal from the firm he will cease to be a partner so far as his rights and duties *inter socios* are concerned, even if the purchaser of his share does not offer himself to take the place of the retiring partner in the firm.[1] More frequently the right of the partner to sell his share in the partnership is guarded by a provision that he shall offer it to his copartners before selling it to a third party and in *Cassels* v. *Stewart* [2] it was held that a provision of that kind did not prevent one of the continuing partners in the firm from purchasing for himself the share of the outgoing partner. In the case of bankruptcy, provision may be made for the bankrupt partner's retirement from the firm under suitable arrangements for paying out his share. In such cases it is not necessary to limit the provisions to bankruptcy in the sense in which the Partnership Act 1890 [3] applies it in Scotland.

---

[1] *Jefferys* v. *Smith* (1827) 3 Russ. 158.
[2] (1881) 8 R.(H.L.) 1. As to the effect of an offer to his copartners collectively, see *Homfray* v. *Fothergill* (1866) L.R. 1 Eq. 567. Such cases do not conflict with the feature of *delectus personae* present in the relation of partnership, since by their express agreement the partners have removed the implication that it applies in the cases governed by their agreement. See Chap. I, *supra* pp. 16–23.
[3] s. 47.

The clauses of the agreement may provide for the retirement of a partner if he becomes insolvent and, unless that term is otherwise to be interpreted in the light of the context in which it is used in the agreement, it will be taken to mean practical insolvency, *i.e.* inability to pay his debts when due and demanded even though on realisation of all his assets he might be able to meet his liabilities in full.[4]

Cases not expressly provided for in the partnership agreement

In cases where there is no express provision for a partner retiring from the firm or where his death or bankruptcy is not provided for in the partnership agreement, the occurrence of any of these events entails a dissolution of the firm and a winding up of its affairs unless the partners are able to arrive at an *ad hoc* agreement as to the future of the business of the partnership. If therefore a partner wishes to retire and there is no provision in the partnership agreement enabling him to do so, his only right is to insist on a dissolution and winding up of the partnership at the expiry of its agreed period of endurance, if any, or on giving notice if it is a partnership at will. It will frequently happen that his copartners will desire to continue the partnership business under the firm name after his retirement and will enter some agreement with him as to satisfaction of his share which will obviate the need for a winding up; and these cases have already been considered.[5] But in the absence of any such arrangements the affairs of the partnership must be wound up, its assets realised, its liabilities discharged and the balance, if any, distributed among the partners according to their respective shares in the partnership.

Continuing authority of the partners for purposes of winding up

While the dissolution of the partnership terminates the relationship of the partners one to another in the association which they have entered into for the conduct of the business venture, that dissolution will in the great majority of cases take place at a date when many matters relating to the prior activities of the firm are not yet fully disposed of and when the realisation of the assets of the firm and the payment of its debts have not yet been accomplished. There remains therefore an area of activity within the partnership where there is a need for some form of continuing authority in the partners to bind the firm in a limited class of transactions. The need for such continuing, if limited, authority might be obviated if, on winding up, the affairs of every partnership were committed to the charge of an official, such as a judicial factor in Scotland or a receiver in England, in order that the partnership may be wound up by an official responsible to the court. This expedient is available to the partners in many cases,[6]

---

[4] *Bayly* v. *Schofield* (1813) 1 M. & S. 338 *per* Le Blanc J. For a provision for dissolution on the " declared insolvency " of any of the partners, see *Hannan* v. *Henderson* (1879) 7 R. 380.

[5] *Supra* Chap. XI, pp. 497–499; and see also *infra* pp. 517–519.

[6] See *infra* pp. 520 *et seq.*

but it would be inappropriate to make it of universal application. In many cases where there are no issues of contention among the partners it is preferable that they should be permitted to wind up the affairs of the firm at their own hands, both because thereby unnecessary expense will be avoided and because the partners who have been engaged in the conduct of the business may be expected to take at least as expert a view of the decisions entailed in completing performance of the firm's contracts, or realising its assets to best advantage and of settling with its creditors, as might be taken by an official unfamiliar with the previous conduct of the business of the firm.

It was accordingly part of the common law in both Scotland and England that this continuing authority remained with the partners after the dissolution of the firm. "The partnership is dissolved in so far as the power of contracting new debts is concerned, but continued to the effect of levying the debts, paying the engagements of the company, and calling on the partners to answer the demands." [7]   The rule is now presented in section 38 of the Partnership Act 1890—

> "38. After the dissolution of a partnership the authority of each partner to bind the firm and the other rights and obligations of the partners continue, notwithstanding the dissolution, so far as may be necessary to wind up the affairs of the partnership, and to complete transactions begun but unfinished at the time of dissolution, but not otherwise.
>
> Provided that the firm is in no case bound by the acts of a partner who has become bankrupt; but this proviso does not affect the liability of any person who has after the bankruptcy represented himself or knowingly suffered himself to be represented as a partner of the bankrupt."

Limitation of the continuing authority

The general effect of section 38 in limiting the continuing authority of the partners is clear, and is closely in accord with the former law of Scotland as expounded by Bell in the passage above quoted.[8]   The obligations undertaken by the firm prior to dissolution must still, so far as outstanding, be implemented and the continuing authority of the partners extends to binding the firm after its dissolution for the expense incurred in so doing.[9]   While the basis of the limitation is clear, it is not, however,

---

[7] Bell, *Comm.* II, 527; *Gordon* v. *Douglas Heron & Co.* (1795) 3 Pat.App. 428.   In England certain dicta in the judgments in earlier cases appear to confer a wider authority on the partners but the decisions themselves conform to the Scottish rule: *Ex p. Williams* (1805) 11 Ves. 3; *Peacock* v. *Peacock* (1808) 16 Ves. 49; *Crawshay* v. *Collins* (1826) 2 Russ. 325; *Wilson* v. *Greenwood* (1818) 1 Swanst. 471; *Butchart* v. *Dresser* (1853) 4 De G.M. & G. 542.

[8] *Supra* n. 7.

[9] Bell, *Comm.* II, 527–528.   But see *Bagel* v. *Miller* [1903] 2 K.B. 212 (firm not liable for goods ordered prior to death of one of partners but delivered to remaining partner after the death).

always easy to draw the dividing line in individual cases. It is not usually in relation to the implementation of obligations undertaken by the firm prior to dissolution that the main difficulty arises. In regard to the performance of such obligations the Scottish courts have taken a liberal view of the continuing authority of the partners. In *Dickson* v. *National Bank of Scotland*[10] a firm of solicitors had been dissolved. Among the matters uncompleted at the date of dissolution was a deposit receipt made payable to the firm in respect of trust funds held by the firm. Eight years after the date of dissolution the sum in the deposit receipt was uplifted by one of the former partners of the firm who subsequently misappropriated the money. In an action raised by the beneficiaries in the trust against the bank for recovery of the sums paid to the former partner of the firm of solicitors the court held that the bank were entitled to give effect to the continuing authority of the partner to act in the winding up of the firm's affairs and that his indorsement of the firm name on the deposit receipt discharged the bank. The decisions relating to transactions of the firm upon bills of exchange subsequent to the dissolution of the firm raise more subtle distinctions but on examination will be found to rest upon the same principle, *i.e.* that if the transaction is merely in implement of the firm's obligation on a bill of exchange drawn, accepted or negotiated by the firm prior to dissolution, that transaction will fall within the partner's continuing authority in the winding up of the firm and will bind the firm; and apparently notice of dishonour given to one of the partners in such circumstances is sufficient to render the firm and the other partners liable on a bill drawn by the firm prior to dissolution.[11] That decision seems to entail that in a winding up, not only is the authority of the partners as agents of their firm under section 5 of the Partnership Act 1890 continued to a limited extent under section 38 but the provisions of section 16 as to notice " to any partner who habitually acts in the partnership business " are likewise continued during the period of winding up and for the purposes of such winding up. On the other hand, after dissolution of the firm no partner has continuing authority to bind the firm and his copartners by his signature on a bill of exchange as evidencing the drawing of the bill by the firm [12] or on a promissory note as binding the firm as the maker of the note [13]; and it appears that even if the debt in respect of which the partner adhibited the firm signature to the negotiable instrument subsisted before the dissolution of the partnership it will not be held to be within that partner's continuing authority for purposes of winding up the firm's affairs to engage the liability of the firm in the obligations consequent upon the drawing, accepting or making of the negotiable instrument, at least if the prior debt has not been constituted against the firm before the dissolution

---

[10] 1917 S.C.(H.L.) 50.   See also *Welsh & Another* v. *Knarston & Others*, 1972 S.L.T. 96 (liability of retired partners for professional negligence in allowing an action to become time-barred, although the negligence occurred after they had retired from the firm).
[11] *Goldfarb* v. *Bartlett & Kremer* [1920] 1 K.B. 639.
[12] *Snodgrass* v. *Hair* (1848) 8 D. 390.
[13] *Goodwin & Others* v. *Industrial & General Trust Ltd. & Another* (1890) 18 R. 193.

occurred.[14]   The principle, which is approved by Bell,[15] is clearly stated
by Lord Medwyn.[16]

> " After the dissolution of a company it is true that it [*i.e.* the partner's
> authority] subsists to a certain effect, and that the partners, and more
> especially the partner who is appointed to wind up the concern, may
> use the firm in gathering in the effects and discharging the obligations
> of the company; he may receive payment, and grant a discharge in
> name of the company; he may draw a bill upon a debtor, and indorse
> it; nay, he may pay a debt due by the company funds in his hands, and
> these funds may be the produce of such bills, or even the bills them-
> selves, provided always the debts paid be just debts; and he will be
> liable to his partners if he act improperly, and admit debts as just
> against the company which are not so.   Now all such acts fall under
> the character of acts in the necessary administrative powers for
> winding up the concern.   But I think such powers go no further, and
> they do not extend to the effect of constituting a debt by granting a
> bill for it, thus giving the creditor of the dissolved company rights
> and privileges which he had not acquired during the subsistence of
> the company, giving *parata executio* against the partners, not in the
> least necessary for winding up the concern."

The enumeration by Lord Medwyn in the above quotation of the
continuing powers of a partner in the winding up of the partnership, in
itself, indicates the sort of difficulty which may arise in determining whether
a particular action by such partner is " necessary to wind up the affairs
of the partnership and to complete transactions, begun but unfinished at
the time of the dissolution."   Lord Medwyn clearly envisages that in the
course of winding up a partner may competently on behalf of the firm
" draw a bill upon a debtor, and indorse it " or pay a firm debt by a
process involving the negotiation of bills held by the firm.   In both cases
the indorsation may involve the firm in liability upon the bill; and Bell
states categorically,[17] " After dissolution, no valid draft, acceptance, or
endorsation can be made by the firm; and it is no authority to do so if
one partner is in the notice empowered to receive and pay the debts of
the company.   The endorsation, draft, or acceptance must be done by all
the partners, or by one specially empowered so to act for them."   There
is an obvious conflict between Bell's broadly stated rule and the dictum of
Lord Medwyn.   In spite of certain dicta in English cases [18] which appear
to support Bell's statement, it is thought that, in view of the Scottish
cases decided subsequently to the publication of the *Commentaries*,[19]
his rule must be taken to be inapplicable to the indorsation or renewal of

---

[14] *Snodgrass* v. *Hair, supra.*
[15] *Comm.* II, 534.
[16] *Snodgrass* v. *Hair, supra* at pp. 397–398.   See also *per* the Lord Justice-Clerk (Hope) at
pp. 395–396; *per* Lord Cockburn at p. 399.
[17] *Loc. cit.*
[18] *Kilgour* v. *Finlyson* (1789) 1 H.Bl. 155 *per* Lord Kenyon; *Abel* v. *Sutton* (1800) 3 Esp. 108
per Lord Kenyon.
[19] *Snodgrass* v. *Hair* (1848) 8 D. 390; *Gordon* v. *McCubbin* (1851) 13 D. 1154.

bills to which the firm was a party prior to its dissolution.[20]   In such cases, the transactions relating to the bills appear to come within the winding up of the affairs of the partnership, and there would appear to be little in equity or in law to justify the extension of the rule to cover them, since if a partner to whom the task of winding up the firm is committed, discounts its bills and applies the proceeds in payment of the firm's liabilities (the situation envisaged by Lord Medwyn) and if one of these bills is later returned dishonoured, the other partners ought in equity to be liable on the indorsation of the partner who has been constituted their agent for the purpose of winding up.   It is therefore more in accordance with the Scottish reported decisions that Bell's statement should be read as restricted to cases where new obligations are purported to be undertaken by bill after the dissolution of the firm.   In these limited circumstances it has been suggested by Lord Kenyon in an English case that even where the indorsation is placed upon the bill before the firm is dissolved but is not put into circulation until after the date of dissolution, such an indorsation might not be a valid indorsation of the firm unless signed by all partners.[21] The same sort of questions may arise as to the accepting or drawing of bills in the firm name after the date of its dissolution.   It has been held in England that an acceptance by a partner of a bill drawn and accepted subsequently to the appearance of notice of dissolution in the *Gazette*, did not bind his copartner.[22]   On the other hand, in *Usher* v. *Dauncey* [23] the partnership in a brewery were in the habit of drawing bills on a firm in London in order to raise finance.   These bills were drawn in blank and filled up as they became required for the purpose.   One of the partners drew and indorsed a number of those blank bills which he handed to a clerk to be filled up and used for the purposes of the partnership as occasion arose.   The partner who had signed and indorsed the bills died, thus dissolving the partnership.   Some time later one of the bills was filled up by the clerk, accepted and thereafter discounted.   Lord Ellenborough held that the power emanated from the partnership while subsisting, and that after the death of the partner who had signed the bill in blank, that bill might be filled up and as completed would bind the firm.   The Court of King's Bench refused to set aside the verdict arrived at in the trial presided over by Lord Ellenborough.[24]

Other instances of new contracts.   On the same ratio it is not within the continuing authority of a partner to bind his firm after its dissolution by admitting liability for a debt which was not constituted against the firm while the partnership still subsisted before its dissolution.[25]   In a

[20] *Muir* v. *Dickson* (1860) 22 D. 1070; *Lewis* v. *Reilly* (1841) 1 Q.B. 349; *Spenceley* v. *Greenwood* (1858) 1 F. & F. 297.
[21] *Abel* v. *Sutton, supra.*
[22] *Wrightson* v. *Pullan* (1816) 1 Stark. 375.
[23] (1814) 4 Camp. 97.
[24] It will be noted, however, that this case is very special as to its facts and while it is relevant to the validity of the bill *after dissolution* it is not in point as to continuing authority *in a winding up* which was not involved in the case.
[25] *McNab* v. *Lockhart* (1843) 5 D. 1014.

case where the application of the triennial prescription to the professional account of a solicitor was in issue, the question arose whether such an account which extended over the period before dissolution of the partnership and continued after the dissolution could be regarded as a continuous account.   Lord Neaves said,[26]

> " I am of opinion that, in order to found a plea of continuity in the account against which prescription is pleaded, there must be an identite of the creditor throughout. . . . Then we have another principle in our law, which has settled that the formation of a company by the assumption of a *bona fide* partner makes a new *persona*. . . . The continuity is, in like manner, broken when the partnership once formed is dissolved by the retirement of one of the partners.   I do not say that there may not be specialities which may alter the general rule, as, for instance, if the client had been communicated with and informed that the account is to be treated as one account; but, apart from specialities, and assuming the change to be known and *bona fide*, I cannot doubt that the assumption or retirement of a partner breaks the continuity of an account."

As appears from that dictum the mere fact of a dissolution through retirement or through assumption of a partner may not in every case suffice to destroy any continuity between the transactions carried through before the change in the firm and those carried through subsequently.   The decision of the question may well be of the nature of a jury question taking into account all the circumstances,—the " specialities " to which Lord Neaves refers.   But, in any event, that sort of consideration as to continuity has only limited relevance in a question relating to a winding up.   In a case where after a dissolution of a firm, its business continues to be carried on by others the question is paramount in importance.   But where on dissolution the firm proceeds to a winding up of its affairs, the relevance of questions of continuity is directed to continuing authority to bind the dissolved firm and will rather be concerned with determining whether what is done further under the winding up is a " continuance " in the sense that it is necessary " to complete transactions begun but unfinished at the time of the dissolution."   In the case of a business of the nature carried on by a firm of solicitors the determination of questions of that kind may be difficult and doubtful in some instances.

" So far as may be necessary to wind up the affairs of the partnership "

The range of the application of these words has already been, to some extent indicated and is described in more particularity by Lord Neaves in the introductory words of the passage quoted from his judgment in *Wotherspoon* v. *Henderson's Trustees*.[27]   It has likewise already been mentioned that a

---

[26] *Wotherspoon* v. *Henderson's Trs.* (1868) 6 M. 1052 at p. 1061.
[27] See *supra* n. 26.

notice of dishonour of a bill of exchange given to one of the partners of a dissolved firm is sufficient to bind the firm and the remaining copartners.[28] A partner will have continuing authority to bind the firm in a sale of its assets [29] or to pledge the assets of the firm if necessary to complete a transaction already commenced before dissolution [30] or to secure a debt incurred by the firm prior to dissolution [31] or its overdraft on current account with a bank.[32] He has continuing authority to uplift sums at credit of the firm in deposit receipt with a bank.[33] Where a company was dissolved and as provided in the contract of copartnery a meeting of the partners was held at which A, one of their number, was appointed to wind up the firm's affairs with power of suing and being sued for the firm which traded under a descriptive name, A was held to have title to sue for reduction of a deed granted by one of his copartners to a third party in fraud of creditors.[34] In some of these specific cases the inter-action between the two provisions of section 38 of the Partnership Act 1890 limiting the authority becomes apparent, and they cannot be regarded as mutually exclusive. In *Butchart* v. *Dresser*,[35] for example, the two partners of a firm of share-brokers contracted for the purchase of certain shares. The firm was dissolved before the purchase had been completed and one of the partners pledged the shares to the bank in security of facilities provided by the bank to enable him to pay for the shares. He also authorised the bank, who were aware that the partnership had been dissolved, to sell the shares to indemnify themselves in respect of the sums advanced by them. The other partner claimed that this arrangement was made without his authority and that since the bank knew of the dissolution they could not regard the pledge of the shares as binding upon him. The court upheld the authority of the partner to pledge the shares after dissolution in order (if one may anachronistically use the words of section 38) " to complete transactions begun but unfinished at the time of the dissolution." But the transaction may equally be regarded as one " necessary to wind up the affairs of the partnership," and indeed in many cases a large common area may be covered by those two provisions.

Continuance of partnership business

Questions of the continuing authority of a partner to bind the firm after dissolution frequently arise not in the course of winding up the affairs of the dissolved partnership but in the continuance by some of the partners of the business formerly carried on by the dissolved partnership. While in such cases the partner carrying through the transaction clearly has authority under section 5 to do so on behalf of the new firm, a third

[28] *Goldfarb* v. *Bartlett & Kremer* [1920] 1 K.B. 639.
[29] *Morgan* v. *Marquis* (1853) 9 Ex. 145.
[30] *Butchart* v. *Dresser* (1853) 10 Hare 453.
[31] *Re Clough, Bradford Commercial Banking Co.* v. *Cure* (1885) 31 Ch.D. 324.
[32] *Re Bourne, Bourne* v. *Bourne* [1906] 1 Ch. 113; [1906] 2 Ch. 427.
[33] *Dickson* v. *National Bank of Scotland*, 1917 S.C.(H.L.) 50.
[34] *Jameson* v. *Watson* (1852) 14 D. 1021.
[35] (1853) 10 Hare 453.

party dealing with him may do so in the reasonable belief that he is acting as a partner of the old firm in virtue of his continuing authority under section 38; for the mere fact that the transaction relates to the continued carrying on of the business formerly conducted by the dissolved partnership is not necessarily inconsistent with the transaction being necessary for the winding up of the partnership affairs.   In the process of realisation of the partnership property in a winding up it is within a partner's continuing authority to carry on the business of the dissolved partnership if it is necessary to do so for a reasonable realisation of that property,[36] and it may also be necessary to continue to carry on the business, at least to some extent, in order to complete contracts begun but unfinished at the time of the dissolution.[37]   But in such cases it is always necessary to examine the transaction closely in order to ascertain whether in fact it may truly be said to arise from the conduct of the dissolved partnership for such purposes or whether it is attributable to some other relationship among the former partners.   In *Ault* v. *Goodrich* [38] a difficult question of this nature arose for decision and the difficulties of reconciling the case are perhaps enhanced by the inadequacy of the report of the decision.   Two persons, a father and his son, were in partnership as timber merchants and entered into a joint adventure with Ault and another person for the purchase and re-sale of some trees.   The son was chiefly concerned in the management of the adventure and before it was completed, he and his father dissolved their partnership.   It appears that the son had misapplied some money which he received on account of the joint adventure.   The court held that the father was responsible for the dealings of his son and partner during the continuance of the partnership and that, as there was no evidence of a new agreement among the parties after the dissolution as to the joint adventure, the other co-adventurers were entitled to rely upon the joint liability of the father and the son for the son's transactions and therefore the father was held liable for his son's conduct after the dissolution of their partnership.   Lindley [39] finds difficulty with this case because of the unsatisfactory terms of the report but considers that the father's responsibility for his son's conduct after the dissolution did not turn upon the fact that they were partners in a partnership now dissolved but on the fact that they were jointly entrusted with the management of the joint adventure in the tree speculation.   In this way he seeks to distinguish the decision from cases like *Butchart* v. *Dresser* and *Re Bourne, Bourne* v. *Bourne.*   It is submitted with diffidence and respect that so far as can be gathered from the report *Ault* v. *Goodrich* may alternatively be regarded as a case of continuing authority in a partner to complete a contract begun but unfinished at the date of dissolution; for if, as seems from the report to be the case, the joint adventure was entered into by the partnership, then upon the dissolution of the partnership and in the process of winding up its

---

[36] *Re Bourne, Bourne* v. *Bourne* [1906] 2 Ch. 427, *per* Vaughan Williams L.J. at p. 430.
[37] *Butchart* v. *Dresser* (1853) 10 Hare 453.
[38] (1828) 4 Russ. 430.
[39] *Op. cit.* pp. 252–253.

affairs, it became necessary to complete and discharge the obligations of the partnership under the joint adventure and to ingather the proceeds thereof so far as falling to the partnership. In those matters the son as a partner had clear authority to bind the partnership even after the dissolution and hence to render his father liable. In any event, in Scotland, where the added complication would be present that the partnership on entering the joint adventure would be regarded as a separate *persona*, it appears likely that the alternative approach to the problem might be preferred.

Dissolved firm not bound by actings of bankrupt partner

In terms of the proviso to section 38 of the Partnership Act 1890, the continuing authority of a partner to bind the firm after its dissolution is further limited by the rule that the firm is in no case bound by the acts of a partner who has become bankrupt. That rule is itself subjected to further exception in that it does not prejudice the liability of any partner who after the bankruptcy represented himself or knowingly suffered himself to be represented as a partner of the bankrupt. It will be borne in mind that in Scotland the bankruptcy of an individual, when referred to in the Partnership Act 1890 means his sequestration under the Bankruptcy (Scotland) Acts.[40] If, therefore, a partner of a firm becomes bankrupt, thus bringing about the dissolution of the partnership, or if, either contemporaneously with, or subsequently to, the dissolution he is rendered bankrupt, in the sense that his own separate estate is sequestrated in bankruptcy, his bankruptcy is a public fact and there is no room for an assumption by a third party who is in actual fact unaware of the bankruptcy that that partner has continuing authority to act for the partnership in the winding up of the firm's affairs. Nor does the wording of the exception to the proviso to section 38 in any way militate against the general rule stated in the proviso; for what is secured by the wording of that exception is that no partner will escape the general liability which attaches to him under section 14 (1) of the Partnership Act 1890 if by his representations or conduct he causes third parties to believe that he and the bankrupt are partners after the dissolution of their partnership. In a case where liability is imposed in terms of section 14 (1), it is not imposed upon the ground that the person so affected is in fact a partner but on the ground that the equitable consequence of his conduct is that he ought to be liable as if he were a partner. The lurking semantic difficulty of the proviso is dispelled if it be recollected that " partnership is as effectively terminated by sequestration as by death " [41] and while after the dissolution of a partnership for any cause, a residual and continuing authority subsists in the partners for the purpose of winding up the affairs of the firm, the partnership relation is no less terminated at dissolution though the consequential and practical needs of winding up require the existence of a limited continuing authority.

[40] Partnership Act 1890, s. 47 (1).
[41] Bell, *Comm.* II, 530.

For the purposes of liability on holding out, the partners after the dissolution are no longer partners and any liability imposed on them by virtue of section 14 (1) is imposed upon them just as if they were strangers to the partnership who had so held themselves out or suffered themselves to be held out. The exception for the case of holding out in the proviso to section 38 reflects the law applied in the earlier English decision in *Lacy* v. *Woolcott*.[42]

Appointment of judicial factor to wind up affairs of the partnership

While in the normal case the process of the winding up of the business of the partnership will be in the hands of the partners themselves, or some of them, in some circumstances the court may regard it as expedient to appoint a judicial factor to administer the affairs of the firm during winding up. At common law, two distinct situations may arise in which a judicial factor may be appointed. Irrespective altogether of the process of winding up the partnership, it is in the discretion of the court to sequestrate the estates of a partnership and to appoint a judicial factor of the sequestrated estates. In such circumstances the judicial factor is normally appointed, not for the purpose of carrying on the business during winding up but in order to protect the firm assets until the firm shall be dissolved [43] or where a serious difference exists between the partners which may materially prejudice the affairs of the partnership.[44] Where a petition is presented for the appointment of a judicial factor on the partnership estate, a crave for sequestration of the estate should also be included in the petition [45]; and a judicial factor may be appointed *ad interim*. Interim appointment has been described as a rare occurrence and in most cases it is either made final or recalled within a comparatively short time. It has been laid down that in future cases there will be incorporated in the interlocutor making the interim appointment a direction to the judicial factor requiring him to report at intervals of not more than one month to the Accountant of Court so long as his appointment stands as an interim appointment.[46]

As has already been mentioned [47] any partner is entitled, upon the dissolution of the partnership, to apply to the court to wind up the business and affairs of the firm and that right extends to the representatives of a partner.[48] A similar right was recognised before the passing of the Partnership Act 1890 and its nature and extent was explained by the Lord President (Inglis) as follows [49]:

" (1) When all the partners in a copartnery are dead, this court

---

[42] (1823) 2 D. & R. 458.
[43] *McCulloch* v. *McCulloch*, 1953 S.C. 189.
[44] *Carabine* v. *Carabine*, 1949 S.C. 521.
[45] *Booth* v. *Mackinnon* (1908) 15 S.L.T. 848.
[46] See *McCulloch* v. *McCulloch, supra, per* the Lord President (Cooper) at p. 192.
[47] *Supra* Chap. IX, p. 406.
[48] Partnership Act 1890, s. 39.
[49] *Dickie* v. *Mitchell* (1874) 1 R. 1030 at p. 1033.

has the power, and will exercise it, of appointing a factor to wind up the partnership estate. . . .[50]

" (2) If there are surviving partners, then, if there is no fault or incapacity on the part of them or any of them, preventing them carrying on their business, this court will not interfere, but will leave the surviving partners to extricate their affairs in their own way. . . .[51]

" (3) Where there is a surviving partner or partners, but these partners are unfitted either for carrying on or winding up the affairs of the partnership, whether from failure of duty, or incapacity of any one or more of them, then this court can, and, if satisfied of the necessity, will, appoint a factor. All such cases are in their nature cases of circumstances, but if the circumstances are strong enough, it is within the competency of the court to make the appointment."

These guiding rules are not altered in essence by the terms of section 39 of the Partnership Act 1890, and it is in the area of discretion afforded by the third of the Lord President's rules that the Scottish decisions both before and after the passing of the Act are helpful. Such decisions cannot be regarded as in the strict sense binding precedents. They are merely examples of the manner in which the court has exercised its discretion in particular cases; but they are of assistance as a guide to the probable response of the court to future situations of a similar kind. Thus in *Macpherson* v. *Richmond* [52] a judicial factor was appointed to wind up the firm's affairs where a petition was presented on the grounds that one of their number had persistently overdrawn from his capital account with the firm, had absented himself from business for a prolonged period alleging as his reason for his absence the prohibition placed upon him of further drawing on his capital account, and on his return to business refused to carry out duties which had normally hitherto fallen to his care. If there is a danger that if the winding up remains in the control of a partner his copartner may not be afforded his rights or his due rights may be defeated, that will be a circumstance which the court will take into account in deciding whether to appoint a judicial factor,[53] even where this involves the court remitting the partnership accounts to an accountant for report as to whether the allegation which was disputed by the respondent partner was true.[54] An issue between the partners of this kind need not raise any question of oppressive conduct on the part of the respondent but merely a difference between the partners in which, on a winding up, the partner in charge of the affairs is in effect continuing the business as a going concern rather than merely in order to realise the partnership property to best advantage in the course of the winding up.[55] In a case,

[50] *Dixon* v. *Dixon* (1831) 10 S. 178; affd. (1832) 6 W. & S. 229.
[51] *Collins & Feely* v. *Young* (1853) 1 Macq. 385.
[52] (1869) 6 S.L.R. 348.
[53] *Allan & Another* v. *Gronmeyer* (1891) 18 R. 784; *Carabine* v. *Carabine*, 1949 S.C. 521.
[54] *Allan & Another* v. *Gronmeyer, supra.* For the type of issue between the partners which may be appropriately determined by these means, see the observations of Lord McLaren at p. 788.
[55] *Allan & Another* v. *Gronmeyer, supra.*

very special upon its facts,[56] the court appears to have exercised its discretion under the third principle enunciated by Lord President Inglis, to the fullest extent. A judicial factor had been appointed *ad interim* for the protection of the partnership estate upon averments by one partner that because of disputes with her son, the other partner who managed the business, she had served six months' notice on him to dissolve the partnership and that she had reasonable cause to fear for the partnership property while it remained in her son's control during that period. The judicial factor took no active steps on his appointment, beyond finding caution and intimating his appointment to the firm's bankers. In the meantime the partners reached agreement as to the settlement of their dispute and the winding up of the firm independently of the judicial factor, and in these circumstances the son submitted that the interim appointment of the judicial factor should be recalled. The court, however, refused to do so, holding that in view of the laxity which had already occurred, it was essential that " what remains to be done should be carried out strictly under the eyes of the court." [57]   Where the partners are incapacitated from administering,[58] or are unfitted to administer,[59] the winding up, the court will appoint a judicial factor as will also be done if the partners have died.[60]   Unfitness of the partners to conduct the winding up may be attributable to advanced age,[61] or to physical or mental incapacity,[62] or it may arise from extravagance [63] or improvidence [64] of a partner. Since the court will not normally appoint a judicial factor if there is a partner or if there are partners capable of winding up the firm, the grounds of unfitness and incapacity alleged in the case of each partner who is, as it were, discarded for the purpose, may vary in the case of each, as in *Dickie* v. *Mitchell* [65] where one of the partners was unfitted by reason of age for the task, while the other, his son-in-law, had been reckless and improvident in managing the partnership business. Disputes and differences among the partners are features which may be considered by the court particularly if they are likely to lead, or have led, to a deadlock.[66]   The court will, however, not intervene in those cases without compelling cause.

" The jurisdiction of the courts to dissolve a partnership, and to appoint a receiver or judicial factor to wind up, is one of great delicacy, and which is only exercised where a very clear case for interposition

[56] *McCulloch* v. *McCulloch*, 1953 S.C. 189.
[57] *Ibid. per* the Lord President (Cooper) at p. 193.
[58] But not, apparently, where the legal incapacity has been incurred by one of the partners as a result of her own voluntary act: *Russell* v. *Russell* (1874) 2 R. 93, *per* Lord Deas at p. 94.
[59] *Dickie* v. *Mitchell* (1874) 1 R. 1030.
[60] *Dixon* v. *Dixon* (1832) 6 W. & S. 229.
[61] *Dickie* v. *Mitchell* (1874) 1 R. 1030.
[62] *Eadie* v. *MacBean's Curator* (1885) 12 R. 660; *Cleghorn* (1901) 8 S.L.T. 409; *Whitwell* v. *Arthur* (1865) 35 Beav. 140.
[63] But see *A.B., Petitioner* (1884) 22 S.L.R. 294.
[64] *Dickie* v. *Mitchell, supra.*
[65] (1874) 1 R. 1030.
[66] *Re Yenidje Tobacco Co. Ltd.* [1916] 2 Ch. 426; *Baird* v. *Lees*, 1924 S.C. 83, cases decided on the similar provision as to application for liquidation under the Companies Acts.

has arisen. To dissolve a partnership or appoint a factor on account of a mere squabble or explosion of bad feeling amongst the partners, would be to punish all for, it might be, the fault of one; and it would rather seem that, to justify an application to the court, the partner complaining must show a case of fraud or abuse of power on the part of the defenders." [67]

In these cases, and also where the grounds of the petition are that the petitioner is himself unfitted, or unable, to undertake the winding up, whereas his copartner's conduct has been such as to occasion the application for dissolution and winding up, it is regarded as more appropriate, where the petition is opposed, that the issue should be brought before the court in an ordinary action and not by way of summary application.[68] But if the differences relate purely to questions of accounting the court will not normally regard these as justifying the appointment of a judicial factor.[69]

The state of the partnership business itself, at the time of the application, may be a matter to be taken into consideration. " It is said to be a stronger thing to appoint a judicial factor in a going concern than in one which exists only for the purpose of winding up, and the petitioner's counsel went so far as to put it in the last case as a matter of right. But I can conceive stronger reasons for the appointment when the business is going on than when it has come to an end." [70] No rigorous rule can be stated as to the grant or the refusal of the appointment on these grounds alone. The whole circumstances must be taken into account; and when this is done, it may be found that the arguments in favour of appointment may be even stronger in the case of a going concern where the partnership business may continue to be conducted in a way prejudicial to, or even disastrous for, the petitioner, than where the partnership merely continues for purposes of winding up, and the scope of the liability likely to attach to the partners as a result is more circumscribed.[71]

Effect of arbitration clause in contract of copartnery

The question whether an arbiter, appointed under a general arbitration clause in the partnership agreement to refer all differences and disputes among the partners, may by his award dissolve the partnership has already been considered.[72] It has been held in the English courts that under such a clause the arbitrator may take part in the process of winding up the firm to a limited extent by allotting the assets of the partnership among the partners,[73] ordering one partner to pay or to give security for payment of

[67] See McLaren's note to Bell's *Comm.* II, 527; *Collins and Feely* v. *Young* (1853) 1 Macq. 385; and compare *Elder* v. *Elder & Watson*, 1952 S.C. 49, *per* Lord Cooper at p. 55.
[68] See *supra* Chap. X, pp. 455–456.
[69] *Gow* v. *Schulze* (1877) 4 R. 928; *Elliott* v. *Cassils* (1907) 15 S.L.T. 190.
[70] *Per* Lord Deas in *Gow* v. *Schulze* (1877) 4 R. 928 at p. 933.
[71] *Dickie* v. *Mitchell* (1874) 1 R. 1030 was a case of the latter kind.
[72] See *supra* Chap. X, pp. 480–484.
[73] *Lingood* v. *Eade* (1747) 2 Atk. 505; *Wood* v. *Wilson* (1835) 2 Cr.M. & R. 241; *Wilkinson* v. *Page* (1842) 1 Hare 276.

a specified sum to his copartners,[74] putting a value on the goodwill of the partnership business,[75] or imposing restraints on the extent to which a partner may continue to carry on the business.[76]   In spite of the differing attitudes taken by Scottish and English courts as to arbitration, it is thought that these decisions might receive consideration as persuasive authority in Scotland, since they are concerned with the *fines compromissi* on a true construction of the arbitration clause; but any force which they possess will be subordinated to a close examination of the actual terms of the clause before the court in order to construe its import and effect.   The arbitrator in England apparently is not empowered to appoint a receiver [77] but a receiver has been appointed in some cases of this kind.[78]   In Scotland, it is abundantly clear that in no circumstances will an arbiter have power to appoint a judicial factor since this is a matter entirely for the court.   It is, however, possible that the court will entertain an application for the appointment of a judicial factor to conduct the winding up, if the situation among the partners, including the award of the arbiter so far as touching upon the winding up, appear to the court to warrant their exercise of their discretionary power of appointment.   But where the question arises upon an application for dissolution of the partnership under section 35 of the Partnership Act 1890 there are dicta of Roxburgh J. in *Olver* v. *Hillier* [79] which suggest that the English courts may disregard the arbitrator's award.   On its facts, however, the case does not require that to be decided.   In the facts before the court in *Olver* v. *Hillier* the dispute had not been submitted to an arbitrator.   One partner applied to the court for dissolution and the other partner asked for a stay of the proceedings in order that the dispute might be referred under the arbitration clause.   It was held that since the dissolution of the partnership involved the exercise of a power which was expressly conferred upon the court under section 35 and might involve the appointment of a receiver and manager, the matter was most conveniently left in the hands of the court.

Right of partner's representatives in a winding up of the partnership

It will be noticed that in terms of section 39 of the Partnership Act 1890 the right conferred upon " every partner " on a dissolution of the partnership to insist on having the property of the firm applied in payment of its debts and liabilities and the surplus assets thereafter in payment of what may be due to the partners is not extended to the representatives of a partner although the partner himself may exercise the right against his copartners " and all persons claiming through them in respect of their

---

[74] *Simmonds* v. *Swaine* (1809) 1 Taunt. 549.
[75] *Re David & Matthews* [1899] 1 Ch. 378.
[76] *Morley* v. *Newman* (1824) 5 D. & R. 317.
[77] *Lingood* v. *Eade, supra*; *Re Mackay* (1834) 2 A. & E. 356; *Cook* v. *Catchpole* (1864) 10 Jur.(N.S.) 1068.
[78] *Routh* v. *Peach* (1795) 2 Anstr. 519; (1796) 3 Anstr. 637; *Olver* v. *Hillier* [1959] 2 All E.R. 220.
[79] [1959] 2 All E.R. 220 at p. 221.

interests as partners." That right is closely akin to a right to insist on a proper winding up of the firm's affairs and appears to be limited to a person who is a partner, and the more so since, while the entitlement is so restricted, the right is expressly stated to be maintainable at the instance of the partner not only against his copartners but also against those claiming through the copartners. On the other hand those words are immediately followed in section 39 by the words " and for that purpose [*i.e.* the winding up of the firm] any partner *or his representatives* may on the termination of the partnership apply to the court to wind up the business and affairs of the firm." (The italics have been supplied.) The first part of section 39 giving the entitlement to insist on a winding up is essential to ensure that the partner's lien or right of retention against the partnership property is made effective.[80] Though the terms in which the first clause of section 39 is couched suggest a possible doubt, it appears probable that the right to insist on a winding up is extended to the representatives of the partner in terms of the second clause thereof. That construction of section 39 is at least consistent with the previous law in both countries.[81] It would be difficult, in any event, to maintain a distinction between the right apparently conferred on the partner himself under the first clause and the derivative right conferred upon his representatives under the second, since in the last resort the right whether maintained by the partner or by his representatives may require to be vindicated in court. It may be that in the drafting of the section the distinction which is intended to be preserved is that between a winding up insisted upon by a partner, where the partner may himself conduct, or at least take part in, the process of the winding up and a winding up at the instance of a representative of a partner who will not as such representative be entitled to take part in the actual winding up.

Assignee of partner's share

A partner will be entitled in terms of section 39 to insist upon a winding up of the partnership business as against the assignee of the share of his copartner since the assignee clearly comes within the description of a person claiming through the copartner in respect of his interest as partner.[82] The assignee of a partner's share, however, will not be entitled himself to insist upon a winding up of the partnership. His rights, after a dissolution of the partnership, are expressly dealt with in section 31 (2) of the Partnership Act 1890 and are confined to receiving " the share of the partnership assets to which the assigning partner is entitled as between himself and the other partners, and, for the purpose of ascertaining that

---

[80] *Supra* Chap. IX, pp. 406–409. See *Keith* v. *Penn* (1840) 2 D. 633; *West* v. *Skip* (1749) 1 Ves.Sen. 239.

[81] See, for Scotland, Bell, *Comm.* II, 535; *Marshall*, Feb. 23, 1816, F.C.; *Stewart* v. *Simpson* (1835) 14 S. 72; for English law, *Stocken* v. *Dawson* (1845) 9 Beav. 239; *West* v. *Skip*, *supra.*

[82] *Cavander* v. *Bulteel* (1873) L.R. 9 Ch. 79. These words will similarly include the executors of a deceased partner and the trustee on the sequestrated estate of a bankrupt partner: *Croft* v. *Pyke* (1733) 3 P.Wms. 180. But they will not cover a person who is a bona fide purchaser from one of the partners of partnership property: *Re Langmead's Trusts* (1855) 20 Beav. 20; 7 De G.M. & G. 353.

share, to an account as from the date of the dissolution." [83]   But the
right conferred by section 31 (2) after dissolution is not of the same order
of ineffectiveness as that conferred in section 31 (1) in the case of a continuing partnership business.   In *Watts* v. *Driscoll* [84] Lord Alverstone
C.J. said,

> " Up to the passing of the [Partnership] Act there was some doubt
> whether the assignee of a share in a partnership had a right to call on
> the other partner to account to him.   I think that it was intended by
> section 31 to determine the rights of the parties under such circum-
> stances.   It is provided by subsection (1), in accordance with the old
> decisions, that during the continuance of the partnership the assignee
> cannot impeach the account of profits agreed to by the partners.
> Then subsection (2) refers to the case of a dissolution of partnership.
> We were pressed by counsel . . . to say that the words in subsection
> (2), ' the share of the partnership assets to which the assigning partner
> is entitled as between himself and the other partners,' include the
> share according to any bargain made in the absence of fraud between
> an outgoing partner and the other partners on the basis of which the
> dissolution takes place; and that whatever the terms of the bargain were
> on which the dissolution took place, even though it had no reference to
> the amount of the partnership assets to which the outgoing partner
> was entitled, and there was no provision for ascertaining the amount
> of the share of the partner who had assigned his interest, or for taking
> accounts of the partnership, the mortgagee or assignee was bound by
> it. . . . I think it was intended to give the assignee a right to have the
> account taken whenever the unexpected event happened. . . ."

Effect of section 39 on right to apply for appointment of judicial factor

The question was at one time raised whether the second clause of
section 39 of the Partnership Act 1890 alters the previous law under which
the appointment of a judicial factor to act on the winding up was a matter
within the discretion of the court and now entitles any partner of a dissolved firm, or the representatives of any such partner, to apply as of
right for the appointment of a judicial factor even where competent and
reliable copartners are available to conduct the winding up. [85]   While the
wording of the clause is not inconsistent with that view, there has been no
suggestion in any of the cases decided since the passing of the Act [86] that
the Scottish courts regard the appointment otherwise than as a matter
within their discretion; and it must be taken to be the better view that the
former rules of the common law shall apply.   It cannot be said, however,

---

[83] See *Whetham* v. *Davey* (1885) 30 Ch.D. 574.
[84] [1901] 1 Ch. 294.
[85] See Professor Lorimer's comments in the *Supplement to Lindley on Partnership* (1891),
p. 104.   See also Lindley, *op. cit.* (6th ed. 1893), p. 806.
[86] *Gatherer* (1893) 1 S.L.T. 401; *Thomson* (1893) 1 S.L.T. 59; *Paterson* (1894) 1 S.L.T. 564;
Robertson (1902) 10 S.L.T. 417; *Carabine* v. *Carabine*, 1949 S.C. 521; *McCulloch* v.
McCulloch, 1953 S.C. 189.

that the cases cited entirely dispose of the argument that section 39 may have altered the former law. Lord McKay in *Carabine* v. *Carabine* seems to favour the view that the function of the courts may have altered since the passing of the Partnership Act 1890. Of the remaining cases *Robertson* seems clearly to support the view that the court still may exercise a discretion in such circumstances as does *Thomson*. In *Gatherer* there was in fact no partnership, whereas in both *Paterson* and *McCulloch* v. *McCulloch* a judicial factor was in fact appointed.

Distribution of assets on final settlement of accounts in winding up

The application of the assets of the partnership on a winding up of its affairs is regulated by the terms of the agreement made among the partners themselves. Any such agreement will not, of course, limit the rights of third parties who are creditors of the firm and who are entitled to claim upon the partnership property to satisfy their claims, since the partners hold the partnership property in trust for the purposes of the partnership,[87] and thus, according to Bell,[88] it " is held by the partners jointly for the uses of the partnership, and is directly answerable as a stock for the payment of its debts." The partners, however, may agree *inter se* as to the proportion in which any surplus remaining after settling with the firm's creditors will be distributed among them, and likewise as to the manner in which any short-fall in the assets of the partnership in satisfying the firm debts will be apportioned among them, though in the latter arrangement the right of creditors to proceed against any partner or partners and to leave him to operate his recourse against his copartners under the partnership agreement will not be affected.

Section 44 of the Partnership Act 1890 lays down general rules for observance in settling accounts *between the partners*, which shall apply subject to any agreement made by the partners themselves.

> " 44. In settling accounts between the partners after a dissolution of partnership, the following rules shall, subject to any agreement, be observed:
>
> (*a*) Losses, including losses and deficiencies of capital, shall be paid first out of profits, next out of capital, and lastly, if necessary, by the partners individually in the proportion in which they were entitled to share profits:
>
> (*b*) The assets of the firm, including the sums, if any, contributed by the partners to make up losses or deficiencies of capital, shall be applied in the following manner and order:
>
> 1. In paying the debts and liabilities of the firm to persons who are not partners therein;
> 2. In paying to each partner rateably what is due from the firm to him for advances as distinguished from capital;

---

[87] Partnership Act 1890, s. 20 (1).
[88] *Comm.* II, 500.

3. In paying to each partner rateably what is due from
    the firm to him in respect of capital;
4. The ultimate residue, if any, shall be divided among
    the partners in the proportions in which profits are
    divisible."

"*Subject to any agreement.*"   It has been emphasised that in a question
of settlement of accounts among the partners themselves, which is the
question which section 44 seeks to regulate, the governing principle is to
ascertain what is the true construction of the agreement among the
partners; and section 44 recognises that principle by making the rules
which it sets forth " subject to any agreement."   The fact that the partners have regulated by an express term of their agreement the basis of
accounting among them may not, however, in every case be sufficient to
solve the problems arising on a winding up of the partnership, since such
a provision in the contract of copartnery will first need to be examined in
order to ascertain whether on a true construction of its terms it may be
regarded as truly intended to cover the settlement of accounts on a winding up of the firm or even on the dissolution of the firm by the retirement
of one of the partners, or whether its true intention is simply to regulate
accounting among the partners while the partnership is a going concern.
It is frequently provided in contracts of copartnery that an account when
signed shall be taken as conclusive among the partners and not reopened
except for a manifest error later discovered and even in that case the contract may provide for reopening of the account on that ground within a
limited period of time.   But even where such provisions occur they must
be closely examined in their context to decide whether they are intended
to be effective in all accounting arising among the partners or merely in
accounting which takes place during the conduct of the continuing
business of the partnership.   While the partners are associated with each
other in a continuing business the periodical accounts of the partnership
may be prepared on the basis of " book " or " written down " values for
the assets of the partnership and omitting any item in respect of goodwill.
Where the business is a continuing one and the real purpose of the accounting is to arrive at the profit or loss attributable to the business during the
period of accounting and to apportion it among the partners, there is no
real objection to accounts of that kind being made conclusive and incapable of being reopened in terms of some suitably drafted provision of
the partnership agreement.   But it does not follow from this that an
account which is conclusive for that purpose will be conclusive for the
purpose of ascertainment of the partners' rights on a winding up.   In
many cases of professional partnerships, where it is intended that the
partnership business shall continue despite the death or retirement of any
partner and where the fixed assets, apart possibly from goodwill, consist
mainly of the partnership premises and office furnishings, it may not be
out of place to settle with a retiring partner or with the representatives of
a deceased partner, on the basis of the last " conclusive " account in the

partnership. But where the affairs of the firm are in process of being wound up accounts taken during the continuing partnership, which omit any item for goodwill or which include the property of the firm at book values, will not necessarily, even when declared to be conclusive for that purpose, establish an agreement that in a winding up the goodwill of the business is to be disregarded or the assets taken at the value appearing against them in the earlier accounts of the partnership. In spite of provisions of this kind in the partnership agreement it may still be possible for a partner to obtain, on a true construction of the agreement, a share of the proceeds of the sale of the goodwill or of a valuation representing the notional proceeds thereof on a winding up of partnership even upon its dissolution through the death or retirement, when the remaining partners continue to carry on the business of the former firm.[89] But such a result will depend upon the true construction of the terms of the partnership agreement and will not arise from extraneous considerations of law such as *e.g.* the legal rights of the widow and children of a deceased partner.[90] Nor can the decisions upon liability for estate duty [91] prevail as against the situation *inter socios* which is established on a true construction of the contract of partnership.[92] It may likewise be possible for a retired partner or the representatives of a deceased partner to have the assets of the partnership properly valued on a winding up, even if, in the accounts of the partnership, while still in business, the assets were included at book values only.[93] A similar accounting difficulty arises from the fact that it does not necessarily follow that because profits and losses have been equally distributed among the partners in the annual accounts of the partnership as a going concern, these will fall to be treated in the same way in a winding up, without reference to the amount of capital contributed by the partners respectively.[94] In the task of arriving at the true intention of the partners as to the method of accounting to be applied *inter socios*, it has been repeatedly recognised by the courts that the manner in which accounts are prepared for the purposes of a subsisting partnership, albeit satisfactory for those purposes, may be inappropriate as a basis of accounting in a final winding up or even in the ascertainment of an individual partner's share on a dissolution of the firm.[95]

" *Losses, including losses and deficiencies of capital.*" Other difficulties as to the correct basis of accounting among partners in a winding up of the firm may arise in regard to the manner in which losses are to be made good. Here again the terms of the partnership agreement must be

---

[89] *Wade* v. *Jenkins* (1860) 2 Giff. 509. But *cf. Steuart* v. *Gladstone* (1878) 10 Ch.D. 626; *Hunter* v. *Dowling* [1895] 2 Ch. 223.

[90] *Ventisei* v. *Ventisei's Exors.*, 1966 S.C. 21.

[91] *Att.-Gen.* v. *Boden* [1912] 1 K.B. 539; *Perpetual Executors & Trustees Association of Australia Ltd.* v. *Commissioner of Taxes of the Commonwealth of Australia* [1954] A.C. 114, *per* Lord Cohen at pp. 130–131.

[92] *Ventisei* v. *Ventisei's Exors, supra.*

[93] *Cruickshank* v. *Sutherland* (1922) 92 L.J.Ch. 136; *Noble* v. *Noble*, 1965 S.L.T. 415.

[94] *Binney* v. *Mutrie* (1886) 12 App.Cas. 160; *Wood* v. *Scoles* (1866) L.R. 1 Ch. 369; *Macredie's Trs.* v. *Lamond* (1886) 24 S.L.R. 114.

[95] *Coventry* v. *Barclay* (1863) 3 De G.J. & Sm. 320; *Ex p. Barber* (1870) L.R. 5 Ch.App. 687.

considered and construed but questions may also arise as to the applicability of any provision of the partnership agreement to the case where the partnership is in process of being wound up. The agreed provisions may be construed as appropriate to a continuing partnership only and not to a process of winding up.[96] Moreover, the term " net profits " may be construed differently in different contexts in the partnership agreement [97] with a consequentially different view as to losses. Thus while in the strictest sense profit represents the excess of receipts over expenditure [98] and accordingly, in winding up the firm, nothing may properly be distributed as profits which does not accord with that description, there is maintained in the carrying on of a going concern a distinction between receipts and expenses which are either ordinary or extraordinary, and the ordinary expenditure will frequently be paid out of capital or money borrowed for the purpose. The treatment of any particular item of expenditure or of receipt as extraordinary or as ordinary reflects a matter of commercial judgment upon which differing opinions may honestly be held and which in the case of difference may properly be decided by a majority of the partners [99]; and thus in a continuing partnership the excess of the trading receipts for any year over the trading expenditure for that year may be distributed as profits without first applying the surplus in replacing capital which has been lost or is not represented by realisable assets.[1] It will be obvious, therefore, that a clause in the partnership agreement which is designed to regulate the rights of partners during the continuance of the firm as a going concern may not be applicable to the case where the firm is in process of being wound up. One of the problems which may arise in the latter case is whether on a winding up any part of the proceeds of the partnership assets may be regarded as a profit until the contributions of the partners to capital have been repaid to them or may be regarded as a loss until the capital contributions of the partners have been utilised and exhausted. The situation may be further complicated where the partners are held to share equally in profit and contribute equally to losses in virtue of the general presumption in favour of equal participation and not in virtue of any express term of the agreement, because that presumption in favour of equality of participation may co-exist with unequal contribution by the partners to the capital stock of the partnership.[2] It is to meet such difficulties that the words " losses, including losses and deficiencies of capital " are introduced in the general rule laid down in section 44 of the Partnership Act 1890 where the rights of the partners *inter se* on a winding up are not otherwise regulated by agreement among them. The words quoted do not, however, entirely resolve

---

[96] *Re Bridgewater Navigation Co. Ltd., Birch* v. *Cropper* (1889) 14 App.Cas. 525; *Lawes* v. *Lawes* (1878) 9 Ch.D. 98; *Re London India Rubber Co.* (1868) L.R. 5 Eq. 519.
[97] *Watson* v. *Haggitt* [1928] A.C. 127.
[98] *Re Spanish Prospecting Co. Ltd.* [1911] 1 Ch. 92.
[99] Partnership Act 1890, s. 24 (8).
[1] For a full discussion of the question in the analogous case of a limited company, see Palmer, *Company Law* (21st ed.), p. 666 and pp. 671–673 and cases there cited.
[2] See *supra* Chap. IX, pp. 400 *et seq.*

the difficulty.   It seems clear that if the assets of the partnership are insufficient to pay the claims of the firm's creditors in full, the resulting shortfall is to be treated as a loss and the partners will be liable *inter se* to make up the shortfall in the ratio in which they have agreed to share profits and make good losses.   In such a case, if the presumption as to equality of sharing applies and if the partners originally contributed un-equal amounts to the capital of the firm, the loss will be apportioned among the partners equally and not in proportion to their unequal contributions to capital since *ex hypothesi* the contributions to capital will have already been devoted to the payment of the claims of third parties and what is now under consideration is an overall loss occurring in the conduct of the business, a matter affecting the fortunes of the partnership in which all the partners have agreed, or are presumed to have agreed, to participate equally.   The position becomes more complex where a surplus remains after satisfying the claims of the firm's creditors who are not partners, but that surplus is insufficient to satisfy in full the advances made by the partners to the firm and the original capital contributions of the partners to the firm.   In the general case, the wording of section 44 is adequate to meet that situation.   If the surplus which remains is in-sufficient to meet the advances made by the partners, as distinct from their contributions to capital, the deficit will be treated as a loss which will be made good in the last resort by the partners themselves in the ratio in which they are entitled to share in profits.   The deficit on the sums advanced by each partner will still be treated as a firm debt which is payable to that partner.[3]   If there is a surplus after both the claims of third parties against the firm and the partners' claims for advances have been paid, and that surplus is not enough to pay each partner his capital in full, then the balances of capital remaining due to each partner should be treated as losses and met by contribution from the partners rateably in the same proportions as other losses are met.   Under section 44 there is no difference in the treatment laid down for a loss representing a shortfall on the amounts advanced by the partners as compared with one on the amounts of capital contributed except that advances are to be repaid in priority to capital.   In each case they are treated as losses and the partners are liable to make them good on the same footing as other losses.   That, however, is the extent of the rule and it does not, where one of the partners is insolvent, impose on the other partners a liability to make up his share of the losses of capital and advances after all the firm's liabilities to third parties have been met.[4]

Capital contributions unequal but losses borne equally

In cases where the partners have made unequal contributions to the capital of the firm but have agreed, or are presumed to have agreed, to

[3] This was also the position before the passing of the Partnership Act 1890. See *Wood* v. *Scoles* (1866) L.R. 1 Ch. 369.
[4] *Garner* v. *Murray* [1904] 1 Ch. 57.

share the profits and bear the losses in equal proportions the application
of the rule in section 44 (*a*) of the Partnership Act 1890 becomes more
difficult, and that difficulty may be further complicated where instead of
having actually contributed unequal sums to the capital of the firm, the
partners are merely under an obligation to do so which remains un-
implemented at least in part.   When this is the basic situation and the
agreement goes no further, then a shortfall on capital is to be treated like
any other loss.   The only speciality is that the actual contributions to
capital are themselves unequal and the precise interpretation to be given
to section 44 (*a*) as to preserving equitable distribution of a deficiency in
capital among the respective partners requires closer examination.   " . . .
When the Act says losses are to be borne equally it means losses sustained
by the firm.   It cannot mean that the individual loss sustained by each
partner is to be of equal amount " [5]; and though in point of fact section
44 (*a*) of the Partnership Act 1890, which Joyce J. had under consideration, does not expressly say that losses are to be borne equally, that, in
appropriate circumstances, will be the effect of its direction that " losses
. . . shall be paid . . . lastly . . . by the partners individually in the proportion
in which they were entitled to share profits."

It is, however, in the assessment of the actual deficit in capital which
the partners are liable to contribute in equal shares or otherwise in such
shares as they were entitled to share in profits that the real notion of
equality of treatment resides and not in a mere mechanical and arithmetical application of the ratio of profit sharing to the shortfall on capital
account.   If the partners are entitled to share in the profits equally but A
has contributed £5,000 to the capital, whereas B has contributed £3,000
and C £1,000 and if after satisfying all other claims against the firm and
cost of winding up, there remains in the coffers of the partnership £6,000,
a loss of capital contributed has arisen amounting to £3,000.   How is
that loss to be dealt with in a winding up?   The Partnership Act 1890
appears to direct that, subject to agreement otherwise among the partners,
all three partners must contribute to the loss equally.   But what is
" equally " in this context?   If the arithmetical approach is adopted each
will be called upon for a further £1,000 and the capital fund having been
restored to its original amount of £9,000 by this means, each will receive
the amount of his original contribution therefrom.   In practical terms,
this will mean that each partner will be regarded as having notionally
contributed his £1,000 which will then be deducted upon the settlement of
his capital account.   A thus will receive £4,000, being his original capital
of £5,000 after deduction of his contribution of £1,000.   B will similarly
receive £2,000; and C will receive nothing since his original capital and
the amount of his contribution equal each other.   It can be said in one
sense that the partners here have contributed to the loss on the capital of
the firm in the proportion in which they were entitled to share in the
profits, *i.e.* equally, but it may require closer analysis before it can be said

[5] *Per* Joyce J. in *Garner* v. *Murray* [1904] 1 Ch. 57 at p. 60.

that each has borne an equal share of the loss upon his individual share of the capital; for A has received in fact 80 per cent. of his original contribution to capital.   B has received 66⅔ per cent. of his original contribution; and C has received nothing.

In a situation such as that envisaged above, it has been stated [6] that " the assets remaining after payment of all debts and advances must be distributed amongst the partners so as to make each partner's loss of capital equal; and if the assets are not sufficient, there must be such a contribution amongst the partners, or some of them, as to put all on an equality."   If there had been a clear surplus sufficient to pay all the sums contributed to the firm by the various partners, then that surplus would have been applied in repaying that capital before the partners came to share equally in any balance remaining.   But a loss has occurred in that the surplus remaining in the hands of the partnership is not sufficient to pay in full the sums originally contributed to the capital.   The rule propounded by Lindley has both good sense and equity to commend it.   It also finds support in some of the earlier decisions.[7]   Of these decisions, two were concerned with proceedings in the winding up of companies under the Companies Act 1862 [8] but in these decisions the earlier law in the partnership cases was examined and applied.

" It seems to me," said North J., " that this £25,000 must be distributed in the way in which the surplus assets were distributed in *Ex p. Maude* [9]—that is, after satisfying all claims for costs etc., the remaining surplus must be applied, first, in levelling down the shares —in returning to those shareholders who have paid £10 per share the sum necessary to bring them down to the level of those who have paid only £3 and that which is left must be divided equally among the shareholders in proportion to the number of their shares.   In *Birch v. Cropper* [10] there was a clear surplus of profit for division.   In the present case there is no profit: on the contrary there is a loss; and the only question is, in what proportion is it to be borne by the shareholders? "

The initial process of " levelling down " referred to by North J. in *Re Weymouth Steam Packet Co.*[11] presents little difficulty in its application to the shares of a joint stock company, but its operation in the case of unequal contributions to the capital of a firm is not discernible so immediately.   If an analogous process of levelling down were applied in the

---

[6] Lindley, *op. cit.* p. 613.
[7] *Re Wakefield Rolling Stock Co.* [1892] 3 Ch. 165; *Re Weymouth Steam Packet Co.* [1891] 1 Ch. 66; *Re Braginton, ex p. Maude* (1867) L.R. 2 Ch. 550.
[8] *Re Wakefield Rolling Stock Co., supra*; *Re Weymouth Steam Packet Co., supra.*
[9] (1867) L.R. 2 Ch. 550.
[10] (1889) 14 App.Cas. 525.
[11] [1891] 1 Ch. 66.   In *Re Wakefield Rolling Stock Co.* [1892] 3 Ch. 165 the levelling down in a case where the £5 shares were paid up to the extent of £1 only, whereas the £1 shares were fully paid up, was accomplished (a) by repayment to the £1 shareholders of 16s. per share to bring them into parity of treatment with the £5 shareholders and (b) after that had been done, distributing the surplus rateably among the shareholders, treating the £5 share holder for the purpose as if he were for each £5 share the owner of five £1 shares.

partnership example already given [12] the capital contributions of each
partner would first be reduced to the level of the smallest contribution,
i.e. £1,000 by paying to the partner with higher contributions of capital
the excess of that contribution over £1,000.   A would thus receive as a
prior payment £4,000, B £2,000 and C could receive nothing since his is
the level to which A and B are both levelled down.   Moreover, since the
prior payments made to A and B exhaust the funds available, C, in
common with A and B, can receive no " equal share " in the distribution
of capital after the levelling down has taken place.   Nevertheless, the
process has resulted in an equality of treatment since A, B and C have all
suffered an equal loss of capital, *i.e.* £1,000.

It therefore appears that the result achieved by levelling down coin-
cides with the result produced simply by striking the loss, or shortfall, on
capital account and dividing that equally among the three partners.   But
it may be that the coincidence in result is fortuitous and it is necessary to
test it by other examples.   This may be done by taking two alternative
situations—

(1) where the fund available in the hands of the firm is inadequate to
compass complete levelling down; and

(2) where the fund is such that a surplus is left after levelling down
but that surplus is not sufficient to pay off the partners' contributions to capital in full.

(1) In the former situation assume the circumstances of the previous
example but that £3,000 only is available in the hands of the partnership.
The shortfall on capital account is now £6,000.   If the arithmetical
approach is adopted, each partner will contribute £2,000 to make up the
capital fund and at the distribution A will receive £5,000 less his contribution of £2,000, *i.e.* £3,000, B will receive £3,000 less £2,000, *i.e.* £1,000 and
C will be called upon to pay £1,000 so that the fund is adequate to make
the foregoing payments to A and B.   But if the levelling down process is
adopted the entire capital fund available in the hands of the partnership
before any further contribution is called for from the partners is only
£3,000 which is insufficient to permit both A and B drawing sufficient from
it to level their capital down to the level of C's £1,000, and there is no
assistance to be derived from section 44 as to the manner in which the
inadequate fund is to be apportioned between A and B.   Nor can it be
said that C should simply be called upon to contribute £3,000 to the fund
to enable A and B's shares to be levelled down to his because that would
be to call upon C to contribute more to the capital of the firm than he
originally agreed to contribute.   The fact is that the actual loss of capital
cannot be redressed in this case by levelling down and the only method
available is to take the total loss on capital and apportion it equally.
Each then has to contribute £2,000 to the *loss* which will leave A with
£3,000, B with £1,000 and C liable to pay £1,000.

[12] *Supra* pp. 532–533.

(2) In the second situation, assume the same capital held by the partners respectively but the funds available in the partnership to be £7,500. There is still a total shortfall on capital of £1,500. If the arithmetical approach be adopted each partner will pay £500 towards the loss. A will then receive £5,000 less £500, or £4,500, B £3,000 less £500, or £2,500, and C £1,000 less £500, or £500. If A and B's shares are levelled down A will receive in priority £4,000 and B will receive in priority £2,000. There will remain £1,500 in the fund which will be shared equally among A, B and C who will then receive the same ultimate amounts as are brought out under the arithmetical process. One cannot readily appeal to the direction that the apportionment is to be "in the proportion in which they were entitled to share in the profits," because there has been interjected an intermediate stage of levelling down which might be thought in itself to conflict with that direction viewed as a general instruction, and while in the general interests of equitable distribution it can be maintained that levelling down must first take place before the general direction in the section is given effect to, it then becomes scarcely possible to appeal to the general direction which has been discarded in the process of levelling down. This objection is met when the direction in section 44 (*b*) (3) is read along with the general direction in section 44 (*a*) since in terms of section 44 (*b*) (3) the assets of the firm, *including the sums, if any, contributed by the partners to make up losses or deficiencies of capital,* shall be applied . . . in paying to each partner rateably what is due from the firm to him in respect of capital. The use of the word "rateably" in this provision, and in the provision of section 44 (*b*) (2) relating to advances, is in contrast with the provision in section 44 (*b*) (4) which alone of all the provisions relating to payment to partners out of the assets of the firm states that the ultimate residue, if any, shall be divided among them " *in the proportions in which profits are divisible.*" It seems clear, therefore, that the scheme of the section as a whole is to treat partners' advances and capital as debts due to the partners from the firm, though debts which are postponed to the debts owed to third party creditors. Section 44 (*a*) is concerned with the making up of losses and deficiencies in capital, a process in which the partners must contribute in the proportion in which they were entitled to share profits. But the sharing among the partners of any surplus remaining after the third party creditors of the firm have been satisfied, is not automatically, and in every case, to be upon the same ratio. It would be manifestly inequitable that the total advances made by the partners to the firm should simply be massed together and distributed among the partners in the proportion in which they share in the profits since the sums so advanced by the respective partners may differ and the difference may not reflect the difference, if any, in their entitlement to participate in profits. The same may be true of the sums contributed by the respective partners as capital. Therefore when section 44 (*b*) comes to deal with the distribution of the surplus assets among the partners, each is regarded as a creditor of the firm in the actual sums advanced or contributed to the capital and

each is entitled to rank upon the surplus rateably in respect of advances made or capital contributed to the firm. But while the general principle is that a partner is regarded as a postponed creditor in respect of advances and capital contributions, the amount of the firm's indebtedness to him in respect of these can only be ascertained upon an accounting where there are insufficient funds remaining to pay these or either of them in full.[13] In respect of advances it has been held in England that since the partner advances some of the money to himself the only way in which he can recover the money that he has advanced is by taking the accounts of the partnership.[14] It seems doubtful whether that decision has any authority in Scotland, however, since it proceeds upon the *ratio* that in English law the firm has no separate existence apart from the partners who comprise it. Under Scots law where the firm is a separate *persona*, there appears to be no reason why an individual partner should not sue the firm for the recovery of sums advanced by him to the firm and the need for proceeding by way of an action of accounting need only arise where there is an insufficiency of partnership assets and the rights of the partners *inter se* require a mutual accounting to be carried out in order to establish the sum due rateably to each partner.[15] The occasions when a right of recovery of this kind will arise in such circumstances of isolation as to support a petitory action directed against the firm will be infrequent. On a dissolution and winding up of the partnership an accounting will normally be necessary. The matters involved in the accounting are summarised by Bell.[16] " In taking an account between the partners themselves, the state of the stock is to be taken as at the dissolution (death, for instance) and the proceeds thereof until it is got in; and each is to be allowed whatever he has advanced to the partnership and to be charged with what he has failed to bring in, or has drawn out more than his just proportion."

Making up losses or deficiencies

The operation of section 44 of the Partnership Act 1890 thus involves the bringing into account of all sums or property contributed by the partners and the division of that or of any surplus remaining after settling the firm's indebtedness to third parties (1) in repayment to the partners, if necessary rateably, the amount of the sums advanced by them to the firm and (2) thereafter in repayment to them of their respective contributions to capital, again, if necessary, rateably to the amount of their respective contributions. If, however, the contribution to capital of one partner is represented by a payment in cash while that of the other is represented by property, such as the furniture and books of a professional partnership, which has been taken over by the partnership at an agreed value, the

---

[13] *Johnston* v. *Losh* (1844) 6 D. 626; *Garner* v. *Murray* [1904] 1 Ch. 57.
[14] *Green* v. *Hertzog* [1954] 1 W.L.R. 1309.
[15] *Green* v. *Hertzog* (*supra*) is, however, apparently regarded by Gow, *Mercantile and Industrial Law of Scotland*, p. 559 n. 62, as authoritative in Scotland since it is cited by him without comment.
[16] *Comm.* II, 535.

question of the value to be ascribed to the latter contribution on a winding up has still to be considered; for it may be that the value at the date of winding up of such property will have either increased or diminished as compared with the value set against it in the partnership agreement.   How then is that particular contribution to be dealt with in the winding up of the partnership?   In the first place, it should be noticed that whatever the value realised from the property on winding up, the partner's original contribution to the capital of the firm is not changed thereby.   That contribution still stands at the figure originally agreed between the partners when the partnership agreement was entered into.   But the value realised may be less than the value originally put upon the property in the agreement.   Is the partner who originally contributed the property to be allowed a rateable claim on the assets of the partnership based upon the agreed value of his original contribution or upon the value actually realised for the property which represents his contribution?   He is allowed to rank rateably in respect of the agreed value of his original contribution.[17]   The diminution in value of his original contribution is to be regarded as a loss of capital incurred by the firm.   Similarly if on realisation an enhanced value be obtained for the property, he is still restricted in his claim for repayment of capital to the agreed amount of his original contribution, since the enhanced value represents a capital profit to the partnership in which both partners will participate in the proportion in which they share in the profits.

Effect of error in compilation of docqueted accounts

In considering the settlement of accounts among the partners on a winding up, the effect of accounts previously settled among them may be of importance.   The questions which may arise may reflect a situation where the partnership agreement itself makes provision for such accounts being regarded as conclusive, *e.g.* where on the death of a partner his share is to be taken at its value according to the last annual account preceding his death [18] or at the mean between his share as appearing in that account and his share as appearing in the annual account prepared after his death.[19] Again the partnership deed may contain a provision, recommended as useful and prudent by Lindley,[20] that an account when signed by the partners shall be conclusive and shall not be reopened except for a manifest error discovered and objected to within a specified time limit.   If the matter is regulated by an agreed term of the partnership the task of the court will be restricted to construing that term in the light of what may reasonably be regarded as the intention of the partners in coming to their agreement.   Thus where the share of a deceased partner was to be determined on the basis of the last annual accounts prepared and signed by

---

[17] *Macredie's Trs.* v. *Lamond* (1886) 24 S.L.R. 114.
[18] *Coventry* v. *Barclay* (1863) 3 De G. & Sim. 320.
[19] *Russel* v. *Glen* (1827) 5 S. 221.
[20] *Op. cit.* p. 435; and see *London Financial Association* v. *Kelk* (1884) L.R. 26 Ch.D. 107, *per* Bacon V.-C. at p. 151.

the partners prior to the death, and such an account had been bona fide prepared and sent to a partner who later died without signing it but he at no time intimated disapproval, it was held that his executors were bound by the account so prepared.   The accounts, having been compiled in good faith and in the usual way and no objection having been taken to them on the ground of error, the absence of the deceased partner's signature was regarded as of no importance since he could not legitimately have refused to sign them.[21]   But no partner will be regarded as bound by his signature to an account if it has been obtained as a result of fraud or if he has been dishonestly kept in ignorance of the material circumstances by his co-partners.[22]   The power to reopen the accounts to correct manifest errors, where the clause contains such a power, applies only to *errores calculi* or such other palpable and obvious errors as are apparent on the face of the accounts, and the means of correcting which are to be found in the writings themselves.[23]   The phrase " manifest errors " is construed to include a more limited scope of errors than might be considered to be covered by its terms; for many errors can be regarded as manifest once they are dis-discovered but the courts have interpreted this and similar expressions occurring in the contract of copartnery as intended to be restricted to omissions or blunders too apparent to permit of real differences of opinion as to their nature.   " Nothing short of an error which is patent on the face of the writings themselves and the means of correcting which are to be found in the writings themselves can be looked to." [24]   The expression will, therefore, not be held to include errors in judgment reflected in the accounts, such as treating as good debts, debts which ultimately are discovered to be bad or failing to take account of losses which at the time of compiling the accounts were not known to have been incurred.[25]

Where there is no such agreed term in the partnership, the rule against reopening past accounts is not so strictly applied, but the onus will be on the party seeking to reopen the account to prove that it is affected by error, particularly when the account has remained unchallenged for a long period of time.[26]   It seems that, even in the absence of a clause declaring past accounts to be conclusive, a partner will not be permitted to found on errors of judgment reflected in the accounts when the errors were made

---

[21] *Coventry* v. *Barclay, supra.*   See also *Ex p. Barber* (1870) L.R. 5 Ch.App. 687; *Hunter* v. *Dowling* [1893] 1 Ch. 391; affd. [1893] 3 Ch. 212 and see [1895] 2 Ch. 223.   In *Coventry* v. *Barclay* the custom of the partners was to place a nominal value on plant and stock in trade and carry over part of their profits to reserve to meet unforeseen losses.   The executors were held bound by the nominal value for plant and stock in trade appearing in the accounts but Lord Westbury held that they were entitled to a share of the reserve fund after paying the losses to meet which the reserve had been created.

[22] *Oldaker* v. *Lavender* (1833) 6 Sim. 239; *Blisset* v. *Daniel* (1853) 10 Hare 493.

[23] *Law and others* v. *Liddell's Trs.* (1862) 24 D. 577, *per* the Lord Justice-Clerk (Inglis) at p. 584 and Lord Benholme at p. 585.

[24] *Law and others* v. *Liddell's Trs., supra per* the Lord Justice-Clerk, *loc. cit.*

[25] *Ex p. Barber* (1870) L.R. 5 Ch.App. 687.

[26] *Findlay Bannatyne & Co.'s Assignee* v. *Donaldson* (1865) 2 M.(H.L.) 86; *Blair* v. *Russell* (1828) 6 S. 836.

bone fide,[27] but the line to be drawn here may at times be a narrow one and if the objector discharges the onus resting on him to prove an error e.g. involving the treatment as good of certain debts which were in fact never recovered and were entirely lost,[28] he may be allowed to reopen the accounts.

Assets accruing after dissolution

In regulating the disposal of the assets of the firm on winding up its affairs section 44 (b) of the Partnership Act 1890 refers simply to " the assets of the firm " without providing expressly for the case of assets or claims which arise after dissolution.   In view of the continuing authority vested in the partners under section 38 to bind the firm and the continuance of the other rights and obligations of the partners, " so far as may be necessary to wind up the affairs of the partnership," a distinction of that sort is not in general necessary to ensure that in the final winding up assets accruing, and claims arising, after dissolution are properly brought into account on a final winding up.   But there are certain special matters which deserve notice.   In *Coventry* v. *Barclay* [29] where the executors of a deceased partner were held bound by the treatment of the valuation of plant and stock in trade in past settled accounts, it was held by Lord Westbury that the reserve fund established in those accounts from profits appropriated to it in order to meet unforeseen losses would still enure to the deceased partner, to the extent of his share, if after satisfying the losses for which it was created a surplus remained in the reserve fund.[30]   While a partner is, in the absence of agreement to the contrary, not entitled to remuneration, apart from his share of profits, for acting in the management of the firm,[31] it has been held in England that where one of the partners carries on the business of the partnership after dissolution in order to wind it up on behalf of his copartners and himself he is entitled to claim remuneration for his services.[32]   The claim will not be allowed if no profit has been made in carrying on the business [33] or where there is a special reason, apart altogether from the law of partnership, why he should not be allowed remuneration, e.g. where he is also the executor of the other partner who is deceased.[34]   On the other hand, where in the winding up of a partnership after dissolution on the death of one of the partners, the

---

[27] *Laing* v. *Campbell* (1865) 36 Beav. 3.
[28] *Findlay Bannatyne & Co.'s Assignee* v. *Donaldson, supra.*   This case was, however, special on its facts since the error occurred in the settled accounts of the old firm and resulted in calls being made on the members of the new firm which took over the business on the basis of those accounts in respect of the loss incurred on the bad debts and the expense of trying to recover them.
[29] (1863) 1 De G. & Sm. 320.
[30] See *supra* n. 21.
[31] Partnership Act 1890, s. 24 (6).   As to special agreement entitling a partner to remuneration see *Faulds* v. *Roxburgh* (1867) 5 M. 373.
[32] *Re Aldridge* [1894] 2 Ch. 97; *Meyer & Co.* v. *Faber* (No. 2) [1923] 2 Ch. 421 at pp. 450–451, *per* Younger L.J.
[33] *Re Aldridge, supra.*
[34] *Burden* v. *Burden* (1813) 1 Ves. & B. 170; *Stocken* v. *Dawson* (1843) 6 Beav. 371; but *cf. Forster* v. *Ridley* (1864) 4 De G.J. & S. 452.

survivors claimed compensation on the ground that the deceased had not attended to the business during a portion of the partnership and had thus thrown the whole conduct of the business upon them, it was held that they could maintain no such claim, since if the deceased were unable or un- willing to carry out his part of the contract, they ought to have sought their remedy by dissolution of the partnership when it became clear that the deceased could not perform his part in the partnership affairs.[35]

Questions as to property accruing and claims incurred after dissolution which are specially provided for in the Partnership Act 1890

While, as has already been mentioned, there is no necessity for a distinction to be preserved for the purposes of winding up between property acquired and liabilities incurred at or before dissolution on the one hand, and those accruing or incurred after dissolution and before winding up is complete on the other hand, the Partnership Act 1890 makes provision for two special cases in sections 40, 41 and 42. Section 41, which deals with the partner's lien on, or right of retention of, the surplus of the partnership assets after satisfying the partnership liabilities on a dissolution as a result of the rescission of the contract of partnership for fraud or misrepresenta- tion has already been examined,[36] and no further or special questions arise for discussion in relation to the process of winding up itself. Section 42 has also previously been under examination [37] but since its operation may vary according to the circumstances surrounding the partners in the wind- ing up process it will require some further study. Likewise some further consideration should be given to the effect of section 40 in the winding up of the firm.

Effect of section 42 where there has been no settlement with a person who has ceased to be a partner

Section 42, as has already been noticed, where a partner has died or otherwise ceased to be a member of the firm and the surviving or remaining partners continue to carry on the business of the firm with its capital or assets without any final settlement of accounts between the firm and the outgoing partner, gives the outgoing partner or his estate a right to recover from the firm at his option either (a) such share of the profits made since the dissolution as the court finds to be attributable to the use of his share of the partnership assets or (b) interest at 5 per cent. per annum on the amount of his share. That optional right may be displaced by agreement to a contrary effect among the partners themselves or in the case of a deceased partner, where his executors lend the deceased's share to the continuing partners at interest.[38] But the earlier authorities appear to

---

[35] *Macredie's Trs.* v. *Lamond* (1886) 24 S.L.R. 114. So held in the Outer House by Lord Fraser and acquiesced in.
[36] *Supra* p. 163.
[37] *Supra* p. 373.
[38] *Stroud* v. *Gwyer* (1860) 28 Beav. 130.

govern the latter exception only where the executors are not themselves members of the firm.[39] If the executors are also members of the firm, it is doubtful in English law whether the optional right now reflected in section 42 (1) of the Partnership Act 1890 still is available. The rights are alternative not cumulative, the choice of the most favourable right being at the option of the outgoing partner or his representatives, but, although both profits and interest cannot be claimed, it appears that in Scotland the action may competently sue alternatively for each of the remedies.[40] The remedy by way of claim of a share of the profits attributable to the continuing use of the outgoing partner's share involves a discretionary decision by the court in which there are a number of factors to be weighed—the nature of the business itself, the amount of capital employed in it, the skill of those partners who conduct its management and general considerations of the conduct and activities of the partners in the partnership.[41] On a consideration of these factors the court may arrive at the conclusion that no share of the profits made is justifiably attributable to the use of the outgoing partner's share and that his claim is restricted to interest on the use of his money,[42] and the share of profits received by the partner before he ceased to be a member of the firm will have little relevance in the decision of the court.[43] Apart altogether from the relative overall contributions of skill and capital to the making of the firm's profits, there appears to be a constant factor to be allowed for in such cases in respect of the fact that the continuing partners are responsible for the conduct and management of the business whereas the outgoing partner no longer has any such responsibility. Section 42 (1) of the Partnership Act 1890 makes no express mention of this factor but since the section leaves the decision in the discretion of the court and since in the pre-statute decisions it was usual in these cases to allow remuneration to the continuing partners when arriving at the portion of the profits attributable to the outgoing partner's share,[44] it seems that this factor will still be a proper one for the court to take into account. But where the continuing partner is also a trustee of the outgoing (deceased) partner and has been guilty of breach of trust, no such remuneration will be allowed for in the calculation.[45]

Attributable to use of share or attributable to skill. The most anxious discrimination of the court in deciding such claims is required in deciding the more general question—how far is the profit made attributable to the skill of the continuing partners and how far to the employment of the funds of the outgoing partner in the business? It is because of the need for such discrimination that the share of profits previously enjoyed by the outgoing partner, while he was still a member of the firm is an irrelevant

---

[39] *Vyse* v. *Foster* (1872) L.R. 8 Ch.App. 309 at p. 334; affd. (1874) L.R. 7 H.L. 318.
[40] *Cochrane* v. *Black* (1855) 17 D. 321; (1857) 19 D. 1019.
[41] *Cochrane* v. *Black supra*; *Simpson* v. *Chapman* (1853) 4 De G.M. & G. 154.
[42] *Simpson* v. *Chapman supra*; *Wedderburn* v. *Wedderburn* (1836) 2 Keen 722.
[43] *Yates* v. *Finn* (1880) L.R. 13 Ch.D. 839.   [44] *Yates* v. *Finn, supra.*
[45] *Stocken* v. *Dawson* (1843) 6 Beav. 371; (1845) 9 Beav. 239; affd. (1848) 17 L.J.Ch. 282.

consideration in such cases.[46]   The nature of the problem is explained by
Romer J. in *Manley* v. *Sartori*.[47]   In the course of his observations,
he said—

> " It may well be that in a particular case profits have been earned
> by the surviving partner not by reason of the use of any asset of the
> partnership, but purely and solely by reason of the exercise of skill
> and diligence by the surviving partner; or it may appear that the profits
> have been wholly or partly earned not by reason of the use of the
> assets of the partnership, but by reason of the fact that the surviving
> partner himself provided further assets and further capital by means
> of which the profit has been earned.   Those profits, so far as earned
> by sources outside the partnership assets, are not profits in which the
> executors of the deceased partner could be entitled to any share . . .
> " The executors of the deceased partner are prima facie entitled
> to a share of the profits proportionate to his share in the assets of the
> partnership.   It is for the surviving partners to show, if they can, that
> the profits have been earned wholly or partly by means other than the
> utilisation of the partnership assets."

That dictum clearly brings out the sort of considerations which may be
weighed by the court in determining the claim of the outgoing partners;
and it will be observed that Romer J. places the onus of advancing and
establishing such considerations upon the surviving or continuing partners.
This appears to be clearly in accord with the terms of section 42 (1) of the
Partnership Act 1890 which asserts the right of the outgoing partner to a
share in the profits made but leaves it to the court to decide what is properly
attributable to the use of the outgoing partner's share.   But the views
advanced by Romer J. will not preclude the outgoing partner's claim to
the extent that it is attributable to the goodwill of the business.[48]

The alternative claim for interest.   The object of section 42 is to compensate an outgoing partner for the retention and use of his money in a
business with which he has ceased to be associated as a partner.   It
follows that this object might not be achieved if the outgoing partner were
solely dependent for his compensation upon such portion of the profits
earned as are found to be attributable to the funds belonging to him which
continue to be employed in the business; for the business may in fact
make no profit or a profit which represents very much less return than
would be afforded by interest on the money at the market rate, and the
outgoing partner in such cases has been deprived of the opportunity of
putting his money out on the market on more advantageous terms.   It is
with this broad notion of compensation in view that section 42 (1) of the
Partnership Act 1890 provides for the alternative remedy that the outgoing

---

[46] *Supra* n. 43.
[47] [1927] 1 Ch. 157 at pp. 163–166.
[48] *Manley* v. *Sartori, supra.*   However, such a claim may be precluded by the terms of the
  partnership agreement, if these provide that on dissolution an outgoing partner will have
  no right to a share in goodwill.

partner may at his option claim interest at 5 per cent. per annum on his
money still employed in the business. It is true that the rate of interest
prescribed in the section has somewhat Victorian echoes when considered
in relation to market rates in the present-day money market, but at least
when the outgoing partner's money has been employed in a failing
business, something may be reclaimed from the impending wreck by
prompt and adroit use of the alternative remedy. The interest allowed by
the section is simple interest. Where the continuing partners are also
trustees of the deceased former partner they may in certain circumstances
be liable in compound interest [49] but that liability will rest upon them in
their character as trustees and not *qua* partners.

Choice of remedy under section 42 (1). Commenting upon the situation produced by the English decisions on the portion of the profit attributable to the outgoing partner's share, Lindley [50] refers to the considerations
to be weighed by the court as laid down in the earlier decisions, particularly
Willett v. *Blanford*,[51] and concludes that " an element of uncertainty has
been introduced into an already difficult and complicated branch of the
law " particularly in view of the subsequent decisions in which profits
made after the death of a partner have been held to be attributable wholly
or partly to the skill and diligence of the continuing partners.[52] He continues, " Moreover, experience shows that judgments for an account of
profits after dissolution are fearfully oppressive; and there appears to be
no instance in which such a judgment has been worked out and has
resulted beneficially to the person in whose favour it was made." Without in any way endorsing the strictures, which in any event seem a trifle
petulant, applied to the courts in that passage it must always be kept in
mind that the element of work and skill will be present in such cases, in
some to a preponderating degree and in all to a significant degree. The
uncertainty which besets the partner who opts for a claim on the profits
made must therefore always be real and considerable; for the evaluation
of the contribution made by skill and labour as compared with capital can
never be reduced to a formula. On the other hand if the option is exercised in favour of the alternative claim for interest the situation is much
less fraught with uncertainty and the only question *in dubio* is the value of
the outgoing partner's share which may be brought out in an accounting.

The Scottish decisions. Though the Scottish cases are neither so
numerous nor so varied in their facts as the English authorities discussed
above, they are sufficiently in line with section 42 (1) of the Partnership
Act 1890 and with the earlier English authorities to suggest that the two
systems of law are in agreement in this area of the law and that the English
decisions will have strongly persuasive authority in the Scottish courts.
In *Minto and Another* v. *Kirkpatrick* [53] the question arose on a claim of

[49] See *Stocken* v. *Dawson, supra.*   [50] *Op. cit.* p. 605.
[51] (1842) 1 Hare 253; but see also *Crawshay* v. *Collins* (1820) 1 J. & W. 267; (1826) 2 Russ.
325, particularly *per* Lord Eldon.
[52] *Page* v. *Ratcliffe* (1897) 75 L.T. 371; *Manley* v. *Sartori* [1927] 1 Ch. 157.
[53] (1833) 11 S. 632.

legitim maintained against the estate of a partner who had deceased and whose share in the partnership continued to be employed in the business by his copartner, his son. Though the pursuers argued for an entitlement to a share of the profits of the business attributable to the amount of the legitim,[54] the court awarded legal interest on the claim. In *Laird* v. *Laird* [55] a partner of a trading company died and left a settlement whereby he appointed one of his partners as *inter alios* a trustee and ordered his funds to be realised and divided within twelve months. In terms of the partnership agreement the interest of a deceased partner was to be realised and paid out by instalments to his representatives within eighteen months. In fact the portion of the trust funds which consisted of his interest in the partnership was not realised but remained in the hands of the firm for some years. It was held that the copartner who was a trustee was liable for the profits earned by the firm so far as attributable to the deceased's funds employed in the business, the case was remitted to the Lord Ordinary and the court ordered such inquiry and investigation before an accountant as the Lord Ordinary might find necessary. The question of liability of the other trustees was expressly reserved and the liability for the profits was imposed on Laird in his character as a partner and on the authority of *Crawshay* v. *Collins*.[56] In *McMurray* v. *McMurray's Trustees* [57] the claim was again in respect of legitim from a deceased's estate where his trustees had carried on the business conducted by the deceased under a power in his settlement. The pursuer was held to be entitled to interest only, apparently on the reasoning that the legitim was a debt to be measured by the amount of the legitim fund at the deceased's death and did not infer a right to participate in the profits earned by the application of the fund after his death. This case, however, does not appear to be concerned with the principle of the law of partnership here discussed. The trustees had not been partners in the deceased's business along with the deceased. They were merely carrying on that business after his death under a power conferred by the deceased upon them. The decision consequently seems to depend rather on principles of the law of trusts and succession. In *Cochrane* v. *Black* [58] where the beneficiaries under a trust deed raised an action of count and reckoning against the trustees who were partners in a mercantile firm in which they had invested the trust funds contrary to the deceased's directions, it was held that it was competent to maintain in these circumstances that the trustees must account for the actual profits realised by employment of the trust funds. In this case, again, the principle of the law of partnership reflected in section 42 (1) of the Partnership Act 1890 is not clearly involved since the deceased himself was never a partner in the firm. That firm had acted as

---

[54] Citing as authority, Bell, *Comm.* II, 501; *Montague on Partnership* I, pp. 24 *et seq.* and pp. 98–99; *Crawshay* v. *Collins* (1808) 15 Ves. 218; *Brown* v. *Vidler* (1797) 15 Ves. 223.

[55] (1855) 17 D. 984.

[56] *Per* Lord Ivory at p. 993.

[57] (1852) 14 D. 1048.

[58] (1855) 17 D. 321; (1857) 19 D. 1019.

his " cashiers " and the partners of the firm, who were his trustees, had after his death employed the funds standing to the deceased's credit in account with the firm in the business of their firm. The case is thus essentially one decided on principles of the law of trust though some of the partnership cases were considered in the judgments.[59] It is interesting to note, however, the reason advanced for the alternative claim to interest on the money by Lord Wood [60]: " At all events...I proceed on the footing that this claim for profits is for an equal proportionate share of the gains made in the business, supposing the trust-money to have formed part of the capital, and the beneficiaries to have to that extent been interested as partners.   These gains having *ex hypothesi* exceeded the sum required to pay 5 per cent. on the capital and trust-money, as a whole, are the pursuers entitled or not to share proportionally in this excess?"

It is difficult to extract from the Scottish decisions any clear application of the rule applied by the English courts under which the profits made are closely analysed to see what may be regarded as attributable to the labour and skill of the continuing partners and what is attributable solely to the employment of the capital.   Indeed in the later report of *Cochrane* v. *Black* [61] in which the proportion of profits applicable to the employment of the trust funds was considered, there is no clear indication in the close and careful analyses of the capital structure of the business undertaken by the Lord Justice-Clerk (Hope) and by Lord Wood that the court considered the question of the portion of profits attributable to the partners' skill in conducting the business in any significant degree, though Lord Murray [62] appears to raise the issue only to dismiss it, and Lord Cowan [63] seems entirely to discard it when he observes, " The question to be solved—what profits were realised by the defenders on the £1,000 of trust-money employed by them in trade?—seems in itself sufficiently simple.   And it would be so, in fact, had the trade been carried on exclusively with the £1,000.   In that case, however large the value of the transactions carried on in the course of the year, the whole profits must, as I apprehend, have been accounted for to the beneficiaries."   If that approach may be taken as the approach of the Scottish courts in deciding questions under section 42 (1) of the Partnership Act 1890, then it represents a marked difference in outlook as compared with that of the English courts.   It is thought, however, that the decision cannot be taken to carry any such implications.   It is repeatedly emphasised in the judgments delivered that the issue before the Scottish court was one of trust and was in no way one of partnership.[64] What the court was deciding in *Cochrane* v. *Black* was the extent of the liability of trustees

---

[59] *e.g. Wedderburn* v. *Wedderburn* (1836) 2 Keen 722.
[60] *Cochrane* v. *Black, supra,* at pp. 335–336.
[61] (1857) 19 D. 1019.
[62] *Ibid.* at p. 1027.
[63] *Ibid.* at p. 1031.
[64] *Ibid. per* the Lord Justice-Clerk at p. 1026; *per* Lord Murray at p. 1027; Lord Wood at pp. 1027–1028.

who had invested the trust funds under their charge in breach of trust and so as to become *auctores in rem suam* as a result. In that context of law, it is well established that the trustees must account for the profit they have made as a result of the breach of trust; but that rule of law has no relevant application even by way of analogy to the right accorded to an outgoing partner under section 42 (1) of the Partnership Act 1890. The earlier decisions by the English courts which have been discussed appear to have been received and considered by the Scottish courts where the question for determination is one purely of partnership and its consequences in law and there appears to be nothing in the decision in *Cochrane* v. *Black* to disturb this.

Exceptions to the rule

The alternative claims provided for in section 42 (1) of the Partnership Act 1890 are inherently qualified in that they are created only " in the absence of any agreement to the contrary," a qualification which has already been commented upon.[65] A further qualification, however, is introduced in section 42 (2) which states—

> " (2). Provided that where by the partnership contract an option is given to surviving or continuing partners to purchase the interest of a deceased or outgoing partner, and that option is duly exercised, the estate of the deceased partner, or the outgoing partner or his estate, as the case may be, is not entitled to any further or other share of profits; but if any partner assuming to act in exercise of the option does not in all material respects comply with the terms thereof, he is liable to account under the foregoing provisions of this section."

No Scottish decision, reported either before or after the passing of the Act, deals with the circumstances envisaged in section 42 (2) which appears to be based upon the law as stated by Lord Cairns in *Vyse* v. *Foster*.[66] The arrangements with which the subsection deals are an option to purchase the outgoing or deceased partner's share.[67] It is not concerned with the case of an executed contract to purchase the share.[68] The distinction may be important, since in the case of an executed contract to purchase, the continuing partners, in the absence of fraud, are not liable to account for profits, unless by neglecting to implement some condition, or not complying with some stipulation of the essence of the contract, or in some other way, they repudiate the contract or give the representatives of the deceased partner a right to rescind the contract.[69] Difficulty may arise in the construction of clauses in the partnership deed affording such an opportunity to purchase.[70]

---

[65] *Supra* pp. 540–541.
[66] (1874) L.R. 7 H.L. 318 at p. 329.
[67] *Willett* v. *Blanford* (1842) 1 Hare 253.
[68] *Vyse* v. *Foster, supra.*
[69] *Vyse* v. *Foster* (1874) L.R. 7 H.L. 318, *per* Lord Cairns at pp. 334–335.
[70] Lindley, *op. cit.* pp. 441–442.

Rights arising where the partnership is dissolved for fraud or misrepresentation

In a winding up of a partnership which has been dissolved on the ground of fraud or misrepresentation, the terms of section 41 of the Partnership Act 1890 may be of considerable importance.

> " 41. Where a partnership contract is rescinded on the ground of the fraud or misrepresentation of one of the parties thereto, the party entitled to rescind is, without prejudice to any other right, entitled—
>
> (*a*) to a lien on, or right of retention of, the surplus of the partnership assets, after satisfying the partnership liabilities, for any sum of money paid by him for the purchase of a share in the partnership and for any capital contributed by him, and is
>
> (*b*) to stand in the place of the creditors of the firm for any payments made by him in respect of the partnership liabilities, and
>
> (*c*) to be indemnified by the person guilty of the fraud or making the representation against all the debts and liabilities of the firm."

Action for rescission

It will be observed that section 41 is concerned with the rights of the pursuer who seeks to rescind the contract of copartnery on the ground that he has been induced to enter into it by the fraud or misrepresentation of one of the parties to the contract. The purpose of the section is, therefore, to explain the consequential rights which will enure to the pursuer in a successful action to rescind the contract of partnership. It may be that the circumstances in which he has been induced to enter the partnership are sufficient to found an action for damages for fraud against the person through whose false representations he has been induced to become a partner, but if the pursuer's action is laid in damages on averments of fraud, the provisions of section 41 add nothing to his remedies at common law. Thus where, a contract of copartnery having been entered into between A and B and having endured for several years, A then raised an action against B for payment of the capital contributed by him to the firm under deduction of the sums he had received from the business, or alternatively for damages, the court assoilzied B. There was no conclusion for reduction of the contract of copartnery and although A averred that he had been induced to enter the contract by reason of B's fraud and misrepresentations the court held that fraud had not been proved and further that A was not entitled to restitution of his capital unless he reduced the contract of copartnery. Neither was he entitled to damages against B for his loss if that was caused by B's innocent misrepresentation.[71] In contrast to that decision, where the pursuer

---

[71] *Manners* v. *Whitehead* (1898) 1 F. 171.

raised an action for reduction of the agreement to enter a partnership
averring and proving that he had been induced by the defender's erroneous
statements as to the profits made from the business, it was held that the
agreement fell to be reduced albeit that there was no evidence that the
defender's misstatements were fraudulently made.[72] These decisions,
however, were reached entirely independently of section 41 of the
Partnership Act 1890 and upon the principles of the common law. In
regard to section 41 they merely serve to emphasise that the use of the
words " fraud or misrepresentation " in that section must be read in
the context of the rescission of the contract and in no way extend the
pursuer's rights and remedies in an action for damages based upon the
misrepresentations of his partner.

Consequential right arising under section 41

The section is founded upon the common law as applied in the
English courts prior to the passing of the Act.[73] While the pre-statute
decisions upon this aspect of the law of partnership are exclusively English
they have been regarded as in consonance with principles of Scots law [74]
and it seems clear that section 41 raises no question as to replacing the
earlier Scots law with material based upon principles which are foreign
to it. The rights afforded under the section to the party who has been
induced by fraud or misrepresentation to enter the agreement of partnership depend upon his claiming to rescind the contract and are consequential upon that claim. They furnish him with certain rights against
the partnership and its property in a question between him and his partners.
He has a lien on, or right of retention of, the surplus of the partnership
assets for the sum paid by him for his share in the partnership and the
capital contributed by him. If he makes any payment to the creditors
of the firm in respect of firm liabilities, he is entitled to take the place of
the creditors whose claims he has thus satisfied in a question between
him and his partners; and he is entitled to an indemnity from the person
responsible for the fraud or misrepresentation against his being called
upon in respect of the debts and liabilities of the firm. These rights
are available to him if he was in fact induced by fraud or misrepresentation to enter the partnership agreement which he now seeks to rescind
even if he had the means available of learning the truth and did not
avail himself of them at the time of entering the partnership.[75]

Without prejudice to any other right

The introduction of those qualifying words as governing the rights
specially mentioned in section 41 seems to preserve to the person induced

[72] *Ferguson* v. *Wilson* (1904) 6 F. 779.
[73] *Pillans* v. *Harkness* (1713) Colles 442; *Rawlins* v. *Wickham* (1858) 3 De G. & J. 304;
     Mycock v. *Beatson* (1879) 13 Ch.D. 384; *Adam* v. *Newbigging* (1888) 13 App.Cas. 308.
[74] See Clark, *op. cit.* I, p. 355.
[75] *Rawlins* v. *Wickham* (1858) 3 De G. & J. 304.

by fraud or misrepresentation to enter into the partnership the other remedies, not mentioned in the section, but which have been held to be available to him at common law. They may indeed have the effect of extending the apparent scope of the lien provided for in section 41 (*a*); for whereas section 41 (*a*) affords him a lien only in respect of the price paid by him for his partnership and the capital contributed by him to it, at common law it has been held that his lien extends to his claim for interest on sums so paid or contributed by him from the date of payment and also to his expenses in the action for rescission of the contract.[76] Moreover, in addition to his lien and to his other rights under section 41 he has been held to be entitled to an order against the person who received the price or the capital contributed making the recipient liable in repayment with interest.[77] It appears that at common law he may claim interest on payments which he has made in respect of liabilities of the partnership.[78] As already mentioned, if he has been induced to enter the partnership by fraud he will have an action for damages against the person whose fraud has induced him to enter the partnership agreement.[79] In some cases that remedy may be more valuable to him than the right of indemnity conferred under section 41 (*c*).[80] If therefore the fraud has been committed by the other party to the partnership agreement, the pursuer will normally have the option of holding to the contract or of rescinding it, and in either event he will be entitled to damages against the person whose fraud has induced him to associate himself in partnership for any loss he may have sustained as a consequence. But that principle operates only in regard to those associated with one another in the partnership. If the fraud which has induced the partnership agreement is perpetrated by a third party and is not in law imputable to the other partner, then no such option is available; for the person defrauded is not then in a position to rescind the contract on the ground of the fraud; he is entitled only to sue in damages the person whose fraud induced him to enter the contract.

Indemnity against all the debts and liabilities of the firm

Section 41 (*c*) of the Partnership Act 1890 confers a right on the person induced to enter a partnership by fraud or misrepresentation to be indemnified by the person guilty of the fraud or making the representation against all the debts and liabilities of the firm. This provision settles a question which was left open to some doubt in *Adam* v. *Newbigging* [81]

---

[76] *Mycock* v. *Beatson* (1879) 13 Ch.D. 384, where interest was allowed at 5 per cent. per annum.
[77] *Adam* v. *Newbigging* (1888) 13 App.Cas. 308; *Rawlins* v. *Wickham, supra.* In both cases interest was allowed at 4 per cent. per annum.
[78] *Rawlins* v. *Wickham, supra.*
[79] *Manners* v. *Whitehead* (1898) 1 F. 171; *Small* v. *Attwood* (1832) Younge 507; *Pulsford* v. *Richards* (1853) 17 Beav. 87; *Cruikshank* v. *McVicar* (1844) 8 Beav. 106.
[80] See *Newbigging* v. *Adam* (1886) 34 Ch.D. 582 and the judgments delivered in the Court of Appeal at that stage of the case.
[81] (1888) 13 App.Cas. 308.

as to the extent of the indemnity available to him in such circumstances
and declares the law in agreement with the decision of the Court of
Appeal in that case.[82]   The right of indemnity conferred is expressed in
general terms to be against the person responsible for the fraud or
misrepresentation and is not necessarily restricted to a partner of the
pursuer. But the right is conferred only " when a partnership contract
is rescinded on the ground of the fraud or misrepresentation of one of
the parties thereto."   Accordingly, the indemnity will operate only when
the other partner is himself the perpetrator of the fraud or the maker of
the representation or when that partner is legally liable for the action
of a third party in perpetrating the fraud or making the representation.

Restitutio in integrum

It will be noticed that section 41 (*a*) provides unqualifiedly for the
lien on the surplus of the partnership assets being in respect of " any
sum of money paid . . . for the purchase of a share in the partnership
and for any capital contributed by him," and that the right of indemnity
conferred in section 41 (*c*) is expressed to be " against all the debts and
liabilities of the firm."   Likewise the right under section 41 (*b*) to stand
in the place of the creditors of the firm for any payments made by the
pursuer in respect of the partnership liabilities is unqualified. All those
rights, however, come into play " where a partnership contract is rescinded," and it is thought that, construed as a whole, the section should
not be regarded as displacing the general principle of the common law
that on rescission of the contract the aim of the court is to restore parties
to their original position before the contract was entered into.   The
principle was explained by Lord Kinnear in relation to a contract induced
by fraud in the following words—

> " It is very clear in law that a contract induced by fraud is not
> null and void, but voidable. It is valid until it is rescinded, and
> accordingly the party defrauded has in general the option, when he
> discovers the fraud, of rescinding the contract or of affirming it.
> But he must do either one or other. He cannot take the benefit
> of the contract in so far as it is beneficial to himself, and reject it
> in so far as it is burdensome to him. If he affirms it, he must affirm
> it in all its terms. If he reduces [rescinds] it, he must give up any
> benefit he may have had before the fraud was discovered." [83]

It appears therefore that the rights conferred by section 41 on the partner
seeking rescission of the contract will be limited by that over-riding
principle even though the words in which those rights are expressed are
unqualified. That certainly was the position in law prior to the passing
of the Partnership Act 1890, it having been held that the partner seeking
his remedy by way of rescission against the firm and his other partner, is

[82] (1886) 34 Ch.D. 582.
[83] *Smyth* v. *Muir* (1891) 19 R. 81 at p. 89.   See also *Urquhart* v. *McPherson* (1878) 3 App.Cas.
831.

entitled to reimbursement of the payments made by him in respect of partnership liabilities, with interest on such payments, but that he must give credit, again with interest, for all profits which he had received under the contract which he seeks to rescind.[84]

Rescinding of contract made on dissolution of partnership

Section 41 of the Partnership Act 1890 is concerned solely with the rights available where a party to the original partnership agreement has rescinded the contract of partnership itself on the ground of fraud or misrepresentation. Questions may, however, come before the court as to rescission of contracts made among the partners during the currency of the partnership or, more especially, upon its dissolution. Since section 41 is in its terms restricted to questions arising as to the formation of the partnership, it is of no service in cases arising in these circumstances which must be disposed of in accordance with the general principles of the common law, the only specialty arising in the case of a contract among partners being the obligations of honour and scrupulous dealing among partners which the law imposes. But while the law insists upon the maintenance of scrupulous honesty in dealings among partners, it does not go so far as to allow any partner to challenge a transaction entered into between his copartner and himself merely upon the ground that he has made a bad bargain. If the partners are both of legal capacity and if there has been no fraud, misrepresentation or concealment, then the agreement made will be binding although it may later be found to have been disadvantageous to one of them. The line to be drawn in such cases can be a narrow one and much will depend upon the view taken by the court of the actings of those partners seeking to uphold the agreement. In *Knight* v. *Marjoribanks* [85] the plaintiff was one of a partnership engaged in a speculation in Australia which was at first unsuccessful and necessitated the contribution by the partners of considerable additional sums of money to enable it to be continued. The plaintiff was pressed for money and unable to contribute his share of these additional sums. It was stated that he was due to pay more than £5,000 to the firm and he did not question the accuracy of that figure nor did he examine, or seek to examine, the books of the firm to verify it. Instead he agreed to assign his interest to the other partners in consideration of the extinction of his liability for the £5,000 and a payment to him of £250 in cash. Subsequently the adventure proved profitable and he raised an action to set aside the transaction regarding his share on the ground of fraud and inadequacy of consideration. The court, however, held the transaction to be binding on the grounds that no fraud had been established, that the plaintiff himself knew, or had the opportunity of knowing, the facts upon which to make his decision

---

[84] *Rawlins* v. *Wickham* (1858) 3 De G. & J. 304; and see the observations of Lord McLaren in *Manners* v. *Whitehead* (1898) 1 F. 171 at pp. 176–177. *Gordon* v. *Howden* (1849) 12 D. 253.
[85] (1848) 11 Beav. 322.

and had agreed to dispose of his rights without an accounting, and that although his copartners knew of his difficult financial situation they had taken no unfair advantage of it.   It is evident from that decision that the issues upon which the court will require to be satisfied will range over the whole circumstances of the particular case.   It may not be too much to state that in cases involving such arrangements among partners, the court will be vigilant to see that there has been no violation of the standard of fair and honest dealing which should subsist among partners, but if satisfied on that score, the court will not upset the arrangement made simply because it has turned out to be a bad bargain for the plaintiff.[86]

Agreements based on false accounts

While the plaintiff in *Knight* v. *Marjoribanks* [87] was held to an agreement into which conceivably he would not have entered had he investigated the accounts of the partnership, the situation is different where an agreement is made with a retiring partner and is based upon accounts which are false.   The position where the accounts, in terms of the partnership agreement are to be regarded as conclusive has already been examined.[88] Where, however, the rights of a partner upon a dissolution of the firm are agreed on the basis of accounts drawn up, the good faith and open dealing which partners are entitled to expect from each other necessitates that the accounts be prepared with scrupulous fairness and if the agreement on dissolution can be shown to have been entered into in error as a result of false accounts [89] or if there has been fraud, whether by misrepresentation or by concealment of the true state of affairs,[90] then it may be set aside.   Even when the contract of a joint stock company provided that the company would be dissolved if a certain proportion of the capital were lost, and that the loss of that proportion of capital would be ascertained by balances annually declared by the directors, a shareholder was allowed an action for a declaration that the company was dissolved on account of losses in spite of the fact that the declared annual balance showed the contrary.[91]

---

[86] See also *Blay* v. *Pollard & Morris* [1930] 1 K.B. 628 where the agreement was upheld in circumstances even stronger in favour of a reduction.

[87] *Supra* n. 85.   Similarly his right to an accounting may be barred by acquiescence; *Flowerdew* v. *Laing* (1843) 5 D. 440.

[88] *Supra* pp. 537–539.

[89] *Chandler* v. *Dorsett* (1679) Rep.temp. Finch 431; *Maddeford* v. *Austwick* (1826) 1 Sim. 89; *Law* v. *Law* [1905] 1 Ch. 140.

[90] *Spittal* v. *Smith* (1829) Taml. 45.

[91] *North British Bank* v. *Collins* (1852) 15 D.(H.L.) 29.

CHAPTER XIII

THE FIRM AND THE PARTNERS
IN BANKRUPTCY

WHILE the bankruptcy of a partner is considered in the Partnership Act 1890 it is examined only as a cause of dissolution of the firm [1] or as a feature affecting the continuing authority of the partner in a winding up of the firm's affairs.[2] The interaction on the firm of bankruptcy proceedings against a partner and on the partners of bankruptcy proceedings taken against the firm is not specially provided for in the Act but is left to be regulated by the common law and the relevant legislation as to bankruptcy without more specialised treatment than is there accorded to the situation in bankruptcy of a firm and its partners. Indeed the Partnership Act 1890 expressly provides that nothing in its terms shall alter the rules of the law of Scotland relating to the bankruptcy of a firm or of the individual partners thereof.[3] In a sense, therefore, the examination of the partnership in bankruptcy pertains rather to a study of the law of bankruptcy than to the law of partnership, but the relation of partnership itself presents some specialities which are relevant to the position of the firm and its partners in bankruptcy and which may conveniently be considered at this stage.

The rules of the law of Scotland as to the bankruptcy of a firm or of its partners have already been summarised,[4] and the special treatment of such questions under Scots law depends, as is the case with many other aspects of the Scots law of partnership, upon the basic principle that the Scottish firm is regarded as a person distinct from the individual partners who comprise it. Since the firm is a legal person or *quasi* person, it is subject to proceedings in bankruptcy in the same way as an individual may be. Similarly, the law respecting gratuitous alienations [5] and illegal or fraudulent preferences [6] is applicable to transactions of the firm just as it may be to those of an individual.[7] As a result of the separate personality of the firm, three different situations may be envisaged in bankruptcy proceedings which involve a partnership:

(1) the bankruptcy of the firm itself without any of the partners being rendered bankrupt;

---

[1] Partnership Act 1890, s. 33 (1).

[2] *Ibid.* s. 38.

[3] Partnership Act 1890, s. 47 (2).

[4] *Supra* Chap. X, pp. 448–449.

[5] Bell, *Comm.* II, 170–171 (common law); Act 1621, c. 18.

[6] See Bell, *Comm.* II, 226 *et seq.* for the position at common law; Act 1696, c. 5; Bankruptcy (Scotland) Act 1913, ss. 5, 6 and 11.

[7] In the case of a challenge of a gratuitous alienation by a firm under the Act 1621, c. 18, the donee can, of course, only be a " confident " and not a " conjunct " person.

(2) the bankruptcy of a partner without the firm being rendered bankrupt; and

(3) the bankruptcy of both the firm and its partners.

In all these cases, the fortunes of the firm and its partners are so interwoven that it is impossible to regard the bankruptcy of one as entirely divorced from any effect upon the others, even when the bankruptcy proceedings have been taken against the firm alone or against one of the partners alone.

(1) Where the firm is sequestrated while the partners remain solvent

In considering the choice of proceedings available to a creditor against a partnership, Bell [8] writes—

" 1. Sequestration may proceed in a combined process against the company, and also against the individuals, where the individuals are insolvent; or it may proceed against the firm alone, and the estate belonging to the company.

" 2. Even where one of the partners is able to pay the whole debts, the sequestration of the company estate may proceed alone; and in that way only can it with certainty be discovered what is the true amount of the debts, so as to give the solvent partners assurance against future responsibility.

" 3. Where the sequestration includes the estates of the company alone, being directed only against the firm, the company stock may be distributed, and the trustee exonerated, leaving the creditors to seek the unpaid balance of their debts from the separate estates of the partners. . . ."

In many cases where the firm is insolvent, while the partners themselves remain solvent, the firm may be rescued from the consequences of insolvency by the partners who may agree to contribute additional sums to the capital of the firm so that it may continue in business. Since a partner is in any event liable personally to the full extent of the firm's debts incurred while he is a partner,[9] he can in no way escape that liability simply because the firm alone is sequestrated, and thus, if he desires to carry on the business of the firm, there will often be no advantage to him in allowing the firm's estates to be sequestrated. But circumstances may arise where the desire to continue the business of the firm is not present, or at least is not present in the breast of every partner. The firm may have undergone a period of constant and continuous losses, and some of the partners may have successfully applied for an order of the court dissolving the partnership on that ground,[10] or in the face of continuing losses all the partners may have agreed to the dissolution of the firm. Again the firm may be dissolved by the death of one of the partners, while its affairs are embarrassed financially,

---

[8] *Comm.* II, 561–562.
[9] Partnership Act 1890, s. 9.
[10] Partnership Act 1890, s. 35 (*e*); *Handyside* v. *Campbell* (1901) 17 T.L.R. 623; and see *supra* Chap. X, pp. 470–472.

even though all, or some of, the partners are themselves solvent.   In many of these cases, it is true, the liabilities of the firm may be met by the partners contributing in the agreed ratio the sums required to make good the short-fall on the assets of the firm as against its liabilities to creditors, instead of permitting its affairs to be wound up in bankruptcy and the creditors subsequently to claim against the partners, or any of them, personally.   If that process were allowed to take place and all the partners were solvent then the interaction of the partners' liability *singuli in solidum* and the right of relief afforded to a partner who has discharged a debt of the firm [11] would achieve the same result.   Even where some of the partners are solvent and have been called upon by the creditors of the firm to make good any outstanding liability they will be entitled to rank on the estates of the partners who are insolvent for the proportion due from those partners in relief of the payment that they have made.[12]   In neither case need the situation of the partners who have met the firm's liabilities so far as outstanding after sequestration of the firm's estates be any worse than it would have been if the firm had been rescued from sequestration by agreement among the partners to contribute further capital.   Where the affairs of the insolvent firm are complicated and involved, however, the considerations advanced by Bell in the passage above quoted may make it advisable that the estates of the firm be wound up under separate proceedings in sequestration, in order that the partners may ascertain the extent of their personal liability and be freed from any indeterminate future obligation.

Discharge

It will have been noticed that in the passage quoted Bell refers to the exoneration of the trustee where the firm alone is proceeded against in bankruptcy.   No mention is made by him of the possibility of the firm itself being discharged in bankruptcy.   When the firm is insolvent and its assets are inadequate to pay the creditors in full, it would usually be inappropriate to discharge the firm while the cautionary obligations of the partners still subsist, although it has been held that a discharge of the firm does not release the partners of the obligations incurred by them as individuals where they have not been discharged as individuals.[13]   But even where that situation occurs in the combined sequestration of the firm and the individual partners, it is not customary to discharge the firm.[14]

Application of the firm for sequestration

It is implicit in Bell's statement that the partners should be able themselves to apply for the sequestration of the firm in order to secure the advantage which he mentions as tending in some cases to make this

---

[11] Partnership Act 1890, s. 4 (2).

[12] On the same footing as would obtain in the case of joint cautioners.   See *infra* pp.576–577.

[13] *Mellis* v. *Royal Bank of Scotland*, June 22, 1815, F.C.

[14] *Steel & Company* (1855) 18 D. 34; and see *infra* pp. 568–571.   It is not regarded as incompetent to discharge the firm but it is not the practice to do so—Goudy, *Bankruptcy* (4th ed.) p. 393.

THE FIRM AND THE PARTNERS IN BANKRUPTCY

advisable. Since the firm is recognised as a person in Scots law, there is no distinction to be drawn in theory between its sequestration on its own application and on the application of a creditor.[15] The real question is in regard to what application on the part of the individual partners of the firm represents the firm itself as an independent *persona*. Sequestration has been awarded on the petition of one of the partners where the other partner had fled the country to avoid arrest on a criminal charge [16]; and in a case where the partnership had been dissolved by the death of one of the partners, sequestration of the firm's estates was awarded on the petition of the surviving partners with the concurrence of a creditor whose debt was sufficient in amount to have allowed him to apply himself for an award of sequestration.[17] Sequestration was also awarded against the estates of a firm consisting of two partners on an application by one of them in the name of the firm, though he had no special mandate from the other partner to apply for sequestration. The other partner, who was abroad, had, however, given the petitioner full power to manage the firm's affairs.[18]

Authority to present a petition on behalf of the firm for its sequestration

The authority last cited raises an issue of some importance. An application for sequestration of the firm's estates, if it be presented in the name of the firm itself, gives rise to questions of legal difficulty. Upon these the Bankruptcy (Scotland) Act 1913 offers no precise guidance. Section 11 of that Act allows sequestration to be awarded " in the case of a living debtor subject to the jurisdiction of the Supreme Courts of Scotland " on his own petition with the concurrence of a creditor or creditors duly qualified under the Act. The firm is regarded as an artificial person in the eyes of the Scots law, but the Act offers no guidance whether an artificial person of the nature of a firm is to be embraced within the description, " a living debtor,"—a description which, on first impression at least, is not apt to include an artificial person at law. In the succeeding part of the section the case of the firm is expressly legislated for, but that relates exclusively to the case where the firm is sequestrated on the petition of a creditor or creditors.[19] Yet it has been traditionally regarded as appropriate for a firm to be treated as a person so as to permit of its applying for its own sequestration. An early Bankruptcy Act [20] provided that the company " may be sequestrated provided that the company shall petition for the sequestration . . . and if the position is not agreed by the company, a mandate signed by such company, or those entitled to act for it, authorising such petition shall be therewith produced." In a yet earlier Act, the Bankrupts Act 1772,[21] it was provided that an award of sequestration

---

[15] Goudy, *op. cit.* p. 118; Wallace, *Bankruptcy* (2nd ed.) p. 60.
[16] *Buchanan* (1849) 11 D. 510.
[17] *Campbell* (1830) 8 S. 625.
[18] *McLean & Son* (1824) 3 S. 122.
[19] See *infra* pp. 559 *et seq.*
[20] 2 & 3 Vict. c. 41.
[21] 12 Geo. 3, c. 47.

could be made " upon the application of those entitled to act for them,"
i.e. for the company, or firm. Although more specific guidance is offered
in both of those early Acts, it is nonetheless incomplete. Commenting
on the provisions of the Bankruptcy Act 1772, Bell asks the pertinent
question, "But who is entitled to act for a company in a matter so
extraordinary?"; and he goes on to state the following propositions—

" 1. A mandate signed by all the partners will be good to authorise
the application. . . .

" 2. A mandate signed by the firm is questionable, as, necessarily,
it must be written by the hand of a single partner; and being an act of the
most extraordinary administration, extinguishing the very life of the
company, it can have no support from the presumed *praepositura*.
But where it is an act of the whole company, legitimately assembled,
or the result of a signed minute expressive of their resolution to
terminate their career, the desire of the petition will on proper
evidence be granted.

" 3. If one of the partners be abroad the rest have no power
without delegation to apply for sequestration . . .

" 4. Where a power is given by the express mandate of an absent
partner to the rest to take the entire management it will be effectual
to authorise a petition." [22]

It appears to have become accepted as settled that Bell's first proposition
is sound. Indeed Wallace [23] baldly states it as a proposition of universal
application. " Where a company, other than a registered company, is the
petitioner, the petition must be presented with the concurrence of *all* the
partners." Under the statutory provisions previously in force Bell's
second proposition also seems well founded. In a matter where the
question of the continuance of the partnership is concerned, it is obviously
difficult to argue that the apparent authority of any individual partner will
extend to cover an application for the sequestration of the firm. The
Partnership Act 1890 [24] permits differences arising as to ordinary matters
connected with the partnership business to be decided by a majority of the
partners but provides that " no change may be made in the nature of the
partnership business without the consent of all existing partners." The
words, " change in the nature of the partnership business " are perhaps
not the most apt to cover a complete cutting off of that business. At the
same time it can be argued with some semblance of cogency that a change
from a partnership business which is a going concern to one which is in a
state of suspended animation and exists merely in order to be wound up
in the interests primarily of its creditors may reasonably be described as a
change in the nature of the partnership business. In any event it is clear
that a decision of the kind involved can hardly be described as an ordinary
matter connected with the partnership business and thus the majority

[22] *Comm.* II, 562–563.
[23] *Manual of the Law of Bankruptcy in Scotland* (2nd ed.) p. 61. Goudy, *op. cit.* p. 118.
[24] s. 24 (8).

have no power under the Partnership Act 1890 to impose their will as to sequestration of the firm upon the minority. The provisions of the Partnership Act 1890 as to the powers of a majority have force only where the partnership agreement makes no contrary provision. But if the partnership agreement provides that a majority of the partners, or an individual partner, e.g. the senior partner, shall have the power to apply for the sequestration of the firm, the partner or partners to whom that power has been committed has a clear mandate from all the partners and thus falls within the terms of Bell's second proposition. The problem, who should sign the mandate for the presentation of the petition, or the petition itself, arises only where the partners are not unanimous as to the desirability of that step. If they in fact are all in agreement, then even if the mandate be signed by one of them in the firm name or takes the form of a minute signed by one of them as chairman recording the unanimous decision of a meeting of all the partners, *cadit quaestio*. The unanimous consent in fact exists and it is thought that the petition would be received if the court were satisfied as to the circumstances.

More doubt attaches to Wallace's statement when it is considered in relation to Bell's third and fourth propositions. When one of the two partners of a firm had fled abroad to avoid apprehension on a charge of forgery, and the remaining partner presented a petition for the sequestration of the firm, the Lord Ordinary ordered notice of the petition to be served at the office of the partnership. On that having been done, he reported the case to the Inner House who held that he might grant the petition in the circumstances.[25] In *McLean & Son*[26] the court held where a son who was abroad had granted a mandate to his father who was in partnership with him to manage the affairs of the firm in his absence, the father could present a petition for the sequestration of the firm.

The foregoing discussion, however, proceeds upon the basis of the law as it existed prior to the Bankruptcy (Scotland) Act 1913 and it has still to be considered whether section 11 of that Act is so expressed as to permit of the presentation of a petition by the partners for the sequestration of the firm. This appears to be accepted as competent in practice but as a matter of construction section 11 enables a petition to be presented by or on behalf of the debtor only where he is a " living debtor." The doubt is tentatively suggested whether a firm properly comes within that description and the doubt is perhaps supported by the fact that when the section proceeds to deal with sequestration on the petition of a qualified creditor, the position of the firm is made subject to express provision to allow for the difference between an artificial person and an individual. It is sincerely hoped that the doubt here raised is not merely mischievously academic. It seems clear from what may be termed the archaeology of the Bankruptcy Acts that, if section 11 of the Bankruptcy (Scotland) Act 1913 has the effect of excluding the petition of a firm for its own

---

[25] *Buchanan* (1849) 11 D. 510.
[26] (1824) 3 S. 122.

sequestration, that is unlikely to have been the intention of the legislature when the section was enacted. Yet the fact remains that it seems possible to regard the firm as a " living debtor " only if one regards it as the collection of a number of separate individual partners each of whom might acceptably be described as a " living debtor." But so to regard the firm involves a complete departure from the fundamental theory of the Scots law as to the nature of a partnership.[27]

Application by creditor for sequestration of firm

A creditor who applies for sequestration of the firm's estates will require to satisfy the court of his qualification to present the petition as he will require to do in the case of an application for the sequestration of the estates of a natural person. In terms of the Bankruptcy (Scotland) Act 1913, s. 11, sequestration is competent on the petition of a qualified creditor or creditors,[28] provided the firm be notour bankrupt and have within a year before the presentation of the petition carried on business in Scotland and any partner have resided or had a dwelling house in Scotland within the said period of one year " or if the company have had a place of business in Scotland." [29] The firm may therefore be sequestrated by an award of the Scottish courts either (a) if within the period of a year before presentation of the petition it has carried on business in Scotland *and* within the same period at least one of its partners has resided or had a dwelling house in Scotland *or* (b) if the firm had a place of business in Scotland. Under either provision it is possible that competing jurisdictions may exist for the purpose of regulating the affairs of the firm in bankruptcy.[30] In both cases it is a prerequisite to the creditor's petition that in addition to the circumstances establishing

[27] It is possible to argue that as a matter of construction the modifying words applicable to a firm, " or otherwise in the case of a company being notour bankrupt . . . place of business in Scotland " are intended to apply to both A and B of the 1st case of s. 11 of the Bankruptcy (Scotland) Act 1913 and that approach is not excluded by *Stewart & McDonald* v. *Brown* (1898) 25 R. 1042, a case where the competency of a petition by a creditor of the firm under the corresponding provision of the Bankruptcy (Scotland) Act 1856 was under consideration. (See *infra* n. 35). The point was not adverted to, however, in the judgments of the court, though they appear to have assumed that the firm might petition for its own sequestration, but equally they seem to declare quite firmly that it is not acceptable to regard the firm, metaphorically, as a " living debtor." A construction which invokes the aid of the special mention of the position of the firm after the provision for sequestration at the instance of a creditor and interprets that as recognising the competency of a petition at the instance of the firm perhaps is impaired by the consideration that the specific mention of the position of the firm is introduced in the case of a firm " being notour bankrupt " a stipulation which appears to be entirely inappropriate in relation to the case of a firm petitioning for its own sequestration. It is to be noticed that the word " debtor " is to be interpreted as applying to companies (including partnerships)—Bankruptcy (Scotland) Act 1913, s. 2; but that is not helpful since, applying that interpretation to s. 11, a " living debtor " simply becomes " a living partnership " and the difficulty remains.

[28] See Bankruptcy (Scotland) Act 1913, s. 12.

[29] In the Bankruptcy (Scotland) Act 1913, s. 11, the provisions in regard to sequestration of an artificial person are expressed in relation to a " company " which is defined (s. 2) as including " bodies corporate, politic, collegiate and partnerships " but they do not apply to a company registered under the Companies Acts: *Standard Property Investment Co. Ltd.* v. *Dunblane Hydropathic* (1884) 12 R. 328. But see *Fraser* (1971) S.L.T. 146.

[30] On this point see *infra* p. 572.

the jurisdiction of the Scottish courts to award sequestration, the firm must be notour bankrupt. The notour bankruptcy of a firm is established either (1) in any of the ways set forth in section 5 of the Bankruptcy (Scotland) Act 1913 for the constitution of the notour bankruptcy of an individual or (2) " by any of the partners being rendered notour bankrupt for a company debt." [31] Though in the first branch of the section the notour bankruptcy of the firm may be established in " any of the ways " in which it may be established in the case of an individual, section 5 of the Bankruptcy (Scotland) Act 1913, which sets out the various ways in which an individual debtor may be rendered notour bankrupt, requires modification before its terms can be applied to the case of an artificial person such as a firm; for it is obvious the reference to imprisonment in section 5 is inappropriate. The additional ground of the notour bankruptcy of the firm provided for in section 6 is in accordance with the underlying Scottish theory of partnership. Although the individual partner has himself been rendered notour bankrupt under section 5 and that, by itself, is a matter entirely separate from the fortunes of the firm, the notour bankruptcy of the firm itself follows as a consequence thereof but only if the notour bankruptcy of the partner arises in consequence of a company debt in respect of which recourse has been taken against the partner. It is thus implicit that the debt in question has already been constituted against the firm itself. [32] The historical difficulty which arose on a construction of the Bankruptcy (Scotland) Act 1856, ss. 7 and 8, and the Debtors (Scotland) Act 1880, s. 6, [33] no longer exists since the Bankruptcy (Scotland) Act 1913, s. 5, makes it a ground of notour bankruptcy that insolvency exists " concurring with a duly executed charge for payment . . . followed by the expiry of the days of charge without payment," and section 6 inter alia makes that a ground for the constitution of notour bankruptcy in respect of a firm.

While the effect is, broadly speaking, to equate the artificial person represented by the firm to an individual, the equation cannot be applied with rigid literalness. It cannot be applied to subject the firm to something which as an artificial person it cannot undergo, namely imprisonment. Nor can the figurative language involved in treating any abstraction of the law as a person be pressed to equate by analogy events in the existence of the firm with the normal incidence of mortality which befalls a natural person. It is not uncommon to hear the dissolution of a firm referred to as equivalent to the death of a natural person. But, while the Bankruptcy (Scotland) Act 1913 provides in section 11 for award of sequestration of the estates of a deceased debtor who at the date of his death was subject to the jurisdiction of the Supreme Courts of Scotland

[31] Bankruptcy (Scotland) Act 1913, s. 6.
[32] If the firm has been dissolved, the debt need no longer be constituted against it but no one partner " may be sued without calling all the others, so far as that is possible unless the company obligation has been previously constituted by writing or decree ": per the Lord President (Inglis) in Neilson v. Wilson (1890) 17 R. 608 at p. 612.
[33] For a discussion of this see Stewart's Tr. v. Salvesen & Company (1900) 2 F. 983

on the petition of a qualified creditor or creditors, a dissolved firm is not a " deceased debtor " for this purpose and its estates cannot be sequestrated in the petition of a creditor unless the firm is notour bankrupt.[34]   Lord McLaren said,

> " We are invited to interpret the words ' deceased debtor ' as being equivalent to ' dissolved company,' and the word ' death ' as being equivalent to ' dissolution of partnership.'   I am not sure that I understand the theory or principle of construction under which the suggested readings are admissible; but I think it must be a theory in which fancy takes the place of logic, and in which the question proposed is, how the statute is to be made to fit the case, and not whether the conditions of the case fit the statute." [35]

The petitioning creditor.   It is essential that the creditor who petitions for sequestration of the firm or who concurs in such a petition should be what Bell describes as " a proper creditor of the partnership." [36]   In the case of third party creditors it will not usually be difficult to establish this, but difficulty may arise where the transaction in which the claim originates has been with a partner and where there is dubiety whether in that transaction he acted for himself as an individual or for the partnership.   If the transaction with the third party was entered into by the partner not in his character as partner but as an individual, then the fact that he has subsequently applied the benefits of the transaction for the uses of his firm will not of itself suffice to make the third party " a proper creditor of the partnership."   If a person who is a partner in a firm receives a loan from a third party which he later employs for the use of the firm, that supervening circumstance will not make the lender a creditor of the firm.   The partner himself will be the firm's creditor and he will remain the debtor of the third party.[37]   But if the firm, while still solvent, has recognised the loan as a firm debt, Bell considers that the third party who lent the money will be regarded as a proper creditor by the firm.[38]   He founds that opinion on the decision in *Ex parte Clowes*,[39] apparently following Cooke's view of that decision.[40]   The

---

[34] *Stewart & McDonald* v. *Brown* (1898) 25 R. 1042.   This case and particularly the opinion of Lord McLaren on the construction of s. 13 of the Bankruptcy (Scotland) Act 1856 lends some support to the point already submitted (*supra* p. 558) that a firm cannot be regarded as a " living debtor " and the real question of construction is whether the modification introduced in respect of a firm where the section is dealing with sequestration on the petition of a creditor is intended also to apply to cases of sequestration on a petition by the firm itself.   The analogy between the death of a natural person and the dissolution of a corporation is to some extent supported by *Salton* v. *New Beeston Cycle Co.* [1900] 1 Ch. 43, but not, it is submitted, to the extent of equating a corporate or quasi-corporate *persona* with a " living debtor."

[35] *Ibid.* at p. 1045.

[36] Bell, *Comm.* II, 563.

[37] *Ex p. Wheatly*, Cooke's *Bankruptcy Law* (8th ed.) p. 534.   See also Bell, *Comm.* II, 563; Pothier, *Traité du Contrat de Société* § 101.

[38] *Comm.* II, 563.

[39] (1789) 2 Bro.C.C. 595.

[40] *Bankruptcy Law* (8th ed.) p. 534.

decision is described by Lindley as a " very peculiar case " and he adds
that " if it was ever an authority for the doctrine that a separate debt
can, as between the partners and the creditor, become a joint debt, or
vice versa, without the privity of the creditor, the case must be considered
as no longer law." [41]   The correct basis for any such change in the position
of the third party creditor seems clearly to rest upon the principle of delegation and it is thought that a more precise formulation of the doctrine is
contained in the words of Lindley [42]: " Upon precisely similar grounds,
a creditor of one person does not become the joint creditor of him and
another who enters into partnership with him, merely because the two
partners have agreed between themselves that the debts of each shall be
the debts of both.   Unless the creditor accedes to that arrangement, he
is not bound by it, nor can he avail himself of it; his position in fact is
unaltered, he does not lose his old right, nor does he gain any new one."
It is not possible for the lender to claim as a creditor of the firm indirectly
as coming in place of the partner to whom he lent the money and who
has applied the loan to the purposes of the firm. A claim by the third
party to be regarded as a creditor of the firm thus indirectly or, as Bell
puts it, " by a circuity " was allowed by Lord Hardwicke " after much
doubt " in *Ex parte Hunter*,[43] but as Bell himself recognises,[44] that
decision has long been regarded as overruled in England.[45] It is moreover a decision which it would be difficult to reconcile with the Scottish
concept of a partnership.

(2) Where the firm is solvent but one of the partners is bankrupt

The bankruptcy of one of the partners of the firm may be an occasion
for the dissolution of the firm [46] or it may give rise to a right in the other
partners, if so provided in the partnership agreement, to continue the
business of the firm on stipulated terms as to paying out the bankrupt
partner.[47]   In either event the bankrupt partner may be a creditor of
the firm in some respects and a debtor of the firm in others. He may
also be a creditor of or a debtor to his partners, or some of them, as
individuals. In dealing with the creditors of the bankrupt partner the
firm will consider the overall position of the bankrupt partner *as regards
the firm*; *i.e.* whether on a balancing of what is owed to him by the firm
against his own indebtedness to the firm, he proves to be a debtor or a
creditor in the resulting balance. When he proves to be a creditor of
the firm in the balance thus brought out, then on a dissolution of the
firm, his creditors will be entitled to his share of the stock and profits of

---

[41] *Op. cit.* p. 736 n. 57.
[42] *Op. cit.* p. 736; and see on this point *Heritable Securities Investment Association* v.
Wingates (1891) 29 S.L.R. 904.
[43] (1741) 1 Atk. 223.
[44] *Comm.* II, 563.
[45] See *Ex p. Harris* (1813) 1 Rose 438 *per* Lord Eldon.
[46] Partnership Act 1890, s. 33 (1).
[47] See *supra* Chap. X, pp. 446–447.

the firm and to repayment of any sums which he has advanced to be used for the purposes of the firm's business. But they will be entitled to these claims only after the debts due by the firm to its own creditors have been deducted, since the right of the bankrupt partner himself, which is being claimed for his creditors, is postponed to that of the creditors of his firm.[48] Moreover, what may be claimed by the creditors is the bankrupt partner's interest in the partnership, and consequently the firm is due to pay to the trustee only the balance due to the partner on a settlement of accounts with him since the trustee takes the interest *tantum et tale* as it was held by the bankrupt partner.[49] In *Borthwick* v. *Wright* [50] a partner of a firm who was also its manager discounted bills belonging to the firm with a bank. The bills were dishonoured and the partner retired them with funds belonging to him as an individual. This he did within sixty days of his being personally rendered bankrupt. On retiring the bills, he made an entry in the books of the firm whereby in consideration of so employing his own funds he extinguished a debt owed by him to the firm. The transaction was challenged by his trustee as an illegal preference to the firm under the Act of 1695, c. 5; but the court held that, since it appeared that the partner had funds belonging to the firm sufficient to retire the bills and it was his duty as manager prior to the sixty days' period to have paid his debt due to the firm, the transaction was not reducible. The argument in challenging the transaction was that the bills were due *to* the firm, not *by* it, and that the bankrupt's name did not appear on them as an individual. Therefore, on retiring them with his own funds, he acquired right to them and was not entitled to deliver them to his partners but should have retained them for the benefit of his private creditors. The problem of settlement of accounts in the partnership thus arose in an acute form under the challenge. Lord Balgray, however, disposed of the question without difficulty. He said,[51]

> " The question therefore comes to be whether, at the period of retiring them, he was possessed of funds belonging to the company? It appears that in his private capacity he was debtor for sums to the company which he ought to have paid prior to the period of sixty days from his bankruptcy; and it was therefore his duty, as manager of the company, to have recovered that sum; or, in other words, to have entered it as having been then paid by him to the company. If he had done so there would have been no room for this question; and I apprehend that we are bound to hold that although he did not make that entry, yet that he thenceforth held that sum in his capacity of manager of the company. If so, then he had sufficient funds in his hands when the bills fell due out of which to retire them, and it was his duty to do so."

[48] Partnership Act 1890, s. 44 (*b*) (1).
[49] Goudy, *Bankruptcy* (4th ed.) p. 582.
[50] (1827) 5 S. 293.
[51] *Ibid.* at pp. 295–296.

Bankrupt partner as creditor of the firm

If there is no agreement to the contrary the firm is dissolved on the date on which the " bankruptcy " of the partner occurred [52] and bankruptcy in this context means sequestration under the Bankruptcy (Scotland) Acts.[53]   Therefore, where the settlement of accounts between the firm and the bankrupt partner shows him to be a creditor of the firm, the amount of his claim will be determined at the date of award of sequestration of his estates unless his rights are otherwise regulated by the partnership agreement.   The amount then shown as due to him will not be varied after that date,[54] save in so far as the variation reflects the result of transactions properly carried through in the course of the winding up of the firm's affairs.[55]   Claims at the instance of the solvent partner or partners personally against the bankrupt partner may not be taken into account and deducted in arriving at the amount due by the firm to the bankrupt partner.   His claim against the firm must be met in full because there is no *concursus debiti et crediti* which will permit of set-off of the solvent partner's claim against him.[56]

Bankrupt partner a debtor to the firm

When the bankrupt partner is indebted to the firm, the firm will rank on his estate for the amount of that indebtedness as it is ascertained after set-off of the amount of his share in the partnership determined at the date of the dissolution.   Where the bankrupt partner is indebted to his firm but has a claim against one of his co-partners who is solvent, there is no compensation between the debt owed to the firm and the debt owed to the bankrupt by the solvent partner.   The latter must pay his debt to the bankrupt partner's estate.   He is not allowed to discharge his debt by paying it to the firm and presenting the firm's discharge thereof in answer to a demand by the bankrupt partner's trustee against him for payment.[57]   Where a partner owed a debt to his firm, it was questioned in *Scott* v. *Ker* [58] whether sequestration could be awarded against his estates on the application of his copartners.   The point arose in the hearing before the House of Lords where it was argued that the sequestration, proceeding upon a debt due by the appellant to himself and his co-partners, was to that extent a sequestration directed by the appellant against himself which, for his part, he had not sought. That argument gave rise to some concern in the House of Lords, perhaps because it is more formidable when viewed against the concept of the partnership in English law than when the Scottish conception of the firm is kept in mind.   On postponed consideration of the case, the Lord

[52] Partnership Act 1890, s. 33 (1).
[53] *Ibid.* s. 47 (1).
[54] Since the firm is then dissolved (subject to agreement to the contrary).   *Ibid.* s. 33 (1).
[55] Partnership Act 1890, s. 38.
[56] *Galdie* v. *Gray* (1774) Mor. 14598; and see *infra* p. 565.
[57] Bell, *Comm.* II, 548.
[58] (1832) 6 W. & S. 214.

Chancellor (Lord Brougham) said, " I have the satisfaction of knowing that the same learned persons whom I consulted upon the practice of the [Scottish] courts . . . are of opinion that the objection founded on the circumstance of the sequestration issuing at the instance of some of the partners of a bank against one of their partners would not, according to the Scotch law, have availed the party, even if taken in time in that court." On the other hand, if the bankrupt partner is indebted to the firm, the firm may set against that indebtedness the amount of the bankrupt's share of the profits and assets of the firm at the date of dissolution and rank on the bankrupt's estate for the balance, if any. In thus compensating the claim of the firm against the bankrupt partner and the interest of the bankrupt in the partnership, it is not, however, competent for the firm to take the process of adjustment of claims further and require a solvent partner who is indebted to the bankrupt to pay the amount of that indebtedness to the firm. The solvent partner so indebted can only be discharged by paying the amount of his debt into the bankrupt partner's estate and he is not permitted to produce a discharge of the debt owed by the bankrupt partner to the firm as a defence to the demand made by the bankrupt partner's trustee against him.[59]

(3) Where the firm and the partners are all bankrupt

If both the firm and all its partners are sequestrated in bankruptcy the entire assets of the firm are available to meet the claims of the creditors of the firm, and until those creditors have received payment in full, the creditors of the individual partners are excluded from any claim upon the firm's assets in respect of the bankrupt partner's share and interest in them. For the same reason, *i.e.* that the partner's interest in the assets of the firm arises only after payment of all debts due by the firm to third party creditors,[60] where any partner owes a debt to his firm, the firm's trustee may rank on that partner's estate *pari passu* with the private creditors of the partner and without deducting the value of the partner's interest in the firm.[61] On the other hand, third party creditors of the firm may rank on the estates of the individual partners for any balance of their claim against the firm which remains unsatisfied, *pari passu* with the private creditors of the partner concerned, provided they deduct from the amount of their claim the sums received by them from the bankrupt estate of the firm or value the amount so to be received if it has not yet been paid to them.[62] A different rule applies in England

---

[59] *Galdie* v. *Gray* (1774) Mor. 14598.

[60] Partnership Act 1890, s. 44 (*b*); *Keith* v. *Penn* (1840) 2 D. 633; Bell, *Comm.* II, 502; *Johnson* v. *Losh* (1844) 6 D. 626.

[61] *Dunlop* v. *Speirs* (1776) Mor. 14610; (1777) 2 Pat.App. 437. But in the House of Lords it was further held that where the claim was lodged after a dividend had been declared and most of the creditors paid, it would not be allowed to disturb or affect dividends paid before notice had been received of the new claim, but the new claim was entitled to be paid up equal to the other creditors before the latter received any further dividend.

[62] *Nicol* v. *Christie* (1827) 5 S. 882; Bankruptcy (Scotland) Act 1913, s. 62.

where, in the words of Lord King,[63] " it is settled, and is a resolution of convenience, that the joint creditors shall be first paid out of the partnership or joint estate, and the separate creditors out of the separate estate of each partner; and if there be a surplus of the joint estate, besides what will pay the joint creditors, the same shall be applied to pay the separate creditors; and if there be, on the other hand, a surplus of the separate estate beyond what will satisfy the separate creditors, it shall go to supply any deficiency that may remain as to the joint creditors." The rule as stated by Lord King still holds force in England and is enacted in the Bankruptcy Act 1914.[64]   It is a consequence of the English concept of a partnership as a mere congeries of the individual partners with the resulting need for equitable rules for the distribution of the estates which the partners hold in different characters.   But there is no room for the application of the English rule in Scotland, since the Partnership Act 1890 expressly preserves " the rules of the law of Scotland relating to the bankruptcy of a firm or of the individual partners thereof," [65] and since, in virtue of the Scottish concept of the firm as a separate *persona* and the partners as cautioners for the firm, there is not the same theoretical basis for distinguishing the joint estate of the partnership from the individual estates of the partners, the situation being basically that of principal and accessory obligations in cautionry.   For the same reasons, the Scottish rule is applicable only in the case of partnership, properly so described, and will not apply where an individual trades under a firm name.   In that case he is merely conducting a business under a descriptive name or one which suggests a partnership which both in fact and in law is non-existent.   Accordingly his estates on bankruptcy, whether derived from the assets of the business or from assets belonging to him otherwise, are combined and all his creditors, whether their claims arise from personal dealings with him or from transactions in the course of carrying on his business, will rank together on the combined estate.[66]

Identity of the firm for purposes of sequestration

It may on occasion be a matter of some difficulty in contemplating proceedings for the sequestration of a firm to decide whether all the activities upon which the claims of the creditors have arisen and sequestration is sought are embraced within the artificial *persona* of the one firm. To a large extent that question will require to be answered upon an assessment of the circumstances of the individual case but the mere fact that the individual partners are common to two firms will not suffice to permit of their being sequestrated under the one sequestration.   Thus firms which consisted of the same partners but carried on different businesses were held to be different and separate firms and in bankruptcy

[63] *Ex p. Cook* (1728) 2 P.Wms. 500.
[64] s. 36 (6); and see *Lacey* v. *Hill* (1876) 4 Ch.D. 537.
[65] s. 47 (2).
[66] *Cullen* v. *Macfarlane* (1842) 4 D. 1522.

their estates were held to be separate estates.[67] " Although an individual cannot form different establishments in trade, having each a separate stock, and debts peculiar and distinct, a plurality of partners may so arrange their contracts, and constitute their mutual trusts, as to form several distinct companies, composed of the very same individuals. And these companies may hold separate estates, and be liable each to sequestration by itself, provided there is a real and perceptible distinction of trade and establishment between the several partnerships." [68] In *Commercial Bank of Scotland* v. *Tod's Trustees* two firms of paper manufacturers, one operating from Polton and the other from Lasswade, had petitioned jointly for sequestration. Both firms were comprised of the same partners but both carried on business from separate premises, kept separate books and accounts and to some extent, although there were customers common to both, had different customers. Lord Low approved the statement of the law above quoted and considered the earlier decisions upon which it was founded.[69] He held that the fact of the identity of partners in the two firms was not conclusive. " Inquiry still remains," he said, " whether the companies are essentially different or, as Mr. Bell puts it, whether there is a real and perceptible distinction of trade and establishment between them." The two firms were entirely separate in origin and though they had come to consist of the same partners, the businesses remained in every other respect distinct. An alteration in the constitution of one firm would not have affected the other. Accordingly Lord Low held that the sequestration of the two firms must proceed as separate sequestrations and their estates could not be massed together in one sequestration to meet the claims of the creditors of both firms. Even when the distinction is not immediately perceptible if it be a real distinction, it is thought that the partnerships will be treated as separate. In *McLaren & Company* v. *Pendreigh's Trustee* [70] two partnerships carried on business under the same firm name of J. & G. Pendreigh. The businesses conducted were different, one that of grain merchants and the other that of brewers. Some of the partners were common to both firms but the members of each firm were not identical. The two partnerships became insolvent and their estates were separately sequestrated as were the estates of the individual partners. An offer of composition was made to the creditors of both firms upon the basis of massing together the assets and liabilities of both and treating the creditors of both as creditors in the one massed estate. The offer of composition was held to be incompetent in terms of section 139 of the Bankruptcy Act 1856.[71]

---

[67] *Commercial Bank of Scotland* v. *Tod's Tr.* (1895) 33 S.L.R. 161 (O.H.).
[68] Bell, *Comm.* II, 515.
[69] *Creditors of P. & F. Forrester* v. *Sir W. Forbes & Co.* (1798) not reported save by Bell, *loc. cit.* See also *Bertram Gardner & Co.* (1795) only reported Bell, *loc. cit.* n. 1; *Royal Bank of Scotland* v. *Stein, Smith & Co.*, Jan. 20, 1813, F.C.
[70] (1869) 7 M. 926.
[71] s. 136 of the Bankruptcy (Scotland) Act 1913 is identical in its terms except that it requires approval by three-fourths in value of the creditors whereas the former Act required the consent of four-fifths in value.

Lord Kinloch, after examining some of the practical objections to treating the estates of the two firms as massed together in the one sequestration, observed, " These illustrations might be largely multiplied. In substance, they all evolve themselves from the primary objection, that two separate sequestrated estates cannot be competently massed to the effect of giving all the creditors on both estates their united funds for an indiscriminate dividend." [72] On the other hand, if two separate firms are established, having the same partners and identical objects and line of business, they will be regarded in bankruptcy as one and the same and their assets and liabilities will be massed together in sequestration.[73]

Offer of composition

Although the offer of composition in *McLaren & Company* v. *Pendreigh's Trustee* was held to be incompetent, that decision was based upon the special considerations which have been discussed. In the case of a partnership an offer of composition in the firm's sequestration may be made by one or more of the partners.[74] The offer may stipulate as a condition that its acceptance shall discharge the partners or only those who make the offer of composition.[75] The creditor may accept the offer and discharge the partners while refusing to discharge the firm [76] or it may be accepted so far as regards the partner making it and his discharge granted while it is refused so far as regards the other partners, the sequestration continuing against them and the firm.[77] An offer of composition by a partner may stipulate for assignation to him of the claims of the creditors against the remaining partners,[78] while on their part the creditors in accepting such an offer may expressly reserve their claims against the remaining partners. It will not be presumed that the creditors have reserved those claims in the absence of express stipulation, unless the offer of composition with its stipulation for the discharge of the partner making it is acquiesced in by the remaining partners.[79]

Discharge

It has already been mentioned that, while it is not incompetent to discharge the firm in bankruptcy, it is not generally the practice to do so.[80] It has been held competent to grant a discharge to the partners upon their offering a composition while the sequestration remains effective

---

[72] *McLaren & Co.* v. *Pendreigh's Tr.*, *supra* at p. 930.

[73] *Royal Bank of Scotland* v. *Assignees of Stein, Smith & Co.*, Jan. 20, 1813, F.C.; Bell, *Comm.* II, 515.

[74] Bankruptcy (Scotland) Act 1913, ss. 134 and 136; *Sinclair & McIntyre's Sequestration* (1885) 1 Sh.Ct.Rep. 279.

[75] *Steel & Co., Petrs.* (1855) 18 D. 34. This decision, however, has its peculiar aspect since Steel was the " sole partner " of James Steel & Company so that the latter was not a true firm but merely a name under which he conducted his trade.

[76] *Smith, Petr.* (1827) 5 S. 357; *Taylor & Paterson, Petrs.* (1840) 2 D. 952.

[77] *Grant, Petr.*, Dec. 21, 1811, F.C.

[78] *Shand & Co.* v. *Winton* (1848) 11 D. 162.

[79] Bell, *Comm.* II, 567.

[80] *Supra* p. 555.

against the firm.[81] If a partner has offered and paid a composition on
the debts of the firm, the firm's creditors may not call upon him as an
individual for payment of any balance outstanding and unpaid from
the funds of the firm; nor may any one or more of the firm's creditors
insist on such a claim if the offer of composition has been accepted by the
requisite majority of the firm's creditors. But the situation is different
if he is bound in an obligation of the firm both as an individual and as
a partner or where he is subject to a personal obligation or to the transaction independently from his liability as a partner of the firm, as, for
instance, where he has drawn a bill of exchange upon the firm and the
firm has accepted it. In these circumstances it has been held that the
contract of composition, while discharging the partner from his obligation
qua partner for the firm's debts, will not suffice to discharge him of an
obligation separately undertaken by him specifically as an individual.[82]
Bell states the view that " there does not seem to be authority under the
statute to conclude a composition contract, without the concurrence of
all the bankrupts, if it shall not be accompanied by a discharge to them
all. Each one of the bankrupts is entitled to insist that the estate shall
be managed and brought to sale and division under the sequestration
as being the best mode of deriving the true value from the estate and he
has an interest so to insist, unless his person and his separate estate
shall be discharged." [83] Bell's view is founded on the reasoning that
the bankruptcy statute then in force authorised a composition only where
it was proposed by the bankrupt, which in the case of a partnership must
comprehend the firm and its partners, or by " his friends " which must
imply that in the case of an individual bankrupt it is with his concurrence,
and in the case of a firm with the concurrence of each partner, that the
composition is offered. The requirements of the Bankruptcy (Scotland)
Act 1913 [84] still retain the features of the earlier statute so far as relied
on by Bell but the Bankruptcy (Scotland) Act 1913 following the Act of
1856 expressly provides that the offer may be made in the case of a
" company " by one or more of the partners thereof. That, of itself,
does not necessarily militate against Bell's view that the offer must have
the concurrence of each partner but since the Act itself does not require
such concurrence in the case of an offer made by one of the partners, it
is not entirely consistent with Bell's theory. It is possible that the
apparent conflict may be resolved on two entirely separate grounds. In
the first place, where the offer of composition is made by one of the
partners, he has a separate and personal interest to serve in addition to
that of the firm in that he will desire to free himself by means of the
composition from his personal, and as yet unquantified, liability as a

[81] *Smith & Jones, Petrs.* (1827) 5 S. 357. The decision, while establishing the competency of
such proceedings, afforded no strong authority for asserting the right of the partners to a
discharge in those circumstances, since the court decided the case " in respect of no
objection."
[82] *Mellis* v. *Royal Bank of Scotland*, June 22, 1815, F.C.; and see Bell, *Comm.* II, 567.
[83] *Comm.* II, 567.
[84] ss. 134 and 136.

cautioner for his firm. That this personal interest is relevant in the determination of the question may be seen in the decisions as to the effect of an offer of composition by one of the partners conditional upon his own discharge, though not upon the discharge of the partners who have not joined in making the offer, or conditional upon the partner who makes the offer receiving an assignation of the creditors' rights against the firm and the remaining partners. These aspects and the decisions on which they are founded have already been mentioned.[85] But in the second place, it is clear that in either case the question for decision by the court resolves itself in some degree into one of title and interest to sue either on the arrangement or on the objections by non-participating partners in it. Thus, where an offer which stipulates for the discharge of the partner who makes the offer, and no other partner, is acquiesced in by the remaining partners, the creditors are presumed to reserve their remedies against the individual estates of the remaining partners.[86] Again where the partner who makes the offer stipulates for an assignation of the creditor's right against the remaining partners, the partner obtaining that assignation is not entitled to demand from his copartners more than the share of what he can prove that he has paid towards the debts of the firm without having been reimbursed from the firm's assets.[87]

(4) Claims against solvent partner where firm's estates have been sequestrated while one or more partners are insolvent and one or more solvent

It is clear that in spite of the sequestration of the firm a solvent partner will remain liable to the creditors of the firm in so far as their claims are not met out of the firm's sequestrated estates. That liability is an accessory one of the nature of cautionry and it does not appear to be possible to found upon it so as to permit of the trustee on the sequestrated estates of the firm calling upon the solvent partner to contribute to the sequestration the sums required to make it possible to pay the firm's creditors in full. The point was raised in *Laing Brothers & Company's Trustee* v. *Low* [88] but did not need to be decided since the court held that the arrangements made between the parties did not infer a partnership between them. Lord McLaren, however, took notice of the point and, while finding it unnecessary to decide it, expressed in very cogent terms the objections in law to the competency of such a claim on the part of the trustee. He said,

> " In the clause of the Partnership Act constituting the special law of Scotland on this subject [89] all that is said is that the firm is a separate person in law, but that a partner is liable to be charged to meet the

---

[85] *Supra* pp. 568 *et seq.*
[86] Bell, *Comm.* II, 567. Wallace, *Manual of Bankruptcy Law in Scotland* (1st ed. 1907) p. 197 states the rule to the opposite effect but as he cites the same passage from Bell's *Commentaries* as authority, he appears to have mis-read it. See Goudy, *op. cit.* p. 393.
[87] Bell, *loc. cit.*
[88] (1896) 23 R. 1105.
[89] Partnership Act 1890, s. 4 (2).

obligations of the firm. Now, sequestration is not a process for rendering a party liable to meet the obligations of a firm—it is a process for attaching the assets of those who are members of the firm and who have been made bankrupt, and I am unable to see how this sequestration is to be converted into an active title for the purpose of putting persons under the trust who are not named in the trustee's appointment." [90]

That view, it is submitted with respect, appears to be incontrovertible. The trustee on the sequestrated estate of a firm has not in that capacity any title to sue a solvent partner of that firm in virtue of the liability imposed on that partner under section 4 (2) of the Partnership Act 1890; for the trustee is vested *tantum et tale* in the assets of the bankrupt firm and in no sense can the terms of section 4 (2) be construed to create a right of recourse in the firm against the solvent partner. There is, in Lord McLaren's words, no " active title " in the trustee for that purpose. Nor will it improve the position of the trustee if in addition to the firm's estates, the estates of the partners, other than the solvent partner, have been sequestrated. It is true that in such cases the sequestrated estates of a partner will have a *pro rata* right of relief against the solvent partner under the section for the amount which these estates have had to pay in excess of the partner's agreed share towards the firm's obligations. This point is to be examined at a later stage. But it is not a right of relief of that kind which is involved in the question which Lord McLaren had under consideration. It is rather a claim to make good the total shortfall in payment of the firm's creditors which has occurred after they have received all that is available to them from the sequestrated estates of the firm and the bankrupt partners. The position of the trustee is different if he is claiming from the solvent partner a sum which the latter has agreed to contribute to the capital or stock of the partnership itself. In that case the agreed or promised contribution is an asset of the partnership estate and the trustee has a clear title to sue for its recovery.

Sequestrated firm a partner in another partnership or joint adventure

If a partner is a creditor of his firm, his claim is postponed until the trade creditors of the firm have been paid in full [91] at least where his claim is for his share of the capital contributed, the advances made on loan to the firm and his share of profits.[92] The trade creditors of the firm may be those creditors to whom the firm has become indebted in the course of the conduct of its business, and these will include the trade creditors of any partnership or joint adventure in which the sequestrated firm has become a partner along with other firms or individuals. The trade creditors of that further partnership or joint adventure will look

---

[90] *Laing Bros. & Co.'s Tr.* v. *Low, supra*, at p. 1116.
[91] *Cullen* v. *Macfarlane* (1842) 4 D. 1522.
[92] Partnership Act 1890, s. 44 (*b*).

first for payment to the estate of that partnership or joint adventure. If that estate is insufficient to pay their claims in full, they will then treat the sequestrated firm as a partner of the joint adventure and rank upon the sequestrated estate for their claim after deducting what they have received towards it from the joint adventure. If their claim still remains unsatisfied to any extent they may have recourse against the estates of the individual partners for the balance.[93]

Competing jurisdictions in bankruptcy of the firm and its partners

Where the firm and its partners are both bankrupt, the situation may arise where the courts of different countries share jurisdiction in the bankruptcy of the different persons involved. Section 122 of the Bankruptcy Act 1914 imposes a duty to give aid to courts of another country in which jurisdiction in bankruptcy has been effectively constituted. Although the Bankruptcy Act 1914 is predominantly an English Act, the duty laid down in section 122 is imposed on " the High Court, the county courts, the courts having jurisdiction in Scotland and every British court elsewhere having jurisdiction in bankruptcy or insolvency." In *Scrivenor* (*Home's Trustee*) v. *Home's Trustees*[94] an order was made by a South African court seeking the aid of the Scottish court to recover assets in Scotland belonging to a deceased partner of a partnership the estates of which had been sequestrated in South Africa. The trustee on the sequestrated estates both of the firm and of the deceased partner raised an action of accounting against the testamentary trustees of the deceased partner who administered the deceased's property in Scotland. It was held by Lord Ashmore in the Outer House that effect must be given to the order of the South African court seeking aid and the defenders, the testamentary trustees, were appointed to lodge an account.

Trust deed for creditors

There is nothing in law to impede the winding up of the affairs of a bankrupt firm and its partners extra-judicially by means of a trust deed for creditors, or an extra-judicial composition contract. Since, however, such arrangements must be regarded as matters outwith the ordinary course of the firm's business, the deed should be executed by all the partners of the firm. The implied authority of a partner will not extend to cover an act of this nature, so that his execution of the contract would not bind the firm; nor, it is thought, would execution of the deed by a majority of the partners, since this does not appear to be a matter on which the decision of the majority will bind the minority, unless the partnership agreement has expressly given the majority a mandate to act in the matter. Since the winding up of the firm's affairs may involve questions of complexity as to the rights and liabilities of the partners *inter se* in relation

[93] *Infra* pp. 576 *et seq.*
[94] 1926 S.L.T. 214; and see *Braga* v. *Taylor*, 1930 S.N. 158 (O.H.).

to the partnership, it will be prudent to make detailed provision in the trust deed or in the contract of composition for the apportionment of liabilities among the partners and for their rights to a discharge.[95]

Challenge of transactions of the partnership

The creditors of a bankrupt firm have the same rights of challenge as the creditors of an individual with respect to gratuitous alienations or illegal preferences granted by the bankrupt. These rights of challenge as in the case of an individual bankrupt may be maintained under the common law or under the Acts 1621, c. 18, and 1696, c. 5, respectively. The specialities which appear in regard to the partnership in these questions relate to the artificial *persona* of the firm and to the consequential feature that any such challengeable transactions must be effected in the name of the firm by the partners as its agents, or by one or more of them as such agents. These two distinct aspects of speciality are, of course, inter-related and may on occasion become merged. Thus it has already been suggested that a challenge under the Act 1621, c. 18, of a gratuitous alienation by the firm may be supported only where the alienation is to a " confident person " since the firm itself can have no natural relationship of blood or affinity to a natural person who is the donee in the transaction such as would characterise the donee as a " conjunct person " with the firm.[96] But that statement though sufficiently self-evident in general terms may become blurred when those acting as the hand of the firm in the transaction in question are conjunct persons with the alienee. It is clear upon analysis of the facts in *Witham and Others* v. *Teenan's Trustee* [97] that no question of the firm being a conjunct person with the gratuitous alienee is involved. Teenan and his son had been in partnership in the firm of Teenan & Son and the estates of Teenan, the father, were sequestrated. The son claimed to vote in the sequestration in respect of a cheque granted by his father in his favour some seven years previously, explaining that it had been granted in security of an advance made by the son to enable his father to pay off another debt. The sheriff substitute, in an interlocutor which was approved by Lord President Inglis both as to its conclusions and its reasoning, held that the son's claim was insufficiently vouched, and the observation was made that the son was a conjunct and confident person, as son and partner, with his father and that his claim must therefore be very narrowly examined.[98] This case has accordingly no relevance as a decision affecting the challenge of a partnership transaction. It is concerned with a transaction between the father and the son (conjunct persons) as individuals and the question of the partnership subsisting between them arises only because that circumstance rendered the father and son confident persons also.[99]

[95] Bell, *Comm.* II, 561.
[96] *Supra* pp. 568–570.
[97] (1884) 11 R. 776.
[98] *Per* Lord Shand in *Tytler* (*Walker's Tr.*) v. *Walker* (1883) 10 R. 699 at p. 704.
[99] Bell, *Comm.* II, 175.

Challenge of illegal preferences under the Act 1696, c. 5

It is not proposed to examine the general law affecting the reduction of illegal preferences, a subject which pertains to the law of bankruptcy rather than to the law of partnership. The transactions of a partnership, like those of an individual, may be subjected to a challenge on the ground that they seek to confer an unfair preference upon a selected creditor or selected creditors of the firm. If the challenge is made under the Act 1696, c. 5, it must be established that it was carried through by the debtor at or after his becoming notour bankrupt or within six months prior thereto [1] and was a voluntary transaction whereby a preference has been or can be directly or indirectly conferred on a creditor in satisfaction or further security of his claim. The circumstances in which a " company " which includes for the purpose a partnership,[2] may be made notour bankrupt are set forth in the Bankruptcy (Scotland) Act 1913, s. 5, and have already been examined.[3]

Transactions in the ordinary course of business

Possibly the most important point to be noticed in the application of the general law as to illegal preferences in bankruptcy to a bankrupt partnership is the exception made in respect of transactions by the bankrupt which are transactions in the ordinary course of business.[4] It will be recollected that the ambit of the ostensible authority of a partner to bind his firm extends to acts done by him " for carrying on in the usual way business of the kind carried on by the firm of which he is a member," [5] and the two concepts (1) of transactions in the ordinary course of business and (2) of transactions for " carrying on in the usual way business of the kind carried on by the firm . . ." are sufficiently similar to prompt closer examination of them. In one sense they converge because if an act of a partner is not done for the carrying on in the usual way business of the kind carried on by his firm it will not be binding on the firm and thus prima facie at least will not be a transaction of the firm which is challengeable on the firm's bankruptcy. The preference, if any, gained by the transaction will still be reducible but it will be reducible on other grounds, namely that the partner had no authority, actual or apparent, to effect the transaction on behalf of the firm. Hence no security over the firm's estate or preferential payment by the firm is notionally involved. That solution of the problem is, however, imperfect since the partner may have actual authority from his copartners to perform the act even though it is not an act for carrying

---

[1] Originally sixty days under the Act 1696, c. 5, now increased to six months: Companies Act 1947, s. 115 (3).

[2] Bankruptcy (Scotland) Act 1913, s. 2.

[3] *Supra* p. 560.

[4] Bell, *Comm.* II, 228: " Payment of a debt in the ordinary course does not indicate failure," but see *Horsbrugh* v. *Ramsay & Co.* (1885) 12 R. 1171.

[5] Partnership Act 1890, s. 5.

on in the usual way business of the kind carried on by the firm. In that case his act will be binding on the firm. It will be a transaction of the firm and if it involves an illegal preference the only mode whereby it may be reduced is by a challenge either at common law or under the Act 1696, c. 5. The situation where a partner, albeit acting beyond the scope of his apparent authority, has actually made a preferential payment to a creditor out of the coffers of the bankrupt firm, is, it is submitted, no exception to the general rule that the transaction may be reduced on the ground that it is not binding on the firm and recoverable from the creditor; for, though payment *de facto* has been made from the firm's estate, it has been made as a result of a transaction in which the partner had no authority to bind the firm.

The more difficult question is whether an act done by a partner within his ostensible authority, *i.e.* done for the carrying on in the usual way of business of the kind carried on by the firm, will *ipso facto* be a transaction in the ordinary course of business so as to exempt it from challenge as an illegal preference. The question whether an act can be said to have been done in carrying on a business in the way in which it is usually carried on is one to which no universally applicable answer can be given. The answer may obviously vary as the nature of the business and the practice of persons engaged in that kind of business is examined. It is only where it can be said that the act is one without which no business can be carried on or conversely that it is an act which is entirely unnecessary for the carrying on of *any* business that any test of universal application can be used in relation to section 5 of the Partnership Act 1890.[6] On the other hand, where the courts have had regard to the question whether a transaction is exempt from challenge as an illegal preference because it is a transaction in the ordinary course of business, the test applied is one of universal application to the conduct of business in general. This is implicit in the words of the Lord President (Inglis) in *Horsbrugh* v. *Ramsay & Company*,[7] a case where a trader whose affairs were embarrassed carried on his business for some years, paying his creditors in cash when he could but frequently by indorsing over to them bills which he received from customers, and within sixty days of notour bankruptcy indorsed three bills, not yet due and received from his customers in payment of the price of goods he had sold to them, to a firm of wholesale leather merchants in payment of goods which he, the debtor, previously received from them. The Lord President said,

" It is, however, urged that this mode of dealing was in the ordinary course of business, and that if so it does not matter whether the words of the statute apply to it or not, for transactions in the ordinary course of business are, in practice, excepted from the operation of the statute. It does not, however, appear to me that these bills were indorsed in the ordinary course of business. The ordinary course of business

---

[6] This point is more fully discussed *supra* Chap. VII, pp. 208–213.
[7] (1885) 12 R. 1171 at p. 1176.

in the case of a trader who is in a state of solvency would have been that every one of these bills should have been lodged with his banker, and placed to his credit, and when he paid his creditors he would have paid them by cheque on his banker."

It is not suggested that a course of dealing within the partnership business such as the debtor indulged in in the case of *Horsbrugh* v. *Ramsay & Company* would enlarge the ambit of the ostensible authority of a partner as it is defined in section 5 of the Partnership Act 1890. If that course of dealing were appealed to the third party would require to establish that the partner had been held out to him in a course of dealing with him as possessing the authority. But section 5 is concerned with what a third party is entitled to assume the ostensible authority of a partner to be and the measure of that authority is not what is usually done in the conduct of the partnership business but what is usually done in the conduct of a business *of the kind* carried on by the partnership. Nevertheless, the test applied by the Lord President for the purpose of transactions in the ordinary course of business is an even more general one than that contained in section 5 of the Partnership Act 1890. It is the test of what would be the normal conduct of the business of a trader and not the normal conduct of any particular kind of trade; and that is the appropriate test in a question of illegal preference where the consideration to be given effect to is not the authority to carry through the transaction, nor even necessarily the state of mind of the debtor when he carried it through [8] but the principle that a debtor whose affairs are embarrassed must act equitably in the interests of the general body of his creditors.[9]

It may therefore be said to follow that while a transaction by a partner on behalf of his firm must always be within his ostensible authority if it is a transaction in the ordinary course of business, in the sense explained by Lord President Inglis, the converse is not necessarily true. It is conceivable that a transaction falling within the partner's ostensible authority under section 5 of the Partnership Act 1890 may yet be reducible as an illegal preference in the bankruptcy of his firm; a transaction for carrying on in the usual way business of the kind carried on by his firm, while in many cases it will be exempt from challenge as a transaction in the ordinary course of business, may not in every case measure up to the wide view of business taken where exemption from challenge is being considered.

The ranking of claims against a partnership

The rules of the law of bankruptcy as to ranking of claims in the sequestration of the firm and its partners are based on the principle that the primary obligation for the debts of the partnership falls upon the firm, the partners being liable in an accessory obligation of *quasi*

---

[8] " It is not to be affected by what passes in the mind of the bankrupt ": *per* Lord Mansfield in *Rust* v. *Cooper* (1777) Cowp. 634; quoted with approval, Bell, *Comm.* II; 228–229, n. 6.
[9] Bell, *Comm.* II, 226–227.

cautionry.[10] In claiming against the sequestrated estate of the firm the creditor need not value and deduct his claim against the partners. He claims and ranks on the firm's estate for the full amount of the debt. The partners are in effect co-obligants with their firm and the creditor's claim against the partners is indistinguishable from a claim against any other co-obligant. While the creditor must, in his affidavit, specify the partners as co-obligants for the debt, he does not need to value or deduct the value of their obligation.[11] In the event, however, of any of the partners holding a security over any part of the firm's estate he must account to the trustee " as if he had paid the debt to the creditor and thereafter ranked on the sequestrated estate under deduction of the value of such security." [12]

Valuation of claims against the firm and its partners for purposes of voting

There is a general duty placed upon a creditor who " has an obligant bound with but liable in relief to the bankrupt " to put a specified value on the obligation of such obligant and deduct that value from the amount of his claim in his affidavit. The creditor is entitled to vote in the sequestration only in respect of the balance thus arrived at.[13] That general duty, however, applies where the co-obligant of the bankrupt is also liable in relief to the bankrupt. In the case of a firm and its partners the firm is primarily liable for the firm debt and the partners undertake liability as cautioners for their firm. The partners are thus co-obligants with their firm but are not co-obligants against whom the firm has any right of relief, whereas if the bankrupt against whom the creditor makes the claim is one of the partners and the claim arises from a firm debt, then the firm and its other partners are co-obligants with the bankrupt partner and also are liable in affording relief to him. The special position of the firm and its partners is provided for in section 57 of the Bankruptcy (Scotland) Act 1913 which provides—

"57. *Valuation of claims against a company and partners.*—A creditor on the estate of a company shall not be bound, for the purpose of voting on the company's estate, to deduct from his claim the value which he may be entitled to draw from the estates of the partners; but, if he claim on the estate of a partner, he shall, before voting, in his oath put a specified value on his claim against the estate of the company and also against the other partners thereof, in so far as they are liable to relieve such partner, and deduct such value from his debt and specify the balance, and he shall be entitled

---

[10] Bell, *Comm.* II, 564; " It is only in the case where the ranking is on the estate of the primary obligant and who is bound to relieve the other obligants that it is not necessary to value the claims against the collateral obligants; but here the company is the primary obligant and George and Francis [the partners] stand in the situation of collateral obligants and entitled to relief out of the funds of the company for proper company debts ": *per* Lord Gillies in *Nicol* v. *Christie* (1827) 5 S. 882.

[11] *University of Glasgow* v. *Yuill's Tr.* (1882) 9 R. 643.

[12] Bankruptcy (Scotland) Act 1913, s. 61.

[13] *Ibid.* s. 56.

to vote as a creditor for the said balance, and no more, without prejudice to the amount of his debt in other respects."

Valuation of claims against the firm and its partners for ranking

This aspect is dealt with separately in section 62 of the Bankruptcy (Scotland) Act 1913 which reads—

" 62. *Value of claim against a company to be deducted from claim against partners.*—When a creditor claims on the estate of the partner of a company in respect of a debt due by such company, the trustee on the estate of such partner shall, before ranking such creditor, put a valuation on the estate of the company, and deduct from the claim of such creditor such estimated value, and rank and pay to him a dividend only on the balance."

It is difficult to resist the impression that Homer, in the shape of the legislature, has in this section indulged in one of the cat-naps which we are told are occasional, if infrequent, in the writings of that great poet. What the section directs the trustee on the sequestrated estate to do is to put a valuation on the estate of the company and deduct that estimated value from the claim of the creditor in the sequestration of the partner. Such a proceeding will lead to very odd results and if it resulted in an equity of treatment of the creditor, that equity would appear to be an entirely accidental outcome. It is thought that what Parliament intended to lay down in this section was that the trustee in the partner's sequestration should value and deduct from the creditor's claim the estimated amount of the dividend which might be claimed by him in respect of his debt in the sequestration of the firm or the estimated amount which the creditor might be expected to obtain from the firm itself in respect of the debt. That is the accepted view taken upon the purport of the section [14]; and it is in accordance with the law as it existed prior to 1913.[15] The decisions on which that view was based [15] were concerned with a claim by the trustee on the sequestrated estates of the firm in the sequestrated estate of the partner. The trustee for the firm was thus claiming as representing the general body of the creditors of the firm and the rule expressed in section 62 of the Bankruptcy (Scotland) Act 1913, which itself reflects the similar provision in section 66 of the Bankruptcy (Scotland) Act 1856, is appropriate for that situation. But section 62 of the Bankruptcy (Scotland) Act 1913 in its terms covers a claim by an individual creditor of the firm in the sequestration of the partner. It will, of course, be necessary for the partner's trustee, as the section directs, to " put a valuation on the estate of the company." In doing so he will require to estimate not only the assets but also the liabilities of the firm. Having done so, he is in a position to estimate the dividend which the creditor might receive from the firm estate and it is thought that

---

[14] See Goudy, *Bankruptcy* (4th ed.) p. 322.
[15] Bell, *Comm.* II, 550–551; *Tr. for Carlyle & Co.'s Creditors* v. *Tr. for Dunlop's Creditors* (1776) Mor. 14610; affd. (1777) 2 Pat.App. 437; *Nicol* v. *Christie* (1827) 5 S. 882.

it is this dividend which should be deducted from the individual creditor's claim in the sequestration of the partner. However, that is not what section 62 directs the trustee to do. He is directed to deduct from the creditor's claim " such estimated value," *i.e.* the estimated value of the estate of the firm, and where the individual creditor for the firm debt is an ordinary creditor the deduction of the estimated total net estate of the firm from his claim in the partner's sequestration would in many cases serve entirely to extinguish that claim and in most cases would result in a deduction larger than the sum which he may be expected to receive from the firm estate in respect of his claim.

" The estate of the company "

It has already been mentioned that in terms of section 2 of the Bankruptcy (Scotland) Act 1913 the word " company " when used in the Act includes partnerships. It was argued in *Brickmann's Trustee* v. *Commercial Bank* [16] that, on a construction of the similar provisions of the Bankruptcy Act 1856,[17] the term " company " was not to be interpreted as including a joint adventure as distinguished from a partnership. The court found it unnecessary to deal with this point, since it disposed of the case upon grounds which rendered that particular issue irrelevant. It is submitted, however, that the argument has little merit. The attempted distinction between a partnership and a joint adventure has found little favour both before [18] and after [19] the argument was advanced, and it would be difficult to suggest any general considerations which might induce the court to construe the term " partnership " in the Bankruptcy (Scotland) Act 1913 as limited in its effect to exclude a joint adventure since the mention of the " genus " (to adopt Lord President Cooper's phrase) must be regarded as including the " species."

Treatment in a partner's sequestration of the creditor's claims against the copartners

Section 62 of the Bankruptcy (Scotland) Act 1913 is confined in its terms to a direction that in ranking a creditor's claim for a firm debt on the sequestration of a partner, the trustee in the partner's sequestration must put a valuation " on the estate of the company " (more properly, as has been submitted, on the dividend obtainable by the creditor from the estate of the company), deduct that and rank the creditor only to the extent of the balance of his debt. No specific mention is made of the treatment of the creditor's claims, or rights of recourse, against the other

[16] (1901) 38 S.L.R. 766.
[17] ss. 65 and 66.
[18] " A joint adventure . . . differs in no respect except its transient nature . . . from an ordinary mercantile partnership." More, Notes to Stair, p. xcviii.
[19] " A joint adventure is simply a species of the genus partnership, differentiated by its limited purpose and duration . . . but in all other essential respects indistinguishable from any other partnership "—*per* the Lord President (Cooper) in *Mair* v. *Wood,* 1948 S.C. 83 at p. 86; and see *infra* Chap. XV, pp. 610 *et seq.*

partners in the firm. Provided the debt has been constituted against the firm, the creditor may, of course, make his own decision as to whether he will claim against the firm or its partners and if he chooses to proceed against the partners he may proceed against any one or more of these. These rights, however, operate only where there is at least one of the partners who is solvent and may be called upon to pay the debt in full and operate his own relief against the firm and his copartners in terms of section 4 (2) of the Partnership Act 1890. When the estates of the firm and all its partners are in sequestration, another rule comes into operation which modifies the general situation under section 4 (2) of the Partnership Act 1890. It was stated by Lord Kinnear in *Brickmann's Trustee* v. *Commercial Bank* [20] in these words: ". . . it is clear that the creditor cannot by any means of ranking obtain more than full payment of his debt." If the creditor were allowed to rank for dividend for the full amount of the firm debt upon the estates of the firm and of each of the partners, the total of the dividends received might exceed the amount of his initial claim, and even if that were not the result, the general body of the creditors in each of the separate sequestrations would have received inequitable treatment in that the creditor in question would have in relation to them received a double or even a multiple ranking for the one claim. On the other hand, he, as a creditor for a debt of the partnership, is in the special position that he may seek payment from the firm and in addition has the supporting accessory obligations of the individual partners *singuli in solidum*. But in the sequestrated estate of any one of those partners he should not be allowed to inflate his claim by failing to take into account what he may receive from the other obligants.

It has been seen that in the case of his claim against the firm express, though perhaps imprecise, direction is given for the valuation and deduction from his claim of the dividend which he may expect from the estate of the firm. While there is no mention in section 62 of the Bankruptcy (Scotland) Act 1913 of a direction similarly to value and deduct in respect of the creditor's claim against the estates of the bankrupt partner's copartners, it is clear that these copartners are co-obligants with the bankrupt partner and also that they are bound in an obligation of relief to him. The creditor in a firm debt who is claiming in the sequestration of one of the partners is, as has already been noted, bound for the purpose of voting to value and deduct his claim against the firm " and also against the other partners thereof, in so far as they are liable to relieve " the partner in whose sequestration he is claiming.[21] But the Act makes no direction that this proceeding is to be followed in valuing his claim for the purposes of ranking and dividend and indeed the amount of the creditor's debt in the partner's sequestration for purposes other than voting is expressly stated in section 57 of the Bankruptcy (Scotland) Act 1913 not to be prejudiced.

[20] (1901) 38 S.L.R. 766 at p. 769.
[21] Bankruptcy (Scotland) Act 1913, s. 57.

In the absence of express provision in the Bankruptcy (Scotland) Act 1913 on this point it is submitted that the common law is still in force. In terms of the common law it appears settled that the creditor must also value and deduct his claim against the other partners in so far as they are liable in relief.[22] The valuation of such claims will thus depend upon the extent of the liability of the copartners to recoup the partner in whose sequestration the claim is made and that liability will presumably be determined by the terms of the partnership agreement or in the absence of such terms, in accordance with the provisions of the Partnership Act 1890.[23]

The circumstances in which a question of valuation and deduction of the creditor's rights against the other partners as co-obligants arises may be complex and require close analysis. In *Brickmann's Trustee* v. *Commercial Bank* [24] a firm, I. W. & O. Brickmann, drew bills on Dawson which Dawson accepted. The bills were discounted by the bank at Messrs. Brickmann's request. Messrs. Brickmann explained that the bills covered goods held by them and Dawson on joint account and enclosed delivery orders in the bank's favour in respect of certain whisky which was so held on joint account. The bank were to hold the delivery orders in security of the specific transaction referred to and it alone and these delivery orders were to be returned or transferred to the party taking up the bills. The estates of I. W. & O. Brickmann were sequestrated during the currency of the bills and the bank claimed a ranking in the sequestration for the total amount of the bills without deducting the value of their security. It was held that they were not bound to value and deduct the security in terms of section 65 of the Bankruptcy Act 1856 [25] and since the whisky did not form part of the bankrupt firm's estate no question arose of valuing it and deducting the value from the claim in terms of section 66 of that Act [25] unless it could be established, as the trustee attempted to argue, that there was a partnership between Messrs. Brickmann and Dawson and that the whisky held in security formed part of the estate of a company in which Brickmanns were a partner. Lord Kinnear said,[26]

> " I cannot think it doubtful that the case the Legislature intended to meet by that section was that of an insolvent and sequestrated partner of an insolvent and sequestrated company; because if the company were solvent, it would be able to pay the claim in full, and the creditor would have neither title nor interest to ask for a ranking on the estate of an individual partner. The sole purpose of the section was to give effect to a general rule which was established long before the Bankruptcy Act of 1856, namely that in bankruptcy no claim could be made on the separate estate of a partner of a company

---

[22] *McCubbin* v. *Turnbull* (1850) 12 D. 1123; *Nicol* v. *Christie* (1827) 5 S. 882.
[23] s. 24 (1).
[24] (1901) 38 S.L.R. 766.
[25] Now represented by ss. 61 and 62 respectively of the Bankruptcy (Scotland) Act 1913.
[26] *Brickmann's Tr.* v. *Commercial Bank, supra,* at pp. 768–769.

for a company debt except for the balance which remained after deduction of all that could be drawn from the company's estate."

In any event in the case under consideration there was no evidence of partnership or joint adventure nor was the bank's claim based on joint adventure; it was based on the direct liability of the endorser of the bills. While property had been pledged in security of that liability it was not the property of the bankrupt firm nor of a further partnership or joint adventure in which the bankrupt firm was a partner.

CHAPTER XIV

THE LIMITED PARTNERSHIP

THE liability of the members of a partnership *singuli in solidum* for the debts incurred by the firm made it unsafe for persons who would otherwise be willing to invest capital in a firm to assume the risk that by doing so they might be held to be partners of the firm. It is true that both under Bovill's Act [1] and the Partnership Act 1890 [2] it is provided that the lending of money to a firm or to a person carrying on a business on condition that the lender receive a share of the profits or a rate of interest varying with the profit earned by the business does not of itself make the lender a partner if the contract is in writing and signed by the parties or on their behalf. To that extent it might be contended that these Acts have already legislated for the situation for which later legislation [3] provides. But his situation was still perilous, if he took any part in the transaction of the business of the firm, such as intervening in its proposed purchases, or indeed if he even apparently took part as an interested party in the firm's business. Such activity on his part would not necessarily involve him as a partner, since a lender whose money is at risk in the fortunes of a firm has a legitimate interest to be served in his character as lender. His position is, however, ambiguous and the decision whether in his actions he sustains the character of lender or the character of partner will often be one of degree, so that the lender in such circumstances may find himself in an area of doubt and indecision how far he may intervene in the business of the firm for the purpose of protecting his own investment. If he crosses a line which is not clearly and sharply drawn, he may find himself declared to be a partner with unlimited liability for the debts of the firm in which he has invested his money. [4]

The reason for the attitude of the courts and the resulting dilemma in which the lender is placed is evident. A loan of money to a business, though an entirely different thing in theory from a contribution to the capital stock of a firm, may not always be so clearly differentiated in actual business practice and, were the law to adopt anything but an attitude of the strictest scrutiny in such cases, it would be possible for the moneyed member of a firm, while enjoying all the rights of a partner in questions arising within the firm, to masquerade in questions affecting third parties as a mere investor in, or lender to, the firm. Yet there are cases where such loans may be entirely bona fide, *e.g.* where friends or relatives finance a young man setting up in business, or where an

[1] 28 & 29 Vict. c. 86.
[2] s. 2 (3) (*d*).
[3] Limited Partnerships Act 1907.
[4] See *supra* Chap. III, pp. 88–92.

established business requires further capital for its development and wishes to raise this by means of a loan from a person they do not intend to assume as a partner.

That type of situation has been recognised for many years in France in the *société en commandite*, but while it is possible to see some resemblance to the *commanditaire* in the lender to a firm who received a share of the profits and who successfully maintained his character solely as a lender under the Partnership Act 1890, yet in Britain there was always the possible duality of character with the consequential possibility of un-limited liability whereas in France both those engaged in running the business, the *commandités*, and those merely investing their money in it, the *commanditaires*, were recognised as members of the association, the *liability* of each class being, however, sharply distinguished.

The Limited Partnerships Act 1907 sought to remove the ambiguity of the position of a person who is interested in the fortunes of the partner-ship purely as an investor of his capital in the firm and without taking any active part in the business of the firm. In its approach to the problem of the partner with limited liability the influence of the French *société en commandite* may be discerned. A person who lends or invests his money in the firm need not thereby expose himself to the perils attendant upon a duality of character originally as lender or investor and subsequently, if he fails to act with the utmost discretion, possibly as a partner. Since the return on the money that he has invested or lent is linked up with the profits of the firm in which he has invested, it is now possible for him to be from the outset a member of the partnership but one who incurs only limited liability provided the terms of the Limited Partnerships Act 1907 are observed.

The Limited Partnerships Act 1907 was hailed as a major advance in the law. Some of the utterances made immediately after its enactment read rather strangely today. A commentator on the Act writing in 1907 observed, " It is more than probable that the effect of this Act may be to exercise a small revolution in the trading world." [5] Later the same writer states, ". . . there can be little doubt that a few years hence will see this system of limited firms very largely adopted throughout the three Kingdoms." [6] It is of course a matter of history that those prognostica-tions have been almost completely falsified. The limited partnership has not proved a highly popular form of association in the business world and, in those cases where its provisions sought to temper the law of partnership to meet the difficulties of the investor in a firm, resort has much more frequently been had to the private limited company. The trouble and expense in establishing such a company is little more than what is involved in setting up a limited partnership and it has the great advantage that the liability of *all* members of the company is limited to the amount of capital which they have agreed to subscribe, whether

[5] Hurrell, *The Limited Partnerships Act* 1907, p. 7.
[6] *Ibid.* p. 8.

those members take an active part in the management of the company or remain more passively interested as shareholders. In a limited partnership there must be at least one partner, called a general partner, who actively conducts the business of the partnership, and he, or, in the case of a number of general partners, they, incur unlimited liability for the debts of the partnership.[7] The advantages of the private limited company in this respect are very marked and when in addition it was possible, as it was for sixty years after the passing of the Limited Partnerships Act 1907, to avoid by means of the " exempt private company " [8] the necessity for filing on the public register of companies particulars of the yearly accounts and balance sheet of the company, it is hardly surprising that in most cases where problems arose of the kind that the Limited Partnerships Act 1907 was designed to meet, it was deemed more expedient to set up a private limited company.

The future of the limited partnership

While in many cases the advantages of the private limited company will still ensure that it is resorted to in preference to the limited partnership, it is possible that more use will be made of the limited partnership in future. Two fairly recent developments may have a bearing on the choice. (1) The introduction of the corporation tax to which the private limited company is liable, whereas the partnership, including the limited partnership, is not [9] is one factor which may have a bearing, and certainly ought to be considered, in making the choice. (2) The abolition of the exempt private company [10] will render it necessary to resort to the limited partnership, if it is desired to withhold from the public the accounts and balance sheet of the concern. There may well be circumstances where either or both of those circumstances exercise a cogent influence upon the decision which is taken. It is thought, however, that in most situations the marked advantage of the private limited company as to the liability of the members will still prove the compelling consideration and that the private limited company will continue to be the favoured type of association. With the example of Mr. Hurrell still vividly before one's mind, however, that prophecy is made with diffidence and with a keen sense of the possibility of fallibility.

The constitution of the limited partnership

A limited partnership may be formed " in the manner and subject to the conditions " provided by the Limited Partnerships Act 1907.[11] In their application for its particular purposes, the general provisions of the

---

[7] Limited Partnerships Act 1907, s. 4 (2).
[8] Companies Act 1948, s. 129 and Sched. VII.
[9] Income and Corporation Taxes Act 1970, ss. 238 (1) and 526 (1). But where one of the partners is a company see s. 155.
[10] Companies Act 1967, s. 2.
[11] Limited Partnerships Act 1907, s. 4 (1).

Partnership Act 1890 as to the meaning of " firm," " firm name " and
" business " are adopted.[12]　Thus a limited partnership, like an ordinary
partnership, may carry on any " business " with a view of profit [13] and
the term " business " will include any trade, occupation or profession.[14]
Similarly a limited partnership is referred to *passim* in the Limited
Partnerships Act 1907 as a " firm " [15] and since the Act provides in
section 3 that that term is to have the meaning assigned to it in the
Partnership Act 1890, it follows that a limited partnership in Scotland
is a *quasi* person in law distinct from the partners who comprise it.[16]

General and limited partners

A limited partnership must comprise two classes of partners (1) one
or more general partners who are liable for all the debts and obligations
of the firm, and (2) one or more limited partners, who at the time of
entering the partnership contribute to the partnership either a capital
sum or property valued at a stated amount and who shall not be liable
for the debts or obligations of the firm beyond the amount so contributed.[17]
During the continuance of the limited partnership a limited partner is not
permitted, directly or indirectly, to withdraw any part of the contribution
which he has made.　If he does so, he remains liable for the firm's debts
and obligations up to the amount which he has withdrawn or which has
been repaid to him.[18]　As in the case of an unlimited partnership a body
corporate may be a limited partner.[19]

Number of members

In the relevant provisions of the Companies Acts 1948 and 1967 as to
restrictions upon the number of partners [19a] the general word " partnership " is employed.　The restrictions as to number of members applies
equally to limited partnerships.

The limited partner

The Limited Partnerships Act 1907, s. 6 (1), provides—

> " 6.—(1) A limited partner shall not take part in the manage-
> ment of the partnership business, and shall have no power to bind
> the firm:
> 　　Provided that a limited partner may by himself or his agent at

---

[12] *Ibid.* s. 3.
[13] Partnership Act 1890, s. 1 (1).
[14] *Ibid.* s. 45.
[15] See *e.g.* ss. 4 (2) and (3), 6 (1), 9 (1), 10 (1), 11, 13.
[16] Partnership Act 1890, s. 4 (2).
[17] Limited Partnerships Act 1907, s. 4 (2).
[18] *Ibid.* s. 4 (3).
[19] *Ibid.* s. 4 (4).
[19a] Companies Act 1948, ss. 429 and 434, as amended by Companies Act 1967, ss. 119 and
120 respectively.　See also Limited Partnerships (Unrestricted Size) No. 1 Regulations,
1971 (S.I. 782 of 1971).

any time inspect the books of the firm and examine into the state and prospects of the partnership business, and may advise with the partners thereon.

If a limited partner takes part in the management of the partnership business he shall be liable for all debts and obligations of the firm incurred while he so takes part in the management as though he were a general partner."

The general purport of the subsection is plain. A limited partner must refrain from interfering in the actual management of the business of the firm; otherwise he will lose his character as a limited partner so long as he continues to interfere in the management. He may, however, " advise with the partners " upon " the state and prospects of the partnership business " and to enable him to take an effective part in discussions of that nature, he is given the right both to inspect the books and to " examine into " the state and prospects of the business. The distinction drawn between actual management and advising with the partners appears to be maintained between activities in which third parties are involved with the firm and discussions among the partners themselves. For the practical purposes of the Act, that basis of distinction is probably a workable one. It might be possible to envisage a situation where a limited partner of strong personality prevailed upon his partners that a certain course of action which he favoured should be adopted. If that process involved his converting his partners to his view, which they had not previously held, it might be difficult to maintain in a general way that he was not taking part in the management. However, the subsection is clearly concerned only with precluding him from taking any active step to carry his own views into effect and thus limits his right to advising with his partners. He is thus restricted to persuading the general partner or partners to adopt his views and the Act regards the management of the business as the conduct necessary to make these views effective in transactions with third parties, activities from which the limited partner is precluded.

It will also be noticed that where the limited partner infringes the subsection and intervenes in the management, the liability which he incurs, while unlimited, is not necessarily co-extensive with unlimited liability for the future but only with the liability for the debts and obligations of the firm incurred " while he so takes part in the management." The moment he ceases to intervene in the management he incurs no further unlimited liability. The qualifying words are important, because if they were not present and the limited partner by intervening in the management became unqualifiedly liable as a general partner, he would continue to be so liable for firm obligations incurred after he had ceased to take part in the business and might even be liable for debts incurred after he had left the firm.[20]

[20] See Limited Partnerships Act 1907, s. 10 and *infra* pp. 595–596.

" And shall not have power to bind the firm "

It is a corollary of the prohibition of the limited partner's taking part in the management of the business that any acts which he purports to perform in that management will not bind the firm. The application of that principle is clear in questions among the partners themselves. A limited partner who intervened in the management would be acting entirely beyond the scope of the authority committed to him as a member of the firm and would be personally answerable to his copartners. The effect of the words upon claims of third parties against the firm founded upon their dealings with a limited partner is not so clear. The words of section 6 (1) " and shall have no power to bind the firm " are clearly susceptible of the construction that no claim against the firm can arise where a limited partner has transacted the business on behalf of the firm, but it is difficult to reconcile that with the equitable rights of a third party in his dealings with a firm under the general law of partnership.[21] While the limited partnership must be registered as such [22] and the particulars to be registered will include the disclosure of those partners who are limited partners,[23] the Limited Partnerships Act 1907 contains no provision that the firm must disclose in its stationery, letter and bill and invoice headings and the like a statement that it is a limited partnership. There consequently appears to be no certitude that a third party dealing with a limited partner will be aware that he is a limited partner or indeed be sufficiently put on his enquiry by notice of the fact that the partnership is a limited one to make it incumbent on him as a reasonable man to consult the public register in order to inform himself of the situation. The position under the Act is even more perplexing, because, although upon registration of the limited partnership, the registrar must send by post to the firm so registered a certificate of registration as a limited partnership,[24] there is no duty laid upon the firm to exhibit the certificate on its premises; and, therefore, it is conceivable that a third party of an alert and observant type, who was in the habit of actually visiting the firm's premises might find nothing on view there which would put him on his enquiry. Nor does the provision of the Act that any person is entitled to inspect the public register and require a certificate of the registration of the partnership or a certified copy or extract from any statement filed by the firm [25] alter the situation of a third party dealing with the firm without being aware that it has been so registered. The drafter of the Limited Partnerships Act 1907 appears to have contented himself with a rather rough and ready equivalence between the situation of the limited partner and that of a " sleeping partner " under the general law of partnership. Hurrell notices this point but also notices the

[21] Partnership Act 1890, s. 5 and see *supra* Chap. VII, pp. 210–211.
[22] Limited Partnerships Act 1907, s. 5.
[23] *Ibid.* s. 8 (*f*).
[24] Limited Partnerships Act 1907, s. 13.
[25] *Ibid.* s. 16 (1).

important aspect in which the equivalence breaks down.[26] If that be
the reason for the rather inexplicable looseness of the statutory provisions
in regard to effective notice to third parties of the nature of the partnership
with which they are dealing, then it must be criticised as a disastrously
facile and unanalysed approach, because the problem of the latent, or
dormant or sleeping partner, does not arise from his acting in the management of the firm's business but rather from the fact that his existence is
unsuspected by the third party dealing with the firm. If a dormant
partner were to emerge from his seclusion and purport to transact business
for the firm, section 5 of the Partnership Act 1890 might prove an
inadequate safeguard for a third party who incautiously dealt with him
on the faith of his representation that he was acting for the firm, since
the third party could hardly claim that he knew or believed a dormant
partner to be a partner of the firm and it might well be that the dormant
partner had no actual authority from his copartners to transact the
business.[27] The position of the limited partner is entirely different. He
is known to be a partner. What may not be known, without inspecting
the public register is that he is a *limited* partner.

It may be, therefore, that, if the question should arise for decision,
some difficulty will be experienced over the true construction of the words
" and shall not have power to bind the firm " which occur in section 6 (1)
of the Limited Partnerships Act 1907. If the third party seeking to hold
the firm liable actually knew that the person with whom he dealt was
a limited partner, no such difficulty need arise; for if he was aware of the
fact, he must make reasonable enquiry of the firm to satisfy himself that
the limited partner was authorised so to act, a situation which is unlikely
though perhaps not inconceivable. In any event, if the third party makes
no such enquiry or insufficient enquiry, there is no violence done to the
general law and equity governing partnership dealings, if he is denied
his claim against that firm. But if the third party is simply dealing with
a " partner " with no knowledge that he is a limited partner or indeed
that the firm is a limited partnership, it is thought that the courts would
be reluctant to read the words " and shall not have power to bind the
firm " as precluding such a third party's claim against the firm. Indeed
it would be difficult so to construe the words when they are read along
with subsequent words occurring in section 6 (1): " If a limited partner
takes part in the management of the partnership business he shall be
liable for all debts and obligations of the firm incurred while he so takes
part in the management as though he were a general partner." It is
possible to construe those words as imposing on the limited partner, in
addition to his sole and personal liability for the transactions which he
has himself carried through, an unlimited liability for all transactions
otherwise carried through in name of the firm during the period when

[26] " A limited partner resembles a sleeping partner, with this important difference that his
liability is limited to the amount of his contribution, whereas a sleeping partner's liability
is unlimited."—*Op. cit.* p. 26.
[27] See Partnership Act 1890, s. 5.

he was dealing as a partner of the firm. Such a construction appears
strained, however. It is thought that the construction of section 6 (1)
as a whole, and along with the general provision in section 7 [28] that
subject to the provisions of the Limited Partnerships Act 1907, the
Partnership Act 1890 and the rules of equity and the common law which
are preserved thereunder will apply to the limited partnership, may induce
the courts to give a somewhat restricted effect to the words occurring in
the first sentence of section 6 (1) of the Limited Partnerships Act 1907.
In that case the question of the rights of the third party against the
limited partnership might possibly be decided on the same lines as adopted
in dealing with similar questions under the general law of partnership
where the particulars registered in terms of the Registration of Business
Names Act 1916 are appealed to.[29]

Registration of the limited partnership

Under section 5 of the Limited Partnerships Act 1907 every limited
partnership must be registered as such in accordance with the provisions
of the Act, or in default thereof it shall be deemed to be a general
partnership, and every limited partner shall be deemed to be a general
partner. The protection and privileges of a limited partner are thus
dependent upon registration in compliance with the provisions of the
Act and any default in compliance will deprive him of his protection.
The requirements of the Act as to registration are contained in section 8.
It is effected by sending by post or delivering to the registrar at the registry
office " in that part of the United Kingdom in which the principal place
of business of the limited partnership is situated or proposed to be
situated " a statement signed by the partners containing certain specified
particulars. In the case of limited partnerships having their principal
place of business in Scotland the registrar of companies is the registrar
of limited partnerships, and the office for the registration of companies
in Edinburgh is the appropriate office to which the statement must be
sent.[30] Though the Limited Partnerships Act 1907 [31] merely stipulates
for " a statement signed by the partners," this should probably be
construed to mean that it must be signed by *all* the partners and that is
the accepted practice.

The particulars to be registered

The statement must include [32]—

    (a) the firm name;
    (b) the general nature of the business;
    (c) the principal place of business;

[28] See *infra* pp. 597–598.
[29] *Tower Cabinet Co. Ltd.* v. *Ingram* [1949] 2 K.B. 397 and see *supra* Chap. V, pp. 152–153.
[30] Limited Partnerships Act 1907, s. 15.
[31] s. 8.
[32] Limited Partnerships Act 1907, s. 8.

(d) the full name of each of the partners;

(e) the term, if any, for which the partnership is entered into, and the date of its commencement;

(f) a statement that the partnership is limited, and the description of every limited partner as such;

(g) the sum contributed by each limited partner, and whether paid in cash, or how otherwise.

In order to supply particulars as to " the general nature of the business " it is accepted practice to insert a copy of the relevant clause in the partnership agreement though if this is too lengthy it may be abridged provided the utmost care is taken to ensure that the resulting statement adequately covers the nature of the business to be conducted in all its aspects. As to the particulars required under paragraph (e), if there is no term of duration fixed for the partnership, it is a partnership at will. In such partnerships any general partner may terminate the partnership at any time on giving reasonable notice.[33] A limited partner will not have this right unless it is expressly provided for in the partnership agreement. In most cases it will be desirable in the interests of the limited partner that this right be stipulated for. If the partnership agreement does not expressly provide for the date of commencement of the partnership, it is held to commence at the date of making the partnership agreement [34] and that date may be included in the particulars.

The particulars required by the Act are those required for registration " in accordance with the Act." It is therefore important that a limited partner should ensure that those particulars are accurately stated. If they are inaccurate, the question may well arise whether the limited partnership has in fact been registered " in accordance with the Act," and if that question is decided adversely the registration will be of no effect to provide his statutory protection as a limited partner. How far inaccuracy in the particulars given would have this result has not been decided, but, since the Act requires the particulars to be given for purposes of registration, it is thought that the courts would not regard the registration as " in accordance with the Act " unless the particulars given are at least accurate in substance.

Registration of changes in limited partnerships

By section 9 of the Limited Partnerships Act 1907 it is provided—

" (1) If during the continuance of a limited partnership any change is made or occurs in—

(a) the firm name,

(b) the general nature of the business,

(c) the principal place of business,

(d) the partners or the name of any partner,

---

[33] Partnership Act 1890, s. 26. For the right of the limited partner, see Limited Partnerships Act 1907, s. 6 (5) (e).
[34] *Williams* v. *Jones* (1826) 5 B. & C. 108.

  (e) the term or character of the partnership,

  (f) the sum contributed by any limited partner,

  (g) the liability of any partner by reason of his becoming a
    limited instead of a general partner or a general instead of a
    limited partner,

a statement signed by the firm, specifying the nature of the change
shall within seven days be sent by post or delivered to the registrar
at the register office in that part of the United Kingdom in which
the partnership is registered.

  " (2) If default is made in compliance with the requirements of
this section each of the general partners shall on conviction under
the Summary Jurisdiction Acts be liable to a fine not exceeding
one pound for each day during which the default continues."

  There are several points of importance to notice in the wording of
section 9. In the first place, it will be observed that the penalty for
default is imposed on the general partners alone. There are no repercussions in the event of default in compliance with the requirements of the
section upon the limited partners. If the limited partnership has initially
been validly registered as such, failure to notify a change subsequently
occuring in the partnership will not involve a limited partner losing his
protection as such under the Act. Secondly, the statement of the notice
of the change is required to be signed " by the firm," whereas the statement required for the initial registration of the limited partnership is
required by section 8 to be signed by " the partners." It appears, therefore, that a statement of changes in the limited partnership may be
signed by a general partner in the firm name. The change envisaged
under section 9 (1) (f) entails that a limited partner may, from time to
time, increase the amount of his original contribution if the capital needs
of the firm increase. It is unlikely that he will agree to do so except on
condition of a larger share in the profits of the firm. As section 9 (1) (f)
is worded, it seems to be envisaged that a limited partner may also
decrease the amount of his original contribution. That, however, would
normally entail that he withdraw or " receive back " part of his original
contribution and if he does so he remains liable for the debts of the firm
up to the amount so withdrawn or received back,[35] so that registration
of a decrease in the amount of his contribution in such circumstances
would be of little practical advantage to the limited partner. Thirdly,
under section 9 (1) (c) provision is made for notification of a change in
the " principal place of business of the partnership." That notification
as in the case of other changes, is to be made to the register office " in
that part of the United Kingdom in which the partnership is registered."
Section 9 probably has in view a change in the location of the principal
place of business from one location in, for example, Scotland to another
location in the same country. The consequences of changing the principal

---

[35] Limited Partnerships Act 1907, s. 4 (3).

place of business from a location in Scotland to one in England are not expressly provided for in the Act. Presumably, a limited partnership already registered in Scotland would require to register itself *de novo* in England[35a] to be assured of its status as a limited partnership in the eyes of the English courts; but this is not entirely free from doubt, since registration under section 8 in the part of the United Kingdom in which the principal place of business of the limited partnership is initially situated appears to confer the status of a limited partnership upon the association [36] and, while section 9 (1) provides for notification of a change in the location of the principal place of business, it does not make any special provision in the case of a change from one part of the United Kingdom to another. Lastly, section 9 (1) (*e*) permits notification of a change in " the term or character of the partnership." The term of endurance of the partnership may be varied by agreement of all the partners,[37] and such a change would clearly require to be notified to the registrar. But a partnership originally entered into for a specified period may be continued after the expiry of that period at will.[38] It is not clear whether any such continuation of the term of the partnership requires notification or whether it may be regarded as a normal incident of a partnership for a specified period and thus covered in terms of the initial registration. If it is decided *ob majorem cautelam* to advise the registrar on the expiry of the specified period that the partnership now continues at will, one such notification would appear to be sufficient, since, even for initial registration, it is sufficient to give particulars of " the term, if any, for which the partnership is entered into." [39]

Registration of Business Names Act 1916

This Act applies to " every firm having a place of business in the United Kingdom and carrying on business under a business name which does not consist of the true surnames of all partners who are individuals and the corporate names of all partners who are corporations without any addition other than the true Christian names of individual partners or initials of such Christian names." [39a] It is, therefore, unrestricted in its application whether the partnership in question be a limited or a general partnership. Neither the Act nor the Business Names Rules 1949 [39b] make express reference to limited partnerships as such and no particulars are required to be lodged on the Business Names Register to distinguish a limited from a general partnership. The distinctive nature of the limited

---

[35a] Lindley, *op. cit.* pp. 794–795 appears to hold this view which is supported by the terms of section 15 of the Limited Partnerships Act 1907. The situation which he has in mind, however, is not one of removal of the principal place of business from one country to the other but rather the addition of a further principal place of business in England to one already existing in Scotland or *vice versa*.
[36] *Ibid.* s. 5.
[37] Partnership Act 1890, s. 19.
[38] Partnership Act 1890, s. 27 (1).
[39] Limited Partnerships Act 1907, s. 8 (*e*).
[39a] Registration of Business Names Act 1916 s. 1 (*a*).
[39b] S.I. 1949 No. 2441.

partnership is notified only in the particulars lodged upon its registration as a limited partnership.[39c]

Effect of registration in the Limited Partnerships Act 1907 as notice

It has already been suggested that the Limited Partnerships Act 1907 is defective in the provision which it makes to direct the attention of third parties to the nature of the partnership with which they are dealing. It might be possible to argue that registration under the Act is itself public notice of the limited nature of the partnership but that view rests upon an insecure basis since the Act itself recognises that registration of the requisite particulars is not in all cases to be regarded as adequate notice of the facts contained in the particulars so registered. In some cases, *e.g.* where a general partner ceases to be a general partner and becomes a limited partner, then the change is not only one which is required to be registered [39d]; it must also be " forthwith advertised " in the *Gazette*.[39e] Even publication of notice in the *Gazette* may not always be sufficient notice of the change. The view is expressed by Lindley [39f] that where A and B are partners of an ordinary partnership of which C is a customer and where the partnership is later converted into a limited partnership in which A ceases to be a general, and becomes a limited, partner, due registration being effected and advertisement published in the *Gazette*, but C is given no more specific notice and remains unaware of the change, then C may still hold A liable as an ordinary partner and is not restricted in his recourse to the amount to which A has now limited his liability. Section 7 of the Limited Partnerships Act 1907 and section 36 (1) of the Partnership Act 1890 are cited by the learned editor in support of that view which appears convincing; for A still remains an " apparent member " of his former firm in terms of section 36 (1) of the Partnership Act 1890, and in terms of section 7 of the Limited Partnerships Act 1907 that provision appears to be applicable even in the case of the new limited partnership.

Change in status from general to limited partner

If a person who has been active as a general partner in a limited partnership, arranges for the future to become a limited partner, it is equitable in the interests of third parties that public notice should be given of the change. The Limited Partnerships Act 1907 recognises this by providing that " notice of any arrangement or transaction under which any person will cease to be a general partner in any firm, and will become a limited partner in that firm . . . shall be forthwith advertised in the *Gazette*, and until notice of the arrangement or transaction is so advertised, the arrangement or transaction shall, for the purposes of this Act be deemed to be of no effect." [40]   In the case of a Scottish limited partnership, the

[39c] Limited Partnerships Act 1907 ss. 5 and 8.
[39d] *Ibid.* s. 9 (1) (*g*).
[39e] *Ibid.* s. 10 (1).
[39f] *Op. cit.* pp. 797–798.
[40] *Ibid.* s. 10 (1).

advertisement must be inserted in the *Edinburgh Gazette*.[41] The public notice required of the change is thus similar to that required in the case of a partner who retires from a general partnership,[42] but it will be observed that the Limited Partnerships Act 1907 does not lay an additional duty of personal notification to those who have had prior dealings with the firm, as is required under the Partnership Act 1890 in the case of a retiring partner. It is not inconsistent with the provisions of section 10 of the Limited Partnerships Act 1907 that such additional notification should be given to persons who had dealings with the firm while the partner in question was a general partner and in view of the terms of section 7 of the Limited Partnerships Act 1907 it may be prudent to do so.

Section 10 (1) of the Limited Partnerships Act 1907 refers generally to " any arrangement or transaction." It is not easy to contemplate any situation in which a general partner may change his status to that of a limited partner in regard to one individual transaction of the firm. Section 10 (1) is concerned not only with a change of status from general to limited partner but also with the case of an assignment of the share of a limited partner [43] and it is probably for the purpose of the latter case that the word " transaction " is included.

The subsection makes no provision for advertisement of a change of status from limited to general partner. Since the Limited Partnerships Act 1907 is designed to afford a statutory protection to the limited partner, it is understandable that no such change of status is treated as a matter of formal notification by advertisement. The circumstances in which a person who has been granted the protection afforded to a limited partner may by his conduct forfeit that protection have already been mentioned.[44]

Assignation of share of limited partner

A limited partner, like any other partner, may assign his share in the partnership to a third party. If the partnership agreement is silent on the point, then he may only do so with the consent of the general partners.[45] This requirement, which is more stringent than that enjoined in the Partnership Act 1890 [46] arises from the different legal consequences of the assignation. In a general partnership the assignation of a partner's share does not make the assignee a partner of the firm but merely affords him certain limited rights to claim the share which would have fallen to his cedent as a partner of the firm. The effect of the assignation by a limited partner of his share is to make the assignee a limited partner " with all the rights of the assignor." [47] He is thus entitled to inspect the

---

[41] *Ibid.* s. 10 (2).
[42] Partnership Act 1890, ss. 36 and 37.
[43] See *infra.*
[44] *Supra* p. 586.
[45] Limited Partnerships Act 1907, s. 6 (5) (*b*).
[46] s. 31.
[47] Limited Partnerships Act 1907, s. 6 (5) (*b*).

firm's books and " examine into the state and prospects of the partnership business " and he is entitled to advise with the partners upon those matters.[48] The consequences of the assignation of a limited partner's share have, therefore, a more direct relevance to the principle of *delectus personae* than those of an assignation of a share in a partnership under the Partnership Act 1890; and the Limited Partnerships Act 1907 has recognised this by requiring " subject to any agreement expressed or implied between the partners " that such an assignation be with the consent of the general partners. On the other hand, the limited partner is a person whose rights in regard to the partnership business are restricted. He may not take part in the management of the business and his only effective rights are to have access to the books and any data which bear upon the state and prospects of the business, and in consultation with the general partners to attempt to persuade them to adopt his views as to the policy of management. There is thus no very significant violation of the principle of *delectus personae* if his assignee is accorded the same rights, and a limited partner should, when agreeing to enter the partnership, consider whether the agreement should stipulate for his right to assign his share without consent of his copartners. It may be, however, that, with the pattern set by the restriction of transfer of shares in most private companies to appeal to as justification, the general partners will be unwilling to concede so untrammelled a right of assignation.

Where an assignation of a limited partner's share has been carried through, either with the consent of the other partners under the Act or by the limited partner's assignation without such consent under the provisions of the partnership agreement, the assignation will still require to be advertised in the *Edinburgh Gazette*.   Until that is done it is of no effect.[49]

Stamp duties

The statement of the amount contributed by a limited partner to the capital of the partnership and the statement of any increase in that amount sent for registration under the Limited Partnerships Act 1907 is charged with *ad valorem* stamp duty. Originally the *ad valorem* rate was five shillings " for every one hundred pounds and any fraction of one hundred pounds over any multiple of one hundred pounds, of the amount so contributed." [50]   The rate has now been doubled.[51]   Although assessed in respect of the contribution made by the limited partner, the liability for payment thereof rests on the firm and on default the duty with interest thereon at 5 per cent. per annum from the date when the statement was delivered is a joint and several debt recoverable from the partners, or any of them, who are named in the statement lodged for the

---

[48] *Ibid.* s. 6 (1).
[49] Limited Partnerships Act 1907, s. 10 (1).
[50] *Ibid.* s. 11.
[51] Finance Act 1920, s. 39; Finance Act 1933, s. 41 (1).

initial registration of the limited partnership. In the case of a statement of increase in the contribution the duty and interest, on default in payment, may be recovered from all or any of the partners " whose discontinuance in the firm shall not, before the date of delivery of such statement of increase, have been duly notified to the registrar." [52]

Statement of false particulars for registration

Any person who makes, signs, sends or delivers for the purpose of registration under the Act, any false statement, known by him to be false, is guilty of an offence and liable to imprisonment for a term not exceeding two years.[53]

Applicability of the general law of partnership

Section 7 of the Limited Partnerships Act 1907 provides—

> " Subject to the provisions of this Act, the Partnership Act 1890, and the rules of equity and of common law applicable to partnerships, except so far as they are inconsistent with the provisions of the last mentioned Act, shall apply to limited partnerships."

The section has already been referred to in discussing the effect to be given to the words " and shall have no power to bind the firm " occurring in section 6 (1) of the Limited Partnerships Act 1907.[54] Section 7, however, has obviously a much wider connotation than that. When rules of the common law or of equity are invoked in relation to a limited partnership, it will be observed that a dual task of construction is involved. The rule must first be examined to ensure that it is not inconsistent with the express provisions of the Partnership Act 1890. If the rule passes this test, it must then be read subject to the provisions of the Limited Partnerships Act 1907 if it is to be applied to a limited partnership. Since the Limited Partnerships Act 1907 is closely confined in its terms to the provisions necessary for the introduction of the limited partnership, there is a wide area in the affairs of such a partnership which is left to be governed by the general law of partnership; yet in applying the general law of partnership at any point in these affairs the nature of the limited partnership and the provisions of the Limited Partnerships Act 1907 directed towards regulating it require close and anxious examination. Unhappily this problem has not been before the courts for judicial consideration in a sufficient number of cases to permit of its being dealt with in any terms save those of the widest generality. Indeed there appears to be only one case reported where the Court has been called upon to supply the rules governing a limited partnership from the general code affecting partnership.[55] It is, therefore, scarcely possible to do

---

[52] Limited Partnerships Act 1907, s. 11.
[53] *Ibid.* s. 12.
[54] See *supra* pp. 589–590.
[55] *Re Hughes & Co.* [1911] 1 Ch. 342, on which see *infra* pp. 603–604. *Re Barnard* [1932] 1 Ch. 269 also raised issues of a general nature as to the effect of the rules of distribution of assets in bankruptcy upon the special position of the limited partner.

more than to quote, with respectful approval, the prudent advice given by Lindley,[56] when considering the effect of section 7. " This," say the learned editors of the work, " renders a formal partnership agreement almost indispensable in the case of a limited partnership; in the absence of such an agreement the partners are sure to find that their rights are not what they intended."

Matters to be implied in a limited partnership failing agreement to the contrary

The Limited Partnerships Act 1907 provides in section 6 (5)—

" (5) Subject to any agreement expressed or implied, between the partners—

(a) Any difference arising as to ordinary matters connected with the partnership business may be decided by a majority of the general partners.

(b) A limited partner may, with the consent of the general partners, assign his share in the partnership, and upon such an assignment the assignee shall become a limited partner with all the rights of the assignor.

(c) The other partners shall not be entitled to dissolve the partnership by reason of any limited partner suffering his share to be charged for his separate debt.

(d) A person may be introduced as a partner without the consent of the existing limited partners.

(e) A limited partner shall not be entitled to dissolve the partnership by notice."

The first of those implied terms appears to be reasonably in accord with the nature of a limited partnership in which the management is exclusively entrusted to the general partners and the general partners' decision on such matters will presumably bind the limited partners even where they have neither been consulted nor given any opportunity of expressing their own views.[57] It does not appear unreasonable that the general partners should take decisions as to the running of the business from day to day without intimating these to the limited partners, who may not always be readily available, before implementing them. The decision of the majority of the general partners is, however, expressly restricted to disputes as to " ordinary matters connected with the partnership business " and would not embrace a power to decide by a majority to, do something outside the scope of the ordinary management or to change the nature of the partnership business without enlisting the consent of the limited partners or indeed the unanimous consent of the general partners. As to acts beyond the ordinary management, the general partners have no authority to perform them unless specifically authorised by their

---

[56] *Op. cit.* p. 788.
[57] Lindley, *op. cit.* p. 807.

copartners [58] and a change in the nature of the partnership business requires, failing agreement to the contrary, the consent of all the existing partners.[59]   There does not seem to be anything in the provisions of the Limited Partnerships Act 1907 which is inconsistent with the application of those rules derived from the Partnership Act 1890 to the limited partnership and it is thought that they are imported into the law applicable to the limited partnership.[60]   Similarly, the provisions of section 19 of the Partnership Act 1890 would appear to preclude the general partners trom varying the terms of the partnership agreement without the consent of all partners, both general and limited.   Even where the dispute is one as to ordinary matters connected with the partnership the decision of the general partners, to be upheld, must be taken in the utmost good faith.[61]

The implied term introduced in section 6 (5) (*b*) has already been considered.[62]

The implied term contained in section 6 (5) (*c*) seems to relate to English partnerships only.   Under the Partnership Act 1890, s. 23, it is provided—

> " 23.—(1) After the commencement of this Act a writ of execution shall not issue against any partnership property except on a judgment against the firm.
>
> (2) The High Court, or a judge thereof, or the Chancery Court of the county palatine of Lancaster, or a county court, may, on the application by summons of any judgment creditor of a partner, make an order charging that partner's interest in the partnership property and profits with payment of the amount of the judgment debt and interest thereon, and may by the same or a subsequent order appoint a receiver of that partner's share of profits (whether already declared or accruing), and of any other money which may be coming to him in respect of the partnership, and direct all accounts and inquiries, and give all other orders and directions which might have been directed or given if the charge had been made in favour of the judgment creditor by the partner, or which the circumstances of the case may require.
>
> (3) The other partner or partners shall be at liberty at any time to redeem the interest charged, or in case of a sale being directed, to purchase the same.
>
> (4) This section shall apply in the case of a cost-book company [63] as if the company were a partnership within the meaning of this Act.
>
> (5) This section shall not apply to Scotland."

By section 33 (2) of the Partnership Act 1890 it is provided—

---

[58] Partnership Act 1890, s. 5.
[59] *Ibid.* s. 24 (8).
[60] Limited Partnerships Act 1907, s. 7.
[61] *Supra* Chap. VI, pp. 180 *et seq.*
[62] *Supra* pp. 595–596.
[63] See *Hawtayne* v. *Bourne* (1841) 7 M. & W. 595.

" (2) A partnership may, at the option of the other partners, be dissolved if any partner suffers his share of the partnership property to be charged under this Act for his separate debt."

Section 23 of the Partnership Act 1890 does not apply to Scotland since as a consequence of the separate *persona* of the firm in Scotland the interest of a partner in the partnership concern " is a portion of the *universitas*: it forms a debt or demand against the company, so as to be arrestable in the hands of the company." [64] It is not, as in England an aliquot share in the joint property of the partnership and in Scotland the creditors of a partner can only affect his share of the balance of the partnership property which remains after the firm debts have been paid. " The principle is that a partner has no right to claim any particular portion of the assets as belonging exclusively to him and neither his assignees nor his separate creditors can have any higher right against the joint property than the debtor or cedent from whom they derive their interest." [65] The ground of dissolution of the partnership afforded in section 33 (2) of the Partnership Act 1890 is dependent on the procedure laid down for England in section 23 and consequentially is not applicable in Scotland.

In England, therefore, a limited partnership differs from an ordinary partnership in that, unless the limited partner agrees, his copartners will not have the option to dissolve the partnership, upon the limited partner's share having been made the subject of a charge for his separate debt, but that distinction has no place in Scottish legal theory.

The implied term contained in section 6 (5) (*d*) has already been covered by the discussion of the effect of section 6 (5) (*b*).[66]

In section 6 (5) (*e*) it is provided that a limited partner shall not be entitled to dissolve the partnership by notice. This sharply contrasts with the position in an ordinary partnership where in the absence of agreement otherwise among the partners, if the partnership is entered into for an undefined term, the partnership may be dissolved by any partner giving notice to his copartners of his intention to dissolve the partnership.[67] The special term introduced in respect of the limited partner under the Limited Partnerships Act 1907, no doubt, was enacted as a sort of logical extension of the principle that the limited partner is not entitled to take part in the management. Nevertheless, he has an interest in the partnership and his capital is at risk, nor is he effectually protected if he withdraws his capital during the continuance of the partnership.[68] In the interests of the limited partner, therefore, it seems prudent to insist where possible on a stipulated right in the agreement allowing him to give notice of dissolution where the partnership is entered into for an undefined term.

[64] Bell, *Comm.* II, 536.
[65] *Per* the Lord Ordinary (Kinnear) in *Parnell* v. *Walter* (1889) 16 R. 917 at p. 925.
[66] See *supra* pp. 595–596.
[67] Partnership Act 1890, s. 32 (*c*).
[68] Limited Partnerships Act 1907, s. 4 (3).

Dissolution

Section 6 (2) of the Limited Partnerships Act 1907 provides—

" A limited partnership shall not be dissolved by the death or bankruptcy of a limited partner, and the lunacy of a limited partner shall not be a ground for dissolution of the partnership unless the lunatic's share cannot be otherwise ascertained and realised."

The divergence here from the law relating to an ordinary partnership should be noted. Subject to any agreement between the partners an ordinary partnership is dissolved by the death or bankruptcy of any partner.[69] This would also be applicable in the case of the death or bankruptcy of a general partner in a limited partnership since there is nothing in the Limited Partnerships Act 1907 which displaces the general rule in his case. In the case of the death or bankruptcy of a limited partner, however, it is expressly provided that neither of those events will dissolve the partnership. The statutory provision is not guarded with introductory words making them applicable " subject to any agreement between the partners " as is the case in section 6 (5) (c) and (e) of the Limited Partnerships Act 1907 and section 33 of the Partnership Act 1890. It would therefore appear to be inappropriate for the partners to include in the partnership agreement a provision that the partnership shall be dissolved on the death or bankruptcy of a limited partner. The Act permits the formation of limited partnerships only " in the manner and subject to the conditions by this Act provided " [70]; and since section 6 (2) is unqualified in its terms, it must be regarded as one of the conditions to be complied with before a limited partnership may be formed.

Continuing use of the share of a deceased or outgoing partner

In an ordinary partnership, where any member of a partnership has died or has otherwise ceased to be a partner, and the surviving or continuing partners continue to carry on the business with its capital or assets without any final settlement of accounts between the firm and that partner, then, unless otherwise agreed to the contrary, that partner or his representatives have the option to claim either the share of the subsequent profits made by the firm which the court finds attributable to the use of his share or interest at 5 per cent. per annum on the amount thereof.[71] That provision would be applicable to a limited partnership where there were two or more general partners, one of whom had died and whose share continued to be used without a settlement of accounts. It would not seem to be applicable on the death of a limited partner since section 6 (2) declares that his death will not dissolve the firm. The representatives of the deceased limited partner would, it is thought, be entitled to claim the share of profits falling to the deceased limited

[69] Partnership Act 1890, s. 33.
[70] Limited Partnerships Act 1907, s. 4 (1).
[71] Partnership Act 1890, s. 42 (1) and see *supra* Chap. XII, pp. 540 *et seq.*

partner in respect of his contribution but if the subsequent trading of the firm had resulted in a loss, the representatives would not be able to avail themselves of the alternative claim for interest at 5 per cent. per annum on his contribution, since the limited partnership has not been dissolved by the death.

Death of the general partner

As has already been stated,[72] the ordinary rules of partnership will apply to a limited partnership where a general partner dies, *i.e.* the firm will be dissolved unless the partnership agreement has provided otherwise. What the Limited Partnerships Act 1907 does not make clear is the position where there is only one general partner and he predeceases the limited partners. In such circumstances one of two situations will arise, either (1) the partnership deed may provide for dissolution of the partnership or may be silent on the point, in which case the firm will be dissolved, or (2) the partnership deed may expressly provide that the partnership shall not be dissolved on the death of the general partner, though that would be a most unlikely and imprudent provision to make where there had been only one general partner from the outset. In both cases there is no effective means of continuing the partnership, which in the first case will require to continue for purposes of winding up and in the second case will continue as a going concern. In neither case have the surviving limited partners or partner the right to interfere in the management of the business, on pain of losing their protection as limited partners.[73] It is true that the protection is lost only for debts and obligations of the firm incurred while he takes part in the management and it is possible where the death of the general partner has dissolved the firm and it is clearly solvent, that a limited partner may be courageous enough to carry on the business in order to wind it up, realising that he exposes himself to no real peril by doing so; but the situation of the firm on dissolution may not be such as to make any such clear-cut appreciation possible, while if the firm is not dissolved by the death of the general partner, a limited partner who intervenes in order to carry on its management as a going concern is forfeiting the very protection which motivated him in becoming a partner in the first place. There is no solution to this problem suggested in the Limited Partnerships Act 1907 and possibly the only course left open to a limited partner in such circumstances, if he desires to retain his protection, will be to petition the court in the exercise of the *nobile officium* (1) in the case where the death has dissolved the partnership to make appropriate arrangements for the winding up of the firm, possibly by the appointment of a judicial factor,[74] or (2) in the case where the death has not in terms of the partnership agreement, occasioned the

---

[72] *Supra* p. 601.
[73] Limited Partnerships Act 1907, s. 6 (1).
[74] The appointment of a judicial factor was held to be competent in the case of winding up a limited partnership though in the case cited that course was not followed: *Muirhead* v. *Borland*, 1925 S.C. 474.

dissolution of the partnership, to order the dissolution thereof and to make appropriate arrangements for its winding up.

Bankruptcy

The observations made regarding the effects of death of a limited or a general partner apply *mutatis mutandis* in the case of bankruptcy.[75]

Lunacy

Under the Partnership Act 1890 the lunacy of one of the partners in an ordinary partnership does not dissolve it though it may afford grounds for an application to the court to dissolve the partnership. The application may be made on behalf of the lunatic partner himself or by any of his copartners.[76] If a general partner in a limited partnership becomes lunatic, there is nothing in section 6 (2) of the Limited Partnerships Act 1907 which prevents an application to the court for dissolution of the partnership and it would seem that the application could be made by a limited partner. An application to dissolve the partnership on the ground of the lunacy of a limited partner, however, would require to be supported by averments that the lunatic's share in the partnership cannot be ascertained and realised otherwise than by dissolving the firm.

Dissolution by order of the court in other cases

Though the only case expressly referred to in the Limited Partnerships Act 1907 is the case of the lunacy of a limited partner, a limited partnership may be dissolved by the court in other circumstances and the grounds of application for the dissolution of an ordinary partnership [77] are in a wide sense applicable to a limited partnership. When a limited partnership is involved, however, its special nature and the distinctive functions of the general as opposed to the limited partner must be taken into consideration. The ground of application in section 35 (*a*) of the Partnership Act 1890 will be available in a limited partnership so far as regards the lunacy of a general partner, but so far as regards the lunacy of a limited partner it is replaced by section 6 (2) of the Limited Partnerships Act 1907. But even in application to the limited partnership of the remaining grounds of petition mentioned in section 35 of the Partnership Act 1890 it may be necessary to keep in view the peculiar position of the limited partner either (a) where his conduct forms the ground of the application or (b) where he is himself the applicant to the court. No decision appears to be reported where an application has been made to the court in consequence of something complained of in the conduct of a limited partner or of some disability which relates to him. It is likely, however, that the courts will be more reluctant to order dissolution in such cases

---

[75] For a discussion of the effects of the bankruptcy of a partner in an ordinary partnership, see *supra* Chap. X, pp. 446–448.

[76] Partnership Act 1890, s. 35 (*a*); and see *supra* Chap. X, pp. 456–461.

[77] Partnership Act 1890, s. 35.

in view of the restricted influence which such a partner can exert over the fortunes of the firm. Where a limited partner is himself the applicant for dissolution of the firm, the restricted nature of his rights and interest in the firm will likewise be taken into consideration by the court in exercising its discretion to make or to refuse the order, but an order will be made on the application of a limited partner if the court considers it just and equitable to do so.[78]

Winding up

It is provided by the Limited Partnerships Act 1907 [79] that—

"In the event of the dissolution of a limited partnership its affairs shall be wound up by the general partners unless the court otherwise orders."

In cases where no real dispute arises among the partners the winding up will be conducted by the general partners who will have a continuing authority, after the dissolution of the partnership, to bind the firm " so far as may be necessary to wind up the affairs of the partnership and to complete transactions began but unfinished at the time of the dissolution, but not otherwise." [80] That mode of winding up will in general be resorted to and will be in the interest of all the partners on the ground of saving of expense. Where, however, there is contention among the partners it may be desired to have the arrangements for the winding up made by the court and not committed to a general partner of the firm. Moreover, in the peculiar nature of the limited partnership other situations may arise where it will be necessary to apply to the court for an order as to the winding up of the partnership. The situation where there is only one general partner and his death has brought about the dissolution of the firm has already been referred to [81] but another situation which will require an application to the court may arise where the only general partner to whom winding up might be committed under section 6 (3) is or becomes bankrupt; for if that occurs, his continuing authority to bind the firm in transactions for the winding up of its affairs will cease.[82]

Applications to the court

Section 6 (4) of the Limited Partnerships Act 1907 reads—

"(4) Applications to the court to wind up a limited partnership shall be by petition under the Companies Acts 1862 to 1900, and the provisions of those Acts relating to the winding up of companies by the court and of the rules made thereunder (including provisions as

---

[78] *Re Hughes & Company* [1911] 1 Ch. 342. In *Muirhead* v. *Borland*, 1925 S.C. 474 the issue between the general and the limited partner was not as to dissolution which both were agreed should take place but as to the manner in which the partnership affairs should be wound up.
[79] s. 6 (3).
[80] Partnership Act 1890, s. 38.
[81] *Supra* pp. 602–603.
[82] Partnership Act 1890, s. 38, proviso.

to fees) shall, subject to such modifications (if any) as the Lord Chancellor, with the concurrence of the President of the Board of Trade, may by rules provide, apply to the winding up by the court of limited partnerships, with the substitution of general partners for directors."

The arrangements as to winding up thus inaugurated by the Limited Partnerships Act 1907 have had a long and somewhat complicated subsequent history. Section 6 (4) itself was repealed by the Companies (Consolidation) Act 1908.[83] Limited partnerships could then be dissolved and wound up by the court as in the case of ordinary partnerships. In England the provisions of the Companies (Consolidation) Act 1908 were repealed so far as regards the winding up of limited partnerships by the Bankruptcy Act 1913 [84] with effect from January 1, 1914. Under the Companies Act 1948, Part IX, dealing with the winding up of unregistered companies, unregistered companies did not include " a limited partnership registered in England or Northern Ireland " but the position of a limited partnership registered in Scotland is not expressly provided for.[85] Under the same section of the Companies Act 1948, however, *any* partnership, whether limited or general, which consists of less than eight members and is not a foreign partnership, is not to be treated as an unregistered company for the purposes of winding up by the court. The effect of section 398 seems to be that a limited partnership registered in England or Northern Ireland may in no case be wound up by the court under the Companies Act 1948. In Scotland it appears that if the limited partnership consists of less than eight members, it is subject to the general exception of partnerships so restricted in numbers and may not be so wound up, while if the Scottish limited partnership consists of not less than eight members it will be regarded as an unregistered company which may be wound up by the court under the Companies Act 1948. The reason for the distinction is not clear and makes any approach to the true construction of section 398 an hazardous enterprise. It has been suggested as alternative interpretations of section 398 read as a whole either (1) that limited partnerships are not regarded as partnerships within the meaning of the section or (2) that the express exclusion of limited partnerships registered in England and Northern Ireland (irrespective of the number of their members) from those unregistered companies which may be wound up under the Act, carries with it the inference that all limited partnerships registered in Scotland, whatever the number of their members, are included within those unregistered companies which may be wound up under the Act.[86] While it cannot be maintained that the position of the Scottish limited partnership is lucidly explained under section 398, it is thought that the construction first suggested is preferable

[83] s. 286.
[84] s. 24.
[85] Companies Act 1948, s. 398.
[86] Lindley, *op. cit.* (12th ed.) p. 805. The passage is not repeated in the thirteenth edition though the same view of the law is stated.

to either of the alternatives proposed by Lindley. In both those alternatives it is implicit that one should regard the section as treating the limited partnership as something entirely distinct from the ordinary partnership and as using the word " partnership " to denote the ordinary partnership alone. That construction immediately collides with the opening words of the section: " For the purposes of this Part of this Act, the expression ' unregistered company ' shall include any trustee savings bank . . . and any partnership, whether limited or not, . . ." In the face of those express words it appears a somewhat strained construction to put upon the section that it treats limited partnerships as if they were not partnerships within the meaning of the section.

Whatever the construction to be placed upon section 398 of the Companies Act 1948, the change introduced in the later legislation in the approach of the courts should be noticed. Under the provisions of section 6 (4) of the Limited Partnerships Act 1907 the words were mandatory: " Applications to the court to wind up a limited partnership *shall* be by petition under the Companies Acts 1862 to 1900 . . ."; but under the Companies (Consolidation) Act 1908 [87] the formula used is permissive. The permissive form of words persists in the Companies Act 1948.[88] The distinction is of importance as was shown in *Muirhead* v. *Borland* [89] where the issue to be decided was whether on an application to wind up a limited partnership, the court should order the winding up to proceed under the Companies Acts or should appoint a judicial factor. Under the provisions of section 6 (4) of the Limited Partnerships Act 1907 the court would have had no alternative but to order winding up under the Companies Acts 1862 to 1900, but under the permissive provisions of section 268 of the Companies (Consolidation) Act 1908 it was regarded by the court as open to them to appoint a judicial factor to conduct the winding up, although in the circumstances of the case they ordered the winding up to proceed under the Companies (Consolidation) Act 1908 and appointed a liquidator.[90]

---

[87] s. 268.
[88] s. 399 (1): ". . . any unregistered company may be wound up under this Act . . ."
[89] 1925 S.C. 474.
[90] See *per* the Lord President (Clyde) at pp. 476–477.

CHAPTER XV

THE JOINT ADVENTURE

A JOINT adventure is a form of association for business purposes which, though distinguished traditionally in Scots law from a partnership or firm,[1] still resembles a partnership closely in nature and in its legal consequences. It is an association formed for the limited purposes of a particular commercial adventure, such as a voyage or a speculative course of dealing in a particular commodity or commodities, but it remains in essence " the relation which subsists between persons carrying on a business in common with a view of profit." [2] It is therefore clearly a species of partnership though the restricted purposes for which it is set up may distinguish it in practical terms from the partnership or firm which is established to carry on a continuing business and these restricted purposes may give rise to legal consequences which are peculiar to the joint adventure. These legal consequences, however, do not entail any divergence in legal theory from that which governs the partnership proper but rather reflect in the application of the general principles, and in particular those relating to the apparent authority of the joint adventurers, the limits of the commercial enterprise which is undertaken. Indeed the Partnership Act 1890 takes no special notice of the joint adventure and leaves it to be regulated within the general provisions of the Act, recognising the joint adventure as a particular form of association only in section 32 (b) which provides that—

> " Subject to any agreement between the partners, a partnership is dissolved—
>
> . . .
>
> (b) If entered into for a single adventure or undertaking, by the termination of that adventure or undertaking;
>
> . . ."

The limits of the joint adventure

While the limited nature of the association is regarded as the distinguishing feature of the joint adventure, there is more difficulty in stating with any degree of precision what limits must be set to the enterprise before it is regarded as a joint adventure rather than a partnership in the fullest and most unqualified sense. The type of association more frequently encountered in the commercial activity of the nineteenth century, where persons, otherwise unassociated with one another, combined to carry through a single specified transaction, often though not

---

[1] See Erskine, *Inst.* III: 3: 29: Bell, *Comm.* II, 538–539, *Prin.* § 392.
[2] Partnership Act 1890, s. 1 (1).

always related to a particular voyage [3] was clearly a joint adventure and
was treated by some writers as a separate contract. Erskine [4] so treated
the joint adventure or, as he called it, the joint trade. Having described
a partnership as " a collective and permanent society, in which all the
socii are, in regard to strangers, considered as one person, and consequently are bound *singuli in solidum* for the company's debts," he went
on to describe a joint trade as " only a momentary contract, where two
or more persons agree to put a sum of money into a common stock, to
be employed as an adventure in a particular course of trade, the produce
of which, after the trading voyage is finished, is to be divided among them
according to their several shares in the adventure." That view was
effectively criticised by Bell [5] who pointed out that in a joint adventure,
as in a partnership, the stock and property are common, the partners
being responsible *singuli in solidum* for the engagements of the active
partners in the adventure, by reason of the " express or presumed
mandate " of the last named, and the creditors, on bankruptcy, having
their claim on the estate of the adventure, " with a demand against the
individuals only for the balance, after deducting what they receive from
the common stock." Bell continues,[6] " The great peculiarity in the doctrine of joint trade . . . is, that, unless where the joint concern is avowed,
and a credit raised on the combined responsibility, the liability being the
result of the discovery of a partnership which was not relied on as regulating the credit, the limits of the contract are fixed by the actual agreement
between the parties; whereas in partnership there is universal responsibility for every engagement *bona fide* relied on, and not beyond the
limits of the company's line of trade."

While the limited nature of the joint adventure is constantly appealed
to as its salient feature, the type of limitation imposed on the association
may vary considerably. The traditional concept of the single adventure
—Erskine's " momentary contract "—is shown in the attempt, not
always successful, to apply it to such cases as *e.g.* trading voyages,[7]
fishing expeditions arranged on the " deal " system,[8] arrangements
between fish-curers and the crew of their " flit-boats," [9] trading [10] and

---

[3] See *e.g. Clements* v. *Macaulay* (1866) 4 M. 583 where the joint adventure was between
the major and quartermaster of the Confederate States Army, representing the Government of the Confederate States and a New Orleans merchant for a voyage charter of a
vessel to load cotton for the West Indies and to return to a port in the Confederate States
with a cargo of arms and medical supplies for the Confederate States Army.

[4] *Inst.* iii: 3: 29.

[5] *Comm.* II, 539; see also Clark, *op. cit.* I, p. 40.

[6] *Loc. cit.*

[7] *Clements* v. *Macaulay* (1866) 4 M. 583: *Montgomery* v. *Forrester & Co.* (1791) Hume 748;
Saville v. *Robertson* (1792) 4 T.R. 720.

[8] *Lockhart* v. *Brown* (1888) 15 R. 742; *Hay* v. *Douglas*, 1922 S.L.T. 365; *Mair* v. *Wood*,
1948 S.C. 83; *Parker* v. *Walker*, 1961 S.L.T 252.

[9] *Clark* v. *Jamieson*, 1909 S.C. 132.

[10] *McCaul's Creditors* v. *Ramsay & Ritchie* (1740) Mor. 14608; *Withers Birch & Co.* v. *Cowan*
(1790) n. r., but see Bell, *Comm.* II, 540; *Logy* v. *Durham* (1697) Mor. 14566; *Wilkie* v.
Johnstone Bannatyne & Co. (1808) 5 Pat.App. 191; *Samuel & Co.* v. *Brown* (1842) 4 D. 1518.

industrial [11] enterprises, ventures which combined both trading and industrial aspects,[12] a publishing venture,[13] the running of a music hall,[14] a public-house,[15] and a grazing farm [16] and the joint purchase of a ticket in a foreign lottery.[17] Even the rather indeterminate arrangements, under which the family business in *Aitchison* v. *Aitchison* [18] was conducted, were ascribed, though perhaps somewhat tentatively to joint adventure; and there have been a number of decisions as to joint adventures in the purchase and development of land,[19] in operations on the stock exchange,[20] in an association of riparian owners of mills and works to maintain reservoirs,[21] in the laying of a water supply pipe line to a town in Peru,[22] in the running of a stage coach between Glasgow and Edinburgh [23] and in the purchase and working of steamers on the River Clyde.[24] It may be affirmed that the constant feature in all such cases is that the joint adventure is of a more restricted nature than an ordinary firm or partnership: yet the considerable differences in the limiting features which have been appealed to as maintaining the distinction suggest that what is being defined is not so much an absolute as a practical expedient. Different limiting features are invoked as characterising the joint adventure in different cases. In some cases it is clearly recognisable in terms of the " momentary contract," the commercial adventure in a single voyage or a single transaction. In others it is possible to see the parties' agreement as governing the type of association under which a number of successive joint adventures are undertaken. The cases as to fishing boats given out on the " deal " system are perhaps of this kind. In another tract of the case law on the subject, it appears to be possible to carry on something of the nature of a continuing business under a joint adventure and the reason for describing the association of parties as such seems to be the limited nature of the continuing business so carried on rather than what might be called its episodic nature. Within this last class there is also a range of variation from those cases where the association can only with difficulty be distinguished from the second class of cases,[25] to those where it becomes difficult to distinguish them from a continuing business conducted under a proper partnership.[26]

[11] *Miller* v. *Walker* (1875) 3 R. 242; *Moore* v. *Dempster* (1879) 6 R. 930; *Beresford's Tr.* v. *Argyll Assessor* (1884) 11 R. 818.   [12] *Lockhart* v. *Moodie* (1877) 4 R. 859.
[13] *Venables* v. *Wood* (1839) 1 D. 659.
[14] *Cooke's Circus Buildings Co. Ltd.* v. *Welding* (1894) 21 R. 339.
[15] *Adam* v. *Adam*, 1962 S.L.T. 332.
[16] *Cameron* v. *Young* (1871) 9 M. 786.
[17] *Clayton* v. *Clayton*, 1937 S.C. 619.
[18] (1877) 4 R. 899. See *supra* Chap. III, pp. 57 *et seq.*
[19] *White* v. *McIntyre* (1841) 3 D. 334; *Keith* v. *Penn* (1840) 2 D. 633; *Fowler* v. *Paterson's Trs.* (1896) 3 S.L.T. 305.
[20] *Mollison* v. *Noltie* (1889) 16 R. 350.
[21] *Orr* v. *Pollock* (1840) 2 D. 1092.
[22] *Stewart* v. *North* (1893) 20 R. 260.
[23] *Jardine* v. *Macfarlane* (1828) 6 S. 564.
[24] *Davie* v. *Buchanan* (1880) 8 R. 319.
[25] *e.g.* some of the land development cases, particularly *Livingstone* v. *Allans* (1900) 3 F. 233; *Keith* v. *Penn* (1840) 2 D. 633.
[26] *Adam* v. *Adam*, 1962 S.L.T. 332; *Jardine* v. *Macfarlane* (1828) 6 S. 564; *Miller* v. *Walker* (1875) 3 R. 242.

Joint ownership distinguished from joint adventure

The essence of joint adventure is some form of joint trading. It is in this aspect of the association of the parties together in a joint business enterprise that the resemblance of the joint adventure to a partnership consists, and as under the general law of partnership joint ownership of itself will not be sufficient to establish a partnership [27] so joint ownership by itself does not constitute a joint adventure. In *Hoare* v. *Dawes* [28] the parties joined together in the purchase of a quantity of tea lying at the India House in terms that it would subsequently be divided among them. It was held that there was no element of partnership or joint adventure in that arrangement. Lord Mansfield distinguished the case from one of joint adventure on the grounds that to make one of the *socii* in such cases liable for the firm there would need to be additional circumstances either that he had agreed with the other parties to share in profits or loss arising from the disposal of the tea or that he had permitted his associates to use his credit and hold him out as jointly answerable. The same rule had earlier been applied in Scotland in cases of joint purchase.[29] In the terms chosen by the older Scottish lawyers such a transaction is merely *emptio rei facta a pluribus ementibus* and no partnership is to be inferred from it in the absence of *contributio lucri et damni*.[30] The same question may arise in other cases of joint holdings and the decision will involve an assessment of all the facts including that of the joint holding.[31] In *Dickson* v. *Dickson* [32] two parties obtained a lease in their favour jointly and to " their heirs and successors whomsoever." One of the original parties having died during the currency of the lease the pursuer was served heir in general to him and raised an action for declarator and count and reckoning. He sought a declarator that he was entitled to the joint possession and management, along with the defender, of the lands leased and of the lime works, etc. situated thereon and to half the profits arising from the lands and limeworks after the death of the original joint tenant and he then concluded for count and reckoning. The Lord Ordinary (Pitmilly) granted decree as concluded for and a petition was presented to the Second Division on the ground that, though the pursuer might be entitled to a share of the fruits of the land, yet since the original tenants had engaged, independently of the lease, in the trade of farmers and lime dealers, he had no right to any share of the profits of that trade merely by virtue of his coming as heir in place of one of the original tenants in the lease. The court refused the petition but seem to have done so on the reasoning that the question raised in it was still left open in the accounting, without their pronouncing at that stage upon

[27] Partnership Act 1890, s. 2 (1).
[28] (1780) 1 Doug. 371.
[29] *Neilson* v. *McDougal* (1682) Mor. 14551.
[30] Bell, *Comm.* II, 544.
[31] *Supra* Chap. III, p. 67.
[32] (1821) 1 S. 113.

the rights of the parties under the arrangements made between the original tenants.

Joint adventure a separate persona

With variations of so wide a kind occurring within the associations generally described as joint adventures, it is hardly surprising that any legal consequences which may be ascribed to it, as distinct from a proper partnership, tend to be imprecise and tentative. There is, however, one feature which may be regarded as universally applicable to such forms of association. In *Clements* v. *Macaulay* [33] the Lord Justice-Clerk (Inglis) referred to it in these words—" A partnership has a local situation, because it has a place of business. This was a mere adventure, in which parties of different countries were temporarily connected. . . ." The point made as to the international character of the joint adventure is of course not universal but was directed to the facts of the particular case, though it is sometimes a point of importance in determining the legality or otherwise of the association. [34] The more general point that the joint adventure has no " local situation " from which it is carried on, is one which raises a wider issue, namely, is the joint adventure such an association of the parties as to give rise to a " firm " with a legal *persona* distinct from those of the individual co-adventurers? Bell firmly advances the view that there is no such independent *persona*, [35] and in *Pyper* v. *Christie* [36] the Lord Justice-Clerk (Moncreiff) said, " But the distinction of a proper copartnery and a joint adventure is simply this, that in the case of a proper copartnery the company is a separate *persona* and subsists in that capacity for the purposes of winding up, while a joint adventure, when completed, is resolved into its elements, and each may maintain his own interests in the common funds by direct action in his own name without the co-operation of the rest." These words are, however, closely related to the situation of the joint adventure on termination of it and only inferentially applicable to the situation while the adventure is in operation. In *Orr* v. *Pollock* [37] the association of the millowners appears to have been regarded by the Lord Ordinary (Lord Moncreiff) as a person in law having implied powers to levy assessments on its members, and in *Livingstone* v. *Allans*, [38] the Lord President (Balfour), while reiterating the distinction that the association under consideration was " not technically a partnership, as no separate legal *persona* was created in whom the common stock could be vested," yet pointed out that the case of the joint adventure was very similar to that of the partnership since the property comprised in a joint adventure may not be effectively

---

[33] (1866) 4 M. 583 at p. 593.
[34] See *infra* pp. 621–623.
[35] *Comm.* II, 539: ". . . there is no firm, and no general responsibility beyond the limited agreement of the parties."
[36] (1878) 6 R. 143 at p. 144.
[37] (1840) 2 D. 1092.
[38] (1900) 3 F. 233.

assigned until all the liabilities of the joint adventure have been satisfied.[39]
In *Mair* v. *Wood* [40] the question was again examined and certain passages
in the opinions of the judges suggest that the views quoted above were
not approved, though, from the report, no argument appears to have
been directed to the point nor were the court referred to the authorities
previously cited.   The Lord President's opinion lends no support whatever
to the view that a joint adventure is not a *persona* distinct from the co-
adventurers.   " A joint adventure is simply a species of the genus partnership, differentiated by its limited purpose and duration (which necessarily
affect the extent of the rights and liabilities flowing from the relationship),
but in all other essential respects indistinguishable from any other
partnership." [41]   Lord Keith is even more emphatic in support of that
view.

> " This would appear to be a partnership, or joint adventure, without
> any firm name.   In addition it seems that it has now come to an end.
> In my opinion, where it is desired to constitute a claim such as the
> present against such a partnership, all the partners, or at least all the
> surviving partners, so far as known, should be called as defenders
> and be designed as partners of a joint adventure that has terminated.
> This is necessary not only from the fact that a partnership, or joint
> adventure, has a separate *persona* by Scots law, but also for the reason
> that questions of relief may arise as between partners, and in any
> decree that may pass against the defenders it is proper that the
> character in which the obligation was incurred should be made
> clear." [42]

It is thought that no argument based upon the passage quoted from
Bell's *Commentaries* [43] and the dictum of Lord Justice-Clerk Moncreiff
in *Pyper* v. *Christie* [44] would now be likely to find acceptance.   There is
a danger of misinterpreting Bell's statement, " There is no firm," since
at the time when he wrote the expression " firm " was used sometimes to
denote the firm name rather than the association itself, viewed as a
separate person.[45]   It is possible, therefore, to explain Bell's statement as
meaning no more than that the joint adventure is " without any firm
name " and thus to reconcile it with the passage quoted from Lord Keith's
judgment.   Lord Justice-Clerk Moncreiff in *Pyper* v. *Christie* [46] is more
pointed in distinguishing a partnership which has a separate legal *persona*
from a joint adventure which is not similarly endowed but it will be noted

[39] *Keith* v. *Penn* (1840) 2 D. 633; *McCaul's Creditors* v. *Ramsay & Ritchie* (1740) Mor. 14608.
[40] 1948 S.C. 83.
[41] *Ibid. per* Lord President Cooper at p. 86.
[42] *Ibid.* at p. 89.
[43] *Supra* n. 35.
[44] *Supra* n. 36.
[45] See *e.g.* Bell, *Comm.* II, 506: " It has been held that the company was bound where a
partner signed the firm of the company to a guarantee. . . ."   See also II, 507–508: " As
a separate person the company is known and recognised in obligations and contracts by
its separate name or firm, as its personal appellation."
[46] (1878) 6 R. 143 at p. 144.

that his dictum is addressed to the specialities of a situation where the joint adventure is completed and the issue remaining is the title of an individual co-adventurer to sue for vindication of his right to his share; and, in the immediately succeeding words of his opinion the Lord Justice-Clerk lays stress upon this when he continues, " While the joint adventure is in operation the contract may of course provide that action may proceed against the debtors to the adventure at the instance of one or more of them, but when the adventure is finished and nothing remains but a division of the funds, each joint adventurer is simply a proprietor of his share of the funds and may vindicate them from the official or manager in whose hands they remain, who holds them on his account." His opinion is silent upon the converse situation in which the question of the *persona* of the joint adventure is likely to arise, *i.e.* where a third party seeks to enforce a debt which has been incurred in the operation of the joint adventure. That was the aspect which the judges had before them in *Mair* v. *Wood* and in the light of the views expressed by them, it is thought that a joint adventure must be regarded as possessing an independent *persona* in Scots law equally with any other firm of partnership.

Differences arising from the inherent nature of the joint adventure

In the passage quoted from the opinion of the Lord President (Cooper) in *Mair* v. *Wood* [47] reference is made to the differentiation of the joint adventure in terms of its limited purpose and duration with the comment that those matters " necessarily affect the extent of the rights and liabilities flowing from the relationship." The nature of a joint adventure as opposed to a partnership proper and the nature of the practical needs which it is designed to serve have repercussions at some points on the legal consequences to be derived from the relationship. The general principles of the law of partnership will apply to the joint adventure [48] but at some points those general principles themselves reflect a response to varying facts and circumstances which may arise within the partnership. The modifications and qualifications which arise in the application of those principles to the joint adventure are similarly responsive to the surrounding circumstances. To that extent they may be said to be not so much qualifications of the general principles as illustrations of their application to particular cases. Since, however, the joint adventure has certain constant features connected with its restricted scope of activity it may be of some profit to discuss the particular aspects in which those features have exerted some influence upon the general principles.

Authority to act on behalf of the joint adventure

Each co-adventurer has authority to transact business on behalf of the joint adventure. He is held out to the public as invested with the

[47] *Supra* p. 612.
[48] Bell, *Comm.* II, 539; *Mair* v. *Wood*, 1948 S.C. 83, *per* the Lord President at p. 86.

authority or alternatively he is *praepositus negotiis societatis* and has either express or tacit authority to bind those associated with him in the joint adventure " for the whole furnishings made to the concern." [49] While his authority thus resembles that of an ordinary partner, it is affected by the limited nature of the joint adventure in two ways. In the first place it is restricted to transactions for " furnishings made to the concern." The co-adventurers do not, therefore, have an ostensible authority co-extensive with that of the partners of a firm. " In proper copartnery *socii* are liable for the actings of one another even where not *in rem versum*, while joint adventurers are so liable only for furnishings made to the concern." [50] " Furnishings to the concern " may comprise goods purchased on its behalf or money borrowed for its use.[51] The liability of the concern for the transactions of a co-adventurer thus depends upon the fact that the joint adventure has had the benefit of the goods or money secured. In the case of money borrowed it will not be necessary to follow and identify the money in the hands of the joint adventure if it can be proved that the association has profited through the application of the money to its purpose.[52] The speciality of treatment of liability in the case of the joint adventure may be regarded as a limitation of the more general liability imposed in partnership proper arising from the restricted nature of the activities of the joint adventure. That explanation, however, merely emphasises the factual situation and tends to mask an important difference in underlying legal principle. In partnership proper the basis of the liability of the partners for the transactions of a copartner is that the latter has contracted in his character of partner and the third party dealing with him has, in consequence, done so in reliance on the credit of his firm. A joint adventure rarely has a firm name [53] and a co-adventurer transacting its business may do so without disclosing the existence of the joint adventure. In such circumstances the third party is dealing with him entirely on the faith of his own credit and not that of the association. Yet if the transaction effected is *in rem versum* of the joint adventure all the co-adventurers will be liable upon it. " If all agree to share in goods to be purchased, and in consequence of that agreement one of them go into the market and make the purchase, it is the same for this purpose [*i.e.* for the liability of the *socii*] as if all the names had been announced to the seller; and therefore all are liable for the value of them." [54] As expressed by Bell,[55] " It is a purchase by the society, whatever credit may have been relied on."

In the second place, however, the liability of the co-adventurers is strictly circumscribed by the limits of the joint adventure itself. " The great peculiarity in the doctrine of joint trade . . . is that unless where the

[49] Bell, *Comm.* II, 543.
[50] *Withers Birch & Co.* v. *Cowan*, Nov. 16, 1790 (not reported). See Bell, *Comm.* II, 539–540.
[51] Bell, *Comm.* II, 544; *Cameron* v. *Young* (1871) 9 M. 786.
[52] Bell, *Comm.* II, 544.
[53] But see *Pyper* v. *Christie* (1878) 6 R. 143.
[54] *Gouthwaite* v. *Duckworth* (1811) 12 East 421, *per* Lord Ellenborough at p. 426.
[55] Bell, *Comm.* II, 539.

joint concern is avowed, and a credit raised on the combined responsibility, the liability being the result of the discovery of a partnership which was not relied on as regulating the credit, the limits of the contract are fixed by the actual agreement between the parties; whereas in partnership there is a universal responsibility for every engagement *bona fide* relied on, and not beyond the limits of the company's line of trade." [56] This aspect of the rule of liability in joint adventure may be said to be the obverse side of the rule enunciated above in the first place. Whereas the first rule goes beyond the basic concept in partnership proper, which is founded upon the equity that third parties must be regarded as dealing on the faith of the credit of the firm, and imposes liability on the joint adventure where the third party was ignorant of its existence and hence did not rely upon its credit, provided the transaction effected was *in rem versum* of the joint adventure, the liability of the *socii* to a third party who is unaware of the existence of the joint adventure at the time when he contracts with one of the co-adventurers, is confined within the terms of the agreement setting up the joint adventure. [57] Indeed, since the ground of liability is that the transaction was effected for the purpose of the joint adventure, and hence was *in rem versum* thereof, it would be difficult to argue that a transaction which did not fall within the limits of the agreement would entitle a third party to sue the co-adventurers in respect of it. Both aspects of the rule are illustrated in *British Linen Co. v. Alexander* [58] where three parties entered into a joint adventure for the purchase of shares in the South Wales Railway Company, each having a one-third share of the profit earned or loss incurred. They agreed that the second and third parties should " provide the funds " by drawing upon the first party, discounting the bills and remitting the proceeds to the first party to be employed by him in the purchase of the shares. The second and third parties each drew separately on the first party who accepted the bills which the drawers then separately discounted, remitting the proceeds to the first party as agreed. The second and third parties became bankrupt and the holder of the second party's bill claimed payment from the first party. The bill was, of course, clearly an accommodation bill but it was held that since the proceeds of the bill had been applied in the prosecution of the joint adventure, the first party was liable in payment thereof. It is more difficult to state what wider liability is imposed if it is disclosed at the time of the transaction that it is entered into on behalf of the joint adventure. It is stated by Erskine that there can be no contract with a joint adventure as such. [59] It seems clear,

---

[56] Bell, *Comm.* II, 539.

[57] *White* v. *McIntyre* (1841) 3 D. 334; *Logy* v. *Durham* (1697) Mor. 14566.

[58] (1853) 15 D. 277. ". . . according to the import of the agreement of the parties, the raising the money in the manner covenanted between them (by discounting bills) was a proper part of the joint adventure ": *per* Lord Fullerton at p. 281.

[59] Erskine, *Inst.* III, 3, 29: ". . . no adventurer can be hurt by any deed not subscribed by himself, though it should be signed by a co-adventurer in his name; for where there is no proper copartnership, there is no subscription by a firm, the establishment of which, by an unanimous resolution of the company, is the only ground upon which the deed of one partner can induce an obligation upon the rest."

however, that Erskine is concerned with the problem of a written agreement purporting to be signed on behalf of the joint adventure by one of the parties to it, and that the use of the term " firm " in the passage quoted,[59] contrasted as it is with the term " company " in the same passage denotes the firm name in which a contract is executed. The ambivalence of the word " firm " as used by the older legal writers has already been noticed,[60] and the quotation from Erskine's *Institutes* does not necessarily refer to transactions entered into by word of mouth by one party to a joint adventure on behalf of the association. Indeed it is clear that Bell, in the qualifying words which he inserted in the quotation from the *Commentaries*,[61] clearly envisages that a co-adventurer may transact business with a third party in such a manner that the third party is apprised of the existence of the joint adventure and relies upon its credit. He does not, however, make it clear what he intends the effect of that qualification to be. In principle it is thought that where the co-adventurer expressly makes known that the transaction is on behalf of the joint adventure he purports to act as its agent, and thus the responsibility of the co-adventurers may be more closely assimilated to that of copartners in a proper copartnership. Yet a joint adventure is of itself not equiparate to a proper copartnership. Its very existence gives notice to the third party that its scope of business is restricted. The third party, therefore, is to some extent put on his inquiry and if the transaction effected is beyond the scope envisaged in the agreement setting up the joint adventure, he may have some difficulty in bringing himself within an equitable rule entitling him to hold the co-adventurers liable.

Contribution by parties to the common stock of the joint adventure

A distinction must be maintained between cases where goods are purchased by one of the co-adventurers on behalf of the adventure and cases where in terms of the agreement setting up the joint adventure each party is taken bound to contribute his quota to the common stock. In the latter case the mere fact that the co-adventurers have purchased from a third party the goods which they are under obligation to contribute to the common stock will involve no one but the individual purchasers in liability. Thus where A, B and C agree each to supply goods to the value of £3,000 to be shipped on a joint trading adventure, and the profits whereof are to be divided among them in accordance with the value of the goods contributed by them, this does not make B and C responsible for the goods purchased by A in order to provide his quota of the cargo forming the common stock of the adventure.[62] That principle is equally applicable in the case of a partnership proper where one of the partners

---

[60] *Supra* p. 612.
[61] *Supra* p. 615, n. 59.
[62] *Heap* v. *Dobson* (1863) 15 C.B.(N.S.) 460; *Smith* v. *Craven* (1831) 1 Cr. & J. 500; 35 R.R. 764; and see *White* v. *McIntyre* (1841) 3 D. 334; *Lockhart* v. *Brown* (1888) 15 R. 742.

transacts with a third party in order to obtain the goods or money which he has agreed to contribute to the property of the partnership as a condition of his becoming a partner. There is no partnership among the parties in relation to transactions entered into by each individually in order to obtain the capital contribution which he must make to the firm in order to become a partner.[63] When one of the parties raises the money which he is under obligation to contribute to the joint stock, by arrangement with a third party, the same rule applies and his copartners or co-adventurers are not liable under any such arrangement.[64] But where the money is raised for the purposes of the joint adventure and not as the contribution of one co-adventurer to the common stock, all the co-adventurers will be liable on the transaction.[65]

Basis of liability where the transaction is on behalf of the joint adventure

Where goods are supplied, or money obtained, from a third party by one of the co-adventurers but for the purposes of the adventure, though that is not disclosed to the third party, there is difficulty in reconciling the basis of the liability of the co-adventurers with the general principle of the implied agency resulting from a species of partnership. If the existence of the joint adventure is not disclosed to the third party, then, so far as the liability of those associated in the adventure is concerned, the terms of section 5 of the Partnership Act 1890 do not cause undue difficulty in spite of the exception from the implied agency occurring in the concluding words of the section—" unless the partner so acting has in fact no authority to act for the firm in the particular matter, and the person with whom he is dealing either knows that he has no authority or does not know or believe him to be a partner." In the case relating to the joint adventure which is under consideration the third party comes within the concluding words. He does not know or believe the person with whom he is dealing to be a partner, or co-adventurer, but before the implied agency provided for in section 5 can be denied, the first part of the saving clause must also apply, *i.e.* it must be established that he had in fact no authority to act for the association comprised in the joint adventure. This he has and consequently the liability of the co-adventurers can be ascribed to the general principle of implied agency in partnership. However, that reasoning rests upon the assumption that at the date when the transaction is carried through the joint adventure is actually in existence. In many cases the transaction will be effected by one of the co-adventurers for the purpose of securing the goods which are to be the subject of the joint adventure. In these cases it is difficult to bring the resultant liability of the co-adventurers within the doctrine

---

[63] *Dickinson* v. *Valpy* (1829) 10 B. & C. 128; *Wilson* v. *Whitehead* (1842) 10 M. & W. 503; and see *supra* Chap. VII, pp. 258–263.

[64] *Dickinson* v. *Valpy, supra.*

[65] *British Linen Co.* v. *Alexander* (1853) 15 D. 277. Compare *North British Bank* v. *Ayrshire Iron Co.* (1853) 15 D. 782.

of implied agency in partnership, because until the goods have been procured there is nothing of the nature of a partnership or joint adventure
in existence. *Gouthwaite* v. *Duckworth* [66] appears to have been decided
on the ground that the adventure commenced with the purchase of the
goods but it is difficult to reconcile the decision with that in *Saville* v.
Robertson [67] save on the ground that in the former case it was never
intended that the individual co-adventurer who bought the goods should
contribute them to the adventure at his own cost exclusively; but that
reasoning does not elide the difficulty in applying the principle of implied
agency in a partnership which is said to have commenced only when the
purchase was completed. The problem is noticed by Lindley [68] who
suggests that the real ground of liability in this case rests upon implied
agency altogether independent of partnership. While as between the
co-adventurers a stipulation that the adventurer who purchased the goods
was to be reimbursed by his co-adventurers might be regarded as merely
operating a right of relief *inter socios*, it does not necessarily destroy the
implication that, if one *socius* effected the purchase, he did so as agent for
and on the credit of all the *socii*. *Gouthwaite* v. *Duckworth* raised the
issue in perhaps its most extreme form, since two of the adventurers,
Browne and Powell, were indebted to the third, Duckworth, and the terms
of the joint adventure were that Browne and Powell should purchase,
pay for and ship the goods and that the proceeds of the joint adventure
would be remitted to Duckworth who, after deducting therefrom the
amount of Browne and Powell's indebtedness to him, would share the
profit with them or would share in any loss which was incurred. Though
Browne actually bought the goods all three co-adventurers were held
liable for the price.

In questions of implied agency arising under a joint adventure, the
stipulated limits of the adventure must, however, be carefully considered;
for these may be held to imply an individual responsibility on the part of
the adventurer dealing with the third party, where under the wider scope
of implied agency which obtains in partnership proper the firm and its
partners would have been held jointly and severally liable. In *Barton* v.
Hanson [69] the action was for the recovery of the price of corn and hay
supplied for the horses on a particular stage in the journey of a stage
coach, and was raised against the concern and the *socii* jointly, on the
ground that, as part of the joint concern, all the *socii* on the different
stages of the run benefited by the use of the horses on that particular
stage, and indeed the Lord Chief Baron (McDonald) so directed the
jury. The Court of Common Pleas, however, corrected that direction,[70]
holding that, in terms of the express provisions of the agreement among
the parties to the joint adventure, the provision of the horses for each

---

[66] (1811) 12 East 421.
[67] (1792) 4 T.R. 720.
[68] *Op. cit.* p. 238.
[69] (1809) 2 Camp. 97; 11 R.R. 524.
[70] (1809) 2 Taunt. 49.

stage was the responsibility of the individual parties, who then were at liberty to hire the horses to the joint adventure and that the individual parties and not the joint adventure were liable. A similar approach to the question of liability was taken by the Scottish courts in a case concerning a joint adventure in the running of a stage coach, when the rent of a coach office taken on let by one of the adventurers and used by him for the purpose of selling tickets was held to be his individual liability.[71]

Liability joint and several

Where goods are purchased or money is borrowed on behalf of the joint adventure in virtue of the implied mandate discussed above, the liability of the co-adventurers therefor is joint and several.[72]

Liability in delict

As in a proper partnership, those associated in a joint adventure incur a joint and several liability to third parties for the wrongful acts or the negligence of one of their number while conducting the affairs of the joint adventure.[73] The test of such liability is explained by Lord Trayner in *McGee* v. *Anderson*.[74] He said:

" The act which was done (which, I take it, was beyond question wrongful) was done . . . for the benefit of all concerned, and all concerned shared that benefit, according to the terms of their joint bargain. It was said, further, that the defender Anderson could not in any view be liable for the delict or wrong of his joint adventurers, because he had not authorised it. But then the thing done was in pursuance of the joint adventure; it was done to protect the joint interest, and to enhance the joint profit, and all profited by it more or less. Anderson cannot take the benefit of the act by which profit was earned or secured (as he has done in point of fact) and then repudiate the act or means by which that profit was gained."

While Lord Trayner's words are helpful in explaining the region of activity within which a vicarious responsibility may arise for the delict of an individual adventurer, it is thought that his insistence on the feature that those so held liable have as a condition of liability in fact profited by the wrongful act cannot be accepted as a necessary condition of the vicarious liability of co-adventurers. It was a feature which was present in the case which his Lordship had under consideration, and it is a feature which may frequently assist in defining the area of activity within which vicarious liability may arise. But it is submitted that there is nothing in the law regarding vicarious liability for wrongs, whether that liability arise in relation to partnership, or agency, or employment, which

---

[71] *Jardine* v. *Macfarlane* (1828) 6 S. 564. See also *White* v. *McIntyre* (1841) 3 D. 334.
[72] Bell, *Prin.* § 395; *Mollison* v. *Noltie* (1889) 16 R. 350; *Fowler* v. *Paterson's Trs.* (1896) 3 S.L.T. 305; *Hay* v. *Douglas*, 1922 S.L.T. 365.
[73] *McGee* v. *Anderson* (1895) 22 R. 274; *Mair* v. *Wood*, 1948 S.C. 83.
[74] *Supra cit.* at p. 277.

demands as a condition of that liability being imposed that he who is
held vicariously liable should have profited by the wrongful act. The
corporation of Glasgow can in no sense be held to profit by the heedless
driving on the part of one of its bus drivers, as a consequence of which a
passer-by is injured; yet it is trite law that the corporation will in such
circumstances be vicariously liable for its driver's lack of care. Nor does
there appear to be any speciality in the application of the doctrine to the
joint adventure which postulates as a condition of its application that the
co-adventurers must have benefited from the wrongful act. In *Mair* v.
Wood,[75] a case where vicarious liability was excluded on a different
ground which is noticed below,[76] Lord President Cooper [77] and Lord
Keith [78] both treated the question of vicarious liability in the joint
adventure precisely as if it arose in a partnership proper. Neither makes
any mention of a condition that the persons held vicariously liable should
have benefited from the wrongful act. The case before them was such
that it could not reasonably have been contended that any such benefit
accrued and if vicarious liability is to be imposed on the joint adventure
on similar terms to those in which it is imposed on a partnership, then
there is nothing in the Partnership Act 1890 to justify Lord Trayner's
condition that benefit be derived from the wrongful act.[79] The only
relevance of the element of benefit is that, since the limits of the joint
adventure are more confined than those of the partnership, the determination that a particular wrong was done in pursuance of the joint adventure
may be assisted if it can be shown, as it was possible to show in *McGee* v.
Anderson,[80] that the consequences of that wrong enured to the benefit
of the co-adventurers. But that is a very different thing from saying
that before the co-adventurers can be held vicariously liable, they must
have derived profit or benefit from the wrong.

No vicarious liability for wrong done by one co-adventurer to another

As in partnership proper a partner may not hold the firm and his
copartners vicariously liable for a wrong which he has suffered at the
hands of a fellow-partner, so in the case of a joint adventure one of the
adventurers similarly circumstanced has no remedy save against the delinquent co-adventurer.[81] The law applicable to a partnership cannot in
this respect be usefully distinguished from that applicable to the joint
adventure. In both cases the association, in the words of Lord Keith,
is " merely the occasion of the pursuer's loss, not its cause, and his claim
has no basis on the ground of re-imbursement." [82]

[75] 1948 S.C. 83.
[76] See *infra* n. 82.
[77] 1948 S.C. 83 at p. 87.
[78] *Ibid.* at pp. 89–90.
[79] Partnership Act 1890, s. 10.
[80] (1895) 22 R. 274.
[81] *Mair* v. *Wood, supra*; Partnership Act 1890, s. 10.
[82] *Mair* v. *Wood, supra* at p. 93.

Illegality of adventure

As in the case of a partnership proper,[83] a joint adventure the object of which is illegal or, being legal, is sought to be attained in a way which is illegal will not be enforced as a contract between the parties. The onus of establishing the illegality of the adventure rests upon those who challenge its legality. Illegality is not presumed to exist in any circumstances, but the court will raise the question *ex proprio motu* if illegality of the joint adventure is to be seen on the face of the record or emerges clearly in the course of the trial of the case even where neither party has sought to rely upon the illegality, provided the court is satisfied that no further evidence can cure the illegality so detected.[84] The mere fact that an illegal act has been committed in the pursuance of the joint adventure will not of itself render the contract of joint adventure illegal and consequently unenforceable[85] and, although certain provisions of the agreement are illegal, it does not necessarily follow that the joint adventure as a whole will be regarded as illegal.[86] If the illegal parts of the contract are severable from those which are legal, then the latter will be enforced though the former will fall. The real problem in such cases is to decide whether the legal and the illegal parts of the contract are truly independent and severable. If they are inextricably interlaced one with another, then to enforce the legal provisions and to ignore the illegal would be to hold the parties to a contract which they did not engage themselves to perform, but where the provisions are truly severable the illegality of one or more of them does not necessarily taint the other and legal provisions.[87]

Gambling

The differing grounds upon which an association of persons may be regarded as formed for an illegal purpose have already been considered.[88] It is important to analyse the situation arising in the joint adventure where its activities appear to be concerned with gaming or wagering transactions. Gloag[89] expresses the view that, despite one dictum to the contrary,[90] gaming transactions are not inherently illegal, save in so far as they have infringed statutory provisions in the manner in which they

---

[83] See *supra* Chap. IV.
[84] Gloag, *Contract* (2nd ed.) p. 549; *Hamilton* v. *McLauchlan* (1908) 16 S.L.T. 341; *Lipton* v. *Powell* [1921] 2 K.B. 51; *Rawlings* v. *General Trading Co.* [1921] 1 K.B. 635; *North West Salt Co.* v. *Electrolytic Alkali Co.* [1914] A.C. 461; *Scott* v. *Brown, Doering & Co.* [1892] 2 Q.B. 724; *Gedge* v. *Royal Exchange Assurance Corporation* [1900] 2 Q.B. 214.
[85] *Thwaites* v. *Coulthwaite* [1896] 1 Ch. 496; *Armstrong* v. *Armstrong* (1834) 3 Myl. & K. 45; *Longworth's Executor's Case* (1859) 1 De G.F. & J. 17 *per* Lord Campbell.
[86] Gloag, *Contract* (2nd ed.) p. 589.
[87] " If the consideration is tainted with illegality, either in whole or in part, all the promises depending on that consideration must fail; but if the consideration be not tainted with illegality, either wholly or in part, then if one of the several promises depending upon it be illegal in itself and the others legal, the legal promises stand ": *per* A. L. Smith L.J. in *Kearney* v. *Whitehaven Colliery Co.* [1893] 1 Q.B. 700 at p. 714.
[88] See *supra*, Chap. IV.
[89] *Contract* (2nd ed.) p. 582.
[90] *Per* Lord Justice-Clerk Moncreiff in *Calder* v. *Stevens* (1871) 9 M. 1074 at p. 1076.

have been conducted, and that their unenforceability results not from illegality but from the fact that they are regarded as *sponsiones ludicrae* undeserving of notice by the courts. Be that as it may, the agreement to conduct a joint adventure in gaming transactions is not itself a gaming transaction and a challenge of the joint adventure as illegal on grounds of gaming or as a *sponsio ludicra* will not succeed merely because it has been proved that the object of the adventure was to enter into gaming transactions. In *Mollison* v. *Noltie* [91] two persons entered into a joint adventure to sell stock in the Grand Trunk Railway of Canada, the transactions being effected in the name of one of them. They did not hold the stock at the date at which they sold it but intended to buy it in at an advantageous price before they were required to deliver it in implement of the contracts of sale. The market, however, rose and thus a loss was incurred. The joint adventurer, who had incurred the loss through entering into the transactions in his own name, sued his co-adventurer to recover half of the loss incurred and was held to be entitled to recover. The Lord Justice-Clerk (Macdonald) [92] first examined the transaction between the sellers and the purchasers of the shares. This was not a wagering transaction: for a wager requires two parties and the purchaser was an ordinary purchaser offering to buy stock and intending to obtain that stock. Nor could the stockbroker through whom the sale was effected be regarded as engaged in a wager with the joint adventurers. His whole interest was to earn his commission and to be kept free of personal liability to the purchaser. As between the two joint adventurers the Lord Justice-Clerk likewise considered that there was no wager. He founded upon the opinion of Lord Wood in *Foulds* v. *Thomson*,[93] where a distinction was drawn between a contract for payment of " differences " in the price of shares on the stock exchange and " a bona fide onerous purchase or sale from or to a party to whom a personal obligation was undertaken to fulfil the contract, which he was entitled to enforce, and in which the responsibility of the pursuer as broker for the defenders did not terminate until the stocks bought or sold were either delivered or paid for." In the relation between the joint adventurers there was no element of gaming because under no circumstances could one joint adventurer be better or worse off than the other.

In *Clayton* v. *Clayton* [94] a somewhat similar question arose in regard to a joint adventure but the issue before the court was more closely related to a possible statutory illegality in the objects of the association than to an objection that the activities of the joint adventure were *sponsiones ludicrae*. Four parties contributed in equal shares to the purchase of a ticket in a foreign lottery upon terms that any winnings were to be equally divided among them. The Betting and Lotteries Act

[91] (1889) 16 R. 350.
[92] *Ibid.* at pp. 352–353.
[93] (1857) 19 D. 803.
[94] 1937 S.C. 619.

1934 [95] provided that " all lotteries are unlawful " and further that
" every person who in connection with any lottery promoted . . . either
in Great Britain or elsewhere— . . . (b) sells or distributes . . . any tickets
or chances in the lottery . . . shall be guilty of an offence." The court
held (1) that a lottery was not illegal by the common law of Scotland,
though one of the judges, Lord Morison, expressed his doubt as to that
proposition; (2) that on a consideration of the Betting and Lotteries Act
1934 as a whole section 21 is to be interpreted as pronouncing upon the
illegality of lotteries that have a locus within Great Britain where the
money is collected and the drawing takes place and did not, and could
not, be read as pronouncing upon the illegality of a lottery which the
British Parliament had no power to declare legal or illegal; (3) that
section 22 (1) applied to foreign lotteries but was addressed to rendering
trafficking in tickets in foreign lotteries within Great Britain illegal, and
did not render the purchase of a ticket in a foreign lottery or the setting
up of a partnership to purchase one illegal. Accordingly the court held
that the contract of joint adventure was capable of lawful performance
and allowed the pursuers who were suing for payment of their shares of
the winnings a proof before answer of their averments. It may be
questioned whether the issue as to the legality of lotteries in Scotland
arose in the case under consideration. The joint adventure was not set
up to conduct a lottery but to purchase a ticket. It is true that the
provision of section 21 of the Act is expressed in very general terms—
" all lotteries are unlawful "—and that may suggest that any activity of
a joint adventure connected with a lottery is an unlawful activity. That
view is supported neither by the Betting and Lotteries Act 1934 itself,
which goes on in section 22 to mention specific activities in relation to a
lottery, short of actually conducting it, which are to be regarded as unlawful, nor by the opinions of the judges who seem clearly to have regarded
the terms of section 21 as referring to the conduct of lotteries. [96] The
court, in ordering a proof before answer, clearly had in mind that on the
averments on record the transaction on which the joint adventure was
founded was either a sale in Great Britain by the defender to the pursuers
of shares in the lottery ticket, in which case it would be unlawful in terms
of section 22 (1) (b) of the Act, or its nature was that the four adventurers
contributed money to enable the pursuer to purchase in the Free State
of Ireland the lottery ticket, in which case no taint of illegality attached
to the joint adventure.

Rights of the joint adventurers inter se

In the absence of express provision as to the respective shares of the
parties in the profits of a joint adventure, the joint adventurers will be
presumed to be entitled to equal shares in the profits. [97] This is in

[95] s. 21 and s. 22 (1).
[96] See *e.g. per* the Lord President (Normand) in *Clayton* v. *Clayton, supra* at p. 628.
[97] *Aitchison* v. *Aitchison* (1877) 4 R. 899; *Fergusson* v. *Graham's Trs.* (1836) 14 S. 871.

accordance with the presumption generally prevailing in partnership under the common law and now declared and enacted in section 24 (1) of the Partnership Act 1890. That section also declares the counteracting presumption (in the absence of express provision) that the partners shall be liable to contribute equally to losses incurred by the firm. Since the majority of the decisions concerned with the joint adventure have arisen on the action of a third party against one or more of the adventurers for payment of a debt incurred by the joint adventure, in which circumstances all the joint adventurers are jointly and severally bound so far as respects the third party, it is not possible to point to any decision where the presumption of equal contribution to losses by the adventurers *inter se* has been clearly declared. There appears to be little doubt, however, that the general rule in partnership will apply and that the joint adventurers will be regarded as equally liable to contribute *inter se* towards losses.[98]

Rights of reimbursement and recompense for special trouble

Where one of the joint adventurers has incurred liability or outlays in pursuance of the joint adventure he is entitled to proportionate relief according to the agreement from his co-adventurers.[99] The rule is of general application in partnership.[1] The rule in partnership is a specialised illustration of the general rule in agency and arises from the partner's position as *praepositus rebus societatis*. In the case of the joint adventure, while the principle is equally valid, the nature of the actual payment made or obligation undertaken will require scrutiny to ensure that it is in fact one made on behalf of the *socii* in pursuance of the joint adventure and is not merely one whereby the individual adventurer has equipped himself with the contribution which he is under obligation to make to the joint adventure.[2] If however it can be shown that one of the adventurers has in the course of the adventure and in pursuance of it properly incurred expense on his own personal account he will be entitled to proportionate relief from his co-adventurers and if the proceeds of the adventure come into his hands, he has a right of retention of these until his claim is satisfied.[3] It has been held that a partner in a joint adventure may, in exceptional circumstances, be entitled to recompense from his fellow adventurers for personal trouble connected with the conduct of

---

[98] That was the decision in *Mollison* v. *Noltie* (1889) 16 R. 350 but the report does not indicate whether the decision proceeded upon an express or a presumed liability to contribute. See also *Logan* v. *Brown* (1824) 3 S. 15. In this report the share of the contribution to losses is not specified. See also Bell, *Prin.* § 396.

[99] *McCaul's Creditors* v. *Ramsay & Ritchie* (1740) Mor. 14608; *Crooks* v. *Tawse* (1779) Mor. 14596.

[1] "The firm must indemnify every partner in respect of payments made and personal liabilities incurred by him—(a) in the ordinary proper conduct of the business of the firm; or (b) in or about anything necessarily done for the preservation of the business or property of the firm."—Partnership Act 1890, s. 24 (2).

[2] See *e.g. White* v. *McIntyre* (1841) 3 D. 334, as an illustration of the kind of problem involved.

[3] *Keith* v. *Penn* (1840) 2 D. 633.

the joint adventure though no provision for this appeared in the agreement between the parties.[4] The circumstances of that case were, however, very special and induced the court to the view that the absence of provision for recompensing him was a *casus improvisus*, and it is not to be relied on as authority for any general right to claim recompense in such circumstances. On its own facts, however, the decision is an arresting one; for the adventure in question having proved ruinous and consequently been terminated the court held the partner entitled to indemnity from his co-adventurers for the recompense in respect of the trouble which he personally had taken.

Compensation

The general principles of the law of partnership as to compensation or set off of claims as between third parties on the one hand and the firm and its partners on the other are—(1) that if the firm sues a third party for a debt due to the firm the third party may not plead compensation in respect of a debt due to him by an individual member of the firm; but (2) if a claim is made by a third party against the firm, the firm may plead compensation in respect of a debt due by the third party to an individual member of the firm. These rules have been touched upon elsewhere in this treatise [5] in their application to a partnership proper. At this stage it is intended to examine only the bearing of the rules upon the joint adventure. The legal theory on which the rules in partnership are based depends upon the independence of the firm as a *quasi*-person from the individual partners who comprise the firm, which entails that the firm, and not the individual partners, is the creditor in debts due to the firm, and accounts for the first principle above set out. But each individual partner is a debtor, albeit an accessory debtor, in all debts due by the firm, and in recognition of that relationship the second principle has been admitted though the decisions have not been entirely unanimous as to the underlying reasoning by means of which that conclusion is reached.[6] In regard to the joint adventure some doubt exists whether the association represented by the joint adventure is a firm, *i.e.* a *persona* distinct from the individual co-adventurers.[7] The opinion has earlier been hazarded that these doubts should perhaps be regarded as dispelled on a consideration of the dicta of the judges in cases arising subsequently to the publication of Bell's *Commentaries*. If the view be still held that a joint adventure does not possess a *persona* independent from those of the co-adventurers, then the underlying reason for the first principle of compensation of debts in partnership disappears in the joint adventure and one might expect it to be argued that a third party sued for a debt due by him to the joint adventure would be allowed to plead compensation

---

[4] *Beath* v. *Campbell Rivers & Co.* (1824) 3 S. 353.
[5] *Supra* Chap. XIII, p. 564.
[6] See Gloag, *Contract* (2nd ed.) p. 648.
[7] See Walker, *Principles of Scottish Private Law* I, p. 370; Bell, *Comm.* II, 539.

in respect of a claim which he has against an individual co-adventurer. The argument is not free from fallacy but one would expect at least that the alleged distinction between partnership and joint adventure would have been explored. In *Thom* v. *North British Banking Company*,[8] however, it was held that compensation cannot be pleaded on a private debt due by a co-adventurer against a debt owed to the joint adventure. No distinction between that case and one involving a partnership was suggested. Lord Fullerton said, " But holding . . . that this was a joint adventure, and known to be so by the defenders, the direction in law sought for from the Judge was that, whatever the state of accounts between the joint adventurers might be, the defenders, though in full knowledge of the joint adventure, were entitled to retain to the extent of one half of the balance in respect of their private claims against [the firm of] Inglis & Knox, one of the two individual joint adventurers. According to all the authorities, that would have been wrong." Lord Fullerton does not specify the authorities on which he relies nor are any mentioned in the report. An unsuccessful search has been made for any prior case in which the point was decided in relation to a joint adventure. The inference appears to be that the decisions on attempted compensation of claims due by individual partners against a claim due to the firm itself were relied upon and that the court saw no reason to distinguish the case of a joint adventure from one of partnership in this particular. On termination of the joint adventure,[9] the general principle applicable in partnership proper appears likely to be applied in the case of the joint adventure. When a solvent partnership is dissolved a debt due to the partnership becomes the property of the partners as individuals; consequently in an action for recovery of the debt due to the partnership, the defender may plead compensation of a debt due to him by an individual partner up to the amount of that partner's share in the debt due by the third party to the firm.[10] A similar right to plead compensation will arise on the termination of a joint adventure when the association has been held to be resolved into its elements, each adventurer being entitled to sue in his own name for his interest in the common funds of the joint adventure without conjoining his co-adventurers in the action.[11] *Concursus debiti et crediti* to the extent of the share of each individual adventurer, therefore, appears to arise at the date of termination of the joint adventure.

There is perhaps more difficulty in applying the second rule of partnership as to compensation to the case of the joint adventure. The right of a firm to plead set off of a debt owed to one of its partners in answer to a claim by a third party against the firm has been justified on two alternative grounds—

---

[8] (1850) 13 D. 134.
[9] See *infra* p. 628.
[10] *Mitchell* v. *The Canal Basin Foundry Co.* (1869) 7 M. 480.
[11] *Pyper* v. *Christie* (1878) 6 R. 143; and see *infra* p. 628.

(1) that in such cases there is implied an assignation of his debt by the partner to the firm which gives rise to *concursus debiti et crediti* between the firm and the third party; or

(2) that no assignation need be implied since the partner is himself a debtor in the debts due by his firm and consequently *concursus debiti et crediti* already exists without any necessity for assignation by him of his debt to the firm.[12] It appears to be a somewhat bold use of analogy to invoke the first reason as a justification of the rule in the case of a joint adventure. The limited nature of the association involved entails that any implication of an assignation by an individual adventurer of his private claims is difficult to justify. The second ground has much more to commend it in any attempt to extend it by analogy to the joint adventure. Whether it be accepted that the joint adventure is in law a separate *persona,* or not, the individual adventurer is jointly and severally bound along with his co-adventurers in liability for the debts incurred in pursuance of the adventure.[13] It may therefore be argued that the question of the separate *persona* of the joint adventure is irrelevant in a consideration whether there is such a *concursus debiti et crediti* as to give rise to the plea of compensation. If it be so, the analogy with partnership seems complete. If it be not so, the individual adventurer is still jointly and severally bound in the debt claimed by the third party and *concursus debiti et crediti* exists between the creditor and himself personally. It will be noted, however, that in those circumstances and on that assumption, the plea of compensation becomes one which is personal to the individual adventurer and where the third party sues the adventurers jointly and severally it is doubtful whether the association as such may plead compensation without his consent. In some cases this may hardly emerge as a practical issue. It is difficult to envisage circumstances where an individual adventurer even if he is the only one remaining solvent will find it less advantageous to plead compensation than to submit to a decree for payment against the co-adventurers jointly and severally and sue the third party in a separate action for recovery of his private debt. This aspect of the law of compensation in partnership does not appear to have been before the courts in any reported decision in its relation to the joint adventure and its application in such cases must therefore be regarded as attended with some doubt. The doubt, however, it is submitted does not attach to the right *of the individual adventurer* himself to plead compensation but to the right of his co-adventurers to plead it in respect of his private claim against the creditor without his consent.

The rules in partnership as to the obverse side of the picture, *i.e.* where the individual partner is sued for a private debt, appear to be broadly

[12] Lord Kinloch founded so strongly upon the second ground as to hold that compensation might be pleaded by the firm even where the partner to whom the debt was owed refused his consent to the firm's plea: *Raleigh* v. *Hughson & Dobson* (1861) 23 D. 352, but this was doubted in the Inner House.

[13] *Supra* p. 619.

applicable in the case of a joint adventure, but may depend in some degree for their application to the joint adventure upon the view which is taken as to the *persona* of the joint adventure. If the joint adventure be regarded as a mere aggregation of the *personae* of the individual adventurers it may be difficult to apply the rule under which an individual partner who is sued for a private debt is precluded from pleading in compensation a debt due by the pursuer to his firm since that rule is based upon the theory that in his character as an individual partner he is not a creditor in debts which are due to his firm.[14] The modification of that principle where the firm has been dissolved but is not bankrupt and the individual partner thereupon becomes the creditor in his proportionate share of the debt due to the dissolved firm has already been noticed and it has been suggested that that modified rule will be equally applicable in the joint adventure.[15] In such circumstances the nature of the *persona* of the firm or the joint adventure no longer enters into the consideration of the case. What is now in issue is whether the dissolution of the firm or the termination of the joint adventure has altered the character of the debt originally owed to the association so that it has become partially a debt owed to the *socius* and a transformation of that kind may be as confidently asserted to take place on the termination of the joint adventure as on the dissolution of the partnership.[16] In the other aspect of compensation where a partner sues for a private debt owed to him and is met by a set-off by the defender in respect of a claim against the pursuer's firm, compensation is pleadable in cases of partnership proper, since the partner is a debtor in all debts due by his firm and there is thus *concursus debiti et crediti* between the private debt for which he sues as an individual and the debt set off which, though primarily a debt of his firm, is one for which he and his copartners are jointly and severally liable to the defender.[17] Again, therefore, it appears that the issue whether the joint adventure, like the firm, has a separate *persona* is not a material one, because the real question affecting the *concursus debiti et crediti* is the joint and several liability of the *socii* for the debt of the association which is pleaded in compensation. Indeed the interposition of the *persona* of the firm in cases of partnership proper may serve to restrict the application of the doctrine in such cases. The liability of the partners for the firm debts is a secondary one in the nature of cautionry and in the case where a firm debt is pleaded in set off against a private debt due to an individual partner the firm debt must first be constituted against the firm as a condition of that secondary liability arising. This may not have happened and thus the *concursus debiti et crediti* may not yet have taken place. It is at least worthy of notice that in *Russell* v. *McNab* the debtor firm was bankrupt and both it and its

---

[14] Gloag, *Contract* (2nd ed.) p. 648.

[15] *Supra* p. 626. See also *Heggie* v. *Heggie* (1858) 21 D. 31.

[16] *Supra* p. 626.

[17] *Russell* v. *McNab* (1824) 3 S. 63.

partners had been sequestrated.[18] If it be contended that the joint adventure has no separate *persona* that difficulty is removed and the operation of compensation based on the joint and several liability of the individual adventurer for a debt incurred to his debtor in pursuance of the joint adventure would be unrestricted.

Personal bar as affecting the assertion of rights of a joint adventurer

Since personal bar is an equitable doctrine of general application in contract, it follows that a co-adventurer may be precluded from the vindication of his rights in the joint adventure either through conduct which will raise a plea of personal bar against him in its classic form [19] or in its more specialised applications shown in cases of *e.g.* waiver, acquiescence, or mora and taciturnity. In *Stewart* v. *North* [20] a co-adventurer in a joint adventure to exploit a concession for supplying water to a town in Peru by means of pipes laid from a source of supply in the interior of the country raised an action against his partner in the adventure alleging that the latter had secured for himself and exploited along with a third person a rival scheme for supplying the same town with water from another source carried by means of steamships. The pursuer claimed that he was entitled to an accounting of the profits made by the rival scheme as falling to the joint adventure. It was held that if he had claimed within a reasonable time he would have been entitled to share in the profits of the rival scheme but that his claim could not be allowed because of his delay in asserting it. There is some dubiety as to the precise ground in law on which the claim was disallowed. The defender's plea in law was that any claims competent had been abandoned. The Lord President (Robertson) appears to found his judgment upon mora but appears to treat it as extinguishing the claim.[21] On the other hand, Lord Kinnear clearly decides the issue on the ground of personal bar:

> " I think it clear, upon the grounds which your Lordships have stated, that that lapse of time is an insuperable bar to the present claim. If the pursuer had been in a position to say that Cockburn [the original party to the joint adventure in respect of whom the claim to an accounting was made] was left entirely ignorant or kept in ignorance of the material facts upon which his claim is founded, I could understand that there might have been a different question." [22]

[18] For a fuller discussion of this point see *supra* pp. 565 *et seq.*

[19] " If a man, either by words or by conduct, has intimated that he consents to an act which has been done, and that he will offer no opposition to it, although it could not have been lawfully done without his consent, and he thereby induces others to do that from which they otherwise might have abstained, he cannot question the legality of the act he had so sanctioned to the prejudice of those who have given faith to his words or to the fair inference to be drawn from his conduct "—*Cairncross* v. *Lorimer* (1860) 3 Macq. 827, *per* the Lord Chancellor (Campbell) at p. 829.

[20] (1893) 20 R. 260.

[21] *Ibid.* at p. 269. Lord Adam (p. 271) and Lord McLaren (p. 271) concurred in substance with the Lord President.

[22] *Ibid.* at p. 272.

The property of the joint adventure

" The stock of the concern is common property, and (as in partnership proper) is held in trust for the creditors of the concern." [23] The Lord Ordinary in *Keith* v. *Penn*,[24] a case of a joint adventure in the purchase of heritable property, is reported as saying, ". . . it will not be disputed that if an heritable subject be really made part of the stock of a trading company and be used by them as such, it will be liable to the claims of the company's creditors in preference to those of the mere personal creditors of the individual partners. . . ." Thus in *Livingstone* v. *Allans* [25] a title to lands was taken to two persons as trustees for themselves each to the extent of one-half *pro indiviso*. One of these parties conveyed to an onerous assignee by a disposition in *ex facie* absolute terms his one-half *pro indiviso* share. The heritable subjects were sold; the remaining joint proprietor received his one-half share of the proceeds but he also claimed to retain the other half-share falling to his co-owner in terms of the original title on the grounds that they had been parties to a joint adventure in acquiring the land for speculative building and that his share must be applied in repayment of his indebtedness to the joint adventure. It was held that (1) the title of the disponee under the *ex facie* absolute disposition was qualified by the trust disclosed in his disponer's title, (2) that the purposes of that trust might be proved by parole, (3) that by such evidence the joint adventure was established and the disposition of one-half share *pro indiviso* was effectual only to the extent of the disponer's interest in the joint adventure, *i.e.* to the extent of one-half of the *free* balance on an accounting with the co-adventurer.

The common stock

As in partnership this will consist of capital and goods originally contributed by the parties to the joint adventure and property subsequently purchased by the joint adventure in pursuance of, and used for the purposes of, the joint adventure. The position appears to be indistinguishable from that in a partnership proper and section 20 (1) of the Partnership Act 1890 appears to be applicable in terms to the joint adventure, regarded as a species of partnership.[26] No difference in theoretical approach to the legal problems arising in relation to the common stock of the joint adventure can be discerned in the decisions but the restricted nature of the joint adventure and the fact that it is

---

[23] Bell, *Prin.* § 396.
[24] (1840) 2 D. 633. See also *McCaul's Creditors* v. *Ramsay & Ritchie* (1740) Mor. 14608; *Fergusson* v. *Graham's Trs.* (1836) 14 S. 871; *Buchanan* v. *Lennox* (1838) 16 S. 824;. *Livingstone* v. *Allans* (1900) 3 F. 233.
[25] (1900) 3 F. 233.
[26] " 20. *Partnership property*. (1) All property and rights and interests in property originally brought into the partnership stock or acquired whether by purchase or otherwise, on account of the firm, or for the purposes and in the course of the partnership business, are called in this Act partnership property and must be held and applied by the partners exclusively for the purposes of the partnership and in accordance with the partnership agreement."

often, if not indeed normally, an association of persons who are simultaneously engaged in other business activities, often of a similar nature but dissociated from the joint adventure, tend to complicate the issues as to the property of the joint adventure particularly when it is acquired in the course of the adventure. The practical questions which may arise are illustrated in *Wilson* v. *Threshie* [27] where on a consideration of the whole circumstances of the case the court held that property purchased by the partners in a joint adventure and used for the purposes of the concern was not the property of the joint adventure. The theoretical considerations as modified by what may be termed the practical ones are felicitously considered by Lord Glenlee,[28] who said,

> " I have no sort of doubt that, so far as it extends, a joint adventure has the same legal consequences with a regular partnership; so that if it is once ascertained that anything forms part of the joint adventure stock, the same rules must apply to it. But when the question is, whether a certain heritable property is in fact part of the stock, it makes a considerable difference, whether the concern is of the nature of a joint adventure or a copartnery; because it is not at all likely that parties would purchase heritage to form part of the stock of an adventure which has no current existence. It is a very different case where the property is not for behoof of the joint adventure but is itself the subject of it. . . ."

Proof that property held on behalf of the adventure

Similar questions may arise in a joint adventure as arise in a partnership proper, regarding the admissibility of evidence establishing the conditions on which the property is held. In this respect the principles to be applied are identical in the case of both types of association and the reader is referred to the treatment of the subject in Chapter IX.[29]

Termination of the joint adventure

In the normal case where parties have agreed to embark upon a joint adventure, the association will be at an end once the object of the adventure has been achieved.[30] While that rule is applicable to the traditional case of the joint trading adventure where the parties associate together for the attainment of one strictly limited purpose, cases occur where the association thus inaugurated is continued to achieve a series of trading enterprises. In such cases the association among the adventurers should perhaps rather be considered as a sort of vehicle for a series of separate joint adventures each in itself self-contained, though, admittedly, it is difficult to disentangle the overriding association from the joint adventures carried on under it. But a joint adventure may, although

[27] (1825) 4 S. 361.
[28] *Ibid.* at p. 364.
[29] *Supra* pp. 382–387.
[30] Partnership Act 1890, s. 32 (*b*).

limited in the character of its objectives and having no firm name or local
habitation, approach otherwise closely to the running of a continuous
business either indefinitely [31] or for a limited period of years.[32] It is
probably in that sort of case that the rule that a joint adventure is
terminable at will of the parties has its application.[33] But since the
continued association of a person with a joint adventure, even for a
single enterprise will involve him in joint and several liability with his
co-adventurers until he terminates the association the rule may be applied
even to a single adventure so that an individual adventurer may terminate
his connection with it on giving reasonable notice. In such a case the
purpose must be to free the individual from further liability to third
parties and not from making his original and stipulated contribution to
the adventure, since if he refused to make his agreed contribution he
would clearly be in breach of contract with his co-adventurers, whether
he gave them reasonable notice or not. It is clear, however, that a joint
adventure which is undertaken for a specified purpose and for a specified
period may be terminated by a partner in the joint adventure if the
original purpose has proved unsuccessful and his co-adventurers propose
to use the resources of the joint adventure for an enterprise not in
contemplation when the agreement was originally entered into,[34] or even
where the original enterprise is still carried on but it is established to the
satisfaction of the court that it has proved unprofitable and that there
is no reasonable prospect of profit in the future.[35] In most cases
determination of the question will involve in some degree a necessity to
put a proper construction upon the terms upon which the parties agreed
to embark on the joint adventure and where the joint adventure is itself
extended beyond the scope originally in contemplation, but still along
the natural lines of its development, the decision will entail an assessment
of what the parties might reasonably be held to have had in contemplation
when they embarked upon the adventure. In these cases it seems that
it would clearly be within the right of any of the parties to terminate the
joint adventure at will but where he has not done so, it may still be a
matter of degree whether there is an extension of the adventure for which
he is involved in liability or the subsequent activities are not comprised
within the original adventure. This sort of problem arose for solution
in *Davie* v. *Buchanan* [36] where three parties entered a joint adventure to
purchase a river steamer and employ her on pleasure sailings on the
River Clyde. Three years later a second steamer was purchased for the

---

[31] *Davie* v. *Buchanan* (1880) 8 R. 319.
[32] *Montgomery* v. *Forrester & Co.* (1791) Hume 748.
[33] *Young* v. *Dougans* (1887) 14 R. 490, *per* the Lord Justice-Clerk (Moncreiff) at p. 495:
"... I think that when one man contributed an invention, and another all the expense,
the contract could not endure longer than the pleasure of both parties: either of them
should have the power of determining it."
[34] *Montgomery* v. *Forrester & Co.* (1791) Hume 748.
[35] *Miller* v. *Walker* (1875) 3 R. 242, though there were other features of this case which
may have played their part in the decision. There is, however, a dictum at p. 249 lending
support for the adventurer's right to terminate where the risk is increased.
[36] (1880) 8 R. 319.

same trade.   No question arose at this stage since it was established that she had been purchased on the credit of the joint adventure and for the purpose of its continuing trade.   However, eleven years later, when the position of the parties and their relations one with another had changed, a third steamer was purchased, and the price was raised with the help of a loan secured over the first steamer.   All these transactions had been carried through by one of the partners in the joint adventure and one of his co-adventurers raised an action against him for an accounting and for payment of his share in the adventure.   The court held, so far as the second steamer was concerned, that the presumption that it had been acquired as the property of the joint adventure had not been rebutted but that, in regard to the third, there was not sufficient evidence of either joint ownership or partnership.

The right to an accounting

The words of Lord Justice-Clerk Moncreiff in *Pyper* v. *Christie* [37] where he pointed out that a joint adventure on its termination does not continue as a separate person for purposes of winding up but " is resolved into its elements," have already been considered. [38]   While in a partnership proper also the individual partner has a right to an accounting, [39] the right assumes an even greater significance in the joint adventure where in the absence of an agreed distribution of the proceeds of the adventure upon its termination, the only way in which an individual adventurer may vindicate his right to his share will be by an action of accounting against his co-adventurer or co-adventurers in whose hands the proceeds of the joint adventure are held.

Delectus personae

The joint adventure closely resembles a partnership in the importance which attaches to the personal qualities of those who associate together in a joint adventure.   It would, it is submitted, be impossible to conceive that, in the absence of an express agreement among the joint adventurers to the contrary, any one of the co-adventurers would be entitled to introduce a new party to the adventure without the consent of all the existing co-adventurers.   In the arrangements under which certain joint trading adventures are embarked upon, invitation may be addressed to outside parties to join in the adventure. [40]   Such cases do not, however, militate in any way against the application of *delectus personae* in cases of joint adventure as in cases of proper partnership.   On examination it will be found either (1) that the invitations so addressed are the offer of one party to associate himself with others in the joint adventure or (2) if there are already two or more co-adventurers, that the invitation addressed

[37] (1878) 6 R. 143 at p. 144.
[38] *Supra* pp. 611–613.
[39] Partnership Act 1890, s. 28.
[40] See *e.g. Withers Birch & Co.* v. *Cowan*, Nov. 16, 1790.   This case is not reported but the facts are related at some length in Bell, *Comm.* II, 540–541.

by one of them to further parties has the approval of those who already
are joint adventurers. The provisions of the Partnership Act 1890 [41]
which prohibit the introduction of a new partner into the partnership
unless all existing partners consent are therefore entirely applicable to
the case of a joint adventure.

Assignation of share

A joint adventurer, like a partner, may assign to a third party his
share and interest in the joint adventure, but, as in the case of a partnership, this will not make the assignee a partner in the joint adventure,
though it will entitle him on termination of the adventure to an accounting
and to payment of the share so assigned. [42]

---

[41] s. 24 (7).
[42] Partnership Act 1890, s. 31.   No reported decision as to a joint adventure has been traced
which is directly in point.   *Livingstone* v. *Allans* (1900) 3 F. 233, though concerned primarily with another issue, appears, however, to have been decided upon the basis that
the rule in partnership applies with equal validity to the joint adventure.

APPENDIX

Contents

1. The Partnership Act 1890.

2. The Limited Partnerships Act 1907.

3. The Limited Partnerships Rules 1907.

4. The Companies Act 1948.
   section 429
   section 434

5. The Companies Act 1967.
   Part IV

6. The Partnerships (Unrestricted Size) No. 1
   Regulations 1968
   (S.I. 1968 No. 1222)

7. The Partnerships (Unrestricted Size) No. 2
   Regulations 1970
   (S.I. 1970 No. 835)

8. The Partnerships (Unrestricted Size) No. 3
   Regulations 1970
   (S.I. 1970 No. 992)

9. The Partnerships (Unrestricted Size) No. 4
   Regulations 1970
   (S.I. 1970 No. 1319)

10. The Limited Partnerships (Unrestricted Size)
    No. 1 Regulations 1971
    (S.I. 1971 No. 782)

Partnership Act 1890

(53 & 54 *Vict. c.* 39)

An Act to declare and amend the Law of Partnership

[14th August 1890] [1]

Nature of Partnership

1. *Definition of partnership.*—(1) Partnership is the relation which subsists between persons carrying on a business in common with a view of profit.

(2) But the relation between members of any company or association which is—

(*a*) Registered as a company under the Companies Act 1862, or any other Act of Parliament for the time being in force and relating to the registration of joint stock companies; or

(*b*) Formed or incorporated by or in pursuance of any other Act of Parliament or letters patent, or Royal Charter; or

(*c*) A company engaged in working mines within and subject to the jurisdiction of the Stannaries:

is not a partnership within the meaning of this Act.

2. *Rules for determining existence of partnership.*—In determining whether a partnership does or does not exist, regard shall be had to the following rules:—

(1) Joint tenancy, tenancy in common, joint property, common property, or part ownership does not of itself create a partnership as to anything so held or owned, whether the tenants or owners do or do not share any profits made by the use thereof.

(2) The sharing of gross returns does not of itself create a partnership, whether the persons sharing such returns have or have not a joint or common right or interest in any property from which or from the use of which the returns are derived.

(3) The receipt by a person of a share of the profits of a business is *prima facie* evidence that he is a partner in the business, but the receipt of such a share, or of a payment contingent on or varying with the profits of a business, does not of itself make him a partner in the business; and in particular—

(*a*) The receipt by a person of a debt or other liquidated amount by instalments or otherwise out of the accruing profits of a business does not of itself make him a partner in the business or liable as such:

(*b*) A contract for the remuneration of a servant or agent of a person engaged in a business by a share of the profits of the business does not of itself make the servant or agent a partner in the business or liable as such:

(*c*) A person being the widow or child of a deceased partner, and receiving by way of annuity a portion of the profits made

---

[1] Applied to limited partnerships by 7 Edw. 7, c. 24, s. 7.

in the business in which the deceased person was a partner, is not by reason only of such receipt a partner in the business or liable as such:

(*d*) The advance of money by way of loan to a person engaged or about to engage in any business on a contract with that person that the lender shall receive a rate of interest varying with the profits, or shall receive a share of the profits arising from carrying on the business, does not of itself make the lender a partner with the person or persons carrying on the business or liable as such: Provided that the contract is in writing, and signed by or on behalf of all the parties thereto:

(*e*) A person receiving by way of annuity or otherwise a portion of the profits of a business in consideration of the sale by him of the goodwill of the business is not by reason only of such receipt a partner in the business or liable as such.

3. *Postponement of rights of person lending or selling in consideration of share of profits in case of insolvency.*—In the event of any person to whom money has been advanced by way of loan upon such a contract as is mentioned in the last foregoing section, or of any buyer of a goodwill in consideration of a share of the profits of the business, being adjudged a bankrupt, entering into an arrangement to pay his creditors less than twenty shillings in the pound, or dying in insolvent circumstances, the lender of the loan shall not be entitled to recover anything in respect of his loan, and the seller of the goodwill shall not be entitled to recover anything in respect of the share of profits contracted for, until the claims of the other creditors of the borrower or buyer for valuable consideration in money or money's worth have been satisfied.

4. *Meaning of firm.*—(1) Persons who have entered into partnership with one another are for the purposes of this Act called collectively a firm, and the name under which their business is carried on is called the firm-name.

(2) In Scotland a firm is a legal person distinct from the partners of whom it is composed, but an individual partner may be charged on a decree or diligence directed against the firm, and on payment of the debts is entitled to relief *pro rata* from the firm and its other members.

Relations of Partners to persons dealing with them

5. *Power of partner to bind the firm.*—Every partner is an agent of the firm and his other partners for the purpose of the business of the partnership; and the acts of every partner who does any act for carrying on in the usual way business of the kind carried on by the firm of which he is a member bind the firm and his partners, unless the partner so acting has in fact no authority to act for the firm in the particular matter, and the person with whom he is dealing either knows that he has no authority, or does not know or believe him to be a partner.

6. *Partners bound by acts on behalf of firm.*—An act or instrument relating to the business of the firm and done or executed in the firm-name, or in any other manner showing an intention to bind the firm, by any person thereto authorised, whether a partner or not, is binding on the firm and all the partners.

Provided that this section shall not affect any general rule of law relating to the execution of deeds or negotiable instruments.

7. *Partner using credit of firm for private purposes.*—Where one partner pledges the credit of the firm for a purpose apparently not connected with the firm's ordinary course of business, the firm is not bound, unless he is in fact specially authorised by the other partners; but this section does not affect any personal liability incurred by an individual partner.

8. *Effect of notice that firm will not be bound by acts of partner.*—If it has been agreed between the partners that any restriction shall be placed on the power of any one or more of them to bind the firm, no act done in contravention of the agreement is binding on the firm with respect to persons having notice of the agreement.

9. *Liability of partners.*—Every partner in a firm is liable jointly with the other partners, and in Scotland severally also, for all debts and obligations of the firm incurred while he is a partner; and after his death his estate is also severally liable in due course of administration for such debts and obligations, so far as they remain unsatisfied, but subject in England or Ireland to the prior payment of his separate debts.

10. *Liability of the firm for wrongs.*—Where, by any wrongful act or omission of any partner acting in the ordinary course of the business of the firm, or with the authority of his co-partners, loss or injury is caused to any person not being a partner in the firm, or any penalty is incurred, the firm is liable therefor to the same extent as the partner so acting or omitting to act.

11. *Misapplication of money or property received for or in custody of the firm.*—In the following cases; namely—

(a) Where one partner acting within the scope of his apparent authority receives the money or property of a third person and misapplies it; and

(b) Where a firm in the course of its business receives money or property of a third person, and the money or property so received is misapplied by one or more of the partners while it is in the custody of the firm;

the firm is liable to make good the loss.

12. *Liability for wrongs joint and several.*—Every partner is liable jointly with his co-partners and also severally for everything for which the firm while he is a partner therein becomes liable under either of the two last preceding sections.

13. *Improper employment of trust-property for partnership purposes.*— If a partner, being a trustee, improperly employs trust-property in the business or on the account of the partnership, no other partner is liable for the trust-property to the persons beneficially interested therein: Provided as follows:—

(1) This section shall not affect any liability incurred by any partner by reason of his having notice of a breach of trust; and

(2) Nothing in this section shall prevent trust money from being followed and recovered from the firm if still in its possession or under its control.

14. *Persons liable by " holding out ".*—(1) Every one who by words spoken or written or by conduct represents himself, or who knowingly suffers himself to be represented, as a partner in a particular firm, is liable as a partner to any one who has on the faith of any such representation given credit to the firm, whether the representation has or has not been made or communicated to the person so giving credit by or with the knowledge of the apparent partner making the representation or suffering it to be made.

(2) Provided that where after a partner's death the partnership business is continued in the old firm-name, the continued use of that name or of the deceased partner's name as part thereof shall not of itself make his executors or administrators estate or effects liable for any partnership debts contracted after his death.

15. *Admissions and representations of partners.*—An admission or representation made by any partner concerning the partnership affairs, and in the ordinary course of its business, is evidence against the firm.

16. *Notice to acting partner to be notice to the firm.*—Notice to any partner who habitually acts in the partnership business of any matter relating to partnership affairs operates as notice to the firm, except in the case of a fraud on the firm committed by or with the consent of that partner.

17. *Liabilities of incoming and outgoing partners.*—(1) A person who is admitted as a partner into an existing firm does not thereby become liable to the creditors of the firm for anything done before he became a partner.

(2) A partner who retires from a firm does not thereby cease to be liable for partnership debts or obligations incurred before his retirement.

(3) A retiring partner may be discharged from any existing liabilities, by an agreement to that effect between himself and the members of the firm as newly constituted and the creditors, and this agreement may be either express or inferred as a fact from the course of dealing between the creditors and the firm as newly constituted.

18. *Revocation of continuing guaranty by change in firm.*—A continuing guaranty or cautionary obligation given either to a firm or to a third person in respect of the transactions of a firm is, in the absence of agreement to the contrary, revoked as to future transactions by any change in the constitution of the firm to which, or of the firm in respect of the transactions of which, the guaranty or obligation was given.

Relations of Partners to one another

19. *Variation by consent of terms of partnership.*—The mutual rights and duties of partners, whether ascertained by agreement or defined by this Act, may be varied by the consent of all the partners, and such consent may be either express or inferred from a course of dealing.

20. *Partnership property.*—(1) All property and rights and interests in property originally brought into the partnership stock or acquired, whether by purchase or otherwise, on account of the firm, or for the purposes and in the course of the partnership business, are called in this Act partnership property, and must be held and applied by the partners exclusively for the purposes of the partnership and in accordance with the partnership agreement.

(2) Provided that the legal estate or interest in any land, or in Scotland the title to and interest in any heritable estate, which belongs to the partnership shall devolve according to the nature and tenure thereof, and the general rules of law thereto applicable, but in trust, so far as necessary, for the persons beneficially interested in the land under this section.

(3) Where co-owners of an estate or interest in any land, or in Scotland of any heritable estate, not being itself partnership property, are partners as to profits made by the use of that land or estate, and purchase other land or estate out of the profits to be used in like manner, the land or estate so purchased belongs to them, in the absence of an agreement to the contrary, not as partners, but as co-owners for the same respective estates and interests as are held by them in the land or estate first mentioned at the date of the purchase.

21. *Property bought with partnership money.*—Unless the contrary intention appears, property bought with money belonging to the firm is deemed to have been bought on account of the firm.

22. *Conversion into personal estate of land held as partnership property.* —Where land or any heritable interest therein has become partnership property, it shall, unless the contrary intention appears, be treated as between the partners (including the representatives of a deceased partner), and also as between the heirs of a deceased partner and his executors or administrators, as personal or moveable and not real or heritable estate.

[2] **23.** *Procedure against partnership property for a partner's separate judgment debt.*—(1) . . . A writ of execution shall not issue against any partnership property except on a judgment against the firm.

(2) The High Court, or a judge thereof, or the Chancery Court of the county palatine of Lancaster, or a county court, may, on the application by summons of any judgment creditor of a partner, make an order charging that partner's interest in the partnership property and profits with payment of the amount of the judgment debt and interest thereon, and may by the same or a subsequent order appoint a receiver of that partner's share of profits (whether already declared or accruing), and of any other money which may be coming to him in respect of the partnership, and direct all accounts and inquiries, and give all other orders and directions which might have been directed or given if the charge had been made in favour of the judgment creditor by the partner, or which the circumstances of the case may require.

(3) The other partner or partners shall be at liberty at any time to redeem the interest charged, or in case of a sale being directed, to purchase the same.

(4) This section shall apply in the case of a cost-book company as if the company were a partnership within the meaning of this Act.

(5) This section shall not apply to Scotland.

24. *Rules as to interests and duties of partners subject to special agreement.*—The interests of partners in the partnership property and their rights and duties in relation to the partnership shall be determined, subject to any agreement express or implied between the partners, by the following rules:

    (1) All the partners are entitled to share equally in the capital and profits of the business, and must contribute equally towards the losses whether of capital or otherwise sustained by the firm.

    (2) The firm must indemnify every partner in respect of payments made and personal liabilities incurred by him—

        (*a*) In the ordinary and proper conduct of the business of the firm; or

---

[2] As repealed in part by S.L.R. 1908.

    (*b*) In or about anything necessarily done for the preservation of the business or property of the firm.

(3) A partner making, for the purpose of the partnership, any actual payment or advance beyond the amount of capital which he has agreed to subscribe, is entitled to interest at the rate of five per cent. per annum from the date of the payment or advance.

(4) A partner is not entitled, before the ascertainment of profits, to interest on the capital subscribed by him.

(5) Every partner may take part in the management of the partnership business.

(6) No partner shall be entitled to remuneration for acting in the partnership business.

(7) No person may be introduced as a partner without the consent of all existing partners.

(8) Any difference arising as to ordinary matters connected with the partnership business may be decided by a majority of the partners, but no change may be made in the nature of the partnership business without the consent of all existing partners.

(9) The partnership books are to be kept at the place of business of the partnership (or the principal place, if there is more than one), and every partner may, when he thinks fit, have access to and inspect and copy any of them.

25. *Expulsion of partner.*—No majority of the partners can expel any partner unless a power to do so has been conferred by express agreement between the partners.

26. *Retirement from partnership at will.*—(1) Where no fixed term has been agreed upon for the duration of the partnership, any partner may determine the partnership at any time on giving notice of his intention so to do to all the other partners.

(2) Where the partnership has originally been constituted by deed, a notice in writing, signed by the partner giving it, shall be sufficient for this purpose.

27. *Where partnership for term is continued over, continuance on old terms presumed.*—(1) Where a partnership entered into for a fixed term is continued after the term has expired, and without any express new agreement, the rights and duties of the partners remain the same as they were at the expiration of the term, so far as is consistent with the incidents of a partnership at will.

(2) A continuance of the business by the partners, or such of them as habitually acted therein during the term, without any settlement or liquidation of the partnership affairs, is presumed to be a continuance of the partnership.

28. *Duty of partners to render accounts, etc.*—Partners are bound to render true accounts and full information of all things affecting the partnership to any partner or his legal representatives.

29. *Accountability of partners for private profits.*—(1) Every partner must account to the firm for any benefit derived by him without the consent of the other partners from any transaction concerning the partnership, or from any use by him of the partnership property, name, or business connection.

(2) This section applies also to transactions undertaken after a partnership has been dissolved by the death of a partner, and before the affairs

thereof have been completely wound up, either by any surviving partner or by the representatives of the deceased partner.

30. *Duty of partner not to compete with firm.*—If a partner, without the consent of the other partners, carries on any business of the same nature as and competing with that of the firm, he must account for and pay over to the firm all profits made by him in that business.

31. *Rights of assignee of share in partnership.*—(1) An assignment by any partner of his share in the partnership, either absolute or by way of mortgage or redeemable charge, does not, as against the other partners, entitle the assignee, during the continuance of the partnership, to interfere in the management or administration of the partnership business or affairs, or to require any accounts of the partnership transactions, or to inspect the partnership books, but entitles the assignee only to receive the share of profits to which the assigning partner would otherwise be entitled, and the assignee must accept the account of profits agreed to by the partners.

(2) In case of a dissolution of the partnership, whether as respects all the partners or as respects the assigning partner, the assignee is entitled to receive the share of the partnership assets to which the assigning partner is entitled as between himself and the other partners, and, for the purpose of ascertaining that share, to an account as from the date of the dissolution.

Dissolution of Partnership, and its consequences

32. *Dissolution by expiration or notice.*—Subject to any agreement between the partners, a partnership is dissolved—

(a) If entered into for a fixed term, by the expiration of that term:

(b) If entered into for a single adventure or undertaking, by the termination of that adventure or undertaking:

(c) If entered into for an undefined time, by any partner giving notice to the other or others of his intention to dissolve the partnership.

In the last-mentioned case the partnership is dissolved as from the date mentioned in the notice as the date of dissolution, or, if no date is so mentioned, as from the date of the communication of the notice.

33. *Dissolution by bankruptcy, death, or charge.*—(1) Subject to any agreement between the partners, every partnership is dissolved as regards all the partners by the death or bankruptcy of any partner.

(2) A partnership may, at the option of the other partners, be dissolved if any partner suffers his share of the partnership property to be charged under this Act for his separate debt.

34. *Dissolution by illegality of partnership.*—A partnership is in every case dissolved by the happening of any event which makes it unlawful for the business of the firm to be carried on or for the members of the firm to carry it on in partnership.

35. *Dissolution by the Court.*—On application by a partner the Court may decree a dissolution of the partnership in any of the following cases:

[3] (a) When a partner is found lunatic by inquisition, or in Scotland by cognition, or is shown to the satisfaction of the Court to be of

---

[3] Repealed as regards England and Wales by the Mental Health Act 1959, Sch. 8, I.

permanently unsound mind, in either of which cases the application may be made as well on behalf of that partner by his committee or next friend or person having title to intervene as by any other partner:

(b) When a partner, other than the partner suing, becomes in any other way permanently incapable of performing his part of the partnership contract:

(c) When a partner, other than the partner suing, has been guilty of such conduct as, in the opinion of the Court, regard being had to the nature of the business, is calculated to prejudicially affect the carrying on of the business:

(d) When a partner, other than the partner suing, wilfully or persistently commits a breach of the partnership agreement, or otherwise so conducts himself in matters relating to the partnership business that it is not reasonably practicable for the other partner or partners to carry on the business in partnership with him:

(e) When the business of the partnership can only be carried on at a loss:

[4](f) Whenever in any case circumstances have arisen which, in the opinion of the Court, render it just and equitable that the partnership be dissolved.

36. *Rights of persons dealing with firm against apparent members of firm.* —(1) Where a person deals with a firm after a change in its constitution he is entitled to treat all apparent members of the old firm as still being members of the firm until he has notice of the change.

(2) An advertisement in the *London Gazette* as to a firm whose principal place of business is in England or Wales, in the *Edinburgh Gazette* as to a firm whose principal place of business is in Scotland, and in the *Dublin Gazette* as to a firm whose principal place of business is in Ireland, shall be notice as to persons who had not dealings with the firm before the date of the dissolution or change so advertised.

(3) The estate of a partner who dies, or who becomes bankrupt, or of a partner who, not having been known to the person dealing with the firm to be a partner, retires from the firm, is not liable for partnership debts contracted after the date of the death, bankruptcy, or retirement respectively.

37. *Right of partners to notify dissolution.*—On the dissolution of a partnership or retirement of a partner any partner may publicly notify the same, and may require the other partner or partners to concur for that purpose in all necessary or proper acts, if any, which cannot be done without his or their concurrence.

38. *Continuing authority of partners for purposes of winding up.*—After the dissolution of a partnership the authority of each partner to bind the firm, and the other rights and obligations of the partners, continue notwithstanding the dissolution so far as may be necessary to wind up the affairs of the partnership, and to complete transactions begun but unfinished at the time of the dissolution, but not otherwise.

Provided that the firm is in no case bound by the acts of a partner who has become bankrupt; but this proviso does not affect the liability of any

---

[4] Amendment. See National Health Service (Amendment) Act 1949, s. 7 (4) (N.H.S. medical partnerships).

person who has after the bankruptcy represented himself or knowingly suffered himself to be represented as a partner of the bankrupt.

39. *Rights of partners as to application of partnership property.*—On the dissolution of a partnership every partner is entitled, as against the other partners in the firm, and all persons claiming through them in respect of their interests as partners, to have the property of the partnership applied in payment of the debts and liabilities of the firm, and to have the surplus assets after such payment applied in payment of what may be due to the partners respectively after deducting what may be due from them as partners to the firm; and for that purpose any partner or his representatives may, on the termination of the partnership, apply to the Court to wind up the business and affairs of the firm.

40. *Apportionment of premium where partnership prematurely dissolved.*—Where one partner has paid a premium to another on entering into a partnership for a fixed term, and the partnership is dissolved before the expiration of that term otherwise than by the death of a partner, the Court may order the repayment of the premium, or of such part thereof as it thinks just, having regard to the terms of the partnership contract and to the length of time during which the partnership has continued; unless

(*a*) the dissolution is, in the judgment of the Court, wholly or chiefly due to the misconduct of the partner who paid the premium, or

(*b*) the partnership has been dissolved by an agreement containing no provision for a return of any part of the premium.

41. *Rights where partnership dissolved for fraud or misrepresentation.*—Where a partnership contract is rescinded on the ground of the fraud or misrepresentation of one of the parties thereto, the party entitled to rescind is, without prejudice to any other right, entitled—

(*a*) to a lien on, or right of retention of, the surplus of the partnership assets, after satisfying the partnership liabilities, for any sum of money paid by him for the purchase of a share in the partnership and for any capital contributed by him, and is

(*b*) to stand in the place of the creditors of the firm for any payments made by him in respect of the partnership liabilities, and

(*c*) to be indemnified by the person guilty of the fraud or making the representation against all the debts and liabilities of the firm.

42. *Right of outgoing partner in certain cases to share profits made after dissolution.*—(1) Where any member of a firm has died or otherwise ceased to be a partner, and the surviving or continuing partners carry on the business of the firm with its capital or assets without any final settlement of accounts as between the firm and the outgoing partner or his estate, then, in the absence of any agreement to the contrary, the outgoing partner or his estate is entitled at the option of himself or his representatives to such share of the profits made since the dissolution as the Court may find to be attributable to the use of his share of the partnership assets, or to interest at the rate of five per cent. per annum on the amount of his share of the partnership assets.

(2) Provided that where by the partnership contract an option is given to surviving or continuing partners to purchase the interest of a deceased or outgoing partner, and that option is duly exercised, the estate of the deceased partner, or the outgoing partner or his estate, as the case may be, is not entitled to any further or other share of profits; but if any partner

assuming to act in exercise of the option does not in all material respects comply with the terms thereof, he is liable to account under the foregoing provisions of this section.

43. *Retiring or deceased partner's share to be a debt.*—Subject to any agreement between the partners, the amount due from surviving or continuing partners to an outgoing partner or the representatives of a deceased partner in respect of the outgoing or deceased partner's share is a debt accruing at the date of the dissolution or death.

44. *Rule for distribution of assets on final settlement of accounts.*—In settling accounts between the partners after a dissolution of partnership, the following rules shall, subject to any agreement, be observed:

(*a*) Losses, including losses and deficiencies of capital, shall be paid first out of profits, next out of capital, and lastly, if necessary, by the partners individually in the proportion in which they were entitled to share profits:

(*b*) The assets of the firm including the sums, if any, contributed by the partners to make up losses or deficiencies of capital, shall be applied in the following manner and order:
  1. In paying the debts and liabilities of the firm to persons who are not partners therein:
  2. In paying to each partner rateably what is due from the firm to him for advances as distinguished from capital:
  3. In paying to each partner rateably what is due from the firm to him in respect of capital:
  4. The ultimate residue, if any, shall be divided among the partners in the proportion in which profits are divisible.

Supplemental

45. *Definitions of " court " and " business ".*—In this Act, unless the contrary intention appears,—

The expression " court " includes every court and judge having jurisdiction in the case:
The expression " business " includes every trade, occupation, or profession.

46. *Saving for rules of equity and common law.*—The rules of equity and of common law applicable to partnership shall continue in force except so far as they are inconsistent with the express provisions of this Act.

47. *Provision as to bankruptcy in Scotland.*—(1) In the application of this Act to Scotland the bankruptcy of a firm or of an individual shall mean sequestration under the Bankruptcy (Scotland) Acts, and also in the case of an individual the issue against him of a decree of cessio bonorum.

(2) Nothing in this Act shall alter the rules of the law of Scotland relating to the bankruptcy of a firm or of the individual partners thereof.

48 and **49.** (Repealed by S.L.R. 1908.)

50. *Short title.*—This Act may be cited as the Partnership Act 1890.

GENERAL NOTE—In the Limited Partnerships Act 1907 and the Limited Partnerships Rules 1907 which follow there must be substituted for references in the text to sterling the equivalent in decimal currency as provided in the Decimal Currency Act 1969, section 10 and Schedule 2.

Limited Partnerships Act 1907
(7 *Edw.* 7, *c.* 24)

An Act to establish Limited Partnerships

[28th August, 1907]

1. *Short title.*—This Act may be cited for all purposes as the Limited Partnerships Act 1907.

2. *Commencement of Act.*—This Act shall come into operation on the first day of January, one thousand nine hundred and eight.

3. *Interpretation of terms.*—In the construction of this Act the following words and expressions shall have the meanings respectively assigned to them in this section, unless there be something in the subject or context repugnant to such construction:—

" Firm," " firm name," and " business " have the same meanings as in the Partnership Act 1890.

" General partner" shall mean any partner who is not a limited partner as defined by this Act.

4. *Definition and constitution of limited partnership.*—(1) From and after the commencement of this Act limited partnerships may be formed in the manner and subject to the conditions by this Act provided.

(2) A limited partnership shall not consist, in the case of a partnership carrying on the business of banking, of more than ten persons, and, in the case of any other partnership, of more than twenty persons, [1] and must consist of one or more persons called general partners, who shall be liable for all debts and obligations of the firm, and one or more persons to be called limited partners, who shall at the time of entering into such partnership contribute thereto a sum or sums as capital or property valued at a stated amount, and who shall not be liable for the debts and obligations of the firm beyond the amount so contributed.

(3) A limited partner shall not during the continuance of the partnership, either directly or indirectly, draw out or receive back any part of his contribution, and if he does so draw out or receive back any such part shall be liable for the debts and obligations of the firm up to the amount so drawn out or received back.

(4) A body corporate may be a limited partner.

5. *Registration of limited partnership required.*—Every limited partnership must be registered as such in accordance with the provisions of this Act, or in default thereof it shall be deemed to be a general partnership, and every limited partner shall be deemed to be a general partner.

6. *Modifications of general law in case of limited partnerships.*—(1) A limited partner shall not take part in the management of the partnership business, and shall not have power to bind the firm:

Provided that a limited partner may by himself or his agent at any time inspect the books of the firm and examine into the state and prospects of the partnership business, and may advise with the partners thereon.

---

[1] Now amended. See Companies Act 1967, s. 121; Limited Partnerships (Unrestricted Size) No. 1 Regulations 1971.

If a limited partner takes part in the management of the partnership business he shall be liable for all debts and obligations of the firm incurred while he so takes part in the management as though he were a general partner.

(2) A limited partnership shall not be dissolved by the death or bankruptcy of a limited partner, and the lunacy of a limited partner shall not be a ground for dissolution of the partnership by the court unless the lunatic's share cannot be otherwise ascertained and realised.

(3) In the event of the dissolution of a limited partnership its affairs shall be wound up by the general partners unless the court otherwise orders.

(4) Applications to the court to wind up a limited partnership shall be by petition under the Companies Acts 1862 to 1900, and the provisions of those Acts relating to the winding up of companies by the court and of the rules made thereunder (including provisions as to fees) shall, subject to such modifications (if any) as the Lord Chancellor, with the concurrence of the President of the Board of Trade, may by rules provide, apply to the winding up by the court of limited partnerships, with the substitution of general partners for directors. [2]

(5) Subject to any agreement expressed or implied between the partners—

(a) Any difference arising as to ordinary matters connected with the partnership business may be decided by a majority of the general partners.

(b) A limited partner may, with the consent of the general partners, assign his share in the partnership, and upon such an assignment the assignee shall become a limited partner with all the rights of the assignor.

(c) The other partners shall not be entitled to dissolve the partnership by reason of any limited partner suffering his share to be charged for his separate debt. [3]

(d) A person may be introduced as a partner without the consent of the existing limited partners.

(e) A limited partner shall not be entitled to dissolve the partnership by notice.

7. *Law as to private partnerships to apply where not excluded by this Act.* —Subject to the provisions of this Act, the Partnership Act 1890, and the rules of equity and of common law applicable to partnerships, except so far as they are inconsistent with the express provisions of the last-mentioned Act, shall apply to limited partnerships.

8. *Manner and particulars of registration.*—The registration of a limited partnership shall be effected by sending by post or delivering to the registrar at the register office in that part of the United Kingdom in which the principal place of business of the limited partnership is situated or proposed to be situated a statement signed by the partners containing the following particulars:—

(a) The firm name;
(b) The general nature of the business;
(c) The principal place of business;

---

[2] Repealed, Companies (Consolidation) Act 1908, s. 286 and Sched. 6, Part I. See *supra* pp. 604–606.

[3] This provision is not apt to govern conditions in a Scottish limited partnership. See *supra.* Chap. X, pp. 452–453.

(*d*) The full name of each of the partners;

(*e*) The term, if any, for which the partnership is entered into, and the date of its commencement;

(*f*) A statement that the partnership is limited, and the description of every limited partner as such;

(*g*) The sum contributed by each limited partner and whether paid in cash or how otherwise.

9. *Registration of changes in partnerships.*—(1) If during the continuance of a limited partnership any change is made or occurs in—

(*a*) The firm name,

(*b*) The general nature of the business,

(*c*) The principal place of business,

(*d*) The partners or the name of any partner,

(*e*) The term or character of the partnership,

(*f*) The sum contributed by any limited partner,

(*g*) The liability of any partner by reason of his becoming a limited instead of a general partner or a general instead of a limited partner,

a statement, signed by the firm, specifying the nature of the change shall within seven days be sent by post or delivered to the registrar at the register office in that part of the United Kingdom in which the partnership is registered.

(2) If default is made in compliance with the requirements of this section each of the general partners shall on conviction under the Summary Jurisdiction Acts be liable to a fine not exceeding one pound for each day during which the default continues.

10. *Advertisement in Gazette of statement of general partner becoming a limited partner and of assignment of share of limited partner.*—(1) Notice of any arrangement or transaction under which any person will cease to be a general partner in any firm, and will become a limited partner in that firm, or under which the share of a limited partner in a firm will be assigned to any person, shall be forthwith advertised in the Gazette, and until notice of the arrangement or transaction is so advertised, the arrangement or transaction shall, for the purposes of this Act, be deemed to be of no effect.

(2) For the purposes of this section, the expression " the Gazette " means—

In the case of a limited partnership registered in England, the London Gazette;

In the case of a limited partnership registered in Scotland, the Edinburgh Gazette;

In the case of a limited partnership registered in Ireland, the Dublin Gazette.

11. *Ad valorem stamp duty on contributions by limited partners.*—The statement of the amount contributed by a limited partner, and a statement of any increase in that amount, sent to the registrar for registration under this Act, shall be charged with an ad valorem stamp duty of five shillings [4] for every one hundred pounds, and any fraction of one hundred pounds over any multiple of one hundred pounds, of the amount so contributed, or of the increase of that amount, as the case may be; and, in default of

[4] Now 50p. Finance Act 1920, s. 30 (1): Finance Act 1933, s. 41 (1).

payment of stamp duty thereon as herein required, the duty with interest thereon at the rate of five per cent. per annum from the date of delivery of such statement shall be a joint and several debt to His Majesty, recoverable from the partners, or any of them, in the said statements named, or, in the case of an increase, from all or any of the said partners whose discontinuance in the firm shall not, before the date of delivery of such statement of increase, have been duly notified to the registrar.

12. *Making false returns to be misdemeanor.*—Every one commits a misdemeanor, and shall be liable to imprisonment [with hard labour][5] for a term not exceeding two years, who makes, signs, sends, or delivers for the purpose of registration under this Act any false statement known by him to be false.

13. *Registrar to file statement and issue certificate of registration.*—On receiving any statement made in pursuance of this Act, the registrar shall cause the same to be filed, and he shall send by post to the firm from whom such statement shall have been received a certificate of the registration thereof.

14. *Register and index to be kept.*—At each of the register offices hereinafter referred to the registrar shall keep, in proper books to be provided for the purpose, a register and an index of all the limited partnerships registered as aforesaid, and of all the statements registered in relation to such partnerships.

15. *Registrar of joint stock companies to be registrar under Act.*—The registrar of joint stock companies shall be the registrar of limited partnerships, and the several offices for the registration of joint stock companies in London, Edinburgh, and Dublin shall be the offices for the registration of limited partnerships carrying on business within those parts of the United Kingdom in which they are respectively situated.

16. *Inspection of statements registered.*—(1) Any person may inspect the statements filed by the registrar in the register offices aforesaid, and there shall be paid for such inspection such fees as may be appointed by the Board of Trade,[6] not exceeding one shilling for each inspection; and any person may require a certificate of the registration of any limited partnership, or a copy of or extract from any registered statement, to be certified by the registrar, and there shall be paid for such certificate of registration, certified copy, or extract such fees as the Board of Trade[6] may appoint, not exceeding two shillings for the certificate of registration, and not exceeding sixpence for each folio of seventy-two words, or in Scotland for each sheet of two hundred words.

(2) A certificate of registration, or a copy of or extract from any statement registered under this Act, if duly certified to be a true copy under the hand of the registrar or one of the assistant registrars (whom it shall not be necessary to prove to be the registrar or assistant registrar) shall, in all legal proceedings, civil or criminal, and in all cases whatsoever be received in evidence.

17. *Power to Board of Trade to make rules.*—The Board of Trade[7] may

---

[5] These words are now repealed. See Criminal Justice (Scotland) Act 1949, s. 16 (2).
[6] Now the Department of Trade and Industry.
[7] Now the Department of Trade and Industry.

make rules (but as to fees with the concurrence of the Treasury) concerning any of the following matters:—

(a) The fees to be paid to the registrar under this Act, so that they do not exceed in the case of the original registration of a limited partnership the sum of two pounds, and in any other case the sum of five shillings;

(b) The duties or additional duties to be performed by the registrar for the purposes of this Act;

(c) The performance by assistant registrars and other officers of acts by this Act required to be done by the registrar;

(d) The forms to be used for the purposes of this Act;

(e) Generally the conduct and regulation of registration under this Act and any matters incidental thereto.

The Limited Partnerships Rules 1907
(*December* 17, 1907)
(*S.R. & O.* 1970 *No.* 1020)

1. " The Act " means the Limited Partnerships Act 1907.

2. Whenever any act is by the Act directed to be done to or by the registrar such act shall be done in England to or by the Registrar of Joint Stock Companies or in his absence to or by such person as the Board of Trade[1] may for the time being authorise; in Scotland to or by the existing Registrar of Joint Stock Companies in Scotland; and in Ireland to or by the existing Assistant Registrar of Joint Stock Companies for Ireland or by such person as the Board of Trade[1] may for the time being authorise in Scotland or Ireland in the absence of the registrar; but in the event of the Board of Trade[1] altering the constitution of the existing Joint Stock Companies Registry Office such act shall be done to or by such officer or officers and at such place or places with reference to the local situation of the principal place of business of the limited partnership to be registered as the Board of Trade[1] may appoint.

3. The fees to be paid to the registrar under the Act shall be as follows:—

(a) on the original registration of a limited partnership the sum of two pounds,

(b) on the registration of a statement of any change within the meaning of section 9 (1) of the Act occurring during the continuance of a limited partnership the sum of five shillings,

(c) by any person inspecting the statements filed by the registrar in the register office the sum of one shilling for each inspection,

(d) by any person requiring a certificate of the registration of any limited partnership or a certified copy of or extract from any registered statement the sum of two shillings for each certificate and for such certified copy or extract the sum of sixpence for each folio of seventy-two words or in Scotland for each sheet of two hundred words.

[1] Now the Department of Trade and Industry.

4. The forms in the appendix hereto with such variations as the circumstances of each case may require shall be the forms to be used for the purposes of the Act.

APPENDIX

Forms to be used for the purposes of the Act

No. of Certificate   Form No. L.P. 1.

LIMITED PARTNERSHIPS ACT 1907   [A £2 fee
                                       stamp must
Application for Registration of a   be impressed
Limited Partnership   here.]

We, the undersigned, being the partners of the firm   hereby apply for registration as a limited partnership, and for that purpose supply the following particulars, pursuant to sect. 8 of the Limited Partnerships Act 1907:—

The firm }
name   }

The general }
nature of   }
the business}

The principal }
place of   }
business   }

The term, if any, for)   Term (if any)   years.
which the partnership)   If no definite term,
is entered into, and the} the conditions of
date of its commence-) existence of the part-
ment   ) nership

Date of Commencement

The Partnership is Limited

Presented or forwarded for filing by

Full name and Address of | ²Amount contributed by each
each of the Partners | Limited Partner, and whether
                            | paid in cash, or how otherwise.
General partners |

Limited partners |

Signatures }
of all the }
partners   }
                                              Date

² A separate statement (Form L.P. 3) of the amounts contributed must accompany this application, for the purpose of capital duty, pursuant to s. 11 of the Act. See now the Finance Act, 1933, s. 41 (2), *supra*, p. 648, n. 4.

No. of Certificate						Form No. L.P. 2.

LIMITED PARTNERSHIPS ACT 1907					[A 5s. fee
									stamp must
Notice of change in the Limited				be impressed
Partnership							here.]

(*)————

Notice is hereby given, pursuant to section 9 of the Limited Partnerships Act 1907, that the changes below have occurred in this limited partnership—						[See note at foot of next page.]†

(*a*) Change in the firm name
{ Previous name

New name

(*b*) Change in the general nature of the business
{ General nature of business as previously carried on

General nature of business as now carried on

(*c*) Change in the principal place of business
{ Previous place of business

New place of business

Presented or forwarded for filing by

(*d*) Change in the partners, or the name of any partner

NOTE.—Changes brought about by death, by transfer of interests, by increase in the number of partners, or by change of name of any partner, must be here notified.

(*e*) Change in the term or character of the partnership
{ Previous term (if any), but, if no definite term, then the conditions under which the partnership was constituted

New term (if any), but, if no definite term, then the conditions under which the partnership is now constituted

(*) Here insert name of firm or limited partnership.
(†) So stated on form. For note referred to see p. 653.

(*f*) Change
    in the
    sum con-
    tributed
    by any
    limited
    partner

NOTE.—Any variation in the sum contributed by any limited partner must be here stated. A statement (Form L.P. 4) of any increase in the amount of the partnership capital, whether arising from an increase of contributions, or from introduction of fresh partners, must be made on a separate form, for the purpose of payment of capital duty, pursuant to sect. 11 of the Act.

(*g*) Change
    in the
    liability
    of any
    partner
    by reason
    of his
    becoming
    a limited
    instead of
    a general
    partner, or
    a general
    instead of
    a limited
    partner

Signature of firm

Date

NOTE.—Each change must be entered in the proper division (*a*), (*b*), (*c*) (*d*), (*e*), (*f*), or (*g*), as the case may be.

Provision is made in this form for notifying all the changes required by the Act to be notified, but it will frequently happen that only one item of change, such as change in the principal place of business, for instance, has, to be notified. In any such case the word " nil " should be inserted in the other divisions.

The statement must be signed at the end by the firm, and delivered for registration within seven days of the change or changes taking place.

No. of Certificate   Form No. L.P. 3.

LIMITED PARTNERSHIPS ACT 1907

(*)————

Statement of the Capital contributed by Limited Partners made
pursuant to section 11 of the Limited Partnerships Act 1907

The amounts contributed in cash or otherwise by the limited partners of the firm (†)   are as follows:—

(*) Here insert name of firm or limited partnership.
(†) Here insert name of firm or limited partnership.

Names and Addresses of Limited Partners	Amounts contributed in cash or otherwise. (If otherwise than in cash, that fact, with particulars, must be stated.)

Signature of a general partner

Date

NOTE.—The stamp duty on the nominal capital is five shillings[2] for every £100, or fraction of £100, contributed by each limited partner.

This statement must accompany the application form L.P. 1 for registration of a limited partnership.

Presented or forwarded for registration by

No. of Certificate   Form No. L.P. 4.

LIMITED PARTNERSHIPS ACT 1907

(*)————

Statement of Increase of Capital contributed in cash, or otherwise, by limited partners, pursuant to section 11 of the Limited Partnerships Act 1907

The capital of the limited partnership (†)   has been increased by the addition thereto of sums contributed, in cash or otherwise, by the limited partners, as follows:—

Names of Limited Partners	Increase or additional sum now contributed. (If otherwise than in cash, that fact, with particulars, must be stated.)	Total amount contributed. (If otherwise than in cash, that fact, with particulars, must be stated.)

[2] Now fifty pence. See Finance Act 1933, s. 41 (2).
(*) Here insert name of firm or limited partnership.
(†) Here insert name of firm or limited partnership.

Signature of a general partner

Date

NOTE.—In the case of a new limited partner, the first and third columns only will be used.

The stamp duty on an increase of capital is five shillings [3] for every £100, or fraction of £100, contributed by each limited partner.

This statement is to filed within 7 days of the increase taking place.

Presented or forwarded for registration by

No. of Certificate

CERTIFICATE OF REGISTRATION OF A LIMITED PARTNERSHIP

I hereby certify, that the firm   having lodged a statement of particulars pursuant to section 8 of the Limited Partnerships Act 1907, is this day registered as a limited partnership.

Given under my hand at London this   day of   one thousand nine hundred and

Fee stamps £

Stamp duty on capital £

Registrar of Limited Partnerships.

PURSUANT TO SECTION 10 OF THE LIMITED PARTNERSHIPS ACT 1907

Notice is hereby given that under an arrangement entered into on the   day of   , 19 ,   ceases to be a general partner and becomes a limited partner in the firm of   carrying on business as   at   .

Dated this   day of   , 19 .

Signature

Witness to the signature of   .

(Name)   .

(Address)   .

PURSUANT TO SECTION 10 OF THE LIMITED PARTNERSHIPS ACT 1907

Notice is hereby given that under an arrangement entered into on the   day of   , 19 ,   of the firm of   carrying on business as   at   has assigned his share as a limited partner in the above-named firm to   .

Dated this   day of   , 19 .

Signature

[3] Now £1. See Finance Act 1933, s. 41 (2).

Witness to the signature of   .

      (Name)   .

      (Address)   .

The Companies Act 1948
(11 & 12 *Geo.* 6, *c.* 38)

. . . . .

429. *Prohibition of banking partnerships with more than ten members.*— No company, association, or partnership consisting of more than ten persons shall be formed for the purpose of carrying on the business of banking, unless it is registered as a company under this Act, or is formed in pursuance of some other Act of Parliament, or of letters patent.

. . . . . .

434. *Prohibition of partnerships with more than twenty members.*—(1) No company, association, or partnership consisting of more than twenty persons shall be formed for the purpose of carrying on any business (other than the business of banking) that has for its object the acquisition of gain by the company, association, or partnership, or by the individual members thereof, unless it is registered as a company under this Act, or is formed in pursuance of some other Act of Parliament, or of letters patent, or is a company engaged in working mines within the stannaries and subject to the jurisdiction of the court exercising the stannaries jurisdiction.

(2) This section shall not apply in relation to any body of persons for the time being approved for the purposes of Part I of the War Risks Insurance Act 1939, by the Minister of Transport, being a body the objects of which are or include the carrying on of business by way of the re-insurance of risks which may be re-insured under any agreement for the purpose mentioned in paragraph (b) of subsection (i) of section one of that Act.

The Companies Act 1967
(*c.* 81)

. . . . .

PART IV

PARTNERSHIPS

119. *Exemption from prohibition imposed by section 429 of the Companies Act 1948 of formation of banking partnerships with more than ten members.* Section 429 of the Companies Act 1948 (which prohibits the formation of a company, association or partnership consisting of more than ten persons for the purpose of carrying on the business of banking unless it is registered as a company under the Companies Act 1948, or is formed in pursuance of some other Act, or of letters patent) shall not prohibit the formation of a partnership consisting of not more than twenty persons each of whom is for the time being authorised by the Board of Trade to be a member of a partnership formed for that purpose and consisting of not more than twenty persons.

120. *Exemptions from prohibition imposed by section 434 of the Companies Act* 1948 *of the formation of other partnerships with more than twenty members.*—(1) Section 434 of the Companies Act 1948 (which prohibits the formation of a company, association or partnership consisting of more than twenty persons for the purpose of carrying on a business (other than the business of banking) for gain as therein mentioned unless it is registered as a company under the Companies Act 1948, or is formed in pursuance of some other Act or of letters patent, or is such a company as is therein mentioned working mines within the stannaries) shall not prohibit the formation—

(*a*) for the purpose of carrying on practice as solicitors, of a partnership consisting of persons each of whom is a solicitor;

(*b*) for the purpose of carrying on practice as accountants, of a partnership consisting of persons each of whom falls within either paragraph (*a*) or paragraph (*b*) of section 161 (1) of the Companies Act 1948;

(*c*) for the purpose of carrying on business as members of a recognised stock exchange, of a partnership consisting of persons each of whom is a member of that exchange.

(2) The Board of Trade may by regulations made by statutory instrument provide that the said section 434 shall not apply to the formation (otherwise than as permitted by virtue of the foregoing subsection), for a purpose specified in the regulations, of a partnership of a description so specified.

(3) In this section " recognised stock exchange " means any body of persons which is for the time being a recognised stock exchange for the purposes of the Prevention of Fraud (Investments) Act 1958, and " solicitor," in relation to England and Wales, means solicitor of the Supreme Court, and, in relation to Scotland, means a person enrolled or deemed to have been enrolled as a solicitor in pursuance of the Solicitors (Scotland) Act 1933.

121. *Exemptions from prohibition imposed by section 4 of the Limited Partnerships Act* 1907 *of limited partnerships with more than twenty members.*—(1) So much of section 4 (2) of the Limited Partnerships Act 1907 as provides that a limited partnership (other than a partnership carrying on the business of banking) shall not consist of more than twenty persons shall not apply—

(*a*) to a partnership carrying on practice as solicitors and consisting of persons each of whom is a solicitor;

(*b*) to a partnership carrying on practice as accountants and consisting of persons each of whom falls within either paragraph (*a*) or paragraph (*b*) of section 161 (1) of the Companies Act 1948;

(*c*) to a partnership carrying on business as members of a recognised stock exchange and consisting of persons each of whom is a member of that exchange.

(2) The Board of Trade may by regulations made by statutory instrument provide that so much of section 4 (2) of the said Act of 1907 as provides that a limited partnership (other than a partnership carrying on the business of banking) shall not consist of more than twenty persons shall not apply to a partnership (other than one permitted by virtue of the fore-

going subsection) carrying on business of a description specified in the
regulations, being a partnership of a description so specified.

(3) In this section " recognised stock exchange " and " solicitor " have
the same meanings respectively as in the last foregoing section.

122. *Extent of Part IV.* This Part of this Act shall not extend to
Northern Ireland.

The Partnerships (Unrestricted Size) No. 1 Regulations 1968
(*July* 30, 1968)
(*S.I.* 1968 *No.* 1222)

The Board of Trade in pursuance of the powers conferred upon them
by section 120 (2) of the Companies Act 1967 (c.81) hereby make the
following Regulations:—

1. Section 434 of the Companies Act 1948 (c.38) shall not apply to the
formation—

    (*a*) for the purpose of carrying on practice as patent agents, of a
        partnership consisting of persons each of whom is registered
        as a patent agent in the register of patent agents maintained
        pursuant to the Patents Act 1949 (c.87);

    (*b*) for the purpose of carrying on one or more of the activities men-
        tioned in Part I of the Schedule hereto, of a partnership con-
        sisting of persons not less than three-quarters of the total
        number of whom are members of one or more of the bodies
        mentioned in Part II of that Schedule.

2. These regulations may be cited as the Partnerships (Unrestricted
Size) No. 1 Regulations 1968 and shall come into operation on 7th August
1968.

SCHEDULE

PART I

1. Surveying.
2. Auctioneering.
3. Valuing.
4. Estate Agency.
5. Land Agency.
6. Estate Management.

PART II

1. The Royal Institution of Chartered Surveyors.
2. The Chartered Land Agents' Society.
3. The Chartered Auctioneers' and Estate Agents' Institute.
4. The Incorporated Society of Valuers and Auctioneers.

The Partnerships (Unrestricted Size) No. 2 Regulations 1970
(*May* 28, 1970)
(*S.I.* 1970 *No.* 835)

The Board of Trade in pursuance of the powers conferred upon them by section 120 (2) of the Companies Act 1967 (c.81) hereby make the following Regulations:—

1. These Regulations may be cited as the Partnerships (Unrestricted Size) No. 2 Regulations 1970.

2. Section 434 of the Companies Act 1948 (c.38) shall not apply to the formation for the purpose of carrying on practice as actuaries of a partnership consisting of persons each of whom is either a Fellow of the Institute of Actuaries or a Fellow of the Faculty of Actuaries.

The Partnerships (Unrestricted Size) No. 3 Regulations 1970
(*July* 1, 1970)
(*S.I.* 1970 *No.* 992)

The Board of Trade in pursuance of the powers conferred upon them by section 120 (2) of the Companies Act 1967 (c.81) hereby make the following Regulations:—

1. These Regulations may be cited as the Partnerships (Unrestricted Size) No. 3 Regulations 1970.

2. Section 434 of the Companies Act 1948 (c.38) shall not apply to the formation for the purpose of carrying on practice as consulting engineers of a partnership consisting of persons the majority of whom are recognised by the Council of Engineering Institutions as Chartered Engineers.

The Partnerships (Unrestricted Size) No. 4 Regulations 1970
(*September* 4, 1970)
(*S.I.* 1970 *No.* 1319)

The Board of Trade in pursuance of the powers conferred upon them by section 120 (2) of the Companies Act 1967 (c.81) hereby make the following Regulations:—

1. These Regulations may be cited as the Partnerships (Unrestricted Size) No. 4 Regulations 1970.

2. Section 434 of the Companies Act 1948 (c.38) shall not apply to the formation for the purpose of carrying on practice as building designers of a partnership consisting of persons not less than three-quarters of whom are persons each of whom is either registered under the Architects (Registration) Act 1931 (c.33) or is recognised by the Council of Engineering Institutions as a Chartered Engineer or by the Royal Institution of Chartered Surveyors as a Chartered Surveyor.

The Limited Partnerships (Unrestricted Size) No. 1 Regulations 1971
(*May* 11, 1971)
(*S.I.* 1971 *No*. 782)

The Secretary of State, in exercise of his powers under section 121 (2) of the Companies Act 1967 (c.81), hereby orders as follows:—

1. These Regulations may be cited as the Limited Partnerships (Unrestricted Size) No. 1 Regulations 1971.

2. So much of section 4 (2) of the Limited Partnerships Act 1907 (c. 24) as provides that a limited partnership (other than a partnership carrying on the business of banking) shall not consist of more than twenty persons shall not apply to a limited partnership carrying on one or more of the activities mentioned in Part I of the Schedule hereto and consisting of persons not less than three-quarters of the total number of whom are members of one of the bodies mentioned in Part II of that Schedule and not more than one-quarter of the total number of whom are limited partners within the meaning of section 4 of the Limited Partnerships Act 1907

SCHEDULE

PART I

1. Surveying.
2. Auctioneering.
3. Valuing.
4. Estate Agency.
5. Land Agency.
6. Estate Management.

PART II

1. The Royal Institution of Chartered Surveyors.
2. The Incorporated Society of Valuers and Auctioneers.

INDEX

ACCOUNT CURRENT, 285

ACCOUNTANTS,
limited partnership of, unrestricted as to number, 657
partnership of, unrestricted as to number, 657
unrestricted number of partners in firm of, 13

ACCOUNTING,
assignee of partner's share, right of, 201–202
joint adventurer's right to, 633
partner's breach of fiduciary duty, liability of firm for, 367
partner's right to, 164 et seq., 193, 198–199, 611
secret profits, for, 165–180, 191–193
settlement of accounts among partners, 404–406, 527–537
See also SETTLING ACCOUNTS BETWEEN PARTNERS.

ACCOUNTS,
book values, 528
conclusive as to partner's share, 537
error—
in docqueted accounts, 537
manifest, 538
errores calculi, 538
false, agreements based on, 552
joint adventure, in, 633
partner's duty to render, 641
settling of, after dissolution, 527
written down value, 528–529
See also SETTLING ACCOUNTS BETWEEN PARTNERS.

ACTUARIES,
partnerships of, unrestricted in size, 659

ADMISSIONS,
made by partner, evidence against firm, 217, 639

ADVANCES,
distinguished from capital, 404
firm, to, 404–405
treatment of, on dissolution, 405

ADVERTISEMENT,
bankruptcy, 508, 643
change in firm, 145, 500, 643
death, 507, 643
dissolution, 288, 290, 500, 643
firm freed from liability for acts of former partner by, 292
limited partnerships—
assignment of limited partner's share, 595–596, 648
general partner, becoming limited partner,, 594–595, 648
notice by, 300

ADVERTISEMENT—cont.
partner's right to notify by, 288, 508, 643
retirement, 145, 508, 643

ADVOCATES,
partnership between, prohibited, 2

AGENCY,
agent using confidential information for own benefit, 172–173
delict, vicarious liability in, 302
fraud of agent, 317–318
mutual, among partners, 158
negative criterion of existence of partnership, 55–56
notice of revocation of authority, 287–288
notice to agent imputed to principal, 218–220
See also AGENCY OF NECESSITY, NEGOTIORUM GESTIO.

AGENCY OF NECESSITY, 214

AGENT. See PROFITS, PARTICIPATION IN.

AGREEMENT,
accounts—
conclusive as to partner's share, 537
method of settling, 527
arbitration clause, 480
based on false accounts, 552
continuation of business, provision for, 510
"fair share of work," partner incapable of performing, 463
"flagrant breach of duties," provision for dissolution on, 465
not to continue business in competition, 420
implied from dissolution agreement etc., 422
partnership, providing for right to assign share, 417
provisions as to valuation of goodwill, 432
share—
agreement for settling, construction of, 528
sale of, right of, 510
terms implied in absence of special, 640–641
to take unequal shares not displaced by retirement of some of the original partners, 402
variation of partnership, 287, 378, 414, 639

ALIENS,
alien ami, 46
alien enemy, 47

ALIENS—*cont.*
  effect on contracts of outbreak of war, 49
  executory contracts, 49
  position at common law, 48
  position under emergency legislation, 48
  trading with enemy, 47

ANNUITY,
  widow or child of deceased partner, to 85–86, 636–637

APPARENT PARTNER, 288, 500, 643
  contrasted with stranger held out as partner, 290–292
  dormant, 503
  effect of Registration of Business Names Act 1916...297
  holding out, 146
  liability of, 500–501
  meaning, 501
  notice, effect of, 505–507

APPOINTMENTS,
  held by partner, treatment of profits of, 166

APPROPRIATION OF PAYMENTS. *See* CLAYTON'S CASE, RULE IN.

ARRESTMENT,
  of partner's share in hands of firm, 395 *et seq.*

ARBITRATION,
  arbiter, power of, to award dissolution under s. 35...480–482
  construction of arbitration clause, 481
  fraud, questions of, involved in submission, 482
  just and equitable ground of dissolution, 483–484
  winding up, effect on, 523–524

ASSIGNATION,
  assignee accepted by other partners as copartner, 418
  delectus personae 414
  position of assignee on dissolution of partnership, 413
  position of assignee while partnership in operation, 412
  rights of assignee, 642
    against other partners, 415
    on winding up, 525
  socius mei socii non est socius meus, 412
  transfer of *jus crediti*, 412

ASSIGNATION OF PARTNER'S SHARE, 201–204, 411–417, 642
  agreement, effect of, on, 414, 417
  limited partner, 595, 647, 648

ASSOCIATION,
  formed for the purpose of carrying on business for acquisition of gain, 6

AUCTIONEERS,
  limited partnership of, conditions on which unrestricted in size, 660

AUCTIONEERS—*cont.*
  partnerships of, unrestricted in size where not less than three-quarters of partners members of approved bodies, 658

AUTHOR AND PUBLISHER, 72

AUTHORITY OF PARTNER, 637
  actual, 158, 209
  admissions and representations made by, 217
  agent for the firm, as, 208
  apparent, 158, 209
    appeal to, to establish implied authority, 210
    effect of exceeding, 236
    extent of, 241–243
    representations by partner as to, 252
    third party put on inquiry as to, 248
    warranty, in case of, 240
  associate his copartners in another business, to, 212
  "business of the firm," for the purpose of, 208
  emergency, in case of, 214
  execute written contracts on behalf of firm, to, 221
  execute written obligations on behalf of firm, to, 222–225
  generally, 212
  implied, 209
  inducement to another to become partner, 254
  limits of, 158, 235
  non-trading firm, 212
  ostensible, 158
  restrictions on, in partnership agreement, 209
  revocation of, during subsistence of partnership, 287
  trading firm, 210–212
  transactions with partner as individual, 244

BANKERS, 111

BANKING,
  restriction of number of partners in firm, 13, 656

BANKRUPTCY,
  acquirenda, 43
  capacity to enter partnership, as affecting bankrupt, 42
  occurring during subsistence of partnership, 41–42
  of firm,
    application for sequestration, 555
      authority to apply on behalf of firm, 556
    by creditor, 559
    competing jurisdictions, 559, 572
    discharge, 555
    joint adventure, whether included, 579
    "living debtor," 558
    means sequestration, 645

BANKRUPTCY—*cont.*
of firm—*cont.*
   notour bankruptcy, 559–560
   petitioning creditor, 561
   postponement of claim of lender in, 93–96, 637
   postponement of claim of seller of goodwill in, 93–96, 637
   " proper creditor of the partnership," 561
   reasons for, while partners solvent, 554–555
of firm and insolvent partners—
   solvent partner, claims against, 570
of firm and partners, 565–566
   discharge, 568
   double ranking, 579–582
   identity of firm for purposes of sequestration, 566
   ranking—
      of claims, 576
      on firm's estate, 565
      on partners' estates, 565
   separate firms with partners in common, 566–568
   valuation of claims—
      for ranking, 578
      for voting, 577
of firm or of its partners, rules as to summarised, 448–449
of partner, 562–565
   date of dissolution, 451
   dissolution of firm upon, 294, 444, 446, 642
   effect of foreign bankruptcy proceedings, 450
   extent of interest claimable for his creditors, 563
   firm, position of, in questions with partner's creditors, 562
   means sequestration, 294, 447, 645
   no continuing authority to act in winding up, 519
   partner as creditor of firm, 564
   partner as debtor to firm, 564
   provisions of partnership agreement as to, 447
   set off, 564
Scots law as to, unaltered by Partnership Act 1890...447–448, 645
sequestrated firm a partner in another partnership, 571
trust deed for creditors, 572
See also COMPOSITION, GRATUITOUS ALIENATIONS, ILLEGAL PREFERENCES, INSOLVENCY OF PARTNER.

BARRISTERS,
partnership between, prohibited, 2

BILLS OF EXCHANGE,
acceptance by firm met by one of partners, 197
acceptance in unqualified terms by partner, 197
acceptor of bill drawn by firm claiming no value received, 225
adhibiting of firm's name to, 227, 244–245

BILLS OF EXCHANGE—*cont.*
authority of partner to deal with firm's bills, 209, 210, 211, 212
benefit of transaction accruing to firm, 256
bills belonging to firm—
   discount of, 563
   retirement of, by partner from own funds, 563
bona fide holder for value of, 252
constitute debt against firm, 161
deceased partner signing firm name on blank bills later used, 293–294
firm, liability of, on, 244–245
firm name, consisting of name of one of partners, on, 248
firm's bill—
   given by new firm for debt of former firm, 271–272
   substituted for former obligation by persons proposing to form partnership, 259–260
incidental advantage gained by firm in regard to, 227–228
joint adventure, accommodation bills, 615
retired partner, liability for acceptance in firm name, 291
winding up, transactions in course of, relating to, 513–515
See also PROMISSORY NOTE.

BOARD OF TRADE. See DEPARTMENT OF TRADE AND INDUSTRY.

BOOKMAKERS, 108
illegal partnership of, 111

BOOKS,
of partnership to be kept at its place of business, 641

BORROWING,
authority of partner to borrow—
   for trading firm, 211, 212
   for non-trading firm, 211, 212
   in emergency, 214–217
without authority but applied in paying firm debts, 256–257

BOVILL'S ACT, 61

BREACH OF TRUST. See TRUST, BREACH OF.

BRIBERY,
firm's right—
   to damages, 167
   to recover bribe from partner, 167
   to rescind contract, 167
property received as bribe, assessment of value, 168

BUSINESS,
" carrying on a business," 2
includes trade, occupation or profession, 2, 645
need not be of continuing nature, 3
number of persons engaged in management of, 4

BUSINESS OF THE FIRM,
actual authority of partner, 209
apparent authority of partner, 209

BUSINESS OF THE FIRM—*cont.*
  authority of partner—
    to associate copartners in another
      business, 212
    to carry on, 209
  implied authority of partner, 209

BUILDING DESIGNERS,
  partnerships of, unrestricted in size
    when not lesss than three-quarters
    of partners recognised by approved
    bodies, 659

CAPACITY TO ENTER PARTNERSHIP,
  aliens, 46–50
  bankrupts, 41–43
  corporations, 44
  firms, 45–46
  insanity, 38–39
  intoxication, 40–41
  married women, 43–44
  minors, 29–38
  pupil children, 24–29

CAPITAL,
  advances beyond amount of capital
    contribution, 641
  contribution to, unequal, 531
  deficiencies of—
    making up, 536
    on winding up, 527–531
  input capital as element in deter-
    mination of shares of partners, 401
  interest on, 641
  levelling down of contributions to,
    on winding up, 533
  losses of, partner's contribution to,
    400, 640
  of deceased etc. partner—
    alternative claim for interest on,
      542
    attribution of profit to share of
      partner, 541
    attribution of profit to skill of
      continuing partners, 541
    choice of remedy, 543
    continuing to be used, 540
    option to purchase interest of, 546
  of partner—
    share a debt accruing at date of
      dissolution, 645
    share of—
      continuing to be used in busi-
      ness, 644
      option to purchase, 644
  not same as property or assets of
    partnership, 404
  treatment of capital contribution
    where presumption of equality
    applies, 404

CAUTIONARY OBLIGATIONS,
  appropriation of payments under
    guarantee of firm transactions, 283
  Clayton's case, rule in, 283
  effect of change on incorporation of
    firm, 282–283
  in respect of debt of firm, 281
  right to combine accounts, 284
  See also CLAYTON'S CASE, RULE IN.

CESSIO BONORUM, 447

CHANGE IN FIRM,
  compared with dissolution, 451
  revocation of continuing guarantees,
    639

CHANGE IN PARTNERSHIP,
  notice of, 505–509

CHARGE,
  against partnership property for
    individual partner's debt, 394, 640
  share of partner for his separate
    debt, 452, 642
  writ of execution against partnership
    property available in England only
    for firm debt, 394

CHARTERED ENGINEERS,
  partnerships of, unrestricted in size
    where majority of partners are
    recognised by Council of, 659

CHEQUES,
  descriptive firm name, signature of
    cheques, 223–224

CHILD OF DECEASED PARTNER,
  annuity to, 85, 636–637

CLAYTON'S CASE, RULE IN, 272, 283
  rebutted by intention of parties, 285
  right to combine accounts, 284

CLUBS,
  basis of liability of members, 5
  not partnerships, 5

COMMON PARTNERS,
  firms having, 566–568

COMMON PROPERTY,
  and part ownership distinguished,
    65–66
  as evidence of partnership, 65

COMMUNITY OF PROFIT AND LOSS,
  as evidencing partnership, 55

COMPANIES, 14
  See also JOINT STOCK COMPANY,
    QUASI-PARTNERSHIP.

COMPENSATION OF CLAIMS. *See* DEBTS,
  set off.

COMPOSITION,
  extra-judicial composition contract,
    572
  firm's sequestration, offer in, 568

CONTRACTS,
  execution of written contract on
    behalf of firm, 220–229

CONTRIBUTION,
  business connection, of, 401
  captial, of, 401
  failing agreement, contribution of
    partners to losses equal, 400
  losses of firm, to, 405
  losses, of partners to, 400
  property, of, 401
  services, of, 401
  skill, of, 401

CONVICTION AS GROUND OF EXPUL-
  SION, 182, 193

Co-Ownership,
  criterion of partnership in property jointly owned, 65–66
  distinction maintained between partnership in property and partnership in profits thereof, 66–69
  heritable estate used by partnership, in, 388
  mines, of, 69
  partnership in the profits of property jointly owned, 67
  property not used in business, 67
  property used in business, 67
  See also Estate Duty.

Corporate Body,
  as partner,
    dissolution of, equivalent to death of individual partner? 446
  may be limited partner, 646

Corporation,
  distinguished from firm, 14–16
  may be partner in firm, 44
  power to enter partnership should be contained in objects clause, 45
  unlimited liability in partnership, yet limited liability within corporation, 45
  where partner of firm, applicability of certain provisions of Partnership Act 1890...44

Costbook Companies, 14, 395, 636

Covenants. See Restrictive Covenant, Restrictive Covenants in Partnership Agreement.

Culpa Tenet Suos Auctores, 308

Customers of Firm,
  retired partner, holding out of, to, 146, 147
  right of, to notice of change in firm, 145, 500–503, 643

Death Duty,
  effect of, on partnership property, 389

Death of Partner,
  agreement as to continuance of firm in event of, 444
  dissolution on, 444
    date of, 451

Debts,
  admission of, by partner, 217
  appropriation of payments, 272, 283
  authority of partner as to, 236–238
  delegation, 149–150
  due by partner to firm, 407–408
  firm debts—
    agreement to take over, 269
    compromise of, 210
    discharge of, 276
    liability of incoming partner for
      See Incoming Partner
    liability of partner for, 160, 638
  guarantees, 227, 280–283
  incurred in ordinary course of business, 575–576

Debts—cont.
  limited partnership, 586–587, 646, 647
    See also Limited Partners, Limited Partnership.
  novation, 149–150
  retiring partner, liability of, 500–508, 639, 643
  set off, 564–565, 625–629
    See also Admissions, Authority of Partner, Clayton's Case, Rule in, Holding Out, Receipts.

Deceased Partner,
  annuity to widow or child of, 85, 636–637
  firm name—
    continuing of partner's name in, 639
    use of, when his name forms part of, 427, 639
  See also Accounts, Capital, Winding Up.

Decimal Currency Act 1969,
  equivalents of sterling in decimal currency, 645

Defamation,
  direct liability of partner acting maliciously, 309
  malice on part of some of partners, 309
  qualified privilege, 309

Delectus Personae, 16, 204, 413, 415, 641
  agreement, effect of, on—
    assignee, introduction of, 17
    new partner, introduction of, 18
    trustees of deceased partner, 19–23
  assignation of partner's share, effect of, 17
  construction of clauses in partnership agreement excluding, 23
  dissolution, effect of, on contracts involving, 497
  implication of, yields to agreement express or implied, 17
  legal effect of, examined, 21–22
  no particular mode or time for consent displacing, 18
  views of institutional writers, 17

Delegation,
  of liability of firm, 276
    outgoing partner, 275
  on change in composition of firm, 148–150

Delict,
  liability of firm in, 302 et seq., 638
  liability of partners inter se in, 206

Dentist,
  entering partnership with unqualified person, 110

Department of Trade and Industry,
  orders respecting partnerships of unrestricted size, 13, 656–657, 658–660

Disclosure, Duty of,
  partners', 161–164

DISSOLUTION,
accounts, settling of, 527
agreement for, rescinding of, 551
arbitration clause, effect of, 480
assignation intimated to copartners
no longer operates as dissolution,
478–480
bankruptcy of partner, 444, 446, 642
provisions of partnership agreement, 447
compared with change in composition, 451
consent, by, 435
date of, when arising on—
bankruptcy, 451
death, 451
insanity, 459
death of partner, 444, 642
distinguished from expulsion, 489
expiry of—
contractual term, 436
notice, 438–444, 642
fraud or misrepresentation, on, 547
rights of partner, 547–552, 644
illegality of partnership business,
453–455, 642
notice, by, 438
notice of, effect of, 505
notice, terms of, 438–439
order of the court, by, 455, 642–643
business can only be carried on at
a loss, 470
date of dissolution, 473
conduct destroying mutual confidence, 466
bad temper, 467
embezzlement, 468
extravagance, 468
habitual hostility, 469
quarrels, 469
conduct prejudicially affecting,
" calculated to prejudicially
affect," 465
carrying on of the business, 464
censure of governing body of
profession, 464–465
flagrant breach of duties, 465
gambling transactions, 464
intemperance, 466
negligent disregard of duties, 464
suicide, 464
violence, 466
date of, when notice served prior
to application, 478
incapable of performing partnership contract, 461
" fair share of the work," 463
partner may not plead own incapacity, 462
insanity of partner, 457
expenses of application, 461
See also INSANITY OF PARTNER.
" just and equitable," 473
abuse of powers, 476
date of dissolution, 478
deadlock, 476

DISSOLUTION—cont.
order of the court, by—cont.
" just and equitable "—cont.
impairment of confidence, 476
not construed ejusdem generis,
473–474
"... that partnership be dissolved," 473–474
persistent breach of partnership
agreement, 466
procedure, 455
partner's right to notify, 643
partner's share charged for his separate debt, 452
premature, return of portion of
premium, 644
treatment of goodwill, 421
See also APPARENT PARTNER, ARBI-
TRATION, CHANGE IN PARTNERSHIP,
DISSOLUTION, EFFECTS OF, NOTICE.

DISSOLUTION, EFFECTS OF,
contracts—
generally, 494–499
involving delectus personae, 497
dormant partner, on, 503
new contracts, 498
option to purchase share of deceased
etc. partner, 644
share of deceased etc. partner—
a debt accruing at date of dissolution, 645
continuing to be used in business,
540, 644
third parties, on, 499

DISSOLUTION OF FIRM,
liability of partner on, 288

DISTINCT TRADES,
firm carrying on, with same partners,
566–568

DORMANT PARTNER,
basis of liability, 213
carrying on business, 4
liability of, on dissolution, 503
position of, in regard to loan to
firm, 90
retiral of, 151

DOUBLE RANKING, 579–582
See also BANKRUPTCY.

DURATION OF LIABILITY. See INCOM-
ING PARTNER, OUTGOING PARTNER.

DURATION OF PARTNERSHIP,
expiration of fixed term of, 436

DUTIES OF PARTNERS. See FIDUCIARY
DUTY, UBERRIMA FIDES.

EDINBURGH GAZETTE. See LIMITED
PARTNERSHIP, NOTICE.

ELECTION,
between former firm and continuing
firm, 146–148

EMBEZZLEMENT,
liability of firm for—
embezzlement by partner, 339–351,
638

EMBEZZLEMENT—*cont.*
  liability of firm for—*cont.*
    misapplication by partner of—
      property in hands of firm, 339–345, 638
      property received for firm, 345–351, 638
      trust funds in his charge, 358–363, 638
    Solicitors' Accounts Rules, effect of, upon firm's liability, 363–366
    See also FOLLOWING THE TRUST MONEY, SOLICITORS' ACCOUNTS RULES, TRUST, BREACH OF.

EQUALITY OF SHARE AND CONTRIBUTION,
  meaning of, 404 *et seq.*

EMPTIO REI FACTA A PLURIBUS EMENTIBUS,
  not partnership, 6

ESTATE AGENTS,
  limited partnership of, conditions in which unrestricted in size, 660
  partnership of, unrestricted in size where not less than three-quarters of partners are members of approved bodies, 658

ESTATE DUTY,
  heritable estate jointly owned, 389
  partnership property, 389

ESTATE MANAGERS,
  limited partnership of, conditions in which unrestricted in size, 660
  partnership of, unrestricted in size where not less than three-quarters of partners are members of approved bodies, 658

ESTATE OF DECEASED PARTNER. *See* DEATH OF PARTNER, DECEASED PARTNER.

ESTOPPEL. *See* PERSONAL BAR, REI INTERVENTUS.

EVIDENCE OF CONSTITUTION OF PARTNERSHIP,
  actual conditions of partnership, 51
  conduct of partners, 53
  existence of partnership, fact of, 51
  facts and circumstances, 53, 54
  formal deed, 51
  heads of agreement, 51
  letters, 51
  mutual agency, 55–56
  parole or circumstantial proof, 52 *et seq.*
  question of mixed fact and law, 54
  statutory definition of partnership, effect of, 55
  statutory rules, effect of, 53
  written evidence, 51

EVIDENCE OF EXISTENCE OF PARTNERSHIP,
  agent remunerated by share of profits, 83–85, 636
  annuity to widow or child of deceased partner, 85–86, 636–637

EVIDENCE OF EXISTENCE OF PARTNERSHIP—*cont.*
  business managed within a family, 56–60
  common property, 65–70, 636
  debt repayable out of profits, 82–83, 636
  express declaration by parties, 59–60
  express denial of partnership, effect of, 59–60
  gross returns, 70–77, 636
  loan repayable by share of profits, 87–92, 637
  participation in profits, 77–82, 636
    in consideration of sale of goodwill, 92–93, 637
  servant remunerated by share of profits, 83–85, 636
  statements by alleged partners, 56
  statutory rules in Partnership Act 1890...63–65, 636–637
  witness's belief that parties are acting as partners, 56
  See also CO-OWNERSHIP, GROSS RETURNS, SHARING OF, PROFITS, PARTICIPATION IN.

EXECUTOR OF DECEASED PARTNER,
  duty owed where also a partner of firm, 190

EXPULSION, 641
  distinguished from—
    dissolution, 489
    power to dissolve partnership, 485
  duty to act fairly and honestly, 188
  expulsion clause after expiry of stipulated term, effect of, 492
  good faith in exercise of power of. 490
  notice of, 487
  oblique motive, 486
  power of,
    abuse of, 486
    must be expressly conferred, 484, 641
    used for oblique motive, 188, 486
  proceedings similar in effect to, 491
  right to be heard. 487
  right to have notice of complaint, 487
  wrongful, 492

FIDUCIARY DUTY,
  breach of, with knowledge of co-partners, 323
  resting on partner personally and not on firm, 324

FIRM,
  accessory liability of partners for, 15–16
  incorporation of, as affecting cautionary obligation. 282–283
  knowledge of, 232
  knowledge of partner who habitually acts in partnership business, 234
  liability of, under contracts in writing, 224–225
  may be partner with other persons in separate venture, 45–46

FIRM—*cont.*
meaning of, 637
persona of, distinct from partners, 1, 15

FIRM NAME,
continued use of, after death of partner, 427
execution of deeds in, 221
execution of deeds in descriptive name, 221
use of, 425

FOLLOWING THE TRUST MONEY, 370–375
extent of right, 371
nature of right, 373–375
recovery from firm, 370
right to profits earned by trust funds, 372

FOREIGN BANKRUPTCY,
competing jurisdiction in, 572

FOREIGN FIRM,
effect of partners, or some of them, becoming enemy aliens, 48 *et seq.*

FOREIGN PARTNER,
in firm situated in—
enemy country, 49 *et seq.*
neutral country, 48
Scotland, 48

FRAUD,
committed with knowledge of co-partners, 323
constructive fraud, 319
liability of principal for agent's, 318
nature of, 319
no profit by, 330–332
of partner, imputed to firm, 321
personal nature of, 321–322
effect of vicarious liability, 332–333

FRAUDULENT PREFERENCES,
by firm, 574–576

GAMING AND WAGERING,
joint adventure in, 621–623
partnership engaged in, 107–108

GAZETTE, NOTICE IN. *See* NOTICE.

GOOD FAITH. *See* DISCLOSURE, DUTY OF, FIDUCIARY DUTY, UBERRIMA FIDES.

GOODWILL,
agreement not to continue in same business, 421
as partnership property, 423–425
attaching to business premises, 425
businesses which possess, 424
dissolution of partnership, on, 421–423
nature of, 419
payment for, by share of profits, 86, 92–93, 637
provisions as to valuation of, 432
right of sale of, 423
unsaleable, 424
use of firm name, 425

GOODWILL—*cont.*
valuation of, 433
agreed valuation of, 424, 432–433

GOODWILL, SALE OF,
as affecting continuance in business, 420
in consideration of share of profits, 92, 637
partly in consideration thereof, 95
postponement of rights on insolvency of firm, 93–96, 637

GRATUITOUS ALIENATIONS,
by firm, 573

GROSS RETURNS,
net profits distinguished, 70

GROSS RETURNS, SHARING OF,
associated with holding of common property, 71
by itself inconclusive of partnership, 72, 636
"half commission" agreements, 75
other factors which taken along with, may imply partnership, 77
share fishing, 76
theatre lettings, 74
whaling voyages, 76
See also ROYALTIES ON BOOK SALES.

GUARANTEES,
changes in firm as affecting continuing guarantees, 280
revocation of continuing, by change in firm, 639
See also CAUTIONARY OBLIGATIONS.

HALF-COMMISSION, AGREEMENTS FOR, 75–76

HIGHWAYMEN, PARTNERSHIP OF, 97–98

HOLDING OUT, 127–157, 638–639
active holding out by party, 136
apparent partner, 146
aspect of personal bar, as an, 130–131
cases where facts suggest either partnership or holding out, 130
change in composition of firm, 144–145
circumstances amounting to, 130–135
distinction of s. 14 (1) and s. 36 of Partnership Act 1890...290–292
dormant or sleeping partner, 151
facts supporting, may be sufficient to establish partnership, 134
fraudulent inducement as defence to, 143
intention to became a partner, 142–143
"knowingly suffers," 133–142
holding out by others, 131
legal effect of, 135
liability in delict, 153
liability of firm, 154–157
notice of retirement, effect of upon subsequent holding out, 296–297
passive holding out by party, 137

HOLDING OUT—*cont.*
pleadable only by those aware of it, 129
quasi-partnership, 128
registration, effect of, under Registration of Business Names Act 1916...152–153
representation must be made known to person relying on, 132
retired partner, 145, 290
steps by party held out to dissociate himself, 137–142
unnamed but identified party, of, 133
use of firm name after death of partner, 427
words or conduct, 132
See also APPARENT PARTNER, CHANGE IN PARTNERSHIP.

IDENTITY OF FIRM. See BANKRUPTCY, DISTINCT TRADES.

ILLEGAL PARTNERSHIP,
bankers, 111
claims against, 125
concealment of illegality, 124
dentists, 110
exceeding maximum permitted number, 13–14
fraudulent misrepresentation as to legality, 124–125
illegal purpose, for, 102
immoral purposes, for, 102
infringing statutes providing business to be carried on by qualified persons, 108–111
insurers, 111
medical practitioners, 110
moneylenders, 111
newspaper proprietors, 111
objects—
blasphemous, 99
contra bonos mores, 97
contrary to established religion, 98
contrary to public policy, 100–102
illegal by statute, 103 *et seq.*
opposed to current notions of morality, 98
severability of, 118–119
to " subvert the constitution," 99–100
partners not *in pari delicto*, 123–124
partnerships initially illegal, 105–108
patent agents, 111
pawnbrokers, 111
See also PAWNBROKERS.
solicitors, 109
theatrical employers, 111
trade unions, 111
violation of revenue laws, 102–103
See also ILLEGALITY, ILLEGALITY BY STATUTE.

ILLEGAL PREFERENCES,
acts within ostensible authority of partner, 575
by firm, 574
notour bankruptcy of firm, 560

ILLEGAL PREFERENCES—*cont.*
transactions in ordinary course of business, 574

ILLEGALITY,
actings upon illegal contract, 126
contract for illegal purpose, 97
dissolution of partnership through, 453–455, 642
objection by court *ex proprio motu*, 126

ILLEGALITY BY STATUTE,
construction of statutory provisions, 104
directory provisions, 103
mala in se, 103
mala prohibita, 103
prohibitory provisions, 103
provisions—
creating illegality to protect particular class of public, 112
in general public interest, 112
rendering certain transactions illegal, 111
Registration of Business Names Act 1916...113–118
requirement of registration, 111

ILLEGALITY OF PARTNERSHIP,
as affecting partner's lien, 411
dissolution on ground of, 453

IMMORALITY,
partnership for immoral purposes, 102–103

IMPLIED POWERS OF PARTNERS. See AUTHORITY OF PARTNER.

INCHOATE ASSOCIATIONS, 142–143, 259

INCOME TAX,
assessment in partnership name, 313
liability of firm and partners to, 205
precedent partner, 314
return of income of firm, 313

INCOMING PARTNER,
liability—
for firm debts, 258, 639
for previous transactions of firm, 271
of partner joining established firm, 263

INDEMNITY OF PARTNER,
for payment of liabilities incurred for firm, 640–641
on rescission of contract for fraud etc., 644

INDUCEMENT TO BECOME PARTNER, 254

INDORSEMENT,
authority of partner to indorse firm bills, 212

INSANITY,
contracts of partnership with lunatic or congenital imbecile void, 38
incapacitating party from entering partnership, 38
liability of lunatic under contracts for necessaries, 38
matter of degree, 39

INSANITY—*cont.*
money advanced to lunatic and expended for his benefit, 38–39
not a status fixed and determinable
as to duration, 38
other contracting party unaware he
was contracting with lunatic, 39
supervening, 39–40

INSANITY OF PARTNER,
date of dissolution of firm on, 459–
460
expenses of application for dissolution, 461
ground of dissolution of partnership,
as, 457, 642–643
representation of insane partner's
interests, 461

INSOLVENCY OF FIRM,
postponement—
of rights of person lending or
selling in consideration of share
of profits, 93–96, 637
not applicable in case of loan on
condition that another person
receive share of profits, 94
rights—
of cautioner of party lending to
firm not postponed, 94–95
of lender postponed even where
agreement not in writing, 95–96

INSOLVENCY OF PARTNER,
" declared insolvency," 449–450

INSURERS, 111

INTENTION OF PARTIES,
express declaration of intention to
enter partnership, 59
express term denying intention to
enter partnership, 59–60
no single factor to be taken in
isolation, 59

INTERDICT,
where remedy may be granted on
breach of partnership agreement,
195–196

INTOXICATION,
necessity of repudiating contract so
soon as sober, 41
partial, no ground for repudiation of
contract; but may vitiate contract
on ground that no contract seriously intended, 41
test applied in deciding whether
contract voidable, 40

JOINT ADVENTURE,
accounting, right to, 633
assignation of share, 634
authority of co-adventurers, 613–616
common stock, 630
contribution to, 616
delectus personae, 633
dissolution of, 607, 631, 642
distinguished from a partnership, 613
for purposes of transaction offending
against statute, 111n.

JOINT ADVENTURE—*cont.*
illegality of, 621
gambling, 621
joint ownership distinguished, 610
liability—
in delict, 619–620
joint and several, 619
of co-adventurers, basis of, 617
limits of, 607–609
nature of, 3, 607
personal bar, 629
presumption of equal shares applies,
403
property of, 630–631
reimbursement for special trouble,
624–625
rights of co-adventurers *inter se*,
623–624
rule as to equality where joint
adventure between firm and individual, 403–404
separate *persona* of, 611–613
sequestrated, whether it may be, 579
set-off, 625–629
termination of, 631–633
trade mark indicating, 430–431
transaction *in rem versum*, 614
wrong done by one co-adventurer to
another, 620

JOINT AND SEVERAL LIABILITY OF
PARTNERS,
breach of trust by copartner, for,
367–369
delict, in, 357–358
firm, for, 351 *et seq.*
termination of, 277

JOINT OWNERSHIP,
of investments, 3
of racehorse, 3
of trade mark, 430–432
not of itself partnership, 3, 636

JOINT PROPERTY,
as evidence of partnership, 65–70,
636

JOINT STOCK COMPANY,
pupil introduced as member of, 27

JOINT TENANCY, 66, 636

JUDICIAL FACTOR,
appointment of, 520 *et seq.*
right to apply for, 526–527

LAND AGENTS,
limited partnership of, conditions on
which unrestricted in size, 660
partnerships of, unrestricted in size
where not less than three-quarters
of partners are members of approved bodies, 658

LATENT PARTNER,
retirement of, 151

LEASES,
partner securing for himself lease of
firm premises, 170–171

LESION, 31

LIABILITY OF FIRM,
actings of former partner binding continuing firm, 292–293
acts within apparent authority of partner, 243
breach of fiduciary duty with knowledge of copartners, 323–326
continuing guarantees, 280, 639
defamation, 308–311
delict, 302 *et seq.*, 638
  committed with authority of his copartners, 308, 638
  contrasted with liability in contract, 307
  joint and several liability on, 638
discharge of firm's obligations, 276
firm receiving benefit from wrongful act, 326–327
fraud—
  committed with knowledge of copartners, 323 *et seq.*
  of partner, 317 *et seq.*
improper employment of trustt—a, money, 328–333, 339–351, 638
malicious prosecution, 312
misapplication of money or property, 339–351, 638
on ground that firm has had benefit of contract, 256
partner acting for private purposes, 306–307, 638
partner who is director of company, 367
penalty imposed on partner under Taxes Management Act 1970...314
penalty incurred by partner, 313, 638
profiting by a partner's fraud, 330 *et seq.*
quantum lucratus, 257, 327
rei interventus, 229
untrue statements—
  as to nature and extent of business, 322
  as to partner's authority, 322
whether written contract binds firm, 225
wilful wrong of partner, 311
See also EMBEZZLEMENT, FOLLOWING THE TRUST MONEY, MISAPPLICATION OF MONEY OR PROPERTY, TRUST, BREACH OF

LIABILITY OF PARTNERS IN DELICT, 638
basis of, 357–358
copartner's delict, for, 351

LIBEL. *See* DEFAMATION.

LICENSING (SCOTLAND) ACT 1959...316

LIEN, PARTNER'S,
circumstances in which right may be lost, 409
debts in respect of which asserted, 407
extent of partnership property affected, 407
illegality of partnership as affecting, 411
nature of, 406, 644
persons against whom lien may be asserted, 408

LIEN, PARTNER'S—*cont.*
rescission of partnership for fraud etc., on, 644
winding up, in, 540

LIMITED PARTNER,
assignation of share, 595, 647
  advertisment of, 596, 648
authority, 586–590
bankruptcy of, 647
body corporate, 646
contribution not to be withdrawn, 586, 646
death of, 647
dissolution of firm, 598, 600–604, 647
insanity of, 603
liability of, 587
management, taking part in, 587, 647
not entitled to dissolve partnership by notice, 598, 600, 647
not permitted to withdraw capital, 586
rights of, 646
suffering share to be charged for his debt, 598–599, 600, 647

LIMITED PARTNERSHIP, 583 *et seq.*
advantages of, 583–584
agreement, need for formal, 598
application of general law of partnership to, 597, 647
assignation of share, 598
assumption of partners, 647
" business," meaning of, 585–586, 646
constitution of, 585–586
continuing use of share of deceased or outgoing partner, 601
definition, 646
dissolution, 598, 600, 601
  by order of court, 603–604
  not dissolved by death or bankruptcy of limited partner, 601, 647
false particulars registered, 597
" firm," meaning of, 646
" firm name," meaning of, 646
France, in, 584
future of, 585
general partner, 586, 646
  advertisement of his becoming limited partner, 594, 648
  bankruptcy of, 603
  becoming limited partner, 594
  death of, 602
  insanity of, 603
  meaning of, 646
  powers of management, 647
index of, 649
management, 598, 646, 647
modification of general law in case of, 597 *et seq.*, 646
new partner, introduction of, 598
number of members, 586, 657, 659–660
particulars to be registered, 590–591
register of, 649
  inspection of, 649
registration of, 590, 646, 651
  certificate of, 649

LIMITED PARTNERSHIP—*cont.*
  registration of—*cont.*
    changes in, 591–593, 648, 652
    default in, 648
    effect of, as notice, 594
    false returns, 649
    manner of, 647
    particulars of, 590–591, 647
    Registration of Business Names Act
      1916...593
    restriction on number of members—
      banking, 646, 657, 660
      trading, 646
  rules, power to make, 649–650
  stamp duties, 596, 648
  unrestricted number of partners,
    conditions for, 657, 660
  winding up, 604–606, 647
    application to court for, 604–606
LIMITED PARTNERSHIPS ACT 1907...
  646–650
LIMITED PARTNERSHIP RULES 1907...
  650–656
  fees, 650
  forms, 651–656
  registrar, who may act as, 650
LIMITED PARTNERSHIPS (UNRESTRICTED
  SIZE) No. 1 REGULATIONS 1971...
  660
LOAN,
  agreement to repay by share of
    profits must be in writing, 87
  by dormant partner to firm, 90
  facts tending to suggest partnership
    rather than, 90–91
  indeterminate line between partner-
    ship and loan, 89
  partially in consideration of share of
    profits and partially otherwise, 95
  possibility of disguising partnership
    as agreement to lend to business,
    87
  postponement of rights of lender in
    insolvency of firm, 93–96
  relation of partner and lender to
    firm not mutually exclusive, 91
  repayable by share of profits, 637
  variation of term that lender receives
    share of profits, 95
  whether fact agreement not in writ-
    ing sufficient to create partnership,
    88
LOSSES,
  borne in proportion to entitlement to
    share profits, 532, 645
  making up, 536
  partners to contribute equally to, 640
  winding up, treatment of, 529 *et seq.*
LOTTERY,
  purchase by parties of ticket in
    foreign lottery, 108
LUNACY. *See* INSANITY.

MAJORITIES,
  decision ruling ordinary matters, 641

MAJORITY OF PARTNERS. *See* MAN-
  AGEMENT OF PARTNERSHIP.
MALICE,
  where imputed to firm, 310
MALICIOUS PROSECUTION,
  by partner, 312
MANAGEMENT OF PARTNERSHIP,
  bona fide consideration of minority
    view, 186
  observance of prescribed procedures
    for arriving at majority decision,
    187
  partner's right to take part in, 641
  powers—
    exercisable by single partner, 182
    of majorities, 183
  presumption for *status quo* where
    partners equally divided, 186
MARRIED WOMAN,
  capable of entering partnership with
    her husband, 43–44
MARRIED WOMEN'S PROPERTY (SCOT-
  LAND) ACT 1920,
  effect of, 44
MEDICAL PRACTITIONERS,
  entering partnership with unqualified
    person, 110
  partnerships between, 2–3
  sharing of gross returns in medical
    partnerships, 72
MEETINGS OF PARTNERS,
  bona fide decision at, 186–187
  observance of procedure prescribed
    for, 187–188
  voting at, 183
  See also MANAGEMENT OF PARTNER-
    SHIP.
MINES,
  co-ownership of, 69
  partnership in, 69
  See also COSTBOOK COMPANIES,
    STANNARIES.
MINOR,
  acting as agent, 30
  capacity to enter partnership when
    he has no curator, 29
  engaging in trade, 31–34
  entitled to challenge on grounds of
    lesion in question with partners,
    31
    but not as against creditors of
      firm, 31
  extent of right to challenge contract
    of partnership, 35–38
  minor who has curator purporting to
    enter partnership without curator's
    consent, 29–30
  misrepresentation as to age, 34–35
  power to enter partnership where he
    has a curator, 29
  transaction *in rem versum,* 31, 33
MISAPPLICATION OF MONEY OR PRO-
  PERTY,
  firm's liability for partner's, 339

MISAPPLICATION OF MONEY OR PRO-
PERTY—*cont.*
improper employment of trust property for partnership purposes, 358
in custody of firm, 343–345, 347–348
money received by firm " in the
course of its business," 348–351
received by partner and misapplied,
339, 343–345
See also EMBEZZLEMENT, FRAUD,
TRUST, BREACH OF.

MISCONDUCT,
dissolution, ground for, 192–193, 464
et seq., 643
See also, DISSOLUTION
interdict restraining, 195–196
premium, return of, on account of,
254–255, 644

MISTAKES IN ACCOUNTS. *See* ACCOUNTS

MONEYLENDERS, 111

MORA AND TACITURNITY,
partner's claim for accounting, 171,
629

MUTUAL INSURANCE SOCIETY,
not partnership, 6

NAME. *See* FIRM NAME, REGISTRA-
TION OF BUSINESS NAMES ACT
1916.

NEGOTIABLE INSTRUMENTS. *See* BILLS
OF EXCHANGE.

NEGOTIORUM GESTIO, 214
whether doctrine operates to extend
authority of one who is already
an agent, 215

NEWSPAPER PROPRIETORS, 111

NOTICE,
acting partner, to, 218, 639
advertisement, by, 300
change in firm, 292–297, 643
date at which notice imputed to
firm, 219
dissolution of partnership by, 436,
642
effects—
of altered name on stationery of
firm, 297, 300–301
of notice that firm will not be
bound by partner's acts, 638
of Registration of Business Names
Act, 1916...297
expulsion, of, 487
knowledge of one partner knowledge of all partners, 220
partner, to, as notice to firm, 218
public generally, to, 298–299
registration under Registration of
Business Names Act 1916 not
public notice, 301
retiring partner, by, 289

NOTICE OF DISSOLUTION, 438
cases where not required, 507
communication of, 442
intention of parties as to period of,
440

NOTICE OF DISSOLUTION—*cont.*
may be prospective, 439
must be explicit, 439
no period of reasonable notice
required, 439
not to be used unfairly, 439
right of partner to give, 288, 510,
643
special notice to former customers of
firm, 299
sufficient if proven that received, 299
third party's rights, effect on, 505

NOVATION,
on change in composition of firm,
148–150

OBLIGATIONS OF PARTNER,
accounts, 641
" any benefit derived," 166–170
attention to business of firm, 193
bankruptcy of partner relieves his
estate from continuing liability for
firm debts, 294
bound by acts on behalf of firm, 637
business connections, use of, 172–173
cautioners for firm, as, 159–161
competing business carried on by
him, 164–165, 178, 642
confidential information—
application of rules in agency,
174–177
use of, 172 *et seq.*
connection of firm, use of, 172, 177,
641
constitution of debt against firm, 277
continuing guarantees, 280
discharge of firm's obligation, 276
dishonest or immoral conduct unconnected with business of firm,
192–193
dissolution of firm, on, 288
duty of honesty, 180
in dealing with third parties, 182
equal contribution to losses in
absence of contrary agreement,
400
expulsion, 188 .
fiduciary relationship of partners,
162
firm name, use of, 171–172, 641
incidence of losses, 527 *et seq.*
incoming partner, 258, 263, 271, 639
insanity of partner, 286
leases, 170–171
liability—
endurance of, 274
for past acts, 274
limits of partner's duty of disclosure,
191–192
outgoing partner, 274, 275, 639
release of one partner as affecting
copartners, 277–278
requirement of *uberrima fides inter
se*, 161
secret profits, 165–166

OBLIGATIONS OF PARTNER—*cont.*
    to account for benefit derived from
        partnership, 164–165, 641–642
    See also PROFESSIONAL NEGLIGENCE.
OPTION,
    dissolve partnership, to, 484–485
    purchase share, to, 546, 644–645
OUTGOING PARTNER,
    continuing liability for firm debts,
        274
    delegation of liability of firm, 275
    option to purchase share of, 546,
        644–645
    right of, to receive profits attribut-
        able to use of his share, 540–543,
        644
        See also CAPITAL.
    share of, a debt accruing at date of
        dissolution, 645

PACTUM ILLICITUM,
    unenforceable in court, 97
PART OWNERSHIP,
    evidence of partnership, as, 65
    part owners not joint proprietors, 66
PARTICIPATION IN PROFITS,
    partners subject to special provision
        as to sharing in profits, 12
    salaried partners, 12
PARTNERS,
    restriction on number of, 13
        accountants, 13, 657
        actuaries, 659
        auctioneers, 658
        banking partnerships, 13, 656
        building designers, 659
        chartered engineers, 659
        estate agents, 658
        estate managers, 658
        land agents, 658
        limited partnerships, in, 586, 646,
            657, 660
        patent agents, 658
        solicitors, 13, 657
        stockbrokers, 13, 657
        surveyors, 658
        trading partnerships, 13, 656
PARTNERSHIP,
    assumption of partners, 641
    definition of, 2 *et seq.*, 636
    illegality of partnership exceeding
        restricted number, 13
    logical difficulties of claiming par-
        ticipation in profit as essential
        element in, 9–10
    necessity for participation by part-
        ners in profits, 7–12
    participation in profits, of essence
        of, 2, 8–12
    property jointly owned, in, 67
    restriction of number of partners, 13
PARTNERSHIP ACT 1890,
    not a codifying Act, 1
    object of, 7

PARTNERSHIP ACT 1890—*cont.*
    saving of rules of equity and com-
        mon law, 2
    use of pre-statute decisions to ex-
        plain, 2
PARTNERSHIP AT WILL,
    communication of notice of dis-
        solution, 442
    continuance of partnership business
        after expiry of term, 437, 641
    dissolution by notice, 437, 438–442
    duration, where no term set for, 436
    expulsion clause, 438, 492
    notice of dissolution—
        effect on third parties, 443
        intention of partners as to period
            of notice, 440
        may be prospective, 439
        must be explicit, 439
        reasonable period of notice not
            required, 439
        right instantly to dissolve, 441
    retirement from, 437, 641
    right of pre-emption, 442
    terms of original partnership con-
        sistent with, 437, 641
PARTNERSHIP PROPERTY, 376 *et seq.*,
        639–640
    " acquired...on account of the firm,"
        378
    Act 1696, cap. 25...382 *et seq.*
    agreement—
        among partners as to what is, 377
        effect of, on nature of partners'
            rights, 391–392
    bought with money belonging to
        firm, 378, 640
    difference of treatment under Scots
        and English law, 394–398
    effect of intent of partners contrary
        to terms of Act, 379–381
    goodwill, 423–425
    heritable estate—
        belonging to partnership, 387
        conversion of, into moveable
            estate, 389, 640
        used by partnership, co-owners in,
            388
    in questions *inter socios*, 376
    in questions with firm's creditors,
        376
    parole proof of mandate to acquire
        property for partnership, 385
    presumption of equality of partners'
        rights, 398–400
    pro indiviso right of partners in
        common stock, 390–391
    proof of trust as regards property
        held for firm, 382 *et seq.*
    proof *prout de jure* as to partner-
        ship property held by individual,
        382, 385
    property acquired by partner as
        personal property, 381
    property held by individual *ex facie*
        absolutely but in trust for firm,
        382 *et seq.*

PARTNERSHIP PROPERTY—*cont.*
protection against charge for partner's separate debt, 394–398, 640
qualification for voting, as, 392
rights of partners *inter se* in, 398–400
trade marks, 428–432
See also ESTATE DUTY, LIEN, PARTNER'S, TRADE MARKS.

PARTNERSHIPS (UNRESTRICTED SIZE) NO. 1 REGULATIONS 1968...658

PARTNERSHIPS (UNRESTRICTED SIZE) NO. 2 REGULATIONS 1970...659

PARTNERSHIPS (UNRESTRICTED SIZE) NO. 3 REGULATIONS 1970...659

PARTNERSHIPS (UNRESTRICTED SIZE) NO. 4 REGULATIONS 1970...659

PARTNERSHIPS, LIMITED (UNRESTRICTED SIZE) NO. 1 REGULATIONS 1970 660

PATENT AGENTS, 111
partnerships of, unrestricted as to number, 658

PAWNBROKERS,
illegal partnerships among, 106–108, 111

PERPETUAL SUCCESSION,
doctrine of, in corporations, 435

PERSONAL BAR,
against firm on admission or representation of partner, 217
holding out an aspect of, 130–131
joint adventure, as affecting rights in, 629

PERSONAL REPRESENTATIVES. *See* EXECUTOR OF DECEASED PARTNER.

PRE-EMPTION, RIGHT OF,
consistent with partnership at will, 438, 442

PREMIUM,
apportionment of, on premature dissolution of partnership, 254–255, 644

PRESCRIPTION,
triennial, 516

PRESUMPTION OF EQUALITY AMONG PARTNERS,
doubts arising as to presumption in early cases, 402
effect of intention upon, 402
joint adventure in, 403
not displaced by change in partnership, 402

PROFESSIONAL NEGLIGENCE,
liability of retired partners for, 275

PROFITS,
accountability of partner for private profits, 165–166, 641–642
community of, 6
legal nature of, 4
net profits, meaning of, 530
participation by partners in, 640

PROFITS—*cont.*
partners to share equally in, 640
where no contrary agreement, 400–402

PROFITS, PARTICIPATION IN,
agents' remuneration by share of profits, 83
annuity to widow, etc. of deceased partner, 85
apparent inconsistency in Partnership Act, s. 2, rule 3...80–82
common law as to, as inferring partnership, 88–89
concerned with net profits, 78
debt paid out of accruing profits, 82
does not of itself set up partnership, 80
implication of partnership in losses examined, 78
indication of intention to set up partnership, 79
loan repayable—
by share of profits, 87
with interest varying with profits, 87
prima facie evidence of partnership, 79
salaried partners, 84–85
sale of goodwill of business, on, 92
servants' remuneration by share of profits, 83
See also INSOLVENCY OF FIRM.

PROMISSORY NOTE,
retired partner, liability for note granted in firm name, 291

PROOF OF PARTNERSHIP. *See* EVIDENCE OF EXISTENCE OF PARTNERSHIP.

PROPERTY,
not defined in Act, 377
See also PARTNERSHIP PROPERTY.

PUBLIC POLICY,
objects of partnership opposed to, 100–102

PUBLISHER AND AUTHOR, 72

PUPIL CHILDREN,
acting as agent, 30
contract of partnership with tutor on pupil's behalf reducible, 25
contracts made without reference to tutor void, 24
contracts made by pupil void, 24
discussion of theory that parents or guardians entering pupils as partners are themselves liable, 25–29
introduced by tutor into joint stock company, 27
may they be partners? 28–29
tutor has no power to engage the pupil's property in speculation, 24–25

QUADRIENNIUM UTILE,
minor, 32
pupil, 25, 28–29

QUANTUM LUCRATUS, 257

QUASI-PARTNERSHIP, 60–63, 76, 79
dissolution of company—
on deadlock, 476
unfair abuse of powers, 476
former application of, examined, 62–63
holding out, by, 60, 128
meaning of—
prior to Partnership Act 1890...60
since passing of Partnership Act 1890...62
participation in profits—
creating, as, 61
does not lead necessarily to inference of partnership at law, 61
involving participation in loss, as, 61
treatment of private limited company as, 474–478

QUASI-PERSONA,
of firm, 16

QUI FACIT PER ALIUM FACIT PER SE, 303, 308

RATIFICATION,
acts of partners, of, 159
incoming partner, by, 259 et seq.

RECEIPTS,
authority of partner to give, 212, 514

RECOMPENSE, 327–330

REGISTRATION OF BUSINESS NAMES ACT 1916,
disability,
extent of, on default in registration, 113–114
relief from, 114–115
effect of—
as notice of change in partnership, 301
as notice of dissociation from partnership, 301
limited partnerships, 593
misleading names, 115
offences and penalties, 115–117
publication of true names, 117
registration under, not public notice, 301

REI INTERVENTUS, 229–235
as affecting conduct in setting up partnership, 52

RELIEF, RIGHT OF,
among partners, 196–198, 637

REMEDIES,
breach of obligation by partner, 193–196
damages, 194–195
dissolution, 193–194
interdict, 194, 195

REPRESENTATION,
by partner—
as to his apparent authority, 252–254
evidence against firm, 217, 639

RESCISSION OF PARTNERSHIP,
action for, 547–548
consequential rights, 548
fraud or misrepresentation, 547 et seq., 644
indemnity against firm liabilities, 549
rescinding of agreement of dissolution, 551
restitutio in integrum, 550
rights of partner induced to enter partnership, 547
"without prejudice to any other right," 548–549, 644

RESPONDEAT SUPERIOR, 303, 304–306, 308

RESTITUTION. See RESCISSION OF PARTNERSHIP.

RESTRAINT OF TRADE. See RESTRICTIVE COVENANT, RESTRICTIVE COVENANTS IN PARTNERSHIP AGREEMENT.

RESTRICTIVE COVENANT, 119–120
on retiring partner bought out by continuing partners, 421
not objectionable because seeks to protect from competition, 421–423

RESTRICTIVE COVENANTS IN PARTNERSHIP AGREEMENT,
construction of, 120–123
similar to those between seller and purchaser of goodwill, 120

RETENTION, PARTNER'S RIGHT OF, 644
See also LIEN, PARTNER'S.

REVENUE LAWS,
partnership contravening foreign, 102–103

REVOCATION,
of authority of partner, 287

RIGHT OF FIRM TO SERVICES OF PARTNER, 205

RIGHTS OF PARTNER,
access to firm's books, 198
accounts, agreed restriction on right to inspect, 198
delectus personae, 204
dissolution for fraud or misrepresentation, 547
distribution of assets, 527 et seq.
equal participation in profits, 400 et seq.
expressed in partnership agreement, 158
expulsion, 188
goodwill, 423
limit on mutual obligations of good faith, 189
management, 182 et seq., 641
nature and extent of his share in firm, 199
partnership property inter socios, 398
pro indiviso right in common stock or fund of partnership, 390
relief inter socios, of, 196

RIGHTS OF PARTNER—*cont.*
   remedies for breach of obligation by
      copartner, 193
   remuneration, 641
      joint adventure, for special trouble
         connected with, 624–625
   share, to assign his, 201–203
   sub-partnership, 203–204
   See also RIGHT OF FIRM TO SERVICES
      OF PARTNER, SALARIED PARTNERS.

ROYALTIES ON BOOK SALES,
   as evidence of partnership, 72

SALARIED PARTNERS,
   receiving salary and/or share of
      profits, 84
   where no agreed share of profits, 85

SECRET PARTNERS. *See* LATENT PART-
   NER.

SEQUESTRATION. *See* BANKRUPTCY.

SERVANT,
   partner, right of—
      to dismiss, 186
      to engage, 186, 210
   See PROFITS, PARTICIPATION IN.

SERVICE,
   whether contract of, or partnership,
      83–84

SET OFF,
   between firm and individual partners,
      564–565
   between firm and third parties, 625–
      629

SETTLING ACCOUNTS BETWEEN PART-
   NERS, 404–405, 645
   advances, treatment of, 405
   capital, treatment of partner's con-
      tributions to, 405
   distribution of assets in final, 404–
      405, 645
   losses, contribution to, 404–405
   profits, treatment of, 405
   See also ACCOUNTS, ACCOUNTING.

SHARE OF PARTNER,
   agreement as to unequal shares,
      401–402
      not displaced by retirement of
         some partners, 402
   agreement for ascertainment of, 528
      et seq.
      determined by custom of trade, as,
         402
   failing agreement, shares of partners
      to be equal, 400–401, 640

SHIP,
   ownership of shares in, not of itself
      partnership, 3

SI QUID SOCIETATI DEBETUR SINGULIS
   DEBETUR, 15

SI QUID UNIVERSITATI DEBETUR
   SINGULIS NON DEBETUR, 14

SLEEPING PARTNERS. *See* DORMANT
   PARTNER, LATENT PARTNER.

SOCIETIES,
   basis of liability of members, 5
   not partnerships, 5

SOCIUS MEI SOCII NON EST SOCIUS
   MEUS, 412

SOLE PARTNER, 3–4

SOLICITORS,
   advice by firm of, leading to breach
      of trust, 366
   entering partnership with unqualified
      person, 109
   limited partnership of, unrestricted
      as to numbers, 657
   partnership of, unrestricted as to
      number, 13, 656–657

SOLICITORS ACCOUNTS RULES,
   effect of, 363 *et seq.*

SPECULATION,
   in investments jointly owned, 3

STAMP DUTIES,
   capital contributed to limited part-
      nership, 596–597, 648

STANNARIES, 14

STOCKBROKERS,
   limited partnership of, unrestricted
      as to numbers, 657
   partnership of, unrestricted as to
      number, 13, 656–657

SUB-PARTNERSHIP, 203–204

SURGEONS, 110

SURVEYORS,
   conditions on which numbers unre-
      stricted—
      limited partnership, 660
      ordinary partnership, 658

SURVIVING PARTNERS,
   accounts, 527–531
      duty to account—
         former partner, to, 540–541
         executor of deceased partner, to,
            539
      subsequent profits, for, 539–541
   authority of, 517–519
   breach of trust by, 363n.
   goodwill, 420 *et seq.*
   holding out, 144–145
   share of deceased partner, 540–546,
      644
      option to purchase, 546, 644–645
   where trustee of deceased partner,
      190

TACIT RELOCATION OF PARTNERSHIP,
   expulsion clause, 492
   partnership at will, as, 437
   terms of original partnership, con-
      sistent with partnership at will, 437

TAXES MANAGEMENT ACT 1970...314

TENANCY IN COMMON, 66

TERMINATION OF LIABILITY,
 for future acts, 274 *et seq.*
  bankruptcy, 294, 643–644
  death, 293, 643
  dissolution of partnership, 288 *et
   seq.*, 643
  retirement, 274–275, 639, 643

TERMINATION OF PARTNERSHIP. *See*
 DISSOLUTION.

THEATRE LETS, 74–75

THEATRICAL EMPLOYERS, 111

TRADE MARKS,
 assignation rendering use deceptive,
  429
 expunging from register, 429
 formerly assignable only along with
  goodwill, 429
 indicating joint adventure, 430–432
 joint ownership of, 430 *et seq.*
 nature of, 428
 registered, 428
  assignability of, 428
 splitting of rights in, 430
 transmissibility of, 428
 unregistered, 428
  assignability of, 428

TRADE SECRETS,
 partner accountable to firm for profits derived from, 172–175

TRADE UNIONS, 111

TRADING PARTNERSHIPS,
 restriction on number of partners in,
  13, 656

TRUCK ACTS, 314–316

TRUST, BREACH OF,
 advice of firm of solicitors leading
  to, 366
 firm's liability for, 358–363
 See also FOLLOWING THE TRUST
  MONEY.

TRUSTEES OF DECEASED PARTNER,
 collective power of management
  when introduced in place of
  deceased, 19–22
 " constitutional " position of, when
  introduced into partnership, 21
 construction of provisions entitling
  them to be introduced as partners,
  23
 extent of powers when introduced
  as partners, 19–23
 practical inability to act collectively
  as partner, 23
 when entitled to act as partners in
  the firm, 19

UBERRIMA FIDES,
 and fiduciary duty examined, 162–
  164
 application to partnership, in its, 161
 effect on contract of copartnery
  discussed, 41
 negotiations to enter partnership, in,
  163

UNINCORPORATED COMPANY, 5–6

USURY,
 previous tendency to regard usurious
  contract as partnership, 88–90

VALUATION,
 goodwill, of, 433
 partner's share, of, 537

VALUERS,
 limited partnership of, conditions on
  which unrestricted in size, 660
 partnerships of, unrestricted in size
  where not less than three-quarters
  of partners are members of
  approved bodies, 658

VARIATION,
 of terms of partnership, 287, 378,
  414, 639
 See also LOAN.

VICARIOUS LIABILITY OF FIRM,
 advice by firm of solicitors leading
  to breach of trust, 366
 agency, 302
 contract of employment, in, 302
 development of doctrine, 303
 distinction between liability under
  s. 11 and s. 13 of Partnership Act
  1890...360
 effect of Solicitors Accounts Rules
  on, 363–366
 false accounts rendered by a partner,
  for, 341
 improper employment of trust funds
  in firm's business, 358
 joint and several liability of partners
  in delict, 356
 merging of ideas of delict and
  authority in, 336
 misapplication of money or property
  of third party, 339
 offence, for commission of, 313–317
 ordinary course of firm's business,
  335
 partner " acting in the ordinary
  course of the business of the
  firm," 306
 partner's delict, for, 302
 partner's wrongful act other than
  fraud, for, 334
 personal nature of fraud as affecting,
  332
 " to the same extent as the partner...," 337
 whether existence of firm can be
  established, 334
 wrong committed without authority
  and not in ordinary course of the
  business, 335
 wrongful act causing injury to copartner, 338
 See also FIDUCIARY DUTY, FRAUD,
  MISAPPLICATION OF MONEY OR
  PROPERTY.

VOTING,
partners' meetings, at, 183
partnership property as qualification for, 392

WAGERING. *See* GAMING AND WAGERING.

WARRANTY OF AUTHORITY,
by partner, 240–241

WIDOW OF PARTNER,
annuity, 85

WILL, PARTNERSHIP AT. *See* PARTNERSHIP AT WILL.

WINDING UP,
accounts—
conclusive as to partners' shares, 537
errors in, 538
arbitration clause, effect of, 523
assets—
accruing after dissolution, 539
distribution of, 527
assignee, right of, 525
bills of exchange, 513
capital—
deficiencies of, 529–533
levelling down, 533
continuance of partnership business, 517
continuing authority of partners, 511, 643
continuity of accounts, 516
distribution of assets on, 527, 645
firm not bound by bankrupt partner, 519
judicial factor—
appointment of, 520
circumstances in which may be appointed, 520–523
lien of partner, 540
limits of continuing authority, 512
losses—
ratio of contribution to, 532
treatment of, 529
new contracts, 515–516
realisation of partnership property, 518
representatives of partner, right of, 524
rescission for fraud or misrepresentation, 547–552, 644
settling accounts, 527
share of outgoing partner—
alternative claim for interest on, 542
attribution of profit—
to skill of continuing partners, 541

WINDING UP—*cont.*
share of outgoing partner—*cont.*
attribution of profit—*cont.*
to use of capital, 541
choice of remedy, 543
share of partner, ascertainment of, 528
"so far as may be necessary to wind up the affairs...," 516–517
See also ACCOUNTS, JUDICIAL FACTOR, RESCISSION OF PARTNERSHIP.

WORDS AND PHRASES,
"acquired on account of the firm," 378
"any benefit derived," 166–170
"association formed for the purpose of carrying on a business with the object of acquisition of gain...," 6
"business," 2–3, 645
"calculated to prejudicially affect," 464–465
"carrying on a business," 2
"declared insolvency," 449
"*emptio rei facta a pluribus ementibus*," 6
"fair share of the work," 463
"firm," 637
"firm name," 637
"flagrant breach of duties," 465
"in the course of its business," 348–351
"just and equitable," 476
"knowingly suffers," 135–142
"living debtor," 558–559
"or any penalty is incurred," 302, 313–317, 638
"proper creditor of the partnership," 561
"*qui facit per alium facit per se*," 303, 308
"*respondeat superior*," 303, 304–306, 308
"*si quid societati debetur singulis debetur*," 15
"*si quid universitati debetur singulis non debetur*," 14
"so far as necessary to wind up the affairs...," 516–517
"*socius mei socii meus socius non est*," 412
"to subvert the constitution," 99–100
"to the same extent as the partner...," 337
"with a view of profit," 4–6
"without prejudice to any other right," 548–549